MIDDLE EAST
PATTERNS

FIFTH EDITION

FIFTH EDITION

MIDDLE EAST PATTERNS

Places, Peoples, and Politics

COLBERT C. HELD
Baylor University

AND

JOHN THOMAS CUMMINGS
Former USAID Economist

Cartography by John V. Cotter

WESTVIEW
PRESS
A Member of the Perseus Books Group

Library of Congress Cataloging-in-Publication Data
Held, Colbert C.
    Middle East patterns : places, peoples, and politics / Colbert C. Held and John Thomas Cummings ; cartography by John V. Cotter. — 5th ed.
        p.   cm.
    Includes bibliographical references and index.
    ISBN: 978-0-8133-4401-0 (alk. paper)
    1. Middle East.   2. Middle East—Geography.   3. Middle East—Social conditions.
4. Middle East—Politics and government.   I. Cummings, John Thomas.   II. Cotter, John V.
III. Title.
    DS44.H418 2011
    915.6—dc22
                                                                        2010007783

10 9 8 7 6 5 4 3 2 1

To
Mildred McDonald Held
With love and with gratitude from both authors and their families
for her support through the years during Middle East perils and
pleasures and during realization of the several editions of this book

Contents

PART ONE

PHYSICAL AND CULTURAL GEOGRAPHY

1 Tricontinental Junction: An Introduction   3

2 The Face of the Earth   13

3 Patterns of Time: Historical-Geographical Foundations   61

4 Patterns of Peoples, Cultures, and Settlements   83

5 The Desert and the Sown: Land Use   139

6 Riches Beneath the Earth   159

7 Manufacturing and Transportation   187

PART TWO

REGIONAL GEOGRAPHY

19 Iran: Complex Republic on the Plateau

Tables and Illustrations

Maps

Figures

Tables

Graphs

Preface and Acknowledgments to the Fifth Edition

As with each of its four earlier versions, this fifth edition of *Middle East Patterns* has been completely updated and extensively rewritten to take into account the many notable developments during the past five years in the complex region analyzed in this study. Forty maps have been revised and three newly prepared by Dr. Cotter, cartographer for all editions; the hundreds of data in all 16 tables have been completely updated; 3 graphs have been redone; and 16 of the 126 photographs are new. Many of the endnotes and bibliographic references reflect the explosive growth of Internet sources and reporting media.

Previous editions of the book were the outgrowth of Dr. Held's nearly fifty years of diplomatic assignments and academic fieldwork in the Middle East, along with teaching and research about the region. During his sixteen years in the Foreign Service with the Department of State beginning in 1957 he was not only assigned to Lebanon, Saudi Arabia, and Iran, as well as to the State Department in Washington, but also to successive, extended temporary duty in all Middle East countries. During his service in the region and on return trips for fieldwork, he took more than 19,000 Kodachrome slides over a period of fifty years, and most of the photographs in this study are from those slides.

This fifth edition of *Middle East Patterns* is not only updated and improved in maps, tables, and photographs, but more important adds as coauthor John Thomas Cummings, an experienced Middle East specialist with emphasis on economics. Dr. Cummings's relationship with the region began in the mid-1960s in Baghdad, where he taught for two years. Later, he received his doctorate in economics at Tufts University and taught at Suffolk University, Tufts University, and the University of Texas in Austin, presenting many courses related to economic development in the Middle East, and authored or coauthored four books and numerous journal articles on related subjects. Leaving academia for the region, he then spent twenty-seven years, mostly with the U.S. Department of Treasury, the U.S. Agency for International Development (USAID), and the UK Department for International Development, in Riyadh, Addis Ababa, Nicosia, Cairo, Baghdad, Kabul, and Jerusalem. During several of these assignments, he consulted with Dr. Held on parts of the earlier editions of this book, and he brings a fresh dynamic to this edition. He has also traveled extensively in every country in the region and in many of those bordering it and thus brings a wealth of direct experience in many geographical and professional sectors of the Middle East.

Together, we two authors have served nearly fifty years in official positions in nine Middle East countries, with fieldwork and intensive travel in all the other countries of the region. With Dr. Held having begun his diplomatic career in Beirut in 1957 and Dr. Cummings having taught in Baghdad in 1965, we have thus had the opportunity to experience intimately the emergence of this intriguing area, from an underestimated and underdeveloped corner of the world before major exploitation of its oil resources to the dynamic and diverse region it had become by 2010. As coauthors we also have the advantage that Dr. Cummings is married to Dr. Held's younger daughter, Joanne, who herself has a master's degree in geography and has spent forty-five years in the Middle East. She is now an experienced Foreign Service Officer specializing in the region and has contributed to all editions of *Middle East Patterns*.

The book is aimed at both midlevel college students and general readers who seek understanding of the spatial dynamics of the Middle East, especially those preparing to visit or work in the Middle East. We have reduced technical terminology to a minimum and have also included a glossary for convenient reference. Although we focus primarily on spatial patterns, we interweave economic, historical, and ethnographic elements of the regional mosaic. The book is therefore useful for courses not only in the geography of the Middle East but also in economics, political science, history, security studies, and anthropology.

Middle East Patterns remains the only comprehensive and up-to-date regional study of the Middle East from a spatial perspective by an American geographer since 1960, and it is unique in its breadth of coverage and its wealth of original maps, photographs, tables, and graphs. Like past editions, it reflects the topical and regional duality of the discipline of geography: Eight chapters in Part One cover the Middle East from a topical or systematic perspective (biophysical, historical, ethnographic, economic, and geopolitical), and eleven chapters in Part Two cover the area from a regional viewpoint, country by country.

Many discussions in Part One refer to the "broader" or "extended" Middle East, comprising North Africa, the trans-Caucasus republics, the Central Asian "stans," and Afghanistan and Pakistan on the eastern periphery. Throughout, the focus on human and cultural aspects of the area is balanced with correlated attention to the physical and biological elements. Analysis of regional topics and states considers the evolving geopolitical and geoeconomic dynamics, with careful and balanced attention to the shifting ramifications of the Palestinian-Israeli conflict.

Every edition of *Middle East Patterns* has involved a great range of assistance and support by more people and agencies than we can possibly thank individually; however, invaluable help from some individuals must be acknowledged. Foreign Service colleagues have provided major assistance: Ambassadors James Akins, Charles Cecil, April Glaspie, Nathaniel Howell, Andrew Killgore, David Newton, Richard Parker, and the late Nicholas Thacher; and Foreign Service Officers Thomas Carolan, Philip Griffin, the late Robert Houghton, Clay Nettles, and Douglas Silliman. The late Dr. Arthur L. Burt, retired chief of the State Department Map Library, also facilitated Dr. Held's fieldwork in earlier years. These special colleagues extended not only assistance but also hospitality and insight during numerous trips throughout the Middle East.

Academic colleagues have likewise been generous in sharing their expertise, and they deserve deep appreciation: Dr. John Wilson of the Baylor University Library and Dr. William Baker, also of Baylor; Dr. Gwyn Rowley of the University of Sheffield, England; and Dr. John W. Fox of the American University of Sharjah (UAE).

Over the years Dr. Held's fieldwork has been greatly facilitated by nongovernmental organizations and other agencies, including oil companies, in virtually every Middle East country, especially Crescent Petroleum Company of Sharjah and its president, Hamid Jafar; Saudi Arabian Oil Company (Saudi Aramco), which provided numerous briefings and arranged visits to many of its facilities through the years, and assisted with photographs through Arthur Clark and Sarah Miller of Aramco Services; and Bahrain Petroleum Company (Bapco), Petroleum Development Oman (PDO), Dubai Petroleum Company (Dupetco), and Amoco Egypt, each of which provided informative briefings. In addition, American Embassy officers in every country have kindly given both of us extended and informative briefings, as have many local government officials.

Knowledgeable friends who have lent their expertise to editions of *Middle East Patterns* include the late Peter Speers, formerly of Aramco, who unstintingly supervised the fine points of Arabic and Arabic place-names through four editions, and with his loss in January 2010 he will be greatly missed; James Mandaville, also a former Aramcon, who has generously vetted chapters and consulted on plant geography; and Dr. Munir Shammaa, distinguished physician with the American University of Beirut Hospital, who provided profound insights about the region. Dr. Cummings is particularly grateful to his son Liam and friends Molly and Rick for their support at critical points in the preparation of this edition.

Baylor University student assistant Kayla Ritter patiently pored over hundreds of data researching statistics with which she ably updated the tables. Westview editors and technicians through the years have patiently led Dr. Held and now both of us through the intricacies of book preparation and publishing, with Karl Yambert and Kay Mariea the latest in an admirable line of talented and supportive editors who deserve warm thanks. Above all, Annette Wenda performed consummate copyediting of a complex manuscript for which we are deeply grateful.

Finally, a note about the preparation of *Middle East Patterns* as something of a family enterprise, with both of our wives—Mildred McDonald Held and Joanne Held Cummings—contributing substantively to the book in many ways. Mildred especially helped to the degree of collaborating on earlier editions. The other Held daughter, Melinda Brunger, who has a law practice with expertise in the energy industry, has also consulted on the book project, editing and in some cases drafting many sections of earlier editions. Dr. Cummings's son John T. M. Cummings added his energy and his excellent computer skills to help with locating relevant photographs and, more important, to assist with bibliographic entries. A family enterprise indeed.

Particular thanks go to Christopher Brunger, who served as a research and editorial assistant who carefully read the entire manuscript with an invaluable critical eye. Thanks go to him also for drafting the country summaries and for research on economics and financial topics.

Notwithstanding all the deeply appreciated contributions and support by colleagues, officials, friends, editors, and family, we joint authors assume complete responsibility for every aspect of *Middle East Patterns*, including errors and oversights. We invite readers to bring to our attention any inaccuracies, and we welcome all comments and suggestions.

C.C.H.
J.T.C.
March 2010

A Note on Transliteration

For transliteration of place-names from Arabic, Hebrew, and Greek, we have generally followed the recommendations of the U.S. Board on Geographic Names (BGN), except that we elected to omit diacritical marks on transliterations from those three languages. We retained diacritics in Turkish words (except the undotted capital "I," as in Istanbul), since Turkish uses a basically Roman alphabet in which diacritics are an integral part of the written language. Indicating the ain and the hamza in Arabic words merely confuses the general reader who knows no Arabic and adds little of essence for readers who do. We have deliberately accepted inconsistency in using conventional forms and spellings for certain names—Cairo (rather than al-Qahirah), Damascus (al-Dimashq), Yemen (al-Yaman), Bab el-Mandeb (Bab al-Mandab), Dubai (Dubayyah), Medina (al-Madinah), Doha (al-Dawhah), Bekaa (Biqa), and others. We have also dropped the definite article (*al*) in many names (Aqabah, Riyadh, Qatif), and where we have retained it we have used it only in the basic form, not in the form modified by "sun letters" (Sharm al-Shaykh, not Sharm ash-Shaykh; Jabal al-Ruwaq, not Jabal ar-Ruwaq). Occasionally, we have deliberately been inconsistent in using the standard BGN transliteration in general discussion and then following the spelling employed in proper names, as in "amirates" and "United Arab Emirates" and in "Zayid" and "Shaykh Zayed Road." We have also retained certain spellings that have become ingrained through use by oil companies.

Some names create certain problems. For example, the Gulf is called the Persian Gulf by Iran and many other countries and the Arabian Gulf by Arab states and some other countries. Many names in former Palestine—and the use of the name Palestine itself—imply particular biases: West Bank versus Samaria and Judea, Gulf of Aqabah versus Gulf of Elat, al-Quds or Jerusalem versus Yerushalayyem, and others. Jordan's disengagement from the West Bank in July–August 1988 has rendered even the applicability of the term "West Bank" a question mark. Revolutionary Iran changed many place-names because they connoted the Pahlavi royal family: For example, Bandar-e Pahlavi is now Bandar-e Anzali, Rezaiyeh is Urumiyeh (conventional: Urmia), and Bandar-e Shahpur is Bandar-e Khomeyni. We have used the new names that have been publicly announced.

C.C.H.
J.T.C.

PART ONE

PHYSICAL AND CULTURAL GEOGRAPHY

1

Tricontinental Junction

An Introduction

MIDDLE EAST PREVIEW

Located at the tricontinental hub of Europe, Asia, and Africa, the Middle East is unique both historically and geopolitically. It is the cradle of civilization, birthplace of the three great monotheistic religions, crossroads of movement and trade, base of extensive empires, resource area for 56 percent of the world's petroleum, home to more than 350 million people in sixteen countries, source of political and ideological ferment, and locus of intractable and explosive conflicts since World War II. Major developments in the region resonate worldwide, and no country can disregard them.

The Middle East has featured prominently in the news almost daily through more than six decades of warfare: five major Arab-Israeli wars plus several more limited conflicts; the almost uninterrupted cycle of violence involving Arabs and Israelis; internecine fighting in Lebanon in 1958 (ended by landing of U.S. forces) and from 1975 to 1991 (involving U.S. forces on two occasions); Turkey's invasion and partial occupation of Cyprus beginning in 1974; Iraq's war with Iran in the 1980s, its invasion of and consequent expulsion from Kuwait in 1990–1991, the international sanctions imposed on it afterward, and its occupation by the U.S.-led coalition from 2003 onward; U.S. operations

in Afghanistan after September 11, 2001; and civil wars and insurgencies in Yemen in the 1960s, 1994, and the late 2000s. Beyond open fighting, there has been an ongoing Arab-Israeli "Peace Process" dating to Henry Kissinger's "Shuttle Diplomacy" in the mid-1970s, hostage taking in Lebanon in the 1970s and 1980s, the overthrow of the shah and the American Embassy hostage crisis in Tehran in 1979–1980, terrorist attacks in most of the countries in the region, Cold War crises ranging from Iran and Turkey in the 1940s to peripheral Afghanistan in the 1980s, and dozens of other headline-worthy events.

In the past two decades, reporting on the Middle East has become more extensive, even, in many cases, more nuanced. But the media are limited in their ability to offer in-depth, objective analyses of the region's complex underlying patterns of regions, peoples, cultures, politics, and aspirations. More significantly, for various domestic reasons—political, religious, economic, historical, and others—the media frequently fail to balance their coverage with viewpoints across the multiplicity of countries, ethnic and religious groups, economic factors, and regional sources of information. As a result, many Americans have perceived the Muslim Middle East, and particularly the Arab Middle East, in negative terms since the late 1940s, reinforcing prejudices and stereotypes that have roots going as far back as the Crusades. Especially after the attacks of September 11, 2002 ("9/11") on the New York World Trade Center and Pentagon, American antagonisms increased almost exponentially, with little or no distinction made between the violent objectives of extremist groups such as al-Qaida and those of the many peaceful cultural and political elements in the region. While it is still too early for a full appraisal of the thinking and planning behind the U.S. policies that led to the unexpected reactions of the various elements of Iraqi society after the 2003 invasion, it is obvious that future policy-making must be grounded in a much better understanding of the region's ethnic, cultural, religious, and geopolitical complexity. These, in turn, are all grounded in the fundamental geographic and economic factors that are analyzed in this study.

For much of the world, including both industrialized and developing countries, the unfolding of economic and political events is closely tied to the resources found in the Middle East and to the factors that affect the availability and movement of those resources. These factors derive from the histories, traditions, aspirations, value systems, problems of development and change, regional and international linkages, and agendas of the peoples and states of the region. The collapse of the Soviet Union, the consequent realignment of transnational relationships in Eurasia, the events following 9/11, the escalating global demand for hydrocarbon fuels and by-products—all these have led to the Middle East's becoming the geopolitical focus not just of the West but of the rest of the world as well.

In view of the foregoing, it is the aim of this book to examine the natural and cultural patterns of the Middle East and their influence on political and economic developments; to analyze and interpret the more significant national, regional, and global relations; and thus to afford a greater knowledge of and deeper insights into this crucial region.

MAP 1.1 The Middle East as tricontinental hub, centrally located at the heart of the World-Island.

World-Island

Because of its tricontinental location (Map 1.1) and its central position in the "World-Island" (see Chap. 8), the region has historically been a global crossroads, as reflected in the title of the late Professor George B. Cressey's 1960 study of Middle East geography. Despite the multifaceted character that has evolved from its crossroads role, the region is often perceived in highly particularistic terms—of petroleum or terrorism or Islamic resurgence or Israeli security or regime change or other single issues—thus obscuring its breadth and complexity. Short-term, simplistic perceptions are also misleading; for example, they imply that the Middle East has become important only recently or that it is typified by the oil crisis of 1973, or the Iranian Revolution of 1979, or the situation in Iraq after 1991 or 2003, or rich oil shaykhs in desert principalities, or fanatical suicide bombers. In fact, the region blends a diverse geography, rich historical traditions, and complex cultural, national, and religious groupings to produce dynamic patterns that evolve and change over time. The text and illustrations in this book depict some of these complexities and contrasts (Figs. 1.1 and 1.2).

FIGURE 1.1 Barren, wind-rippled dunes in Saudi Arabia's Rub al-Khali (Empty Quarter).

FIGURE 1.2 Village surrounded by green fields of corn (maize) and well-forested slopes in Turkey's Pontic Mountains, an area of moderately heavy precipitation just south of the Black Sea.

One significance of the location of the Middle East derives from its irregular shape. Seas penetrate deeply into the land and alternate with peninsulas and land bridges around the Syrian-Mesopotamian core. The Red, Mediterranean, Black, and Caspian seas, plus the Persian/Arabian Gulf, have facilitated maritime movements of the peoples of the area for more than 5,000 years, provided access to the region, and, conversely, served as natural insulation between regional cultural groups.

Cradle of Civilization

Evidence of the earliest known humans has been found in eastern Africa, and the migration of their descendants to the rest of the world clearly traversed the Middle East. Thus, this region has had human inhabitants for scores of millennia, and it seems to have produced the earliest integrated civilizations, agricultural villages and developed towns, and religious-political systems. Although very old human skeletons and tools have been found in other areas, it is the Middle East that is commonly known as the "cradle of civilization." As will be discussed in Chapter 3, these civilizations evolved in the Fertile Crescent, an arc of fertile land that extends along the Levant and around the Syrian Desert to the Gulf and particularly through the Mesopotamian Basin, the depression occupied by the Tigris and Euphrates rivers (see Map 3.1). From this geographical core, the ideas, techniques, and implements of the Fertile Crescent diffused to other similar environments—westward to the Nile Valley in Egypt, eastward to the Indus Valley in present-day Pakistan, and beyond, mixing with advanced civilizations in those areas.

More than 5,000 years ago, the seminal culture hearth of Mesopotamia produced the earliest known writing, along with high levels of science and mathematics. The Middle East thus became a matrix for later Western and Oriental civilizations. The cultural complex that spread outward from the Mesopotamian core also gave rise to successive confrontations among expanding ancient empires. The high level of civilization achieved by successive empires suggests a capacity for adaptation that is still evident in the region. Several power foci, which will be discussed in Chapter 3, emerged through the centuries and have persisted for more than 4,500 years to the present.

Religious Societies

In addition to clashes among successive empires, the Middle East gave rise to the three major monotheistic religions: Judaism, Christianity, and Islam. Each is rooted in earlier religions, yet each is distinctive and each became global in extent. Their respective origins within the region provide one measure of the cultural richness and unique significance of the Middle East.

Just as Christianity gave rise to a general civilization referred to as Christendom, so Islam engendered the Islamic civilization. The cradle of both the religion of Islam and the corollary culture of Islam, the Middle East remains the heartland of the Islamic culture realm. The original core area of this culture—Mecca and Medina in western Saudi Arabia—is the goal of the annual Muslim *hajj*, or pilgrimage, and is a religious focus for most Muslims, who pray daily facing Mecca.

Islamic civilization is the most pervasive unifying factor in the Middle East, and the correlation between religion and culture, on the one hand, and geographical area and environment, on the other, is a major element in any study of the region. This civilization of the Middle East region served two influential roles during medieval times. During the so-called Dark Ages in Europe, while the Byzantine Empire engaged in political and theological disputes, the Islamic Middle East was translating and interpreting classical writings—literary, philosophical, and scientific—thus preserving the classical heritage, much of which might otherwise have been lost. Also, contemporaneously, the Middle East served as a remarkable commercial crossroads, maintaining contacts with potent East Asian civilizations, partly through Muslim missionaries, and later linking those civilizations with a revived Mediterranean area and Renaissance Europe.

Twenty-First-Century Importance

Aside from the region's historical importance, five contemporary facets dominate global perceptions of the Middle East: unequaled petroleum resources, the ongoing Arab-Israeli conflict and related cycles of violence and war, terrorism, rivalries among leaders and states, and extremism among zealous Muslims, Jews, and Christians. This study will treat each of these five, but introductory mentions of oil and the cycles of warfare are appropriate at this point.

Most of the Middle East's petroleum—some three-fifths of the world's known reserves—is found in a broad depression extending southeastward from near Elazığ, Turkey, along the axis of the Gulf, to the Arabian Sea coast of Oman. Of the 70.5 million barrels of daily global petroleum production in 2009, 21.8 million barrels, or about 31 percent, originated in this region. On the other hand, the oil producers depend heavily upon imports of goods and technical and managerial expertise from industrialized countries. Interdependence has increased as the industrialized countries seek stable energy supplies—as the oil crisis of 2008 demonstrated—and as the oil-producing countries continue to require Western technology for development.

The Arab-Israeli wars in 1948–1949, 1956, 1967, 1973, 1982, and 2006, the first and second intifadahs, and the attack on Hamas in Gaza in 2008–2009 resulted in thousands of casualties and the diversion of billions of dollars needed on all sides for development. The oil boycott in 1973, periodic outbreaks of fighting in the Levant, and nearly continuous international efforts to broker a peace process all attest to the destabilizing effects of the Arab-Israeli conflict. Farther east, the internecine Gulf wars of 1980–1988, 1990–1991, 2003, and after resulted in many more casualties and damage to infrastructure than earlier battles in the Levant.

THE MIDDLE EAST: DEFINITION AND DELIMITATION

Definition

What exactly is the proper designation of the Middle East, and what does the root term mean? Terms used historically have almost all been Eurocentric in origin—"the East," "the Orient," "the Outremer," "the Levant," "the Near East," "the Middle East."[1] All indicate an area across the sea and east of those European countries whose political and economic empires increasingly dominated the world from the fifteenth century on into the mid-twentieth century. During the sixteenth century, Ottoman Empire realms became known as the "Near East" in contrast to the "Far East" of East and Southeast Asia; not until World War II and after was "Near East" generally supplanted by "Middle East." Even so, "Near East" survives in some usages, including the designation of the U.S. Department of State bureau responsible for the general area, the Bureau of Near Eastern Affairs.

Delimitation

Scholars universally accept that the Fertile Crescent is the nucleus of the Middle East, and they widely consider the core region to comprise the general area from Northeast Africa to South Asia. Here we will follow the broad consensus that the region extends from the western border of Egypt to the eastern border of Iran and from the Black Sea to the Arabian Sea (see Map 1.2). Because the peripheral regions of our sixteen-state core affect and interact with the core, this study also includes some consideration of the broader region.

Our core area could well have also embraced states such as Libya and the Sudan on

MAP 1.2 Map delineating Middle East boundaries as defined for this book. The map shows only international boundaries, country names, capital cities, and seas. The radius of the circle is 1,250 mi/2,012 km. Note central location of Baghdad.

the basis of their location and close links to states that have been included. Other states like Afghanistan or even Somalia also have links with our sixteen-state Middle East through ongoing political and military events. Still others like the Central Asian "stans" and the Trans-Caucasus nations with similarly hydrocarbon-dominated economies interact with our core region.

The importance of both the historical and the contemporary interconnections between the Middle East and North Africa demands recognition. From the Atlantic to the Nile, the lands of North Africa have for millennia maintained relations with the Middle East heartland. The ties strengthened profoundly after the seventh-century Muslim conquest of North Africa, and although later European colonialism disturbed the relations, ties have been renewed to varying degrees in recent years.

The western extension is considered to comprise the five North African states of Morocco, Algeria, Tunisia, Libya, and Sudan, all also Arab and Muslim. The area of northwestern Africa is referred to as the Maghrib (or Maghreb, "west"), and, less commonly, the Arab lands east of Libya are termed the Mashriq ("east"). Many scholars and observers maintain that the links between the two areas create an Arab unit, a Greater Middle East, a Middle East/North Africa (MENA) unit. Chapter 8 includes a brief discussion of the "Broader Middle East" concept in a general context.

Despite religious and historical links, North Africa and the Middle East proper have differing historical influences, interests, and agendas. The Mashriq has had more intimate relations with Turks and Persians. Lands west of the Nile have had their own regional influences and, unlike the Mashriq, were subject to direct European colonization in the nineteenth century. Especially since World War II, the Arab states of the Mashriq have increasingly interacted with one another, despite periodic divisive influences. Israel on the west, Iran on the east, and Turkey on the north—all non-Arab—are of greater concern to the Middle East than to North Africa. It is for these reasons that this study focuses on the sixteen-state core Middle East delimited above.

In the following chapters it will be shown that, despite obvious diversity, there is a basic geographic, historic, political, and economic unity across the core region—a unity that lessens in the periphery.

REGIONAL UNITY OF EMPIRES

Interwoven historical-political-geographical developments have, over many centuries, exercised integrating influences on the region. For 4,000 years, up to the end of World War I, the Middle East experienced varying degrees of control by a series of great empires centered in several power cores, or foci, in the region. The empires echo many familiar names: Babylonian, Hittite, Egyptian, Assyrian, Chaldean, Persian, Seleucid, Ptolemaic, Roman, Byzantine, Parthian, Sassanian, Umayyad, Abbasid, and Ottoman. A score of other, smaller empires are less familiar: Aramaean, Phoenician, Sabaean, Nabataean, Fatimid, and others.

Except for the Roman Empire, governed from outside the Middle East, the major empires centered in four focal points of power: Mesopotamia, Asia Minor, the Nile Valley, and the Iranian Plateau, with the Syrian realm a possible fifth. Each of the power foci has functioned two or three times as an imperial power center over the millennia, and at one time or another each major part of the Middle East has controlled most or much of the rest of the region. Conversely, almost every part of the Middle East has been controlled by each of the other major parts. During periods of close political unity, an interchange of ideas, mores, goods, and people among areas added to a unifying cultural identity. These power foci and additional minor cores are a major theme of this book and will be analyzed in both their historical and their geopolitical contexts (see Chaps. 3 and 8).

AIMS AND CONCEPTS: A GLANCE

In recognition of the reciprocal relationships between geography and history, this book integrates historical highlights with a geographical analysis of patterns, particularly cultural patterns, as the title of the work indicates. These cultural patterns are especially influenced by time, so that process becomes an essential element in the several analyses. Biophysical patterns—the patterns of fundamental natural elements—generally change more slowly than cultural ones, but they, too, yield to noteworthy processes. We therefore examine the interaction of people and biophysical phenomena, not only in the context of their spatial relations but also in the context of their historical processes over time.

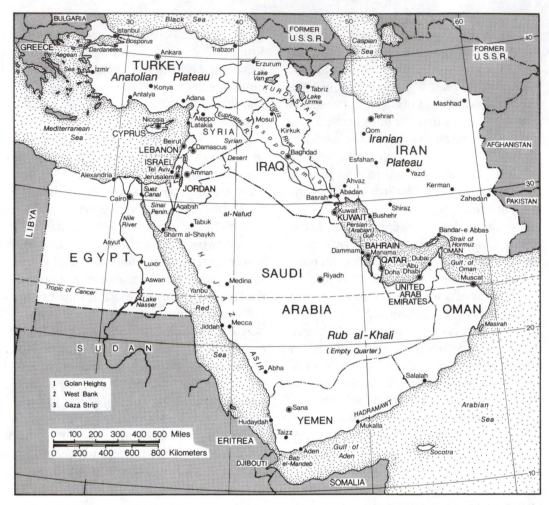

MAP 1.3 Reference map showing most of the names frequently used in this book. Note latitudes and interpenetration of land and water.

Further, geography emphasizes the complementary character of the patterns of human activity and natural elements, revealing the discipline's dual character—cultural and physical. Human or cultural elements include both people (their number, distribution, ethnic types, and other group characteristics, including their sense of identity) and their great variety of works (settlements, agriculture and related facilities, transportation routes and facilities, industries, and other cultural features). Major biophysical or natural elements include landforms, water resources, climate, soils, vegetation, animal life, mineral resources, and economic characteristics.

Following a survey of patterns of the biophysical elements of the Middle East in Chapter 2 from both a systematic and a regional perspective, Chapter 3 reviews the historical foundations. Chapters 4 through 8 examine the area from a broad systematic or topical perspective, examining thematic patterns, both natural and cultural. Chapters 9 through 19 shift perspective and focus on individual countries of the Middle East. In this regional approach, the overall Middle East region is subdivided into meaningful segments (subregions or minor regions) that are examined both as individual units and as interrelated parts of the whole. For the purposes of this book, the main regional unit of analysis is the sovereign nation, or state (Map 1.3). Therefore, this book studies the Middle East not only as a whole, in terms of elements or topics, but also as sixteen states/regions. Within each country, the component "landscapes" or third-order regions (that is, sub-subregions) are identified and numbered on particular country maps. Two summary tables in Chapter 8 suggest some major characteristics of each country in the extended areas of North Africa, the Trans-Caucasus, and Central Asia.

Perceptions of environment vary from one cultural group to another and change over time. For example, to the Bedouin of eastern Saudi Arabia during the early twentieth century, their habitat was a typical desert area in which they, as nomadic pastoralists, could migrate with their flocks in search of pasturage. By contrast, petroleum geologists and engineers after the mid-1930s, concentrating on subsurface features, perceived that same desert as an area of vast potential petroleum resources. This book incorporates such varying environmental perceptions.

In summary, this book is a broadly geographical study of the Middle East that focuses on spatial relations among peoples, human activities, biophysical elements, and economic resources—their overall configuration and also microlevel interactions. In the process, analysis of the region reveals both variations and similarities, and synthesis reveals its unity and diversity, with an overall focus on those factors that produce the remarkable panorama of interacting patterns in the contemporary Middle East.

NOTES

1. French *Outremer* = overseas. *Levant*, from Latin = the rising.

2

The Face of the Earth

AN OVERVIEW

A basic tenet of geography is that physical features on the earth's surface and their related bioclimatic elements reciprocally interact with patterns of population, peoples, and human activities. Although the physical environment should not be said to determine the human condition, it must nevertheless be understood to influence, sometimes powerfully, many aspects of human activities. Such influence can readily be seen to affect Middle East societies' modes of living, urban development, transportation, access to irrigation water, and share of energy resources. Furthermore, each environmental factor interacts with every other factor: Precipitation affects vegetation, elevation affects temperature, type of bedrock affects soils, and so on. We hardly need to be reminded of the impact on human lives of earthquakes, volcanic eruptions, tsunamis, hurricanes, sandstorms, tornadoes, floods, mudslides, and other phenomena that show that the environment is not simply a passive stage on which the human drama is enacted.

A reasonable appreciation of the Middle East physical environment and its influences is essential for an understanding of the regional culture, history, economy, and political development. From such a viewpoint, this chapter focuses on the basic physical environmental aspects of the Middle East—landforms, climate, soils, and natural vegetation. Chapters 3–8—that is, the remainder of Part One—consider history, peoples, and the range of human activities. Major influences of these factors on the peripheral areas of North Africa and Central Asia mentioned in Chapter 1 will be touched upon. Since the related factors of geomorphology (landforms) and climate have the greatest effects on cultural and economic patterns, those two factors are examined first.

FORMS OF THE LANDS

General Patterns

Map 2.1 and Figure 2.1 show that land and sea areas alternate like broad spokes around the Middle East hub, with four land areas forming great promontories into the seas and, conversely, five seas penetrating deeply into the land. In the northwest, Asia Minor, embracing the Anatolian Plateau, serves as a peninsular bridge to southeastern Europe. Tracing the earth patterns on a map, the observer sees that southeastward from eastern Anatolia, the Iranian Plateau extends into Asia proper. Farther clockwise, one sees the massive rectangular Arabian Peninsula, which split from Africa along the axis of the Red Sea, beyond which Egypt occupies the square northeastern corner of the continent

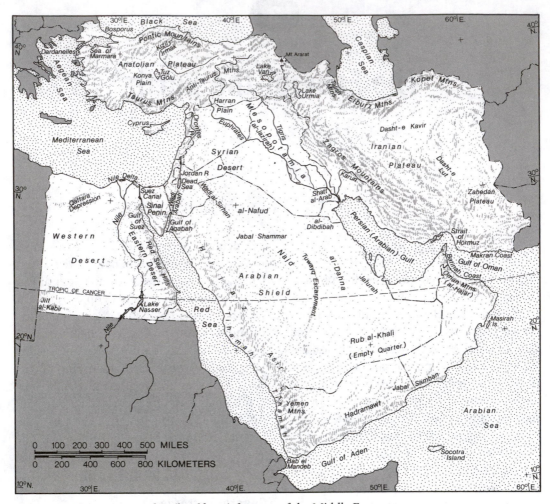

MAP 2.1 Major geomorphic (landform) features of the Middle East.

of Africa. Finally, in the center, the regional hub consists of the Fertile Crescent area, which constitutes the zone between the northern (Anatolian-Iranian) and southern (Egyptian-Arabian) belts of the region.

The largest of the five water bodies reaching into Middle East lands, the deep Mediterranean Sea on the west washes the shores of six of the core Middle East states as well as the four Arab Maghrib countries of North Africa. The Black Sea, to the north of Asia Minor, lies between Turkey and the other five littoral states and overflows to the Mediterranean through the fabled and picturesque straits of the Bosporus and Dardanelles. The

Caspian Sea to the northeast is in fact an inland lake with no outlet to the sea and with its surface well below sea level. The Persian/Arabian Gulf—or usually just "the Gulf"—occupies the drowned, downbuckled tectonic trough between Arabia and Iran. The Red Sea, with its two extensions to the north and the related Gulf of Aden to the south, floods the great rift (linear split) that separates the Arabian Peninsula from Africa (Fig. 2.2) and connects with the Mediterranean through the artificial Suez Canal.

Penetration of seas into the land has several major consequences. Physically, the seas—the Mediterranean especially—intersperse

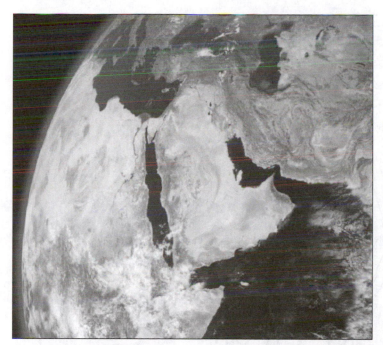

FIGURE 2.1
Image from space of the
Eastern Hemisphere, enlarged
to emphasize the Middle East.
(Photograph courtesy of
National Aeronautics and
Space Administration)

FIGURE 2.2 Image from space looking northeast across the Sinai Peninsula, with the Gulf of Suez on the west (*lower edge of figure*) and the Gulf of Aqabah on the east. The great Levant Rift System extends from lower right to upper left and cradles the Dead Sea and Sea of Galilee. The Suez Canal is left center, and the Mediterranean Sea is in the upper left corner. Dark, rugged, ancient basement rocks are exposed in the southern Sinai and along the eastern coast of the Gulf of Aqabah. (Photograph courtesy of National Aeronautics and Space Administration)

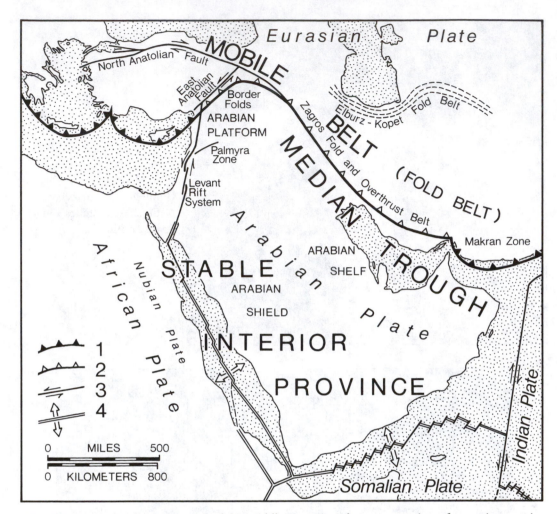

MAP 2.2 Generalized tectonic map of the Middle East. Note the concentration of tectonic zones in eastern Anatolia. *Symbols:* 1 = collision zone involving subduction of sea floor along arcurate plate contacts; 2 = collision zone involving continental overthrusting (western Iran); 3 = horizontal displacement along transform faults (arrows indicate left-lateral or right-lateral); 4 = seafloor spreading, the pulling apart of the ocean's crust.

sources of moisture in areas that would be far more desertic without them. In addition, deep penetration of the seas creates a great deal more coastline, which in turn increases the opportunities for human contacts with the outside world. The seaways provide, as they have for millennia, major routes for trade and movement of peoples.

As elsewhere on earth, major landform provinces and features of the Middle East generally originated because of the tectonic shifting of large segments of the earth's out-ermost crust over millions of years. These crustal segments, or "plates," in the lithosphere[1] jostle one another periodically and in so doing profoundly affect one another's adjacent edges. According to the theory of plate tectonics,[2] at least four, and perhaps six or more, plates have collided or been pulled apart to create the present landform pattern of the Middle East (Map 2.2; see also Fig. 2.1). Typically, contact borders of several plates are marked by major fault zones—in Anatolia and Iran, for example—some of

FIGURE 2.3 Rock-strewn steppe landscape in southwestern Syria—one type of *hamadah*. A thin lava flow has broken down to produce this type of surface. Angularity is typical of weathering in a dry climate area.

which are still active and periodically cause destructive earthquakes. Other pressure contact areas have resulted in compression-folded mountain ranges (the Zagros, for example) or down-folded troughs (the Gulf).

Although most of the gross landforms of the Middle East have evolved directly or indirectly from regional plate movements, smaller and more local forms have been shaped by other factors. Local tectonic movements, erosion by water or wind, and combined wind erosion and deposition are some typical factors. For example, some of the extensive sand deserts of Arabia are reshaped deposits of sand blown in from appreciable distances, sometimes over hundreds of miles.

Elsewhere are broad plains areas of "desert pavement," where the surface is blanketed with a layer of pebbles left behind after finer particles have been blown away by persistent winds. The pebble layer serves as armor for the underlying sand particles so long as the delicate ecological balance is undisturbed. Unfortunately, that equilibrium has been severely upset in extensive Middle East desert areas by modern development and activity, with its wheeled vehicles, construction equipment, bulldozers, and military tanks.

Running water, now relatively limited in the vast arid realms that dominate the region, has profoundly altered some of the desert landforms. Many were shaped by streams that developed in earlier geological ages when rainfall was greater and streams were much larger, with proportionately greater erosive power. Weathering and erosion of rock in arid areas produce a greater angularity and sharpness of outline than is typically found in more humid areas, such as northern Turkey, where the silhouettes are more rounded. Such angularity can be seen on a small scale in many places where thin lava flows have weathered into a rugged cover of sharp boulders, one type of *hamadah* (Fig. 2.3).

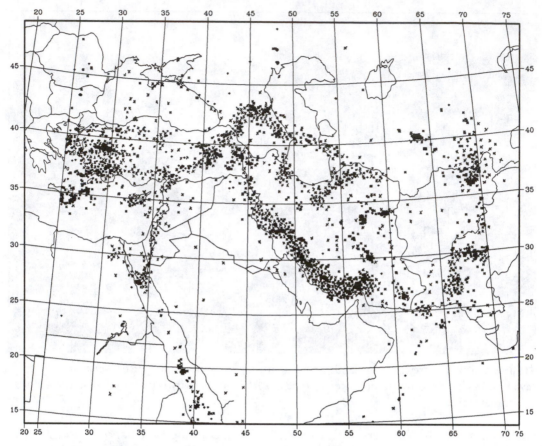

MAP 2.3 Major Middle East earthquakes, 1966–2009 (magnitude of more than 4.5 and depth less than 31 mi/50 km). Note the concentration of seismicity along the Zagros Fold and Overthrust Belt and in western and eastern Anatolian Turkey. Compare with Map 2.2. Boundaries as shown on NEIC compilation. (Updated from USGS Web site on earlier map by special courtesy of National Earthquake Information Center, U.S. Geological Survey)

Usually the result of tectonic plate shifts, significant seismic activity and especially volcanism are widespread in the region. The map of earthquakes (Map 2.3) both indicates zones of actively colliding plates and also illustrates the especially high incidence of seismic events in Anatolia, Iran, and Cyprus. Tectonic plate activity and folding become even more intensive in the junction area of Afghanistan, Iran, and Pakistan, as is clear from space imagery. Colliding plates, separating plates, and some shearing plates generate outpourings of lava either explosively from volcanoes or quietly through vents and fissures. Anatolia has numerous classic volcanic cones, including Mount Ararat, and large areas of southwestern Syria, central Jordan, western Yemen, and especially western Saudi Arabia are buried under extensive lava flows (Fig. 2.4).

Stable Interior Province

On a broad scale, the landform patterns of the Middle East may be grouped into three general structural and landform provinces: the Stable Interior Province, the Mobile Belt, and, intermediate between the two, the Median Trough (see Map 2.2). This threefold division serves as a basis for a survey of major Middle Eastern landforms that will, in turn,

FIGURE 2.4 The extensive volcanic fields of the Western Arabian Shield include al-Wahbah explosion crater (*above center*) and scores of cinder cones, such as the one shown here.

aid in understanding the region's cultural patterns. Maps 2.1 and 2.2 show most of the features mentioned below, but reference to a more detailed map is recommended for the study of this chapter.[3]

Nubian-Arabian Shield. The Stable Interior Province lies in the southwesterly 60 percent of the Middle East proper, its nucleus an extensive area of ancient metamorphic basement rock constituting the Nubian-Arabian Shield. Planed down over millions of years, the shield is primarily a plateau in character but displays many remarkable volcanic features (see Fig. 2.4) as well as scores of faults and mountain ridges along ancient sutures. A prominent uptilt has created mountains on either side of the Red Sea rift.

The shield's ancient basement rocks, most 560–890 million years old or more by radiometric dating, have split open along the Red Sea axis of seafloor spreading and are exposed along both uptilted coasts of this slowly widening rift. After it was well developed, the shield was depressed except to the southwest, and the flanks were covered by thousands of feet of sedimentary rocks, principally limestones. The oldest strata deposited on sea floors more than 500 million years ago, these sedimentaries now outcrop in and underlie the great arc of territory sweeping from northern Egypt through the Fertile Crescent countries and around the eastern and southeastern flanks of the Arabian Peninsula. Some contain huge oil reservoirs.

Arabian Peninsula. In the east, a narrow coastal plain, Tihamah, extends virtually the full length of the Arabian Peninsula's Red Sea coast and is backed by a formidable mountain range. This linear barrier, the Hijaz Mountains, averages 7,000 ft/2,135 m and forms the uptilted western edge of the Arabian

Shield. Back of the Hijaz, the ancient basement rocks of the shield extend in a semicircle, convex eastward, to the heart of the Arabian Peninsula. There, uplift bowed up the shield into the Central Arabian Arch, greatly increasing erosion to cause an eastward retreat of the edge of the older sedimentary cover that formerly blanketed much of western Arabia millions of years ago.

The opening of the Red Sea rift occurred in two stages, the first in the late Oligocene–early Miocene (about 25 million years ago), the second during the Pliocene (about 4–5 million years ago). This rifting and seafloor spreading, plus faulting in the shield, induced extrusion of several extensive flows of basaltic lava—one as large as 7,720 mi²/20,000 km² (see Fig. 2.4). Successive older lava series reach thousands of feet in thickness in the peninsula's southwestern corner and constitute the rugged mountains that give the High Yemen its character (shown in Chaps. 4 and 16).

To the north, northeast, and southeast of central Arabia, the basement is depressed and is buried under layers of sedimentary rock, the Arabian Shelf. These have a vital significance in the world economy, since around and under the Gulf they contain the world's greatest known oil resources.

Sand, wind, aridity, and open space have combined to create three large and several small sand deserts in the Arabian Peninsula. In the south center lies the Rub al-Khali (Empty Quarter), the world's largest single sand dune area (see Fig. 1.1). In the north is the Nafud (or the Great Nafud), one-fifth the size of the Rub al-Khali. Extending in a great arc from the Nafud to the Rub al-Khali through eastern Arabia is a belt of red sand known as the Dahna.

At the southeastern corner of the Arabian Peninsula are the rugged and curious Oman Mountains (or Jabal al-Hajar), with elevations typically around 5,000 ft/1,525 m but peaking at 10,000 ft/3,048 m. They are a product of collision between the Arabian Plate and the Iranian subplate but are a case of the unusual process of obduction (the reverse of subduction). At their northern end, the Oman Mountains culminate in the dramatic Musandam Peninsula, aptly referred to as the Horn of Arabia.[4]

Egyptian Deserts. Between the Red Sea and the Nile Valley, Egypt's Eastern Desert culminates in the Red Sea Hills, a moderately rugged and barren mountain mass of dominantly basement rocks. These ancient crystalline rocks are part of the Nubian Shield, corresponding to the Arabian Shield east of the Red Sea. Unlike the exposed Red Sea Hill rocks, the shield west of the Nile, in the Western Desert, is blanketed with relatively thin sedimentary strata to the south and additional, thicker, younger strata to the north. Along the contact between the two sets of thicknesses of sedimentary cover, depressions cradle five oases, and the profound Qattara Depression in the north descends 436 ft/133 m below sea level. The significance of these depressions is examined in Chapter 17. The Nile River separates the two major deserts, and its great delta lies in a former embayment of the Mediterranean coast.

Central Areas. In the heart of the Middle East, the same general sedimentary sequence found in the eastern Arabian Peninsula overlies the basement rocks in the Fertile Crescent and Syrian Desert areas. However, strata in the central area are more level, and vast expanses of eastern Jordan, eastern and southern Syria, and western Iraq show level to undulating surfaces of Cretaceous limestones.

Jordan Valley and Related Features. A major geomorphic feature of the western Fertile Crescent is the Levant Rift System, a great trench that extends from the northwestern end of the Red Sea up the Gulf of Aqabah and along the axis of the Wadi al-Arabah, Dead Sea, Jordan Valley, and Bekaa of Lebanon to

FIGURE 2.5 The Jordan River meandering across its floodplain (*al-Zor*), flowing sluggishly from upper right (from the Sea of Galilee, just out of the picture) to lower left. The higher terrace level is *al-Ghor*.

the Ghab Depression in northwestern Syria (Fig. 2.5; see also Fig. 2.2). This feature is primarily a transform fault, similar to the San Andreas Fault in California, that resulted chiefly from counterclockwise rotation of the Arabian Plate away from the African Plate.

The system, referred to by various other names—Dead Sea Fault, Jordan–Dead Sea Rift, West Arabian Fault Zone, and others— is a left-lateral fault (showing a leftward shear when viewed across the fault line) that resulted in a total horizontal displacement of 66.5 mi/107 km during two main stages. Thus, the igneous and metamorphic rocks north of Aqabah were formerly adjacent to the center of the east coast of the Sinai Peninsula. The four deeper basins along the fault— the Gulf of Aqabah, Dead Sea, Sea of Galilee, and Huleh Basin—are "pull-apart zones" in which elongated depressions were formed as local grabens. The bottom of the trench is

below sea level from well south of the Dead Sea to north of the Sea of Galilee, with the steadily shrinking Dead Sea the lowest point on the globe (see "Middle East Lakes" section later in this chapter).

The first of the rift system's three main segments comprises the trench and related features extending from the Gulf of Aqabah north to and including the Huleh Basin. A second segment, the most seismically active of the three, begins at the southern border of Lebanon, where the Levant Rift bends to the northeast. This less profound trench with its flat floor of sediments constitutes the Bekaa, a prominent linear depression through eastern Lebanon. In the third segment, beginning at the northern border of Lebanon, the fault zone turns north again and finally disappears just beyond the Ghab Depression in northwestern Syria, the northernmost feature of the system (pictured in Fig. 5.4).

The linear belt between the Mediterranean and the three-segment rift just described is up-warped along a north-south axis for most of its length and is considered by some geologists to be a sliver subplate related to the African Plate. The highlands formed by the upfolded and faulted structures in the belt include, from south to north, the Judean and Samarian hills, the upper Galilee highlands, Mount Lebanon, and the Jabal al-Nusayriyah (sometimes Jabal al-Ansariyah, but officially Jabal al-Sahiliyah). East of the Bekaa are the Anti-Lebanon Mountains, beyond which extend the prominent splayed ridges of the Palmyra Folds, crumpled up and faulted by the counterclockwise rotation of the Arabian Plate.

Mobile Belt

The Mobile Belt (or Fold Belt) is a complex continuous band of folded, faulted, and compressed mountains extending from western to eastern Anatolia and then southeastward across Iran and eastward into the Pamirs and Himalayas. This belt, the middle segment of the vast east-west Alpine-Himalayan mountain system, makes Turkey, northeastern Iraq, and Iran structurally extraordinarily complicated. Some of the folding and complicated structures may be seen in Figure 2.1.

Asia Minor (Anatolia) and Cyprus. South of and generally parallel to the Black Sea coast, the Pontic Mountains (5,000–13,000 ft/1,524–3,962 m) stretch virtually the full length of Turkey. For much of their extent, they lie north of the great North Anatolian Transform Fault (see Map 2.2), the eastern end of a 4,000-mi/6,440-km fault zone that begins at the Mid-Atlantic Rift and transits the northern Maghrib. Periodic slippage along this right-lateral fault produces devastating earthquakes; the most disastrous in the region in recent times occurred south of Istanbul in August 1999 (see Chap. 18).

Rimming the southern side of Asia Minor are the Taurus Mountains (7,000–9,000 ft/

2,135–2,745 m), whose complexity reflects the severity of the compression that formed them. The slightly offset Anti-Taurus Mountains extend eastward to merge with folds that in turn bend southeastward to expand into the Zagros Mountains. The Anti-Taurus generally parallel the East Anatolian Transform Fault, which in turn partially parallels the Southeast Anatolian Suture Zone between the former northern edge of the Arabian Plate and the southeastern edge of the Anatolian subplate (see Map 2.2).

At its southwestern end, the East Anatolian Transform Fault links with both the northern end of the Levant Rift System and the eastern end of the Cyprus Subduction Zone. At its northeastern end, it intersects the North Anatolian Fault. The proximity of these several seismic belts results in frequent and severe earthquakes (see Map 2.3), such as the three catastrophic quakes in the Erzincan area in 1938, 1983, and 1992. South of the suture zone is a complex foreland in which moderate Border Folds merge into the Harran Plain along the Turkish-Syrian boundary.

Located in the junction of these several fault zones, the East Anatolian Accretionary Complex is a jumble of mountains and tilted plateaus (Fig. 2.6), where compression at the junction of plates creates severe seismic movements. Volcanic vents have also opened and are now marked by massive volcanoes (Mount Ararat near the Turkish-Iranian border reaches 16,948 ft/5,166 m), crater lakes, cinder cones, and lava flows. Mineralization along these various plate contacts gives Turkey more nonfuel mineral wealth than any other country in the Middle East, although Iran is similarly wealthy for the same geological reasons. In between this East Anatolian system and the western mountains is the exceedingly complicated central Anatolian intermontane plateau, with its lowest part an almost flat-floored basin occupied by the shallow Tuz Gölü.

FIGURE 2.6 Eastern Anatolian Mountains west of Lake Van—rugged, snow-covered, cloud-shrouded, and geologically very complex. Heavy precipitation makes this mountain area a major hydrographic center spawning such major rivers as the Tigris and Euphrates.

More than 600 mi/965 km to the west, the Aegean coastal zone of extreme western Anatolia is an area of block mountains, alternating uplifted and downdropped masses (horsts and grabens). These structures have produced a series of rugged east-west promontories and deeply indented bays on the Aegean coast, which beckoned Ionian Greeks to settle in the sixth century BCE. In the northwest, a large foundered block flooded to form the Sea of Marmara, which links the Aegean and Black seas through flooded valleys to its southwest and northeast.

About 55 mi/88 km off the Mediterranean coast of Turkey, the island of Cyprus is considered to have been formed as a result of the same plate collision that produced the Taurus range. An exposed granitic intrusion forms the core of the Troodos (6,407 ft/1,953 m),

the highly mineralized mountain mass of southern Cyprus, whereas a linear limestone reef was uplifted to produce the narrow Kyrenia range (3,360 ft/1,025 m), which parallels the northern coast of the island. The depression between the Troodos and Kyrenia highlands is a sediment-filled basin, the Mesaoria, Cyprus's breadbasket.

Iranian Plateau and Ranges. Complex folding in the Mobile Belt extends farther eastward and southeastward from Anatolia into the Iranian mountain and intermontane plateau regions. From the junction of Turkey, Iran, and Iraq to the Arabian Sea, compression and subduction between the Arabian Plate and the Iranian subplate have crumpled, faulted, and thrust-faulted mostly sedimentary rocks along the longest and most

FIGURE 2.7 Denuded pitching anticline in typical structures of the Folded Zagros Mountains of western Iran. In such subsurface folds are found the great petroleum reservoirs of the area. Compare with Figure 8.6, which shows salt domes that also form oil-reservoir structures.

prominent fold belt in the Middle East, the Zagros Mountains (10,000–14,000 ft/3,000–4,300 m) (Fig. 2.7; note caption). In the southern Zagros, scores of salt plugs have been pushed to or near the surface, creating stratigraphic structures that in many instances have entrapped large quantities of petroleum and natural gas. Farther southeast, the Makran range, behind Iran's coast on the Gulf of Oman, is the result of recent uplift of

oceanic crust and exhibits forms that are distinctly different from the Zagros geomorphology and related to the Oman Mountains across the Gulf.

Compressed between the rigid core blocks of Iran and the Russian Platform of the Eurasian Plate, high linear ridges were folded sharply upward all across northern Iran. The Elburz Mountains south of the Caspian Sea and the series of ridges in the Kopet Mountains along the Iran-Turkmenistan border reach elevations of 12,000–15,000 ft/3,660–4,575 m in the Elburz and somewhat less in the Kopet. As in eastern Turkey, plate collision in the Elburz belt squeezed lava out of volcanic vents, with the towering cone of Mount Damavand (18,600 ft/5,669 m) the highest point in the entire Middle East. Scattered volcanoes—including Iran's only recently active vent—appear along the eastern Iranian border near Afghanistan and Pakistan, and complex fold mountains around the Zahedan Plateau enclose the third side of the triangular Iranian Plateau. As in central Anatolia, the lowest part of Iran's inner basin contains ephemeral salt lakes (playas), known in Iran as *kavirs*. Compressional highland chains extend still farther eastward into Central Asia, increasing in complexity and elevations to become the globe's mightiest mountain masses—the Hindu Kush, Tien Shan, and Himalayas, with the Pamir Knot tying them together.

Median Trough

The Mesopotamian-Gulf trough, which is technically the northeastern edge of the Stable Interior Province, lies along the median axis between the Arabian Plate and the Iranian subplate and is one of the most conspicuous geomorphic features of the Middle East. It is also the world's greatest petroleum province, a zone of downbuckling and subsidence on the flanks of the Arabian Shield. The northwestern half of the trough, the Mesopotamian Basin, is above sea level and has two subdivisions: a low plateau northwest of Baghdad and an alluvial-deltaic plain from Baghdad to the Gulf. The southeastern half of the structural trough is drowned by the shallow waters of the Gulf, the sea invading from the Indian Ocean through the Strait of Hormuz. One of the world's most strategic chokepoints, the strait is thus as significant physically as it is economically and strategically. The Gulf and its littorals will be dis-

cussed in detail in various later sections and chapters.

MIDDLE EAST WATERS

Seas and Gulfs

Even after the sea basins of the Middle East reached their approximate present contours, major modifications occurred in response to slight crustal adjustments and climatic variations. Especially during the Pleistocene glacial period, the sea fell to more than 395 ft/120 m below its current level as ice advanced, when millions of cubic meters of ocean water were frozen into sheets. During those same periods of glacial maxima, the Middle East enjoyed pluvial periods, when precipitation increased appreciably. The increased rainfall charged the regional aquifers and induced environmental conditions more favorable for human cultural development during the long Paleolithic period. Eustatic (sea-level) changes during glacial retreats, when the melting of the ice sheets freed water that had been previously locked in the glaciers, brought seas 180–195 ft/55–60 m higher than at present, giving a total differential of more than 590 ft/180 m over the 1.3 million years of the glacial Pleistocene.

The great drop in sea level during glacial maxima left the straits of the region as dry sills between basins—the Strait of Gibraltar, connecting the Mediterranean and the Atlantic; the Bosporus and Dardanelles, connecting the Mediterranean and the Black Sea; and the Strait of Hormuz, connecting the Gulf and the Indian Ocean. With their main water supplies cut off, the basins of the three inland seas became extensive deep desert basins, large-scale versions of today's Death Valley in California. The salt deposited in these basins during periods of evaporation still affects the chemical composition of rocks, water, and soil in the region. As the interglacial thaw induced a rise in sea level, the mounting water crested the formerly dry straits and roared into the empty basins in thunderous cascades, gradually refilling the huge depressions to their former, and approximately present, configurations.

Red Sea and Gulf of Aden. The Red Sea occupies an elongated, escarpment-bounded depression 1,220 mi/1,965 km long and 155–280 mi/250–450 km wide. Tectonically, it is a northward extension of the great African Continental Rift that has its southern origin in Mozambique and in turn extends northward through the Levant Rift to Turkey. As was mentioned earlier, rifting opened the Red Sea in two phases several million years ago, and it is still continuing along the sea's entire length. South of 21° N Lat, a narrow inner axial trough within the sea's main trough is about 6,500 ft/2,000 m deep, formed by seafloor spreading processes during the past 4 million years. North of 25°, the inner axial trough is lacking, and the floor has an irregular, faulted surface. Between the shores and the center axis, a narrow continental shelf extends along both coasts.

Seafloor spreading, especially in the central Red Sea, conveys molten lava into the bottom of the trench. The lava heats the seawater above it and stimulates the formation of hot brines and the development of sludge with high concentrations of zinc, copper, silver, gold, and other metals. Facing each other across these deeps, Saudi Arabia and Sudan formed a Red Sea Commission in 1975 to consider exploitation of the metals. The sludge is not a commercially feasible source at present, but it may well be a major source for the metals in the future.

Rifting along both branches of the Red Sea at the northern end, along the Gulf of Aqabah east of the Sinai Peninsula and the Gulf of Suez west of the peninsula (see Fig. 2.2), is of two different types and ages. With great depths, exceeding 5,900 ft/1,800 m, the Gulf of Aqabah is a pull-apart zone associated with the Levant Rift and is morphologically related to the Dead Sea, the Sea of Galilee, and the Huleh Basin. Much shallower, only about 150 ft/45 m, and a much older structure, the Gulf of Suez split from the Red Sea Hills to the west and subsided over a long period.

At the southern end of the Red Sea, the Gulf of Aden opened by seafloor spreading along a rift at right angles to the Red Sea; it has proceeded further to become an example of a young ocean basin. It exhibits well-defined continental margins, small ocean basins, an oceanic crust floor, an active mid-ocean ridge (Sheba Ridge), and a spreading center characterized by a rift valley and transverse fracture zones. This triple junction of the rifts (see Map 2.2) creates a magnificent laboratory for observing the mechanics and processes of active seafloor spreading, especially in and around Djibouti.

Persian/Arabian Gulf. Lying in a tectonically downfolded basin of Late Pliocene to Pleistocene age, the shallow Gulf (Arabic: *al-Khalij*) is a marginal sea that exhibits striking contrasts with the Red Sea and the Gulf of Aden. It covers approximately 87,000 mi²/226,000 km² and is about 620 mi/1,000 km long and 125–185 mi/201–300 km wide. Although it reaches depths of more than 330 ft/100 m near the Strait of Hormuz, its average depth is only 115 ft/35 m. Since the floor slope and depth are greater on the Iranian side, the basin has a marked bathymetric asymmetry across its axis, reflecting the downfolding between the Arabian Plate and Iranian subplate. Because the Gulf's elongated axis defines this separation between two different geomorphic provinces, the opposite coasts, Arabia to the west and Iran to the east, reflect the contrasting structures. The low surface of the eastern half of the stable Arabian Shelf is a generally level coastal area that slopes gently under the shallow Gulf waters and is fringed with offshore sand islands and sand spits. One such sand spit is Ras Tanura, the location of three large oil installations on the Saudi coast (see Fig. 6.4).

To the east of the anticlinal Qatar Peninsula is a broad, shallow area of the Gulf 33–66 ft/10–20 m deep studded with numerous shoals and salt-dome islands, around which huge petroleum accumulations are exploited. Formerly the world's greatest natural-pearl fishing area, the Great Pearl Bank Barrier extends eastward across this embayment. The concave southern coast of the Gulf is typified by low, evaporitic, supratidal flats (*sabkhahs*), some of which, along the coast of the United Arab Emirates (UAE), are more than 6 mi/10 km wide. On the east, in contrast, the Iranian coast rises steeply and quickly merges with the folded ridges of the Zagros Foreland.

The Gulf varies widely in temperature and salinity because of its considerable supply of fresh water, shallowness, and limited connection with the ocean. In summer, the surface waters are warm and evaporation is high. Even in winter, water temperature is about 68°F/20°C. Salinity varies from 7 percent (twice that of average seawater) in protected Arabian lagoons to less than 3.7 percent near the Strait of Hormuz. The major freshwater influx into the Gulf is the Shatt al-Arab (the combined Tigris and Euphrates rivers), but water also enters from the Karun River in Iran and from short streams descending the western ridges of the Zagros Foreland. Tidal ranges in the western Gulf are moderate, with average maximums of about 8 ft/2.5 m. When the sea level fell during the later Pleistocene glaciation and the Gulf evaporated, the Tigris-Euphrates river system extended eastward, flowed across the dry basin, and emptied into the Arabian Sea through the Strait of Hormuz. About 18,000 years ago, when sea levels again rose from meltwaters from ice sheets warmed by rising temperatures, seawater poured back into the basin, and the present level was reached about 5,000 years ago.

With more than a score of major oil-export terminals in operation in the Gulf virtu-ally around the clock, and with forty to fifty large tankers sailing up or down the Gulf daily, pollution of the waters and beaches has long been a grave concern around the littoral. Despite government monitoring and caveat, and despite appreciable care taken by oil companies and shippers, as many as a quarter of a million barrels of oil pollute the Gulf annually. The rapidly growing population around the littoral discards many tons of waste into the water daily. A major pollution crisis occurred in January 1991, when Iraqi forces retreating from Kuwait engaged in ecoterrorism by dumping several million barrels of crude oil (the amount can only be estimated) into the Gulf off the coast of the amirate. This largest oil spill in history spread south to the Qatar coast within sixty days, killing countless fish, shrimp, crabs, and birds, as well as fouling sea-grass beds and beaches and posing a threat to desalination plant intakes. Although reasonable revival took place in less time than was initially forecast, the crisis was a global wake-up call to the potential catastrophe posed by current oil technology.

Mediterranean Sea. Of complex origin, the Mediterranean is partially a western remnant of the pre-Miocene Tethys Sea and partially a collapsed structure along the collision zone between the African and Eurasian plates. Since its re-creation with the most recent melting of the Pleistocene ice, it has been virtually enclosed (its name means "sea in the middle of the land"), connecting with the global oceans only through the narrow Strait of Gibraltar. An artificial link with the Red Sea opened with construction of the Suez Canal in 1869. The Mediterranean's greatest depth (15,072 ft/4,594 m) is west of Crete, and a basin off the Levant coast is 4,787 ft/1,459 m. Except in the southeast, where Nile sediments are borne seaward and then eastward and northeastward by currents, most Mediterranean coasts descend sharply under the fringing waters. Few ports, therefore, face major dredging problems, unlike virtually all Gulf ports.

The extensive, deep Mediterranean waters exercise profound effects on the climate of much of the Middle East and North Africa, with the elongated basin serving as a conduit for weather-maker low-pressure systems. The sea has carried ships of many nations for thousands of years. Such maritime activity has linked North Africa with Europe and the Levant and has encouraged a variety of interrelations among Mediterranean littoral peoples, producing a "Mediterranean" subrace, diet, agriculture, music, and history. Fishing in this virtually inland sea has supplied a crucial element in the diet of the littoral peoples for millennia.

Black Sea.   Occupying a deeply foundered subplate, the Black Sea (also known as the Euxine Sea, the ancient *Pontus Euxinus*) is relatively shallow near the Danube Delta in the northwest but has depths exceeding 7,000 ft/2,135 m across much of its southern extent. The northern slopes of Turkey's Pontic Mountains plunge steeply into the Black Sea, giving deepwater access to Turkey's many northern ports. Receiving a plentiful freshwater inflow from rivers in the north and several smaller rivers in the south, the Black Sea is only moderately salty. Virtually tideless, it overflows freely through the Bosporus into the Sea of Marmara and thence through the Dardanelles into the Aegean. Commonality of certain interests has led the six Black Sea littoral states to concert their planning and actions—for example, in tackling the increasingly serious problem of the basin's pollution. Pollution and other issues have demanded growing attention since the Black Sea, like the Gulf and the Caspian Sea, has become a major factor in the burgeoning oil industry of the region.

Caspian Sea.   Unlike the other seas, the inland Caspian has no present outlet, and its surface averages about 92 ft/28 m below sea level. The Caspian bottom has two basins divided by a high sill east of the Baku Peninsula. Its floor built up by Volga sediments, the shallower of the basins lies at the northern end and eastern side; the greatest depth is in the southwestern quadrant, 3,363 ft/1,025 m. With most of the fluviatile inflow coming from the Volga at the northern end, the level of the Caspian slowly dropped until the late 1970s as Russia increasingly utilized Volga water for irrigation. The trend reversed in 1977, and by 1995 the Caspian had risen by 8 ft/2.4 m before slowly receding. A railroad ferry crosses from Baku to Türkmenbashy, and other freight and passenger ships utilize the sea; however, most vessels on the Caspian are fishing boats seeking especially the famous Caspian sturgeon, source of the valuable Russian and Iranian caviar.

As in the Persian/Arabian Gulf area, the tectonics of the Caspian Basin created structures favorable for huge accumulations of petroleum and natural gas both around and under the seabed. Indeed, some of the world's earliest major oil production came from the still-active Baku field on the Azerbaijan coast. Prior to 1991, however, the Soviet Union was so negligent in protecting the environment in all its mineral industries that the entire Caspian Basin became frighteningly polluted.[5]

The focus of the very considerable geopolitical significance of the Caspian shifted after 1991 from a bilateral rivalry between the Soviet Union and Iran to more complex multilateral relationships among Russia, Iran, and three former Soviet republics. The three newly independent littorals—Azerbaijan, Kazakhstan, and Turkmenistan—are now major players in the Great Oil Game of the Caspian Basin. One problem has been defining the complicated median lines that specify what areas of the seabed fall to the respective littorals for offshore oil drilling. Increasingly booming after the mid-1990s, the oil industry of the Caspian Basin–Central Asian states is noted in Chapter 6.

Rivers Great and Small

The major river systems in the southwestern and north-central sectors of the Middle East rise in external upstream areas with significant water surpluses because extreme aridity in this region precludes any large-scale, local perennial runoff. Structural conditions in some of the more humid sectors interrupt drainage lines to divert a considerable percentage of the interior runoff into closed basins. In these ways, the major river systems are limited both qualitatively and quantitatively but have played dramatic roles in the long history of the region.

The two largest stream systems in the core Middle East are the Nile in the southwest and the Tigris-Euphrates in the center, with all three rivers crossing deserts for hundreds of miles in their lower reaches but originating in highlands with a water surplus. Along with the Jordan, these most fabled streams in scriptures and ancient history have had renewed roles in current events, particularly in Israel/Palestine, Egypt, and Iraq. In addition, escalating disputes over transboundary waters are among the potentially serious confrontations faced by governments in the region in the twenty-first century (see Chap. 8).[6] The interests of downstream consuming countries (Sudan and Egypt, Syria and Iraq) have long been in competition with those of the better-watered countries controlling the sources of the three major rivers.

In the Middle East, as elsewhere in the world, states face political and economic, as well as geographic, barriers to collaboration over water resources. Upstream Turkey is stronger both militarily and economically than either of the downstream consumers of Euphrates and Tigris waters, although a larger part of the river basin lies in Iraq and Syria, which have historically relied on the rivers for their agricultural production.

Downstream Egypt's investments in hydraulic infrastructure, on the other hand, lead it to demand that the share of the Nile's waters reaching its border is not reduced by the development of hydroelectric and irrigation facilities in the poorer upstream countries of eastern Africa.

Turkey's argument is based on sovereign rights to the water falling on its territory; Egypt's relies on historic productive use. While considerable negotiations stretching over decades have tried to resolve such conflicts, there is not yet an internationally agreed-upon adjudication system for the resolution of these disputes when negotiations fail. The fresh waters of the Nile, Euphrates, and Tigris and the seawaters of the Gulf are shared by many countries that vary in size, strength, and reliance on the waters in question. Negotiations on water use and protection (from contamination and other misuse) fall victim to the same view of water rights as an issue of sovereignty as opposed to interdependence, with the result of increasing transaction costs.

Great streams in peripheral states also have rainy mountain origins: most notably, the Indus in Pakistan, as well as the Syr Darya and Amu Darya in Central Asia, and the Helmand in Afghanistan. In the Arabian Peninsula, not one perennial stream drains any part of the area—compelling confirmation of the stark aridity of this vast realm.

With the major exception of the Nile, virtually all Middle East rivers have a maximum runoff in late spring and a minimum flow in early fall. Most are fed by runoff from snowmelt, which comes later than the actual precipitation maximum, November through February; their minimum flow after the hot, dry summer is supplied primarily by springs and other groundwater discharge. The Nile regime is precisely the reverse, as it floods in late summer and early fall, following the heavy summer monsoon rains in the Ethiopian highlands, and is at its minimum in the spring.

Tigris and Euphrates Rivers. The fabled Tigris (Arabic: Dijlah; Turkish: Dicle) and Euphrates (Arabic: al-Furat; Turkish: Firat) rivers enter the Gulf through a common 100-mi/160-km channel, the Shatt al-Arab, but each is otherwise a separate stream. Both rise in the snowy eastern Anatolian highlands, the hydrographic center of Turkey, with their headwaters only a few miles from each other (see Map 2.1). Additional tributaries augment their flow, but downstream, as they course across the flat desert, they lose water through evaporation and diversion for irrigation purposes. With diminished flow, they lose carrying capacity, drop some of their loads of silt, and continue to build up a common vast deltaic plain, with each channel also building natural levees.[7]

The longer of the two and with the greater drainage basin, the Euphrates begins at the confluence of the Kara and Murat rivers northeast of Malatya in eastern Turkey and ends at its junction with the Tigris at Qurnah, at the head of the Shatt al-Arab. More than 1,700 mi/2,700 km long, it drains a basin of 171,430 mi^2/444,000 km^2. About 28 percent of its basin is in Turkey, 17 percent in Syria, 40 percent in Iraq, and 15 percent in Saudi Arabia. However, more than 90 percent of the actual water flow is from runoff in Turkey. The Balikh and Khabur left-bank tributaries, rising in the Anti-Taurus foothills, join the Euphrates as it flows across Syria, but no tributaries enter it in Iraq. Mean annual flow at Hit, in central Iraq, was formerly 31,820 mn m^3 (million cubic meters) per year; however, damming of the Euphrates at four places in Turkey and at al-Thawrah (formerly Tabaqah) in Syria greatly diminished the river's mean flow after the mid-1990s. The consequent political disputes are considered in Chapter 8.

Although shorter than the Euphrates, the Tigris (1,150 mi/1,850 km) formerly carried an average 42,230 mn m^3 of water per year, 25 percent more than the Euphrates, and

since the Turkish and Syrian diversions of the Euphrates, the difference is even greater. To compensate for the dwindling lower Euphrates, water can be diverted north of Baghdad by the Samarra barrage from the Tigris to the Euphrates by way of Lake Tharthar, a flood-control facility occupying a depression between the two rivers. Other aspects of water management have been enhanced with the completion in late 1992 of Iraq's so-called third river, a 350-mi/563-km canal that extends from Baghdad to Basrah.

Draining an area of more than 43,110 mi^2/111,655 km^2 above Samarra, the Tigris, unlike the Euphrates, receives significant contributions from tributaries in Iraq. Bringing snowmelt and rainwater from the high Zagros in northeastern Iraq, all the tributaries enter along the left bank; they include, from north to south, Great Zab, Little Zab, Udhaym, and Diyala. The Karkheh joins the Tigris at Amarah, upstream from Qurnah. More than the upper Tigris, the lower Tigris is subject to sudden flooding, especially when the Zab rivers flood simultaneously. However, flood-control measures, such as the Tharthar Project, have done much to alleviate the impact of floods. Unlike the Nile, neither river is satisfactory for regular navigation, although the Tigris carried shallow-draft boats in the early 1900s.

The building of the natural Tigris-Euphrates Delta has long been a subject of debate among geomorphologists, particularly regarding how much the head of the Gulf has been depressed by deltaic sediments and when this occurred during the delta's formation. The enormous load of silt carried by the Tigris (about 40 mn m^3 annually past Baghdad), and formerly by the Euphrates (whose silt now largely settles in Turkish and Syrian reservoirs and in flood-control basins between Ramadi and Karbala in Iraq), has built a huge delta beyond Hit on the Euphrates and beyond Samarra on the Tigris. The rivers could logically be expected to continue steady construction of a contemporary common delta; however, building from the east, the much more rapidly advancing combined fan and delta of the Karun River has, in effect, dammed the outlet of the Tigris-Euphrates system into the Gulf. This barrier causes the Tigris-Euphrates streams to slow down and drop their silt load prior to overflowing the barrier.

The silting process created a maze of marshes and channels northwest of Basrah, many of which, after existing for thousands of years, were drained by Saddam Husayn for political reasons (see Chap. 13 for map of drainage and pictures of Marsh Arabs). Thus, the shoreline of the head of the Gulf during Sumerian times, for example, is uncertain. Whereas Ur seems to have been a port during its heyday, 3000 BCE, it may have been a river port, like modern Basrah. Problems regarding delta building and early coastlines at the head of the Gulf merit further investigation.

Nile River. With a length of 4,240 mi/6,825 km, the Nile is the world's longest river. Its drainage basin of 1.15 mn mi^2/2.98 mn km^2 is almost one-tenth the land area of Africa, although the Amazon, Mississippi, and Congo rivers have still larger watersheds. Seen anywhere along its lower course, the Nile, with an average annual flow at Aswan of 83,570 mn m^3 per year, is an amazingly large stream to have traversed the full width of the eastern Sahara. Completion of the Aswan High Dam in 1971 greatly altered the river's millennia-long regime and seasonal rhythm, and today's Nile is quite different from that famed in history.

The Nile's longest tributary, the White Nile, rises in the lake district of East Africa and carries the relatively uniform overflow northward from Lake Victoria. From this lake, whence the river's alternate name of Victoria Nile, the White Nile descends into the Sudd, the world's largest freshwater swamp, in southern Sudan. After dropping its silt load in and being regulated by the Sudd, the river flows northward and crosses progressively more desertic terrain to join the Blue Nile at Khartoum. It is the White Nile that gives the Nile its steady flow.

The Blue Nile is fed by heavy summer monsoon rains on the high Ethiopian Plateau and therefore has a different regime from that of the more uniform White Nile. It was the summer Blue Nile floods that, prior to the two Aswan dams, caused the historically famous annual Nile flood in Egypt, supplying about 80 percent of the river's water. From Khartoum, the Nile flows over a series of five cataracts (a sixth is drowned under Lake Nasser), numbered upstream from the first cataract at Aswan. Still in the Sudan, 200 mi/322 km below the Khartoum confluence, it receives the intermittent Atbara, the river's last tributary. Debouching into the Mediterranean 1,680 mi/2,705 km below the Atbara confluence, the Nile has for thousands of years dropped a great silt load to build up the extensive delta that is an integral part of the country. However, the Aswan High Dam has changed the river regime, and the Nile no longer brings silt to add significantly to its delta. Over the past 150 years, several barrages and major dams have been constructed to regulate the Nile flow, with the climactic structure the Aswan High Dam. Major political problems concerning the Nile are discussed in Chapter 8.

Fold Belt Rivers. Asia Minor and the western Iranian highlands have many perennial streams, only a limited number of which carry sufficient volume to be noteworthy. Clockwise, they include the Büyük Menderes in southwestern Anatolia; Gediz, debouching just north of Izmir; Sakarya, draining the highlands between Ankara and Istanbul and reaching the Black Sea west of Zonguldak; Kızıl, or Kızılırmak (Turkish *ırmak* = river); the ancient Halys, with its basin covering much of north-central Anatolia, making a broad loop before reaching its appreciable delta between Sinop and Samsun; and Yeşil, debouching across its delta east of Samsun. Most of these rivers have been dammed for power generation.

Continuing clockwise, farther east is the Aras, which forms the Turkish-Armenian and Iranian-Azerbaijan borders and empties into the Caspian Sea over the combined Kura-Aras delta south of Baku. In Iran, the Qezel Owzan-Safid drains a considerable area between Tehran and Tabriz and then cuts through a steep-sided gorge in the western Elburz (where it has been dammed) to empty into the southwestern Caspian over an appreciable delta; the Zayandeh, or Zayandeh Rud (Persian *rud* = river), has an importance beyond its physical volume as it irrigates a considerable area around Esfahan before losing itself in a sump southeast of the city; and the Karun carries the largest volume of all Iranian rivers across a huge delta built jointly with its tributary, the Dez, and the nearby Karkheh. In Turkey, the two parallel Ceyhan and Seyhan rivers drain into the northeastern corner of the Mediterranean across the extensive Çukurova (Turkish *ova* = plain), the combined deltaic plain built by the two rivers.

Three Levant Rivers.   Three modest rivers in the Levant have economic and political significance (see Chap. 8) far beyond their physical dimensions. The Jordan River (al-Urdunn) has several headwaters draining southeastern Lebanon, southwestern Syria, and northern Israel; its major tributary, the Yarmuk, enters on the left (east) bank just south of the Sea of Galilee. The Zarqa enters from the plateau south of the Yarmuk. With a low gradient and meandering slowly along the flat rift valley floor, the Jordan has cut through old lakebed deposits laid down in the late Pleistocene pluvial periods, when the ancestral Dead Sea was as much as 655 ft/200 m higher than now (see Fig. 2.5). Increased diversion of the Jor-

dan and its tributary waters for irrigation purposes by Israel and Jordan utilizes most of the river's water, except at flood time, before it reaches the Dead Sea. Thus, both the Jordan River and the Dead Sea are shrinking, leading to serious environmental and economic concerns.

The two other Levant rivers of note, both fed by springs, arise within a few hundred meters of each other near Baalbak in the northern Bekaa of Lebanon and then flow in opposite directions. The Litani, the ancient Leontes, flows southward and below the Qirawn Dam enters a rapidly deepening and colorful gorge before turning sharply westward to the Mediterranean. Its course lies entirely within Lebanon. Israeli water planners have long sought methods by which to divert Litani water into the upper Jordan basin to increase irrigation supplies for Israel. The historic Orontes River (Arabic: Asi) flows northward along the bend in the Levant Rift into Syria and continues through Homs and Hamah, enters the reclaimed Ghab Marshes in a graben at the north end of the rift valley, and after flowing through Antakya (Antioch) in Turkey debouches into the Mediterranean.

Middle East Lakes

Few natural freshwater lakes of any considerable size and significance occur in the Middle East outside the Tigris and Euphrates valleys, where they tend to be shallow and where those in the south are in fact marshes. Large dams constructed on several major rivers during recent decades have impounded impressive freshwater reservoirs that are noted elsewhere. However, five lakes of the Middle East—only one with fresh water—are noteworthy here, and these and others are discussed in more detail in the relevant country chapters.

The two most familiar lakes in the region lie in the Jordan Trench. Although not large, the Sea of Galilee in Israel (also called Lake Tiberias and Lake Kinneret) has both religious-historical significance and crucial contemporary economic and political importance. Covering only 64 mi^2/165 km^2, the lake's surface varies between 685 and 710 ft/209 and 214 m below sea level, and its maximum depth is 138 ft/42 m. The lake occupies one of the enlarged basins in the Levant Rift System (see Fig. 2.2) and, fed mainly by and drained by the Jordan River, is now regulated as the control basin for Israel's national water system. Its generally fresh water is locally briny owing to underwater salt springs, especially near Tiberias on its west coast. Access by Syria to the northeast shore of the lake was an issue of sharp debate in the evolution of the borders of Israel.

Farther south in the Levant Rift lies the Middle East's most famous salt lake, the Dead Sea. The lowest water body on earth, its surface is more than 1,310 ft/400 m below sea level, and its maximum depth is an additional 1,300 ft/396 m lower. Like other inland lakes with no outlet, the Dead Sea has become increasingly saline because of the evaporation from its surface—roughly 96.8 mn ft^3/2.74 mn m^3 per day—and because of the addition of salt from surrounding springs. Its water shows the highest salinity of all the world's water bodies, 35 percent, ten times that of average seawater. As a result, fish cannot survive in the water (hence the name of the lake), and the buoyancy is so great that people cannot sink while swimming in the Dead Sea.

Another result is that dissolved salts are present in such quantities that they are precipitated naturally or in evaporation pans, so that they are "mined" on a large scale in Israel and Jordan. This evaporation and a steadily diminishing inflow of water from the Jordan River in the north—the lake's main supply of fresh water—owing to an increasing use of the river basin's water for irrigation, mean that the lake's surface is steadily dropping. The surface has fallen 75 ft/22.9 m since 1960. One resort on the Israeli side was originally established at the water's edge but by 2008 was a mile from the receding shoreline. At present, the southern basin has shrunk to a small pond, and, essentially separated from the larger and deeper northern basin by the sill extending from the Lisan Peninsula, it is now only a few inches deep.[8]

Numerous large saltwater lakes occupy closed tectonic basins in northwestern Iran and on the Anatolian Plateau. The two largest are Lake Van and Lake Urmia, the two lying on either side of the Turkish-Iranian boundary. Nestled in the rugged eastern Anatolian highlands, Lake Van, whose water is bitter because of several salts, is 82 ft/25 m deep, has a surface elevation of 5,400 ft/1,646 m, and covers 1,434 mi^2/3,714 km^2. Lake Urmia is shallower, not more than 66 ft/20 m deep, and very salty; it expands in size by one-third with the spring runoff to cover 2,317 mi^2/6,000 km^2.

The structurally and topographically complex southwestern part of Anatolia cradles a dozen salt lakes between Denizli on the west and Konya on the east. In northwestern Anatolia, lakes also occupy inland extensions of grabens both east and south of the Sea of Marmara. Tuz Gölü (Turkish: salt lake) is a shallow evaporation pan in the central Anatolian sump that expands and contracts markedly according to seasonal precipitation.

Groundwater

In addition to surface water, underground water is of vital significance in the Middle East and has been for thousands of years. Some groundwater comes to the surface in natural springs—artesian springs (*ayns* in the Arab lands), or contact springs—or emerges from caverns formed in limestone. Other water is tapped by hand-dug wells, familiar from biblical and Quranic accounts, many 50–100 ft/15–30 m deep. Some wells in desert areas, especially those sunk by nomads, may be only a few feet deep, dug into the sand and gravel of a broad wadi or an alluvial fan.

Especially in Iran, but also in other Middle Eastern areas, water in alluvial fans is tapped by a remarkable *qanat* system (also called *foggara, falaj, karez*), underground tunnels with spaced access wells reaching the surface (see Chap. 5). Thus, oases in the desert may be supplied by river water (Nile, Tigris, Euphrates), natural springs (in Egypt's Western Desert and in Saudi Arabia's Hofuf and Qatif oases), or dug wells (many in Iran and Saudi Arabia's Najd).

Rapidly growing populations, greatly increased supplies of capital, and more intense exploitation of the environment in the Middle East focused modern regional and national attention on water resources in general by the 1970s. Vast areas have no dependable surface runoff, but modern hydrogeological studies have discovered that some places have surprisingly large underground water supplies—for example, the great alluvial fans in the UAE. Especially after oil developments, technology has been applied to the search for and exploitation of underground water, with the result that supplies beyond any earlier expectations have been found and are being pumped by electric or internal combustion engines from deep wells. It is now known that much of this water, usually in the deeper aquifers, is nonrenewable fossil water that was accumulated thousands of years ago, especially during the pluvial periods of the Pleistocene. Other aquifers are inexplicably recharged in the short term, even in areas that receive only minimum amounts of precipitation. Modern technology, in the form of ever deeper wells and (subsidized) powerful pumps, permitted such an overuse of these limited water supplies that critical shortages have developed, and without sizable investments in desalination facilities, current living conditions in many countries will become unsustainable within two or three decades.

In the central Arabian Peninsula, outcropping sedimentary strata of the Arabian Shelf contain aquifers that are recharged by the low annual rainfall in Najd and then carry the water at increasing depths underground very slowly eastward toward the Gulf coast. Some of this water emerges in artesian springs in Hofuf, Qatif, and Bahrain, as well as from the Gulf bottom near Bahrain; some is pumped from wells drilled in the recharge area itself. Enormous amounts of fossil water in the Cretaceous Wasia and Biyadh aquifers are being heavily exploited, although recently in decreasing amounts, in central Saudi Arabia. In the Western Desert of Egypt, the widespread Nubian sandstone, which overlies the Nubian Shield, also contains huge amounts of fossil water that is being increasingly exploited. Some of this water emerges in the five oases of the area. Groundwater also plays a vital role in the water supplies of Mount Lebanon, western Jordan, the coastal plain of Israel, and, indeed, every country of the Middle East, as will be discussed in later chapters.

Thus, the significance of the patterns of physical features goes far beyond that of the landforms as such. Great importance attaches to the features' influence on and interaction with other patterns, cultural and biophysical. Topography has always influenced and will always influence where people cultivate their fields, build their settlements, align their transportation routes, construct their ports, fight their battles, and conduct their other activities. Similarly, landforms have interacted with climate, soils, and vegetation to create the infinitely varied natural environment. Above all, the utilization of water has been and is the single most critical aspect of the human experience in the Middle East. Economic and political aspects of the water problem are discussed further in Chapter 8.

Along with geomorphology, climate and its major effects play an important part in Middle East culture and regional developments.

THE SKIES AND THE WINDS: CLIMATE

Climate has as much direct and indirect impact on people and their activities as any geographic factor. It affects the preferred places for human habitation, the clothes people wear, the design of their houses, the vigor of their outdoor labor, the need for energy to cool or heat their homes, where their various crops grow best, and many of their daily activities. In its interaction with other biophysical elements, the climate in a given environment is of pervasive significance. Temperature, precipitation, and winds, for example, influence other natural elements in the landscape—vegetation especially but also soils, landforms, and animal life. In turn, temperature and precipitation types and amounts are influenced by elevation and mountain barriers.

Factors of Middle East Climate

Whereas weather is the sum of day-to-day conditions of the atmosphere, climate is the long-term average of those conditions. Thus, climate may be thought of as "statistical weather." Six basic factors control climates everywhere: latitude, seasonal pressure belts, passing pressure systems, land-water relationships, ocean currents, and landforms.[9] All of these except ocean currents, which are not of major importance in this area, are examined below in their Middle East context.

Latitude. The latitudinal location of a place has two critical direct influences that in turn exercise major indirect influences. First, the latitude determines the angle at which the rays of the sun strike the earth and, thus, basically determines the amount of insolation, or solar radiation, a place receives. Second, as the vertical rays of the sun at noon shift latitudinally with the seasons, belts of atmospheric pressure and winds—and their effects on precipitation—shift accordingly. Located between 13° and 42° N Lat, the Middle East lies in the lower to middle latitudes. For comparison purposes, the lower forty-eight United States lie between 25° and 49° N Lat.

For general discussion purposes, the 35th parallel may be used as a rough dividing line between the more humid northern areas of the Middle East and the more arid southern three-fourths. The Levant coast and other highland areas are, of course, exceptions to this division.

Seasonal Pressure Belts. Atmospheric pressure, whether in a belt or in a cell, influences whether air in a given belt is descending or rising, but far more significantly, pressure in adjacent belts or cells determines the strength, direction, duration, and other characteristics of winds in a given area. In general, two main pressure belts affect Middle East weather conditions.

First, most of the arid southern zone of the Middle East south of the 35th parallel lies much of the year under a subtropical high-pressure belt, a discontinuous east-west zone in which descending dry air heats adiabatically (by compression) and desiccates. The belt itself is marked by calms; however, once the subsiding air reaches the surface, it pours outward both northward and southward. The airflow toward the pole joins the belt of the westerlies, and the flow toward the equator veers counterclockwise to become the northeast trade winds. The dry high pressure and the dry northeast trades produce a desert belt that extends from the Atlantic Ocean eastward across North Africa, including the great Sahara (Arabic *sahra* = desert), then across Arabia and Iran to merge with the interior midlatitude deserts of Central Asia (Fig. 2.8; see also Fig. 2.1).

Second, the more humid areas north of 35°, extending from the Aegean and Mediterranean to northern Iran, are primarily a zone of transition between pressure belts and generally have a typical Mediterranean climate. In this climate type, conditions alternate between hot, dry summers and cool or cold, relatively moist, winters. In summer, this zone lies under dry continental trade winds or descending hot, dry air, a seasonal extension of

FIGURE 2.8 Giant sand dunes in the vast dune field of al-Liwa in southwestern Abu Dhabi, UAE, indicating the extreme desert conditions of the lower Gulf region. Although surficially useless even for nomadic herding, the area has subsurface structures that contain huge petroleum and natural gas reservoirs.

the full desert conditions farther south. In winter, this same zone lies under a belt of stormy westerlies and passing atmospheric depressions that migrates southward during the low-sun season.

An added contrast between winter and summer conditions in the southernmost Middle East results from the seasonal reversal of the great Asian pressure systems and the monsoons (Arabic *mawsim* = seasons). Surface counterclockwise airflow out of the huge Asian high pressure streams northerly over the Middle East in winter ("northeast monsoon"), whereas in summer deflected trade winds flow southwesterly over the Middle East into the deep Asian low ("southwest monsoon"). This seasonal pressure and wind reversal, with the migration of the vertical rays of the sun, involve the corresponding migration of the equatorial low-pressure belt, or doldrums, technically the Intertropical

Convergence Zone (ITCZ). This belt is sometimes referred to as the Near-Equator Trade Wind Convergence, or, more informally, the "monsoon trough," but all the names are indicative of the nature of the belt. Extending across the extreme southern Arabian Peninsula, the ITCZ breeds critical late-spring and early-fall precipitation in Asir and Yemen in the southwestern part of the peninsula and in Dhufar in southern Oman in the southeast. More discussion is given to this phenomenon under the "Precipitation" section below.

Passing Pressure Systems. Passing low-pressure systems—depressions, or "lows"—are the winter weather makers for the northern and central parts of the Middle East. In autumn, as the vertical rays of the sun at noon shift southward, the belt of the stormy westerlies and the mean position of the polar front also shift southward over the northern sector of the region. Within that belt, in response to positioning of the jet stream, cyclonic depressions periodically move from west to east, following several regular tracks across the northern third of the Middle East.

These precipitation producers pass near Cyprus and continue across Lebanon, Syria, and Iraq into Iran, although one track goes north of Asia Minor through the Black Sea. Less frequently, low-pressure systems cross Israel and Jordan and veer southeastward into the Arabian Peninsula. In most of the region, these weather makers bring the winter precipitation that is characteristic of the Mediterranean climate. Similar patterns are found in southern California, Italy, Greece, and elsewhere.

Land-Water Relationships. The land-water patterns in the region are major influences on climatic conditions in the region. Since the sea is the ultimate source of all moisture, the presence of water bodies, especially on the windward side, increases the potential for precipitation and humidity. Because of the high specific heat of water, large bodies of water also moderate the temperature of the air above them, warming onshore winds in winter and cooling them in summer in a heat exchange. This phenomenon influences the coastal rims of all five Middle East seas, but it especially affects the more northern areas, along the Black Sea and Caspian coasts and along the eastern Mediterranean shores.

Landforms. Topography influences every aspect of climate. Highland areas have lower temperatures; mountain barriers intercept winds and wring moisture from them; mountain masses shunt storms to one side or the other; open seas and plains give full play to prevailing winds. Highlands such as the Anatolian Plateau divert passing storms to the north or south, influencing the storm tracks and other climatic elements. Since, in the normal lapse rate, temperature decreases 3.3°F/1.9°C for each 1,000 ft/305 m of elevation, highland areas enjoy temperatures lower than those of adjacent plains. Many favored mountain areas in the Middle East become bustling resort centers during the hot summers.

Highlands may also produce orographic (mountain-induced) precipitation from moisture-laden winds. Mount Lebanon is a classic example: Moist westerly winds from the Mediterranean hit the windward slopes of the north-south mountain range behind Tripoli, Beirut, and Sidon. As they move upslope, they rapidly cool adiabatically at 5.5°F/3.1°C for each 1,000 ft/305 m, reach cloud stage and then dew point as they lose capacity to hold moisture, and precipitate rain at middle elevations and snow on the upper slopes (Fig. 2.9). Similar orographic influences operate on the windward slopes north and south of Mount Lebanon, as well as in the Anatolian, Zagros, Elburz, and Yemen mountains. Areas on the leeward side of mountain chains, by contrast, tend to be drier, or even arid.

Elements of Middle East Climate

The climate factors just reviewed combine to produce various climate characteristics, such as temperature, winds, precipitation, humidity, and evaporation, which in turn produce certain climate types in specific areas: deserts, steppes, and humid temperate zones. Temperature and precipitation patterns are shown in two maps (2.4 and 2.5), and data for those same elements at selected stations are listed in Table 2.1. The table also gives elevation, latitude and longitude, and climate type for each of the stations; the distributional patterns of the climate types are given in Map 2.6.

Temperature. The hallmarks of Middle East climate are without question heat and aridity. Thus, temperature is the premier element in this survey of the regional climate. Markedly high temperatures prevail more than half of the year in most of the lowland areas of the Middle East, especially interior areas or those

FIGURE 2.9 Dahr al-Baydar, a pass in central Mount Lebanon, with its typical heavy winter snow cover. Moist winds blowing off the Mediterranean ascend the steep west-facing slopes and, during January to March, drop several feet of snow at upper elevations. Apple orchards are on the terraces in the foreground. Jabal Baruk is in the distance, with one of the remaining groves of Cedars of Lebanon.

subject to airflow from the interior (Map 2.4A). Although July and August are the hottest months, the period from April through October is warm to hot in most of the region. Afternoon temperatures of 100°F/38°C are registered in the middle Nile Valley and in the interior of Arabia by early March, and such temperatures may continue well into November. Averages of more than 90°F/32°C for the hottest months are common for extensive areas of Iraq (95°F/35°C for July in Baghdad), Iran, and especially the Arabian Peninsula. The cloudless summer skies, typical of desert and Mediterranean climate conditions, add to elevated daytime temperatures.

However, in data for desert stations, the averages mask the extremes of temperature. For example, at Abqaiq, an oil-production center in eastern Saudi Arabia, the mean daily temperature for July and August is a broiling

98°F/37°C—compared, for example, with 91°F/33°C for Yuma, Arizona, in July, one of the highest monthly means in the United States. But even more revealing is the average of Abqaiq's daily *maximum* temperatures (afternoon highs) for July, August, and October— 112°F/44°C, 113°F/45°C, and 114°F/45.5°C, respectively. The station has recorded an absolute maximum of 125°F/52°C in July, and in many years fifteen or twenty consecutive weeks pass during which afternoon highs exceed 100°F/38°C. Baghdad, 600 miles farther north, records average maximum afternoon highs for July of 110°F/43°C, with the absolute July maximum reaching 125°F/52°C.

Before air-conditioning became common in the region, many older homes in the region included an underground room (in Iraq, a *sirdab*) where the family sought relief from the heat. In the hotter areas, especially along

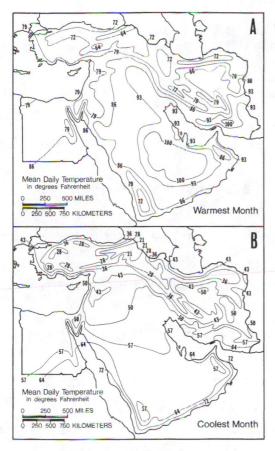

MAP 2.4 Temperatures for warmest and coolest months.

the humid coasts, summer nights bring little respite from the heat of day, either because of a small diurnal range of temperature (difference between day and night), because of high humidity, or both. Many village families and city dwellers slept on the typical flat roof of the home to escape the interior heat, and many still commonly do so in lower-income households. By contrast, at considerable elevations or in open deserts, summer nights can be cool or even chilly (Map 2.4B).

Nevertheless, the temperature of some interior locations is moderated by elevation. Midsummer afternoon readings exceed 100°F/38°C in Damascus, Tehran, and Amman, but at these interior locations and elevations, the heat accumulated during the day radiates back into the cloudless sky and dry air at night, dropping the predawn minimum temperatures to levels 35–40°F/20–22°C below the afternoon maxima. This appreciable diurnal range provides a respite from the enervating, dehydrating heat of the day. Yet the daily means of the warm months mask the extremes and indicate an apparently quite moderate average temperature. Coastal localities generally experience smaller diurnal and seasonal ranges, especially in the eastern Mediterranean.

Several well-endowed mountain areas have become prosperous summer resorts not only for local lowlanders but also for visitors from the Gulf states, Saudi Arabia, and elsewhere. Prominent venues in the mountains behind Beirut and in similar climate areas in the mountains of Syria, Turkey, and Iran offer temperature relief, especially in the evenings. Traditionally, in high summer, key members of the Saudi government move to the city of Taif, at 5,000 ft/1,525 m, in the Hijaz Mountains to escape the furnace heat of Riyadh or the sweltering humidity of Jiddah.

Cities on the Anatolian and Iranian plateaus combine characteristics of dry highland summers, and thus clear nights, with the effects of location at a more northerly latitude. For example, the highest mean at Ankara is 25°F/14°C cooler than that at Dhahran near sea level in Saudi Arabia.

The degree of contrast between summer and winter temperatures depends primarily on latitude, interior location, and elevation. Samsun, on Turkey's northern coast, and Ankara, 115 mi/185 km inland, have the same August mean temperature, but Samsun's January mean is 12°F/7°C higher than Ankara's because of the warming effect of the Black Sea. The uplands of Anatolia and Iran, with higher elevations and more northerly and continental influences, register the coldest winters of the Middle East. These cold conditions are reflected in the data for Erzurum in eastern Anatolia and for Tabriz in northwestern Iran (Table 2.1).

TABLE 2.1 Selected Middle East Temperatures and Precipitation (°C and mm)

CLIMATE STATION			JAN	FEB	MAR	APR	MAY	JNE	JLY	AUG	SPT	OCT	NOV	DEC	ANNUAL
Istanbul, Turkey	40 m		6	6	8	12	17	21	23	23	21	16	11	8	14°C
40°58'N/29°05'E	Csa		94	71	58	43	30	23	18	15	28	54	89	102	625 mm
Izmir, Turkey	25 m		9	9	11	15	20	25	28	27	23	18	14	10	17°C
38°26'N/27°10'E	Csa		141	100	72	43	39	8	3	3	11	41	93	141	695 mm
Ankara, Turkey	894 m		0	1	5	11	16	20	23	23	18	13	7	2	12°C
30°57'N/32°53'E	Csa		37	36	36	37	49	30	14	9	17	24	30	43	362 mm
Rize, Turkey	4 m		7	7	8	11	16	20	22	23	20	16	12	9	14°C
41°02'N/40°30'E	Cfa		259	215	187	97	97	131	150	211	270	299	278	246	2440 mm
Erzurum, Turkey	1863 m		-11	-9	-3	5	10	14	18	18	13	7	0	-7	5°C
39°55'N/41°16'E	Dfb		25	28	35	54	73	54	28	18	25	48	35	22	445 mm
Anzali, Iran	-15 m		8	8	9	13	19	22	26	25	23	18	14	10	16°C
37°28'N/49°28'E	Cfa		133	125	111	75	56	57	45	131	298	326	227	173	1757 mm
Tabriz, Iran	1362 m		-3	-1	5	12	17	22	27	26	22	15	7	1	13°C
38°08'N/46°15'E	BSh		28	28	61	61	46	20	3	5	10	36	25	33	356 mm
Esfahan, Iran	1598 m		4	6	10	16	20	25	28	26	23	16	9	4	16°C
32°37'N/51°40'E	BWh		19	16	18	16	8	1	5	1	0	3	19	20	126 mm
Tehran, Iran	1519 m		2	5	10	17	22	28	31	29	26	19	12	6	17°C
35°37'N/51°40'E	BSh		43	38	38	33	15	3	3	3	3	10	25	30	244 mm
Zahedan, Iran	1370 m		6	12	15	19	23	27	28	26	22	18	12	7	18°C
29°28'N/60°53'E	BWh		30	24	14	16	7	0	0	0	0	0	13	9	113 mm
Nicosia, Cyprus	217 m		11	11	12	17	21	26	28	28	25	21	16	12	19°C
35°09'N/33°17'E	Csa		74	43	37	17	21	9	1	2	7	21	32	75	339 mm
Aleppo, Syria	392 m		6	7	10	16	21	25	28	29	24	19	12	8	17°C
36°11'N/37°13'E	Csa		63	46	36	35	14	4	0	2	0	18	27	74	319 mm
Damascus, Syria	729 m		8	9	12	17	21	25	27	28	24	21	14	9	18°C
33°29'N/36°14'E	Csa		38	33	23	13	5	0	0	0	0	10	25	43	190 mm
Dayr al-Zawr, Sy	203 m		8	10	13	19	24	30	32	32	28	21	14	8	20°C
35°20'N/40°09'E	BSh		35	33	32	20	7	2	0	0	0	3	12	33	177 mm
Beirut, Lebanon	16 m		14	14	15	18	21	24	26	27	26	23	19	16	20°C
33°47'N/35°29'E	Csa		113	80	77	26	10	1	0	0	7	20	78	105	517 mm
Bhamdun, Leb	1130 m		7	7	9	13	17	20	22	22	19	17	13	9	15°C
33°46'N/35°39'E	Csa		302	262	194	95	40	1	1	1	3	54	132	239	1324 mm
Jerusalem, Israel	810 m		9	10	12	16	20	22	23	24	22	20	15	11	17°C
31°47'N/35°13'E	Csa		128	106	85	17	4	0	0	0	1	8	61	76	486 mm

Station	Lat/Long	Elev	Köppen	J	F	M	A	M	J	J	A	S	O	N	D	Year
Elat, Israel	29°33'N/34°57'E	11 m	BWh	16	18	20	24	29	32	34	34	31	27	22	17	25°C
				2	5	5	3	0	0	0	0	0	0	2	9	26 mm
Amman, Jordan	31°57'N/35°57'E	771 m	Csa	8	9	12	16	21	24	26	25	23	21	15	10	18°C
				68	59	44	13	5	0	0	0	0	1	31	48	273 mm
Mosul, Iraq	36°19'N/43°09'E	222 m	Csa	6	9	12	17	24	30	34	33	30	20	13	8	20°C
				70	67	65	55	20	1	0	0	0	7	43	62	390 mm
Baghdad, Iraq	33°20'N/44°24'E	34 m	BWh	10	12	16	22	28	33	35	34	31	25	17	11	23°C
				25	25	29	16	7	0	0	0	0	3	22	26	153 mm
Basrah, Iraq	30°34'N/47°47'E	2 m	BWh	12	14	18	24	29	32	34	33	31	26	19	14	24°C
				26	17	25	22	7	0	0	0	0	1	28	38	164 mm
Kuwait, Kuwait	29°20'N/47°57'E	11 m	BWh	14	16	20	26	31	35	37	37	33	27	21	15	26°C
				15	7	8	11	3	0	0	0	0	0	25	41	110 mm
Hayil, Saudi Arabia	27°31'N/41°44'E	914 m	BWh	12	13	17	20	25	29	31	30	28	23	19	12	22°C
				9	8	6	11	7	0	0	0	0	11	22	3	77 mm
Dhahran, Saudi Ar	26°16'N/50°10'E	25 m	BWh	17	17	22	27	32	35	37	36	34	29	24	18	27°C
				26	15	12	2	3	0	0	0	0	0	4	24	86 mm
Riyadh, Saudi Arab	24°42'N/46°43'E	609 m	BWh	14	17	21	27	32	34	36	36	33	28	22	17	26°C
				13	10	30	30	13	0	0	0	0	0	5	10	111 mm
Jiddah, Saudi Arab	21°30'N/39°12'E	12 m	BWh	23	24	24	27	30	31	32	31	29	29	27	26	28°C
				17	2	13	11	13	1	0	2	0	0	6	12	77 mm
Sharjah, UAE	25°21'N/55°23'E	2 m	BWh	18	18	22	25	28	30	33	34	33	28	24	20	26°C
				34	13	9	18	1	0	0	2	0	0	18	21	116 mm
Muscat, Oman	22°37'N/58°35'E	5 m	BWh	22	22	25	30	34	36	34	32	34	30	26	23	29°C
				28	13	10	10	1	3	1	1	3	1	10	18	99 mm
Aden, Yemen	12°50'N/45°02'E	3 m	BWh	26	26	27	29	31	33	32	32	29	31	26	26	29°C
				7	3	6	0	1	3	7	2	1	1	2	6	39 mm
Sana, Yemen	15°23'N/44°11'E	2350 m	BWh	17	18	20	21	24	24	23	23	24	19	16	16	20°C
				0	4	21	46	20	46	102	20	9	3	0	0	251 mm
Alexandria, Egypt	31°12'N/29°57'E	7 m	BSh	15	15	17	19	20	24	26	26	24	24	21	17	21°C
				44	25	11	3	2	0	0	0	1	7	30	48	172 mm
Cairo, Egypt	30°08'N/31°34'E	74 m	BWh	14	15	18	21	25	28	29	29	28	24	20	16	22°C
				5	5	3	3	0	0	0	0	0	0	3	5	24 mm
Luxor, Egypt	25°40'N/32°42'E	89 m	BWh	14	16	20	25	30	32	32	32	30	27	21	16	25°C
				0	0	0	0	0	0	0	0	0	0	0	0	0 mm

Table includes station latitude and longitude, elevation in meters, and Koeppen classification. See text for explanation of Koeppen symbols. (*Original source: Willy Rudloff, World Climates* [Stuttgart: Wissenschaftliche Verlagsgesellschaft mbH, 1981] [except Bhamdun and Hayil] [with permission]. Twelve stations updated from National Climatic Data Center: www.ncdc.noaa.gov/oa/ncdc.html.)

How the impact of climate change will affect the Middle East is not known exactly, but some predictive models have indicated the drought conditions of recent years may become even more common throughout the eastern Mediterranean. As is true for the world as a whole, more work must be done to discover the definitive trend of temperatures in the region and in the peripheral areas. More discussion of this subject can be found in Chapter 4 ("Patterns: Climate Change").

Precipitation.   The crucial importance of temperature in the Middle East is matched by the significance of precipitation. One clear indication of this is the obvious correlation between the pattern of heavier precipitation, or its runoff, and concentrations of population (compare Map 2.5 and maps of population in Chap. 4). Water plays a vital role even in those regions of the world in which it is plentiful, but its role in the Middle East, where water supplies are marginal in so much of the region, is critical. Water is life.

High seasonal temperatures in much of the region typically accompany low precipitation. Thus, "dryness" is the key word for the climate in most of this region. At the extreme, the interior of the southern half of the Arabian Peninsula, the Rub al-Khali, is probably as dry as any area of comparable size on earth. In some parts of this area, there may be no rainfall for several successive years.

Vast arid areas of the Middle East and of the peripheral areas of the Sahara and Central Asian deserts receive only 1–5 in/25–125 mm of precipitation annually (Map 2.5). This zone of aridity lies too far south to benefit from the west-east passage of rain-bearing depressions in winter and too far north to receive monsoon rain from the ITCZ in summer. The quarter of the Middle East generally north of the 35th parallel is, however, influenced by the westerlies and receives 15–40 in/380–1,015 mm of precipitation. Obviously, a rather sharp contrast exists in rainfall

amounts, and thus in vegetation and agriculture, between the northern one-fourth and the southern half of the region.

Except in the southern Arabian Peninsula and in limited areas in the north, by far most of the Middle East's precipitation falls during the months October–April, which is typical of the Mediterranean climate (cf. Beirut, Jerusalem, and Mosul in Table 2.1), and also characteristic of southern California. Annual totals generally increase with increasing latitude, elevation, and western exposure. The rainfall is concentrated in winter, and the hottest time of the year is dry, with all that implies for people and vegetation, including crops.

The limited precipitation at desert stations varies greatly from year to year, so that the percentage variation can be high because of the meager amounts involved. By its very nature, desert rainfall tends to be sporadic, with long dry spells broken by sudden, brief downpours that are sharply restricted in area. In December 2003, an area southwest of the Dead Sea received its normal total annual rainfall amount in a single one-hour downpour. The sudden rains penetrate quickly into the porous ground in a sand desert area to produce a sudden growth of grass and flowers, which soon attract Bedouin herdsmen with their camels, sheep, or goats. In less absorptive sand areas, and with little vegetation to absorb the rain, the runoff quickly concentrates into the local wadis—dry drainage channels, sometimes so broad and flat that they are hardly perceptible as drainage lines—and causes flash floods.

The mountains in the southwestern corner of Turkey are an example of the orographic influence of west-facing slopes, receiving more than 60 in/1,525 mm of precipitation during the winter. The mountains of northern Lebanon also receive about the same amount, much of it as heavy snows, the basis for several ski resorts, such as the Cedars. Depressions reaching the southeastern corner of the Black Sea rise up mountain slopes and

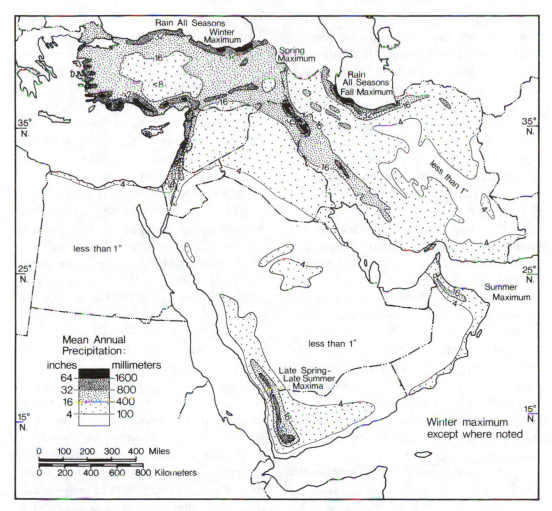

MAP 2.5 Middle East precipitation. Note heavy orographic precipitation on mountains rimming Asia Minor and on other mountain ranges—Elburz, Zagros, Lebanon, Asir, and Oman.

yield more than 90 in/2,285 mm at Rize, probably the highest total precipitation in the Middle East. Inland, 25–40 in/635–1,015 mm of precipitation, much of it as snow, falls on the upper ridges of the Zagros Mountains and the higher slopes of the eastern Anatolian Mountains. The slow melting of the deep snows in the eastern Anatolian hydrographic center during the spring and early summer supplies the runoff for the Tigris and Euphrates rivers and other streams that have their headwaters in these highlands.

Snow falls every winter in the uplands of the Middle East north of about 35° N Lat.

Once or twice in most winters it also falls as far south as the Jerusalem hill country and the Jordanian highlands. After the dry late 1990s, heavy snows blanketed the Levant in successive winters, culminating in 2–3 ft/60–90 cm of snow in Lebanon, Syria, Israel, and Jordan in 2003–2004. The Mesopotamian deserts receive occasional snowfalls, and it has snowed in Riyadh and—in 1987, for the first time in memory or records—even in the Buraymi Oasis on the United Arab Emirates–Oman border.

The seasonal reversal of monsoon winds along the southern fringe of the Arabian

Peninsula gives this limited area a distinctive climate regime, especially regarding precipitation. The rugged Yemen Mountains and their extension into the Asir of Saudi Arabia intercept moisture-laden southwest monsoon winds between April and September, producing 20–40 in/500–1,000 mm of orographic rain on west-facing slopes. Lying equatorward of the Tropic of Cancer (23½° N Lat), the mountains receive monsoon rains in two periods: first, during the migration of the convergence belt northward in late April–early May, and then again during its shift southward in August (see Sana, Table 2.1). Because of this relatively abundant rainfall, the area earned the ancient designation Arabia Felix (Fortunate Arabia). The coastal area of Dhufar in southern Oman also has an unusual regime, with the lingering of the ITCZ during the summer months creating a local cool, cloudy, misty summer that attracts thousands of visitors seeking relief from the heat of the Muscat area and elsewhere. The Oman Mountains similarly receive light rain from these summer conditions.

Winds.   Wind is both a factor and an element in climate. As it transfers large amounts of air from one place to another, wind influences temperature, humidity and precipitation, evaporation, and bodily responses in both people and animals. Higher-velocity winds create or reduce sand dunes by shifting large amounts of sand; also, by using sand and other rock particles as tools, they are major agents in desert erosion. On Middle Eastern waterways, mariners have depended upon the steady winds for centuries. The influence of wind on precipitation is of particular significance. Therefore, it is necessary to examine several aspects of winds in the Middle East, especially their role in influencing precipitation, and to discuss the more significant specific winds.

The ITCZ equatorial low-pressure belt, displaced northward and intensified in its May–August persistence over the Indian subcontinent, controls winds over the entire Middle East for more than four months during the summer. So strong are these southwest monsoon winds that they pull the surface waters away from the south shore of the Arabian Peninsula, causing an upwelling of cool water from the deeps next to the coast and enhancing fishing conditions. Middle East sailors have followed the summer winds eastward to the Indian subcontinent for millennia.

Well to the north of the low-pressure belt, air circulation pulls in the northeast trade winds toward the ITCZ. Blowing on clear, cloudless summer days, these strong northerly winds in the Aegean and the Mediterranean are called *Etesian* (annual) winds by the Greeks and *meltemi* (wind) by the Turks. Useful to sailors when moderate, the *Etesians/meltimi* become hazardous when their velocity is higher.

These prevailing winds continue over the low relief of Egypt as normal northeast trade winds and blow steadily through the Nile Valley for most of the year. They are of great value to Egypt, since they fill the sails of hundreds of riverboats, *faluqas*, as these rugged craft sail upstream against the current. They then furl their sails and drift downstream for the return trip. On the other side of the Arabian Peninsula, blowing down the Mesopotamian trough and the Gulf basin, is the early summer *shamal* (Arabic for "north"). This dry wind blows at 25–30 mph/40–50 kph in June and early July, bringing frequent dust storms from Mesopotamia before moderating to 15–20 mph/25–32 kph in late summer. At higher velocities, the *shamal* poses hazards to small sailing dhows and even to huge oil tankers loading at Gulf terminals. Wind-borne dust is common in all seasons, primarily in the most barren desert areas, which have a minimal vegetative cover to hold the loose surface particles. Seasonal winds, temperatures, and precipitation are often significant factors in military planning

FIGURE 2.10 Persian wind towers (*badgirs*), center, in a historic preservation area of Dubai City, surrounded by modern structures. With air-conditioning now virtually universal in this cheap energy region, only a few preserved *badgirs* remain of the thousands formerly common around the Gulf.

in the region, as in coalition operations in the Gulf in 1991 and 2003.

In various other parts of the Middle East where the strong flow of air during the summer monsoon is especially constant, the wind has many local names. For example, in the eastern Iranian province of Sistan, just west of the seasonal low-pressure center, it is called *bad-e sad-o-bist* (the wind of 120 days). Human ingenuity often puts these prevailing winds to practical use. In southern Iran and along the Gulf coasts, a former architectural feature of many homes was the *badgir*, the so-called Persian wind tower, which uses vertical ducts down four sides of a square tower to direct the air downward into rooms below. These wind towers are disappearing, however, as older homes with *badgirs* are razed for newer structures and as artificial air-conditioning becomes commonplace (Fig. 2.10).

Cool-season conditions are controlled by the southward shift of the belt of the westerlies over the northern Middle East. This belt brings a standard set of meteorological occurrences. As a depression, with its counter-clockwise circulation, approaches the eastern Mediterranean from the west, winds are southerly or southeasterly on the front of the low. Especially in spring and autumn, these winds pull warm or even hot, dry air out of the Sahara into the Mediterranean coastal areas.

Through much of the Mediterranean Basin, the hot, dry wind on the front of a passing low is called a *sirocco*, originally an Italian word derived from the Arabic *sharq* (east). Sirocco-type winds, which are similar to the Santa Anas in California, desiccate the landscape, wither leaves and fruit on trees, render the brush vegetation susceptible to fires, and cause respiratory difficulties for people. As the depression tracks eastward, the winds have local names in the areas through which the system moves: *jibli* (south or southeast) in Libya, *khamsin* (Arabic for "fifty," probably suggesting the average number of days it might blow) in Egypt, *shlur shluq* (southeast) in Lebanon and Syria, *sharqi* in Iraq, *kaws* (the archer) in the Gulf, and *simoon* (poison) in parts of the Gulf area. In the Gulf, strong southwestern winds, known locally as *swahili* (coastal), replace the *kaws*.

When wintertime pressure differentials suck air out of the elevated northern plateaus, wind may begin quite cold but, in descending from the plateaus, warms by compression and raises temperatures rapidly at the foot of the slopes. Such wind is known as a "foehn" in the Alps and as a "chinook" on the eastern slopes of the Rocky Mountains in North America. Strong foehnlike winds known as *raghiehs* blow along the coasts of Turkey and Syria in the northeastern Mediterranean, originating from the plateau north of the Taurus Mountains. *Nashi*, northeasterly winds along the southern coast of Iran, likewise descend from the plateau behind the coast and have a foehn effect.

Humidity.   Three generalizations can be made about humidity in the Middle East. First, generally low humidity characterizes deserts and higher elevations. The low humidity in Egypt has preserved human and animal mummies and delicate inlaid wood for more than 4,000 years. In interior deserts, relative humidity for the three summer months can average between 12 and 18 percent, falling to 5 percent and occasionally even to an extreme 3 percent. Accompanied by high temperatures and brisk winds, as is usual, such low humidity parches the skin, causes nosebleeds, and scorches vegetation.

Second, humidity along the coasts, even in arid areas, tends to be quite high in summer, causing an uncomfortable combination of heat and humidity. Cities on the Levant coast of the Mediterranean, on the Caspian and Red Sea coasts, and all around the Gulf are very humid during August and early September, with average readings of 70–75 percent. One consequence of high coastal humidity: Low predawn temperatures in some areas

produce heavy dew. Along the coast near Tel Aviv, dew falls an average of 200 nights each year, reaching a cumulative total equal to 1.2 in/30 mm of rain.

The third generalization is that humidity is moderate and exercises no remarkable effects in much of Asia Minor. Ankara, Sivas, and Erzurum all have percentages within a moderate range.

Evaporation.   Evaporation plays a key role in determining aridity, but it is difficult to measure precisely, and no universally practiced system has been adopted to record it. If the mean annual water loss exceeds the mean annual precipitation, conditions tend toward aridity. Measurements of evaporation in the central Arabian Peninsula show rates ranging from 35 to 100 times the local mean annual rainfall. Actual evaporation in al-Sulayyil, in the southern Najd, for example, averages 207 in/5,250 mm annually,[10] more than 100 times the mean annual rainfall. Similar conditions exist in southern Egypt—where evaporation from Lake Nasser is a major problem—and southern Iran. However, other influences—season of precipitation, temperature, soil conditions—can be of major importance and can affect the ecology. Other factors being equal, natural vegetation is indicative of aridity and, indirectly, of evaporation.

Climate Regions

The factors and elements of Middle Eastern climates combine to produce specific regional climate types. The widely used classification system for climate types developed by W. Koeppen and R. Geiger can be meaningfully applied to the Middle East, and on this basis regional types may be drawn (Map 2.6).[11] Each of the stations listed in Table 2.1 is assigned its Koeppen climate classification, and it is instructive to see how individual stations (shown on Map 2.6 by letter symbols) fit into the patterns of climate types.

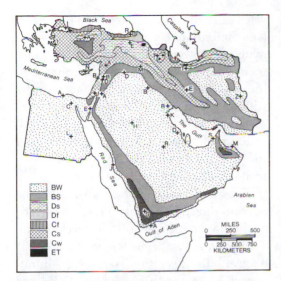

MAP 2.6 Climate types according to modified Koeppen system. BW = desert, BS = steppe. Initials indicate climate stations listed in Table 2.1. See text for explanation of other symbols.

More than 85 percent of the Middle East is dominated by dry or summer-dry climates. In Koeppen's year-round dry (B) climates, evaporation exceeds precipitation; however, degrees of dryness separate B climates into arid (BW) and semiarid or steppe (BS), the latter characteristic of a short grassland vegetation area. Nearly half the Middle East is actual desert, BW; another 18–20 percent is steppe, BS. The division is economically important, since nomadic herding predominates on the dry side of the steppe, whereas barley and even wheat can be grown in most years on the moist side of the steppe. Most of the BW/BS climates are hot in summer and either warm or mild in winter, thus falling into the Koeppen category of BWh or BSh ("h" signifies hot or warm). The dry climates in areas of high elevation fall below the boundary between hot and cold and are therefore BWk or BSk.

Still another third of the region receives sufficient precipitation to balance or outweigh evaporation, although nearly all of it falls during the cool months, November–April. This cool-season precipitation evaporates less than summer moisture and is therefore more effective. These areas of Mediterranean-type climate are designated Cs by Koeppen ("C" indicates a mesothermal, temperate climate; "s" indicates summer dry). The warmer areas of Cs climate are classed as Csa, the cooler areas Csb. The Csa type, the typical Mediterranean climate, is continuous along the shores of the Levant and western and southern Asia Minor. An upland Cs extends along the highland Fertile Crescent, along the Zagros, and into northeastern Iran.

The climate of small areas in Yemen, southern Oman, and the Oman Mountains is similar to the Csa except that the rain comes mostly during the summer monsoon, a condition identified by Koeppen as Cwa ("w" indicates winter dry), a cooler version of the savanna climate. Tundra climate characterizes a few high mountaintops in eastern Anatolia and northern Iran (ET on Map 2.6).

Adding to the complexity of the climates of the Anatolian and Iranian plateaus are four limited areas with conditions unusual for the Middle East. Two each on the southern coasts of the Black Sea and the Caspian receive enough precipitation in summer as well as in winter to be recognized as year-round moist climate areas, Cfa ("f" indicates moist all year). Also unusual are several interior mountain areas in Turkey and Iran with sufficiently cold winters to place them in the Koeppen D category (microthermal, continental climates). This type of climate covers two-thirds of North America, but it is relatively rare in the Middle East.

OTHER ASPECTS OF THE ENVIRONMENT

Soils and Their Ecological Relationships

Elements of the environment exert complex reciprocal effects, and human activities add still other types and degrees of reciprocal influences. These ecological interactions constitute a fundamental dynamic in the geographic system, and it follows that a change in any one element in the ecosystem generates a change in the system as a whole.

A soil is the product of several environmental factors: parent material, climate, vegetation, fauna (especially humans), relief, and time. Comparing this chapter's maps reveals a pattern among the factors that influence the general character of soils in the Middle East. For example, predominant aridity and heat are two of the strongest general influences on the soils of the vast area from Morocco to Pakistan, excluding Asia Minor and the Levant. Limited vegetation cover in this same general area, also largely a consequence of aridity, deprives soils of humus. Extensive rock outcroppings, as well as loose sand, also profoundly affect soil characteristics. Mountain soils are especially influenced by relief, specifically the slope on which they develop. Proper management is important for all soils, and one characteristic that is amenable to management is soil salinity, a serious problem especially in southern Mesopotamia but also in most desert areas where crops are irrigated on poorly drained land.

Large desert areas are totally lacking in true soils—widespread expanses of sand and virtually bare rock are obvious examples. The surface materials in much of the region have not developed a mature soil "profile," a cross section that reveals identifying horizons (the vertical sequence of colors and textures that differentiate soils). Lack of a mature soil profile results from several ecological conditions, including extreme aridity. In arid areas, there is no soil water to move downward and leach chemicals and other materials into the lower horizons of the soil profile.

With little or no organic matter on the surface or in the upper horizon of soils, especially those of desert areas, soils of light color predominate in the region. Light color likewise prevails in soils that have an accumulation of salt near the surface. Around the desert margins, in semiarid and subhumid environments, most of the soils have an ele-

vated calcium content, often from the underlying limestone that is frequently the parent material. However, soil calcium also builds up in moisture-deficient areas because soluble products of weathering accumulate within the upper horizons of the soil to form calcium carbonate and soluble salts. In moderate amounts, both salt and gypsum reduce soil productivity, and in large quantities they render soils unfit for cultivation.

Thus, agriculture in desert areas is limited not only directly by aridity but also indirectly by the effects of aridity on soil development. There are, nevertheless, exceptionally productive soils in certain desert areas—in numerous oases, the Nile Valley and Delta, and the floodplains of the Tigris and Euphrates rivers, for example (Map 2.7). Similarly, such exceptional soils have long been cultivated in the Indus Valley; indeed, the principles of soil patterns reviewed above are generally applicable throughout the broader peripheral areas west and east of the core Middle East.

It is in the coastal plains, plateaus, and rolling lands of the northern and northwestern areas of the Middle East that soils have reached mature development because of humid, temperate conditions. In Asia Minor, western Iran, and the Fertile Crescent, where annual precipitation exceeds 10 in/255 mm and averages perhaps 25 in/635 mm, there are extensive areas of well-developed and productive soils. These regions exhibit greater varieties of soil groups as well as greater variations within the groups.

Middle East Soil Patterns

The systematic classification and nomenclature of soils—soil taxonomy—has presented problems ever since the burgeoning of soil science. Unlike flora, fauna, rocks, and similar landscape elements, soils were often classified and named by different soil scientists according to different characteristics and genetic factors. A general ecological-genetic system developed by the Russians and based

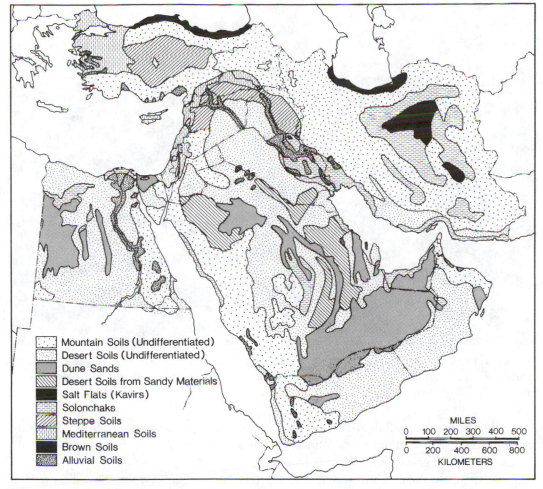

MAP 2.7   Middle East soils. (Adapted from several sources, especially United Nations Educational, Scientific, and Cultural Organization [UNESCO] 1971–1981)

Legend:

- Mountain Soils (Undifferentiated)
- Desert Soils (Undifferentiated)
- Dune Sands
- Desert Soils from Sandy Materials
- Salt Flats (Kavirs)
- Solonchaks
- Steppe Soils
- Mediterranean Soils
- Brown Soils
- Alluvial Soils

MILES
0   100   200   300   400   500

0   200   400   600   800
KILOMETERS

primarily on climate factors was widely used— but also widely debated—for several decades before the 1970s. Of several national systems that have emerged, the "Seventh Approximation," published by the U.S. Department of Agriculture in 1975, has been the most influential. Based on inherent soil characteristics, the classification is highly scientific and precise. However, since its precision introduces technical detail that is confusing to the nonspecialist, the following discussion utilizes a simpler and more familiar taxonomy based on the traditional ecological-genetic concept.

Barren Sands and Rock and Other Non-Soils. Generally speaking, the area of barren land and desert soils in the Middle East lies south of the 35th parallel—that is, southward from the 10-in/250-mm rainfall line (cf. Map 2.5). Approximately half of the area extending from western Egypt across the Arabian Peninsula and the Syrian Desert to eastern Iran is so barren that it lacks either true soil or appreciable vegetation cover on its virtually bare rock or its gravel, loose sand, and dune sand (see Figs. 1.1 and 2.11). Prominent sand areas include western Egypt and, on the Arabian Peninsula, the Great Nafud in the

FIGURE 2.11 Vegetation and soils, eastern Arabia. These *adher* and *rimth* bushes grow on compact, sandy soils southwest of Dhahran. Animal tracks indicate grazing of the vegetation by desert animals.

north and the enormous Rub al-Khali in the south, with the arc of Dahna sands connecting the two. Huge gravel plains lacking true soils extend across the north of the Arabian Peninsula and appear in extensive tracts in the eastern third of the peninsula.

Large areas of Lithosols (rock soils) extend along the east side of the Levant Rift System–Red Sea rift on the basaltic lava outpourings. A particularly common type of landscape in this area is the *hamadah*, typically an extensive plain with barren rock or a surface cover of stones (see Fig. 2.3). Actual soil development is limited, and vegetal cover is generally lacking. Even larger areas of Lithosols extend over the limestones of eastern Syria and Jordan, of Iraq west of the Euphrates, and along the axis of the north-south escarpments in central Arabia shown in Figure 14.2. Soils of the Lithosol group are also intermixed with varied Mountain soils in all the mountainous areas and are

grouped with Undifferentiated Mountain soils on Map 2.7.

True Soils of the Desert.   The other half of the desert areas referred to above contains true soils with developed profiles and vegetation cover: Desert soils, Red Desert soils, Sierozem soils, and Solonchak (salty) soils. All except Solonchaks are grouped as Undifferentiated Desert soils on Map 2.7. Some profiles are weakly developed, and some of the vegetation is thin and scattered, but the landscape is less barren than the desert areas of Egypt, the Nafud, and the Rub al-Khali.

Desert soils are light gray or light brownish gray, low in organic matter, and closely overlie calcareous (calcium-containing) material, typically limestone. They normally support scattered shrubby desert plants but can be quite productive when irrigated. Much the same may be said of the Red Desert soils, although they are reddish, in the upper

FIGURE 2.12 Sabkhat Matti, a typical *sabkhah* (tidal salt flat). With a white crust of silty salt, such flats are inviting to vehicles and aircraft, but using them can be risky, especially after a rain. The soil on the *sabkhah* is a Solonchak, as the salt crust suggests.

part of the profile, as the name suggests, and tend to develop in the hotter parts of the deserts. Sierozems are more widely scattered but are found in two large areas: on the floor of the great central basin of Turkey around Tuz Gölü and in much of northern Syria, where they support scattered short grass and brush as well as desert shrubs.

Solonchak soils are especially found in large interior undrained basins and low-lying areas: the Dasht-e Lut and the even saltier Dasht-e Kavir (Salt Desert) on the Iranian Plateau, the Qattara Depression in north-western Egypt, southern Mesopotamia back from the river floodplains, in the tidal flats (*sabkhahs*) along low coastlines on both sides of the Arabian Peninsula, and over the inland coastal plain of the Gulf (Fig. 2.12; see also Map 2.7). Because of either interior drainage or periodic tides, all these areas have high saltwater tables that supply salty water to the surface; evaporation of this water forms the typical salt crust of Solonchaks. Most Solon-chaks are useless for agriculture, but some

can be made reasonably productive by artifi-cially flushing the salt with fresh water and then applying proper fertilization. One area of special interest suffering seriously from salt accumulation in otherwise irrigable and cultivable soils is southern Iraq.

Alluvial Soils. Alluvial soils—or, more prop-erly, soils on alluvium as a parent material—are among the most intensively cultivated and productive in the world, certainly in the Mid-dle East. Although limited in area, they in-clude the rich soils of the Nile Valley and Delta, floodplains of the Tigris and Euphrates rivers, valleys of west-central Iran, and small scattered oases and larger wadi bottoms of the Arabian Peninsula. They possess young pro-files, are usually of good texture and tillability, and display most of the other characteristics of an ideal agricultural soil. Moreover, water for irrigating the soils is typically nearby.

Soils of the Humid Areas. Except for the ir-rigated alluvial soils, most of the cultivated

FIGURE 2.13 Cultivated Reddish-Chestnut steppe soils in the western Fertile Crescent south of Aleppo, Syria. This is productive wheat country. Archaeological excavations in the foreground are of ancient Ebla.

and agriculturally productive soils of the Middle East are those of Asia Minor, the Fertile Crescent proper, and western Iran. On the inner, less humid side of the curve of the Fertile Crescent, there is an irregular belt of grassland soils that have developed in a zone receiving 6–10 in/150–250 mm of annual precipitation. They belong, in groups of decreasing aridity, to the traditional Reddish-Brown, Chestnut, and Reddish-Chestnut groups (grouped as Steppe soils on Map 2.7; see Fig. 2.13). Such soils vary from well developed and deep to poorly developed and thin on hillsides. Most are calcareous, especially since many overlie the widespread limestones of Jordan, Syria, southeastern Turkey, and Iraq, where they receive sufficient precipitation to permit grain farming without irrigation.

In a major portion of the Mediterranean climate areas, a particular group of soils develops because of the regime of cool, wet winters and hot, dry summers. Usually called Mediterranean soils (as on Map 2.7), they are

of a reddish-brown color, because of their iron content, and are referred to as *terra rossa* (red earth). Especially in early spring, this soil contrasts dramatically with the white limestone hills that surround pockets of the soil in southern Turkey and the Levant. Although badly eroded on limestone slopes in many areas, *terra rossa* has been productive for thousands of years throughout the Mediterranean Basin and is thus more important than is suggested by its limited occurrences.

Rendzina soil is also derived from limestones, usually the softer types, such as marls, and is often associated with *terra rossa*. Usually gray or black, in contrast to the rust of the *terra rossa*, it is calcareous, clayey, and productive. It alternates with *terra rossa* in the uplands inland from the Levant coast from northwestern Syria south to Beer Sheva in Israel (its occurrences are too limited to show on Map 2.7).

Most of the remaining soil pattern is a complex one, forming a mosaic of Noncal-

cic Brown soils, Brown Forest soils, and
Lithosols and other Mountain soils of Anatolia, northwestern Iran, and the mountains
behind the eastern Mediterranean coast.
These soil associations produce a great variety of foods, fodder, and industrial crops,
including timber forests and tree crops of
nuts and fruits, on moderate slopes in the
better climate areas.

Vegetation

As a product of interacting influences on
landscape, the natural vegetation of an area
is often an effective indicator of the general
character of the local ecosystem. Like the region's topography and soils, Middle East
vegetation has undergone natural changes
during recent geological times. Certain
plants are survivals from earlier periods;
other plants from those periods have completely disappeared, from either natural or
human causes, and their former presence is
indicated only by seeds, spores, fruits, or
leaves in old lakebeds or in archaeological
mounds (tells).

Human activities, including agriculture,
have especially altered vegetation as well as
other aspects of the environment in the millennia since the Agricultural Revolution. Unfortunately, the human impact on natural
vegetation in the Middle East has been one of
destruction as well as change. People have
cleared forests not only to gain land for agricultural purposes but also to obtain timber
and fuel. Cedars of Lebanon and other trees
of the Levant supplied timbers for Egyptian
and Phoenician ships, as did trees from Anatolia for ships of the Greeks, Romans, Byzantines, and Ottomans. Wood has also been
used in the Middle East for making charcoal,
long used in heating and cooking and in lime
and pottery kilns. Not only trees but also
grasses, shrubs, and other low vegetation
have been degraded or destroyed because of
human activity and because of overgrazing
by sheep and goats.

Middle East Vegetation Patterns

Varied vegetation types extend from the
dense high forests inland from the Black Sea
and Caspian coasts to the scattered desert
shrub of the Arabian Peninsula and the barren, salty *kavirs* of the interior Iranian
Plateau (Map 2.8). Notwithstanding extensive forests in several northern mountain
areas, the vegetal formations occupying the
greatest expanses of the region are annual
grasses and broadleaf annuals and shrubs of
the steppes and deserts. Rather specialized
scrub forms known as *maquis* and *garigue*,
originally French terms but now more widely
used, are typical of the Mediterranean areas
with their cool, wet winters and hot, rainless
summers (Fig. 2.14).

The phytogeographical (*phyto* = plant)
patterns examined here are primarily the
plant associations, inferred from existing vegetation in noncultivated areas, that would
exist without human interference.[12]

Desert Shrub.   The true desert is the product
of aridity, and its xerophytic (dry plant) vegetation gives the desert its true expression.
This environment supplies plants with favorable warmth and light but then imposes unfavorable moisture conditions. Some plants
tolerate drought, some resist it, and some
avoid it. When water occasionally does become available, plants respond immediately
and profusely.

Areas that are barren of vegetation are
generally coextensive with the areas of barren
sands, rock, and salt surfaces on the soil map
(Map 2.7), as well as with the areas that receive less than 1 in/25 mm of annual rainfall—even so, the Rub al-Khali has areas that
have surprisingly well-developed vegetation.
Deserts that are truly barren of vegetation are
less common than is often supposed, and the
typical desert exhibits at least a scattering of
especially equipped dry bush or shrub (see
Fig. 2.11).

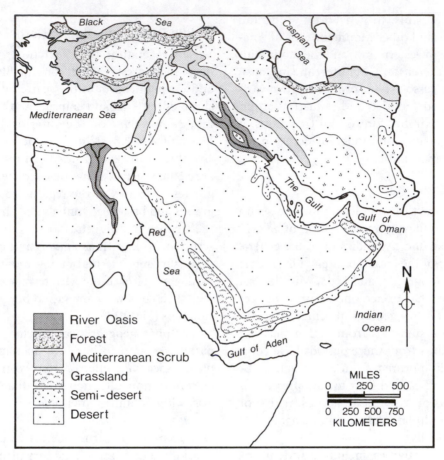

MAP 2.8 Middle East natural vegetation. Both "Grassland" and "Semidesert" may be roughly equivalent to steppe.

Beginning with its small size—3–5 ft/1–1.5 m—and the wide spacing among individual plants to accommodate the limited supply of moisture, xerophytic vegetation has an impressive array of survival devices. With low shoot-to-root ratios, some shrubs have root systems that extend to depths of 30–50 ft/9–15 m. Their leaves are small, are often coated against excess transpiration (moisture loss), and in some species curl or even drop during unusually dry periods. Tough stems resist drought, and the shrubs often have thorns for protection against grazing animals. Some of the lower bushes, 6–18 in/15–46 cm high, have woody or wiry stems and tiny leaves but a deep root system. By con-

trast, other desert plants, such as *Euphorbia*, store water in expandable succulent parts.

Scattered among the perennial and often long-lived shrubby plants are other low vegetal forms (4–12 in/10–30 cm) that sometimes constitute more than two-thirds of the typical desert plant community, including some species of grasses and many herbaceous forms. Some of these small plants are perennial, some are annual, and a few are both, depending upon their ecology. Most of the herbaceous annuals have an ephemeral life cycle of six to ten weeks, after which they lie dormant as seeds that burst into sprouts with the next rain, sometimes several years later. Along with a few of the xeromorphic peren-

FIGURE 2.14 Typical Mediterranean flora on south-facing slopes of the Taurus Mountains of southern Turkey. Growing in limestone-derived soil in this summer-dry climate, the taller vegetative association is maquis; the lower is garigue. The road at lower left fringes the Mediterranean shore.

nial shrubs, they "avoid" the dry season instead of trying to endure it.

Shrubs in extensive fields of eolian (wind-blown) sand may be passive sand dwellers or sand binders; the latter hold the sand around extensive root systems and thus build prominent phytogenic (plant-created) mounds or hillocks. The resulting landscape, usually called *dikakah* or *marbakh* in Arabia, makes cross-country travel difficult. Some salty soils support halophytic (salt plant) vegetation. Over much of the eastern Arabian Peninsula, a common saltbush popularly called *rimth*— useful for fodder and dietary salt for camels and other animals—is usually associated with at least slightly salty groundwater in poorly drained areas (see Fig. 2.11). However, on the true *sabkhahs* along the eastern Arabian Peninsula coast and on the *kavirs* of interior Iran, with their salt crust and briny

subsurface, not even the most salt-tolerant plants can survive (see Fig. 2.12).[13]

The acacia, one of the largest desert shrubs, grades into a modest tree—up to 20 ft/6 m— in moister soils. With its characteristic umbrella crown, it is a prominent and readily identifiable vegetative form in the silts, sands, and gravels in drainage channels or sheets from the central to the southern Arabian Peninsula. Often where no other shade is available from the broiling sun, the acacia offers welcome relief to animals and people.

Grasslands (Steppes). Like most other boundaries in nature, the change from desert to grassland is actually a zone of transition, and the division between the two is difficult to delineate. As moisture increases away from the desert, the more xerophytic species increasingly yield to plants adapted to the greater precipitation and better-developed soils. More important, plant population density increases until the grasses form a virtually continuous vegetal cover.

The steppes constitute a discontinuous belt extending from the Sinai Peninsula northward through western Jordan and Syria, across southeastern Turkey and northern Syria, in an arc around northern Iraq, and along the Zagros piedmont. Some of the region's most extensive steppes are in central Anatolia and smaller areas in scattered locations in west-central Iran. (Steppe and semidesert are much the same in many areas.) With their short-grass vegetation, the steppe lands are thus the core of the Fertile Crescent, with all that fact implies historically and agriculturally.

Mediterranean Zone.   Whereas desert and steppe plants are especially equipped to survive a drought that lasts even many years, Mediterranean floras survive the characteristic summer drought of two to six months and then take advantage of the winter rain. The typical denser flora appears as a low evergreen forest with scattered small trees and more closely spaced bushes and scrub. The height of the plants and the density of their growth increase from the dry side (approximately along the 15-in/380-mm isohyet) to the more humid part of the habitat, where the summer drought is also shorter (see Fig. 2.14). On the dry side, the vegetation zone is similar to the wooded steppe. On the humid side, the zone grades into the full forest of the highlands across the northern sector of the Middle East.

In between is the typical Mediterranean flora, which may be divided into two main groups: garigue, the lower and more degraded of the flora, and maquis, the taller and better-developed association. Some plant geographers also distinguish a third category of Mediterranean vegetation, *batha*, a kind of subgarigue. Both maquis and garigue are found in climate areas across southern Europe and elsewhere. In southern California, for example, similar vegetation is called "chaparral."

Garigue includes primarily a sclerophyllous (hard-leafed) scrub about 3 ft/1 m in height and also smaller shrubs, grass, and, in spring, many colorful flowers—anemone, ranunculus, crocus, iris, and others. Commonly found on steeper, uncultivated hillsides in the Levant and in western and southern Asia Minor, garigue is a last safeguard against soil erosion. Maquis, which is typical of more favorable habitats than is garigue, forms a woodland dominated by low sclerophyllous evergreen trees and shrubs up to about 12 ft/3.7 m in height. In better maquis stands are trees—oaks, pistachios, and pines, especially the widespread Aleppo pine. Culinary herbs, such as thyme, marjoram, and laurel, and flowering bushes, such as oleanders, are associated with both garigue and maquis.

Forests.   Few areas in the Middle East now have woodlands as well developed as those in Europe and North America, but historical evidence indicates that 2,500–3,000 years ago, forests clothed slopes that are now almost bare or are ragged—forests such as the Cedars of Lebanon or the forests of Asia Minor. Current reforestation and afforestation programs in several Middle East states are demonstrating that many previously treeless habitats can, given proper care, produce impressive forests of selected species. The United Arab Emirates, especially Abu Dhabi, is even growing small forests in the desert.

The most extensive high forests extend along the Pontic Mountains from Istanbul eastward to the Iranian border and include impressive stands of beech, mixed with areas of spruce (especially *Picea orientalis*) in the east. On the southern, inner slopes of the Pontic Mountains, and especially in the western highlands, there are extensive areas of oak

FIGURE 2.15 Mediterranean forests in the Troodos Mountains of Cyprus: Wild pine (*Pinus brutia*) and Troodos pine (*P. nigra*) clothe the upper slopes (*foreground*), with a mixed maquis and garigue scrub forest on the slopes in the distance. Summer homes are scattered in the fragrant pine forests.

and pine (*Pinus nigra* and *P. silvestris* in the north and *P. brutia* in the west). *P. nigra* and *P. brutia* dominate the Taurus Mountain forests across southern Anatolia, and oaks predominate in the southeastern mountains west and south of Lake Van.

The great Euxinian Forest of northern Anatolia extends, with some discontinuity, into northern Iran to link up with the Hyrcanian or Caspian Forest in the Elburz Mountains. This humid forest facing the Caspian Sea is almost tropical in its luxuriance, with a rich variety of undergrowth as well as tall trees: linden, ash, oak, beech, elm, hornbeam, walnut, maple, and evergreens. Beech, dominant on the lower open slopes, is gradually replaced higher up, so that at 6,000–8,000 ft/1,830–2,440 m one finds the most magnificent trees in the Middle East—primarily oaks (*Quercus macranthera* and

others) but also elm, ash, hornbeam, and maple.

In the higher elevations of the Zagros chains there is a somewhat dry, deciduous forest in which oaks dominate. With smaller and more widely spaced trees, and with a limited number of species, this Zagrosian Forest differs appreciably from the humid Euxinian and Hyrcanian forests.

In the west, scattered woodlands survive in areas of former extensive forests in the Levant highlands—in Israel, Jordan, Lebanon, and Syria—and on the island of Cyprus (Fig. 2.15). Most of these forests are either small remnants of great expanses of trees in the past, the Cedars of Lebanon, for example, or woodlands planted in recent decades through government programs of reforestation or afforestation. Israel has pursued an especially vigorous program of forestry, including encouraging tourists to purchase and plant seedlings.

The endemic Aleppo pine, *P. halepensis*, is the tree most frequently planted in the regional forestry programs. Sometimes called the "umbrella pine," it has come to be identified with the Levant highlands. Efforts to regenerate forests of Cedars of Lebanon (*Cedrus libani*) have encountered many problems, especially slow growth. The broad-leaved tree most often used in plantation programs is a rapidly growing oak, *Q. ithaburensis*. In drier areas, the pistachio serves well in planted woodlands; in still more arid areas, the tamarisk is utilized. *Tamarix aphylla* is used in group plantings and *T. gallica* as windbreaks.

Animal Life

Historical Changes.　The varied Middle East environments support a rich variety of fauna. Iran alone has approximately the same number of species of mammals as all of Europe west of the pre-1991 Soviet border. Unfortunately, to judge by biblical and other early writings, many larger species have become extinct in the Middle East. Still others have been reduced to a fraction of their former count, are nearing extinction, or now occupy only a remnant of their original range.

Appreciably different environmental conditions in the Middle East during the Tertiary period and the Pleistocene epoch supported animal groups unlike those of modern times. For example, although the ancestor of *Bos taurus*, wild and domesticated cattle, came from the Taurus Mountains of southern Anatolia, there is fossil evidence of *Bos* in the Rub al-Khali during pre-Pleistocene times. Some gazelle were numerous in the steppes and more vegetated deserts, and several species of deer grazed the wooded steppe and open forests. Wild sheep and goats kept to the heights. Lions, tigers, leopards, cheetahs, and other felines were formerly common in parts of the Fertile Crescent and Iran, and other carnivores, such as the wolf, fox, jackal, and hyena, roamed much of the same area.

All of these larger mammals have been decimated by nature and people, and the lion and tiger have virtually disappeared from the region. The crocodile disappeared about 1900, the ostrich in the early 1930s. The ruggedness of the north and the aridity of the south have given refuge to individual survivors and to small groups of gazelle, deer, mountain sheep and goats (including ibex), wild boar, and similar mammals, along with an occasional leopard, wolf, jackal, hyena, or fox. A considerable baboon population is found in the woodlands of Asir in southwestern Arabia. Hundreds of hamadryas baboons scurry through the brush among the granite knobs of the national park along the escarpment west of Abha; they are heedless of park visitors but nimbly steal any food left unattended.

The gazelle population of the Syrian and Arabian deserts has declined precipitously, primarily as a result of hunting with rifles from vehicles. As endangered species, gazelle and oryx (a type of antelope) are now protected. In small numbers, oryx can survive in the arid Rub al-Khali, mainly because they require no water except moisture from the leaves they eat, particularly from early-morning dew. During the 1990s, some governments in the eastern Arabian Peninsula initiated programs for the preservation, scientific breeding, and restoration of the gazelle and oryx populations. By 2004, the programs showed notable success; the Arabian oryx facility in Oman has been declared a World Heritage Site.

The numerous domesticated animals of the Middle East—including sheep, camels, goats, donkeys, and cattle—are of great economic significance and are discussed with land use in Chapter 5.

Some Common Types.　The smaller mammals are much more numerous than the larger animals in both species and population and include hare, squirrel, hedgehog, honey badger, mongoose, and many species of rodents (jerboa, gerbil, hamster, field mouse, sand rat). The many species of reptiles include few harmful types, but there are a few vipers, cobras, and adders.

Lizards, represented by dozens of species, are common in all parts of the Middle East. One common lizard of the Arabian Desert is the burrowing *dabb*, or spiney-tailed lizard, a heavy-bodied herbivorous species that grows to 18–20 in/45–50 cm and is eaten by the Bedouin. The longer but slimmer *waral*, or desert monitor, is carnivorous and more aggressive; unlike the *dabb*, it is not considered edible. The small *tuhayhi*, an agamid lizard, seeks protection by vibrating its body and sinking into loose sand. The sand-swimming skink and other lizards also use submergence in sand as a temperature-regulating device, since lizards—and many other animals— must maintain body temperature within a fairly narrow range. Stinging scorpions are especially numerous in the more arid areas. Since they are nocturnal, they can generally be avoided by the exercise of reasonable care.

Birds. The Middle East has traditionally been rich in bird life and is estimated to have at least 500 species. During spring and fall, the great eastern Mediterranean flyway is used by many flocks of migrating birds. The narrowness of the corridor affords an exceptional opportunity for bird observation but also adds to the vulnerability of the migrating birds to hunters. Marshes along the many coasts attract thousands of waterfowl, and many game birds are present, although now in reduced numbers. Among the common birds of prey are falcons, traditionally used by the Bedouin for hunting. This sport has become increasingly popular in the Arabian Peninsula and the drier areas of the Fertile Crescent. Field birds are especially numerous along the Nile Valley, and cotes for pigeons and doves are a common sight around vil-lages. Doves, which are rarely hunted, are seen everywhere outside the cities in Israel. A variety of songbirds frequent the forests of the Pontic Mountains of northern Turkey and the Elburz in Iran, and birds are often referred to in Persian literature.

Insects. Some insects in the region are major pests and dangers to health. Malaria-spreading mosquitoes remain a serious problem despite intensive pesticide programs. Flies (*Diptera*) are not only a widespread nuisance but also a serious health threat, since they spread eye diseases as well as gastrointestinal disorders. Incredibly, passengers in a vehicle traveling the open desert far from any settlement who stop for a picnic will almost immediately find themselves besieged by clouds of persistent flies. There were formerly plagues of locusts, sometimes catastrophic, but concerted action has reduced the locust danger to a minimum; however, in 2003– 2004, locusts swarmed in Northwest Africa, and small swarms descended on Cyprus, Lebanon, and Israel.

Having surveyed the major aspects of the natural environment, this study turns next to the other side of the coin to examine human patterns.

NOTES

1. Technical terms not explained in the text are defined in the Glossary. See also the simplified geological time chart at the end of the book.

2. The theory of plate tectonics has been a major focus of earth science since the late 1950s. Simplified presentations are given in most leading atlases, and evolving aspects are discussed periodically in many journals, such as *Scientific American*. See National Geographic Society 1983, 2004. No single work in English covers the geomorphology of the Middle East and the peripheral areas, but see Brown and Coleman 1972; U.S. Geological Survey 1966–1967, 1975, and 1989; R. Said 1962; and the very technical Dixon and Robertson 1984. Vita-Finzi 1986 is scientific yet readable and uses many examples and illustrations from the Middle East and North Africa.

3. Two or three National Geographic Society maps are very useful, especially "Heart of the Middle East" (2002), with an excellent space-landscape image map on the reverse. Also useful is "Afghanistan, Pakistan, and the Middle East" (2003). Any good atlas would also be helpful.

4. The term "Horn of Arabia" was used for the first time of which I am aware by Erhard F. Gabriel in Gabriel 1988, 233.

5. See Cullen 1999, which includes a very useful National Geographic map supplement.

6. World Bank 2009.

7. Both rivers are examined in detail in Kolars and Mitchell 1991. See also Rogers and Lydon 1994 (which has a good bibliography); Ventner 1998; Soffer 1999; and Biswas et al. 1997.

8. Kreiger 1988 is a readable account of several aspects of the Dead Sea and includes a useful bibliography.

9. Factors and elements of Middle East climate are examined in Taha et al. 1981 and Rudloff 1981. Interesting data are in the Arabian American Oil Company n.d. (ca. 1978), which is, unfortunately, hard to find. Detailed data for individual major regional stations are available from the National Climatic Data Center Web site, http://ncdc.noaa .gov/oa/climate/afghan/, with factors discussed in the respective country narratives. Additional climate maps and diagrams may be found in most good world atlases.

10. Mandaville 1990, quoting data from Saudi Arabia's Ministry of Agriculture and Water.

11. Several sources describe the system, including the readily available *Goode's World Atlas* (2005).

12. See Zohary 1962 and his many other studies. Hills 1966 has general coverage of vegetation in arid lands. The interrelationships between plants and soils are also examined in Hills. Two sheets of UNESCO's "Soil Map of the World" cover the Middle East: VII-1 and V-2. A major recent contribution to the study of the flora of eastern Arabia is Mandaville 1990.

13. Mandaville 1990, 16; Schulz and Whitney 1986; and Mandaville n.d.

Patterns of Time
Historical-Geographical Foundations

PERSISTENCE OF PATTERNS

Succession of Landscapes

Evolving over thousands of years and over a wide range of physical and cultural environments, the region's cultural mosaic and political patterns are exceedingly complex. Chronologically successive cultures and empires have partially erased yet partially preserved preceding patterns, creating by this long development a marvelous geographical palimpsest. This sequential development, its traces in the modern Middle East, and its significant impact on contemporary human and political affairs are the themes of this chapter, which deals with the historical-political geography of the region.

Evidence of sequent occupance,[1] or the settlement and exploitation of the same region by successive cultures, dates from earliest times and characterizes many Middle Eastern landscapes. In the narrow coastal plain of southern Lebanon, for example, a modern oil pipeline extends along or over Ottoman Turkish buildings, medieval Muslim mosques, a Crusader castle, Byzantine mosaics, Roman tombs, ruins of the Phoenician port of Sidon, Bronze Age pottery shards, and Neolithic flints (Fig. 3.1). The wrinkled hand of the past has fashioned much of the landscape of the Middle East.

Even if ruins and artifacts from the distant past are not visible on the surface, they are often stratified in successively older layers beneath the surface. In the more favorable environments of the Middle East, few excavations fail to yield some kind of evidence of ancient human occupation or use of the land. The past is nearly always present.

Heritage of Patterns

Prior to surveying the evolution of the regional palimpsest, we can gain appreciation of the significance of its long heritage by glancing at six selected topics as examples of that heritage. These examples underscore the relevance of even the distant past to present-day patterns and problems.

1. Religion. Certain sites and towns settled in ancient times had religious motivations or gained religious importance for later groups. Many of the centers have retained their significance or achieved even greater emotional impact, so they attract hundreds of thousands of pilgrims—and, in some cases, secular tourists—annually, thereby maintaining major economic importance. For example, before the development of Saudi Arabia's oil fields, pilgrims to Mecca and Medina provided the major basis for the kingdom's economy. Similarly, control of Jerusalem

FIGURE 3.1 Excavated ruins of Byblos, Lebanon, one of the most significant archaeological sites in the Middle East. Finds date from the Neolithic and include later Egyptian, Amorite, Phoenician, Persian, Roman, and Crusader ruins.

generated foreign exchange for the Ottoman Empire and successor governments. Religious sites often hold significance for multiple religious groups, leading to disputes over which historical "layer" is to be recognized, preserved, or excavated. Such controversies center on several sites in and around Jerusalem, especially the Haram al-Sharif, or Temple Mount. Muslim shrines such as those in Najaf and Karbala in Iraq, Qom and Mashhad in Iran, and Konya in Turkey are especially noteworthy.

2. Infrastructure. Infrastructural features—basic facilities supporting other development, including irrigation systems, caravan routes, and hillside terracing to facilitate farming—have evolved over centuries. Numerous ancient examples still survive, enhancing the value of particular areas and influencing relative levels of prosperity in the region. The middle and lower Tigris-Euphrates Valley, the Nile Valley and Delta, and the Jordan Valley, for example, have been developed over thousands of years into productive irrigated farming areas. Such development required enormous efforts by earlier peoples to achieve the clearing of dense vegetation, drainage, leveling, cultivation, irrigation by means of an elaborately engineered system of canals, and restoration after periodic flooding. Thus, modern economies rely on ancient infrastructures and on the cultural heritage of ancient technologies.

3. Natural Resources. Settlements and human activities have long correlated with patterns of natural resources, notably those of water, fertile soils, metallic ore deposits, and, more recently, oil. Such sites often show signs of a remarkable sequent occupance, with infrastructural elements from Roman aqueducts to modern pipelines. However, some ecological problems also persist. Increasingly serious are problems with salt-impregnated soils resulting from faulty irrigation of poorly drained areas or soil erosion caused by improperly cultivated slopes or overgrazing. Stone tools found along former lakeshores in deserts of the Arabian Peninsula signal environmental deterioration. Meanwhile, new areas have become habitable, with oil providing an economic base and with new technologies, such as pumping and desalination, providing the necessary water. The long history of civilization in the region yields practical information about its patterns of natural resources and their evolution over time.

4. *Strategic Features.* The strategic significance of Middle East seas, straits, coastal plains, mountain passes, river valleys, and major trade and invasion routes was displayed in ancient times and persists at the beginning of the twenty-first century despite modern technology. For example, the Strait of Hormuz and the Gulf are both still important strategically despite the development of sophisticated military aircraft and missiles that can easily cross over them.

5. *Culture and Art.* Virtually every contemporary city in the Middle East is on the site of an ancient town, and excavations for foundations of modern buildings commonly uncover statues, monuments, or other ancient remains. Logically enough, certain locational factors exercise a persistent attraction for human occupation and cross-country routes. Ruins of monuments and other structures, found by the thousands throughout the settled Middle East, have become tourist attractions in many countries, while transportable artifacts, stone and clay inscriptions, documents on papyrus and vellum, and other antiquities are preserved in museums all over the world. Beyond their economic value, such items are valuable to researchers because they provide clues about the historical evolution of the area. Unfortunately, thousands of artifacts have been—and still are—illegally excavated and traded on the black market. The looting of the Iraqi National Museum in 2003 was a cultural tragedy for the world.

6. *Political and Military Models and Conflict.* Sequent occupance over millennia has resulted in competing claims to the same lands and pressure on inhabited areas to accommodate high population growth, refugees, and new immigrants. The founding of the modern state of Israel, in which a Jewish population has largely displaced a Palestinian one, exemplifies this type of political and territorial conflict. The war between Iran and Iraq in the 1980s echoed numerous territorial and religious rivalries of earlier periods along the same fracture zone, as has the contemporary Cyprus struggle. Thus, any analysis of modern conflicts and political antagonisms in the region must take cognizance of the roots of such strife in the area's historical-political geography. Although five former Middle East monarchies are now republics, six states are still monarchies (and another is a republican federation of seven monarchies), a heritage of a long history of kingdoms, empires, and principalities.

EARLY PATTERNS

Primitive Peoples and Pristine Environments

The more favorable Middle East environments attracted human habitation as early as the Paleolithic period, or Old Stone Age, contemporary with Pleistocene glaciation (about 1.6 million years ago to 12,000 BCE). Primitive Paleolithic human (or humanoid) groups were environmentally bound to sites that offered fresh water, easily gathered food, and natural shelters, especially caves. Particularly favorable sites were found in the western and

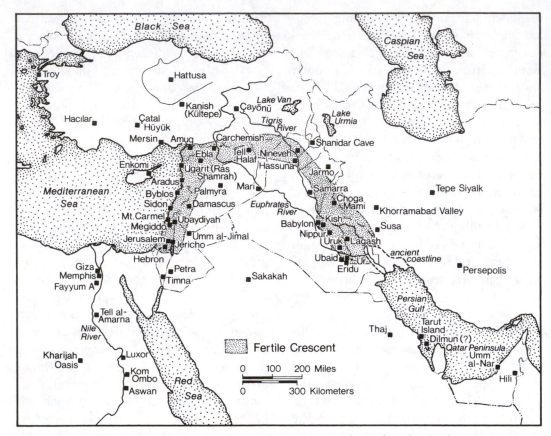

MAP 3.1 Selected major ancient sites. The Fertile Crescent is often referred to in the text.

eastern limbs of the Fertile Crescent (Map 3.1) and adjacent areas of the Anatolian Plateau.[2] The earliest known humanoid site in the region, dating from more than a million years ago, is in northern Saudi Arabia, near the village of Shuwayhitiyah. The study of this site in the mid-1980s introduced an entirely new concept of human migration into Asia from the area of hominid origin in East Africa. Stone tools from several of these extremely ancient sites in Arabia have now been found.[3] Until the 1980s, the earliest site studied dated from 600,000 years ago at Ubaydiyah, on an ancient lakeshore in the Jordan Valley just south of the Sea of Galilee. Numerous Paleolithic sites more than 100,000 years old are scattered from the Nile Valley to the piedmont arc around Mesopotamia and include one being excavated in Sharjah in 2010.

Climatic changes that caused the northward retreat of the last ice sheets in Eurasia beginning about 15,000 years ago also modified the ecology of the Middle East. Open woodlands and grasslands soon characterized the Fertile Crescent, a contrast to the damp forests that invaded Eurasian areas uncovered by the melting and retreating glaciers. As one consequence, the Fertile Crescent population increased and developed, ushering in the Mesolithic period, or Middle Stone Age— sometimes called Epipaleolithic—which began in about 12,000 BCE.

Neolithic Revolution in a Special Environment

Ameliorating climatic conditions after 9000 BCE brought further steady improvements in the Fertile Crescent environment, which encouraged not only an increase in the number of Mesolithic peoples but also the growth and spread of wild plants and animals that made up their food supply. This favorable environment of grasslands with scattered trees became the native habitat of early forms of wheat and barley, varieties of which are still found in the northern Fertile Crescent.[4] Wild varieties of both were widely harvested for many centuries; they were gradually domesticated and cultivated along with other major food plants, including vegetables and nut trees. At about the same time, animals that still dominate the farm scene were domesticated—sheep, goats, cattle, pigs, and dogs. Hence, in about 8000 BCE, in the arc from the Levant to the western Zagros, there occurred the Agricultural Revolution, or Agricultural Transformation, the most important single innovation in human history.

Thus, a particular environment, a special plant community, and an adaptive population combined to initiate the Neolithic period, the New Stone Age. Heralded especially by the Agricultural Revolution, the Neolithic period also saw the systematic development of organized settlements. Such settlements were not feasible prior to the planned cultivation of plants and the domestication of animals, so that the agricultural and urban revolutions functioned reciprocally. Moreover, these stimulated, or at least were accompanied by, a further complex of cultural processes—political administration, organized religion, trade, and, finally, writing—in both Mesopotamia and Egypt.

The Archaeological Tell

Giving mute, fascinating, and vital testimony regarding Neolithic and later settlements is the archaeological mound, a common feature of the Middle East landscape. Usually referred to by the Semitic word *tell*,[5] an archaeological mound marks an ancient site on which successive settlements were established on the debris of earlier ones. Typical tells contain layers of cultural remains accumulated over thousands of years, the height of the mound generally indicating the length of time the site was occupied. With characteristically flat tops and sharply sloping sides, tells are prime targets for archaeological excavations. Correlation of finds among tells reveals patterns of cultures and settlement, including economic and political relations, that existed more than 5,000 years ago.

Many of the thousands of tells scattered over the Middle East are world renowned and attract scores of scholars and thousands of tourists annually. Familiar examples include Troy in northwestern Asia Minor, Babylon in central Mesopotamia, and Jericho in the Jordan Valley (all shown on Map 3.1).

Agriculture, Cities, and Civilization

The human advance from food gathering to food producing in about 7000 BCE[6] and the consequent expansion of the food supply accompanied a great increase in population in more favorable areas. As well as providing a more balanced diet, agriculture also permitted production of a food surplus for nonproductive seasons and for famines. In addition, farming permitted and encouraged experimentation, cooperative planning, and a concentration of people into villages, which resulted in a widening of social exchange, organization, and trade within and among settlements. Food-storage facilities, key evidence of early agriculture, and food-preservation techniques required group planning.

About 5500 BCE, Fertile Crescent farmers took another giant step forward—minimizing dependence on local rainfall: They extended, then gradually shifted, farming from the Zagros piedmonts above the Tigris-Euphrates Basin down to the Mesopotamian plain along the riverbanks. The new agriculture was irrigated cultivation, utilizing a system of canals to feed river water to the planted fields.

Along with the earlier rainfed farming advances, irrigated farming accompanied or had a "feedback" effect on key social developments in Mesopotamia: cooperative planning; organized engineering; expanded storage facilities for harvest surpluses; trade relations to exchange excess food for other items; cities to accommodate people, goods, and expanded activities, as well as to permit specialization of labor; defenses for the protection of food supplies, irrigation works, settlements, and temples; centralized administration to apportion water and to coordinate activities; and for inventories and trade, a system of writing, the basis for future law, literature, and long-distance communication.

Evidence of origins of agriculture in areas outside Mesopotamia is contradictory. Rather than having been borrowed from the Tigris-Euphrates Basin, systematic agriculture in the Nile Valley may have had independent beginnings. Certainly, farming—and, by necessity, irrigation—began very early in Egypt, as it did also in Southeast Asia. However, evidence for Mesopotamia as the source area for the diffusion of settled agriculture remains strong.

Specific innovations developed as Mesopotamian irrigation agriculture evolved. With all dates BCE, the plow appeared in about 3000–4000; the wheel was well known in Mesopotamia by 3500, but apparently not in Egypt until 1700; and stamp and cylinder seals (possibly ancestors of writing) had appeared in some quantity by 3500. Impressive temples had been constructed in Uruk (Erech of the Old Testament, Warka in modern Iraq) by 3300; earliest evidences of writing also appeared about 3300, and cuneiform (wedge-shaped) writing on clay was common by 2400;[7] and a dozen major Sumerian cities, and many more villages, existed in Mesopotamia by 2700.

Excavations of early Mesopotamian cities reveal cultural achievements and urban developments that were remarkably advanced for their time (4000–3500 BCE). The ruins of Uruk, southeast of Baghdad (see Map 3.1),

suggest a population of 50,000, and the outline of the walls extends for 5.6 mi/9 km. Impressive temples, some on stepped platforms, and terraced towers, or ziggurats, dominated several cities on the Mesopotamian plain, and the Hanging Gardens of Babylon and the Tower of Babel of the Old Testament were almost certainly ziggurats. Regrettably, many of the great Mesopotamian sites were damaged, some very badly, during the fighting and looting of 2003 and the period following.

The building of terraced or stepped towers in Mesopotamia was generally contemporary with pyramid construction in Egypt, and the stepped design of the Pyramid of Zoser at Saqqara, the oldest known pyramid along the Nile, suggests that it was borrowed from the Mesopotamian ziggurat concept. Thus, evidence from 5,000 years ago clearly shows remarkable interaction between peoples and environment in the Tigris-Euphrates Basin. Irrigation farming and urban development were twin manifestations of the evolving and expanding early culture.[8]

Another major factor in the human-environmental relationship was the availability of building materials for the growing number of structures erected in Mesopotamia. In the southern part of the basin, only the clays and silts laid down by the Tigris and Euphrates rivers on their lower alluvial plain were directly available for building. Unshaped river mud (*tawf*) supplied the material for the earlier structures in the area, and it is still a common construction material for houses in villages of southern Iraq. Later structures were of sun-dried mud brick, and still later buildings were faced with fired brick. Southern Mesopotamian ziggurats, temples, and palaces of the third and second millennia BCE are therefore less well preserved than are the massive Egyptian temples and pyramids, which were constructed of the limestone plentiful in the Nile Valley (Fig. 3.2). Similarly, Assyrian palaces in northern Mesopotamia, built of limestone

FIGURE 3.2 Temple of Hatshepsut (Dayr al-Bahari), in ancient Thebes, Egypt. The temple (fifteenth century BCE) faces east toward the Nile and Karnak and Luxor on the east bank of the river. Behind the cliff, to the west, is the Valley of the Kings.

from nearby quarries, have survived remarkably well.

HISTORICAL-POLITICAL EVOLUTION

The rise and expansion of Middle East empires after 4000 BCE display political-geographical pattern dynamics that are still relevant today. For this reason, the following condensed survey of the evolution of ancient and medieval patterns serves as a prelude to studying the modern region. Obviously, in this brief survey, only the more noteworthy developments can be considered; few of the extremely important migrations of peoples, especially those into the region, can be given the attention they merit.

Early Mesopotamian States

Middle East recorded history begins in the fourth millennium BCE in southern Meso-

potamia with the Sumerians, whose origins are unknown and whose written language is unrelated to any other known language. Earliest records show them in control of the irrigation works and related settlements in ancient Sumer, remembered as Shinar in the biblical account found in Genesis 10 and 11. Functioning as city-states, the major cities of Sumer in the middle of the third millennium BCE were Eridu, Uruk, Ur (later Ur of the Chaldees, home of Abraham of both the Old Testament and the Quran), and others (shown on Map 3.2). The partially excavated ruins of these famous settlements of 4,500–5,000 years ago now lie well away from any river, but the towns were originally established along the banks of the Euphrates, which later changed course. The Euphrates, with its slower, more manageable flow, offered advantages for the siting of cities and fields that the more rapidly flowing Tigris could not provide.

MAP 3.2 Mesopotamia and adjacent lands, showing earliest known states as well as earliest known cities—Uruk, Eridu, Ur, Lagash, and others. The dashed line indicates approximate limits of the Old Babylonian Empire.

North of Sumer lived the Akkadians, the first of many Semitic groups to enter Mesopotamia. They probably came from the Arabian Peninsula, a source region for successive waves of Semites into the Fertile Crescent for 3,000 years. They overwhelmed the Sumerians in about 2335 BCE, unified the former city-states, and developed the first known empire. In the realm extending from the Zagros Mountains westward to the Mediterranean, their language became the lingua franca, or common language, of the civilized Middle East for centuries. After a short but productive period, the Akkadian heartland was overrun briefly in about 2200 BCE by the Gutians from the Zagros Mountains. This invasion was a precursor of many later conflicts between powers based in the adjacent strongholds of the Tigris-Euphrates Basin and Za-

gros Mountains–Iranian Plateau—the latest in the 1980s.

Reemerging as a culturally mixed people, the persistent Sumerians established a United Sumer and Akkad with a capital at Ur. This empire reached its peak of brilliance in about 2000 BCE, developing a thriving trade with the Indus Valley peoples and establishing ports of call on the sea route to the Indus. Ruins of such ports have been found along the shores of the modern UAE and Oman and on islands in the Gulf, especially on Bahrain. There, excavations have uncovered well-preserved, impressive ruins of what is believed to have been the *Dilmun* referred to in Sumerian records.[9]

The first Babylonian Empire emerged soon after 2000 BCE and absorbed Sumer. It was created by another Semitic group, the Amorites (which means "westerners" in Amorite), who migrated into central Mesopotamia from the Syrian Desert in about 2000 BCE. From their power center in Babylon, they controlled all of Mesopotamia, and between 1792 and 1750 BCE they were ruled by one of the most famous kings in Oriental history, Hammurabi (or Hammurapi) the Great. His famous legal code collected and systematized Sumerian and Akkadian laws from earlier centuries and brought a new sophistication to political administration and control. Babylonians developed advanced mathematical calculations that were used for more than a millennium; their sexagesimal system is still standard in our sixty-second minute, sixty-minute hour, and 360° circle. Babylon and Babylonia played important roles in Mesopotamia for more than 2,000 years.[10]

Other noteworthy power centers evolved and expanded in several parts of the region after 1700 BCE, demonstrating the persistence of imperial realms in certain environments. Mesopotamia lost its isolated self-sufficiency as peoples with new languages and new cultures entered Asia Minor, the Iranian Plateau, the Levant, and the Caucasus. These included the Indo-European Hittites, who controlled Asia Minor for more than 400 years from their stronghold of Hattusa (or Hattushash) in Anatolia. They destroyed Babylon during an incursion in the sixteenth century BCE but mysteriously withdrew following their triumph, after which the Indo-European Kassites, in another instance of a basin-mountain clash, emerged from the Zagros Mountains to rule the weakened Babylonian area for more than four centuries. Another group, the Hurrians (biblical Horites), spoke a language that was neither Semitic nor Indo-European and relied on an Indo-European warrior aristocracy and horse-drawn chariots to build the Kingdom of Mitanni in about 1500 BCE. Hurrian military power pushed the borders of Mitanni control westward to the Mediterranean and eastward to the Zagros.

However, of all the ancient Middle East civilizations and empires outside Mesopotamia, none could match the fabled culture of the Nile, the Pharaonic kingdoms of Upper and Lower Egypt.

Early Egypt

The steadily evolving Mesopotamian culture of the late Neolithic period and early Bronze Age diffused not only eastward to the Indus Valley and beyond but also westward to the Nile Valley. Ancient well-developed cultures already present there adapted Mesopotamian influences and made them distinctly "Egyptian." For example, the writing developed in Sumer as a practical method of recording inventories and trade transactions was a relatively simple technique that required only quick incisions with a reed stylus on damp clay, with both reed and clay widely available. The concept of writing was apparently borrowed by the Egyptians, who used their familiar materials, bronze chisel and stone, to carve elaborate hieroglyphics (lit., "sacred carving") for religious or royal inscriptions.[11]

Basic environmental differences between Mesopotamia and Egypt influenced other historical and cultural differences. Both rivers of Mesopotamia, the Tigris and the Euphrates, have irregular flow regimes, run in shallow beds, flood unpredictably (or did so especially before the hydraulic works of the twentieth century), shift courses, and generally lack a dependable rhythm. The Nile, in contrast, has eroded a wall-bounded valley in the rock desert, has a regular floodplain and flood time (late summer), seldom shifts course, and follows a regular rhythm documented over centuries.

Although links between culture and environment can be overstated, certain correlations can be drawn for the early Nile civilization. Egyptian cultural stability followed the rhythm of the river and was influenced by the relative isolation enforced by the desert beyond the Nile Valley. The Nile's physical unity facilitated early political unity after a certain cultural level developed along the river (Map 3.3). Well before 3000 BCE, sailboats proceeded upstream, blown by the northeast trade winds, and drifted downstream, carried by the river's current. Only limited east-west traffic left the Nile Valley, since regular commercial movement over the deserts flanking the valley was hazardous.

Also, a unified administration coordinated efforts to construct and maintain major canals, allocate water, protect riparian rights of access to the Nile, resurvey fields after the annual floods that deposited the fertile silt, and maintain a god-king leadership figure.[12] The continuity and stability of the cosmos were dominant concepts among the ancient Egyptians; the fact that wood, cloth, and papyrus, even the desiccated remains of people and animals, were naturally preserved in their hot, dry climate may have influenced their perception of life as a benevolent rhythm.

The Egyptians constructed temples and tombs and other advanced architectural works that are stunning even today. They created sophisticated jewelry, inlaid ornaments,

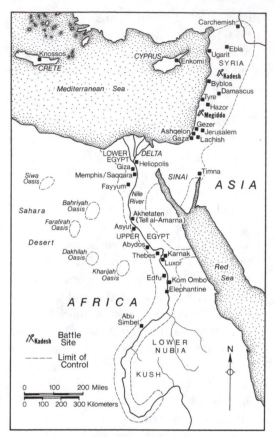

MAP 3.3 Ancient Egypt and the Levant, showing major ancient sites. The dashed line shows the approximate maximum limit of the New Kingdom control.

vases, and sculpture. New discoveries during the 1990s and later have further enhanced the already fabulous corpus of well-preserved artifacts from tombs and temples. To obtain such materials as gold, ebony, cedar, and turquoise, the Egyptians carried on active trade, especially with peoples of the upper Nile, along the Red Sea, and in the eastern Mediterranean—including Minoans, Mycenaeans, Hittites, Canaanites, and others. Along with such trade, sustained Egyptian military and imperial activities in the Levant and elsewhere engendered a cross-fertilization of ideas and techniques. Enriched by these contacts, Egyptian culture in turn influenced Greek and Roman development, and thereby Western civilization.

Egyptian power declined after about 1090 BCE and succumbed to outside control as Libyans, Ethiopians, and Assyrians imposed their respective dynasties. The Persians then conquered Egypt in 525 BCE and, with only a brief interruption, held it for 200 years until it submitted to Alexander the Great in 332 BCE . Under Alexander's Hellenistic successors, the Greek-Macedonian Ptolemies, Egypt achieved independence again for 250 years and experienced a cultural resurgence before passing to Roman control in 30 BCE. Although it enjoyed long periods of autonomy under successive hegemons, Egypt was not to achieve true sovereignty again for almost 2,000 years, until after World War II.

Mesopotamia to the Roman Conquests

Assyrian Empire.   Along with Babylonia, Assyria was one of the most persistent of Fertile Crescent imperial states. It emerged about 1350 BCE, centered in the upper Tigris Basin, and dominated the Middle East for 300 years after 935 BCE as the prototypical Oriental monarchy (Map 3.4A). The Assyrian Empire maintained control by means of its sternness, organization, efficiency, engineering, commerce, communications, and record keeping. During its eighth-century expansion, Assyria mastered the Levant, conquered the biblical kingdom of Israel, and in the latter case dispersed the population, a practice the Assyrians often followed with vanquished peoples. Assyria disappeared from history after being overwhelmed by Babylonians and Medes, who took Nineveh in 612 BCE.

Discoveries of superbly detailed bas-relief friezes and other finds in the ruins of Assyrian palace complexes at Khorsabad, Nimrud, and Nineveh in the early nineteenth century launched modern systematic archaeology. They also stimulated an appreciation of ancient Mesopotamian history as it emerged from the translation of some of the 22,000 clay tablets found in the palace library at Nineveh.

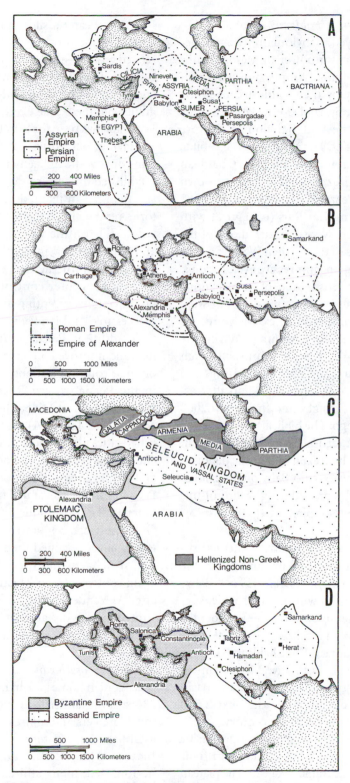

MAP 3.4 Major Middle East–Mediterranean empires from before 1000 BCE to the rise of Islam.

Neo-Babylonian (Chaldean) Empire. With Assyria destroyed, Babylonia once again became the dominant power in Mesopotamia. This Neo-Babylonian Empire was led for almost a century by the Chaldeans, a Semitic people from the Syrian Desert, like the Semitic Amorites of the Old Babylonian Empire 1,400 years earlier. The great imperial capital, Babylon, was revitalized by the Chaldean king Nebuchadrezzar the Great (also known as Nebuchadnezzar), who reigned 604–562 BCE. Its Hanging Gardens (a ziggurat with planted terraces) were considered one of the Seven Wonders of the Ancient World, and the Ishtar Gate remains impressive even in ruins. The excavated extensive ruins of Nebuchadrezzar's palace were very impressive but were rather debased by unduly extensive reconstruction by the Iraqi government during the 1980s. Babylon's excavated ruins, although damaged during the fighting, looting, and subsequent occupation in 2003 and after, afford significant insight into the life of 2,000 to 4,000 years ago. The biblical account of the destruction of Jerusalem and other Judean cities by Nebuchadnezzar and of the deportation of the Judeans into Babylonian exile in 586 BCE provides an enduring record of this monarch and his empire.

Persian (Achaemenid) Empire. After its brilliant Chaldean revival, Babylonia fell to the Persian king Cyrus the Great in 539 BCE. Babylon itself, captured without a struggle, survived for another six centuries—Alexander the Great died there in 323 BCE—but by 100 CE it had been abandoned. The Chaldean Babylonian Empire was the last native Mesopotamian state of antiquity. The Tigris-Euphrates Basin was ruled by outsiders for the next 2,500 years, well into the twentieth century.

The Persians were an Indo-European tribe that swept down on Babylonia from their stronghold on the Iranian Plateau. The plateau had already disgorged the Gutians and the Indo-European Kassites and Medes, and from it later erupted other conquering Persian-related groups—the Parthians, Sassanians, and Safavids. Thus, the plateau has been the source area for Indo-European conquerors and immigrants into the Fertile Crescent as the Arabian Peninsula has been for Semitic invaders.

Having merged with the Medes, the Persians during the Achaemenid dynasty swiftly established an empire that was more extensive than any of its predecessors. Their territories reached from the Balkan Peninsula and Nile Valley on the west to the Indus Valley and Turanian Basin on the east (see Map 3.4A). Thus, for the first time, one Middle East power center controlled all the other power centers, excepting only the barren and inaccessible Arabian Peninsula.

In addition, Persia profited from, inherited, and improved on Assyrian efficiency and on their communications, as was exemplified in the Persian Royal Road from Susa (in southwestern Iran) to Sardis (in western Asia Minor; see Map 3.4A). Some already established cities played more powerful roles, especially Susa, Ecbatana (modern Hamadan), and the legendary Persepolis (Fig. 3.3). The Persian Empire continued for more than 200 years until it was conquered by Alexander the Great between 334 and 326 BCE. Although Persia never regained the territorial dominion of Achaemenid times, Iranian peoples again controlled the plateau within a century after Alexander's death. They have demonstrated for 2,300 years that they are a culturally and politically significant power.

The Empire of Alexander. Leaving his small Macedonian home base in northern Greece in 334 BCE, Alexander the Great had conquered the entire Persian Empire by 326 BCE and had established his eastern frontier beyond the Indus (see Map 3.4B). Of the dozens of cities he founded, many still carry forms of his name—Alexandria (al-Iskandariyah), Egypt;

FIGURE 3.3 Persepolis in modern Iran. The wonderfully detailed bas-reliefs on the staircase and platform of the Apadana (fifth century BCE), built by Darius the Great and his son Xerxes, depict representatives of subject peoples and reveal much about the social and political situation of the time.

Iskenderun, Turkey; Qandahar, Afghanistan; and others. He engendered cultural interchange, encouraged ethnic intermixing, and spread Hellenistic ideas and practices while expanding his own empire. His death in Babylon at age thirty-three left a power vacuum, and imperial lands were parceled out among Alexander's top generals. Ultimately, a threefold division emerged that, alongside revived Persian power, survived for 250 years.

Seleucid and Ptolemaic Empires. With slightly shifting boundaries, the two most important Hellenistic states in the Middle East were the Seleucid and the Ptolemaic (see Map 3.4C), and ruins and other physical and cultural vestiges of these empires are still evident in scores of sites in Egypt and the Levant. Asia Minor fragmented into a complex mosaic of kingdoms. An Armenian state persisted for centuries and became the base for an Armenian national identity that still endures. The northeastern Iranian Plateau area embraced the Iranian Parthian kingdom, and a Hellenized Greco-Bactrian kingdom dominated lands farther east.

Hellenistic cultural influences continued into the Roman and Byzantine empires in the Middle East, spanning a period of almost a millennium. Two Hellenistic cities in the Middle East are noteworthy: Antioch (now Antakya, Turkey), on the lower Orontes River, became a prominent regional center in the Seleucid realm and continued a rich history up to today; and in the Ptolemaic kingdom, Alexandria, founded in 331 BCE by Alexander near the mouth of the Nile, became a brilliant center of Hellenism with a large Greek population. Its lighthouse (Pharos), built in about 300 BCE, was one of the Seven Wonders of the Ancient World and aided navigation for 1,600 years. The Ptolemaic Empire ended with Cleopatra's suicide in 30 BCE, when Egypt entered 673 years of control by the Roman and eastern Roman empires. The Seleucid Empire also collapsed before the advancing Romans, and Syria became a Roman province in 64 BCE.

Smaller Semitic Kingdoms.   Other noteworthy cultures contemporaneous with these extensive empires include those of the Hebrews, Canaanite-Phoenicians, and Aramaeans. The Hebrews, a Semitic tribe, appear to have emerged from the Arabian Desert, as did other Semites mentioned earlier. Legends of their early culture and migrations, typical of many tribal groups of the time, are recorded in the book of Genesis. These biblical narratives yield insights into both the Hebrew culture and also many of the attitudes of the time.[13] In Canaan, the Hebrews not only confronted the native Canaanites in the hill country; they were also long kept from the southern coast by other recent arrivals—the Sea Peoples, especially the Philistines, from the Aegean region. Archaeological discoveries have now shown that the Philistine civilization was not the uncouth culture traditionally associated with the name Philistine, but was, indeed, generally superior to that of their Israelite neighbors.[14] It was from Philistia, land of the Philistines, that the later name Falastina, or Palestine, was derived.

The biblical narrative indicates that a unified Israelite kingdom finally emerged (about 1020 BCE) and lasted almost a century, dividing in 922 BCE after the death of Solomon. The northern kingdom, Israel, lasted less than 200 years and was conquered by the Assyrians in 722 BCE, its people dispersed as the ten lost tribes. Judah, the southern kingdom, with Jerusalem as its capital, survived Israel by 136 years but fell to Nebuchadrezzar in 586 BCE, when thousands of Judeans were deported to Babylon. Many returned to Judea

after 50 years of Babylonian captivity, but others remained, forming a thriving Jewish colony in Mesopotamia that lasted 2,500 years. It may be noted that from 922 BCE until the twentieth century, the Palestine area has been a sovereign state under a native administration in de jure control of a unified territory for only a few decades under the Hasmoneans (Maccabees), a reign that was ended by the Romans in 63 BCE. Most of the Jews of Palestine had been dispersed over the Mediterranean Basin and the Middle East by the middle of the second century CE.[15]

The "land of Canaan" comprised the general area of the western Syria–Palestine realm. Although the individualistic Canaanite city-states maintained active common cultural and economic ties, including an intermingling of some elements of their language and religion along with trade, they failed to unify politically or militarily. Thus, because they were vulnerable to invading Egyptians, Amorites, Israelites, Assyrians, and others, the more extended Canaanite civilization declined after about the eleventh century BCE.

The Canaanite cultural genius, however, long stimulated and diversified through interaction with the advanced Egyptian civilization, now became concentrated among the northern coastal groups, who became known as Phoenicians. These extraordinary innovators developed remarkable city-states around ports at Tyre, Sidon, Beirut, Byblos, Tripoli, and Aradus. Because they were crowded into an isolated coastal plain with limited agricultural land, the Phoenicians turned to the sea, developing an aggressive maritime trade, which reached as far as the western Mediterranean, and founding colonies over a wide area. Their most powerful colony, Carthage, founded in about 800 BCE, challenged Rome itself for supremacy in the three Punic (Phoenician) Wars of the second and third centuries BCE. While conducting their wide-ranging trade, the Phoenicians simplified and carried with them the first true alphabet, derived from characters developed by Semitic peoples in the Levant. This alphabet was subsequently adapted by the Greeks, Etruscans, and Romans.[16]

The Aramaeans, who—like the neighboring Canaanites—were long indigenous, were inland traders who diffused their culture along with their Semitic language. The Aramaic tongue spread along land trading routes and became the lingua franca of commerce and diplomacy from Egypt to Mesopotamia. It was still spoken in Syria and Palestine at the time of Christ. According to Old Testament accounts, Damascus and other Aramaean city-states, the biblical Aram, were overcome by the Hebrew King David. However, they regained their independence and continued as Aramaean centers until conquered by the Assyrians in 732 BCE. The Aramaean culture gradually faded, but dialects of the Aramaic language continued into the present time in several church liturgies and are still spoken in northern Iraq and in villages north of Damascus.

Roman and Successor Empires

Roman. Although Hellenistic control over much of the Middle East originated from an outside area (Macedonia), Rome was the first power from outside the region to maintain hegemony over large areas of the region for a lengthy period. However, extensive as it was, Roman territorial control never equaled that of the Persian and Hellenistic empires (see Map 3.4). Even so, Egypt and Syria-Palestine felt the lingering Roman influence until the seventh century CE, and Asia Minor did so for several centuries longer.

Roman legions failed to venture beyond Mesopotamia. They contended with Iranian-based armies along the Euphrates and in Armenia but were never successful in sustained desert operations. To symbolize their military presence, however, they constructed lines of forts and boundary markers to form the

Limes Arabicus (Arabian Boundary), similar to the *limes* constructed in central Europe. In northwestern Syria, well-preserved stretches of Roman roads still exist, a part of ancient infrastructure underlying the modern Middle East. Vestiges of their presence—roads, forts, theaters, temples, aqueducts, baths—are prominent features in the landscapes of Asia Minor, the Levant, Egypt, and across North Africa, partly because Roman construction in those areas was monumental and well engineered (Figs. 3.4 and 3.5). Some structures combine Hellenistic, Roman, and Byzantine construction from different periods, and these Greco-Roman ruins, from Istanbul in the northwest to Dura Europos on the upper Euphrates in the east, attract many visitors from around the world.[17]

Parthian. Although Alexander destroyed the Persian Empire, the Iranian identity reasserted itself a century later through the Iranian Parthians. Emerging as a native kingdom in 248 BCE, the Parthian Kingdom became an empire within 75 years, extending over the Iranian Plateau and Mesopotamia. Observing the historic strategic value of the narrowest width of the middle Tigris-Euphrates interfluve, the Parthians established twin capital cities—Seleucia and Ctesiphon—near modern Baghdad.

Sassanian. The Parthian Empire was overthrown in 226 CE and was succeeded by another Iranian empire, the Sassanian (or Sassanid). The powerful Sassanians expanded northeastward across the Oxus River (modern Amu Darya, between the contemporary republics of Turkmenistan and Uzbekistan) and eastward to the Indus, as well as across the Gulf into the Qatif area of Arabia and into Oman (see Map 3.4D). They maintained Ctesiphon as a capital (Fig. 3.6) and also inherited Rome and its Byzantine successor as a perennial territorial adversary in Syria-Mesopotamia. The Sassanian Empire collapsed

FIGURE 3.4 Famous Greco-Roman ruins: the dramatic amphitheater on a cliff side in Pergamum (modern Bergama, Turkey).

FIGURE 3.5 Another well-known Greco-Roman ruin: colonnaded street in the ruins of Jarash, north of Amman, a great Roman provincial city. Note the paved street, which has a well-engineered storm drain underneath.

FIGURE 3.6 Ruins of the great vaulted hall (al-Madain) in Ctesiphon, the Sassanian capital (see Map 3.4D), on the left bank of the Tigris River southeast of Baghdad. The brick vault of the third century is one of the highest freestanding brick arches ever constructed. Note two figures standing right of lower center.

entirely under the assault of invading Arab Muslims in the 630s and 640s.

Byzantine.   Although the Western Roman Empire and its formerly great capital declined after the fourth century CE, the eastern empire and its capital thrived. Founded by the first eastern emperor, Constantine, and named after its founder, Constantinople was earlier Byzantium and later Istanbul. Steadily orientalized, the eastern empire became less Latin and more Greek and after the fall of Rome in 476 was referred to as the Byzantine Empire. It gradually expanded to embrace the Italian and Balkan peninsulas in Europe, Egypt and the southern Mediterranean coast in North Africa, and Asia Minor and the Levant in between. After holding these extensive lands for many centuries (see Map 3.4D), it gradually contracted, until the only remaining territory was an enfeebled Constantinople and its environs, which fell to the Ottomans in the watershed year of 1453. Allowing for expansions and contractions, it survived for 1,123 years, longer than any other empire in the Middle East.[18]

Having battled each other to a standstill for control of the Fertile Crescent, the mutually exhausted Byzantines and Sassanians suddenly faced a common Arab invader. The weakened Byzantines lost Egypt and the Levant in the 630s to the Muslim assault but were able to hold on to their Anatolian stronghold. The Sassanians were forced to surrender not only Mesopotamia but also their entire Iranian Plateau power base, and both areas experienced profound and permanent transformation. The Middle East had entered a new era, that of Islam.

Islamic Empires

The Arab irruption into Mesopotamia and Syria-Palestine in 633 was another in the series of Semitic waves from interior Arabia

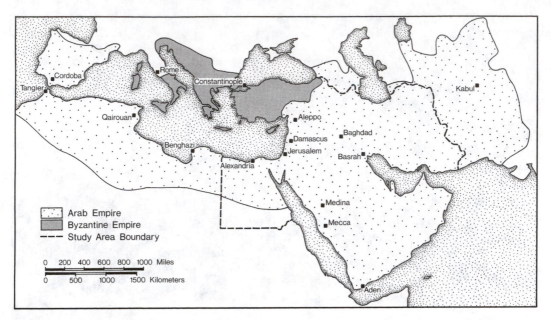

MAP 3.5 Arab Empire at its maximum extent, late eighth century. Arabs never succeeded in conquering Asia Minor.

extending back over 3,000 years. This particular invasion, however, was more purposeful, involved many more people and far more territory than had previous ones, and had incalculably greater ramifications. With it, the present cultural patterns of the region began to emerge.

The founder of Islam, the Prophet Muhammad, had unified the Arabs of the Hijaz (western Arabia) and then of the entire Arabian Peninsula. This he achieved on three levels: a new religion (the adherents of which were called Muslims—see Chap. 4), a political organization (virtually a theocracy), and ethnic identity. Precepts for all three are found in the Muslim scriptures, the Quran. After Muhammad's death in 632, dedicated Muslims poured northward to spread the faith and to seize new lands for its flowering. Within a century, Muslim forces appeared before Tours in France, the high point of their westward spread, while other Muslims held Central Asia. At its maximum extent in the eighth century, the Arab Empire exceeded in size all previous Middle East empires and compared

with the Roman Empire at its maximum (cf. Maps 3.4 and 3.5). The Muslim invasion marked the first Semitic conquest of the Iranian Plateau, although the conquerors imposed only the religion of Islam and their alphabet, not their Semitic language, Arab identity, or physical characteristics.

However, even more than the Roman Empire, the Arab Empire and its successor Muslim empires and kingdoms shifted capitals and cores, broke into parts, recombined in different patterns, and changed composition. But unified or fragmented, the region retained one enduring characteristic—Islam as religion and culture. The development of the Muslim religion and the Islamic state were two highly integrated aspects of the same phenomenon. These aspects not only still thrive but, having been remolded in the contemporary state system, have become resurgent traditions.[19]

With the founding of the Umayyad Empire in 661, power shifted from the Hijaz to Syria, with the new capital in Damascus. The character of the Muslim state altered accordingly, from a religion-centered theocracy to an empire imitative of Byzantine and Persian courts.

In 750, the Abbasid dynasty seized control of the Arab Empire and transferred the center from Damascus to Mesopotamia. After governing from several centers, the Abbasids built their new capital, Baghdad, on the narrowest segment of the Tigris-Euphrates interfluve, which had been occupied earlier by a succession of imperial capital cities. The next century brought the reign of Harun al-Rashid, the Abbasid caliph of Arabian Nights fame.[20] During the same century, however, evidence of the decline of the Abbasids appeared as the court weakened and breakaway kingdoms rose, expanded, and were absorbed.[21]

Seljuks, Crusaders, and Mongols

Seljuks. Besides the breakaway states, several other kingdoms were established by invaders from outside the Middle East. Islamized Seljuk Turks from Central Asia moved into the Iranian Plateau and entered Baghdad in 1055 but left the Abbasid caliphs as figureheads. From Mesopotamia they forced their way westward and, in the watershed battle of Manzikert north of Lake Van (1071), defeated Byzantine armies. They then carried Islam into inner Anatolia for the first time. Islam gradually expanded over all of Asia Minor, and it has remained entrenched there ever since. With the way open into Anatolia, the Seljuks established the Sultanate of Rum (Rum = Rome, that is, Europe) and indirectly paved the way for the later expansion of the Turkish Ottoman Empire.

Crusaders. The second group of states established by outside invaders arose primarily in response to the Seljuk incursions and their threat to the Byzantines (see Fig. 9.3). After the Byzantines' defeat at Manzikert, and with Seljuk territorial control continuing to expand, the Byzantines petitioned for help from the Roman Catholic feudal states of western Europe. Successive waves of Christians—

French, English, German, Italian, and other Europeans, all labeled "Franks" by the Middle East Muslims—surged eastward in response to the Byzantine request. The human waves became known as the Crusades. The First Crusade began in 1096; succeeding ones started in 1147, 1189, 1202, 1218, and 1228, and there were others unconnected with the original purpose.

The First Crusade established several Crusader kingdoms that occupied a relatively small area along a coastal strip at the eastern end of the Mediterranean. After two centuries, Muslim resistance finally expelled the occupiers, and the last Crusader foothold, Acre, fell in 1291. Although the Crusades had only a modest impact on the Middle East at the time, the reverse effects were momentous, since they were a major stimulus for the European Renaissance. The movement became a major chapter in European medieval history, embellished with adventure and romance, while establishing hostility toward Muslims as the Western norm for centuries to come. Among Middle East Muslims, the rankling memories of these successive European invasions have recently become rekindled—especially among Palestinians, to whom even the word "Crusades" is painful. In the Levant, numerous ruined Crusader castles remain as romantic symbols of early European imperialism in the Middle East. Some castles, like other more ancient Middle East monuments, served military purposes intermittently into the twenty-first century because of their massive walls and strategic sites.[22]

Mongols. In the thirteenth century, invading horse-mounted Mongol and Tatar-Mongol archers made far-ranging territorial conquests in the Middle East to add to their vast empires in Asia. Generally short-lived, the conquests nevertheless yielded the Il-Khanid dynasty in Persia (1256–1349) through Genghis Khan's grandson Hulagu. Genghis Khan, Hulagu (who sacked Baghdad in 1258), and

Tamerlane (Timur Leng, who took Baghdad in 1393) successively laid waste to extensive areas of the Middle East. So devastating was Hulagu's ravaging of Mesopotamia that the complex, centuries-old irrigation system and roads were not restored to their former efficiency until the twentieth century.

Ottoman Empire and Contemporaries

Like the Seljuks, the Ottomans were a Turkish tribe who converted to Islam in Central Asia and then migrated into the plateaus of Iran and Anatolia. Beginning in the early fourteenth century, the Ottomans steadily expanded from their small principality in northwestern Asia Minor until they controlled a vast area from the Danube to Yemen (see Map 8.3). The Ottoman Middle East holdings remained fairly constant from the early 1600s until World War I—with the notable exception of Egypt, which gradually disengaged itself. Like the Byzantines, whom they displaced, the Ottomans gained and lost territories, but they were remarkable for their political longevity: An unbroken dynasty held the sultanate for 600 years. Chapters 8 and 18 explain how the Ottoman Empire had a crucial impact on regional developments in the early twentieth century.

Reviving Persian political organization once again, a kingdom under the Safavids emerged in the Iranian Plateau in 1500. With changes in dynasty in 1736 (Afshars), 1750 (Zands), 1794 (Qajars), and 1925 (Pahlavis), Persia steadily progressed—periodically contending with the Ottomans over Mesopotamia—as a monarchy until early 1979. It changed its official name from Persia to Iran in 1935 and to the Islamic Republic of Iran after the 1979 revolution.

Thus, from about 1500 until World War I, two major powers, each based in one of the two strongest power foci, contended with each other, primarily along the line of the Zagros piedmont: the Ottoman Empire, based in Anatolia, and the Persian Empire, based on the Iranian Plateau. Still occupying a third power focus, but with limits on its former greatness, Egypt gradually eased away from direct Ottoman control during the early nineteenth century but was under British protection by World War I. The interior of the Arabian Peninsula escaped Ottoman control and remained tribally fragmented until the 1930s, when most of the peninsula was unified as Saudi Arabia.

SOME INFERENCES: POWER CORES

The foregoing review of the evolution of political-geographical patterns of the Middle East reveals several broad, persistent factors. Significant lessons to be drawn from the review are relevant not only as a basis for the rest of this book, and thus for better understanding the Middle East, but also as parameters for formulating practical foreign policies in the region.

1. Four major power foci, or cores, and two minor ones have appeared and reappeared in the Middle East throughout history: The Anatolian Plateau (Asia Minor), Iranian Plateau, Tigris-Euphrates Basin (Mesopotamia), and Nile Valley are the four major cores, and the western Fertile Crescent and central and western Arabian Peninsula are the two minor cores. Lesser centers of strength have been the Yemen and Oman areas (Map 3.6).[23]

2. The two most persistently powerful foci, and the two from which the most extensive geographical areas have usually been controlled, have been the two intermontane plateaus, Anatolia and Iran. These two mountain-rimmed centers now host two of the three most populous states—which are also among the most powerful states—in the Middle East: Turkey, Iran, and Egypt.

3. No one power has ever succeeded in conquering and occupying the entire core Middle East as the region is defined in Chapter 1. Regardless of the extent of the existing imperial power during any given period,

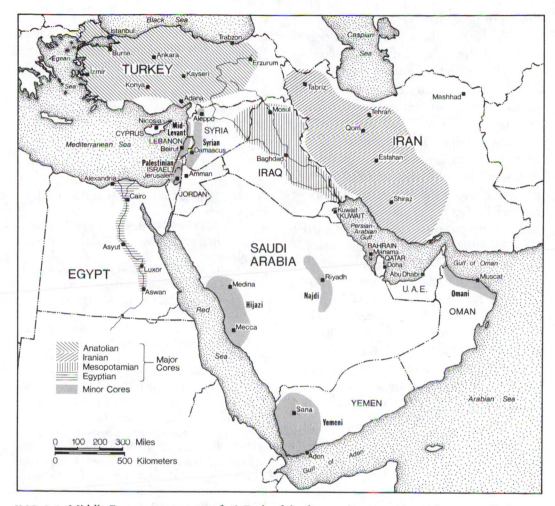

MAP 3.6 Middle East power cores, or foci. Each of the four main power centers has controlled most of the Middle East at some time, but none has controlled all other cores simultaneously.

some other part of the region maintained its independence.

4. The one area that has always been able to maintain its independence, or at least its separateness, from outside powers is the interior of the Arabian Peninsula (Najd). The peninsula was a center of imperial territorial control during the middle of the seventh century, but otherwise it has been relatively isolated, except as a source of migrants who appeared in Syria and Mesopotamia between 2500 BCE and 700 CE.

5. Although Mesopotamia was the earliest power focus and remained the main core for 1,700 years, it gradually weakened as a sepa-

rate center and later functioned as a focus of power only when connected to the Iranian Plateau center. Under the sovereignty of Iraq, Mesopotamia demonstrated renewed potency beginning in the 1980s.

6. The political-geographical history of the Middle East has, to a great extent, revolved around the cyclic interaction of the powers occupying Asia Minor and the Iranian Plateau. Each power often sought control of Mesopotamia, which was sometimes used as a springboard against the power on the other side of the basin.

7. Powers centered in the three northern foci have controlled the Nile Valley at various

times, but never has the Nile Valley power controlled any one of the three major northern foci. Rather, sustained Egyptian control outside Egypt has been limited to the western limb of the Fertile Crescent (Syria-Palestine realm) plus some brief inroads into southeastern Anatolia by Egyptian forces in the 1830s.

Neither history nor geography can dictate the future. Changing technology, fervent ideologies, outside influences, or other developments might alter the relative significance of the several power foci in the Middle East. Since the 1950s, the emergence of Israel and the rise of the Middle East's petroleum age have unquestionably reorchestrated political, military, and economic interrelationships. Yet to consider historical and geographical factors in the region's role as mere academic curiosities is to misread vital lessons and to risk repetition of the mistakes of the past. The roles of the centers at the present time are revisited in Chapter 8, which examines contemporary Middle Eastern political-geographical development.

NOTES

1. Whittlesey 1929.
2. Remarkable archaeological discoveries in southeastern Anatolia during the late 1900s and early 2000s found new evidence of early civilization in several sites.
3. Whalen and Pease 1992. In line with these discoveries, a humanoid jawbone was found in 1991 near Tbilisi, Georgia, that was dated to 900,000 years ago. Another dating gave the bone an age of 1.6 million years. *New York Times,* Feb. 3, 1992.
4. See Redman 1978. Recent additional evidence is given in Heun et al. 1997 and is covered in the *New York Times,* Nov. 18, 1997.
5. A *tell* is termed a *tepe* or *chega* in Persian, *hüyük* in Turkish, and *kom* in Egyptian usage.
6. The Wendorf team found evidence that indicated, through laboratory dating, much earlier cultivation in the Nile Valley. See Wendorf and Schild 1980.
7. See Schmandt-Bessarat 1978 and other articles by her. See also the readable but scholarly Redman 1978,

with its attention to environmental factors; Robinson 1995, 8–13, 58–87; and *New York Times,* Apr. 6, 1999.
8. See Redman 1978, along with Redman 1994; Burenhult 1993; and Saggs 1989.
9. See Bibby 1969.
10. Among scores of accounts of Mesopotamian prehistory and early historical geography, many are in scarce technical journals. Available accounts are in Redman 1978; Saggs 1995; Burenhult 1994, 16–59; and Potts 1997.
11. German archaeologists claimed in late 1989 that some inscriptions found at Abydos gave radiocarbon dates of 3200–3400 BCE, thus predating Mesopotamian writing.
12. See Butzer 1976, which has its critics but is generally accepted by others and is informative and stimulating.
13. See Finkelstein and Silberman 2001, which examines recent discoveries and theories about ancient cultures in the Levant, especially with reference to biblical narratives.
14. See Tubb 1998, Chaps. 7–8; and *New York Times,* Sept. 29, 1992, and July 23, 1996.
15. Among myriad books and articles on ancient Israel, see Aharoni 1967; Baly 1957; and G. Smith 1935 for consideration of geographical factors. See also Finkelstein and Silberman 2001 and R. Friedman 1997. A readable history is Grant 1984.
16. For more recent treatment, see Gore 2004.
17. Kennedy and Riley 1990 has fascinating aerial photographs of Roman roads and ruins in the region.
18. Among several excellent accounts of the Byzantines, see the standard Shaw 1976; Shaw and Shaw 1977; and Norwich 1997.
19. B. Lewis 1973.
20. The original title of *Tales of the Arabian Nights* was *The Thousand and One Nights.* These charming stories, which include such familiar tales as those about Sindbad the Sailor and Ali Baba and the Forty Thieves, reveal many aspects of medieval Islamic culture. For good historical coverage of this period, see S. Fisher and Ochsenwald 1997 and Hourani 1991.
21. Many good histories cover the Islamic Arab empires and later developments. The older classic is Brockelmann 1949. A useful recent one is Hourani 1991.
22. The standard work on the Crusades is Runciman 1954.
23. Based on "Middle East Power Foci and Their Persistence," paper given by author Held, Apr. 15, 1991, to the Association of American Geographers in Miami.

Patterns of Peoples, Cultures, and Settlements
A Demographic Overview

A DEMOGRAPHIC OVERVIEW

The exceedingly complex patterns of distribution of population and peoples in the Middle East are shaped by many interacting biophysical, cultural, and historical influences. Obviously highly correlated are the geographical patterns of population and precipitation and water supply; other factors have constantly been at work to shape unique patterns of peoples, languages, religions, and ethnic groups. Ethnic complexity, for example, often suggests that alternating mountains and valleys compartmentalize different groups of peoples or give refuge to weaker groups.

Enumerating populations is difficult in most Middle East countries, and quantifying religions and linguistic groups is even more of a problem because it often confronts sensitive issues. Governments may attempt to obscure the number—and therefore the influence—of minority ethnic groups, such as Kurds in Turkey (and other countries overlapping "Kurdistan"), or expatriates in Saudi Arabia. Similarly, official enumerators may manipulate religious minority data—for example, Egypt with the Copts and Iran with Armenians, Zoroastrians, and Bahai. Therefore, figures vary widely, even in the best reports, and the following discussion and related tables represent a careful compromise among several authoritative sources. Data in the text are usually kept consistent with those in the tables and the country summaries, although more recent figures are occasionally introduced.

Censuses in some Middle East countries face various problems: Nomads are difficult to locate, technical difficulties can limit accuracy, and sensitivity may cause some results to be withheld for perceived security or political reasons. Although advanced in many ways, Lebanon, with its multiplicity of antagonistic religious communities and associated political factions, has not taken a census since 1932. Saudi Arabia conducted only basic demographic sampling until its 1974 partial census, and it was reticent about some data collected in subsequent efforts. Rapid growth in oil states like Kuwait, the United Arab Emirates, and Saudi Arabia often rendered statistics obsolete before they were published. The Iraqi invasion of Kuwait in August 1990 prompted the exodus of hundreds of thousands of the amirate's inhabitants, greatly altering its demographics. Qatar took its first census in 1986, and Oman in 1993. Even the statistics-conscious state of Israel experienced difficulty in maintaining reliable data during the influx of immigrants from the Former Soviet Union (FSU) beginning in 1989. Although it has quietly manipulated emigration data, Israel has an excellent

Central Bureau of Statistics. Bahrain, Cyprus, Egypt, and Turkey also regularly collect and publish good country statistics.

Middle East governments have made enormous and admirable improvement since the 1960s and 1970s in gathering statistical data and making at least much of it available to the public—Lebanon excepted. In view of the foregoing, however, it is obvious that accurate, extensive, intensive quantitative analyses of the region are impossible and that there is appreciable statistical unevenness across the Middle East.[1] In the extended region, statistics in North African reporting are reasonably reliable, while those in the Central Asian "stans" are still evolving, especially in Afghanistan. Figures from Pakistan are quite good except for the northwestern tribal areas.

The core sixteen countries of the Middle East had an estimated 2008 population total of 350 million, about 5.3 percent of the estimated world population of 6.71 billion. This was four and a half times the 1950 total of 79.7 million, prior to the explosive population growth accompanying the oil boom. During the nearly sixty-year period after 1950, population increased by almost twenty-two times in Kuwait and by an astonishing fifty times in the UAE, and the population in most of the other states—including in the countries of the extended region—increased at least three- or fourfold.

Two comparisons regarding Muslim and Arab populations may be noted. First, of approximately 1.57 billion Muslims in the world, about 26.7 percent are in the core Middle East and another 23.8 percent in the fifteen extended region states. Second, of the estimated 2008 total population of all twenty-two Arab League states (including Palestine) of 340.9 million, 202.1 million are in the twelve Middle East member states (plus Palestine). For these and other geographical and historical reasons, the core Middle East constitutes the center of Islamic and Arab identity.[2] But it should always be kept in mind that most Muslims are not Arabs and not all Arabs are Muslims.

The following discussion of patterns of Middle Eastern peoples reveals the richness and complexity of the region's cultural patterns and gives insights into the human dynamics behind major trends and events in the area: the underlying political patterns, historical and contemporary conflicts, traditional group hostilities, changing cultural patterns, migrations of ethnic and religious groups, and irredentist claims. Although these patterns have long demonstrated their critical impact on geopolitical interactions, their impact in Iraq has appeared in news headlines daily since 2003 as world attention suddenly began to focus on, for example, the patterns of Kurds, Sunnis, Shii, Turkmans, and others.

PATTERNS: POPULATION

Distribution

The distribution of population in the Middle East (see Maps 4.1 and 4.2, Fig. 4.1, and, later in this chapter, Map 4.7 on urban population) is not only of great significance in itself; it also reflects where are found the more favorable environments and greater economic opportunities—twin magnets that attract people. The degree of urbanization (Map 4.1) reflects both the historical role of cities in the Middle East and the rapid urbanization after 1950. The region is more urbanized than may be assumed.

By 2010, about 300 cities in the region had more than 100,000 people, and some 30 cities exceeded 1 million.[3] Cities with between 100,000 and 500,000 have become more numerous since the 1970s and are found in almost all Middle East countries and peripheral states. Nevertheless, despite the trend of increasing urbanization, a high proportion of the people of the extended region still live in villages.

Some of the scattered dots on Map 4.2 represent nomadic pastoralists, whose numbers can only be estimated. Their high mobility

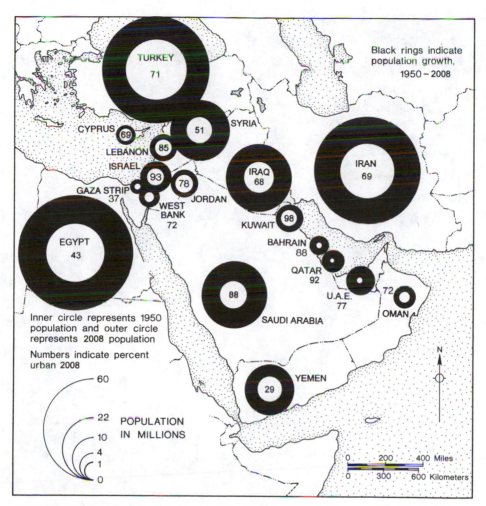

TURKEY
71

CYPRUS
69
LEBANON
85
ISRAEL
93
GAZA STRIP
37
WEST
BANK
72

SYRIA
51

IRAQ
68

JORDAN
78

KUWAIT
98

BAHRAIN
88

QATAR
92

U.A.E.
77

IRAN
69

OMAN
72

Black rings indicate
population growth,
1950 – 2008

EGYPT
43

SAUDI ARABIA
88

Inner circle represents 1950
population and outer circle
represents 2008 population

Numbers indicate percent
urban 2008

YEMEN
29

POPULATION
IN MILLIONS

60
22
10
4
1
0

N

0   200   400 Miles
0   300   600 Kilometers

MAP 4.1 Middle East population growth, 1950–2008. The dominance of the "big three"—Turkey, Egypt, and Iran—in population size is obvious. The thickness of the outer ring indicates the population increase during the past half century.

makes them difficult to count, but their numbers have been steadily decreasing. Several hundred thousand Bedouin of the Arabian Peninsula are known to have settled between 1960 and 2009, and the same is happening with Bedouin elsewhere, partly because of official pressures and incentives. Rough estimates for the region are 600,000 Bedouin, 1.5 million other nomads, and 2.5 million who move their livestock between mountain and lowland pastures with the seasons—a lifestyle called "transhumance" or "vertical nomadism" (Fig. 4.2).

Populations of the extended region's states vary greatly, as Table 4.1 and Graph 4.1 indicate for the sixteen core states. As is true anywhere, population variations can be traced to six major factors: quality of the geographical environment, range and quality of natural resources, effectiveness of the national economy (and outside aid)—including food supply and health care—social and political pressures for or against population increase, incidental or planned (and even forced) immigration and emigration, and territorial size. In Part Two, these factors are explored

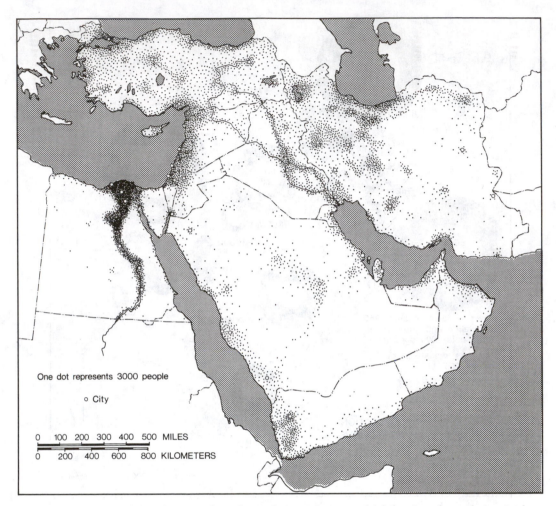

MAP 4.2 Dot map of distribution of rural population. The proverbial density of population in the Nile Valley and Delta is clearly shown. Scattered smaller villages are underrepresented. Compare with Figure 4.1.

for each country, but some quantitative comparisons can be made here.

In 2008, all three of the largest populations were close to 75 million—Egypt, Iran, and Turkey (see Graph 4.1); they are among the four geographically biggest countries and are also three of the four major power cores (see Map 3.6). Iraq has the fourth-largest population and is the fourth major power core. Only slightly smaller, the fifth-largest population inhabits the geographically biggest state in the region—Saudi Arabia. Yemen and Syria, next in size, have moderately large populations for

their partly rugged and partly arid environments. Israel's population growth has depended on periodically explosive immigration and capital transfers. Of the remaining countries, Jordan, the UAE, and Oman have relatively small populations for their size because of extensive barren areas with small numbers of nomads. Kuwait, Cyprus, Qatar, and Bahrain are still smaller with prosperous populations.

Density

Along with the basic patterns of population distribution, those of population density—

FIGURE 4.1 Image from space of the Middle East and adjacent areas at night. The concentrations of lights indicate concentrations of population (cf. Maps 4.2 and 4.7). The gray spots show reddish natural gas flares, especially offshore facilities in the Gulf area. (Copyright 2004, National Geographic Society, Washington, D.C., July 2004. Used with NGS permission.)

FIGURE 4.2
Bedouin in Saudi Arabia, watering their camels at wells in the broad Wadi Sahba, west of Harad, enjoy a joke with author Held.

TABLE 4.1 Area and Demography

Country	1 Area in sq. mi.	2 Area in sq. km.	3 Pop in 1000s	4 Density per sq. mi.	5 Density per sq. km.	6 % Pop. Urban	7 % Annual Growth
Bahrain	281	728	1,084	3,857.7	1,489.0	88.4	7.4
Cyprus[a]	3,572	9,251	1,076	301.2	116.3	68.8	2.4
Egypt	385,229	997,739	74,805	194.2	75.0	42.6	2.0
Iran	636,374	1,648,200	72,269	113.6	43.8	68.5	1.6
Iraq	167,618	434,128	29,492	173.0	66.8	67.9	1.9
Israel	8,357[b]	21,643	7,018[c]	839.8	324.3	92.9	1.7
Jordan[d]	34,277	88,778	5,844	170.5	65.8	78.3	2.2
Kuwait	6,880	17,818	3,530	513.1	198.1	98.3	7.3
Lebanon	4,016	10,400	4,142	1,031.4	398.3	85.0	1.1
Oman	119,500	309,500	2,651	22.2	8.6	71.5	1.5
Qatar	4,184	10,836	1,448	346.1	133.6	92.0	14.8
Saudi Arabia	830,000	2,149,690	24,780	29.9	11.5	87.7	2.4
Syria	71,498	185,180	19,514	272.9	105.4	50.6	2.5
Turkey	302,535	783,562	71,002	234.7	90.6	70.5	1.2
UAE	32,280	83,600	4,660	144.4	55.7	76.7	5.6
Yemen	203,891	528,076	23,013	112.9	43.6	28.6	3.5
Gaza	140	363	1,444	10,314.3	3,978.0	—	3.3
West Bank	2,278	5,900	2,656	1,165.9	450.2	71.6	2.5
TOTAL/AVG.	2,812,910	7,285,392	350,428	124.6	48.1	72.9	3.6
United Kingdom	93,851	243,073	61,446	654.7	252.8	89.5	0.6
Venezuela	353,841	916,445	27,884	78.8	30.4	87.2	1.7

Area includes internal waters. Population data are estimates for 2008. Percentage of population that is urban (Column 6) from most recent census. Percentage of annual growth rate (Column 7) is average for the period 2003–2008. [a]Data are for the entire island. [b]Excludes West Bank, East Jerusalem, Gaza Strip, and Golan Heights. [c]Includes Golan Heights and East Jerusalem, and excludes Israelis in the West Bank and Gaza Strip. [d]Excludes West Bank, formerly under Jordanian administration. (*Source*: *Britannica World Data*, 2009 [with permission].)

the number of persons per unit of area—are also significant. However, these figures for most regional countries are not comparable to those for European countries, where few extensive areas are uninhabited. As the dots in Map 4.2 show, Middle Easterners congregate heavily in a few locales, and there are large extents that are uninhabited or have only a few nomads or widely scattered villages. Thus, aside from favored areas like Asia Minor and the Levant, concentrations are in "islands" of better environments.

Some small oases may be widely scattered, with only a few families occupying each, as in the Jiwa (Liwa) oases in western Abu Dhabi;

by contrast, millions of people may be crowded into a narrow, intensively cultivated valley, like that of the Nile. In both cases, only a small percentage of total state area is actually occupied. For example, Egypt's 74.8 million people have an overall density of 194.2 per mi²/75.0 per km². However, population density based on the area actually inhabited and cultivated, about 3.5 percent of Egypt's total area, soars to more than 5,550 per mi²/2,140 per km². The overall density on the small island of Bahrain is very high, and it is two to three times higher in the areas actually occupied. The anomalous density in the Gaza Strip—more than 10,300 per mi²/3,970 per

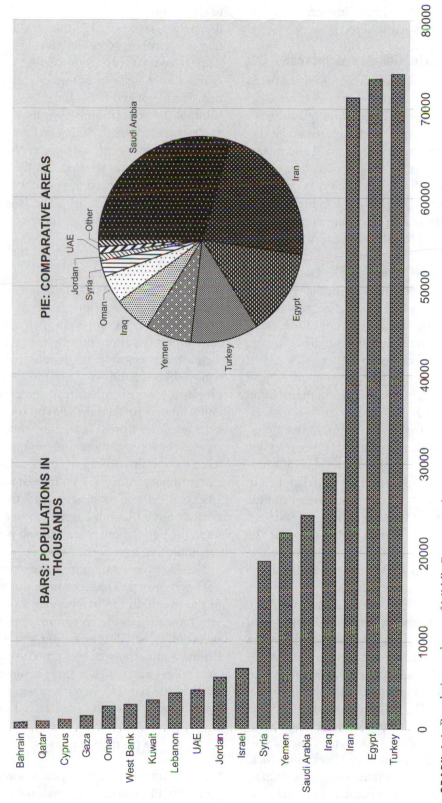

GRAPH 4.1 Population and area of Middle East countries.

km², reflects the appalling crowding of refugees in this artificial territory.

Rates of Birth, Death, and Increase

Statistics show a sharp decline over the twentieth century in crude death rates (deaths per 1,000 population) in developing countries. Better hygiene, health education, and health-care facilities have lowered infant and maternal mortality and lengthened the average human life. Birthrates have not really increased overall (those for live births have, however), but death rates have decreased notably in many countries. The result has been a marked rise in population.

As shown in Table 4.1, the growth rates of the sixteen core countries, plus the West Bank and Gaza, show high population growth, due to high birthrates and immigration rates. Whereas the crude birthrates of Syria, Oman, and Yemen all exceeded 40 per 1,000 several years ago—similar to rates in many African countries—only Yemen's rate remained that high into the 2000s. Some countries, particularly Egypt, Turkey, and Iran, have emphasized government-supported family-planning programs, but some groups resist because traditional customs encourage large families. In Israel, where as a group Jews have one of the lowest birthrates in the region, the state encourages more Jewish births to offset the higher Arab birthrate—but aside from ultra-religious groups and some West Bank settlers, success has been limited.

Birthrates vary both from country to country and among groups and classes—for example, across religious and ethnic groups (sometimes equivalent to economic classes) in all Middle East countries. The rate is substantially lower among Coptic Christians than Muslims in Egypt, lower among Maronites than Shii in Lebanon, lower among secular Jews than ultra-Orthodox and Oriental Jews in Israel, and lower among Greeks than Turks in Cyprus. These differences can accentuate political antagonisms because they might lead to changes in the balance of power. Population pyramids (Graph 4.2) show the distribution of age cohorts (see Glossary), varying in shape from country to country depending on factors like changes in birthrates and migration. For Egypt and Syria, the relative overall youth of the population is obvious. For Syria and especially Iran, declining birthrates have slowed population growth; under the shah, family planning was stressed, but the Islamic Republic at first reversed this policy before reinstating it (see Chap. 19). The UAE (like other Gulf states) has a large number of male expatriates of working age.

Migration

All three basic aspects of migration—immigration, emigration, and internal migration—play major roles in defining the contemporary pattern of peoples in the Middle East. For example, immigration into the region (by Jews and South Asians, for example) and migration within the region (by Palestinians, Jordanians, Egyptians, Jews, Lebanese, and Kurds) have dramatically increased some populations and profoundly altered the ethnic makeup of some states. The extraordinary influx of Jews into Israel from 1945 to 1951 and again after 1989 from the Former Soviet Union completely reconstituted the population, character, and political orientation of traditional Palestine.

Generally, emigration from the region has not been so large. However, since the middle of the twentieth century, hundreds of thousands have fled limited economic opportunities, conflict, and discrimination, going to the United States, Canada, Western Europe, and Australia—particularly Turks, Palestinian Arabs, Christian Lebanese, Syrians, Jordanians, Kurds, Israelis—and, in the 2000s, Iraqis.

PATTERNS: PEOPLES

It is the cultural differentiation among peoples—variations in language, religion, customs

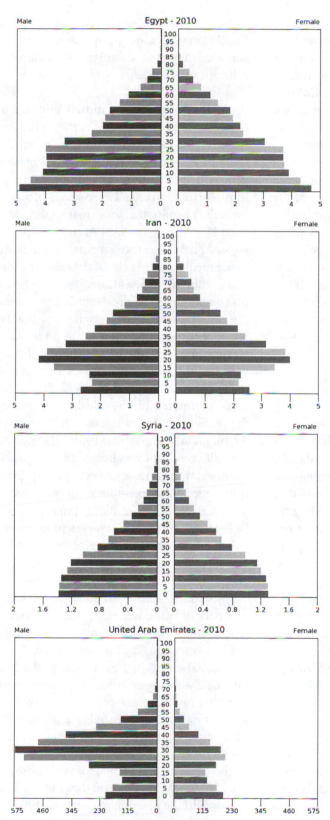

GRAPH 4.2
Contrasting population pyramids of four Middle East countries (population in millions).
(*Source*: U.S. Census Bureau, International Data Base)

and dress, values, and historical experiences—that creates separate group identities and nations. Thus, examination of the mosaic of peoples, or ethnic groups, is a major component of this analysis of the region. Cultural patterns are, in effect, shuffled three times. The two dominant cultural ones, language and religion, deserve individual attention; sections on those are followed by a survey of ethnic groups. Two salient points about the patterns of peoples are worth noting at the outset: About half the population of the region is non-Arab (although twelve countries are Arab), and within its essential theological unity, Islam carries ethnic and political imprints and has several sectarian variations. Thus, the region has great cultural diversity.[4] When the extended Middle East states are considered, even greater variety appears—a major factor hindering regional unity.

PATTERNS: LANGUAGES

Language is the principal criterion for defining ethnic groups, particularly if the distinction is an ethnolinguistic one. Thus, Map 4.3 summarizes one of the most revealing patterns in the cultural geography of the Middle East. The depiction of only six main linguistic groupings should not obscure the presence of about twenty-five other language groups in less accessible basins, valleys, and plateaus. Some of these languages appear on Map 4.3, but many others are covered in the listing of ethnic groups later in the chapter, and some of them are discussed in this section. The principal languages of the region are, in order of speaker populations: Arabic, Turkish, Farsi, Kurdish, Azeri, and Hebrew.

Semitic and Berber

The Semitic language group includes Arabic, the numerically predominant regional language; Hebrew, spoken in Israel; and vestiges of Aramaic, formerly spoken widely throughout the Middle East going back more than 2,500 years. The North African Berber and Coptic languages are grouped here with the Semitic languages, although they belong to different subfamilies.

Arabic.   Arabic is the national language of twelve of the core countries of the region and is spoken by more than half the total population of the core countries, about 172 million people. It is spoken by an additional 85 million North Africans. Three levels of usage prevail: (1) colloquial, informal spoken Arabic; (2) modern standard Arabic, or "newspaper Arabic," the more formal version used in the media; and (3) classical Arabic, the formal and highly conventionalized style based on the language of pre-Islamic poetry, the Quran, and writings from the first few Islamic centuries. Educated Arabs understand all three, but the uneducated have difficulty with the two more formal levels. In addition, there are four major dialects in the twelve Arab countries in the Mashriq: those of Egypt, Syria (western Arabic), Iraq (eastern Arabic), and the Arabian Peninsula. Significant differences of vocabulary and pronunciation exist among, and even within, these four. One major example is the pronunciation in Egypt of the Arabic "j" (*jiim*) as a hard "g." Thus, *jabal* (mountain) is pronounced *gabal* in Egypt: this creates problems transliterating place-names. Variants in North Africa (the Maghrib) are even further removed.

Speaking Arabic as a mother tongue is the hallmark of being an Arab. Since it is the language of the Quran, the holy book of Islam, it has a mystical quality for many Arabs. It has additional emotional overtones as the language in which speeches and documents on Arab nationalism are prepared. In written form, it even plays a central role in art, since calligraphy is widely used in traditional decorative motifs in lieu of the sometimes proscribed human and animal forms; it is one of the highest Islamic fine arts. (See the excellent example in the opening pages of this book.)

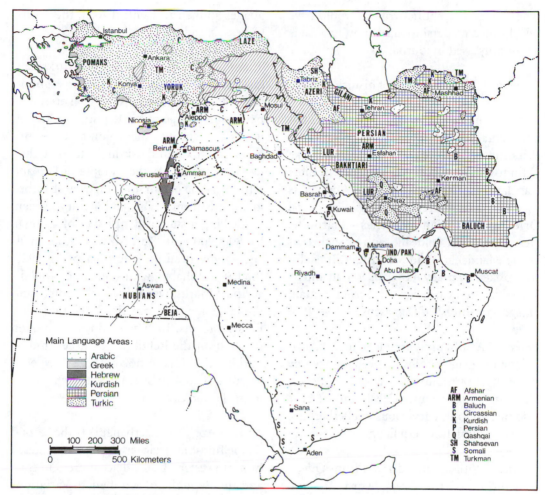

MAP 4.3 Middle East languages, indicating ethnolinguistic groups. This pattern has been the basis for numerous political developments and regional conflicts. Note that the complexity of the pattern of languages is greatest in mountain areas, especially in Iran.

Hebrew. Compared with Arabic, Hebrew is the mother tongue in a relatively limited area for a comparatively small number of people, a little more than 5 million—not of all the Jews in the region or even all Israeli Jews. An ancient language, it was the vernacular for more than 1,000 years in the traditional Old Testament area of Israel. It ceased to be a working language centuries ago, but for Jewish communities it remained the language of religion, much as Latin, Greek, and Syriac are used in Christian liturgies. As a scriptural language, like Arabic for Muslims, it has a mystical quality

for religious Jews. For the ultrareligious, it is so sacred that it is reserved only for rituals; some regard as near blasphemy its vernacular use and employ instead Yiddish or other languages. Many recent FSU emigrants have resisted adopting Hebrew, holding on to Russian.

Hebrew was revived in the late nineteenth century under the stimulus of the Zionist movement—because a unifying language was needed as an added stimulus for Jewish immigrants to Palestine. Contemporary usage has required adaptation of old terms and the coinage of new ones. Because Israeli scholarly and scientific writings would have only limited readership in Hebrew, English is commonly used in journals.

Aramaic.   Now primarily of historical interest, Aramaic served for more than 1,500 years as the lingua franca of the Fertile Crescent; it had replaced Hebrew as the language of Palestine well before the time of Christ. Like Latin to the West, Aramaic was used in Bible translations. The Syriac form of Aramaic is used in the scriptures and liturgies of several Oriental Christian churches—Maronite, Nestorian, and Chaldean—and by such sects as the Mandaeans and Samaritans. It is also still spoken by many Assyrians in Iraq and by a few hundred Christians in three mountain villages northwest of Damascus.

Berber.   A subfamily language in the Afro-Asiatic language family, Berber is spoken by more than 14 million North Africans, especially in Morocco and Algeria. In the core Middle East, only a few thousand Berbers live in oases in northwestern Egypt.

Coptic.   With a name derived from *Qibt*, a corruption of the Greek word *Aigyptos* (Egypt), Coptic was the latest form of the ancient Egyptian language. Greek influenced it during the Hellenistic period, but it was Egypt's vernacular until, over the centuries, it was gradually supplanted by Arabic after the Muslim conquest. The discovery that many Coptic words came directly from ancient Egyptian aided in the deciphering of hieroglyphics. By the sixteenth century, it was used primarily in the liturgy of the Coptic Christian church in Egypt; that remains the case today.

Altaic Turkic Languages

The Altaic family includes a large number of languages spoken in the FSU and in China, as well as Magyar (Hungarian) and Finnish in Europe and more than a score of Turkic languages spoken in Central Asia, the Trans-Caucasus, and the Middle East.

Turkish.   The best known of the Turkic languages, Turkish is spoken by the largest number of Turkic-language speakers. The national language of the Republic of Turkey, it was brought into the region by tribes migrating from Central Asia in the tenth to thirteenth centuries. As they adopted Islam and settled in Asia Minor, the language absorbed loanwords from Arabic and literary Persian.

Lacking a standard alphabet of its own, for 800–900 years Turkish was rather inadequately written in Arabic script. In 1928, the Latin alphabet, with some borrowed diacritical marks, was officially adopted, and the language was "purified" of Arabic and Persian terms. In the region, it is spoken throughout the Republic of Turkey and by Turkish Cypriots in northern Cyprus; elsewhere, it is spoken by small scattered groups in the Fertile Crescent.

Azeri.   Azeri (or Azerbaijani) is the second major Turkic language in the region, centered in northwestern Iran, adjacent areas in Iraq, and the Republic of Azerbaijan. Variations appear in the western Elburz and the southern Caspian littoral among the Afshar, Shahsavan (now called Ilsavan), and Qajar groups. Like Turkish, Azeri entered with migrating tribes during the Abbasid era.

Other Turkic languages, spoken by several hundred thousand people each in Iran, Turkey, and Iraq, include Qashqai (spoken by tribes in the southern Zagros Mountains of Iran) and various Turkman dialects spoken by scattered peoples in the Anatolian-Iranian mountains and basins and in small areas in northeastern Iraq. Still others are the national tongues of peripheral "stan" states: Turkman in Turkmenistan and northern Afghanistan, Uzbek in Uzbekistan and northern Afghanistan, Kazakh in Kazakhstan, and Kirghiz in Kyrgyzstan.

Indo-European Languages

The Indo-European languages of the region include more than a score of Indo-Iranian tongues, the main ones being Farsi (Persian), Kurdish, Baluchi, and Luri (with its related dialect of Bakhtiari). Armenian and Greek—in the Indo-European family—are spoken by several hundred thousand people each. Four other languages in this family, which are spoken by millions of people in the eastern areas of the peripheral states, are also discussed below.

Farsi (Persian). The primary Indo-Iranian language is Farsi, a name taken from the ancient Iranian province of Fars. After Arabic and Turkish, it is spoken by the third-largest language group in the region. The Persian languages were brought to the Iranian Plateau more than 1,500 years before Turkic languages were heard in the area. After the Muslim conquest of Iran in the seventh century, Persian, like Turkish, incorporated hundreds of Arabic loanwords, adopting a modified Arabic script.

It is the primary language of Iran, although nearly half of Iranians speak another mother tongue—Azeri, Kurdish, Gilaki, Luri, Baluchi, Arabic, and others. However, as the official language and that used by the mass media, government, and educational institutions, Farsi is a second language for most minority groups. Persian literature has a rich history dating from the Zoroastrian scriptures, the *Avesta*, written before 500 BCE.

Kurdish. The second most common Indo-Iranian language in the region, Kurdish is found across a geographical range extending from the streets of Beirut eastward to remote valleys in Afghanistan, though its main concentration of more than 20 million speakers is in the mountains of Kurdistan. It is grammatically and lexically distinct from Persian, and two major dialects may be distinguished. The

pattern of Kurdish speakers exploded into a major factor in Iraq after 2003. Reflecting the extension of Kurdistan into several hegemonies, Kurdish is written with the Arabic alphabet in Iraq, the adapted Arabic alphabet in Iran, and the Latin alphabet in Turkey.

Other Indo-Iranian Languages. Baluchi is spoken in Baluchistan in southeastern and eastern Iran; even more speakers are in the adjacent areas of Pakistan and Afghanistan. It is also spoken by several thousand Baluch across the Gulf in the UAE and Oman. Luri, a dialect of Persian, is spoken by nomadic tribes in the central Zagros, both by the Lur themselves and also, in a slightly different dialect, by their Bakhtiari neighbors. Sometimes called "Caspian" languages, a half-dozen Indo-Iranian dialects, mixed with one or two Turkic tongues, are spoken along the southern Caspian coast and on the northern slopes of the Elburz Mountains. Indo-European languages—some spoken by as many as 50 million people—common in the peripheral countries include Tajik in Tajikistan, Pushtun (or Pashtu or Pakto) in Afghanistan and Pakistan, Punjabi (or Panjabi) in Pakistan, and Dari (closely related to Farsi) and Hazara in Afghanistan.

Armenian and Greek. Armenian and Greek, two Indo-European languages, were formerly spoken over more extensive areas in the region than at present. Armenian was the dominant language for more than 2,000 years in the area of historical Armenia—the highlands at the junction of Turkey, Iran, and the Republic of Armenia. However, Armenian speakers in the core Middle East are now found mainly in urban centers, such as Istanbul, Aleppo, Damascus, Beirut, Nicosia, Tehran, Cairo, Baghdad, and Jerusalem. The language is, of course, the national tongue of the adjacent Republic of Armenia.

Similarly, Greek was a major language in western Asia Minor 2,000 years before Turks arrived in significant numbers, and it took root on numerous Mediterranean islands, including Cyprus. As the urban and intellectual language of the Levant for centuries after Alexander the Great, Greek was the original language for much of the New Testament.[5] However, only a few thousand Greek speakers remain in Asia Minor, the Levant, and Egypt; the main concentration is now in southern Cyprus.

PATTERNS: RELIGIONS

Complexity of Patterns of Religion

At first glance, the pattern of religions appears simple: Islam embraces more than 90 percent of the people of the core Middle East. This pattern, however, is complicated by the interwoven and disparate segments of Islam, by the basic divisions within Islam between Sunni and Shii, and by the splintering of Shii sects.

Divisions within Christianity, which developed in the region, are even more numerous. Differing theological interpretations resulted in major schisms, which were later only partly mended by the church in Rome, until more than a dozen sects claimed sole possession of Christian truth.

Several million Jews are now concentrated in Israel, where ethnic and sectarian subdivisions periodically dispute such issues as conversion and observation of the Sabbath. Ancient or syncretic religions—Zoroastrian, Yazidi, Mandaean, Alawi, Druze, and Bahai—constitute small Middle Eastern minorities.

Religious divisions have long played, and now increasingly play, significant cultural-political-geographical roles in the Middle East. In recent decades, political instability and social violence have increasingly devolved from intensification of religious and ethnic consciousness. In turn, political polarization resulting from religious fervor has inflamed communal feelings and weakened national bonds. The increasing linkages between politics and religion have been a cause of growing apprehension since the 1970s, and especially after 9/11. This topic is explored in Chapter 8.

The pattern of religions has been strongly influenced by two historical factors in modern times. First, when Muslims conquered the area from the Nile River to the Iranian Plateau in the seventh century, there were millions of Christians and Zoroastrians, scores of thousands of Jews, thousands of Mandaeans, and other smaller groups. In general, the Muslim invaders proselytized these conquered peoples. However, the Quran taught that Jews and Christians were *ahl al-kitab* (people of the book), permitted to keep their religions and communities under certain conditions. Later, Mandaeans, Zoroastrians, and even Berbers were accepted as people of the book. Therefore, religious groups had a strong group identity linked with their courts, areas of residence, occupations and usually language, as well as religion. This group identity persists, and it continues to affect regional relationships and the internal politics of Middle East states.

In a second historical development, the concept of people of the book was codified in the Ottoman Empire into the *millet* system (from *millah*, "religion" or "religious community"), and *millets* further imprinted group consciousness on the non-Muslims of the Middle East. Religious affiliation assumed great cultural-political significance, and identity cards in Lebanon and Israel, for example, still indicate in some way the individual's religion.[6]

Three Monotheistic World Religions

The Middle East is familiarly and significantly known as the birthplace of the world's three major monotheistic religions, all of which worship the same God: Judaism, Christianity, and Islam (Map 4.4; Fig. 4.3). Judaism and Christianity both began in the hills between the Mediterranean coastal plain

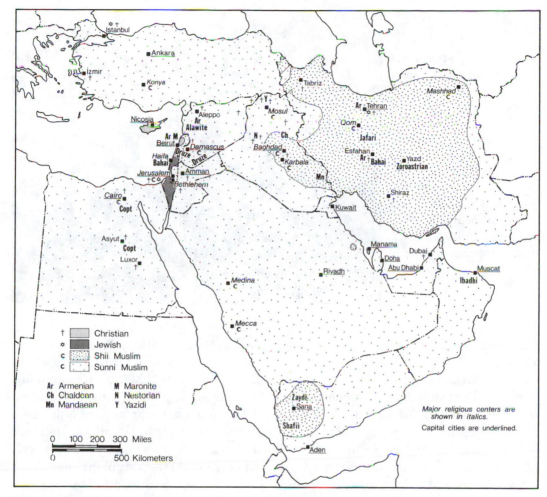

MAP 4.4 Middle East religions. Note the overwhelming dominance of Islam and the extension of Shiism into southern Iraq.

and the Jordan Valley, and Islam originated 700 mi/1,125 km to the southeast in the heights inland from the Red Sea. As Judaism borrowed from Mesopotamian and Canaanite traditions, so Christianity evolved from Judaic and other practices of the region, and Islam borrowed heavily from Judaism, Christianity, and local Hijazi customs. In the late 2000s, Muslims number about 320 million, about 92 percent of the population of the region. Christianity is the second-largest religion, with approximately 15 million adherents, and Judaism third with approximately 6 million.

The following discussion focuses on spatial relations rather than historical evolution or theology. Islam is examined first and in somewhat more detail because of its greater geographical and quantitative importance in the region and because it is less well known or understood outside the Muslim world.

Islam. The Arabic word "Islam" signifies submitting oneself to God's will, and a Muslim is "one who submits." The term "Muhammadan" is a misnomer, since it suggests a parallel with "Christian"—a worshiper of Christ—whereas Muslims do not worship

FIGURE 4.3
Mosque of St. Sophia (Greek: Haghia Sophia; Turkish: Aya Sofya [Divine Wisdom]) in Istanbul. Originally a Byzantine church, it was converted into a mosque when Constantinople was captured by the Ottomans in 1453. Deconsecrated in the 1930s, it is now a museum open to the public.

Muhammad. Rather, they revere him and his teachings, and they consider him the Seal of the Prophets, that is, the last and greatest of the prophets, a line that had stretched from Adam and Noah to John the Baptist and Jesus.[7]

The origins of Islam are regional in character. Mecca, the Arabian town in which Islam evolved, was an important caravan post between Yemen and Syria. Its importance was enhanced by the Well of Zamzam, since water was scarce along Tihamah, the barren Red Sea coastal plain followed by the caravans. It was also the site of an ancient shrine, the *Kaabah*, which contained an array of idols and housed the revered Black Stone (a meteorite). Rapid development in the sixth century stimulated intellectual exchange, as townspeople and Bedouin from the Hijaz mingled with the caravan travelers from Syria, Yemen, and elsewhere.

One Mecca merchant who was inspired by the ideas being discussed was Muhammad ibn Abdullah, a member of the Hashim clan of the Quraysh tribe.[8] While meditating in a nearby cave, he received what he later explained were dictations from the Angel Gabriel of the Holy Word of the one God (Arabic *Allah* = the God). Preaching his revelations, he denounced the Kaabah idols and thereby endangered Mecca's pilgrim trade. Harassed by local merchants, Muhammad and his followers—the original Muslims—emigrated to Yathrib, 210 mi/340 km north of Mecca. Yathrib later became known as al-Madinat al-Nabi (the City of the Prophet), or simply al-Madina (the City). The migration was in 622 CE, which became the first year of the Islamic calendar. Muslim years, comprising twelve lunar months (eleven days shorter than Gregorian or solar years), are designated as anno Hegirae (AH), year of the Hegira (Arabic *hijrah* = flight).

In Medina, the Prophet recited dictations from the Angel to his followers until his death in 632. These were assembled in 651 into the Muslim scriptures, the Quran (Koran), meaning "recitation"—the essential core of Islam. Accepted by Muslims as the exact Word of God linking God and believers, the Quran uses poetic language reflecting the Hijaz and village and Bedouin traditions, just as the Old and New Testaments refer to the desert traditions of Sinai and the Syro-Palestinian area.

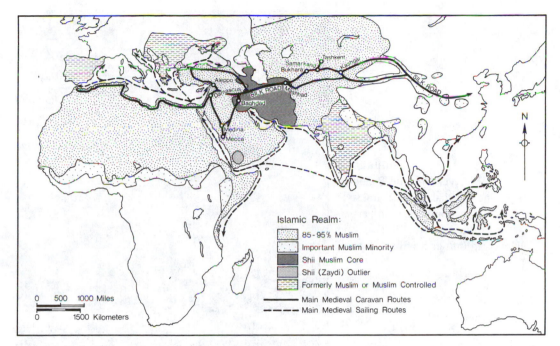

MAP 4.5 Present extent of Islam, with major medieval caravan and sea routes that contributed to the spread and persistence of Islam.

Translation of the Quran from Arabic was long strongly discouraged, since that would mean altering the direct Word of God, and converts perforce had to learn the language in order to understand the scriptures. As Islam spread throughout the Middle East and North Africa to Spain and into Central Asia (Map 4.5), the Arabic language also spread, with crucial historical and political-geographical consequences.

The Muslim place of worship is the mosque (from Arabic *masjid,* "place of worship"). Each mosque has an exterior minaret and interior mihrab, which indicates where worshipers should direct their prayers—toward Mecca. Figure 4.4 pictures one type of mosque; styles are nearly unlimited. Over the centuries, thousands of shrines have been built all over the Islamic world; they are interesting and moving features in many otherwise barren landscapes (Fig. 4.5).

Although, like all religions, Islam has elaborated a complex and subtle body of theol-ogy, both its essential message and its practice are simple and straightforward, and that is one of the reasons for its rapidly growing numbers. Its one fundamental essential is that a convert express and believe the *shahadah,* or profession of faith: "There is no god but God; Muhammad is the messenger of God," a translation of the euphonious Arabic *La ilaha illa Allah; Muhammadun rasulu Allah.* The *shahadah* and four additional primary obligations constitute the five pillars of Islam, which have profoundly affected regional character in the Islamic world: *salah,* devotional worship or prayer five times a day facing toward the Kaabah, the House of God, in Mecca (Fig. 4.6); *zakah,* religious tax (and *sadaqah,* voluntary almsgiving, additionally meritorious); *sawm,* fasting during the holy month of Ramadan, ninth in the year; and, for those who have the means, the *hajj,* the pilgrimage to Mecca.

The Quran underlies Sharia, the sacred law of Islam, which covers all aspects of the

FIGURE 4.4
Martyrs' Mosque, Baghdad.
The unusual architectural style
incorporates certain Persian
influences from the east and
Umayyad influences from the west.

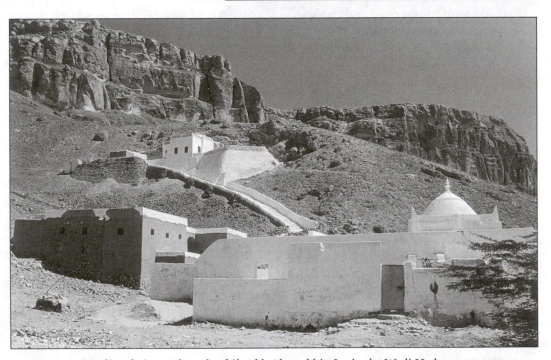

FIGURE 4.5 Muslim shrine and tomb of Shaykh Ahmad bin Isa in the Wadi Hadramawt, eastern
Yemen. A visit to the tomb is a poignant experience, and many such shrines are found throughout
the Middle East.

lives of Muslims—not only religious and private but also political and public, social and economic. Sharia still plays an important role in the legal systems of several Middle East countries—notably Saudi Arabia, Qatar, and Iran—and complements the more Westernized legal codes of countries such as Egypt, Syria, and Iraq. Resurgent Islamic fundamentalism, which has received so much attention since 9/11, has brought a renewed interest in Sharia, especially since it is at times in conflict with modern secular trends in the region.

Islam was for many centuries both religion and government, and when Sharia was compiled, it combined religious and civil matters. The caliph (Arabic *khalifah* = successor) thus led both the community of believers (the *ummah*) and the Islamic state. Although subsequent schisms placed severe strains on the unity of religion and state, resurgent fundamentalism—Islamism—has revived ferment for Islamized control in several states, from Morocco to Afghanistan and Pakistan.

The most momentous dispute within Islam occurred with the seventh-century division between Sunni and Shii.[9] It has led to wars, assassinations, civil conflict, and rancor throughout the Muslim world for more than 1,300 years and has major repercussions in the Middle East today. The Sunni (or Sunnites)—*ahl al-sunnah wa-l-jamaah*, "the people of custom and community"—consider themselves the original orthodox Muslims and have always been in the overwhelming majority. They believe that caliphs should be chosen by leaders of the *ummah* primarily to be secular leaders. The Shii (or Shiites or Shiah)—*shiat Ali*, "partisans (or supporters) of Ali"—separated beginning in 657, holding that only descendants of Muhammad, through his daughter Fatima and son-in-law Ali, were legitimate successors to the Prophet. To Shii, these successors are divinely guided, sinless, infallible religious leaders (imams) with authority to interpret the Prophet's spiritual knowledge. The schism has accentuated

political, social, and cultural divisions both historically and currently—perhaps as bitterly today as at any time in the past—in Iraq particularly, but also in Lebanon, Yemen, Saudi Arabia, and Bahrain, as well as in peripheral Pakistan (see Chap. 8).

After the initial split, the Shii further divided over succession issues (Table 4.2):

1. The predominant group accepted Ali and eleven of his descendants as the true imams and became known as Twelvers (also *Ithna Ashari*, *Imamis*, and *Jafaris*). They are concentrated in Iran and Iraq, but at least some are found in every Middle East country.

2. A smaller group preferred a different seventh imam, Ismail, and became known as Seveners (also *Ismailis*). Many of them split off into heterodox sects such as the Druze and the Alawi. They had political power between the tenth and thirteenth centuries. Early Ismaili dynasties ruled in Syria and Bahrain, and the Fatimids, named for Muhammad's daughter, achieved an Egyptian renaissance during the tenth to twelfth centuries. Ismaili "assassins" engaged in political sabotage and murder, primarily in northern Iran. Found mainly in India, Syria, the Gulf area, and East Africa, contemporary Ismailis form three communities—the largest is headed by the Agha Khan.

Two Ismaili offshoots mentioned above deserve attention. The Druze originated in Cairo in 1017 with followers of the Fatimid caliph al-Hakim. Although they called themselves *Muwahhidun* (Unitarists), outsiders called them Druze after the name of an early missionary. They won large numbers of converts among isolated mountain peoples in southern Lebanon and adjacent areas, and they are still concentrated in that region. They are an esoteric and nonproselytizing sect, and their present connections to the rest of Islam are tenuous at best.

The second offshoot sect, the Alawis (or Alawites, also known as *Nusayris* and sometimes *Ansariyahs*) are concentrated in northwestern Syria and nearby parts of Turkey.

FIGURE 4.6 Muslim members of the Jordanian Desert Patrol performing one of the five daily prayers, near Petra. (Tor Eigeland, *Saudi Aramco World*, SAWDIA)

Although "Alawi" indicates "followers of Ali," the rituals of their esoteric religion include pre-Christian, Christian, and Sabian elements as well as Shii practices. Using neither mosques nor churches, Alawis conduct rites at shrines near revered tombs and sacred groves. In Turkey they are called Alevi; they include Arabs, Turks, and Kurds, and they often conceal their heterodoxy.

3. A third group of Shii chose a different fifth imam, Zayd, and became known as Fivers (also *Zaydis*). They are concentrated in Yemen, where Zaydi secular imams held power until the overthrow of Imam al-Badr in the mid-1960s. Yemeni Shii links originated in the support given Ali by Yemeni tribesmen settling in southern Mesopotamia after the Arab Muslim conquest of the area.

An isolated, little-known group of Muslims, the Ibadhis, live in Inner Oman, where they were banished from southern Iraq in the seventh century. They are descendants of the Kharijites (*khawarij* = those who went out), who assassinated Ali and differed with both Sunni and Shii beliefs regarding caliphal succession. They maintained their imamate in Inner Oman and periodically fought for control of Muscat and all of Oman into the mid-twentieth century. With Nazwa as their main center, they are now a conservative group integrated into Omani development.

To briefly summarize some basic statistics, a comprehensive report on global Islam published in 2009 makes the following points relevant to this study: These sixteen countries are home to about 22.6 percent of the world's 1.57 billion Muslims, the twenty-two members of the Arab League have about 20.3 percent, the vast majority of Muslims are neither Arab nor live in the Middle East, between 10 and 13 percent of Muslims worldwide and of Muslims in our core area are members of one

TABLE 4.2 Religions of the Middle East

Religion, Church, Sect (Including Alternate Names)	Main Center or Pat. Seat	Liturgical Language	Main Areas in Which Found in Mideast
— ISLAM —			
Sunni Islam (largest sect by far)	None (Mecca)	>Ar; Turk, Farsi	Most of Mideast
Shii Islam (second-largest sect by far)	None (Mecca, Karbala)	Farsi, Arabic	Iran, Southern Iraq, South Lebanon
Imamis (Jafaris, "Twelvers," Ithna Ashari)	——	Farsi, Arabic	Iran, Iraq
Ismailis ("Seveners")	——	Arabic	Levant
Zaydis ("Fivers")	——	Arabic	Yemen
Alawis/Alevis (Alawites, Nusayris, Ansaris)	None	Arabic, Turkish	W Syria, Turkey
Druzes (Muwahhidun ["Unitarians"])	None	Arabic	S Syr, C Leb, N Isr
Ibadhis	Nazwa, Oman	Arabic	Inner Oman, <Iran
— CHRISTIANITY —			
Churches with no outside affiliation			
Coptic Orthodox Church (C O C, Alexandria)	Cairo	Coptic, Arabic	C and N Egypt
Armenian Orthodox Ch. (Arm. Georgian Church)	Antilyas, Leb	Armenian	C Middle East
Syrian Orth. Ch. (Jacobite Ch., W Syr. Church)	Damascus	Syriac, Arabic	Syria, Iraq
Ethiopian Orthodox Church (Ethiopian Church)	Addis Ababa	Geez	Egypt
Church of the East (Nestorian Church, East Syrian Church, Assyrian Church)	Baghdad (official)	Syriac	Syria, Iraq
Churches affiliated with the Patriarchate of Constantinople			
Orthodox Patriarchate of Constantinople (Greek Orthodox Church of Const., The Great Church)	Istanbul	Greek	Levant
Greek Orth. Church of Antioch (Rum Orth., etc.)	Damascus	Arabic	Levant
Greek Orth. Church of Alexandria (Ch. of Alex.)	Alexandria	Greek, Arabic	Egypt
Greek Orth. Church of Jerusalem (Ch. of Jerus.)	Jerusalem	Arabic, Greek	Levant
Greek Orthodox (Several other names)	(Several)	(Several)	Levant
Uniate Churches: Churches united with the Roman Catholic Church			
Coptic Catholic Church (Coptic Cath. Ch. of Alex.)	Cairo	Coptic, Arabic	Egypt
Maronite Church (Maronite Church of Antioch)	Bkirke, Leb	Syriac, Arabic	Central Lebanon
Syrian Catholic Ch. (Patriarchate of Antioch)	Beirut, Leb	Syriac, Arabic	Levant
Armenian Cath. Church (Arm. Cath. Ch. Cilicia)	Bzummar, Leb	Armenian	Levant
Chaldean Catholic Church (Chaldean Church)	Baghdad	Syriac, Arabic	Iraq
Melkite Church (Rum Catholic Church, Greek Catholic Church of Antioch)	Damascus	Arabic	Syria
Western churches			
Roman Catholic Church	Rome	(Various)	Mideast exc Arabia
Protestant Churches (Presbyterians, Methodists, Baptists, Anglicans, several others)	——	English, others	Mideast exc Arabia
— JUDAISM —			
Orthodox Judaism	(Jerusalem)	Hebrew	Israel, <other ME
Hasidic Judaism [ultra-Orthodox Judaism]	(Jerusalem)	Hebrew	Israel
(Samaritanism [offshoot of Judaism])	Nabulus, Holon	Aramaic	West Bank, Israel
— OTHERS —			
Yazidism (erroneously: "Devil Worship")	None	Kurdish, Ar	NW Iraq, NE Syria
Mandaeism (Sabianism, Mendaism)	None	Aramaic dial.	Baghdad, S Iraq
Bahaism	Haifa	(Several)	Iran, Levant
Zoroastrianism	None	Farsi	Central Iran

"Pat." = Patriarchal. Some liturgies use local languages (Arabic, Turkish, Farsi [Persian]) in addition to the traditional languages. Syriac is a form of Aramaic. Memberships vary widely, from more than 320 million Muslims to about 709 Samaritans. (*Sources*: Various, including Joseph 1983; *Britannica World Data 2009*; *CIA World Factbook*; *Background Notes* 2009 and 2010; and authors' field research.)

of the Shii sects, and about 65 percent of all Shii live in the sixteen countries of this study.[10]

Christianity.   Middle East Christianity today embraces more than a dozen sects centered on the spiritual and ethical teachings of Jesus of Nazareth, who is believed to have lived and taught in Palestine 2,000 years ago.[11] In the Occidental world, calendar years are designated (with an inadvertent error of about four years) as anno Domini (AD), indicating years that have elapsed since the birth of Jesus. A religiously neutral term is CE, Common Era, as in this book.

Although other religions share the messianic concept, Christianity preaches, as a central belief, that Jesus was the long-awaited Messiah (Greek *Christos* = "the anointed"). The early apostles compiled his teachings in the Gospels (good tidings) and added their own preachings and letters. Assembled, these writings form the New Testament (New Covenant), the main Christian scriptures— coupled with the Old Testament to constitute the Christian Bible. From its earliest years, Christianity incorporated influences from the region's several cultures—Jewish, Greek, Roman, and Aramaic.

By New Testament accounts, Jesus was acclaimed during his three-year ministry in Judea, Galilee, and nearby places. However, only a few of his followers, mainly converted Jews, remained faithful after his crucifixion by the Roman authorities. From the beginning, Jews who followed Jesus were on uneasy terms with the Jewish religious establishment, and when in 66 CE these early Christians refused to support the Jewish revolt, they were effectively cut off from their former compatriots.

Even before this breach, the apostle-missionaries preached to the Gentiles (Greeks) in Asia Minor and Syria. Antioch was the first Christian center, soon followed by Edessa (modern Şanlıurfa) farther east. Suppressed for more than 200 years by Roman authori-

ties as inimical to the imperial religion, it was officially permitted by the Edict of Milan (313), then accepted by Emperor Constantine after the imperial capital was moved from Rome to Constantinople in 330, and became the state religion of the empire in 380. A series of ecumenical councils, convened in or near the new capital, debated heresies and sought unity but often actually engendered fragmentation. Christianity was the dominant religion of the Middle East outside Iran and the Arabian Peninsula from the fourth to seventh centuries, but today it is a minority faith in an overwhelmingly Muslim area (Fig. 4.7).

The approximately 15 million Christians in the Middle East are divided among more than a dozen Orthodox and Catholic sects; a small number are Protestants (see Table 4.2). Although exact figures are unknown, it is possible to estimate the number of Christians in the main groups. Copts, about 10 percent of Egypt's population, are the largest; most are Orthodox,[12] some are Catholics, and a few are Protestants. The second-largest group is found in Syria—about 2 million adherents of several Orthodox and Catholic sects. Third are the Christians of Lebanon—perhaps 1.6 million, The Maronites (Catholics) are the most prominent, not only religiously but politically and economically as well. There are about 1 million Iraqi Christians, but the post-2003 insurrection has seen many emigrate; most are Assyrians, divided into Catholic and Nestorian sects. Fifth largest is the Greek Orthodox community of Cyprus— more than 700,000 who are nearly 100 percent of the population of the southern part of the island. Finally, Israel/Palestine, Turkey, Iran, and Jordan each have sizable Christian minorities: at least 400,000 in Israel/Palestine, about 300,000 each in Turkey and Iran, and 210,000 in Jordan.[13] Antagonisms among Christian sects persisted for centuries, but in the past 50 years or so, these have lessened, both because of global ecumenism and the

FIGURE 4.7 The famous St. Katherine's Monastery, an Orthodox monastery of the sixth century, nestled at the foot of Mount Sinai (Jabal Musa) in the southern Sinai Peninsula.

need of minorities to make common cause to preserve their rights.

Judaism. The oldest of the three great monotheistic religions, Judaism evolved over a period of more than 1,500 years, a development that is the theme of the Old Testament. It takes its name from Judah, the tribe of King David, from which the term "Jew" is also derived. The patriarch Jacob, whose religious name was Israel, is the eponymous ancestor of the *Bnai Yisrael*, or Children (lit. "Sons") of Israel.[14]

Judaism's roots lie in the traditions of a seminomadic Aramaean tribe personified in the patriarch Abraham. In the Old Testament narrative, the original group migrated from southern Mesopotamia, Ur of the Chaldees, up the Euphrates Valley to the Harran and then, traditionally around 1700 BCE, southwestward to the southern hills of Canaan. Abraham's grandson Jacob (Israel) migrated to Egypt, where his descendants multiplied;

later, perhaps in the thirteenth century BCE, they made their "Exodus" from Egypt to claim Canaan. In the biblical account, it was out of the tribal growth and development of the *Bnai Yisrael* during the Exodus that evolved the monotheistic religion that came to be known as Judaism. It revolved around the one God (Yahweh), the covenant between God and the people of Israel, the comprehensive law, and, for many Jews, the land.

Missionary activity among the Hebrews (referred to as Jews after the 50-year Babylonian Exile) following the return of many exiles in 538 BCE reflected the belief in Israel's election by God to mediate divine blessings to all nations. By the time of Jesus, Judaism was winning many converts throughout the Roman Empire. However, after the Romans destroyed the temple in Jerusalem in 70 CE and dispersed many Palestinian Jews, proselytizing almost ceased. Particularism and separatism, as opposed to universalism, increasingly characterized Judaism, which then had a mostly token presence in its original territory for more than eighteen centuries.

Different interpretations of the Torah (the Law, the Pentateuch, the first five books of the Old Testament) and the Talmud (a body of commentary and guidance) have led to various groupings within Judaism. In modern times, it embraces such groups as the ultra-Orthodox Hasidim ("those who are pious"), Orthodox, Conservative, Reform, and Reconstructionist Judaism. Neither Reform Judaism, which seeks to bring the faith into modern Western life, nor Conservative Judaism, taking a middle position, achieved any recognition in Israel until the 1970s; in the new century, non-Orthodox Judaism still has a second-class status because of the overwhelming preeminence of the Orthodox establishment. This is the cause of much bitterness on the part of the many American and other Jews in the diaspora who are not Orthodox. The debate is especially relevant to individuals converted to Judaism by liberal rabbis and who emigrate to Israel where their conversions are not recognized.

Nevertheless, Judaism has not experienced the degree of institutionalized sectarian fragmentation suffered by Christianity and Islam. Reimplanted in its native locale in the mid-twentieth century, Judaism has become for many of its adherents a belief system that is quite different from its original theology. Surveys have shown that only a minority of Israeli Jews actually practice the religion, and distinctions must be drawn among Jews, practitioners of Judaism, Zionists, and Israelis. The cleavage between ultra-Orthodox and secular Jews in Israel is discussed in Chapter 12.

Two ancient Jewish sects also have a presence in Israel. The Karaites differ from other Jews by holding that Moses did not receive any oral law at Mount Sinai; they therefore do not accept the Talmud as authoritative. They also use patrilineal, not matrilineal, descent to determine who is a Jew. There are perhaps 25,000 Karaites in Israel. A much older and smaller sect is the Samaritans who trace their origins to the refusal of some Israelites to obey King David's command that all temple worship must be in Jerusalem. They now number about 709, half in Israel, half on the West Bank near their historic shrine on Mount Gerizim.

Other Religions

The primarily Kurdish Yazidis (or Yezidis), who are scattered across northern Syria and northern Iraq and in adjacent areas of Turkey and Iran, call themselves *Dawasin*, and are called *Dasnayis* by the Syrians; they are strictly self-segregated and endogamous. Their highly syncretic religion borrows heavily from Zoroastrianism, Judaism, Nestorian Christianity, and Islam; prominent in their beliefs is a repentant and pardoned Satan, the Peacock King. Their practice of "prudent propitiation" of the Peacock King has been mistakenly interpreted as devil worship.

Zoroastrianism is named after its traditional founder, Zoroaster (Greek form of Zarathustra), who is believed to have lived in the sixth century BCE. It was the established religion of the Achaemenid and Sassanian empires. Essentially monotheistic in its worship of *Ahura Mazda* (Lord Wisdom), its characteristic dualism significantly influenced both Judaism and Christianity. Taught by magi as priests, it emphasizes the eternal cosmic contest between good and evil, falsehood and truth, darkness and light. Traditional practices include veneration of fire—the life energy—and exposure of the dead to vultures on "towers of silence" (*dakhmes* or *qala-e khamushan*) to avoid polluting either the earth or fire. Its scripture is the *Avesta*, supplemented by the commentary *Zend-Avesta*. Out of favor after the seventh-century Muslim invasion, many eventually converted to Islam. Although their religion is officially recognized, Iranian Zoroastrians are at a definite disadvantage under the current fundamentalist government; they survive primarily in the Yazd and Kerman areas of central Iran. Coreligionists include the Parsees in India and other diasporic communities.

A small religious group concentrated in Iraq that has received renewed attention since 2003 is the Mandaeans (from Aramaic *manda,* "knowledge"), also called Sabians (baptizers) and "John the Baptist Christians." Although they are not Christians, John the Baptist is a central figure in this highly syncretic religion, which has Jewish, Iranian, Babylonian, Gnostic, and Christian elements. Because they stress the importance of regular absolutions, they live near running water, mostly along the lower Tigris River. Their scriptures and liturgy are in Syriac.

A fairly new eclectic faith, Bahai, arose in Iran in the 1840s as an offshoot of Shii Islam. Mysticism spread rapidly after a Shii religious leader was acclaimed the *bab* (gate) between the worldly and the spiritual realms. Advocating a universalistic faith synthesizing Islam, Judaism, and Christianity, Bahai has spread widely in Europe and North America. Its world center is on Mount Carmel in Haifa, Israel, and its members number tens of thousands in the Middle East, chiefly in central Iran, where they have been persecuted as apostates since the Islamic revolution and where their situation has become increasingly dire in the new century.[15]

PATTERNS: ETHNIC GROUPS

Aspects of language and religion patterns may now be merged in a survey of ethnic groups (Table 4.3), examining four major aggregates—Arabs, Turks, Persians, and Jews—briefly discussing related smaller groups associated with each. The relationship between primary group and associated groups may involve language, religion, cultural affinity, or geographical proximity, including shared nationality. For example, the Lur and the Bakhtiari are considered with Persians, since

all three live in Iran, speak Indo-Iranian languages, and are Shii Muslims. Similarly, the Maronites and Druze are considered with Arabs, since both are associated with Lebanon and speak Arabic, even though the Maronites are Christians and the Druze are a heretical offshoot of Shii Islam. Given cultural and historical complexities, the categories used are not always exclusive. The significance of minority ethnic groups in the region's various bodies politic is directly addressed in Chapter 8.[16]

Arabs and Related Groups

Arabs. Even with diverse traits and distribution over vast distances, the ethnic identity of the Arabs is one of the basic realities of the pattern of peoples in the region. Numbering about 172.0 million, not only are Arabs the overwhelmingly dominant ethnolinguistic group in the twelve Arab countries of our sixteen core states, but they also include at least 1 million nationals in three other countries—Israel, Turkey, and Iran—and are numerically negligible only in Cyprus. In the five Arab countries in North Africa plus Sudan, they number another 97.2 million.

All Arabs share two cultural elements, and most share a third. First, the Arabic language provides an element common to all, despite dialect variations. As the language of the Quran, it has deep religious and cultural significance for most Arabs. Second, the Islamic cultural heritage embodied in architecture, design, calligraphy, and art provides a common Arab history—Muslim and Christian, orthodox and heterodox, Bedouin and city dweller, Syrian and Qatari, Moroccan and Egyptian. It underlies modern Arab political identity, relevant in many modern problems and conflicts (Chap. 8). Third, since more than 92 percent of Middle East Arabs are Muslim, Islam links the majority.[17]

Copts. Coptic ethnic identity derives primarily from religion. About 10 percent of the

TABLE 4.3 Ethnic Groups of the Middle East (with Ethnolinguistic Groupings)

Ethnic Group (and Alt. Names)	Main Lang.	Main Religion	No., 1,000s	Main Areas/Comments
— AFRO-ASIATIC: Semitic and Berber —				
ALAWIS (Alawites, Nusayris)	Arabic	Alawi	2,203	W Syria, N Lebanon
ARABS	Arabic	Islam (>Sunni)	172,000	Mid East, N Africa
ASSYRIANS (Aissores)	Syriac, Arabic	Christn (Nest., Cath.)	? 1,000	NE Syria, N Iraq
COPTS	Arabic	Christn (Coptic)	7,450	C and N Egypt
DRUZES (Muwahhidun)	Arabic	Druze	1,000	S Syr, C Leb, N Israel
JEWS (Yahudis)	Hebrew, Ar.	Judaism	6,000	Israel, Iran, Turkey
MANDAEANS (Sabians, Mendai)	Ar., Aramaic	Mandaean	25	Baghdad, S Iraq, Iran
MARONITES	Ar., French	Christn (Maronite)	1,150	NC and C Lebanon
(MUTAWALIS) (Metouali)	(Arabic)	(Shii Islam)	1,350	(C and S Lebanon)
SAMARITANS	Ar. , Aram. di.	Samaritan	<1	709 in Nablus, Holon
BERBERS	Berber	Sunni Islam	1,000	NW Egypt (mils. to W)
— URAL-ALTAIC: Turkic —				
AFSHAR (includes several groups)	Azeri	Shii Islam	? 750	NW Iran, SC Iran
AZERIS (Azerbaijanis)	Azeri	Shii Islam	13,500	NW Iran
QAJARS (includes several groups)	Azeri	Shii Islam	? 250	SE Caspian Coast
QASHQAI	Qashqai	Shii Islam	? 950	Iran: C Zagros Mts.
ILSAVAN/SHAHSAVAN (sev.)	Azeri	Shii Islam	? 410	NW Iran, other Iran
TATARS ("Tartars")	Tatar Turkic	Sunni Islam	? 1,000	E Turkey, N Iran
TURKS	Turkish	Sunni Islam	62,000	Turkey; few scattered
TURKMANS (Turcomans)	Turkman	Sunni Islam	2,300	N Iran, NE Iraq, Trky
YORUK	Turkish	Sunni Islam	? 1,500	W and SE Turkey
— INDO-EUROPEAN: Indo-Iranian, Armenian, and Greek —				
BAKHTIARI	Luri	Shii Islam	1,500	Iran: C Zagros Mts.
BALUCH (Baluchis)	Baluchi	Sunni Islam	2,000	SE Iran (& Pak & Afgh)
GILANI/GILAKI (inc. sev. grps)	Gilaki	Shii Islam	? 3,500	SW Caspian Coast
HAZARAS (Berberis)	Hazaragi	Shii Islam	? 300	E Iran; >in Afgh, Pak
KURDS	Kurdish	Sunni Islam	24,500	Iran, Iraq, Syria, Trky
LUR (includes several groups)	Luri	Shii Islam	2,500	C Zagros Mts., E Iraq
MAZANDARANI (incl. sev. grps)	Mazandarani	Shii Islam	? 3,500	SW Caspian Coast
PERSIANS	Farsi (Persian)	Shii Islam	37,000	C & N Iran; <Iraq, UAE
PUSHTUN (Pukhtun, Pathans)	Pashto	Sunni Islam	250	E Iran (mils. to E)
YAZIDIS (Dasnayi, Asdais)	Kurdish	Yazidi	? 300	N Iraq, NW Syria
ZOROASTRIANS (Parsis, Gabres, Zardoshti)	Farsi (Persian)	Zoroastrian	? 160	SC Iran (Yazd), Tehran (also many in India)
ARMENIANS (Hai)	Armenian	Christn (>Arm Orth)	900	Leb, Syria, Iran, Trky
GREEKS (Elleniki)	Greek	Christn (Orthodox)	825	Cyprus, Istanbul, Egypt
— CAUCASIC —				
CIRCASSIANS (Adyghe, Cherkes)	Circassian	>Sunni Islam	150	Trky, Syria, Jrdn, Israel
GEORGIANS	Georgian	>Sunni Islam	? 65	N Turkey, WC Iran
LAZE (Laz, Chan)	Laz, Turkish	Sunni Islam	? 100	SE Black Sea Coast
— MISCELLANEOUS —				
BEJA	Beja	Sunni Islam	<20	<SE Egypt (>NE Sudn)
GYPSIES (Rom, many others)	Romany, etc.	Various	? 1,300	Scattered
NUBIANS	Nubian, Ar.	Sunni Islam	150	<S Egypt (>N Sudan)

Groups may overlap and are, therefore, not necessarily mutually exclusive (e.g., Druzes and Alawis are Arabs). Some categories are basically religious groups that have also become ethnically differentiated (e.g., Copts). Some groups are closely related (e.g., Gilani/Gilaki and Mazandarani). Mutawali are Lebanese Shii Muslims; the name is from the nineteenth century. Numbers can be only rough estimates in some cases and may not match data in other sections because of rounding. (*Source*: Data from *Britannica World Data 2009*; *World Factbook 2009*; *Ethnologue 2005*; Weekes 1984; Department of State *Background Notes* 2009–2010; and the authors' field research.)

population of Egypt, Copts are the largest non-Muslim ethnic group in the region, a remnant of the ancient Hamitic Egyptians who became Christians. Practicing endogamy and segregation from other Egyptians and from invaders, they preserved their Monophysite Christianity[18] as well as a sometimes disputed genetic physical kinship with early Egyptians. Their language survived as the vernacular until supplanted by Arabic 1,000 years after the Islamic conquest. Outside the urban centers of Cairo and Alexandria, they are concentrated in Upper Egypt. Friction with the majority Muslims is discussed in Chapter 17.

Maronites. Like the Copts, Maronites are differentiated primarily on the basis of religion. However, geographical isolation in the Lebanon Mountains encouraged independence and endogamy, producing cultural differentiation and substantial political autonomy. Arabic supplanted Syriac during the eighteenth century as a working language, and historic ties with the French culminating in the mandate years (1920–1943) promoted French as a second language. The determined separatism of the Maronites has been a compelling dynamic in Lebanese political-geographical events (see Chap. 10).

Oppressed for adherence to a Christian heresy, they left Syria in the tenth century and settled in the mountains around Qadisha Gorge. Their cooperation with the Crusader invaders alienated them from the Muslim population, and a small group of Maronites left with the retreating Crusaders to settle in Cyprus, where a community remains. The exact origins of their long adherence to the Church of Rome are in dispute. Many thousands began to emigrate in the late nineteenth century, and the civil conflicts of the last half of the twentieth century accelerated emigration again. As many as 1 million Maronites remain in the Levant, most in Lebanon but a few in Cyprus, Syria, and Israel.

Druze. Druze identity also originated in religion, with cultural and physical differentiations developing over the centuries. Originating in Egypt, the Druze won adherents in the Mount Hermon area, where they are still centered. Additional contemporary concentrations are in the Shuf area in central Mount Lebanon and in the Jabal al-Druze (officially now Jabal al-Arab) of southern Syria.

As heretics, the Druze were alienated from other Shii and even more from Sunnis; they clashed with Maronites as both groups migrated into central Mount Lebanon 1,000 years ago. Rejected by their neighbors, they separated themselves through endogamy. Their fierce sense of independence and separatism gave them a military orientation, which they exhibited against opposing Crusaders, against Maronites in the 1840s–1850s and 1958, and in the 1975–1991 civil conflict in Lebanon.[19] Druze in Israel generally accepted the Jewish government in 1948–1949; they are the only Arabs permitted to serve in the Israeli army. Even so, Druze-Israeli relations deteriorated after Israel's annexation of the Golan Heights in 1981 and the Israeli occupation of southern Lebanon in 1978–2000.

Alawi. The Alawi are also primarily distinguished by religion, and they too have developed distinct cultural attributes through segregation and endogamy. They are concentrated in and around the Jabal al-Sahiliyah in northwestern Syria and constitute about 11 percent of the population.

The Alawi have preserved no ancient language and use Arabic. Although criticized by other Syrians for cooperating with French-mandate authorities, after World War II they were trusted in the army and in government because of their minority status. A climax of the group's role came in 1969, when Syrian Air Force general Hafiz al-Asad, an Alawi, seized power in Damascus. He held the presidency from 1971 until his death in June 2000, when he was succeeded by his Alawi son. In religion, but not necessarily in other ways, they are kin to the more numerous Alevi in Turkey (Chap. 18).[20]

Assyrians.   Distinguished principally by their religion and, for many, their language, Assyrians preserve certain Nestorian and Jacobite traditions. They consider themselves to be ethnic descendants of ancient Mesopotamians. A Christological controversy in the fifth century cost them communion with the rest of Christendom; they remained outside and east of the Byzantine Empire. A considerable number retained their identity in Mesopotamia and remain there and in adjacent areas today; those in Iraq constitute the country's largest group of Christians.

One group of Assyrians separated from the Nestorian church in 1551, reuniting with Rome in the uniate Chaldean Catholic Church—now the larger sect. The original Nestorian Assyrians have retained their ancient independence. Both, along with related groups, have preserved a common ethnic identity, and all retained Syriac in their liturgies; however, the Chaldeans and certain Suryanis have increasingly adopted the local language in church and in the home— mostly Arabic but also, in adjacent areas, Turkish or Farsi. A large number of Nestorian Assyrians still use neo-Aramaic (or Syriac) as a vernacular.

With the sects well intermixed in much of their common area, Assyrians number as many as 1 million by some estimates. Many live in Baghdad, but others continue to live in northern Iraq (especially in Kirkuk, Irbil, Mosul, and adjacent areas), eastern Syria, and northwestern Iran. They have periodically suffered persecution; thousands fled decimation in Iraq, notably after the 1933 massacre in the north. Many have fled Islamist and Kurdish oppression since 2003. Assyrians in the West may outnumber the core population by as much as four or five times.[21]

Circassians.   Half a million Circassians migrated into the region from the Caucasus when czarist Russia seized their homeland after the Congress of Berlin in 1878. A non-Semitic Islamic people, they were permitted by the Ottomans to settle along an axis from Damascus southward to Amman and beyond, as well as in Asia Minor and in the mountains of Kurdistan. They still live in these areas and play modest roles in Syria, Jordan, and northern Israel. Prior to its destruction by the Israelis, Qunaytirah, in the Golan Heights, was a center of Circassian settlement.

Yazidis.   The Yazidis have Kurdish ethnic roots (some in the group dispute this) but are mainly distinguished by their heterodox religion. They are settled farmers concentrated in the Jabal Sinjar west of Mosul and in the hills northwest of Aleppo, with scattered groups in adjacent states. Yazidis do not interact with neighboring tribes; they practice endogamy and prohibit conversion into the group.

Nubians.   Nubians lived in the area between Aswan, Egypt, and the Dongola region of Sudan for perhaps 3,000 years before the construction of the Aswan High Dam. More African in appearance than the Egyptians farther north on the Nile, the Nubians converted to Christianity in the sixth century and resisted Islam until 1366. Nearly all speak the Nubian language, but most of them also speak Arabic. Of the total Nubian population in Egypt and the Sudan, about one-third live in Egypt and are Sunni Muslims. (See more about them in Chap. 17.)

Others.   Smaller ethnic groups interrelate with the dominant Arab group because of geographical proximity. Some are differentiated by language, some by religion, and some by both.

The Beja are nomadic pastoralists migrating seasonally into southeastern Egypt from northeastern Sudan. The Berbers are a major ethnic group in North Africa, numbering more than 11 million from Egypt westward to the Atlantic. However, only a few thousand live in the Middle East as covered in this study, primarily in Egypt's long-isolated Siwa Oasis. The Romans called them *barbari* (barbarians)—hence their name. The Mandaeans are a dwindling group in Iraq living in al-Amarah, Suq al-Shuyukh, and Baghdad. The Shabak are another small group in the "ethnic shatter zone" of northern Iraq. Originally Sufi mystics in the fourteenth and fifteenth centuries, they became secretive and heretical, practiced endogamy, and became a closed and isolated community.

The Sulaba (or Sulayb) are a nomadic people in the Arabian Peninsula who, in small groups, follow Bedouin tribes in their migrations and serve as tinkers, musicians, and entertainers for the Bedouin and villagers. They are not considered Arabs, and they are so ostracized that their origins and traditions are little known. Gypsies wander by the thousands in many parts of the Middle East as traditional migrants. Many claim to be Muslims, but others engage in varied religious practices. They probably originated in northwestern India and share linguistic roots with other Gypsies, speaking dialects of Romany, an Indic branch of Indo-Iranian, as well as, in many cases, local languages.

Chechens migrated into the region from the northern Caucasus in the mid-nineteenth century, when 40,000 arrived in Turkey, where most have been assimilated. Later, other small groups of Chechens settled farther south in the Ottoman Empire; more than 2,000, sometimes called Shishanis, still live in west-central Jordan alongside their fellow Caucasians, the Circassians.

Turks and Related Groups

Turks. The second-largest ethnolinguistic group in the core Middle East (after the Arabs), ethnic Turks number about 50 million, somewhat more than one-third of the total number of Turkic-speaking peoples of the world. Generally, they speak Turkish as a primary language, are Muslims (90 percent are Sunni), claim a Turkish heritage, and are patriotic about the Republic of Turkey. Culturally, they combined Persian, Arab, Byzantine, and Anatolian cultural elements with their former nomadic Central Asian culture. Turks, Tatars, and Turkmans are difficult to differentiate, in spite of distinctive characteristics, partly because of intermarriage and cultural assimilation.[22]

Four groups of Turks can be identified through cultural and geographical differences. First, the Anatolian Turks in Asia Minor are a thorough biological mixture of earlier Anatolian peoples. Second, the Rumelian Turks (from Rum, meaning "Roman," or European) are European Turks who remained in Europe after Ottoman days but later returned to Turkey. More than 400,000 were expelled from Greece in the 1920s with a similar number of Greeks forced from Turkey; many thousands more arrived later in Turkey from Bulgaria, Romania, and Yugoslavia. Also from Bulgaria came about 150,000 Pomaks—Bulgar converts to Islam when the Ottomans controlled the Balkans. Now highly Turkified, they live in western Anatolia. Third are descendants of Turks who stayed in various parts of the Middle East separated from the Ottoman Empire after World War I. They are steadily becoming Arabized. Fourth are some 200,000 Turkish Cypriots, descendants either of Turks who moved to the island after the Ottoman conquest in the sixteenth century or of Cypriot converts to Islam. They have been joined by more than 50,000 Turks from the mainland since 1974, along with 35,000–40,000 Turkish troops.

Azeris. Azeris are the second-largest Turkic group and the fifth-largest ethnolinguistic group in the region. They live to the north and east of the more numerous Kurds; related groups—including the Ilsavan/Shahsavan, Afshar, and Qajars—live farther to the east. Some Azeris live in Turkey and Iraq—perhaps a million. They are the dominant group—some 11.5 million—in two provinces (East and West Azerbaijan) of northwestern Iran. Another 7.5 million live in the oil-rich Azerbaijan Republic. Like the Persians, and unlike most Turks, they are Shii Muslims. Tabriz is an Azeri center, although its population is ethnically complex.

Turkmans (also Turkmens or Turkomans). Despite having a similar Turkic language, Turkmans are distinct from Turks and Tatars. Most live in historic Turkistan—primarily in the Republic of Turkmenistan, north of Iran and east of the Caspian. Highly tribalized, their tribal names are commonly known as designations for their traditional hand-knotted rugs. One of the most widely scattered ethnic groups in the region, there are concentrations in central and eastern Anatolia, northeastern Iraq in the foothills near Mosul and Kirkuk, and across northern Iran, particularly in the northeastern mountains of Khorasan. They tend to live in mountainous areas and to preserve their nomadism for both economic and defensive reasons; however, as with most nomadic groups, the Turkmans are integrating into the sedentary economy. They are all Muslims, about two-thirds Sunni and one-third Shii.

Yoruk (or Yörük). The Yoruk are descendants of some of the earliest Turkish tribes to enter Asia Minor; as evidence, their Turkish language has been less influenced by Arabic and Persian than has the national Turkish language. Nominally Muslim, their Islam is unorthodox, with neither clergy nor mosques. The changes in Yoruk habitat and lifestyle are indicative of development in the region. Under the Ottomans, they were nomads in western Anatolia in the uplands between Konya and Bursa. Intensive government proj-

ects during the 1920s and 1930s to develop pastures and to improve agriculture interfered with their seasonal migrations, producing gradual sedentarization. But in the mid-twentieth century, several thousand migrated to southeastern Turkey, where they resumed nomadic pastoralism, using trucks rather than camels. Rug knotting is a traditional skill.

Ilsavan/Shahsavan. The name Shahsavan (shah lovers) was impolitic after the 1979 overthrow of the monarchy, and so they became the Ilsavan (tribe lovers). They are a large nomadic group closely related to the Azeris and Afshars, traditionally sharing territory and migrations to some extent. Like those groups, the Ilsavan are Shii. They were given special tribal status in the seventeenth century because they were loyal to the shah, and they traditionally supported the ruling dynasty; however, they seem to have accepted the revolutionary government.

Qashqai. The Qashqai are descendants of Turkic tribes who left Central Asia in the eleventh century and moved into the Zagros Mountains in the fifteenth century. Like the great majority of Iranian ethnic groups, they are Shii. Their persistent nomadism, both horizontal and vertical (transhumance), is legendary. Herding large flocks of sheep, they make an arduous seasonal migration, over distances up to 350 mi/560 km, between summer and winter pastures. Incomes are supplemented by making knotted rugs, *kilims* (woven rugs), and bags in traditional patterns.[23]

Afshars. The Afshars are another Turkic group that probably moved from Turkistan onto the Iranian Plateau during the Middle Ages. Like the Ilsavan (with whom they at times migrate), they are sometimes considered a subdivision of the Azeris: All three speak related dialects, practice Shii Islam, and engage in nomadism. They are widely distributed in the northern Zagros Mountains, from north of Tabriz to Hamadan, and there are two other concentrations—in Iran in the mountains south of Kerman and in Turkey east of Kayseri.

Qajars. The Turkic-speaking Qajars are one of several interlocked ethnic groups in northwestern Iran and the southern Caspian littoral. Some related groups belong to the Turkic family and others to the Iranian-language family. The Qajars supplied a dynasty that ruled Persia from 1794 to 1925. Mostly settled farmers, with small groups of seasonal nomads, they form a small enclave among the more numerous Mazandarani along the southeastern Caspian coast.

Tatars. Sometimes incorrectly called "Tartars," the Tatars (archers) were named after (but not directly descended from) the Ta-Ta Mongols who invaded the region in the thirteenth century. Over time, they intermarried with Turks, resulting in a widespread Turko-Tatar group. Turks, Turkmans, Tatars, Turko-Tatars, and Mongols are often confused in historical writings. The Tatars north of the Black and Caspian seas are far more numerous than those in the Middle East. Thousands emigrated from Russia to Turkey during the nineteenth century; they have since become assimilated. Tatars speak a Turkic Kipchak language rather than a Mongolic tongue, and virtually all are Muslim, most of them Sunni.

Peripheral Turkish Groups. Millions of members of additional Turkic peoples have long inhabited the steppes and mountain valleys of Central Asia. Their homelands became independent republics after 1991. Some of the groups received particular attention after the global focus shifted to Afghanistan and its neighbors following the 9/11 attacks. Noteworthy are Uzbeks, Kirghiz, and Kazakhs.

Persians and Related Groups

Persians are the third-largest ethnolinguistic group after Arabs and Turks. Indo-Iranians entered the mountains and basins south and southwest of the Caspian during the second millennium BCE. One branch went southeastward into the Indus Valley and eventually dominated the subcontinent; others halted in the rugged folds of the Zagros Mountains and settled in western Iran. Those south of the Caspian became the Medes (or Medians); those in the southern Zagros became Persians. They called themselves Aryans (nobles) and named their new homeland after themselves—Iran.

Persians. After a thousand years in the folds of the Zagros, the Persians emerged as a unified sedentary people in the sixth century BCE and built an unprecedented empire (see Chap. 3). Although later defeated by Alexander the Great and then overwhelmed by Arab Muslims in the seventh century, they repeatedly restored a power base on the intermontane Iranian Plateau. Since World War I, the Persians have become the leading ethnic group in Iran, filling most government, industrial, professional, and cultural positions. By the 1970s, most educated Persians spoke French or English in addition to Farsi, and many were educated in the United States or Europe; however, after the Islamic Revolution, the authorities discouraged Westernization, forcing a return to Islamic fundamentalism.

More than 95 percent of Persians adhere to the Twelver (*Jafari*) sect of Shii Islam, for nationalistic as much as for theological reasons. A small but significant number are Zoroastrians and Bahai. Living throughout Iran, Persians are the majority of the population in many of the foothills, valleys, basins, and plateaus and predominate in the cities of Hamadan, Qom, Tehran, Shiraz, and Kerman.

In addition to the approximately 34 million Persians in Iran (about half the population), another million live on the west side of the Gulf, in the Qatif and al-Hasa oases in the Eastern Province of Saudi Arabia (where they are Arabized), and near the Shii shrines in Iraq. Wherever they live, they proudly differentiate themselves by their language, Shii religion, history, 2,000 years of literature, and distinctive arts. The cleavage between Persians and Arabs along the Zagros piedmont has periodically erupted over the centuries, most recently in the bloody 1980–1988 Iran-Iraq War.[24]

Kurds. The fourth-largest ethnolinguistic group, the Kurds occupy a historic mountain homeland—politically fragmented Kurdistan—at the junction of and comprising parts of Turkey, Iran, Iraq, and Syria (see Map 4.3). They not only predominate there but also mix with neighboring Azeris and Armenians, as well as with Turks, Turkmans, Arabs, Assyrians, and others. Both their total population and its distribution among the countries that share Kurdistan can only be estimated subject to controversy. Kurdish leaders claim much higher numbers than officials and scholars accept. Reasonable figures in the 2000s suggest about 24 million in "Kurdistan"—11.5 million in Turkey, 6 million in Iran, 5 million in Iraq, and perhaps 1 million in Syria—plus others in Armenia, Lebanon, central Anatolia, the central Zagros Mountains, and the Elburz and Kopet mountains.

Language, heritage, culture, and a fierce sense of independence combine to define Kurdishness, along with physical attributes; many consider themselves descendants of the Medes, while others believe they were formerly part of the Lur. Most are Sunni Muslims, separating them from the Shii Persians, although some in Iran and Iraq are Shii. Retaining a tribal structure, they are settled farmers, herdsmen, and townsmen. Especially in their core mountain home area, they

have historically resisted outside authority. Those in Iraq have notably battled for self-government, especially in 1974–1975, during the 1980s Iran-Iraq War, during and after the 1991 Gulf War, and after 2003. Similarly, Kurds in Turkey engaged in a decadelong fight for recognition in which 30,000 died during the 1980s and 1990s.

Both the historical and the contemporary plights of the Kurds became the focus of intensive media coverage after the Gulf War of 1990–1991, and again in the 2000s. Further details on the situation of the Kurds in the respective countries that share Kurdistan are given in Chapters 14, 17, and 18, and the general Kurdish problem is discussed in Chapter 8.[25]

Baluch. Like the Kurds, the Baluch (sometimes Baloch) are primarily Sunni, speak an Indo-Iranian language, and have a relatively isolated traditional homeland—Baluchistan—at the junction of three countries: Iran, Pakistan, and Afghanistan. However, it is arid, and they are much more nomadic or seminomadic than the Kurds, with only a few in impoverished villages. Tribal organization remains strong among them, but the tribes are not closely integrated. In their spare desert and mountain environment, they are the poorest and most neglected major group in Iran. Probably a mixture of Dravidians from India and Arab invaders, they are culturally more closely related to Pakistanis and the Pushtun of Afghanistan than to the Persians.

Emigrants from poverty, they crossed the Gulf of Oman to both Oman and the present UAE, where their round tents originally provided a contrast to the rectangular Arab tents. They serve in large numbers in the various military forces of the southeastern Arabian Peninsula. Since 2000, Baluch separatist groups have become active in both Pakistan and Iran.

Lur. Of uncertain origin, the Lur speak a dialect of Persian and are linguistically and culturally related to the Persians and the nearby Bakhtiari. They occupy Lorestan, a homeland in the central Zagros Mountains between Bakhtaran (Kermanshah) and Shiraz, and are racially mixed.

The basic social unit among the Lur is the tribe (*il*). Some nomadic tribes are summer migrants to the high mountains; other tribes have become sedentary or semisedentary, especially in the eastern valleys, and have adopted Persian (Farsi) as a second language. Tribal structure has gradually become less rigid as the power of the chiefs (*khans*) has been undermined by the central government. Most Lur are Shii but hold some beliefs that are inconsistent with Persian and Bakhtiari Shiism. Of the Lur who have spilled over into Iraq, a few roam the Zagros piedmont in the Mandali area east of Baghdad, while others work in towns along the Tigris. Estimates of their numbers vary widely.

Bakhtiari. Tribes in the *Il-e Bakhtiari* confederation relate geographically and culturally not only to the nearby Lur but also to the Turkic Qashqai. Like the latter, the Bakhtiari are tribally organized, disciplined, and still largely nomadic. Historically having a powerful role in Iranian politics, Bakhtiari leaders often held high government positions until the 1920s; the political influence of the *khans* was restricted by the central government after World War I. They had a long tradition of services in the Iranian army. Their ethnic dress evokes statues and bas-reliefs of Parthians of 2,000 years ago. Like many Iranian tribes, they produce handmade rugs with distinctive designs.

Zoroastrians. Zoroastrians are probably the least physically mixed ethnic Persians in Iran, comparable to the Copts in Egypt—so sharply distinguished by their religion that they constitute a distinct ethnic group like the Maronites or Druze in the Levant. By adhering to a definite geographical area, practicing endogamy, and exercising group determination, they have survived and preserved their identity despite persecution. There may be as many as 100,000 in Iran.[26] Many fled to western India after the Arab invasion in the seventh century where they became known as Parsees; concentrated in Bombay, they include some of the major industrialist families of southern Asia. There is also a diaspora in Europe and the United States.

Others. Another score of ethnic groups related to the Persians are found in pockets on the Iranian Plateau, further illustrating the complexity of the ethnic pattern in the eastern Middle East. Two are fairly large— numbering about three million each; neither are sharply differentiated from their neighbors, and both are farmers and fishermen along the Caspian shore. The Gilani live along the southwestern shore around Rasht; the Mazandarani are in the coastal lowlands and adjacent mountains to the southeast.

Jews and Samaritans

Jews. After a series of unsuccessful revolts against the Romans and the destruction of the Temple built by Herod, many Jews were deported from Palestine. In this second dispersion of the Jews (the first was to Babylon), the exiles joined the many sizable Jewish communities already established around the Mediterranean. For example, the community in Alexandria in Egypt thrived for more than 2,200 years until after World War II; it was here that the Old Testament was translated into Greek—the famous Septuagint—in the third century BCE, for the use of non-Palestinian Jews and Gentiles attracted to Judaism but unfamiliar with Hebrew. For Muslims, Jews (like Christians) were *ahl al-kitab*— "people of the book"; under the Ottomans, they constituted a *millet*, and their minority rights were sufficiently protected that tens of thousands of Sephardic (Spanish) Jews fleeing the Inquisition in the sixteenth century settled in the Ottoman Empire. They thus became citizens of successor Arab states after 1918.

Ashkenazi (German) Jews from Europe migrated to the Middle East rather recently, from the late nineteenth century into the twentieth, especially in waves of immigration (*aliyah*) after World War II. After the establishment of Israel in 1948, most of the Jews in Middle East Arab countries emigrated, largely to Israel—an estimated 300,000 from Egypt, Lebanon, Syria, Iraq, and Yemen by the early 1990s. Smaller proportions of the Turkish and Iranian Jewish communities also have emigrated.

Despite generally endogamous traditions, Jewish immigrants in Israel exhibited physical differences related to their countries of origin, plus a variety of linguistic, political-geographical (or national), and ideological backgrounds. Subethnic divisions emerged between Ashkenazis and Mizrahim (Oriental or Eastern Jews, including Sephardim). Sabras—native-born Israelis—form another subgroup. The continuing question "Who is a Jew?" and the distinctions among observant Jews, nonobservant (or nonpracticing) Jews, Halakhic Jews (strict adherents to religious law), assimilated Jews, and even Christian Jews complicate citizenship problems regarding the Law of Return. Of a world total of about 14.5 million Jews, about 6.0 million lived in Israel in 2008. About 35,000 more lived in the rest of the Middle East (out of about 1 million pre–World War II), mainly in Iran and Turkey.[27]

Samaritans.   The Samaritans, mentioned in the New Testament, are a tiny but very interesting group. They are descended from Israelites who remained in Samaria during the Babylonian Exile and, through intermarriage with other groups, emerged as a new people. They found themselves estranged from the much changed Jews who returned from Babylon, and the two groups remain theolog-

ically incompatible even today. Decimated in battles with the Romans and Byzantines, they were almost extinct a century ago (155 members in 1908) and still numbered only 709 in the late 2000s. About half of them today live in Nabulus, north of Jerusalem, and the other half in Holon, near Tel Aviv.[28] The group scarcely reproduces itself but maintains a strict policy of endogamy. Many Palestinians are probably descendants of Samaritans who converted to Christianity and Islam.[29]

Armenians, Greeks, and Others

Armenians.   Armenians date back more than 3,000 years, to about the time the Hittites disappeared from Anatolia. Prior to World War I, they were centered in the Lake Van area and surrounding eastern Anatolian mountains, long referred to as Armenia. The ancient kingdom of Armenia, located in the same area, was the first state to adopt Christianity as its official religion.

Although Armenians were once an influential *millet* in the Ottoman Empire, relations between Armenians and Turks became hostile after 1878, and there were battles in 1895–1896, 1909, 1915–1917, and 1920–1921. In a confused, complex, and disputed series of circumstances (including Kurdish-Armenian-Turkish-Russian relations), hundreds of thousands of Armenians in central and eastern Asia Minor were persecuted, massacred, and deported; thousands more fled into adjacent lands for safety. A post–World War I Armenian republic was proposed by the Allies at the Paris Peace Conference, but a sustained independent Armenia materialized only in 1991.

Although the Armenians survived in their traditional homeland only under Ottoman and Russian overlords, they have maintained a strong, separate ethnic identity, language, and religion, partly through a tradition of endogamy. They center on the church (usually Orthodox, some Catholics), school, newspaper, and businesses, and have a cultural emphasis on education and achievement. In the core Middle East they total about 900,000—in Syria (more than 2 percent of the population, found especially in Aleppo and Damascus), Lebanon, Jordan, Iran, Turkey, and Iraq. The Armenian Republic, independent since 1991 from the Soviet Union, has more than 3 million people, and thousands of Middle East Armenians have emigrated there as well as to the West since World War II.

Greeks. Greek migrants have settled in different areas of the Middle East for millennia. They occupied the Aegean Sea fringe of Asia Minor beginning around 1000 BCE, reaching a population of some 2 million before World War I. Following the failure of a Greek military expedition against the new Turkish Republic in 1922, another in a centuries-long series of hostilities between Greeks and Turks, many fled or were expelled, while others were exchanged for Turks in Greece. Only a few thousand remain in Turkey—mostly in Istanbul. Greeks lived in Egypt and Syria-Palestine from the time of Alexander the Great; thousands left Egypt because of nationalist pressure during the 1950s and 1960s. Jerusalem has a small Greek colony, considerably Arabized. A religious presence remains in the form of historic Greek Orthodox Patriarchates in Istanbul, Alexandria, Antioch, and Jerusalem. More than 700 thousand Greeks live in Cyprus, the largest concentration in the region today. They maintain their strong identity not only through the Greek language but also through close ties with Greece, with which many sought *enosis* (union) during the civil war of the 1950s (see Chap. 10).

Georgians. A Christian group in the ethnically complex southern Caucasus Mountains, the Georgians kept to their historic homeland, although many were dispersed over Asia Minor and Iran from the seventeenth

century on, when some became Muslims. Like Armenians and Azeris, the Georgians had their own republic in the former USSR; it became independent in 1991 with a population of nearly 5 million. Small communities of Georgians live in Turkey and are being gradually assimilated.

Laze. Many Laze left the southern Caucasus after 1878 following Russia's seizure of the area, settling across the border in northeastern Turkey. Traditionally seafarers and fishermen living on or near the Black Sea coast, where Rize is a Laze center, they often serve on Black Sea ships or in the Turkish navy. They speak their own language, Laz, which is akin to Georgian.

PATTERNS: HUMAN DEVELOPMENT— WOMEN, MEN, CHILDREN

Over the past two generations, there has been considerable improvement in the living standards of the people who inhabit the Middle East. Within the region, there were notable differences before the oil boom took off, and differences are still there—but there have been significant changes in the intraregional and intergender patterns of these differences.

In 2008, a panel of social scientists, including five Nobel laureates in economics, was commissioned by the French government to examine methods of measuring "well-being" that were more comprehensive than commonly used parameters—the most common of which is gross domestic product (GDP) per capita. Their extensive report was divided into three parts: The first dealt with the familiar shortcomings of GDP, the second enumerated a number of measures of "quality of life," and the third examined the well-being of future generations. Though the panel made no specific recommendations for replacing GDP as a measure, there are some tested statistics that we can consider in the quest to identify changes in the quality of the lives of Middle Easterners over the past generation.[30]

Since 1990, the UN Development Programme (UNDP) has published the Human Development Index,[31] with components representing health, education, and income. Beginning in 1995, it used the technique to consider differences between the genders with the Gender-related Development Index (GDI). To examine regional patterns here, we will look briefly at a number of indicators in the health and education sectors, noting gender differences as appropriate where data are available.[32]

Health

Life expectancy at birth is the statistic most employed with regard to gains over time and patterns across countries as far as health is concerned. From the early 1950s through the late 2000s, there were major advances in this regard in all regional countries. The median male life expectancy some 60 years ago was 41.95 years, and for females it was 44.00 years; more recently, for men it was 70.25 years and for women 73.55 years—gains of 67.5 percent and 67.2 percent, respectively. But there remain significant differences across countries—Yemen especially lags behind the rest of the region, and Cyprus is well out in front.[33] Almost as significant as these gains was the fact that women in the Middle East now show the same pattern of living notably longer than men as do women in the developed world—a historical advantage of about 4.00 years. In the 1950s, the median difference between the genders in the region was only 2.10 years; recently this has risen to 3.95 years.

Much of this increased advantage of women relative to men has to do with a reduction in maternal mortality, but the span of years for which data are available is unfortunately shorter. Still, the numbers are illustrative: In 1988, the median for the region was 200 deaths per 100,000 live births, and by

2005 this figure had fallen to 63. But the extent of the recent range remains troubling—as low as 4 in Israel and Kuwait and 10 in Cyprus, but as high as 300 in war-ravaged Iraq and 430 in Yemen.

Among the health measures that can show how the situation of children has changed is the mortality rate in the first five years of life. In 1960, the median rate was 233 per 1,000 births; by 2007, this had fallen to 24, a decline of 92 percent. In both years there was a sizable spread across the region—in 1960, rates above 250 were seen in Egypt, Saudi Arabia, Oman, and Yemen; some narrowing has occurred, and in 2007 the rates ranged from 5 in Cyprus and Israel and 8 in the UAE to 44 in Iraq and 73 in Yemen. The rate in Iraq soared in the late 1990s and early 2000s to more than 120, so some recovery is apparent recently. Improvements also are notable in the access to clean water and the polio-immunization rate. In the early 1990s, in Iraq, Yemen, Egypt, Turkey, Oman, and Iran, less than 85 percent had clean water available and less than 85 percent of children were immunized in Yemen, Iraq, and Turkey. By 2006, only in Yemen and Iraq were less than 85 percent without clean water, and less than 85 percent of children had been immunized only in Iraq and Lebanon. By way of contrast, twelve countries had access rates and immunization levels above 95 percent.[34]

Female Genital Mutilation

A further point regarding women's welfare and health must be mentioned—female genital mutilation (FGM), sometimes and less accurately called female circumcision.[35] Although we have no data available to show changes in FGM prevalence over time, there is a definite geographic pattern associated with it historically, and it is not unreasonable to assume this has not changed much over time. It is almost entirely an African phenomenon, and aside from Egypt, the only other places in this region where it has until recently been known to be significantly present are along the Red Sea coast of extreme southwestern Saudi Arabia and adjoining parts of Yemen—areas with close historical ties to Africa. In Egypt, where there has been considerable study of FGM in recent years, as well as major efforts to curb the practice, it is estimated that well over 90 percent of today's adult women have been subjected to it.[36] It crosses social and economic lines—more important, it crosses religious lines: Coptic Christian women are as likely as their Muslim sisters to have undergone FGM. It is not clear whether the practice originated in Egypt, but there is evidence from mummies that it was known in Pharaonic times (as was male circumcision). In the past two decades, campaigns to keep young women from having to follow in the footsteps of their mothers and older sisters have secured the active cooperation of both Egypt's late Grand Mufti Tantawi and the Coptic Pope Shenouda III; each repeatedly denied that the practice has any religious sanction—that, in fact, it is contrary to both Islamic and Christian principles.

In the past few years, the extent of FGM among the Kurds in Iran and Iraq has become apparent, but no clear explanation for this phenomenon has yet emerged. It has been suggested that the canons of the Shafei school of Islamic law[37] (which prevails in Egypt, Sudan, and Somalia where FGM is common) can be interpreted so as to highly recommend FGM, and this is also the school favored by Kurds in these two countries. By way of contrast, Kurds in Turkey and Syria generally follow the Hanafi school, which opposes the practice, and it does not seem to be much practiced among them.

Education

There are a number of available measures illustrating educational progress. Female adult literacy in the region in 1970 was generally low; in half the countries the rate was less than 20 percent, and the median rate for the region was only 30 percent. By the mid-2000s, the median had risen to 82 percent—still quite low in Yemen (30 percent) but above 70 percent in all but three countries. The percentage of girls among secondary school students has risen sharply even as total secondary enrollment has grown faster than population. In the late 1960s, a rate of 31.95 percent was the median; by 2005 this had climbed to 48.10 percent. In every country except Israel the annual growth rate for girls in secondary education was higher than the growth of total enrollment. In thirteen countries (including Palestine), the percentage of girls from the relevant age cohorts attending secondary school in 2005 was greater than or about equal to the corresponding percentage of boys; in twelve countries, this percentage of girls exceeded 75 percent. Again, both Yemen and Iraq are the outliers, with the proportions of both girls and boys receiving secondary training well below the rest of the region.

How good the education Middle Eastern children are actually receiving is another question entirely. One bit of evidence can be seen in a poll taken by the Global Economic Forum in 2009 that included twelve of the region's countries. When asked how the respondents rated their own countries' educational systems, with a few exceptions, their answers pointed to mediocrity—with a median score of 3.8 out of 7.0.[38]

In summary, the pattern that emerges from considering these indicators is one of improved living standards over the past generation or so, with women and children being particular beneficiaries of health and educational advances. However, the cross-regional picture is mixed. Not surprisingly, the richest countries have uniformly registered impressive gains, but Jordan and, to a lesser extent, Syria and Lebanon also have seen considerable improvement. War-plagued Iraq has a great deal of catching up to do following the restoration of relative peace, but it also has the

FIGURE 4.8 One type of traditional agricultural village in the Middle East: mud village with open pattern in northwestern Iran, with dung patties for fuel in foreground.

oil income to do so. Yemen, on the other hand, will advance the welfare of its people only with considerable outside assistance.

PATTERNS: SETTLEMENTS

Variety of Patterns

The Middle East has a wide range of settlement types, forms, and functions within a great variety of environments, historical traditions, and state systems. The variety is greatly increased when peripheral North Africa and Central Asia are considered. In size, settlements range from hamlets of a dozen families to one of the largest cities in the world (Cairo). Villages by the scores of thousands dot the rural landscape, from European Turkey to the cultivated valleys of northeastern Iran (see Figs. 4.8, 4.9, and 4.10), and more than 300 cities have passed the 100,000 population mark. In morphology, settlements have traditionally exhibited

a wide variety of forms, from very compact to widely dispersed, depending on topography, water supply, and other influences.[39]

In intensively irrigated areas like the Nile Valley and Delta, settlements are compact to conserve valuable farmland (Chap. 17), whereas villages on Syrian and Iranian steppes are more dispersed (see Fig. 4.8). Settlements that were—or still are—walled exhibit the usual crowding of enclosed places, but expansion since World War II has tended to open the texture on the fringes, and newly established suburbs are more dispersed than settlements of earlier centuries (Map 4.6). The typical Middle East urban structure has certain characteristics traditionally designated as "Islamic" (see "Internal Structures of Cities" below).

The agricultural-settlement landscapes of the region differ markedly from those of humid western Europe and eastern North America. From house design and construction

FIGURE 4.9 More compact traditional "cellular" mud village of Majmaah in the Sudayr area of Najd, central Saudi Arabia. Majmaah has been greatly modernized since this 1965 view.

FIGURE 4.10 Kurdish village in open steppe landscape of southeastern Turkey.

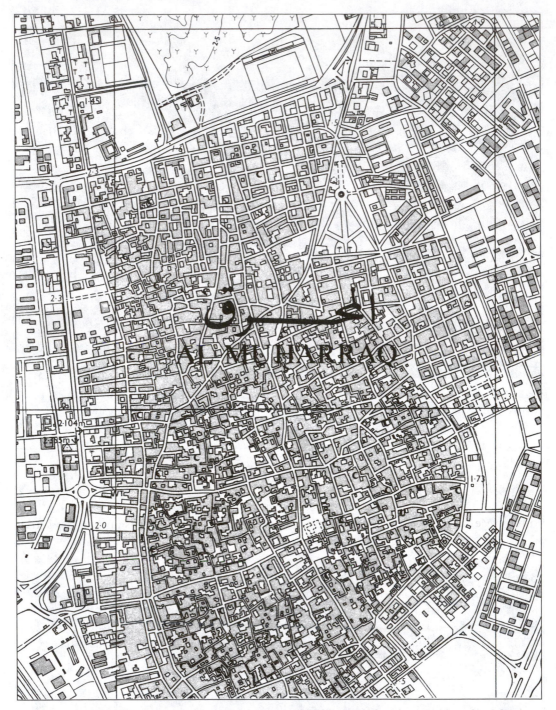

MAP 4.6 Traditional street pattern, Muharraq, Bahrain. The core of Muharraq, like other Islamic cities, is unplanned, narrow, and winding. On the edges of the old core are planned right-angle streets with larger blocks from the post-1960 period. The area shown is the same as that in Fig. 4.12. (Map courtesy of Survey Directorate, Bahrain)

FIGURE 4.11 Yemeni agricultural hamlet perched on mountain shoulder, surrounded by steep, terraced slopes of escarpment west of Sana. Well protected from surprise attack, settlements in these areas are small and close together, since farmers prefer not to have to walk very far to their fields in such rugged topography.

materials to street patterns and connecting roads, they express their regional context, and are somewhat comparable to those in northern Mexico and the southwestern United States. The irregular fields around the agricultural villages on the Jordanian steppe contrast sharply with the geometric grid of the U.S. Corn Belt, and the pattern of wheat and barley fields in the inner Fertile Crescent bears little resemblance to those in intensively irrigated Egypt. Similarly, Iranian agricultural villages and their surrounding fields, irrigated by *qanats*, contrast with villages perched on terraced slopes in Lebanon and Yemen (Fig. 4.11).

Five Types of Patterns

Five patterns have evolved: (1) the house and its elements (courtyard, storage facilities, garden—perhaps even its construction mate-

rials); (2) houses and other structures within the settlement; (3) distribution of settlements and their fields over the landscape; (4) interdependent relationships among the settlements (central places); and (5) links (roads and paths) between settlements. Although there is much more complexity since the 1950s, these fundamental categories are the same.

However managed, these five settlement patterns interact and are interrelated in a regional spatial system. Nomads or scattered peasants are interdependent with nearby villages and cities, villages with their central city, cities with their hinterland villages, and so on up and down the hierarchy. Since no one element is an isolate, each can be fully understood only in its regional context.[40]

Many factors influence patterns of distribution, density, and dispersion of human groupings and their structures. Water supply is always a basic consideration, but other ecological factors are also significant: topography, vegetation, climate, and soils. Cultural factors are often equally influential: traditions (including religion), aesthetics, transportation facilities, government support and other political aspects, regional function, defense, citizen action, and industrial relationships. Such considerations condition a settlement's size, shape, morphology, function, and position within the regional hierarchy of places. Moreover, as Middle East settlements have vividly demonstrated since World War II, the historical-technological context is a compelling factor.

Obviously, then, how people group themselves and their structures says much about how they manage the space in which they live. Countryside, village, and city are a spatial system, an ensemble of interacting subsystems combining in a dynamic whole. None is a discrete realm unto itself.

Overall Settlement Pattern

Population distribution has been examined above (see Map 4.2). Map 4.7 shows the main settlement concentrations in the Nile Valley and Delta, Asia Minor, western Iran, and the Levant, with secondary loci along the Tigris and Euphrates rivers. Map 4.2 indicates the virtually uninhabited areas of the region, emphasizing the repelling influence of extreme aridity on permanent human settlement. Figure 4.1 dramatically portrays the pattern of settlements and the concentration of cities, not only in the core Middle East but also in Libya, the Trans-Caucasus, Central Asia, and the Indus Valley.

Until the mid-twentieth century, the overwhelming majority of Middle Easterners lived in villages. With the exception of nomads, whose mode of "settlement" is a special case, the isolated rural resident was rare, found only in some Asia Minor and northwestern Iran locales. Although cities had long

been important in the region's socioeconomic pattern, they had declined in number, size, and importance after the sixteenth century. Modernization, especially in the newly wealthy oil states, reversed the rural-urban percentages, giving rise to rapid urbanization (see Maps 4.1 and 4.7 and Fig. 4.1).

Urbanization

By the late 1980s, about 50 percent of the population of the Middle East lived in cities; by the late 2000s, the percentage was about 62.5 percent in rapidly growing population. The urban trend was primarily the result of internal migrations from the villages to the cities and, in the Gulf, of labor flow and immigration from areas such as India, Pakistan, Jordan, and Yemen.

Unusual circumstances have created extraordinary urban percentages in some areas. Petroleum development attracted concentrations in city-states on the western coastal fringe of the Gulf, which once supported only fishing hamlets on the coast and scattered nomads in the hinterland. Now almost the entire population here is technically urban. Kuwait, for example, exploded from about 50,000 people in 1940 to 3.5 million in 2008, about 88 percent of whom lived in Kuwait City and its suburbs. Similar urbanization has occurred in Bahrain, Qatar, and the UAE since the 1960s.

For different reasons, urbanization is also high in Israel, despite the existence of scores of small settlements. Even Egypt, the agricultural country par excellence, has 43 percent urbanization. Surplus workers from the villages have migrated into Cairo especially, swelling the population of the Greater Cairo region to 18 million. Alexandria and other cities have likewise expanded. In Iran, a similar inpouring of villagers into Greater Tehran has caused its population to surge to close to 10 million, with Mashhad about 2.5 million and Esfahan, Karaj, Tabriz, and Shiraz more than 1.2 million each. Saudi Arabia experienced remark-

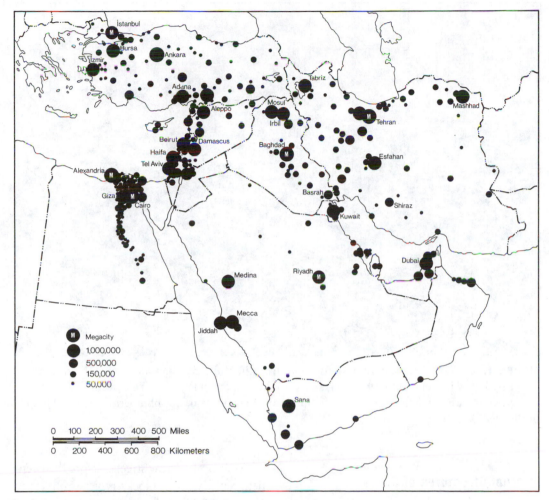

MAP 4.7 Pattern of distribution of urban population. Note the concentration of cities in the northern half of the region, in the Levant, and especially in the Nile Valley and Delta. Istanbul, Ankara, Tehran, Baghdad, Alexandria, Cairo, and Riyadh are in the multimillion population category.

able urbanization during the 1970s and 1980s. Dammam and nearby fishing villages rocketed from a few hundred dwellers to a conurbation of more than 1 million population. In the interior, Greater Riyadh, a desert capital of 30,000 before World War II, exploded during the oil boom and was estimated to have more than 4.5 million inhabitants in 2009.

Similarly, the urbanization that has characterized population movements in much of the world over half a century has resulted in permutations peculiar to the Middle East and some of the peripheral countries. Millions of

expatriates swelled the populations of the Gulf cities—Kuwait, Dammam, al-Khobar, Manama, Doha, Abu Dhabi, Dubai, Ahvaz, and Bandar-e Abbas—while hundreds of thousands of nomads have abandoned their lifestyle to become city dwellers. Sedentarization has been one of the major socioeconomic phenomena of the region for several decades. It has gone hand in hand with a reduction of nomad numbers to near insignificance. However, former nomads remarkably retain their tribal consciousness and relationships for many years, after becoming urbanized.

FIGURE 4.12 Traditional pattern of houses and streets in Muharraq, Bahrain, a small Islamic city. This aerial view from the mid-1960s looks southwest along the old causeway connecting Muharraq (*foreground*) with Manama, capital of Bahrain. Compare patterns in this photograph with the map of the area (Map 4.6).

Internal Structures of Cities

The internal morphological and structural patterns of settlements reflect interaction between urban development and historical-geographical influences. These include the street pattern, placement of central squares and other open areas, siting of religious and government structures, location and shape of the central market and commercial activities, and presence and character of ethnic concentrations. Identification and analysis of such characteristics aid understanding the initial role intended for a settlement in its regional system, as well as subsequent accretions to its functions, successive modifications of the urban morphology, and the interrelations between it and its neighbors.

For centuries, the traditional settlement, whether village or city, has had a highly irregu-lar pattern of narrow streets. Before the twentieth century, house blocks, typically uneven in size, were "cellular" with an open courtyard usual in each (Fig. 4.12; see also Fig. 4.9). Such an appearance identifies the older core of virtually every city and typifies villages that predate the nineteenth century. The fundamental compactness of settlements in hot arid areas minimized the length of water conduits and reduced heat from the direct sun. Streets were pathways among the houses; wheeled vehicles were rarely used when most towns evolved morphologically; the narrow lanes were sufficient for pedestrians and animals.

Urban Core Elements. Except in Israel, Cyprus, and parts of Lebanon, virtually every older town and city follows the traditional Islamic pattern of a core area comprising six elements: (1) a large Friday Mosque (*Masjid al-Jami*); (2) the city's principal educational facilities, the madrasah, typically conjoined to the mosque; (3) the main public water-based facilities—drinking fountains, latrines, and baths (*hammams*); (4) courts and other institutions of justice (*al-adl*) along with related administrative institutions, depending upon the city's role; (5) the citadel (*al-qalah*), often large and well fortified; and (6) most extensive of all in area, the commercial district.

The last element—the characteristic Middle Eastern *suq* (Arabic), *bazaar* (Persian), or *çarsı* (Turkish)—may surround the other core elements or radiate along one main axis in an alignment conditioned by environmental factors. A major *suq* includes numerous craft shops in which artisans produce such items as copper- and brassware, leather goods, textiles, jewelry, and perhaps such specialty goods as inlaid woods. Inns (*caravanserais* and *khans*), used to house travelers and their animals, were included in or were adjacent to the *suq*. Offices for levying customs (*gumruk*), banking facilities—especially for currency exchange—and related financial offices were usually in the commercial core, and some still are. A quiet stroll through any of the traditional *suqs* or *bazaars* of Istanbul, Cairo, Aleppo, Damascus, Baghdad, Mosul, Tehran, or Esfahan becomes a brief education in local history, geographical relationships, economy, customs, and culture of the area.

Urban Quarters. Although the system is declining, the city in the Middle East and the periphery has traditionally been divided into "quarters" (*harat, rayyat, mahallat, akhtat*). Many such quarters were closely knit and homogeneous communities in which people sought safety and protection among others of their own kind. Such group protection was the main or only recourse during many periods, and identity factors included religion, ethnicity, and village of origin. There were commonly quarters, among religions, for Christians, Jews, and Muslims; among Muslims, for Kurds, Turkmans, Persians, and Turks; among Arab Muslims, for Sunni, Shii, Druze, or migrants from specific villages.

The contemporary quarters in most older cities had their genesis during the tenth century, 200 or 300 years after the entrenchment of Islam in most of the region. It was during this time that the concept of "clients" (*mawali*) and "people of the book" (*ahl al-kitab*) became firm. There were as many as thirty-seven quarters in medieval Cairo, forty in Jerusalem (but only nine major ones), fifty in Aleppo, and seventy in Damascus. Sectors for Europeans were long set aside in the Galatea section of Constantinople by both Byzantines and Ottomans. Similar European quarters evolved in other cities after 1900, especially in Beirut, Damascus, Cairo, Baghdad, Tehran, and major Gulf cities. Thus, the concept and pattern of quarters became deeply ingrained in the region. Even with the less sharp definition of boundaries, the expansion of cities on a vast scale, and the growing homogeneity of population in the various *mahallat*, the designation of quarters often continues as a tradition.

The expansion of diplomatic communities added to the "foreign" quarters and in some cases created predominantly *corps diplomatique* enclaves. When Saudi Arabia permitted the shift of embassies from Jiddah to Riyadh in the early 1980s, it set aside a spacious new area for a splendid exclusive diplomatic quarter, even assisting poorer countries to build there. The Omani government established a handsome diplomatic quarter in the new suburb of al-Khuwayr, west of Muscat, where both government ministries and embassies are concentrated.

In most cities in the region, each major quarter replicated the city core on a reduced scale. When most major Middle East cities evolved, a neighborhood mosque was required every few blocks so the *azan* (alternatively, *adhan*—the call to prayer), given by the *muazzin* from the minaret, could be heard by all. A hierarchy of mosques often developed, with the main mosque in a quarter becoming the hub for smaller versions of the institutions and facilities found in the city core. In addition to the mosque, facilities needed for a quarter's social life were a *suq*, including bakeries, greengrocers, spice and ghee merchants, and a public kitchen or restaurant; a *hammam*; and a *khan*. Spacing among mosques increased in the twentieth century as amplifiers and loudspeakers increased the distance over which the *muazzin* could be heard. Indeed, the *azan* and Quranic readings have increasingly been recorded, even televised.

In several Islamic cities, as in many cities in Christendom, the urban nucleus is a religious monument or shrine dedicated to a religious leader or saint. The shrine attracts the usual array of ancillary facilities and institutions, particularly to service visitors. Mecca is the prime pilgrimage destination in Islam; it had an important shrine and served a significant commercial function prior to the time of Muhammad. Other major shrine cities are Medina, with the tomb of the Prophet Muhammad; Karbala and al-Najaf, just west of the Euphrates in Iraq, with the two main Shii shrines; Kadhimiya and Samarra in Iraq, and Mashhad and Qom in Iran, all with important Shii tombs; and such multifunctional cities as Jerusalem, Damascus, Konya, and Istanbul with major sites attracting thousands of pilgrims annually.

Significant as mosques and related elements may be, residences obviously occupy most of a city. Here the texture is finer and more uniform than in the grosser pattern of the core. Traditional houses, although not necessarily contemporary dwellings, in the Middle Eastern city are modest in size, with walls built to the edge of the property line, an open courtyard in the center or to one side, and different living quarters for males and females. The men of the family have more open quarters; women's quarters have shuttered windows and greater privacy. Typically,

the house is one or two stories high, and the staircase to the second story, if any, is in the courtyard. A flat roof is often surrounded by a low parapet and is regularly used by the family as a sleeping area during the summer, which is also the dry season in most of the region. The overall pattern of such houses, built wall against wall in small blocks divided by narrow zigzagging streets, is one of cellular regularity (see Fig. 4.12).

These traditional characteristics have been appreciably modified as settlements have expanded and modernized virtually everywhere in the Middle East since 1950. New and old have come face-to-face. Although the traditional has yielded to modern technology, the heritage of the past in many cities, but not in all parts and not in all cities, is often still perceptible in both architecture and city planning. Villages especially retain the character of fortified compounds and protected sites (see Fig. 4.11).

Air-conditioning is now almost universal in the Gulf amirates and Saudi Arabia; here, the ancient tradition of sleeping on the roof during the summer has almost disappeared; it is still common in many other parts of the region, particularly in villages. Air-conditioning permits flexibility in house design, especially in window arrangement, and in many ways middle- and upper-middle-class residences in many cities would be acclaimed by Westerners of comparable income levels. Nevertheless, the construction of walls along property lines, the preference for courtyards, and limited yard or garden areas remain. The broad green lawns of an American suburb are impractical in the water-deficient region, although smaller ones are seen around many homes in well-watered Tehran and some mansions in Riyadh, and in Jewish settlements in occupied territories, for example.

A more striking departure from tradition is seen in urban street design. With very high automobile ownership per family in much of the region, especially in the Gulf, Cyprus, and

FIGURE 4.13 Central Business District of Kuwait City, entirely developed since the late 1950s.

Israel, new streets are generously wide. Cities like Kuwait, Doha, Riyadh, Dammam, and Dubai had ample areas of desert into which to expand, and planners took advantage of the space to provide broad boulevards and wide secondary and tertiary streets in new sections, in contrast to the traditional narrow lanes in older quarters.

Blending traditional and modern also characterizes the commercial sections of many cities. The *suq* is too deeply ingrained in tradition and has served the purpose too well and too long to be discarded entirely for foreign mercantile fashions. The old vaulted aisles or palm frond–covered lanes lined with shops still exist in less affluent areas or in carefully preserved places. Centuries-old markets retain their distinct traditional mystique in Istanbul, Esfahan, Aleppo, Damascus, Sana, and Cairo, as well as in peripheral cities like Casablanca, Samarkand, Kabul, and Peshawar.

However, many old *suqs* have been supplanted in the most extensively modernized cities with attractive air-conditioned commercial centers. These combine the traditional *suq* with the shopping-mall concept—itself a twentieth-century adaptation of the *suq*. The range of goods traditionally offered for sale has also been enormously expanded, so that shops in Beirut, Riyadh, Doha, Abu Dhabi, Tehran, and Ankara now also offer virtually every type of consumer goods: Japanese and Swiss watches, mobile telephones, laptops, iPods, Xboxes, and so on. Dubai has complemented its wide range of *suqs* with superluxury shops, catering to the very wealthy from the UAE and other Gulf states.

Urban areas planned and constructed since 1960 display a markedly different morphology from older sectors, and dramatic changes in structural and textural patterns designate the lines beyond which the new planning has been carried out (see Map 4.6). Such changes are obvious in Damascus, Jerusalem, Ankara, and Tehran; the urban morphology of the West is especially evident in Gulf cities from Kuwait (Fig. 4.13) to Dubai, but also in Istanbul, Cairo, Beirut, and Tel Aviv. High-rise office and apartment buildings, extensive suburbs, the coalescence of cities into conurbations, divided freeways (dual carriageways), and futuristic airports became commonplace in only two decades.

Urban Problems and Prospects

In many cities where expansion was extreme, whether in Ankara, Amman, Abu Dhabi, Beirut, Baghdad, or a score of other explosively growing metropolises, newcomers poured into the urban fringe and erected spontaneous (squatter) settlements faster than adequate housing could be planned and constructed. In much of the Gulf area, government oil funds were fortunately available for adequate public housing to replace the squatter huts, although construction initially lagged behind the influx of new population. Lacking oil income, Turkey, Lebanon, Jordan, and Egypt have found it difficult to fund housing in expanding areas. Jordan, Lebanon, Syria, and the Palestinian areas faced the special problem of having both unofficial and official Palestinian refugee camps spring up around Jericho, Amman, Irbid, Sidon, Beirut, and Dara. Official camps were given basic support from the United Nations Relief and Works Agency (UNRWA). Improved refugee housing was financially and politically difficult to provide over more than six decades.

Israel is a special case in that foreign aid from both private and government sources supplied reasonably adequate amounts for housing—after some delay—the flood of immigrants in the late 1940s and the 1950s. Later *olim* (immigrants) were very well housed, and impressive homes were built— a large number in settlements in the occupied West Bank and Gaza—for many of the hundreds of thousands who arrived from the FSU during the 1990s. Principal funding came from controversial multibillion-dollar

U.S.-guaranteed loans in 1991–1992 and 2003.

Spontaneous settlements in Turkey, *gecekondus*, were first built when rural families began migrating into main urban centers—Istanbul, Izmir, Ankara—after World War II. They erected simple huts on the urban fringes, and under Turkish law a house built and roofed before the authorities prohibit further construction must be allowed to stand where and as built. Most of the huts were constructed between dusk and dawn to avoid observation, hence the name *gecekondu* (built overnight), and the government generally did not prohibit these self-built settlements.

Under similar circumstances in Iraq, when villagers and Bedouin poured into Baghdad in search of employment and improved living standards during the 1950s, authorities were overwhelmed in their limited efforts to provide funding, planning, space, and quarters for thousands of migrants. The settlers themselves built the same type of mud huts that members of lower economic groups had built in Mesopotamia for thousands of years—solid mud walls, with palm fronds and reed mats forming a pitched roof. Spaced only a few feet apart and lacking basic amenities, these *sarifahs* multiplied into sprawling settlements until they were replaced by public housing as oil income increased.

Despite the problems, town planning in the Middle East has been on a scale unprecedented in the region's history and impressive on a world scale. The reconstruction of war-devastated cities in Europe during the 1950s demanded extraordinary town-planning efforts, and expertise developed at that time was later applied to the unparalleled urban expansion in the Gulf area. Initially, urban planners had to be imported by most of the rapidly expanding Middle East countries, since their own experts were few in number and relatively inexperienced in such large-scale planning.

Most of the Gulf states turned to the British for expertise, since these countries had been under British tutelage prior to gaining independence in the 1960s and early 1970s. One consequence is that major Gulf cities bear the unmistakable stamp of British town-planning concepts—for example, the traffic "roundabout," known as a rotary or traffic circle in the United States, where it is rarely used. Local technicians were rapidly trained in town planning, and governments soon took over the enormous task of planning their own cities and villages. Some of the designs are striking, having been facilitated by the fact that cost was often no object.

Planning in Israel was unique in that a high degree of expertise developed among Jewish newcomers under the mandate; also, many planning experts emigrated to the Jewish state. As the new state grew, there was a highly coordinated and well-financed planning program at every level. The site of each settlement was carefully selected, whether on or near a razed Arab village, a restoration of a known or supposed biblical site, or completely new. Once the site was chosen, the internal design was drawn up and a selection of house types was supplied by the planners. This ensured balanced distribution of immigrants, efficient use of water, economic activity for the new inhabitants, and a systematic security pattern in the expanding state.[41] The category of settlement for a given site was also determined by the central planners—*kibbutz, moshav, nahal,* or multifunction town (see Chap. 12). Similar planning went into the scores of highly controversial "settlements" built in the Israeli-occupied West Bank and Gaza Strip.

Despite planning, virtually every Middle Eastern city—especially those with more than 500,000 inhabitants—has found itself faced with the same problems as similar cities elsewhere, particularly in developing countries. Traffic problems often top the list: Increasing affluence may double or triple the

number of vehicles crowding into the space allotted to them, which expands only slowly. Crowded streets; inexperienced drivers; lack of parking facilities and adequate traffic policing; narrow streets in the older sections, often the commercial core; problems with traffic lights; and, in some cities (Cairo, for example), admixtures of animals and carts— all combine to create traffic nightmares. Tehran, Beirut, Cairo, and Istanbul rank high on a world traveler's list of cities with the worst traffic. Cairo, Istanbul, and Tehran now have metro systems that alleviate some of the surface chaos.

Along with traffic, some big cities struggle with serious shortages of water, gas, electricity, sewerage facilities, telephones, and other utilities and services; urban populations are growing, while per capita water resources are declining. Increasing unpredictability of precipitation and stream flow due to climate change adds more stress to both rural and urban systems. Even cities in the more humid areas—Istanbul, Beirut, Haifa—suffer water shortages during long dry summers because distribution systems are inadequate. Cairo, even with a plentiful source of water in the Nile, has the same problem. For many years, municipal water was supplied in Ankara for only brief periods two or three times a day. Jiddah has periodically gone waterless in the summer, but the intense downpour in November 2009 generated floods that killed at least 120 and left thousands homeless after 3.55 in/90 mm fell in four hours. In Beirut, apartment houses, even in normal times, are, by design, supplied with water through such small pipes that it must be stored during the night in roof tanks, one for each apartment. Similarly, homes in Cyprus have prominent but essential water tanks on their roofs next to solar panels for hot water. Residents of Amman, capital of water-poor Jordan, store water when they receive scheduled deliveries.

Coastal cities in Israel recycle treated sewage to stretch the water supply, pumping it back into the aquifers under the coastal plain from which much of the supply is obtained. Continuous recycling without plentiful recharging by natural runoff in dry years affects the taste of drinking water in the Tel Aviv area and worries some Israeli planners, but the procedure is a conservational success—in 2004, 189 mn gal/0.71 mn m³ of treated wastewater were available daily. Occasional wet seasons, such as the winters of 1997–1998, 2002–2003, and 2009–2010, help counteract some of the problem, but Israel, like the entire eastern Mediterranean, has seen a very dry period since 2003.

Kuwait City is unique in having developed with virtually no natural surface or underground water. In earlier times, the small village on Kuwait Bay brought most of its fresh water in goatskins and other similar containers by boat from the Shatt al-Arab, south of Basrah. When oil revenues exploded, Kuwait took advantage of large supplies of fuel (and funds) to distill seawater. In the mid-1950s, a gallon of water delivered by tanker truck cost the same as a gallon of gasoline. As the population doubled and redoubled, Kuwait installed additional and more efficient distillation facilities, while exploiting newly discovered groundwater supplies. Desalination has been increasingly important in other Gulf cities and on the Red Sea coast since 1970. By the late 1990s, Saudi Arabia—which annually uses 936 percent of its total renewable water resources—had installed more than thirty large desalination plants, providing 70 percent of the drinking-water supply. Nearly forty more such plants were to be in operation in the region by the end of the 2000s.[42] In 2004, some 275 bn gal/1.033 bn m³ were produced through desalination and another 45 bn gal/0.133 bn m³ through wastewater treatment.

Governments in the region have struggled with their stewardship of water resources, balancing political expediency against optimal service provision and sustainable use. As water becomes increasingly scarce, especially in relation to the growing demands of demographic and lifestyle changes, competition among users will create challenges for still developing institutional processes. In countries relying on externally sourced rivers, desalination, and highly variable precipitation, patterns of unproductive water use and squandered public finances contribute to potential conflict.

While the specific impacts of climate change are still being evaluated, the key points of agreement regarding the Middle East include reduced stream flow, less precipitation, and higher temperatures. Areas with lower precipitation already have high variability, and this uncertainty over water availability strains relations among resource users, like agriculture, industry, urban dwellers, and the basic needs of the environment.[43] At a bare minimum, one person requires 1 cubic meter—265 gallons—of drinking water per year; that same amount of water will produce only 1 kilogram of grain in arid-land irrigated agriculture.[44] The latter sector, which claims 80 to 90 percent of water in most countries of the region, will demand even more with higher temperatures and lower soil moisture; cities, growing in size and prosperity, will cut into the resources available for rural areas. Competition between the enormous agricultural base in Egypt, with its still memorable land redistribution to smallholders, and the ponderous Cairo metropolis exemplifies the political quandary facing some countries in the region.

The agricultural experience of millennia has enabled farmers in Egypt, Yemen, Iraq, and other areas to develop modifications of simple technologies, allying traditional social relations with relatively predictable arrivals of water. While limited technology imposed certain constraints, the development of new mechanisms to create and provide fresh water has posed problems for user communities over the social and political structures necessary to ensure just and efficient distribution. From an economic perspective, large hydraulic projects required the significant financing available only to national governments. In some cases, this permitted elite groups to "capture" water resources, restricting access and increasing costs for the rest of the population.

Partly because of a failure to modernize, for either financial or technical reasons, and partly because of problems with distribution networks, many Middle East cities, and far more towns and villages, have water that cannot be safely relied upon. Since many residents nevertheless drink the water, intestinal parasitic diseases are endemic. Whereas Istanbul, Nicosia, Cairo, Damascus, Riyadh, and Tel Aviv supply relatively safe potable water, Ankara, Beirut, Amman, and wartime Baghdad,[45] among other capitals, do not. Bottled water is preferred, or essential, in much of the region. People living in areas not served by a piped distribution system in good repair must either take water from a possibly polluted source or buy it from private tankers, costing the poor much more than the wealthy may be paying for city water.

Nearly all Middle East cities have the capacity to supply reasonably reliable electrical power to their citizens. The electricity age has thoroughly pervaded the region and, indeed, has swept the Levant and the Gulf as much as it has western Europe and North America. Nearly inexhaustible supplies of energy in the Gulf deliver to virtually every urban household the electricity to operate air-conditioning, refrigerators, and a full range of household appliances. With plentiful electricity, main city streets—and even intercity highways—are well lighted, such as the 100-mi/161-km motorway between Abu Dhabi and al-Ayn.

Settlement morphology in the Middle East since the 1950s has evolved under unique conditions. Explosive development accompanying the oil boom has had pro-

found effects on settlements in the region, especially in the Gulf area. There the impact of Western technological influence on traditional cities created a certain dichotomy of urban planning and execution: A major dilemma has been how to modernize and provide the desired conveniences without destroying or detracting from the charm and historical values of a Jerusalem, Cairo, Istanbul, or Damascus. Charm and tradition have too often yielded to technology, economic demands, and the urge to modernize; historic structures and quarters have been razed for modular high-rise office and apartment blocks of little architectural value.

Hardly a city has escaped overuse of the bulldozer blade, leveling old buildings and quarters in Jiddah, Kuwait, Baghdad, Tehran, Beirut, and Jerusalem in seeming haphazard fashion sometimes. Sharp debate has accompanied such changes, particularly in Jerusalem, a city sacred to three great world religions. Plans to rebuild the war-damaged core of Beirut were fiercely disputed in the early 1990s before the design for the area was adopted. Reconstruction was virtually completed by 2005, although many outlying neighborhoods still had damaged structures when, during the "Summer War" of 2006 between Israel and Hizballah, some were hit with renewed aerial bombardment by the Israeli Air Force—a circumstance against which even the most careful planner is helpless. Similarly, parts of Kuwait City required rebuilding after the 1990–1991 Gulf War. In Iraq, enormous reconstruction programs will be required to restore thousands of structures, transportation facilities, factories, utilities, and similar resources that were destroyed or damaged in 2003 and afterward.

The dilemma for urban planners in the Middle East had no simple solution: Central Business Districts had to be either modernized or overwhelmed with automobile traffic. Vigorous efforts of conservationists have rather successfully preserved most of the picturesque charm of the old cores of Sana, Istanbul, Esfahan, and Damascus. The entire town of Shibam, in the Wadi Hadramawt of eastern Yemen, as well as Sana's Old City have been declared world historic sites by the United Nations Educational, Scientific, and Cultural Organization (UNESCO) (see Chap. 6).

PATTERNS: CLIMATE CHANGE

Climate has been one of the major factors that historically has determined how the Middle East has been settled and how its societies and economies have developed. Within relatively recent times, changes in climate have had dramatic effects on settlement patterns, as archaeological evidence increasingly shows. For example, before about the eighth millennium BCE, what is now the Sahara was a grassland, where nomadic peoples wandered with their flocks. Marvelous petroglyphs in numerous caves[46] in western Egypt and northwestern Sudan depict lakes, boats, fish, and even swimmers. As the climate became warmer and drier, the grasses withered, and over time the nomads settled in the nearby Nile Valley.

In the twenty-first century, the Middle East, along with the rest of the world, faces the prospect of rapid changes in climate induced by human activity—specifically, increasing temperatures due to rising levels of gases like carbon dioxide in the atmosphere. Ironically, much of this is due to profligate use of fossil fuels, like the petroleum and natural gas that forms so much of the basis of the Middle East's modern economy. While this is not the place to discuss at length such a complex subject or to engage in speculation about exactly how, where, and when the region will be affected by climate change,[47] there are two different kinds of effects it may experience in the coming decades that we can at least consider at this time.

First, the Middle East, like other parts of the planet, will be directly impacted by any changes in temperature, rainfall, humidity, wind patterns, and sea levels. Second, if the prospect of unfavorable climate shifts actually results in serious reductions in the use of hydrocarbon fuels, the economies of many of the region's states (and not just the petro-exporters) will encounter major challenges to the continuation of living standards that have depended on the sale of these fuels.

Seven or eight millennia ago, hotter and drier conditions shifted the desert northward until in places it reached the Mediterranean. One scenario for the future envisages Saharan aridity spreading to the Levant, Turkey, and southern Europe, with possibly increased rainfall to the east along the slopes of the Zagros, resulting in a wetter Mesopotamia.[48] Whether the drought conditions in the eastern Mediterranean over the past two decades are harbingers of such a shift is still unclear. What is obvious, however, is that this area is already short of the water it needs to support its population and the still important agricultural sector upon which many depend for their livelihoods.[49] Similarly, an unfavorable shift in the extent of the summer monsoon in the Ethiopian highlands could severely reduce the water that the Nile brings to Egyptian farmers. It is not difficult to see how such changed circumstances would exacerbate the region's political conflicts. Rising sea levels would negatively affect low-lying productive areas like the Nile Delta and southern Iraq. In other parts of the region, the extensive coastal infrastructure for petro-exports would be affected, and along all the littorals, seawater would increasingly impinge on freshwater aquifers.

On the other hand, if global sentiment supports a serious reduction in the use of fossil fuels, then within one or two decades, the lifeblood of several of the region's economies would begin to be constricted. The smaller Gulf states have for some time been amassing revenues in excess of their current needs, and by the time oil demand might slacken noticeably, they might all be able to provide their citizens with a high standard of living from their foreign investment earnings. That would not be the case, however, for the "Big Three" in terms of both population and oil reserves—Saudi Arabia, Iran, and Iraq. To the extent they have engaged in long-range planning (for the time when their reserves are exhausted), they have thought in terms of having several decades to prepare for a post-petroeconomy.

Perhaps the actions of Saudi Arabia in the late 2000s best illustrate the confused state of thinking on climate change in the region. On the one hand, the kingdom actually has a history of making alternative-energy investments—not surprisingly, solar-power development has been high on its agenda. Additionally, it has been pursuing ways of burying greenhouse gases in near-depleted oil fields. But in 2009, its representatives put forward its claim for compensation from consuming states in the event of a decline in demand for its hydrocarbon exports. At the UN Climate Summit in Copenhagen that year, its delegation went so far as to deny the existence of any link between human activity and climate change. To outside observers, both these actions seemed designed to prevent any meaningful agreement to reduce greenhouse gases from emerging from these negotiations.

Meanwhile at the summit, the UAE issued a strong joint statement with five other small countries, calling on the developed nations to make deep cuts in greenhouse gases and focus on the worldwide problem of insufficient fresh water. Breaking with the general tendency of major oil exporters to downplay the issue, the UAE, with its colleagues, pledged to increase its domestic efforts to promote clean-energy approaches. The joint statement succinctly described the specific situation that the Middle East may soon be facing: "Scientific evidence clearly shows that anthropogenic greenhouse gas emissions contribute significantly to global warming. The potential risks of unmitigated climate change are enormous. . . . The prospects are grim. Rising temperatures will cause major crop declines . . . and significant changes in the availability of water resources. . . . Storms, droughts, forest fires and floods will cause irreversible environmental degradation and desertification, affecting the food supply of millions and causing massive migration flows."[50] Pope Benedict XVI made the same point even more succinctly in December 2009: "If you want to cultivate peace, protect creation."[51]

NOTES

1. A recent study of how differing population estimates can seriously affect government policy decisions was summarized in *Orient Planet*, Jan. 4, 2010, www.orientplanet.com/Press_Release_Jan4.htm.

2. The Pew Forum on Religion and Public Life 2009.

3. Because across our group of countries the latest available estimates are for different dates and because countries define "city" in different ways, these numbers are approximate.

4. Of several useful studies of peoples, religions, and languages of the Middle East, a particularly helpful one is Weekes 1984, which includes a bibliography for each people. Non-Muslims are included in D. Bates and Rassam 1983; Eickelman 1981; Gulick 1983; and Bengio and Ben-Dor 1999. Minorities are discussed in Nisan 2002. Relatively up-to-date statistics of peoples within individual countries are given in the Encyclopaedia Britannica's annual *Britannica World Data* and the Central Intelligence Agency's *World Factbook*. For languages especially, see the excellent Grimes et al. 1996; and www.ethnologue.org.

5. Greek was also the language of the Septuagint, the oldest surviving version of the Old Testament.

6. In addition to Weekes 1984 and the Encyclopaedia Britannica's annual *Britannica World Data*, religions are studied in Nisan 2002 and J. Joseph 1983.

7. Of the scores of studies of Islam, useful ones include the classic W. Smith 1957; B. Lewis 1973; Esposito 1995; and Fuller 2003. Many books on Islam appeared after the 1991 Gulf War, and still more followed 9/11 and the 2003 war in Iraq.

8. A good and readable biography is Armstrong 1992.

9. A recent study of the Shii is Fuller and Francke 2001.

10. The Pew Forum on Religion and Public Life 2009.

11. Among thousands of references on Christianity, two handy studies are McManners 1990 and D. Barrett et al. 2001. Comparative treatment is given in H. Smith 1991.

12. Technically, Orthodox communities are those in full communion with the Ecumenical Patriarchate (Greek) in Istanbul/Constantinople. Copts, Armenians, Nestorians, and the Jacobites of Syria are not; thus, they are sometimes termed "Oriental" or "Oriental Orthodox" communities. To simplify matters here, the term "Orthodox" is used for all these groups to distinguish them from Catholics (that is, those in communion with Rome).

13. Large but difficult to estimate are the proportions of the expatriate populations of Saudi Arabia and the Gulf states that are at least nominally Christian; the same is true for many of the FSU immigrants to Israel since 1990 (see "Multicultures: Who Is a Jew?" in Chap. 12).

14. As with Christianity, thousands of studies examine Judaism and its ramifications. In addition to H. Smith 1991, see Blau 1966 and Wigoder et al. 2002.

15. Radio Free Europe/Radio Liberty, Mar. 9, 2010, www.rferl.org/content/Bahai_faith_iran_persecution/1077789.html.

16. In addition to the general references given in note 4, the studies of Middle East peoples include Gonen 1993 and National Geographic Society 2001.

17. Of scores of studies of Arabs, useful are the classic Hourani 1991; Baker 2003; Khashan 2000; Hoyland 2001; and Rogan 2009.

18. Most ethnic Copts are Orthodox in religious affiliation, but some are Catholic or Protestant.

19. Betts 1988 is a concise and useful study of the Druze. For more details, see Nisan 2002, Chap. 5.

20. Nisan 2002, Chap. 6.

21. Ibid., Chap. 9.

22. See *Turkey* Country Study 1995; B. Lewis 1968; and D. Howard 2001.

23. An intensive study of the Qashqai is Beck 1986.

24. The Persians are examined in W. Fisher 1968; *Iran* Country Study 1989; and Hunter 1990.

25. The plight of the Kurds is widely examined. See *Iraq* Country Study 1990; Ghareeb 1981; and O'Shea 2003.

26. Hinnels 2005, 6.

27. See *New York Times,* July 25, 1999, for an in-depth study of the subject, plus Simon, Laskier, and Reguer 2003; and Nisan 2002, Chaps. 12 and 13.

28. *Christian Science Monitor,* Jan. 16, 1998; www.the-samaritans.com.

29. This relationship is being studied by geneticists—for example, P. Shen et al. 2004.

30. Stiglitz, Sen, and Fitoussi 2009.

31. UNDP, *Human Development Report,* 1990–2009.

32. We have chosen not to look at the GDI itself but only at health and education components like those used for the GDI. This index also uses estimates for gender differences in income that, for several of the countries in this study, are of questionable reliability.

33. Israel was omitted in this case because of a lack of comparable early data.

34. Data in this section are derived from *United Nations Statistical Yearbook*, published annually (New York); *United Nations Demographic Yearbook*, published annually (New York); UNDP, *Human Development Report*, 1990–2009; United Nations Children's Fund (UNICEF), *The State of the World's Children*, published annually (New York); Save the Children, *State of the World's Mothers*, published annually (Westport, CT); and World Economic Forum, *The Global Gender Gap, 2009* (Geneva, Switzerland).

35. Basic facts on FGM can be found at www.who.int/mediacentre/factsheets/fs241/en/print.html.

36. Morgan 2007.

37. There are four schools of law among Sunnis; all are considered equally legitimate in authority, but historically one school tends to dominate in an area and each school has its own "territory." The Shafei school is favored in eastern Africa from the Mediterranean south to Tanzania, in Yemen, and in Indonesia (where FGM is also found); the Hanifi school in the Levant, Turkey, the Balkans, Central Asia, and the subcontinent; the Maliki school across Muslim Africa west of Egypt and the Sudan; and the Hanbali school in Saudi Arabia. See also Ahmad n.d.

38. World Economic Forum 2009a, 390.

39. Several works on Middle East cities have appeared since the mid-1960s, most of which have been collections of papers given at conferences and symposia. See, for example, Serjeant 1980, with especially stimulating and authoritative perspectives on the Islamic city at a UNESCO colloquium; Saqqaf 1987, which focuses on the ancient-modern confrontation; and Blake and Lawless 1980. Bonine 1977 contemplates the Islamic urban experience. Antoniou 1981 is another UNESCO look at the Islamic city from the aspect of conservation. English 1966, Bonine 1979, and Kheirabadi 1991 focus on Iranian urban development; Grill 1984 looks at Arabian Peninsula urbanization; and Altorki and Cole 1989 analyze the special

case of Unayzah. Abu-Lughod 1971, Rodenbeck 1998, Ghannam 2002, and Raymond 2000 examine Cairo. Ragette 1983 considers the reconstruction of Beirut, as does Gavin and Maluf 1996. AlSayyad 1991 looks at the genesis of Arab Muslim urbanism. MacAdam 2002 studies Roman settlement patterns.

40. Walter Christaller's classical theory of central places (1966), the most widely applied model for the study of the hierarchy of settlements, is of limited applicability in much of the Middle East.

41. See Soffer and Minghi 1986.

42. The vulnerability of these vital plants was emphasized in August 2009 when a technical failure at a Kuwaiti sewage treatment plant resulted in the release of untreated wastewater into the Gulf close to an intake for a desalination facility. Sabotage, of course, is another danger.

43. B. Bates 2008.

44. Jaganathan, Mohammed, and Kremer 2009.

45. Author Cummings remembers from personal experience in the 1960s when Baghdad's tap water was quite potable.

46. The most famous of which is the Cave of the Swimmers in Egypt's Gilf al-Kabir region. Featured in the film *The English Patient*, its fame has unfortunately attracted many visitors, and some have vandalized the petroglyphs. On a visit to the region in 2004, author Cummings saw several examples of such vandalism.

47. For a balanced discussion of the relative uncertainties of the science of climate change and the need to be cognizant of the consequences of inaction, see "The Clouds of Unknowing," *Economist*, Mar. 20, 2010.

48. As postulated in a study conducted at the University of New South Wales Climate Change Research Center, and reported in *Science Daily*, Aug. 13, 2008, www.sciencedaily.com.

49. The danger of recurring "water wars" on a local basis was, for example, reported for Lebanon in "Climate Change and Politics" 2009.

50. The statement was signed also by Cape Verde, Costa Rica, Iceland, Singapore, and Slovenia. "Joint Statement of the Foreign Ministers 2009."

51. Pope Benedict XVI 2009.

5

The Desert and the Sown
Land Use

Agricultural conditions, systems, and products differ strikingly across the Middle East. Landscapes vary from irrigated plots in the Nile Valley to Mediterranean croplands and fruit orchards in the Levant and from extensive wheat fields in interior Anatolia to desert rangelands of Arabia's wandering herdsmen. Anatolian and Iranian mountain slopes and valleys are reminiscent of the European Alps. In contrast, vast arid expanses of interior Arabia and Iran appear barren. Although some areas, such as the Rub al-Khali, have little to offer agriculturally, other large desert stretches are used effectively by nomadic herders. The same generalizations apply to North Africa and Central Asia, with much of the Trans-Caucasus region better watered and more similar to northern Turkey and northern Iran.

Agricultural lands in the region fall into three broad types—not all mutually exclusive—according to the availability of moisture: (1) subhumid and humid areas suitable for rainfed crops, from wheat and barley on the drier margin to maize and tea with more rainfall; (2) irrigated areas located primarily in deserts and semideserts but also increasingly as enclaves in the more humid areas; and (3) arid and semiarid lands used by pastoralists for grazing their animals. This chapter surveys these patterns of land use (Table 5.1), forestry and fishing, and land tenure and reform from a regional perspective.

AGRICULTURE

Before the oil boom began in the mid-1950s, the Middle East was by every criterion overwhelmingly an agricultural and fishing area. The manufacturing and services sectors were at best only minimally developed. Though agricultural yields were modest, the region was a net exporter of food. By the 1990s, however, these sixteen states were importing more than 50 percent of their food requirements; this percentage continues to rise as the population grows, acquires more purchasing power, and shifts from agricultural employment to more varied economic activity.

The decline in agricultural employment has been especially marked in the petroleum-producing areas, most significantly in the areas around the Gulf. There is still some fishing in the city-states that once relied heavily on this activity, but its economic contribution is now negligible, as is the percentage of the workforce employed in fishing. (The percentage of workers in the major sectors is seen in Table 7.1, which also shows the relative importance of agriculture in each country.)

Even in those countries with a relatively high percentage of the economically active

TABLE 5.1 Land Use: General

Country	1 Total Area Arable and Perm. Crops	2 Area Under Irrigation Total	3 % of Cult. Area	4 Arable Land	5 Perm Mdw & Pasture	6 Forest, Woodland	7 Waste, other
				Percentage of Total Area Under:			
Bahrain	6	4	67	3	5	<1	83
Cyprus	156	46	29	12	<1	19	64
Egypt	3,538	3,530	99	3	—	<1	96
Iran	18,549	8,856	48	10	18	7	63
Iraq	5,450	3,525	65	12	9	2	77
Israel	376	225	60	14	6	8	69
Jordan	221	81	37	2	8	<1	88
Kuwait	18	9	50	<1	8	<1	91
Lebanon	287	104	36	14	38	13	19
Oman	99	59	60	<1	5	<1	94
Qatar	21	13	62	2	5	<1	92
Saudi Arabia	3,625	1,731	48	2	79	<1	18
Syria	5,683	1,396	25	26	44	3	22
Turkey	24,837	5,215	21	28	19	13	35
UAE	290	227	78	<1	4	4	89
Yemen	1,625	680	42	3	42	<1	54
Gaza	—	—	—	—	—	—	—
West Bank	—	—	—	—	—	—	—
TOTAL/AVG.	64,781	25,701	40	—	—	—	—

Data in Columns 1 and 2 are in thousands of hectares (2007). Percentages in Columns 3-7 calculated from FAO data. (*Source*: UN Food and Agriculture Org., www.fao.org/corp/statistics.)

population still engaged in agriculture, its percentage of GDP may be smaller. For example, in Egypt, 24.8 percent of the workforce is in agriculture and fishing, but only about 14 percent of GDP comes from these sources. In Yemen, the 48.0 percent of the workforce engaged in agriculture and fishing contributes 9.0 percent to GDP, while from the 4.0 percent engaged in manufacturing and mining comes 9.6 percent. Moreover, manufacturing now surpasses agriculture as the leading employer in some formerly agricultural countries.

The relative decline of agriculture may obscure government efforts to develop the sector's potential. Agriculture is such a vital element that all regional states are conducting systematic, wide-ranging development programs. Oil income may taper off in a few years, but meanwhile some of that capital can be invested in irrigation and high-tech projects that will make long-term returns.

Some General Aspects

By its very nature, agriculture is so highly interactive with ecological factors and cultural traditions that it differs from one area to another as well as within an area. For example, the mixed farming practiced in the United States and western Europe is not often found in the Middle East; it would not be very suitable for a farmer to grow what he then feeds to his animals in an environment with more grazing land than grain surpluses. Livestock income—including dairy, eggs, meat, and meat by-products—accounts for less than one-third of the agricultural income in the region. Nevertheless, animals play a significant role in the cycle, providing income between harvests. Traditional livestock herding

FIGURE 5.1 Agricultural development in the Syrian Jazirah, east of the Euphrates River: harvesting a bumper wheat crop by hand (note sickle in the woman's right hand).

by nomadic pastoralists, however, is steadily declining not only in the deserts of the oil states but also in the mountains of Iran, Turkey, and Central Asia.

Wheat is found throughout the region, leading all crops in area sown (Fig. 5.1). Specialized crops are produced in scattered areas: coffee and the mildly narcotic *qat* in Yemen, frankincense in southern Oman and Yemen, tea in northeastern Turkey and northwestern Iran, dates around the Gulf (Fig. 5.2), licorice in southern Iraq, and pine nuts in Lebanon.

Food crops occupy most of the cultivated area, but industrial crops (cotton, tobacco, sugarcane, sugar beets, linseed, sesame) have also been locally important for more than a century. Cotton and flax have been major crops in Egypt since Pharaonic times. Where ecological conditions are favorable, industrial crops have been promoted by governments since the 1950s—for example, sugar beets in

Syria and Turkey and cotton in Israel and Turkey.

Except for intensively irrigated lands (like in Egypt), parts of Israel, and a few other scattered areas, low crop yields still typify agriculture, although there have been notable increases since the 1950s. For example, high-yield wheats have markedly raised output; wheat is usually grown on lands with highly variable precipitation. Until the 1960s, mechanization was uncommon, but cooperative programs have increased machine use, especially tractors (see Table 5.2, Col. 7). Farming in Israel is especially highly mechanized, and it is becoming progressively more so in Turkey, Iran, and Syria, as is seen by the large number of tractors.

Small farms (often tenant operated) characterize the region—one reason for limited mechanization. Along with efforts to improve yields, farmers and governments have made systematic attempts to improve crop

FIGURE 5.2 Extensive date groves inland from Suhar, Oman, seen from a tower of the old fort.

quality (and of the produce that reaches the consumer), conservation, efficiency, and other agricultural practices. Such programs produce a regionwide dynamic of change, with uneven but sometimes excellent results.

Physical Factors

1. Climate.   Moisture supply is the main factor in much of the region, and except in parts of Turkey and in some mountain areas it is inadequate, seasonally concentrated, and unreliable. Where climate is marginal, drought years are frequent and severe, and such areas experience wide swings in grain production. For example, in the dry year of 1984, Jordan produced only 15,000 mt (metric tons) of wheat; in unusually wet 1980, the crop was 134,000 mt—793 percent greater.

Only 7 percent of the region can regularly support rainfed agriculture (note isohyets on Map 2.5 and see Table 2.1). Approximate precipitation parameters for agriculture are the 5-in/125-mm isohyet as the minimum

for grains and the 12-in/300-mm isohyet as the lower limit for other crops. Irrigation can extend the cultivated area, but only to a limited extent, and it must be developed at great expense and effort for the most intensive and effective methods of water use. Available water is finite, and irrigable land is limited. Despite the problem of aridity, crops benefit from the long growing season, prevailingly clear skies, and favorable light for plant growth.

2. Soils.   Because naturally productive soils are limited, higher yields need good farm management, including intensive fertilization, good drainage, improved fallowing, and wise crop rotation. Salinity buildup is an ever-present problem in drier areas, notably in southern Iraq.

3. Relief.   Mountainous areas and rough terrain reduce the amount of land naturally suitable for cultivation. Although valuable for

TABLE 5.2 Land Use: Major Ground Crops and Number of Tractors

Country	1 Wheat Area	2 Wheat Prod.	3 All Vegetables	4 Tomatoes	5 Seed Cotton	6 Grapes	7 Tractors
Bahrain	—	—	2	5	—	—	13
Cyprus	5	11	5	29	—	34	1,170
Egypt	1,139	7,379	580	7,550	560	1,485	99,300
Iran	4,045	9,500	1,750	5,000	300	3,000	265,000
Iraq	2,203	2,228	105	830	18	184	72,800
Israel	86	159	188	434	48	113	24,500
Jordan	16	20	71	617	—	20	—
Kuwait	—	1	49	56	—	—	105
Lebanon	53	116	23	305	—	119	8,300
Oman	—	1	99	41	—	—	215
Qatar	—	—	15	12	—	—	60
Saudi Arabia	450	2,630	400	478	—	144	9,930
Syria	1,668	4,041	192	733	711	273	107,946
Turkey	8,098	17,234	290	9,945	2,275	3,613	1,037,383
UAE	—	—	140	215	—	—	380
Yemen	142	219	55	212	24	126	6,500
Gaza	—	—	—	—	—	—	—
West Bank	—	—	—	—	—	—	—
TOTAL	17,905	43,539	3,964	26,462	3,936	9,111	1,633,602

Wheat area, Column 1, is in thousands of hectares. Crop production, Columns 2–6, is in thousands of metric tons. Tractors are in units. Data for 2007. (*Source*: UN Food and Agriculture Org., www.fao.org/corp/statistics.)

their cooler climate and as major sources of runoff for irrigation water, mountains have only limited agricultural potential (see Fig. 2.6). However, in places, laborious terracing and other techniques have made production of specialty crops possible. Nevertheless, population pressure on the land long ago induced cultivators to plow highland slopes; the resulting loss of shrubs and trees that slowed runoff and protected the soil seriously escalated soil erosion. For their part, the low-lying plains and plateaus, which are appropriate for cultivation, are often areas of inadequate moisture and less productive soils.

Traditions, Techniques, and Technology

Improvements have been hindered by persistent traditional practices inimical to better farming and marketing. Until recently, farm input costs (fertilizer, pesticides, machinery)

were only 25 percent of the gross output value, in contrast to 70 percent in the United States. Thus, value added per agricultural worker has been generally low, but the situation is improving markedly. The rapidly expanding production of horticultural crops in plastic greenhouses impresses even the casual observer, not only in the Fertile Crescent but also in Egypt, Saudi Arabia, and the Gulf amirates. Although more costly, greenhouse production of tomatoes, beans, peppers, eggplant, strawberries, and similar crops permits earlier marketing, much higher yields, more attractive produce, and higher revenues.

Ironically, the countries that have the resources needed for capital-intensive agriculture have, with some exceptions, the lowest agricultural potential: Oman, Saudi Arabia, and the Gulf states. Iraq and Iran have both oil income and agricultural potential but have squandered much of their wealth on weaponry. However, every Middle Eastern government has an active, if not uniformly effective, national program for upgrading agriculture, and oil-producing states with a limited agricultural potential have given financial assistance to their less wealthy Arab neighbors who have greater crop possibilities. Such aid is mutually beneficial, as it produces a multiplier effect, and regional agricultural progress has been appreciably stimulated.

Perceptible mechanization has come late and slowly, and because it needs a systems approach that has been neglected, the mere adoption of machines does not optimize benefits. Even the greatly increased use of internal-combustion engines, common even in remote areas for irrigation, can be a mixed blessing because of overpumping. Tractors have become steadily more common; regionally, their number grew by more than 750 percent between 1970 and 2007, led by a tenfold increase in the number in Turkey, which has more than 66 percent of the region's total. Iran is second, with 17 percent (see Table 5.2). More sophisticated and expensive machines—cotton pickers, maize pickers, wheat combines—are still relatively unusual. Milking machines were rare until the 1990s, except in Israel, but by 2006 Turkey had almost 156,000 compared to an estimate of only 150 in 1970.

With major financial aid from the United States and international Jewish agencies, Israel devotes even higher capital inputs per unit area to land reclamation and improvement than do the Gulf states with oil income but desert environments. In proportion to its size, Israel has executed the most intensive programs in the region; one of its major reclamation projects, the drainage and cultivation of the Huleh Marshes in extreme northern Israel, was undertaken as early as the 1950s. It should be noted that by the 1990s, it was realized that this project had damaging ecological side effects, and parts of the marsh were reflooded. Whereas "making

the desert bloom" has actually been accomplished only in limited "oasis" areas in the dry Negev, scores of projects have improved cropland or rangeland, irrigated cultivated areas, drained marshes, and installed systems for drip irrigation.

Some areas, especially in Turkey, have good rainfed yields on average, but in most of the region irrigation is either essential, as in Egypt, or highly beneficial, as on the Levant coastal plains. Since water is usually the critical input, governments have prioritized projects harnessing more of their water, distributing it to improved cultivable areas, and utilizing more efficient techniques. Some of the world's major irrigation projects, with construction of world-class dams, have been undertaken in the region: the Southeast Anatolia Project (GAP) in Turkey, the Jazirah Project in Syria, and the Aswan High Dam in Egypt. Political problems ensuing from these projects are examined in Chapter 8.

Feeding the People

In the Middle East, where the climate is often less than favorable and water is increasingly scarce—and where climate-change projections indicate agricultural circumstances may worsen—it is not surprising that imports supply an increasing share of edible consumables. But that is not to say that agriculture in the region has not achieved advances with improved technology and better husbandry. For example, food-production per capita indexes reveal impressive gains in some of the countries where agriculture is significant. Over more than four decades from the early 1960s to the mid-2000s, per capita food output grew by 121.0 percent in Iran, 88.1 percent in Egypt, 56.0 percent in Lebanon, 24.8 percent in Syria, 22.0 percent in Jordan, and 20.8 percent in Cyprus. More modest but still positive growth was realized in Israel (9.4 percent) and Turkey (6.0 percent). On the other hand, per capita output in Yemen fell by 12.5 percent—perhaps illustrating the lure of *qat* cultivation over food crops in allocating scarce water resources; in war-ravaged Iraq, the index declined by 36.8 percent. (By way of comparison, food output per capita in the United States over the same period rose by 35.9 percent).[1]

This per capita increase does not imply, of course, anything like self-sufficiency, and the region's trade figures show increasing food imports across the board. For the six mostly desert countries of the peninsula, producing even a modest proportion of their food needs domestically is out of the question—thus, here there has been a significant movement toward investment in agriculture in countries with more favorable growing conditions. For example, in 2008, the UAE announced its interest in projects in Kazakhstan and the Sudan, as well as in purchasing farmland in Southeast Asia and Latin America.[2] A Saudi Arabian firm, the Al-Amoudi Group, was proceeding in 2009 with plans to develop as much as 1.24 mn ac (acres)/500,000 ha (hectares) in Ethiopia.[3] Also in 2009, several Gulf States announced the expansion of the capital of the Arab Authority for Agricultural Investment and Development (AAAID) by $2 billion.[4] The AAAID was founded in 1977 with the intention primarily of investing in the Sudan. The political instability of that country and other factors had kept the organization's activities quite modest until this renewal of interest.[5]

LANDHOLDINGS AND LAND REFORM

Land Tenure

Land tenure is an essential socioeconomic aspect of agricultural patterns and is extraordinarily complex in the Middle East—partly because there are sixteen different national systems and partly from the various legal systems of earlier rulers. The prevailing system developed in an Islamic context after the seventh century, modified over four centuries under the Ottoman Empire (excluding Iran).

Islamic law deals with land-related issues extensively, and so they are often intimately connected to religion.

In simplified terms, landholdings everywhere, except in Cyprus and parts of Israel, fall into three major categories: (1) state-owned land, the most common type, with strong usufruct rights vested in the occupant (*miri* lands, called *khaliseh* in Iran); (2) freehold or privately owned land (*mulk*); and (3) land in a religious trust (*waqf*), a unique Islamic trusteeship for the endowment of some religious or other social purpose, such as a mosque or school. The amount of *waqf* land is steadily decreasing; the trusts are discouraged by modern governments because they are difficult to control or tax. Despite reverence for the institution, *waqf* land has been widely expropriated in land-reform programs.

Two subcategories of land tenure play important roles in agriculture. The nomadic tribal grazing range (*dirah*) is based on the concept of land as territory rather than land as property. In its *dirah*, a major tribe considers that it has priority rights to the communal range and to access to water sources. Hundreds of thousands of square miles are nomadic tribal ranges in the region as a whole. A second subcategory, the communal village—*musha* in Syria and Palestine—permits villagers in marginal areas to shift between sedentarism and nomadism as circumstances dictate.[6]

Large state landholdings often passed quietly into private control during the post–World War I period; when the mandatory powers took over from the Ottomans, they often applied European concepts of private landownership. Taking advantage of the situation, trustees under the old system took title to tracts of *miri* land under their own names; tribal leaders especially were registered as "owners" of extensive communal areas by the mandatories. This later caused considerable problems, particularly in Iraq (see below).

In Palestine, traditional systems changed sharply between the world wars; the Jewish

National Fund (JNF) acquired land from Arab titleholders, often absentees, evicted the usufruct tenants, and turned it over to Zionist immigrants. The new arrangement suggested aspects of the Islamic *miri* and *waqf* systems—the JNF, as trustee, took title "in the name of the Jewish people" and leased it for nominal sums to the colonists. More significantly, in the course of the fighting in 1948 and 1949, Israel confiscated about 1,112,000 ac/450,000 ha of cultivated land from Palestinian Arab owners who had become refugees. Absorbed by the state or the quasi-official JNF, it was then leased to Jewish settlers. After 1967, as the occupying power, Israel expropriated major swaths of land in the West Bank and Gaza, to establish Jewish settlements, build strategic roads, and set up military outposts, all very controversial.

Holdings and Reform

Landholding size is another significant aspect of land tenure and agricultural patterns; it has had a major impact on the social and political stability of several countries in the region. Since World War II, reform-minded governments have pursued land-reform programs, breaking up holdings considered to be excessively large and lessening the influence of powerful landlords.

Even before land reform, smallholdings were typical in the Middle East, especially in irrigated areas where land is scarce, highly desirable, and expensive, and this is still the case. In Egypt, for example, where all cultivated land must be irrigated, farms of less than 2.5 ac/1 ha make up 96 percent of all agricultural land. Such smallholdings occupy only 15 percent of the nonirrigated areas in Syria.

Before reform programs began in the mid-1950s, small numbers of wealthy landlords possessed huge holdings in Egypt, Syria, Iraq, and Iran. In Iraq, for example, a study by the UN Food and Agriculture Organization (FAO) revealed that 2 percent of the landowners held 66 percent of the land in

the mid-1950s; in Iran, large owners and tribal leaders controlled 50 percent of the land. Following the model of revolutionary republican Egypt under Gamal Abd al-Nasser, Syria and Iraq initiated reform programs during the late 1950s and early 1960s. One result of redistribution: The number of great landlords in the Middle East declined sharply. The same reforms changed landowning patterns: Individual ownership replaced many of the tribal rights to planting and pasture, and consolidation programs reduced fragmented, scattered holdings.

RAINFED CROP FARMING

Extensive Grain Farming

As the mean annual rainfall increases to about 5 in/125 mm along the inner margin of the Fertile Crescent, desert and semiarid grasslands give way to subhumid cropland (Map 5.1). Cereal grains in this subhumid belt—wheat, barley, and millet—are in fact highly bred grasses. Here, though poor rain years are frequent, grains grown without irrigation yield moderately good crops in wet years and at least minimum crops in drought years. Wheat yields might range between 2.5 and 15 bu (bushels) per ac/165 and 1,000 kg per ha; barley does as well or better. Yields have increased significantly since the new dwarf wheats were introduced.

Crop failures in marginal lands are frequent. With a comprehensive range-management program, it could be better if the more drought-prone areas grew high-quality forage grasses to increase meat production, but changing might be difficult, since some nomadic groups on the margins of grain-farming areas operate as both wandering herdsmen and part-time grain farmers. In a wet cycle, they settle down, shifting back to nomadic herding in a dry cycle, as in the *musha* village. In each cycle, a few more families tend to remain sedentary, so nomad numbers gradually diminish.

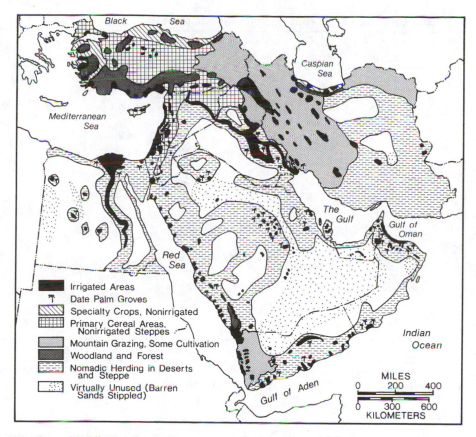

MAP 5.1 Middle East land use. Note the large amount of area virtually unused or useful only for nomadic herding.

Whether grown on the dry margins or in the more humid areas, it is all winter wheat, planted in autumn to get the cool-season rainfall, then harvested in the early days of the warm, dry summer.

Mediterranean Agriculture

Wheat and Other Cereals. In the rainfed agriculture of the more humid Mediterranean climate areas, wheat is still the dominant crop, but there is considerable variety, including specialized arboriculture (tree crops), viticulture (grape cultivation), and a great range of irrigated crops. Wheat is more intensively cultivated in this wetter area where yields are higher and more reliable than in the steppes (14–17 bu per ac/940–

1,145 kg per ha is typical). Millet and barley are also common.

Vegetables and Fruits. Mediterranean-type agricultural conditions are ecologically suitable, particularly with supplementary irrigation, for a variety of vegetables and fruits, many of which evolved in the area. Coastal plains from western Turkey to southern Israel and in Cyprus are veritable vegetable gardens and fruit orchards. Irrigation supports citrus groves, especially oranges, in segments all along the coastal belt; bananas are grown in southern Turkey, Cyprus, Lebanon, and Israel. Oranges in Lebanon, Israel (the Jaffa orange), and Gaza are prime products, although Iran, Egypt, and Turkey greatly exceed the Levant in production (Table 5.3 and Fig. 5.3). Soft

TABLE 5.3 Land Use: Tree Crops, Timber (Roundwood), and Fish

Country	1 All Fruits	2 Oranges	3 Tree Nuts	4 Olives	5 Dates	6 Timber	7 Fish
Bahrain	18	—	—	—	15	—	7.0
Cyprus	194	42	1	14	—	12	4.7
Egypt	9,356	1,800	34	318	1,130	268	982.1
Iran	13,604	2,300	529	40	1,000	800	548.7
Iraq	878	73	4	2	440	59	73.2
Israel	1,378	190	7	30	17	25	25.6
Jordan	220	32	1	125	5	4	1.0
Kuwait	15	—	—	—	15	—	3.2
Lebanon	950	229	32	76	—	7	4.5
Oman	299	—	—	—	256	—	140.2
Qatar	23	—	—	—	22	—	15.0
Saudi Arabia	1,664	—	—	—	983	—	58.6
Syria	2,006	603	139	495	4	40	17.6
Turkey	12,289	1,427	882	1,076	9	13,019	697.3
UAE	785	—	1	—	755	—	86.9
Yemen	915	129	—	—	50	—	169.2
Gaza	—	—	—	—	—	—	—
West Bank	—	—	—	—	—	—	—
TOTALS	44,594	6,825	1,630	2,176	4,701	14,234	2,834.8

All data are for 2007. Crops and fish are in thousands of metric tons. Roundwood is in thousands of cubic meters. Column 1 excludes melons. (*Source*: UN Food and Agriculture Org., www.fao.org/corp/statistics.)

fruits—peaches, apricots, plums, pears, and cherries—and vines are grown higher up, at cooler and more humid elevations. Two especially important perennials, olives and grapes, occupy 40 percent of the region's fruit area. Less favorable lower hillsides are clothed with olive groves well into the interior, even east of the Bekaa–Jordan Rift. On dry, stony slopes in much of the eastern Mediterranean and on the Zagros in Iran, nut trees such as almonds, walnuts, and pistachios thrive, despite the dry, hot summers. Figs appear where irrigation permits; Smyrna (Izmir) figs, rich and purple and large as lemons, are world renowned.

Fruits, vegetables, and nuts are also specialties in favorable areas well away from the coasts and far into the interior of Anatolia, Syria, and Iran. The Bekaa-Galilee-Jordan trench shelters fruit orchards, including bananas. The Damascus oasis, the Ghutah, is a fabled garden, and well-tended groves flourish in protected basins and valleys in Turkey and Iran, where harvested fruits are spread on rooftops and roadsides to dry under the summer sun. Dried apricots and a variety of pistachios from Iran are widely marketed. Oilseeds, including sunflower, sesame, and safflower, are commonly grown in large fields in the all-season rain areas of northwestern Turkey.

The Olive: A Special Note.   The most widespread tree crop is, as it has been for thousands of years, the olive—hallmark of true Mediterranean conditions (Fig. 5.4). With a very long taproot, as deep as 30 ft/9 m, and a small, waxy leaf, the evergreen tree is well adapted to cool, wet winters and warm, rainless summers. Adapted to soil characteristics, it requires no irrigation and only modest attention to live for more than 1,500 years and to produce plentiful crops for centuries. The tree bears an average 90 lbs/40 kg in alternate years, with yield varying with soil moisture.[7] Peoples of the Mediterranean Basin, including North Africa,

FIGURE 5.3 Sorting oranges and tangerines in a grove in the Egyptian Delta north of Cairo.

FIGURE 5.4 New olive groves on west-facing slopes of Jabal al-Zawiyah, near the northern end of the Ghab Depression in northwestern Syria. Syria is conducting a major campaign of increasing olive production in its agricultural development.

have for millennia depended upon the olive for both food and oil: the basic oil for cooking, soap, cosmetics, food preservation, and even for greasing wagon wheels.

Industrial Crops.   To compensate for the dry conditions in summer, farmers in Mediterranean climate areas use supplementary irrigation where feasible to produce industrial crops—cotton, tobacco, sugar beet, sugarcane (more common in warmer Upper Egypt), linseed, and hemp. Egyptian long-staple cotton, an improved variety of a crop cultivated for thousands of years, is in wide demand globally. Cotton has been greatly expanded in Turkey, Syria, and Israel, as has the sugar beet in Turkey and Syria.

Carob, or "locust trees," grow on dry, uncultivated hillsides. A major crop in southern Cyprus, carob beans are exported for use as cattle feed, varnish base, and a health-food substitute for chocolate. The trees also grow along the southern coast of Turkey and in the Levant.

Agriculture in Year-Round Rain Areas

Compared with the steppe and Mediterranean areas, a different crop ecology characterizes northern Turkey and northwestern Iran, where appreciable amounts of summer rain complement that of winter. The landscape exhibits fields of maize in Turkey (see Fig. 1.2), tea plantations in both Turkey (on the southeastern Black Sea coast) and Iran (south of the Caspian), rice (sometimes with supplementary irrigation) in the same areas, and the world's greatest hazelnut (filbert) groves on the seaward-facing slopes around Trabzon in Turkey. The famous Turkish tobacco predominates farther west along the Black Sea, and still farther west are extensive fields of sunflowers.

The High Yemen also gets summer precipitation, as does the Asir north of Yemen. Utilizing the monsoonal rains to grow grain sorghum (milo maize), a summer crop, Yemen is the region's leading producer. The highlands also produce small amounts of

Yemen's famous coffee, which, however, is yielding to *qat*, another specialty crop of the remarkable steep terraces (Fig. 5.5). Two other specialty crops of the Middle East are narcotic—opium poppies in western Turkey and Iran, grown under government control, and hashish grown illegally in Lebanon and Iran. In Afghanistan, unregulated poppy growing gives it the invidious distinction of being the world's leading producer.

WATER IN THE DESERT: IRRIGATION

As it has for more than 8,000 years, irrigation plays a vital role in the life of the Middle East, as well as in the extended areas to the east and west, where more than three-fourths of the area is arid or semiarid. It helps remedy the deficiency, seasonality, and variability of rainfall to maximize the benefits of a long, frost-free growing season. Much of it is supplementary, rather than the only source of water, and rainfed and irrigated cultivation intermingle in many areas. If irrigation is possible year-round in an area with a long growing season, two and even three crops a year are grown, as in Egypt.

Sources of Water

Life from the Rivers.   Most irrigation water comes from rivers (see Chap. 2). The Nile, Tigris, and Euphrates are the three main sources, but scores of smaller rivers and hundreds of streamlets also supply water. Fed by runoff from rains and snows on highlands adjacent to the desert valleys, their flow depends on the timing of the rainfall and snowmelt. Some rivers are tapped indirectly— from dammed reservoirs, shallow wells in alluvium adjacent to riverbanks, underground tunnels, or diversion canals—but the river remains the primary source.

Groundwater.   Second most important for irrigation source are aquifers tapped primarily with wells. Some are only a few feet deep,

FIGURE 5.5 Typical terraced agriculture on steep slopes west of Sana, Yemen. The main crop is *qat* (discussed in Chap. 16), although some coffee is also grown here. Agricultural villages are perched on narrow mountain ridges.

but some ancient hand-dug wells reach 300–400 ft/90–120 m; modern drilling reaches 2,000–3,000 ft/610–915 m. In many instances, water has been found when exploring for oil, as in the great Wasia aquifer in central Arabia. Elsewhere, modern hydrogeological technology has found moderately productive aquifers in areas long considered hopelessly waterless—Egypt's Western Desert, western and eastern Arabia, Inner Oman, and landward from the UAE coast.

Springs. Naturally flowing springs are a third source. They usually occur where the water table intersects the ground surface, often in a series along a stratum outcrop or fault line. Nearly every state has at least some springs, thousands of which are used to irrigate plots ranging in size from a few square feet to a score or more acres. Some issue from horizontal solution channels, as in Mount Lebanon, others from vertical solution shafts in limestone karst regions, as in eastern Arabia. Artesian springs bring water from appreciable depths to support several extensive oases. Saudi Arabia's three largest oases—Hofuf, Qatif, and al-Kharj—are irrigated in this way, as are oases in Bahrain and Egypt.

Irrigation methods depend on the water source as well as on the technology available. Since World War II, huge dams, elevated concrete water chutes (Fig. 5.6), drilled wells, and mechanical pumps have rapidly replaced traditional techniques, yet the old methods survive in many areas. Gravity-flow canals, hand-bucket transfer of water, counterpoised buckets (Egypt's *shadufs*), Archimedes' screws, and water wheels (the picturesque *noriahs* of Hamah, on the Orontes in Syria) are still to be seen.

A more complicated traditional method for transporting irrigation water under certain

FIGURE 5.6 Elevated precast concrete irrigation channel in a recently irrigated area, part of the major Syrian Jazirah development scheme.

conditions is the *qanat* system (see Fig. 19.3), which taps water at an upslope source and conducts it downslope through an underground tunnel. The ideal environment is a large alluvial fan, the cone of gravel deposited by a stream emerging from a constricted valley onto a piedmont. Originating in Persia millennia ago, the concept spread eastward to Central Asia and westward through Arabia to Morocco—and, indeed, eventually was applied by Spanish colonists on a small scale in the Western Hemisphere. It has other names in different places—*karez, falaj, foggara.*

Excavation involves both horizontal and vertical digging to construct a carefully controlled, gently sloping tunnel to carry the water, as well as regularly spaced vertical shafts down to the tunnel. On the surface, a telltale alignment of holes, each surrounded by a circular spoil ridge, reveals a *qanat.* Scores of thousands tunnel through alluvial fans at the foot of mountains in Iran and surrounding countries, especially Oman. Although many still supply water to towns, villages, and fields, increasing numbers are abandoned each year for cheaper and more easily maintained pipelines.

Irrigation Technology. Modern technology has introduced efficient methods of applying water directly to crops, including overhead sprinkler systems and drip (trickle) irrigation. The latter sends moisture—sometimes mixed with fertilizer—to each individual plant via spaced openings. Although expensive initially, it makes very efficient use of water, fertilizer, and labor, and it is being utilized on an increasing scale. Overhead sprinklers, although more efficient than basin and furrow methods, lose some water to evaporation both in the air and on the surface. They also require sizable investment, but both movable impulse sprinklers and self-propelled center-pivot circular sprinklers are nevertheless widely found; the latter were used on a grand scale in the wheat fields of central Saudi Arabia.

FIGURE 5.7 Aerial view of irrigated agriculture in the Nile Valley, central Egypt. The dividing line between verdant irrigated crops and barren desert is knife sharp. The photograph illustrates Rudyard Kipling's comment on the Nile as "that little damp trickle of life."

Irrigated Lands

A Quantitative View. In 1980, irrigated cropland covered 55,360 mi²/143,380 km², which was 1.9 percent of all the land and 20 percent of the agricultural land in the sixteen states. In 2007, the total was 99,232 mi²/257,010 km²—4 percent of the total area and 40 percent of the cropland—a 74 percent increase in twenty-seven years. This clearly indicates regionwide efforts to intensify agriculture. The value of crops raised by artificial watering constitutes a disproportionate percentage of the value of total production, perhaps as much as three-fourths. One explanation is that all cultivated land is irrigated in Egypt (Fig. 5.7), which ranks as the second most agriculturally productive country in the Middle East (Turkey is first). From one-quarter to one-half of the cultivated land in most other major agricultural countries in the region is irrigated (see Table 5.1); in Turkey, with 21 percent so watered, and Syria, with 25 percent, irrigated crops are more than 38 and 65 percent of production, respectively.

Although expanding irrigation is obvious for increasing production, this encounters four serious obstacles: decreasing availability of water, increasing expense in terms of cost-effectiveness, competition for land availability, and conflicts over riparian rights. Although high expenditures per unit area in Israel, Saudi Arabia, and some of the Gulf states have produced excellent returns, such expenditure levels are of questionable cost-effectiveness, and they are not practicable in most parts of the region. In southern Iraq, expanding irrigation presents its own problems, including salination. Drainage, both surface and underground tile, may offer more benefit than irrigation in some areas.

Dates: A Special Note.   Dates play an even more crucial role in traditional desert agriculture than do olives along the Mediterranean. The date palm (*Phoenix dactylifera*) is the most familiar and historically important plant of the entire North African–Middle Eastern–South Asian desert region.[8] Throughout this zone, from Morocco to the Indian subcontinent, it provides a staple food, construction material, and fiber for weaving baskets and mats. It is so fundamental in the Middle East that it appears on stamps, currency, coins, and Saudi Arabia's royal flag. It has been a basic food in desert areas for millennia; the tree survives searing heat and lasts for generations, thriving on minimal water in large groves in oases (see Fig. 5.2). Its fruit can be preserved for months, with high nutritional value and a range of vitamins. Its essential role has diminished as modern transportation and trade have brought both unlimited amounts of food and also refrigeration to even once remote desert areas.

ROLE OF ANIMALS

Livestock raising, dating to 8000 BCE, is common in all three types of land, differing from one area to another. Nomadic herding in the desert or in the Zagros Mountains is quite different from raising animals on farms, especially on irrigated farms. Available statistics do not distinguish between farm animals and those herded by nomads, so the following cited data pertain to all types of livestock.

Commercial animal husbandry is most intensive in specialized agricultural settlements in Israel. In addition, commercial raising of small animals has made rapid strides elsewhere since 1950. Chicken farming, for example, surged sharply during the 1970s and has expanded in every country, especially in Iran, Turkey, Saudi Arabia, and Egypt. With no religious or social-consumption taboos, their production has increased in Turkey, for example, from 59 million in 1988 to 345 million in 2007. Although no figures are available, pigeons are raised in large numbers in towns and villages as well as by farmers in many areas, especially in Egypt. Fish farming is an important aspect of land use in Israel and has begun in Saudi Arabia and other Gulf countries.

Meat animals are produced in large numbers (Table 5.4). Poultry, sheep, goats, and cattle (*Bos taurus*) are the most numerous (Fig. 5.8). Hogs are raised in Cyprus, Israel, Egypt, Lebanon, and Turkey, although pork cannot be marketed in conservative Muslim or Jewish areas. In one of the world's most poorly informed official actions of 2009, the Egyptian government ordered all the hogs in the country to be slaughtered to appease fears of the H1N1 (or swine) influenza.[9] Sheep have been numerous for millennia and are an important source, not only of meat, wool, and skins but also of milk and cheese. Iran, Turkey, and Syria together have almost 80 percent of the region's sheep.

Goats are about half as numerous as sheep. Despite their reputation for destroying vegetation, properly managed, goats are hardly more damaging than sheep or cows, and are uniquely valuable in their grazing of the poorer types of forage. Vegetation can best be protected by excluding them from designated areas, and goat-exclusion laws have been very successful in Cyprus, Israel, and Turkey. Angora goats in Turkey are especially valuable for their unique hair, used in making mohair.

The number of camels was slowly declining, from more than 1 million in 1969–1971 to 763,000 in 1985; however, it had risen to 1.35 million by 2007 as interest in camels revived—for the sport of camel racing, for example. The traditional significance of the camel, including its use for feasts, suggests that it will continue to play an important, if diminished, role well into the twenty-first century.

Cattle numbers increased steadily with population and the standard of living from the

TABLE 5.4 Domestic Animals (Thousands of Head)

Country	1 Camels	2 Cattle	3 Sheep	4 Hogs	5 Chickens	6 Goats	7 Buffaloes
Bahrain	1	9	41	—	470	23	—
Cyprus	—	55	259	450	3,100	339	—
Egypt	120	4,550	6	30	96,000	3,980	3,977
Iran	152	7,609	53,800	—	420,000	25,531	620
Iraq	10	1,500	6,200	—	33,000	1,650	120
Israel	5	394	433	206	37,000	87	—
Jordan	18	69	2,496	—	25,000	434	—
Kuwait	5	28	900	—	32,500	160	—
Lebanon	>1	77	340	15	35,000	495	—
Oman	122	314	366	—	4,200	1,620	—
Qatar	14	8	120	—	4,500	160	—
Saudi Arabia	260	372	7,000	—	145,000	2,200	—
Syria	25	1,168	22,865	—	24,500	1,561	5
Turkey	1	10,871	25,462	1	344,820	6,286	101
UAE	260	125	615	—	15,500	1,570	—
Yemen	361	1,480	8,420	—	51,000	8,414	—
Gaza	—	—	—	—	—	—	—
West Bank	—	—	—	—	—	—	—
TOTAL	1,354	28,629	129,323	702	1,271,590	54,510	4,823

Data for 2007. Animal raising has always been a major economic-cultural activity in the region, and numbers have increased appreciably during the last two decades. Chickens have tripled in numbers. (*Source*: UN Food and Agriculture Org., www.fao.org/corp/statistics.)

FIGURE 5.8 Anatolian shepherd with sheep and goats on steppe lands east of Ankara. Some of the goats are of the famous Angora (Ankara) breed.

early 1960s to the mid-1980s when farmers in Turkey and Egypt turned to raising crops and concentrating on smaller animals. Numbers stabilized during the 1990s, and the quality of cattle improved as farmers turned to better breeds. With dairy cattle, this has greatly improved milk yield. A growing awareness of the nutritional benefits of milk has encouraged dairying in many areas; Ras al-Khaymah now produces cow's milk for the UAE's urban areas. Israel has imported and bred some of the best dairy cattle in the world, and it leads the region in milk output per animal by a wide margin. Egyptian farms, with plenty of water in which buffalo can submerge themselves, have three-fourths of the region's stock (*Bubalus bubalis*, or water buffalo, quite different from the American bison). They were common in the marshes of southern Iraq until these were drained by Saddam Husayn after 1991; they seem to be slowly returning in the 2000s.

Horse populations have declined sharply in every state, with the exceptions of Saudi Arabia and Qatar, as the workhorse has been displaced by the tractor and the truck. Fine Arabian show horses constitute only a small percentage of the equine population; after becoming rare in the region by the mid-twentieth century, they are again being bred by a few wealthy Saudis and other Arabs.

Nomadic Pastoralism

Nomadic pastoralism is an essential aspect of the Middle East in the popular perception and also in fact. Animal herding by nomads involves a wide range of periodic migrations by tribal groups and their animals in search of grass and water. These periodic movements, both across country and vertically to higher or lower elevations, resulted in the interrelated triad of nonsedentary herding—nomadism, pastoralism, and tribalism. Nomadic pastoralism extends over a larger area than any other type of agricultural activity—more, in fact, than all other types combined. It dominates dry areas not only in the core Middle East,

from Egypt's Western Desert across the Arabian Peninsula to Iranian Baluchistan, but also in North Africa and Central Asia.

Major nomadic pastoral groups include the Arab Bedouin of the deserts and steppes (see Fig. 4.2), Qashqai and Bakhtiari of the High Zagros, Turkmans of the Kopet ranges, Baluch of southeastern Iran, and in the extended eastern area Turkmans, Uzbek, and Kazakh in Central Asia and the Berber in North Africa. Although the numbers engaged in nomadic herding are steadily decreasing, it remains a significant aspect of tradition, culture, and economic life, especially in the Arabian Peninsula and Syrian Desert in the core region and in vast areas of the peripheral countries.

Using marginal resources and very basic technology, Bedouin are well suited to their environment, primarily through a symbiotic relationship with their animals. Alone on the open desert in summer, a Bedouin family could survive only a day or two, as there would be no water, food, or shelter. But the family's camels, which feed on salty shrubs, supply milk consumed as liquid, yogurt, or cheese; hair for weaving; hides and leather; dung for fuel; in an emergency, meat; and, of course, transportation.

Most contemporary Bedouin also herd sheep and goats for wool, milk, hides, and meat. Their essential characteristic is their geographically cyclic movements to sustain their herds and flocks. Other nomads follow cycles that may vary in frequency, types of animals, and other details.

The Remarkable Camel

The domesticated camel appeared about 2000 BCE. Although the two-humped Bactrian camel (*Camelus bactrianus*) is common in parts of Anatolia and Iran and dominant in Central Asia, the Arabian camel, or dromedary (*C. dromedarius*), with one hump, has long been herded in the Arabian Peninsula, North Africa, and adjacent lands. In the Syrian Desert, Mesopotamia,

FIGURE 5.9 Camels watering at wells in the broad Wadi Sahba, west of Harad, eastern Saudi Arabia.

Anatolia, and Iran, sheep and goats are common, whereas camels are less so—indeed, there are none at all in mountainous areas.

The camel adapts especially well to desert life with its remarkable ability to conserve water in hot weather and low water requirements in winter (Fig. 5.9). Its long neck allows it to graze both surface vegetation and tree leaves. Its soft padded feet operate like snowshoes and enable it to walk over drift sand without sinking and over hot surfaces without pain.

Traversing terrain that other beasts cannot, the "ship of the desert" can carry heavier loads through greater heat and aridity for a longer working life than oxen, horses, or donkeys. Using camel caravans, Arabs monopolized ancient trade routes and laid the bases for mercantile cities over a wide area. The camel actually delayed the development of desert roads in the region, since wagons and carts drawn by oxen or horses were less efficient than camels. However, after the mid-twentieth century, motor vehicles, aircraft, and railroads displaced the camel as transport, certainly for long distances, and modern Bedouin even transport their camels and other animals by the omnipresent Toyota pickup.[10]

FOREST PRODUCTS

Forestry plays a minor role in the region, as is suggested by the sparse forest vegetation (see Map 2.8). Only Turkey and Iran have noteworthy industries, and extensive systematic timber exploitation is found only in Turkey. Production in the high Pontus in the north, the high Taurus in the south, and the highlands between Istanbul and Ankara yields 459 mn ft³/13 mn m³ of roundwood a year (see Table 5.3). Iran's 2008 output was only one-eighth of its 1995 figure. No other country in the region produces even 10.6 mn ft³/0.3 mn m³.

FISHING

Surrounded and deeply penetrated by seas, and with a total coastline exceeding 14,585 mi/23,470 km, Middle East countries have an appreciable potential for a fisheries industry (Fig. 5.10). However, other factors inhibit progress toward reaching that potential, including overfishing and pollution.

Facing three seas and with vigorous maritime activity, Turkey had long led the sixteen countries in fish landed. However, Egypt has

FIGURE 5.10 Daily fish auction in the small port of Khasab, Oman, near the Strait of Hormuz. Note prows of tour dhows to the left. See also smugglers' boats in Khasab in Figure 16.1.

overtaken Turkey, partly by increasing its freshwater catch. Iran ranks third, followed by Yemen, Oman, and the UAE (see Table 5.3). Iran exploits its long coastline on the Gulf, as well as on the Gulf of Oman and the Caspian Sea. It takes nearly 550,000 mt annually, and it reaps a notably valuable—but decreasing—harvest of caviar (fish roe) from the Caspian. Access to rich fisheries associated with the upwelling waters along the southern coast of the Arabian Peninsula provides Yemen and neighboring Oman with their considerable catches. All the leading fishing states increased their landings during the 2000s.

NOTES

1. Production indexes are drawn from the UN Food and Agriculture Organization *Production Yearbook*, published annually.

2. *Food Business Review*, July 16, 2008.

3. *Addis Fortune*, Oct. 12, 2009.

4. Reuters, Oct. 11, 2009.

5. See www.aaaid.org/ for further information.

6. J. Held 1979. Studies of Middle East land use that are more general include Askari and Cummings 1976 and Beaumont and McLachlan 1985. The crucial role of water is studied in Rogers and Lydon 1994; Ventner 1998; Biswas et al. 1997; Soffer 1999; and Fox 2003. The Encyclopaedia Britannica's *Britannica World Data* is very useful for production figures, and the UN's FAO *Production Yearbook*, published annually, is indispensable for production data, more promptly available on the excellent FAO Web site, www.faostat.fao.org.

7. *The Daily Star* (Beirut), Nov. 11, 2004.

8. This paragraph is based on *Saudi Aramco and Its World* 1995, 15.

9. *The Guardian*, Apr. 30, 2009. For Cairo, this meant the disastrous evisceration of its garbage-collection system, dependent on poor Christians, the *zebaleen*, who fed the refuse to their pigs; see *Los Angeles Times*, May 29, 2009.

10. For interesting discussions of Bedouin and camels, see Dickson 1949; Hills 1966; Bulliet 1975; Jabbur 1995; and *Saudi Aramco and Its World* 1995.

6

Riches Beneath the Earth

A PERSPECTIVE

With its enormous hydrocarbon wealth, the Middle East is without equal and perforce has a unique global role.[1] Moreover, the region's share of the world's oil and gas reserves and production is certain to increase, since the relatively smaller reserves elsewhere are being more rapidly depleted by intensive exploitation. At the outset, natural gas must be given special attention, because recent discoveries mean that the Gulf province has surpassed Russia as having the world's largest gas resources and because production can be easily exported as LNG (liquefied natural gas) to meet rapidly mounting world demand. In economic terms, never before in history has a region achieved such explosive large-scale development so quickly as this area did during the decades following World War II.

Western cognizance of the vital importance of Middle East oil was manifest in 1990 when U.S. and European forces responded immediately to the imperilment of Kuwaiti and Saudi oil fields. By the mid-1990s, these more dramatic aspects of the Gulf "oil boom" had subsided, and immense production came to be routine. The region and its huge energy output were taken for granted, and some Western powers—especially the United States—refocused their main atten-

tion on the emerging (and reemerging) Caspian oil province, partly to offset the supremacy of the Middle East.

Notwithstanding the importance of energy reserves, emphasis on oil should not obscure the region's other important characteristics. The Middle East also has historical, geopolitical, political, geographical, human, and nonenergy economic significance. The gravity of these other aspects is often overlooked or is subordinated to petroleum and more limited regional interests. This chapter focuses on oil, but the book as a whole aims to weigh the region's variety and achieve a more balanced perspective.

Petroleum, natural gas, and petroproducts are virtually the sole items produced and exported on any scale by several Middle East countries. At the three-year average production rate in the mid-2000s, regional petroleum resources will last for about ninety years if there are no further discoveries. Unlikely as this may be, these countries are well aware of the singularity on which their wealth is based and of its eventual depletion. They also know that external forces influence the production, transportation, and marketing of their most important product. In view of the relatively rapid exhaustibility of this unique resource, and with the lessons of other boom-and-bust situations to guide them, they have sought to control their own destinies—through the Organization of Petroleum Exporting Countries (OPEC), for example. In pursuit of long-term economic viability, they are undertaking intensive diversification programs, including agricultural development, as discussed in Chapter 5.

With a few exceptions, the overall percentage of the world's supply of underground resources other than petroleum in the region is relatively modest. Nevertheless, nonenergy minerals are major items in several countries with limited oil output. Non-oil minerals are or have been of historic importance in Turkey, Iran, and Cyprus; now this is also true for Jordan, Egypt, Syria, and Israel.

PETROLEUM: HISTORICAL DEVELOPMENT

Asphalt, gas, and oil seeps from underground hydrocarbon deposits have been known for millennia at numerous sites in the Middle East—in northern Mesopotamia, near Hit on the Euphrates, on both sides of the head of the Persian/Arabian Gulf, under the Dead Sea, at the northern end of the Gulf of Suez, and in a dozen other places. Bitumen (asphalt, pitch, tar) is mentioned several times in the Old Testament: Noah used pitch in constructing the ark, and Moses's mother used bitumen and pitch to line the basket in which she floated her baby on the Nile. Bitumen was used as mortar in the construction of brick walls, ziggurats, and other buildings in Sumerian and Babylonian times and can still be identified in many ruins in Iraq and western Iran.

The biblical "fiery furnace" of Shadrach, Meshach, and Abednego may refer to the still-burning gas seepage known as the "eternal fires" near Kirkuk in northern Iraq. Gas flares were the focal points of fire-reverencing religions of ancient Persia, and fire temples were numerous. Oil from seeps and oozes was collected for lamps, and it was used in warfare long before the Christian era. Thus, twentieth-century oil explorers had historical indicators for siting their early wildcat wells. Politically, subsurface oil and gas fields are indifferent to human (and mutable) surface authority and boundaries, and reservoirs may extend under two or more nations.

Financed by a British syndicate, William Knox D'Arcy, a British subject, obtained a concession in 1901 to drill in western Iran; his crew made the Middle East's first major strike in 1908. The initial discovery was in the Masjed-e Soleyman field, the first of many fabulous reservoirs (Map 6.1). The next year, the D'Arcy group formed the Anglo-Persian Oil Company (APOC), which became the Anglo-Iranian Oil Company (AIOC) in 1935 and British Petroleum (BP) in 1951. APOC made the first shipment of oil in 1912 from Abadan on the Shatt al-Arab, today still a major oil center. World War I proved the superiority of oil over coal for fueling naval and commercial vessels and accelerated development of the industry. Demand for oil spiraled upward and is still mounting.

Other European entrepreneurs sought exploration rights across the border in Mesopotamia after the find in Iran. The Turkish Petroleum Company (TPC), formed before World War I by British, German, and Dutch interests[2] found oil in 1927 by drilling a few hundred meters from the "eternal fires." This discovery near Kirkuk opened what remains one of the world's major oil fields. In 1928, the United States made its first entry into the region's oil race when the Near East Development Corporation (NEDC) obtained an equity interest in TPC, renamed Iraq Petroleum Company (IPC) in 1929. NEDC originally comprised five companies but later was equally divided between Standard of New Jersey (now Exxon) and Socony Vacuum (later Mobil, which merged with Exxon in 1999).

From the early years of exploration, agreements among companies divided up operating areas. One accord was the Red Line Agreement, reached in 1928, which covered

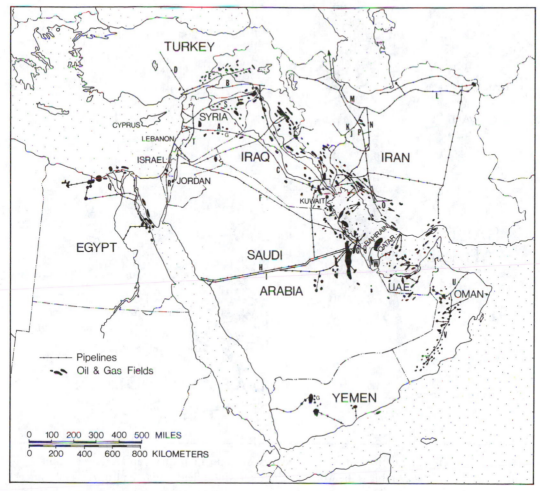

MAP 6.1 Major petroleum and natural gas fields and pipelines in the Middle East, 2010. Gulf fields are detailed on Map 6.2. (Adapted from several sources)

former Ottoman possessions, excluding Kuwait and Egypt. It provided that any oil deals involving areas within the Red Line must be unanimously approved by all companies operating there. Although later rescinded, this agreement regulated concession patterns in much of the region over a critical period.

Neither the worldwide depression nor discoveries of other large supplies of oil, like the East Texas field, slowed intensive exploration in the 1930s. By World War II, exploration had revealed the presence of huge quantities of oil beyond southern Iraq in the Mesopotamian-Gulf trough (Map 6.2).

The modest but historically important Bahrain field, found in 1932, was the first discovered in the Gulf area proper, outside Iran and Iraq. It was also the scene of the region's first all-U.S. oil venture. A subsidiary of Standard Oil of California (Socal—later in partnership with Texaco), the Bahrain Petroleum Company (Bapco) was chartered in Canada in order to meet the requirement that concessions in British territories be granted to "British companies." From the hills on the upturned strata of Bahrain's structural dome, U.S. geologists using binoculars studied Dammam Dome on the mainland 20

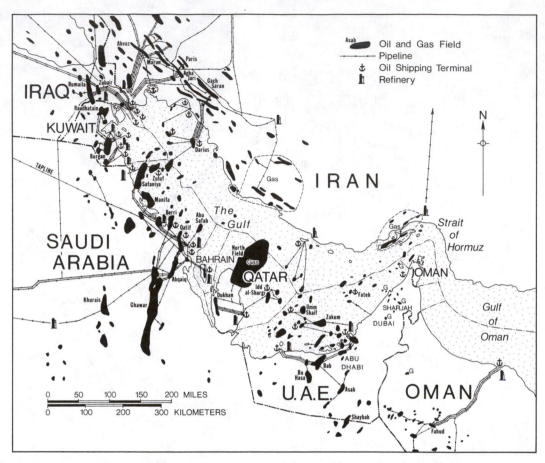

MAP 6.2 Petroleum and natural gas fields, pipelines, oil-export terminals, and refineries, Gulf region. Ghawar in Saudi Arabia is the world's richest known oil field. (Adapted from several sources)

mi/32 km away, becoming convinced that a likely oil reservoir lay under it.

Urged by these geologists, Socal obtained a concession in 1933 for the eastern part of the newly united Kingdom of Saudi Arabia; it then operated there as California Arabian Standard Oil Company (Casoc) and found oil in 1938 in Dammam Dome as predicted. A new and more appropriate name—Arabian American Oil Company (familiarly known as Aramco)—was adopted in 1944. Even after it became a national company—officially, the Saudi Arabian Oil Company—in 1988 it retained the well-known acronym as "Saudi Aramco" (Fig. 6.1). In the 1930s, the Kuwait Oil Company—formed by APOC (BP) and Gulf (later merged

with Chevron)—discovered the rich Burgan reservoir in the amirate.

Growing realization of the oil potential accelerated exploration in the lower Gulf, and after World War II more than a score of new enterprises were exploring on land and offshore. British, Dutch, French, and U.S. "majors" had dominated the industry for forty years; now they were joined by firms from Italy, Germany, Spain, Japan, Brazil, India, and elsewhere. Still later, producing countries formed their own companies and gradually took over most or all the operations within their borders.

The Dukhan field in western Qatar was discovered in 1940 by an IPC subsidiary that later became the Qatar Petroleum Company, but production was delayed until 1949. Companies with multiple and international ownerships were given concessions in offshore areas of Abu Dhabi; others received onshore concessions. These huge oil and gas resources are now generally under the Abu Dhabi National Oil Company (ADNOC). The offshore Umm Shaif field, in Abu Dhabi territorial waters, was the first of many major offshore discoveries to complement the onshore fields in the lower Gulf. This field was found in 1958, but it did not produce until 1962 because of difficulties producing, transporting, and storing offshore oil. The large onshore Bab field opened in 1963, and production began in other amirates several years later, primarily by smaller companies. In Oman, after successive concession companies had disappointing results, Petroleum Development (Oman), or PDO, hit oil in 1963 and 1964, and production began in 1967. PDO is now 60 percent government owned, with Shell holding 34 percent, and is responsible for more than 90 percent of the sultanate's output. Several other companies operate on a limited scale in Oman, and production is from 106 mostly small fields.

In the western part of the region, exploration—which began early in Egypt—has shown that resources are comparatively modest. Oil seepages near the mouth of the Gulf of Suez, known from Roman times, attracted attention soon after the opening of the petroleum age, and, indeed, the first well drilled in Egypt (1886) was the earliest in the Middle East. However, commercial production did not begin until 1913, a year after the first Iranian oil shipment, and major output levels were not reached until the 1960s. Major natural gas fields offshore from the Nile Delta now dominate the Egyptian energy scene. In addition to the public-sector Egyptian General Petroleum Company, more than a score of international companies operate in Egypt, including BP, Shell, Agip, and British Gas. As

in Oman, production in Egypt is from many small fields.

Syria finally made a small find in 1956 and began commercial production in 1959 in the far northeast (in segments of the Fold Belt in which the Kirkuk field had been found in Iraq), but production was delayed until pipelines could be laid. After new discoveries in the mid-1980s, Syria undertook an intensive and successful search for new fields, especially around Dayr al-Zawr.

To the south, drilling in Jordan in the mid-1950s, when the kingdom controlled the West Bank, found nothing on either side of the river, and more efforts in the 1980s have resulted in only negligible production. With further exploration, modest gas deposits have been found near the Iraqi border. In Lebanon, a test well in the 1940s showed no likely prospects; no further development has been undertaken. In Israel, hydrocarbon indications in and around the Dead Sea attracted surveys, but only minor resources have been found. Modest amounts of gas offshore from southern Israel and Gaza began to feed a gas-fired power plant in 2003. A more promising field was identified off Haifa in 2009, but its extent remains to be reliably evaluated.

The latest discoveries in new areas were made in the two Yemens in the 1980s before their merger in 1990. Earlier tests in the west of the then Yemen Arab Republic (YAR) had been negative, but a U.S. company (Hunt) made a major oil strike in 1984 in the Marib Basin area in the east. Production and export began in late 1987. The Marib success encouraged the People's Democratic Republic of Yemen (PDRY) to drill in an extension of the structure south of the border, and tests found oil in appreciable quantities that by the early 1990s far exceeded the reserves found in the original strikes to the north. Total discovered reserves are modest but domestically important.

Turkey found oil in 1940, and development there achieved a steady pace in the 1960s and is continuing. Results have been

FIGURE 6.1 Large crude carriers (oil tankers) taking on crude oil at a Saudi Aramco loading pier in the Gulf. With exports sometimes of more than 10 mn bpd (barrels per day), Saudi loading facilities must be extensive. (B. H. Moody, *Saudi Aramco World*, SAWDIA)

only limited, since the extreme folding and faulting typical of this area fragment the reservoirs and cause the individual fields to be small and scattered, as in Oman. Shell and Mobil have each joined efforts with the Turkish national oil company, as have other smaller companies. Finally, exploration on Cyprus during the 1940s and 1950s found no promising structures, indicating that Cyprus, like Lebanon, is unlikely to have onshore oil. However, both countries raised hopes for offshore gas finds in the late 2000s, encouraged by Egypt's successes north of the Nile Delta and the discovery off Haifa in 2009.

PATTERNS OF RESERVES

As of 2010, 757.3 bn bbl (billion barrels) of oil—about 56 percent of the world's proved reserves—lay under the Middle East, most of it around and under the Gulf and to the northwest along the Tigris and Euphrates (Map 6.3; see also Map 6.1). Exploration in recent decades continues to be intensive: New discoveries during just the years 1987–1991 augmented reserves by nearly 40 percent. In the 2000s, reserves increased only by about 11 percent, but the new discoveries totaled about 78 bn bbl, or an amount equivalent to 410 percent of U.S. reserves.

Around the Gulf Trough

By far the largest in both the Middle East and the world, Saudi reserves of 259.9 bn bbl equal the total of all the rest of the world outside the Middle East, excepting Venezuela, Mexico, and Brazil (for Canada, see below). After Saudi Arabia, the second through fifth

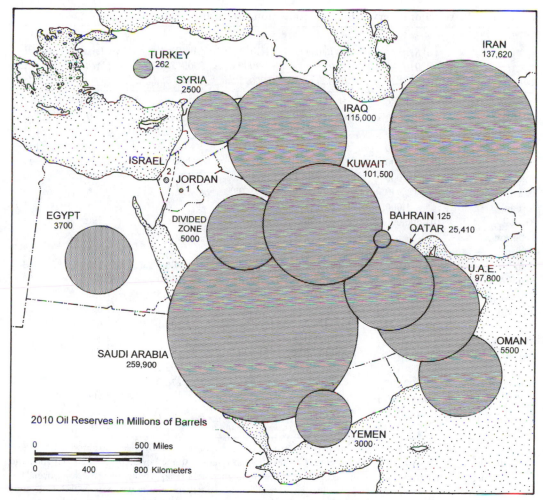

MAP 6.3 Proved petroleum reserves in the Middle East, by country. Proportional circles show amount of proved reserves in millions of barrels as of 2010. (From data in *Oil and Gas Journal*, Dec. 21, 2009, and in U.S. Department of Energy, Energy Information Administration (EIA), *Country Analysis Briefs*, 2009–2010, www.eia.doe.gov/emeu/cabs/cabsme.html)

rankings (regionally and globally) go to Iran, Iraq, Kuwait, and the UAE (Table 6.1 and Graph 6.1). These four shift in rank among themselves periodically; Iran claimed a large increase in 2002–2003 that put it in second place. (Reserves data became somewhat confused in 2002 when a trade group argued that Canada should be credited with estimates of the oil recoverable from bitumen in the tar sands of Alberta. Some databases adjusted accordingly, rocketing Canada from 5 bn bbl to 178 bn bbl, into second place behind Saudi

Arabia. A similar adjustment could reasonably be made for Venezuela's tar sands.)[3] The next five ranking countries are widely scattered geographically: Venezuela, 99 bn bbl of proven reserves; Russia, 60 bn; Libya, 44 bn; Nigeria, 37 bn; and the United States, 19 bn.

Eastern Saudi Arabia has more than a third of the region's reserves, distributed over fifty fields, onshore and offshore, extending from Kuwait south to the Abu Dhabi border (Map 6.2). Prominent is the large, linear Ghawar field, the world's greatest single oil

TABLE 6.1 Petroleum: Reserves, Recent Production, Wells, and Fields

Country	1 Oil Resrvs 2010 1,000s Bbl	2 Gas Resrvs 2010 Bills Ft.³	3 Production 2009 1,000s Bpd	4 Av. Prod. 2005–2007 1,000s Bpd	5 No. Prod. Oil Wells 2008	6 Number of Fields 2004
Bahrain	124,560	3,250	29.5	172.8	496	1
Cyprus	0	0	0.0	0.0	0	0
(Divided Zone)[a]	5,000,000	1,000	540.0	570.0	578	5
Egypt	3,700,000	58,500	680.0	667.3	1,491	134
Iran[b]	137,620,000	1,045,670	3,725.0	3,899.5	1,128	41
Iraq[c]	115,000,000	111,940	2,400.0	1,930.0	1,685	20
Israel	1,940	1,075	0.0	5.7	6	6
Jordan	1,000	213	0.0	0.0	4	1
Kuwait	101,500,000	63,000	2,010.0	2,166.7	790	8
Lebanon	0	0	0.0	0.0	0	0
Oman	5,500,000	30,000	800.0	735.2	2,298	106
Qatar	25,410,000	899,325	765.0	806.9	421	8
Saudi Arabia	255,900,000	257,970	7,920.0	8,805.0	1,560	50
Syria	2,500,000	8,500	365.0	422.8	136	17
Turkey	262,200	215	45.0	41.3	897	79
UAE	97,800,000	214,400	2,378.7	2,508.1	1,456	24
Yemen	3,000,000	16,900	270.0	379.0	1,649	27
TOTALS	753,319,700	2,711,958	21,928.2	23,104.7	14,595	527
Abu Dhabi	92,200,000	198,500	2,135.0	2,273.0	1,200	14
Dubai	4,000,000	4,000	200.0	184.4	200	5
Ras al-Khaymah	100,000	1,200	0.7	0.7	7	1
Sharjah	1,500,000	10,700	43.0	50.0	49	4

The question of oil reserves has become a matter of vigorous debate in recent years. [a]Divided Zone production is normally divided between Kuwait and Saudi Arabia. [b]Claimed Iranian reserves jumped by 35 bn bbl between 2002 and 2003, which, if correct, replace Iraq's as the second largest reserves in the world. [c]Iraq production was below normal because of internal attacks on pipelines and of still-damaged facilities subsequent to fighting after March 2003. Note units used in Columns 1–4. The last four rows give data on the four amirates of the UAE that produce petroleum. (*Sources: Oil and Gas Journal*, Dec. 21, 2009 [Columns 1–3 and 5]; Energy Information Administration, www.eia.doe.gov [Column 4]; *International Petroleum Encyclopedia 2003* [Column 6].)

reservoir. The gently folded and domed structures of northeastern Arabia continue northward into Kuwait, with which Saudi Arabia shares the world's biggest offshore field, Safaniya-Khafji. The Arabian-Kuwait structures then extend into Iraq joining the northwest-southeast trend of the Zagros fold reservoirs in southern Iraq. One particular field, the Rumaila, straddles the border and was significant in the lead-up to the invasion of Kuwait in 1990 and in boundary revisions in 1992. In Iraq, with 115 bn bbl of reserves, oil reservoirs have been found in subsurface folds from Ain Zalah in the far north through the Kirkuk and Baghdad reservoirs to Rumaila and Zubair in the extreme south.

In the southern Gulf (Fig. 6.2), most of the major fields lie in Abu Dhabi, largest and westernmost of the seven component shaykhdoms of the UAE. In 2010, it had nearly five times the reserves of the United States. Onshore in the north, Kuwait has the fabulous Burgan field, with more oil per unit of surface area than any other field known. With Saudi Arabia and Kuwait holding half shares in the oil of the Divided Zone (the former Neutral Zone), Kuwait's 104.0 bn bbl accord it fourth rank in reserves in the Middle East and the world.

MIDDLE EAST PETROLEUM RESERVES, 2010

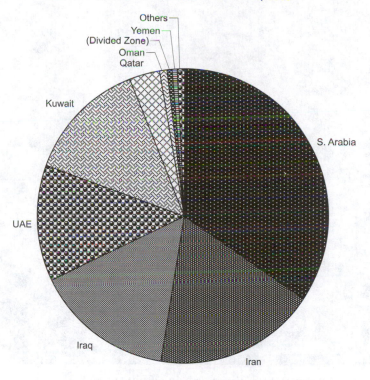

WORLD REGIONS PETROLEUM RESERVES, 2010

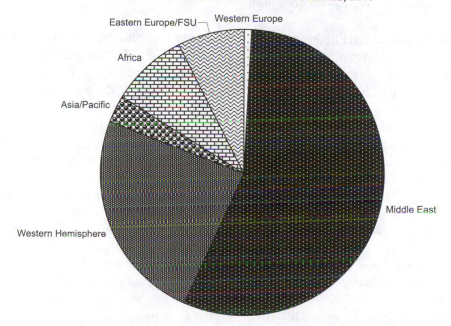

GRAPH 6.1 Petroleum reserves of Middle East countries (*top*) and of world regions (*bottom*). (From data in *Oil and Gas Journal*, Dec. 21, 2009, and in U.S. Department of Energy, Energy Information Administration, *Country Analysis Briefs*, 2009–2010, www.eia.doe.gov/emeu/cabs/cabsme.html)

FIGURE 6.2 Some of the surface facilities of Dubai's offshore Fateh field, 56 mi/90 km from the coast. Resting on the seabed are huge bell-shaped tanks that store oil from surrounding wells until it can be loaded onto tankers such as the one shown.

Iran formerly was ranked fifth in reserves, but it now claims to be second (Canadian tar sands excluded), with 137.6 bn bbl, even after producing some 70.0 bn bbl over the century since oil was discovered in 1908. Virtually all of the country's fields follow the trend of folds in the Zagros Mountains in western Iran, from Kermanshah in the northwest to Bandar-e Abbas in the southeast at the Strait of Hormuz. Lying in the southeastern part of the sedimentary basin, opposite the Qatar Peninsula and east toward the Strait of Hormuz, are more than a dozen rich gas fields. Like Saudi Arabia and Kuwait, Iran also possesses offshore fields with impressive reserves and production.

Qatar's reserves in its onshore Dukhan field and three offshore fields were, until 2000, about equal to those of Egypt and Yemen, but then new discoveries raised the total to 25.4 bn bbl. But its relatively modest oil reserves are richly supplemented by the supergiant gas reservoir in the North Field, the world's largest, which alone gives it the world's third-greatest gas reserves after Russia and Iran (see Table 6.1). Development of this field and of the systems to distribute its production were some of the region's most active energy projects in the 2000s.

Oman was the last of the Gulf area states to achieve significant levels of petroleum production. The original discoveries in 1963 and 1964 were followed by more than 100 other scattered modest discoveries by the 2000s. Although none are as rich as the fields in less complex structures farther northwest up the Gulf trough, Oman is now credited with 5.5 bn bbl of proved reserves.

Bahrain, although the earliest of the actual Gulf producers, has the smallest reserves.

During deep-test drilling for oil in 1949, Bapco was first to find gas in the Khuff formation (Permian Age), which is now known to have enormous gas reserves. Commercial development of Bahrain's Khuff deep gas began in 1969. Most of Bahrain's oil comes from Abu Safa, an offshore field primarily in Saudi Arabian waters west of the island. Its output of 140,000 barrels per day has been donated to Bahrain by the field's Saudi operators, and production doubled in 2002–2004, although only half of the new output will be donated.[4]

In the Levant

Although reserves on the western side of the region are only a minor part of the regional total, sizable fields have been found and are yielding roughly 1.8 mn bpd. Production is primarily from Egypt, Syria, and Yemen, with limited output from Turkey.

Egypt ranks ninth in reserves, just after Yemen, in the region. Petroleum and gas are found in more than 135 fields in and on both sides of the Gulf of Suez, in many small fields in the Western Desert, and, particularly nonassociated gas, in recently discovered fields in the northern Nile Delta and offshore. With increasingly large gas finds, Egypt's reserves are becoming significant on the western side of the region. These reservoirs are in completely separate basins from those of the Gulf.

Syria's older fields lie in the extreme northeastern corner of the country, just west of the Tigris River, and are an integral part of the structures containing the Batman fields of southeastern Turkey and the fields of northern Iraq. A significant discovery in late 1984 near Dayr al-Zawr initiated a modest boom in eastern Syria that spread to the center of the country, opening some small new fields, for a country total of 17. Lacking new discoveries, Syria's reserves are steadily diminishing.

Jordan's recently found Hamzah field, near al-Azraq, has shown only limited poten-

tial. Yemen's reserves are greater but still modest at 3 bn bbl, placing it between Egypt and Syria; this poorest corner of the Middle East desperately needs oil income.

Turkey's small fields lie at the upper end of structures reaching northwestward from Oman up the Gulf trough and through the Mesopotamian depression. About 80 minor fields have been found on the upper Tigris and, more recently, on the upper Euphrates; total reserves are only 300 mn bbl.

PETROLEUM PRODUCTION

Some Influences on Production

Whereas reserves reveal the production potential of individual fields and countries, the trend of actual production and marketing is volatile and reflects a combination of complex factors. Production may move upward as new reserves are exploited, as in Saudi Arabia for thirty-five virtually unbroken years after World War II. Conversely, production may drop steadily as reserves are depleted, as in Bahrain after 1970. In Kuwait, daily production was deliberately reduced by government fiat in 1972 to extend the life of the reserves. Production may drop in a country because of labor unrest, political tensions, natural disasters, or wartime conditions, as in Iran and Iraq in the 1980s and in Iraq and Kuwait in the early 1990s. Iraqi output dropped to a fraction of its normal level in 1991–1992 because of UN-imposed sanctions, and it continued to produce below its 1989 "normal" level until it collapsed in 2003. By the end of the decade, Iraq had seen some recovery, but a combination of factors—pipeline sabotage, obsolete facilities, insecure working conditions—has kept output below 3 mn bpd.

Global production was transformed by advances in offshore drilling techniques, which allowed operations in ever-deeper and rougher waters. Greatly upgraded exploration techniques and data interpretation have led to new discoveries. Output has increasingly been affected by less dramatic innovation and technology to raise production in mature fields: enhanced oil recovery (EOR) methods, such as horizontal drilling, waterflooding, gas injection, fracture stimulation, and improved output transportation. Investments in new techniques and procedures have been encouraged as even slight improvements in discovery efforts and small increases in output translate into much higher returns with rising prices. Old wells, producing only 2–3 bpd, that had been shut in are reopened as strip wells when prices exceed operating costs.

However, along with these factors, market demand is obviously a crucial influence on production levels. (See "Markets and Marketing" later in this chapter.) After more than twenty-five years of steadily and even dramatically increasing production as unparalleled industrial development occurred in much of the world, Middle East output curves became erratic in the early 1970s. Noteworthy was the impact of the 1973 Arab-Israeli war and the subsequent Arab oil boycott (which was aimed at the United States after it began resupplying armaments to Israel during the war);[5] the sharp rise in oil prices as OPEC and other producers increasingly took control of the output and marketing of their own resources; the growing realization among oil-consuming nations that they must both conserve and substitute for petroleum and natural gas; the market entry of new producing areas in the North Sea, Alaska, and the Soviet Union; and the OPEC decision to vary production to support prices.

The impact of market demand was dramatically demonstrated in the price spike of 2004–2005 and even more so in 2008, when soaring demand in China and India (and likely intense speculative activity) drove spot prices to record levels close to $150 a barrel before collapsing in the face of global reces-

sion (and the apparent withdrawal of speculators from the market). Producer cuts in output did little to stem the decline as demand shrank, and it is not clear whether high prices contributed to the recession. But when the air had been let out of the bubble, prices recovered somewhat in 2009. Still, average annual prices fell from about $100 a barrel in 2008 to less than $62 in 2009.[6]

Noteworthy on the technical level: An oil or gas field has an optimal production level that theoretically permits maximum production over a maximum time period. In the Middle East, this can be more readily determined and followed than in the United States—in virtually all Middle East fields, exploration and production are controlled by one operator, whereas U.S. fields are typically developed by many different companies competing for oil underlying a checkerboard of leases. A statistical comparison shows the consequence: In the Middle East, 21.8 mn bpd came from 14,595 wells in 2009, an average of 1,494 bpd per well, while in the United States, production of 5.3 mn bpd was obtained from 512,560 wells, an average of 10.3 bpd per well. U.S. production costs are thus appreciably higher, and oil-recovery percentages are lower without expensive secondary recovery procedures.

Natural Gas

Natural gas reserves include both "associated" and "nonassociated" gas. The former is found with petroleum and reaches the surface along with the oil in which it is dissolved. Nonassociated gas occurs separately in underground reservoirs and is produced only as gas. The distinction is significant in several ways, including the availability to consumers of one kind of gas or the other.

Associated gas must be separated from crude oil as soon as the mixture reaches the surface. In the early years of Middle East production, the demand was for oil; since associated gas had no market, it was separated and immediately burned off ("flared"). Gradually, as increased population and economic development created a major market demand for gas, flaring diminished, and it was piped to nearby markets. Rapidly increasing oil production made enormous amounts of associated gas available after separation. These seemingly inexhaustible supplies came to be taken for granted by local consumers—power companies, fertilizer companies, water desalination plants, aluminum smelters, and residential customers. Gas was utilized in more sophisticated ways—after being broken down into its major components of methane, ethane, propane, butane, and heavier hydrocarbons.

Thus, when oil production decreased sharply in the early 1980s, not only did the exporters suffer reduced oil income, but they also suddenly had insufficient supplies of the gas that had become a fringe benefit of high production levels. This impelled increased searches for and production of nonassociated gas, which could be exploited independently of the demand for oil.

After Bahrain found a major gas reservoir in the deep Khuff formation in 1949, its neighbors also drilled into the Khuff and likewise found enormous amounts of nonassociated gas. Qatar's huge North Field reservoir is in the same zone; all Gulf states have found large reserves both there and in other deep reservoirs. The fields discovered by Iran since the late 1970s, many in the Khuff zone (it shares the offshore North Field, the world's largest), raised its reserves to 1,046 tcf (trillion cubic feet), by far the largest reserves outside Russia. Qatar, with the major share of the North Field, has about 899 tcf, and is third in rank behind Iran. At the end of 2009, the region had about 41 percent of world reserves. Thus, as in other places, gas is assuming an increasingly significant role in the region's energy pattern. Gas exports from the Arab countries alone were reported to have grown almost 55 percent between 2004 and 2009, with Qatar responsible for most of the

increase.[7] Middle East gas, as much as its oil, may well power much of the world's industry in the twenty-first century and beyond; however, if new technologies satisfy environmental and cost concerns, extensive deposits of gas-bearing shale in both North America and Europe could make those markets self-sufficient for many years.

Production Comparisons

Map 6.4 presents a graphic comparison of petroleum production by Middle East countries in thousands of barrels per day in 2009. Saudi Arabia ranked second or third during the 1970s and 1980s, behind the Soviet Union and the United States, but it moved into first place in 1991 and has kept that position. It hit a world record in 2003—an average of 9.8 mn bpd. The kingdom has a history of varying output in response to market conditions, and was expected to reach its goal of having a production capacity of 12.5 mn bpd by the end of 2009. Iran reached peaks of more than 6 mn bpd in 1974 and 5.9 mn bpd in 1976 before tumbling to 1.37 mn bpd in the war year of 1981. Under stable conditions, Iran, which hovered around 3.8 mn bpd during the late 2000s, could probably sustain an average daily production of 5 mn bbl for many years.

Iraq moved up to third from fourth in 1975, surpassing Kuwait; it exceeded 1 mn bpd from 1960 on, with a peak of 3.4 mn bpd in 1979 (its last "normal" production year for the next three decades). Output dropped periodically during the early 1970s, when confrontations with Syria interrupted pipeline throughput to the Mediterranean. This situation happened again in the early 1980s during the Iran-Iraq War; it averaged less than 1 mn bpd in 1981–1983. Output reached 3 mn bpd in mid-1990, when Iraq bitterly disputed quotas and over-quota production with its OPEC comembers. These and other oil issues were part of its stated rationale for invading Kuwait. When the coalition went into action,

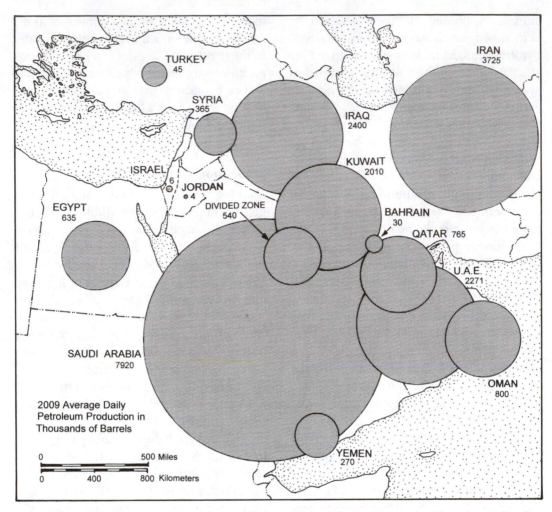

MAP 6.4 Petroleum production in the Middle East, by country, in thousands of barrels per day, for 2009. (From data in *Oil and Gas Journal*, Dec. 21, 2009, and in U.S. Department of Energy, Energy Information Administration, *Country Analysis Briefs*, 2009–2010, www.eia.doe.gov/emeu/cabs/cabsme.html)

Iraq suffered heavy bomb damage and was temporarily forced to shut down all exports. For the next six years, UN controls limited official production to 305,000–600,000 bpd, then after 1997 to 2 mn–2.4 mn bpd. Output collapsed following the 2003 invasion but recovered quickly to 2 mn bpd by year's end. It continued at that level through 2007, and in 2009 it hit 2.4 mn bpd. The goal of 3 mn bpd has remained elusive, as continued insecurity and field-equipment obsolescence remained as hindrances; in 2009, the government insti-

tuted a policy of aggressively seeking contractual arrangements with large international oil companies with a view to overcoming these difficulties (see Chap. 13) .

The next-largest producer in the Gulf and in the Middle East is the UAE, where production rose from a negligible amount in 1963 to 2 mn bpd in 1977 before joining the regional downward trend. Before UAE independence in 1971, oil was produced only in Abu Dhabi, still by far the federation's major producer. Dubai's offshore Fateh field contributed a growing share of the total until output fell after 2001. UAE production in 2009 was 2.27 mn bpd.

Kuwait led Middle East production from 1954 to 1966; it peaked in 1972 at 3 mn bpd, and then, for conservation purposes, output was intentionally reduced (dropping it to fourth or fifth place), and fell to 675,000 bpd in 1982 due to the oil crisis, rebounding to more than 1.5 mn bpd in 1989. It was interrupted, of course, with the Iraqi invasion in 1990 (see Chap. 15) but recovered to average 1.9 mn bpd during the remainder of the 1990s. Output increased after 2003 to supplement the needs of the U.S.-U.K. forces in Iraq, and was 2.28 mn bpd in 2009.

Production in Oman, which is not a member of OPEC, quickly reached stride in the late 1960s; production ranged between 300,000 and 400,000 bpd before falling off. Then new discoveries and improved recovery techniques led to gains—from 283,000 bpd in 1980 to a peak of 933,000 bpd in 2000. Production declined gradually to about 720,000 bpd in 2007 before Oman's major investments in enhanced oil recovery techniques resulted in increases in output in both 2008 and 2009.

Egypt, also not constrained by OPEC quotas, varied between 800,000 and 900,000 bpd in most years through the 1980s and 1990s but lost ground in the 2000s. Sector earnings were boosted by growing gas production. Syria's very heavy crude output varied from 160,000 to 175,000 bpd in the late 1970s and early 1980s. The discovery in eastern Syria of a light sweet crude oil in the mid-1980s more than tripled output by 2000 before the level dropped to 365,000 bpd in 2009. The country had been exporting one-third of production, but growing domestic demand is eating into exports. Far to the south, Yemeni production peaked in 2005 at 413,000 bpd, but as in Syria output fell and by the end of the decade was about 270,000 bpd. Israel's negligible output vies with Jordan's as the smallest of all producers.

In assessing the Middle East's long-range significance in this sector, two production ratios are important: the ratio of its annual production to its reserves and the ratio of its percentage of world production to its percentage of world reserves. Middle East production in 2009, for example, was 1.1 percent of its reserves, while in the United States it was 10.1 percent, and in Western Europe 11.5 percent. That same year, Middle East production amounted to 30.9 percent of the world total, from 55.9 percent of the world's petroleum reserves; Western Hemisphere production was 23.6 percent of the world total, from only 13.2 percent of the world's reserves (omitting Canadian oil sands); and corresponding figures for other petro-provinces showed the same high ratio of production to reserves. The vital lesson: More intensive exploitation of oil resources will exhaust reserves more rapidly in areas outside the Middle East.

Thus, the world will be even more highly dependent on the Middle East for oil by the mid-twenty-first century than it is at present because of its remarkably high ratio of reserves to production; however, in the event that concerns about climate change result in a serious medium-term decline in consumption, then a very different consumer-supplier situation will evolve (see Chap. 4's "Patterns: Climate Change"). It should be noted that in 2009, the International Energy Agency, the members of which are the major consuming countries, seems to have determined that the time horizon for so-called peak oil may be as soon as 2020—which suggests that in a decade or so, the global output of conventional oil will begin to decline, assuming that demand continues to grow as it has in recent years.[8]

MAJOR OIL FACILITIES

Raising petroleum and gas to the wellhead is only the beginning of a complex handling and processing procedure. The crude oil must be gathered from the field; associated gas must be separated and either flared in the field or piped to a consuming or processing facility. The degassed crude may then require "sweetening" before it is transported to an export terminal or a nearby refinery. Refining "cracks" the crude into a series of hydrocarbons, from the lightest fractions at one end (naphtha and gasoline), through the middle distillates (kerosene and aviation jet fuel) to heavy fractions like fuel oil and asphalt. Each product requires separate handling and has its own market. A salient development in the regional petroleum industry during the past two decades was the marked expansion of the petrochemical sector, especially in the major producing countries. Saudi Arabia, Iran, the UAE, and—because of its huge gas resources—Qatar have been constructing large plants and expanding existing plants. Petrochemical facilities utilize a plentiful raw material, add greatly to its value, and supply a profitable export. Moreover, oil production processed in these plants is not included in a country's OPEC quota (discussed in the section "OPEC: Pricing and Participation" later in this chapter).[9]

In the early years, most of the Middle East's degassed crude petroleum was directly exported by tanker ships to overseas consumers. Much production is still exported in the same way. However, over the years, increasing amounts have been refined in the region and the products either consumed locally by the larger and more affluent populations or else exported in a more valuable refined form. Refineries were built in Iran, Bahrain, and Saudi Arabia soon after production began in each country, and refining is now a significant industry in every state.

A fairly high correlation exists between the patterns of producing fields and of handling and processing facilities—particularly with regard to pipelines and export terminals, but not necessarily refineries and petrochemical industries. Crude feedstock can be transported hundreds of miles by pipeline to refineries far distant from an oil field; more frequently, it is transported by tanker ship to coastal refineries in more heavily populated industrial states. Major pipelines, export terminals, and refineries are shown on Maps 6.1 and 6.2.

Pipelines

Pipelines are the arteries of the petroleum industry. Indeed, they are a unique transportation system from the time the oil approaches the surface of the ground until it arrives at the interconnected refinery or shipping terminal. Since oil is of little value until it is moved from the well to an export or processing facility, pipelines are integral and vital links in the industry.

Numerous factors greatly influence the routes and costs of long-distance pipelines, such as topography, surface rock, population density, and environmental sensitivities (Fig. 6.3). Increasingly important is the security of the pipelines and of the oil passing through them, the attitude of authorities concerned, and the political stability of the areas traversed. International pipelines have been particularly susceptible to shutdowns because of disputes among states along the routes and, more seriously, because of sabotage by dissident groups.

More than 10,000 mi/16,093 km of large-diameter pipelines transport crude petroleum from major fields to regional shipping terminals and refineries. Three systems merit attention because of the leading roles they play or have played and because they exemplify the problems that can affect pipelines and other oil facilities as a result of the regional crosscurrents.

Iraq's pipeline systems illustrate the problems of an interior location and the importance of good relations with neighboring states. For more than forty years, Iraq exported through IPC lines from Kirkuk across

FIGURE 6.3 Constructing a pipeline through the mountains of the Hijaz in western Saudi Arabia. (Michael J. Isaac, Saudi Aramco)

Syria to the Mediterranean, the oldest long-distance network in the region. Opening in 1934, they ran parallel from Kirkuk to Ha-dithah on the Euphrates, where they divided with one line crossing Trans-Jordan to Haifa, in the British mandate of Palestine, and the other, via Syria, terminating in Tripoli, in the French mandate of Lebanon. By 1950, new political circumstances decreed abandoning Haifa as a destination, and the IPC laid pipe to Baniyas in Syria. Heightened "family quarrels" between the Baathi regimes in Iraq and Syria led to the latter's closing all IPC lines crossing its territory in 1982, but not before Iraq had undertaken alternatives lessening its dependence on the Syrian connections.

In the 1970s, Iraq built two new networks. In 1975, it finished an entirely internal line to terminals at the head of the Gulf, where the export facilities were highly concentrated on its narrow strip of coast. This arrangement was soon disrupted when the terminals were destroyed in 1980–1981, early in the war with Iran. Fortunately, Iraq supplemented its Gulf outlet with a new 603-mi/970-km, 40-in/102-cm line from Kirkuk through Turkey to Yumurtalık on the Mediterranean near Iskenderun, which opened in 1977. Its capacity was increased in 1984, and a parallel 46-in/117-cm line was opened in 1987, giving the system through Turkey a capacity of 1.6 mn bpd, although throughput was about 500,000 bpd in early 2010.

Still concerned about depending on only one neighboring country, Iraq discussed with Jordan and Saudi Arabia possible routes through their territories to Aqabah and Yanbu, respectively. Iraq eventually rejected Aqabah, just across the border from Elat in Israel and an easy target for Israeli artillery or air strikes. Instead, construction went ahead on a 500,000-bpd 48-in/122-cm line (IPSA-I) to connect with Petroline, the huge Saudi crude oil line. Balked at exporting through Syria and through its own terminals on the Gulf, Iraq could then send crude through Turkey and Saudi Arabia for the remaining years of its war with Iran. Later, a separate 48-in/122-cm line, IPSA-II, parallel to the Saudi lines across the peninsula to a separate Red Sea export terminal, Muajjil, 30 mi/48 km south of Yanbu, opened in January 1990, with a capacity of 1.65 mn bpd.

Thus, in 1990 Iraq had an export capacity of 3.15 mn bpd through Turkey and Saudi Arabia and 800,000 bpd through its own Gulf terminals when they were in operation, plus the potential for 1.25 mn bpd across Syria through the old IPC lines. However, its dependence on the goodwill of its neighbors for its exports became dramatically evident once again later that year when Saddam inexplicably disdained all favorable neighborly ties and invaded Kuwait. Complying with UN sanctions against Iraq, both Turkey and Saudi Arabia closed the lines crossing their territories, vowing to keep them shut in as long as UN sanctions required it. Thus, Iraq had no lines through which to export—the price of being virtually landlocked and of not maintaining friendly relations with at least some of its neighbors. The invasion also quickly led to a coalition blockade to exports from its own terminals.

By the mid-1990s, UN sanctions were modified to allow oil to flow through the Turkish lines, but by the end of the 2000s Saudi Arabia had still not relented on its closure of IPSA. Exports were interrupted again in March 2003; when pumping through Turkey was resumed after formal hostilities ceased, sabotage frequently interfered.

The second international petroleum pipeline of major significance was the Trans-Arabian Pipe Line (Tapline), which extended 1,068 mi/1,718 km from eastern Saudi Arabia to the Mediterranean in southern Lebanon. Although the line was shut in by the early 1980s, Tapline played a noteworthy role in Middle East oil developments over three decades, and it provides an excellent case study in geographic petroleum economics.

Plans were considered during World War II and completed by 1946 for a Gulf-to-Mediterranean route—a shortcut avoiding the long, slow voyage around the Arabian Peninsula and through the Suez Canal. Compared with the route of the original IPC lines across the Syrian Desert, the proposed route was much longer and its environment much more barren, virtually uninhabited except for small numbers of Bedouin, across almost unknown terrain. Tapline's diameter of 30–31 in/76–79 cm was also much larger than that of its predecessors.

Opened in December 1950, it crossed Saudi Arabia, Jordan, Syria, and Lebanon (see F, Map 6.1). Five large pump stations were needed to move the eventual capacity of 500,000 bpd, and a given barrel of oil required eleven days to transit the line to the Zahrani loading terminal near Sidon. Most of the oil was exported, but feedstock was also supplied to refineries in Zarqa in Jordan and Sidon in Lebanon. Tapline was a signal success for many years, but its situation became awkward after June 1967, when control over part of it passed to Israel, which had occupied the Golan Heights. Problems ranging from sabotage to disputes over royalties were exacerbated after the 1973 Arab-Israeli war.

Another difficulty was that closure of the Suez Canal after the 1967 war stimulated the construction and use of increasingly larger oil tankers. Very Large Crude Carriers (VLCCs) could transport crude from the Gulf around southern Africa to western Europe and North America even more cheaply than could the smaller tankers that had formerly followed either the Red Sea–Suez Canal–Mediterranean route or, more important for Tapline, lifted crude from the Zahrani terminal. With mount-

FIGURE 6.4 One of the world's largest tank farms, on a sand spit at Saudi Aramco's Ras Tanura export terminal on the Gulf coast. The terminal is one of the world's largest. (Shaikh M. Amin, Saudi Aramco)

ing operational problems and expenses, after February 1975 the fabled line was no longer used for exports—oil lifted at Ras Tanura (Fig. 6.4) could be landed at English Channel ports by VLCCs at a rate more than $2 per barrel cheaper than oil lifted from Zahrani.

Thus, technology, economics, politics, and geography combined to render Tapline obsolete after twenty-five years of operation. Using only a small fraction of its capacity, it did continue to move less than 100,000 bpd to supply the refinery at Zarqa to maintain Saudi Arabian goodwill toward Jordan. These shipments gradually lessened, partly because of nonpayment, and they stopped entirely in August 1990 when Jordan hesitated in support of UN actions against Iraq (see Chap. 11). After 1990, Tapline fell into disuse. By the early 2000s, its physical condition had deteriorated, and a possible reopening to Jordan was estimated to require an investment of as much as $400 million. No

action had been taken by the end of the decade.

A third noteworthy line began as an internal facility but gained international connections. In 1981, Saudi Arabia opened the largest-diameter long-distance crude oil line in the region, the 48-in/122-cm Petroline from the Eastern Province to the Red Sea at Yanbu, with a new export facility, refinery, and petrochemical complex. The original capacity of 1.85 mn bpd was raised to 3.3 mn bpd with the opening of a 56-in/142-cm parallel interconnected (looped) line in 1987. This East-West system was further upgraded during the early 1990s to a capacity of 4.8 mn bpd to ensure a protected outlet during crisis periods in the Gulf. Normally, it carries only a fraction of its capacity but is sufficient to supply Yanbu's facilities and small amounts for export. During crises, it can deliver about half the kingdom's output to the Red Sea for export via tanker, either northward through the Suez Canal or to Egypt's "Sumed" lines or southward through the Bab el-Mandeb.

In the late 1990s, after the oil-producing former Soviet republics became independent, questions arose as to how to bring output from the Caspian petro-province to export terminals; controversies slowed determining the routing of new pipelines. A partial and temporary solution was the limited 115,000-bpd line that opened in 1999 connecting the Baku fields with Supsa in Georgia on the Black Sea. From there, tankers deliver oil to other Black Sea ports or transit the Turkish Straits to the Mediterranean. This line could have been paralleled by a large-capacity line, but Turkey strongly objected for two reasons: first, the growing environmental threat from already heavy tanker traffic through the narrow Bosporus, and, second, Turkey's desire—supported by others—for a new line to transit its own territory. Proposed was a route from Baku to Tbilisi, Georgia, and then through Erzurum in eastern Anatolia to a port near Ceyhan on the Gulf of Iskenderun.

The United States gave top priority to the Baku-Tbilisi-Ceyhan (BTC) route to decrease reliance on Middle East oil and to have a route crossing friendly countries, avoiding Iran and Russia (see Map 6.1). It therefore put determined pressure on the countries and companies concerned. With its growing friendship with Turkey, Israel was a key supporter for the Ceyhan outlet, which would be close to its import facilities. The project was finally approved, and BTC construction began through very difficult terrain. The 1,040-mi/1,674-km line with a capacity of 1 mn bpd became operational in 2005.

Another important aspect of the pipeline network is the large—and steadily growing—number of natural gas lines in the region. Most are internal, but several major gas pipelines are being laid across international borders. Notably, Turkey increased its gas imports in 2002 through new lines from Iran and Russia: a large line from Tabriz into east-

ern Turkey and the dual "Blue Stream" line from Russia under the Black Sea to Samsun. Turkey is now so well supplied with gas that a planned line from Baku to Erzurum, paralleling the BTC, is being held in abeyance. However, Turkey and the European Union (EU) agreed in 2009 to build the Nabucco gas pipeline designed to carry gas 2,000 mi/3,220 km from the Caspian region to Austria. Gas from Qatar's supergiant North Field will inevitably be exported in great quantities, and the necessary infrastructure is already under construction. Europe, Turkey, the Levant, the UAE, Oman, Pakistan, and India have been suggested as potential markets. A UAE group has evolved the Dolphin initiative for an $8–$10 billion project for piping Qatar gas to Abu Dhabi, Dubai, Suhar (Oman), and later on to Pakistan. The export of Egyptian gas began in 2003 through a pipeline under the Gulf of Aqabah to Jordan; this has now been extended north to Syria and Lebanon.

Other Pipelines, Terminals, and Refineries

In addition to the major long lines just described, several internal pipelines are of noteworthy regional importance and have a significant impact on international movements of Middle East petroleum. Both Egypt and Israel provide shortcuts that permit oil to move from the Red Sea to the Mediterranean, serving tankers that are too large for the Suez Canal or that prefer to avoid the canal. Egypt's Suez-Mediterranean system (Sumed) consists of twin parallel 42-in/107-cm lines that run to a terminal just west of Alexandria. Israel's 42-in/107-cm Trans-Israel Pipeline (Tipline) runs 158 mi/254 km from Elat to a terminal at Ashqelon. It opened in 1968 in a deal with Iran under the monarchy to supply Israel secretly with petroleum, but became largely moribund after the Islamic Revolution. Since 2004, however, the flow has been in the opposite direction, competing with the Suez Canal—Russian oil bound for Asian

TABLE 6.2 Petroleum: Refineries and Refining Activity

Country	1 Number of Refineries	2 Total Refinery Capacity (Bpd)	3 Largest Refinery in Respective Country	4 Main Refinery Capacity (Bpd)
Bahrain	1	262,000	Sitra	263,000
Cyprus	0	—	—	—
(Divided Zone)	0	—	—	—
Egypt	9	726,000	Suez	146,300
Iran	9	1,451,000	Abadan	350,000
Iraq	8	598,500	Baiji	310,000
Israel	2	220,000	Haifa	180,000
Jordan	1	90,000	Zarqa	90,400
Kuwait	3	936,000	Mina al-Ahmadi	466,000
Lebanon	0	—	—	—
Oman	2	222,000	Sohar	116,000
Qatar	2	346,000	Umm Said	200,000
Saudi Arabia	7	2,080,000	Ras Tanura	550,000
Syria	2	240,000	Baniyas	132,725
Turkey	6	714,000	Izmit	230,440
UAE	5	781,000	Ruwais	350,000
Yemen	2	140,000	Little Aden	120,000
TOTAL	59	8,806,500	—	3,504,865

Data as of 2009. (*Source*: Energy Information Administration, www.eia.doe.gov.)

markets. Plans to expand its capacity of 400,000 bpd to 1.1 mn bpd are reported, as is a direct marine pipeline connection from Ceyhan in Turkey to Ashqelon.[10] Details on the more important oil-export terminals and refineries are given in the individual country chapters. However, Table 6.2 gives comparative data on refineries.

MARKETS AND MARKETING

Early developers of Middle East petroleum fields—all from western Europe and North America—envisaged exploiting the resources for export to their respective home countries or for fueling naval ships. Local consumption was limited. However, as the pace of regional development increased, demand for the petro-products mounted in the Middle East as elsewhere, and governments in oil-exporting countries gained control over the exploitation and marketing of their highly valuable and sometimes sole resource and

then contracted for local basic processing facilities.

Marketing large amounts of petroleum has traditionally been through long-term contracts. Concessionary companies operating in a producing country were often the direct sellers, disposing of their product within a stable if highly complex global system. For decades, the system was essentially controlled by a few major companies—the "Seven Sisters": Jersey Standard (Exxon), British Petroleum, Royal Dutch/Shell, Standard of California (Chevron), Texaco (which merged with Chevron), Socony-Vacuum (Mobil, now merged with Exxon), and Gulf (which merged with Chevron). Italian, Spanish, Brazilian, and Japanese companies later joined in, thereby gaining international marketing influence.

Until 1970, the main importers of Middle East crude were industrial countries that required supplies beyond their own production capacity, including those countries that held major concessions in the region. Some importers had only limited or even no known petroleum resources of their own. Virtually every major oil exporter in the Middle East in the 1960s and 1970s counted the same half-dozen purchasers among its top ten customers: Britain, France, West Germany, Japan, the Netherlands, and the United States. Secondary buyers included Italy, Spain, Canada, and Brazil; Australia, India, Sweden, and Switzerland were also regular customers.

After 1970, steadily increasing production from new offshore fields on the continental shelves of Britain and other North Sea littoral countries afforded northwestern Europe a large supply of local oil and gas. As one result, the demand for Middle East crude by these countries dropped by more than 3 mn bpd as both Britain and Norway became net exporters, completely redirecting the world oil industry. Another significant development in the 1990s was the opening of the Caspian petro-province—with particular impetus from the United States—to commercial exploration and exploitation. From the early 1970s on, the trend of oil exports from the Middle East from year to year has been markedly more variable than that during the previous decades. The import pattern of the United States also changed and varies considerably: In 1977, the United States imported 46 percent of its oil, about 18 percent from the Middle East; in 1983, it imported only 28 percent of its oil requirements, just 4 percent from the Middle East; in 1988, it imported about 41 percent, about 11 percent from the Middle East; in 1999, it imported 55 percent, about 20 percent from the Middle East; and by 2008, it imported 57 percent, but only 18 percent from the Middle East.

In addition to increased local use of petroleum, natural gas consumption in the Middle East has also grown dramatically. Whereas in 1972 more than two-thirds of the gas produced in association with oil was either flared or reinjected (pumped back into the oil reservoir), by 1982 only half of the gas was being flared, and utilization had increased by 38 percent. Flaring dropped below 10 percent by the mid-2000s.

OPEC: PRICING AND PARTICIPATION

In the 1940s and 1950s, companies operating concessions in the Middle East generally determined output and prices, taking into account production costs and world demand. With little input from the countries involved, they periodically set and publicly stated posted prices as the "list" prices at which various grades of crude would be sold at Gulf terminals. Highly complex arrangements, royalties, taxes, deductions, and discounts affected government revenues and company profits.

When posted prices fell in 1960, governments of major producing countries became disgruntled, and in an effort to gain greater control over pricing they met in Baghdad in September 1960 and created the Organization of Petroleum Exporting Countries (based in Vienna). Charter OPEC members were Saudi Arabia, Iran, Iraq, Kuwait, and Venezuela; other members would be: Algeria (joining in 1969), Angola (2007), Ecuador (1973, inactive from 1992 to 2007), Gabon (1975, withdrew 1995), Indonesia (1962, withdrew 2008), Libya (1962), Nigeria (1971), Qatar (1961), and the UAE (joined as Abu Dhabi in 1967). Of the twelve current members, six are in the region considered in this work, and five are Arab countries. Bahrain, Oman, Egypt, Yemen, and Syria have never been members. In the aftermath of the 1967 Arab-Israeli War, three Arab exporters—Kuwait, Libya, and Saudi Arabia—formed a parallel group, the Organization of Arab Petroleum Exporting Countries (OAPEC, headquartered in Kuwait), which now includes all Arab members of OPEC plus Bahrain, Egypt, Syria, and Tunisia (membership suspended in 1988). OAPEC has not played a consistently significant role in the regional oil industry. Oman and Yemen have not joined either group.

Prices of virtually all other commodities rose steadily from the late 1940s, but petroleum was increasingly underpriced into the early 1970s. Not until late in 1973 was the free-on-board price of the benchmark Arabian light crude at Ras Tanura to surge decisively above $3 per barrel. (All prices and sales were, and still are, in U.S. dollars, although whenever the dollar weakens there is nervous speculation about substituting the euro.) Mounting determination by OPEC members to strengthen their hold on the pricing and handling of their petroleum was sharpened by the 1973 Arab-Israeli war, and OAPEC members embargoed oil shipments to the United States and the Netherlands in retaliation for actions or policies considered supportive of Israel.

Late 1973 was the turning point in company-government relations, as company-set "posted prices" were abandoned in favor of OPEC-announced prices. The posted price had increased from the long-set $1.80/bbl in 1970 to $2.18 in 1971, then three times in six months—to $2.90 in mid-1973, $5.12 in October, and in one historic jump $11.65 in December. OPEC had arrived.[11] The price then rose gradually to $13.34 at the beginning of 1979, doubled in one year to $26.00, and peaked at $34.00 in October 1981 with Iran-Iraq War jitters. Unified pricing, however, was often disregarded by sellers—increasingly so into the mid- and late 1980s, until the price fell to about $13.00 a barrel.

The 1973–1974 price escalation (which proceeded independently of the OAPEC embargo) broke the previously steady and often rapid growth of global petroleum consumption since 1945. Shaken by a tenfold price increase from late 1973 to early 1981, major consuming countries tried to minimize the shock not only by promoting conservation and more efficient use of oil but also by using alternative forms of energy. In addition, increased prices stimulated development of resources and higher production in non-OPEC countries, depressing demand for OPEC oil. The changing balance dropped OPEC's share of world production from 56 percent in 1973 to 29 percent in 1985. However, it rebounded and averaged about 40 percent in the mid-1990s. The seemingly insatiable demand for oil into the late 1970s, despite escalating prices, had created surplus productive capacity, which in turn exerted downward pressure on market prices and caused financial stress in several OPEC states.

In the early 1990s, OPEC continued to struggle with the difficult problem of apportioning quotas among cartel members and hence with price maintenance. As in any such arrangement, members try to maximize revenues, but are often unwilling to adhere to assigned quotas—the sine qua non for success. OPEC had mixed results during the 1990s, and prices fell with the crash of Asian economies until they were less than $10/bbl in early 1999, an all-time low in adjusted real prices. However, at a meeting in March 1999, OPEC managed to get both members and nonmembers to lower output to realistic levels, and average prices rose considerably over the following years, averaging about $25/bbl over 2000 to 2003. Then the average annual price rose steadily to a high of nearly $100/bbl in 2008, before falling after the bursting of a speculative bubble and the onset of global recession.

During the late 1990s, market forces made clear the dilemma faced by both companies and producing countries. If controls are meaningful, artificially reduced production has a push-pull effect: It extends field life and supports higher prices, but it also reduces consumption (especially in poorer countries), drives conservation, encourages the search for alternative sources of energy, and lowers the threshold for exploiting unconventional oil resources like heavy oil, tar sands, and shale. Moreover, standard cartel theory holds as inevitable that there will be greater centrifugal forces and cheating on quotas; this induces a breakdown in the production and pricing structure, and the cycle starts all over again.

When the price falls below a certain optimum (not just a certain minimum), the income squeeze on producing countries and oil companies seriously impacts the entire world economy. Similarly, an excessively high price depletes the budgets of the poorer nonproducing states and creates resistance from main consumers. Most consumer states now have some flexibility in switching among various fuels for such major requirements as generating electricity guided by relative cost considerations.

One repercussion of an excessively low price during the late 1990s was a startling series of mergers of major Western oil companies in an effort to stay economically healthy. Some of the mergers involved exchanges of stock worth tens of billions of dollars. British Petroleum acquired Amoco in late 1998 to become BP Amoco, absorbing in 1999 Arco (which had acquired Union a year earlier), and is now just plain BP; ExxonMobil was formed in 1999 in a megamerger of corporate giants; Total (French) and Fina (Belgian) merged and added Elf Aquitaine in 1999 to become the world's fourth-largest oil company; Chevron (which had already acquired Gulf) and Texaco combined in 2001 and picked up Unocal in 2005; Conoco and Phillips merged in 2002 to form the third-largest U.S. oil company and acquired Burlington Resources in 2006. All of these companies have long been very much involved in the Middle East.

While Middle East producers were pooling the marketing prices of their output in OPEC in the 1960s and 1970s, each individual government steadily increased its "participation" in the private companies holding concessions in its country. By 1980, most OPEC countries had complete ownership of local producing operations through national oil companies. Since then, these companies have increased their downstream operations (refining, distributing, retailing) both domestically and in customer countries, thus expanding interdependence between producers and consumers.

OTHER MINERALS

The production and utilization of petroleum and natural gas have been the focal point of economic mineral activity in the Middle East for decades. However, several areas are highly mineralized, have produced limited to modest quantities of ores for many centuries, and are now the focus of intensified mineral exploration activities (Map 6.5). The oil-producing countries have joined their neighbors in intensively searching for commercially useful deposits.

Even limited production can bring significant benefit to a local area, especially one lacking petroleum; conversely, processing ores in areas like western Iran and northern Oman can be relatively economical because of the availability of large amounts of local gas. Additionally, many minerals industries are more labor intensive than the petro-sector and therefore can create many jobs. Income from mining and quarrying industries is expected to increase appreciably in the near future.

Turkey and Iran, which lie across the mineralized Fold Belt, have long produced large amounts of a wide variety of solid minerals. Cyprus is part of the belt and has been a considerable mineral producer historically, although it faces approaching depletion of its once appreciable resources of copper, iron pyrites, and chromite. Jordan, Syria, Israel, Egypt, and Iraq produce phosphate rock in significant quantities, and Israel and Jordan also have noteworthy potash output from the Dead Sea. Both Saudi Arabia and Egypt hope to revive and expand mining in the crystalline shield areas in their territories.[12]

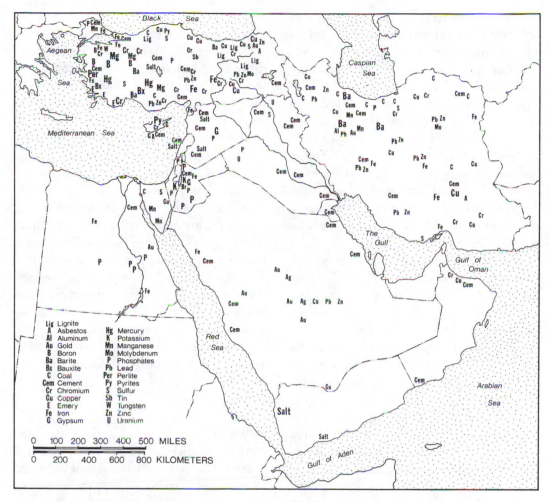

MAP 6.5 Distribution of more important deposits of solid minerals in the Middle East. Note the richness of mineral occurrences in the zones of tectonic plate contacts in Turkey, Iran, and Cyprus. (Adapted from several maps in U.S. Geological Survey, *Minerals Information*, 2002 and 2003 and from maps and reports of 2009 in http://minerals.usgs.gov/minerals/pubs/country)

Solid Fuels

Although sparse coal resources retarded Middle East industrial development in the nineteenth century, the problem has diminished since World War II. Only Turkey, Iran, and Egypt have noteworthy coal reserves, and only Turkey's production is significant, with Iran's now gradually increasing.

Turkey compensates for its small petroleum output by intensively exploiting its considerable coal (1.4 bn mt) and lignite (8 bn mt) resources. Solid fuels production in 2007 was 74 mn mt, 95 percent of which was lignite. Although Iran's coal reserves are in some of the same structures that contain coal beds in Turkey, production has lagged—about 2.0 mn mt per year—because of its enormous hydrocarbon reserves. Egypt's more modest coal production is useful locally, and production is increasing in newly opened mines in northern Sinai.[13]

Metals

Most (although not all) metallic ores occur in mineralized igneous and crystalline rocks.

They cannot, therefore, be normally expected in the extensive sedimentary areas of the Fertile Crescent countries or the Arabian Peninsula. Certain metals may be found in either class of rocks, and, indeed, some limited deposits of iron, lead, and zinc are found in the sedimentary strata just mentioned. Concentrated mineralization is found primarily in three specific areas of the region—the complex rocks of the Anatolian and Iranian plateaus, the shield blocks on either side of the Red Sea, and the unusual Oman Mountains—and it is mainly these areas that have been exploited for their metals.

As is the case for solid minerals in general, Turkey possesses by far the greatest variety and quantity of metal ores, and Iran is second. Several ores in Turkey are minable by large-scale methods: bauxite, chromite, copper, zinc, gold, iron, and silver. Only its chromite production ranks on a world scale—a comfortable second. More significant, however, are a number of industrial minerals; it is one of the world's leading producers for several of these: barite, boron, kaolin and other clays, magnesite, pumice, and strontium. Its minerals exports, including cement, now exceed $2.5 billion annually. Iran, emphasizing hydrocarbons, has not given commensurate effort to solid mineral production. However, it has developed some major deposits and is a significant producer of copper, chromium, iron ore, lead, zinc, and molybdenum. Iran, Turkey, and Egypt, leaders in iron ore resources, also share leadership in the production of pig iron and steel. The Hittites exploited Anatolian iron before 1800 BCE; they had a near monopoly on ironworking for centuries. Iran's iron reserves are twice those of Turkey and Egypt combined, but its production is appreciably less than Turkey's.

Nonferrous metals regularly produced in noteworthy quantities in the region include especially copper, but also lead, zinc, mercury, and bauxite (aluminum ore). Histori-cally, Turkey, Cyprus, and Iran have been the region's leading copper producers; since the early 1980s, Iran has taken first place after more than a decade of developing its resources. Oman appeared as a copper producer for the first time in 1983 and ranks third, after Turkey, in output, although its quite limited reserves are nearly exhausted. Production from Cyprus's ancient mines varies and in some years ceases to be commercially worthwhile.

Iran normally leads in the output of lead and zinc, with Turkey in second place. Turkey is the region's only producer of bauxite and mercury worth noting, and it has significant reserves of uranium, unexploited at the present time. Israel, however, produces small amounts of uranium from its Negev phosphate deposits for supplementary use in the reactor at nearby Dimona, the center of its nuclear weaponry program. Jordan signed an agreement in 2010 with a French firm to begin uranium mining.

Nonmetals

Certain nonmetallic minerals may be found in several different rock environments, others are found only in sedimentary rocks, and still others occur only in igneous rocks. Thus, the Middle East's nonmetallic ores are more widely distributed over the region than are its metallic resources and may even be processed from sea- or lake water.

The most widely produced solid mineral is salt, produced in virtually every country in the region but in especially large quantities in Turkey, Egypt, and Iran. Lebanon, Yemen, Egypt, and Iraq produce salt by evaporating seawater in small ponds or evaporation pans along the shore. Others evaporate surface or underground brines, and Iran and Yemen mine rock salt from underground salt plugs that have pushed their way toward the surface from deep subsurface strata.

Regional output of phosphate rock, valuable for making chemical fertilizers, is of con-

FIGURE 6.5 Open-pit mining of phosphates near Palmyra in central Syria. Phosphate-rich beds extend through much of the area of Syria, Jordan, Iraq, and Israel.

siderable significance on the global scale, as demand for phosphate rock has mounted sharply with the growing need for soil fertilizers to increase productivity. Middle East resources have therefore been vigorously exploited, with production steadily growing through the late 1970s and 1980s. The region's leading producer is Jordan, which in 2007 also ranked seventh in the world, with output of 5.54 mn mt. Three neighboring states are significant producers from similar rock strata: in order, Syria (Fig. 6.5), Israel, and Egypt.

Other nonmetallic minerals of the region may be noted, especially with regard to the unusual aspects of several of them. For example, meerschaum is found in significant commercial quantities only in Turkey. Despite its name ("sea foam" in German), it is a hydrous magnesium silicate—a fine white clayey mineral—used to make special kinds of smoking pipe bowls, many of which are elaborately carved and highly prized. Potash is produced in large amounts from Dead Sea water by both Israel and Jordan, with the newer Jordanian plant having world rank. Among other minerals Israel produces from the Dead Sea is bromine; output is about one-third of the world total. Asbestos has long been a major product of the metamorphic rocks of Cyprus and is produced from related structures in Turkey and Egypt. However, output has decreased sharply because of health dangers arising from its use.

NOTES

1. Hundreds of sources cover various aspects of Middle East oil, both in general and for respective producing countries. For detailed early development of the Gulf oil industry, see Marlowe 1962. Peterson 1983 discusses the politics of oil. An excellent source for current data on petroleum, natural gas, and coal is

U.S. Department of Energy, Energy Information Administration (EIA), at www.eia.doe.gov/emeu/cabs/. PennWell's weekly *Oil and Gas Journal* is almost indispensable, and PennWell's annual *International Petroleum Encyclopedia* (IPE) is also very useful. *Saudi Aramco and Its World* 1995 and earlier editions are authoritative and available. The BP annual statistical report, found at www.bp.com, is useful. For solid minerals, refer to the U.S. Geological Survey (USGS) *Minerals Yearbook*, which also includes some petroleum information. It is published every year or two, and some of the latest editions may also be found at http://minerals.usgs.gov/minerals. For a readable best-seller account of the oil industry, see Yergin 1991, and a recent opinion piece by the same author, "It's Still the One," *Foreign Policy Special Report*, Aug. 24, 2009, www.foreignpolicy.com/articles/2009/08/17/its_still_the_one. Aspects of U.S. dependence on oil are covered in Roberts 2004 and Klare 2004.

2. See note 16, Chap. 13.

3. See *New York Times,* June 18, 2003, and Aug. 14, 2003, and especially Aug. 31, 2004. The Alberta sands could contain more than 1 trillion bbl, but recoverable amounts are questionable. Statistics on reserves and production differ among sources, and criteria for estimating reserves vary among companies and countries. "Proved" reserves are those that engineering evidence indicates can be commercially produced with reasonable certainty with normal techniques. "Probable" reserves are those whose existence is less well known but that are expected to be commercial in the future. Some companies also include "possible" reserves. The EIA Web site is one standard and available source regarding reserves, although later data appear in the annual *International Petroleum Encyclopedia* as well as in the year-end issue of the *Oil and Gas Journal*. Most countries report reserves (and production) in barrels of 42 U.S. gallons, but some report in metric tons, and equivalents are not always precise. One mt is equal to 7.31 bbl of average gravity crude but may vary considerably with variations in gravity. Also, some information may be kept confidential, thus skewing other information. Finally, it must be noted that after about 2000, considerable debate arose regarding the validity of reserves data announced by some companies and some countries.

4. EIA *Country Analysis Briefs: Bahrain*, Nov. 2004 and Mar. 2008.

5. The boycott was eventually extended to the Netherlands, Portugal, South Africa, and Rhodesia: The last three were targeted as a gesture against lingering colonialism in Africa.

6. EIA, "Short Term Energy Outlook," Feb. 10, 2010.

7. *Oil and Gas Journal*, Dec. 30, 2009. Qatar was close to replacing Algeria, the longtime Arab leading gas exporter.

8. As reported in *Economist* 2009b.

9. For Saudi Arabia's petrochemical industry, see *Oil and Gas Journal*, Aug. 16, 1999, 65–71. For Iran, see same issue, 20–24. For an excellent worldwide review of gas processing, see several articles in *Oil and Gas Journal*, June 28, 2004.

10. *Journal of Energy Security*, Feb. 19, 2009, www.ensec.org.

11. See *Oil and Gas Journal*, Dec. 28, 1998, 18–23; and EIA, *OPEC Fact Sheet*, Jan. 2005 (also available at www.eia.doe.gov/emeu/cabs/).

12. The best source for solid minerals information is the USGS, formerly in various editions of the *Minerals Yearbook*, mentioned in note 1, but now at http://minerals.usgs.gov/minerals/pubs/country/index.html#pubs.

13. USGS Minerals Yearbook.

7

Manufacturing and Transportation

PRELIMINARY VIEW

The Stimulus of Oil

The unparalleled petroleum development surveyed in the previous chapter naturally stimulated growth in other economic sectors. Although the entire region benefited from the ripple effect on a grand scale, the expansion was most remarkable along the Gulf. Along the coast, tiny fishing villages like Abu Dhabi and Doha became within a few years capitals of nations with some of the world's highest per capita incomes. Farther inland, caravan trails and rutted tracks became motorways threading across rolling deserts. By the early 1990s, the Gulf states and Saudi Arabia had achieved stunning material progress that was awesome to local inhabitant and outside specialist alike. By the 2000s, the splendor and even opulence of public buildings, hotels, airport terminals, shopping centers, and universities were matched by the number and complexity of technologically advanced gas-oil separating facilities, shipping terminals, oil refineries, petrochemical plants, dry docks, aluminum smelters, and similar installations that seemed to have sprung out of the desert.[1]

Several states have built modest to appreciable industrial foundations and have developed impressively diversified producing sectors. Even so, none of the major oil exporters is a true "industrial" state, in the Western sense, although prerevolutionary Iran as well as Iraq aspired to high levels of industrialization. Modern manufacturing started earlier in the eastern Mediterranean, especially in Egypt, where it began in the early 1800s under Muhammad Ali, and in Turkey, where it originated in the nineteenth century Ottoman New Order. Economic evolution during the regional oil boom and the emergence of Israel contributed to the pattern of manufacturing discussed later in this chapter, which reveals the importance of manufacturing in the older areas of Turkey, Iran, and Egypt as well as more recently in Syria, Israel, and Iraq, and on a smaller scale Cyprus and Lebanon.

Quantification of the industrialization of states in the region is difficult because of the shortage of meaningful and comparable statistics. Determining the values of the usual criteria used to analyze the degree of industrialization—percentage of GDP derived from manufacturing and other industrial output, percentage of the workforce employed in manufacturing and other industries, and per capita energy consumption, steel output, and other indicators—is thus problematic. For example, the region is unique in that its high consumption of electric energy is not closely linked to industrial activity. Additionally, much of the industry is capital intensive, highly automated, and labor extensive: A refinery is a huge facility with high output, but it employs few workers.

Since the overwhelming emphasis is on petroleum exploitation, the Gulf's recently evolved economic patterns and activities differ from those of neighboring non-oil areas. There are considerable gaps in the per capita income between the Gulf and the eastern Mediterranean—except Israel—but the ripple effect of oil income in part of the region has been noteworthy in other parts. In Cyprus, Jordan, and—before 1975—Lebanon, the ripple effect has been impressive. Israel's dramatic development has been independent of the regional oil boom; it has been heavily financed by capital transfers—grants, especially from the United States and Germany—and by other favored treatment by the United States. Capital availability from oil revenues has set the pace throughout the region, even though development has been uneven among the states and sectors of their economies. In any given year over the past thirty years, Saudi Arabia expended $250–$275 billion (in 2009 dollars) for development in a large area with a relatively small population, whereas Egypt had only one-tenth that amount for a small inhabited area with a population three to four times that of the kingdom.

Rapidly developing Gulf states soaked up surplus labor not only from Yemen, Egypt, Lebanon, Jordan, and Syria but also from India, Pakistan, and other Asian countries. At the same time, a reverse flow of cash in grants, loans, and worker remittances transferred a share of oil profits to nonproducing areas or to smaller producers. From Baghdad to Beirut, Kuwait to Cairo, Dubai to Damascus, capital and development fever became the common denominators. Contractors, artisans, and consultants came by the thousands and laborers by the millions to take advantage of the boom.

Historical Perspective

During the golden age of Islam in the ninth and tenth centuries, the Middle East boasted the world's best-developed economy and flourishing trade. High-quality textiles were a specialty—linens from Egypt, damask from Damascus, silks from Kufah, brocades from Shiraz, and muslin from Mosul, as well as carpets from Iran, Bukhara, and elsewhere. Colored glass from Syria, decorated tiles from many places, pottery, porcelain, inlaid and decorated wood, embossed and inlaid brass and copper (damascene), engraved gold and silver jewelry, leather wares, and fine soaps and perfumes were produced in the small workshops of the *suqs*, or bazaars. Products moved between Spain on the west and Samarkand on the east and as far as Scandinavia and China.

Some goods moved by sea, with Basrah a preeminent port. However, more of the traffic was overland, and great dromedary caravans plodded eastward from Baghdad to Samarkand, where loads were transferred to the Bactrian camels of the Mongols and Chinese (see Map 4.5). Towns favorably located as trade centers thrived; some of them have kept their fame and prosperity to the present.

However, with the age of discovery, ships flying the flags of Portugal, Holland, and Britain sailed around Africa, gaining control of trade routes to southern and eastern Asia. Middle East arts and crafts declined and, their markets lost, continued only at a survival level. By the eighteenth century, the great caravans along the Silk Road between the Islamic world and China were only a memory.

Renewed European interest in the Middle East in the nineteenth century revived some aspects of the region's economic activity—carpet making, metalworking, and woodworking. Steamships carried far greater loads than had the earlier small sailing vessels, and European investors built railways from ports into interiors under concessionary terms.

COOPERATION AND AID

Arab Economic Coordination

The ideal of Arab unity has always had an economic component, but economic coordination after World War II has been inhibited by recurrent political tensions and conflict. Numerous successive economic agreements have been negotiated, only to become ineffective in reality. As early as 1953, the Arab League sponsored the signing of the Arab Joint Defense and Economic Cooperation Agreement, but the agreement quietly expired after three or four years. The Arab Economic Unity Agreement of 1956 sought economic union among Egypt, Iraq, Jordan, Kuwait, and Syria. It, too, failed. The same countries, minus Kuwait, motivated by desire for pan-Arab cooperation, formed the Arab Common Market in 1964, but with no new members the effort was officially abandoned in 1971. The fate of these examples is typical of that of other efforts that did not succeed because members were unwilling to subsume national interests to regional ones.[2] Similar friction has hindered regionwide cooperation, and Israel, Iran, and Turkey are excluded from Arab groupings.

One subregional effort has achieved some success: the Cooperation Council of the Arab States of the Gulf, better known as the Gulf Cooperation Council (GCC), created in 1981. The GCC is more than an economic agency, although it has an effective economic component (see Chap. 8). A broader business-oriented grouping intended to link all Middle East states, including Israel, with other countries, the Middle East/North Africa Economic Conference was initiated in 1994 under the auspices of the World Economic Forum, but it has languished in tandem with the peace process.

Economic Aid

A further influence on Middle East economic patterns is that of direct transfers of capital into and within the region. Huge amounts of petrodollars flowed to the exporters after 1972 and were used for development projects by them, as well as for aid to non-oil states.

Going back sixty years, industrialized states have made large grants and loans to many governments in the Middle East. The United States has been the biggest source, primarily to Israel, Turkey, Egypt, and Jordan; however, virtually every country in the region—other than the Gulf amirates—received U.S. aid at some point since the 1940s, including Iran, Iraq, and Saudi Arabia. Israel received—and continues to receive—by far the greatest amounts, up to one-third of all U.S. foreign aid at times, along with generous indirect grants and loans of many types. Most Western European countries—especially Britain, Germany, and France, but also some of the smaller states—have also granted and lent large amounts to regional countries. The Soviet Union gave its client states massive assistance, primarily military but also economic—for example, for major dams in Egypt and Syria. Japan is the leading Asian donor; the People's Republic of China has been active in recent decades.

In addition to bilateral assistance, technical and development aid has also been given to most states through the UN and its agencies; the UN Relief and Works Agency (UNRWA) has funneled large amounts to Palestinian refugees from 1949 to the present. Technical assistance has also gone to the oil states on a reimbursable basis.[3]

Aid from regional donors beginning in the 1960s began a wealth-sharing process; at first, the beneficiaries were poorer Arab states, but within a few years the efforts became global in scope. In 1961, the Kuwait Fund for Arab Economic Development was founded; it had disbursed some $14.4 billion in loans and grants for 760 development projects in 103 countries across the Third World through 2008. Similar funds were created by other oil states—the Abu Dhabi Fund for Arab

Economic Development, the Iraqi Fund for External Development, and the Saudi Fund for Development. Large grants are regularly made by oil states to non-oil states outside the channels of the funds, especially on an emergency basis. Aid to countries assisting the defense of Gulf producers is especially substantial. "Frontline states"—Egypt, Syria, Lebanon, and Jordan—have received billions from the oil producers in the wake of Arab-Israeli conflicts, and Egypt and Syria were rewarded for their participation in the coalition to liberate Kuwait in 2001. Many of the oil-rich rulers, like the late Shaykh Zayid of Abu Dhabi, the sultan of Oman, the amirs of Kuwait and Qatar, and members of the Saudi royal family have donated billions to educational, medical, religious, and developmental institutions in Egypt, Pakistan, Indonesia, and other friendly countries. Multilateral entities from the Islamic Development Bank and the World Bank to the OPEC Fund for International Development, UN-affiliated agencies, and nongovernment charities[4] have also been major recipients.

Kuwait, Saudi Arabia, Qatar, and the UAE paid more than $55 billion of Iraq's wartime expenses during its war with Iran. Kuwait, Saudi Arabia, and the UAE helped defray costs incurred by coalition members (including the United States) in their rollback of the Iraqis in 1991; reimbursements totaled $84 billion, and material support was another $51 billion. They also contributed billions for losses to Turkey, Jordan, and Egypt because of the UN sanctions and coalition actions.[5]

REGIONAL DEVELOPMENT PROBLEMS

Remarkable though it has been, regional development has been hindered by several fundamental problems in addition to the lack of effective coordination and the originally inadequate infrastructure. Shortages of skilled labor required importation of millions of technicians and ordinary workers, and then required time to train indigenous workers and managers to replace expatriates. The original dependence of the Gulf oil states on northwestern Europeans and Americans for oil exploration and development evolved into a relationship involving oil supplies, dollar payments, technological needs, and petrodollar recycling. Nearly everywhere, the shortage of water—and in places, an actual lack of water—has had a serious negative impact on the pattern of economic development.

Therefore, despite its energy resources, the Middle East faced serious problems in the first quarter century of moving toward economic development, yet achieved admirable results. Nevertheless, it still faces difficulties in achieving comprehensive economic development. Progress in certain sectors has been dramatic, but gaining long-term self-sufficiency in balanced economies is more challenging.

Labor and Skills

An insufficient pool of skilled labor initially was the most serious single development deterrent in much of the Middle East, especially in the Gulf states, and the steps taken to meet labor demands have had profound spatial implications. For much of the last half of the twentieth century, there was a sharp contrast in labor availability between the northwestern and southeastern parts of the region. The northwest had a labor surplus and a modest supply of technical and managerial people. By contrast, the Gulf area possessed a sparse and primarily pastoral and fishing population, inadequate in number and unequipped with the skills necessary to meet the needs of a booming oil economy.

Labor requirements in the Gulf states were both qualitative and quantitative. Unskilled workers from nearby areas were available in almost unlimited numbers, but engineers, technicians, managers, and similar professionals were in short supply. As the pace of development increased during the 1960s and

1970s, workers at all levels came from Jordan, Egypt, and Lebanon to Saudi Arabia and the smaller Gulf states. Yemenis filled thousands of unskilled jobs in Saudi Arabia, and Indians, Pakistanis, and Baluch poured into the lower Gulf. By the 2000s, about 11 million migrant workers in Saudi Arabia and the Gulf amirates constituted from one- to two-thirds of the labor force.

Cultural affiliations were important, since Arabic speakers and Muslims tended to adapt most easily in the Gulf. Initially, Pakistanis and Indian Muslims often adjusted more readily than cosmopolitan Lebanese. In addition, technical and managerial positions generally required fluency in English, the lingua franca of the oil industry. As a consequence, the workforce was transformed in size and composition throughout the Gulf within a few years, with a higher percentage of the expatriate workers being Filipinos, Thais, Sri Lankans, and South Koreans. With its almost insatiable demand for additional labor, Saudi Arabia in the late 2000s still had an estimated 5.5 million expatriate workers.

The situation of Palestinian workers in the Gulf is a special one. The demand for skilled workers and professionals was rapidly escalating in Kuwait just when the Palestinian Arabs were forced to leave their homeland. Many moved to Kuwait, and by 1986 the number of Palestinians/Jordanians there had climbed to more than 400,000. In Kuwait, as was true to even a greater extent in Jordan, the Palestinians helped create the economy that absorbed them. However, Kuwait later became concerned about the growing political power of the Palestinians and discouraged further Palestinian immigration. During the Iraqi occupation of Kuwait from August 1990 to February 1991, many Palestinians, among others, evacuated their homes and went elsewhere for the duration of the conflict. When Palestinian leaders either approved Saddam Husayn's invasion or refused to condemn it, Kuwait

was deeply offended, and many of the Palestinians (and other expatriate evacuees) were neither invited back nor permitted to return; indeed, some of the Palestinians who had stayed were accused of collaboration with the enemy. By the late 2000s, the Palestinian population of Kuwait was, although not accurately known, estimated to be about 40,000,[6] less than 10 percent of the number before August 1990. More South Asians were brought in to replace departed Arabs.

The migration of hundreds of thousands of people to the Gulf area exerted a profound effect on the workforce in both the supplying and the receiving countries. For example, more than 20 percent of the population of North Yemen was working in Saudi Arabia during the 1970s and early 1980s. Then some 800,000 were expelled during the Gulf crisis of 1990–1991 because of Saudi anger over Yemen having taken an anticoalition stance. Their lost remittances plunged Yemen into even deeper poverty.

The working and living conditions of foreign workers vary from semiluxury for European and American bankers and Ph.D.'s[7] to penury and close to semislavery for unskilled Somalis or Bangladeshis.[8] The latter are often victimized by both the migration or employment agencies that placed them in jobs[9] and unscrupulous employers who confiscate their passports and cheat them of their earnings. Conditions are worse in some countries than in others, but even in more open societies like Jordan, Lebanon, and Israel exploitative treatment is not uncommon. Israel became dependent on "guest workers" from the mid-1990s, to replace Palestinians especially after the onset of the first intifadah. As many as 300,000—half of them illegal—have been in the country at various times, working in agriculture and construction and as servants and caregivers, and coming from countries ranging from Bolivia to Bulgaria to the Philippines. Cases of abuse have been better documented there because of the presence of human rights nongovernmental organizations and investigative journalists.[10]

Remittances

One measure of the magnitude of the labor migration to the Gulf oil states is the amount of money the migrant workers sent back to their home countries. For example, in 1981, Jordanians working outside their own country sent back more than $1.23 billion, which was equal to 28 percent of the kingdom's GDP, 39 percent of its imports, and 168 percent of its exports. Similarly, in 1982, Egyptians remitted $1.87 billion, which nearly doubled by 1997 to $3.4 billion. Illustrative of the increase in Pakistani workers in the Gulf is the fact that remittances to Pakistan totaled $339 million in 1974–1975 and $2 billion in 1980–1981, a sixfold increase in six years. Remittances to North Yemen also exceeded $2 billion annually in the early 1980s.

When recession hit the oil states in the mid-1980s, many expatriates lost their jobs and returned home; others who remained had lower incomes and sent smaller remittances home. This reduction in income inevitably created economic difficulties for the labor-supplying countries. Even after the partial recovery in the late 1980s, the demand for labor in the Gulf did not return to its earlier levels, since the peak of the construction boom had passed. Since the late 1980s, the service sector has provided many expatriate jobs—for example, for filling the large number of hotel and restaurant positions.

Even more serious than the recession were the economic blows that struck many expatriates as direct and indirect results of the Iraqi invasion of Kuwait. Hundreds of thousands of workers and professionals found themselves without jobs and no longer welcome in their adopted lands, and they were forced to return to depressed economic conditions in their home countries—Jordan, Lebanon, Egypt, and Yemen. Many also lost savings and other assets they had held in Kuwait. By the late 1990s, the Gulf labor market had recovered, and many expatriates were again at work. In the 2000s, the situation was much the same—despite many countries replacing expatriates with indigenous workers. However, when Dubai's economy crashed in 2008, the impact on foreign workers was considerable.[11]

Remittances have become the largest source of capital flows in the Middle East.[12] Jordanian expatriates sent home $3.7 billion officially and perhaps another $3 billion unofficially in 2008. The same degree of remittance growth was realized by Egypt and Pakistan—$9.5 billion and $7.0 billion in 2008, respectively; Yemen, however, was less fortunate, at least as far as officially reported remittances were concerned—only $1.4 billion in 2008[13]—reflecting continuing problems with Saudi Arabia, previously the major employers of unskilled Yemeni workers.[14]

PATTERNS OF INDUSTRY

Factors of Industrial Location

The region's patterns of manufacturing are determined by the classic geographical factors of raw materials, labor supply, transportation, market, and power (energy), along with such intangibles as financial incentives, momentum, tradition, and technology. Concentrations of the greatest number of factors attract the largest ensembles of manufacturing.

Distribution of Centers

Despite the remarkable economic development since 1950, most of the region's industrial complexes other than petroleum processing tend to be relatively modest on a world scale. Originally serving domestic requirements, some manufacturing centers now include plants that export most of their output. Many more textile mills (in Turkey, Egypt, and Israel), clothing factories (not only in the Levant but even in the UAE),

TABLE 7.1 Economically Active Population: Total and Sector Distribution

		1	2	3	4	5	6	7	8
		Econ. Active Population		*Percentage of Economically Active Population in Selected Sectors*					
Country and Year of Data		Total No. in 1,000s	% Total Population	Ag, For, Fishing	Mfg, Mng, Qg	Construc- tion	Trnsp, Comm	Trade, Htl, Rt	Servs, Other
Bahrain	2004	308	47.4	1.5	18.0	8.6	4.5	15.5	26.9
Cyprus[a]	2006	341	49.6	5.0	11.7	10.2	5.1	25.8	23.5
Egypt	2006	19,253	30.0	24.8	12.0	6.7	5.7	13.5	24.7
Iran	2006	16,027	26.7	20.9	17.6	10.3	6.1	12.0	21.1
Iraq	2006	4,757	24.8	11.6	10.6	11.2	6.4	6.8	52.3
Israel	2006	2,610	39.0	1.6	15.2	4.9	5.8	15.6	37.6
Jordan	2006	1,293	23.6	3.0	13.1	5.5	8.5	17.3	33.9
Kuwait	2006	1,364	56.4	1.6	7.3	7.9	3.2	16.1	59.5
Lebanon	2005	1,362	34.0	19.1	18.9	6.2	7.0	16.5	28.8
Oman	2007	737	31.5	7.9	11.4	16.0	3.8	14.8	20.6
Qatar	2006	280	53.7	2.2	18.3	18.4	3.1	13.2	28.2
S. Arabia	2007	7,437	32.8	7.8	11.6	14.6	4.1	14.3	30.2
Syria	2006	5,460	31.9	26.8	12.1	11.6	4.9	13.3	30.3
Turkey	2007	23,641	33.2	30.3	16.3	4.1	4.3	17.1	19.8
UAE	2006	2,191	54.2	7.7	16.6	16.5	6.1	24.1	13.6
Yemen	2006	4,091	24.2	48.0	4.0	5.8	3.0	10.7	19.1
Gaza	—	254	19.0	11.7	6.2	7.0	3.5	11.4	60.2
W. Bank	—	555	23.6	11.6	9.5	9.8	4.3	14.9	39.2
TOTAL/AVG.		91,961	35.3	13.5	12.8	9.7	5.0	15.2	31.6
U.K.	2003	29,595	49.7	1.4	12.8	7.0	6.0	23.2	30.5
Venezuela	2002	11,674	46.4	8.2	10.8	6.7	6.1	22.4	41.5

Sectors include agriculture, forestry, fishing (3); manufacturing, mining, quarrying (4); construction (5); transportation, communications (6); trade, hotels, restaurants (7); and services and other (8). Data among countries are difficult to compare because of varying dates of data. [a]Cyprus data for Republic of Cyprus (Southern Cyprus) only. Corresponding data for United Kingdom and Venezuela given for comparison. (*Source: Britannica World Data, 2009* [with permission].)

wineries (in the Levant and Cyprus), and similar operations cater to foreign markets. Israel is especially export oriented, from diamond cutting and armaments to high-tech electronics and software. Similarly, petrochemical plants in the oil states market output globally.

Although data reporting lags behind development, some comparisons are useful: In absolute terms—ignoring per capita output—Turkey in the 2000s is by far the leading Middle East country in terms of total value added by manufacturing, followed by Israel, Iran, Saudi Arabia, the UAE, and Egypt. Iraq was formerly a ranking industrial state but, after losing many of its factories and much of its

industrial organization in three wars, is now struggling to regain its footing.

Turkey has the largest industrial workforce (3.85 million), followed by Iran (2.82 million) and Egypt (2.31 million)—in each case, from 12 to 18 percent of the workforce (Table 7.1). Turkey and Iran have the largest number of producing enterprises, many of them small. Manufacturing contributes 32 percent of GDP in Egypt, 18 percent Turkey, 13 percent in Israel, and 11 percent in Iran.

Certain industries—including such basic production as processed foods and beverages, construction materials, and clothing—are widespread and are found in every country and in many parts of the larger countries. Less widespread but nevertheless found virtually everywhere are textiles, leather, wood products, cement, printing, cigarettes, metalworking, ceramics, and jewelry. Less common are glass, plastics, chemicals, tools, small appliances, and irrigation pipe and sprinklers. States with significant oil and gas production have evolved an ensemble of industries using hydrocarbons as feedstock or fuel—oil refineries, water distillation plants, electricity generating, petrochemical plants, fertilizer factories, and, in two Gulf states, such energy-dependent operations as aluminum smelters. Leading natural gas producers are expanding gas-processing facilities to meet growing world demand for LNG.

Only in the most industrialized countries are there industries making or assembling motor vehicles, ships, machine tools, major appliances, electronic items, and armaments. Only in Israel, Egypt, and Turkey is there aircraft production, and Israel alone has diamond cutting. Few countries engage in basic research and development to any noteworthy extent, and Israel, which ranks on the world scale, is far in the lead in information technology, developing and producing world-class computer chips and electronic components. During the mid-1990s, UN inspection teams found that Iraq had developed research programs beyond anything that had been expected; however, its industrial complex was brought to a virtual standstill in 2003, except for basic oil processing; recovery has been slow. Turkey, Egypt, Iran, Saudi Arabia, and others are steadily increasing research efforts.

Seven economic zones may be geographically differentiated within the area (Map 7.1; see also Table 7.1). They form a rough arc following the trend of the Fertile Crescent but extending beyond and below it, and each area is separately examined in the country chapters.

1. Nile Delta.   Egypt's manufacturing sector is one of the two earliest and most diversified in the regions and comprises the area bounded by Alexandria-Cairo-Suez–Port Said–Alexandria. Greater Cairo and Alexandria are the most important locales, along with the textile towns in the delta. Served by a thick road and railway net and with one of the world's highest population densities, the area calls upon creative traditions of the ancient, medieval, and modern ages. Besides prized handcrafted items, products range from processed foods and textiles to aluminum, iron and steel, metal products, motor vehicles, fertilizers, refined petroleum products, furniture, light armaments, and helicopter assembly.

2. Levant.   Northeast of the first zone is a grouping of five neighboring but unconnected manufacturing concentrations in the four Levant states and Cyprus.

2A. Israel.   The dense concentration in Israel makes up the most nationally balanced and systematized range of manufacturing facilities in the region. One reason for this variety is that Israel was until the 1990s basically isolated, with few materials moving into or out of it on the landward side, which encouraged autarky. Moreover, Israel has many inventive and technologically advanced people, like technically trained immigrants from the FSU, Europe, and the United States. With considerable support from the United States, Israel has developed leading research laboratories and built a sophisticated military establishment that stimulates and feeds a large high-tech industrial complex. This, in turn, supports a dense population at a high standard of living. Most types of manufacturing are found in Israel, from food processing to one of the world's largest armaments industries (including a controversial nuclear facility at Dimona). Software development was stressed during the 1990s, and now software production has rocketed to a leading position in manufacturing and exports. The coastal conurbation of Greater Tel Aviv and Haifa (Fig. 7.1) comprises the main indus-

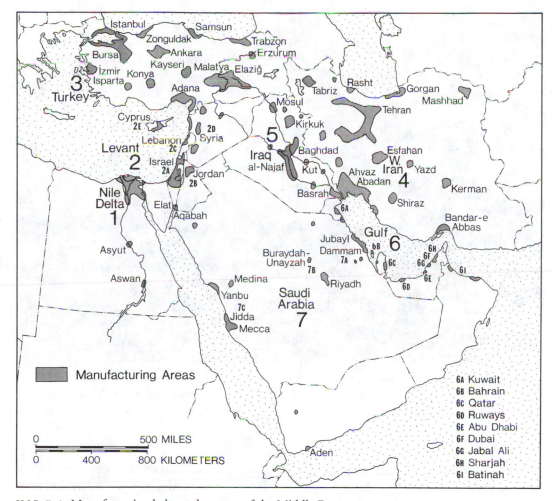

MAP 7.1 Manufacturing belts and centers of the Middle East.

trial concentrations, but manufacturing is widely dispersed for both development and security reasons. Many specialty factories—electronics plants, for example—operate in kibbutzim and other smaller settlements.

2B. Jordan. The industrial area of Jordan has only a modest range of light manufacturing facilities concentrated primarily in the Amman-Zarqa-Irbid triangle in the northwestern part of the country. Aqaba, the only port, is expanding chemical production. Growth rates have been high since 1960, but Jordan started from a very low industrial base. As one benefit Jordan received as a

"peace dividend" for signing a treaty with Israel in 1994, several modest Qualifying Industrial Zones (QIZs) have been set up in northwestern Jordan. Some plants in the QIZs are partly Israeli financed, and their products include Israeli-made content that "qualify" them for duty-free entry into the United States.

2C. Lebanon. Traditionally, Lebanese manufacturing has been consumer oriented, often related to the retail trade, with most activity concentrated in Beirut, Tripoli, and Sidon. As in Egypt and Syria, handcrafted articles are produced in great variety, from

FIGURE 7.1 Main Haifa industrial area, just north of the city of Haifa, Israel, seen from Mount Carmel. The area specializes in petroleum refining and chemical production but makes a broad spectrum of products.

inlaid wood furniture to jewelry. Manufactured products include textiles, clothing, leather items, paints, chemicals, cement, glassware (a tradition dating to Phoenician times), cigarettes (a state monopoly), and raw steel and other metal products. Lebanon's open economy attracted huge amounts of investment capital before 1975, but industrial production dropped sharply with the outbreak of conflict and then limped along. Recovery has been slow, but by the late 2000s there were many encouraging signs.

2D. Syria.   Damascus has been famous for more than 1,200 years for its handcrafted metals (damascene), textiles (damask), inlaid woods, and glass. Since the 1960s, more factory-made goods have been produced on a modest scale: machine-made textiles, clothing, appliances, machinery, cement, chemi-

cals, cigarettes, and similar items. The ancient trade center of Aleppo has modern industry. Expanding petroleum production stimulated industrial growth during the 1980s and 1990s. Homs and Hamah, on the Damascus-Aleppo axis; the coastal centers of Latakia, Baniyas, and Tartus; and the developing centers of Raqqah and Dayr al-Zawr in the Euphrates Valley are also worth noting. A period of more than four decades of Baathi rule has favored large-scale state enterprises over the private sector.

2E. Cyprus.   The main producing areas are around Nicosia and on the south coast in Limassol and Larnaca. Despite the loss of northern Cyprus after 1974, the republic's vitality encouraged the emergence or expansion of plants producing cigarettes, processed foodstuffs, wine, paper products, clothing, shoes, textiles, and cement. The manufacturing sector, like the rest of the economy of the island, has faced the problem of uncertainty in both the south and north, but especially in the north. Cyprus is a member of the EU, giving it access to a market of almost 500 million consumers, and since 2008 uses the euro, the common currency of sixteen EU members.

3. Turkey. Endowed with many elements conducive to industrial development, Turkey's reported total value added by manufacturing equals those of all of this study's countries combined, Israel excepted. Food processing is by far the most important activity and is on a much greater scale than elsewhere in the region. Textiles, leather goods, tobacco products, wood and paper products, ceramics, appliances, chemicals, petroleum products, electronic items, pharmaceuticals, heavy and light machinery, assembled automobiles, railway equipment, farm tractors, small ships, and handmade and machine-made rugs are among its products. Manufacturing is widespread, and most larger cities have several factories. Major centers are Istanbul, Izmir, Zonguldak, Ankara, Kırıkkale, Divriği, Mersin, Adana, and Erzurum, plus the others shown on Map 7.1. Turkey and the EU are in a customs union, considerably enlarging the market available to its manufacturers.

4. Western Iran. Like Turkey, Iran has a large population, workforce, and domestic market, as well as numerous raw materials and other advantages for manufacturing. Unlike Turkey, Iran also has huge oil resources. The two lead the region in numbers of industrial workers and manufacturing plants. With a creative, inventive, and energetic core population, Iran has a long and distinguished history of manufacturing, traditionally producing rugs, textiles, handcrafted metalwares, jewelry, ceramics (especially tiles), and similar items. Its highly diversified modern industrial products—

many made in small five- to ten-employee shops—include fabricated metals (utilitarian wrought iron as well as traditional copper and brass, as shown in Fig. 19.5), jewelry, a wide range of food products, plain and art textiles and leather goods, hand-knotted rugs, and petroleum products and chemicals.

Major areas include Tehran, the Ahvaz-Abadan–Bandar-e Khomeini triangle at the head of the Gulf, Kharg Island, Shiraz, Sar Cheshmeh, Arak, Esfahan, Tabriz, and Gorgan. By the time of the revolution in 1979, Iran had clearly ranked with the moderately large industrial producers. However, the Iran-Iraq War damaged many of its plants, and the Islamist regime's policies retarded broader industrial development and subjected it to international sanctions. Its advanced and controversial nuclear program was of great international concern in the late 2000s (see Chap. 19).

5. Iraq. The amount and variety of manufacturing in Iraq increased steadily after a modest start in the mid-1950s and by the late 1980s had made impressive advances. However, much effort was devoted to the military—indeed, more so than was realized at the time. As one result, coalition bombing targeted and heavily damaged much of its industrial complex in 1991, and the complex was closely inspected by UN technicians for several years after. Many of Iraq's remaining factories—excluding most of the petroleum-related plants—were destroyed or damaged during the American preinvasion bombings in March 2003 or during the ground operations after the invasion. A major rationale given for the attack was that Saddam Husayn's industries produced weapons of mass destruction, although neither the plants nor the weapons were subsequently found. Like much of the rest of the economy, post-2003 industrial recovery has been uneven, with signs of progress at the end of the decade.

FIGURE 7.2 Interior view of one of the several large textile mills in Iraq. The city of Mosul long produced lightweight cotton textiles that became known as muslin. (Nik Wheeler, Saudi Aramco World, SANDIA)

The pattern of its industrial operations and potential persists: Baghdad is the center of a sprawling modern industrial zone, which proved much more developed and sophisticated than expected when UN inspectors checked it in 1991. Government planning had spread facilities to Mosul (Fig. 7.2) and Kirkuk in the north and to Basrah and al-Zubayr in the south. Southern areas were the most heavily damaged in 1980–1988 and 1991, and reconstruction there had proceeded only slowly by 2003. Petrochemicals and other petroleum-related products normally make up a considerable share of the country's industrial output, but Baathi military ambitions also mandated a large and varied armaments industry, now mostly in ruins. Many smaller establishments produce processed foods and beverages, cigarettes, textiles (muslin from Mosul), clothing, shoes, furniture, and metal goods. Traditional handcrafts include silversmithing, copper- and brasswares, textiles, and rug making.

6. Gulf. The Gulf industrial zone, including Oman—but excluding Saudi Arabia, Iraq, and Iran—might be divided into subzones based partly on national boundaries, as was the case with the Levant. Facilities have a substantial degree of similarity and have developed almost entirely since the 1960s, with petro-development stimulating dramatic growth. The core economic activity in every subcenter of the zone is petroleum production and processing, and the main satellite facilities produce related products—petrochemicals, fertilizers, liquefied natural gas derivatives, secondary sulfur, plastics, and a range of refinery products.

However, there is an impressive array of manufacturing in parts of the area; further diversification is under way, with emphasis

FIGURE 7.3 Rusayl Industrial Area on the Batinah Coast of Oman, west of Muscat. The success of this project prompted Oman to develop similar industrial areas in other locations.

on ready-made clothing (see Chap. 15). Because construction has been prominent in the economy since the mid-1950s, construction materials are a major industry. It includes cement, cement blocks, bricks, steel reinforcing rods, and metal frames for windows and doors. Dhow building is still carried on in traditional centers: Kuwait, Bahrain, Ajman, and Ras al-Khaymah. Most larger new industries are capital intensive as well as large energy users.

Major subcenters are (6A) the Kuwait Bay and Gulf coast area, with refineries and petrochemical plants; (6B) northeastern Bahrain, with locational advantages and the earliest industrial development, including the Sitra refinery; (6C) east-central Qatar, with a booming concentration of petro-processing, around Musayid and Doha; (6D–6H) five UAE industrial developments of (6D) al-Ruways near the Jabal Dhanna terminal, (6E)

Abu Dhabi Island with light production, (6F) Dubai City with a wide range of small plants producing consumer goods, (6G) Jabal Ali—a major and still expanding and diversifying heavy industrial center south of Dubai, and (6H) Sharjah with modest manufacturing establishments; and finally (6I) the Batinah coast of Oman, which produced only a few handcrafted articles until the mid-1960s but now includes copper-related plants near Suhar and an impressive industrial estate at Rusayl, west of Muscat (Fig. 7.3). An additional industrial park is in operation in Salalah, where an expanding port is a manufacturing core.

7. Saudi Triad: Al-Hasa, Najd, Hijaz. From a pre-1935 manufacturing production level below that of any other major country in the Middle East, Saudi Arabia by the 1990s had developed a vigorous and diversified range of production. Latest available data on value added by manufacturing show Saudi Arabia ranking fourth in the region, after Turkey, Israel, and Iran. Initially, development focused almost entirely on oil in the Eastern Province, but there are now diversified industries not only in the east but also in both mid-Arabia and the west. Developments include an industrial city and port on each side of the peninsula—Jubayl on the Gulf and Yanbu on the Red Sea. Thus, it now has three main producing centers: (7A) on the Gulf coast along the Jubayl-Dammam-al-Khobar axis, with outliers in the Hofuf-Abqaiq area; (7B) the two centers of Qasim and Riyadh in Najd; and (7C) the Jiddah-Mecca area in the Hijaz, with an outlier in Yanbu.

TRANSPORTATION

Roads were of limited significance before World War I because of centuries of preference for maritime trade whenever possible and transport via camel caravans when land movement was necessary. In 1859–1863, a French company built a 69-mi/111-km road from the Beirut port to Damascus, and an additional 258 mi/415 km of roads had been built in Lebanon by 1900. At the onset of the twentieth century, the French, British, Germans, and—in Iran—Russians were involved in building roads, railroads, and ports in and around the region, mostly under concessionary terms. The Dutch, Portuguese, and British successively controlled the main sealanes after the sixteenth century, and British steamships played a major role in the Gulf until World War II.

Consequently, the mandates and recently independent states of the region had a basic transportation net by the late 1920s that was appreciably improved by the end of World War II. However, it was soon apparent that the net was inadequate for modern development; within the peninsula, there was no semblance of sufficiency. Fortunately, the huge petrodollar influx permitted transformation of the regional communications network—roads, seaports, airports, pipelines, and, more recently, railways.

Two aspects of regional communications patterns are worth noting. First, the region has "islands," or cores of development, separated by uninhabited or sparsely populated deserts, mountain masses, or seas. Before the mid-nineteenth century, these were linked by land caravans or by small vessels, with flexible schedules and capacities and minimum costs. Railway and road nets were not required, nor would they have been profitable, since there was little cargo traffic between the centers. Even today, the two main rail nets, in Turkey and Iran, and two secondary ones, in Egypt and Iraq, are primarily internal, with limited international movement of freight or passengers; in the late 2000s some changes in this regard were under way. However, the three most extensive road nets, in Turkey, Saudi Arabia, and Iran, are increasingly linked with the outside, and both cargo and passengers cross frontiers along roads in steadily growing numbers. In peaceful periods, the main highway border crossings, especially on weekends and holidays, are crowded—between Lebanon and Syria, Syria and Jordan, Turkey and Bulgaria, Turkey and Iran, Kuwait and Iraq, and Saudi Arabia and Bahrain.

Second, airways in parts of the Middle East developed to a significant level while railroads lagged, and airlines serve the "island" pattern of the region's urban centers very well. Aircraft overfly and thereby ignore both the physical-environmental hazards and the political perils—the expanses of desert, sea, and mountains when flying Istanbul-Dubai, Beirut-Tehran, or Cairo-Sana, and the political obstacles of a sanctioned Iraq during the 1990s. Where airlines are locally unavailable or inadequate, the road net serves most purposes. Railways are of less regional importance than other available means of trans-

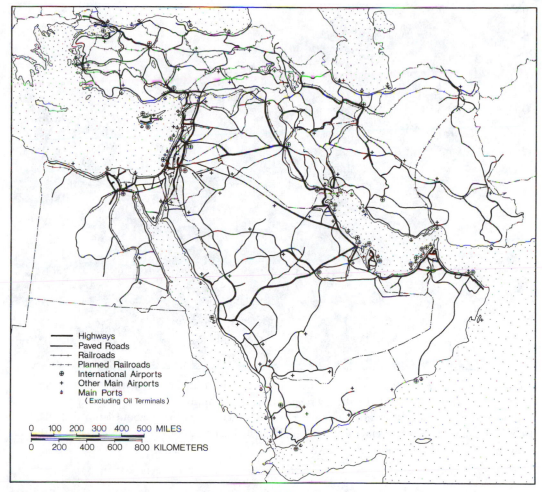

MAP 7.2 Major transportation facilities of the Middle East.

portation (Map 7.2), although this seems likely to change in the coming decade (see "Railways" below).

Highways

Prior to midcentury, most of the road systems in the Middle East were scattered webs around capitals or other primary cities in the Fertile Crescent or in Egypt, Turkey, and Iran. Only a few miles of surfaced roads existed anywhere in the Arabian Peninsula. By the late 2000s, the region had 643,180 mi/1,035,052 km of roads, of which more than three-fourths were paved highways (Fig. 7.4). Barring unexpected

frontier closures, a motorist can now drive on paved roads—mostly first-class highways—from Istanbul over the Bosporus bridges to the Pakistan border via Erzurum, Tabriz, Tehran, and Yazd; or from Istanbul to Aden via Adana, Damascus, Amman, and Jiddah; or turn east at Jiddah and reach Abu Dhabi and Muscat via Riyadh and Dammam. Even Bahrain can now be reached by highway via a causeway opened in 1986 (Fig. 7.5); work on a second one linking it to Qatar was under way in the late 2000s. The planned causeway and bridge across the Strait of Tiran will tie Egyptian roads to Saudi Arabia and the intraregional net.

FIGURE 7.4 Highways old and new. In 1964 in remote areas of the Trucial States in the northern Oman Mountains (*top photo*), the already rugged track (maximum speed, 10 mph/16 kph) degenerated into a rocky streambed in one narrow pass (maximum speed, about 3 mph/5 kph). By 1979 in the same area, a first-class, well-built highway had been built (*bottom photo*)—one of the many blessings of the oil boom in the UAE.

FIGURE 7.5 One of the major highway links in the Middle East: a stretch of open causeway connecting Saudi Arabia and Bahrain, a 15.5-mi/25-km facility opened in 1986 at a cost of more than $1 billion.

The regional network is also linked to the Trans-European Motorway (TEM) through Turkey. When completed, this special integrated, high-grade motorway will run north and south through eastern Europe, from Gdansk on Poland's Baltic coast to Istanbul, then east to Ankara and the Iranian border, about 6,215 mi/10,000 km. Spur roads in Anatolia will extend the main TEM to the borders of Syria and Iraq; 2,235 m/3,600 km of the TEM will be in Turkey.

Israel's extraordinarily dense network of roads is very heavily traveled and has been regularly upgraded, although it is somewhat isolated. Before 1967, there were no connections with the country's neighbors open to the public, although UN and diplomatic personnel could cross in several places, like the famous Mandelbaum Gate in Jerusalem. By 2000, there were moderately traveled cross-border connections with Egypt and Jordan. Virtually 100 percent of Israeli roads are paved.

Cyprus, where driving on the left side of the road is a British legacy, also has a dense road net and an administration that has been divided between north and south since 1974. It has the second-highest ratio of road length to area in the region, behind only the other island state, Bahrain (Table 7.2). Both parts of Cyprus are tied to the Levant's road system by frequent car ferry; the north is also linked the same way directly to the Turkish network. Other ferries transport private cars and trucks, connecting eastern Mediterranean ports like Istanbul, Izmir, and Mersin in Turkey; Latakia, Syria; Beirut and Juniyah in Lebanon; and Alexandria in Egypt. A special truck ferry from Volos in Greece to Tartus in

TABLE 7.2 Transportation: Roads, Railroads, and Merchant Marine

Country	1 Roads: Length in Km	2 % of Roads Paved	3 Km of Roads per Km²	4 Number of Vehicles (all types)	5 Persons per Vehicle	6 RR Track: in Km	7 Airports w/Sched. Flights	8 Merchant Marine 1,000s DWT
Bahrain	3,498	79	4.80	181,849	3.4	—	1	192.5
Cyprus	12,059	65	1.30	343,428	2.4	—	2	36,198.1
Egypt	92,370	81	0.54	1,665,519	37.0	9,525	11	1,685.2
Iran	72,611	92	0.04	1,793,692	24.0	8,565	19	8,345.3
Iraq	45,550	84	0.10	325,664	18.0	580[a]	—	1,578.8
Israel	17,870	100	0.80	1,636,346	3.7	913[a]	7	723.4
Jordan	7,601	100	0.08	293,027	15.0	788	2	113.6
Kuwait	5,720	81	0.32	887,622	2.3	—	1	3,188.5
Lebanon	7,300	85	0.70	1,384,640	2.5	401[b]	1	438.2
Oman	40,116	37	0.13	339,746	6.9	—	6	11.7
Qatar	1,230	90	0.11	190,000	2.9	—	1	744.0
Saudi Arabia	178,946	100	0.08	2,936,000	6.6	1,392[a]	28	1,278.0
Syria	51,967	75	0.26	421,564	37.0	2,711[a]	5	210.4
Turkey	426,914	45	0.44	5,711,096	11.0	8,697	26	7,114.3
UAE	4,080~	100	0.05	257,950	9.6	—	6	1,491.7
Yemen	71,300	9	0.14	531,716	29.0	—	12	13.7
Gaza	—	—	—	45,166	23.0	—	—	—
West Bank	—	—	—	112,380	18.0	—	—	—
TOTAL/AG.	1,039,132	76	—	19,057,405	14.0	33,572	128	63,327.4
U.K.	388,008	100	1.60	25,761,000	2.3	17,156	57	4,355.0
Venezuela	96,200	34	0.41	2,047,000	11.0	768[a]	20	1,355.4

[a]Route length (other railway lengths are for total track length). [b]Little of Lebanon's network is usable. Column 3 is the ratio between the length of roads and the area of each country. Number of vehicles in Column 4 includes automobiles, buses, and trucks. Column 8 is the total of merchant marine ships in thousands of deadweight tons. (*Sources: Britannica World Data*, 2007 [Columns 4, 5, 7, and 8], 2008 [Column 3], and 2009 [Columns 1, 2, and 6] [with permission].)

Syria enables truckers to avoid the long, winding drive through Anatolia.

Predictably, the most densely inhabited areas, if reasonably prosperous, have the densest highway networks, as can be seen in Table 7.2 and Map 7.2. Bahrain, Cyprus, and Israel have the region's densest nets, but these countries are small and absolute road length is limited. Turkey, Saudi Arabia, Egypt, and Iran, in that order, have the greatest total extent of roads.

Some segments of the road net are noteworthy both for their engineering and for their scenic impact. The paved 62-mi/100-km highway from Hudaydah, on Yemen's Red Sea coast, up the steep, rugged escarpment to the capital, Sana, affords magnificent

vistas as it winds past terraced fields and picturesque villages to reach the plateau, 9,000 ft/2,743 m above sea level. Similarly, the highway from Jiddah to Taif offers spectacular views, leaving the heat of the coastal plain and ascending to the cooler height of the Saudi summer capital. The highway from Beirut over the mountains and across the Bekaa toward Damascus is famed for its vistas. Less dramatic with lower elevations, but still interesting, is the drive from Tel Aviv and Jaffa on the Mediterranean to Jerusalem (2,500 ft/762 m) and down the eastern slopes to the Jordan (1,200 ft/365 m below sea level).

The drive along the coast of southern Turkey offers a scenic beauty similar to that of the French and Italian rivieras, as well as sites of major archaeological interest. Another dramatic mountain drive begins in Tehran and proceeds over the Elburz Mountains, at 9,000 ft/2,745 m, to Chalus on the Caspian Sea shore, 80 ft/24 m below sea level. Spectacular scenery also characterizes two roads into northeastern Iraq, the ones climbing into the Ruwanduz Gorge from Irbil and into the Sulaymaniyah area from Kirkuk (see Fig. 13.3). With almost no change in elevation, the drive between Cairo and Alexandria on the Delta Road, through the villages and green landscape of the irrigated delta, provides an interesting contrast to the other Cairo-Alexandria link, the Desert Road.

The region's road net is rapidly achieving maturity. All major cities and towns are now connected, and the need in the twenty-first century is to integrate more of the villages, to construct shorter routes between some major cities, to make dual highways of standard roads in some high-traffic areas, and to continue to densify the net. In Table 7.2, data on all types of vehicles (Col. 4) and persons per vehicle (Col. 5) are revealing in several ways: They may be indicative of a country's standard of living according to income per capita; however, because they include all types of vehicles, they may also suggest the usage level of mass transportation (number of buses) and the degree of automotive transport (number of trucks). The entire population of nine countries could be transported by available vehicles at one time. Kuwait has the smallest number of persons per vehicle (2.3), and Cyprus, Lebanon, Qatar, Bahrain, and Israel have fewer than 4. These six have smaller areas and populations, but they are either oil states (like Kuwait) or have more advanced industrialized economies (like Israel). Syria and Yemen have appreciably more trucks and buses than passenger cars, and Saudi Arabia has equal numbers of cars and heavy vehicles. With the oil industry's requirements and the kingdom's vast expanse, large numbers of heavy trucks are needed.

Railways

Economics did not justify the construction of extensive rail nets in the region during the heyday of railway building elsewhere, and development from the 1960s onward employed the greater flexibility of highways and airways. As in many other areas with numerous long-distance travelers, passenger traffic has been mostly by air, and since most cargo could be shipped by truck, cargo aircraft, ships, or—in the case of petroleum and petroleum products—pipelines, any appreciable expansion of rail nets seemed unlikely and, indeed, unnecessary. However, with the explosive development of the petroleum-exporting Arabian Peninsula states after the 1970s, planning turned toward railway transportation.

In 2009, the total length of railway lines in the Middle East was 20,862 mi/33,572 km, less than 3 percent of the total mileage of paved roads. The region's average 0.0046 km of rail line per square kilometer of area compares with Australia's ratio and roughly the same amount of territory. By contrast, Britain, somewhat smaller than Oman, has 10,563 mi/17,156 km of rails, nearly half of the total Middle East rail length, and with 0.07 km of railway per square kilometer of area.

Map 7.2 shows that the densest net is in Turkey, with nearly one-third of the region's total. Under the Bosporus, the Marmaray tunnel project links Turkey's European and Anatolian lines. The nets of Egypt and Iran are less extensive, but they are nevertheless heavily traveled (Fig. 7.6) and reasonably adequate in length, particularly in view of their extensive, virtually uninhabited desert areas.

In 2009, the entire Arabian Peninsula, with more than 1.30 mn mi²/3.17 mn km², had only 864 mi/1,390 km of railway, all connecting Riyadh with the Dammam economic complex in eastern Saudi Arabia. But by then, an advanced plan was under way for a Gulf

FIGURE 7.6 Railway station in Tanta, Egypt, in the Nile Delta. Railways are heavily utilized in Egypt, especially by passengers.

Cooperation Council $25 billion joint railway network to be tendered in early 2010: It calls for the GCC states to be linked with a 1,315-mi/2,117-km rail net starting in Kuwait and Saudi Arabia before extension of the lines linking Bahrain, Qatar, and the UAE. Target date for completion is 2017.[15] Saudi Arabia had already begun work on a major rail link connecting Riyadh to the Jordan border (and on to Europe) that will begin operations in 2010; this will tie into two lines in the preconstruction phase—one crossing the peninsula from the Red Sea to Riyadh (with a spur linking Mecca to Medina) and the other tying into the GCC net and running north from Dammam to the Kuwait border. In 2010, Kuwait was close to beginning construction of a line running from the Iraqi border to the Saudi border. Urban rail systems are also part of recent activity; Dubai's opened in 2009, and networks for Kuwait City and Mecca are planned;

Cairo, Istanbul, Ankara, Bursa, Izmir, and Tehran already have metros.

Certain rail lines in the Middle East are renowned historically: the Orient Express from France, which technically terminated in Istanbul but actually continued to Konya and Aleppo on a reduced scale (in another change with the times, the famed rail service was officially discontinued in 2009);[16] the Alexandria-Cairo-Luxor-Aswan line, part of the never-completed Cape-to-Cairo railway; the line built in Palestine in 1892 to transport pilgrims from Jaffa to Jerusalem (being replaced in 2010 by a new high-speed intercity line); the Hijaz Railway from Damascus to Medina, which was built by the Ottomans at the beginning of the twentieth century for Muslim pilgrims traveling to Mecca but was destroyed south of Maan by the Arab Revolt in 1916–1917;[17] and the route through the scenic Dez River gorge through the Zagros Mountains in southwestern Iran.

Airways and Airfields

The Middle East's location, astride the land, sea, and air routes crossing the tricontinental hub, led to the establishment of a few transit airports prior to World War II. Rapid petroleum development stimulated demand for air service and airports from the early 1950s, and by the early 1990s the Middle East possessed an excellent pattern of airports (see Map 7.2), including not only the world's largest but some of the world's technologically best equipped. In 2009, Dubai's airport was the seventeenth busiest in the world in terms of passenger traffic.[18] Others, like Jiddah, Istanbul, Cairo, Tehran, and Lod (Tel Aviv), are regularly in the top fifty airports outside the United States in passenger numbers.[19]

After normal air traffic resumed following the attacks of 9/11, "explosive growth" took place in the region, and it became the "world's hottest air transport market."[20] Especially in the Gulf region, carriers and airports underwent billion-dollar expansions. Dubai's sumptuous new airport terminal served 37.4 million passengers in 2008, making it the world's twentieth busiest that year, and has received top ratings for passenger satisfaction. Istanbul, Antalya, Jeddah, and Cairo were also among the hundred airports serving the most passengers globally. Among several other openings, Tehran inaugurated a new airport in 2004, and Qatar is building a facility at Doha that will increase passenger capacity from 4.6 million annually to 60 million by 2020. Israel opened an impressive and efficient new terminal at Ben Gurion (Lod) International Airport in 2004.

Every Middle East country has its own national airline, and some states also have private carriers. Half of the fleets have thirty-five or more jet aircraft each, and Emirates Airlines (Dubai), Saudia (Saudi Arabian Airlines), and THY (Turkish Airlines) rank between twentieth and thirtieth among world airlines in available seat-kilometers (ASK, a key index of airline capacity). Petrodollars and aggressive marketing have combined to advance airlines in the Gulf region. Emirates Airlines, inaugurated in Dubai in 1985, now has the largest fleet in the region; Qatar Airways began only in 1994 and has 153 jets on order to add to the 72 it already operates; and, not to be outdone, Abu Dhabi started Etihad Airways in 2003 as the UAE national carrier—with a fleet of 49 planes and 107 more on order.

Turkey's THY, EgyptAir, and IranAir are large, long-established airlines carrying both domestic and international passengers. El Al, the Israeli national airline, though small, is an important link with international destinations, especially the United States. Gulf Air was an early joint carrier for Bahrain, Qatar, the UAE, and Oman; however, after the 1970s, the last three owners sold their stakes and started their own fleets—Oman Air (the region's smallest), Emirates (Dubai) and Etihad (Abu Dhabi), and Qatar Airways. Gulf Air continues to thrive as Bahrain's state airline. Iraqi Airways collapsed after the 1991 sanctions, but it resumed limited operations in 2004. Most of the region's large international airports have regular flights to Asian, European, and North American destinations, and increasing numbers of them—in Turkey especially—are flying to Central Asia.

Water Transportation and Ports

The people of the Middle East have long made use of the region's interpenetrating seas, another effect of the influence of land-water relationships on human patterns. Only the heart of the Arabian Peninsula, more than 200 mi/322 km from a seacoast, is too far from a body of water for easy access. The seas of the region have been sailed for at least 5,000 years, and numerous ruins of ports from earlier days are found in the Gulf and eastern Mediterranean. Sailing reached a golden age during the Abbasid Empire, notably during the eighth to twelfth centuries.[21]

The basic seagoing craft has long been some version of the ship popularly known as the dhow (from Swahili, *daw*), which is locally called by specific terms designating type of hull—*bum* (boom), *sanbuq, ganja*, and others. As they have been for more than 2,000 years, dhows are still equipped with the lateen sail, a triangular fore-and-aft sail hung from a very long yard. This rigging permits the ship to keep very close to the wind. However, more and more of the vessels are equipped with engines, either auxiliary or primary.

Following tradition, many dhows still sail around the shores of the Gulf, along the coasts of Oman and Yemen, down the east African coast, and on the age-old routes to the mouths of the Indus, the Malabar Coast, and Sri Lanka. Small modern ships are increasingly replacing the picturesque dhows; nevertheless, the latter serve a unique function and are still to be seen by the score anchored in "the Creek" in Dubai (see Fig. 15.7) and in other Gulf ports. They are still built in small numbers in the traditional way in Kuwait, Bahrain, most of the coastal towns of the UAE, and Oman.

Despite construction of the Suez Canal in the 1860s, the Middle East did not enter the mainstream of modern shipping until the mid-twentieth century. Turkey was most active in sailing, having regained its maritime lead after its World War I defeat, and as oil production mounted in the Gulf the leading petroleum states entered the tanker market in order to ship their own exports. Iran and Kuwait developed sizable national fleets, and Egypt, Iraq, the UAE, and Saudi Arabia have a modest tonnage in tankers (see Table 7.2). Offering both a neutral flag of convenience and a long shipping tradition, Cyprus ranks first in the Middle East and fourth in the world in registered fleet tonnage.

With the notable exceptions of the Nile, Tigris, and Euphrates, inland waterways—and therefore inland water transportation—are negligible in the region. The Nile was the main way to move people and goods up and down Egypt's linear axis for more than 5,000 years. Construction of modern rail lines and highways has scarcely diminished either the number of picturesque but practical *faluqas*, the typical Nile sailboat, or the tonnage they transport, and the river carries a fair amount of barge traffic as well. More than 300 modern ships can transport thousands of tourist passengers up and down the river daily, enjoying a holiday between Aswan and Luxor or a sojourn on Lake Nasser.

Shallower and more irregular than the Nile, the Tigris and the Euphrates are little used for navigation since they can accommodate only small boats with very limited draft. Picturesque circular rafts (*balams*), which were waterproofed with bitumen and used to float small loads downstream on the Tigris, have long given way to modern land transportation. By contrast, on the Shatt al-Arab, below the confluence of the Tigris and Euphrates, and on the Karun, which joins the Shatt al-Arab at Khorramshahr, there is normally a fair number of medium-large ships of considerable draft. Basrah, Khorramshahr, and Abadan, all fronting on the Shatt al-Arab, are three of the major river ports, not only of the Gulf but also of the Middle East. Though it was Iraq's only port for decades, Basrah had become inadequate by the 1970s.

Many modern Middle East coastal cities have been ports for hundreds or even thousands of years—Istanbul (Byzantium or Constantinople), Beirut (Berytus), Jaffa, Alexandria, Aden, Muscat, Basrah, and several others along the Gulf. Some famed in antiquity now lack sufficient harborage or depth for modern shipping, such as Sidon and Tyre; other ports have silted up and now lie well inland, as is true of Miletus, Ephesus, and Ur, for example.

By virtue of the tonnage represented by the millions of barrels of oil pumped through an export terminal, large oil-shipping ports exceed even the most major dry-cargo ports in tonnage. (An average barrel of petroleum weighs about 300 lb/136 kg, so that only 7.35 bbl weigh 1 mt.) Petroleum shipments pushed Saudi Arabia to first place and Iran to third place in rankings of export tonnage among all countries of the world by 1982, before the drop in the oil-export market. Thus, the relative ranking of Middle East general-cargo ports differs from the ranking of ports that include oil handling. Leading oil-export terminals are Mina al-Ahmadi and Mina Abdullah, Kuwait; Juaymah and Ras Tanura in eastern Saudi Arabia and Yanbu on the Red Sea; Kharg Island (Darius) and Bandar-e Khomeyni, Iran; Musayid (Umm Said), Qatar; Jabal Dhanna, Abu Dhabi; and Mina al-Fahal, Oman. Export terminals in Yemen, Egypt, and Syria handle smaller tonnages.

Although the container and roll-on/roll-off (Ro-Ro) revolutions in maritime shipping forced older ports to make costly modifications, the advanced technology was accommodated in the planning and construction of the more recent Gulf ports. Also, in the Gulf there was space for the huge storage yards needed for containerization and Ro-Ro operations, whereas such space was at a premium in Istanbul, Beirut, and Alexandria, for example. In addition, several Gulf ports have included dry docks in their port facilities—at Dammam, Bahrain, and Dubai, for example; such repair facilities are also in Jiddah on the Red Sea and Alexandria on the Mediterranean.

By the early 1990s, major modern ports were well distributed among the Middle East states, and in the early 2000s several dry-cargo ports handled well over 5 million tons annually: Shuwaykh, Kuwait; Dubai and Khor Fakkan, UAE (Khor Fakkan is on the Indian Ocean), both important for transshipment; Jiddah, the main Saudi Red Sea port; Alexandria and its auxiliary ports, Dikhaylah and Damietta, and Port Said, Egypt; and Haifa, Israel. (See port symbols on Map 7.2.) Ports that lead in the handling of general cargo include: Dammam, the main general-cargo port for the sprawling oil industry and cities of the Eastern Province of Saudi Arabia; Abu Dhabi, UAE; Muscat/Matrah, Oman; Aqabah, Jordan's only port; Ashdod, Israel; Beirut, Lebanon; and Iskenderun in the northeast Mediterranean, Izmir on the Aegean, and Istanbul, Turkey.

Maritime economics and risk insurance have impacted the port geography on the two sides of the Horn of Arabia. As Dubai augmented its role as an entrepôt (Fig. 7.7) and free port in the Gulf, Oman expanded its southern port, Salalah, on the Indian Ocean. Using it saves time and reduces risk, as ships do not have to enter the Gulf (see Chaps. 15 and 16). Piracy in the western Indian Ocean became a serious problem in the 2000s, with vessels ranging from fishing boats to supertankers falling prey to Somalia-based pirates. The greater risks of traversing this area translate into higher insurance fees and often long detours, increasing shipping costs (see Chap. 8).

TRADE

The external trade of Middle East states has expanded exponentially since the 1960s, particularly under the impetus of petroleum; revenue from its sales created a large market for imports of capital and consumer goods (Table 7.3). Intraregional trade has also expanded greatly; non-oil producers import petroleum from their oil-exporting neighbors, and some exchange food products in return. However, quantitatively, only the oil-short industrialized countries can absorb the enormous exports of the Gulf states, and they turn to their industrialized-country customers for the advanced technology items that constitute the bulk of their nonfood imports (Table 7.4). Thus, intraregional trade is constrained by the fact that neighboring states often produce similar crops, consumer items, or energy products.

FIGURE 7.7 Aerial view of burgeoning container port in Dubai, UAE. Goods arrive in Dubai in bulk and are broken down for smaller onward shipments.

Few of the states in the region include even one other Middle East country as one of their three leading customers according to percentage of value of commodities traded. By contrast, four of Lebanon's top five customers are Middle East states. Isolated as it has been from its neighbors, Israel had no overt trade with its neighbors until the 1978 Camp David accords, which provided that Israel could purchase petroleum from Egypt. That arrangement languished, but other Israel-Egypt trade increased gradually after the peace treaty between the two countries took effect. In the late 2000s, Egypt began sizable sales of natural gas to Israel (see Chap. 17).

It should be noted that even though they are relatively limited, exports from the non-oil states to their neighbors normally form a considerable percentage of their total exports. For example, Jordan may produce only modest amounts of vegetables, pharmaceuti-

cals, and clothing, but export markets are significant. Since the 1994 Israel-Jordan peace accord, Israel has been among those markets under reciprocal arrangements. Iraq was particularly important in Jordan's foreign trade, since it was Jordan's main customer before August 1990 and its main oil supplier after 1990 until the 2003 conflict. The 1990–1991 Gulf crisis adversely affected Jordan's trade with Iraq and Saudi Arabia, and Jordan later worked eagerly to restore trade relations with both. Natural gas exports by Egypt, Saudi Arabia, Qatar, and Iran will reorient some trade patterns over time. Many of the exports from Lebanon, Bahrain, and the UAE are, in fact, re-exports. Such trade has particularly made Dubai and Sharjah lively commercial centers.

Not surprisingly, petroleum is by far the dominant feature of Middle East trade. It is the main export of the area to the rest of the

TABLE 7.3 Foreign Trade: Exports and Imports (Values and Selected Products)

Country and Year of Data		TOTAL VALUE Millions $US		RAW MATERIALS (%)				MANUFACTURED GOODS (%)			
		1	2	3	4	5	6	7	8	9	10
				Agric, Etc.		Fuel/Enr		Total		%Mach/TE	
		Exports	Imports	Exp	Imp	Exp	Imp	Exp	Imp	Exp	Imp
Bahrain	2006	11,662.0	8,957.0	0.7	12.8	65.8	37.2	28.9	43.3	0.7	18.9
Cyprus	2006	1,414.9	7,046.0	30.5	13.8	8.1	10.9	59.4	75.0	27.3	29.6
Egypt	2005-06	18,455.1	30,441.0	2.9	18.1	39.2	4.8	55.5	74.4	1.7	24.1
Iran	2005-06	60,013.0	40,969.0	4.1	11.7	86.5	2.7	9.1	84.8	0.7	47.9
Iraq	2007	39,590.0	18,289.0	0.8	31.5	96.8	0.4	2.1	68.1	0.2	30.3
Israel	2006	46,792.0	47,834.0	5.4	7.0	0.4	9.4	58.5	61.4	28.7	31.5
Jordan	2006	5,164.8	11,443.6	14.4	19.3	0.2	16.5	73.5	63.6	10.7	23.0
Kuwait	2006	63,466.0	17,266.2	0.5	17.8	90.6	0.6	8.6	80.6	1.3	39.7
Lebanon[a]	2005	1,879.8	9,339.0	23.7	18.7	0.2	17.7	71.5	62.0	13.9	23.6
Oman	2007	24,684.4	15,974.4	6.2	22.9	80.5	2.8	13.1	72.6	7.7	39.6
Qatar	2006	34,051.0	16,440.0	0.2	12.7	87.1	0.7	12.6	85.1	1.8	46.9
S. Arabia	2007	233,988.5	90,156.8	1.0	17.0	86.0	0.2	12.8	82.3	1.6	43.6
Syria	2006	10,919.0	11,488.0	16.5	20.1	72.2	3.0	10.5	76.4	0.4	24.1
Turkey	2007	107,213.0	170,057.0	11.1	7.6	2.0	16.6	85.7	72.5	26.6	31.1
UAE	2006	142,602.2	86,179.8	7.3	33.6	64.2	0.9	28.5	65.4	8.8	28.5
Yemen	2006	6,586.3	5,219.8	2.5	37.2	96.5	12.0	0.9	50.7	0.3	20.8
TOTAL/AVG.		808,482.0	587,100.6	8.0	18.9	54.8	8.5	33.2	69.9	8.3	31.5
U. K.	2006	444,439.0	606,428.0	6.3	10.4	8.0	4.6	82.3	82.5	44.4	43.6
Venezuela	2006	61,385.0	30,559.0	1.9	14.0	81.4	2.6	15.8	82.9	2.3	43.1

Columns 3 and 4 include animal and vegetable foods, beverages, and industrial agricultural products (tobacco, cotton, and so on). Columns 5 and 6 (Fuels and Energy materials) include mineral fuels (petroleum, natural gas, coal, lignite), lubricants, and related products. Manufactured goods include all classes of manufactured products, including machinery. "% Mach/TE" indicates the percentage of machinery and transportation equipment included in the percentage total of manufactures. [a]Data for Lebanon in Columns 5 and 6 include minerals. Spread of data over several years makes comparisons difficult and risky. (*Source: Britannica World Data*, 2009 [Columns 1 and 2] and 2007 [Columns 3–10] [with permission].)

world; indeed, petroleum and petroleum products constitute at least 85 percent of the primary exports of all the major oil producers and normally 90–95 percent of the exports of Iraq, Kuwait, Yemen, and the UAE. Petroleum even constitutes one-third of the exports of Egypt and more than two-thirds of those of Syria (see Table 7.3).

Among the top two or three non-oil exports are, by percentage, fruits and vegetables (Cyprus, Turkey, Lebanon, Jordan, Syria, Egypt), chemicals (Israel, Saudi Arabia, Qatar, Turkey, Jordan), textiles (Turkey, Syria, Egypt, Israel), and clothing (Cyprus, Turkey, Jordan, Israel). A few of the region's specialty exports include aluminum (Bahrain, UAE),

footwear (Cyprus), and phosphates (Jordan, Israel, Syria, Egypt, Iraq). A unique export from the region is cut diamonds from Israel, with the gems forming 24 percent of the state's exports. Armaments from Israel are a large but not completely known percentage of its exports—another unusual export item from the regional perspective.

As they are around the world, oil and petroleum products are high on the import lists of the region's non-oil states (see Table 7.3). They constitute about 17–20 percent of Turkey's and Jordan's imports but only 10 percent of Israel's. Although crude petroleum, transported through a direct underwater pipeline from Saudi Arabia, accounts for

TABLE 7.4 Directions of Foreign Trade (Export and Import Percentages)

		1	2	3	4	5	6	7	8	9	10
Country and		*Percentage of Exports to*					*Percentage of Imports from*				
Year of Data		EU	USA	Japan	China	Other	EU	USA	Japan	China	Other
Bahrain	2004	—	3.2	—	—	91.8	10.9	—	6.2	—	70.6
Cyprus	2006	39.7	—	—	—	43.4	46.5	—	—	—	24.5
Egypt	2006	17.0	9.0	—	—	49.7	5.0	8.0	—	6.0	40.3
Iran	2005-06	5.7	—	16.9	11.9	41.8	25.9	—	—	5.5	48.3
Iraq	2006	24.0	40.0	—	—	23.5	—	10.8	—	4.6	35.9
Israel	2006	13.8	38.4	—	5.9[a]	29.4	25.9	12.4	—	5.1	29.0
Jordan	2006	—	25.1	—	—	90.5	7.8	4.7	—	10.4	47.1
Kuwait	2006	—	12.0	20.0	—	53.7	11.2	11.9	7.6	7.0	43.4
Lebanon	2005	6.7	—	—	—	66.0	25.8	5.9	—	7.9	35.5
Oman	2007	—	—	—	28.0	73.8	5.3	5.8	15.8	—	53.5
Qatar	2006	—	—	41.5	—	40.0	18.6	9.9	12.0	5.8	40.8
S. Arabia	2007	—	15.1	16.5	6.3	51.3	13.4	13.6	8.7	9.7	41.4
Syria	2006	32.7	—	—	—	34.3	—	—	—	6.5	44.2
Turkey	2007	31.9	3.9	—	—	29.3	20.8	4.5	—	7.8	25.9
UAE	2006	—	—	25.9	—	53.9	15.8	11.4	5.8	11.0	40.5
Yemen	2000	5.9	5.7	—	22.5	90.6	9.1	—	—	7.3	74.0

EU=member states of the European Union. USA=United States. OTHER=mainly neighboring Middle East states, but also India, Taiwan, Vietnam. Many of the figures are estimates based on data from trading partners. (*Source: Britannica World Data*, 2009 [with permission].)

more than 50 percent of Bahrain's imports, the crude is refined in the island's Sitra refinery and then re-exported.

Food ranks among the three leading imports into virtually all Middle East countries, with the notable exception of Turkey. Of Egypt's imports, 10 percent are foodstuffs, a major shift from the early 1960s. Again with the exception of Turkey, Israel's food import percentage is the lowest in the region. Excluding food, the four leading imports by percentage are usually machinery, motor vehicles, chemicals, and iron and steel. Until the worst years of Lebanon's civil war, that country's second leading import was gold bullion. In Israel, a leading import (19 percent by value) is rough diamonds, which are then cut and re-exported.

NOTES

1. The material covered in this chapter has been the subject of scores of studies since the late 1960s.

For a historical perspective, see Issawi 1982. The latest data on production, transportation, and trade are in the U.S. Department of State's annual *Country Commercial Guides*; the Encyclopaedia Britannica's yearbook, *Britannica World Data*; Central Intelligence Agency, *World Factbook*; U.S. Department of Energy, Energy Information Administration (EIA), *Country Analysis Briefs*; the Department of State's *Background Notes* on different countries, posted periodically; *Middle East and North Africa* 2003; UN annuals; *Middle East Economic Digest*; and *Middle East Economic Survey*.

2. See Owen 1999 and Shafik 1999, both found in M. Hudson 1999. Much of the following section is based on these two studies.

3. For example, the U.S.–Saudi Arabian Joint Commission on Economic Cooperation brought several hundred American specialists from U.S. government agencies and private institutions to work on more than forty projects in the kingdom from the mid-1970s to the mid-1990s, with Saudi Arabia paying all the expenses.

4. For example, Qatar's $100 million donation to the victims of Hurricane Katrina and Abu Dhabi's $150 million endowment for a Washington children's hospital (see Chap. 15).

5. See *New York Times*, Sept. 8, 1992.

6. Plus perhaps as many again with Jordanian passports; see Chapter 15.

7. As author Cummings can personally affirm.

8. See, for example, *The Daily Star* (Beirut), Feb. 7, 2005.

9. *BBC News*, June 4, 2009, http://newsvote.bbc.co.uk/panorama/hi/front_page/newsld_7982000/7982356.stm.

10. See, for example, International Federation for Human Rights 2003 and Sasser 2004.

11. *BBC News*, Dec. 8, 2009.

12. Shafik 1999.

13. World Bank, *World Development Indicators Database*, Apr. 2009.

14. Some Yemeni workers are present illegally in Saudi Arabia, so this official figure for remittances may not be representative of the actual situation.

15. See www.english.globalarabnetwork.com, Jan. 3, 2010.

16. After more than 125 years, the last train to bear the designation "Orient Express" ran in December 2009 (*The Guardian*, Dec. 5, 2009).

17. Discussions of a joint Saudi Arabian–Turkish project to rebuild the line were announced in 2009 (see Chap. 14).

18. This was, of course, before the full brunt of Dubai's financial crisis had hit.

19. See Airport Operators Council International periodic reports, www.airports.org/, and UN International Civil Aviation Organization annual reports, www.icao.int/. These sources are also used in the following analysis.

20. *New York Times*, Apr. 13, 2004.

21. See Hourani 1963.

8

The Earth and the State
Geopolitics

The Middle East has served as a tricontinental hub for millennia. Peoples, armies, merchants, and ideas have flowed to, from, and across the region. Political ideology and processes in the flow were sometimes adapted and sometimes rejected but often influenced the internal evolution of these sixteen states. Externally, the spatial patterns discussed in the five previous chapters profoundly influenced the relationships established among the states, with neighboring areas and with more distant lands. The interaction between these patterns and political behavior—geopolitics—is the theme of this chapter.

In this book, geopolitics concerns the interface between geographical area and political phenomena. Geopolitics is conceptually equivalent to political geography; the terms will be used interchangeably. Although this chapter focuses on the state as a political-geographical phenomenon, it also covers internal and external geopolitical relations of the core Middle East, with periodic references to the broader region extending into North Africa and Central Asia (Map 8.1; see also Tables 8.1 and 8.2).

HUB AND HEARTLAND

Early geopolitical concepts of "Heartland" and "World-Island" appeared in Sir Halford J. Mackinder's paper of 1904[1] with his conceptual modifications in 1919 and 1943. Mackinder defined the Heartland bastion basically as Siberia, which he conceived of as ringed by an Inner Crescent extending from northwestern Europe through southern Asia to northeastern Asia. Beyond the Inner Crescent he viewed an Outer Crescent—the Americas, southern Africa, and Australia. He labeled tricontinental Europe, Asia, and Africa the "World-Island" and proposed in 1919 that:

> Who rules East Europe commands the Heartland;
> Who rules the Heartland commands the World-Island;
> Who rules the World-Island commands the World.

Although the Mackinder dictum has received its just share of criticism, the idea of a World-Island emphasizes the links among the three "inner continents." Emphasizing those links, it coincidentally spotlights the pivotal location of the Middle East in the World-Island.

Mackinder's Heartland concept was challenged by Professor Nicholas John Spykman during World War II. To Spykman, controlling the Heartland is only a strong defensive position; it is control of western and southern Europe, the Middle East, southern and southeastern Asia, China, and Japan that is crucial.

MAP 8.1 The core Middle East, shown inside heavy borders, with related states of North Africa, virtually all Arab and Muslim; adjacent republics of the Trans-Caucasus, none Arab and only one Muslim; the five "stans" of Central Asia, none Arab but all Muslim; plus Afghanistan and Pakistan, both Muslim. The entire area is sometimes referred to as the "Broader Middle East," although that term may apply only to the core Middle East and North Africa.

For Spykman, thus, it was Mackinder's Inner Crescent that was key, calling it "Rimland." He further theorized that, on the one hand, domination of both the Heartland and the Rimland by one superpower or power group would create an unmatched power base. On the other hand, control of the Rimland, or most of it, by one power would offset domination of the Heartland by another. Viewed from such global geopolitical perspectives, the Middle East's location confers enormous strategic importance. Its geostrategic value thus enhances its oil wealth, human resources, and commercial role.

In World War I, Ottomans, Germans, Russians, British, French, and even Greeks and Italians contended for Middle East territory. The British and French emerged dominant

and became the main imperialist powers in the region between the wars. France controlled Syria and Lebanon with a foothold on the Horn of Africa; Britain had control over not only the three mandates of Palestine, Transjordan, and (until 1932) Iraq but also the Gulf shaykhdoms and Aden (and bases as well in Egypt and Cyprus).

In World War II, Germany sought but ultimately failed to gain the Suez Canal and other regional lines of communications on the route to Middle East oil fields.

THE STATE IN THE MIDDLE EAST

A Recent Political Mosaic

Of the sixteen core Middle East states, only seven were independent before 1943—Egypt,

TABLE 8.1 Peripheral States: Selected Representative Data

	1	2	3	4	5	6	7	8
Country	Area in Sq. Miles	Pop. in 1,000s	Pop. per Sq. Mile	Literacy (latest)	GNP/Cap (2006)	Persons Per Veh.	Oil Resrvs (1,000s Bbl)	Oil Prod. Bpd, 2008
Algeria	919,595	34,574	37.6	72.1	3,350	12	12,200,000	1,240,000
Libya	679,362	5,871	8.6	85.4	8,300	4	44,270,000	1,545,000
Morocco	177,117	31,606	178.4	53.5	2,050	19	752	300
Sudan	967,499	39,445	40.8	89.6	900	371	5,000,000	500,000
Tunisia	63,170	10,325	163.4	77.9	2,830	11	425,000	82,000
Sub-Total	*2,806,743*	*121,821*	—	—	—	—	*61,895,752*	*3,367,300*
Armenia	11,484	2,996	260.9	99.4	2,040	—	—	—
Azerbaijan	33,409	8,178	244.8	98.8	2,200	14	7,000,000	1,000,000
Georgia	27,086	4,360	196.0	100.0	1,900	13	35,000	1,000
Sub-Total	*71,979*	*15,534*	—	—	—	—	*7,035,000*	*1,001,000*
Kazakhstan	1,052,090	15,655	14.9	99.5	4,700	9	30,000,000	1,330,000
Kyrgyzstan	77,182	5,281	68.4	98.7	520	—	40,000	1,000
Tajikistan	55,300	6,839	123.7	99.6	520	—	12,000	—
Turkmenistan	188,500	5,180	27.5	99.5	1,230	19	600,000	220,000
Uzbekistan	172,700	27,345	158.3	99.3	600	31	594,000	85,000
Sub-Total	*1,545,772*	*60,300*	—	—	—	—	*31,246,000*	*1,636,000*
Afghanistan	249,347	28,266	113.4	28.1	319	88	—	—
Pakistan	307,374	161,910	526.8	52.0	930	15	339,000	66,000
Sub-Total	*556,721*	*190,176*	—	—	—	—	*339,000*	*66,000*
TOTALS/AVG.	4,981,215	387,831	—	—	—	—	100,515,752	6,070,300

Population in Column 2 is estimate for midyear 2008. Literacy in Column 4 is in percentage over age 15 and is the latest available, although data vary from 2003 to 2007. Oil reserves as of 2010. BPD in Column 8 = production in average number of barrels per day. (*Sources*: Data in Columns 1–6 from *Britannica World Data*, 2009 [with permission]; data in Columns 7 and 8 from *Oil and Gas Journal*, Dec. 21, 2009.)

Turkey, Iraq, Iran, Saudi Arabia, Oman, and Yemen—and Britain still limited the sovereignty of Oman, Iraq, and even Egypt. The area has, therefore, ancient cultures in new states—old wine in new bottles.

Much of the region's recent history reflects the political inexperience and insecurity of newly independent states. Although Kuwait gained its independence in 1961, middle and lower Gulf states achieved sovereignty only in 1971 after decades under British "protection." Following a period of uncertainty, the crown colony of Aden and the adjoining hinterland protectorates merged into an independent entity, the People's Democratic Republic of Yemen (PDRY), in 1967; a united Yemen, with the PDRY merging with the Yemen Arab Republic (YAR), materialized in 1990. Cyprus, a former British

Crown colony, gained independence in 1960, only to face invasion by Turkey in 1974 and the creation of a de facto Turkish republic in the north of the island. The four Levant states achieved independence from mandate status between 1943 and 1948; the fifth mandate (Iraq) had already realized nominal sovereignty in 1932. Saudi Arabia did not become a unified kingdom with that name until 1932, and while Egypt ended formal British protectorate status in 1922, colonial vestiges remained until 1956. Both Turkey and Iran are centuries-old sovereign countries; they declared themselves republics, following long histories of monarchical rule, only in 1923 and 1979, respectively (Iran endured partial occupation by Britain and the Soviet Union during World War II). Egypt, Iraq, and North Yemen (YAR) also replaced monarchies with

TABLE 8.2 Peripheral States: Land Use and Irrigated Land

	1	2	3	4	5	6	7
	Arable &	Area Under	% of Crops	2007 Percentage of Area Under:			
Country	Perm. Crops	Irrigation	Irrigated	Forests	Mdw & Past	Agr. & PC	Other
Algeria	8,390	570	6.8	1.0	13.8	17.7	81.7
Libya	2,050	470	22.9	0.1	7.7	9.0	91.0
Morocco	8,960	1,484	16.6	9.8	47.1	69.1	23.1
Sudan	19,546	1,863	9.5	27.9	49.3	57.7	14.5
Tunisia	4,931	418	8.5	7.0	31.5	77.2	29.7
Sub-Total	*42,877*	*4,805*	—	—	—	—	—
Armenia	460	274	59.6	9.7	41.0	59.2	33.0
Azerbaijan	2,078	1,426	68.6	11.3	32.4	60.3	31.1
Georgia	577	433	75.0	39.7	27.9	37.9	24.1
Sub-Total	*3,115*	*2,133*	—	—	—	—	—
Kazakhstan	22,800	3,556	15.6	1.2	68.6	77.0	21.8
Kyrgyzstan	1,353	1,021	75.5	4.6	48.9	56.3	39.5
Tajikistan	811	722	89.0	2.9	26.9	33.5	64.3
Turkmenistan	1,913	1,800	94.1	8.8	65.3	69.5	21.8
Uzbekistan	4,640	4,281	92.3	7.8	51.7	63.4	29.6
Sub-Total	*31,517*	*11,380*	—	—	—	—	—
Afghanistan	8,661	3,199	36.9	1.2	46.0	59.5	39.5
Pakistan	22,300	19,200	86.1	2.4[a]	6.5	36.5	62.2
Sub-Total	*29,934*	*22,399*	—	—	—	—	—
TOTALS	109,470	40,717	—	—	—	—	—

Data in columns 1 and 2 are in thousands of hectares (2007). Macro land use patterns tend to change slowly. Column 1 is area in cultivated crops (e.g., grains and cotton) and permanent crops (e.g., olives and vineyards). Columns 4-7 calculated from FAO data. [a]Forests in Pakistan are included under Other (Column 7). Column 5 is Meadow and Pasture. Column 6 is equivalent to Column 1, Agriculture and Permanent Crops. (*Source*: UN Food and Agriculture Org., www.fao.org/corp/statistics.)

republics between the early 1950s and early 1960s.

Thus, the political character of the Middle East is a complex of ambiguities, contradictions, and efforts at differentiation. Muslim and especially Arab states have made conceptual efforts toward solidarity, but practical obstacles repeatedly intervene. Because of varied imperial or colonial influences, most have nonindigenous, artificial structures that did not evolve out of their own socioeconomic-political context or culture.[2] Most acquired their institutions and political-geographical boundaries from British-French delineations. Only a handful of initial alignments in the entire region were negotiated entirely by indigenous states on both sides of the border. Boundaries set by outsiders often ignored local, tribal, or traditional considerations, creating resentment against imperialist dictates. Iraqi bitterness over Britain's defining the boundary between it and the then British protectorate of Kuwait has repeatedly manifested itself—as in the invasion of Kuwait in 1990. But in other cases, imposition of borders by outside powers settled territorial disputes of long standing.

World War I Territorial Agreements

Among several such accords, three contradictory agreements from World War I and others in its aftermath profoundly influenced future developments, contemporary political-geographical boundaries and current patterns, crises, and conflicts in the Middle East.

FIGURE 8.1 Topkapı Saray, palace complex of the Ottoman sultans and heart of the Ottoman Empire (see Map 8.3) for more than 550 years. The sultan's private quarters were to the right, harem in the center of the figure, and huge kitchens in the lower wing. The complex is now a world-class museum, with unique collections of porcelain, timepieces, jewels, and tiles.

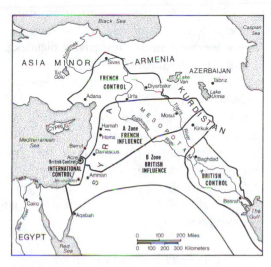

MAP 8.2 Sykes-Picot Agreement territorial allotments that, although later disavowed, became the basis for the post–World War I mandate system.

Britain concluded two conflicting pacts in 1915 and 1916 disposing of Ottoman territories after the war (Fig. 8.1). The 1915 accord was an exchange of official correspondence between Sir Henry McMahon, British high commissioner in Cairo, and Sharif Husayn of Mecca, Ottoman governor of the Hijaz. They agreed that the sharif's Arab followers would revolt against the Turks in Arabia and Syria and that Britain, in return, would support the creation of an independent Arab state in former Ottoman lands after the war. Despite this pledge of independence for most of the Fertile Crescent, Britain then signed the Sykes-Picot Agreement with France and Russia in May 1916, by which the region was to be divided between British and French control and influence (Map 8.2). Basically, the same territory was to be treated in two vastly different ways.

The third contradiction was incorporated into the Balfour Declaration of November 1917, in which Britain unilaterally promised support for a Jewish homeland in Palestine (see "The Arab-Israeli Problem" later in this chapter). With this, a part of the Fertile Crescent was to be disposed of in a way conflicting with both previous agreements.

The Arab Revolt

In accordance with the Husayn-McMahon correspondence, and with British support, the Arab Revolt against the Ottomans began in June 1916. Coordinating the Arab attacks with British operations in Palestine was the legendary Col. T. E. Lawrence, the storied "Lawrence of Arabia" who chronicled the fighting from the Hijaz to Damascus in *Seven Pillars of Wisdom*.[3] The principal Arab leader in the field was Amir Faysal, third son of Sharif Husayn.

The Arabs, having met their obligations under the Husayn-McMahon letters, were dismayed to learn of the Sykes-Picot Agreement and the Balfour Declaration, both of which contradicted Britain's promises to Arab leaders. They had been encouraged by U.S. president Woodrow Wilson's Fourteen Points, the twelfth of which supported self-determination for peoples formerly under Ottoman control. The Arabs came to mistrust Britain, France, and the United States after the Allies reneged on promises to them. In contrast, Jewish groups gained support for their proposed homeland in the Middle East.

PEACE TREATIES AND MANDATES

In the postwar peace conferences, Britain and France dominated decisions on the erstwhile Ottoman territories (Map 8.3).[4] Unable to reconcile the promises made in 1915–1917, they held generally to the Sykes-Picot Agreement and specifically to the Balfour Declaration; for Britain, the aim above all was as it long had been: protect the route to India.[5] The United States did insist on an official inquiry into Arab opinion, and the King-Crane Commission went to the Levant. But its efforts were undermined by Britain and France, and its report—citing the risks of French control in Syria and Zionist goals in Palestine—was disregarded; it was not even published for more than three years.[6]

Middle East mandates under the new League of Nations took shape at the San Remo Conference in April 1920. Territorially, the outlines of the Sykes-Picot Agreement (see Map 8.2) were followed. Historical Greater Syria was divided so that the north (future Syria and Lebanon) passed to France and the south (future Palestine and Jordan) to Britain—which also received the mandate for Mesopotamia (Iraq). Other mandates covered African and western Pacific territories of defeated Germany.

The mandates were to be temporary, emphasizing the importance of the principles of self-determination and calling for early independence for the mandated areas. Uniquely, the provisions for the Palestine mandate were incompatible with the stated purposes of the overall mandate system. It included the essential points of the Balfour Declaration, supported a Jewish homeland in Palestine (a victory for the Zionists), and passed over the goal of self-determination by the majority of the population—the 90 percent who were indigenous Palestinian Arabs.

Following complex territorial trades and further divisions of the areas in question, the mandates became official and de jure in 1923. By that time, Transjordan had been excluded from the Palestine mandate, and Greater Lebanon had been constituted as a separate French mandate.

PRESENT BASIC PATTERNS

The State and Its Location

In political geography, a state's location is the most important single factor in its evolution.

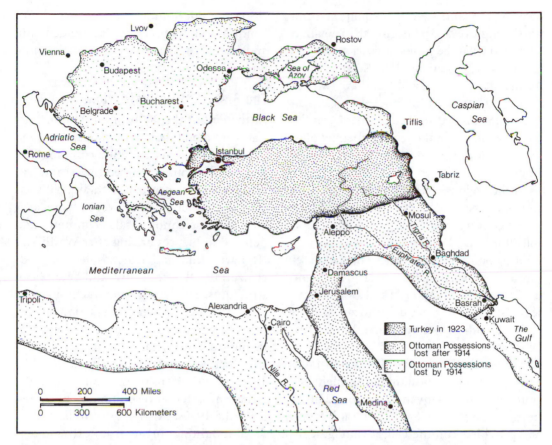

MAP 8.3 The Ottoman Empire at its maximum extent, showing territorial losses by 1914 and after World War I. Losses after 1914 are of special interest in this book.

Other fundamental state geopolitical factors considered below include population and its composition, state institutions, and raison d'être.

Whether the location is a matter of latitude, coastal versus landlocked, island versus mainland, bordering on few or many neighbors, or lying astride a mountain range as opposed to being in an intermontane basin, each aspect influences the state's geopolitical development. Lebanon's à cheval position (lit., "on horseback") astride a linear mountain range, for example, imposes the challenge of how to unite people and link communications on opposite sides of the mountains. Egypt's extension up the Nile Valley to just beyond the first cataract, and its

union of the valley and the delta, is a classic case of a riverine state maintaining linear unity, although the entire Nile Basin has never been united. Iraq, as modern heir to the Tigris-Euphrates Basin, is another classic example of a riverine state. Turkey and Iran illustrate mountain bastions holding long-lasting, independent polities.

Every Middle East state possesses some seacoast, although only Oman, the UAE, and Yemen directly face open ocean (the Indian Ocean). Deep maritime indentations facilitate access, and most states are well endowed with coastlines. Jordan and Iraq are exceptions: Jordan has only 16 mi/26 km on the Red Sea for its Aqabah port; Iraq—with a narrow 36-mi/58-km opening at the marshy head of the Gulf—lacks adequate natural port facilities. Critical during the Iran-Iraq War, Iraq cited the problem in its several attempts to seize part or all of Kuwait. Saudi Arabia, Israel, Egypt, and Iran have two-sea locations (Iran also fronts the inland Caspian Sea for 460 mi/740 km). Turkey has by far the longest seacoast in the region, opening onto the Mediterranean, Aegean, Marmara, and Black seas.

In the region, every state's location has a strategic aspect. Bahrain's situation midway in the Gulf has historically been an asset; it still affords the advantages of an entrepôt and meeting point—now enhanced by the causeway link to the mainland. Similarly, the island of Cyprus benefits from its situation—it can serve as neutral ground for Arabs and Israelis, Middle Easterners and Europeans, Lebanese factions during 1975–1991, and, in better times, Greeks and Turks. On land, Turkey's "bridge" location has brought advantages and disadvantages from Hittite times to the present. Syria's central location has provided commercial advantages, reduced lately by tensions along all its borders.

The State and Its Population

Both demographically and geopolitically, a state's population is significant in terms of number, distribution, density, and composition (see Maps 4.1 and 4.2; Tables 4.1 and 4.3). Each major ethnic group has strong sentiments of nationalism.

Every Middle East state has minorities, and some countries have as many as ten or twelve sizable ethnic groups. A minority's geopolitical significance increases with the extent of its antinational sentiment or separatism. Militant minorities in Lebanon and Cyprus have fractured the basic integrity of those states. Israel considers its Arab minority, a nine-to-one majority in 1920, a threat. In Iraq, Turkey, and Iran, the central governments have periodically faced rebellions by sizable Kurdish minorities. Others have expe-

rienced ethnic conflict—Egypt with Copts, Saudi Arabia with Persian-descended Shii, and Iran with Azeris, Arabs, Baluch, and a dozen other groups.[7]

The State and Its Institutions

At the end of the 2000s, nine Middle East states are republics, six are monarchies, and one—the UAE—is a unique combination. Most of the polities entered the second half of the twentieth century as traditional societies and monarchies. However, those societies faced technological, economic, and political influences arising after World War II.[8] Egypt, Iraq, and Yemen opted for modernization (theoretically) and republican structures. The Iranian monarchy, by contrast, was overthrown in a reaction against modernization and for the restoration of religious traditionalism.

Leftist pressures have declined since the 1970s, when anciens régimes came under internal and external revolutionary pressures; since the 1990s, existing governments have faced mounting threats from extreme religious fundamentalist movements. Egypt fought back—successfully, but too violently, according to many observers. Turkey both resisted and accommodated its Islamists with impressive success, while Oman and especially Jordan adapted through incremental change. The Saudis have faced the dilemma of simultaneous extremist fundamentalist attacks and liberal pressures—along with external coercion—and have responded with small but often significant changes. Individual rulers of Kuwait, Bahrain, and the constituents of the UAE practice economic liberalism while maintaining much political traditionalism.

After 9/11, international attention focused on the region, with the Bush administration claiming that increased democracy would promote political stability in the Middle East and combat terrorism worldwide. Citizen participation levels in the region's republics are highly variable, with democratic processes observed in Israel, Cyprus, Jordan, and Turkey, excluding certain minorities as well as the Israeli-occupied territories. They are the only states that conduct open elections with freedom for most opposition parties. Lebanon's basically sound electoral system has long been marred by Syrian influences. Party activities are limited in other republics so that elections often lack legitimacy. Egypt has a history of political restrictions, but in the 2000s elections were fairly well monitored, and oppositionists gained. Yemeni elections had generally seemed successively more open, as the presidential elections of 1999 and 2006 and the parliamentary voting of 2003 were adjudged by international observers; however, the legislative poll scheduled for 2009 was abruptly postponed, to the dismay of the U.S. State Department.[9] Iraq, of course, has held a widely publicized series of elections since January 2005 (see Chap. 14 for details). Iran has had elections with relatively open voting since 1979, but candidates are prescreened by the conservative clerics. As opposition to the authoritarian clerical rule mounted in Iran, the Council of Guardians nullified the eligibility of more than 2,000 reformist candidates for parliament in both the 2004 and the 2008 elections. The 2009 presidential election was seriously compromised, with rioters protesting the results in many cities and, in consequence, there was a clear loss in the regime's legitimacy.

Among the monarchies, Jordan has held numerous parliamentary elections, the last held in 2007; however, in November 2009 the king dismissed the elected parliament in what many observers saw as a regressive move for Jordanian democracy. Gulf monarchies have slowly relaxed the rigidity of their governance of four and five decades ago, noting warning signs of dethronements in Egypt and Iraq in the 1950s and in Yemen in 1962. Kuwait and Bahrain theoretically became constitutional states and elected parliaments

in 1962 and 1973, respectively. Kuwait has held regular elections for its National Assembly, the latest in 2009, pronounced generally free and fair; women have had the vote since 2005. The amir of Bahrain suppressed the parliament in 1975, but the new ruler, who was elevated to king, supported parliamentary elections in 2002, the first in nearly three decades. Another round was held in 2006, with one woman among the successful candidates.

No national elections have ever been conducted in Saudi Arabia, although one-half of the municipal council members were chosen in stages in early 2005 by an all-male electorate. Qatar's first national election is due in June 2010; a third round of municipal elections was held in 2007, with women voting under the 2004 constitution. Oman's sultan presented a quasi constitution in 1996, and he declared universal suffrage for the 2003 elections to the Consultative Council, which were observed to be free and fair; a second election was held in 2007. The Palestinian Authority (PA) has conducted elections for president and assembly, the latest in December 2004; when the Islamist bloc led by Hamas won, the Bush administration's professed enthusiasm for free elections in the region faded somewhat. New elections scheduled for January 2010 have been postponed indefinitely because of the current split between the West Bank and Gaza. In the UAE, a limited electoral college, including women, chose half the members of the Federal National Council in 2006.[10]

Like Western democracies, which did not spring full-blown from their Greek model, Middle East states will require time to achieve self-identity, social balance, and political maturity. They, too, will likely experience setbacks mixed with periods of forward momentum. Civil rights or human rights, for example, are denied one group or another in every country in the Middle East—including Israel, Turkey, and Cyprus—and this continues to present special challenges.

Raison d'Être

The state idea, or its raison d'être (reason for being), is its basic centripetal force—the unique, distinctive idea seen in the emergence of a particular piece of territory and segment of humanity in a specific unit. As developed by Richard Hartshorne,[11] the raison d'être reflects the dominance of unifying factors over divisive factors—of centripetal over centrifugal forces. The impact of an abstract idea on state evolution was further examined by Stephen B. Jones,[12] who traced the motivating political idea through four subsequent links: decision, movement, field, and political area. Both the raison d'être and the links in Jones's unified-field idea aid us in understanding Middle East state patterns.

Some regional states were created by outside powers in contradiction to British assurances and to pre-1919 Arab expectations. Their evolutions have been hampered by the lack of an indigenous initial idea or a consensus regarding their raison d'être. The mandates of Syria, Iraq, and Palestine, as well as much of the Lebanese and Transjordanian populations, were frustrated by developments after 1920, and independence did not bring consensus on a state idea.

Historically independent areas, in contrast, had a traditional raison d'être that could be adapted and followed. Turkey, under Kemal Atatürk, was clearly motivated by "Turkey for the Turks, and the Turks for Turkey!" Iran under Reza Shah had centuries of Persian culture as a core state concept. Egypt had an extremely long history as a culture and polity. In the south of the region, although ruled by unenlightened monarchs, Oman and Yemen also had a sense of polity going back centuries. To their north, after 1932, the tribal leader in the Arabian Peninsula, Abd al-Aziz Al Saud (Ibn Saud), developed a raison d'être for Saudi Arabia as a Muslim desert monarchy.

The regional state with the most explicit reason for being is the only settler state, Israel, which extended "a national home for the Jewish people" in the Palestine mandate into an independent Jewish state. By contrast, Cyprus has not found a commonality of purpose and modality between its Greek-Cypriot majority and its Turkish-Cypriot minority. The island consists of two de facto Cypruses as polities, although the northern Turkish entity has not gained international recognition. The remarkable UAE, a federal republican union of monarchies, would appear to have no real raison d'être; nevertheless, it is effectively succeeding as a state.

REGIONAL LINKAGES

Bases for Links

Large and diverse, the Middle East faces several centrifugal forces; however, it also possesses some regional centripetal forces, with Islam being the strongest unifying link. Only Israel and South Cyprus lie outside the Islamic realm (*Dar al-Islam*), with Lebanon divided between Muslims and Christians. In times past, Islam has unified all of the area—and more—in one empire (see Map 3.5). Nevertheless, as in times past, localism, ethnic separatism, nationalism, religious zealotry and militancy, and ambitious local leaders disrupt unity. Turkey and Iran sharply distinguish themselves ethnically and linguistically from other states; these in turn counterbalance regional unity with local concerns. Israel does not participate in regional political institutions—indeed, it excludes itself and is excluded from them. Arab unity often yields to national interests and competition among leaders.[13]

Regional and Subregional Organizations

Regional cooperation persists despite differences. Seven agencies exemplify both the benefits and the obstacles to regional cooperation. Five multilateral development funds represent cooperative efforts.

Agencies

1. Organization of the Islamic Conference. The organization that embraces the largest number of Middle East states—fourteen of the sixteen, excluding only Israel and Cyprus[14] but plus Palestine—is the Organization of the Islamic Conference (OIC), headquartered in Jiddah since 1969. It promotes Islamic solidarity and has fifty-seven members, from Suriname in South America to Brunei on Borneo. It thus embraces all of the North African and Central Asian countries in our peripheral extension.

2. Arab League. The twelve Arab states (plus Palestine) of the region are the core of the twenty-two members of the League of Arab States, better known as the Arab League. It includes nine additional African states—Mauritania, Morocco, Algeria, Tunisia, Libya, Sudan, Comoros, Somalia, and Djibouti. Six Middle East states founded the league in 1945, locating its headquarters in Cairo. It has never achieved its intended integrative role, but even so it is the most unifying of the organs of which most of the region's countries are members. Frequent contradictory national interests obstruct league unity, as was apparent during the Gulf crisis in 1990 and during the U.S.-led invasion of Iraq in 2003. The league makes statements on the Arab-Israeli problem and other Arab concerns, but conspicuous differences weaken their impact.

3 and 4. OPEC and OAPEC. Of the organizations dealing with specific aspects of inter-Arab coordination and involving Arab participation in wider groupings, two of the best known are the Organization of Petroleum Exporting Countries (OPEC—of which Iran is also a member) and the Organization of Arab Petroleum Exporting Countries (OAPEC), both discussed in Chapter 6. OPEC plays a particularly important role in the regional economy, although only six Middle East countries are members—Iraq, Iran, Kuwait, Saudi Arabia, Qatar, and the UAE. OAPEC, which also includes Bahrain, Egypt, and Syria, has been less influential.

5. Gulf Cooperation Council. Created in 1981, the Cooperation Council of the Arab States of the Gulf—the Gulf Cooperation Council (GCC)—aims to coordinate economic, cultural, military, and political affairs among its members, Saudi Arabia, Kuwait, Bahrain, Qatar, the UAE, and Oman, with focus on oil policy, development, social problems (including expatriate labor), Gulf trade, resolution of border disputes, and, especially, security. Seeking security for their regimes and preservation of their national sovereignty and territorial integrity, they have cooperated in the antiterrorist efforts of the United States, and four members—Kuwait, Qatar, Bahrain, and Oman—supported U.S. operations against Iraq.

The GCC's revolutionary republican neighbors, Iran and Iraq—at war when it was formed—have at times had hegemonic pretensions over the Gulf. Forming a unified front motivated the GCC's creation, and the members maintain a regional military force. Among their economic goals, the members agreed in 2001 to form a customs union and a single market and adopt a common currency in the following decade, but efforts have lagged. Some members have been dissatisfied with the slowness of the internal and external trade negotiations and have proceeded unilaterally with their own arrangements—for example, Bahrain in 2006 and Oman in 2009 entered into free trade agreements with the United States. A planned currency union to be launched in 2010 has had some difficulties; Oman never joined, the UAE held back in 2009, while Kuwait occasionally voiced some hesitation. The smaller GCC members will have to come to terms with the reality of Saudi Arabian dominance if such a union is to be achieved.[15]

6. *Economic Cooperation Organization.*   In 1964, Turkey, Iran, and Pakistan—members of the pre-1979 Central Treaty Organization (CENTO)—formed the Regional Cooperation for Development (RCD). Initial financial underwriting came primarily from ambitious and oil-wealthy Iran, and it addressed transportation links as well as tourism, postal services, frontier formalities, and other areas of potential coordination. Phased down after the 1979 Iranian Revolution, it was revived in 1985 as the Economic Cooperation Organization (ECO) with expanded goals. In 1992, six new Muslim ex-Soviet republics—Azerbaijan, Kazakhstan, Kyrgyzstan, Tajikistan, Turkmenistan, and Uzbekistan—were admitted, along with Afghanistan. Its members have significant natural resources and potential.

7. *Greater Arab Free Trade Area.*   In keeping with the Arab League's aim of promoting economic unity, there have been several attempts to institutionalize this goal; until recently, none had much success. The Greater Arab Free Trade Area (GAFTA) is the latest and most ambitious—and perhaps is more likely to advance. It began in 1998, but adherence has been gradual, with the last of its seventeen members joining in 2008. Some members have already begun to reduce tariffs on trade among themselves. What makes this attempt at unity different is the concurrent involvement of the European Union with all the members; in one way or another, the EU is negotiating free trade agreements bilaterally with each—through the Euro-Mediterranean Partnership, discussions with the GCC, and separate talks with Iraq and Yemen. Most of them are anxious to affiliate with the EU—which has promoted a GAFTA-like institution as a highly desirable adjunct. The EU's long-term goal is a fully operative FTA en-

compassing all of both Europe and the Middle East by sometime in the 2020s.[16] To promote this goal, the EU funds programs as part of its European Neighborhood Policy under which the countries studied here benefit; for example, for the 2010–2012 period, 5.7 bn euros ($7.8 bn) has been appropriated.[17]

Multilateral Development Funds

1. *Islamic Development Bank.*   In its origin an offshoot of the OIC, the Islamic Development Bank (IDB) began operations in 1975, providing development finance to OIC members that was Islamically acceptable: in short, free of any taint of *riba*—usury or interest. Fourteen of the countries in this study, plus Palestine, are IDB members; collectively, they have subscribed more than 73 percent of the bank's capital of close to $25 billion. Through 2008, the IDB had extended more than 6,700 loans amounting to some $63.4 billion to fifty-six member countries.

2. *Arab Fund for Economic and Social Development.*   Authorized by the Arab League, the Arab Fund for Economic and Social Development (AFESD) commenced operations in 1974. All twenty-two members of the Arab League have contributed to the fund's resources; the twelve countries plus Palestine in this study are the sources of more than 76 percent of the paid-in capital. Through 2008, the AFESD had committed about $20.9 billion in loans and grants to 459 projects in seventeen Arab countries.

3. *Arab Monetary Fund.*   Also originating with the Arab League, the Arab Monetary Fund (AMF) became active in 1976. As with the AFESD, all twenty-two Arab League members have subscribed to the AMF's capital—about $2.8 billion at the end of 2008; of this more than 70 percent had been subscribed by the countries in this study. The AMF is a regional version of the International Monetary Fund and assists members

with balance of payments deficits, structural adjustments, and the reforms needed to offset these problems. Through 2008, it had extended some $5.1 billion in 141 loans to fifteen member countries. The biggest beneficiaries have been Egypt, Morocco, Iraq, and Yemen.

4. OPEC Fund for International Development. The OPEC Fund (OFID) was founded in 1976 with capital from the then thirteen members of OPEC; six are included in this study, and they have contributed about 65 percent of OFID's paid-in capital. Through 2008, 121 developing countries and numerous official and private institutions have benefited from $10.3 billion in OFID loans and grants.

5. International Fund for Agricultural Development. With much of Africa facing famine, the UN convened the World Food Conference in 1973. OPEC spearheaded negotiations with the Organization of Economic Cooperation and Development (OECD), leading to the foundation of the International Fund for Agricultural Development (IFAD) that began operations in 1978 dedicated to alleviating rural poverty. Saudi Arabia has been IFAD's second-largest subscriber of capital, and twelve OPEC members have provided 27 percent of the fund's resources. Through 2008, IFAD had lent $10.8 billion for more than 800 projects in 108 countries.

Most other agencies are economic (many under the aegis of the Council of Arab Economic Unity) and deal with everything from olives to tourism, but some agencies are at the people-to-people level—for example, Arab historians, jurists, or athletes.

Unions: Attempts and Failures

Despite continuing influence by Britain and France and inter-Arab rivalry, Arab states attempted several subregional political mergers between the 1950s and 1980. Notably, the United Arab Republic (UAR) joined Syria and Egypt in 1958, but Syria withdrew in 1961. Yemen nominally federated with the UAR in 1958 to form the short-lived United Arab States, but this alliance also collapsed in 1961.

Jordan and Iraq, ruled at the time by Hashimite monarch cousins, became the Arab Federation in 1958 to counterbalance the UAR, but this dissolved after the overthrow of the Iraqi king the same year. The new Iraqi leader proposed a union of Iraq, Syria, and Jordan, but this never materialized. Other efforts at political unity faded quickly: a resurrection of the United Arab Republic with Egypt, Syria, and Iraq in 1963; plans for a Federation of Arab Republics with Egypt, Syria, and Libya in 1971; and a merger of Egypt and Libya in 1972. Prompted by Egyptian president Anwar Sadat's dramatic visit to Jerusalem in 1977 and ensuing Egyptian-Israeli détente, Syria and Iraq talked seriously in 1978–1979 about unity, but again the plans came to naught.

Before its "East of Suez" withdrawal, Britain set up the Federation of Arab Amirates of the South in 1959 in the Aden Protectorate, which then expanded to became the Federation of South Arabia. It fell to the Marxist People's Democratic Republic of Yemen, which in turn merged with North Yemen in 1990 to form the Republic of Yemen (see Chap. 16). Despite a bloody but short civil war in 1994, the union has endured, although separatism has apparently gained considerable support in the south in the late 2000s.

A different type of union took place two decades earlier on the other side of the Arabian Peninsula. In 1968, before Britain's withdrawal from the Gulf, the seven Trucial States proposed to form a Federation of Arab Amirates with Bahrain and Qatar. The latter opted for separate independence, but the other seven federated in the United Arab Emirates, in which the principalities maintain semisovereignty but voluntarily join in certain common political, economic, cultural, and security structures. The federation—instead of full union—has seen cooperation and stability (see Chap. 15).

The Greater Arab Free Trade Area (discussed above) may offer a more practicable way to further Arab unity by forgoing the political aspects and concentrating on the benefits to be gained on the economic side, particularly within the framework of promoting free trade with the EU.

Alliances and the Baghdad Pact

Regional military alliances—sometimes merely placement of military forces under one command—have formed during emergencies. The impetus for such pacts has usually been a crisis between the Arab frontline states and Israel, and temporary alliances preceded the four major Arab-Israeli wars. The 1990–1991 coalition against Iraq, which mixed Arab and non-Arab states, created tensions between participating and rejectionist states. Similar tensions arose over the degree of support or opposition to the U.S.-led invasion of Iraq in 2003.

The Baghdad Pact, a long-range pact involving the Middle East, originated in 1955, with U.S. and British encouragement, as a cordon sanitaire against Soviet expansionism. Formally termed the Middle East Treaty Organization, it initially included only Turkey and Iraq, but Britain, Pakistan, and Iran later joined. The pact was vigorously opposed by Nasserist Egypt and its allies. Following the monarchy's overthrow in 1958, Iraq withdrew. Renamed the Central Treaty Organization, it was headquartered in Ankara for two decades until it disintegrated in 1979, when revolutionary Iran, and then Pakistan, withdrew. The ECO (see above) is in some respects a successor organization.

REGIONAL CONFLICTS

Once several polities in the region were independent, the Middle East experienced conflicts over such matters as borders, access to scarce resources, competing ideologies, leadership, and self-determination. Geographically, the conflicts may cross frontiers or may be subregional, regional, or between the region and outside forces.

Not all major clashes have arisen between sovereign governments. Some conflicts have been and are between nonstate organizations and states, between paramilitary forces of subnational groups, between religious and secular groups, or between individual leaders. Lebanon was fragmented for more than fifteen years by fighting between the PLO and Kataib,[18] the PLO and Shii, Druze and Kataib, and other intergroup conflicts (see Chap. 10). The PLO also fought Jordanian forces in 1970 and later periodically battled Israeli troops and conducted guerrilla raids in Israel. The 2006 "Summer War" involved Hizballah and Israel, and the latter's target in Gaza in 2008–2009 was Hamas.

Militant extremist groups, claiming to be acting for Islam or representing Islamist organizations, have posed threats to nearly every government in the region. From 1991 to 1997, antigovernment forces mounted a virtual insurgency in Egypt—some seeking political power, some opposed to Egyptian-Israeli détente, some demanding adherence to their version of Islam. The Muslim Brotherhood, originally an Egyptian opposition group, revived and became active not only in Egypt but also in Jordan and Syria. Some organizations have created internal and transnational movements, discussed later. The Baath (Renaissance) party has been influential in the Fertile Crescent states, but opposing factions governed in Syria and Iraq until the fall of Saddam Husayn. The 1964–1975 Dhufar Rebellion in southern Oman pitted an isolated marginalized group—joined by Marxists from South Yemen—against an authoritarian sultan (see Map 16.2). After 9/11, a new era in regional conflicts brought more widespread and intensified terrorism, discussed at the end of this chapter.

Boundary and Territorial Disputes

Most Middle East countries have engaged in disputes with neighbors over the location or demarcation of their boundaries. These disputes have usually been limited to diplomatic exchanges or skirmishes, but three have provoked devastating wars. Virtually no boundary disputes remain active as of 2009; UAE borders with both its neighbors, Saudi Arabia and Oman, have now been formally ratified and demarcated on the ground. Irredentist and nationalist claims retain the potential for conflict and may reassert themselves in the future.

Early Disputes.   Three pre-independence territorial disputes in the Fertile Crescent involved (1) inclusion of the Mosul area in the British mandate of Iraq, (2) delineation of the southern Transjordan–Saudi Arabia border, and (3) status of Alexandretta (Turkish: Iskenderun) in northwestern Syria. The first two were soon resolved, but the third dispute echoed for several years. A 1921 accord provided for the Sanjak (subprovince) of Alexandretta—with a large Turkish minority and port facilities desired by both Turkey and Syria—a special regime within the Syrian mandate. The League of Nations created the separate Republic of Hatay in 1938, but in 1939 France ceded it to Turkey, violating mandate provisions. Syria has still not entirely accepted the loss, and many Syrian-made maps show both the 1936 and 1939 boundaries; both are indicated in Chapter 9 (Map 9.1).

Arabian Peninsula Boundaries.   Saudi Arabia, with the largest number of immediate land neighbors in the region (seven), sought to rationalize most of its boundaries through quiet negotiations during the 1960s and 1970s, although border tensions continue with Yemen.[19] An agreement in 1965 gave Jordan an extra 10 mi/16 km of coastline for the expansion of its port of Aqabah in exchange for an inland desert tract. A settlement with Kuwait in 1969 divided the Saudi Arabia–Kuwait Neutral Zone, and another in 1981, with Iraq, divided the other neutral zone and straightened the boundary extending westward. An agreement with Qatar in 1965, revised in 1992, defined this boundary, and a 1974 accord defined a long-disputed boundary with the UAE involving the Buraymi Oasis.

Final ratification of Saudi boundaries with Iraq, Qatar, and the UAE was delayed for several years, although the delineations were generally accepted and shown as de facto on the official maps of all four countries. The several boundaries were registered with the UN by Saudi Arabia in 1995, and later agreements led to designation of the borders with Iraq and Qatar as de jure. Ratification of the border with the UAE was long delayed but was finally accepted, and the boundary is shown as de jure in this book. A Saudi agreement with Oman in 1982 deferred territorial questions, but in March 1991 the two governments ratified the delimitation of their common border of more than 400 mi/645 km through the eastern part of the barren Rub al-Khali. This has now been demarcated and is de jure.

The border between Saudi Arabia and Yemen has been particularly difficult to settle because of frequent antagonism between the two governments. The 1934 Treaty of Taif resulted in demarcation of a short segment of the boundary between Yemen and the Asir region of the Saudi kingdom, but dispute continued over the remaining part of the border until a boundary treaty was signed in 2000 covering the entire line from the coast to Oman. Demarcation of the new segment was to be undertaken "in an amicable way." General relations between Saudi Arabia and Yemen concurrently improved with the resolution of the boundary problem; in the late

2000s, the Houthi rebellion in northern Yemen recalled the still-troubled nature of this region. One long-standing boundary problem—between the two former Yemens—disappeared with their unification.

Other Boundary and Territorial Problems. Of four other significant Arabian Peninsula boundary disputes, two were readily resolved. In the south, the frontier between Oman and the former South Yemen saw fighting in the 1970s, but in 1992 united Yemen readily agreed to a definitive settlement, ratified in 1998. Similarly, in 1993 Oman and the UAE delineated their long-disputed border. In the north, Iraq and Jordan agreed in 1984 to a slight modification of their boundary to permit an exchange of small parcels of territory;[20] this de jure delineation is shown in several maps in this book. The fourth disputed boundary, between Iraq and Kuwait, included Iraq's claim to the whole of Kuwait. A border defined (but not demarcated) by an agreement between Iraq and Kuwait in 1963 was confirmed and demarcated by a special UN Iraq-Kuwait Boundary Demarcation Commission after Iraq was forced to withdraw from Kuwait in 1991. The commission's work and report were accepted by the UN Security Council (UNSC) in Resolution 833 in 1993. Iraq at first refused to accept the line but agreed to it in November 1994, refused it again briefly in 1999, then accepted it in an apparently final stance.[21] Jordan and Saudi Arabia agreed to demarcate their maritime border in 2007.[22] Thus, at long last, after decades of disputes and negotiations, all political boundaries on the Arabian Peninsula have been formally settled and are internationally accepted as de jure.

Four disputes involving irredentist territories on the Arabian Peninsula and in offshore areas became acute during the period 1961–1991:

1. Iraq denounced British delineations and territorial allotments at the head of the Gulf in 1923, arguing that its access to the Gulf was too narrow for its size and needs. It had received most of the former Ottoman province of Basrah and claimed the remainder, which had been given to Kuwait. Since in other cases former Ottoman administrative units were divided in creating mandates, Iraq's claim was declared invalid by international-law specialists. Although it accepted the status quo in 1932 upon independence, it reasserted its claims during the late 1930s, including threats of military action. With Kuwaiti independence in 1961 and the end of British protection, Iraq moved to annex Kuwait by force, but after a stiff warning by both Britain and the Arab League, it again accepted the status quo. But in 1973–1974, Iraq claimed once again part of Kuwait—the islands of Warba and Bubiyan—to expand its Gulf outlet; once again, it dropped its claims and withdrew its forces.[23] With this history, Saddam Husayn's threat to Kuwait in 1990 initially just appeared to be more posturing.

2. In 1968, as Britain prepared to withdraw from the lower Gulf, Iran moved to fill the impending vacuum and affirm its dominance by reasserting old claims to Bahrain as Iran's "fourteenth province," as well as to several small islands in the southern Gulf. However, in 1970 the shah accepted the UN finding that Bahrainis preferred independence and renounced further claims to Bahrain.

3. On the other hand, Iran's claims in the south continued. On November 30, 1971, the day before Britain withdrew, it occupied three islands in the lower Gulf that had long been understood to belong to Sharjah and Ras al-Khaymah, asserting its need to protect the Strait of Hormuz. Accord was reached regarding Abu Musa—located well away from the strait and closer to Sharjah than to Iran; this included dividing any oil revenue from or around the island between the two parties. In 1992, Iran restricted access to the island, and it periodically reasserts its control, followed by UAE protests. The other two is-

FIGURE 8.2 Internation interaction: an unusual international border crossing, on an artificial island at the median line between Saudi Arabia (*foreground*) and Bahrain on the causeway connecting them (see Fig. 7.5). (Abdulla Y. al-Dobais, Saudi Aramco)

lands, Greater Tunb and Lesser Tunb, nearer the Strait, had been under Ras al-Khaymah sovereignty before 1970, but Iran occupied them prior to the UAE's independence.[24]

4. A lengthy dispute between Bahrain and Qatar also involved Gulf islands. Citing its historic ties to western Qatar, Bahrain claimed the Hawar islands and the Dibal and Jarada shoals off the western coast of the peninsula. In 1996, Qatar took its case to the International Court of Justice, which decided in 2001 that the islands should go to Bahrain, but that Bahrain should quit all claims to mainland territory. Both sides accepted the verdict amicably.

For the Gulf, there are problems of maritime boundaries in this semi-enclosed sea.

As offshore oil discoveries reached mid-Gulf from both sides, delineation became essential. Law of the Sea agreements elsewhere provided precedents for establishing median lines in the central Gulf, as opposed to the north and south, and the lines were surveyed in the late 1950s and the 1960s. In the north, complexities regarding the lines among Iran, Iraq, Kuwait, and the former Neutral Zone have delayed final agreement, and similar problems arose with the UAE's component amirates and Iran in the south. Despite the potential for confrontation over huge offshore oil and gas resources, agreements have been reached relatively promptly, and non-agreed-upon lines have so far caused few difficulties (see Fig. 8.2).[25]

Territorially, there is another problem relative to the Gulf: what it is to be called, not only by the states surrounding or near to it, but by other countries, businesses, and individuals (including writers of books about the Middle East). Iran insists that it is the "Persian" Gulf, and cites long historical usage to back up its claim. The littoral Arab states prefer "Arabian" (or "Arab") Gulf, but have accepted use of just "the Gulf." That this is not a minor matter can be seen from two incidents in early 2010. The second Islamic Solidarity Games (ISG), originally scheduled for October 2009, were to be held at several Iranian venues.[26] When Iran included "Persian Gulf" in the ISG logo and related materials, the Arab states, led by Saudi Arabia, objected; when negotiations failed to yield a solution, the games were finally canceled in January 2010. Then Iran threatened in February 2010 to deny the use of its airspace to any airline that referred to the waterway by any name other than "Persian Gulf." The warning was particularly aimed at airlines based in Gulf Arab countries that have numerous flights to Iranian destinations.[27]

Another continental-shelf dispute concerns determining a median line in the Aegean Sea between Turkey and Greece. Since its territory includes several large islands just off the western and southern coasts of Asia Minor, Greece favors a median line between the islands and the Turkish mainland. However, that would extend its Exclusive Economic Zone rights over practically the entire Aegean Sea, including all potential offshore petroleum resources—a solution Turkey has declared it will not accept.

The conflict over partitioning the Aegean is heightened by the situation in Cyprus. Since both Turkey and Greece are members of the North Atlantic Treaty Organization (NATO), and since Turkey seeks to join Greece (and Cyprus) as a member of the EU, the international community closely monitors any possibility of military action over the Aegean or Cyprus. The Cyprus dispute received intensive attention in 2003 and 2004, culminating in the accession of southern (Greek) Cyprus to the EU in May 2004 and the continued isolation of northern (Turkish) Cyprus. (See Chap. 10.)

Finally, the median line (*thalweg*) river boundary down the Shatt al-Arab between Iraq and Iran involved the two riparian states in disputes and then warfare (discussed later in this chapter in the section "The Iran-Iraq War, 1980–1988").

Hydrogeopolitics

The availability, management, and sharing of the natural resource of water increasingly rival the influence of petroleum in the political geography of the area. Whereas petroleum is a valuable economic resource, water is essential to life itself.

Population increases in many countries have overwhelmed water resources. Rivers, because of their transnational character, automatically become subjects of international concern. Egypt has seen the amount of water in the Nile—rising in other countries to the south—decrease in recent decades by the time the river reaches Lake Nasser. Use of Tigris and Euphrates water by the three riparian states—Turkey, Syria, and Iraq—has dramatically increased since the 1960s. Notable is Turkey's Southeast Anatolia Project (GAP) with the Atatürk Dam on the Euphrates generating electric power and irrigating millions of acres (see Chap. 18) and diminishing downstream flow in Syria and Iraq. Syria's Jazirah Project, with its core facility the Tabaqah Dam on the Euphrates, involves irrigating hundreds of thousands of acres, further decreasing the flow to Iraq. In Iraq, the wars of 1991 and 2003 and cross-border Kurdish-related tensions have stalled meaningful progress in water negotiations. Saudi Arabia overused its groundwater in an ill-advised effort to be self-sufficient in wheat, with the water table dropping by 7 or 8 ft/2.1

or 2.4 m before the program was reduced in the late 1980s.

In part, the effort to gain access to the Jordan, Yarmuk, and Litani rivers and to underground aquifers prompted Israel to seize the Golan Heights and southern Lebanon and to plant settlements in the West Bank. Palestinian-Israeli peace talks have periodically addressed water sharing without significant progress.

The nine states of the Nile Basin discussed regional cooperation in Cairo in June 1990, and the UN Economic Commission for Africa and the UN Development Programme are promoting group water projects. Thus, initial steps have been taken toward water-sharing protocols, but the real problems have yet to be addressed. According to the 1966 Helsinki Rules and a 1972 UN convention, water rights depend on population and need, keeping historical allocations in mind. On the other hand, international law acknowledges the absolute sovereignty of a state over its own resources. Without regional and international agreements, national development plans and the growing thirst of increasing populations will lead to more conflicts over water use in the Middle East.[28]

Religious and Ideological Conflicts

The Role of Religion. Religious movements have strongly impacted the Middle East, and they are of crucial importance in the regional geopolitical equation today. The Islamic state was a theocracy, and religion and politics—"church and state"—are congenitally linked in Muslim concepts. Extreme politicization of Islam divides Muslims and creates some of the region's sharpest cleavages. As with other religious conflicts, the real dissension often arises from national political hostilities, economic competition, ethnolinguistic and cultural dissensions, territorial disputes, and outside interference.

Religious contentions also merge with others in many struggles between religious groups in the Middle East. A closer look at the conflict "between Jews and Muslims" reveals underlying territorial, political, and cultural bases for hostility. The fifteen-year civil war in Lebanon "between Christians and Muslims" reflected dominant-group economic-cultural discrimination and competition as much as religion. Revolutionary activities of Shii in Lebanon and elsewhere reflect not only religion but also historic economic disadvantages and Iranian and Iraqi nationalism.

Modernization since the 1950s has revealed inadequacies in modern industrialized culture, leading to a strong resurgence of an Islamic religious-political framework. Older groups like the Muslim Brotherhood (*Ikhwan al-Muslimun*), founded in Egypt in 1929, have received new impetus. Many newer "fraternities" (*jamaats*) have arisen in Egypt and the Fertile Crescent, advocating revolutionary and antigovernment positions, rejection of modern trends, and a return to traditional Islam. Among the better-known groups are al-Qaida, Hamas, and Hizballah (see below, "Terrorism and Piracy").

Arabism in the Region. Partly an outgrowth of the regional identification of Arabism with Islam and partly a product of anticolonial nationalism, Arab ideologies may display slightly different emphases; they are categorized with such terms as "Arabism," "Arab nationalism," "Arab solidarity," "Arab unity," and "Arab socialism." Under some circumstances, Arab identity transcends state nationalism, prompting coordinated political and economic stands,[29] though differing interpretations of identity periodically create conflict among states. Although Arabs value consensus, political crises led to dissension during 1990–1991 and again with the 2003 invasion of Iraq.

From outside the "Arab system," Iranian Shii fundamentalism has had less impact since the mid-1990s, but it still has an influence. In the late 2000s, Saudi Arabia and the Gulf states, for example, were increasingly concerned at what was called the "Shii Crescent," stretching from Iran through Shii-majority Iraq and Alawi-dominated Syria into Lebanon with the strong presence of Hizballah in government. Also externally, Turkey has seen ideological conflicts between secular and Islamic ideologies, with one indication: the more prevalent wearing of headscarves by women. Nationalism, ideological and political clashes, and religious divisions have also caused internal conflict in Israel.

THE ARAB-ISRAELI PROBLEM

Among geopolitical problems since World War II, the emotionally charged conflict between Arabs and Israelis is unique in its regional impact, its global ramifications, its great-power involvement, its intractability, and its impact on the U.S. role in Middle East affairs. It has many facets: ethnic confrontation, conflicting historical-territorial claims, religious implications, ethical dilemmas, and political and geopolitical repercussions. The problem also has many perspectives, with Arab and Israeli viewpoints fragmented into many subperspectives.[30] From any one of these, the conflict has caused tragic amounts of casualties, suffering, and physical destruction, and it has retarded regional development and wasted human and other resources. This study emphasizes the essentially geographical basis of the conflict, with "geographical" including the human factor (Map 8.4).

The modern conflict began with increasing nationalism among Jews in Europe and Arabs in the Middle East. Jewish nationalism arose in the 1880s, taking shape as Zionism, the aspiration to establish a Jewish polity in "Zion"—a hill in Jerusalem, but by extension Palestine. Its influence and activity expanded until, with support from several sources, it achieved a Jewish state in Palestine in 1948.

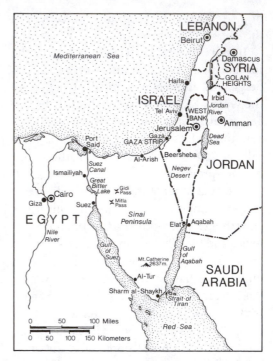

MAP 8.4 Political-geographical setting of the Arab-Israeli problem, showing the territories directly involved in the conflict.

By contrast, Arab nationalisms developed in isolation, based on local situations—of which Palestine was only one—and were weakened and fragmented by colonialism that frustrated their aims.

As Jews in late-nineteenth-century Europe sought a national identity similar to that of the Germans or French, they joined in common efforts to achieve self-determination and group liberation, all according to Enlightenment concepts. Jewish nationalism combined with secularism to direct attention to the Land of Israel (Eretz Yisrael) as the territory of a revived Jewish nation. Leaders stressed links among Jews in the Diaspora and the Land of Israel and focused on Jews as a minority people "in exile," not just a religious group. They encouraged the revival of Hebrew, for centuries strictly a liturgical language, as the literary and linguistically unifying medium of Jewish-Hebrew nationalism.

Evolution of Zionism

In the 1880s, eastern European pogroms against Jews engendered a movement, *Hovevei Tzion* (Lovers of Zion), urging migration to Palestine. It was institutionalized by Theodor Herzl, a Hungarian journalist, who came to believe, after covering the Dreyfus affair in France,[31] that Jews must achieve self-determination territorially. In 1896, in the book *Der Judenstaat* (The Jews' State), he called for an independent state for Jews; in 1897, he organized the First Zionist Congress.

At its meeting, Herzl founded the World Zionist Organization (WZO), which is still a preeminent organization supporting the state of Israel. Herzl directed Jewish and world attention to Zionism, and he galvanized other movements and organizations to support efforts to channel Jews to Palestine. A leading Zionist encouraged his compatriots to "make Jewish Palestine the mother country of world Jewry, with Jewish communities in the Diaspora as the colonies—and not the reverse."[32]

The WZO and subsidiary organizations attracted Jewish settlers to Ottoman Palestine, enlisting the support of world Jewry. Following Jones's "Unified Field Theory," mentioned above, Zionism is the idea that led through decision and movement over a world field to Palestine. One proponent ironically encouraged immigration for "a people without a land for a land without people"[33] in 1901—when more than 400,000 Palestinian Arabs lived in that land: Palestine. The settler effort proceeded, sometimes with Ottoman and British mandatory opposition, and immigrants outnumbered indigenous Arabs within a half century. Colonists immigrated for various reasons, but the predominant goal was a modern, secular, socialist state to serve as a territorial base for Jews as a people more than as a religious group.

The Balfour Declaration

World War I gave Zionist leaders the chance to lay the groundwork for a Jewish state. Foreseeing the end of Ottoman rule, British Zionists pressed Britain to officially support the establishment of a Jewish state in Palestine. Proponents argued this would attract the support of Jews in Germany and motivate Jews in the United States to urge that country to join the Allies against Germany. In response to intensive lobbying, Britain issued the one-sentence Balfour Declaration in 1917:

His Majesty's Government view with favour the establishment in Palestine of a national home for the Jewish people, and will use their best endeavours to facilitate the achievement of this object, it being clearly understood that nothing shall be done which may prejudice the civil and religious rights of existing non-Jewish communities in Palestine, or the rights and political status enjoyed by Jews in any other country.[34]

This sentence, with its two conflicting parts, was as internally contradictory and cynically expedient as some of Britain's other wartime pronouncements, but it has had far more serious and long-lasting implications. For better or worse, it set the course of history for the modern Middle East.[35]

World War I Through World War II

A British white paper sought to clarify the Balfour Declaration in 1922. It stated that although the declaration was a basic factor in establishing the Palestine mandate (Map 8.5A), it did not mean that Britain favored Palestine as a whole becoming a Jewish national home or a strictly Jewish polity or that it intended the "disappearance or subordination" of the indigenous Arab population or its culture.

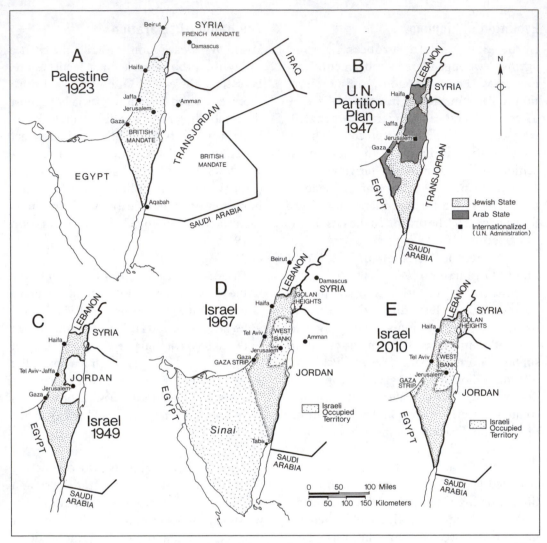

MAP 8.5 The territorial evolution of Israel, from Palestinian mandate to contemporary state, with occupied territories. See also Map 8.7.

The paper stressed that Britain excluded Palestine from the area of Arab independence mentioned in the Husayn-McMahon correspondence. Assurances by Britain and France in 1918 that they would establish in Greater Syria and Mesopotamia "national governments that drew their authority from the initiative and free choice of the native populations" were ignored for Palestine, as were declarations in Wilson's Fourteen Points and in the Covenant of the League of Nations. Palestinians and their Arab sup-

porters found that Zionist influence in London and Jerusalem overrode Arab influence and that only the first half of the Balfour Declaration was being applied. Arab violence followed.

As early as 1919, Palestinians attacked Jewish settlers to forestall further colonization. Periodic forays evoked Jewish counterattacks and the formation of Zionist defense forces, since settlers claimed that the protection given them by the British was inadequate. Whereas Jewish efforts were highly organized, those of the Arabs were fragmented and disorganized, partly because their leaders were divided. Thus began the cycle of violence that continues in the first decade of the new millennium.

Meanwhile, the organization of the Zionists, the inflow of settlers (later, especially, refugees from Nazi Germany), the systematic purchase of prime agricultural land by the Jewish National Fund (JNF), and increasing Jewish support of Zionism created favorable conditions for Herzl's state to emerge. JNF resources not only increased Jewish landholdings but also dispossessed thousands of Palestinian *fellahin* (farmers) and their families. In August 1929, after ten days of mutual provocations and rioting, an Arab attack killed fifty-nine Jews in Hebron, causing Jews to abandon that city. General strikes and uprisings by the Arabs against both British and Jews broke out in 1936. As Britain considered partitioning Palestine, violence upsurged periodically until the outbreak of World War II. Zionist leaders exerted greater pressure against both Arabs and British administrators as the Jewish population grew and as the Zionists gained support because of the brutality of the Hitler regime.

While World War II blazed, Jewish extremists struck at British mandatory authorities in an attempt to seize Palestine. At the end of the war, Zionist recruiters in Europe enabled Jewish refugees to go to Palestine as both fighters and settlers. British efforts to control immigration were unsuccessful and led to more attacks—notably on British mandatory offices in Jerusalem's King David Hotel in July 1946. Conducted by the Jewish terrorist group Irgun Zvai Leumi led by Menachem Begin (Israeli prime minister, 1977–1983), the blast killed ninety-one Britons, Jews, and Arabs. Many observers consider this attack the first case of classic terrorism in Palestine.

The Emergence of Israel

War-weary Britain announced in 1947 that it intended to relinquish the mandate and leave the future of Palestine to the UN. After thirty years, they had tired of trying to resolve the dilemma they had themselves caused with the Balfour Declaration. Zionist pressure came from many directions, especially the United States, with President Harry S. Truman demanding that 100,000 Jews be admitted immediately to Palestine. Arabs demanded that the British adhere to their obligations to the indigenous Palestinians.

As the British prepared to depart, the UN Special Committee on Palestine drew up a Partition Plan for Palestine. The UN General Assembly voted for the plan in November 1947, under U.S. pressure. Although it was never implemented, its provisions still have a certain juridical force and serve as a geopolitical point of reference. It called for three entities: a Jewish state with 56 percent of mandate Palestine; an Arab state, 43 percent; and a small enclave comprising Jerusalem to become a UN-administered international zone (Map 8.5B)—a *corpus separatum* (separate entity), accessible to all faiths and peoples but belonging to neither Arabs nor Jews (Fig. 8.3).

Theoretically based on ethnic distribution, the proposed political-geographical jigsaw reflected the difficulty of equitably partitioning the mandate. Zionists resented not receiving all of Palestine for the Jewish state, in keeping with their interpretation of the Balfour Declaration. Other critics of the plan pointed to its partiality for the Jewish state, which received 56 percent of Palestine although Jews made up only one-third of the population and owned only about 7 percent of the land. The proposed boundaries would have included 407,000 Arabs in the Jewish state and 10,000 Jews in the Arab state, as well as 142,000 Jews and 68,000 Arabs in international Jerusalem.

The Arabs, relying on the principle that a mandate territory could not legally be alienated from the indigenous population, rejected the proposed surrender of more than half their homeland to comparatively recent

FIGURE 8.3 The Dome of the Rock (Qubbat as-Sukhra), originally completed in 691 as a shrine over the Sacred Rock, associated with both the biblical narrative of Abraham's near sacrifice of his son and the account of Solomon's Temple as well as with the Muslim belief of Muhammad's ascent to heaven.

settlers. But the Zionists accepted the proposal, which granted UN legitimacy to their sovereignty over half of Palestine. Jews and Arabs engaged in preliminary fighting, sometimes battling British forces.

The Zionist leadership proclaimed the independent state of Israel, mentioning no boundaries, when the British ended the mandate and withdrew their troops on May 14, 1948. Military units from contiguous Arab states entered the ex-mandate at the same time to aid Palestinians. Only the British-trained Jordanians and Iraqis held their ground in the highlands. Fighting alternated with cease-fires, but the other Arab forces were defeated by better-armed and -organized Jewish fighters.

At the end, Israel controlled not only the area allotted the Jewish state in the Partition Plan but also half the territory of the Arab state. The Jordan Arab Legion, with Iraqi troops on its right flank, held the highlands to the north, south, and east of Jerusalem, and Egyptians held a narrow tract northeast of the Sinai—the Gaza Strip. Jerusalem was split between Jordan and Israel—Jordan with the Old City and most of the holy sites, along with the rest of the West Bank.[36]

Territorial Phases

Theoretically, Israel became an independent state within the borders of the Partition Plan. However, a second "territorial phase" was based on the situation at the end of the fighting—the "cease-fire lines" negotiated by a UN mediator. These expanded Israel's original area by 50 percent and became (and still are) Israel's de facto boundaries (Map 8.5C).

Although Jordan held the eastern part of Jerusalem, including the Old City, Israel unilaterally declared Jerusalem as its national capital in 1950. This was pronounced invalid by the UN because the original Partition Plan had designated Jerusalem as a *corpus separatum* under UN administration. A short-lived third territorial phase came when Israel occupied Sinai during the Israeli-British-French collaborative assault on Suez in 1956. It later pulled out under international pressure, especially from U.S. president Dwight Eisenhower.

The fourth phase of Israel's territorial evolution began after the Six-Day (or June) War in 1967, in which Israel seized Sinai, Gaza, the West Bank, and the southwestern corner of Syria, the Golan Heights (Map 8.5D). This reunited Jerusalem, a major Israeli goal; the boundaries of East Jerusalem were then extended, and the entire area was unilaterally annexed. Only a few small states have recognized that extension, and all major embassies are still located in Tel Aviv. The U.S. Congress, urged by the Israeli lobby, has periodically attempted to force the American Embassy to move to Jerusalem; however, successive presidents have adhered to long-standing commitments and resisted the efforts.

This phase lasted until the beginning of Israel's step-by-step withdrawal from Sinai under agreements mediated by U.S. secretary of state Henry Kissinger. These were reached after the Egyptian-Syrian attacks in occupied Sinai and occupied Golan in 1973—the Yom Kippur/Ramadan War. The withdrawal from the Sinai proceeded under accords reached at Camp David in 1978 and the Egyptian-Israeli peace treaty of 1979. One small sticking point was the Taba enclave in eastern Sinai; it reverted to Egypt in 1988 after binding arbitration.

Israel's annexation of the Golan in 1981 could be termed a fifth phase—an action never recognized by any country. A sixth phase can be seen in Israel's invasions of Lebanon in 1978 and 1982. Although most of its forces were withdrawn by 1984, Israel maintained control of a heavily fortified 440-mi²/1,140-km² "security zone" in Lebanon. Helping patrol the area were the 3,000 Lebanese in the proxy South Lebanon Army (SLA)—organized, trained, armed, paid, and supplied by Israel. The control of southern Lebanon was ostensibly to deter rocket attacks on and infiltration into northern Israel. After twenty-two years and more than 900 casualties, mounting domestic and international criticism, and resistance from Hizballah and other guerrillas, Israel unilaterally withdrew in May 2000.

First called by Israeli "occupied territories," then "administered territories," then simply "territories," four areas—the West Bank, Gaza Strip, Golan Heights, and Sinai—were under Israeli military government from 1967 until the Sinai was evacuated and the Golan Heights was annexed.

The West Bank and East Jerusalem still remain the territorial core—but not the only territorial aspect—of the Arab-Israeli conflict, globally as well as locally. Palestinians are determined to remain in their homes, while Israel builds illegal settlements and expands existing ones in an organized program of Jewish displacement of local inhabitants in the occupied territories (see Fig. 8.4).

Frustrated and marginalized, Palestinians turned to a citizens' rebellion that began in Gaza in 1987. In this first intifadah (literally, "shaking off"), armed soldiers confronted rock-throwing Palestinian youths demonstrating against military occupation and settlement expansion. Unlike more ephemeral earlier protests, it became a full-scale insurgency despite all-out army action. Resistance increased Palestinian confidence, and more extreme groups, such as Hamas, emerged. Although its intensity had lessened by 1991, the coalition partners in the 1990–1991 Gulf crisis realized the need for a genuine peace process, and it subsided with negotiations

FIGURE 8.4 Armed Jewish settlers in the West Bank, in the heart of Hebron, which has theoretically been turned over to the Palestinian Authority (*top*), and a new settlement in 1997 near Hebron in the process of being developed (*bottom*). First come the mobile homes (shown here), then the permanent houses. Both are illegal under the Fourth Geneva Convention, which Israel rejects.

that ended with the Israeli-Palestinian accord in Gaza in September 1993. By then, 1,119 Palestinians had been killed by Israeli soldiers or civilians and more than 100,000 wounded or injured; 124 Israeli soldiers and civilians had been killed.[37]

The second intifadah broke out in September 2000 after a particularly violent clash in Jerusalem. Palestinians hold that the immediate cause was a visit to the Haram al-Sharif/Temple Mount by Likud Party leader Ariel Sharon—about to be elected Israeli prime minister—with a retinue of 1,000 armed police and military personnel. In any case, the flash point was reached, and what Palestinians called the "al-Aqsa intifadah"—after the large and revered mosque in the Haram al-Sharif complex—was under way. Intense passions flared, as seen in heightened militancy and frequent suicide bombings. In turn, heavy-handedness characterized Israeli responses, including targeted assassinations, bulldozing of homes and olive groves by Israeli forces, and destruction of Palestinian government buildings in Ramallah. With no effective curbs on either side's attacks, the cycle of violence escalated to new levels, with many countries urging the United States to exert some constraints. The intifadah was interrupted by the death of Palestinian president Yasser Arafat in November 2004 and the election of Mahmoud Abbas as the new PA president in January 2005. For the most part, relative calm then prevailed, but incidents continued into the late 2000s (see below, "Terrorism and Piracy").

The Palestinians

Although Palestinians are primarily refugees, they may be grouped geographically in seven categories: those who stayed in areas designated by the UN as the Jewish state; those who remained in the Arab areas taken over by Israel in 1948–1949; those who lived in the areas held by the Arab armies (the West Bank and Gaza); those who fled the areas incorporated into Israel in 1948–1949, becoming refugees in adjoining districts (West Bank and Gaza, later occupied by Israel); those who fled to the East Bank between 1947 and the present (granted Jordanian citizenship); those who fled into adjoining countries and have remained there; and those who emigrated to other countries.

Even before the outbreak of full-scale fighting in May 1948, Palestinians had lost the initiative to Zionist forces, and thousands fled from areas in which Arabs and Jews were contending for land and military advantage. They had been especially terrified by the massacre of 254 Palestinian villagers in Deir Yassin, near Jerusalem, by Jewish terrorists in April 1948, which was then widely reported in order to cause panic among the Arabs. Beginning in May, the thousands of refugees became hundreds of thousands as Israeli military units gained the advantage.

By the time fighting subsided in 1949, some 800,000 (estimates run from 720,000 to 960,000) Palestinians had fled or been expelled from their homes and lands by Israeli forces. Arabs refer to these watershed events as *al-nakbah*, "the catastrophe." After studying newly declassified documentation in the mid-1980s, a group of Israeli scholars, who became known as the "New Historians," wrote that inter alia the expulsion of the Palestinians, and the effort to cause panic among them, was more deliberate and common than previously admitted. The New History has been widely accepted.[38]

The largest number sought refuge in the hill country of central Palestine; others continued across the Jordan River to Transjordan. Others crowded into the southwestern corner of Palestine—the Gaza Strip; still others fled to Lebanon and Syria. About 160,000 Arabs, mostly in Galilee, refused to leave their lands and homes and stayed in the Jewish state. These Israeli Arabs have increased in numbers and now constitute more than 20 percent of Israel's population.

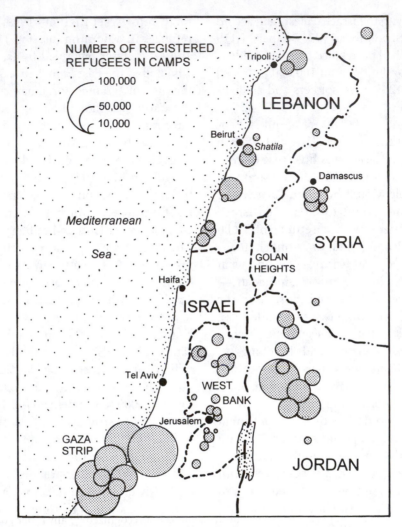

MAP 8.6 Palestinian refugee camps in Gaza, West Bank, Jordan, Syria, and Lebanon, operated by the United Nations Relief and Works Agency (UNRWA). As of 2009, these fifty-nine camps had a population of 1.4 million, a significant portion of the 4.1 million refugees registered with UNRWA.

The refugees expected to return home when the fighting ceased. As it became clear after the 1949 cease-fire that the Israelis would not allow them to return to their homes, the UN created the UN Relief and Works Agency (UNRWA) to provide emergency refugee aid. It set up camps where homeless Palestinians were concentrated: Gaza, the West Bank, the East Bank (Jordan, especially around Amman), southern and central Lebanon (especially around Beirut), and Syria (see Map 8.6). Although UNRWA aid supported only a marginal existence, it sustained—and continues to sustain—thousands of refugees in the fifty-nine camps that the agency continued to administer in 2010. Not all the refugees, of course, call the camps home. Those with professional skills or sufficient funds generally did not register with UNRWA.

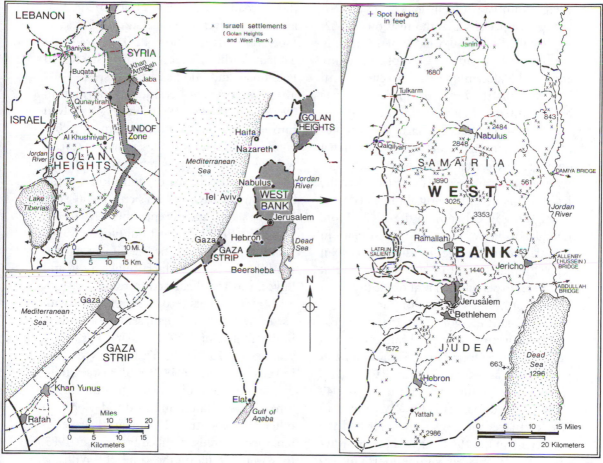

MAP 8.7 Territories occupied by Israel in 1967 and still mostly occupied in early 2010. Israel announced a unilateral withdrawal from Gaza by the end of 2005 but invaded it briefly in December 2008. Israel considers Golan part of Israel, but the claim is not recognized by any other government.

The status of the refugees within their host countries varies. Only Jordan has given full citizenship to them. Syria has extended equal rights (except the right to passports) but maintains strict control. Lebanon accepted them originally, but then feared the impact on that country's internal balance between Christians and Muslims; after 1972, it fought them militarily, and the government has officially declared its intention to refuse them permanent settlement (see Chap. 10). Other Arab countries took in only limited numbers of Palestinians. Many refugees reject integration into their host country's economy and society,

deliberately maintaining their refugee status as a symbol of determination to return to their homeland and regain their patrimony.

With Israel's 1967 conquests (Map 8.7), more than 116,000 original refugees were again uprooted, mostly from the West Bank. Some 100,000 crossed the Jordan to the East Bank ("displaced persons" to UNRWA), 99,000 Syrians took flight from Golan deeper into Syria, and 35,000 Bedouin and villagers in the Sinai fled across the Suez Canal. (As with the earlier figures, these are estimates.) Thousands of the original refugees in southern Lebanon abandoned their camps and villages with Israeli incursions into southern Lebanon, especially after the invasion of 1982.

Unskilled refugees could at best find only menial jobs outside the camps, but many educated Palestinians (often schooled in UNRWA institutions) prospered in their host countries; they were significant in developing the Gulf states. Beirut was a center of Palestinian intellectual activity, Amman a demographic center, and Kuwait a center of Palestinian commercial activity. However, the Palestinians' role in Beirut diminished with the fighting in Lebanon in the 1980s. More notably, of the some 400,000 Palestinians in Kuwait before the Iraqi invasion, fewer than 40,000 remained in the late 2000s—the rest had been expelled or not allowed to return because of Arafat's support of Iraq.

Palestinians categorized in the seven geographical groups mentioned earlier may also be divided into four categories according to their status as refugees: (1) all Palestinians, (2) registered refugees from the 1948–1949 fighting (under specific UNRWA criteria), (3) "displaced persons" who first fled the West Bank in the 1967 war, and (4) those living in the camps—about one-fourth of registered refugees. With these various ways of classifying them, differences in enumeration inevitably arise.[39]

At the end of the 2000s, there were about 4.0 million Palestinians residing in the West Bank, East Jerusalem, and Gaza and about 1.5 million in Israel proper, 2.5 million in Jordan, 0.5 million in Syria, 0.4 million in Lebanon, from 0.4 to 0.5 million in other Middle East countries, and 0.3 million or more elsewhere—for a total of more than 9.5 million.

Facing international inaction after 1949, the Palestinians slowly began to organize. One early major group, founded in 1958, was Fatah (the reverse acronym for Harakat al-Tahrir al-Filastiniyah, Palestinian Liberation Movement), which conducted guerrilla raids by *fedayeen* (literally, "sacrificers") into Israel from neighboring countries. Not until 1964

did a broad-based organization emerge that aimed to recover the homeland, the Palestine Liberation Organization (PLO). It gradually gained a leading if highly controversial role in Palestinian and Middle East affairs, especially after Yasser Arafat became its chairman in 1969. After the late 1960s, the PLO evolved into a complex institution that expanded beyond paramilitary activities, founding several welfare agencies serving refugees.

With Jordan as the organization's initial base, King Husayn saw it as creating a "state within a state," and in September 1970 he defeated the PLO in a short but bloody war—"Black September" to the Palestinians. It then moved to Lebanon, which, unlike Syria and Egypt, was too disunited to resist. In 1974, Arab governments recognized the PLO, with Yasser Arafat as chairman, as the sole official representative of the Palestinians. For twelve years after 1970, the organization was centered in Lebanon, until, in 1982, under Israeli military and Western diplomatic pressure, it was forced to withdraw from Beirut and relocate in other Arab countries. Headquarters were established in Tunis; bombed by Israel in 1985, they were rebuilt on the same site. With the onset of the peace process it moved to Gaza in 1994 as the Palestinian Authority and then to Ramallah in the West Bank; besieged by Israel in 2002, the PA remains there, though Hamas has controlled Gaza since 2007.

In 1988, a year into the first intifadah, the Palestine National Council (PNC) proclaimed an independent State of Palestine in the West Bank and Gaza, with its capital as Jerusalem. The PNC proposed that this would be the Arab state approved, along with the Jewish state, by the UN General Assembly Partition Resolution of 1947 (which also gave Jerusalem the status of *corpus separatum*). More than eighty governments tendered their recognition within a year, but supported by the United States Israel categorically rejected the declaration, refusing to deal with the PLO for several years. By 1992, the PLO could no longer be ignored, as the Israeli government under Yitzhak Rabin acknowledged.

The Peace Process

Renewed attempts to initiate contacts between the Israelis and Palestinians began in 1990, as U.S. and European leaders forged a broad coalition against Iraq. Partly in recognition of the intifadah, they agreed that after Kuwait's liberation the coalition's basic premises would be applied to the Palestine-Israel problem. Thus initiated was a series of diplomatic efforts that continue in the new millennium. The Madrid Conference of October 1991 gave the peace process a vigorous start.

Meanwhile, Israel and the PLO negotiated and initialed a Declaration of Principles in secret bilateral sessions in Oslo, Norway. The famous Rabin-Arafat handshake in Washington marked the formal signing in September 1993. There followed a period of some progress, but stalemate set in when later Israeli prime ministers reneged and Arafat was unable to carry out his commitments.

On the positive side, Israeli troops withdrew from Gaza City and Jericho, allowing Arafat's return and the initiation of the PA as a quasi state. Concurrently, Jordan and Israel signed a peace treaty. Further talks led to the Taba Agreement and PA authority over small areas in the West Bank.

Strong opposition among Israeli extremists climaxed when a Jewish fanatic assassinated Prime Minister Rabin in November 1995. On the Palestinian side, conflict arose between the PA and Islamist rejectionists like Hamas (Harakat al-Muqawamah al-Islamiyya, Islamic Resistance Movement). Founded in 1987, it had initially been supported by Israeli intelligence agencies as a counter to the secular PLO; in a classic case of "blowback," Hamas undertook to sabotage further talks.[40] After Israel assassinated a Hamas leader, its suicide bombers killed sixty-one Israelis.

The peace process thus quickly lost favor among Israelis who elected hard-liner Binyamin Netanyahu prime minister in May 1996. Never one to compromise, he speeded up settlement activity in the West Bank and Jerusalem and undertook actions that provoked armed clashes between Israeli soldiers and Palestinian policemen, claiming a toll of seventy-nine Palestinians and fifteen Israelis. Negotiations faltered for three years, achieving only a partial Israeli withdrawal from Hebron and the Wye River Memorandum brokered by President Clinton to advance previous agreements. Claiming that the PA had failed to control terrorism, Netanyahu refused to implement the Oslo accords and Wye agreement.

Ehud Barak replaced Netanyahu as prime minister in May 1999. Dialogue resumed with notable success on several specifics, encouraging Clinton to bring Barak and Arafat together at Camp David in July 2000. Controversy surrounds why this summit and its follow-up failed to solidify the progress that had been made and to move on to other issues; each side has blamed the other. But other observers have noted that the final U.S.-Israeli offer was subtly inadequate, while the Palestinians missed the opportunity to make a timely counteroffer.[41]

With a suggested plan for regional peace offered by Saudi Arabia at a 2003 Arab League summit in Beirut, with violence at new heights, and with PA president Arafat termed "irrelevant" by Israel and the Bush administration, a "Quartet" composed of the UN, United States, the EU, and Russia developed a "road map" toward peace between Israel and the Palestinians in 2003. It outlined peace by stages, but it was soon waved aside, at least tentatively. An unofficial group of concerned Israelis and Palestinians hopefully offered an informal "Geneva Accord" in 2003, but it, too, failed to prompt movement forward.

Discussions were overshadowed by a new project under way in Israel: construction of a "Separation Fence" designed to enclose the

FIGURE 8.5 One segment of the Israeli "Separation Fence," which Israel claims is essential for its security. A wall in certain stretches, the barrier is actually built almost entirely on Palestinian lands and here divides a village. It has been a matter of continuing controversy.

West Bank (Fig. 8.5). Intended as a "security barrier" against would-be suicide bombers, the complex structure—part wall but mostly fence—is an elaborate system of barriers, watchtowers, and access roads; at a cost of $4 million per mile, it was projected to eventually extend 210 mi/338 km. It was designed to follow the 1967 border for only 11 percent of its length, stretching into the West Bank so that it can "gather in" Israeli settlements along with 15 percent of the area. The serpentine alignment separates villagers from farms and families from relatives.[42] Israel claims the barrier is essential to its security, but an opposing writer cited "its brutality and naked territorial ambition." Even President George W. Bush said it caused problems for the peace process.[43] The UN overwhelmingly condemned its routing of the barrier, and the International Court at The Hague found the routing illegal in July 2004. Israel has largely ignored these criticisms.[44] However, legal appeals within Israel slowed its construction and caused some changes in its route, and by the end of the 2000s, only 57 percent had been completed.[45] During his 2009 pilgrimage, Pope Benedict XVI said, "In a world where more and more borders are being opened up—to trade, to travel, to movement of peoples, to cultural exchanges—it is tragic to see walls still being erected."[46]

In 2004 Israel announced plans for a unilateral pullout from Gaza, including an evacuation of an estimated 8,000 Israeli settlers. The announcement created controversy not only internationally and among the Palestinians but also in Israel and within Prime Minister Ariel Sharon's own Likud Party. But if Gaza was then technically unoccupied, Israel remained in tight control of its borders, and the IDF entered the Strip frequently, before and after Hamas took control in 2007 and Operation Cast Lead began in 2008. At the end of the decade, little had changed on either side of the border (see Chap. 12).[47]

As George W. Bush quite aptly, if a bit inelegantly, put it in January 2008, "Swiss cheese isn't going to work when it comes to the territory of a state."[48]

THE IRAN-IRAQ WAR, 1980–1988

Ancient enmities flared into open conflict along the Zagros piedmont between "Mesopotamians" to the west and "Iranians" to the east with the overthrow of the shah in 1979. For centuries, the Sunni Ottomans were to the west and the Shii Persians held the Zagros and the Iranian Plateau. Post–World War I Iraq and Iran periodically clashed along the ridges and the Shatt al-Arab. The new republic's aggressiveness and apparent instability led Iraq to try forcing Iran to accede to several long-standing demands by invading across the Shatt in September 1980. It soon held several positions inside Iran and called for the return of Gulf islands that Iran had occupied since 1971. Thus began the Iran-Iraq War, which Iraq expected to last a few weeks but which dragged on for eight years.

Iraq aimed to reinstate the pre-1975 boundary along the Shatt. Difficult to delineate equitably, the modern boundary was first drawn in 1847 and slightly modified in 1913–1914. In 1937, it was changed to follow the *thalweg* (the deepest channel) near Abadan but the low-water mark on the east (Iranian) bank (Map 8.8A), in accordance with the 1913–1914 agreement. In 1969, the shah renounced this treaty, and by 1975 a powerful Iran forced Iraq to accept a boundary that followed the *thalweg* along the entire Shatt (Map 8.8B) in return for ceasing to assist the rebellion of Iraq's Kurds.

War operations damaged or destroyed many major facilities in the northern Gulf,

including Iraq's ports and much of the city of Basrah. Air raids and missile attacks struck major cities on both sides, and oil production decreased sharply in both countries. Casualties were tragically high, especially among young Iranians, and combined fatalities were reliably reported to exceed 500,000.[49]

Because of the war, all the Gulf states were affected economically—losses estimated at $200 billion directly and more than $1 trillion indirectly. Oil tankers calling at export terminals were attacked—the "tanker war," which intensified in 1987. The Gulf amirates and Saudi Arabia gave Iraq about $50 billion in aid, and the latter allowed Iraq to build a pipeline connecting to the Saudi East-West line. The United States committed to keeping the Gulf accessible by providing naval escorts to U.S.-registered tankers—actually mostly reflagged Kuwaiti vessels. In the confusion of the Gulf's confined area, mistakes led to the USS *Star*'s being hit by an Iraqi Exocet missile in May 1987, killing 37 of its crew, and to the USS *Vincennes*'s shooting down an Iranian civilian aircraft with a missile in July 1988, with a loss of all 290 people aboard. Both Iraq and the United States agreed to pay damages for their errors.

With both countries exhausted, Iran surprisingly accepted a UN Security Council resolution calling for an immediate cease-fire, possibly because of fears of Iraqi chemical attacks. In March 1988, Iraq used poison gas against the Kurdish village of Halabja, killing several thousands, in reprisal for Kurds having joined Iran in a prior attack. A UN-sponsored armistice took effect in August 1988.

The war engendered some curious transnational relationships. Syria, although Arab and Baathi ruled like Iraq, refused to allow Iraq the use of pipelines across its territory. Despite the Islamic Republic's vociferous condemnations of Israel, the Jewish state followed its principle of aiding an enemy of the Arabs by supplying Iran with spare parts and arms in collusion with the United States,

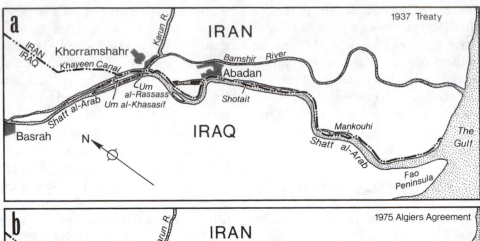

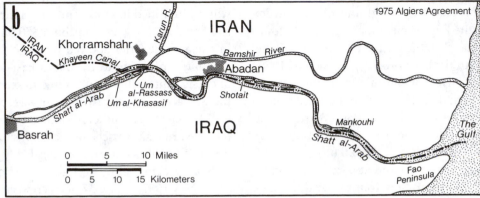

MAP 8.8 Iran-Iraq boundary along the Shatt al-Arab. The boundary shift from the east bank of the river to the deepest part of the channel (the *thalweg*) in 1975 was one reason for the Iran-Iraq War, 1980–1988. (Redrawn from Tareq Y. Ismael, *Iraq and Iran: Roots of Conflict* [Syracuse, NY: Syracuse University Press, 1982], 23. Names as on original. Used with permission.)

as was revealed by the Iran-Contra scandal. Ironically, two of Iraq's biggest financial and logistical supporters, Kuwait and Saudi Arabia, became its victims two years later.

THE GULF CRISIS, 1990–1991

Despite the huge losses from the 1980–1988 fighting, Iraq launched a second Gulf war less than two years later. Saddam Husayn resurrected his country's long-standing claim to Kuwait, demanding that Kuwait forgive the billions in loans it had made to Iraq during the 1980s and cede to Iraq its part of the rich Rumaila oil field; Kuwait rejected these demands. While giving assurances that he would

not attack an Arab country, on August 2, 1990, he ordered the 100,000 troops massed on the border—supposedly only for maneuvers—to advance into Kuwait.[50]

Regional and world reaction varied in kind and degree. Iraq sought support from the more oppressed and militant Arabs, claiming to champion Arabism, Islam, the Palestinians, the overthrow of wealthy monarchies, anti-imperialism, and other popular causes. One Iraqi proposal linked withdrawal from Kuwait with Israeli withdrawal from the occupied territories and Syrian withdrawal from Lebanon. Some frustrated Palestinians cheered these declarations, and the PLO leadership expressed support, as did Yemen, Sudan, Libya,

Algeria, and Tunisia. Jordan, with close economic ties to Iraq, equivocated. Iraq gained Iran's neutrality by hastily accepting the harsh terms Iran had placed in 1988 for a treaty ending their war.

Coalition Response

Acting under the Carter Doctrine, the United States sought and received prompt Saudi permission to dispatch troops to northeastern Saudi Arabia within days of the invasion. Most Western reaction to the invasion was channeled through the UN Security Council. Under its resolutions, thirty-six states joined the U.S./U.K.-led coalition and cooperated in Kuwait's liberation. Germany and Japan sent no troops but contributed large funds; India allowed the use of refueling facilities to coalition forces.

Although Iraq claimed Kuwait as its "rightful nineteenth province," its occupation forces committed many atrocities—executions, widespread mistreatment of hundreds of Kuwaitis, hostage taking, and large-scale looting, including museum collections and $3–4 billion in gold bullion as well as cash in the banks (UN resolutions eventually secured the return of most of the museum collections and gold bullion). The invasion also set in motion a human tide of more than 3 million refugees of many nationalities, and hundreds of Europeans and Americans were held hostage in Baghdad.

The UNSC gave Iraq a deadline of January 15, 1991, to leave Kuwait or face a full-scale military attack in both Kuwait and Iraq. When Iraq did not withdraw, intensive target-specific air strikes were directed at Baghdad and other major cities in Iraq. Saddam refused to capitulate, and the coalition ground attack began on February 24, 1991, overwhelming Iraqi forces in Kuwait in a few days.

Destruction and Ecoterrorism

Details of military operations are well covered elsewhere (see note 50). However, two Iraqi wartime actions are noteworthy. First, thirty-two ground-to-ground Scud missiles were launched at targets in Saudi Arabia and thirty-nine at Israel. Some were destroyed by Patriot antimissile batteries, but others damaged buildings in both countries; one caused twenty-seven U.S. military fatalities in Dammam, Saudi Arabia. Second, after the beginning of hostilities, Iraq employed a new and destructive tactic, appropriately labeled "environmental terrorism" or "ecoterrorism"—dumping and setting fire to oil, thus making a weapon of the one commodity available in abundance. To deter expected coalition offensive operations along the coast, the Iraqis opened the valves of storage facilities in the export terminals and on tankers in the area, deliberately creating the greatest oil spill in history, 4 to 6 million barrels (in comparison, the *Exxon Valdez* spill in Alaska was 258,000 barrels), which worked its way down the Gulf coast, destroying enormous quantities of plant and animal life.

As the Iraqis pulled back in defeat, they escalated the ecoterrorism by blowing up and setting fire to most of the amirate's oil wells. Some 651 wells were set ablaze, and another 60 spewed crude oil under high pressure. By early summer of 1991, about 5.5 million barrels of oil and enormous quantities of natural gas were lost each day—approximately twice the normal average daily production of Kuwait (also of Iraq)—with a value at that time of $75 million. Upon the liberation of Kuwait, the best oil-well firefighting teams in the world arrived to extinguish the blazes and cap the flowing wells, a task that, despite dangers and difficulties, they accomplished by early November.[51]

One positive outcome of the war was that it focused the attention of the Western powers on the Palestinian-Israeli conflict and the possibility of initiating a peace process. On the negative side was the failure of Iraq and the UN coalition—primarily the United States—to resolve the impasse over weapons inspections and other provisions of the sanctions.

There was also the later criticism that "the United States didn't finish the job" and that it should have pushed on to Baghdad to overthrow the Baathi once and for all. This idea might have appealed to its proponents; however, such action would have violated the very specifically worded UN mandate and betrayed the terms of the coalition, instantly transforming partners into enemies.

"OPERATION IRAQI FREEDOM"

Following 9/11 and U.S. president George W. Bush's declaration of a "War on Terror," three developments led up to the invasion of Iraq: the U.S. incursion into Afghanistan in search of Osama bin Laden and other al-Qaida leaders, several months of well-publicized U.S. planning—including presentations to the UN—and revelations of intentions, and several weeks of inspections by UN teams for weapons of mass destruction (WMDs) in Iraq. With a modest coalition—Britain the main partner—of forces in place in Kuwait and the lower Gulf, and with hot weather approaching, the U.S.-led invasion of Iraq began on March 20, 2003, with the code name "Operation Iraqi Freedom."

Reasons given by the U.S. administration and the British prime minister for the preemptive attack included the threat posed to the United States and Britain from the alleged WMDs, supposed links between Iraq and al-Qaida, and the oppression of the Iraqi people by the Saddam Husayn regime. President Bush's letter to Congress justifying the attack stated that its aims were to "protect the national security of the United States, as well as the security of other countries," against the threat of the Iraqi WMDs and to obtain Iraqi compliance with relevant UN resolutions.[52]

The claims and actions surrounding the invasion and the subsequent occupation provoked a vigorous negative international response, with the United States receiving more condemnation than it had in many years. Domestic reaction was bitterly divided, with opinions particularly strong regarding the influence of a small group of prowar "neocons" (neoconservatives) centered in the Department of Defense and the Office of the Vice President.

The operations in late March 2003 achieved their military objectives relatively promptly, and the United States announced the formal end of hostilities in mid-April. Coalition casualties were light in the invasion but increased during the subsequent occupation. Developments in postinvasion Iraq are discussed below in Chapter 13. In concluding this section, it should be pointed out that in Operation Iraqi Freedom, no WMDs were discovered; as to the presence of al-Qaida, there was none until the insurgency brought that group and others like it into Iraq. By the end of the decade, the war had cost the United States nearly 4,400 military fatalities, more than 31,500 physically wounded, and at least 100,000 troops with severe psychological problems. U.S. taxpayers had by then been burdened with about $1 trillion in direct war-related (deficit) spending; this is roughly twenty times what the Bush administration estimated costs would be at the outset, and future U.S. budgets will see another $1 to $2 trillion in long-term expenses (veterans' compensation, military equipment replacement, debt service, and related costs).

On the Iraqi side, it is impossible to pinpoint the losses reliably; the number of civilian and military deaths has been variously estimated at from more than 100,000 to as many as 1.3 million. Some 2.5 million Iraqis fled to safer havens in neighboring countries and farther afield; the number of internally displaced persons in 2008 was estimated to be at least 1.8 million.[53] Nearly one in six Iraqis has been forced to leave their homes, and the economic costs to the country are truly incalculable.

STRATEGIC STRAITS

Five sea passages, four major and one minor, in the region are of geostrategic significance: the Suez Canal, the Turkish Straits (Dardanelles and Bosporus), the Strait of Hormuz, Bab el-Mandeb, and the Strait of Tiran. Some are familiar historically; all have made news in recent decades. The U.S. Department of Energy identifies six major chokepoints for global oil trade; four are in the Middle East (all of the above except Tiran).[54]

Suez Canal

Egypt's Suez Canal was excavated between 1859 and 1869 through the Isthmus of Suez, which linked Africa and Asia. Entirely at sea level with no locks, it is approximately 110 mi/177 km long. It has been enlarged numerous times to a navigational width of 650 ft/198 m and a depth of 62 ft/18.9 m. A ten-year project is under way to widen and deepen the canal so that it can accommodate Very Large Crude Carriers (VLCCs) with a draft of 68 ft/20.7 m and a weight of 350,000 deadweight tons. By the end of 2009, the project had progressed to the point where 64 percent of the world's tankers and 99 percent of all cargo ships could pass through. A combination of global recession and fears of piracy south of the Red Sea led to a decrease in traffic in 2008–2009 as an average of fifty-three ships transited the route daily, down from fifty-eight a year earlier; revenues were off by 7.2 percent to $4.74 billion.[55]

Its opening shortened the sea trip between Britain and India by 5,000 mi/8,000 km, so that after the 1870s most world shipping shifted from the route around Africa to the Mediterranean-Suez–Red Sea route. Suez Canal closures, for six months in 1956 and for eight years prior to June 1975, diverted traffic—including increasing numbers of VLCCs—to other routes, and some shipping never returned to Suez. The canal also faces competition from Egypt's own Sumed pipeline, which carries crude oil from the Red Sea to the Mediterranean, thus bypassing the canal. In 2007, Sumed and the canal together carried 3.2 mn bpd. An underwater extension across the Red Sea to link directly to Saudi Arabia's east-west pipeline at Yanbu is being discussed.

Straits

Turkish Straits. These straits, the Dardanelles to the southwest and the Bosporus to the northeast, are linked up by the Sea of Marmara (Map 8.9) and have been of crucial importance since the Bronze Age. The legend of the Trojan War tells of fighting over the beautiful Helen, a romanticization of the struggle during the twelfth century BCE for control of the entrance to the Black Sea and its rich coastlands. The World War I Gallipoli campaign in 1915 is the most recent clash over control of the straits. International access to the straits was spelled out in the Lausanne Convention of 1923 and again in the Montreux Convention of 1936, which still governs international use of the waterways.[56]

The Bosporus (Greek for "ox-ford"; Turkish: Karadeniz Boğazı) is shorter, narrower, and shallower than the Dardanelles—about 17 mi/28 km long, 2,500 ft/762 m wide at its narrowest, and 100 ft/30 m at its minimum midstream depth. Since the Sea of Marmara is as deep as, and much wider than, the two straits, any ship afloat can make the passage between the Aegean and the Black seas. Although the three bodies of water separate Europe from Asia Minor, the Bosporus was bridged in 1973 and again in 1988. The Marmaray project, including a rail tunnel billed as earthquake proof under the strait, serves both Istanbul's metro system and through trains. A third bridge at the northern end of the Bosporus is scheduled to begin construction in 2010.

The Dardanelles (Turkish: Çanakkale Boğazı), the ancient Hellespont, connects the

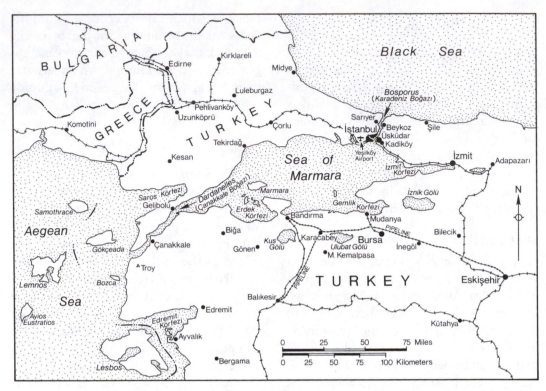

MAP 8.9 The Turkish straits (Bosporus and Dardanelles) and their geographic setting—a major world maritime connection and "chokepoint." The disastrous earthquake of August 17, 1999, was centered just south of Izmit.

Aegean Sea and the Sea of Marmara and lies between the Gallipoli Peninsula on the northwest and Asia Minor to the south. It is about 36 mi/57 km long, 4,000 ft/1,200 m wide at its narrowest, 4 mi/6.4 km at its widest, and 150–300 ft/45–90 m deep.

Traffic through the straits has increased markedly since World War I—international traffic by more than ten times. In the first half of 2009, shipping was feeling the effects of the global recession but still came to about 128 ships a day—about 140 percent above Suez Canal levels. Half the larger ships are tankers, and nearly half of all vessels fly the flags of Russia and other successor states of the FSU, especially Ukraine and Georgia. Straits traffic is expected to increase still more with the further development of Caspian oil fields and the growth of the Danube–Main Rivers waterway. The in-

crease will begin to stretch the capacity of the straits to accommodate tanker traffic. More than 3 mn bpd of crude—twice the amount of the late 1990s—transited the straits daily in the mid-2000s, raising serious concerns about environmental safety. By the end of the decade, transit fell to less than 2.5 mn bpd[57] as new pipelines opened to the Mediterranean (see Chaps. 6 and 18 for discussion of pipelines).

Strait of Hormuz. Connecting the Gulf and the Indian Ocean, the Strait of Hormuz squeezes between Iran to the north and an exclave of Oman on the Musandam Peninsula to the south (Fig. 8.6 and Map 8.10). It is by far the world's most vital oil chokepoint, and although no longer do 90 percent of the region's petroleum exports pass through it, as was true before the various Gulf wars, it still

FIGURE 8.6 Image from space, looking southeast, of the Strait of Hormuz, one of the world's most important economic chokepoints, with Iran to the left, Oman and the UAE to the right. The dark oval areas are salt domes, which often indicate petroleum and gas reservoirs. Compare with Map 8.10. (Photograph courtesy of National Aeronautics and Space Administration)

carries more than 15 mn bpd. Some of its previous traffic is piped to the Red Sea and the Mediterranean, but general cargo is growing. Traffic varies with the world petroleum market, the political climate in the Gulf, and tanker size. Increasing shiploads of natural gas liquids (NGL) and product transit each day.

With a depth of 290 ft/88 m and widths of 28–59 mi/45–95 km, Hormuz is the widest of the significant straits in the Middle East. Nevertheless, it is vulnerable to sabotage and some kinds of weaponry, and its defense is vital to both petroleum exporters and petroleum consumers. Thus, the security of the Gulf and the strait is a major aim of the Western powers and their regional allies.

Bab el-Mandeb. At the opposite corner of the Arabian Peninsula, the Bab el-Mandeb (Gate of Lamentation) connects the Red Sea and Gulf of Aden. The strait is divided into two channels by the small but strategically located Yemeni island of Perim. Two other states, Eritrea and Djibouti, share the territorial waters in the straits. The main channel, with a width of 10 mi/16 km and a depth of 1,056 ft/322 m, is to the west of Perim on the African side, next to Djibouti.

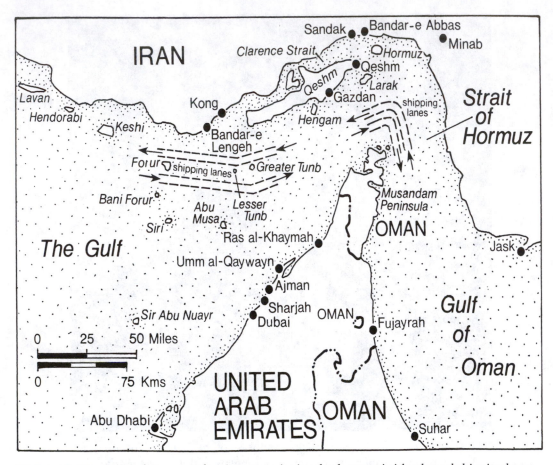

MAP 8.10 The Strait of Hormuz, showing countries involved, strategic islands, and shipping lanes. Compare Figure 8.6.

Bab el-Mandeb's importance grew significantly when the Suez Canal opened, since virtually all shipping transiting the canal also passes through it. Canal traffic developed more ports along the Red Sea, and so the strait was busy even with the canal closed in order to serve Jiddah, Yanbu, and others. Aden, lying a few miles east of the Bab el-Mandeb, owes much of its modern importance to the rise in Suez use. About eighty ships a day transit the strait, with tankers carrying just over 3 mn bpd. Increased piracy in the seas to the south has raised the risks along this route. The hijacking of the Saudi-flagged *Sirius Star* in November 2008 accelerated the trend of tankers to opt for the longer trip around Africa (see below, "Terrorism and Piracy").

Strait of Tiran.   Connecting the Red Sea and the Gulf of Aqabah at the southeastern tip of the Sinai Peninsula, with Egypt on the west and Saudi Arabia on the east, the Strait of Tiran is of relatively minor importance in comparison with the Suez Canal and the straits already described. Nevertheless, its closure was considered a major justification for the Israeli preemptive attack on Egypt in June 1967. The debate over the precise international principles relating to Tiran has not yet resolved the exact status of the strait. In the late 2000s, a $3 billion causeway-bridge system linking Saudi Arabia and Egypt across the strait had reached the planning stage.

GREAT-POWER RIVALRY

Britain and Russia long vied for spheres of influence from the Balkans to the Himalayas. Britain's protective umbrella over the Suez Canal, Aden, and the Gulf defended its lifeline, first, to India and, later, to oil. Russian pressure on the "Northern Tier" diminished during the 1920s and 1930s, but the Soviet Union resumed the historic push into southwestern Asia after World War II. With Britain no longer able to counter the pressure, the United States increasingly took over as protector of the Northern Tier—Turkey and Iran—against Russian expansion into an area of increasingly vital concern. Rivalry between the United States and the USSR in the region became a major dynamic in the global Cold War and in the region's relations and geopolitics for forty-five years. Much of this "Great Game in the Middle East" seemed to have ended with the Soviet collapse and the subsequent cooperation between the United States and some former Soviet republics. However, highlights of the rivalry are worth a brief review.

The policy of "containment" first advocated in a watershed article by "X" (Ambassador George Kennan)[58] was formalized in the Truman Doctrine in March 1947. The declaration signaled a U.S. commitment to maintain the balance of power in the Middle East while Britain withdrew in phases from Greece, India, and the Palestine mandate. Later, Britain lost its influence in Iran, gave up Suez in 1956, and left the Gulf and the periphery of the Arabian Peninsula in 1971–1972. However, it continues to have vital interests in the region and generally coordinates political and military operations with the United States, as it did on a major scale during the 1990–1991 Gulf crisis and its aftermath—including the no-fly zones—and even more prominently in the invasion of Iraq in 2003.

The Eisenhower administration sought to unify regional resistance to Soviet pressure. With U.S. and British encouragement, the Baghdad Pact was formed in 1955, eventually including Turkey, Iraq, Iran, Pakistan, and Britain. The United States was a full member of the economic committee and the major source of pact funding. Consequent to the Suez imbroglio of 1956—the joint Israeli-British-French invasion of Egypt—the Eisenhower Doctrine, announced in January 1957, committed the United States to countering Communist moves in the Middle East. Not always applied consistently, it nonetheless was pursued by succeeding administrations. But while the United States tried to minimize Soviet regional influence, it also adopted policies antagonizing key Arab countries, easing the way for the Soviets.

The Nixon Doctrine encouraged the region's states to be responsible for their own defense, focusing on Iran and, secondarily, Saudi Arabia, to counter the Soviets. In the eastern Mediterranean, Turkey and Greece were NATO's southeastern flank, with the British providing support in Cyprus. In the Fertile Crescent, Israel's so-called special relationship with the United States was strengthened.

The Carter Doctrine, promulgated in 1980 following the Iranian Revolution, collapse of the Central Treaty Organization (the former Baghdad Pact), and the Soviet invasion of Afghanistan in December 1979, emphasized U.S. interests in the Gulf. It laid the groundwork for a Rapid Deployment Force—later the Central Command. The Reagan administration sent U.S. naval forces to the Gulf in 1987 and 1988. The dispatch of U.S. troops to Saudi Arabia in 1990–1991 by the first Bush administration was based on the Carter Doctrine and was an extension of Reagan's support of Kuwait.

The next projection of U.S. policy into the broader region was a major part of the "War on Terror"—the dispatch of coalition troops to Afghanistan in October 2001 after the 9/11 terrorist attacks. A stiffening of U.S. policy toward Iraq also emerged during 2002 based on allegations of Iraqi links to al-Qaida, climaxing with invasion in March 2003. Amid criticism of the actions toward Iraq, President George W. Bush announced a complex policy in November 2003 that, refined and enlarged, became the Broader Middle East and North Africa Initiative. A White House fact sheet in June 2004 gave as the initiative's aims to "advance freedom, democracy, and prosperity" and to "support political, economic, and social reform" in the states of the region. The invasion and subsequent occupation of Iraq were cast as integral parts of furthering the goals of fighting terrorism, suppressing weapons of mass destruction, and promoting freedom and democracy.[59] Viewed with hindsight, the question must be asked as to what extent have any of these goals been realized through U.S. actions in either Afghanistan or Iraq.

In the twenty-first century, there are numerous signs that the "Great Game" may still be being played, perhaps with more players and somewhat different objectives and rules. The resources of the Middle East and the adjoining areas in Central Asia are vital to the prosperity of a world in which the old imperial powers are no longer alone in their ability to participate in regional affairs.

TERRORISM AND PIRACY

Especially with the beginning of the new century, regional nonstate actors increasingly threatened both the citizens and economies of countries far from the Middle East, sometimes with the compliance of rogue states like Taliban Afghanistan and ungoverned Somalia, but often acting on their own. Neither of their methods—terrorism and piracy—were new, but changes in international politics and technology have made them manifest in a number of new ways that have challenged the effectiveness of conventional political and military responses.

Terrorism

In recent decades, violence has been wreaked against civilians to spread fear and terror in many parts of the world; a cult of terrorism has been linked to the Muslim world in general and the Palestinian-Israeli problem in particular. Terrorism—both in concept and in practice—is not new and can be traced to centuries past: for example, the Ismaili Assassins of the eleventh and twelfth centuries and the "Reign of Terror" of the eighteenth-century French Revolution. Modern terrorists are truly global, not only Islamist and Jewish extremists in the Middle East but also Shining Path in Peru, Red Brigades in Italy, the Irish Republican Army, Basque separatists in Spain, Chechen rebels, Tamil Tigers (now quiet), Aum Shinrikyo in Japan, and right-wing bombers in Oklahoma.

The definition of terrorism is crucial, since it can imply responsibility; terrorism is often violence against a favored group by a disfavored group, and there is no single widely accepted definition. In U.S. State Department terms, it is premeditated, politically motivated violence perpetrated against noncombatant targets by subnational groups or clandestine agents, usually intended to influence an audience. The Federal Bureau of Investigation defines it as the unlawful use of force and violence against persons or property to intimidate or coerce a government, the civilian population, or any segment thereof, in furtherance of political or social objectives. The *Encyclopaedia Britannica* and other sources recognize that it can also be a government tool.

Similarly, the application of the very terms "terrorism" or "terrorist" in specific instances can be biased, as some newspapers have stated in their guidelines for reporters, and although useful, the terms are labels and, if employed, should not be tendentious. An act labeled "terrorism" by one side is not necessarily terrorism in an objective sense and may at least more properly be referred to as "alleged terrorism." Distinctions are also drawn between brutal acts committed during open warfare or against military targets and heinous acts committed against innocent civilians in full peacetime. Similar distinctions may sometimes be drawn between acts of unquestionable terrorism and legitimate acts of resistance against an oppressive government or foreign occupation.

In the Middle East, Israel and (generally) the West declare that there is no room for excuses, and they reject that one side's "terrorist" is another's "freedom fighter." Yet all sides agree that an entire people or religious group must not be incriminated because of the violent actions of a few. No one factor can be identified as the cause of terrorism, and it is difficult to specify one that is even broadly comprehensive. After 9/11, scholarship on the subject suffered as public shock and military action overwhelmed research into its root causes and effective antiterrorism strategies. Rational calls have been made for the "War on Terror" to counter terrorist actions with a focus on conditions that produced them, emphasizing that terrorists will continue to emerge from environments of ignored or mounting grievances. Increasingly, policy makers are focusing on the geographical and geopolitical dynamics discussed in this chapter.

Following World War II, Zionist determination to achieve an independent Jewish state gave rise to some of the region's seminal acts of terrorism.[60] Two notable examples were cited above: the bombing of the King David Hotel in 1946 by the Irgun Zvai Leumi to intimidate British mandate authorities, and the Irgun-Lehi-Haganah well-planned massacre of more than 250 Arab villagers in Deir Yassin[61] in April 1948 then widely publicized to panic Palestinians into fleeing. Decades of conflict between Jews and Arab Muslim and Christian populations followed, with cycles of violence sometimes erupting into open warfare before reverting to individual attacks that often killed innocent women and children.

Terrorist practices by Middle East groups spread to Europe (notably the 1972 seizure in Munich of Israeli Olympic athletes, who were killed during a rescue attempt) and Africa (hijacking of airliners in 1976 and bombings at American Embassies in Kenya and Tanzania in 1998). After the most devastating attack of its type in history on September 11, 2001, President Bush announced the "War on Terror" focusing on terrorism by Muslim militant fundamentalists. Britain, Spain, and Russia concentrate on domestic terrorism as well. The U.S. policy has been widely extended, targeting individuals, businesses, organizations, and polities that may be seen to aid, finance, or harbor terrorism, and it has led to debates regarding infringement of civil liberties and cultural biases against Arabs and Muslims. Actual warfare was initiated by U.S. and allied forces in Afghanistan in 2001 and Iraq in 2003.

Israelis claim their strikes against Arabs have been to preserve the safety and security of their citizens and state and thus have been existential; Palestinians argue that suicide bombings and similar attacks have been relatively small-scale desperation measures in response to Israeli actions, to call world attention to their grievances, or to press their rights to lands or resources taken by Israelis. The basic asymmetry between the capabilities of the two sides has been noted by Israelis, Arabs, and foreign observers. The cycles of violence have involved control over allotted lands, holy places, arable land, freedom of access, and water resources in contested areas; cataloging the sequence of terrorist attacks is difficult. By the end of 2005, relative quiet had returned, but sporadic incidents continued. An Israeli source estimates that through December 2008, 1,062 Israelis and 4,907 Palestinians had been killed; there are disputes over the relative numbers of combatant and civilian deaths on both sides, but indications are that civilian casualties were in the majority among Israelis and Palestinians.[62]

Names of some Middle East militant groups have been incorporated into the daily vocabulary of the 2000s, none more so than al-Qaida (or al-Qaeda, "The Camp"), a widespread organization led by Osama bin Laden, who is considered to have coordinated the 9/11 attacks.[63] Ironically in still another example of blowback, the United States and other countries that al-Qaida now targets originally supported it against the Soviet Union in Afghanistan.[64] Other groups include the Palestinian groups Hamas, Islamic Jihad, and the al-Aqsa Martyrs Brigades, which have claimed primary responsibility for the most lethal suicide bombings and other attacks in the Israel/Palestine area; Hizballah (or Hezbollah), a Shii group that arose in opposition to Israel's occupation of Lebanon, that is supported by Iran with Syrian cooperation, and that is an important political force in Lebanon—it engaged Israel in the "Summer War" of 2006 with some success; Jamaat al-Islamiyya (Islamic Fraternity), an Egyptian Islamic organization implicated in the assassination of Anwar Sadat in 1981; and Israeli extremist groups like Kach and Kahane Chai that were part of a movement leading to the assassination of Prime Minister Rabin.

That the question of "terrorist or freedom fighter" is not always clear can be seen in the case of two Iranian groups long opposed to the clerical regime. One, the Mujahideen al-Khalq ("strugglers of the people"), participated in the revolution against the monarchy but was leftist and relatively secular in politics, blending this with Shii theology. Persecuted by the Islamic Republic, many of its members fled to Iraq from which they opposed Tehran during the Iran-Iraq War. It was branded a terrorist organization by Iran; the United States[65] and Canada agreed and gave it the same designation. But in 2009, after it secured considerable support from Europeans who see it as a group seeking Iran's liberation, the EU dropped it from this status.[66] The other group, Jundullah ("soldiers of God"), is Sunni and Baluch nationalist in its makeup. It has undertaken numerous bombings and assassinations aimed at Shii Persians. To Tehran, it naturally is a terrorist group, but there is some evidence it received encouragement and assistance from the United States during the Bush administration.[67]

Although numerous groups commit many kinds of terrorism, specific motivations vary. In the Israeli-Palestinian context, for example, some terrorist attacks have been intended primarily to call attention to a given cause or movement, to terrorize an opposing population into leaving a given piece of territory, to bargain for the release of prisoners held by the targeted group, or to avenge the assassination or execution of members, especially leaders, of the acting group.

Motivations likewise differ on a broader scale: Terrorists carrying out attacks in Saudi Arabia in the early 2000s sought regime change and hoped to intimidate foreign and non-Muslim technicians; daily attacks against civilians in Iraq from 2003 on were designed partly to coerce emerging domestic authorities, partly to terrorize other religious groups and weaken them politically, and partly to further "ethnic cleansing"; regular terrorist attacks in Egypt during the 1990s were attempts to forge a dominant role for Islamists in government; and conflict and terrorism in southeastern Turkey from 1984 to 1999 were part of a Kurdish Workers Party campaign to create an independent Kurdish state. But in much of the militancy of the Muslim world, from the Maghrib to Indonesia, the intra-Islamic search for identity, revival, and dominance is an important underlying theme.

Observers who label the complex patterns of mutual violence as a clash of civilizations or as some similar Islamic onslaught on the West fail to comprehend the fundamental dynamics of this crucial encounter. It is essential that all factions understand the wellsprings of the others' actions. For the more powerful West, this would mean confronting the complex dimensions of the resentment directed against it; for the extremists, it would mean recognizing the counterproductivity of terrorism.

Piracy

Piracy has hit the world's headlines with full force in recent years with images that have displaced the romantic ones of countless Hollywood movies and the stirring reference to "the shores of Tripoli" in the familiar "Marines' Hymn." It is not an activity that ever really went away; for many years, the Strait of Malacca was home to pirates operating from remote Sumatran coves. But it is pirates from Somalia attacking all sorts and sizes of vessels in the waters to the south of the Arabian Peninsula and east of the Horn of Africa that have brought piracy back to the forefront of international problems.[68]

The current situation can be traced to the 1980s when foreign donors, seeking ways to increase the incomes of ordinary Somalis, undertook with some success to develop the country's fishery sector, improving the quality of the local boats and operating methods of the fishermen and financing shore-based facilities to allow the export of the increased catches. In 1991, the despotic Siad Barre regime was overthrown, and the country quickly descended into civil war. From the fishery's viewpoint, two consequences ensued: Exporting capabilities melted away, and the Somali Coast Guard no longer protected the country's maritime economic zone from foreign fishing boats. Faced with a drastic reduction in their incomes, some Somali fishermen began attacking the foreign interlopers. Adding to the resentments of coastal village dwellers were the deals apparently reached by regional warlords with European and Asian companies allowing the latter to dump toxic waste in waters just offshore.

Over time, the Somalis realized that money could be earned from harassing foreign shipping in the very busy sea-lanes that were within reach of their boats, taking hostage both vessels and crews. As ever-larger ransoms were realized, the fishermen/pirates upgraded their working capital—better and faster boats, satellite guidance systems, relatively sophisticated weaponry, and "mother" supply ships stationed so as to allow for longer stays at sea and voyaging greater distances from home ports. By the late 2000s, victims ranged from pleasure yachts to supertankers; there were even ill-advised (and failed) attempts to capture French and Dutch naval frigates.[69] World shipping faced added costs for insurance and/or from the need to follow longer routes that avoided the pirates' expanding operating zones. Modern tankers, which, despite their tremendous size, typically carry very small crews, are a tempting target; it is not clear how many have changed their routes to Europe far southward around Africa—a much more expensive journey.[70] If captured, not only is a tanker a valuable prize, but there is also the strong possibility that any conflict over such a vessel could result in ecological disaster. Regarding the original impetus toward Somali piracy, with foreign fishing fleets largely scared off, small-scale fisherman from the region seem to be enjoying something of a boom.[71]

By 2008, ransoms gained by the pirates reached an estimated $150 million annually, and the international community had begun to mobilize. In 2008, the U.S.-led international naval unit Combined Task Force 150 set up the Maritime Security Patrol Area covering the Gulf of Aden and adjacent waters. The UN Security Council unanimously adopted Resolution 1838, calling upon "states with naval vessels and military aircraft operating in the area . . . to repress acts of piracy."[72] Despite the increase in counterpiracy efforts, 2009 actually saw a near doubling[73] in pirate activities as they spread their operations farther afield.

Still, the international naval force could point to some successes—takeover attempts in the vital Gulf of Aden region were down considerably, and the overall success rate for the pirates had been cut in half.[74]

Part of the problem lies in the reluctance of the states participating in the Task Force to transport the pirates to home territories for trial, lest they claim asylum upon arrival. Kenya and the Seychelles have been willing to try them in their courts, but both countries lack the infrastructure to handle large numbers,[75] and the Seychelles especially could be subject to reprisals from pirate gangs.[76] An international tribunal similar to those employed for trying war-crimes suspects from conflicts in the Balkans and Africa is one possible solution.

There remains the question of whether Somali piracy is related to terrorism in the region.[77] The FBI definition of terrorism stated in the previous section encompassed three elements: unlawful use of force or violence, intention to intimidate or coerce, and the furtherance of political or social objectives. Initially, all three were present in some fashion—the pirates of the 1980s were acting against foreign fishing fleets and toxic-waste dumpers. But the pirates of the twenty-first century seem to be motivated almost solely by the prospect of ransom, and thus they seem more appropriately classified as criminals, despite occasional reiterations of fishing and toxic-dumping grievances. That is not to say that there are no links between the pirates and terrorist organizations (and ties as well to arms and drug smugglers).[78] It has been alleged that the latter have been involved in facilitating money transfers (in return for a share) and in supplying some of the armaments and other equipment needed by pirate gangs. Additionally, the continued status of Somalia as a failed state (and the possibility of this situation spreading across the Bab el-Mandeb to Yemen) offers international terrorist organizations a convenient base of operations. The activities of both pirates and terrorists, actual and potential, seem likely to thrive in the absence of any effective government in Somalia.[79]

NOTES

1. Mackinder 1904, which has been reprinted in several political geography studies. Sir Halford expanded and revised his thoughts in Mackinder 1919 and again in a 1943 *Foreign Affairs* article. An underrated challenge to Mackinder came in Spykman 1944. The Rimland challenge is discussed below.

2. Ayubi 1995 comprehensively examines Arab states and gives realistic insights. See also note 8 below.

3. T. E. Lawrence's personal account appeared in his classic *Seven Pillars of Wisdom: A Triumph*, which appeared in several versions and many editions. He and his saga were much celebrated during the 1920s and had a renaissance in the 1970s and 1980s. In the extensive literature about him, an excellent authorized biography is J. Wilson 1990, which places Lawrence in the context of the momentous events of the period. A recent brief article with maps is Belt 1999.

4. Fromkin 2000 is a comprehensive treatment of how the contemporary Middle East emerged from the dealings of Britain and France with each other and with third parties during and after World War I.

5. Busch 1971 is an excellent study of the interaction between Britain's Indian and Middle East policies during World War I and its aftermath.

6. See H. Howard 1963.

7. Ethnicity and the state have been examined in many studies. For several that focus on the Middle East, see Hourani 1947; Esman and Rabinovich 1988; Bengio and Ben-Dor 1999; Ma'oz 1999; and Nisan 2002.

8. Middle East state development has been analyzed in numerous recent studies. For example, see Salamé 1987; Ayubi 1995; Khashan 2000; Owen 2000b; Hinnebusch 2003; R. Khalidi 2004; and Netton 1986, which focuses on the Gulf.

9. U.S. State Department, *Background Note: Yemen*, Jan. 2010.

10. See the respective country chapters for more details on all these elections.

11. Hartshorne 1950.

12. S. Jones 1954.

13. See several papers in M. Hudson 1999. See also Ayubi 1995 and Kemp and Harkavy 1997. International organizations are listed in the CIA's annual

World Factbook appendix, which includes Middle East regional organizations.

14. North Cyprus has observer status with the OIC.

15. *The Daily Telegraph* (UK), Dec. 15, 2009.

16. See http://ec.europa.eu/external_relations/euromed/index_en.htm for further information.

17. *Global Arab Network*, Mar. 2, 2010.

18. The Kataib is better known in English as the Phalange, a political party and its supporting militia that draws its strength from the Maronites.

19. Several boundaries mentioned in this paragraph are depicted and briefly accounted for in successive issues of the U.S. Department of State's *Geographic Notes*. A general map of the Arabian Peninsula lines as of 1991 is in Bradford Thomas, "Gulf Boundaries," no. 13 (Mar. 1, 1991): 1–5. The Saudi-Iraq boundary is shown on pp. 2–3 of the same issue and is covered again in vol. 2, no. 2 (Summer 1992): 11–12; Saudi-Qatar and Saudi-UAE are covered in vol. 2, no. 4 (Winter 1992–1993): 1–2 and in vol. 3, no. 4 (Winter 1993–1994): 12–13; Saudi-Oman is in vol. 3, no. 1 (Spring 1993): 2–3. All Middle East boundaries are discussed in A. Day 1982, 178–233. A concise review of Arabian Peninsula borders is given in Schofield 1996. Boundaries on Middle East maps in National Geographic Society 2004 are correct.

20. The Oman-Yemen boundary is shown in *Geographic Notes* 3, no. 1 (Spring 1993): 3–5; the Jordan-Iraq line in no. 13 (Mar. 1, 1991): 2; again in vol. 2, no. 4 (Winter 1992–1993): 2–3; and again in vol. 3, no. 4 (Winter 1993–1994): 9–10. See also Schofield 1996, which mentions the Oman-UAE boundary.

21. *Geographic Notes* 3, no. 2 (Summer 1993): 1–2, with more details in vol. 4, no. 2 (Summer 1994): 23–29. For exhaustive studies, see Schofield 1993 and H. Rahman 1997. For concise coverage, see Cordesman and Hashim 1997, 184–189. A useful Kuwaiti summary is at www.kuwait-info.org/borders.html.

22. *Arab News* (Riyadh), Dec. 17, 2007.

23. The Iraq-Kuwait territorial dispute is discussed in Kelly 1980; Crystal 1990; Finnie 1992; and H. Rahman 1997.

24. Details are given in Taryam 1987, which includes a useful bibliographical essay covering good sources on the islands and on the UAE.

25. The Gulf maritime boundaries are succinctly examined in *Geographic Notes*, no. 14 (Oct. 1, 1991): 11–12. See also Blake 1987.

26. *The Daily Telegraph*, Jan. 17, 2010.

27. *The Daily Star* (Beirut), Feb. 23, 2010.

28. Many recent studies examine various aspects of Middle East hydrogeopolitics. See, especially, *Water for the Future* 1999; Biswas et al. 1997; Elmusa 1997; Wolf 1995; Rogers and Lydon 1994; Berkoff 1994; Rowley 1999, 2008; and Fox 2003.

29. The subject is examined from different viewpoints in dozens of studies: for example, Curtis 1981; Salamé 1987; Esman and Rabinovich 1988; Andersen, Seibert, and Wagner 1990; Ajami 1993; M. Hudson 1999; Khashan 2000; Dawisha 2003; and Rubin 2003.

30. Literally thousands of books and articles examine the Palestine/Israel problem from every conceivable perspective. Some are very good even when supporting one viewpoint. Others subtly screen their bias, and many are merely polemic. Students and readers must select sources with a critical eye; many polemics focus on peripheral issues (for example, religious ambiguities) by way of pursuing an agenda. On the overall conflict, a well-regarded and balanced study is C. Smith 2007. A suggested balance of other studies is: Gerner 1994; Tessler 1994; Morris 1989; Pappé 1999, 2004; Newman 1999; Quandt 2001; Laqueur and Rubin 2001; Rogan and Shlaim 2001; Gilbert 2002; Chomsky 2003; N. Finkelstein 2003; Gazit 2003; and Sand 2009. It is worth noting that some of the severest critics of some Israeli actions are Israelis. See also the introductory note to the Bibliography and the Bibliography itself.

31. The Dreyfus trial is covered in numerous encyclopedias and histories of Zionism. See, for example, Sela 2002, s.v. "Zionism"; and Sachar 1976, Chaps. 3 and 4.

32. A. Gordon 1997. Other concepts of Zionism are discussed in Avishai 2002, Hertzberg 2003, and in some readings in W. Khalidi 1971. Pappé 1997 looks favorably on revised Zionism as conceived by the New Historians; it is often called "Post-Zionism," which is vigorously criticized in Karsh 1997.

33. Credited to Zangwill 1901; actually this oft-cited phrase seems to be a slight rearrangement of Zangwill's actual words: "Palestine is a country without a people; the Jews are a people without a country."

34. It is contained in a brief letter from Foreign Secretary A. J. Balfour to Lord Rothschild dated November 2, 1917. An image of the original letter can be seen at http://blog.balder.org/billeder-blog/Balfour-Declaration.jpg.

35. The Balfour Declaration has been analyzed in many books and articles. The massive and authoritative Stein 1983 (a reprint of the 1961 edition), by a man associated with the World Zionist Organization, is the most detailed.

36. For a recent overview, see Gorenberg 2009.

37. Figures are from the Palestine Human Rights Center and *Christian Science Monitor*, Mar. 19, 1993.

Two useful books on the intifadah are Schiff and Yaari 1989 and Peretz 1994. For reviews of the second intifadah, see Ackerman 2001 and Hammami and Tamari 2001.

38. Regarding Deir Yassin, Begin 1977 includes an account by that author and later Israeli prime minister, who then was commander of Irgun Zvai Leumi, the terrorist group that, along with the Stern Gang, conducted the massacre. For a quite different version, see the report by the local Red Cross representative, Jacques de Reynier, in W. Khalidi 1971, 761–766. Deir Yassin is discussed in any good account of events of the period. See, for example, the sources given in note 25 of this chapter, as well as McGowan and Ellis 1998. Some Israeli sources contest the number of villagers killed, claiming it to be nearer 150, while not minimizing the enormity of the massacre. The birth of the Palestinian refugee problem is addressed by a then leading New Historian in Morris 1989, which is vigorously rebutted in Karsh 1997, then re-rebutted in Morris 1998, and finally "revisited" in Morris 2004. See also Pappé 1999.

39. Three relevant articles examine the refugee situation: Kershner 1999; *New York Times*, Apr. 23, 1998; and R. Sayigh 1998. For the latest data, see www.un .org/unrwa/refugees/me.html.

40. See Hroub 2000 for a well-researched study of Hamas, including a review of the Muslim Brotherhood.

41. See Ross 2004 for an insider interpretation of the U.S. side in much of the peace process, including the 2000 Camp David talks. See Hanieh 2001 for a detailed Palestinian version of the Camp David talks by a participant. In Agha and Malley 2001, a Palestinian and an American, who each participated, give their joint view. For an intensive scholarly study of the negotiations, see Swisher 2004.

42. For a view of how the wall affects one well-known Palestinian town, see Ivereigh 2008.

43. See http://georgewbush-whitehouse.archives .gov/news/releases/2003/07/20030725-6.html, in remarks welcoming President Abbas to the White House, July 25, 2003.

44. The barrier has been widely discussed. The quotation is from Lagerquist 2004. See also *New York Times Magazine*, Aug. 3, 2003, 34–37; *New York Times*, Oct. 25, 2003; *Christian Science Monitor*, Oct. 31 and Nov. 14, 2003. *New York Times*, July 7 and 10, 2004, reports the Hague decision. *Jerusalem Report*, Jan. 12, 2004, gives Israeli views on the Hague hearings.

45. *Jerusalem Post*, July 10, 2007; *The Guardian*, Dec. 23, 2009.

46. *Washington Times*, May 14, 2009.

47. *Haaretz*, Dec. 24, 2009.

48. *Jerusalem Post*, Jan. 10, 2008.

49. Among many studies of the origins and ramifications of the Iran-Iraq War, see Chubin and Tripp 1988; Khadduri 1988; Karsh 1990; and Gause 2002.

50. The Gulf crisis and war were intensively covered. A useful full chronology is given in the *Middle East Journal* 45, nos. 1, 2, and 3 (Winter, Spring, and Summer 1991). Also, the *Middle East Journal* 45, no. 1, has four excellent articles pertaining to the Gulf crisis. Standard books on the war are Schwarzkopf 1992 and Khadduri and Ghareeb 1997. See also J. Long 2001.

51. Much of the information on Iraq's "ecoterrorism" is covered in media reports of the period, but a useful, concise report is R. Williams et al. 1991, which has excellent space imagery. See also Earle 1992.

52. See full-page article in the *New York Times*, Mar. 20, 2003. Other pertinent articles are in the Feb. 27 and Sept. 22, 2003, editions. Among the spate of books that appeared over the next eighteen months, see Frum and Perle 2003 for the extreme "neocon" viewpoint, Brzezinski 2004 for an opposite perspective, Blix 2004 for a view from the UN team chief who led the inspections in Iraq before the invasion, and R. Clarke 2004, which rebuts the U.S. claims regarding Iraqi links with al-Qaida. Few events in U.S. history have evoked so many passionate pro and con books and articles—especially on the Internet—in such a short time.

53. Internal Displacement Monitoring Centre, "Challenges of Forced Displacement within Iraq," Dec. 29, 2008, www.internal-displacement.org.

54. See the concise and useful EIA *Country Analysis Briefs: World Oil Transit Chokepoints*, Jan. 2008, at www .eia.doe.gov/cabs/World_Oil_Transit_Chokepoints/Full .html.

55. *Xinhua*, July 26, 2009.

56. See H. Howard 1974.

57. See note 52.

58. Kennan 1987 is a reprint of the widely read 1947 article and is accompanied by comments and a retrospective by that author, who died at age 101 in March 2005.

59. See *New York Times*, May 13 and June 6, 2004. For a broader view, see Murden 2002, especially Chap. 3, "The Pax Americana in the Middle East."

60. An overview of Jewish terrorism from mandate days into the twenty-first century is found in Pedahzur and Perliger 2009.

61. Begin 1977.

62. B'Tselem, www.btselem.org/English/Statistics/ Casualties.asp.

63. In 2009, a U.S. Senate report was released that argued that bin Laden was allowed to escape from U.S. military forces in December 2001 by a decision of then secretary of defense Rumsfeld. See *New York*

Times, Nov. 29, 2009; and "Tora Bora Revisited: How We Failed to Get bin Laden and Why It Matters Today," Report to the Committee on Foreign Relations, United States Senate, Nov. 30, 2009, at http://foreign.senate.gov/imo/media/doc/Tora_Bora_Report.pdf.

64. Bergen and Reynolds 2005.

65. The U.S. military in Iraq has, however, quietly protected group members. See CNN, "U.S. Protects Iranian Opposition Group in Iraq," Apr. 6, 2007. Camp Ashraf outside Baghdad where they were located was turned over to Iraqi control in 2009. See *Christian Science Monitor*, June 25, 2009; and *BBC News*, Aug. 15, 2009.

66. Reuters, Jan. 26, 2009.

67. *BBC News*, Oct. 19, 2009.

68. A good summary is found in Roger Middleton, "Piracy in Somalia: Threatening Global Trade, Feeding Local Wars," *Chatham House Briefing Paper*, Oct. 2008, www.chathamhouse.org.uk/files/12203_1008piracysomalia.pdf. For official U.S. and U.K. positions on the problem, see www.state.gov/t/prm/rls/fs/128540.htm and www.fco.gov.uk/en/global-issues/conflict-prevention/piracy/international-response, respectively.

69. Agence France Presse, Oct. 7, 2009; Associated Press, Mar. 17, 2010.

70. *Business Mirror*, Dec. 9, 2009, www.businessmirror.com.ph/top-news/19580-piracy-indiced-costs-seen-rising.html/.

71. Agence France Presse, Feb. 6, 2010; *The Star* (Toronto), Jan. 10, 2010.

72. www.un.org/News/Press/docs/2008/sc9514.doc.htm.

73. *New York Times*, Dec. 30, 2009.

74. *Washington Post*, Dec. 25, 2009; *Christian Science Monitor*, Mar. 8, 2010.

75. By early 2010, more than 100 piracy suspects had been handed over to Kenyan authorities through arrangements with the United States, the EU, and other countries (Agence France Presse, Mar. 8, 2010). The same problems were experienced in the Seychelles (MSNBC, Mar. 10, 2010).

76. *The Independent*, Oct. 28, 2009, www.independent.co.uk/news/world/africa/is-seychelles-turning-a-blind-eye-to-pirates-1810496.html; *AsiaOne*, Dec. 8, 2009, www.asiaone.com/News/AsiaOne+News/World/Story/A1Story20091208-184709.html; Agence France Presse, Feb. 7, 2010.

77. RAND Corporation, June 5, 2009, www.rand.org/news/press/2008/06/05/.

78. *The East African* (Nairobi), Jan. 10, 2010.

79. Arguing for concentrating on local development as the solution for Somalia's problems is Bruton 2009.

PART TWO

REGIONAL GEOGRAPHY

9

Syria
Middle East Heartland

REGIONAL KEYSTONE

Ancient Role, Modern Role

Historical-geographical Syria, lying between the Mediterranean and the middle Euphrates, has often functioned as the geographical keystone of the Middle East. Not only is its situation central, but also its location near the regional heart is enhanced by patterns of landforms, climates, and travel routes. Damascus and Aleppo have played outstanding roles as commercial and cultural centers for 3,500 years, and Syria's cereal belt has served as a granary for empires over many centuries. Three major corridors cross the Syrian realm: the main one south of the Turkish mountain wall and north of the desert, a second one through the Palmyra Oasis, and a north-south one through western Syria that long served as a segment of the north-south land route between Yemen and Asia Minor. The routes were for thousands of years—indeed, until after World War I—the major passageways through the region for the movement of people and goods.

In this location, it has for millennia seen migrating peoples, marching armies, and multiple political influences. Indigenous Syrians have thereby at various times absorbed several ethnic and cultural groups and have sustained challenges to their capacity for unity and even survival. Periodically during its long history, the Syrian realm has served as a major power base, reaching its apogee during the Damascus-centered Umayyad Empire, 661–750. Later it was a focus of Islamic-Arab aspirations and potentially a modern political-spiritual center of the Arab world. Contemporary Syria, with only moderate size and population, and with limited resources, has a manifest role in the region regardless of the serious problems it faces and despite its shifting relationships with its neighbors and with the Great Powers. Some of its economic difficulties during the past several decades may be traced to its policy planning and relations. Other more general problems arise from the country's ideologically self-imposed isolation, anachronistic restrictions, and illiberal political agenda. Still others stem partly from a mutual failure by Syria and the West to establish meaningful rapport. This chapter will examine its capabilities and role.[1]

The Three Syrias

"Syria" as used in this chapter will usually refer to the Syrian Arab Republic, so named in 1961. The republic is coextensive, except for the Alexandretta (Iskanderun) area, with the French League of Nations mandate (1923–1946). However, "historic Syria" existed for more than 2,000 years and comprised the general area that is now Syria,

SYRIA

Long-form official name, anglicized: Syrian Arab Republic

Official name, transliterated: Al-Jumhuriyah al-Arabiyah as-Suriyah

Form of government: unitary multiparty republic with one legislative house (People's Assembly)

Area: 71,498 mi^2/185,180 km^2 (including 500 mi^2/1,295 km^2 of Israeli-occupied Golan)

Population, 2008: 19,514,000; Literacy (Latest): 78.4%

Ethnic composition (%): Arab 86.2, of which Syrian 74.9, Bedouin 7.4, Palestinian 3.9; Kurd 7.3; Armenian 2.7; other (Circassian, Turkman, Assyrian) 3.8

Religions (%): Sunni Muslim 74; Alawi 11; Christian 10; Druze and other 5

Demography: Life expectancy—69.0 yr (M), 71.7 yr (F); Birthrate (per 1,000)—27.8; Fertility rate—3.4

GDP, 2009: $54.35 billion; purchasing power parity: $102.5 billion; per capita: $4,700

Currency: Syrian pound, US$1 = 44.91 pounds; 1 pound = $0.0213 (March 2010)

Energy reserves: oil—2.5 bn bbl; natural gas—8.5 tn ft^3; coal—nil

Main exports (% of total value, 2006): crude petroleum 33.6; food and live animals 14.9, of which vegetables and fruit 6.0; apparel and clothing accessories 7.9; fabrics and yarns 7.5; refined petroleum 6.7

Main imports (% of total value, 2006): refined petroleum 24.4; food 10.7; vehicles 8.6; iron and steel 8.3; nonelectrical machinery and equipment 7.3

Capital city: Damascus (al-Dimashq, often al-Sham) 1,614,500; other cities: Aleppo (Halab) 1,975,200, Homs (Hims) 800,400, Latakia (al-Ladhiqiyah) 468,700, Hamah 368,800

Lebanon, Jordan, western Iraq, Israel, and the Israeli-occupied parts of Palestine. References to "Syria" in some writings refer to "Greater Syria."

THE PHYSICAL CHALLENGE

Regions of Syria

Syria has six well-differentiated natural regions, indicated on Map 9.1 by encircled numbers. [1] A plain extends the length of the coast, widest in the north behind Latakia and in the south near Lebanon. It is agriculturally productive and the base for the main port of Latakia, the oil-export port of Baniyas (more active when Iraqi pipelines were oper-

ational), and the developing port and oil terminal of Tartus. [2] A succession of mountains lies to the east: in the north is the continuous north-south Jabal al-Sahiliyah ("Coastal Mountains"—the official toponym, formerly Jabal al-Nusayriyah or Jabal al-Ansariyah), in the center are the southwest-northeast Anti-Lebanon Mountains dividing Syria and Lebanon, and in the south is the complex mass of Mount Hermon. The uplifted Jurassic and Cretaceous limestone Jabal al-Sahiliyah is bounded on the east by an impressive fault with both vertical displacement and a strike slip of more than 12 mi/20 km, which is also the west side of the Ghab graben, the northern end of the Levant Rift System.

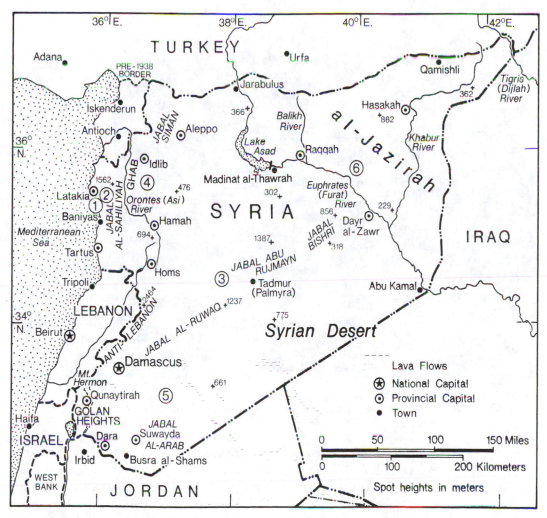

MAP 9.1 General map of Syria with major towns and physical features. Circled numbers indicate geographical regions of the country.

East of the mountains is a large plateau divided by [3] a southwest-northeast zone of complex folding and faulting associated with the Palmyra Folds. There are several local names for sections of the splayed ridges, including Jabal al-Ruwaq northeast of Damascus, Jabal Abu Rajmayn in the center, and Jabal Bishri toward the Euphrates.

North of the Palmyra Folds and west of the Euphrates, the level to rolling steppe land [4] supports a north-south zone of extensive grain cultivation, coextensive with a constellation of settlements, including the cities of Homs (Hims), Hamah, and Aleppo. South of the Palmyra Folds the plateau has a quite different character. Toward the west are [5] extensive basaltic lava flows of several ages, accompanied by numerous cinder cones. Jabal al-Druze (Jebel Druze—officially, Jabal al-Arab) is a huge lava dome that reaches 3,300 ft/1,000 m above the plain and is flanked on the northeast by the wide basalt plain of al-Safa and on the northwest by the thin, scabby, blistered lava flow of al-Laja. The plains to the west of the Jabal are the well-cultivated Hawran (Fig. 9.1), its western

FIGURE 9.1 View over Salkhad, looking generally west over the agricultural Hawran from a volcanic neck in the Jabal al-Druze (now Jabal al-Arab), southwestern Syria.

edge a lava plateau that forms the Golan overlooking the Sea of Galilee. East of the lava belt, the Syrian Desert extends into Iraq, Jordan, and Saudi Arabia, offering little except sparse grasses and bushes for the grazing animals of the Bedouin. In northeastern Syria is [6] the Jazirah, which lies east of the entrenched Euphrates River and continues the level to rolling landscape that lies west of the river. It has been a focus of major economic development since about 1970 following increased exploitation of the oil fields located there and completion of the Euphrates Dam and its associated installations.

The Agricultural Base

On one hand, Syria's share of the Fertile Crescent's climate, soil, landforms, and other beneficial characteristics gives it large areas of relatively productive agricultural land. Making up about one-third of the country, this land supplies the sustained economic base for the country, as it has for 2,500 years. On the other hand, problems of aridity and rough relief in the other two-thirds present a major physical challenge. This challenge and the responses to it are part of the saga of contemporary Syria.

By its very nature, the Fertile Crescent's inner boundary is a zone of marginal precipitation. Cyclical oscillation of the 12-in/300-mm isohyet (see Map 2.5) between wet and dry periods is a tensional element in Syrian agriculture. Consequently, it affects many aspects of economic and social life, including shifts between sedentarism and nomadism along the frontier. In seasonal distribution, rainfall in this typical dry summer Mediterranean climate (Koeppen Csa) is concentrated in the cool months. Annual precipitation ranges from 30 in/750 mm along the coast to 55 in/1,400 mm on the upper west-facing slopes of the Jabal al-Sahiliyah/Jabal al-Nusayriyah, then decreases sharply to the east, in the rain shadow of the mountains, to 22 in/550 mm in the Ghab Depression.

East of the mountains, the north-south subhumid agricultural belt with its steppe soils extends southward from Aleppo well into Jordan, and rainfall typically averages 12–20 in/300–500 mm along this southwestern horn of the Fertile Crescent. Eastward from Aleppo, averages are 10–12 in/250–300 mm, with double those amounts in the extreme northeast. Away from the more humid Crescent, the southeastern two-thirds of the country averages less than 8 in/200 mm, with the driest area, abutting the Jordan panhandle, receiving less than 4 in/100 mm. Here and along the Euphrates in the extreme southeast, mean July temperatures exceed 90°F/32°C. There the Syrian Desert is in full sway.

THE IMPRINT OF TIME

Ancient Patterns

In the western and northern parts of Syria are many of the earliest known settlements, dating well back into the ninth millennium BCE (see Chap. 3). Some of the earliest pottery ever found was discovered on the banks of the Euphrates, and Damascus claims the title of the world's oldest continuously inhabited city. Ugarit just north of Latakia on the coast, Ebla 30 mi/50 km southwest of Aleppo, and Mari on the middle Euphrates are among the most important ancient sites in the region; they were thriving city-states or imperial capitals early in the second millennium BCE (see Map 3.1). The oldest known alphabet—twenty-nine characters in cuneiform script, dating from the fifteenth century BCE—was found during the excavation of Ugarit. Late in the second millennium, the Syrian region became and continued to be for almost 1,000 years a marchland, contested among successive great empires, including the Amorite and the Aramaean (the biblical Aram), which were rooted in Syria itself.

Alexander the Great's conquest of the Persians in 334–326 BCE led to Syria's inclusion in the Seleucid Empire for more than 200 years. After Rome supplanted the Seleucids and made Syria a Roman province in 64 BCE, the Greco-Roman culture became infused with Christianity. The new sect gained its first major foothold in Antioch, flourishing under the eastern Roman and Byzantine empires. Ruins of churches and of entire towns from this period—Syria's several "dead cities"—can be visited in the northwest and south. Impressive Greco-Roman tourist sites are Palmyra (Fig. 9.2), Apamaea, Bosra, and Dura Europos. From 540 CE, Byzantines and Sassanians fought for a century and inflicted severe destruction on the countryside and cities. Ghassanians—Christian Arabs mainly in southern Syria—provided many powerful families in the sixth and seventh centuries CE.

Arab Invasions and After

When the Arab Muslims arrived, war-weakened Byzantines were unable to defend their possessions, and in 636 CE Syria was the first area to fall to the Muslims after their eruption from the Hijaz. Just 25 years later, it entered its 90-year Golden Age when the Islamic Umayyad Empire, with Damascus the capital, was established. The new official language, Arabic, gradually displaced Aramaic and Greek, and Islam became dominant over Christianity, although it never entirely displaced it. As it had before and did later, Syria showed its ability to fuse cultures and evolve into something "Syrian."

When the Abbasids supplanted the Umayyads in 750 and the power center shifted to Baghdad, Syria became a contested land for the next 800 years. Abbasids, Egyptians, Seljuks, Crusaders, and Mongols vied for control. All held Syria, or parts of it, for varying lengths of time, leaving signs of their control in aqueducts, forts, and caravansaries.

FIGURE 9.2 Ruins of the colonnade of Palmyra (modern Tadmur) in central Syria, prosperous oasis trade center under Queen Zenobia in the late third century, as a key caravan station, and briefly a military power.

Ruins of spectacular Crusader castles in western Syria attract both tourists and serious students of medieval architecture (Fig. 9.3). The Ottomans conquered Syria in 1516, controlling it for 400 years until their empire broke up after 1918.

French Mandate

When France took the League of Nations mandate of Syria in the early 1920s, demarcation of the borders signaled the first time in history that a separate, quasi-independent polity of "Syria" had been formally defined. After part of the territory was detached as Lebanon and internal pieces were shifted as France wished, the mandate became the direct precursor of the contemporary state (see Chap. 8).

To inhibit nationalism and unity, France divided the territory into statelets: Aleppo,

Damascus, and Alawite (called Latakia after 1930) in 1920; Jabal al-Druze in 1921; and an autonomous Sanjak (subprovince) of Alexandretta (Turkish: Iskenderun) in 1923. In 1925, Damascus and Aleppo were united, and Alawite and Jabal al-Druze were added in 1936; they were separated again in 1939 and finally reunited in 1942. Revolts and instability typified the mandate, but after World War II Syria became formally and officially an independent state on April 17, 1946.[2] Except for a revised boundary around Alexandretta-Antioch (Iskenderun-Antakya) (see Chap. 8), postindependence Syria embraces virtually the same territory as the mandate after Lebanon's separation (see Map 9.1).

The United Arab Republic

Independent Syria shared with Lebanon and Jordan insecurity and instability after World

FIGURE 9.3 Krak des Chevaliers, Castle of the Knights (Arabic: Qalat al-Husn), an especially well-preserved Crusader castle in the Homs Gap west of Homs in west-central Syria. It was built in the eleventh century. (Photograph courtesy of Liam Cummings)

War II, the sudden assumption of independence, and the trauma of the emergence of an increasingly powerful Israel on a portion of historic "Greater Syria." On several occasions, Syria expressed interest in unions—perhaps manifesting the Greater Syria syndrome—with one or another of its Arab neighbors. Only once did an actual merger transpire—between 1958 and 1961 it linked with Egypt in the United Arab Republic (see Chap. 8). Although it served its original purpose, forestalling a pro-Communist coup in Syria, Egyptian domination offended Syrians, who saw themselves as the standard-bearers of Arab nationalism. After three years of unequal partnership, it withdrew from the UAR. In 1978–1979, there were some merger discussions with Iraq, but they foundered on the issue of leadership.

THE SYRIAN MIXTURE

Patterns of Population

With 19.6 million inhabitants, Syria ranks seventh among the states considered herein. Population doubled between 1963 and 1987,

and its earlier high growth rate, 3.5–4 percent annually, fell to 2.2 percent by 2008. Rapid population growth contributes to such socioeconomic problems as high unemployment, stagnant per capita income, and housing shortages. The surplus population has even begun repopulating the historically important "dead cities," economically important tourist destinations. As in other regional countries, the raw population density figure is misleading, since the population is markedly concentrated in the more humid western area (see Map 4.2 and Table 4.1).

Syria has, from early times, had scattered cities of appreciable size and fame along the Euphrates and especially in the more humid west of the country. Damascus (Fig. 9.4) and Aleppo have long alternated leadership in population, but recently Greater Damascus surpassed Greater Aleppo.

The historical population concentration axis along the humid steppe belt, Damascus-Homs-Hamah-Aleppo, now includes Latakia, the main port. With development of the Euphrates Valley and the Jazirah to the east, cities in those areas have expanded rapidly,

FIGURE 9.4 The "new" downtown Damascus, telephoto view looking east from the top of Mount Qassiun. The multistory buildings date from the 1980s, the uniform-height buildings in the foreground from the French mandate prior to World War II. The Old City of Damascus is slightly above center, surrounding the Umayyad Mosque, whose minarets are plainly visible. The rich, irrigated Ghutah is in the distance but is being encroached upon by the urban sprawl of Damascus.

especially Dayr al-Zawr, Raqqah, Qamishli, and Hasakah. In addition, scores of villages—some of them with populations of 10,000–20,000—are found in the broad, flat-floored river valley and adjacent plateaus consequent to development projects in the area. Suwayda, in the Jabal al-Arab, and Dara, on the Jordan border, are the largest centers in the south. Major universities are located in each of the largest cities.

Human Diversity

Arab Majority and Ethnic Minorities. Although Syria has less religious and ethnic diversity than some of its neighbors, the variety that does exist is both noteworthy and influential in the state function. Among the several ethnolinguistic groups, the dominant one, for more than 1,000 years, has been Syrian Arabs, 82 percent of the population. In-

cluded in this majority are the Bedouin, steadily less nomadic, now less than 8 percent of the total. As in most Arab societies, identity is a double categorization: linguistic (Arabic) and religious (Islam), as Chapter 4 indicates. Syria has several religious and social minorities distinct from the primary group. In addition to Arabs, the national mixture comprises Kurds, Armenians, Circassians, Turkmans, and Assyrians, plus small groups of Azeris, Gypsies, and Jews. After Sunni Muslims, religious minorities include a dozen Christian and at least four heterodox Islamic sects.

With one or two notable exceptions, ethnoreligious social groups have, since the 1960s, exhibited a high degree of intergroup tolerance. Partly because of tight domestic political controls, partly because limited economic potential has not engendered fierce competition for advantage, and partly because the nation has been under external pressures, Syrians have benefited from intercommunal concord. Expressed differently, the government, under rather rigid one-party control, tends to leave its citizens alone if they stay out of politics. Minorities—especially Christians—have enjoyed a degree of stability and security far greater than their counterparts in most other states in the region.[3]

After the Arabs, the largest ethnolinguistic minority in Syria is the Kurds—about 7 percent of the population. Speaking their own language, Kurds are mostly distributed across the north, next to their ethnic homeland of "Kurdistan," with concentrations in the mountains of the northwest and in the northeast. Many of them, along with Armenians, fled from Turkey in the 1920s and early 1930s following a failed insurrection against Turkish authorities in eastern Anatolia. In addition to the main Kurdish belt in the north, several thousand Kurds live in the cities, especially in the Damascus Kurdish Quarter. Although most are Sunni Muslims, some are Shii, Christian, or Yazidi.

The second-largest ethnolinguistic minority is the Armenians, about 3 percent of the population, and the least-assimilated group. Entirely Christian, they fled Turkish Armenia in the 1920s and 1930s and settled in Aleppo, where nearly 75 percent of them live, and Damascus. Educated and skilled, they work in trade, crafts (many jewelry artisans in Damascus are Armenians), small industry, and the professions. Many emigrated in the 1990s in search of better socioeconomic conditions.

Smaller minorities include Turkmans, Circassians, and Jews. Nearly all speak some Arabic, but the Turkmans and Circassians, like Kurds and Armenians, primarily use their own languages. The roughly 110,000 Turkmans, who are Sunnis and Turkic speakers, are mostly seminomadic herdsmen in the Jazirah, but some are settled agriculturalists in the Aleppo area. The particularly distinct Circassians occupy the Hawran in the south, with Druze east and west of them. Only half as numerous as Turkmans, they play a more significant role in the economy and society.

Jews numbered more than 30,000 before World War II, living, like Armenians, mostly in Aleppo and Damascus. Israeli-Syrian hostility after 1948 put them in an ambivalent position; their status periodically led to acute friction between Syria and Israel (and the United States), when Israel asserted, and Syria denied, that they were mistreated. In April 1992, under U.S. pressure, the government declared that any of the 4,000 remaining who wished to emigrate could do so. Only about 400 chose to stay.[4]

Dominant Islam and Other Religions. About 90 percent of the Syrian Arabs are Muslims, reflecting the high correlation of Arabism and Islam. Of these, four-fifths are Sunni. Other Muslim (or quasi-Muslim) sects are mainly heterodox Shii groups—Alawi, Druze, and Ismaili. Largest and, since the 1960s, most important are the Alawis (or Alawites), about 11 percent of the population and more than two-thirds of the inhabitants around the Jabal al-Sahiliyah in the northwest. Prior to the 1960s, they were primarily agriculturalists, but they served in the army in numbers beyond their percentage of the population. The Baath coup in 1963 enhanced their role, especially in the military, and when an Alawi, Hafiz al-Asad, became president in 1971, their position improved decisively. When he died in 2000, his son, Bashar al-Asad, succeeded him, preserving Alawi control.[5]

The Druze played a major political-military role during the mandate period. The Jabal al-Druze was one of the statelets created by France, and periodic Druze revolts were a serious problem for the mandatory. However, the half-million Druze (about 3 percent of the population) are now more subdued. They

FIGURE 9.5
The Greek Orthodox convent of Saydnaya, located 12 mi/20 km north of Damascus at the foot of the Anti-Lebanon Mountains in western Syria. The shrine of the Virgin in the convent was at one time a major attraction for pilgrims and still brings scores of visitors each day, both Muslim and Christian.

are still concentrated in the rough lava dome of the Jabal al-Arab/Jabal al-Druze and in the Mount Hermon area in the south, and are more than 80 percent of the inhabitants in those areas. The Ismailis, less than half as numerous as the Druze, are mostly in the area of Salamiyah east of Hamah and in the mountains west of Hamah, where the Ismaili Assassins were important during the Crusades.[6]

As many as 10 percent of Syrians are Christians, and except for the Armenians, a separate group ethnolinguistically, nearly all are Arabs. Syrian Christian groups trace their tradition to the oldest Christian communities, recalling Paul's conversion near Damascus and the early role of Antioch; their spiritual ancestors predated Islam in Syria by more than 500 years. They congregate in western

Syria's larger cities and are splintered into a dozen sects, the largest of which are the Greek Orthodox (nearly 5 percent of the population), Armenian Orthodox (Gregorians), Syrian Orthodox (Jacobites), and Catholic Uniates. Greek, Latin, Arabic, and Syriac (Aramaic) are liturgical languages; it is worth noting that Aramaic is the spoken language for several thousand Greek Catholics and Orthodox in three mountain villages north of Damascus, including Malula and Saydnaya (Fig. 9.5). Nestorian Assyrians are some of the most recent arrivals in Syria. Fleeing Iraq in 1933, they were settled in a score of villages on the upper Khabur River, west of Hasakah. Historically, Syrian Christians have been prominent in Arab nationalist movements, yet they have also felt an affinity with the West, having been a favored group during the Crusader and mandate periods.

EVOLVING ECONOMIC PATTERNS

Mandate Syria developed modestly during two decades of French economic dominance. Like most of the area, it faced constraints as a new state trying to enter the modern industrial world. Conflict with Israel during and after 1948 substantially slowed development, and it was not until well into the 1960s that there was significant growth and development. Even so, continued confrontation with Israel (and consequently with the United States), has cost it dearly in its efforts to achieve its long-range economic potential. Such constraints were especially acute after the U.S. invasion of Iraq in 2003 when U.S. congressional and UN actions imposed sanctions in 2003–2004.

For several Middle East states in recent decades, growth in the productive sectors has been slowed by internal and regional instability, experimentation with political-economic ideologies, and overconcentration on military buildup. Additionally in Syria, government controls increasingly dictated prices, wages, and what could be produced, imported, and sold. As long as the economy was propped up by foreign funding, socialist management worked to a degree. However, when this support dwindled in the 1990s, the centralized inefficient bureaucracy could not manage the economy in reasonable fashion, and development did not keep pace with potential.

Since 1961, Syria's economy can be described in terms of five stages, each lasting about a decade:

1. The 1960s were a time of buildup, with annual growth increasing from 2 to 3 percent to 6 to 7 percent over the decade. Its traditional laissez-faire economy, controlled by a small urban merchant-landowner class, had reached a turning point during the union with socialist Egypt in the UAR, 1958 to 1961. Land redistribution and nationalization of private enterprises increased in pace into the mid-1960s and early 1970s. More than 100 of the largest enterprises were nationalized, along with the mineral industries, including petroleum, and railways, ports, and the airline (Map 9.2).

2. The second stage, from 1973 until 1982, saw the economy improve, with growth averaging 10 percent annually. The stimulus for this was a huge influx of foreign funding and technical expertise. The crowning achievement was completion in 1973 of the Tabaqah or Euphrates Dam (Fig. 9.6), the region's second-largest dam (after Egypt's Aswan High Dam). It expanded irrigation and land reclamation, an extended transportation system, more diversified manufacturing, and an extensive building program.

3. The third stage, 1982–1990, saw a marked downturn in the economy. The trigger was a sharp drop in oil prices, which halved the income of the Gulf states and reduced Syrian employment there. Oil exports earned less, even as they increased substantially. Foreign aid steadily diminished—aid from the USSR evaporated with its collapse. The currency fell to one-tenth its 1982 value; annual inflation reached 100 percent. Lack of foreign exchange reduced imports of both consumer goods and vital producer goods, and many factories were unable to operate. Military equipment and the partial occupation of Lebanon by Syrian troops were costly. Syria lost credibility in the West because of its actions in Lebanon, its continued ties with the USSR, and its apparent support of terrorist groups. As Israel's main adversary, it was blacklisted by the United States; it offended its Arab neighbors by supporting Iran against Iraq in the 1980s. Europe and the United States applied sanctions. With the Soviet Union unable to supply and support it militarily, Syria began to seek accommodation with the West.[7]

4. During the 1990s, the economy first improved, then declined, and finally leveled off.

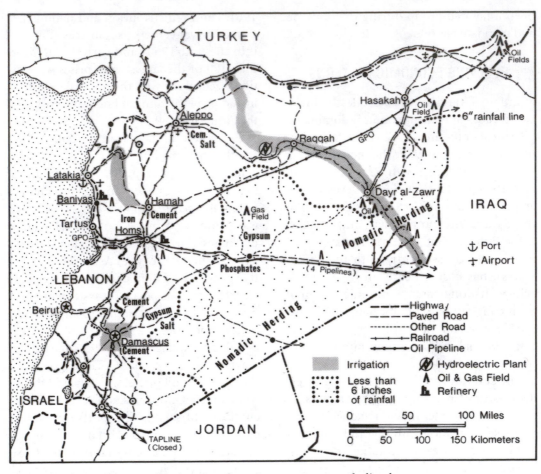

MAP 9.2 Economic map of Syria. Manufacturing centers are underlined.

Syrian relations with both the West and its Arab neighbors improved appreciably. When Iraq invaded Kuwait in 1990, it joined the allies and sent 19,000 troops to join coalition forces. In return, the Gulf states renewed their aid under the Damascus Declaration of 1991. Substantial European and Japanese financial help followed, and the government undertook some economic reforms aimed at improving its long-term prospects. GDP annual growth exceeded 5 percent through 1995. But the peace process stalled, and low oil prices flattened the economy in the late 1990s; in 1999, both peace prospects and oil prices turned up. Slightly increased foreign

investment and returning expatriate capital helped stabilize the otherwise stressed economy. However, the government seemed unable to loosen its control of strategic sectors, including petroleum, electricity, banking, and chemicals. Continued heavy expenditures for military purposes and the twenty-five-year occupation of parts of Lebanon also restrained progress. The economy at century's end was well behind its potential.

5. When Bashar al-Asad acceded to the presidency after his father's death at the start of the new millennium, there was both hope and speculation that this British-educated and technology-oriented younger man would

FIGURE 9.6 Euphrates Dam in northern Syria, key element in the Syrian plan to develop the Jazirah (area east of the Euphrates), including the broad Euphrates Valley itself. Lake Asad is to the left. Note the eastern valley wall in the distance.

at least continue and perhaps even accelerate the modest economic reforms of the 1990s. To no small extent this proved to be true, but Syria's economy felt the impact as well of external events, such as the second intifadah, repercussions of the 9/11 attacks on the United States, and the invasion of Iraq and its aftermath. Relations with the United States under the second Bush administration seriously deteriorated, as Syria seemed to be an annex of the "Axis of Evil." Further reforms included by mid-decade: legalization of privately owned banks, a gradual loosening of foreign-exchange controls, relaxation of onerous import and export procedures, and implementation of a free trade agreement with Turkey. The late 2000s saw an Association Agreement initialed with the EU, legislation creating a stock exchange (opened in 2009), decreased subsidies for gasoline and cement, and securitization of government debt through the issue of treasury bills and bonds.

A barrage of reforms like these and others proclaimed by the government in the 2000s might have set the stage for increased growth by the end of the decade—but this did not happen: in 2008, growth was only an estimated 2.8 percent despite record high oil prices. (By way of contrast, in 2001 and 2002, growth was 3.5 and 4.5 percent, respectively.) The reason for this lackadaisical response to reform was put diplomatically in a recent EU report: "The political and economic reforms announced at the beginning of [President al-Asad's] term are materializing slower than expected, causing frustration among some parts of the population."[8] The problems seem to have a double cause: insufficient follow-through on many economic changes, and strong political resistance to loosening statist controls needed to make reform a success. Still, Syria seemed to weather both increased U.S.-imposed sanctions and the global crisis of 2008 with few discernible effects and seemed to be attracting the interest of foreign investors again in 2009, as both France and, to a lesser extent, the United States moved to improve relations.[9] The EU was prepared to sign an Association Agreement in late 2009, pending Syrian approval of the final text.[10]

Economic growth that lags population growth not only forestalls improvements in the standard of living but also implies that job creation is not keeping pace with the entry of young Syrians into the job market. Officially, in the late 2000s, the government estimated the unemployment rate at about 10 percent; observers of the economy put it much higher—perhaps 20 percent—and increasing. Additionally, corruption is a concern; the 2009 report of Transparency International ranked Syria 126th of 180 countries and 11th in the region; this did represent a considerable improvement over 2008. As regards economic competitiveness, the World Economic Forum publishes the Global Competitiveness Index annually; in 2009, Syria was last of 12 regional countries rated and 94th of 133 internationally. The Fraser Institute, a conservative think tank, ranked it last in the region regarding economic freedom and 125th globally of 141 countries in 2008; there had been considerable improvement noted since 1985, but nearly all of this was registered through 2001.[11]

As to whether economic change has done much for the living standards of the average Syrian, it is difficult to say. Using the Human Development Index (HDI) of the United Nations Development Programme (UNDP), which has components representing health, education, and per capita income, some improvement is apparent. In 2007, it ranked 107th of 182 countries worldwide and 13th of the 16 countries included in this book. The 2007 HDI was 25 percent above what it was in 1980, mostly due to health and education gains.[12]

An unanticipated economic problem arose after the U.S.-led invasion of Iraq—the flood of refugees entering Syria to escape the chaos when coalition forces failed to provide security after toppling Saddam Husayn. The long-standing enmity between the contending Baathi regimes meant Syria had been home to some Iraqi political exiles for decades, but by the late 2000s estimates agreed that at least 1 million Iraqis were domiciled mostly in Damascus and a few other large cities. A sizable fraction registered with the UN High Commission for Refugees (UNHCR); the rest continued to hope to return to their homes. UNHCR statistics show that the largest group was Sunni. However, minorities—Christians, Mandaeans, and Yezidis—seem represented by more than their proportions in Iraq's population; for example, about 12 percent were Christians.[13] Many arrivals were from the middle class who initially supported themselves, but with the passage of time, penury became their state. Not until after 2007 did their plight and that of Syria—a relatively poor country—receive much official international attention. The UNHCR at the end of the decade reported it had only a third of the resources it needed to carry out its tasks and expressed the fear that desperate refugees might turn to illegal activities—even to joining terrorist groups operating in the region.

Emigration from Syria for economic reasons has long been a historic fact, and high domestic unemployment continues to encourage this. As many as 1 million Syrian workers, mostly unskilled, have sought jobs in Lebanon for at least part of most recent years; World Bank figures for emigrant remittances ($824 million in 2007) probably miss much of the flow from Lebanon, thus considerably understating the importance of emigrant wages in the economy.

Agriculture

Traditionally a major element in the economy, agriculture in the late 2000s still engages about 20 percent of the labor force and accounts for about 23 percent of GDP and 15 percent of exports. A large share of the capital investment in development after the late

1960s went into land reclamation, land improvement, irrigation schemes, and agricultural programs. Agriculture and the oil industry are the government's top economic priorities. The recalibrated goal in agriculture is to maximize food self-sufficiency to free limited foreign exchange for essential uses. After 1996, its status shifted from net importer of wheat and flour to net exporter, thus not only saving hard currency but also earning it.[14] Syrian cotton, all handpicked, is considered to be of high quality; some 235,000 mt of cotton lint were produced in 2008–2009; 40,000 mt were exported.

Cyclic variations in rainfall totals and seasonal distribution are a crucial factor in the western Fertile Crescent because they create enormous swings in grain production. Between 1947 and 1960, about every third year was dry, and the wheat crop in the dry year of 1973 was only one-fourth that in the very wet year of 1972. The advantages of and need for expanded irrigation are obvious, and despite financial, technical, and geographical problems, Syria has worked toward that goal. The area under irrigation doubled between 1975 and 1993 and continues to increase steadily, but the expansion of irrigation has not been enough to liberate the far northeastern region from the need for reliable rainfall. After three years of drought, this poorest part of the country was seeing large-scale hunger and outbound migration in 2009–2010.[15]

As is true for the region as a whole, wheat and barley are the dominant crops, claiming nearly three-fourths of cultivation. The more humid agricultural lands produce cotton and sugar beets, and cotton leads in the expanding irrigated areas of the Jazirah. Tomatoes and lentils grow widely, as do more than a score of seasonal vegetables. Permanent tree and vine crops grow both in irrigated areas and on rainfed slopes: citrus on the coastal plain and in the Ghutah (the extensive oasis around Damascus), and olives, figs, and grapes on many slopes in the west, where

they are well adapted to the Mediterranean regime. As part of its agricultural development program, Syria is vigorously expanding olive production (Fig. 5.4), doubling output in the past twenty years. It now vies with Turkey, the longtime leader, as the region's leading olive producer (see Table 5.3). Rice is increasingly grown in the Ghab and in the Jazirah. Overall, from the early 1960s through the mid-2000s, food production per capita rose by about 25 percent.[16]

Syria's climate and its agricultural experience under prevailing climatic conditions led to its being chosen by the Consultative Group on International Agricultural Research (CGIAR)—a major sponsor of efforts to improve living standards in developing countries[17]—as the site for studying water-scarce agriculture. The International Center for Agricultural Research in Dry Areas has been located near Aleppo since 1976; it is internationally renowned and operates a dozen specialized laboratories in fields ranging from biotechnology to virology and soil physics. In addition to concentrating on improving crops traditionally grown in dry areas, its particular concerns include water-use efficiency, rangeland management, and environmental preservation.

Ghab Project. The Ghab Project involved drainage, hydroelectric production, and irrigation and was completed in 1965. It reclaimed 61,780 ac/25,000 ha of former marshland in the Ghab Depression, east of and parallel to the Jabal al-Sahiliyah in northwestern Syria. Roughly 31 mi/50 km long by 9 mi/15 km wide, this northern end of the Levant Rift System was formerly flooded by the lower Orontes River. The basalt lava flow that dammed the Orontes at the Ghab's northern outlet was cut through. Besides the land reclaimed, twice as much other land was improved in the project, and the area now yields cotton, rice, sugar beets, wheat, and barley.

Euphrates Dam.   The most important development project in modern Syria is the Euphrates Dam (sometimes Tabaqah Dam), involving not only the huge dam but also a hydroelectric installation, a long-line electrical distribution net, the lake behind the dam, an extensive irrigation system, a new town, and agricultural development in the Jazirah. Like Egypt's Aswan High Dam, the project was facilitated by Soviet financial and technical assistance. Initiated in 1961 and dedicated in 1973, it is 197 ft/60 m high and 3 mi/4.5 km long (Fig. 9.6). The reservoir, Lake Asad, extends 50 mi/80 km upstream, covers 247 mi^2/640 km^2, storing 12 bn m^3 of water.[18] The power station, opened in 1978, has eight 100,000-kilowatt turbines and at first generated more than 90 percent of Syria's electricity; this share dropped sharply as demand grew rapidly and as new thermal power plants came on line. By the late 2000s, the latter contributed about 80 percent to installed capacity. Gas was gaining on oil as the leading fuel in use, but oil was still slightly in the lead.[19]

A major goal of the project is irrigating 1.58 mn ac/640,000 ha along the Euphrates and its tributaries. It has virtually achieved its original goals—by the mid-2000s, irrigation had nearly tripled in extent. Tabaqah, the village at the original dam site, rapidly expanded and was renamed Madinat al-Thawrah (Revolution City), now with more than 100,000 inhabitants. More than a dozen new villages have been built to accommodate the scores of thousands attracted to the Jazirah.

Nevertheless, several problems have affected the project.[20] The Euphrates enters Syria from Turkey and leaves it for Iraq, so the three states involved have contended sharply over complex water rights (see Chap. 8). After the dam's completion, Syria and Iraq disputed the division of water, bringing them to the verge of war in 1975 before Saudi Arabia mediated resolution. Then Turkey largely ignored Syria in undertaking a triple damming of the river, thus upsetting its timetable for Jazirah irrigation projects. More immediately serious was the revelation that large sections of the intended irrigation areas are underlain by easily soluble gypsum. Since dissolution of the gypsum would both reduce soil quality and result in water loss, elevated concrete-trough channels must be used to carry water, and plans to irrigate some areas have had to be canceled. The 77,170 ac/31,230 ha of irrigated land (and 18,532 ac/7,500 ha of other land) drowned by Lake Asad (its waters displaced nearly sixty villages) must be accounted for in computing the benefits.

Growth of Industry

Minerals.   A dearth of mineral resources hindered economic progress in Syria for centuries.[21] Only recently has modern technology facilitated discovery of two moderately large and important mineral resources, petroleum and phosphates. In the late 2000s the sector, primarily petroleum, accounts for more than 40 percent of export earnings—in 2007, 27 percent of GDP.[22]

Petroleum.   Intensive exploration led to discovery of oil in 1956 in the extreme northeastern corner of Syria, where several small, closely spaced fields align with adjacent fields in Iraq and in Turkey farther north. Following Qaratshuk (Karatshuk), Syria's discovery field, Suwaydiyah was found in 1959. All of these fields unfortunately produce heavy, high-sulfur crude. Major output began only in 1968 after a 404 mi/650 km pipeline opened to the Homs refinery and Tartus terminal.

Until 1986, the heavy crude had to be blended with lighter ones, originally tapped at the Homs refinery from IPC pipelines from Iraq. Following Syria's shutdown of those lines in the early 1980s (see Chap. 6), it blended light crude brought by tanker from Iran to Tartus with its own heavy oil. However, the Tayyim field and some small fields discovered around Dayr al-Zawr after 1984 have very light sweet crude. Production from this cluster is pumped to refineries and export terminals through the appropriated IPC pipelines, thus enabling Syria to meet its own blending requirements.

Average daily production rose from 27,000 bpd in 1968 to a high of 605,000 bpd in 1995, vying with Qatar's daily average before falling back in the following years. Production continued to average 560,000 bpd in the late 1990s but declined steadily to 385,000 bpd by 2009, when oil reserves were 2.5 bn bbl (see Table 6.1). Syria's first refinery, in Homs, originally used feedstock from IPC pipelines. Its throughput of 107,000 bpd is exceeded by the 135,000 bpd capacity of the later Baniyas refinery, built on the coast in 1980. Both blend Syrian heavy and light crudes.

A half-dozen small gas fields south of Lake Asad and others near Palmyra supply power plants and industry. A large field discovered in 1997 in the Abi Rabah area is tied by pipeline to power plants near Aleppo and in Damascus and Homs. A major gas plant near Palmyra was due to begin operations in 2010, producing 95.3 mn ft^3/2.7 mn^3 annually. In addition to expanding its own power-generating capacity, Syria agreed in 1996 to integrate its grid into a regional network with Egypt and Jordan (and eventually Iraq); it was completed for the first three countries in 2001 when Lebanon also became a participant. The Arab Gas Pipeline now carries gas from Egypt via Jordan to Syria. Settling transit fees with Egypt in 2009 allows deliveries to Lebanon as well and eventually to Turkey.

Phosphates. Rock strata comparable to those giving Israel, Jordan, and Iraq enormous reserves of phosphate rock were traced into central Syria in the early 1970s, and production rose from 600,000 mt in 1974 to 3.7 mn mt by 2007, ranking seventh in the world.[23]

Reserves near Palmyra totaling 2 bn mt and sufficient for many years of production merited building a railroad to the mines in the late 1970s (see Map 9.2); they are of lower quality than in neighboring states. Increased exports are planned to help compensate for declining oil revenues. Production of other minerals—salt, gypsum, sulfur from petroleum processing, cement (from two large mills at Tartus and Hamah), and steel from a plant near Hamah—is for domestic use only. All mineral resources were nationalized in 1964, but recent economic reforms promise to open the sector to private investment.

Manufacturing

For many centuries, Damascus and other Syrian cities enjoyed fame for their damascene metalwork, damask fabrics, muslins, linens, silk brocades, tapestries, carpets, tooled leather, carved and inlaid furniture, glassware, pottery, jewelry, mosaics, and similar craft work. Fortunately for Syria and the world, these crafts have survived to the present, and such products are prized as handmade creations; however, they are an inadequate basis for a manufacturing complex in the modern technological world.

Limitations that became apparent in the late 1940s typified industrial development at that time. Management lacked expertise, and labor lacked technical skills. The merchant families were unable or unwilling to invest the amounts needed for expansion, and domestic instability discouraged outside investors. When the Baath government nationalized major industries, investment capital for certain industries became available through government channels. However, in general, all of Syria's political-economic deficiencies converged to inhibit rational industrial development.

Planning and development during the 1970s gave early emphasis to infrastructure and basic industries: highways, railroads, the Euphrates Dam, cement plants, iron and steel mills, and similar industries. Little consideration was given to precision goods or high-technology items. Well into the mid-1990s, heavy industry, sugar production and other food processing, cement, chemicals, textiles, and other enterprises continued as parastatals, as did banking and oil. But with the easing of government restrictions—especially through the 1991 Investment Law No. 10—private investment moved into food processing, pharmaceuticals, textiles, ready-made clothing, and transportation.

By the late 1990s, industry was moving forward more than in the past, but Syria was not gaining on its neighbors. Virtually every city benefited from industrial expansion: Aleppo gained tractor, agricultural machinery, appliance, food-processing, and cement plants; Hamah, iron and steel, textile, and cement operations; Homs, fertilizer plants, using phosphates from near Palmyra; Tartus, the largest cement plant; Baniyas, a refinery bigger than the older Homs facility; and smaller factories in Latakia, Dayr al-Zawr, Hasakah, and Raqqah. Still hampered by regulations, entrepreneurs hoped to gain under the new regime. To some extent this has proved true in the 2000s with the economic reforms mentioned above, plus increased emphasis on the private sector and changes in the laws on corporate governance (in 2008). But at end of the decade, the burden of state control was still heavy.

TRANSPORTATION AND TRADE

As a keystone in the Fertile Crescent, Syria has been the focus of route junctions and crossings for millennia, and in part it still fulfills that function. From the late Neolithic onward, the Damascus-Aleppo axis served routes from the south—the Via Maris (Sea Route) from Egypt and the King's Highway from Arabia; the east—from Persia and Mesopotamia; and the north—through the Cilician Gates from Anatolia. With today's technologically advanced transportation systems, intraregional highway and air routes cross Syria both north-south and east-west.

Syria has a road and rail network (see Table 7.2) adequate for current needs. The more thickly settled areas naturally have the densest network of roads, and only through-routes cross the sparsely inhabited deserts. Modern paved highways now connect all major cities; a four-lane divided throughway extends from Jordan to Turkey through Damascus, Homs, Hamah, and Aleppo. New rail lines facilitate development of the Jazirah and the center of the country. The line from Latakia through Aleppo, Madinat al-Thawrah, Raqqah, Dayr al-Zawr, and Hasakah to Qamishli has been a major factor both in developing northeastern agriculture and Latakia port and in stimulating all the cities it passes. In the late 2000s, plans for the first phase of a metro system in Damascus were under way.

By the late 1940s, with no adequate general-cargo ports of its own, Syria used Beirut, having lost access to Iskenderun in 1939 and Haifa in 1948. The government began a long-range development program for Latakia and, later, Tartus. Baniyas had long been the terminus for Iraq pipelines. Latakia is now a major general-port facility, and Tartus has undergone significant expansion since the 1980s.

Although trade in and through Syria diminished during the last stages of Ottoman rule, it has long been a lively activity. The vigorous retail trade remained in the private sector, though it suffered from government restraints. The *suq* is prominent in every town and city. The bustling Suq Hamidiyah in Damascus and the underground Aleppo *suq* have been famed for centuries; each contains hundreds of small shops selling a wide range of items. One reminder of Syria's commercial traditions is the annual Damascus International Trade Fair, conducted in July since 1954. Foreign commerce is primarily with Western Europe, Lebanon, and Saudi

Arabia. It initialed an association agreement with the EU in 2008. Since 2001, it has been seeking accession to the World Trade Organization (WTO), which would require extensive liberalization. WTO talks had not progressed far by the end of the 2000s (the government blames the United States for this situation, probably accurately), and Syria remains the only Arab League member without even observer status with the WTO.[24] (See Tables 7.3 and 7.4.)

POLITICAL GEOGRAPHY

Internal Relations

Like other parts of the Fertile Crescent, Syria's political and territorial aspirations were formulated at the end of World War I, and, as a mandate, its state form was imposed upon it. Thus, when it achieved independence in 1946, its boundaries were prefixed, and Syrians had to achieve a state idea—raison d'être—within an imposed European context. As one consequence, national memories of the Umayyad Empire and the long-persistent national consciousness of "Greater Syria" resurfaced. Although mandate Syria had been unable to prevent dismemberment of the historical Greater Syria, the independent state could express irredentist claims regarding detached territories.

The most burning issue was Lebanon—for Syria an amputation of an inherent piece of its territory (not until 2009 would the two establish normal diplomatic relations). This stance was revived after 1976 when, as part of the Arab Deterrent Force, it occupied part of Lebanon. The last of its troops finally left eastern Lebanon in 2005 under pressure from the international community led by the United States and France. Syria had contended that, after Israel ended its occupation of southern Lebanon in 2000, its forces helped deter a return. Its presence was also a bargaining chip in negotiations with Israel.[25] A second territorial issue was the transfer of the Sanjak of Alexandretta to Turkey in 1939. More sweeping complaints in the 1920s had argued that the Palestine and Transjordan mandates had also been unlawfully detached from its historic territory to suit the agendas of the mandatories.

With no specific boundaries to influence them, France and Britain delimited mandate Syria for their own ends in rough accord with the Sykes-Picot Agreement (see Map 8.2), with two interesting results: The northern boundary simply followed the line of the Berlin-to-Baghdad railway from north of Aleppo to Nusaybin, some 200 mi/322 km, and the southeastern border is entirely geometrical—from the Jabal al-Druze to the Euphrates a straight line of 275 mi/443 km across the Syrian Desert. Even though Bedouin still seasonally migrate across this line, and although there have been tensions on the Turkish border occasionally, both boundaries have proved to be reasonably satisfactory.

Three sections of the western land boundary have produced problems. The northwestern segment, around Alexandretta, has already been discussed (see "Boundary and Territorial Disputes," Chap. 8). Syria objected to the boundary drawn with Lebanon because some territory given Lebanon was mostly Muslim—its inclusion in a supposedly Christian state could not be justified. At the Sea of Galilee's southeast, it ran several hundred meters back from the water's edge, giving the shore to the Palestine mandate, and the 1949 Armistice Line put this in Israel (which, since 1967, has occupied the Golan).

Golan

Israel's conquest of the strategic and heavily fortified Golan in the 1967 war, occupation of the area after the war, and integration of the area into Israel in 1981 potentially further diminished Syria's territory. Its categorical rejection of Israel's unilateral incorporation of the Golan and its adamant irredentist determination to recover it have been manifest in every Syrian-Israeli negotiation or discussion. Syria considers that it has a strong case: No country has recognized Israel's annexation of the Golan—even the United States has consistently rejected it.

Centrifugal Forces

Not until the early 1970s did Syria stabilize enough politically to achieve national unity and a rational government structure. Prior to that time, it saw more coups d'état than any other regional state. Even with stabilization, the government has had a double-minority power structure. Ideologically, the party in power, the Baath (Arab Renaissance Party), first achieved power in a 1963 coup; ethnically, the father-and-son presidents have been from the relatively small Alawi minority.

Major social competitions acting centrifugally are the periodically acute conflict between liberal and conservative Islam and the opposition of both groups to the secularism of the Baathi-Alawi alliance. The best organized of the fundamentalist groups, the Muslim Brotherhood, seriously challenged the al-Asad regime twice. Reflecting Sunni hatred of the heterodox Alawis, the Brotherhood killed more than sixty Alawi military cadets in Aleppo in 1979. Then, as the Islamic Front, it seized Hamah in February 1982. Responding security forces killed thousands of inhabitants, destroying much of the city in subduing the rebels.[26] This overreaction is the blackest mark against the regime, which otherwise has not evinced massive physical repression. Whereas large Palestinian refugee groups have been centrifugal forces in Lebanon and Jordan, the large number in Syria—approximately 422,000—has been kept under strict control, although assured of sympathy for their cause. The leadership of Hamas, the principal Islamist group among the Palestinians, has long been situated in Damascus, and there is some controversy over how much influence Syria has over the group. Since Hamas won the Palestinian parliamentary elections in January 2006 and especially since it seized sole control of Gaza since June 2007, the dominance of the Damascus leaders has given way to local cadres.

Centripetal Forces

Considering these potent divisive forces, it is noteworthy that two related movements, Syrian nationalism and Arab nationalism, have been effective in offsetting centrifugal forces and bringing Syrians together into a viable national group. The regularity of coups d'état prior to 1963 has been broken, and the public will to stand firm vis-à-vis Israel and against political criticism and insistent opposition from the United States and other Western countries helped it maintain unity into the new century. In the 1990s, the regime survived the loss of its Soviet connection and managed some success rebuilding relationships with the West. Under Bashar al-Asad, it has yielded some of its rigid control, though political openness and the residual internal stresses have yet to be reconciled.

RELATIONS

Regional Relations

Damascus's leading role in Arab nationalism was widely accepted in the Fertile Crescent at the end of World War I. The Arab leadership that backed the Arab Revolt of 1916–1917 had been centered there, and a short-lived kingdom was established under Faysal ibn Husayn in 1920. In taking the mandate, France forced Faysal to abdicate, but Syria never forgot its moment of glory. However, its attempts to assert regional leadership have met resolute resistance from its neighbors.

Observing the mistakes of Nasserist Egypt, Syria balanced backing for Arab socialism and Arab nationalism—already an overcrowded arena—with a focus on Syrian nationalism and domestic development. Showing its support for Palestine in three wars with Israel, it has taken in thousands of

Palestinian refugees. It was a charter member of the Arab League and has played an active role in that organization. The Arab Boycott of Israel office is in Damascus, although by the early 2000s the boycott had lost most of its sting. Although Syria considers itself part of the Islamic world and has participated in the Organization of the Islamic Conference, it, like Iraq and Egypt, advocates and practices a greater degree of secularism than do more conservative Muslim states.

Syria's relations with virtually all of its neighbors since 1950 have been marked by frictions and, in the case of Israel, by successive hostilities. Relations with Lebanon are of special significance, but have already been discussed in Chapter 8 and are further examined in Chapter 10.

Syria and Iraq pursued mutual economic interests until the mid-1960s. For many years, Iraq's only petroleum outlets were its pipelines across Syria, with terminals in Baniyas and in Tripoli, Lebanon. These were vital to Iraq and earned Syria annual royalties of more than $120 million, plus similar discounts on Iraqi crude for the Homs refinery. Nevertheless, ideological disputes between Iraqi and Syrian Baathists and disagreements over oil royalties led to sporadic interruptions in the 1970s and a definitive shutdown in 1982. Syria supported Iran during the Iran-Iraq War, despite its long and vigorous advocacy of Arab unity. Then, defying domestic opposition, the government had little hesitation in 1990 about joining, along with Egypt, the coalition that forced Iraq to withdraw from Kuwait. Renewed détente between the two countries led to their signing a free trade agreement in 2001. Syria was elected a nonpermanent member of the UN Security Council that year and in 2002 supported the resolution requiring Iraq to readmit weapons inspectors. However, in the lead-up to the U.S.-U.K. invasion in 2003, it was part of the large majority on the council that refused to sanction preemptive military action. After

Iraq regained the ability to act independently of the occupying powers, the two countries resumed diplomatic relations in 2006, ending a twenty-four-year hiatus. But at the end of the decade, Iraq was accusing Syria of sheltering hostile Baathis and of allowing terror attacks in Iraq to be launched by them and others. While the first claim is accurate, the second has seemed less likely.

Relations with Jordan on the south have ranged from close to several border closures and even to at least two brief, abortive Syrian invasions of northwestern Jordan. They differed on Iraq's invasion of Kuwait, and Syria condemned the Jordanian-Israeli peace treaty of 1994. However, with the ascension of King Abdullah to Jordan's throne in 1999 and the ascension of Bashar al-Asad to Syria's presidency in 2000, they achieved their closest relations in decades.

Baathi, secular, Alawi-led Syria has had an ambiguous, mostly rocky relationship with conservative, religious, Sunni Saudi Arabia, despite the fact that, as a "frontline state," Syria has been the beneficiary of considerable Saudi financial assistance. On the one hand, its alliance with revolutionary Iran stretching over three decades alarms the kingdom; on the other, Syria was an active participant in the coalition against Iraq when the latter was threatening Saudi territory. In the late 2000s, Saudi King Abdullah seemed to have some rapport with al-Asad, perhaps to offer some counterbalance to Iran and assuage his country's fears of a "Shii Crescent" extending from Iran to Lebanon.

Syria's decades-long dispute with Turkey over Alexandretta (Iskenderun) lost cogency many years ago, although as late as the mid-2000s, maps showed a double border with the area as Syrian. In the 1970s and 1980s, relations were exacerbated by Euphrates problems, but they remained correct until 1998. Triggering tensions then was Syria's support of Kurdish rebels, especially the Kurdish Workers Party (PKK), fighting Turkish troops in southeastern Turkey. It renewed Alexandretta irredentism, denounced interference with the Euphrates, and condemned Turkey for its increasing collaboration with Israel. But following Turkish threats of military action and regional mediation, Syria withdrew its support of the PKK.[27] In the late 2000s, Turkey was actively mediating to revive negotiations between Syria and Israel, much to the displeasure of the Bush administration that actively discouraged Israeli participation.

With non-Arab revolutionary Iran, Syria forged a strategic alliance rooted from the early 1980s in their mutual antipathy toward the Saddam Husayn regime in Iraq (and perhaps maintained after 2003 by Bush's attempts to isolate both from the global arena). On a practical level, the mausoleum of Sayeeda Zeinab, daughter of Ali, the first Shii imam, and sister of Hassan and Husayn, the second and third imams, has drawn hundreds of thousands of Iranian pilgrims (and their business) to Damascus, especially before 2003 when the premier Shii holy places in Iraq were essentially unreachable for Iranians. Increasingly in the 2000s, this alliance has been of concern to Syria's Arab neighbors, and it has been a factor in the Obama administration's early moves to engage Syria in dialogue.

Global Relations

Syria developed special relations with France during the latter's administration of the mandate. Despite its resentment of that country, it inevitably adopted aspects of French culture, and French is still used by some elite groups. Franco-Syrian relations after 1946 gradually diminished to ordinary commercial exchange. However, France was active in pressuring Syria to withdraw from Lebanon, and following the Hariri assassination in 2005, it pushed for an international investigation into possible Syrian involvement. Citing Syria's constructive role in settling the crisis in Lebanon over the presidential succession in 2008, French president

Nicolas Sarkozi and al-Asad exchanged visits later that year.

As was true with Egypt and Iraq, 1950s Syria found its channels with the West highly constricted because of Western—especially U.S.—support of Israel, its main adversary. It turned to the USSR and East Europe for arms, economic aid, and technical assistance, including funding for such projects as the Euphrates Dam. Soviet military advisers and liaison personnel served in Syria for more than three decades. However, it kept communism at home firmly under control and, like Egypt, did not become a Soviet satellite. Disintegration of the USSR in 1991 suddenly deprived it of its politico-economic mainstay and compelled President Hafiz al-Asad to pursue accommodation with the West. Inter alia, he sought greater concord with the EU and with individual European states.

Syria's relations with the United States were friendly early on. In 1919, the King-Crane Commission found a reservoir of goodwill toward the United States, partly because of the work of the Syrian Protestant College (later the American University of Beirut) and partly because of the widely heralded ideals of President Wilson's Fourteen Points. Relations cooled after U.S. endorsement of the Balfour Declaration and support for Zionist colonization in Palestine.

Following the 1948–1949 Arab-Israeli war, and especially after Syria accepted help from the USSR in the mid-1950s, U.S.-Syrian relations ranged from fair to strained until 1990. Indeed, diplomatic relations were actually broken after the 1967 war and resumed only in 1974. The United States and other Western countries criticized its decision to send thousands of troops into Lebanon in 1976, and brief skirmishes erupted between U.S. and Syrian forces in Lebanon in that confused period.

A pragmatic détente followed Syria's internal political moderation in the late 1980s, which coincided with the phasing out of Soviet aid and, concurrently, its participation in the 1990–1991 coalition against Iraq. The United States also welcomed its cooperation in the active peace process of the early 1990s. With foundering of peace negotiations, the United States and Israel accused Syria of harboring leaders of alleged terrorist groups. In response, Syria expelled a number of suspected leaders.[28] Even so, the U.S. State Department retained Syria on its annual list of states sponsoring terrorism, despite finding no evidence that Syrian officials have engaged in terrorist acts since 1986.

Washington-Damascus relations spiraled downward in the 2000s over U.S. allegations that along its long desert border with Iraq, Syria allowed a flow of militiamen intent on joining the insurgency against coalition forces in Iraq.[29] In late 2003 the U.S. Congress passed the Syrian Accountability and Lebanon Sovereignty Restoration Act. The bill endorsed diplomatic and economic sanctions against Syria, although there was little contact to sanction, and demanded that it withdraw from Lebanon.[30] Bitter exchanges followed President Bush's approval of Israel's actions when it bombed a camp north of Damascus in 2003 and assassinated a former Hamas leader in his car in the Syrian capital in 2004. Pressure on Syria continued with UN Security Council Resolution 1559, sponsored primarily by the United States, demanding Syrian withdrawal from Lebanon and respect for Lebanon's independence. It complied in April 2005 by recalling the last of its troops and its intelligence agents.

The assassination of former Lebanese prime minister Rafiq Hariri in February 2005 (as well as a number of other prominent anti-Syrian individuals) strongly indicated the involvement of at least elements of the Damascus regime. The United States and France spearheaded another UN resolution setting up a commission to investigate the attack on Hariri, and its preliminary findings were that it was unlikely that it could have been carried out without the knowledge of Syrian intelligence. Its work continued, with indications that individuals suspected of involvement had been identified; a Special Tribunal was authorized to try them, and in March 2009 the court began operations in The Hague.

In September 2007, Israel carried out an aerial strike on a military site in northern Syria without initial explanation; later it leaked an allegation that it involved a nuclear facility under construction. A few months later, the United States accused North Korea of helping Syria build a secret reactor. Damascus denied the charges and allowed limited access to the site for inspectors from the International Atomic Energy Agency (IAEA). By the end of the decade, the incident remained murky, with the IAEA finding evidence of the presence of some radioactive material, criticizing Syria for its desultory cooperation in its investigations, but indicating that little had emerged from its work so far to support the more expansive aspects of the U.S.-Israeli claims.

In 2009, the new U.S. administration moved to rethink the Bush policies on Syria that led to such rather curious results as opposition to Israeli-Syrian peace talks. High-level officials, including Special Envoy to the Middle East George Mitchell, visited Damascus and conferred with President al-Asad, and in 2010, the administration nominated an ambassador to Syria to fill a five-year vacancy. At the least, Syria no longer seemed to be the unnamed member of the "Axis of Evil."

Despite its own ambiguities, and despite the external efforts to marginalize it, Syria persists as a key historical and geopolitical player in the region.

NOTES

1. P. Khoury 1987 is an excellent account of Syria as mandate. Hopwood 1988 examines independent Syria's political and cultural evolution. *Syria* Country Study 1988 is an excellent general study in an authoritative series. Pipes 1990 is a critical study. Theroux

1996 is a recent useful illustrated *National Geographic* report. *The Economist,* Dec. 31, 2004, has a summary update.

2. Syrians also celebrate May 17, the day on which the last French forces evacuated Syria.

3. *New York Times*, June 8, 2003.

4. *New York Times*, Dec. 15, 1992.

5. See Nisan 2002, Chap. 6.

6. See Bengio and Ben-Dor 1999, Chap. 7.

7. See Perthes 1992.

8. European Commission 2007.

9. *Wall Street Journal* 2009.

10. See http://ec.europa.eu/external_relations/syria/index_en.htm for developments.

11. Transparency International 2009; World Economic Forum 2009a; Fraser Institute 2008.

12. United Nations Development Programme 2009. Each report includes data that lag by two years.

13. International Rescue Committee 2008.

14. *Agricultural Situation Report: Syria*, 1998.

15. *Daily Star* (Beirut), Mar. 7, 2010.

16. UN Food and Agricultural Organization, *Production Yearbook* (Rome), various issues. See also http://faostat.fao.org. For Syria and the countries in the following chapters, changes in per capita food production were calculated using a three-year average in the base period and the average for 2004 to 2006.

17. For further information on CGIAR research facilities, see www.cgiar.org.

18. Data supplied by Syrian engineers at the Euphrates Dam during Held's interview on June 8, 1990.

19. International Energy Agency (IEA), "2006 Energy Balance for Syria," www.iea.org/country/index.asp.

20. See the excellent and detailed analyses in Kolars and Mitchell 1991.

21. For Syria and the other countries in the following chapters, see the country articles in U.S. Geological Survey (USGS), *Minerals Yearbook*, vol. 3, *International* (Washington, DC: USGS, 2008). See also www.usgs.gov.

22. USGS, "The Minerals Industry of Syria," in ibid.

23. Ibid.

24. See U.S. Department of State, *Country Commercial Guide: Syria*, FY 2006; U.S. Department of State, *Background Note: Syria*, Feb. 2010; and U.S. Department of Energy, Energy Information Administration (EIA), *Country Analysis Briefs: Syria*, June 2009, and "Syria Energy Profile," 2009. Plaut 1999 is particular in its invidious perspective. See also *New York Times*, Jan. 27, 2000. Bashar al-Asad, who succeeded his late father as president of Syria in July 2000, was expected to modernize and loosen the economy, but he has not achieved the success expected. See Ghadbian 2001.

25. Salhani 2003.

26. Discussed in many sources at the time, the Hamah conflict is revisited in *Christian Science Monitor*, Oct. 3, 2003, and in *New York Times*, Oct. 24, 2003.

27. See *New York Times*, Oct. 4, 1998.

28. *New York Times*, July 18, 2003. For a background view, see Little 1990. For a broader context, see B. Kaufman 1996. More details are given in *Syria* Country Study 1987; for an update, see Hemmer 2003 and Zunes 2004.

29. *New York Times*, July 15, 2003.

30. *New York Times*, May 12 and May 14, 2004; *Washington Post*, Oct. 7, 2003; *New York Times*, Sept. 27, 2004.

10

Lebanon and Cyprus
A Mountain and an Island

Lebanon

THE CHARACTER OF LEBANON

Lebanon differs strikingly both physically and culturally from the rest of the Middle East. Dominated by the rugged and well-watered range of Mount Lebanon, it is green on the western slopes facing the blue Mediterranean, and brown from the steppes and deserts to the east. It is small enough to be traversed by car in a few hours even on its long axis, yet it displays almost as much landscape diversity as does Turkey, seventy-six times its size. Culturally, it is one of the most highly developed countries in the Middle East and is one of the most liberal, Western, modernized, literate, and education centered, with an open entrepreneurial economy and society. Under normal circumstances, Lebanese engage in enjoying the good life and sharing it with nearly 2 million visitors a year—a pleasant environment, an array of excellent cuisines, and a varied nightlife.

Lebanon is also the region's most multisectarian state, and interconfessional tensions have frequently flared into open conflict. Between 1975 and 1991, these intensified and exploded into externally fueled warfare. With traditionally inadequate military and police forces, and weakened by internal factionalism, it became the confused battleground for its own militias and its neighbors' armies. Lebanon sank steadily into anarchy to become the area's most devastated and endangered country. Once called the Switzerland of the Middle East, in the 1980s it was fragmented, a nation in jeopardy, in the process of collapse. Not until 1991 did internecine killing finally cease under determined pressure from other Arab states. Through 2000, however, it remained an arena in the Arab-Israeli conflict until, after twenty-two years, Israel unilaterally withdrew from the south. For fifteen years after 1991, it made slow but steady progress toward recovery, before losing many of its gains in 2006 when the "Summer War" between Israel and Lebanese Shii militias exploded briefly but intensely on its soil.

RICH PAST, COMPLEX EVOLUTION

The advantages and resources of Lebanon attracted humanoids more than 800,000 years ago during the Mindel glaciation, as is revealed by artifacts found near Sidon and in the high intermontane Bekaa. Byblos and many other sites show evidence of occupancy before and during the Neolithic period, from the ninth to the fourth millennium BCE. "Phoenicia," the name applied to the area after 1200 BCE, is the Greek translation of "Canaan"—land of purple-red. The reference

LEBANON

Long-form official name, anglicized: Republic of Lebanon

Official name, transliterated: Al-Jumhuriyah al-Lubnaniyah

Form of government: unitary multiparty republic with one legislative house (National Assembly)

Area: 4,016 mi^2/10,400 km^2

Population, 2008: 4,142,000; Literacy (Latest): 88.3%

Ethnic composition (%): Arab 84.5, of which Lebanese 71.2, Palestinian 12.1; Armenian 6.8; Kurd 6.1; other 2.6

Religions (%—data approximate): Muslim 53, of which Shii 32, Sunni 21; Christian 39 of which Catholic 26.5 (of which Maronite 20, Greek Catholic or Melkite 4.5), Orthodox 12 (of which Greek Orthodox 6, Armenian Apostolic 5), Protestant 0.5; Druze 7; Alawi 1.

Demography: Life expectancy—70.2 yr (M), 75.2 yr (F); Birthrate (per 1,000)—19.7; Fertility rate—1.92

GDP, 2009: $32.66 billion; purchasing power parity: $47.82 billion; per capita: $11,500

Currency: Lebanese pound, US$1 = 1,495 pounds, 1 pound = $0.00066 (March 2010)

Energy reserves: oil, natural gas, and coal—nil

Main exports (% of total value, 2005): electrical equipment 16.7; base metals 14.7; precious metal (significantly gold) jewelry 11.9; food and live animals 10.7; chemicals and chemical products 8.7

Main imports (% of total value, 2005): mineral products 23.8; electrical equipment 11.4; food and live animals 10.3; chemicals and chemical products 8.8; transport equipment 8.7

Capital city: Beirut (agglomeration) 1,770,000; other cities: Tripoli 212,900; Sidon 149,000; Tyre 117,100; Nabatiyah 89,400

---

is probably to the important export of textiles dyed "royal purple" with secretions from the murex shellfish found in abundance at Sidon and Tyre. The coastal city-states of Tyre, Sidon, Beirut, and Byblos used the famous Cedars of Lebanon for shipbuilding and export to timber-starved Egypt before 2400 BCE. By the thirteenth century BCE, the Phoenicians had also developed, probably for use in their active maritime trade, an alphabet that was gradually adopted, adapted, and diffused throughout the ancient world.[1] Despite repeated invasions and later

control by the Seleucids, Romans, and Byzantines, the area thrived, as monuments and ruins in every part of modern Lebanon attest.

Christianity's strength developed during the Roman-Byzantine centuries and has shaped modern Lebanon. After the Muslim conquest, the confessional balance and, later, the linguistic pattern slowly changed, but Christian dominance in Mount Lebanon persisted through thirteen centuries under the Umayyads, Abbasids, Crusaders, Mamluks, and Ottomans. Under the latter's *millet* system, the region enjoyed considerable autonomy from the sixteenth century onward, and after fighting between Christians and Druze in 1860, it gained a special status that continued through World War I.[2]

Lebanon emerged as a separate entity as a French League of Nations mandate. As was explained in the previous chapter, its territory was detached from the mandate of Syria and was enlarged to create Grand Liban, "Greater Lebanon." This included not only the coastal plain and Mount Lebanon, but also, to the east, the Bekaa, paralleling Mount Lebanon, and the separate Anti-Lebanon mountain ridges (Map 10.1). After two decades of French tutelage, it was declared independent by the Free French in November 1941; independence was reaffirmed on November 22, 1943, now the official independence day. As in Syria, the last French forces did not evacuate the country until 1946.

LEBANON AND THE LEBANESE

Lebanon is synonymous with cultural diversity; virtually every major ethnic and religious group in the Fertile Crescent is represented. However, the underlying diversity is sectarian rather than ethnolinguistic. Moreover, emphasis on antagonisms between Christians and Muslims neglects the tensions within more than a dozen Christian and half a dozen Muslim subgroups. Intercommunal tensions are so complicated that many sects have opposed a census since that of 1932, which showed a Christian majority and, under the system arranged by the French, gave dominant government and military power to the Christians. This arrangement was not changed until 1990, although there had been an obvious Muslim majority for decades. With no new census data since 1932, Lebanon's present demographic details can only be estimated.

The 2009 population of about 4.2 million was a modest increase from the estimated 3 million in 1975, the lowest population

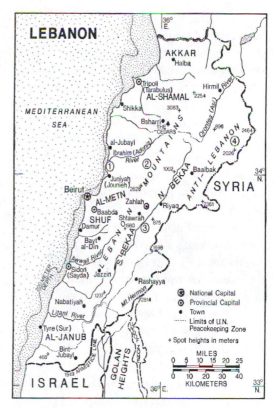

MAP 10.1 General map of Lebanon. Circled numbers identify regions discussed in the text.

growth in the region over that period. This is traceable partly to family choice in a relatively educated society and partly to emigration;[3] during the worst years of fighting, including the 1982 Israeli invasion, as many as 900,000 Lebanese may have left. When the 1989 accord seemed to be holding, many returned, although voluntary emigration has long been a feature of Lebanese history—and of the economy. Remittances from emigrants were $5.8 billion, about 24 percent of GDP, in 2007; one estimate is that these are the equivalent of about $1,400 per Lebanese resident annually.[4]

Ethnolinguistic Groups

Lebanese. Ethnolinguistically, about 85 percent of the Lebanese are Arabs in that their mother tongue is Arabic. However, the cultural variations among Arabs seen elsewhere in the region are especially wide and critical here. Some Maronite Christians, for example, deny Arab ancestry, claiming descent from Phoenicians or Byzantines. Yet other Lebanese Christians resolutely consider themselves Arab, advocating religious tolerance. DNA studies show that the Lebanese—Christians and Muslims—share the genes of Phoenicians and Canaanites.[5] By contrast, Palestinian refugees in Lebanon find their identity, in addition to being Palestinian, in their Arabism and in Islam, or as Palestinian Christians.

The largest non-Arab minority are the Armenians, some 7 percent of the population. Kurds are the second-largest minority, about 6 percent, followed by small numbers of Circassians, Assyrians, Turks, and Jews. There were more than 20,000 Jews a century ago and more than 7,000 in the 1950s; there were fewer than 100 in the 2000s.

Refugees and Foreigners. Although not a separate ethnolinguistic group in Lebanon, the large Palestinian refugee minority (most are Sunni, with a Christian minority) has been a focus of contention since their arrival in 1948. Of the 800,000 who were displaced from Palestine during 1947–1949, about 150,000 crossed into southern Lebanon, most expecting to return home within a short time. More came during the 1967 Arab-Israeli war and after the 1970 fighting in Jordan. They crowded into refugee camps built by the UN Relief and Works Agency (UNRWA) near Tyre, Sidon, Tripoli, Beirut, and Baalbak (see Map 8.6). In June 2009, 422,188 were registered with UNRWA.[6]

A few Palestinians, especially professionals, have obtained citizenship, but most are poor, stateless camp dwellers. The government and a majority of the Lebanese have always rejected settlement or assimilation of the Palestinians, largely because of the sociopolitical threat it would pose to the country's delicate power balance and to the already stressed social fabric. Having witnessed the "Palestinization" of Jordan, suffered repeated Israeli invasions and bombing raids because of Palestinian and pro-Palestinian activity on their soil, and seen the Palestinian role in much of the fighting in the 1970s and 1980s, the Lebanese reject further perpetuation of the more than sixty years' turmoil.[7] In 2002, parliament banned landownership by Palestinians, but in 2005 the Labor Ministry increased the number of professions open to them.

More recent additions to the refugee population are approximately 50,000 Iraqis fleeing the post-2003 chaos of their homeland. Their presence in Lebanon is much smaller than in Syria or Jordan, and only about 10,000 were registered with the Beirut office of the United Nations High Commission for Refugees at the end of 2008. A recent estimate was that 70 percent of the Iraqis are in the country illegally and thus could be imprisoned, deported, or both. A "hidden minority" of sorts are as many as 1 million foreign workers, many of whom are Syrians, mostly unskilled laborers seeking day labor in construction or agriculture. More recently, a sizable number of Asians have found employment here as they have in many oil states. A European–North American colony has reemerged since the 1990s, but its relative size is much smaller than before the 1975–1990 war.

Confessional Groupings

Among the multidimensional and interactive factors in Lebanon's societal matrix, religious affiliation is the most decisive determinant in social intercourse. Among its crucial influences, it is the basis for political organization and state structure, with seats in parliament allocated on a confessional basis.

Christians and Druze enjoyed special status under the Ottomans, and Maronite Christians were the core around which France created mandate Lebanon. Distinct from the Sunni Muslim lands around it, Lebanon—as a mandate and an independent state—evolved under a carefully fabricated balance of confessional elements: The Christian "majority" held key positions, but power sharing and the distribution of offices were designed to produce stability and effectiveness. The system can be better understood by reviewing the religious groupings. Map 10.2 shows the distribution of the major groups before civil war began in 1975; although the information is outdated, it is still instructive.[8]

Muslims.   Muslims make up about 53 percent of the population in the late 2000s, and Sunni and Shii are more evenly divided in Lebanon than elsewhere in the region. More than half are Shii who, excluding the heterodox Druze and Alawi, make up the largest single sect—close to a third of the country's population. Once referred to as Mutawalis, they have also been the most oppressed group. Emerging from passivity in the 1970s, they matched others with their own militias—first, Amal (Hope), in 1974, and Hizballah (Party of God), in 1980. They are concentrated in the south, Beirut's southern slums, and the northern Bekaa. While most Shii are Imamis (or Twelvers), there are also a few thousand Ismailis (or Fivers).

Sunnis, about 21 percent of the population and formerly the largest and most influential Muslim group, are widely distributed, with concentrations in Beirut, Tripoli and the Akkar, the southern Bekaa, and the Shuf (see Map 10.1). More than any other sect, the Sunnis resented the separation of mandate Lebanon from Greater Syria. Still, the quiet sympathies of this conservative, mostly middle-class group today often lie more with moderate Christians than with militant Muslims.

Druze and Alawi.   Two offshoots of Shiism, also part of the Lebanese mosaic, are so distinct in their beliefs and practices that they deserve mention apart from orthodox Muslims. The Druze, despite being only about 7 percent of the population, have loomed large

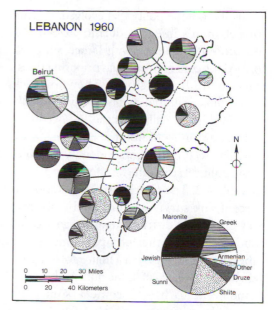

MAP 10.2 Patterns of religions in Lebanon for 1960, the latest year with reliable data. Circles are in proportion to the populations involved, and pie graphs indicate percentages of adherents to the various sects. Figures have, of course, changed over the past fifty years, as discussed in the text, but the graphs still reflect the complexity of communal structure in this small country.

in the area's sociopolitical dynamics for centuries. Concentrated in the mountains southeast of Beirut ("Druzistan") and especially in the Shuf, they played a key role in the fighting of both 1958 and 1975–1991, and they remain very much an appreciable factor in everyday political life. The Alawi have spilled over from their concentration in northwest Syria and number around 60,000, mostly in Tripoli.

Christians.   Among all the sects, Maronites were once the largest and most influential, but they are only about 20 percent in the 2000s. Considering themselves the creators and developers of the state, they assumed the role of guardians of its sovereignty and Christian character. In both mandate and independent Lebanon, they fashioned a Christian haven, and they dominated into the early

1970s the unique polity that evolved. Fearing for Lebanon's integrity during 1975–1991, Maronite Phalangists, with Israeli support, formed the core of the militias opposing Palestinian and Muslim groups. They now lack strong direction, sharing power fairly equally with Sunnis and Shii under the Taif Accords.

In addition to Maronites, another dozen Christian sects have separate identity and roles in the political structure. Most of them appear in Table 4.2. The Greek Orthodox (about 6 percent) are survivors from the Byzantines; they are widely distributed and urge accommodation with other groups. None of the other groups have played a major role in politics, but in the late 2000s the non-Arab Armenians seem to have become a somewhat critical factor in the new politics of coalitions.[9]

A SUBREGIONAL PERSPECTIVE

Looking down at Lebanon, an air passenger flying eastward from Beirut can clearly see the four distinct parallel regions that extend south-southwest to north-northeast: [1] a narrow coastal plain, [2] the Lebanon Mountains core area, [3] the linear flat-floored depression of the Bekaa, and [4] the complex Anti-Lebanon Mountains on the border with Syria (see circled numbers on Map 10.1).

[1] Coastal Plain

Extending the full length of the 140-mi/225-km Mediterranean shore, a narrow plain is partly wave-cut rock platform and partly alluvial fan deposits of streams debouching from deep mountain valleys. Interrupted in five places by mountains reaching the sea, in some places it is wide enough only for the highway and parallel little-used railway. Between Tyre and Sidon it is carpeted by citrus groves for more than 1 mi/1.6 km back from shore; in the extreme north, it widens to 20 mi/32 km in the Plain of Akkar.

Urban sprawl up and down the plain is rapidly supplanting the orchards and market gardens that long characterized the area. Greater Beirut extends more than 20 mi/32 km from Juniyah in the north to Damur in the south. Scenically located on a separate low structural peninsular plateau, one of the few significant protrusions from the eastern Mediterranean coast, Beirut has been occupied since the Neolithic period. A minor Phoenician port and city-state, it achieved greater stature as a Roman city with its famous law school; it was destroyed in an earthquake and tidal wave in 551 CE.

As Lebanon's primate city, Beirut developed rapidly after 1950. Luxury apartment buildings and hotels (Fig. 10.1) contrasted with slums and Palestinian camps. The slums mushroomed with the displacement of poor Shii and others by conflicts on the southern border, especially during the Israeli occupation. In 1991, after sixteen years of division between Christian East and Muslim West, the city felt the old "Beirut élan" was a bit subdued, but it gradually revived in the 1990s and 2000s.

The virtually destroyed city center was almost completely rebuilt according to a controversial and elaborate multibillion-dollar plan by the Lebanese Company for Development and Reconstruction (Solidere).[10] Construction excavations confirmed that for 5,000 years Beirut was indeed the nucleus of successive Canaanite/Phoenician, Roman, Byzantine, and Ottoman cities. Significant remains of each city level are preserved in a fascinating below-street-level "Archaeology Trail."[11]

Toward the north end of the coastal plain lies Lebanon's second city and second port, Tripoli (Arabic: Tarabulus),[12] a Sunni Muslim stronghold. Its basalt and limestone twelfth-century Crusader castle faces fourteenth- and fifteenth-century Mamluk castles, all impressive reminders of its tapestried history. On the southern plain is the Phoenician port of Tyre (Arabic: Sur), overlying and adjoining extensive Greco-Roman ruins. The ruins and Old Tyre are a UNESCO World Heritage Site.

FIGURE 10.1 High-rise apartment buildings in mainly Muslim southern Beirut along Ramlat al-Bayda beach (*top*), and in Juniyah, a Christian area north of Beirut (*bottom*). Juniyah was a village before 1975 that developed very rapidly during the fighting in 1975–1990. The vineyard in the foreground is a remnant of former extensive agricultural exploitation of this west-facing slope.

The Phoenician port of Sidon (Arabic: Sayda) lies north of Tyre, with a picturesque Crusader castle offshore. Also worth noting is the small northern port of Jubayl (better known as Byblos), with its renowned excavations showing civilizations from Neolithic times on (see Fig. 3.1).

[2] Mount Lebanon

The traditional core is Mount Lebanon (Arabic: Jabal Lubnan), technically called Jabal al-Gharbi (Western Mountains). The range divides the coastal plain and western slopes from the eastern slopes and depression, making Lebanon a state that is geopolitically à cheval. Like rugged mountains in many humid areas, it provided isolation and security to several groups, notably Maronites and Druze. Mount Lebanon has thus played a profound role in the area's historical-cultural development.

Lying west of the great Yammunah Fault (see Chap. 2), the range's sedimentary strata were arched up by relatively gentle east-west compressional forces during the Miocene-Pliocene epochs. The resulting arch is a rather open anticlinal structure aligned southwest-northeast and extending from the low Homs Gap at its northern end to the complex tectonic junction in southern Lebanon. The range is affected by several faults along its axis and by many cross faults. Highest elevations are toward the north, reaching 10,129 ft/3,088 m at Qurnat al-Sawda, east-southeast of Tripoli; elevations around 6,500 ft/2,000 m continue southward along the ridgeline to east of Sidon.

A significant hydrogeological feature of Mount Lebanon is the outcropping of extensive aquifers, bringing groundwater to the surface in lines of springs along the outcrops. Some of these springs are exceptionally large, feeding short, swift rivers that have eroded and dissolved spectacular canyons in the western slopes, thus adding to the rugged relief. The springs irrigate the terraces and the more gentle slopes, as well as supply drinking water, some of which is bottled for consumption in Beirut and for export.

The western slopes were originally heavily forested with oak, pine, fir, cedar, and juniper, with the famous Cedars of Lebanon (*Cedrus libani*—the national symbol) forming a belt at elevations between 4,600 and 7,200 ft/1,400 and 2,200 m. Some 4,000 years of exploitation has degraded the vegetation to maquis, although a few small stands of cedars are preserved. The main group is in central Lebanon on Jabal Baruk, but the most famous is in the north, near the ski resort of Bsharri. Plantations of stone pine (*Pinus pinea*) and Aleppo pine (*P. halepensis*) give small areas a wooded aspect (Fig. 10.2), and stone pine yields the edible piñon nut (Arabic: *snubar*).[13]

Maronites and Druze intensified and diversified agriculture on the western slopes, building thousands of terraces. Villages developed on spectacular sites, some formerly Phoenician and Roman settlements, whose ruins often survive. After World War II, many towns in the 2,000–4,500-ft/600–1,475-m zone became summer resorts. At upper levels, around 6,500 ft/2,000 m, ski resorts such as The Cedars and Laqluq thrive between mid-December and late March (see also Fig. 2.9).

[3] The Bekaa

The Bekaa (Arabic: al-Biqa, "basin" or "depression") is a young tectonic intermontane trough, a segment of the Levant Rift System paralleling Mount Lebanon. Along the western side of the Bekaa, the Yammunah fracture slices off Mount Lebanon on its eastern side and creates a vertical displacement of several thousand meters and a left-lateral horizontal displacement of about 4.4 mi/7 km. It is the most seismically active of the many fractures in the Levant. Perceptible earthquakes result from displacement along one or another of

FIGURE 10.2 Typical western slope of Mount Lebanon, showing scattered villages, terraced agriculture, low pine woodlands, and interspersed maquis and garigue flora. The main village shown is Baqlin, located in the Druze area west of Bayt ed-Din.

Lebanon's fault planes every few years. Severe tremors strike once every 100–150 years, with the most recent being in 1956, when 7,000 buildings were destroyed east of Sidon by slippage along the Roum Fault.

The main drainage of the Bekaa, the Litani River, flows southward from near Baalbak, with a flow of 700–900 mn m³ a year at Qirawn (Qaraoun). It has been dammed to create a reservoir, and water is diverted to produce electricity and to supply water for limited irrigation.[14] It is a completely Lebanese river from its source to its mouth in the Mediterranean; it should be noted, however, that Zionist planners as early as 1919 sought it as a water source for the future Jewish state.

A low, barely perceptible divide near Baalbak separates the watersheds of the Litani and the Orontes (Asi) River to the north. The Orontes follows the Bekaa into Syria past Homs and Hamah and through the Ghab Depression. Both rivers are fed by springs on both sides of the Bekaa that attracted Paleolithic wanderers; the tells of at least thirty Neolithic villages are prominent features in the area.

Although the northern Bekaa lies in the rain shadow of the highest segment of Mount Lebanon and receives only 9 in/230 mm of rain a year, the central area around Shtawrah gets 24 in/610 mm, the south even more. The valley was an important granary from Roman times well into the last century, but wheat and barley production has declined as more area is irrigated for fruit trees, sugar beets, and market gardening. Seen from adjacent heights in spring, it is colorful with fruit blossoms, cultivated flowers, green fields, and, when law enforcement is lax, bright-red opium poppies.

[4] Anti-Lebanon

Properly the Jabal al-Sharqi (Eastern Mountains), the Anti-Lebanon Mountains are folded linear highlands east of the Bekaa and along the frontier with Syria; indeed, only the western ridges lie within Lebanon. An anticlinal structure similar to Mount Lebanon, these eastern highlands have several ridges exceeding 6,500 ft/2,000 m, and the summit of volcanic Mount Hermon (Jabal al-Shaykh), a southerly extension of the eastern highlands, reaches 9,230 ft/2,813 m. The Anti-Lebanon Mountains are the least-exploited part of Lebanon and in the north are virtually uninhabited.

ECONOMIC PATTERNS

From Phoenician times, Lebanon's major economic activities have taken advantage of locational and physiographic assets: (1) its central location on the coast, positioning it for trade between the hinterland to the east and Mediterranean lands to the west; (2) its central location in the Middle East, making it an intraregional and interregional crossroad; (3) its well-watered coastal plain and somewhat indented coastline, facilitating port development; (4) its also well-watered mountains, through which passes lead inland; and (5) its original forest cover and agricultural (horticultural) development.

Despite the foregoing advantages, mandate Lebanon had a small population and area and limited agricultural and virtually no mineral resources; the enterprising residents therefore revived their Levantine skills as traders. Further expanding the service economy after 1950, they developed financial and medical services, educational facilities, a modern port and airport, consultative expertise, recreation areas—services then inadequate in most of the region. Foreign embassies and businesses based representatives in "the Paris of the East." When the UN sought a site for its Middle East regional of-fices in 1963, it chose Beirut and returned after a fifteen-year hiatus in 1997.[15]

Beirut functioned for decades as an efficient and thriving service center for the emerging oil areas of the Gulf. But when fighting erupted in this nerve center in 1975, Lebanon lost its economic role, while rapid development was taking place in the wealthy oil states.[16] By the time relative peace and stability returned in the early 1990s, it had much less to offer its former patrons, who in turn had less need for Lebanese goods and services.[17]

By the late 2000s, more than fifteen years after the fighting ended, the economy presented a mixed picture, with much accomplished and much yet to do. One problem has been the persistence of the business methods of the war years and the immediate aftermath. Most regional states have followed world trends and rationalized procedures and relationships, but Lebanon has been slow to catch up. For example, inadequate regulatory procedures led to scandal in 2009 when a prominent Shii businessman was arrested for promoting a Ponzi-like scheme that reportedly bilked local investors out of more than $1 billion; when population differences are considered, this was about the equivalent for Lebanon of the $65 billion Madoff fraud in the United States.[18] Progress is retarded by corruption (in 2009, the rating agency Transparency International ranked it 130th of 180 countries worldwide and twelfth in the region),[19] red tape, archaic legislation, and high taxes. As Lebanon's minister of justice put it in November 2009, "Commercial laws . . . open a broad path to freedom in business contracting but we have to admit that the legal culture in our country lacks the credibility in legislation."[20]

Admirable improvements are offset by serious problems: high unemployment, a bloated bureaucracy, and static wages accompanied by rising prices. Fifteen percent of the population holds 45 percent of the wealth; a third of the population lives in poverty.[21] On the other hand, peace does seem to have had a broad positive effect on living standards. Using the Human Development Index (HDI) computed by the UNDP, Lebanon ranked 83rd out of 182 countries globally and 10th of the 16 in the region in 2007. More important, Lebanon's HDI had risen by 42.7 percent since 1990, when internal warfare was drawing to a close, promoting it into the "high human development" category.[22] The EU and Lebanon signed an Association Agreement that entered into force in 2006, opening the way for it to be fully incorporated into the European Neighborhood Policy.[23]

Services

The service sector drives the modern economy, accounting in 2007 for about 75 percent of GDP. Before 1975, Lebanon offered a full range—from tourism and banking operations to personal services and aircraft engine maintenance. It had excellent educational and medical facilities: In addition to the second-oldest university in the Arab world and one of the best—the American University of Beirut— there was the French Jesuit Université St. Joseph, Beirut University College (formerly Beirut College for Women, now Lebanese American University), Beirut Arab University, Lebanese University, and the Armenian Hagazian College. Medical facilities, especially the American University Hospital and the Hôtel Dieu de France Hospital, both connected to good medical schools, served patients from Lebanon and much of the region. These facilities still offer high-quality medical care, but the Gulf states now enjoy larger and more highly technological facilities.

Lebanon's reputation as the "Switzerland of the Middle East" before 1975 also applied to the extensive banking system, which is being revived, complete with banking secrecy and unrestricted capital movement. Not only were deposits and trusts attracted from Saudi Arabia and the Gulf oil states, but so was cap-

ital from less stable economies like Syria, Egypt, Iraq, and Jordan. This helped fuel remarkable development between 1955 and 1975, and renewed flows are aiding current reconstruction efforts. But as with other parts of its service sector, after years of warfare, Lebanese banking never quite recovered to its former dominant level—in the late 2000s, only two of the region's thirty largest banks were headquartered in Beirut, as opposed to fourteen in the four Gulf states. On the other hand, the country's banks apparently had a justifiably healthy suspicion of the dubious financial instruments that rose to global importance in the 1990s and 2000s; when the crisis struck internationally in 2008, they weathered the storm with sharp increases posted in assets, deposits, and profits. The Lebanese lira (or pound), 90 percent gold-backed and freely convertible, was one of the world's most stable currencies before 1975; however, during the fighting it dropped from 3.2 to the U.S. dollar to as low as a disastrous 3,000 to the dollar in late 1992. Pegged to the U.S. currency in September 1999, it was stable at an average of 1,485 to the dollar over the first quarter of 2010. From the end of 2007, the reserves of Banque du Liban, the central bank, rose from $9.8 billion to $24.1 billion in less than two years, despite the global financial crisis.[24] Its gold reserves ($9.2 billion) are the fifteenth largest in the world and the highest in the region.[25]

Before 1975, tourism was a major industry. While the war raged, wealthy Arabs went elsewhere, vacationing and shopping in the United States and Western Europe. After 9/11, however, they began to return to Lebanon, partly to avoid racial profiling and security delays in the West. As before, Arab visitors feel welcomed and comfortable in the cultural milieu: tourism has recovered to prewar levels—nearly 2 million arrivals in 2009, despite the global recession.[26] The healthy tourism sector helped the country weather the 2008–2009 global recession; economic growth averaged 6.5 percent over the period.

Lebanese entrepreneurs ensure that inducements are plentiful: more than 300 hotels (including several luxury five-star facilities), spacious marinas near coastal hotels, many excellent restaurants, attractive beach resorts, beautiful scenery, both summer and winter mountain resorts, the striking Casino du Liban, shopping galore, relaxed social mores, and a varied nightlife in Beirut—in general, a palpable joie de vivre—along with easy access by land, sea, or air.

Trade and Transportation

Along with services, trade was formerly, and is becoming again, a major economic sector. Significant from Phoenician times, Lebanon's trade began its modern growth under the mandate and burgeoned after the region's oil industry began to boom in the 1950s. Beirut's port, with its duty-free zone, became a break-in-bulk point and an entrepôt to warehouse products for onward shipment. Large stores and small shops handled widely varied articles from Western Europe, the Middle East, and South Asia, including luxury items for super-affluent Gulf clients. Changed circumstances have delayed a return to such halcyon commercial conditions, but trade has shown a marked upswing in the 2000s. The EU-Lebanon Association Agreement entered into force in April 2007, and this was followed within a year by an Action Plan to give bilateral relations a new impetus. It gained observer status with the World Trade Organization in 1999, and had anticipated accession by 2005,[27] but negotiations have gone slowly, and at the end of the decade it was still only an observer.

Because of consumer goods imports, Lebanon's balance of trade in tangible goods has long been negative. However, the balance of payments normally has been positive because of services, financial transactions, diaspora remittances, and other income sources from a wide range of economic activities.

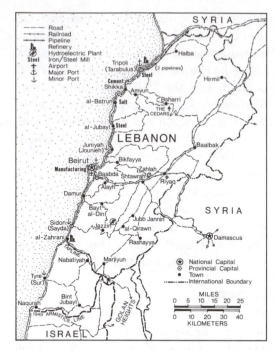

MAP 10.3 Economic map of Lebanon.

Beirut's seaport and airport were ideally situated to serve as gateways to the Levant and beyond. The port, sixteenth busiest in the world in the early 1970s, was often inoperative during the 1975–1990 fighting. It has been rebuilt, expanded, and modernized, but in the changed regional commercial dynamics of the new millennium, it now plays a more modest role. A smaller sister port for central Lebanon is Juniyah (see Map 10.3 for all ports), which developed primarily for importing war matériel during the fighting. At that time, the ancient port of Sidon also expanded to serve the south, but by 2005 it was unloading only one-fourth as many ships as during the 1980s. In the north is Tripoli, Lebanon's second port, formerly the terminus of one of the IPC pipelines from Iraq.

For air transportation, Beirut–Rafiq Hariri International Airport once served as the Middle East's aviation hub for both passengers and cargo. Although squeezed into a narrow strip between mountains and coastline, it was the region's busiest civil airport during the

1960s. Often nonoperational during the 1980s, it embarked on a $500 million modernization and expansion, including a new runway built on a remarkable ramp reclaimed from the Mediterranean. A new terminal opened in 1998, with a capacity of 6 million passengers annually. At the end of the 2000s, the airport was awaiting the return of direct flights to the United States, suspended since 1985.[28]

Middle East Airlines, rescued by the Central Bank in 1996 from closure, slashed one-fourth of its workforce and showed an operating profit in 2004 for the first time in twenty-five years. At the end of the decade it had a fleet of thirteen jets, with six more on order; gradual reprivatization is planned. Trans-Mediterranean Airlines was formerly a major cargo carrier, but suspended operations in 2004 because of safety concerns. With a new owner and new capital, it planned to relaunch service in 2010.

Lebanese rail lines are antiquated and little used. Plans to rehabilitate the coastal line have a low priority, and most goods and passengers move by road. The road net is relatively dense (see Map 10.3), considering the rugged terrain. Many mountain roads are narrow and steep, but most are well surfaced to withstand winter rains and, at higher elevations, deep snows. The Beirut-Damascus highway and the coast road are famously scenic routes, and both have recently been upgraded to accommodate the heavy traffic in this automobile-minded country. Lebanon has a very low 2.5 persons per vehicle.

Manufacturing

Lebanon's modest production of specialized craft items and textiles diversified after 1950 until manufacturing surpassed agriculture in importance. Little heavy industry evolved, however; cement factories and oil refineries constitute this sector. Although severely disrupted by warfare, manufacturing gradually recovered during the 1990s. Although it has

not yet attained its earlier level, it is about 20 percent of GDP. Most establishments, like most shops and service institutions, are small—85 percent employ fewer than twenty-five people. Light industries cluster around Beirut, producing clothing, textiles, processed foods, jewelry, oriental handicrafts, printed materials, cigarettes, paints, and furniture. Three cement plants and two steel plants operate near Tripoli.

The Tripoli and Sidon oil refineries were originally fed by Iraqi and Saudi Arabian pipelines, respectively: When these closed, tanker deliveries took over in the early 1980s. Both refineries were heavily damaged in the fighting, but the Tripoli plant is operational again, using as feedstock Syrian crude delivered through part of the old IPC line. Lebanon relies on imported oil for the generation of about 92 percent of its electricity.[29] In addition to furniture and metal products, Tripoli produces soap from olive oil. The Bekaa has several food-processing plants, including beet-sugar mills and wineries. Two cement plants produced nearly 5 million tons in 2007 to meet increased demand partly due to reconstruction after Israeli bombing raids during the Summer War of 2006.[30]

Agriculture

Lebanon's physical assets allow high-grade varied horticulture. Generations of farmers have harvested fruits, nuts, and vegetables that are scarce in the Middle East. Though precipitation is concentrated in the cool season, hydrogeological conditions permit direct collection of runoff, directly or indirectly through springs, for irrigation well into the summer. Meltwater from heavy snows is particularly useful. Elaborate terracing protects the slopes from erosion from heavy rainfall (50–60 in/1,270–1,525 mm) at this elevation and spreads water from runoff, irrigating crops in the terraces.[31]

Mount Lebanon's upslope offers ecological conditions for subtropical crops along the

FIGURE 10.3 Agriculture on the coastal plain of southern Lebanon, north of Sidon. This fertile strip has been cultivated for millennia (*note foreground*) and now has hundreds of plastic hothouses to aid early yields of horticultural crops.

coast and progressively cooler-environment crops at increasing elevations—vertical zonation on the principle that "altitude equals latitude." In alluvial soils along the coast are irrigated groves of bananas, lemons, oranges, and grapefruit. Hothouses proliferated during the 1990s; their vegetables are in high demand during the winter and early spring in the Gulf states (Fig. 10.3). Slightly higher and on rocky soils are extensive olive and smaller almond groves that need little or no irrigation. Still higher—2,000 to 5,000 ft/610 to 1,525 m—is a vertical succession of irrigated orchards of peaches, apricots, pears, plums, and cherries; vineyards are at several levels. At still higher elevations are apple orchards.

Vineyards have thrived in the Bekaa since Phoenician times, and the three well-known wineries in the Ksara and Zahlah area, on the lower and drier eastern slopes, had by the mid-2000s increased to fifteen. They produce up to 7 million bottles annually, a third for export.[32] Otherwise, crops here are normally of three types: nonirrigated wheat and barley; semi-irrigated sugar beets, onions, potatoes, and melons; and irrigated fruits, tomatoes, and a wide range of other vegetables, especially in the Shtawrah (Chtoura) "oasis." The Bekaa also includes a lively food-processing industry, producing sugar, fruit juices, canned fruits and vegetables, and wine. In the late 2000s, agriculture accounted for only about 5 percent of Lebanon's GDP but 10 percent of its exports. From the early 1960s through the mid-2000s, per capita food production increased by more than 55 percent.[33] On the other hand, the country's dependence on imports for much of its food is shown in the fact that, for agricultural items, imports are about six times the value of exports.

FACTIONS AND TERRITORIES

State Idea and Its Disintegration

When the French separated the semiautonomous Mount Lebanon from Greater Syria in 1920, they intended to create a mandate around the Maronites, the area's dominant sect. But this alone was not an adequate base for a viable state, so to enlarge Lebanon (and fragment Syria further), they appended the coastal plain, the Bekaa, and part of the Anti-Lebanon, along with their Sunni and Shii Muslims, Druze, and non-Maronite Christians. Additional territory may have enhanced economic viability, but it concomitantly increased political vulnerability. Detaching Syrian territory increased resentment among Syrians, leading to ongoing irredentist claims. It also engendered long-lasting animus among Sunnis, Shii, and Druze separated from "Muslim" Syria and included in "Christian" Lebanon.

With some French help, the several groups that merged in the Lebanese confessional confederation after 1920 evolved a unique political structure of pragmatic representative government. Lebanon's raison d'être expanded to embrace the pluralistic society; power sharing, checks and balances, and compromise were the base for preserving the state.

The mechanisms of the system were codified less in the formal constitution than in the informal National Pact of 1943, really an agreement between the two largest sects at the time—the Maronites and the Sunnis. This unwritten "gentlemen's agreement" enshrined political power sharing among confessional groups according to the 1932 census: Maronite president, Sunni prime minister, Shii president (speaker) of parliament, Druze and others ministers, and, not least, a Maronite commander of the armed forces. This formula institutionalized Maronite leadership, but it worked reasonably well so long as economic prosperity melded the factions. It

gradually lost credibility as the Christian-Muslim ratio obviously shifted over the years, which Christians obscured by persistently refusing a census.

The National Pact and related agreements also failed to come to grips with territorial aspects of the groups, each of which originally possessed a fairly defined "turf" (see Map 10.2). When the political equilibrium broke down, territorial patterns solidified into a mosaic of ministates with its own *zaim* (group leader). Territorial sovereignty became as fragmented as the body politic. The system cracked in the 1958 civil war, again in 1968–1969, once more in 1973 with Palestinian–Lebanese Army firefights, and broke down completely in 1975. When Palestinian guerrillas were expelled from Jordan in 1971 after "Black September" and came to Beirut, many Lebanese rejected their attempts to duplicate the "state within a state" they had had in Jordan. But their presence heightened domestic tension, and the fragmented Lebanese were unable to replicate Jordan's military success.[34] It was a Maronite-Palestinian battle in Beirut that precipitated full-scale fighting in 1975.

Proxy "Civil" War in Lebanon

For sixteen years after 1975, Lebanon suffered weeks of terrible killing and destruction alternating with uncertain cease-fires. More than a dozen factions fielded heavily armed militias. Unrestrained by a powerless government, Fatah guerrillas struck into northern Israel; this led to Israeli reprisals, some major, as in March 1978, and to full-scale invasion in June 1982 under Israeli defense minister Ariel Sharon. Ironically named "Operation Peace in Northern Galilee," the air, naval, and ground assaults on already war-weary Lebanon killed more than 17,000 and destroyed hundreds of buildings.[35] By August, Israelis and Palestinians were battling in Beirut's streets; Western mediation forced the evacuation of PLO troops and Syrians.[36] The

Multi-National Force (MNF), including U.S. marines, arrived to help stabilize a chaotic situation, but when it withdrew, Maronite Phalange (*Kataib*) forces, with indirect Israeli support, massacred more than 800 Palestinian civilians in the Sabra-Shatila refugee camps in Beirut in mid-September.[37] This atrocity has been internationally condemned as the most infamous single act of the entire period.

Facing virtual anarchy, the MNF was redeployed in Lebanon, only to face anti-Israeli and anti-Western militants who replaced departed PLO fighters. In a new dimension of suicide extremism, truck bombs destroyed four sites, killing more than 400 Americans, Europeans, and Israelis: the American Embassy in April 1983, killing 46; U.S. marine and French barracks in October, killing 241 Americans and 56 French; and Israeli military headquarters near Tyre in November, killing 60. New Lebanese groups—especially the Shii Hizballah—took guerrilla action against Israelis in southern Lebanon and northern Israel. They, as well as Druze, also fired on MNF troops, particularly U.S. marines. In November and December, in response to the attacks, U.S. and French aircraft struck Syrian and Hizballah positions and the U.S. Navy lobbed huge shells into Druze redoubts. Kidnappings of Westerners became a regular occurrence.

The Lebanese themselves suffered egregiously from the full-scale warfare. By 1991, some 140,000 had been killed and as many wounded. Two presidents had been assassinated, Beirut's center was in ruins, and thousands of buildings around Beirut, in Tripoli, and in towns and villages in the mountains and the south were in shambles, totaling more than $50 billion in losses. A dubious Israeli-Lebanese peace accord brokered by the United States signed in 1983 was predictably abrogated in 1984.[38]

Asked to supply most of the 1976 Arab Deterrent Force, Syria sent large contingents into eastern Lebanon to maintain equilibrium and to discourage potential incursions into Syria through Lebanon. President al-Asad exploited the situation's ambiguity to prolong Syrian occupation, and apparently also to test the possibility of reattaching Grand Liban to "Greater Syria." He later dismissed this idea but kept 35,000–40,000 troops in Lebanon for several years to guarantee Syrian hegemony and to use them in the complex chess game between Israel and Syria and their respective partisans.

Finally, in October 1989, under the aegis of the Arab League and with strong Syrian pressure inside Lebanon, most of the surviving members of the 1972 parliament met in Taif, Saudi Arabia, and agreed on a Document of National Understanding. Weary of death and destruction, the militias agreed to disarm, and a more equable political structure was adopted. The powers of the Maronite president, the Sunni prime minister, and the Shii speaker of parliament were rebalanced, and parliamentary seats were apportioned 50-50 between Christians and Muslims. Confessionalism remained a political factor, but with some promise of phasing it out eventually.

The revived Lebanese Army became more effective, helping to stabilize government control, even to some extent in the far south after Israel's withdrawal in May 2000. There, for twenty-two years, the most militant groups (Hizballah, rejectionist Palestinians, Amal, and Iranian volunteers) had confronted the occupiers and their proxy South Lebanon Army (SLA).[39] Frequent encounters between opponents of Israel, on one side, and Israelis and the SLA, on the other, as well as Hizballah/Amal rocket attacks on northern Israel countered by Israeli attacks into Lebanon, became a persistent cycle of violence. Israeli reactions included air raids well into Lebanon, and occasionally in Beirut.

Before the occupation ended, there were two further major Israeli campaigns: a six-day blitz in July 1993 dubbed "Operation Accountability" and "Operation Grapes of

Wrath" in April 1996. Massive destruction sent an exodus of 400,000 refugees north in 1993, overwhelming Beirut. One account described the operation as "punishing the civilians in order to pressure the politicians."[40] A truce ensued, but the attacks soon resumed.[41] In 1996, an unusually heavy Hizballah rocket attack on northern Israel set off the second—sixteen days of the heaviest shelling, bombing, and gunship fire since 1982. An Israeli artillery attack on a UN post in Qana on April 18 killed 102 civilians taking refuge in this neutral spot; Israel said it was accidental, but firsthand observers and an official UN report judged it deliberate.[42] Retaliatory Hizballah rockets, by Israeli accounts, were ineffective.[43] On into 1990, Lebanon—unable to reclaim its territory in the south or to restrain the militias trying to do so—was the unhappy venue for the only active warfare in the Arab-Israeli conflict.

In May 2000, after twenty-two years of occupation of southern Lebanon, Israel unilaterally withdrew, as had been called for in UN Resolution 425 of 1978; its agent, the SLA, collapsed. Despite occasional exchanges between Hizballah and Israeli forces across the restored border over the next five years, the area was relatively stable. But Lebanon still bore Syrian military occupation and political hegemony until 2005.

The heavy hand of Syria pressured parliament in August 2004 to amend the constitution and extend the term of President Emile Lahoud, a Syrian ally. Widespread opposition led to a political crisis, with Prime Minister Rafiq Hariri resigning in protest.[44] But external forces countered Syria in the form of the U.S.- and French-backed UN Security Council Resolution 1559 in September, calling for "all remaining forces to withdraw from Lebanon" and respect for Lebanon's political independence.

Amid rising tensions in early 2005, a powerful explosion in downtown Beirut killed Hariri and twenty-two others in February. In a country where assassination had been all too common for thirty years, this event galvanized and polarized public opinion like none other during that period. No group claimed responsibility, but there had been several attacks on others known to oppose Syria, so strong suspicion was directed at Damascus, and nearly daily anti-Syrian demonstrations took place in Beirut. On March 9, Syria's tactical ally, Hizballah, organized a pro-Syria rally that drew several hundred thousand of mostly poor Shii: This was countered by an anti-Syrian response that filled the streets with an estimated 1 million people from all groups on March 14—giving the nascent political coalition the name of the March 14th Movement. Headed by Hariri's son Saad, it swept to victory in parliamentary polling held the following May and June.

In the meantime, Syria withdrew its remaining troops at the end of April.[45] Pressed by the United States and France, the UN undertook to investigate the Hariri assassination; the resulting report concluded that the assassination "could not have taken place without the approval of top-ranked Syrian officials and . . . been organized without the collaborations of their counterparts in the Lebanese security forces."[46] A new broad-based government that included Hizballah and Amal ministers took no concrete action but focused on political and economic reforms, endorsing Hizballah as the agent of "national resistance."

This set the stage for the events of July 2006. During one of Hizballah's occasional raids across the border from southern Lebanon, three Israeli soldiers were killed and two were taken captive. A response was to be expected, but the ferocity of it astonished longtime Middle East observers: Israel immediately unleashed sustained air attacks on Lebanon's infrastructure as far as Beirut, and later moved against the guerrillas on the ground. Perhaps even more astonishing was

Hizballah's counterattack: It began launching thousands of rockets, hitting targets far beyond the border area—for example, in Haifa. Calls from the international community for a cease-fire went unheeded, as Israel (with tacit support from the Bush administration) continued its air attacks for thirty-three days. On both sides the brunt of the casualties, damage, and displacement was borne by civilians, and in the end, Hizballah emerged bloodied but unbowed, having proved its ability to wreak serious damage on Israel. (The repercussions on the Israeli side are discussed in Chap. 12.) In the aftermath, donors pledged as much as $8.5 billion to Lebanon, tying the aid to movement on the government's program for fiscal and economic reform. The U.S. Agency for International Development had a $447 million program for the 2007 to 2009 period, about three-fourths for immediate postbombing recovery.[47]

When the government moved to approve the UN plans to try suspects in the Hariri bombing, the Hizballah and Amal ministers resigned in November, setting off eighteen months of conflict, sieges, general strikes, car bombs, and assassinations—culminating in the spectacle of a six-month period of an empty presidency. Finally, Qatar brokered a settlement and the election of army chief Michael Suleiman as president, averting a renewal of civil war. The new president met with his Syrian counterpart, Bashar al-Asad; they agreed to establish for the first time full normal diplomatic relations.

A hard-fought election in June 2009 gave a close victory (in seats but not votes)[48] to the March 14th coalition, and Saad Hariri was named prime minister. It took him until November to form a national unity government, including Hizballah, other opposition parties, and nonparty members named by the president. Pressure from Saudi Arabia and Syria was instrumental in the reaching an agreement, and both Lebanese and foreign observers seemed to feel that Syrian influence was on the upswing,[49] especially after Hariri's year-end visit to Damascus after his new coalition cabinet was in place.[50] Hizballah's successes had lent strength to its political allies.

Cyprus

HISTORICAL GEOGRAPHY

Two geographical facts—that Cyprus is an island and that it is located in the eastern Mediterranean—are the most important aspects of its existence. About the size of Puerto Rico, it is the third-largest Mediterranean island after Sicily and Sardinia. Its mountains are clearly visible across the 43 mi/69 km of water that separate it from Asia Minor, and it lies 65 mi/105 km from Syria and 475 mi/765 km from mainland Greece. Its coastline has several semiprotected bays that have sheltered ships for millennia. Occupied during the Neolithic period, about 9000 BCE, it has been fought for and used as a base for more than 3,500 years,[51] with its original mineral wealth—especially copper—and agricultural resources valuable bonuses. The island was formed during the Tertiary mountain-building period along the arcuate boundary between the African and Eurasian plates (see Map 2.2). Seismic repercussions from continuing plate convergence produce periodic earthquakes, some of them catastrophic.

A third basic geographical fact is the island's division since 1974 between two antagonistic ethnic groups, Greek and Turkish.[52] The imposed separation installed a Turkish regime of ambiguous standing in the island's northern third, while the internationally recognized and overwhelmingly Greek Republic of Cyprus ruled the south.

Developments Before Independence

Six crucial events in the island's long history are fundamental to the contemporary situation. First, timber for shipbuilding and cop-

CYPRUS

Long-form official name, anglicized: Republic of Cyprus (ROC, south) (Turkish Republic of North Cyprus [TRNC] in the north, recognized only by Turkey)

Official name, transliterated (ROC): Kipriaki Dhimokratia (Greek); Kibris Cumhuriyeti (Turkish)

Form of government: unitary multiparty republic with a unicameral legislature (House of Representatives)

Area: 3,572 mi^2/9,251 km^2

Population, 2008: 1,076,000 (entire island); 805,000 (ROC); 271, 000 (TRNC); Literacy (Latest, ROC): 96.9%

Ethnic composition (entire island, %): Greek Cypriot 68.7; Turkish Cypriot 24.4; Armenian 2.5; Arab 2.2, of which Lebanese 1.9; British 1.0; other 1.2

Religions (entire island, %): Greek Orthodox 70.9; Muslim 25.0; Roman Catholic 1.6; Anglican 0.8; other 1.7

Demography: Life expectancy (ROC)—77.0 yr (M), 81.7 yr (F); Birthrate (entire island, per 1,000)—12.4; Fertility rate (entire island)—1.54

GDP: ROC (2009): $23.22 billion; purchasing power parity: $22.85 billion; per capita: $21,200; TRNC (2007): purchasing power parity: $1.83 billion; per capita: $11,700

Currency: Euro, $1 = €0.739, €1 = $1.353 (March 2010)

Energy reserves: oil, natural gas and coal—nil

Main exports (entire island, % of total value, 2006): refined petroleum 17.4; vegetables and fruit 9.9; telecommunications equipment 9.5; road vehicles 9.4; medicines 8.2; tobacco products 4.3; clothing 0.8

Main imports (entire island, % of total value, 2006): machinery and transport equipment 28.3; refined petroleum 15.3; food 9.3

Capital city: Nicosia (ROC) 219,200, (TRNC) 49,237; other cities: Limassol 172,500; Larnaca 77,000

---

per brought Bronze Age Minoans (from Crete) and Mycenaeans (from Greece), a connection emphasized by Greek Cypriots. Successive masters—Assyrians, Egyptians, Persians—ruled Cyprus until the Greco-Roman period, when the second important event occurred: The New Testament tells of Paul and Barnabas preaching Christianity on the island (45 CE), and the religion was reinforced during 800 years of Byzantine rule from 364. Brief Crusader and Frankish episodes preceded its cession in 1489 to Venice, which built the magnificent walls of Old Nicosia.

The third main event was the Ottoman conquest in 1570 and the migration of thousands of Muslims to the island over the next 300 years. These three events set the stage for the modern conflict between Greeks and Turks. The fourth crucial event was the arrival in 1878 of Britain; the island with around 180,000 residents then was to be a base for protecting the new Suez Canal and the route to India; for well or ill, Britain then

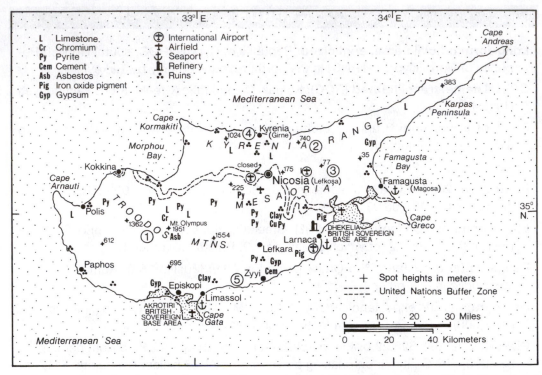

MAP 10.4 General and economic map of Cyprus, showing dividing line between North Cyprus and South Cyprus. Circled numbers indicate the regions discussed in the text.

affected Cypriot fortunes for most of a critical century.

Independence and Its Problems

Formally annexed by Britain in 1914,[53] Cyprus demanded an end to colonial status after World War II; in the 1950s Greek Cypriots revolted. Behind the sometimes savage attacks of the EOKA (National Organization of Cypriot Fighters) guerrillas with support from Greece, the majority wanted union with Greece (enosis), not independence. But after five years of conflict, Britain, Greek and Turkish Cypriots, and the Greek and Turkish governments signed the Zurich-London Agreements, creating the independent Republic of Cyprus (ROC) in August 1960—the fifth crucial event. Britain retains two strategically valuable Sovereign Base Areas (SBAs) on the south coast after fifty years (Map 10.4); they remain British overseas ter-

ritories and constitute about 2.7 percent of the island's area.

The ROC faced predictable dilemmas. Of a total population of 550,000, 79 percent were Greek speaking and Greek Orthodox in religion, and most strongly desired enosis; about 18 percent were Turkish speaking and Sunni Muslims, and sought autonomy under either confederation or partition (*taksim*); 3 percent were descendants of Armenian and Maronite refugees, all Christians, plus a few thousand British and other expatriates. All lived intermingled on the island; though most villages tended to be either Greek or Turkish, some villages and the larger towns were mixed.

Upon independence, a power-sharing agreement prorated political positions seven Greeks to three Turks (six to four in the proposed army), although the demographic ratio was about eight to two; it was not successful.

By the end of 1963, intense frictions led many Turkish Cypriots to withdraw "behind the barricades," and tension heightened between Greece and Turkey. This prompted the UN Security Council to establish the UN Peacekeeping Force in Cyprus in 1964. It has regularly demonstrated its value and has served its purpose for more than forty-five years. Through the 1960s and into the 1970s, Greek Cypriots operated the government virtually alone, with conflicts between those wanting enosis and those content with an independent republic. After further intercommunal violence in 1967–1968, Turkish Cypriots formed a provisional administration of their own.

The ideological struggle among Greek Cypriots culminated in July 1974 in a foolhardy attempted coup by pro-enosis hardliners—supported by the military junta in Athens—against the all-Greek Cyprus government. It quickly failed when the president, Archbishop Makarios, escaped assassination. Nevertheless, Turkey responded quickly, invading under the terms of the 1960 Treaty of Guarantee to protect the Turkish population. Backed by this strong military presence, the Cypriot Turks posthaste divided the island, with the Turkish north ending up with 36 percent of the land, 18 percent of the population, and half of Nicosia. Consequently, some 200,000 Greeks fled south, 45,000 Turks northward, and 6,000–8,000 died—all within a few weeks. This division into a Turkish-Cypriot north, backed by 40,000 Turkish troops, and a Greek-Cypriot south, protected by 6,000 Greek troops, is the sixth and most climactic crucial event affecting today's Cyprus. (Both the consequences of the island's division and economic factors have resulted in there being a sizable Cypriot diaspora—both Greek and Turkish; conservative estimates start at 500,000.)

Divided Cyprus

With the two sides separated by a UN buffer zone, the ROC in the south is the interna-tionally recognized legitimate government. Despite losing much of its productive capacity, it energetically pursued revitalization. It quickly gained more tourists, industrial output, and income from services than the pre-1974 state had islandwide. Through its own efforts and with external assistance, it generated remarkable political and economic development, culminating in its admission to the EU in 2004.

By contrast, North Cyprus has suffered more political ambiguity and has seen less economic development. Under Turkish tutelage, the de facto autonomous administration was recast in February 1975 as a unilaterally declared Turkish Federated State of Cyprus, implying for the future the kind of federation Turkish Cypriots had demanded twenty years earlier. When there was no movement toward a solution, it renamed itself the Turkish Republic of Northern Cyprus (TRNC) in 1983. Internationally isolated, the TRNC has received no recognition by any country other than Turkey. To enhance the north's Turkishness, the Ankara government settled about 55,000 Turks in the TRNC by the mid-2000s.[54]

Despite the early violence and bitterness, the two communities have shown remarkable physical restraint under complex measures either negotiated between them or externally imposed. Attempts to devise institutional arrangements for reunification acceptable to both groups and also to Greece and Turkey have been continuous and were especially vigorous after violence broke out at the dividing line in 1996.[55] In all these negotiations, success has been elusive, with four basic sticking points: (1) the constitutional character of a reunified government, (2) the territorial extent of each entity; (3) the right of return of refugees to their pre-1974 homes, and (4) troop strength in each territory.

With fits and starts, the UN got the two sides to negotiate, led by their "community leaders," thus avoiding the political overtones of "presidents," and when this failed to achieve a mutually agreed solution, the UN secretary-general proposed his own—the so-called Annan Plan: a united republic of two states in confederation, limited right of return for refugees with some border adjustments, and a continued presence of Greek and Turkish military; the plan was to be voted on separately by the two communities. In the meantime, the ROC was one of a group of nine countries, mostly ex-Communist, ready for EU membership. The EU was eager to admit the eastern European states promptly and knew that Greece would delay this unless the ROC was guaranteed admission regardless of whether a settlement for the island was reached before admission. So it capitulated to Greece—thus losing whatever leverage it might have had to forward the Annan Plan.

In 2003, to offset his earlier inflexibility Turkish Cypriot leader Rauf Denktash suddenly opened the border between North and South to crossings in both directions for all islanders, and within a year more than 3 million crossings were recorded, markedly improving the intercommunal atmosphere. But when the time came to vote on the plan in April 2004, the improved attitude was to no avail, despite backing from the United States, the EU, Greece, and Turkey. The Turks (eager for inclusion in the EU) accepted it by 65 percent, but the Greeks, led by a hard-line president, rejected it by 75 percent, knowing full well that the ROC would enter the EU in any case a few days after the vote. In consolation, the EU promised the TRNC about $311 million in development aid, and the ROC was roundly criticized internationally for rejecting the proposals.[56]

In 2008, Greek Cypriots chose a new, more conciliatory president who campaigned promising to restart negotiations. He quickly met with his Turkish counterpart in the first of many sessions between them, and there were even more meetings between joint working groups; in the first year, more than twenty confidence-building measures were agreed upon. Intra-island trade rose from zero in 2003 to $12.4 million in 2008, and personal shopping by Cypriots visiting the "other side" was easily several times higher. At the end of the 2000s, prospects for forward movement were much brighter; after a late-2009 election, the new government in Athens was headed by a prime minister who espoused a federal solution for Cyprus. Intensified intercommunal negotiations were set for 2010;[57] the major sticking points in negotiations remain security for the Turks and the status of property ownership for the Greeks.[58]

With this political-geographical background, we can now analyze the basic character of the island.

TWO MOUNTAINS, THREE PLAINS

With a remarkably varied landscape for such a small area, the island has five distinct regions: two east-west mountain ranges in the north and south, a broad basin in between, and narrow plains along north and south coasts (see Map 10.4). In the southwest are [1] the Troodos Mountains, the oval geomorphic nucleus of the island and a true massif, with an intruded granite core exposed by erosion. Mount Olympus, the island's highest elevation, reaches 6,400 ft/1,951 m. Extensive mineralization accompanied the intrusions, and breakdown of the Troodos rocks produced fertile soils. Stretching the length of the northern edge of the island is [2] the Kyrenia Range, a narrow, steep mountain ridge primarily of Cretaceous limestone that attains 3,360 ft/1,024 m. Some igneous patches occur, and metamorphism has produced marble in places. Much of the range is porous because of solution cavities and is a source of springwater. Its ridges are rough and craggy, appropriately wild for the Crusader castle ruins that cling to its pinnacles.

Nestled between the Kyrenia Range and the Troodos is [3] the Mesaoria, the island's breadbasket, an alluvial plain with fertile soils with a platform of upturned sedimentaries between the Kyrenia ridge and the lower basin. Open at both east and west ends, the Mesaoria slopes primarily eastward, from about 700 ft/215 m to sea level on the coast. Nicosia, the divided primate city of the island and capital of both the ROC and the TRNC, nestles in the center. North of the Kyrenia Range, [4] a narrow coastal plain separates the steep northern slopes from the shore, with citrus groves in irrigated areas and rain-fed crops elsewhere. [5] The coastal plain south of the Troodos is generally wider but more irregular. It is also more densely populated and more industrially developed, with three centers, Limassol, Larnaca, and Paphos, plus the two British SBAs—Akrotiri and Dhekelia.

MEDITERRANEAN CLIMATE, MEDITERRANEAN CROPS

Cyprus has a typical Mediterranean climate, with hot, dry summers and mild, moist winters. It receives 75 percent of possible sunshine in an average year, attracting tourists with its warmth, scenic sites, and well-developed resorts; tourism is the primary economic sector, with 2.4 million arrivals in 2008. With only 13 in/340 mm of rainfall at Nicosia on the Mesaoria (see data for Nicosia in Table 2.1), crops other than the dominant grains must be irrigated. The upper Troodos slopes exert the typical orographic effect and wring up to 45 in/1,145 mm of moisture from winter's westerly winds, much of it as snow, allowing a modest skiing season most years. Much of the runoff from the impermeable igneous rocks is captured in reservoirs or aquifers to be used for irrigation during the summer. With cool temperatures and appreciable moisture, the slopes are forested with pine, cedar, cypress, and poplar (Fig. 10.4).

These woodlands contrast sharply with the typical low, open maquis and garigue typical of Mediterranean lowlands in much of Cyprus. Resorts do double duty in summer and winter.

With assets of climate, relief, and soils, the island has had a favorable agricultural base for centuries. However, during the past thirty-five years, agriculture has fallen to less than 3 percent of GDP and 9 percent of the labor force. Produce includes several tree crops—olives, carobs (it leads the region in carob-bean exports), almonds, citrus, and other fruits—and especially grapes. Its wine, although not of premium quality, is quite good, and extensive vineyards occupy the Troodos southern midslopes. Table grapes, raisins, and wines are major products and exports, as are citrus fruits of all types. Potatoes rank with citrus and grapes in tonnage and are also a major export. More than half of farms have some irrigation, mostly from shallow wells; 35 percent of cultivated land is irrigated.

Water supply and pollution are increasingly serious problems, not only for agriculture, but also crucially for the vital tourist economy and for households; it is not altogether an exaggeration to state that at the end of the 2000s, the water deficit of the entire island was close to replacing its political division as its most serious problem. A prolonged drought during the 1990s gravely upset the island's water balance, reducing the level in the artificial reservoirs to less than 15 percent of normal in 1997–1999. Heavy rainfall in 2001–2003 broke the ten-year drought and refilled most of the reservoirs, but a return of dry years led to water rationing in 2007. Both Greek and Turkish sides have been seeking drastic new solutions to the problem, ranging from building offshore desalinization facilities to importing water by ship and pipeline from Greece and Turkey. At the end of the decade, Cyprus was on many lists of the world's most water-distressed countries.

FIGURE 10.4 Typical landscape on south-facing slopes of the Troodos, western Cyprus. A well-varied area, with olive groves (*right foreground*), vineyards (*left foreground*), terraced cultivation (*middle distance*), and scrub oak and pine forest (*slopes in the distance*).

NONAGRICULTURAL ECONOMY

Mineralization in the Troodos during the igneous intrusions and the accompanying metamorphism gave the island major resources of copper, iron pyrites, chrome, asbestos, and iron-oxide pigments as well as lesser amounts of gold, silver, and zinc. Deposits of copper, the main metal in bronze, were exploited as early as the third millennium BCE and became a major source of the metal for the eastern Mediterranean during the Bronze Age. Indeed, the Greek and Latin words for copper are related to the island's name. In modern times, mining was second only to agriculture during the 1950s and 1960s, but the major older deposits of copper and chrome had been virtually exhausted by the late 1970s. Feasibility studies on exploiting other possible deposits were undertaken in the late 2000s,[59] by which time the island produced only modest tonnages of pyrite, iron-oxide pigments (for paints), bentonite clays, celestite, and gypsum. After long exploiting large asbestos reserves in the Troodos, the Amiantos mine closed in 1989 because of decreased world demand. Thus, the island's once-considerable income from mineral exports is now negligible, although asbestos, bentonite, celestite, chromite, copper, gypsum, iron-oxide pigments, pyrite, and salt resources are still noteworthy. Cyprus and Lebanon are the only countries in the region with no known petroleum or natural gas resources.[60] All of the island's electricity is generated in plants fired with imported oil.[61]

Currently, the republic has a thriving open, free-market, service-based economy, with manufactured products (foods, clothing, tex-

FIGURE 10.5 Pleasant outdoor café on Kyrenia harbor, North Cyprus's premier resort area.

tiles, chemicals) constituting 54 percent of the exports in 2007. Taking advantage of an educated and English-speaking population, good airline and maritime connections, and exceptional telecommunications, it makes a "bridge" of its geography. Contributing 78 percent to GDP is the service sector, including tourism, employing 71 percent of the labor force. Tourism was hit fairly hard by the global recession—2009 earnings were down more than 15 percent. It has become an international business hub—more stable than Beirut—and attracts regional offices, banks, and investments; adopting the euro as its currency in 2008, it is well integrated into the EU. Transparency International gave Cyprus a quite good rating regarding corruption—second in the region and twelfth in the EU; with regard to economic freedom, it was rated third in the region and fifteenth in the EU.[62] On paper, it seems to be a major participant in international shipping: actually, nearly all ships flying its flag do so only for economic advantage—Cyprus's maritime registry is the world's seventh-largest supplier of a "flag of convenience" to the industry.

The ROC's per capita GDP of $21,200 in 2009 is one of the three highest in the region. In 2007, it ranked 32nd of 182 countries globally (and 3rd in the region) according to the UNDP's Human Development Index, placing it among the very high human development countries.[63]

The economic disparity between north and south is obvious. Although the TRNC also has a free-market economy, political and economic uncertainty has discouraged investment. The mid-2000s did see several years of strong growth led by construction. Compared to the south, tourism is relatively modest, concentrated around the beautiful port of Kyrenia (Fig. 10.5); most visitors are British or Turkish. Its economy relies on agriculture and government services, which together employ more than half the workforce. Lack of skilled labor and inflation have hurt the economy, which is closely tied to that of Turkey. Since the sectoral border opened in

2003, several thousand northerners have found employment in the south. Per capita GDP is about half that in the ROC, and it is heavily dependent on its patron for most of its trade and financial assistance—$400 million annually in the late 2000s.

RELATIONS

Though of little international influence politically or economically, the ROC has surprisingly complex relations, particularly as a result of the intra-island discord. Traditionally nonaligned in foreign policy, it has consistently identified with the West culturally. It has long had close associations with Greece and Britain (though the SBAs are an irritant); as an EU member, it is moving more toward broader European concerns. The US Agency for International Development has long had a small economic assistance program to support intercommunal activities; from 2006 to 2008 it totaled about $32 million. The TRNC remains fairly isolated, but assistance from the EU after the ROC became a member has increased contacts in that direction. It has observer status but not membership in the Organization of the Islamic Conference.

Our focus now returns to the Levant mainland for a contrasting view of the Kingdom of Jordan.

NOTES

1. See Gore 2004.

2. W. Harris 2003, Chaps. 2 and 3.

3. Estimates of the Lebanese diaspora vary widely. A conservative figure would be in the range of 4 to 5 million, but much larger numbers are claimed elsewhere—for example, 12.4 million in September 2009 in http://identitychef.wordpress.com/2009/09/06/lebanese-diaspora-worldwide-geographical-distribution/.

4. *New York Times*, Dec. 24, 2007.

5. Gore 2004.

6. Estimates of the Palestinian population vary widely for any country but especially for Lebanon (and, after the early 1990s, for Kuwait). The UNRWA

figures for their Field of Operation—where they maintain refugee camps—are based on registered Palestinians. See www.un.org/unrwa/refugees/lebanon.html for the 2009 estimate.

7. See S. Haddad 2003, Pt. 1.

8. See also Cobban 1985; *Lebanon* Country Study 1988; and Zamir 1999.

9. Gambill 2009. See also Sanjan 2009.

10. Ragette 1983; *New York Times*, Feb. 23, 1997; *Christian Science Monitor*, Jan. 5, 1999; the elaborate Gavin and Maluf 1996; Meadows 1994.

11. See Abbott 1994.

12. Gulick 1967. Maps in the book show the differences between street patterns of the old city and modern developments.

13. Mikesell 1969.

14. J. Hudson 1971.

15. Beirut is now the permanent home of the UN Economic and Social Commission for Western Asia.

16. See *Lebanon* Country Study 1988.

17. Although the fighting in Lebanon was not across international boundaries and was "internal" or "civil" in many ways, one or another faction was continually and openly stimulated and supported by outside states and groups, especially Israel, Syria, Libya, Iraq, Iran, Saudi Arabia, and other Gulf states, not to mention most of the Great Powers.

18. *New York Times*, Sept. 16, 2009.

19. Transparency International 2009.

20. *The Daily Star* (Beirut), Nov. 25, 2009.

21. *The Daily Star*, Apr. 15, 2004; U.S. Department of State, *Background Note: Lebanon*, 2003.

22. United Nations Development Programme 2009.

23. For further details on the relationship, see "EU-Lebanon Action Plan," http://ec.europa.eu/world/enp/pdf/lebanon_enp_ap_final_en.pdf; and European Commission, "Lebanese Republic: Country Strategy Paper, 2007–2013."

24. *The Daily Star*, Dec. 21, 2009. As a result, Moody's Investors Services changed its outlook for the government's bonds from stable to positive.

25. *The Daily Star*, Feb. 23, 2010.

26. There were complaints, though, that 2009 visitors were spending less money (*The Daily Star*, Dec. 18, 2009).

27. U.S. Department of State, *Background Note: Lebanon*, Jan. 2009 and *Country Commercial Guide: Lebanon* 2010; U.S. Department of Energy, Energy Information Administration (EIA), *Lebanon*, Aug. 2004; *The Daily Star*, Apr. 15, 2004.

28. *The Daily Star*, Dec. 17, 2009.

29. IEA, "2006 Energy Balance for Lebanon," www.iea.org/country/index.asp.

30. USGS, "The Mineral Industry of Lebanon," in *Minerals Yearbook* 2008.

31. N. Lewis 1953.

32. *The Daily Star*, Oct. 13, 2004.

33. FAO, *Production Yearbook*, various editions.

34. Many studies analyze Lebanon's problems leading up to and during the civil war of the 1970s and 1980s, although readers must beware of some authors' biases. Useful are W. Haddad 1985, which is concise and philosophical but insightful; Rabinovich 1985, giving a moderate Israeli scholar's analysis; the entire issue of the *Middle East Journal* 38, no. 2 (Spring 1984); T. Friedman 1989 and Fisk 1990, two very good journalistic accounts, one American and one British; D. Gordon 1983 and Salibi 1988, two concise general studies of Lebanon; and Norton 1987.

35. It is worth noting that Osama bin Laden claimed in his videotape of late October 2004 that "as I watched [TV coverage of] the destroyed towers in Lebanon, it occurred to me to . . . destroy towers in America so that it can taste some of what we are tasting" (*New York Times*, Oct. 30, 2004).

36. See T. Friedman 1989; Fisk 1990; and Rabinovich 1985.

37. See the Israeli government's Kahan Commission 1983; its official report charged Sharon with "personal responsibility" and recommended his removal from office. In January 2002, Elie Hobeika, a onetime minister in the Lebanese government and the leader of a pro-Israeli Christian militia implicated in the massacre, was assassinated after he claimed that he had proof of his innocence and was willing to testify in legal proceedings seeking an indictment of Sharon, by then Israeli prime minister.

38. The U.S. role and related events are traced in detail in Parker 1993, Pt. 3.

39. *Lebanon Report* (Spring 1998): 28–42.

40. *Christian Science Monitor*, Aug. 2, 1993.

41. *Economist*, July 15, 1995.

42. See *New York Times*, Apr. 19, Apr. 28, May 1, and May 8, 1996.

43. The depressing cycle of violence is seen in the detailed *Middle East Journal* chronology. For events in "Grapes of Wrath," see vol. 50, nos. 3 and 4 (Summer and Autumn 1996).

44. See *New York Times*, Sept. 4, 2004; and *Christian Science Monitor*, Oct. 5 and Oct. 25, 2004.

45. *New York Times*, Feb. 15, Mar. 1, 2, and 3, 2005; *Christian Science Monitor*, Feb. 25, 2005, 43, and Mar. 11, 2005, 24–26.

46. *BBC News*, Oct. 21, 2005.

47. See www.usaid.gov/lb/programs/index.html.

48. Muhanna 2009. The article estimates that the March 14th coalition secured only 43.4 percent of the vote while the opposition gained 53.4 percent.

49. *BBC News*, Nov. 25, 2009.

50. *New York Times*, Dec. 21 2009.

51. Hundreds of antiquities from 9500 BCE to the late Roman period, along with ruins from medieval times, are scattered over the island and are among the most important attractions of Cyprus. Especially famous are the Greco-Roman mosaic floors in Paphos, in southwest Cyprus, and the Greco-Roman city of Salamis on the east coast.

52. Even straightforward geographical writings on Cyprus by Cypriots show how viewpoints often differ sharply between Greek Cypriots and Turkish Cypriots. Denktash 1982 is an opposing view by the leader of the Turkish Cypriot community. See also *Cyprus* Country Study 1993 and the brief presentation in Central Intelligence Agency 1973 for a concise coverage of the island before the emergence of North Cyprus, and Reddaway 1986. Stasis and Mavrocordatos 1989 is a secondary school–level book but is still useful. Karouzis and Karouzis 1997 is actually a practical geography of Cyprus written by Greek Cypriot geographers. Also U.S. Department of State, *Background Note: Cyprus*, June 2009, and *Country Commercial Guide* 2009.

53. In some ways, a harbinger of British wartime Middle East policies designed to protect the route to India; see Busch 1971.

54. *Cyprus Mail*, Aug. 8, 2004.

55. *New York Times*, Aug. 12, 16, and 18, 1996.

56. *New York Times*, Apr. 27, 2003, Feb. 14, 2004, and Apr. 1, 21, 24, and 25, 2004; *Christian Science Monitor*, Apr. 23, 2004.

57. Reuters 2009. A major negotiating problem on each side remains: With the Turks, President Talat is far more open to a settlement than the TRNC prime minister; with the Greeks, can any agreement be approved in the necessary referendum? See *Hurriyet: Daily News and Economic Review* 2009a, 2009b.

58. *Economist*, Dec. 2, 2009.

59. USGS, "The Mineral Industry of Cyprus," in *Minerals Yearbook* 2008.

60. *New York Times* editorial, Apr. 27, 2004; Associated Press report in *Waco Tribune-Herald*, Apr. 27, 2004. However, recent gas-field discoveries off the Israeli coast allow the possibility that there may be gas off Cyprus as well.

61. IEA, "2006 Energy Balance for Cyprus," www.iea.org/country/index.asp.

62. Transparency International 2009; Fraser Institute 2008.

63. United Nations Development Programme 2009.

11

Jordan
The Land Beyond and Between

During its long history, the area of the modern Kingdom of Jordan has undergone many changes in name, political status, and economic level. One result of these shifts, especially during the twentieth century, is confusion regarding Jordan's political geography, specifically its territorial base, and because of the ancient use of "Jordan" for the famed river and valley and as the name of the country.

The autonomous polity of Transjordan was created in the early 1920s, in lands taken from the Turks during World War I, as a British mandate under the League of Nations. The Amirate of Transjordan, its name for twenty-five years, became independent in May 1946. Attachment of the West Bank, part of the former Palestine mandate, to the kingdom in 1948 (officially 1950) made "Transjordan" a misnomer and led to the adoption of the Hashimite Kingdom of Jordan as its official designation. Israel's occupation of the West Bank in 1967 led to more ambiguity until Jordan announced its disengagement from the West Bank in 1988.

For the sake of clarity, we will use terms for this area in this way: The expression trans-Jordan basically indicates direction, "beyond the Jordan River," as opposed to cis-Jordan, "this side of the river"—from the European perspective. The term "Transjordan" refers to the polity occupying a specific area east of the river between 1923 and 1948–1950 as a mandate and then as a kingdom. With no political implications, trans-Jordania revives an old regional name. It could be said that Transjordan was a trans-Jordan polity in trans-Jordania.

Four general aspects of spatial relations are noteworthy. First, whatever its name or status, its location "beyond the Jordan" has been a significant factor in its geography and history. The physical barriers of the deep Jordan Trench to the west and the desert expanses to the east were serious obstacles to the movement of peoples and goods, although caravans had some useful routes. Second, the narrow, better-watered, and most densely populated highland zone squeezed between trench and desert was a north-south transit route, the eastern counterpart of the Trunk Road or Via Maris (Way of the Sea) extending from Egypt through Gaza and Megiddo to Damascus. Caravans followed either of two routes in trans-Jordania: the King's Highway past Petra, Karak, and Amman to Damascus, or the generally level Desert Road, 18 mi/29 km farther to the east out on the plateau (Map 11.1).

Third, the area's transitional character is another very basic geographical aspect. It has been the "land between"—never a significant power center or a major part of one. Conflict

JORDAN

Long-form official name, anglicized: Hashimite Kingdom of Jordan

Official name, transliterated: Al-Mamlakah al-Urdunniyah al-Hashimiyah

Form of government: constitutional monarchy with two legislative houses (Senate, House of Representatives)

Area: 34,495 mi^2/89,342 km^2

Population, 2008: 5,844,000; Literacy (Latest): 91.1%

Ethnic composition (%): Arab 97.8, of which Jordanian 32.4, Palestinian 32.2, Iraqi 14.0, Bedouin 12.8; Circassian 1.2; Armenian and other 1.0

Religions (%): Sunni Muslim 92; Christian 6; other (including small numbers of Shii and Druze) 2

Demography: Life expectancy—70.6 yr (M), 72.4 yr (F); Birthrate (per 1,000)—29.1; Fertility rate—2.71

GDP, 2009: $22.56 billion; purchasing power parity: $33.06 billion; per capita: $5,300

Currency: Jordanian dinar, US$1 = 0.7035 dinars, 1 dinar = $1.402 (March 2010)

Energy reserves: oil—1 mn bbl; natural gas—213 bn ft^3; coal—nil

Main exports (% of total value, 2006): clothing 24.3; machinery and apparatus 9.2; potash 8.0; medicines 5.9; gold 5.4; vegetables and fruit 4.2; phosphates 4.1; precious jewelry 3.8

Main imports (% of total value, 2006): crude petroleum 17.7; machinery and apparatus 14.8; food 12.9; vehicles 8.8; chemicals and chemical products 8.7

Capital city: Amman 1,036,330; other cities: Zarqa 395,227; Irbid 250,645; Rusayfah 227,735; Quwaysimah 135,500; Wadi as-Sir 122,032

---

between "the desert and the sown," between nomads and settlements, inhibited development east of the Jordan Valley. It embraced petty kingdoms such as Rabboth-Ammon and Moab 3,000 years ago, and places like Gilead had regional identity, but the area lacked specific regional unity until after World War I.

The *raison de création* of mandate Transjordan, beyond the purely political goals mentioned below, destined it to be a buffer state. To keep French control north of the Yarmuk, to hold back Saudis from the Jordan Valley, and to focus Iraqis on Mesopotamia, the mandate was designed, delineated, and operated by Britain as a buffer. With Israel's creation in 1948, independent Transjordan—a bit smaller than the U.S. state of Indiana—became the archetypal buffer among its neighbors, its fate inextricably linked to the vagaries of conflict between Israel and the Palestinians and other Arabs. Jordan not only has the longest border with Israel of all the Arab states, but it has long been targeted by Israeli extremists as the future home for all the Arabs remaining in Israel and the occupied territories. Indeed, the western and better-watered part of trans-Jordania has been envisioned by some Zionists as part of Greater Israel.

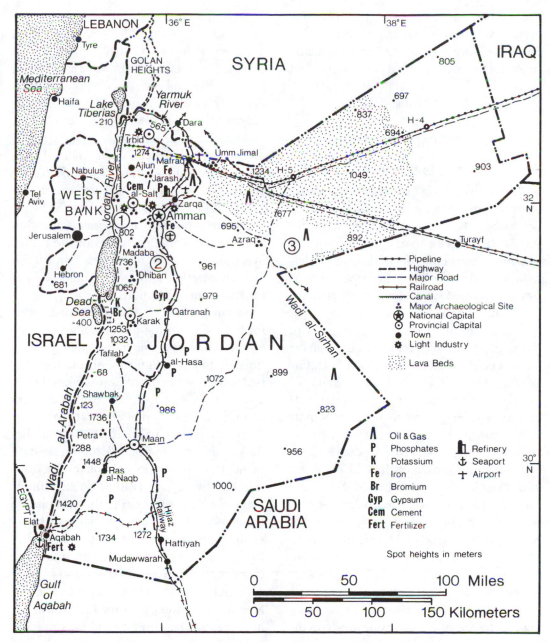

MAP 11.1 General and economic map of Jordan. Circled numbers indicate regions discussed in text. Note concentration of settlement and development in western Jordan.

The fourth aspect concerns Jordan's territorial stability and integrity. During the mandate and its first independent years, it lay entirely east of the river—its Arabic name then was Sharq al-Urdunn (East of the Jor-

dan). In 1950, incorporation of the central Palestine hill country (the West Bank) expanded its territorial base by a very important 2,270 mi²/5,880 km², but this was lost to Israeli conquest and occupation in the June

War of 1967. After twenty-one years of uncertainty, it renounced claims to the West
Bank; therefore, description, data, and analysis of Jordan here pertain only to the East
Bank—in effect, to virtually the same territory as the 1923–1946 mandate.[1]

HISTORICAL EVOLUTION

From Early Times to the Muslim Conquest

Vestiges of the early history of the area are
sharply etched into the landscape of the western fourth of contemporary Jordan. In this
settled part of the country, one is rarely out
of sight of some reminder of the past—a dol-
men, tell, ruined building, Roman milestone,
or the excavated ruins of an entire city, such
as Jarash, Umm al-Jimal, or Petra.

Trans-Jordania's golden age began with
the Seleucids of Syria, continued through the
Roman era, and extended into the Byzantine
period (about 200 BCE–600 CE), when it benefited from thriving caravan routes and trade
centers. Prominent traders were the Semitic
Nabataeans, who operated from their extraordinary capital of Petra. Modern Amman
was Rabboth Ammon of the Old Testament
and then Greco-Roman Philadelphia. It and
Jarash (see Fig. 3.5) were two major members
of the Decapolis, a ten-city league formed to
resist nomadic attacks. Mosaic floors from
Byzantine Christian churches and other
buildings of the fifth and sixth centuries are
found in many sites. Especially remarkable
are those in the small highland town of Madaba, southwest of Amman; one preserves the
famous Madaba Map, which shows in intricate detail Palestine and adjacent areas, including a recognizable plan of Jerusalem.[2]

From Muslim Conquest to the Present

This golden age waned with Byzantium's
ejection by invading Arabs in 634–636. Traditional routes lost stability and security; the
profitable land trade dwindled and virtually
disappeared by the ninth century—especially

undermined as maritime traders linked the
Indian Ocean and the Mediterranean. Cities
declined, villages vanished, and Bedouin
overwhelmed settled areas. Not until the Ottoman Hijaz Railway reused the corridor in
the early 1900s was the area economically
reawakened even marginally. Then World
War I action and, a few years later, the mem-
oirs of T. E. Lawrence (*Seven Pillars of Wisdom*), reintroduced trans-Jordania to the
West. This vague undefined area east of the
Jordan Trench sprawled beyond its highland
backbone out into its desert realms, merging
into the barren wildernesses of the future
Syria on the north, the future Iraq on the
east, and, to the south, what would become
the Kingdom of Saudi Arabia.

Britain, as League of Nations mandatory
for both sides of the Jordan Valley, initially
oversaw the area through the fledgling Palestinian mandate administration, but it promised self-government to East Bank notables
at al-Salt in August 1920. British experts
meeting with Colonial Secretary Winston
Churchill in Cairo in March 1921 agreed that
the inchoate region would become a separate
mandate, ruled by Amir Abdullah. The decision had two aims: (1) to be a token fulfill-
ment of British promises to the Arabs in the
Husayn-McMahon correspondence of 1915–
1916 (see Chap. 8) and (2) to placate the
Hashimite family—direct descendants of the
Prophet Muhammad—in the person of Amir
Abdullah ibn Husayn, son of the sharif of
Mecca and brother of Amir Faysal, who simultaneously became king of Iraq. Churchill
met Abdullah in Jerusalem to inform him of
the plan, regularized with the official launch
of the Middle East mandates in September
1923.[3] The penurious amirate gained independence in 1946 with Abdullah as king.

The political-geographical, demographic,
economic, and social character of the kingdom altered dramatically and permanently
after the advent of Israel on May 14, 1948:
Scores of thousands of Palestinian refugees

crossed over the Jordan River to Transjordan, Abdullah provisionally annexed the West Bank, and Jordan was pulled into the vortex that has characterized Arab-Israeli relations into the new millennium. Partly because of his confidential dealings with the Israelis[4]—an ill-kept secret—he was assassinated in Jerusalem in 1951. His son Talal succeeded him briefly, but in 1952 his then only sixteen-year-old grandson, Husayn, ascended the throne.[5]

King Husayn (or Hussein) deftly balanced the many conflicting forces impinging on his vulnerable realm, having learned from his grandfather how to walk a geopolitical tightrope. He usually chose the moderate and often mediating role, seeking consensus, sometimes at great risk. However, he made the first of two costly strategic mistakes when he joined Egypt and Syria against Israel in the 1967 June War. Jordan suffered heavy military and territorial losses in the debacle, losing all areas west of the Jordan to conquest, more than a third of the kingdom's most educated population, much of its arable land, and its Holy Land sites. Territorially, it returned to its trans-Jordan status of pre-1948, a status confirmed by Husayn when he renounced all legal ties with the West Bank in 1988.

Cyclic turbulence has characterized Jordan's situation from independence to the present: the 1948–1949 war with Israel, the 1967 disaster, periodic border clashes, internal engagements between army and insurgents, many coup attempts, terrorist attacks, and persistent socioeconomic turmoil in its efforts to balance transnational interests with its relations with Palestinians on both sides of the Jordan Valley. In the name of stability, martial law was imposed from 1967 to 1989. The most serious internal conflict was the showdown between the government and Palestinian *fedayeen* in September 1970 ("Black September" to Palestinians); an estimated 3,300 were killed on both sides. In this civil war, the army gained control, forcing the *fedayeen* to withdraw, mostly to Lebanon (see Chap. 10). Husayn later reconciled with PLO leader Yasser Arafat, but relations remained strained.

The king moved toward a limited democracy, balancing the interests of his "guest" Palestinian constituents and his still somewhat tribalized native East Bank subjects. In parliamentary elections in 1989 and 1993, he expanded political limits but still controlled the process.[6] The year 1990 brought a grave dilemma when Iraq invaded Kuwait. Jordan would be isolated politically and economically from the international community if he failed to censure Saddam, but he would risk his throne if he denounced Iraq and joined the coalition. In making his second costly strategic mistake, he opted for neutrality and was, indeed, immediately isolated, losing all aid from the Gulf states, the United States, and Europe; thousands of Jordanian/Palestinian expatriate workers in the Gulf were expelled, returning home to a shattered economy. But domestically the king's popularity was affirmed and the national consensus solidified—even under the stresses his choice had imposed.

After skillfully managing the 1993 parliamentary elections, Husayn again took a chance—signing a peace treaty with Israel, then under moderate prime minister Yitzhak Rabin, in 1994. The measure refurbished relations with the United States, bringing some economic rewards. The treaty also promised "peace dividends"; in practice, short-term returns were disappointing. The deteriorating economy provoked riots in 1996 and led to the suspension of parliament. Both for economic and for political reasons, popular opposition to rapprochement with Israel mounted, especially when Rabin's successor, Binyamin Netanyahu, stalled on implementation.[7] As an antinormalization movement gained momentum, Husayn died in February 1999, ending a reign of forty-seven years. He was succeeded by his son, Abdullah II, who reaffirmed his father's stance for peace and moderation, ties to the West, and links to Arab neighbors.[8]

The new king was tested by repeated crises during the following years. Focusing on both political stability and economic reform, he pushed for a "Jordan First" program and further privatization of state enterprises. When an increasingly assertive parliament seemed to be moving beyond acceptable limits in 2001, Abdullah dissolved it. Two years later, the first elections since 1997 went well despite tensions from the invasion of Iraq in 2003. Elections in 2007 resulted in a reduced Islamist presence in the 110-seat parliament, largely due to reducing the representation of urban areas in favor of rural areas that then elected independents loyal to the monarchy; seven women were among the members. This parliament, criticized for inaction during the global economic crisis, was dissolved by Abdullah in November 2009; his actions continued the drift of Jordan away from democracy.

Having cooperated after 9/11 in the fight against terrorism, the king faced another dilemma with the invasion of Iraq. However, he held tighter reins and managed public reaction skillfully: his "Jordan First" program emphasized the kingdom's security, while he personally expressed opposition to the invasion, even to President Bush.[9] He declined to send troops, but offset this refusal by offering use of Jordan for several coalition operations, granting overflights for military aircraft, providing rest and recreational opportunities for coalition troops, and opening Aqabah port for their use. Jordan thus became a valuable partner in the aftermath, profiting economically and offsetting other losses. For Iraq's postinvasion economy, Aqabah again became an important link in transit trade. Security conditions on the highway to Iraq in the mid-2000s varied between somewhat chancy and absolutely terrible, but the route continued to be an important conduit. Amman

quickly became the headquarters of many official delegations, international institutions, and business firms that had interests in Iraq but preferred the city as a far more agreeable location than Baghdad. Further, Jordan opened its doors to Iraqis fleeing the deteriorating situations they encountered at home (more on this below).

PEOPLES:
ARABS, MINORITIES, AND REFUGEES

Arabs

During the millennium prior to World War I, the inhabitants of trans-Jordania were, as now, overwhelmingly Arab ethnolinguistically and predominantly Sunni Muslim in religion. The mandate population of the 1920s was entirely made up of villagers and Bedouin, but the nomads gradually became sedentarized. Jordan is now more than 80 percent urbanized, and villagers enjoy most modern amenities, often commuting to work in nearby towns.

More than half of urbanized Jordanians live on one or another of the several *jabals* (hills) of Amman, the capital and primate city (Fig. 11.1). These residents, many of whom are Palestinians, flourished along with the rapid growth and development of the economy. Many have been educated abroad and speak English as a second language, and an appreciable number of them are Christian. Rusayfah and Zarqa to the east of Amman are actually large suburbs of the capital. Irbid is the population node in the northwest, and Aqabah in the southwest is the kingdom's thriving single port.

Before 1900, tribal Bedouin constituted most of the population, but like Bedouin in neighboring countries, they gradually shifted away from nomadism. Nevertheless, a sense of tribal identity and heritage remains significant in both society and political culture. Bedouin in the army repeatedly showed traditional loyalty during crises to their para-

FIGURE 11.1 Amman, capital of Jordan. The amphitheater was the heart of Roman Philadelphia. Beyond the theater is a modern residential area on Jabal al-Jawfa; to the right is Jabal al-Ashrafiyah. This older area of Amman is yielding to the post-1980 urban development farther west.

mount chieftain, the king, thereby maintaining the political structure. The tribal element in Jordan's society persists and periodically asserts itself.[10]

Minorities

Both ethnic and religious minorities play noteworthy but amicable roles in the Jordanian political and social systems. About 45,000 Circassians (see Chap. 4) live in villages around Amman and in the capital itself. As many as 15,000 Chechens (sometimes called Shishanis) preserve their language and culture, brought with them a century ago. Several hundred Armenians sought refuge in Jordan between the 1880s and 1920s; perhaps 30,000 of their descendants remain unassimilated in the population. The expatriate community, small and almost entirely British before World War II, has grown steadily, is much broader in composition, and numbers in the tens of thousands.

Jordan's social fabric is not torn by intersectarian conflict, like Lebanon's; relations between the Sunni Muslims (more than 92 percent of the population) and the Christians (about 6 percent) have always been good. Christians are mostly Greek Orthodox but also include Armenian Orthodox, Greek and Roman Catholics, Syrian Orthodox, and Copts. They constitute a community that dates back to the earliest spread of Christianity in the second century. Some towns are Christian centers—Karak, Madaba, and al-Salt—and Amman also has a high percentage of Christians.

Ethnic and religious distinctions aside, it is the division between native "East Bankers" and "Jordanian Palestinians" that is the crucial dynamic in Jordan's sociopolitical system.

Both East Bankers and Palestinians are Arab, speak Arabic, are mostly Sunni Muslim, and have other characteristics in common. But the essential difference is that the Palestinians are refugees, having been dispossessed of their homeland, property, and national identity, and therefore have profoundly different national sentiments and aspirations from those of indigenous Jordanians.[11]

Refugees

The 300,000 population of the Transjordan mandate in 1921 had increased to only 433,000 by 1946 and independence. However, this figure increased dramatically in 1948–1949 with the influx of about 132,000 Palestinian refugees to the East Bank. Another 365,000 took refuge among the 400,000 permanent inhabitants of the West Bank, which was defended against Israel by Jordan's Arab Legion and its allies. In a matter of weeks, the East Bank population increased nearly one-third, and subsequent annexation of the West Bank increased it by another 765,000. With an overall jump during that brief period of more than 200 percent on the East Bank, the original inhabitants found themselves outnumbered two to one by Palestinians. Furthermore, half of the West Bankers were also refugees, displaced by Israeli conquest from their lands and livelihood, and both the refugees and the natives in the West Bank resented Jordanian annexation.

The kingdom's demographic—and territorial—status again altered radically with Israel's 1967 conquest of the West Bank. Jordan lost territory with tourist attractions and arable lands; half its population lived on the West Bank. Then, of these, more than 125,000 West Bank "old refugees" became twice displaced, fleeing invading Israeli forces to the East Bank, followed by 100,000 West Bank residents and 45,000 from Gaza—"new refugees" or "displaced persons." Thus, 270,000 new Palestinians augmented the refugees of the late 1940s, their children, and others that had arrived between 1949 to 1967. A small population flow from West Bank to East Bank continued after 1967, while Israeli extremists loudly contended that all Arabs west of the Jordan River must eventually be expelled to Jordan. Of Jordan's 5.8 million people in 2008, about two-thirds were Palestinians; about 950,000 were officially registered refugees, one-third living in ten UNRWA camps.[12] Most Palestinians have taken Jordanian citizenship; Jordan is the only Arab country to have granted such status to all its refugee population.

A new and in some ways even more pressing refugee problem followed the invasion of Iraq. During the Saddam Husayn regime, Jordan had an Iraqi exile population, and other Iraqis lived there because of family or business connections. But as the failure of the United States to provide domestic security became increasingly obvious, the trickle of Iraqis arriving in Amman became a flood in 2004 and 2005. By 2007, at least 700,000 were in Jordan (by some estimates as many as 1 million); most were Sunnis fleeing the battle zones of Baghdad or western Iraq, but a large percentage were from minorities—of those registered with UNHCR, 16 percent were Christians and 6 percent were Mandaeans. (By way of contrast, the United States had accepted fewer than 1,000 Iraqi refugees to that point.) Although many were from the middle class, able at first to support themselves, as their exile lengthened, their situations became more straitened. Jordan, despite its extensive experience in dealing with large population displacements, is still a relatively poor country, and not until almost five years after the invasion did its problems in this regard (and similar ones in Syria) receive much official attention abroad.

PHYSICAL RESOURCE BASE

Regions of Jordan

Jordan has exhibited remarkable flexibility during the changes in its territory and population, particularly in view of its limited physical resource base. A brief survey of this and the state's exploitation of its resources will aid in understanding the challenges to this buffer kingdom.[13]

An east-west cross-section shows a three-fold physical division (see circled numbers on Map 11.1): [1] Along the western edge is the Jordan Valley and its continuation southward in the Wadi Arabah, a major part of the Levant Rift System, with the lowest continental elevations on earth along the Dead Sea. [2] Immediately east of the valley is a north-south belt of highlands—4,100 ft/1,250 m in the north and the highest elevations in the Palestine-Jordan area, 5,575 ft/1,700 m in the south. [3] Extending eastward at a level of 2,625–2,950 ft/800–900 m is the Eastern Desert, occupying 85 percent of Jordan with a surface that is variously flat, rolling, or exhibiting erosional remnants.

[1] Jordan Valley. The Jordan Valley (Arabic *al-Ghor*), 65 mi/104 km long, may be subdivided into four narrow parallel belts.

(1) The river itself (see Fig. 2.5), winding in tight meanders in a narrow bed, joins the Yarmuk River just south of the Sea of Galilee and falls to the Dead Sea, 1,385 ft/422 m below sea level at the end of the 2000s (recently, the sea's level seems to be falling even faster than what had been an annual average of 3.3 ft/1 m). (2) The floodplain (Arabic *al-Zor*), with a mantle of rank vegetation called "thicket of the Jordan" in biblical passages, has a level surface that is just a few meters above the river level. (3) The upper terrace level, the *Ghor*, is several hundred meters wide and is divided from the *Zor* by a narrow, eroded slope. The King Abdullah Canal (originally East Ghor Canal) was constructed on the gently sloping upper terrace level (see "Water: The Vital Resource" below), enabling development of the most productive farmland in Jordan. The East Ghor is an archaeologist's paradise, with 224 sites identified. (4) A high, ruggedly eroded escarpment—with a total rise of more than 4,265 ft/1,300 m within 1.2 mi/2 km—forms the eastern wall of the great trench that extends from the Sea of Galilee to and beyond the Gulf of Aqabah (see Chap. 2 and Fig. 2.2).

[2] Highland Belt. Extending from the Yarmuk in the north to the Gulf of Aqabah in the south, the highland belt receives the country's most precipitation and therefore has always served as the core of settlement, development, and culture east of the valley. It varies markedly in width and relief, and there are fundamental differences in rocks and structure among its northern, central, and southern thirds. Because of their basic significance and clear differentiation, the five principal subregions of the highland belt require examination in some detail.

(1) With an average 24–30 in/600–750 mm of precipitation, moderate slopes, productive soils, and a remarkable number of flowing springs, the Ajlun Highland is the best-watered and most naturally productive part of Jordan. It extends from the Yarmuk southward to the deep, broad valley of the Wadi Zarqa, the biblical River Jabbock, which cuts through a long sequence of geological strata. It supports the densest population in the greatest number of villages outside the Amman metropolitan area. Along with cultivated crops, natural woodland has been legendary since ancient times, when resin of trees on these hills yielded the celebrated "balm in Gilead" (Fig. 11.2).

On the plateau north of the Ajlun Dome lies Irbid (ancient Arbela), the third-largest city. East of Irbid is Ramtha (ancient Ramoth or Ramoth Gilead), an old caravan station. Until relatively recently, it was the main border crossing between Syria and Jordan; this is now on the north-south motorway to the east. Along the eastern flank is the ancient city of Jarash, with a well-preserved gate, colonnaded main street, forum, theaters, and temples spanning Hellenistic, Roman, and

FIGURE 11.2 The humid northwest of Jordan: contemporary scrub oak and pine woodland in the formerly forested, moist Ajlun Highland, biblical Gilead.

Byzantine times (see Fig. 3.5). Rising near Amman, the Zarqa joins the Jordan after a descent of 3,580 ft/1,090 m. The King Talal Dam, Jordan's largest, was built on the lower Zarqa in 1977; its reservoir supplies Amman.

(2) South of the Wadi Zarqa is the Northern Balqa Highland, sometimes called the Amman Highland. On its western slope is al-Salt, the main center of trans-Jordania before the mandate. On its southeastern edge is Amman, the capital and administrative, economic, communications, industrial, and cultural center of Jordan. With buildings of limestone and chalk dimension stone covering the steep slopes of the several *jabals*, the city's morphology is dramatic (see Fig. 11.1). From a population of some 6,000 in the 1920s, Greater Amman was edging toward 2.5 million by the late 2000s.

(3) The Southern Balqa lies south of the Northern Balqa/Amman Highland on the partly dissected Karak Plateau, an area of grain cultivation and seminomadic pastoralism. This is the biblical Land of Moab and the classical Peraea ("on the other side"). It is bounded on the south by a spectacular gash, the Wadi Mujib, the biblical River Arnon (Fig. 11.3). Winding across the plateau is the scenic descendant of the historic King's Highway, connecting the cities of Hisban (ancient Heshbon), Madaba, Dhiban (ancient Dibon), and Karak (ancient Kir Hareseth, chief Moabite city)—all mentioned in biblical accounts and all with archaeological remains dating to that period. Northwest of Madaba is Mount Nebo, from which the biblical narrative relates that Moses viewed the Promised Land.

(4) The most rugged part of Jordan, the Shara Mountains (from *seir* = rock) traverse the ancient land of Edom (red). The King's Highway continues southward along the crest of the Shara to the Hisma, passing fewer villages as aridity increases. The village of Wadi

FIGURE 11.3 Modern highway winding its way down into the Wadi Mujib, the biblical River Arnon, in the semidesert near Karak, southern Jordan.

Musa adjoins and services the fabulous archaeological site of Petra,[14] referred to by a British poet as the "rose-red city, half as old as time," hidden in the colorful mesas of Nubian sandstone on the Shara's western edge (Fig. 11.4). Petra is justifiably Jordan's most frequented tourist site, around which is a national park.

(5) The Hisma landscape includes the Hisma Depression itself, with broad sand corridors winding their way among vertical-sided mesas and buttes of red Nubian sandstone—the dramatic, silent land of the Wadi Ram (sometimes Rum). From the Wadi Ram, a rugged highway and railway corridor reaches the Red Sea at Aqabah. The town has grown from a fishing village of fewer than 2,000 people in 1945 to 95,000 in 2008. Although, like the adjacent Israeli port of Elat, it is off the main sea-lanes, it has expanded into a bustling modern port, chemical-processing center, and resort city, serving as the anchor for Jordan's short coastline, 16 mi/26 km.

[3] Eastern Desert. Stretching eastward from the highland belt is the Eastern Desert, the Badia, traditional realm of the Bedouin. A dry tableland at the northwest of the Syro-Arabian Desert, it is, except in one or two depressions, everywhere more than 2,000 ft/610 m. Even so, it lies nearly 1,000 ft/305 m below the general level of the highland belt. Thus, it is in the rain shadow and receives only 2–8 in/50–200 mm of precipitation annually. Its western margin is Jordan's phosphate belt; a small oil field and a natural gas field are farther east. One former notable feature of economic importance is the Hijaz Railway,[15] built by the Ottomans in the early 1900s along the line between the sown region on the west and the desert on the east.

Of the Eastern Desert's several subdivisions, two have served historic roles: The broad, shallow depression of Wadi al-Sirhan extending southeastward along the Jordan–Saudi Arabia boundary was a traditional

FIGURE 11.4
Its original name and purpose unknown, this famous monument in Petra was carved out of a vertical red sandstone cliff about 2,000 years ago. It is fancifully referred to in modern times as al-Khaznah ("The Treasury").

route for caravans for centuries and is still used for Bedouin migrations; and Azraq Oasis—shallow pools and marshes forming the only permanent body of water in the Jordan desert—provides sanctuary for enormous flocks of migrating birds during the spring and fall along the great Levant flyway. Much of the north-central desert is a barren lava plain (see Map 11.1), a *hamadah*; angular lava boulders constitute the surface. (See Fig. 2.3 for a related *hamadah* in Syria.)

WATER: THE VITAL RESOURCE

As in other Middle East countries, Jordan's water balance is increasingly a high-priority national issue, not just in agriculture but also for human survival. It is entirely dependent on limited and variable winter rainfall, with no major rivers to dam or draw from (but see section on Yarmuk below), and no aquifers to bring artesian water from well-watered areas. The two perennial streams worth noting flow along a sensitive border—the Jordan on the west and the Yarmuk on the north.[16] With average annual precipitation generally less than 5 in/125 mm, Jordan's average annual water resources are about 875 mn m³, ranking it tenth among the world's water-poor states. Daily per capita consumption has averaged 85 liters per day recently and is declining—compared with 300 in Israel and 600 in Europe and America. Severe droughts, like the one that began in 2005, cause not only crop failures but also industrial emergencies and domestic water interruptions during the summer season.

Government projects and other various efforts to increase water supply and to conserve what is available involve controversial remedies and offer few long-term solutions. There has been one benefit: Because irrigation is the biggest consumer, farmers are required to use more efficient systems, particularly drip irrigation. Since Jordan's dependency ratio—the percentage of renewable water received from or shared with other countries (primarily Syria and Israel)—is about 23 percent, water-allocation agreements among the neighboring riparian states are critical. The Israeli-Jordanian peace treaty gives Jordan a specific allotment from the Sea of Galilee, designed to encourage cooperative efforts to develop, conserve, and expand water resources for both countries. The high variability of precipitation and stream flow, likely to increase with climate change, highlights the lack of a clear mechanism for sharing shortages and point to potential conflicts. Improved Syrian-Jordanian relations have revived cooperation on the Unity Dam on the Yarmuk, completed in 2006 after delays due to Israeli challenges and disputes between Jordan and Syria over allocations. While the dam increases storage capacity and electricity generation, it has been criticized for further damaging the Jordan River.

Drawing water from the Yarmuk, the King Abdullah Canal—usually called the East Ghor Canal—supplies about three-fourths of Jordan's irrigated area. Begun in 1959 and opened in stages between the 1960s and 1980s, it diverts Yarmuk water into a canal along the level *Ghor* between the floodplain and the eastern wall of the valley. This takes advantage of the greater hydraulic head at its elevation and uses Yarmuk water before it mixes with the much saltier and diminishing Jordan River water. By the mid-1980s, the canal had been extended, in three stages, to reach a length of 72 mi/116 km to the Dead Sea, and the irrigated area was steadily increasing (see next section).

ECONOMIC GEOGRAPHY

Independent Transjordan of 1946, soon to be overwhelmed with thousands of destitute refugees, faced bleak prospects. It had limited agricultural potential, minimal water supplies, virtually no developed resources, no industry, a very poor population, and a penniless government. But with moderate inflows of aid, vigorous effort from its inhabitants, and the stimulus from annexing the West Bank, the renamed Jordan developed into a politically and economically viable polity. It has achieved remarkable economic progress but still struggles with some of the same constraints. It exploits phosphate and potash resources (important exports), has an expanding manufacturing sector, promotes tourism, confronts high population growth, and participates in world organizations, international trade agreements, and regional schemes to share electric power.[17] In the late 2000s, it struggled with inflation and persistent budget deficits; as a result, it agreed with the International Monetary Fund to end subsidies on petroleum and several consumer goods, adding to the cost of living for most residents and possibly heightening the appeal of radical Islamic political groups.

Compared to most of its neighbors, Jordan enjoys the reputation of being less corrupt: Ratings agency Transparency International in 2009 ranked it 49th out of 180 countries globally and 7th in the region—behind only the Gulf states and the much richer Cyprus and Israel. The same is true considering the World Economic Forum's Global Competitiveness Index: Jordan is the region's 8th most competitive economy (behind only its much richer and more developed neighbors) and in 2009 ranked 50th of 133 countries globally. In the same vein, the Fraser Institute, a conservative

FIGURE 11.5 Irrigated citrus groves south of Karamah on East Ghor, Jordan Valley. The white structures in the distance are hothouses for producing early vegetables.

think tank, gave Jordan fairly high marks regarding economic freedom in 2008, ranking it 45th of 141 countries globally and 6th regionally, behind only the Gulf states and Cyprus.[18]

The Human Development Index (HDI)—calculated by the UNDP to allow comparisons of living standards on a global basis using measures of life expectancy, educational levels, and per capita income—in 2007 ranked Jordan 96th of 182 countries and 12th of the 16 included in this book. The HDI showed a significant increase—a gain of 22.2 percent since 1980 based on notable improvements in all three components of the index. Jordan used the UNDP method on a national basis to compute variation across governorates; urban Amman, Aqabah, and Irbid had the highest HDIs and rural Tafila, Mafraq, and Maan the lowest, but the spread between the highest and lowest was only 7.2 percent.[19]

Agriculture

Less than 5 percent of Jordan is arable; three-fourths of this area is rainfed, producing relatively low-yield crops of wheat and barley.[20] By far most food—and 90 percent of exported food—comes from irrigated lands, mostly in the valley. The exceptional climate there permits intensive production of such crops as citrus and bananas; specialty crops are grown in hothouses (Fig. 11.5). Although agriculture accounts for only 3.6 percent of GDP (2008) and employs only 2.7 percent of the labor force, it is still a significant sector of the economy—high-value horticultural products provide 6 percent of exports. Wheat imports, with the United States the biggest supplier, average 660,000 mt, since domestic production at best meets only one month of demand. With the heavy rainfall of 2001–2002, wheat production was 70,000 mt, compared to 12,000 mt in the dry following season. The prolonged drought that has gripped the region beginning in 2005 has hit hard at nonirrigated production; it has also emphasized the urgent need for determining which crops offer the greatest return per unit of water required. From about 1970 to the mid-2000s, food production per capita rose by more than 20 percent despite the handicaps under which the sector operates.[21]

Mining

Phosphates underlie extensive areas of Jordan, generally along the axis of the Hijaz Railway—almost 1 billion tons of high-grade phosphate rock. Since mining began in 1934, exports have steadily increased in response to growing world demand and higher prices. It is now among the world's four leading exporters, shipping more than 7 million tons annually to thirty countries, especially India. Production from the largest deposit—at al-Shidiyah, northeast of Aqabah—is being expanded to 7.5 mn mt per year and more if demand continues to be strong. The nearly exhausted al-Hasa and Wadi al-Abyad sites are being phased out. On the Dead Sea, Jordan opened a $425 million processing complex in 1982 to recover chemicals from brines. The plant is one of the world's largest, with output of 1.8 million tons of potash and associated bromine and magnesium annually. These plus phosphates constitute a major share of Jordan's exports.[22]

Despite fifty years of hydrocarbon exploration, findings have been scant. Of some fifty exploratory oil and gas wells drilled, only a few have yielded even meager output. The small Hamzah oil field, near Azraq, produces only 40 bpd, about one-tenth of its peak output in the mid-1980s. Modest natural gas resources have been developed in the Rishah area, near the Iraq border, where output powers one nearby power plant. British Petroleum was exploring further for gas near Rishah in 2009. In 2003, Jordan began importing natural gas from Egypt's increasingly abundant production by pipeline to a power plant in Aqabah. The line has been extended to Amman and northern Jordan, connecting to Syria's network and beyond. In 2001, Egypt, Syria, and Jordan inaugurated power lines that link their national electric grids; later linkages to the Lebanese and Turkish grids were added. Natural gas generates about 70 percent of Jordan's electricity, with oil powering nearly all the rest.[23] In 2010, Jordan signed an agreement with a French firm to begin uranium mining and began discussions with France about building nuclear power plants.[24]

Formerly fed by Saudi crude via Tapline but cut off in 1990, the Zarqa refinery (90,400 bpd capacity) was thereafter supplied for twelve years with Iraqi crude: Under dispensation from the UN embargo, Jordan transported its requirements 600 mi/965 km by highway from Iraq with a fleet of 1,600 tanker trucks because a more efficient pipeline could not be financed. After the invasion of Iraq in 2003, Jordan turned to Kuwait, Saudi Arabia, and the UAE for its needs. Ideally, Jordan could be supplied by Tapline deliveries; however, after years of disuse, the line needs extensive and expensive renovation, and since Jordan's daily requirements are only one-fifth of the line's capacity, startup and operating costs would substantially exceed benefits. Processing oil shale from the kingdom's considerable resources, perhaps up to 40 bn mt, could become a more attractive prospect as higher prices make it more nearly cost-effective; however, the existing technology for treating shale is rather water intensive and thus problematic for Jordan.[25]

Manufacturing and Trade

Better to accommodate the vast number of refugees, to emerge from a preindustrial agricultural economy after the 1950s, and to change from a rentier to at least a semirentier situation, Jordan sought diversification and the opening of appropriate manufacturing plants. Small and simple early enterprises produced processed foods, detergents, paper products, batteries, and similar items; they clustered around the Amman-Zarqa area, which soon added cement plants and the oil refinery. By the 1980s and 1990s, several larger and more complex plants opened in Irbid (diversified industries) and Aqabah (fertilizers, other chemicals), as well as in Greater Amman. Along with the Israel-Jordan peace treaty in 1994, followed by the 1995 Amman Economic Summit, the United States brokered formal economic relations between the two signatories in an effort to afford Jordan a tangible "peace dividend."

One consequence was the special Qualifying Industrial Zones (QIZs) with factories that would produce goods with partly Israeli-made content. Such goods would then be allowed free trade access, as formalized in a 2001 Free Trade Agreement (FTA), to the United States, the latter's first such agreement with an Arab country. Five QIZs were operating in 2009, but they have not been without controversy and opposition. Many plants operating in the zones are Indian- and Chinese-owned, and a considerable percentage of the workers in them are South Asian. There has been measurable benefit to Jordan, however, as exports to the United States have climbed sharply. Low-price items, like electronic components, textiles, and ready-made clothing, provided an 84 percent increase in exports to the United States between 2001 and 2002 alone.[26]

Light industrial exports are now the major driving force in Jordan's current economic growth, and exports are spurred by the growing number of trade arrangements. Not only QIZ products enter the U.S. tariff and quota free; nearly all goods and services are covered in the FTA. When the Jordan-European Union Association Agreement came into force in 2002, the parties began implement-ing an FTA over a twelve-year period. Jordan entered the World Trade Organization in 2000. Total exports have grown more than fivefold in the past fifteen years to an estimated $6.5 billion in 2008.

Transportation

Jordan's highway system satisfactorily serves the kingdom's needs. Along the basic routes earlier established, roads were significantly extended and upgraded during the 1980s and 1990s. The main north-south route is a well-engineered four-lane divided motorway that runs from Syria to Aqabah. Another highway extends northward from Aqabah through the Wadi Arabah and along the eastern shore of the Dead Sea; there is also a connector tying the main Baghdad highway to Azraq, Maan, and Aqabah.

The historic Hijaz Railway (or Pilgrim Railway), inherited from the Ottomans and made famous by the Lawrence of Arabia legend, has been upgraded, and passenger express rail service was opened between Amman and Damascus in 1999.[27] It is mostly used for freight and consists of narrow-gauge trackage. A similar link connects phosphate mines near Maan with Aqabah, where territorial exchanges with Saudi Arabia permitted extension of Jordan's coastline and expansion of the port. With extensive facilities for the export of phosphate rock and potash, Aqabah has expanded its capacity for handling general cargo and is a major link in Iraq's trade as well. In the late 2000s, Jordan announced plans for a major expansion of its rail network and began seeking some $6 billion in finance for the 671 mi/1,080 km effort. The north-south phase, scheduled to begin in 2010, will connect the Syrian system through Amman and Maan to Aqabah. An east-west line will run from Amman to the Saudi Arabian border, where it will link with that country's ongoing rail expansion program (see Chap. 14); a branch of this same line will also reach the Iraqi border.[28] A light rail metro system for the Amman-Zarqa area is also part of the plan, with the design contract due to be awarded in 2010.[29]

The kingdom's national air carrier, Royal Jordanian Airlines (RJA), is headquartered at Queen Alia International Airport, south of Amman, and operates about forty jets with worldwide routes. RJA plays a major role in the growing tourism sector, built around the country's archaeological treasures, such as Petra, Jarash, Umm Qais, Kerak, and Ajloun; resorts on the Gulf of Aqabah and the Dead Sea; and religious destinations like Mount Nebo, Madaba, Machaerus, and the Jordan River baptismal site. In 2008, Jordan saw 3.7 million visitor arrivals and, despite the global recession, was one of a very small number of countries to register a tourist gain in 2009. In the 2000s, Amman built a regional reputation as a medical center staffed by well-trained multilingual personnel; "medical tourism" saw an estimated 210,000 foreigners treated in private Jordanian hospitals.

Finances and Aid

During the mandate years, domestic finances were woefully inadequate. For decades, Jordan survived only as a rentier polity: Britain provided basic budgetary support through 1957, and then the United States became its main supporter. Saudi Arabia, Kuwait, and other Arab states rewarded the kingdom's role in the 1967 war with hundreds of millions of dollars in aid that promoted development during the 1970s and early 1980s. This support ceased when Husayn tilted toward Iraq, losing Jordan billions in remittances, trade, and services. With soaring unemployment, he acceded to U.S. pressure, signing a peace treaty with Israel in 1994. The "peace dividends" were limited but brought eventual improvement, as was explained earlier, but Jordan's graduation from semirentier status will take time.

Remittances from Jordanians working abroad have always been a major source of national income. In 2003, they were equal to 765 percent of export revenues and 337 percent of tourism receipts.[30] In 2009, they were expected to fall slightly because of the global economic situation, but still amounted to $3.8 billion, a fifth of GDP.

RELATIONS

Jordan has primarily followed a pro-Western foreign policy—sometimes to its disadvantage and with inevitable ups and downs. Close ties between mandate Transjordan and Britain continued after the polity's independence, and they continue still. Britain has regularly supplied aid, and in 1958 it sent paratroopers to the kingdom after the coup in Iraq. Beginning in the 1950s, the United States gradually became Jordan's main benefactor, providing more than $9 billion in military and economic aid through the late 2000s.[31] U.S. support helped preserve the kingdom when government forces and Palestinian *fedayeen* were battling in 1970–1971. Rapport slowed in the late 1970s when the perception was that the United States was buying Jordan's pliability in the Arab-Israel problem with minimum support, compared with tenfold greater aid to Israel. Improvements in the 1980s cooled in 1990 when King Husayn waffled on Iraq's Kuwait misadventure, but warmed after the mid-1990s when he formalized ties to Israel, devoting his last days to the peace process. Relations have been warm with Abdullah, who, however, had reservations about the invasion of Iraq. There has a been a steep price to pay for these close U.S. ties, however; in November 2005, an Iraqi al-Qaida cell carried out three coordinated and nearly simultaneous hotel bombings in Amman that killed some sixty people, mostly Jordanians and other Arabs.

U.S. development assistance began in the 1950s, and the U.S. Agency for International Development (USAID) still has an active program that in the past has ranged from fighting malaria to building water-treatment plants to supporting restoration at major tourist sites like Petra and Umm Qais. In the 2000s, considerable attention has gone to one of the most persistent problems—high unemployment; for example, to help create jobs, more than 175,000 microfinance loans have gone to small entrepreneurs, while others with slightly larger businesses have been trained in how to take advantage of the U.S. FTA and find export markets for their products.[32] Jordan has good relations with several European countries that have given appreciable aid. As mentioned above, Jordan has an Association Agreement with the EU[33] and a Jordan–United States FTA is being implemented.[34]

Jordan is not a prime mover in the Arab world, but it has periodically mediated and moderated frictions in the region. It is a founding member of the Arab League and is interlinked with its neighbors in economic, political, and cultural associations. Relations with Syria should be very close under geopolitical logic, but they have been bewilderingly uneven.[35] Saudi Arabia and Hashimite Jordan viewed each other with suspicion for several decades; however, the Saudis aided Jordan magnanimously during the 1970s and 1980s not only with monetary grants and crude oil through Tapline but also with small military forces. The break in 1990 over Saddam Husayn's aggression was mended after Abdullah's accession. Relations with Kuwait had been very close, with Kuwait supplying Jordan with hundreds of millions of dollars and employing 250,000 expatriate Jordanians/Palestinians, but aid ceased and the Jordanian expatriates (most in professional or semiprofessional capacities) were no longer welcome after Iraq's defeat. However, Kuwait reopened its embassy in Amman in 1999, signaling a return to normalcy.[36]

From the inception of the Transjordan and Iraq mandates in the early 1920s, relations between the two were special because

Hashimite brothers occupied both thrones. Successor Hashimite cousins briefly united the kingdoms in the Arab Federation in 1958, but this quickly collapsed when King Faysal II of Iraq was assassinated in a violent coup. Encouraged by the West and by its neighbors, Jordan established a symbiotic economic relationship with Iraq during the Iran-Iraq War and prospered from the transit of Iraqi imports and exports. This was one reason for Husayn's reluctance to judge Iraq in 1990;[37] during the Gulf War he straddled the fence by giving humanitarian aid to Iraq and quiet moral support to the coalition. When Abdullah faced much the same quandary in 2003, he avoided conflict with Iraq but cooperated with the coalition and quickly resumed economic links with Iraq by mid-2003. In August 2003, Jordan's embassy in Baghdad was bombed, leaving eleven dead. Nonetheless, it continued to assist reconstruction efforts—for example, by facilitating the training of more than 50,000 police cadets and corrections officers in Jordan. In 2008, a Jordanian ambassador returned to Baghdad to strengthen bilateral ties, and King Abdullah became the first Arab leader to visit Iraq since 2003.

Having had a close association with mandate Palestine, Jordan has believed it must maintain a relationship with Israel. Husayn pragmatically and realistically conducted clandestine contacts;[38] after the 1994 peace treaty, talks continued more openly. Despite fighting each other in two costly wars, their generally correct relations culminated in that treaty. Recent history has shown that Jordan—the buffer, the "land between" and "land beyond"—is in a geopolitical quandary: This Arab state in an Arab world must maintain multiple associations with that world while relating to its powerful neighbor Israel and to the West, and all parties must make the best of it. In 2008, tripartite talks among Jordan, Israel, and the World Bank revived the idea of a canal or pipeline carrying water from the Gulf of Aqabah to the rapidly shrinking Dead Sea, with electricity generation and desalination possibilities; a pilot project to test the feasibility of the controversial effort was announced in 2009.[39]

Finally, a major political consideration remains just as it was sixty years ago—the government's ability to balance its obligations to its Palestinian population, its indigenous East Bankers, West Bank Palestinians and the Palestinian Authority, the Palestinian diaspora, and other Arabs, as well as the United States and Israel. The earlier and once not unreasonable idea of a confederation between Jordan (the "East Bank") and the Palestinian Authority (the "West Bank") has now been overtaken by events. Jordan can only hope that extremist elements in Israel will not try to force it to accommodate, either gradually or in another catastrophe, the 4.5 million Palestinians from west of the Jordan River. Meanwhile, the kingdom continues to seek the equilibrium essential to its survival and prosperity.

NOTES

1. In addition to relying on extensive field research by author Held during more than a score of visits to Jordan over a period of forty years, *Jordan* Country Study 1991; Naval Intelligence Division 1943; Fathi 1994; Baly 1957; Orni and Efrat 1980; and Salibi 1998 (with a strong geographical approach) have been employed. See also www.nic.gov.jo/.

2. Useful for information on this period are G. Smith 1935; Naval Intelligence Division 1943; Baly 1957; and Aharoni 1974. A good recent history of Jordan is Robins 2004.

3. See Naval Intelligence Division 1943; M. Wilson 1987; Sachar 1976, 126–127; Yapp 1996, 139–143; Robins 2004; and Shlaim 1990.

4. These connections are the main subject of Shlaim 1990.

5. Talal bin Abdullah (1909–1972) abdicated for health reasons (probably schizophrenia) after a reign of only thirteen months. Queen Zein, his wife and mother of Husayn, was very influential during his reign and the early years of her son's.

6. L. Adams 1996, 527.

7. *Christian Science Monitor*, Oct. 30, 1997. A detailed study with a longer perspective is Lucas 2004.

8. Lengthy coverage, including extensive background material, is given in the *New York Times*, Feb. 8, 1999, with additional coverage on Jan. 26 and Feb. 6 and 19, 1999.

9. Greenwood 2003.

10. Tribalism is discussed at some length in *Jordan* Country Study 1991. See also Salibi 1998 and Fathi 1994. For a case study, see Jungen 2002.

11. The economic aspects of the split are examined in Reiter 2004.

12. See UNRWA Web site: www.un.org/unrwa/.

13. In addition to sources listed in note 1, see the old but classic G. Smith 1935.

14. An older but readable and well-done study on Petra is Browning 1977. Continuous excavations have produced numerous remarkable archaeological finds at the site during the past two decades.

15. And possibly of future importance: Turkey and Saudi Arabia have recently indicated an interest in rebuilding the line with standard-gauge tracks to link up with Saudi plans to connect Jiddah, Riyadh, and Medinah by rail (*Arab News* [Riyadh], Feb. 5, 2009; see also Chap. 14).

16. See Salameh 1990; Kolars 1990; Wolf 1995; El-musa 1997; *Water for the Future* 1999; and Soffer 1999. Jordan's increasingly alarming water problem is studied in Ferragina 2002.

17. Economic aspects are covered in Gubser 1983; the U.S. Department of State's *Country Commercial Guide: Jordan*, FY 2008, and *Background Note: Jordan*, Jan. 2010; *Jordan* Country Study 1991; U.S. Department of Energy, Energy Information Administration, *EIA: Jordan*, Apr. 2004; and *CIA World Factbook* 2009.

18. Transparency International 2009; World Economic Forum 2009a; Fraser Institute 2008.

19. United Nations Development Programme 2009; Ministry of Planning and International Cooperation, *Jordan Human Development Report, 2004: Building Sustainable Livelihoods* (Amman, Jordan).

20. This section on agriculture is partly from *Agricultural Situation Report: Jordan* 1997, 2004.

21. FAO, various issues. For Jordan, unlike the other countries in this study, the base years for this calculation were 1969 to 1971, after Jordan lost much of its agricultural land to Israeli occupation in 1967.

22. USGS, "The Mineral Industry of Jordan," in *Minerals Yearbook* 2008. Jordan is the world's third-largest bromine producer.

23. IEA, "2006 Energy Balance for Jordan," www.iea.org/country/index.asp.

24. *The Daily Star* (Beirut), Feb. 22, 2010.

25. For details of Jordan's minerals industries, see *Minerals Yearbook: Jordan* 1997; "Mineral Industries of Jordan, Lebanon, and Syria," in *Minerals Yearbook* 2008; EIA, *Jordan*, Aug. 1999 and Apr. 2004; and U.S. Department of State, *Background Note: Jordan*, Oct. 2004 and Jan. 2010.

26. The U.S. economic initiative, its progress in Jordan, and the QIZs are examined in P. Moore and Schrank 2003.

27. See note 15.

28. In 2003, thirteen Arab countries approved a railway linkage agreement that would be implemented by the end of the 2010s; the Jordan-Saudi Arabian and Iraqi-Kuwaiti lines would extend to the Gulf states.

29. See http://amman-metro.com/press/ for details.

30. *The Daily Star*, May 11, 2004.

31. See U.S. Department of State, *Background Note: Jordan*, Oct. 2004, Feb. 2009, and Jan. 2010, from which several aspects of this section are drawn, along with Greenwood 2003 and Lucas 2004.

32. USAID Mission/Jordan: http://jordan.usaid.gov/.

33. See EU, European Commission, External Relations Directorate, *Jordan Strategy Paper, 2007–2013* and *National Indicative Programme, 2007–2010*, http://ec.europa.eu/world/enp/pdf/country/2011_enpi_nip_jordan_en.pdf.

34. See www.ustr.gov/trade-agreements/free-trade-agreements/jordan-fta. Duties on nearly all traded products will be eliminated by 2010.

35. *Christian Science Monitor*, Apr. 23, 1999.

36. *New York Times*, Mar. 5 and Sept. 7, 1999.

37. The delicate position of Jordan at this time is discussed in Bouillon 2002.

38. The not-so-secret contacts are treated at length in Shlaim 1990.

39. *Jerusalem Post*, June 28, 2009.

12

Israel, Palestine, and Disputed Territories

Israel

Among the 124 states that have gained independence since 1943, 10 of them in the Middle East, Israel has generated an unprecedented level of international involvement, both in support and in opposition. Chapter 8 examines the Arab-Israeli conflict, the geopolitics of the Jewish state and of the territories it has occupied since 1967, and the problem of the use of names regarding these areas. This section focuses on Israel itself, followed by discussion of the local aspects of the Occupied Territories. In 2010, there was little certainty—even after more than sixty years—regarding the parameters of a Palestinian entity, and the disposition of the Golan Heights remained undetermined.

One of Israel's leaders once commented that Israel is in, but not of, the Middle East. It is, indeed, distinct by virtually every criterion—political, ethnographic, geographic, economic, military. The circumstances of its founding and early evolution kept it isolated, relating to its neighbors only in military operations for decades. Regionally perceived as a European nationalistic colony, the Jewish state was long a pariah to its Arab neighbors. Yet Israel has, with strong U.S. support, signed peace treaties with Egypt and Jordan, and off and on has had working relationships with other Arab countries. Conflict remains, however, with the Palestinians, Syria, and Lebanon.[1]

HISTORICAL NOTE

The long history of Palestine[2] holds a special significance for Christians and Muslims as well as for Jews because of biblical and Quranic associations with the land. For many Jews, the Old Testament accounts support modern Zionist claims to the land, whereas more recent history underlies the often conflicting claims of Muslims and Christians.

As outlined in Chapter 8, the Ottoman defeat in World War I was followed by British occupation of Palestine and the Trans-Jordan area and later by establishment of the British mandate under the League of Nations that simultaneously promised a Jewish homeland and the safeguarding of the rights of indigenous Palestinians. After absorbing thousands of Jewish immigrants, the mandate was theoretically partitioned by the United Nations in 1947. However, when the state of Israel was proclaimed on May 14, 1948, fighting erupted between Jews and Arabs; Israel—the Jewish-controlled area—expanded by 50 percent with the Arab defeat. The subsequent history is discussed in Chapter 8, and Israel's territorial evolution is shown in Map 8.5.

ISRAEL

Long-form official name, anglicized: State of Israel

Official name, transliterated: Medinat Yisra'el (Hebrew); Isra'il (Arabic)

Form of government: multiparty republic with one legislative house (Knesset)

Area: 7,886 mi^2/20,425 km^2 (de jure Israel; excludes occupied areas)

Population, 2008: 7,018,000; Literacy (Latest): 95.4%

Ethnic composition (%): Jewish 76.2; Arab and other 23.8

Religions (%): Jewish 76.2, of which "secular" ca. 33, "traditional" ca. 30, Orthodox ca. 7, and ultra-Orthodox ca. 6; Muslim (mostly Sunni) 16.1; Christian 2.1; Druze 1.6; other 3.9

Demography: Life expectancy—78.5 yr (M), 82.2 yr (F); Birthrate (per 1,000)—21.1; Fertility rate—2.90

GDP, 2009: Israel: $215.7 billion; purchasing power parity: $205.2 billion; per capita: $28,400; West Bank and Gaza: $6.64 billion; purchasing power parity: $11.95 billion; per capita: $2,800

Currency: Israeli shekel, US$1 = 3.732 shekels, 1 shekel = $0.268 (March 2010)

Energy reserves: oil—1.9 mn bbl; natural gas—1.08 tn ft^3; coal—nil

Main exports (% of total value, 2006): worked diamonds 27.7; machinery and apparatus 16.1; rough diamonds 6.7; medicines 6.4; professional/scientific equipment 2.9

Main imports (% of total value, 2006): machinery and apparatus 20.6; diamonds 18.9; chemicals and chemical products 11.2; crude petroleum 10.0; transport vehicles 5.6

Capital city: Jerusalem (seat of government) 729,100 (excludes East Jerusalem); other major cities: Tel Aviv–Yafo (agglomeration) 3,040,400; Haifa 267,000; Rishon LeZiyyon 221,500

VARIED LANDSCAPES

Regions and Climate

Long latitudinally and narrow longitudinally, the whole of historic Palestine is 265 mi/425 km long and 47 mi/76 km wide (Map 12.1). The irregular shape of Israel proper gives the narrowest corridor north of Tel Aviv a width of less than 10 miles. Although the territory is small, it straddles several climate zones, and with its contrasting landforms, it embraces a wide range of environments relative to its size.[3]

The area exhibits a simple regional pattern, with three parallel linear belts extending along a north-south axis (circled numbers on Map 12.1): [1] a moderately broad Mediterranean plain, [2] a wider arch of limestone hills down the center, and [3] the deep Jordan–Dead Sea–Arabah trench on the east. In addition, [4] the desertic Negev in the south is a complex area of cross-folds and basins, with a maximum elevation of 3,390 ft/1,035 m. In the north, the hills rise to 3,963 ft/1,208 m in Upper Galilee (the highest summit in all of historic Palestine); Jerusalem in the

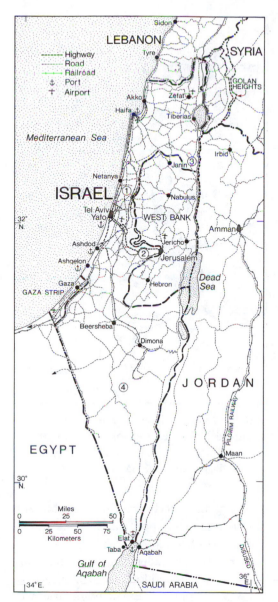

MAP 12.1 General map of Israel, with main transportation routes. Circled numbers indicate regions mentioned in text.

The latitude and climate are similar to those of southern California, with a Mediterranean climate (Koeppen Csa) phasing southward into low-latitude steppe (BSh) and desert (BWh). Although summers are hot and dry, with no rainfall, Tel Aviv on the Mediterranean coast is uncomfortably humid in August. Higher elevations are hot during the cloudless summer days, with low humidity, but are cool at night. January is comfortable in the lowlands but can be raw in the hills. Snow falls most years around Jerusalem and in Upper Galilee, occasionally heavily, and heavy rains may flood lower elevations. The coastal plain has a long crop season, and frosts are rare.

As in Syria and Lebanon, rainfall decreases from north to south and from the coast inland: Acre receives 26 in/650 mm, Tel Aviv 20.8 in/529 mm, Gaza 10.5 in/263 mm, and Elat only 1 in/26 mm. A site halfway up the western slopes of the Samarian Hills receives twice as much as one at the same elevation and latitude in the rain shadow on the eastern slopes. Agriculture in coastal areas has the bonus of 200 dew nights, which contribute an additional 1.2 in/30 mm of moisture. Much of the arable land has moderate to appreciable rainfall, with only the southern Negev and the southern Jordan Valley having actual desert climate.

Soils and Vegetation

The patterns of soils and vegetation in Israel/Palestine are, because of the area's varied environments, notably complex.[4] Characteristic *terra rossa* soils developed on most of the hard carbonates (limestone and dolomite) in the hills, but many soils have long ago been eroded away. Similarly, Rendzinas that formed on the softer carbonate outcrops (marls and chalks) east and west of the main *terra rossas* have also been seriously eroded. These losses have exposed bare rock, often exhibiting *lapies* (fluting and grooving by solution processes), the common hill landscape of the Holy Land.

central hills is at 2,500 ft/762 m. Eastern slopes descend to the Jordan Trench, with the Sea of Galilee at 692 ft/211 m below sea level and the Dead Sea at 1,385 ft/422 m below sea level. Water surface levels in both bodies vary, and the Dead Sea water level has lately been falling by more than 3.3 ft/ 1 m annually.

Alluvial soils dominate the Huleh and Jezreel valleys and much of the coastal plain, with *hamra* (red) clayey-sandy soils alternating with alluvials on the plain. Many basins in the uplands, especially in the Galilee and Samarian hills, contain alluvial soils derived from *terra rossas* and Rendzinas eroded from the slopes above. Productive loessal soils (loess is fine windblown material) occupy the Beer Sheva Basin and adjoin a belt of moderately fertile but dry steppe soil; however, the rest of the Negev has mostly sandy or stony desert soils, including *hamadahs*. Dark soils on basaltic lava occupy small areas north and southwest of the Sea of Galilee. Partly owing to reclamation work since World War I, the best agricultural areas are in the coastal plain and other plains areas, including the northern Negev, the plains and valleys of Jezreel and the Huleh, and the major basins.

The maquis, garigue, and *batha* vegetation (see Chap. 2) of the hills is the Mediterranean landscape most familiar to visitors. However, in Palestine three major phytogeographical zones meet—Mediterranean in more humid areas, desertic Saharo-Sindian in the southern Negev and the southern rift valley, and transitional Irano-Turanian in between—and display an exceptional variety of plants. About 2,500 plant species are known in Israel, compared with, for example, 1,700 in Britain. The vegetative landscape has been greatly modified over the past fifty years by the active Israeli planting of pine trees in the humid north and center and of eucalyptus trees on the lower slopes and plains, including the northern Negev. However, true desert areas remain quite barren, with widely scattered bean caper bushes, broom, and, where more moisture is available at depth, acacia trees.

Water

Water is crucial throughout the region. In Israel, planning and development rely on a high level of consumption of water, so water supply is of particular significance, involving

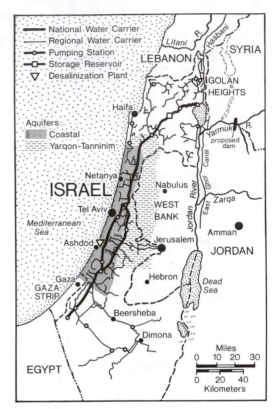

MAP 12.2 Water situation in Israel, the Occupied Territories, and adjacent areas. (Adapted from map in *Geographic Notes*, no. 13, U.S. Department of State)

not only major technical challenges but also significant social, political, territorial, and military controversies.[5]

Early Zionist leaders sought to maximize water resources and lobbied Britain successfully to extend the mandate boundaries well to the north to include the Sea of Galilee, Lake Huleh, and some of the Jordan's headwaters. However, they did not gain control over all these water sources, as some of the Jordan headwaters were apportioned to other mandates: for example, the much sought-after Lower and Upper Litani went to Lebanon (Map 12.2). With the conquest of the Golan and occupation of the West Bank in 1967, Israel gained much of what had been sought in 1919. While conquering and holding these areas has been justified in the name of national security, control of these water resources is a major factor.[6] Control led to the foundation of Jewish settlements in the occupied areas, slowly at first in the late 1960s and 1970s, then at an increasingly faster pace under Israeli governments of all political orientations.

Water is an increasingly contentious issue in any negotiations with Jordan, the Palestinians, and Syria.[7] One practical problem faced in these negotiations is that the city of Tiberias is dumping its sewage into the Jordan River, negatively impacting all downstream users—Israelis, Palestinians, and Jordanians alike. Israel is dependent on surface water and groundwater that originate outside its boundaries for more than half its water supply, a growing stress as per capita consumption increases and per capita resources decline in all the countries to which it is hydrologically connected.[8]

The Israeli government estimates total annual renewable resources to be 60 bn ft^3/1.7 bn m^3, an adequate amount for a Levantine country.[9] However, demand is so heavy that even with efficient use of all the water in the state and the occupied areas, Israel regularly consumes 95 percent of the resources. A growing population and ever-increasing water use inexorably signify that, as stated by an Israeli geographer, unless proper action is taken promptly, "Israel is on the threshold of a catastrophe."[10]

Some planners urge a serious de-emphasis of agriculture, which claims almost 60 percent of total water withdrawal. Industry—using just under 6 percent—has a much higher economic return per unit of water. However, the farm lobby is very powerful, and governments have so far considered it to be political suicide to decrease support of agriculture. However, water tariffs have been raised, and rationing has been imposed during critical shortages.[11] To maximize efficiency, Israel concentrates research, development, and planning on agriculture (see "Agriculture" below) and seeks to extend availability with processed effluents, saline water, and seawater. Two desalination plants are operating, and three more are due by 2012, despite their heavy energy use.

Coastal plain aquifers are extensions of strata underlying the West Bank, where they receive most of their water charge. Thus, allocation of underground water in the hill country is an issue of major contention between Jewish settlers and West Bank Arabs. Similarly, water sharing is a contentious issue in the comprehensive negotiations between Israel and the Palestinian Authority. Jewish settlers receive and use substantially more water per capita than do the indigenous Arabs, provoking the Palestinian claim that they are systematically deprived of their rightful share of water—or of any water at all—needed for their lands and villages.[12]

The state's biggest project was the National Water Carrier. Partly a canal, mostly a massive underground pipeline 8.86 ft/2.7 m in diameter, it runs from Tabagha on the Sea of Galilee to the Negev (see Map 12.2). Opened in 1964, the project spans 140 mi/225 km and can deliver nearly 400 mn m^3 per year, most of it during the summer months, from the water-surplus north to the water-deficient south. Drought years may reduce delivery to only 160 mn m^3, as in 1986 when the Sea of Galilee's level was 20 in/0.5 m below the acceptable minimum. A prolonged dry period extended through the 2000s; by 2009, the level was so critical that pumping was occasionally suspended. The relatively wet winter of 2009–2010 restored the lake level up to the lowest level of acceptability and, downstream, raised the Dead Sea level—which had fallen for thirteen consecutive years—but by only 3.1 in/8 cm.[13]

The Water Commission of Israel before 1967 controlled all sources within the existing boundaries; following occupation of the West Bank in 1967, it took over surface water and groundwater throughout the West Bank. Jewish settlements were linked to the National

Water Carrier, limiting Palestinian rights to water resources, including the Jordan River. Water use in the West Bank settlements is similar to, or even higher than, that within Israel proper, and of the approximately 75 mn m³ supplied to the settlements annually, about 60 percent comes from wells under Israeli control within the West Bank.[14] The Water Commission's power over withdrawals derives from government ownership of wells, and it controls not only the amount but also the location and allocation of withdrawals.

On the coastal plain, groundwater is pumped from shallow aquifers fed by moderate rainfall and runoff from the slopes to the east (see Map 12.2). It augments water piped from Galilee and the rehabilitated Yarqon River for urban consumption and intensive irrigation. Decades of overpumping have steadily depleted aquifers, despite increasingly efficient irrigation and vigorous recycling of urban wastewater back into the aquifers. With record dry conditions in the 2000s, warnings of the consequences of overuse became increasingly dire. As an Israeli water expert said, "The water crisis is entirely of our own doing. ... The government allocated funds for desalination plants but failed to allocate the resources for conservation."[15] What was billed as "Israel's worst-ever water pollution" was reported in 2010; it resulted from dumping rocket fuel and the remains of explosives by Israel Military Industries into the aquifer at Ramat Hasheron, a Tel Aviv suburb.[16]

POPULATION AND PEOPLES

Immigration

Zionism in the 1920s required a rapid increase in the *yishuv* ("settlement," the Jewish community) to create a Jewish majority by the end of the mandate period. Each stage of immigration—or Aliyah ("ascent," to Palestine)—added thousands of *olim* (ascenders), culminating in the Fifth Aliyah in the 1930s with the arrival of more than 250,000 as anti-

Semitism grew in Europe. Unrestricted immigration, essential to the Zionist program, was a serious problem for the British, who were as equally obligated under the Balfour Declaration to protect the rights of the native Arabs as they were to permit immigration. Palestinians saw the inflow as an invasion of European outsiders, displacing the indigenous population.

"Ingathering" After Independence.   With independence in 1948, Jews around the world were urged to come and fulfill the ideological goal of "the ingathering of the exiles." The resulting influx had long been anticipated, and exceptional organization permitted the flood of 686,748 arrivals by the end of 1951 to be processed, housed, and fed. Special operations by air brought in virtually entire communities. More than 121,000 of the 130,000 Jews in Iraq, descended from an ancient community dating to the Babylonian Captivity, were brought to Israel, as were 44,000 of the 45,000 Jews in Yemen. Another 810,000 came between 1952 and 1972.[17] Until the mid-1970s, immigrants constituted more than half of the population. The level fell over the next decade, but arrivals of Former Soviet Union (FSU) immigrants restored it to nearly 40 percent at the start of the new century. By then, the population had been drawn from more than 100 countries.

Immigration after independence diminished as the supply of would-be Israelis decreased and as word spread about the difficulty of life in Israel. Olim fell from 239,076 in 1949 to some 25,000–35,000 annually, while a new phenomenon—significant emigration, including *Sabras*, native-born Israelis—set in.[18] But emigration is difficult to quantify: Few who left officially declared their intention, and many Israelis have a second passport from their own or their ancestors' native country and simply return there; others leave as tourists and remain in their destination. In any case, no longer are emigrants stigmatized by their ex-countrymen as they were in the state's first decades, when they earned the derogatory designation *yordim* (those who "go down") for having done *yenda* ("descent"), the opposite of *aliyah*.

Jews from the Former Soviet Union. With the USSR's collapse, an opportunity to offset the growing departures came with the entry of large numbers of FSU Jews. Free emigration of Jews from the USSR had been demanded for more than twenty-five years, and the United States, pressed by Israel, had linked it to other negotiations with the Soviets. Once restrictions were lifted, about 350,000 poured into Israel between late 1989 and early 1992—peaking at 35,000 in December 1990. By 1992, when both Israel's absorptive capacity and the urge to leave the FSU had abated, immigration fell to one-third the peak.[19] Though arrival numbers decreased steadily over the next years, by 1999 nearly 900,000 had come. To accommodate them, Israel turned in 1992 to the United States for a $10 billion loan guarantee. In return, the new Labor government promised to reverse the policy of expanding Jewish settlements on the West Bank. However, settlement building soon resumed, as it had on previous occasions, and it continued through the 2000s, despite condemnation both within Israel and by the international community.

Immigration in the 2000s slowed, at least partly because of the second intifadah, dropping from 50,000 to about 14,000 in 2007, when it was exceeded by emigration—an estimated 20,000 that year. A report in 2008 indicated that half of official emigrants were FSU Jews.[20]

Present Population Structure

Immigration has created a unique multiethnic, multicultural, multilingual, and multireligious society, with a rich and complex structure and vigorous, if not always amicable, sociopolitical relationships within Israel.

The greatest numbers of immigrants have come from the FSU, Morocco, Romania, Poland, Iraq, and Iran. Many and diverse languages persist in Israel, reflecting both the immigrants' national origins and the perseverance of mother tongues: Russian (and other Slavic languages), Romanian, Western and Eastern Arabic, German, French, Spanish, Ladino (the language of Sephardic Jews), English, and Yiddish—hence, the great variety of periodicals seen on newsstands. In addition to language and sometimes costume, the wide range of physical characteristics—the Ethiopian features of Falashas, the southern Arabian appearance of Yemenis, and the blond, blue-eyed Germans—attests to the varied origins of Israelis.

Multicultures: Who Is a Jew?

In 1950, the Knesset passed the Law of Return, granting immediate citizenship to any Jew settling in Israel. However, the law's vagueness led to questions about the criteria for citizenship, and debate continues on the so-called "Who is a Jew?" question. Landmark court cases have narrowed but not resolved the issue. A 1970 amendment to the law included non-Jewish children, grandchildren, and spouses of Jews. Under the law, a Jew must have a Jewish mother or a mother converted to Judaism in accordance with traditional Jewish law (Halakhah) or must convert in an approved way. Those converted by non-Orthodox rabbis face barriers, as do some groups (e.g., Ethiopians) whose historic links with Judaism are questioned by religious authorities.

Religious practice is not required for citizenship. Studies show that approximately half of Israeli Jews are "nonobservant" or secular; however, ethnic Jews who have converted to another religion are not eligible for citizenship under the Law of Return. It is significant that family descent has become the standard, reinforcing the ethnicity of Jewishness. The influx of FSU *olim* brought, for the first time, thousands of non-Jews—Russians who envisioned greater promise in a more affluent society. Many of them were spouses, children, or grandchildren of acknowledged Jews. Some 25 percent of all FSU immigrants as of 1999 were not Jewish by *Halakah* standards; by the late 1990s, more than half of those arriving from the FSU were non-Jews, creating additional tensions regarding Russians.[21] A decade into the new century, the Russians remain a highly distinct group; many resist speaking Hebrew and vote for Russian-dominated political parties.[22] They are also subject to commonly-held negative stereotypes—for example, that they are disproportionately involved in criminal activities.[23]

Intergroup Conflicts. Imbued with European nationalism, secularism, and socialism, European Jews—the Ashkenazim (from the Hebrew for "Germany")—established a Zionist state defined in terms of European principles. With large-scale immigration, however, groups from other regions and cultures brought new and often very different political, social and religious concepts with them and tenaciously maintained them. The melting-pot idea dissipated. The unified monocultural Jewish society of the early Ashkenazi Zionists gradually became multidimensionally varied, transformed into a factionalized body politic and conversely a vigorous, stimulating society, on the other.

The cleavages—some abstruse—were ethnic: Ashkenazi/Sephardi/Mizrahi/Russian/Ethiopian/Arab; political: left/right/center; religious: ultra-Orthodox/Orthodox/Conservative/Reform/Kabbalist/secular; economic: rich/middle class/poor; philosophical: Western/Eastern and modern/traditional; and residential location: inside pre-1967 Israel/West Bank settlements. Cutting across all the above categories are hawkish/moderate/dovish orientations toward the peace process. All polarizations become acute in elections, when more than a score of parties contest for Knesset seats. Although cleavages should not be overemphasized, neither should they be underestimated. The Ashkenazi/Mizrahi, Jewish/Arab, and Orthodox/secular dichotomies are particularly important.

As immigration increased, Oriental Jews from North Africa, the Middle East, and southern Asia came to outnumber the Ashkenazim. Sometimes called "Sephardim" (from the Hebrew for "Spain"), and more recently (and more accurately) "Mizrahim" ("Orientals" or "Easterners"), for more than thirty years they integrated poorly into political and economic life; many were first sent to remote frontier settlements. By the late 1980s, they were 54 percent of the population but a far smaller proportion in upper employment and education ranks, and they saw themselves as "Jews in the form of Arabs," "imported" to outnumber Palestinian Arabs and as cheap labor for the elite Ashkenazim. The Sephardim/Mizrahim protested their second-class citizenship not only by demonstrating but also by voting against the historic liberal Ashkenazi establishment (Labor Party) for right-wing parties, but by 1992 they were also at odds with the Right as well.

Alienation and frustration are still serious problems, and some Ashkenazis worry that higher Mizrahi birthrates will combine with the even higher Arab birthrates to relegate European/North American Jews to an increasingly minor role. The Ashkenazis, largely secular in outlook, also face challenges from the growing number of ultra-Orthodox (Hebrew: *Haredim*), who have the country's highest birthrate. Mindful of the need to amalgamate groups from diverse cultural backgrounds, the government has relied heavily on service in the Israeli Defense Forces (IDF) for national integration. This is supplemented by intensive training in Hebrew for all *olim* and general education to "Israelize" the newcomers—which Mizrahim understand but resent when it means diminishing their historic cultural identity.

Broad historical, religious, and cultural differences underline the interethnic conflict between the majority Jews and the minority Palestinian Arabs.[24] Although most Palestinians fled in 1947–1949 (see Chap. 8), about 160,000 remained, with major concentrations in Galilee. With a high average birthrate, Arabs within Israel numbered more than 1.4 million in 2009, about 20 percent of the population. Distrust and resentment, as well as mutual preference for segregation, characterize contemporary Jewish-Arab attitudes, with some notable exceptions on both sides. Most Arab population centers are surrounded by "mirror" government-planned Jewish housing. Budget allocations (five times higher for Jewish communities than for Arab ones) and government grants to municipalities (three times higher for Jewish municipalities) have led to inequities in housing, economic development, education, employment, welfare, and general services.[25] Arab university graduates have difficulty finding suitable employment. Even so, entrepreneurial Arabs have developed small industries in Arab areas, and some have become reasonably successful (see Map 12.3).[26] The common belief that Israeli Arabs have lower incomes on average than Jews is difficult to show statistically, but they are demonstrably at a disadvantage as regards health care: In 2001, average life expectancy for Arabs was 3.5 years less than for their Jewish fellow citizens.[27]

Many Israeli Jews call for equal treatment of Israeli Arabs and for mutual tolerance. But there are also many Jewish extremists, such as the Kach Party's founder, the late U.S. rabbi Meyer Kahane, who openly expressed determination to "cleanse" Israel of all Arabs.[28] A similar stance is taken by the right-wing Yisrael Beytenu (Israel Is Our Home) party, supported in the 2009 election by many "Russians" and afterward a major partner in the coalition government.[29]

In the late 1980s, the "New History" debate emerged among Israeli intellectuals and led by young historians who examined official documents from the 1940s and 1950s that had been declassified in the 1980s.[30] They argued that many events around the birth and early evolution of the state had long been misrepresented for nationalistic reasons, reporting distortions about, inter alia, the motivations of early Zionist leaders, the 1948–1949 war, and the onset of the Palestinian refugee problem long embedded in the "mythology" of Israel's early years. Their reinterpretation of traditional historiography had a major impact on the country and on Jews elsewhere in the world.[31] In the late 1990s, some Israeli schoolbooks were rewritten to incorporate the revised history, and *Tkuma* (Rebirth), a twenty-two-part television series produced for the fiftieth anniversary celebration, included many New History segments.[32]

Another fiercely debated topic concerns Israel as a "Jewish and democratic" state, as stated in the Basic Laws (which continue to serve in place of a formal constitution). The subject has been taken up by Israelis opposed to the indefinite continuation of de facto rule over the Occupied Territories where the number of voiceless Palestinians will soon equal the Jewish population in Israel and the Occupied Territories combined. Even within Israel's pre-1967 boundaries, non-Jews are more than 20 percent of the population. In a democracy, all citizens are equal before the law, but in many ways this principle does not hold true for Israeli Arabs on a day-to-day basis. For example, Arab municipalities are funded at a much lower level than Jewish ones, and land owned by the state and the Jewish National Fund (JNF) is available only to Jews. In early 2010, legislation was moving forward in the Knesset allowing towns to exclude certain kinds of residents while requiring Arab members of the body to swear allegiance to Israel as a Jewish state.[33] Respected jurist and former chief justice of the Israeli Supreme Court Aharon Barak argued in 2009 for a state both Jewish and truly democratic: "Only a national home

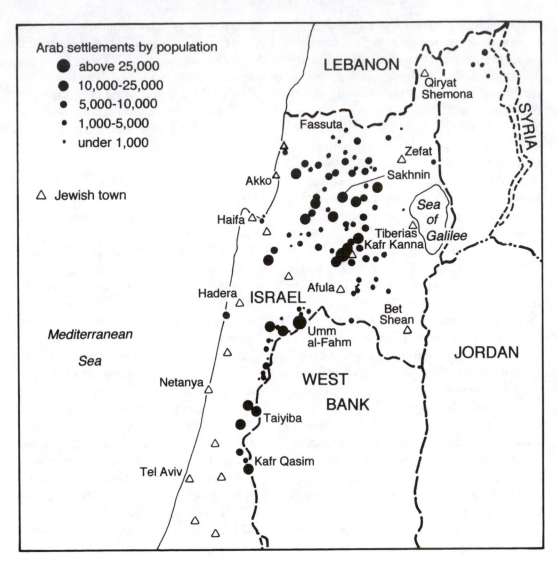

MAP 12.3 Areas of continued Palestinian Arab settlement in Israel, indicating centers of Arab manufacturing enterprises. (Adapted from Izhak Schnell, Itzhak Benenson, and Michael Sofer, "The Spatial Pattern of Arab Industrial Markets in Israel," *Annals* [Association of American Geographers] 89, no. 2 [June 1999]: 312–337. Used with permission.)

built on foundations of equality and respect for the individual can endure over time. Only a state that relates in an equal manner to all its children can win acceptance in the society of freedom-loving nations. Only a society based on principles of equality can live in peace with itself."[34]

Religions and Religious Frictions.   In 2008, 76 percent of the population were Jews and 16 percent were Muslims, mostly Sunni. Frictions between Jews and Muslims (and Christians) are grave enough, but frictions among Jewish groups are more serious and sensitive. Somewhat as in Lebanon, religious communities, sects, and subsects are critical per se and determine governmental structure, as elections repeatedly demonstrate.

Debate between religious conservatives and liberals, evident in diverse religious groups throughout the Middle East, is particularly intense in Israel. Noteworthy, in view of the crucial support given Israel by the U.S. Jewish community, is the rift between Conservative and Reform Jews—the great majority in the United States—on the one hand, and Israeli Orthodox rabbis, on the other. Orthodox leaders reject conversions, weddings, and other rites performed by non-Orthodox rabbis, a position opposed by more liberal U.S. Jews, who favor a more pluralistic Jewish society. In 2009, an Israeli woman was arrested while reading from a Torah scroll to a group of Conservative women at the Western Wall, thereby infringing on rules enforced there by the Orthodox Rabbinate.[35] Similarly, the imposition of gender segregation by Haredim on bus routes primarily serving their neighborhoods in Jerusalem provoked demonstrations by secular women in 2010.[36]

Public confrontations between Haredim and secular Israelis seemed to occur with increased frequency in the 2000s. Haredim seek to impose religious law on all phases of life, while secular citizens demand freedom of choice. Secular groups also oppose rising amounts of government subsidies to ultra-Orthodox sects. Many Haredim emphasize spiritual redemption and reserve Hebrew only for religious purposes: Some sects even oppose Zionism, completely eschew political participation, and believe a Jewish state must await the coming of the Messiah (*Moshiach*). Other groups believe that the Torah (the Pentateuch) supports Jewish claims to the land of Israel and participate in the state's political life.

Adherents of two ancient sects outside mainstream Judaism also live in the state. Karaites, as many as 25,000 mostly around Ramla, Ashdod, and Beer Sheva, reject the Oral Law of rabbinic Judaism, holding only to what is written in the Torah. Some sources trace their origin to the Saducees, the opponents of the Pharisees, the progenitors of rabbinic Judaism. Most Orthodox consider Karaites to be Jews according to the Halakhah, but controversies remain, partly because they are patrilineal in defining Jewishness, unlike matrilineal descent in the mainstream. A much smaller and more ancient group is the Samaritans, whose break with historic Judaism dates to King David's decree that all temple worship must be in Jerusalem. Claiming a direct link to those Israelites not taken into exile in Babylon and maintaining their own sacred site on Mount Gerizim, they have dwindled to fewer than 725, divided between the Tel Aviv suburb of Holon and a village on Mount Gerizim in the West Bank.

Religions of Non-Jews. Of the non-Jews in Israel, most are Arabs, of whom four-fifths are Sunni Muslims. Recognized as a separate group since 1957, the 120,000 Druze stand out because many remained through the hostilities in both 1948 (in Galilee) and 1967 (in the Golan); many serve in the Israeli Defense Forces. A few thousand Shii who came from Lebanon several decades ago dwell in the north, along with a few hundred Alawis. About 3,000 Circassians, non-Semitic Muslims with their own language, live primarily in two Galilee villages, Kafr Kama and Rihaniya, and also serve in the IDF. The eclectic Bahai, with origins in Shiism, have their impressive world center on Mount Carmel, overlooking Haifa, but have only a few hundred members of varied ethnic backgrounds.

Because of the close ties between Christianity and the Holy Land, at least thirty different Christian sects, representing many nationalities, are found in Israel. They congregate in Jerusalem and the Galilee, maintaining centuries-old churches, monasteries, hostelries, and schools. But the approximately 140,000 Christians in official figures are mostly Arabs; there are also perhaps 25,000 Europeans and Americans, many connected with ecclesiastical or charitable institutions.

Harder to classify are as many as 300,000 aliens, some with work permits but many illegal; they are largely from Asia, the Balkans, and Latin America and include Christians, Hindus, and Buddhists. As many as one-third of the FSU emigrants (or another 300,000) are not Jewish by religion, ethnicity, or tradition; unless they undergo conversion according to Halakhah, their personal status is ambiguous.

Nearly three-fourths of indigenous Christians are Greek Orthodox and Greek Catholics. Roman Catholics, third in number, have a patriarch in Jerusalem and supervise many of the Christian holy sites. A bewildering variety of other Christian denominations maintain at least small congregations in the Holy Land. Anglicans and Lutherans have had a long-time presence. Draft laws have been submitted to the Knesset to make proselytizing among Jews by Christian groups illegal, and so-called Messianic Jews face great difficulties on a daily basis. A U.S. State Department 2009 report was critical of the status of religious freedom in Israel, citing, inter alia, the situation of non-Orthodox religious Jews, non-Jewish FSU emigrants, and Christians, as well as the lack of protection accorded by the state to sacred sites of Christians and Muslims (of the 137 recognized such sites, all are Jewish).[37]

SETTLEMENTS

Settlement patterns are particularly relevant because of the quintessential role of settlement of the land in Zionist ideology. They are also significant in the landscape's rapid transformation and because of the unique aspects of settlement preplanning, design, functions, and interrelations with inhabitants. The societal organization foreseen by planners called for collective and cooperative rural settlements. *Olim* of similar cultural background were assigned to the same settlement to maximize group effort, and the land, owned by the JNF, would be leased to the group, not individuals.

Three Rural Types

Three rural settlement types evolved: the kibbutz, moshav, and moshav *shittufi* (collective moshav). The kibbutz, the first of which was established in 1921, is a commune based on agriculture but with the potential to become an industrial collective. Eventually numbering more than 300 (down by 2008 to 256 with a population of 106,000), kibbutzim became one of the two main forms of Jewish rural settlement. Originally communes in every respect—holding land and other property in common, with a common mess hall and child-care center—the kibbutz was a great attraction. But as society evolved, kibbutzim became less communalized, and few now dine or care for children in common. Some are still agricultural, but many now earn income in other ways—polishing diamonds, producing electronic goods, maintaining tourist facilities, or by serving as commuter towns near major cities.

The moshav is a smallholders' cooperative settlement, on JNF or government land, in which each family has an individual home and a plot of ground to work (Fig. 12.1). Marketing of produce, however, is done cooperatively. Moshavim became the main rural settlement type and in the late 2000s numbered about 400 with a total population close to 210,000. The moshav *shittufi* combine features of the moshav and the kibbutz: Members have individual homesteads but conduct agriculture and economy as a collective unit. Two other agricultural settlement types, the *moshava* and *moshav ovdim*, are found in limited numbers. A new form of rural settlement is the *yeshuv kehilati*; numbering 107 in 2008, their members live independent economic lives, usually working outside the community.

FIGURE 12.1 Margaliyot, 1958 and 1990. A moshav founded in 1954 on a dramatic site on the Galilee Heights overlooking the Huleh Valley, Margaliyot replaced the old Arab village of Hunin, ruins of which are seen in the background (*top*). By 1990, the moshav had been largely rebuilt two or three times, and Hunin had virtually disappeared (*bottom*). It was even more changed in 1997, but bad weather prevented photography.

Urban Planning

Of more than 650 Arab villages before and during the mandate years, 394 were destroyed by the Israelis in 1948; only a modest number remain within Israel's pre-1967 boundaries. Many had few residents after the flight and expulsion of Palestinian refugees in 1947–1949; many occupied villages were sequestered by military authorities after independence. Since these sites usually had locational assets—water supply, good soil, defensibility, transportation—new Jewish settlements were usually built adjacent to or atop them (Fig. 12.1).

Despite the early Zionist emphasis on rural settlement, the flow of immigrants to towns made urban planning also necessary. New separate quarters for Jews were established outside the older sections of existing towns as far back as the late 1800s, and in 1909 the new town of Tel Aviv, the planned modern hub of the state, was founded north of Jaffa. New designed extensions of Haifa and Jerusalem followed. Major institutions and monuments were planned for hilltop sites in Jerusalem: Hebrew University, the Knesset, other government buildings, memorials, and similar structures. The government built high-rise apartments in strategic locations around East Jerusalem after Israel took the West Bank in 1967 and in a controversial move extended the municipal boundaries of the city.

The Jewish Quarter inside the Old City of Jerusalem was largely cleared of centuries-old houses and rebuilt after 1967; one large block was bulldozed for the Wailing Wall plaza. As in many historical cities worldwide, construction has often occurred at the expense of traditional architecture and communities. In Haifa, several sites on Mount Carmel became Jewish residential areas, resorts, and institutions, including two universities. As nearly 1 million *olim* poured into an already densely populated Israel during the 1990s, urban housing was in short supply and consequently became more expensive. New apartment buildings were built taller, while in West Bank settlements individual houses were erected by the thousands to attract residents; most Israelis, however, preferred the greater certainty of towns inside Israel proper.

ECONOMIC PATTERNS

A General Economic Perspective

Israel's economic distinctiveness is as marked as its political and religious differentiations. Initial planning, including economic planning, predated the immigration that began at the turn of the last century. The base institution was the World Zionist Organization (WZO), founded in 1897 at the First Zionist Congress. The JNF (Hebrew: Keren Kayemeth Leisrael, familiar as KKL) was founded in 1901 to obtain and manage land for Zionist colonies. The Keren Hayesod was founded in 1920 as the main Zionist international fund-raising agency; the United Jewish Appeal serves this function in the United States. The Jewish Agency, founded in 1919, served as an informal government under the mandate, and it continues, along with WZO, to work hand in hand with the government.

Specialized planning and research agencies coordinated virtually every phase of the economy before the major socioeconomic changes of the 1990s. Similar planning addressed defense, science, education, and the arts. All this rested on interlocking national institutions (government, JNF, Jewish Agency) and the central labor organization (Histadrut), which until its status declined in the mid-1990s controlled not only labor activities but also industries and economic institutions. Although lacking petroleum resources, this diverse base led to a society that, with the advantage of billions of dollars yearly in aid, achieved the most advanced and balanced economic development and the highest general standard of living in the region.

Success was also based on the complex politico-economic agreements that Israel has made with the EU, Turkey, and other states, now including Egypt and Jordan, as well as with the United States. Israel's transformation into a developed economy is seen in its accession to membership in the Organization for Economic Cooperation and Development (OECD—the "rich countries' club") due in 2010;[38] however, Israel has been warned that it must step up its anticorruption efforts to meet OECD standards.[39]

More economic stimulus came from the FSU immigrants—highly trained producers and eager consumers. The peace treaties with Egypt and Jordan and apparent progress on agreements with the Palestinians and Syria converged to produce a boom during the 1990s. Israel's regional isolation has eased, and aid from the United States, Jewish organizations, and individual donors continues in large amounts. These resources maintain not only its high per capita GDP but also its military-industrial complex, ambitious technological research, and development more characteristic of a world power (information technology, nuclear weapons and energy, space technology, missiles and antimissile weapons, and biological and chemical technologies), a wide-ranging intelligence and diplomatic agenda, massive welfare programs, and an extensive bureaucracy.[40] In the 2000s, after a slowdown brought on by the second intifadah and troubles in the high-technology sector, the economy recovered and grew at a robust average of about 5 percent annually until 2008. The global recession at the end of the 2000s hit hard at diamond and high-technology exports, and tourism was also negatively impacted.

The business environment in the 2000s is facing a growing perception of high-level corruption, culminating in the spectacle at the end of the decade of both the previous prime minister and the previous president facing criminal charges. These events were only the latest in a long series of trials involving ministers from all parts of the political spectrum, as well as senior municipal officials and civil servants and have been particularly damaging to the business climate domestically[41] and internationally. Over the decade Transparency International's annual Corruption Perceptions Index (CPI) has shown steady erosion for Israel both in its CPI value and its relative ranking; as indicated above, the OECD has recently indicated its concern in this regard. Additionally, according to the World Economic Forum, Israel has been losing some of its competitive edge; using the WEF's Global Competitiveness Index, Israel has seen a slow decline and in 2009 was only 3rd in the region and 27th of 133 countries rated globally. On the other hand, the Fraser Institute has found a steady increase in economic freedom in Israel (its index value rising from 4.92 in 1970 to 6.63 in 2006); still, it ranked only 8th in the region behind Egypt and just ahead of Iran, and 76th of 141 countries globally.[42] A World Bank study on the ease of doing business was more favorable in assessing Israel—2nd in the region and 29th globally.[43]

Another problem, usually seen as political—the settlements in the Occupied Territories—has strong economic implications as well. Because the costs of building and maintaining the settlements have been spread out among a plethora of budget categories, it is difficult to put an exact figure on how much revenue goes to support them.[44] One study estimated that through 2003, the nonmilitary total ran to $10 billion; another has put the annual figure in the 2000s at some $550 million, with additional military expenditures of $350 to $500 million yearly. Settlers are subsidized with low-cost housing and utilities—and, until recently, with tax breaks—and any government that seeks to change four decades of settlement policies faces vested interests of some 500,000 highly vocal and organized constituents. On the other hand, the cost of subsidizing the settlements is borne by the rest of the country, and as was recently pointed out by the Israeli Central Bureau of Statistics, the settlers enjoy family incomes 10 percent above the national average and have an unemployment rate 1.5 percent below the average.[45]

Agriculture

In the original Zionist plan for Palestine, agriculture was not just a routine economic activity or a necessity to provide employment and food to the immigrants. Above all, it represented an ideological and mystical bonding of the Jewish people to the Land of Israel. Nevertheless, the practical side of farming was very much emphasized, with stress on research, experimentation, and efficiency. Thus, Israeli agriculture has become the region's most scientifically planned, organized, systematized, modernized, and mechanized, ranking among the most productive in the world.

The range of crops, however, differs little from that in other Mediterranean lands. As in Lebanon, citrus is prominent: along with grapefruit, the famous Jaffa oranges grown for centuries on the coastal plain supply one of Israel's most recognized exports. Market-oriented horticulture is especially highly developed, systematized by area, growing techniques, and exact dates so that specialty crops can be rushed to European markets earlier than those from other areas. In the relentless quest for maximum yield from each unit of land, agricultural researchers have promoted new varieties of plants, use of best patterns of planting (such as growing tender crops on gentle slopes for cold air drainage), and, above all, maximizing water efficiency (including use of slightly saline water or purified effluents) and drip irrigation—which was invented by Israelis—to apply water and liquid fertilizers. As has been mentioned above, tightening water constraints are the biggest threat to agriculture; even the most

optimistic projections for efficiency gains indicate that the state will have to rethink and radically revise historic agricultural policies. Many crops now grown are too water intensive and will inevitably be phased out (some quite soon). From the early 1960s to the mid-2000s, per capita food production increased by about 9.5 percent, a relatively small gain that reflects the comparatively high level of agricultural technology already employed in the 1960s base period.[46]

As with crops, the dairying, fishing, and forestry sectors are also scientifically planned and conducted. For example, the milk yield of dairy cows is the highest in the world. In forestry, more than 115 million trees have been planted in forests and woodlands as well as along roads, in windbreaks, and along frontiers and in other security areas.

Whereas virtually all Jewish agriculture is institutionalized and cooperative, Arab farms, located primarily in Galilee, are generally individual and traditional. Lacking the technological assistance and funding given the Zionist rural communities and without access to Jewish marketing cooperatives, they remain less mechanized, more conservative, less prosperous, and more subject to water problems. About 170,000 Bedouin pastoralists in the Negev have resisted settlement in an effort to preserve their traditional way of life. However, increasing numbers have shifted to sedentary living and have surrendered their *dirahs* for use as airfields, settlements, and mining areas.

Mining and Energy

Mining activity has two major foci: phosphates mining and Dead Sea water evaporation. A third focus is technically a mineral industry: production of cut and polished diamonds, which provides a leading export. In the early 2000s, modest discoveries of natural gas offshore from southern Israel and Gaza suggested an extension of Egypt's rich gas reservoirs north of the Nile Delta. Since 2003, a pipeline from one offshore field has fed a gas-fired power plant in Ashdod. A promising find about 60 mi/97 km off west of Haifa was reported in 2009, and while its extent is still under evaluation,[47] early indications were that it could supply the country's needs for up to twenty years.[48] After resolving several problems, not all political, Israel and Egypt built a gas pipeline from Arish in Sinai to Ashqelon; deliveries started in 2008 and are expected to reach more than 60 bcf (billion cubic feet)/1.7 bcm (billion cubic meters) per year. Onshore oil resources are negligible, and the only known onshore hydrocarbon deposit of potential interest is oil shale in the northern Negev, where there may be more than 1 bn mt. Meanwhile, 99 percent of oil imports come from several sources—increasingly from Russia and the Caspian Basin. Utilizing Israel's two-sea location is a 42-in/107 cm oil pipeline (Trans-Israel Pipeline—Tipline) with a 400,000 bpd capacity that connects Elat on the Red Sea with Ashqelon on the Mediterranean, permitting tankers to bypass the Suez Canal (see Chap. 6).

As a heavy energy consumer, Israel exploits a range of sources. It is a world leader in solar technology, and 80 percent of homes have solar panels on their roofs to heat water. In 2006, about 70 percent of the country's electricity was generated using coal, 18 percent using gas, and the rest oil. Gas is gradually supplanting coal and oil. The coal-fired plants required 12 mn mt of imported coal yearly, about half from South Africa; these plants add to local pollution. Israel has studied the possibility of building a nuclear power plant in the Negev; in 2009, it had reportedly requested U.S. approval, indicating it would allow international inspection of the proposed plant, but not of its "other nuclear capabilities," referring to the nuclear weapons facility at Dimona (see "Manufacturing" section).[49]

Israel's major subsurface mineral resource is phosphorite (phosphate-bearing rock),

MAP 12.4 General and economic map of Israel, without transportation routes, which are shown on Map 12.1.

part of the great regional belt of late Cretaceous phosphates. Extensive open-pit mining of high-grade ore is concentrated in the northern Negev, where Oron is the main center (see Map 12.4). Phosphate production of 3.1 mn mt in 2007, third in the region after Syria and Jordan, was shipped by rail to Ashdod for export.

Evaporation of Dead Sea water in extensive ponds at Sedom at the lake's southern end yields large quantities of bromine, potash, and magnesium chloride, plus smaller amounts of other chemicals. Israel is normally the world's second-largest producer of bromine and bromine compounds and sixth-largest producer of potash. Continued evaporation, combined with curtailed inflow of the Jordan River, is drying up the southern third (Map 12.4): a third of the lake's previous surface area has been lost since 1960 as the water level has dropped an incredible 75 ft/22.9 m.

Manufacturing

Even more than agriculture, manufacturing differentiates Israel from its neighbors in organization, scope, technical level, and marketing. In spite of a limited resource base and dependence on imported energy, its industrial development is by far the most diversified and technologically advanced in the region. Expertise brought by European and FSU immigrants, along with imported technology and research and engineering advances in Israel, yielded rapid development. Early industries produced basic items: processed food and beverages, textiles, clothing, and similar light articles. Increased population, with its notable "brain gain," and transfers of both capital and technology, led to far more complex production than Israel's age as a state and its population, size, geographical area, and resource base would otherwise suggest. Research in universities and elsewhere—especially at Technion, the Weizmann Institute, the Soreq and Dimona nuclear facilities, the Nes Ziyyona Israel Institute for Biological Research, and several military research facilities—has carried scientific and industrial technology well beyond that learned from immigrant researchers and outside sources.[50] Five Israelis—three scientists and two economists—were awarded Nobel prizes in the 2000s, and the country is among the top five globally in patents granted per capita.

With a diversified, technologically advanced economy, Israel specializes in high-technology electronic and biomedical equipment, optical and other precision goods, safety and security items, and military equipment. Its computer software and hardware industry has boomed just as competition from cheaper Asian sources has undercut polished diamonds, long one of the most important exports. In the global arms trade, it ranks fourth in the world. Although the Israel Aircraft Industries (IAI), partnered with South Africa, failed in the mid-1980s to meet a commitment to produce the Lavi fighter aircraft in which the United States had invested nearly $1.5 billion, IAI did produce a Lavi-type aircraft and then reportedly sold its electronics system to China. The United States objected to that sale and again in late 1999 when IAI sold sophisticated radar systems, also to China.[51] IAI produces combat and civil aircraft as well as armored cars, missiles, patrol boats, and similar military items. Specific armaments exports include the Uzi submachine gun, missiles, artillery shells, armored vehicles, and naval craft.

Israel's most famous weapons plant is the Dimona nuclear facility, built secretly in the mid-1950s with French assistance. The uranium found in the nearby phosphorite rocks is supplemented with ore imported from South Africa. Indeed, it collaborated with South Africa on nuclear weapons development; the partners may have tested a weapon in 1979.[52] Israel's nuclear capability and possession of a sizable number of nuclear devices were revealed in 1986 when Mordechai Vanunu, an Israeli former technician at Dimona, gave photographs and details of the underground operations to a London newspaper.[53] As a member of the exclusive nuclear club—although refusing to sign the Nuclear Nonproliferation Treaty—the Jewish state is far more technically advanced and militarily powerful than any of its neighbors or many industrialized states.[54]

The main concentration of industry is along the coast from Haifa to Ashdod; outliers are Ashqelon and the Negev centers of Beer Sheva, Dimona, Arad, Sedom, and Elat. Haifa has the greatest single concentration, including oil refining, chemicals, fertilizers, shipbuilding, and more (see Fig. 7.1). Tel Aviv has a variety of lighter industries, and IAI, the state's largest employer, operates near Ben Gurion Airport.

Most domestic production comes from large enterprises. Most are either state owned or owned jointly by government and quasi-government agencies, though some privatization has occurred. A growing proportion comes from small establishments; many develop in kibbutzim turning from agriculture to light industry. Manufacturing is increasingly dispersed, both for security and for local employment reasons, into and around small settlements literally from Dan to Beer Sheva.

Transportation

Palestine has long been a land bridge; by contrast, independent Israel was largely isolated within its boundaries until the border with Egypt opened in the 1980s and with Jordan after 1994. Traffic flow with both neighbors is still limited, although increasing. In any case, Israel recognized that isolation before 1980 underscored the necessity of good air and sea connections with the outside world, and it vigorously maintained them. It has also developed in its limited territory an effective integrated domestic transportation system; although traffic around Tel Aviv has strained facilities, upgraded mass transit is easing the problem. Urban as well as intercity bus operations are frequent and exceptionally efficient. The Negev corridor to the head of the Gulf of Aqabah gives it an outlet to the Red Sea and on to the Indian Ocean, and it serves as a land link between the Red Sea and the Mediterranean (Map 12.1). Israel has plans for a railway over that link, used since 1968 for the Tipline, but this is a project for

the mid-2010s at the earliest. Conversely, the Negev triangle, with its apex at the head of the Gulf of Aqabah, divides the Arab states of the Fertile Crescent from those of North Africa, a matter of immense economic and strategic significance.[55]

Highways. North of Beer Sheva, Israel maintains an extraordinarily dense road net that is entirely paved, and heavily traveled sections east and north of Tel Aviv are divided throughways (Map 12.1). The main north-south trunk route extends southward from the Ladder of Tyre, north of Akko (Acre) in the northwest, along the coastal plain through Haifa, Tel Aviv, and Ashqelon to Gaza, cutting southeastward across the Negev to Elat. A parallel north-south route 30 mi/48 km to the east runs from Metullah at Israel's northern tip down the west side of the Jordan rift to Elat. Similarly, a main-crest road runs the length of the occupied West Bank hill country; other hill country roads are also integrated into the highway net of Israel. In the early 2000s, an ambitious plan for a 190 mi/300 km trans-Israel multilane freeway down the coastal plain was adopted, and large parts of it are now in service. Excellent though the present highway system is, the great density of population and the high standard of living had overcrowded the roads with more than 1.6 million vehicles by 2008.

Railways. Rail lines have been used primarily for transporting heavy bulk freight—such as phosphates and other minerals, grains, fuel, and citrus. However, they are increasingly carrying passengers in the central metropolitan area. Building on the modest rail net of the British mandate, new standard-gauge lines have been constructed—from Hadera (south of Haifa) to Tel Aviv in 1953, to Beer Sheva in 1956 (with a branch line to Ashdod), on to Dimona in 1965, then to Oron and the phosphate pits in the Har Zin area. A final extension to Elat remains in the planning stage. A new Tel Aviv–Ben Gurion Airport high-speed intercity line, opened in 2004, joins the main north-south line (Tel Aviv–Haifa-Nahariyya) at Tel Aviv. An extension to Jerusalem was under construction in the late 2000s. Light rail systems for both Tel Aviv and Jerusalem have been authorized, but for different reasons, at the end of the 2000s, implementation was encountering difficulties in both cities.

Ports and Shipping. Supplanting Jaffa (Yafo), a major harbor since the Bronze Age, Haifa became the dominant port after 1900 and has become one of the busiest general-cargo ports in the Middle East. Ashdod, 20 mi/32 km south of Tel Aviv and formerly of negligible importance, has developed as a second major Mediterranean deepwater port to handle exports of phosphates and Dead Sea chemicals and imports for south-central Israel. Ashqelon, south of Ashdod, is primarily a specialty port for handling imported coal and petroleum. Elat, the country's fourth major port, serves the Indian Ocean trade and handles petroleum moving through the Tipline.

Airlines. As was mentioned earlier, full and effective air service was for several decades of particular importance for Israel because of its isolation from its land-side neighbors. Continuing to be important for strategic reasons, it early became the channel for the immense flow of tourists.

A commercial airport built in 1936 at Lydda (Lod) on the coastal plain southeast of Tel Aviv became Lod Airport after 1948 and later Ben Gurion International Airport. It handles virtually all of Israel's international air traffic and ranks third among the Middle East's airports in the number of monthly aircraft departures. Small airports are located at Elat, Rosh Pina in the north, and near Tel Aviv for light aircraft. El Al is Israel's international airline, and Arkia is a primarily internal airline.

COMMERCE AND SERVICES

Israel is one of the most trade-dependent countries in the world and was a founding member of the World Trade Organization. It has FTAs with the United States, the EU,[56] its main trading partners, and many other countries. Much of its merchandise trade is with the EU—$37.5 billion in 2007—but the United States is its largest individual partner. Exports and imports are listed in the country summary box early in this chapter, and other data are given in Tables 7.3 and 7.4. The unique role of diamonds is noteworthy: In recent years, rough diamonds have been about one-fifth of imports; cut and polished diamonds (worth about $13 billion) are about one-fourth of exports. But with strong competition from lower-cost countries like India, output decreased from 20 percent of world production in 2003 to 12 percent in 2007. Domestic trade is significant: Small businesses still thrive, but larger stores are gaining ground, and many large Western-style shopping malls have appeared since the mid-1980s.

A full range of services has developed, with banking and tourism as major segments after public services. The state's banking system has worldwide connections, and two banks are among the world's top 100 institutions, with branches in the United States and Europe. The highly regulated banking sector, formerly state owned, is easing restrictions somewhat, and a controlling stake in the largest bank, Bank Hapoalim, has been privatized.

With some of the world's most important religious, historical, and scientific sites (Figs. 12.2 and 12.3), Israel has a vigorous tourist sector that the government intensively exploits. From 4,000 in 1948, tourist numbers rose to 2 million annually during the late 1990s, contributing $3 billion to the economy. However, the convergence of the second intifadah, the impact of 9/11, and a soft economy cut tourism by 60 percent in the early

FIGURE 12.2 Jerusalem, looking west from the Mount of Olives. The view shows the eastern wall of the Old City at bottom, the Dome of the Rock and other buildings of the Old City in the middle ground, and the ever-increasing new high-rise buildings of the burgeoning West Jerusalem in the distance (1997).

FIGURE 12.3
View in the Old City of Jerusalem: the Via Dolorosa in the Christian Quarter. To the left is the Ecce Homo Arch. The church is part of the Convent of the Sisters of Zion. (Photograph by Mildred M. Held)

2000s. Recovery was gradual, only to be hit again by the slump of 2009.

Reflecting historic Jewish emphasis on education and medical care, Israel has built major universities and hospitals. Supported both by the government and by contributions from abroad, there are seven universities in Israel (excluding the Occupied Territories), the largest in Tel Aviv and Jerusalem. Hebrew University is best known and is one of the finest in the Middle East. The Israel Institute of Technology (Technion) in Haifa was founded in 1924, a year before Hebrew University. Hadassah Hospital, on a hilltop in West Jerusalem, is a world-class medical facility.

RELATIONS

Regional Relations

Because of hostilities between Israel and its neighbors over the circumstances of its establishment and expansion, as well as the impact of the Palestinian refugee populations, relations between the Jewish state and most of the region have generally been antagonistic since the 1940s. Details of the several wars and of relations between Israel and Egypt, Jordan, and Syria are given in Chapter 8 and in the respective country chapters, along with the history of Israeli incursions into Lebanon. Only after the U.S.-mediated Israeli-Egyptian peace treaty in 1979 did Israel have diplomatic relations with any adjacent state. Once the peace process was set in motion in 1991, the level of regional tensions decreased, and the 1994 peace treaty with Jordan opened Israel's longest border.

Egypt. Before 1979, Egypt was Israel's most persistent and powerful military enemy, but since then it has often cooperated with Israel in various peace efforts and other regional initiatives. Having normalized diplomatic relations, the two have realized mutual peace dividends replacing periodic destructive military operations; there are frequent visits back and forth between their officials.[57] Tens of thousands of Israeli tourists visit resorts in the Sinai every year.

Jordan. Israel and Jordan had a half century of covert contacts; after two wars and with U.S. mediation, the 1994 treaty led to the most nearly normal relations Israel enjoys with any neighbor. In 2009, the two announced that they would move ahead with planning an expensive and highly controversial canal between the Red and Dead seas, designed to slow the recession of the latter, generate electric power, and desalinate some of the incoming water. There are numerous objections to the plan—economic, technical, and environmental—and despite the apparent interest of the World Bank in the proposal, its execution is far from certain. In both Jordan and Egypt are Qualified Industrial Zones from which products can be exported tariff free to the United States if they contain a certain percentage of Israeli inputs.

Syria. Israel and Syria have not only fought three wars but have also shown the most persistent hostility in their day-to-day affairs, with control of the Golan Heights an issue of constant dispute. In the late 2000s, Turkey mediated between the two to restart negotiations, despite strong opposition from the Bush administration. But the results of the 2009 election and the reemergence of a government led by Binyamin Netanyahu seemed not to augur well for these efforts, since this government, unlike its predecessor, flatly insists on Israel's retention of the Golan.

Lebanon. Curiously, it has been with vulnerable Lebanon, which has numerous internal factions and little real control over its own domain, that Israel has had some of the most variable relations. Its troop withdrawal in May 2000 after twenty-two years of occupation of southern Lebanon should have opened opportunities for détente, but Syrian influence intervened. Israel considered its opponent in the 2006 "Summer War"—Hizballah—to be a Syrian proxy.[58] Hizballah's successes in launching rockets into population centers like Haifa and Tiberias severely embarrassed the government and prompted a major bombing campaign as far into Lebanon as the Shii-dominated southern suburbs of Beirut. Despite heavy damage and loss of life, Hizballah claimed victory because it had "stood up" to Israel's advanced technology. In Israel, the conduct of the war was examined by an independent commission, which found that there were "serious failings and flaws in the lack of strategic thinking and planning in both the political and military echelons." The finding was very damaging to Israel's prime minister, Ehud Olmert, already weakened by serious allegations of personal corruption, who was said to be responsible for "a severe failure in exercising judgment, responsibility and prudence."[59]

Iraq. Israel's relations with Iraq were hostile beginning with Iraq's fighting alongside the Jordan Arab Legion in 1948–1949; the subsequent war of words was heightened by overt actions, like Israel's bombing of the Osirak nuclear reactor in June 1981 and Iraq's launching of Scud missiles against Israel in 1991. The Israel lobby in the United States supported the coalition against Iraq in 1990–1991, and Israel and pro-Israel U.S. groups (which had links with some prominent Iraqi exiles)[60] were leading advocates for invading Iraq in 2003. Former UK prime minister Tony Blair revealed in testimony he gave to a parliamentary inquiry in 2010 that, when he and President George W. Bush were in the early planning stages in 2002 for the invasion, Israel was a major consideration and that "there may have been conversations that we had even with Israelis, the two of us, whilst we were there."[61] Postinvasion Iraq has shown little interest in détente with Israel without a settlement of the Palestinian problem, despite pressure from the Bush administration.

Iran. Israeli-Iranian relations are now strongly adversarial, although they were very friendly under the shah's regime, when their security establishments collaborated closely. Israel supported Iran during the Iran-Iraq War, and one elaborate scheme to aid Iran involved the United States in the Iran-Contra scandal revealed in 1987.[62] After Iraq's defeat, Israel and its supporters argued for a U.S. policy of "dual containment" of Iraq and Iran. In the 2000s, Israel and the United States acted together in arguing that Iran's nuclear program was extremely dangerous. Israel bluntly let it be known it was prepared to take unilateral military action against Iran. Without ruling out the military option, the United States has preferred to act with the EU, Russia, and China on the diplomatic front, since precipitate Israeli actions would obviously endanger U.S. troops in Iraq and Afghanistan. Israel's long status as the region's only state with nuclear weapons and its leading role in the campaign against Iran had in 2009 the negative result of the IAEA membership voting for the first time in nearly twenty years for a resolution calling on Israel to sign the Non-Proliferation Treaty and put all its nuclear sites under UN inspection.[63] Hostility toward Iran has led Israel to growing links with Azerbaijan, which has an uneasy relationship with the Islamic Republic, where a majority of Azeris live.[64]

Turkey. Israel's closest rapport in the region has been with Turkey—Muslim and non-Arab—with which it has had a long history of diplomatic, economic, and military relations, dating to Turkish recognition of the state in 1949. They exchanged ambassadors in 1991, signed a Free Trade Agreement in 1996, and increasingly engaged in military collaboration, technical exchanges, and cooperation on water and oil projects (see Chap.

18). In the 2000s, Turkey became deeply involved as a mediator between Israel and Syria, and the Israeli government showed considerable interest. In 2009, the Gaza offensive and the Netanyahu victory in Israel distanced the two countries. The future of Israeli-Turkish relations was very clouded at the end of the decade.

Palestine.   For many years, dealing with the Palestine Liberation Organization (PLO) was a criminal offense under Israeli law. From the 1970s on, to undermine the secular PLO, Israel encouraged Islamic elements. (Ironically, these same elements, in a classic case of "blowback" or the "law of unintended consequences," coalesced into such groups as Hamas and Islamic Jihad—and Hamas in the 2006 election defeated Fatah, the biggest party in the PLO, seizing power in the Gaza Strip the next year.) The law was repealed in 1993 in the context of the ongoing peace talks, which later that year led to mutual recognition and the transition of the PLO into a Palestinian authority. Certainly, the relations between Israel and the Palestinians have been and will be the critical external issue in Israeli politics for the foreseeable future, as is further discussed below under "Occupied Territories."

Global Relations

Although isolated from its neighbors in the 1960s and 1970s, Israel steadily developed relations with more distant states and had diplomatic relations with 160 countries in 2009.

Great Britain.   In Europe, Britain was the most involved with early Zionist agencies and independent Israel. It issued the Balfour Declaration in 1917 (see Chap. 8), and controlled the mandate in Palestine until 1948. In 1956, it acted with France and Israel in the Suez invasion. More recently, because of its other regional interests, especially in petroleum, Britain has followed a more balanced regional policy. It has been active in the peace process, and upon his resignation as prime minister in 2007, Tony Blair became the official envoy of the Quartet on the Middle East—the UN, the United States, the EU, and Russia. In 2010, Britain expelled a senior diplomat (the Mossad London station chief) attached to the Israeli embassy, because of the use of several forged British passports in connection with the assassination of a Hamas official in Dubai (see Chap. 15).[65]

Germany.   The enormous loss of life by Jews at the hands of the Nazis remains an overwhelming political, ethnic, and religious event in Israeli life. Postwar West German authorities not only expressed remorse but also paid more than $4 billion in reparations to Israel, in development loans and as restitution to individuals who suffered under the Nazis. United Germany continued to make amends. In the 2000s, Germany allied with France and other EU states in a more balanced Middle East policy and opposed the preemptive war against Iraq in 2003.

France and Others.   The French Jewish banking family of Rothschild was the first major supporter of Jewish colonization in Palestine in the early 1880s. In the 1950s, France helped Israel build the Dimona nuclear facility and sold it fighter aircraft and other military equipment. More recent French-Israeli relations have been occasionally thorny, despite France's large and influential Jewish population. Israel criticized France when the latter joined Germany in opposing the invasion of Iraq, and it expressed concern over the apparent rise in anti-Jewish sentiment in France in the mid-2000s.

The Netherlands is often bracketed with the United States as Israel's strongest supporter globally. However, the crash in 1992 of an El Al cargo plane carrying, it was eventually revealed, the makings for sarin gas, not only killed many on the ground but also caused widespread illnesses among rescue workers and others near the crash site. The incident negatively affected the two countries' relationship for many years when Israel refused to supply details about the plane's cargo.[66]

Belgium and South Africa have strong links with Israel based on the diamond industry. With South Africa there are also ties dating to when it and Israel were pariahs in their respective regions. They shared military interests and, as mentioned above, cooperated in developing nuclear weapons; the postapartheid South African government renounced all its efforts in this matter.

Longtime antagonists Russia and China now have good relations with Israel, which sends and receives sophisticated arms to and from both. With nearly 1 million former Soviet citizens—mostly Russians—in Israel, and with Russia now supplying much of Israel's oil imports, Israel-Russia relations are increasingly close. These ties are particularly interesting in view of the years of nonrecognition (1967–1990) and the decades of Soviet military support for Israel's Arab neighbors. Israel has invested heavily in China's booming economy.

A centuries-long conflict between Jews and Roman Catholics continues to influence relations between Israel and the Vatican. Accusing the Vatican of anti-Jewish policies and actions, Israel demanded that the pope apologize for and renounce those policies. The Vatican modified its stance on doctrinal issues, and Vatican-Israeli diplomatic relations were established in 1993. However, questions regarding the status of church property that the Vatican believed would be settled promptly after the opening of relations remained unresolved at the end of the 2000s.[67] John Paul II visited Israel in 2000, and although the pope refused to meet all Israeli demands, the Sharon government eulogized him upon his death in April 2005. His successor, Benedict XVI, made a pilgrimage that included Israel in 2009.

United States. There is no formal alliance between the United States and Israel, but their so-called special relationship has been much closer than ties with almost any other country and has been a source of crucial diplomatic and economic resources for Israel.[68] Zionist lobbying in 1917 brought American endorsement of the Balfour Declaration. President Truman granted recognition eleven minutes after independence was declared. Since then, U.S. support has steadily escalated quantitatively and qualitatively.[69] Despite Israel's high per capita GDP, the United States extended direct grants of more than $85 billion between 1949 and the late 2000s. These transfers were made "up front," in cash at the beginning of the fiscal year for general budget support; few of the strings attached to most U.S. foreign assistance apply. Often, one-fourth of all direct foreign assistance has gone to Israel and another one-fifth to Egypt to continue its peace with Israel.[70] In addition, there have been sizable subsidies from U.S. government agencies for research and development—such as the Lavi fighter and joint work on missiles and antimissile missiles. Additionally, tax-deductible private donations to Israel by individuals and by organizations like the United Jewish Appeal, along with sales of Israeli bonds, have been considerable. The United States underwrote intelligence activities conducted by Israel, often as a U.S. surrogate, especially during the Cold War.[71]

The numerous issues on which the United States differs with Israel, even when serious, have almost invariably been discussed quietly, so as not to disturb the special relationship. Disputes usually arise from broad strategic U.S. interests, often connected to UN commitments. The United States rejects Israel's unilateral annexation of the Golan Heights, and it warned against incorporating the West Bank and Gaza Strip, which would violate several U.S. declarations and the Fourth Geneva Convention, and the United

States has promoted Palestinian rights in the Occupied Territories so that the peace process could proceed.

After the 1990–1991 Gulf crisis, both the United States and the United Nations were morally and logically obligated, after waiting twenty-five years for progress on UN Resolution 242, to press for the initiation of peace talks. The United States was also obligated to pursue a firm position on Jewish settlements in the Occupied Territories in keeping with its long-term opposition to these settlements, but the second Bush administration softened the U.S. position. Israel complained bitterly in 2009 when the Obama administration seemed to be reverting to the pre-Bush level of U.S. opposition to settlement building. Although Netanyahu announced a temporary freeze on some settlement construction, supposedly to promote resumption of talks with the Palestinians, there was some doubt about what the promise really meant;[72] to the dismay of the United States, he then followed it with an announcement that 700 new apartments were to be built in East Jerusalem.[73]

His government is heavily dependent on parties opposed to any concessions regarding the settlements, and to assuage them he openly affirmed the temporary nature of the freeze and that planning for the new units and the provision of some supporting infrastructure would proceed in the meantime. Also, the IDF has indicated that it might be unable to carry out any major settlement closures because of the growing influence that irredentist rabbis have on ordinary troops.[74]

In March 2010, during a visit by U.S. vice president Joseph Biden to both Israel and the West Bank to encourage renewed peace negotiations, an official Israeli government announcement was released detailing plans for a further 1,600 Jewish homes in East Jerusalem. The U.S. response was a series of plainly displeased diplomatic protests, including claims that Biden had been deliberately insulted. Both the White House and the State Department demanded that the new construction plans be canceled, reiterating the long-held United States position that the final status of Jerusalem is subject to negotiation between the parties involved and is not to be determined by unilateral actions on Israel's part. Unused to hearing public criticism from the American side, Israel and Netanyahu's government reacted with a combination of confusion and defiance. The Palestinians indicated that the housing plans ruled out resumption of peace talks.

At this writing, it is not clear whether the peace process can somehow be put back on track or whether the dispute signals a shift in the "special relationship" between the two states.[75] Additionally, and probably much more important for the future of peace negotiations, Israeli officials announced later in March that 50,000 new housing units for Jewish occupancy in East Jerusalem and nearby areas are in various stages of preparation and approval. The construction of 20,000 units were said already to be in the advanced stages of implementation.[76]

Occupied Territories

As was shown in Chapter 8, Israel captured four pieces of land, at least one from each of its foes, in the 1967 war: Sinai and the Gaza Strip from Egypt, the West Bank from Jordan, and the Golan from Syria. Neither Sinai nor the Golan had been part of mandate Palestine; hence, they were not in the 1947 UN partition. However, both the West Bank and Gaza had been integral parts of Palestine, and both were included in the half of the mandate allotted to the proposed Arab state in 1947. In keeping with "exchanging a piece of land for a land of peace," as urged from several sides, Israel withdrew from the Sinai—which is two-thirds larger than Israel itself—pursuant to the peace treaty with Egypt.

However, Israel still controls the three remaining areas. Not until the Gulf crisis in 1990–1991 galvanized the peace process did the status of the West Bank and Gaza begin to change with the signing of the Oslo Agreement. Solidly Arab, they became a microcosm of the Arab-Israeli problem. It was in Gaza that the first intifadah, the Palestinian uprising, escalated during 1987–1992, and in the West Bank that the second intifadah spread. The two regions became the geographical and human symbols of the struggle for the land itself. Israeli extremists claimed both as part of Eretz Israel; asserting what they believe is their right to settle there, they insisted on "creating facts on the ground"— by creeping annexation through building settlements, Israel would achieve permanent control without having to declare outright annexation. They reject the applicability of the Fourth Geneva Convention of 1949 to these settlements, but the international community, including the United States, holds to the convention's relevance.

FROM WEST BANK AND GAZA TO THE PALESTINIAN AUTHORITY

During the 1990s, the West Bank and Gaza underwent a dramatic and historic transformation. Change came in slow, small steps, but by early 2000 both of the areas were constituent parts of a fragmented Palestinian Authority (PA), a state-in-becoming. Progress was reversed in September 2000 with the outbreak of the second intifadah and the renewed cycle of violence through the following decade at the end of which contending Palestinian regimes prevailed in the two parts of the putative state.

West Bank

Since the end of World War II, the West Bank has been: (1) part of mandate Palestine, (2) a remnant annexed by Jordan, (3) a territory taken and occupied by Israel in 1967, (4) a fragmented self-governing area under the PA in the 1990s, and (5) an even more fragmented area with increasing settler population in the 2000s—with Palestinian inhabitants progressively more resolved to resist further inroads.

Defended in 1948–1949 from Israeli conquest by Arab forces and then annexed by Transjordan (the East Bank), it became known as the West Bank. Deeply indented on the west by the Jerusalem salient, the northern part includes the Samarian Hills, with Nabulus as a center, and the southern the Judean Hills, with a center at Hebron (Fig. 12.4). The kidney-shaped area of 2,270-mi^2/5,900-km^2 (see Map 8.7) was militarily occupied and administered by Israel after 1967, but it is neither de jure nor de facto under Israeli sovereignty. The boundary with Israel is the Armistice Line ("Green Line") agreed to in 1949, prominent in the controversy over the siting of Israel's "security fence" (Map 12.5).

Severed in 1949 from the rest of Palestine, the West Bank was technically held by Transjordan in trust for the Palestinians pending an eventual treaty. Israel took the area in 1967, renaming it Judea and Samaria, placing it under strict military control and bringing in settlers. Jordan claimed it until 1988, when King Husayn renounced all hold on it. This renunciation, the first intifadah, and the aftermath of the Gulf crisis brought the beginnings of self-government to the West Bank in the late 1990s.

Demography. The population in 1947 was estimated to be 400,000. This number increased in 1948 through the influx of 365,000 refugees from areas taken by Israel. By May 1967, 845,000 was the estimated total, despite outmigration, mostly to the East Bank, of more than 400,000. By September 1967 there were only 596,000, as refugees fled across the Jordan ahead of approaching Israeli forces. The 1997 census found a total of 1,873,476, excluding Jewish settlers, and a mid-2008

FIGURE 12.4 Barbs of discord: Jewish settlement impinging on an indigenous Palestinian neighborhood in Hebron. Kiryat Arba, across the road in the distance, is one of the most controversial of all Jewish settlements in the occupied areas and is expanding into an area to the right in the foreground. Note the Israeli soldier to the left.

estimate suggested 2.4 million; additionally, about a half million settlers are now living there (including East Jerusalem). The Arabs live in about 450 towns and villages; about 30 percent live in 25 larger towns and some 10 percent in 19 UNRWA refugee camps. Besides East Jerusalem, main towns include Ramallah, Nabulus, Hebron (al-Khalil), Bethlehem, Jericho, Janin, al-Birah, Tulkarm, and Halhul.

As recounted in Chapter 8, the establishment of Jewish settlements in the West Bank, virtually without interruption since the 1970s, has been at the center of the territorial dispute. By 2009, about 150 official settlements plus another 100 or so "outposts" marked the terrain of the West Bank and East Jerusalem. Strategically and meticulously patterned to consolidate Israeli holdings and to fragment Palestinian lands, they are con-

nected by strategic "access and bypass roads" that cause still more fragmentation (see Map 12.6). Overwhelming international opinion sees the settlements as violating the Fourth Geneva Convention—a situation reaffirmed in 1999—but Israel rejects the convention's applicability. The status of Jerusalem,[77] particularly East Jerusalem, and the settlements were both sticking points in the 2000 Camp David negotiations and remained so through the following decade. In 2005, Israel invoked a 1950 policy to confiscate hundreds of Palestinian properties in East Jerusalem, and this has proceeded apace over the next several years.[78] Hopes for flexibility on the settlement question were set back by the return of Netanyahu as prime minister in 2009, despite his announcement of a temporary freeze on construction in some areas.

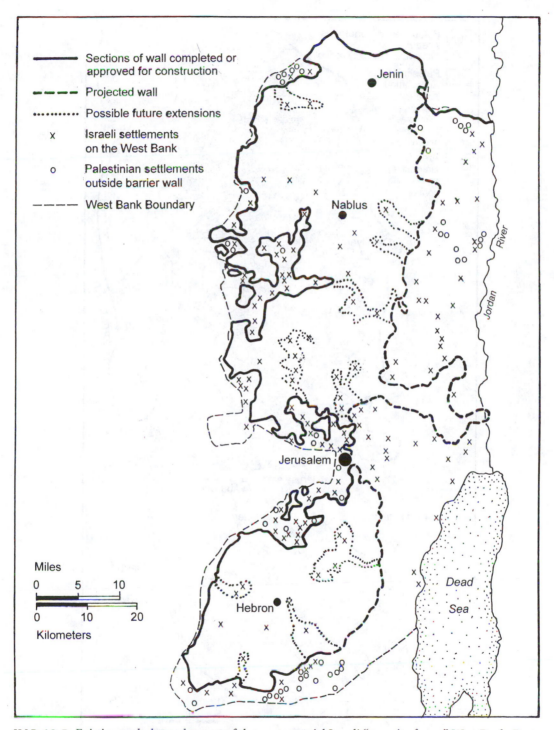

Legend:

- ——— Sections of wall completed or approved for construction
- – – – Projected wall
- ·········· Possible future extensions
- x Israeli settlements on the West Bank
- o Palestinian settlements outside barrier wall
- — — West Bank Boundary

Jenin

Nablus

Jordan River

Jerusalem

Dead Sea

Hebron

Miles
0   5   10

0   10   20
Kilometers

MAP 12.5 Existing and planned extent of the controversial Israeli "security fence," West Bank. Part of the alignment was judged illegal in 2004 by the International Court of Justice in The Hague. Only selected Jewish settlements are shown.

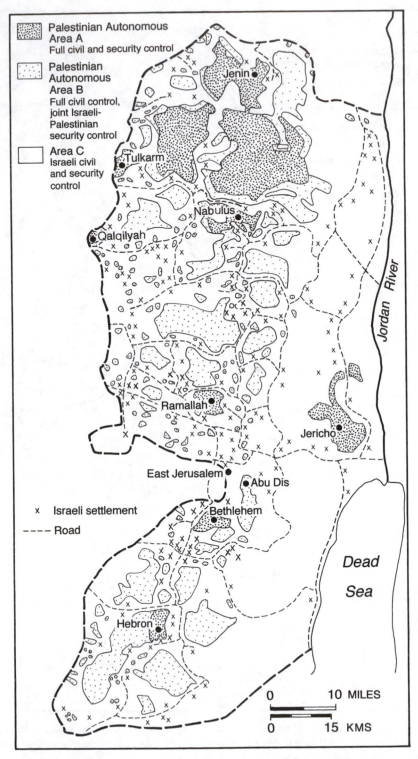

MAP 12.6 Areas A, B, and C, West Bank, with Jewish settlements and strategic roads. Rapid developments around East Jerusalem have changed the earlier situation shown here.

Water and Land. In addition to land itself, water is the basis for many conflicts between Israelis and Palestinians, at the official and the individual levels. Disputes arise not only in the allocation of daily supplies but also in the exercise of control over aquifers that supply both the West Bank and the densely populated Israeli coastal plain. Runoff from the considerable winter rainfall accumulates in these aquifers, some yielding water in springs, others feeding wells. Possessing the hydrogeological information, the technology, and official authority, Israel and Israeli settlers increasingly dominate water resources as well, leaving many Arab farmers with little or no water for farming or domestic use.[79]

Concomitantly, settlers have taken over land in various ways. Many settlements are on land that was state owned under Jordan before 1967, requisitioned as security areas or nature reserves. With insufficient water for farm and family use, encircled by settlements, and living under a military government that gives preference to settlers, some Arab farmers eventually sell their plots to Israeli agents. Claims that some farmers have no legal proof of their long ownership, due to the failure of past governments—Turkish, British, and Jordanian—to establish complete and accurate cadastres (official landownership registers) transfer more land to settlers. A former Israeli official in the West Bank wrote: "Redemption of the land (*geulat haqarqa*) is a fundamental Zionist concept. . . . The history of the Zionist enterprise is an account of physical *faits accomplis* through land acquisitions and settlement, created to achieve national, political, and military objectives. . . . The Palestinians, attaching the same macronational and symbolic value to the land, resist Israeli land acquisition efforts with whatever means they can muster. The unequal strength of the conflicting parties, however, dictates the results."[80]

The Economy. The West Bank has long suffered from uncertainty and instability, mini-

mal private investment and governmental inputs, constrained industrial development, corruption, high unemployment, and, consequently, limited economic development. Before 1967, the region received little in the way of resources promoting development either from the limited resources of the Jordanian government or from international donors.

After 1967 the modest agricultural sector saw loss of land to growing Jewish settlements and fragmentation of what remained, inadequate irrigation water,[81] obsolete equipment, lack of access to land by cultivators, shortage of capital, and limited markets. The only employment for many West Bankers and Gazans was menial labor in the settlements and nearby Israeli towns, or building the settlements that were consuming their territorial heritage. Addressing this irony finally in the late 1990s, the PA barred Palestinians from construction work in the settlements. Because Israel had in any case periodically placed curfews on both territories, it imported some 300,000 foreign workers as menials.

Although the West Bank and Gaza were to be PA autonomous areas, pledges of several billion dollars by the EU and United States had only limited impact. In 2007, according to the Human Development Index, the Occupied Territories were ranked only 110th of 182 countries, 14th of those in included in this study, and less than 79 percent of the HDI of Israel proper.[82]

A Palestinian State. With the Declaration of Principles signed by Israel and the PLO in September 1993 (Oslo I) and the Cairo Agreement eight months later, preliminary steps toward self-rule in the West Bank and Gaza began in May 1994. The PA became a virtual government of a quasi state at first composed of Gaza (excluding Jewish settlements) and the Jericho area. Oslo II in September 1995 began troop withdrawals from part of the West Bank areas, extending full PA control to six cities and scattered rural areas (Area A, Map 12.6). The Israeli

Defense Forces and PA shared jurisdiction over a few more noncontiguous locations (Area B), but the IDF had complete control of most of the region (Area C).

The first Palestinian election in January 1996 made PLO chairman Yasser Arafat president of the PA and chose the Palestine Legislative Council (PLC). Following the assassination of Yitzhak Rabin in 1995, Netanyahu became prime minister for the first time in 1996. For the next three years, he pursued his long-declared views—noncooperation with Palestinians—signing several agreements, notably the Wye River Memorandum of October 1998, but then equivocating on implementation. Ehud Barak defeated him in the 1999 elections, and movement toward a comprehensive settlement resumed, but it remained elusive at Camp David in late 2000.

Emerging in the 1990s as a quasi state, the PA encountered the complexities of establishing a political entity. Revolutionaries had to adjust to the realities of governance, including balancing authority with democratic processes. Graft and corruption were too common, but some of the institutions of statehood gradually appeared. Private efforts to promote the economy helped in the short term. In 1997 the PA and the EU signed an interim Association Agreement that provided duty-free access to the EU for Palestinian exports. President Bill Clinton dedicated a new international airport in Gaza in 1998, although Israeli bulldozers destroyed the runways in 2001 after the outbreak of the second intifadah and most of the terminal in the 2009 bombing campaign against Hamas. To save taxes and delays at Israel's Ashqelon port, the PA opened a modest but highly symbolic seaport in Gaza. With financial and political support from the United States[83] and Europe, and mutual accommodation between Israel and the PA, full statehood appeared to be achievable.

However, the PA's status regressed with the second intifadah following the visit of Ariel Sharon to the Haram al-Sharif/Temple Mount and with his consequent election victory in 2001. Sharon declared Arafat to be "irrelevant," and communication all but ceased. The IDF retook most of Areas A and B and laid siege to the PA compound in Ramallah, rendering the already crippled administration helpless—leaving the field open to factions espousing terrorism like Hamas to consolidate popular support. Arafat died in late 2004, and Mahmoud Abbas was elected to be his successor. Sharon suffered a stroke in January 2006, leaving him in a permanent vegetative state; he was succeeded by his deputy, Ehud Olmert.

That same month, reacting against PA ineffectiveness and rampant corruption, voters gave a narrow plurality and a clear majority of PLC seats to a mostly Islamist list headed by Hamas over the long-dominant Fatah faction of Arafat and Abbas.[84] Despite previous calls for free elections in the Middle East, the Bush administration's reaction, taken up by Israel, was that a Hamas-led government was unacceptable because of its nonrecognition of Israel. Abbas attempted to form a coalition, but all efforts failed. When Hamas militants seized control of Gaza in June 2007, Abbas appointed a cabinet excluding Hamas to govern the West Bank, effectively splitting the PA territory in two. In 2008, discussions between Olmert and Abbas led to the former offering a land swap—in return for settlement blocs on the West Bank, Israel would compensate the Palestinians with areas adjacent to Gaza and the southern part of the West Bank. The two sides were scheduled to come together in Washington in January 2009, but Israel's military campaign in Gaza intervened.

Economic and security reforms improved the West Bank's situation: The new Fatah-led government has overseen a mini economic boom. The 2009 party elections replaced many veteran leaders with new faces on the Central Committee, strengthening Abbas and a faction led by the popular Marwan Barghouti (imprisoned in Israel);[85] polls gave Fatah considerably more voter support than Hamas.

FIGURE 12.5 Birzeit University, leading Palestinian institution located near Ramallah, fifteen miles north of Jerusalem. Many major Palestinian figures are graduates of Birzeit.

In this atmosphere, a relatively confident PA prime minister Salam Fayyad announced his administration's intention to set up a de facto Palestinian state within two years. Abbas resumed negotiations with the Israelis in 2007, and some progress was reported at first, but at the end of the decade, with the Gaza offensive in January 2009, the subsequent return of Netanyahu to the prime ministership, and the continuation of settlement building, the long stalemate resumed. The tenures of both the PLC and Abbas were nearing their end, but the division between the West Bank and Gaza precluded holding the election, which was postponed with the incumbents' terms extended.

There were some positive economic signs, for the West Bank at least, at the end of the decade. First, the International Monetary Fund estimated growth to be about 7 percent for 2009, projecting an optimistic picture for the near term.[86] Second, the PA was seeking full observer status with the World Trade Organization.[87] Third, with the backing of the United States and the World Bank, Wataniya Palestine launched its mobile phone service while awaiting Israeli approval of the full range of frequencies agreed upon for its network.[88] Fourth, Palestine's first planned community, Rawabi, commenced construction on a site north of Ramallah (Fig. 12.5); The new town is to provide modern housing for 40,000 residents;[89] its construction has aroused opposition from the politically powerful Israeli settler movement. In each case, observers agreed, success will depend upon Israeli cooperation, fully testing the Netanyahu pledge to move rapidly to establish "economic peace" with the PA.[90] A 2010 World Bank–supervised report identified the difficulty that the Palestinians have in attracting badly needed foreign investment when Israel controls the entry and movement of potential investors.[91]

Gaza

The Gaza Strip is a small area along the Mediterranean coast, sandwiched between

Egypt and Israel, that Egyptian military forces held through the end of the 1948–1949 fighting. Separated from settled Egypt by the Sinai, it was under military control[92] until it was captured by Israel in the abortive tripartite Suez invasion in 1956. It reverted to Egypt after Israel was forced to withdraw from the Sinai and Gaza in early 1957, but it was again taken by Israel in the 1967 assault and remained under Israeli military occupation thereafter. Little economic development occurred under either regime.

Because of its small size and isolated location, the Gaza Strip (see Map 8.7) and its human and political importance were often overlooked until clashes between Gazans and Israeli troops in late 1987 provoked the outbreak of the first intifadah. It is only 25 mi/40 km long and 5.6 mi/9 km wide—about twice the size of the U.S. District of Columbia—yet it shelters a population of more than 1.5 million, giving it the markedly high density of 10,790 people per mi^2/4,170 per km^2. Such densities usually characterize urban areas or extraordinarily rich agricultural lands, whereas Gaza is in neither category. With an extremely circumscribed economy, more than 50 percent unemployment, and little industry, the crowded Strip was described by Sara Roy as "concentrated misery."[93]

The Gaza Strip is part of the Sinai-Palestine coastal plain, with high sand dunes along the shore backed by areas with good soils of sandy clay, silt, and loess. Marginal annual rainfall of 12 in/300 mm is supplemented by wells tapping the appreciable groundwater supplies. To support the high population, agriculture is intensely irrigated; as a result, aquifers have been overused, endangering both the amount and the quality of groundwater. The water table has been lowered near the seacoast, reducing aquifer resistance to seawater intrusion and raising the salinity level.

The area has long been agriculturally productive. Citrus is a primary crop; other tree products include dates, almonds, grapes, and olives, plus vegetables and field crops. With close to half the area under crops, agriculture is still a major sector of the economy. It has, however, been surpassed as employer and contributor to GDP by public and other services and by construction. Much of GDP has come from remittances from workers employed abroad, UNRWA's minimal support of refugees, private charities, and, at times, the wages of 30,000–35,000 day laborers in Israel, mostly in construction and agriculture.[94] Tensions during the first intifadah provoked periodic Israeli curfews and prohibitions against Gazans entering Israel—again the case since Hamas took control. Unemployment is 40 and 50 percent even during "normal" times.

The second intifadah produced more intense violence, with Israel demolishing homes and buildings as collective punishment for militant actions against Israelis. UNRWA saved Gazans from starvation: More than two-thirds of them are registered with UNRWA as refugees. No visitor to this concentration of human misery can disagree with one writer's characterization of Gaza in 1988 as "a pressure-cooker ready to explode"—which indeed it did in both intifadahs. It is plagued, he wrote, by "overcrowding, poverty, hatred, violence, oppression, poor sanitation, anger, frustration, drugs, and crime."[95] Full of despair and feeling dispossessed, many Gazans turned to radical fundamentalism—the Islamic Resistance Movement (Hamas) and Islamic Jihad—sometimes employing terrorist methods, which in turn generated Israeli suppression in an unending cycle of violence. Israel was relieved to turn this quagmire over to nominal PA control in 1994; attacks on the few Jewish settlements brought the IDF back, leading to armed resistance.

Despite the Strip's overcrowding, Jewish settlements sprung up, though in much smaller numbers than on the West Bank. Some 8,500 settlers lived in twenty-one communities, taking up 30 percent of the area for 0.4 percent of the population. In spacious surroundings with paved and lighted streets, irrigated lawns, swimming pools, and riding stables,[96] they needed about 3,000 Israeli troops to provide them security. Though Sharon was cool toward the "road map to peace" put forward by the "Quartet" (the UN, the United States, the EU, and Russia), he decided in 2004 to withdraw unilaterally from Gaza, evacuating the settlements that cost tens of millions of dollars each year to maintain, while keeping control over land, air, and sea access to the narrow area and compensating the settlers up to $500,000 per family. Despite conflicts that split the governing coalition, he carried his plan through by September 2005.

The following months were marked by violent clashes between partisans of Hamas and Fatah; in the 2006 election, Hamas prevailed with heavy support in Gaza City and Hebron, the two largest constituencies.[97] Sporadic fighting continued even after formation of a Hamas-led government. Israel blockaded the entry points to the area with varying degrees of severity until a Hamas faction seized control in June 2007; after that, Israel permitted only limited shipments for humanitarian purposes to enter. Gaza may have become technically unoccupied, but Israel was still almost fully in control.

From April 2001, rockets and mortars were fired into Israeli territory—about 3,400 until an informal cease-fire went into effect in July 2008. It was to last six months, and in the first four months attacks virtually ceased. But in November, an Israeli raid killed six Hamas fighters, the cease-fire faltered, and the firings resumed. On December 27, Israel struck back with Operation Cast Lead, inflicting major damage and casualties on the city and its inhabitants. While the IDF stated it minimized civilian casualties and that only 25.3 percent of the fatalities—296 out of 1,196—were noncombatants, the Israeli human rights group B'Tselem conducted a survey that showed much higher numbers—773 out of a total of 1,387, or 55.7 percent.[98] Official Israeli statistics indicate that from April 2001 through August 2009, some 4,400 Gazan rockets and mortars caused the deaths of 15 Israeli civilians. An investigation headed by respected South African jurist Richard Goldstone for the UN Human Rights Council found evidence that both sides had committed war crimes during the campaign.[99] Despite voices inside Israel calling for an independent inquiry into the IDF's actions in Gaza, like the one conducted after the 2006 Summer War, Netanyahu dismissed the Goldstone report as biased and anti-Semitic—although Judge Goldstone is himself Jewish—claiming that the IDF's investigations of its own actions were sufficient.

As of early 2010, Gaza remained under an almost complete blockade with frequent military incursions, under as much Israeli control as before Sharon's pullout in 2005. Whatever bright signs might exist for the West Bank economy in 2010 did not extend to Gaza.

GOLAN HEIGHTS

Of the three territories, in addition to Jerusalem, that are still occupied by Israel, Golan is the only one that was and still is indisputably de jure part of another sovereign state, Syria (see Chaps. 8 and 9). Yet the Golan is the only one of the territories captured in 1967 that Israel has annexed, simply by announcing in December 1981 that Israeli law would apply in the Golan. This unilateral declaration, like the annexation of East Jerusalem and its detachment from the West Bank, has received no international recognition and has been widely condemned.

Having simmered mostly in the background of the Arab-Israel conflict, the Golan problem was seriously discussed when Yitzhak Rabin was prime minister, but was then put aside until late 1999. At that time, Prime Minister Ehud Barak and President Hafiz al-Asad agreed to negotiate normalizing relations in tandem with Israeli withdrawal from Golan territories. Sessions were held in Washington in late 1999 and early 2000, with President Clinton offering encouragement.[100] However, negotiators reached no agreements, and talks were suspended. Since his accession in June 2000, the current Syrian leader, Bashar al-Asad, has insisted on return of the seized territory as the sine qua non for normalizing relations. The second intifadah put further discussions on hold, but talks resumed in the mid-2000s with the mediation of Turkey, despite the Bush administration's opposition. Little concrete progress was apparent by the time the Israeli Right returned to power in 2009; the Netanyahu government has indicated interest in resuming negotiations only if all previous conditions agreed to by the two parties are rescinded, while Syria holds that renewed discussions should build on what has already been done.

Israel's settlement of the Golan occurred following the expulsion of more than 90 percent of the area's 93,000 inhabitants (other estimates run as high as 250,000) with the 1967 fighting. This left only 5,875 Druze, 385 Alawis, and a few hundred others, mostly Circassians, in Qunaytirah. By 2005, about 16,500 Israelis occupied thirty-three settlements, and 19,000 Druze resided in the only four towns to escape demolition after 1967. With heavy financial support, the settlers have developed considerable water resources, expanded vineyards, installed a winery, and intensified agriculture. The IDF placed sophisticated radar equipment on the shoulder of Mount Hermon to monitor military movements inside Syria. Ski resorts were established on the mountain's upper slopes.

The present eastern border of the Golan was determined in the disengagement agreements between Israel and Syria following the 1973 war. It is actually a variable-width buffer zone, up to 5.5 mi/9 km wide and as narrow as 0.2 mi/0.32 km, between lines A and B (see Map 8.7), supervised by UN observers. Within the buffer zone, the agreement called for Israeli evacuation of Qunaytirah, which Israeli forces demolished prior to their pullback.

Extending about 40 mi/64 km north-south and 8–16 mi/13–26 km east-west, the Golan covers about 445 mi^2/1,150 km^2. Mainly a basaltic plateau rising from 985 ft/300 m to 3,935 ft/1,200 m, highest in the north, the Golan is a tilted tableland sloping toward Israel. A high escarpment, 1,310–2,625 ft/400–800 m—again, highest in the north—overlooks Israel on the west, matched by the Galilee escarpment across the Huleh Basin and the Sea of Galilee.

The Golan thus possesses a traditional strategic advantage. During the 1950s, Syria fortified it with both gun emplacements and bunkers on the brow of the heights, anticipating an eventual conflict, but these fortifications did little to impede the Israeli advance in the June 1967 fighting. Syrian gunners and Israeli artillery periodically exchanged fire during the early 1950s and early 1960s, usually over Israeli construction or agricultural work in the forbidden Demilitarized Zones (DMZs). Claims and counterclaims regarding these hundreds of incidents accumulated and eventually escalated into a major motivation of the 1967 war. In a 1976 interview, Gen. Moshe Dayan (Israeli defense minister 1967–1974) commented that 80 percent of the attacks were provoked by the Israelis and that the Golan was seized to add land to the state.[101] Control after 1967 denied Syria the elevation advantage and, in contrast, gave Israel the benefit of a glacis, a territorial cushion, placing it on Mount Hermon with command of the whole four-state junction—southeastern Lebanon, southwestern Syria, northwestern Jordan, and, of course, northeastern Israel. However, military technology has advanced so much since 1967 that it is not clear that the erstwhile strategic value of the highlands is still significant; discussions in the 2000s with Syria about returning Golan seemed to have aroused little concern in the Israeli military.

Syrian-Israeli negotiations clearly must grapple with difficult issues—settlements, water, mutual security, economic implications, precise border demarcations, national emotions, historical claims, geopolitical strategy, and quid pro quo. Some arguments may appear trivial to outsiders, but grand strategy can be a matter of centimeters of horizontal or vertical earth and cubic centimeters of water. Progress in any bilateral negotiations will need the determined efforts of a third party acceptable to both sides. The Bush administration's scornful opposition to Syria ruled the United States out of this role;[102] as mentioned, Turkey then stepped into the breach, while Washington curiously pressured Israel not to participate. By the end of the decade, Turkey backed away somewhat, largely because of its citizenry's negative reaction to the 2009 Gaza offensive, but France indicated some interest in working with the two parties, and Syria was showing interest in engaging the United States as a mediator.[103] The situation was helped in March 2010 by the Obama decision to return a ranking ambassador to Damascus.

NOTES

1. The complex history of Israel's development has been covered in unprecedented detail by thousands of books and articles. The problem is to distinguish the polemics for and against from the reasonably balanced accounts that also put the story in context. See Sachar 1976, 1987; *Israel* Country Study 1990; Goldschmidt 2010; Peretz 1994; Reich and Kieval 1993; and Bregman 2003. Many specific aspects of Israel are covered in sources given in notes below.

2. "Palestine" is universally used, even by Israeli writers, to apply historically to the general area between the Mediterranean Sea and the Jordan River and from Metullah at the northern tip of Israel to Elat at the head of the Gulf of Aqabah. The term includes contemporary Israel and all Occupied Territories but excludes Golan.

3. Few of the books on Israel focus on regional coverage. Survey of Israel (*Atlas of Israel*) 1985 is invaluable, and it is complemented by Baly 1957; Orni and Efrat 1980; and Efrat 1996. Also useful is *Israel: The*

Historical Atlas 1997 and the small but authoritative Israel Pocket Library 1973.

4. The best coverage of this topic is found in Zohary 1962.

5. Israel's water problems are treated in many studies, but see Dillman 1989; Rogers and Lydon 1994; Hof 1997; Rouyer 2000; *Water for the Future* 1999; Soffer 1999; *Near East Report*, Sept. 6, 1999; Amery and Wolf 2000; Rowley 1999 and especially 2009; and Dolatyar and Gray 2000.

6. *Near East Report*, Feb. 17, 1992, 44; Dillman 1989.

7. The critical nature of water in Israeli-Palestinian negotiations is emphasized in a recent World Bank report, "Assessment of Restrictions on Palestinian Water Sector Development," Report no. 47657-GZ, Apr. 2009, which concluded that, on average, an Israeli gets four times as much water as a Palestinian as Israel uses 80 percent of the mountain aquifer supply and that the Palestinian water system is "nearing catastrophe." See also *Ha'aretz*, Apr. 20, 2009.

8. FAO Aquastat *Water Report no. 34*, 2009, www.fao.org/nr/water/aquaatat/water_res/index.stm.

9. A recent comprehensive profile of Israel's water situation can be found in ibid.

10. University of Haifa geographer Arnon Soffer, quoted in *Christian Science Monitor*, Mar. 14, 1990; he expands on his thesis in Soffer 1999. See also Dillman 1989.

11. As in other states in the region, Israeli observers have called for an assessment of what crops should be grown with the dwindling water supplies. See Beyth 2006.

12. *Ha'aretz*, Oct. 27, 2009; *BBC News*, Oct. 27, 2009, reporting on a study from Amnesty International (2009), which blames the Oslo Accords for institutionalizing Israeli control over Palestinian water resources.

13. *Ha'aretz*, Mar. 4, 2010.

14. World Bank 2009.

15. Dr. Peretz Dar quoted in *Ha'aretz*, Nov. 3, 2008.

16. *Ha'aretz*, Feb. 24, 2010.

17. See sections 3–5 in the Israel Pocket Library's *Immigration and Settlement* volume. Sachar 1976, 395–424, gives slightly different figures. For current data, see Central Bureau of Statistics, *Statistical Abstract of Israel*, www.cbs.gov.il.

18. Some reports put the number of emigrants as high as 500,000, many in the United States; see Sachar 1976, 833–835, 232–234; Israel Country Study 1990, 88–91; and the Israel Pocket Library's *Immigration and Settlement* volume, 59–61.

19. See the five-part series on Soviet Jewish immigration in the *Christian Science Monitor*, July 25–Aug. 1, 1991.

20. Philippov 2008.

21. *New York Times*, Dec. 6, 1999; *Jerusalem Post*, North American Edition, Nov. 5, 1999. The "Who is a Jew?" question became acute regarding Falash Mura Ethiopians. See *Christian Science Monitor*, Jan. 9, 2004.

22. The resentment of some Israelis toward the Russians, especially those who remain Christian, is obvious on virulent blogs like http://samsonblinded.org/blog/the-russians-have-come.htm and http://jewishisrael.ning.com/profiles/blogs/tbn-christian-missionary. There may be as many as 250,000 Russians of nominal Christian background and unaccounted for in official statistics. See Sandro Magister, "The Invisible Christians of the Holy Land," http://chiesa.espresso.repubblica.it/articolo/26006?eng=y.

23. *Ha'aretz*, Feb. 18, 2010.

24. See Lustick 1980; Hazony 2000; Bisharah 2002; Efron 2003; Ghanem 2001; Goldscheider 2002; and M. Ellis 2002.

25. A recent attempt to measure the extent of social, economic, health, and educational gaps between Jewish and Arab Israelis was reported in *Jerusalem Post*, Nov. 19, 2009. The study, which is based on official statistics and indicates the gaps are growing, was carried out by Sikkuy, the Association for the Advancement of Civic Equality, and is available at www.sikkuy.org.il/english/en2007/sikkuy2007.pdf.

26. See Falah 1992 regarding "mirror housing" and other discrimination. For discrimination in employment, see the *Jerusalem Post*, International Edition, Nov. 23, 1991. For Arab industries, see Schnell, Benenson, and Sofer 1999.

27. See Chernichovsky 2005.

28. Kahane 1981 voices a radical view but articulates demands by many Israeli extremists that all Arabs must be expelled from Eretz Yisrael. Kahane, who was formerly leader of the U.S. extremist Jewish Defense League, was assassinated in New York in 1991.

29. *Jerusalem Post*, Feb. 10, 2009. The housing minister warned that "populations that should not mix are spreading" and that it was no less than a national responsibility to keep Arabs from moving into "Jewish areas" (*Ha'aretz*, July 2, 2009).

30. An early revelation by the New Historians was Morris 1989 (first published in 1987). Morris followed with several other critical writings, including "Falsifying the Record" in a 1995 issue of the *Journal of Palestine Studies*. Efraim Karsh led the attack on the New Historians in Karsh 1997 and 1999. For more by a New Historian, see Pappé 1999, 2004. Morris backtracks somewhat in Morris 2004. See also Morris 2008, 2009; and Thomas 2007. On the related issue of a growing critical reassessment of Zionism, see Pappé 1997 and Wurmser's 1999 defense of traditional Zionism. See also Sternhell 1998. For a lengthy analysis, see

"The Battle over History," *Jerusalem Post*, North American Edition, Nov. 5, 1999.

31. A more recent treatment of much the same subject is found in Sand 2009. For a discussion of the book and the author's provocative title, *The Invention of the Jewish People*, see *New York Times*, Nov. 24, 2009; and *Ha'aretz*, Nov. 27, 2009.

32. *Tkuma* is discussed in the *New York Times*, Apr. 10, 1998.

33. At the same time, a bill requiring equal access to state lands for all citizens was rejected (*Ha'aretz* Dec. 22, 2009, and Jan. 3, 2010). On the oath, see *Jerusalem Post*, Jan. 3, 2010.

34. See article from *Forward* at www.myjewish learning.com/israel/Contemporary_Life/Politics/Supreme_Court/Democratic_and_Jewish_State.shtml.

35. *Ha'aretz*, Nov. 18, 2009. The group of women returned to pray at the wall the following month without incident and without the scroll (*New York Times*, Dec. 22, 2009; see also *Forward*, Jan. 1, 2010).

36. Mandelbaum 2010.

37. U.S. Department of State 2009. There have been numerous reports of increased vandalism of Christian sites in Jerusalem (*Asia News*, Dec. 16, 2009) and of an upswing in the harassment of Christian clergy (*Jerusalem Post*, Nov. 27, 2009), in both cases by Haredi youth.

38. For details regarding Israel's joining the OECD, see www.mfa.gov.il/MFA/Government/Communiques/2007/Israel+to+join+OECD+16-May-2007.htm.

39. www.oecd.org/dataoecd/60/10/44253914.pdf, reported in *Ha'aretz*, Dec. 17, 2009.

40. Because the Israeli economy is highly varied and changes rapidly, it requires close monitoring. Among the available sources are the *New York Times*, *Christian Science Monitor*, *Washington Post*, and *Ha'aretz*. See also the U.S. Department of State's *Country Commercial Guide: Israel*, July 2004, and *Background Note: Israel*, Dec. 2009; U.S. Department of Energy, Energy Information Administration, *Country Analysis Briefs: Israel*, Apr. 2004; and Central Bureau of Statistics, *Statistical Abstract of Israel*, www.cbs.gov.il.

41. A University of Haifa poll found that a majority of Israelis feel that the last two governments rank as equally corrupt and that the last three prime ministers have been the most corrupt in the country's history (*Ha'aretz*, Mar. 16, 2010).

42. Transparency International 2009; World Economic Forum 2009a; Fraser Institute 2008.

43. World Bank and the International Finance Corporation, "Doing Business, 2008," www.doingbusiness.org/features/DB2008Report.aspx.

44. A recent study showed that while Jewish municipalities within Israel proper get 35 percent of their re-

sources from the central government, the settlements get 64 percent (*Ha'aretz*, July 21, 2009).

45. *Ha'aretz*, Dec. 22, 2009.

46. FAO, various issues. Still, the highly developed agricultural sector in the United States saw a 36 percent gain in per capita food output over the same period.

47. A preliminary estimate was 5.7 tcf/0.161 tcm, which would increase Israeli gas reserves by more than 500 percent (*Oil and Gas Journal*, Dec. 17, 2009).

48. A company building a power plant to begin operations in 2013 has signed a contract to use gas from this field (*Oil and Gas Journal*, Dec. 15, 2009).

49. Israel's "least-kept secret"—its nuclear arsenal—and the revelations made by Israeli nuclear technician Mordechai Vanunu about this subject are treated in Gaffney 1989 and Y. Cohen 2003; see also Federation of American Scientists, "Nuclear Weapons," www.fas.org/nuke/guide/israel/nuke/; and several articles in the *Bulletin of Atomic Scientists*, www.thebulletin.org/.

50. The subject is discussed in detail in *Israel* Country Study 1990, especially in Chaps. 3 and 5. See also Black and Morris 1991; Hersch 1991; Cockburn and Cockburn 1991; and, on the secret Israel Institute for Biological Research, *Jerusalem Report*, Dec. 21, 1998, 16–21. This institute was the intended destination of the sarin-gas components that were aboard the El Al cargo plane that crashed in Holland on October 4, 1992, also covered in the latter source.

51. See *Israel* Country Study 1990, 316; Cockburn and Cockburn 1991, 291–292; *New York Times*, Mar. 14, 1992; and, on later sales, *New York Times*, Nov. 11 and Dec. 2, 1999.

52. See *Ha'aretz*, Aug. 2, 2009. South Africa later acknowledged that it had produced several nuclear weapons but that it had dismantled them at the time the apartheid regime ended; it then signed the Nuclear Nonproliferation Treaty. Several studies of Israel's role in South Africa's program are available: among them are Farr 1999 and McCreal 2006a, 2006b.

53. The revelations were widely covered in news media at the time. See Hersch 1991; Black and Morris 1991, 437–443; *Israel* Country Study 1990, 317–318; *Jerusalem Post*, North American Edition, Dec. 3, 1999; and A. Cohen 1998. Imprisoned for eighteen years, Vanunu was released in April 2004 and called for the destruction of the Dimona reactor. Since his release, he has been refused permission to leave Israel or to have any contact with foreigners, although author Held had several long interviews with him and his brother in Jerusalem in 1997. See Y. Cohen 2003; *New York Times*, Apr. 20 and July 5, 2004; and *The Telegraph*, Dec. 29, 2009.

54. For further details on Israel's arsenal, see www.nti.org/db/disarmament/country_israel.html.

55. Egyptian–Saudi Arabian plans for a causeway and bridge spanning the Strait of Tiran would remedy this situation somewhat; as plans progressed, Israel expressed its concern in terms of the security of shipping to Elat (*The Times* [London], May 4, 2007).

56. For further information, see www.ustr.gov/trade-agreements/free-trade-agreements for the United States, and for the EU, see http://ec.europa.eu/trade/creating-opportunities/bilateral-relations/countries/israel/.

57. Netanyahu on December 28, 2009, made his third visit to Egypt since becoming prime minister nine months earlier.

58. For a treatment of how the events played out, see Harel and Issacharoff 2009.

59. Full text of the summary of the commission's report is in *New York Times*, Jan. 30, 2008.

60. Particularly with the Iraq National Congress and its founder Ahmad Chalabi. See Chapter 13.

61. As quoted in *Foreign Policy*, Feb. 8, 2010, www.foreignpolicy.com/posts/2010/02/08/I_dont_mean_to_say_I_told_you_so_ but.

62. Fully reported in the news media during late 1986 and early 1987, the affair may be studied in Tower 1987.

63. Reuters, Sept. 18, 2009.

64. *Radio Free Europe/Radio Liberty*, Mar. 9, 2010, www.rferl.org/content/ The_Blooming_Relationship_Between_Azerbaijan_And_Israel/1978312.html.

65. *BBC News*, Mar. 23, 2010; *Ha'aretz*, Mar. 25, 2010.

66. The first reports of the crash in early October 1992 included nothing about the cargo inventory. For information that finally emerged six years later, see *Jerusalem Report*, Dec. 21, 1998; and *New York Times*, Jan. 29, 1999.

67. This situation was denounced as "outrageous" by Rabbi David Rosen, a prominent leader in Jewish-Catholic dialogue efforts (*Ha'aretz*, Jan. 18, 2010).

68. See Mearsheimer and Walt 2008.

69. See Miller 2008.

70. See Stauffer 2003 and Israeli Web sites, such as www.mfa.gov.il/MFA and www.jewishvirtuallibrary.org/. Spiegel 1985 is also an academic study of relations, examined administration by administration. Lenczowski 1990, written by a longtime scholar of Middle East affairs, looks at successive presidential policies also academically but from a somewhat different viewpoint than Spiegel. Among his several well-balanced studies, Quandt 2001 focuses on the critical peace process. For later analyses, see Zunes 2004; *Middle East Quarterly* 1998; *Congressional Quarterly* 2007, Chap. 3; Ball 1992; and S. Lewis 1999. An editor of the *Near East Report*, published by the American Israel Public Affairs

Committee (AIPAC), the Israeli lobby in Washington, recounts AIPAC's achievements in Bard 1991. An opposing view is presented in two works: Curtiss 1996, written by the editor of the *Washington Report on Middle East Affairs*, and Findley 1989. Opposing views on U.S.-Israeli relations are given in the biweekly *Near East Report* and the American Educational Trust's monthly *Washington Report on Middle East Affairs*.

71. See Cockburn and Cockburn 1991 and *Washington Report on Middle East Affairs* 11, no. 5 (Nov. 1992): 12, 86.

72. See Gorenberg 2009.

73. *The Daily Star* (Beirut), Dec. 28, 2009.

74. *BBC News*, Sept. 7, 2009; *Ha'aretz*, Oct. 23 and Nov. 16, 2009.

75. The Israeli lobby in the United States was quick off the mark to fix the entire blame for the situation on President Obama. See, for example, *Foreign Policy*, Apr. 2, 2010, www.foreignpolicy.com/articles/2010/04/01/obama_s_foolish_settlements_ultimatum? See also *New York Times*, Mar. 21, 2010.

76. *Ha'aretz*, Mar 11, 2010.

77. For one treatment of the city's complexity, see Armstrong 1997.

78. Like data on Palestinians, those on Jewish settlers and settlements are problematic. Inclusion or exclusion of figures on East Jerusalem makes a huge difference. Israel insists that the East Jerusalem as enlarged unilaterally by Israel in 1967 is part of Israel itself, but the claim is rejected by the United Nations and virtually all of its members except Israel. Large-scale land seizures were reported in the *New York Times*, Jan. 25, 2005. Settlements are monitored in detail in the bimonthly publication by the Foundation for Middle East Peace, *Report on Israeli Settlement in the Occupied Territories*, and the Foundation for Middle East Peace (FMEP) Web site, www.fmep.org. Much of the same material appears in the quarterly *Journal of Palestine Studies* under "Settlement Monitor," usually prepared by FMEP editor Geoffrey Aronson. See also *New York Times*, Mar. 17, 1999. Regarding Jerusalem, see Lustick 1997; Rempel 1997; Abu Odeh 1992; and Emmett 1996. For differing accounts of Camp David in 2000, see Ross 2004 and Hanieh 2001.

79. Nakhleh 1988; *Christian Science Monitor*, Sept. 14, 1992; *Water for the Future* 1999; Rouyer 2000; Soffer 1999; Ventner 1998; Frederiksen 2003; more recently, World Bank 2009.

80. Benvenisti 1984, 19.

81. The scope of the water problem is addressed in World Bank 2009.

82. United Nations Development Programme 2009.

83. USAID funds programs on the West Bank and Gaza. Since 1993, some $1.7 billion has gone to the economic growth, education, health, and water sectors. See www.usaid.gov/wbg/Programs.html.

84. Hamas and allies received 44.4 percent, Fatah 41.4 percent. Hamas won seventy-four seats, Fatah forty-five. Voting was on two levels—for party lists and for individual candidates. Hamas prevailed because, of the individual seats, it gained forty-five to Fatah's seventeen.

85. *New York Times*, Aug. 12, 2009.

86. International Monetary Fund 2009.

87. *Media Line*, Jan. 5, 2010.

88. *Reuters*, Nov. 1, 2009. The company's difficulties were highlighted in an interview aired on NPR, Sept. 7, 2009.

89. *The Guardian*, Sept. 8, 2009; *Media Line*, Jan. 5, 2010.

90. *Ha'aretz*, Mar. 26, 2009.

91. PalTrade, "Obtaining Visas for Investors," Feb. 2010; *The Daily Star*, Mar. 9, 2010.

92. Unlike Jordan with the West Bank, Egypt never annexed the Gaza Strip. It was administered as a totally separate territory, and its residents had neither Egyptian citizenship nor ready access to Egypt itself.

93. S. Roy 1995.

94. See ibid.

95. Nakhleh 1988, 210.

96. S. Roy 1995.

97. See above, note 84. The two parties split the sixteen electoral districts evenly.

98. www.btselem.org/Download/20090909_Cast_Lead_Fatalities_Eng.pdf.

99. See www2.ohchr.org/english/bodies/hrcouncil/docs/12session/A-HRC-12-48_ADVANCE1.pdf and www2.ohchr.org/english/bodies/hrcouncil/docs/12session/A-HRC-12-48_ADVANCE2.pdf for the executive summary and the recommendations and conclusions, respectively.

100. For a full account of Rabin negotiations, see Rabinovich 1998. For basic considerations in both earlier and the 1999–2000 talks, see BenMeir 1994, 1997. Regarding the importance of water in the Golan context, see Hof 1997. The same scholar examines the delicate issue of a new border (based on previous lines) in Hof 1999 and the new boundary drawn by the UN in 2000 in Hof 2001. For news accounts of the 1999–2000 meetings, see *Christian Science Monitor*, Dec. 15, 1999, and Jan. 13, 2000. For an in-depth account, with a map, see *New York Times*, Jan. 16, 2000.

101. Dayan's comments have been extensively covered. See Hof 1999.

102. Kastner 2008.

103. Mideast Peace Pulse 2009.

13

Iraq
Modern Mesopotamia

IRAQ AND ITS ANTECEDENTS

Modern Iraq emerged as an independent kingdom in 1932, its boundaries and major institutions defined while it was a League of Nations mandate under British tutelage. In accordance with the 1920 San Remo talks and the 1923 Treaty of Lausanne, mandate Iraq incorporated three former Ottoman *vilayets* (provinces)—Mosul, Baghdad, and (partially) Basrah. With the exception of the western desert and the northeastern mountains, it was coextensive with the traditional geographical region of Mesopotamia (literally, "between the rivers"). The Arabic name *al-Iraq* (literally, "the cliff") had been applied geographically to lower Mesopotamia; for the first time, it designated a state occupying the basin.

Whether traditional Mesopotamia or modern state, Iraq is the land of two rivers, the Tigris and Euphrates, two of the three great rivers in the Middle East. The earliest known civilizations were born in this eastern limb of the Fertile Crescent. It served as the culture hearth from which the first ideas of sedentary agriculture, domestication of animals, the wheel, writing, and urban development diffused westward to the Nile Valley and eastward to the Indus Valley. Evidence of the Neolithic Agricultural Revolution is scattered along the Zagros piedmont east of the lower Tigris, and ruins of the world's first cities have been uncovered between the two rivers south of Baghdad (see Chap. 3). Sumer, Akkad, Babylonia, and Assyria are part of Iraq's historical and cultural heritage, and their remains are a major element in the landscape, attracting modern scientists and tourists alike in peacetime.

Mesopotamia has been one of the major political and military power bases of the region (see "Power Cores," Chap. 3). For 2,000 years after Cyrus the Great, it was usually linked with the adjacent plateau to the east, and the basin—rather than the plateau—was the core of the combined areas from the Persian Achaemenids to the Arab Muslims. Twice in the five decades after 633, the Euphrates Valley saw conflict over the Islamic caliphate (see Chap. 4), resulting in the martyrdoms of Ali and his son Husayn, whose tombs in al-Najaf and Karbala, respectively, are major Shii shrines.

Only a province of the Umayyad Empire after 661, Mesopotamia supplanted Syria as the Muslim imperial heartland in 750. With the Abbasid Empire, it was the nucleus of cultural efflorescence under Caliph Harun al-Rashid (r. 786–809) of *Arabian Nights* fame. Decline followed this golden age; Baghdad was sacked by Mongols—first by Helagu, grandson of Genghis Khan, in 1258, then in 1393 by Tamerlane, who killed or enslaved the intellectual cadre of savants,

IRAQ

Long-form official name, anglicized: Republic of Iraq

Official name, transliterated: Al-Jumhuriyah al-Iraqiyah

Form of government: Multiparty republic with one legislative house (Council of Representatives)

Area: 167,618 mi^2/434,128 km^2

Population, 2008: 29,492,000; Literacy (Latest): 74.1%

Ethnic composition (%): Arab 75–80; Kurd 15–20; other 5

Religions (%): Muslim 97, of which Shii 60–65, Sunni 32–37; Christian 3 (primarily Chaldean rite and Syrian rite Catholic, and Nestorian)

Demography: Life expectancy—68.6 yr (M), 71.3 yr (F); Birthrate (per 1,000)—30.1; Fertility rate—3.86

GDP, 2009: $70.1 billion; purchasing power parity: $112.0 billion; per capita: $3,600

Currency: Iraqi dinar, US$1 = 1,115 dinars, 1 dinar = $0.00084 (March 2010)

Energy reserves: oil—115.0 bn bbl (ranking with those of Iran as second or third largest in the Middle East and world); gas—111.94 tn ft^3; coal—nil

Main exports (% of total value, 2007): crude petroleum 95.4; refined petroleum products 4.0

Main imports (% of total value, 2007): government imports 44.3, of which refined petroleum 7.9; capital goods 41.8; consumer goods 13.9

Capital city: Baghdad 5,054,000; other cities: Mosul 1,316,000; Irbil 926,000; Basrah 870,000; Sulaymaniyah 825,000; Kirkuk 750,000

---

artisans, writers, and engineers. Both conquerors destroyed its extensive irrigation systems, built over millennia, as well as cities, craft shops, and trade routes. Ottomans and Persians later contended for the ravaged basin, with the Ottomans finally triumphing in 1638. Shifting political weight toward the west ended the long politico-economic symbiosis between the Mesopotamian Basin and the Iranian Plateau.

Since then, the Zagros piedmont has been the fault line of tension between Arab and Iranian culture and territorial aspiration. Ottoman rule continued until World War I, when British and Indian forces drove the Turks back into Anatolia, and Britain received the mandate over the newly created Iraq in the early 1920s.[1]

In a complex and carefully crafted scheme for British hegemony over most of the Middle East, Colonial Secretary Winston Churchill and his team of regional specialists put Hashimite prince Faysal bin Husayn on the throne of the new kingdom. A plebiscite seemed to legitimize his accession, but resistance to Britain increased, with a bloody insurgency lasting several months. After a decade of tension, Iraq was the first mandate to gain independence, becoming a sovereign state (with British-imposed limitations) in 1932.

Before proceeding with the evolution of independent Iraq, we must examine the foundations and resources that formed a basis for the contemporary state and that will enable post-2003 Iraq to rebuild.

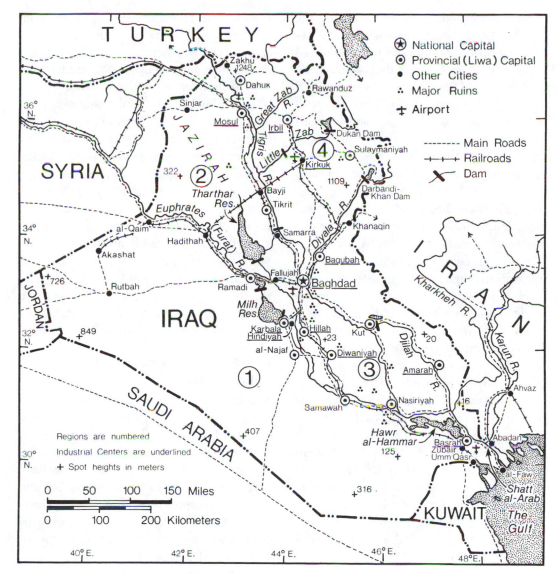

MAP 13.1 General map of Iraq, with main cities, transportation, and antiquity sites. Circled numbers designate regions. The 33rd and 36th parallels marked UN "no-fly zones" after the 1990–1991 Gulf War, but the zones were irrelevant after March 2003.

REGIONAL PATTERNS

Cradled in the land segment of the great tectonic trough downfolded between the Arabian Platform to the southwest and the Zagros ridges to the northeast, Iraq has four distinct natural regions, with identifiable roles in Mesopotamian political and economic life: [1] western and southwestern desert plateau, [2] Jazirah or northern Mesopotamian upland, [3] southern Mesopotamian alluvial plain, and [4] northeastern uplands and Zagros Mountains (see circled numbers on Map 13.1).

[1] Western and Southwestern Deserts

This extension of the Syrian and Arabian deserts west of the Euphrates Valley is the barren western third of Iraq—mostly the province of al-Anbar. The few thousand remaining Bedouin live in this least-populated and least-developed part of the country. It is a continuation of the Jordanian desert platform and the Arabian area of al-Widyan, furrowed with numerous east-west wadis and traversed by an express motorway from Baghdad to Amman, Aqabah, and Damascus. Rutbah developed from a dusty way station in the 1950s into a bustling highway junction, trading center, and military checkpoint. The highway was a vital link to Aqabah during the Iran-Iraq War and the aftermath of the 1991 Gulf War; it again became especially crowded as the ground link between Baghdad and Amman after 2003.

Farther east is al-Hajarah, a limestone platform strewn with flint and chert, crossed by the centuries-old caravan trail of the Darb Zubaydah for pilgrims to Mecca. Farther southeast is the sandy, gravelly plain of Dibdibah, cut by the prominent Wadi al-Batin forming Kuwait's western boundary. The open desert to the west was used by U.S. and coalition forces moving north from Saudi Arabia in February 1991 to outflank and encircle Iraqi forces in Kuwait. The far west gained a place in history when it was used to launch nearly eighty Scud missiles into Saudi Arabia and Israel in 1991; it saw intense conflict from 2003 until tribal leaders were able to establish social control by 2008.

[2] Jazirah: Northern Mesopotamian Upland

Most of the Jazirah upland, extending from Syria into central Iraq, is a desert plateau descending from 1,475 ft/450 m in the northeast to 260 ft/79 m at Baghdad. Except for the floodplains and the area northwest of Mosul, population in this broad interfluve is sparse. In the extreme north, a prominent outlying ridge of the Zagros–Anti-Taurus folds, the Jabal Sinjar, extends westward from Mosul.

The region is drained from north to south by the steep-banked Wadi Tharthar, empty-ing into the Tharthar Depression between the Tigris and Euphrates. In the 1950s, an artificial lake was developed to hold Tigris floodwaters diverted by the Samara Barrage; any overflow moves southward into the Euphrates. North of Jabal Sinjar, the undulating plateau has rainfed cultivation of wheat and barley; modern Iraq's granary, it was vital to ancient empires. The plateau is bisected by the rail line to Baghdad. Jazirah development plans include significant irrigation like that in the Syrian part of the region. Mosul, on the site of Nineveh in the heart of ancient Assyria, has grown steadily over the past sixty years. Iraq's second-largest city, it lies on the Jazirah's northeast periphery but serves as the thriving main center for the northern third of the country; its complex ethnic makeup is key to post-2003 political stability.

[3] Southern Mesopotamian Alluvial Plain

Southeastward from Ramadi on the Euphrates and south of Samarra on the Tigris is essential Iraq, a flat alluvial plain that in recent geological time grew Gulfward from silt dropped in the coalesced deltas of four rivers: primarily the Tigris and Euphrates, but also the Karkheh and Karun. The original shoreline is marked by a sinuous cliff, probably the feature for which Iraq is named; it extends from Ramadi to near Samarra. Along and between the lower courses of the two rivers, ancient empires thrived, and ruins of the world's most ancient cities still stand; here is the cultural and economic core of modern Iraq. On the western edge lie the two most sacred Shii shrines, the tombs of the martyred Husayn in Karbala and Ali—Husayn's father, the fourth caliph and first Shii imam—in al-Najaf.

The northern end of the alluvial plain, where the rivers come closest, is one of the historically most strategic sites in the region. Its importance is shown in many ways: A major trade route has transited the narrow

FIGURE 13.1 Liberation Monument, Baghdad, by Iraqi artist Jawad Salim, erected following the 1958 revolution.

interfluve since Neolithic times; successive primate cities were here—Akkad (its exact site is uncertain), Babylon, Seleucia, Ctesiphon, and Baghdad; it has developed irrigation agriculture for centuries; and, of greatest current significance, its advantages and attractions for modern industry are many. Temperatures during the dry summers average 95°F/35°C in July, soaring in daytime to more than 122°F/50°C. Winter rainfall averages only 5.5 in/140 mm. Elevations and relief are low, heights ranging from 80 ft/25 m in the north to sea level in the south. Some areas beyond the natural levees are actually below sea level upstream from the still-growing deltas of the Karkheh and Karun rivers debouching from Iran into the Shatt al-Arab.

Modern Baghdad, heir to famed empires of the past, was founded in 754 as the Abbasid capital. Legendary in the *Arabian Nights* (see Chap. 3), it thrived for 500 years before being sacked in 1258 and again in 1401, then sinking into 500 years of obscurity. Until 1991, even until 2003, contemporary Baghdad was a vibrant, multifaceted capital (Fig. 13.1), with major universities and one of the world's finest antiquities museums. Its unique collection was deplorably looted in April 2003 in the chaos following the U.S. capture of the city, and it may never recover all its treasures. Pre-2003 emphasis on militarism is seen in the capitals monuments with martial themes. Under U.S. occupation, with all the problems of a foreign military presence, Baghdad struggled to maintain human existence.

Southeast of Baghdad, the central interfluve was for centuries mostly wasteland or saline marshes because of the high water table and inadequate drainage. To drain the marshes, where dissidents lived among the Madan—the Marsh Arabs—and to reclaim

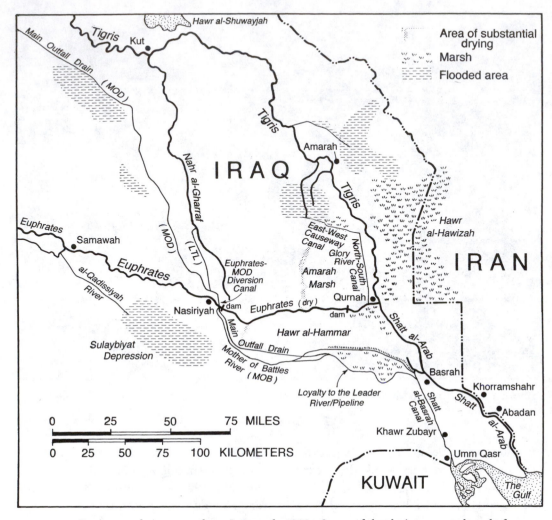

MAP 13.2 Drainage schemes, southern Iraq, early 1990s. Some of the drainage was altered after March 2003, when some Marsh Arabs returned to their traditional homeland.

the arable land, the government built the 350-mi/563-km Main Outfall Drain (MOD) in 1992 along the interfluve's axis (Map 13.2). Sometimes called the Third River, the MOD drained the central marshes and destroyed the Madan homeland.[2] On the same axis is a north-south express motorway.

Traces of abandoned channels of the Tigris and Euphrates indicate radical course changes by the rivers, as do the sites of ancient cities—Kish, Nippur, Uruk, Ur, and others—no longer on riverbanks along which they originally lay. Both settlement

and cultivation exhibit a ribbon pattern, concentrated along the rivers and canals, strikingly green against the desert tan. Cultivation is due both to the proximity of water and, more important, to the better drainage on the low, broad natural levees built up on the banks during regular overflow. Where the stream has bifurcated, naturally or artificially, as the Euphrates has in several places below Hit, agriculture and settlement have been especially intensive.

Between Nasiriyah and the confluence of the Euphrates with the Tigris at Qurnah lies an area once unique—the marshes of the Madan, the Marsh Arabs, with their own unique culture. For thousands of years, they used reeds (*qasab*) growing there to build homes on artificial islands (Fig. 13.2A) and to construct their council houses (*mudhifs*) (Fig. 13.2B). They caught the plentiful fish; raised water buffalo for milk, yogurt, and hides; and moved between houses and villages in the high-prowed *mashhuf* (shown in Fig. 13.2A), poling through the shallows.[3] Shii fugitives took refuge in the marshes in 1991–1992, accelerating Saddam's determination to drain the marshes and corral the Madan. Their environment destroyed, thousands fled their homes, many to Iran; the remainder were forced into collective villages, as were Kurds in the late 1980s.[4] This remarkable group's millennia-old unique way of life disappeared for a decade, but many displaced Madan chose to return to their familiar but much degraded environs after 2003 when the levees holding back the water were cut, allowing some of the area to be reflooded. Although there has been significant progress in restoring the ecosystem, full recovery may not be possible.[5]

East of the marshes and the Hawr al-Hammar, the confluence of the two rivers creates the Shatt al-Arab, which flows 100 mi/160 km to the Gulf. For much of the Shatt's length, a broad belt of date-palm groves paralleled both riverbanks, naturally irrigated by freshwater in an intricate canal network subject to the daily tides. Most of this productive landscape was obliterated during the Iran-Iraq War, leaving shattered stumps in place of great groves. Some replanting was undertaken in the 2000s.

Midway up the Shatt on its west bank lies Basrah, Iraq's main port. This historic trade center is a Shii stronghold, and its older quarters attest to the longtime influence of India. Heavily damaged during the Iran-Iraq War, it was devastated again in 1991, with still further destruction during the Shii insurrection in 1991 and 1992, and yet more beginning in

2003. The government pointedly neglected it after 1991, leaving the once thriving port city shabby and intensifying animosity between southern Shii and central Sunni. Under the post-2004 Shii-majority government, Basrah has received more attention, damage has been repaired, and airport and seaport have been refurbished.

However, tensions and disputes with both Iran and Kuwait over land, sea, and river boundaries that rub shoulders at the narrow head of the Gulf are still sticking points in bilateral relationships and development. In a tit-for-tat restriction of water, small dams have been built on both sides of the Iraq-Iran border, and disagreements of exact boundary lines have come close to conflict over oil wells (with Iran) and fishing and sea transit (with Kuwait).

Two of Iraq's main oil fields—Zubair and Rumaila—lie in the desert west of the Shatt. Rumaila was the center of acrimonious dispute between Iraq and Kuwait in the 1980s. West of the Shatt's mouth is Iraq's narrow window on the Gulf, 36 mi/58 km of coastline at the lower end of the Iraq "funnel."

In this strategic outlet to the sea is an increasing concentration of oil activity, heavier industries, and multiple port developments (discussed later in this chapter). It is also the focus of Iraq's historic grievance against Britain's delineation of boundaries in the early 1920s, and it is thus the basis of its territorial complaints and claims against Iran and Kuwait. From here it lashed out in 1980 and 1990. The details of its claims regarding the Shatt and the Kuwait boundaries are in Chapter 8 (see Map 8.8).

The physical geography of the extreme southeast is as much influenced by the southwestward-building deltas of the Karun and Karkheh rivers as by the southeastward-building deltas of the Tigris and Euphrates and their common outlet, the Shatt al-Arab. The spread of these deltas has had three geomorphic effects: It has aided in filling in the head

FIGURE 13.2 An all-reed village (*top*) and a typical *mudhif*, or all-reed council house (*bottom*), in the lower Euphrates marshes east of Nasiriyah, in 1979. The boat is a typical *mashuf*. Government drainage of the marshes in the early 1990s transformed the ecology of the area and displaced the marsh-dwelling Arabs (al-Madan) from their unique homes of many centuries. However, they began returning and restoring their ecology after mid-2003.

of the Gulf, it has forced the Tigris and Euphrates together into the Shatt, and it has simultaneously blocked some of the combined drainage and thus contributed to the formation of extensive and invaluable wetlands of lakes, intermittent lakes, and marshes—some below sea level—that sprawl over much of the deltas of the four rivers.[6] Some of these marshes were among those fully or partly drained during the 1990s.

[4] Northeastern Uplands and Zagros Mountains

Uplands, piedmont, and rugged mountains rising northeastward from the upper Tigris contrast sharply with most of the country. Except for a few prominent ridges near the Tigris, the highlands lie northeast of a line connecting Zakhu, Mosul, Irbil, Kirkuk, and Khanaqin. Elevations rise from 655 ft/200 m on the lower piedmont just east of the Tigris to 3,000 ft/915 m in the foothills, then reach 5,900 ft/1,800 m on the ridgetops and 11,808 ft/3,600 m on the Iranian border east of Ruwanduz. Lying at 36° N Lat, only 6° farther north than Iraq's torrid Gulf coast, the heights are blanketed with snow half the year and can be cool on summer nights. At lower elevations, Irbil and Kirkuk are hot in summer, but they get 15 in/385 mm of winter precipitation compared to Basrah's 6.5 in/164 mm. In the foothills and on the piedmont are Iraq's third- and sixth-largest cities: Irbil (sometimes Arbil or Erbil) with 926,000 people, and Kirkuk, still a great oil center after seventy-seven years of production, with 750,000. Both because of oil beneath it and because of its mixed ethnicity, Kirkuk has long been a center of contention, where dominant Sunni Arabs oppressed Sunni Kurds during the Baath regime and where tensions flared following restoration of Kurdish influence after 2003. Well up into the mountains is Sulaymaniyah, competing with Irbil as a Kurdish political center, its population of 825,000 ranking fifth in Iraq.

Ridges in the far north extend east-west, following the trend of folding in the Taurus and Anti-Taurus mountains, whereas tectonic trends south of Ruwanduz turn southeast and thence combine with the dominant Zagros folds. The same forces that created the ridges and linear foothills also produced the subsurface structures in which petroleum and gas accumulated. Several streams follow deep gorges parallel to the folds in their upper courses and then cross the grain of the ridges to join the Tigris: the Khabur, Great Zab, Little Zab, Udhaym, and Diyala. The highest ridges contain Iraq's only forests, some quite extensive, preserved by the area's isolation and ruggedness. Most of the slopes permit only grazing, lower and gentler slopes support fruit and nut trees, and the broad valley bottoms are intensively cultivated. Access to the heights is limited, and passes through the Zagros into Iran are few. Most famous of these routes is the Ruwanduz River Gorge (Fig. 13.3), with the spectacular Spilak Pass and Ali Beg Gorge west of Ruwanduz and the Shinak Pass near the border.

Some of Iraq's earliest and largest hydraulic projects were developed in the 1950s in these well-watered, rugged mountain areas, where deep gorges and solid rock offered ideal sites for construction. The Dukan Dam and its large reservoir were built on the upper Little Zab, the Darbandikhan Dam and reservoir on the upper Diyala, and, later, the Dibs Dam on the Little Zab. The Great Zab's potential was finally harnessed in the late 1980s with the construction of a large dam in its upper course.

Apart from its landforms, the northeast is also noteworthy as a refuge for minorities, a political-cultural buffer and frontier, and an underground reservoir of hydrocarbons. It is the Iraqi segment of Greater Kurdistan, the much larger area through which Kurdish tribesmen normally move freely across Iraq, Iran, and Turkey. With their main center in

FIGURE 13.3 Western entrance of the dramatic and strategic Ruwanduz (sometimes Rawanduz or Rawandoz) River Gorge, northeastern Iraq. The gorge carries the main road from Irbil to Iran—the only route linking the two countries through the rugged northern Zagros Mountains.

Sulaymaniyah, Kurds are overwhelmingly the dominant group in the area (see Chap. 4). They have used the ruggedness and isolation of the elevated Zagros as their fortress and refuge in their successive wars for autonomy— including in 1991–1992. In the lower hills are many Turkmans and smaller numbers of Assyrians, Sarliyyas, Yazidis, and others.

POPULATION AND PEOPLES

Population Patterns

Iraq's estimated population of 29.5 million in 2008 was nearly six times what it was in 1950. Growth occurred through natural increase, unlike the much greater percentage upsurges primarily from immigration in the Gulf amirates. Maps 4.2 and 13.3 and Figure 4.1 show that population is found in linear patterns along the banks of rivers and canals on the plains but is more generally distributed in the villages and towns of the northeastern uplands and mountains.

The greatest single concentration of population, about half the total, begins north and west of Baghdad, sprawls westward and southward across the mid-Iraq interfluve— encompassing the well-publicized "Sunni Triangle"—and then follows the Euphrates and its branches along the west side of the alluvial plain to Samawah. A highly mixed mélange of ethnic and religious groups, metropolitan Baghdad has almost one-fifth of Iraq's population. West of Baghdad is Fallujah, a major center of Sunni insurgency and the site of a weeklong offensive against insurgents in November 2004. Farther south are the Shii shrine cities of al-Najaf and Karbala, each with about 500,000 people; Hillah, one of the main date-producing cen-

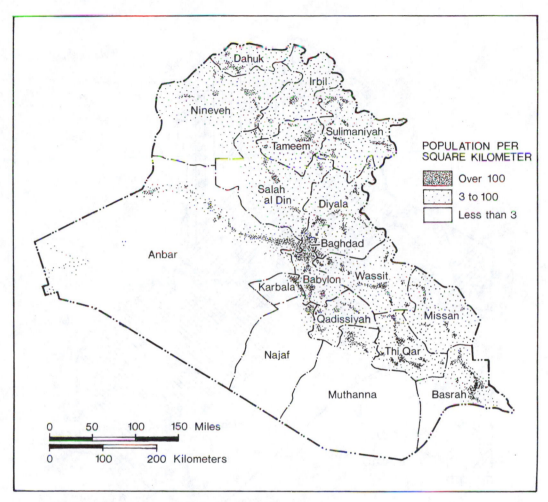

MAP 13.3 Provinces and population density, Iraq.

ters in Iraq; Diwaniyah; and, farthest south, Nasiriyah.

Secondary concentrations are found (1) in the south, where population in Basrah, the marshes between Basrah and Nasiriyah, and Amarah fluctuated wildly during the three wars of 1980–1988, 1990–1991, and 2003 and afterward; (2) around Mosul in the north; and (3) in the northeastern piedmont, with its twin nodes of Irbil and Kirkuk, and the outlying city of Sulaymaniyah.

Ethnolinguistic Groups

Some groups within Iraq's borders have maintained their separateness for many cen-

turies, to the extent that group identities compete with Iraqi nationalism. The complexity of the country's ethnic and religious mosaic, along with the crucial significance of that complexity, has been emphasized by political geographers and other regional specialists for decades. The true relevance of the intricacy became abundantly clear after 2003. Although the primary ethnic conflict is between Arab and Kurd, equally significant is the religious rift between Sunni and Shii, discussed below. Smaller ethnic minorities—Turkman, Assyrian, Armenian, Yazidi, Lur and smaller Persian-speaking groups, Mandaean, and others—remain distinctive but,

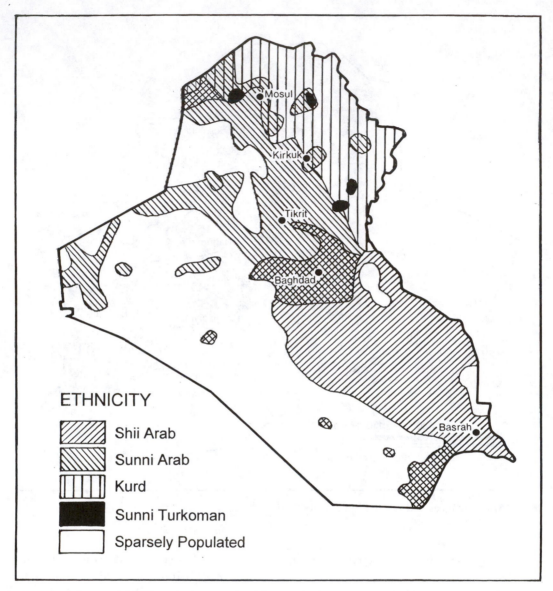

MAP 13.4 Pattern of major ethnic groupings, Iraq.

except for the Assyrians between the world wars and some of the Persians in the 1980s, are not actively separatist or antinational.

The geographic pattern of the three large adversarial groups in Iraq has always constituted an issue crucial to the country's internal and external policies (Map 13.4). With the highly nationalistic Kurds concentrated in the north and the restive Shii in the south, the minority Sunni elite in between kept control of the government and economy. This three-cornered conflict governed coalition actions against Iraq for the decade following 1991. Indeed, the brutal Sunni suppression of the Shii in the south and of the Kurds in the north in the early 1990s prompted the establishment of the southern and northern no-fly zones (see "Kurds" below). It became the single greatest problem facing the U.S.-led occupation after April 2003.

Arabs. Composing some 75 percent of the population, Arabs have been the largest ethnic group numerically for 1,000 years. During most of that period, they have considered themselves the eastern bulwark against non-Arab influences. Iraqi Arabs actually represent a biological mixture of many peoples over thousands of years.

Although perhaps only about a fourth of the Arabs are Sunni, they have dominated politics and the economy for centuries. Since Shii have long been associated with Iran and Iranians, Sunnis have considered themselves the "loyalists," with strong ties to other (and mostly Sunni) Arab countries. When Sunni Ottomans were in control, Shii became alienated, isolated through endogamy, and deprived through decreased cultural and economic opportunities. The majority of the Kurds are also Sunni, so that the combined Sunni groups make up a bit more than a third of the total population.

Shiism, based on Ali's faction, emerged in southern Iraq during the seventh century. Growing among the tribes, its strength there continued up to the present time, although Iran has had the largest Shii concentration since the sixteenth century. The Shii are some 60 percent of the population, mainly in the south and around Baghdad area. The roles of the Shii, Sunnis, and Kurds after 2003 are examined later.

Kurds. The Kurds, mostly Sunni and about a fifth of the population, live primarily in the northeast uplands and Zagros Mountains—Iraqi Kurdistan (see Chap. 4); they are also well represented in Baghdad. After 1927, petroleum development around Kirkuk, on the Kurdish periphery, prompted a new interaction between plain and mountain. The government and the Kurds never reached accommodation, leading to a seemingly unending cycle of internecine conflicts from the mandate period onward—in 1919–1930, 1943–1946, 1961–1970, 1974–1975, during the Iran-Iraq War, the late 1980s, and then the fateful months in 1991–1992 after the Gulf War, when more than 1 million Kurds fled military attacks before the no-fly rules were imposed.

The last two cycles were unique. The first was a climax to bitter fighting along the Iranian border in early 1988, when local Kurdish *peshmerga* (guerrillas) supported an Iranian attack inside Iraq. As Iraqi forces had on previous occasions when they were seriously threatened, they used poison gas both in the battle and against civilians in the Kurdish town of Halabjah, where several thousand died.[7]

The government then razed Kurdish villages, expelling thousands of Kurds into the northern region, and resettling others in cement-block collective settlements, expecting this to solve the Kurdish problem definitively.[8] During Iraq's venture into Kuwait, Kurds took advantage of the situation and sought control of their "homeland." Iraqi forces using helicopter gunships and bombers responded ferociously after withdrawing from Kuwait, driving more than 1 million to seek safety in Turkey and Iran. Through UN resolutions, the United States and Britain declared an air exclusion, or no-fly zone, for fixed-wing aircraft north of the 36th parallel and enforced it until the 2003 invasion.

Protected by the zone, Kurds held elections in 1992, setting the stage for autonomy. In a power struggle between the two major groups, the Barzani faction allied with Saddam against the Talibani faction, supported by Iran. After establishing an autonomous area in the 1990s, even issuing their own currency, the Kurds were in a strong position when the Baathi regime collapsed. They assisted U.S. forces during the fighting, working cautiously with them during the occupation and, in some cases, taking revenge against their erstwhile Sunni oppressors.

By 2003, the Kurdish region was the fief of a coalition of two tribe-based parties—the

Kurdish Democratic Party (KDP—Barzanis) and the Patriotic Union of Kurdistan (PUK—Talabanis). The Iraqi constitution, ratified in 2005, was federal in nature; the Kurdistan Regional Government (KRG—recognized ad interim under the Coalition Provisional Authority [CPA]) then reconstituted itself as a federal region within the republic, officially composed of three provinces.[9] Also in 2005, elections gave the coalition and its allies 104 of the 111 seats in the Kurdish National Assembly (KNA)[10] and chose its candidate, Massoud Barzani, as president. In the late 2000s, the KRG sometimes acted as a state in federal Iraq and sometimes as an almost independent entity. Controversial contracts were signed with foreign oil companies with little regard for Baghdad's theoretical authority, the KRG agenda of annexing parts of Kirkuk and three other provinces outside its official boundaries was forwarded, and elements of the Kurdish Workers Party (PKK—see Chap. 18) were given de facto asylum. Some PKK militants conducted cross-border raids into Turkey, embroiling the central government in a seriously inflammatory situation with its powerful northern neighbor. Although these policies and others of similarly nationalistic derivation were undoubtedly popular among most Kurdish voters, the KDP-PUK coalition's growing reputation for cronyism and corruption was less so: In 2009, elections for the KNA saw an impressive showing by a newcomer party, Goran—the Change List—which garnered 23 percent of the vote to the disadvantage particularly of the PUK. Indications were that the KNA would now have a real opposition grouping of perhaps more than 40 members to counterbalance the governing coalition.

The minority Fayli Kurds are not associated with the KRG but vote primarily for Shii parties. Living along the Iraq-Iran border, they have been persecuted by both countries and often denied citizenship by each. Despite their Kurdish ethnicity and because their struggle with Saddam Husayn was outside the KDP-PUK context, they have benefited little from the increased status of the KRG.

Turkmans (sometimes Turkmens or Turkomens). Making up more than 2 percent of the Iraqi population, Turkmans live in the piedmont and foothills of the northeast. Settled between the Arabs of Mesopotamia and the Kurds of the Zagros, they are numerous in both Kirkuk and Irbil as well as in piedmont villages. They are both Sunni and Shii, live in agricultural villages, and are middle class, as well as constituting part of the urban population. Their ethnicity gives them an influential external protector that shares their serious concerns about Kurdish dominance—Turkey.[11]

Other Ethnic Minorities. Smaller minorities include Persian-speaking Shii with strong ties to Iran, many of whom were expelled to Iran in the early 1980s when they voiced pro-Iranian sentiments. Their strongholds were the shrine cities and neighborhoods of Karbala, al-Najaf, and al-Kazimiyah (near Baghdad), as well as Basrah. Another Persian-speaking group, the Lur, are concentrated in tribal villages near the Iranian frontier.

Jews numbered 118,000 in the 1947 census but were probably more numerous, since in 1951 about 121,000 emigrated to Israel and several thousand went to Iran. They generally had lived in urban areas, often as merchants, professionals, and government officials in Baghdad. A few thousand remained in Iraq in the mid-1980s, but most of them emigrated later. After 2003, a few Iraqi Jews went to Israel from Iraq, while small numbers of Israelis and other Jews filtered into Iraq, especially in the north and in Baghdad. The small group of Mandaeans—also called Sabians or John the Baptist Christians—are an interesting ancient people of uncertain origin who are differentiated primarily by their Gnostic religion but also are physically distinct (see Chap. 4). The heterodox Yazidis, kin to groups in Syria and Turkey, live in villages along the Jabal Sinjar west of Mosul; they are generally considered to be ethnic Kurds, but many of them stress their separate identity. Their situation has become precarious because of their reputation (erroneous) as devil worshipers: In 2007, two Yazidi villages were attacked by Muslim militants.[12]

Christian Minorities. Christians have had a strong presence from early in the Christian era. The earliest and largest of the Christian groups are the Assyrians, numbering more than half a million, distributed from the Syrian border to Irbil and Kirkuk, as well as in Baghdad; religiously, they are divided into Nestorian and Chaldean (Catholic) sects. Armenians number about 20,000 and are usually urban dwellers. Christians have come under siege for their general liberalism (their shops sell alcohol, for example), beginning with the months of insecurity following the invasion, and Christian emigration has been very high since 2003.[13] The kidnapping and murder of the Chaldean archbishop of Mosul in February 2008 intensified the fears of remaining Christians.[14]

ECONOMIC PATTERNS AND PROBLEMS

Economic Interrelations

Mandate Iraq was, like its Arab neighbors, overwhelmingly agricultural. Despite its enviable agricultural potential, its actual land development and production were limited. Manufacturing was confined to handicrafts such as metalworking, weaving, and food processing.

Emerging from centuries of Ottoman colonial control, the new Iraq, with British help, steadily evolved a more diversified economy. The discovery of oil in 1927 brought a preeminent dimension to the economy; Iraq possessed superior economic potential—with plentiful water and arable land, on the one hand, and enormous energy resources, on the other, and a growing supply of productive labor to exploit them. Independent Iraq gradually took its place in the region's emerging political pattern and steadily developed its infrastructure: roads, railways, ports, dams, schools, and related structures. After the 1958 coup, major industries were transferred to the public sector, and nationalization of the petroleum industry began in 1972. By the late 1970s, Iraq had achieved considerable development but was squandering huge sums on military armaments and weapons industries. As was explained earlier, the 1980–1988 Iran-Iraq War and the invasion of Kuwait in 1990–1991 consumed capital and labor, diverted national energies, and destroyed much of the new infrastructure and industry.

Iraq's geographical vulnerability was exposed in the late 1970s as relations with neighbors deteriorated. First, intra-Baathi disputes led Syria to shut down Iraq's export oil pipelines to the Mediterranean, and, although Iraq gained a Turkish outlet in 1977, it still needed the export terminals on the Gulf. Then war with Iran destroyed those facilities. Before the country could catch its breath after the Iran-Iraq War, Saddam Husayn turned on Kuwait. With every chance to withdraw, he defied the UN coalition, and Iraq paid heavily for his third major blunder, as the new pipeline outlet opened across Saudi Arabia in 1985 was lost consequent to this invasion. It seemed that every prospect for economic takeoff was blocked by some costly political or military miscalculation.

The postinvasion Iraqi economy at the end of the 2000s was sorely in need of foreign direct investment (FDI), and not just because of the capital it would add; more important is the technology transfer and the upgrading of domestic labor skills that can accompany FDI. Unfortunately, decades of misrule through 2003 and the frequent chaos since then discourage investors—for obvious security-based reasons, of course, but also because of a prevailing atmosphere of corruption. In 2008, Transparency International ranked Iraq 176th of 180 countries and worst of the Middle East states.[15]

Agriculture

Although it was the country's major economic activity in the 1920s, agriculture contributed only an estimated 5 percent in 2006. A new village revitalization program now in place promises to advance the sector. Of the country's total area, about 13 percent is arable. A surprising 53 percent of the arable land is rainfed, nearly all of it in the mainly Kurdish north and northeast, although most of the actual production is from the intensively cultivated areas of the irrigated plains.

Major crops are grown on both the irrigated plains and the rainfed northern uplands—barley, wheat, cotton, potatoes, tobacco, millet, and sorghum. Wheat and barley are winter crops, utilizing the rains of the Mediterranean climate, whereas the other plants are summer grown, with some irrigation in the north. Other crops, especially rice and dates, are found in the southern irrigated areas along the rivers and canals, with citrus flourishing in the shade of date palms—thousands of which were destroyed by warfare. A complete range of temperate and subtropical fruits and vegetables is also grown.

By the 1970s, Iraq had shifted from net food exporter to food importer, a shift prompted by several factors: population increase, a rising standard of living, increased industrialization, migration of farmworkers to the cities and to military service, punitive destruction of villages, and a loss of soil productivity in poorly drained, irrigated areas of the south. Ambitious land reclamation projects were accelerated after 1988, especially in the Jazirah along the East Euphrates channel and in the Third River Project in the southern interfluve. Irrigated area was thus greatly increased in the late 1980s, and agricultural efficiency improved as collectivized farms

were privatized. Iraq is dependent on external upstream sources for just over half of its renewable water resources, primarily Turkey, and to a lesser extent, Syria and Iran. Turkey's increasing preemption of Euphrates and Tigris water (see Chaps. 8 and 18) has created significant tensions between the two countries, at a time when other stresses (Kurdish ambitions, oil pipelines, regional relationships) require immediate attention. The reduced flow has challenged Iraqi inventiveness and has caused serious problems for irrigated agriculture. Iraq must balance concerns about water with its need for the oil pipeline through Turkey to the Mediterranean. If security gains prove permanent, it may be able to adopt less water-intensive agricultural practices and begin to approach its great potential in this sector.

Petroleum

The first well drilled in Iraq, by the Turkish Petroleum Company (TPC, later the Iraq Petroleum Company, or IPC—a British-dominated consortium with Dutch, American, and French partners),[16] struck a major reservoir at Baba Gur, north of Kirkuk, in 1927. However, exports were delayed for seven years pending completion of pipelines. The government believed—correctly, as records later showed—that IPC slowed development in Britain's political-economic interests, and relations with IPC were discordant until Iraq nationalized the company in 1975. Iraq was a founding member of OPEC in 1960; it passed Law 80 in 1961, reclaiming all concession areas not in production, and created the Iraq National Oil Company. These frictions in the country's oil operations continued even after nationalization of IPC, to the detriment of national development.

Long ranked with Saudi Arabia, Iran, and Kuwait as the region's big four in reserves, Iraq is conservatively credited with at least 115 billion barrels of proved conventional crude resources, placing it second in the re-

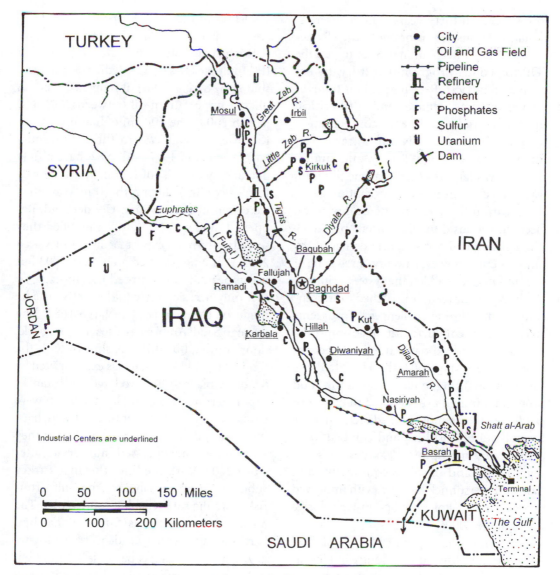

MAP 13.5 Economic map of Iraq, with major pipelines, oil fields, mineral deposits, ports, and airports.

gion and in the world after Saudi Arabia until recently, when Iran upped its reserves to 137.6 bn bbl (see Table 6.1). Many geologists believe that further exploration will give Iraq an additional 45–100 bn bbl. Known gas reserves, primarily associated gas, are 112 tn ft³/3.1 tn m³. Fields are scattered from the northern border to the Shatt al-Arab (Map 13.5; see also Map 6.1). However, only seventeen of the fields are developed, primarily the

multibillion-barrel reservoirs: current production is from only 1,685 wells.

Iraqi production has never been commensurate with its known reserves. Output peaked at 3.4 mn bpd in 1979 but has since fluctuated greatly, based mostly on the impact of Saddam Husayn's military adventures. After sharp drops during the war with Iran, production approached 3 mn bpd in 1989, only to drop to 283,000 bpd in 1991, its lowest level in forty years. Under international sanctions, it was not until the UN Security Council Resolution 986 setting up the "Oil for Food" program that it legally exported oil in 1997. Receipts paid for humanitarian imports (later extended to critical machinery and equipment), compensation to Gulf War victims, UN teams, transit fees for pipelines through Turkey, and similar costs. It was later revealed that the program was often circumvented by corruption.[17]

As with other parts of the economy, oil faced enormous difficulties after April 2003. The fighting had not seriously damaged the infrastructure; however, twenty-three years of war and neglect had left the system crippled. Coalition repair teams dispatched to Iraq encountered daunting challenges.[18] Insurgents systematically conducted sabotage, impeding production and exports, targeting pipelines especially. In May 2003, the UN lifted the sanctions and then ended the Oil for Food program. Limited production and export of crude resumed almost immediately after the formal end of hostilities and climbed to an average of 2 mn bpd in 2004, despite sabotage, faulty and obsolete equipment, and danger to personnel. But even with improved security, the goal of 3 mn bpd proved elusive through the 2000s.

Iraq's refining capacity of 598,500 bpd throughput is distributed among eight installations, geographically distributed between Kirkuk and Basrah. The two largest are in the center: Bayji with 310,000 bpd north of Baghdad and Dawrah with 100,000 bpd in Greater Baghdad. The Basrah refinery, with 150,000 bpd normal capacity, serves the south. All refineries were operating well below capacity, were sorely in need of repair and upgrading, and were frequently attacked by insurgents. Through the 2000s, gasoline, kerosene, and other refined products were constantly in short supply. At the end of the decade, the country was still importing about a quarter of its needs of some products.

Details of the several pipeline complexes are given in the "Pipelines" section of Chapter 6. It is worth noting that, although the old IPC multiple lines to the Mediterranean were shut in by Syria in 1982, it reopened them to illicitly import Iraqi oil between 2001 and March 2003. The 600-mile dual lines from Kirkuk across southeastern Turkey to Yumurtalık, opened in 1977 and 1987, have a fully operational capacity of 1.1 mn bpd and saved Iraq's economy during the Iran War; they were shut in after 1990 at UN demand. Reopened under UN Resolution 986, they served as the main export facility until March 2003. Pumping resumed after April 2003 but was repeatedly interrupted by sabotage, so that only occasionally could effective use be made of the facility. The large IPSA line through Saudi Arabia was also a major "backdoor" outlet, but this was shut in with the Iraqi attack on Kuwait; it was expropriated by Saudi Arabia in 2001. Two large trestle tanker export terminals off the Shatt al-Arab were damaged in the 1980s fighting but were back in partial operation by the late 1990s; they were immediately pressed into service after April 2003. With the lines through Turkey subject to insurgent sabotage, the Gulf terminals were the sole reliable export outlet. The al-Basrah terminal has four 400,000 bpd berths for Very Large Crude Carriers; Khawr al-Amaya's handling capacity is 1.2 mn bpd.

Soon after the formal end of hostilities in 2003, the coalition declared that oil income would restore the economy and social structure. By the end of the 2000s, the sector had yet to realize its potential. But despite frequent interruptions of exports due to sabotage or the failure of aging petro-infrastructure, output in the late 2000s was at its highest since the invasion—earning Iraq the 2008 high-price windfall. However, at 2.4 mn bpd in 2009, it was still well below peak output in the late 1970s. Revenues in 2009 were off by about a third from the record level of $61 billion the year previously.

Iraq's ten-year strategy (2008–2017) calls for 4.0 mn bpd by 2012 and 6.0 mn bpd by 2017. In December 2009, the minister of petroleum claimed Iraq could eventually produce 12 mn bpd,[19] but there was skepticism that so much expansion will occur in the first five years, given regulatory, administrative, and political constraints.[20] Hoping to accelerate increases, in late 2009 Iraq signed several service contracts with foreign oil firms for developments in the rich southern fields of Rumaila and Zubair; ironically, one of the partners in the first deal was British Petroleum (BP), an original shareholder in IPC. Then ExxonMobil and Royal Dutch Shell, also ex-IPC shareholders, signed a similar contract; they will be paid a set fee for each barrel they produce.[21] The veterans are being joined by new players, like Russia's Lukoil, a partner in opening Iraq's vast and untapped West Qurna field, which alone could produce 1.8 mn bpd.[22] Even Angola's state oil company, Sonangol, has signed on to develop two fields.[23] The major internationals are clearly looking to the future in Iraq; they see this in the south, and they want to be in on the ground floor.[24] With its eye on greatly increased output in the not too distant future, Iraq indicated it will not discuss its place in the OPEC quota system until 2012.[25]

Other Minerals

The nonfuel mineral resources of Iraq have so far proved to be relatively limited compared with those of Turkey and Iran; only sulfur and phosphates are noteworthy. In addition to by-product sulfur from its refineries, one of the world's biggest deposits of mineral sulfur—130 million metric tons—is at Mishraq south of Mosul—and nearby plants produce a range of acids and other products. Phosphate mining at Akashat on the Euphrates near the Syrian border was expanded several times after the late 1970s, and a large plant at al-Qaim processes some of the phosphates for acids and fertilizers. Both the sulfur and phosphates, along with their derivative products, are normally important exports.

Water Resources

Iraq, like Egypt, is formed by its rivers; however, water is of the greatest value when it comes in the right amounts and at the right time. The steady flow of the Tigris and Euphrates has historically provided for irrigation and domestic needs, but since 1991 the deterioration of infrastructure has led to a decline in the access to safe water and sanitation in both urban and rural areas. Before 1991, 95 percent of urban dwellers had clean drinking water; by 2007, this percentage had dropped to 73 percent as a result of war, sabotage, and lack of maintenance. Additionally, many Iraqis had taken refuge from the insurgency outside the existing service areas. Rural facilities suffered even more, from both physical damage and deterioration, with dependable service dropping from 75 to 43 percent over the same period.[26] Damage to distribution systems results in half the water's being lost before reaching its intended destinations. Sanitation has also been hard hit—outside of the KRG's domain, less than 10 percent of wastewater gets any sort of treatment. The rest flows directly into rivers and aquifers, contaminating drinking and irrigation water. Since the necessary large-scale infrastructure projects are expensive and have been slow to construct, stopgap measures have been used with mixed results.

Manufacturing

Most industrial development has occurred since 1960 and is concentrated around Baghdad, with its large market and labor supply but also with advantages in transportation and energy, and, in the south, around Basrah, with its import-export advantages and proximity to the oil and gas sector. Increased hydrocarbon production in the north stimulated industrial growth in the Mosul-Irbil-Kirkuk triangle, giving Iraq its third manufacturing region (see Map 7.1). The more important manufacturing centers are underlined on Map 13.1, although many smaller towns pursue various crafts.

Textiles have been a traditional product for centuries, with Mosul—which gave its name to muslin—still a center. Food and beverage processing have been major activities for decades. Increased oil production in the 1950s generated many enterprises exploiting energy or using hydrocarbons as raw materials. Concentration in the center intensified as additional plants produced a wide range of items—pharmaceuticals, paper and plastic products, household appliances, clothing, assembled automobiles and trucks, and, before 1991, large amounts of military weaponry and support systems.

The mid-Iraq interfluve continues to be the country's industrial heartland. Before bombing by Iran during the 1980s and by the coalition in 1990–1991 and again in 2003, the strategic southern corridor was a center for petrochemicals and heavy industry—iron and steel, steel fabrication products, oil pipe, salt, and fertilizers and other chemicals. Oil revenues financed generous subsidies to socialized industries, giving rise to several large (and often inefficient) state-owned enterprises (SOEs). Postinvasion Iraq saw attempts to privatize some SOEs, but there had been little success by the end of the 2000s. Foreign investment has been sought by the government, but aside from the oil sector and opportunities in the KRG, there has not been much interest; potential investors cite both security concerns and a pervading atmosphere of corruption.[27]

Increasing emphasis on military prowess in the 1970s and 1980s (with Soviet cooperation) spurred development of a sophisticated weapons industry. For most of the 1990s, the nature, location, capacity, and level of readiness of this industry were issues central to a grim cat-and-mouse game between Iraqi authorities and weapons inspectors from the UN Special Commission (UNSCOM) team. UNSCOM inspections were conducted under UN Resolution 687 of April 1991, setting the terms for the ceasefire between Iraq and the coalition, for Iraq's disarmament, and for prohibition of the possession or production of chemical, biological, and nuclear weapons. Following a serious confrontation in December 1998, Iraq refused to cooperate further with UNSCOM, and the United States and Britain launched a punishing four-day air attack on December 16–19.[28] Not until November 2002 did inspectors return to Iraq, this time as the United Nations Monitoring, Verification, and Inspection Commission (UNMOVIC), under UN Resolution 1441, to search for weapons of mass destruction (WMD) or the facilities producing them. UNMOVIC had found no evidence of either by the time the U.S.-led invasion was launched in March 2003; neither did the intensive search by the United States after the invasion ever turn up any trace of WMDs.

Transportation and Trade

Roads. Iraq's physical geography and early development—mostly along the two northwest-southeast axes of the Tigris and Euphrates—imposed a pattern on road and railroad development. Major roads generally parallel both rivers. The main north-south motorway from Mosul to Baghdad goes along the Tigris, but then takes the interfluve directly to Basrah and Kuwait (see Map 13.1). In addition to this motorway, three highways converge on Baghdad from the north and west: from Sulaymaniyah, from Irbil through Kirkuk, and from the Jordan border. The latter is an express motorway joined by the Euphrates highway from Syria. Highways also follow both rivers south of Baghdad.

The links to north, west, and south brought in essential food and military matériel during the Iran-Iraq War, especially from Jordan's Aqabah port through Rutbah and Ramadi to Baghdad. Dozens of bridges and road junctions destroyed or damaged in 1991 and again in 2003 were gradually repaired or replaced after mid-2003, although regularly sabotaged. The highway system was heavily utilized for the U.S.-led invasion and then by resupply and reconstruction trucks afterward. So regular were the supply runs that convoys were frequently attacked, especially by remote-controlled "improvised explosive devices" (IEDs) set by insurgents. The IEDs became such dangers to convoy personnel that ordinary trucks and vans had to be armored; nonetheless, there were many casualties among Iraqi civilians and Iraqi and Coalition security forces.

Railways. The Berlin-to-Baghdad railway was a German goal during the heyday of railroad building; it enters Iraq northwest of Mosul, parallels the Tigris to Baghdad, and then follows the Euphrates to Basrah and the Gulf. It was the country's only railway until development of phosphate deposits near al-Qaim prompted construction of a 318-mi/512-km link, completed in 1984, down the Euphrates and across to Baghdad. Another line, 156 mi/252 km long, finished in 1987, parallels the major pipelines from Kirkuk to Hadithah on the Euphrates, where it joins the line from al-Qaim to Baghdad. A third line into Baghdad links Irbil and Kirkuk with the capital. During the 1990s, the main lines were repaired, upgraded, and double-tracked between Baghdad and Basrah. Like those in Egypt, Iraqi railways normally carry a heavy passenger load. In 2008, the popular Baghdad-Basrah route was back in operation. At the end of the 2000s, the government was pursuing plans for a Baghdad metro system with two lines. As Kuwait is planning a rail line from its border with Iraq to that with Saudi Arabia (see Chap. 15), an extension of the Iraqi system to tie in with this will be needed.

Airlines. Although Iraqi Airways (IA), founded in 1946, evolved into a modestly successful operation, with twenty-three aircraft in the 1970s, it was virtually dormant after 1990. It ambitiously resumed flights to Amman and Damascus with one plane in October 2004. However, flights into Baghdad were such potential targets for insurgents that IA was little used during the early postinvasion period, but as the decade progressed a more normal schedule became possible. Basrah Airport, built in the 1980s by Saddam Husayn, went largely unused because of the sanctions after 1991 until civilian traffic resumed in 2005; the British military departed in 2009 and returned it to Iraqi control. Kurdistan Airlines was launched in 2005; the KRG opened Sulaimaniyah International Airport the same year, and Irbil's Hawler International Airport was expanded to accommodate the largest passenger jets. Al-Najaf's airport does a thriving business in religious tourism.

Ports. The narrowness of Iraq's Gulf window—only 36 mi/58 km—restricts potential port sites: only the exploitation of indentations (drowned estuaries, called *khawrs* or *khors*) has enabled useful port development. Although several ports are needed because of the scale and variety of imports and exports, Basrah served for centuries as the only port, but its location on the relatively shallow Shatt al-Arab limited growth and led to congestion. Oil development and economic expansion after the 1950s demanded additional facilities, including (1) an oil terminal at al-Faw, down the Shatt al-Arab from Basrah; (2) two general-cargo ports, Khawr al-Zubair and Umm Qasr, on a drowned estuary near the Kuwait border, with Umm Qasr also serving as a naval base; and (3) two oil-export terminals—Mina al-Bakr (now called al-Basrah) and Khawr al-Amayah—on trestle causeways into the deeper water at the head of the Gulf. Even before the war with Iran, the ports were overloaded, and

Iraq imported through Aqabah, Kuwait, and other Gulf ports. Iran destroyed the domestic complexes in the early 1980s, necessitating Iraq's greater reliance on Kuwait and especially Aqabah, both of which were denied to Iraq during the 1990–1991 war. Restored in the 1990s, the domestic ports suffered only limited damage in 2003; Umm Qasr was quickly made usable, and the trestles were soon put into limited operation.

Trade. Crude petroleum has long constituted 90–95 percent of Iraqi exports, along with some processed dates and fertilizers. Like other aspects of the economy, trade was greatly affected by the three wars between 1980 and 2003. UN Resolution 661 of August 1990 imposed sanctions that remained in effect until May 2003. In the early 1990s, only a minimum flow—some smuggled—entered or left Iraq; 80,000–100,000 bpd of oil was trucked to Jordan under special exemption. In a desperate situation, Iraq finally agreed to the terms of the Oil for Food Resolution 986 of 1995. Exports then generated funds for food and medicine; essential machinery and equipment were later permitted. The program was renewed every six months until sanctions were lifted. Immediately after April 2003, trade was of course abnormal: Only oil was exported—under coalition control—and the only official imports came under coalition orders. However, a lively "informal" trade across all land borders brought in great quantities, including automobiles, electronic goods, and large appliances, satisfying demands pent up since 1990. Gradually, as security and the domestic economy improved, importing became more normalized.

Retail trade is still largely conducted in typical Arab small-shop operations. The traditional covered *suq* is found in most urban centers, and after some delay a few large Western-type malls have evolved in the biggest cities, especially in the KRG. The mer-

chant class declined sharply under the Baathis, and although business and free enterprise were encouraged after 2003, merchants faced looting, kidnapping of family members for ransom, and threats from insurgents if goods were considered forbidden by fundamentalist Muslims (liquor and Western videos, for example). The once-strong Iraqi dinar (equal to about US$3.20 in the 1970s) collapsed after the two Gulf wars and by mid-2003 was worth only US$0.0005. Since the locally printed currency was easily counterfeited, the occupation authorities quickly replaced it in October 2003 with conventionally engraved notes, restoring confidence in the money supply.

Debt and Reparations

Any discussion of Iraq's current economy and its prospects would be incomplete without taking note of an enormous problem the current government inherited from more than three decades of Baathi despotism and specifically from the Saddam regime. To finance the military framework he deemed necessary to further his ambitions, he incurred huge debts, against future oil revenues, with obligations owed to foreign governments and armament suppliers from all parts of the political spectrum. Then using what he acquired in two disastrously undertaken aggressions against Iran and Kuwait that ended in defeat, he obligated Iraq to make massive reparations for the havoc wreaked on his opponents and to others who could claim collateral damages. Within a few months of Saddam's toppling, Iraqi officials were aware of the enormity of the problem they were facing, although its exact size was difficult to identify—estimates ran as high as more than $350 billion if all potential reparations claims were considered.

Possibly because the United States was eager for Iraq's oil revenues to be used as soon as possible for reconstruction, it began to call for debt forgiveness very soon after the fall of Baghdad through the Club of Paris, an informal group of the largest creditor countries. In 2004, a compromise resulted in the forgiveness of 80 percent of Iraq's debt to club members. Some creditors forgave more—for example, the United States all of its $4.1 billion and Russia 93 percent of about $13 billion. The members tied forgiveness to a package of reforms to be undertaken by Iraq, as did the International Monetary Fund when it extended a series of Stand-By Arrangements beginning in 2005—the third of which was for $5.5 billion in 2009. During the Iran war, Iraq borrowed very heavily from Gulf Cooperation Council (GCC) states, and at the end of the 2000s it was not clear how much progress it had made on this front, aside from the UAE's announcing in 2008 the cancellation of $7 billion. In 2009, Iraq asked China to forgive $8.5 billion.

Reparations are separate from debt: In 1991, Iraq was required by the UN to put aside 5 percent of all future oil revenues to pay more than $50 billion to Kuwait for damages during the occupation. In June 2008, Iraq said it had already paid more than $27 billion and petitioned the UN to reduce the percentage it had to put aside, thus lengthening the time to complete reparations. Iran has claims as well; although these do not have official backing, the UN did estimate in 1991 that about $100 billion was due to Iran. At the end of the 2000s, there were indications that, while Iran was still pressing its claims, it perhaps was more interested in establishing strong links with a Shii-dominated Iraqi government and in settling long-standing issues like demarcating their long mutual border as was originally agreed under the Algiers Accord in 1975 (see "Regional Conflicts," Chapter 8).

Having reviewed Iraq's fundamental physical and resource patterns in the preceding sections, we can now examine highlights of the country's evolution following establishment of the monarchy.

MONARCHY, REPUBLIC, DESPOTRY, AND BEYOND

Pre-2003. Under British tutelage, mandate Iraq developed only slowly, partly because of constraints imposed on oil exploration and production. Even after independence in 1932, British officials continued in key positions.[29] During the 1950s, the autocratic pro-Western prime minister, Nuri al-Said, linked Iraq with the West and led his country into the Baghdad Pact (see Chap. 8) as the only Arab member. At the time, Nasserist Arabism was sweeping the Middle East and inspiring Iraqi nationalists to resist Western ties, and the Baghdad Pact was a move squarely against Nasser's view of Arab unity. In the uncertainty, a military coup d'état violently overthrew the Iraqi monarchy in July 1958, and King Faysal II, along with most of his family and closest advisers (including Nuri al-Said) were murdered. The coup leader, Gen. Abd al-Karim Qasim (Kassem), established a republic that, born in brutality, experienced successive decades of intermittent violence.

The Qasim regime fell, in turn, to a coup in 1963 that first brought power to the Baath (Arab Renaissance) Party; it was ousted within months by nationalist officers. Coup attempts in 1965 and 1966 failed before the party decisively regained power in July 1968. It remained dominant, with strongman Saddam Husayn increasingly in control until he seized the presidency in 1979, holding the office until April 2003. (Baath control in Syria also began in 1963; after 1966, the party split into two feuding factions—Syrian and Iraqi).[30]

From the moment of the mandate's imposition, Iraqis felt marginalized and deprived of their proper place in the Arab sun. Resisting mandate status, they clamored for independence, and afterward continued to object to British influence until the monarchy was overthrown in 1958 when, however unstable the government, they finally felt they had achieved real independence. They possessed a rich culture and often embraced political and cultural pluralism, regardless of the uncertain political situation in their country. Over the past eighty years, Iraqis have pursued many avenues to demonstrate political potency and to offset perceived external denigration. As Chapter 8 explained, Iraq has long asserted its claim to Kuwait and a larger share of the Gulf coast. For forty years, the government accused oil companies of acting against Iraqi interests—not a groundless charge—and later led the successful organization of OPEC. When Britain withdrew from the Gulf in 1971, Iraq promptly asserted its claim to be the new hegemon. However, when challenged by Iran, it prudently yielded to its more powerful neighbor, then under the shah and supported by the United States. But these claims served notice of the ambitions that led to war against Iran and the invasion of Kuwait.

During the 1970s, prevailing high oil prices benefited Iraq, and the country achieved marked progress. When the Baath formally selected Saddam Husayn as president in 1979, Iraq was personified in the most ambitious and aggressive leader since its creation. Within a year, it was at war with Iran—the first of his several major miscalculations; by 1988, it had suffered not only hundreds of thousands of casualties but also the destruction of much of its new infrastructure. During the war, it received billions of dollars in aid from Gulf oil states, as well as assistance and encouragement from the United States; some sectors of the economy actually advanced during the 1980s. After the cease-fire, Iraq rebuilt and rearmed, borrowing tens of billions of dollars, with future oil production as collateral.

In August 1990, he once again miscalculated and invaded Kuwait. When he refused to withdraw and coalition aircraft attacked Iraqi targets, the damage inflicted on Iraq's main cities and infrastructure during just a few weeks exceeded that dealt by Iran over eight years. In a decade-long stalemate with the UN—and specifically with the United States—over conditions for lifting sanctions, Iraq fell to its lowest standard of living since the 1920s. It appeared that, by choice, the leadership preferred pride and penury over perceived submission and prosperity. The cat-and-mouse game that the regime played with UNSCOM was later revealed to be mainly a device to keep Iran and Israel guessing as to its military capabilities, which in fact were largely imaginary. Nevertheless, when UN inspectors returned in 2002 after a four-year hiatus, Iraq's responses over several months were declared to be inadequate by the UN. The U.S. administration under George W. Bush had decided that the putative weapons of mass destruction were a casus belli. A U.S. ultimatum was predictably rejected, and coalition attacks began on March 20, 2003 (see Chap. 8).[31]

Post-2003: Occupation Rule. Beginning with the coalition's formal declaration of the end of major combat activity on May 1, Iraq entered the most crucial months of its existence as an independent state under an occupation authority largely unprepared for whatever followed military victory. Iraqis toppled dozens of self-aggrandizing monuments to Saddam, and thousands of his life-size portraits were torn from their mountings; hundreds of his palaces, government buildings, and party offices had been reduced to bombed-out hulks. Rioters and looters seemed to rule the day in Baghdad and other cities. The Coalition Provisional Authority exercised power with U.S./coalition military backing and appointed twenty-five Iraqis to a temporary Governing Council (GC), including many exiles with close ties to the invading forces. With the old regime ousted, many Iraqis who had lost family members sought help in finding remains in the mass burials known to exist. Tens of thousands of bodies were discovered, and human rights groups estimated that as many as 300,000 missing Iraqis had been executed by the Mukhabarat, the Baathist intelligence service.[32]

A growing insurgency used increasingly destructive devices, from AK-47s, mortars, and rocket-propelled grenades to suicide bombers and car and truck bombs; these deadly vehicles destroyed the Jordanian Embassy and the UN headquarters in Baghdad in August and killed hundreds in al-Najaf, Karbala, and Baghdad. Improvised explosive devices caused hundreds of roadside blasts, unnerving military and civilian drivers alike. In December, Saddam was found in a small underground hiding place near his clan stronghold of Tikrit. After a dramatic trial, he was executed a year later.

With the restoration of political and economic structures interrupted and sometimes offset by sabotage and attacks, Iraq moved haltingly toward revival. Despite its low level of credibility, the Governing Council drew up a Transitional Administrative Law, and the CPA surrendered state sovereignty to the appointed Iraqi Interim Government (IIG) replacing the Governing Council on June 28, 2004. The UN had already authorized ending the formal occupation. The interim government displayed some signs of exercising sovereignty, although it was obviously dependent on the coalition for security and solvency.

Post-2003: Regaining Autonomy.   The caretaker IIG scheduled national and local elections for January 30, 2005, the first of several political events in a momentous year. Despite multiple daily insurgent attacks on Iraqi and coalition forces, preparations for the first free elections in Iraq in fifty years were not disrupted. Even a quadrupled level of assaults on election day did not prevent fairly successful polling, as 8.45 million voters—59 percent of those eligible—cast their ballots. As expected, the Shii list won the largest number

of seats (140 with 47 percent of the vote) in the 275-member Iraqi National Assembly (INA) and the Kurds the next largest (75 with 25 percent). With many Sunnis boycotting the polling, the Iraqi List—hoping to draw on Sunni voters—won only 40 seats and 14 percent.

The new parliament was charged with drafting a permanent constitution to replace the transitional law by August 15, arranging for a national vote on the constitution on October 15 and—if it was approved—conducting elections for a full-term government on December 15. It was also to choose an interim president and two vice presidents, who would decide on a prime minister. These offices were split among Kurds (president), Sunni Arabs (one vice president plus parliament speaker), and Shii (one vice president and prime minister).[33] Overwhelming Kurdish and Shii support gave 79 percent approval to the constitution; it provided for (but did not require) a federal structure, thus institutionalizing the KRG. By the end of the 2000s, the proposal to divide the rest of Iraq into two more states—in the south a predominantly Shii entity and in the center one with a Sunni majority—remained unrealized, with strong Sunni opposition and less than united support from the Shii.

The December 2005 election for the Iraqi Council of Representatives saw notably more Sunni voters—more than 70 percent of eligible voters took part; the Shii and Kurdish lists lost seats (securing 128 and 53, respectively), a new Sunni coalition emerged (59 seats), and the more secular cross-community Iraqi List declined (25 seats). Losing their majority, the Shii parties allied with the Kurds and eventually selected Nuri al-Maliki as prime minister;[34] his cabinet also included members of Sunni parties. Provincial elections in January 2009 rewarded the prime minister's faction and notably weakened the influence of groups with pro-Iranian coloring. For the Council of Representatives elections set for

March 2010, al-Maliki broke his link to the main Shii bloc and formed a broad coalition, State of Law, made up of Shii, Sunni, Kurdish, Christian, and secular elements.[35] Agreeing on a law governing this election proved troublesome, in part because of disagreement over exactly who was entitled to vote in Kirkuk. A final compromise included representation for the large numbers who had fled to neighboring countries; predictably, setting a date for the elections was followed by an expected surge in bombings by those trying to sabotage the process.

The results seem to indicate a swing away from sectarian-dominated parties, with two broad-based blocs, respectively Iraqiya, led by former prime minister Ayad Allawi, and State of Law, headed by current prime minister Nuri al-Maliki, gaining the largest number of seats (91 and 89, respectively—a majority, actually, between them); both the two leaders are nationalists and proponents of a strong central government, but they have important differences as well.[36] Al-Maliki's gains came somewhat at the expense of the Iraq National Alliance (INA), an almost entirely Shii grouping with ties to Iran.[37] However, the process of producing a viable coalition government is bound to be arduous, and an alliance between al-Maliki and the INA leading to a Shii-dominated regime that shut out the Sunnis could lead to renewed insurgency.[38] This would be more likely if an Iranian hand was detected as clearly at work in forming the resulting government.[39] On the other hand, both the INA and the Kurds are potential spoilers if they feel excluded. Of course, if the situation involving Iran's nuclear ambitions were to escalate sharply, then the prospects for an orderly transition in Iraq would clearly be impacted.

The multitude of elections since 2004 has sometimes seemed confusing to both Iraqis and foreigners; they have not been totally devoid of controversy, but they have generally been free of the electoral fraud that was so apparent in the 2009 pollings in Afghanistan and Iran. The 2010 election's results will provide the greatest test so far for Iraq's fragile democracy.

On the military side at the end of the 2000s, the situation seemed better than it had four years earlier, but it was difficult to evaluate future prospects. What the Bush administration in 2003 thought would be a short campaign followed by the emergence of a stable, democratic Iraq supported by oil exports had turned into the United States' third longest war (after Vietnam and Afghanistan), which by March 2010 had cost nearly 4,400 American lives and about $1 trillion dollars in direct outlays. For Iraq, the loss was far worse, though much harder to quantify with precision: quite likely more deaths than the estimated 500,000 suffered in the war with Iran and more hundreds of billions of dollars in economic damage than was inflicted between 1980 and 2003.

Seven years after the invasion, more than 1 in 6 Iraqis remained dislocated from their former homes, some 1.9 million were internally displaced persons (IDPs), and at least 2 million had left the country as refugees.[40] The IDP problem has intensified ethic/sectarian conflicts—for example, in Kirkuk and in many Baghdad and Mosul neighborhoods—and the government ministry tasked with mitigating the situation has been perennially underfunded. The refugees have increasingly become a burden in those countries that have offered sanctuary to the largest numbers of them—Syria and Jordan (see Chaps. 9 and 11).

"The New Way Forward" (commonly referred to as "the Surge") undertaken in the spring of 2007 was essentially a counterinsurgency campaign with limited objectives; on the whole, it seemed to accomplish these objectives, especially in Baghdad and in areas where units related to al-Qaida had been strong.[41] In February 2009, the Obama administration decided that the situation allowed a phased drawdown of U.S. troops with Iraqi forces taking charge of urban areas by midyear, a U.S. transition from combat and counterinsurgency to training and support by August 2010, and a redeployment of all U.S. forces by the end of 2010.

RELATIONS

Iraq's earliest relations were perforce with Britain, the mandatory that also controlled the Iraq Petroleum Company, and links remained close—if not always friendly—until 1958. Relations were distant after the 1958 coup, and British forces guarded newly independent Kuwait against Iraqi threats. Britain was a leading member of both coalitions in 1990 and 2003 and was a partner in air patrols of the no-fly zones.

Iraq has had significant relations with many states, both neighbors and distant countries. With all its immediate neighbors, these have been unusually dynamic relations. Indeed, it has been at war with all of them except Jordan and has directly fought Iran and Kuwait. Syrian, Saudi, and Turkish forces joined the 1990–1991 coalition but not the coalition of 2003. With all neighbors, relations have swung from friendly to antagonistic and sometimes back again in a single decade.

Between 1958 and 1990, Iraq's primary foreign policy concern was to affirm and strengthen its Arab credentials and to assert leadership in the region. It supplied troops in the 1948–1949 war between Arab countries and Israel, and it did so again in 1967. It consistently supported the Palestinian cause, winning appreciation among Palestinians and other Arabs on the street, especially in Jordan and Yemen. As implacable opponents and genuine threats to each other's security, Iraq and Israel have viewed each other as major foes. Israel bombed Iraq's Osirak nuclear reactor in 1981, and Iraq struck back against the Jewish state in

1991 when it fired thirty-nine Scud missiles into Israel during the coalition's response to the invasion of Kuwait. Israel gave military assistance to Iran during the Iran-Iraq War, waged an effective war of words against Iraq, and was active through its supporters in the United States in urging and prioritizing the 2003 invasion. Ahmed Chalabi, founder of the exile group the Iraq National Congress and putative candidate of the neocons in the Bush administration to head postinvasion Iraq, was believed by them to favor signing a peace treaty with Israel once he was in power.[42]

Especially after the 1958 revolution, Iraq emphasized its historical role in Islam (Fig. 13.4), despite the dominance of the secularist Baath; it considers itself the eastern anchor of the Arab world and the natural eastern flank of the Mashriq, the Arab Middle East, with Egypt the western flank. As a member of the Arab League, it was regularly militant, a "rejectionist" state, under Saddam Husayn and its earlier leaders, often advocating more aggressive stands than the majority of members. Its direct relations with Egypt have blown hot and cold since 1958. Other Arab states of the Mashriq have been ambivalent toward Iraq: They condemned the aggression against Kuwait and its firing Scud missiles into Saudi Arabia, but they still recognized its support of Arabism, its stand against Iran, its defiance of the vestiges of imperialism, and its opposition to Israel. Because of rifts between the Baath factions in Damascus and Baghdad, relations with Syria deteriorated when the Baath came to power in Iraq—especially after Syria supported Iran in the 1980s and joined the 1990–1991 coalition. However, both countries found closer relations to be expedient later in the 1990s. The United States repeatedly accused Syria of aiding Iraq up to 2003 and insurgent groups afterward. At the end of the decade, Iraq voiced concerns that Syria-based terrorists had carried out several major bombing attacks, but no

FIGURE 13.4 Spiral minaret (al-Mawiyah), Samarra, Iraq, built in the ninth century while Samarra was the capital of the Abbasid Empire. Figures at base give the scale of this unusual minaret, 171 ft/52 m high, which served the Friday Mosque, glimpsed at lower left.

direct evidence of infiltrators crossing the long desert border had been uncovered.

Iraq's relations with Jordan between 1923 and 1958 rested on the kinship of the Hashimite kings of the two countries. Although meaningful implementation of the proposed Arab Federation between the two kingdoms was prevented by the 1958 revolu-tion, mutual interests restored relations. The link proved to be critical to Iraq in the 1990–1991 crisis and through the following decade, as well as being economically bene-ficial to Jordan, as was shown in Chapter 11 and earlier in this chapter. Jordan's embassy in Baghdad was struck by insurgents in 2003, leaving eleven dead. Full relations between the two neighbors were restored in 2008 with the visit of King Abdullah, the first Arab head of state to visit since 2003.

It is with its Arab neighbors of the Gulf that Iraq's relations are the most critical and sometimes ambiguous. When the Gulf states and Saudi Arabia organized the GCC, they excluded Iraq. Yet after invading Iran and proclaiming itself the bastion of Arabism against Persian designs, when Iraq desperately required assistance all the GCC states came to its aid with billions in finance and other assistance. Kuwait and Saudi Arabia were especially helpful. In addition, they helped with proxy shipments of oil on Iraq's OPEC quota and account, and Saudi Arabia agreed to construct the IPSA pipeline to the Red Sea across its territory. Iraq's about-face invasion of Kuwait and its attacks on Saudi Arabia during the Gulf war thus seemed all the more inexplicable, and these actions contradicted its vociferous claims to be a leading supporter of Arab unity. Both Kuwait and Saudi Arabia supported U.S. and UK air patrols of the no-fly zones, and Kuwait was a key factor, beginning in 2003, in operations connected with the invasion and occupation. But, along with other Arab states, even Kuwait was skeptical about the motivation of the United States regarding its role in the Gulf and the wider Middle East. As Iraq regained its sovereignty, relations with its southern neighbors improved, but there has been a strong undercurrent among them of dismay at the militant Shiism manifesting itself in Iraq, as well as concern about the perceived close ties between the al-Maliki government and Iran.

Alienated from the West after 1958, Iraq turned to the USSR, receiving military supplies denied by the West, while keeping domestic Communists under strict control. It intermittently resisted other relations with the Soviets and, over time, attempted to balance its East-West relations, positioning itself to receive assistance from the West as the So-

viet Union disintegrated. Russia supported the coalition in 1990–1991 but was sympathetic to Iraq's plight under sanctions and U.S. and UK air attacks. It opposed the U.S.-led invasion, perhaps hoping to better position Russian companies bidding for oil and other contracts. Russia canceled 93 percent of Iraqi debt owed it in 2008.

Relations with Turkey were quiet for decades, but they were reinvigorated in the 1970s by the agreement on the pipeline from Kirkuk to Yumurtalık. They were further improved by later arrangements to double the line, with Turkey receiving its oil supplies through the lines. However, this rapport collapsed in August 1990 when Turkey shut in the lines in accordance with UN sanctions against Iraq. Relations between Turkey and Iraq were on a roller coaster in the early 1990s, especially regarding the Kurds, and the Kurdish issue became a very serious problem in the period before and after March 2003.[43] Underneath the relations regarding oil and Kurds, running tension also persists over Turkey's reduction of Euphrates water to downstream riparians, as well as over Turkey's increasing support of Turkmans who are scattered among Iraqi Kurds. Ironically, Turkey has benefited considerably from a great increase in its exports to Iraq, especially to the Kurdish region.

The historical antagonism between the people of the Mesopotamian Basin and those of the Iranian Plateau intensified after the 1979 Iranian Revolution and broke into open warfare between Iran and Iraq in September 1980 (see Chap. 8). After eight years of combat and two years of bickering, Iraq made an uneasy peace with Iran in 1990 in order to ensure Iran's neutrality and to avert the danger of having to fight on two fronts. After the early 1990s, Iranian-Iraqi relations remained uneasily quiescent, and after 2003 Iranian Shii pilgrims flooded into al-Najaf and Karbala for the first time in nearly twenty-five years. Official relations have been cordial, but even the Shii-led government has been concerned by the links between certain factions in Iran and some Shii militias/political parties in Iraq. Despite the religious commonality, there is a transcending ambiguity based on historic Arab-Persian antagonisms.

Crucial as Iraq's links were with its neighbors, its relations with the United States have proved to be the most decisive. U.S.-Iraqi relations following the 1958 revolution were little more than "correct," and along with several other Arab governments Iraq broke relations after the 1967 Arab-Israeli war on the grounds that the United States had assisted Israel during that conflict. Quiet negotiations based on anti-Iran concerns finally led to a resumption of full diplomatic relations in December 1984. The détente survived several crises, with the United States making a number of gestures toward Iraq in the late 1980s. Opponents in both countries resisted rapprochement, and the U.S. advances were heavily criticized, especially after Iraq invaded Kuwait in 1990; however, diplomatic observers emphasized that such efforts are standard and have been used with considerable success in many circumstances.

Although relations were patently low in 1990–1991, with the United States leading the coalition against Iraq, they worsened as sanctions remained year after year, largely at U.S. insistence. By 1998, the United States had virtually co-opted the UN role in responding to Iraqi actions, despite increasing criticism from other Security Council members. With the expulsion of UNSCOM inspectors in late 1998, the almost daily bombing by U.S. planes became a war of attrition; Iraq gained appreciable, if grudging, sympathy from its Arab neighbors and other countries. With the United States demanding full compliance with UN relations before lifting sanctions, implying that only "regime change" could meet these requirements, and with its increasing support for exile opposition groups, the intensified air campaign was criticized in the Arab world as "sinister" and exhibiting "sheer savage vigor of supremacy."[44]

The hard-line Clinton administration policies set the stage for covert planning by neoconservatives who came to power with the Bush administration pressing for an early invasion of Iraq; preparations became more overt after September 11, 2001. The Bush administration alleged Iraqi links to al-Qaida and proclaimed as established fact that Saddam had secret caches of "weapons of mass destruction." The unlikelihood of secular Baathis allying with ultrafundamentalists was ignored, and the fact that the recently returned UNMOVIC inspectors found no evidence of WMDs was dismissed, as were their pleas for additional time.[45]

The events following the invasion of 2003 have been described above (in "Monarchy, Republic, Despotry, and Beyond"). Only in 2006 did real diminution of U.S. civil authority over the country begin to take hold, and in 2007 Iraq and the United States agreed to negotiate the framework for a long-term relationship.[46] In 2008, the two reached a Security Agreement, basically covering the conditions under which the U.S. military would stay in the country during a phased drawdown. Additionally, a Security Framework Agreement was reached governing civil relations—on issues of an economic, cultural, scientific, technological, health, and trade nature. To secure parliamentary passage of the agreement, Prime Minister al-Maliki agreed to submit it to a referendum in 2010; remaining implacably opposed were those Shii elements allied with Muqtada al-Sadr.

In 2007, Iraq and the UN, with support from the World Bank, formally launched the International Compact with Iraq at a meeting at Sharm al-Sheikh, Egypt, attended by representatives of more than seventy countries and international organizations. The compact is a five-year program to help Iraq solidify its goal of establishing a unified federal democratic state, achieve economic self-sufficiency, and become an active member of regional and international organizations.[47]

The foregoing analysis of Iraq should make clear that, despite the country's complex situation at the end of the 2000s, it is a land with many enduring physical and human assets. Although it has been tragically misguided and misgoverned, it should have the right to seize—and should seize—this opportunity to develop its great national potential.

NOTES

1. The creation of Iraq is recounted in several studies. A detailed account is Catherwood 2004. More background is given in Klieman 1970, Chap. 7. Busch 1971 discusses the military campaign and its aftermath in the framework of the sometimes competing interests of London and British India. The accounts of the crises of the early 1920s were revived in 2003–2004, when the resistance seemed to be replicated against the coalition. See *New York Times*, July 20, 2003; and *Christian Science Monitor*, Mar. 11, 2004.

2. See *New York Times*, Jan. 24, 1993. For a later, more detailed study, see also Malinowski 2004, and for the most intensive studies of all, made from an environmental viewpoint, see United Nations Environment Programme (UNEP) 2001, 2003.

3. The fascinating story of the former ecological symbiosis between marsh and Madan is recounted in the classic account Thesiger 1964. It has been republished and reprinted several times. For an excellent detailed recent study, see UNEP 2001.

4. These remarks are based partly on Edwards and Yamashita 1999 and partly on updates in *Economist*, Mar. 4, 2005, 77–78, and in a detailed, well-illustrated article in the *New York Times*, Mar. 8, 2005. A recent Reuters account of how drought has affected the area is in *Dawn* (Pakistan), Feb. 4, 2009, www.dawn.com/2009/02/04/int21.htm.

5. See *Washington Post*, July 23, 2009, for a marvelous photo montage: www.washingtonpost.com/wp-dyn/content/gallery/2009/07/23/GA2009072303612.html.

6. Discussed in Lees and Falcon 1952.

7. Though in the run-up to the 2003 invasion, the Bush administration used the Halabjah gassing as proof of the Saddam regime's perfidy, in 1988 the Reagan administration echoed Iraqi claims and tried to shift the blame to Iran (*New York Times*, Jan. 17, 2003). See also Silverstein 2007 at www.harpers.org/archive/2007/07/hbc-90000448, for an interview with Joost Hilterman, author of *A Poisonous Affair: America, Iraq, and the Gassing of Halabja* (2007).

8. Journalistic reports on the Kurds appeared daily during the spring and summer of 1991 and resumed in 2003. A spate of books on the Kurds has also appeared during the past twenty-five years. A good study by a veteran journalist is Randal 1998. More scholarly studies include Ghareeb 1981; Entessar 1992; Gunter 1999; McDowall 2000; and O'Shea 2003. During field observations in Kurdistan in mid-1990, author Held visited the ruins of scores of the razed Kurdish villages and observed several of the new settlements. The sight left no doubt as to the scale of the project or the government's determination to subdue the Kurds through reversing the geographical advantage. With some protection under the no-fly operations, the Kurds returned to their villages after the mid-1990s.

9. Dohuk, Irbil, and Sulaymaniyah. The KRG claims and has de facto control over parts of Nineveh, Tamim, and Diyalah as well; this would give the KRG the cities of Kirkuk and Mosul.

10. To the central government, the KNA is known as the Iraqi Kurdistan Parliament.

11. For the Turkmans, the biggest source of contention with the Kurds is Kirkuk, where many of the former live and which the latter claim as the "Kurdish Jerusalem."

12. See http://chiesa.espresso.repubblica.it/articolo/162781?eng=y.

13. See Chapters 9 and 11 for estimates of Christians among Iraqi refugees in those countries.

14. Some 1,960 Christians were reported killed in Iraq from 2003 through the end of 2009 (*Asia News*, Dec. 31, 2009).

15. Transparency International 2009.

16. TPC originally included German interests; after World War I, as confiscated enemy property, this share went to France. U.S. companies protested their exclusion and eventually joined the consortium.

17. The Independent Inquiry Committee was appointed to investigate charges of corruption; its report is available at www.iic-offp.org/documents/IIC%20Final%20Report%2027Oct2005.pdf.

18. See *Oil and Gas Journal*, July 7, July 30, and Dec. 15, 2003. See also *New York Times*, Nov. 3, 2002, Dec. 14, 2003, and June 6 and June 21, 2004. An excellent account of the oil industry is U.S. Department of Energy, Energy Information Administration, *Country Analysis Briefs: Iraq*, Nov. 2004. See also articles on Iraq in recent volumes of the annual *International Petroleum Encyclopedia*.

19. *BBC News*, Dec. 12, 2009.

20. Expressed by the International Energy Agency as reported by Reuters, July 1, 2009, in *Iraq Directory*, www.iraqdirectory.com/.

21. *New York Times*, Oct. 14 and Dec. 12, 2009; *BBC News*, Dec. 11, 2009.

22. *New York Times*, Dec. 30, 2009.

23. At much higher production fees because the fields are in the still dangerous northern province of Nineveh (*BBC News*, Dec. 30, 2009).

24. *New York Times*, Dec. 1, 2009.

25. *Business Week*, Mar. 16, 2010.

26. World Bank 2009.

27. *New York Times*, Sept. 28 and Oct. 29, 2009.

28. For the 1998 crisis, see *New York Times*, Dec. 29, 1998. For a study of Iraq's armaments industry before 1998, see Cordesman and Hashim 1997, Chaps. 7 and 15. For a partisan account by an UNSCOM member, see Ritter 1999; for a different and later view by an UNSCOM chief, see Butler 2000.

29. Among several good histories of Iraq, see Helms 1984; Farouk-Sluglett and Sluglett 2001; Tripp 2002; and the especially good Marr 2004. *Iraq* Country Study 1990, like all volumes in that series, gives excellent broad coverage. Cordesman and Hashim 1997 studies the post-1991 situation. A useful summary is U.S. Department of State, *Background Note: Iraq*, March 2010.

30. For a treatment of the shift from monarchy to republic, see Kimball 1972.

31. There are almost innumerable treatments already available on these and consequent events; a sampling in alphabetic order: Ajami 2006; Allawi 2007; Bacevich 2008; Bremer 2006; Chandrasekaran 2006; Diamond 2005; Galbraith 2007; Goldberg 2008a; Haas 2009, Packer 2005; Phillips 2005; Pollack 2002; Ricks 2007; Shadid 2005; and Zinni 2006. See also review article by Terrill 2009.

32. *New York Times*, July 29 and Aug. 8, 2003.

33. The June turnover was discussed fully in the *Christian Science Monitor* and *New York Times*, June 29, 2004. The January elections and the new parliament's early actions were covered in *Economist*, Feb. 11, 2005, 43–46.

34. The Council of Representatives elected Jalal Talabani, head of the Kurdish PUK party, to the national presidency.

35. *New York Times*, Oct. 2, 2009.

36. Both are Shii also, but Allawi is secular in reputation and outlook; the voters supporting his bloc seem to have been predominantly Sunni.

37. The Iraqi Independent High Electoral Commission released the preliminary results on March 26; of the 325 seats, the INA took 70 and the Kurdistan Alliance (the joint list of the KDP and the PUK) 43, with the rest going to minor parties. The UN Security Council accepted these results on March 31and called on Iraqis to accept them.

38. The case for forming a government that is *national in character* as opposed to a *national unity government* was laid out in an interview with Meagan O'Sullivan in Council of Foreign Relations, Apr. 2, 2010, at www.cfr.org/publications/21755/after_the_elections.html.

39. Leading the attempts to disqualify Sunni parliamentarians by classifying them as ex-Baathists was Ahmed Chalabi, erstwhile ally of U.S. neocons in the run-up to the 2003 invasion, but more recently tied to pro-Iranian Shii parties.

40. Internal Displacement Monitoring Centre; see http://internal-displacement.org/countries/Iraq. Other estimates of IDPs range as high as 2.65 million in 2009. Some Iraqis were originally displaced before 2003—especially Kurds, Madan, and Shii by Saddam as group punishment—but have yet to find their permanent and/or original homes.

41. See Ricks 2009.

42. Dizard 2004.

43. See de Bellaigue 2007.

44. See *Christian Science Monitor*, Nov. 30, 1998; and *New York Times*, Nov. 2, 1999. The quotation is from *New York Times*, Dec. 20, 1996.

45. See Hiro 2004.

46. See Brumley and Campbell 2007.

47. For further information, see www.un.org/News/Press/docs//2007/note6078.doc.htm and www.un.org/News/Press/docs//2007/note6078.doc.htm.

14

Saudi Arabia
Development in the Desert

The Arabian Peninsula (Arabic: Jazirat al-Arab, "Island of the Arabs") has played a significant role through 7,000 years of Middle East history. Three especially important points need emphasis. One, it served as the source area for Semitic peoples who migrated into the Fertile Crescent as Akkadians, Amorites, Assyrians, Aramaeans, Chaldeans; as smaller groups that included Canaanites, Hebrews, Edomites, Nabataeans; and, of particular interest, as Arabs in the seventh century. Two, it is the cradle of Islam, the religion of more than 1.25 billion people, and the destination of more than 2.5 million pilgrims every year, while hundreds of millions of Muslims face Mecca for prayer five times daily. Three, under its eastern margin lie 45 percent of the world's known petroleum reserves. Seven states occupy the peninsula: Saudi Arabia, the four Gulf states (see Chap. 15), and Oman and Yemen (see Chap. 16).

A PREVIEW

Saudi Arabia's geography and economy place it prominently in international rankings. It is the largest of the sixteen countries in the core region treated here,[1] and it ranks twelfth in size in the world. It possesses the world's largest oil reserves, largest single oil reservoir, largest-capacity oil-export terminal, largest oil storage tanks, longest natural gas liquids pipeline, largest-capacity seawater desalination plant, and largest airport. Its Red Sea coast is longest of all the littoral states; its Gulf coast is second after Iran's. It abuts every state on the peninsula plus Jordan and Iraq. Although it normally keeps a low profile politically and militarily, it tries to serve as a regional balancing factor and to maintain a modest defense capability.

While Saudi Arabia is most known for oil and Islam, these are not its only significant characteristics. Politically conservative and internationally oriented toward the West, its economic power reinforces its independence and the development of its distinctive assets. Funded with petrodollars, it progressed rapidly after 1960, employing millions of foreign consultants, managers, and laborers, yet it sought zealously to preserve its deeply religious and traditional character. Nevertheless, its people demonstrated socioeconomic resilience in their adaptation both to decades of affluence and to years of recession, as well as to nearby periods of warfare. Eight five-year economic plans have focused on "Saudiization," the development of human services and resources—planners, managers, and workers—to replace expatriates with a new generation of educated Saudis trained in the skills needed by the nation.

Saudi Arabia is a young nation, founded in 1932 on a core dating from earlier in the

SAUDI ARABIA

Long-form official name, anglicized: Kingdom of Saudi Arabia

Official name, transliterated: al-Mamlakah al-'Arabiyah as-Sa'udiyah

Form of government: monarchy

Area: 830,000 mi^2/2,149,690 km^2

Population, 2008: 24,780,000; Literacy (Latest): 80.4%

Ethnic composition (%): Saudi 74; expatriate 26, of which Indian 5, Bangladeshi 3.5, Filipino 3.5, Egyptian 3, Palestinian 1, other about 10.

Religions (%): Muslim 94, of which Sunni 84, Shii 10; Christian 3.5; Hindu 1; other 1.5

Demography: Life expectancy—73.7 yr (M), 77.8 yr (F); Birthrate (per 1,000)—24.5; Fertility rate—3.17

GDP, 2008: $469.4 billion; purchasing power parity: $577.9 billion; per capita: $20,500

Currency: Saudi riyal, US$1/3.75 Saudi riyals (January 2010)

Energy reserves: oil—259.9 bn bbl (largest in the world); natural gas—263 tn ft^3; coal—nil

Main exports (% of total value, 2007): crude petroleum 75.8; refined petroleum 12.2; other fuel 6.2

Main imports (% of total value, 2007): machinery and apparatus 29.5; transport equipment 17.6; base and fabricated metals 15.0; food and live animals 13.3; chemicals and chemical products 11.8

Capital city: Riyadh 4,465,000; other cities: Jiddah 3,012,000; Mecca 1,385,000; Medina 1,010,000; Dammam 822,000

---

century. It was born of a special combination of circumstances and has adhered to many of the traditions that were an integral part of its raison d'être. Such conservatism has mixed consequences: It strengthens the social fabric but both inhibits social evolution and attracts foreign and domestic criticism. Its contrasts received global attention when it hosted several hundred thousand foreign troops and media personnel from thirty-three countries during the 1990–1991 Gulf crisis. Saudis realized that the forces were there as protectors, but they were apprehensive about the social mores and values being introduced. But not just foreign influences on domestic standards have been worrisome; the kingdom aspires to

build a modern economy based on sound market principles and a thriving business sector, yet evidence of corruption hindering this goal is apparent. Using the Corruption Perceptions Index of the rating agency Transparency International, its score was only 4.3 out of 10, well below all its Gulf Cooperation Council (GCC) partners in 2009, 80th out of 180 countries globally, and 10th in the region.[2]

HISTORICAL-POLITICAL GEOGRAPHY

Limited earlier archaeological exploration had found evidence of widespread ancient occupation, settlement sites, and burial mounds. Dramatic discoveries in the mid-

1980s confirmed that bands of *Homo erectus* had brought their Developed Oldowan tool culture from the Olduvai Gorge area in East Africa to western Arabia more than 1 million years ago (see Chap. 3). Late Paleolithic and Neolithic tools found in the now-barren Rub al-Khali were left by hunters or settlers along old lakeshores more than 17,000 years ago and again 10,000–5,000 years ago.[3] Finds along the northeastern coast and on Tarut Island reveal ties with Mesopotamian civilizations of 2500 BCE and earlier (see Map 3.1).

A retracing of old trade routes has shown that many towns depended economically on serving one or more caravan tracks. The major ancient route from Aden led northward through Asir and the Hijaz to the caravansary and watering point of Mecca before continuing northward. Traffic along this route in the early seventh century influenced the emergence of Islam.

When Islam's focus of power passed from Mecca and Medina to Damascus in the seventh century and later to Baghdad, the role of the Hijaz diminished for centuries. Most of Arabia was a frontier zone, isolated and tribally fragmented. In 1258, Mamluk Egyptian control of the holy places replaced Abbasid suzerainty; this passed to the Ottomans who conquered Egypt in 1517. The interior evolved separately, leading to the emergence in the eighteenth century of the Al Sauds. Battling other clans, they gained a leading role in Najd, the peninsula's core and still the nucleus of Saudi power.

In the mid-eighteenth century, the Al Saud leader Muhammad ibn Saud led his family into alliance with a religious reformer, Muhammad ibn Abd al-Wahhab, linking Saudi political-military power and Muslim puritanism. The bond still persists as a strong symbiosis, a hallmark of the kingdom's political-religious identity. The religious element is sometimes called "unitarian" (less appropriately, Wahhabism). From their center in al-Diriyah near Riyadh, the alliance controlled most of the peninsula by the early 1800s. The wary Ottomans ordered Muhammad Ali of Egypt to overthrow the Al Sauds and to reestablish imperial authority over the holy places. Al-Diriyah was captured in 1818, and although Al Saud dominance was interrupted it was not eradicated. This invasion of the heartland was one of very few such successful penetrations into the deep interior in history, but it was only briefly effective. A few years later, the Sauds regained their lost territories, except in the Hijaz, and established a new capital in Riyadh, where it has remained.

When Saudi leadership was later weakened by family disputes, the Ottomans occupied al-Hasa in the east, with the Rashids, a rival clan, gaining control over much of Najd. The Sauds fled to Kuwait, from which a young member of the family, Abd al-Aziz ibn Abd al-Rahman, reconquered Riyadh and Najd in 1902. He organized Bedouin into groups of *ikhwan* (brethren) and gradually reclaimed most of the peninsula, annexing the last major area in 1925 when his warriors conquered the Hijaz—the western highlands and coast of the peninsula, which had been the domain of the Hashimite family of Sharif Husayn, of Arab Revolt fame. With control of the holy cities of Mecca and Medina, Abd al-Aziz became "Custodian of the Two Holy Mosques." Each royal successor has used this official title, comparable to the British monarch's designation as "Defender of the Faith."

In January 1927, Abd al-Aziz was officially proclaimed "King of the Hijaz and Najd and Its Dependencies," with Mecca and Riyadh as his capitals. In the Treaty of Jiddah (1927), Britain recognized the status quo in Arabia. In September 1932, Abd al-Aziz, who became known in the West as Ibn Saud, renamed the country the Kingdom of Saudi Arabia, still the official designation.[4]

Uneducated but pragmatic, he accepted modernization and skillfully persuaded conservative religious leaders to accept new technologies: automobiles, radios, telephones, and aircraft. After fifty years of adroit rule, guiding his kingdom in unprecedented transformation, he died in 1953 and has been succeeded by five sons—Saud ibn Abd al-Aziz (1953–1964), Faysal ibn Abd al-Aziz (1964–1975), Khalid ibn Abd al-Aziz (1975–1982), Fahd ibn Abd al-Aziz (1982–2005), and, since 2005, Abdullah ibn Abd al-Aziz (regent from 1997 following Fahd's incapacitation from a stroke).

Details of governance are unusually important in Saudi Arabia and deserve some attention. Reflecting the joint power structure, it is controlled by the Al Sauds, in the person of the king, and by the religious leaders, the ulama (sometimes ulema). They intervene if the king departs from conservative Islam. In 1953, Abd al-Aziz appointed the first cabinet; the Council of Ministers—about 30 by the 2000s—is the basic organ of state. In 1993, Fahd responded to pressure for liberalization, reviving the Consultative Council (Majlis al-Shura) originated by his father, with 150 members since 2005. Similar provincial bodies were also formed. Although formation of such groups represents a limited step forward, it is a significant one, as has been demonstrated in the council's frequent meetings and relations with the king and his ministers.[5]

The Basic Law of 1992 codified the monarchy and its powers, declared the Holy Quran to be the country's constitution, and stated that government must observe Islamic law (Sharia). In 2006, Abdullah established the Allegiance Commission made up of senior family members to select the crown prince in the future. The king faces many constraints on his policies and actions, including those concerning modernization. As a consequence, reform has been slow, and it has been widely criticized, especially since 9/11, both by less conservative Saudis and by Western media.

The steps taken to broaden political institutions have not only been cautious but also consistent with the Saudi practice of evolution rather than revolution. There are no po-

litical parties or national elections, and the king leads as a shaykh of shaykhs in a male-dominated, largely tribal society. Tradition—not Islamic law—demands that women be severely limited socially, with some exceptions for foreigners: They may not dine alone in a restaurant, drive an automobile, or work in an open public office, and they must be segregated in schools and completely covered in public. Under the kingdom's raison d'être, there is no separation of religion and state. The religious police (*mutawwiin*) enforce adherence to Islamic norms by monitoring public behavior. According to a U.S. Department of State summary, "Saudi law severely limits freedom of speech and press. Authorities do not countenance criticism of Islam, the ruling family, or the Government."[6]

Saudi Arabia took a small but important step forward in 2005 when it held its first nationwide elections. In three stages, half the members of 178 municipal councils were elected, the other half to be appointed by the king. Women (and members of the military) were not allowed to run for the council or to vote,[7] and less than one-third of the males eligible to cast ballots actually registered. Government spokesmen explained that steps toward wider elections had to be taken slowly so that the conservative society could adapt to the procedures. Time will tell whether sociopolitical changes in the kingdom can be made quantitatively and qualitatively at the pace demanded by circumstances.

PHYSICAL PATTERNS

Diversity in the Desert

Despite the preponderance of sand deserts, Saudi Arabia's landforms exhibit great diversity, even in the sizes, shapes, and colors of dunes.[8] Although there are some northern and eastern areas of vast seeming sameness, subtle differences exist and are of great significance to the Bedouin who roam these realms—although in steadily decreasing numbers. The relatively green mountains of Asir in the southwest are especially differentiated from the rest of the country. Scarped sedimentary Najd in the center, crystalline shield Najd farther west, lava-covered areas in the north and the west, and immense sand seas in north, south, and east contrast with one another in both geomorphology and cultural character.

The gross geomorphological characteristics of the peninsula are influenced by its formation as a separate tectonic plate that split from northeastern Africa along the Red Sea rift during the Tertiary period (see Chap. 2). The west-central third of the peninsula is a massive crystalline block of Precambrian igneous and metamorphic rocks, overlain with extensive young basalts on the west. Eastward, sedimentary layers cover the rest of the peninsula, except in al-Hajar in Oman, with strata dipping generally eastward and with successively younger outcrops toward the Gulf. Sand seas and sand dunes blanket more than one-third of the peninsula, including the Nafud in the north, the vast Rub al-Khali in the south, and the arc of the Dahna dunes connecting the two.

Regions

[1] Tihamah. Starting on the west, the first natural region (see circled numbers on Map 14.1) consists of a sandy-gravelly coastal plain, Tihamah, which extends virtually the full length of the Red Sea coast. Squeezed between the coastline and the rugged Hijaz range, it varies in width from a few meters at the Gulf of Aqabah to more than 25 mi/40 km near Jaizan in the south. The plain is referred to in the north as Tihamat al-Sham, in the center as Tihamat al-Hijaz, and in the south as Tihamat Asir. Although it is naturally barren and forbidding, is almost waterless between infrequent rains, and lacks significant harbor indentations, it has been a major route of passage for centuries. During that time, small ports—Wajh, Yanbu, Jiddah,

Jaizan—somehow persevered, supported by fishing and limited trade, with Jiddah the port for Mecca pilgrims after the seventh century. It is now the kingdom's leading general port, and the once small fishing villages are huge industrial ports. A first-class highway now extends along the ancient caravan route from Jordan to Yemen.

[2] Hijaz-Asir Mountains. East of the coastal plain is a mountain belt ranging in width from 25 to 87 mi/40 to 140 km. It is generally low in the north but increases in elevation toward the south, with crest elevations reaching 6,987 ft/2,130 m northwest of Medina and 9,840 ft/3,000 m near Abha. A gap in the ridges near Mecca has carried a travel route for centuries. From this formidable uplifted crystalline mountain block comes the name for the western region—al-Hijaz (the barrier). The elevated southern segment is the Asir, the best-watered part of the country, with 12–20 in/300–500 mm of rain annually, much of it during the summer monsoon. Moderate slopes echoing the dramatic terraces farther south in Yemen (Fig. 14.1) have long supported warm-season crops. In addition to the Asir rainfall, the Hijaz crest line receives the most winter rain of any part of the kingdom. Nestled in barren volcanic basins in the center are Islam's sacred cities, Mecca and Medina, as well as al-Taif, the traditional summer capital. In the unique and fascinating Asir are the rapidly expanding agricultural and resort area around Abha, the military area of Khamis Mushayt, and the pleasant Najran district. A national park attracts thousands of visitors, enjoying spectacular views down the great seaward-facing escarpment populated by hundreds of hamadryas baboons that scamper through the wooded uplands.

[3] Najd. Continuing eastward from the central segment of the uplifted highland and extending to the middle of the peninsula is

MAP 14.1 Reference map of Saudi Arabia. Circled numbers refer to regions discussed in the text. Petroleum, solid minerals, transportation, and other topics are shown on maps in relevant chapters (Maps 6.1, 6.2, 6.5, 7.2, and others).

the crystalline block of the Arabian Shield. It comprises granites, gabbros, gneisses, schists, marbles, and related rocks. Like most shield areas, it has mineralized areas, with deposits of copper, gold, silver, lead, zinc, and other metals. Amounts of most of these minerals are limited, although numerous ancient gold and silver workings have been found through intensive searches by U.S., French, and Saudi geologists. Persistent exploration has found more than a score of deposits worth large-

scale exploitation, and several major mines are now operating. A contract was awarded in 2007 to develop phosphate deposits.[9]

Along the shield's western edge are six major lava fields, 390–7,720 mi²/1,000– 20,000 km² in extent, dotted with numerous lava cones and cinder cones in north-south alignments (see Fig. 2.4). A relatively young basalt flow near Medina dates from as recently as 1250 CE. As Map 4.2 shows, extensive areas of the crystalline shield between the

FIGURE 14.1 An unusual landscape in overwhelmingly desertic Saudi Arabia: terraced agriculture in the Asir, the best-watered region of the kingdom, just north of Yemen.

Hijaz Mountains and central Najd are virtually uninhabited.

East of the shield and distinctly contrasting with it is sedimentary Najd, part of the central plateau with outcropping sedimentary rocks in a great curved belt around the eastern edge of the crystalline basement. Escarpments, ridges, and buttes, each with a resistant cap, are characteristic features around this Central Arabian Arch. One particular escarpment, an Upper Jurassic limestone cuesta extending along a 1,000-mi/1,600-km crescent, forms Jabal Tuwayq, the most prominent physiographic feature of central Arabia. All of these outcropping strata dip eastward and are found at depths several thousand feet below the surface in the eastern oil fields. The layers of sedimentary rocks in eastern Najd both serve as catchment rocks for aquifers that are tapped in the Eastern Province and also provide

conditions for many local contact springs. These gave rise to numerous ancient and still-persisting Najd settlements, and their presence prompted the drilling of water wells in modern times.

Groups of villages around several central places and coordination of agricultural activity have resulted in a subregional consciousness along Jabal Tuwayq. The main subregion in the north is al-Qasim, located west of the Tuwayq cuesta and centered on the large towns of Buraydah and Unayzah, southeast of Hayil.[10] South-southeast of al-Qasim and west of Jabal Tuwayq is the Washm subregion, with several small towns and an expansive agricultural economy. East of al-Qasim, on the backslope of the Tuwayq escarpment, is the Sudayr, centered on Majmaah (see Fig. 4.9), less populated than al-Qasim. All three districts experienced remarkable development of irrigation agriculture during the

1980s, as well as road-net intensification, population increase, and urban development.

Southeast of Riyadh is the subregion of al-Kharj, with significant solution springs and one of the largest oases in the peninsula. For many years, one of the most important of several concentrations of U.S. military personnel was here, until all were withdrawn in 2003. Extending southward from al-Kharj along a secondary cuesta are two well-defined subregions: al-Hawtah, with the villages of al-Hillah and al-Hilway, and, farther south, al-Aflaj, centered on Layla. Al-Aflaj refers to the irrigation system that formerly supported extensive gardens around Layla. The Hawtah subregion was launched into a local oil boom in the period 1989–1991 with the discovery of completely new resources of superlight petroleum in fields extending 47 mi/75 km from the southern Hawtah to al-Dilam, south of al-Kharj.

[4] *Dahna, Summan, and the Coastal Plain.* Between Najd and the Gulf coast lie three belts that generally parallel the arcuate Jabal Tuwayq. All are generally considered to be in the Eastern Province, and they contain most of Saudi Arabia's oil fields: (1) the Dahna, a great arc of rust-colored sand dunes 30 mi/48 km wide and extending 800 mi/1,290 km from the Nafud in the north to the Rub al-Khali in the south; (2) al-Summan plateau, with escarpments and buttes on its eastern margins; and (3) near the Gulf coast, an irregular plain terminating in a ragged coastline of *sabkhahs* (see Fig. 2.12), sand spits, and offshore sandbars.

Under the plateau and coastal plain, as well as offshore, are the world's greatest petroleum reservoirs, now well delineated and intensively exploited. Except for the Hofuf and Qatif oases and a few small coastal villages, this vast area was the haunt of Bedouin and their herds prior to World War II. Now it throbs with hundreds of oil wells flowing under high-pressure, gas-oil separator plants,

flow lines, pump stations, heavy road traffic, oil-related industries, sprawling cities, bustling ports, and an expanding economy. The nerve center of the vast operation is the oil company headquarters in Dhahran, near which are located the King Fahd University of Petroleum and Minerals, the older international airport, and the huge new airport; on the coast are the expanding cities of Dammam (the provincial capital) and al-Khobar, creating an agglomeration of varied population and economy. North of Dammam is the great oil-export terminal and refinery of Ras Tanura (see Fig. 6.4), farther north the newer and equally large export terminal of Juaymah, and north of that the industrial city of Jubayl.

[5] *Rub al-Khali.*   Vast seas of sand in the north and south of the country constitute two of the most distinctive physical features on the peninsula. The largest single dune field in the world, the Rub al-Khali (Empty Quarter), covers more than 230,000 mi^2/600,000 km^2. Referred to simply as al-Rimal (the Sands) by Bedouin, the Rub al-Khali comprises almost entirely loose, dry sand shaped into dunes that vary depending upon the wind. Three types predominate: numerous linear or longitudinal dunes (*uruq*; singular, *irq*), some of them 60 mi/100 km long, in the western half (see Fig. 1.1); barchans or crescent dunes in the northeast; and giant dunes, the remarkable Sand Mountains, along the eastern and southern margins. Formless "sand seas" fill other areas. A few areas exhibit some vegetation, but the loose sands are barren; because few wells exist in the area, even Bedouin generally avoid it. Al Murrah and occasional other tribesmen move along the edges, infrequently crossing it.[11] The eastern area has been opened by development of the rich Shaybah oil field on the UAE border during the 1990s.

[6] *The Nafud.*   In the northwest is the great desert called by the Bedouin simply al-

Nafud, the northern term for "sandy desert." Characterized by complex dune forms including deep pits, the reddish sands cover 45,000 mi²/116,550 km². The sediment source for the sand is an extensive area of poorly cemented Paleozoic sandstones that lie upwind from it. The area is sparsely inhabited but constitutes an important seasonal grazing area.

[7] Northern Regions. In the northern reaches of the country are a sequence of varied landscapes, each with its own identification. In the extreme northwest, at the northern end of the Red Sea, is the rugged area of Midyan (biblical Midian), which drops eastward to the plain around the military cantonment town of Tabuk. Farther east is the mountain mass of al-Tubayq, which sinks northeastward to the Wadi al-Sirhan, the great northwest-southeast depression extending from al-Azraq in Jordan to the oasis of al-Jawf in Saudi Arabia. The depression is more than 200 mi/322 km long, about 25 mi/40 km wide, and 1,000 ft/305 m below the level of the plateau. To the northeast are the extensive lava fields and cinder cones of al-Harrah, southeast of which extend al-Hamad, al-Widyan, and al-Hajarah, stony plains traversed by the abandoned Trans-Arabian Pipe Line (Tapline). Southwest of Kuwait is the well-marked Wadi al-Batin and the gravel plain of the Dibdibah.

Most of this vast expanse was virtually uninhabited before 1950, when Tapline spanned the desert and gradually opened the sandy-gravelly plains to development. Towns grew up around the five pump stations, and truck drivers and other travelers followed the pipeline track, later blacktopped and then upgraded to a major highway. Each town now exceeds 25,000 in population and functions as a service center for traffic along the long highway. The military cantonment of Hafar al-Batin built near Qaysumah was key to ground-force operations during the Gulf War in 1990–1991.

POPULATION AND PEOPLES

Census taking is both a complicated procedure and a sensitive matter. It is complicated because the population is widely scattered, Bedouin move frequently and try to avoid government attention, urban populations shift rapidly, and expatriates present special problems of enumeration: They change fairly frequently, both individually and in total number, and the kingdom has been reluctant to acknowledge its large foreign population. A 1963 sampling suggested a total population of about 3.3 million; a 1992 census showed 16,929,294, about 30 percent expatriate; and in the late 2000s, an estimated 28.1 million included more than 5.5 million expatriates. Census taking is sensitive because rich Saudi Arabia is surrounded by poorer neighbors with considerable military capability. Overall population growth rate is about 3 percent annually. Although it has been declining, the total fertility rate—the number of children the average woman will have—remains high in the late 2000s at 4.05, fourth highest in the region after Yemen, Oman, and Iraq, so population will continue to grow rapidly for the foreseeable future.

Saudi Arabia has three principal population nuclei and several outliers, all separated by empty or sparsely settled desert. Most populous is Najd, the Saudi heartland, with its node in Greater Riyadh, which now has about 4.4 million inhabitants and remarkably contemporary institutions and buildings (Figs. 14.2 and 14.3). Relatively concentrated Najd settlements extend from Hayil and Buraydah in the north southeastward to al-Kharj, and there are a score of towns of small to medium size in the irrigated depressions on the plateau and along the escarpments.

In the west, the Hijaz-Asir nucleus is aligned on the Jiddah-Mecca-Taif axis. The extended area reaches from Yanbu and Medina in the north to Jaizan and Najran in the south and includes Abha and Khamis Mushayt in

FIGURE 14.2 Young students attending the Visitors' Center for Environmental Awareness in Riyadh, suggesting a great advance from the former Bedouin culture of the peninsula—although Bedouin were acutely aware of their desert environment! Note that only males are in this class group. (Abdullah Y. Al-Dobais, *Saudi Aramco World*, SAWDIA)

FIGURE 14.3 Modern and unusual high-rise buildings in Riyadh are replacing virtually all of the traditional and often charming structures of the pre-1950s capital.

the rapidly developing Asir. Across the peninsula, the Eastern Province population centers on Dammam Municipality (which includes Qatif, Dammam, Dhahran, al-Khobar, and al-Thuqbah). The extended agglomeration extends from the new industrial port city of Jubayl on the north to Hofuf in al-Hasa Oasis on the south and includes Qatif Oasis, the oil terminals of Juaymah and Ras Tanura, and the oil-producing center of Abqaiq.

Outliers with sizable populations include Tabuk, in the northwestern corner of the kingdom, with more than 350,000 population; the Hayil Oasis, south of the Nafud, with about 150,000; al-Jawf Oasis, north of the Nafud; settlements along Tapline; and the smaller settlements of al-Khamasin and al-Sulayyil toward the southern end of the Jabal Tuwayq.

Although the indigenous Saudi population is relatively uniform ethnically, it includes varied tribal affiliations. During the thirteen centuries of annual pilgrimages to Mecca some pilgrims have remained, and they and their descendants have added to the Saudi mixture strains from Indonesia to Morocco, Central Asia to West Africa—evident especially in the Hijaz. In coastal Asir, some have African physical traits, combined with characteristics that are neither typically Arab nor typically African. In the Qatif and Hofuf oases of the Eastern Province, there are descendants of Iranians who settled there centuries ago, bringing Shii Islam to the predominantly Sunni peninsula. Expatriates come from all corners of the globe.

Clothing is traditional, and centuries-old styles are very much maintained despite modernization. Males wear the loose-fitting, ankle-length white *thawb* (sometimes *thobe*) (see Fig. 4.2). In cool weather and on more formal occasions, a cloak (*bisht* or *mishlah*) is worn over the *thawb*. The head covering both outdoors and indoors is the ubiquitous *ghutrah* (called a *kufiyah* in the Levant), a head cloth with a double ring of black cord

(*igal*) to hold it in place. In the oil industry and industrial plants, workers commonly wear Western work clothing during the day, and increasing numbers of young men prefer Western styles. A female in public wears the loose, floor-length *abayah* over her head and body. It may cover a dress similar to the *thawb*, except that it is usually colorful, or the latest Paris fashion. Any of several types of veil or partial face covering may be added to the *abayah*.

Centuries ago, the marginal economy and lack of unity and security prompted many kinship groups to seek localized order in tribalism. Although modernization has weakened this tribalism, tribal identity is retained by many Saudis, especially Bedouin. Village organization and tribal affiliation remain basic social factors among both settled and nomadic populations.

Foreign workers were drawn to the oil fields and cities as early as the 1940s, arriving in large numbers in the 1970s. Uneasy that there are so many non-Muslims in the cradle of Islam, the government strictly controls who enters, for what reason, and for how long; each must have a responsible local person or institution as sponsor. Early expatriates developed petroleum resources; later arrivals were brought in to expand the infrastructure and to maintain going concerns unable to find qualified or willing Saudi employees. Rising standards of living created demand for millions of custodial and domestic workers, available in seemingly unlimited numbers from Asia. For many decades, a rewarding symbiosis existed between Saudi Arabia and the large Yemeni labor pool—more than a million worked in the kingdom during the 1980s before they were expelled because of Yemen's stance on Iraq's invasion of Kuwait; they are still officially banned twenty years later. In the past decade, restrictions against casual visitors have been eased to admit organized groups of tourists eager to see such rarely visited sites as Medain Saleh in the northern Hejaz, which is second only to Petra as a monument to the Nabateans who dominated the trade route from Yemen to Syria 2,000 years ago. In 2010 it was reported that the government had set a goal of increasing tourism receipts by more than 350 percent to $64 billion by 2019.[12]

SETTLEMENTS

Although nomadic traditions are strong in the peninsula, sedentarism preceded nomadism. Until after World War II, the typical settlement pattern was widely scattered oasis villages and occasional towns in a symbiotic relationship with nomadic Bedouin living in their long, rectangular tents. Nor were the two lifestyles mutually exclusive: During severe droughts, Bedouin moved into villages; conversely, in less dry years, villagers—especially former nomads—sometimes moved into the desert. Before the petroleum age, an estimated 60 percent of the population was at least partly nomadic. Settling the Bedouin has been a deliberate state policy since Abd al-Aziz's time. Oil stimulated sedentarization, and by the 1990s Bedouin had decreased to less than 4 percent of the population. Permanently settled nomads consider themselves *hadar*—that is, no longer Bedouin.

Since World War II, urbanization has accelerated in Saudi Arabia, as elsewhere, increasing with petroleum development. By the 2000s, nearly 80 percent of the population was urban. No extensive preindustrial cities had evolved, and even the largest settlements—Mecca and Medina, for example—were moderate-size towns of 30,000 each in the 1930s. But few of today's towns or cities are on completely new sites; even Jubayl and Yanbu are extensions of earlier villages. Transformation of the landscape, epitomized in the metamorphosis of the urban scene, has had minimal outside cognizance; such is one of the drawbacks to the Saudi policy of admitting few Western scholars and reporters. Those who visited Jiddah, Riyadh, and Dammam in the 1950s, when all three were small with few amenities, marvel at what unlimited funds and reasonably intelligent planning have accomplished. Many unique, charming, and historic structures—palaces, forts, walls, and houses—were unfortunately swept away in the rush to modernize; many buildings, especially in Riyadh, were of mud and could not be saved, although a few major sites have been preserved, most of them in Riyadh and Jiddah. Generally, there is more than enough space in the surrounding desert for urban expansion.

Traditional Islamic architectural themes are often employed in new urban centers, universities, and museums. A wide variety of contemporary designs have characterized major new structures that, with generous funding, need not employ monotonous modular techniques. Indeed, Saudi structures are a great architectural success when Islamic traditions are combined with other Arabian features in a contemporary mode. In the mountain villages of Asir, unique exterior house walls typically show alternating courses of mud and projecting rock, with the rock ledges deflecting rain to prevent erosion of the primarily mud walls. Building walls in Najd are topped by decorative battlements, vestiges of military architecture. In Najd, but also in other parts of the country, the wooden doors of many houses are decorated with elaborate geometric designs.

ECONOMIC PATTERNS

Economic patterns had been stable for centuries when discovery of petroleum in 1938 initiated a literally fabulous transformation. Before then, remote and poor Arabia survived on limited pastoralism and oasis agriculture, coastal fishing, pilgrimage earnings, and meager trade. With modest but increasing oil production during the 1950s and 1960s, the kingdom had a glimpse of things to come—the development explosion of the 1970s. National income from oil exceeded $300 million per day between 1977 and 1981, supplying billions of dollars for perhaps the most complete transformation in history of a large country on a grand scale and in a short time. With urban and systems planners, design engineers, architects, contractors, educators, and workers from Western Europe, North America, the Middle East, and South Asia, Saudi Arabia virtually built an entire country, from infrastructure to complete universities and U.S.-style fast-food shops. Private capital contributed retail centers, many of the smaller industries, and most of the agricultural expansion.[13]

Much of the development has been guided by a series of five-year plans, with a peak during the $195 billion second plan, 1975–1980; twenty-eight dams, four ports, 175,000 new homes, 15,000 mi/24,000 km of roads, and the Jiddah airport (the world's largest until Riyadh's opened) were completed. Water projects, industrial developments, petroleum operations, infrastructure, and the billion-dollar causeway to Bahrain were constructed or greatly expanded. The fourth plan, 1985–1990, was curtailed following the sharp drop in the oil market in 1982. Daily oil sales dropped from $364.8 million in 1980 to $36.3 million in 1985—and the value of the dollar was also shrinking. The fifth plan, 1990–1995, budgeted for $100 billion, focused especially on the needs of the country's defenses arising from the Gulf War. The sixth plan, 1995–2000, emphasized government efficiency, more training, a more diverse economy—especially in industry and agriculture—and greater Saudiization of the labor force. The seventh (2000–2005) and eighth plans (2005–2010) focused on diversification and the private sector.

Each plan has sought to reduce dependence on crude petroleum, to increase self-sufficiency and reduce imports, and, in the long run, to develop national viability for the inevitable end of petroleum-based prosperity when the wells run dry. A secondary goal is to ensure that the enviable and highly efficient infrastructure, systematically developed at the cost of many hundreds of billions of dollars, is properly maintained, repaired, and upgraded.[14] While in many ways it is obvious how much the living standards for Saudi citizens have improved, using the Human Development Index computed by the UNDP illustrates the manner in which this has happened. The kingdom's rose by 13.3 percent between 1990 and 2007 because of major increases in the life expectancy and education components of the index. In 2007, it ranked 59th out of 182 countries globally and 8th regionally.[15]

Agriculture

Agriculture's share in the economy decreased sharply after 1960, falling to only 3 percent by the mid-1970s. It jumped to 13 percent a decade later when fuel subsidies pushed a rapid expansion of irrigated crop production, but it gradually returned to 3 percent by the late 2000s. In 2008, the government reversed its policy of self-sufficiency in wheat, formulated in the tense 1970s, in recognition of the devastating effect massive irrigation projects have had on the rapidly dwindling supply of nonrenewable groundwater. Rain-fed agriculture dominates in Asir, where highlands intercept summer monsoon rains and the water is efficiently utilized on terraced plots (see Fig. 14.1).

As a result of planning for agricultural self-sufficiency, with the government offering many times the world market price for wheat produced domestically, and with subsidies for well drilling and pump fuel, wheat acreage rocketed from an average of 175,400 ac/71,000 ha 1979–1981 to 2.02 mn ac/816,000 ha in 1989–1991, and production increased from 180,000 mt to 3.69 mn mt.[16] The Najdi landscape was transformed in the 1980s with hundreds of startlingly green circles of wheat, watered by self-propelled center-pivot sprinkler systems, appearing against the tawny sands. Because domestic demand was only 800,000 mt, the excess was exported or donated—in effect, "virtual water" was being exported from the desert kingdom. As the aquifer water level plummeted from overuse, and cost accounting showed the real costs involved, the government decreased subsidies and reduced quotas. In 2006, the agricultural sector used 88 percent of domestic water resources; the proportion had been declining slowly with the changes in the incentive structure. Wheat production had fallen sharply, and by the late 2000s was about 2.6 mn mt, when the most important commodities by value were meat, fruits, milk, eggs, and vegetables.

Of the many oases in the kingdom, the two largest—both in the Eastern Province—are classic examples. Hofuf (al-Hasa),[17] the largest on the peninsula and the largest groundwater-fed oasis in the world, is watered by 159 springs, including 8 major artesian springs (*ayns*) that flow a total of more than 1,900 gal/7,190 l per second. The largest single spring has a flow of 475 gal/1,800 l per second. A major project in the early 1970s modernized and systematized the irrigation and drainage, replacing ditches with concrete conduits. The greater drawdown is lowering the water table alarmingly. Qatif, a few miles north of Dammam, received much of the same modernization. Both oases have been improved and upgraded in successive development projects. Large areas of former date-palm groves are now devoted to fruit trees and vegetable production in plastic greenhouses. The transformation is another instance of the steady disappearance of the traditional and fascinating before the march of modernization and the imperative for efficiency.

Although their numbers are decreasing, many Bedouin still pursue a nomadic lifestyle and continue to supply animals and animal products to the economy. Increasing numbers of families divide their time between nomadism and raising crops or other economic pursuits in villages on the perimeters of their tribal *dirahs*. As have nomads in other parts of the Middle East, many have electric generators, televisions, and refrigerators in their tents, parking their pickup trucks alongside.

Water studies have yielded approximations of the water balance, permitting systematic efforts for more effective use of renewable resources. Hydrogeological studies reveal that much of the deep aquifer water in Najd is "fossil water," stored as long ago as 40,000 years, and that water in the relatively shallow aquifers of the Eastern Province is 18,000–28,000 years old. Thus, using this water amounts to "mining" nonrenewable resources, and systematic efforts must be made to substitute renewable water for fossil water in irrigation—particularly in the production of subsidized wheat, for example. The Disi aquifer, spanning the Saudi-Jordan border, is being used by both countries in a "race to the bottom," with little apparent regard for conservation; generally, with aquifers, it is difficult to determine how much water there is and how much can be withdrawn.

Fundamental to the agricultural program has been a series of water development projects that added more than 200 dams with a capacity of 29.5 bn ft³/836 mn m³, several hundred deep wells, and many miles of irrigation conduits. Most of the dams were constructed in Najd and particularly in Asir, where the Wadi Bishah Dam is one of the largest in the Middle East outside Turkey and Egypt.

The domestic water supply also relies on desalination. Availability of huge amounts of fuel prompted the initiation in 1965 of a massive construction program of large-scale plants. Within two decades, the kingdom had the world's greatest desalination complex and led the world in the production of potable water. In the mid-2000s, thirty facilities pumped desalted water through 2,300 mi/3,700 km of pipelines to supply 70 percent of the kingdom's potable water. With more large plants recently completed, the country has a daily capacity of 800 mn gal/3 mn m^3. The Jubayl operation is the world's largest and pumps millions of gallons of distilled water daily to Riyadh;[18] however, prodigal use often creates shortages in summer months. Potable water, like many commodities, is heavily subsidized, and it is often not metered; thus, it is frequently wasted. More seriously for the future, eventually plentiful cheap energy will be depleted, the population will have certainly doubled or more, and the country will face a crucial threat to its survival.

Fishing

Important on both coasts for centuries, fishing since the 1950s has been especially developed on the east coast. Traditional methods have been replaced by modernized techniques and equipment. Ships operate primarily out of Dammam, and there are processing and freezing plants in Dammam and al-Khobar. Additional facilities were built in the new port of Jubayl. With all of the Gulf littoral states intensifying fishing efforts, overfishing has occurred, and the total Gulf catch peaked in 1967–1968.

Petroleum Industry

Beneath the deserts of eastern Arabia, the world's largest petroleum reserves lay unrecognized until the 1930s.[19] King Abd al-Aziz had granted a concession to a British syndicate in 1923, but it did not pursue exploration and lost the concession. In 1933, he gave Standard Oil of California (Socal) the exclusive right to prospect for and produce oil in eastern Arabia, along with preferential rights in other parts of the kingdom, originally for a period of sixty years. California Arabian Standard Oil Company (Casoc), a new subsidiary, took up the concession in 1934. Socal (which later became Chevron) agreed to a 50-50 ownership deal in Casoc

with the Texas Company (which merged with Chevron in 2001) in 1937. In 1944, Casoc was renamed Arabian American Oil Company, with the now world-famous acronym Aramco, which is still used even for the Saudi-owned company. In 1948, the Standard Oil Company of New Jersey (later named Esso and then Exxon) and the Socony-Vacuum Oil Company (later named Mobil) joined in the Aramco ownership (they merged and become ExxonMobil in 1999). The four owner companies formed the all-U.S. capital and technical force behind oil development in mainland Saudi Arabia until 1973.

Socal started drilling in April 1935 in Dammam Dome near the Gulf coast; the first discovery came in March 1938. (The discovery well, Dammam Number 7, was finally shut down only in 1983 after producing 1,600 bpd for 45 years.) Exports started in May 1939 at Ras Tanura, eventually one of the world's great oil-export terminals (see Fig. 6.4). Exploration—which still continues—soon showed that the Eastern Province contained the world's largest fields. The first segment of Ghawar, the largest of these, was found in 1948, and Safaniya, the largest offshore field in the world, was discovered in 1951. By 2004, eighty commercial oil and gas fields had been discovered (see Maps 6.1 and 6.2), including the remarkable Shaybah oil and gas structure along the UAE southern border in the remote Rub al-Khali. In full operation by 1998, it produces 500,000 bpd of especially valuable extra-light crude and huge amounts of nonassociated gas (see Fig. 14-4). A cumulative total of about 125 bn bbl has been produced just by Aramco since 1938, yet reserves were 260 bn bbl in 2010 and were expected to increase; reserves of natural gas exceeded 263.0 tn ft^3/7.45 tn m^3 (fourth largest in the world), and major projects were under way to upgrade scores of facilities all over the kingdom.

FIGURE 14.4 A triumph of technology: the major crude-processing facility built in "the middle of nowhere"—at Shaybah in Sand Hills of the Empty Quarter. The relatively recently discovered field lies just south of the southern UAE border. (Abdullah Y. Al-Dobais, *Saudi Aramco World*, SAWDIA)

In 1973, the government took a 25 percent ownership of Aramco, increasing it to 60 percent in 1974 and to 100 percent in 1980; the U.S. partners were bought out. Designated the Saudi Arabian Oil Company (Saudi Aramco) in 1988, it continues to be known in the industry by its familiar acronym and is both operator for Saudi production and intermediate contractor for a range of engineering and construction projects. The company first served this function in 1949, overseeing construction of the Dammam-Riyadh railway, and more recently the implementation of the Master Gas Plan.

Aramco took its first major step into downstream operations in 1988 in a joint venture with Texaco for refining, distributing, and marketing in the eastern and Gulf coast regions of the United States. It has since purchased or joined enterprises in South Korea and other Asian countries. Its funda-

mental structure and function changed greatly during the 1990s consequent to a royal decree of July 1, 1993. Entirely government owned, it was charged with all government oil operations in the kingdom, upstream and downstream, from exploration to marketing. It took over Tapline (originally a separate company), Petroline (East-West Crude Oil Line), all government-owned refineries, and Petromin retail marketing outlets. Thus, it is no longer simply an upstream company producing oil and gas but a fully integrated, diversified company with refining and shipping interests and worldwide joint-venture marketing operations. Its reserves, production capacity, production facilities, transport lines, markets, and workforce size (58,000) make it one of the world's four-largest integrated oil companies.

As explained in Chapter 8, the former Saudi Arabia–Kuwait Neutral Zone was partitioned between the two neighbors in 1965, demarcated in 1970, and divided approximately equally. To avoid confusion, the two governments agreed to share equally the zone's oil reserves and revenues. Although parastatal Aramco was sole operator in the kingdom, U.S.-owned Texaco had the concession for the zone (held by Getty Oil Company before 1984), and after 1957 the Japanese-owned Arabian Oil Company held offshore rights until it lost them in 2000. Proved reserves are 5 bn bbl; production averages 600,000 bpd.

As sole operator in its concession area, Aramco drilled only the optimum number of wells, without having to be concerned about leases and offset drilling; even after sixty years, none of them requires pumping. Reservoir pressure is maintained by reinjecting natural gas and by a huge water-injection system—more than 10 mn bbl of nonpotable water is pumped daily into major reservoirs as oil is withdrawn. Much of the water is brought to the great Ghawar field by three large pipelines 60 mi/100 km from the Gulf. About 1,560 flowing wells produce up to 9.1 mn bpd, or about 5,833 bpd each, compared with an average 10.4 bpd from each of the 512,560 wells in the United States.

Handling, transporting, and processing the petroleum require a complex of facilities all across eastern Arabia—strung together with more than 13,050 mi/21,000 km of pipelines. Each of more than 70 gas-oil separator plants serves several wells within a considerable radius via flow lines, each well showing its fiery flare—now reduced to conserve natural gas—against the sky. Stabilizers in Abqaiq and Juaymah "sweeten" sour crude, and natural gas liquids (NGL) plants produce propane, butane, and natural gasoline. There are numerous large petroleum-related industrial plants along the Gulf coast, especially in the industrial city of Jubayl. Huge oil-export terminals operate at Ras Tanura and Juaymah, with crude and product storage capacities

of 30 mn bbl and 25 mn bbl, respectively, as well as at Yanbu on the Red Sea, with 12.5 mn bbl storage capacity—two and a half times the average daily production in the United States.

The kingdom has seven active refineries with a total throughput of 2.1 mn bpd. In the east, the largest are in Ras Tanura, 550,000 bpd, and Jubayl, 290,000; in the west, in Rabigh, 400,000, and in Yanbu, 400,000 and 235,000; and in Najd, Riyadh, 120,000.[20] As Chapter 6 explained, the great 500,000 bpd Trans-Arabian Pipe Line (Tapline) that opened in 1951 was beset by political problems and became unprofitable during the 1970s. It ceased pumping to Sidon in 1983 and to the Zarqa refinery in Jordan in 1990; it is now unusable without major new investment.

However, the concept of an outlet to the west was strategically revived for insurance against potential dangers to shipping in the Gulf and at the Hormuz chokepoint, leading in the 1980s to a billion-dollar project spanning the peninsula, from the eastern fields to Yanbu on the Red Sea, with three pipelines. The East-West NGL pipeline, 726 mi/1,170 km long and 26–30 in/66–76 cm in diameter, was commissioned in 1981. The first component of a dual East-West Crude Oil Pipeline, 48 in/122 cm in diameter, was commissioned the same year; a huge second one, 56 in/142 cm in diameter and a "loop" of the first line, opened in 1987. Both are 745 mi/1,200 km long. The addition of pumps and the expansion of facilities at each end of this system in 1991 raised capacity to nearly 5 mn bpd—ten times Tapline's capacity and half of Aramco's production capacity. The parallel NGL line carries 270,000 bpd of ethane and natural gas liquids. This gives the kingdom an entirely domestic secure route, reducing the cutoff threat, although exports from Yanbu are still subject to interdiction at either end of the Red Sea. After the invasion of Kuwait in 1990, the government closed the 2.35 mn bpd IPSA pipelines, an Iraqi-owned facility, from southern Iraq to the Red Sea after less than one year in service; it was seized by the Saudis in 2001 and remains shut in (see Chap. 6).

During the 1960s, Aramco realized that the kingdom's combined natural gas resources, associated and nonassociated, were an asset rivaling oil wealth. By the late 2000s, total proven gas reserves (more than 250 tn ft^3) ranked fourth in the world (after Russia, Iran, and Qatar, and ahead of the United States). In the late 1970s, the kingdom undertook the ambitious Master Gas System. Formerly flared associated gas (about 57 percent of proven reserves) now supplies power-generating stations, water desalination plants, numerous factories, and domestic lines—or is reinjected to maintain oil-field pressure. Huge reservoirs of nonassociated gas—including deep Khuff gas under the great Ghawar oil field—are yielding gas for the industrial cities of Jubayl and Yanbu as fuel and feedstock for oil refineries, petrochemical and fertilizer plants, steel plants and rolling mills, and other industries. Serious attention is being given to the considerable potential for large-scale exports. Jubayl and Yanbu together account for 10 percent of the world's petrochemical production and are further expanding their output. Now collecting and processing more than 5.67 bn ft^3/161 mn m^3 of gas per day, the system can add the equivalent of more than 1.25 mn bbl of crude oil a day to the world's supply of energy. In the late 2000s, about half the kingdom's electricity was generated using gas, and this proportion was increasing.

The increasing importance of natural gas in both the domestic and the world economies prompted Saudi Arabia to complement the Master Gas Plan of the 1980s with a $20 billion Saudi Gas Initiative (SGI). The SGI is opening new gas fields and constructing processing facilities, all with foreign investment participation—the first since nationalization in the 1970s. Both newcomers and old Middle East hands are among the firms that have sought and won exploration concessions in joint ventures with Saudi Aramco. Successful contenders include Royal Dutch/Shell, ENI of Italy in partnership with Repsol YPF of Spain, Lukoil of Russia, and Sinopec of China; much of their efforts are directed to the previously underexplored Rub al-Khali.

Saudi Arabia is a charter member of both OPEC and OAPEC (see Chap. 6) and has played a particularly major role in the former since its founding. As its production constituted an increasingly greater share of the OPEC and world totals, it played a "swing role" in influencing the world price of petroleum for several years by varying its output. As the world's leading producer, it was the only country with sufficient spare capacity to increase output significantly enough—1.5 to 2 mn bpd—to stabilize or bring down oil prices. Through the mid-2000s, along with pressing all OPEC members to adhere to their quotas, the kingdom's role as a market maker still held up—for example, during the 2003–2004 oil crisis. The Saudi increase in mid-2004 was, indeed, helpful in causing prices to retreat from the record highs up to that time. However, during the oil-price spike later that year, not even maximum output from all producers could force the price to return to the $30–$40 range from its sustained record high—up to that time—in the $50-plus-a-barrel bracket.[21]

By the late 2000s, the world oil market seemed to have entered a new stage, with the result that prices hit all-time record highs close to $150 a barrel in the summer of 2008. Whether this was due to escalating demand in the two largest countries, China and India, or speculative manipulations in the market or a combination of both was not clear. What was obvious was that neither increased Saudi output nor the Bush administration's all-purpose prescription for whatever happened in world oil markets—more drilling in the United States—could dampen the rapid escalation. Similarly, when prices fell even more precipitously in the fall of that year, whether due to the deepening global economic crisis or speculators retiring from the market with enormous profits, it was equally clear Saudi output variations were not a factor. Those record prices earned the kingdom an estimated $284.5 billion for 2008; however, with the decline in prices and global recession in 2009, revenues declined by more that 45 percent to an estimated $154.2 billion.

In the face of opposition from Venezuela and Iran, the Saudis have remained a strong supporter of continuing the practice of pricing oil in dollars, reiterating in 2010 that it would keep the riyal linked directly to the dollar.[22] A study based on data from the International Energy Agency showed that, along with the UAE, Saudi Arabia has hewn most closely to its assigned OPEC production quota; these two states were in compliance about 98 percent of the time, while the overall average compliance rate was only 56 percent.[23]

Other Industries

In the 1950s, manufacturing expanded with four key developments: expansion and diversification of oil operations and the industry's workforce, a rapid increase in population and consumer demand, growth in available private and government capital, and an increase in foreign company joint ventures with Saudi partners—including the government. Succeeding decades saw a marked increase in the number, size, and diversity of producing establishments. At first they turned out processed foods, paper and plastic items, clothing, and basic furniture. From the 1970s, they added items such as paints, air conditioners, aluminum prefabricated buildings, steel rods, and a number of products using oil and gas as feedstocks and fuel. It is products like petrochemicals and other chemicals, fertilizers, and by-product sulfur that have become the multibillion-dollar core of the industrial-complex output. The coun-

try still lacks sophisticated industries such as electronics, optics, and other precision goods.

Unlike the Gulf states, Saudi Arabia has not tried to link its domestic financial services sector too closely to the international market for a number of reasons: a history of tight banking regulations, a long-held policy of keeping the riyal from being internationalized, the sensitivity of having an interest-based system in the cradle of Islam, and the ability to let the domestic system enjoy most of the benefits accruing from corporate ties to some of the world's biggest banks. Nevertheless, the need for a modern and efficient financial system has long been recognized, and the domestic sector is extensive and a major employer; eight of its twelve banks are among the thirty largest in the Arab world.

With a shortage of indigenous technological experience and trained labor, the kingdom relied on foreigners for technology, equipment, and labor for construction and industrialization projects—often on a turnkey basis (see Chap. 7). For many major efforts, contracts were on a build-operate-maintain (BOM) basis. However, educational and vocational programs have provided more trained local workers, and Saudiization is raising the percentage of Saudis in the labor force. More important is the large-scale development of education, including technical training, under the five-year plans.

The King Fahd University of Petroleum and Minerals (Fig. 14.5) is an example of the major institutions established since the 1960s. In 2009, two major new universities were launched. On a Red Sea coast campus, the King Abdullah University of Science and Technology began with an enrollment of some 800 students from more than sixty countries, all on full scholarships; women will attend classes with men and need not be veiled.[24] The Princess Noura bint Abdulrahman University in a Riyadh suburb will eventually enroll 40,000 women students, offering

FIGURE 14.5 University of Petroleum and Minerals in Dhahran, Eastern Province. Built in the 1960s on a stretch of sand and rock south of Aramco headquarters, it was the first of several new universities built in Saudi Arabia with some of the rising oil income and represents the plans for a modernized and technological segment in Saudi society.

courses that they would have difficulty studying at gender-segregated institutions. By the end of 2000s, the kingdom had more than fifty institutions of higher learning, located in every major city in the country.

Investing the high petrodollar income of the 1970s, Saudi Arabia built the two model industrial cities mentioned earlier, Jubayl on the Gulf and Yanbu on the Red Sea. Focusing on industries based on oil and gas, both have refineries and plants producing petrochemicals and other chemicals, fertilizers, plastics, steel, and plastic and metal goods. Facilities now include ports and airports, huge dual-purpose systems combining seawater desalination and power generation, and satellite industrial and consumer goods plants. Integrated planning and construction included both service and residential sectors in contemporary architectural designs.[25]

By the 2000s, manufacturing was contributing more than 10 percent to GDP. Many incentives attracted both local capital and joint ventures by foreign companies. The government established Saudi Arabian Basic Industries Corporation (now partially privatized) in 1976 to develop large petrochemical and steel plants. In 2008, it was reported that nearly 4,000 factories were capitalized at $81.7 billion and that petrochemicals were the most rapidly expanding industry.

Transportation

Highways. With sparse population and a preindustrial economy, Arabia before the mid-twentieth century had no road network to move people and goods over the deserts. Camels plodding along ancient caravan trails continued to be the common mode of transport, especially of goods, until after World

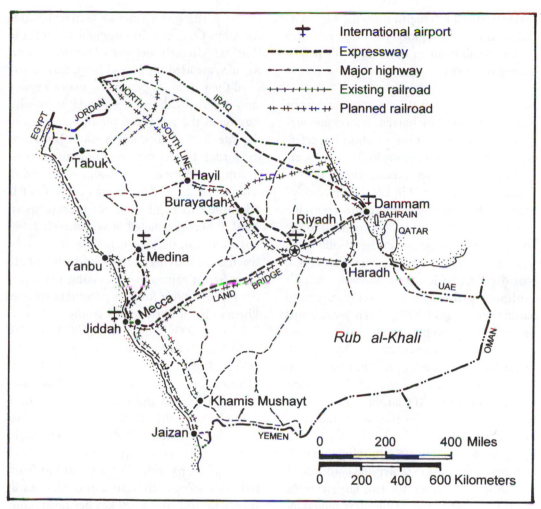

MAP 14.2 Transportation and other economic aspects of Saudi Arabia. Roads are shown in greater detail than in Map 7.2, and planned rail lines are indicated.

War II. A few automobiles drove across the open deserts, following old caravan routes, but they often foundered in deep sand before the advent of four-wheel drive and sand tires.

Petroleum development called for establishment and expansion of a road net, and the first surfaced roads linked the main towns and oil facilities in the Eastern Province. Highway construction peaked in the early 1980s; by the late 1990s, highways extended to every town, and remote villages were tied into the network by branch rural roads (Map 14.2; see also Map 7.2). A four-lane divided highway connects the Red Sea and the Gulf

(Jiddah-Mecca-Riyadh-Dammam), with a spur to Medina in the west and another to Unayzah and Buraydah in the northern Najd. At the Gulf end, the highway crosses the 15.5-mi/25-km King Fahd Causeway to Bahrain that opened in 1986 (see Fig. 7.5), carrying unbroken lines of cars on Thursdays and Fridays, the Saudi weekend. It has been so successful that at the end of the 2000s, serious planning was under way for a $3 billion 31.1-mi/50-km causeway and bridge project across the Strait of Tiran to connect Saudi Arabia and Egypt's Sinai Peninsula, with Tiran Island as the midway link.[26] Several major north-south highways in the west, central, and eastern regions tie the population centers to all eight of the kingdom's neighboring countries.

Air Facilities.   Population concentrations widely separated by barren deserts encouraged the use of air transportation in preference to railways and roads in the early years of the country's development. Saudia, the national airline, founded in 1945, evolved originally under a management contract with the U.S. airline TWA. It steadily expanded to become the largest airline in the Middle East, with more than 140 jet aircraft serving a worldwide traffic net; however, Dubai's Emirates Airline's fleet markedly surpassed Saudia's in the mid-2000s. A ten-year airport building program has supplied all cities and major towns in the country with modern airports, their runways accommodating at least medium-size jet aircraft. In the new century, more than 200 airports, 25 with regular commercial service, served Saudi cities and towns.

Between 1981 and 1984, the kingdom built two new international airports—in Jiddah and in Riyadh—then the two largest in the world. Jiddah's covers 40 mi^2/103km^2 and includes a separate facility for up to 2 million Muslims making the annual pilgrimage to nearby Mecca. Three times the size of that in Jiddah, the opulent Riyadh airport opened in 1984, and its four terminals can handle 15 million passengers a year. In 1999, an even larger facility covering 300 mi^2/780 km^2 opened in the Eastern Province, 22 mi/57 km northwest of Dammam, replacing the kingdom's first modern airport in Dhahran.

Railways.   The Saudi Government Railroad, opened in 1951, links the port of Dammam with Riyadh via Hofuf, Harad, and al-Kharj. This 360-mi/580-km link was the sole operating rail line in the kingdom—and the entire peninsula—for thirty years.

In 1985, the government's General Saudi Railways Organization opened a dual line that ran directly between Dammam and Riyadh, avoided the Harad loop, and shortened the trip by 20 percent. A major expansion of the Saudi rail net was either under way or in the advanced planning stages in the late 2000s.[27] The north-south line from the Jordan border (and ongoing routes connecting to Europe) to Riyadh via Buraydah with a branch to Ras Azwar on the Gulf is scheduled to begin limited operations in 2010. When completed, it will stretch 1,490 mi/2,400 km; the line is mainly for freight (including moving bauxite and phosphate from Saudi mines to processing plants),[28] but plans provide for later passenger service. The Saudi Landbridge will connect the Red Sea with the Gulf via a 590 mi/945 km line from Jiddah to Riyadh, an upgrade of the existing Riyadh-Dammam link, and a 70 mi/115 km connector between Dammam and Jubayl; a link to the Kuwaiti system now being built is also planned. The first contracts were signed in 2008. The Haramain (Two Sanctuaries) High Speed line will speed pilgrims some 273 mi/440 km from Jeddah's airport to Mecca and Medina at speeds up to 200 mi/320 km per hour; construction was to begin in 2009.[29] A Chinese-French combine signed a contract also in 2009 to connect central Mecca with outlying pilgrimage sites with a monorail.[30] Finally, in late 2009, construction was to begin on a light-rail metro system in Riyadh; two lines are planned for the first phase.[31] The legendary Hijaz Railway—sometimes Pilgrim Railway—stopped operating after World War I, and much of its trackage no longer exists (see Chap. 7). However, again in 2009, during a visit of the Turkish president, the Saudis announced that the two countries would undertake a feasibility study for rebuilding the century-old line as a standard-gauge line linking Turkey's network with the new Saudi line to Medina.[32] Recognizing the historic regional significance of the railway, two museums, in Madain Salih and Medina, featuring old trains and other equipment, opened in 2006.[33]

Ports and Shipping. Beginning in the 1950s, the earliest infrastructural preparation for the enormous development ahead was the expansion of ports on both sides of the peninsula. Jiddah had for centuries served as the entry port for pilgrims to nearby Mecca as well as for the limited cargo to Hijaz. When dredging through coral reefs and the manifold expansions of docks, handling facilities, and storage areas were completed, Jiddah became one of the leading ports in the region for containerized and bulk cargo. A new pilgrim terminal, Jiddah Islamic Port, was added to its facilities. In the east, Dammam evolved into the Gulf coast equivalent of Jiddah. Large, newer specialized ports were built during 1975–1985 in the industrial cities of Jubayl on the Gulf and Yanbu on the Red Sea. As was noted earlier, two of the world's largest oil-export terminals were developed in Ras Tanura (an impressive 6 mn bpd capacity) and Juaymah, followed by Yanbu on the west.

Trade

Formerly limited by the sparse and low-income population, domestic trade is now a significant segment in the economy with an affluent population of avid consumers. The traditional Middle East *suq*, with multiple small, specialized shops, characterized Saudi Arabian marketing through the 1960s. As consumer spending boomed, outlets also changed, stimulated by modern retailing practices; urban shops became larger and similar to those in Western cities. New opulent complexes in Riyadh and Jiddah equal major shopping malls in North America in facilities and inventory. Foreigners do find it disconcerting that shops close for thirty minutes several times a day for prayers—another indicator of conservative religious practices. In small settlements, open-air *suqs* still thrive. The large, well-stocked supermarkets that operate in every city offer most brands on the international market as well as a wide range of specialty products favored by expatriates from Asian countries. Fresh fruits and vegetables arrive by road and air from horticultural centers as far as 1,500 mi/2,410 km away. As in the Gulf area, large automobile dealerships offer all major makes of cars, and Saudis are very much automobile minded, with the second-largest number of cars in the region after Turkey.

The kingdom's imports are diversified by both type and source. They range from heavy equipment used by oil companies and contractors to large amounts of armaments and military support equipment and a wide variety of consumer products. Exports once were 99 percent petroleum and petroleum products, but they are becoming increasingly varied (see country summary). Saudi Arabia now ranks as both the world's leading producer and leading exporter of petroleum. The United States normally imports more than 1.75 mn bpd from Saudi Arabia, which thus ranks among its leading suppliers, along with Canada, Mexico, and Venezuela. Oil exports, which are currently about 1.5 mn bpd less than production figures, rose from about 2 mn bpd in the early 1960s to an average of nearly 9 mn bpd in 1979–1981, fell to less than half that total in 1988, then averaged about 8.9 mn bpd in 2007. Major export destinations in the late 2000s were Japan, Taiwan, the United States, and the EU; in 2007, export values amounted to 65 percent of GDP. Major suppliers of the kingdom's imports are the EU, the United States, China, and Japan. The six countries of the Gulf Cooperation Council launched a customs union in 2003; it was due to be fully implemented by the end of 2009. In 2005, Saudi Arabia gained accession to the World Trade Organization.

RELATIONS

As a large, strategically located country with some of the world's most vitally valuable resources, Saudi Arabia inevitably has especially sensitive relations with its neighbors and with its global partners. This would be true regardless of the structure and policies of the country's government. It is particularly applicable in view of the Saudi kingdom's monarchal system of governance and its unusually rigid conservatism. The monarchy has been subjected to heavy criticism for several years, both cautiously within the country and vigorously on the world scene.

As the kingdom emerged in the 1950s from long isolation, it sought to maintain its national interests within the Arab world, within the Islamic community, and among other oil-producing—and oil-consuming—countries. It was a charter member of the United Nations, and it has supported the Arab League, Organization of the Islamic Conference, Gulf Cooperation Council (headquartered in Saudi Arabia), International Monetary Fund, World Bank, International Fund for Agricultural Development, African Development Bank, Islamic Development Bank, OPEC, OAPEC, and other economic agencies. It is a member of the so-called G-20, the principal economic and financial forum of the world's wealthiest economies that in 2009 supplanted the more restricted G-8 in this role.[34] In both absolute and percentage of GDP terms, it is one of the leading donor countries. Despite its natural dominance among its neighbors, it rarely plays a combative or hawkish role, preferring a more defensive posture as home of the Two Holy Mosques.

The kingdom has, since its inception in 1932, maintained generally peaceful relations with its eight neighbors, although not uniformly so. Prior to the 1990–1991 Gulf crisis, the most notable exceptions were a short war with Yemen in 1934, a dispute with Abu Dhabi and Oman over the Buraymi Oasis during the 1940s and 1950s, and tensions over Saudi support of the imam of Inner Oman against the sultan of Oman during the late 1950s and 1960s. The kingdom has also had running boundary disputes with Qatar. Border problems have similarly created periodic tensions with the UAE, Oman, and Yemen, but they have been smoothed over, and all of the kingdom's boundaries are de jure (see Chap. 8). Membership in the GCC and other shared developments have warmed relations with Qatar, the UAE, and Oman.

Conflict with Yemen arose in 1962–1969, when Saudi Arabia supported the royalists during the Yemen civil war, as well as in 1990, when it made efforts to hinder unification of the two Yemens. Border discords flared during the 1990s; there was even a one-day battle in July 1998 over the tiny island of Duwaima.[35] Activities by rebel Yemeni tribes along the border north of Sadah in 2009–2010 provoked Saudi military responses. Yemen's refusal to condemn Iraq's invasion of Kuwait (Yemen was a rotating member of the UN Security Council at the time) caused Saudi ire, and 800,000 Yemeni workers were expelled and forced to return home. Tensions over the 1,300-mi/2,100-km border flared in the late 1990s, but then eased. Similarly, Jordan's ambivalent stance regarding Iraq derailed the rapport between the two moderate monarchies. Financial support ceased along with major purchases, crude oil exports via Tapline stopped, and thousands of Jordanians lost their employment. With the visit of then Crown Prince Abdullah in 1996, bilateral relations with Jordan began to improve.[36]

Saudi support for Iraq in its war against Iran beginning in 1980 was both financial and political, including agreement for the IPSA pipeline to be built from southern Iraq to the Red Sea. Saudi Arabia turned bitterly against Saddam Husayn after he invaded Kuwait in 1990, and it closed the IPSA line, supplied bases for the coalition forces against

Iraq, and joined in the coalition. The kingdom incurred considerable financial costs during the war—an estimated $55 billion in direct payments to some of the coalition partners ($15 billion to the United States alone), foregone oil revenues, and donated supplies. During the 1990s, Saudi Arabia supported general enforcement of sanctions against Iraq but balked at the heavier attacks later in the decade. It was also notably less involved in the Anglo-American invasion of Iraq, and later in 2003 the United States pulled its troops that had been stationed in the kingdom since 1990.

It has had good relations with Kuwait, sharing the Divided Zone and assisting Kuwait on a grand scale when it was invaded by Iraq in 1990. Good Saudi-Bahraini relations are evident in the fact that modest amounts of crude oil have been pumped to Bahrain for refining from the early years, and more so in Saudi generosity in donating to Bahrain most of the income from the off-shore Abu Safah field near the two states' median line. Further evidence is the successful construction and operation of the causeway, financed by Saudi Arabia and completed in 1986, linking Bahrain to the mainland.

Financial support from Saudi Arabia and the other Gulf states was for many years the Palestine Liberation Organization's main source of income, although some of the PLO actions contrasted with Saudi Arabia's basically nonviolent political philosophy and moderate stance. The PLO lost that support when its chairman, the late Yasser Arafat, chose not to condemn Iraq's invasion of Kuwait, though the government and the PLO later reached an outward rapprochement. Since the mid-1970s, the kingdom has extended considerable bilateral assistance to developing countries; part of this assistance has been channeled through the Saudi Fund for Development (SFD) that by 2008 had financed 430 projects and programs in seventy-three countries with total funding of $7.7

billion.[37] It has also been a major source of capital for other development agencies including the World Bank, African Development Bank, Islamic Development Bank, OPEC Fund, and Arab Fund for Economic and Social Development.[38] Its capital subscriptions to the World Bank and the International Monetary Fund are high enough to earn it a permanent seat on these organizations' boards of executive directors.

Overall, British-Saudi relations have remained good, with Britain filling multibillion-dollar arms contracts after U.S. sales to the kingdom halted because of pressure by pro-Israeli groups in the United States. Increasing numbers of Britons are serving in a wide range of professional, managerial, and technical capacities, especially as more British military equipment is utilized in the kingdom. In addition, Saudi Arabia, through the GCC, is drawing closer to the EU in general.

Saudi Arabia's close relations with the United States began with Aramco's exploration for petroleum in the 1930s. Diplomatic relations were established in 1933, and an American Embassy opened in Jiddah in 1944, the same year that a consulate general opened in Dhahran to service the burgeoning American community in the oil industry. It is still the only diplomatic post allowed east of Riyadh. Although Riyadh had been the royal capital for decades, all foreign embassies were restricted to Jiddah until the mid-1980s, when an elaborate new diplomatic quarter opened in Riyadh.

As Aramco's operations expanded, thousands of U.S. employees and their dependents came to the Eastern Province. They have lived in Aramco camps for decades, devoting their entire working lives to the ongoing project. Both Aramco and its four U.S. corporate owners before 1973 maintained excellent relations with the provincial and central governments.

The United States and Saudi Arabia also cooperated in other technical areas during the heyday of their relations: The U.S. Geological Survey conducted geological and mineral studies in the western shield area for many years and cooperated in the production of geographical and geological maps. In 1974, the US–Saudi Arabia Joint Commission for Economic Cooperation (JECOR), funded by the Saudi Arabian government, was established for research into issues of mutual interest and for technical assistance. Funded entirely by the kingdom, more than thirty development projects under the JECOR umbrella—ranging from establishing a national park in the Asir and bolstering the capabilities of Saudi Customs authorities to staffing an economic "think tank" in the Ministry of Finance and National Economy— were carried out by several hundred American consultants seconded to it by the U.S. Department of the Treasury and other agencies.[39] As many as 65,000 U.S. citizens lived and worked in the kingdom in the early 1980s, but the number has steadily decreased, especially after 9/11.

In 1942, King Abd al-Aziz agreed to the construction of a U.S. air base south of Dhahran, which was a combined military-civilian airfield until 1999. It then reverted to a Saudi military air base, and a huge new civil airport opened farther north. In 1953, the U.S. Military Training Mission began training elements of the Saudi air force, army, and navy, and that program continues on a small scale. The United States has also been the kingdom's major supplier of military equipment and services—amounting to billions of dollars annually—and provides consultant and supervisory services by the U.S. Army Corps of Engineers for military construction. The Saudi government compensated the allies $16.8 billion in war costs during the 1990–1991 Gulf crisis, in addition to supplying airfields, facilities, and logistical support. After the Gulf war, about 5,000 U.S. troops remained in the kingdom as rapid deployment forces in case Iraq attacked again.

However, the Saudi and regional reaction to a non-Muslim military presence, especially American, in Muslim lands made the presence untenable. Car-bomb attacks killed twenty-six Americans in 1995–1996. Anti-American sentiment increased—as it did elsewhere in the region—after the beginning of the second intifadah in 2000, and the resentment became mutual in the days after 9/11, when news reports surfaced revealing that fifteen of the terrorists involved in the 9/11 attack had been Saudi citizens. Terrorist attacks in Riyadh in 2003 killed more than fifty people, including nine Americans, and a full-scale assault on the U.S. Consulate General in Jiddah in December 2004 killed four non-American staff members.

By early 2005, U.S.-Saudi relations were under tension from both directions, with each side aware that the attacks were directed against both the Saudi regime and the United States. Although both acknowledged that the symbiotic relationship must be preserved, inevitably there have been misgivings on both sides—as in all Arab and virtually all Muslim states—because of the "special relationship" between the United States and Israel.

The kingdom supports a peaceful resolution of the Arab-Israeli conflict but is firm in its support of justice for the Palestinians and in support of UN Resolution 242 calling for Israel's withdrawal from territories occupied in 1967. In 2002, then Crown Prince Abdullah proposed at an Arab League summit what has come to be known as the Arab Peace Initiative (API); to end the Arab-Israeli conflict, it proposes to normalize relations between all the Arab countries and Israel, in exchange for a complete Israeli withdrawal from the occupied territories (including East Jerusalem) and a "just settlement" of the Palestinian refugee problem. As king, Abdullah has continued to promote the API, and when, after the inauguration of President Obama, the United States finally showed real interest in its possibilities, reports indicated that revisions to make it more palatable to Israel were under consideration: demilitarization of the future Palestinian state and a refugee settlement not involving a large-scale return to Israel proper.

Saudi Arabia's intentions to broaden its contacts in the world were demonstrated in the early 1990s, when the kingdom established diplomatic relations with long-shunned Russia and China; reestablished relations with Iran, which had been broken off in 1988; and indicated plans to exchange diplomats with East European countries. In addition, the Saudis have given numerous contracts to Russian and Chinese companies for major construction and natural gas exploration contracts.

In a move unique in Saudi history, King Abdullah met with Pope Benedict XVI in 2007[40] and followed this with a call for dialogue among the three main monotheistic faiths—Judaism, Christianity, and Islam—and for mutual tolerance and cooperation. With his active support, 2008 saw the convening of three unusual conferences of religious leaders: The first was in June in Mecca with Muslim participants pledging to improve Sunni-Shii relations, the second was cosponsored by Spain in July with Jewish and Christian representatives, and the third was in November at the United Nations in New York, bringing political leaders together with attendees from the three faiths. King Abdullah addressed all three meetings, telling the third session, "Terrorism and criminality are the enemies of every religion and every civilization. They would not have emerged except for the absence of the principle of tolerance."[41]

NOTES

1. Kazakhstan in Central Asia and Sudan and Algeria in North Africa are larger.

2. Transparency International 2009.

3. One of the first Saudi monographs on the country's archaeology is the elaborately illustrated al-Ansary 1982. Whalen and Pease 1992 discusses the Developed Oldowan tool findings.

4. The history of the interior of the Arabian Peninsula was little known until oil developments brought Arabia to world attention, and accurate, detailed history of the area is still limited. Useful, concise accounts are in *Saudi Arabia* Country Study 1995, *Saudi Aramco and Its World* 1995, and *A Land Transformed* 2006. For more details, see Holden and Johns 1982. More recent recommended studies are Barger 2000, an intimate presentation by a former president of Aramco; Vasiliev 2000 and al-Rasheed 2002, good histories; Champion 2003; and Lippman 2004. Some popular accounts are fanciful or spiteful.

5. These reforms and the council are analyzed in Dekmejian 1998.

6. U.S. Department of State, *Country Commercial Guide: Saudi Arabia*, Aug. 2004.

7. Two women were elected, however, to the board of Jiddah's influential chamber of commerce and industry (*BBC News*, Nov. 30, 2005).

8. Coverage of Arabian regions and physical aspects is in Ministry of Agriculture and Water 1984; U.S. Geological Survey 1966–1967, 1975, 1989; McKee 1979; Holm 1960; Brown and Coleman 1972; Brown 1972; Scoville 1979; *Saudi Aramco and Its World* 1995; and Farsi 1989.

9. USGS, "The Mineral Industry of Saudi Arabia," in *Minerals Yearbook* 2008. Minerals development is a major incentive to the recent railroad building program.

10. Shamekh 1975 discusses Bedouin in the Qasim, and Altorki and Cole 1989 discusses development connected with Unayzah.

11. The readable Thesiger 1959 on the Rub al-Khali realm has become a classic.

12. *Global Arab Network*, Feb. 7, 2010.

13. The rapidly changing development of Saudi Arabia must be followed closely in relevant periodicals. It is well covered in the *Middle East Economic Survey* and the *Middle East Economic Digest*. *Country Commercial Guide: Saudi Arabia* 2009 is very helpful. The economy is covered in context in U.S. Department of State, *Background Note: Saudi Arabia*, Jan. 2009. Comprehensive statistics are given in the Kingdom of Saudi Arabia's *Statistical Year Book*. Oil developments are given in the authoritative *Saudi Aramco and Its World* 1995 and *A Land Transformed* 2006; U.S. Department of Energy, Energy Information Administration, *Country Analysis Briefs: Saudi Arabia*, Nov. 2009; *Minerals Yearbook: Saudi Arabia* 2002; http://minerals.usgs.gov/minerals/; *Oil and Gas Journal*; the annual *International Petroleum Encyclopedia*; P. Woodward 1988; Nabir 1988; and Saudi Aramco, *Annual Report*, various years.

14. See U.S. Department of State, *Background Note: Saudi Arabia*, Jan. 2009.

15. United Nations Development Programme 2009.

16. See the Statistical Databases Web site of the UN Food and Agriculture Organization (FAO) at http://faostat.fao.org/.

17. See the well-regarded Vidal 1955, although the oases have been greatly transformed since the study was made.

18. Additionally, about 120 mn gal/0.45 mn m^3 in treated wastewater was available daily (FAO Aquastat 2009).

19. The history, development, and recent situation of the Saudi oil industry are authoritatively covered in *Saudi Aramco and Its World* 1995 and *A Land Transformed* 2006. Other sidelights are in Yergin 1991. For detailed current information see EIA, Aug. 2008.

20. U.S. Department of Energy, Energy Information Administration, *Country Analysis Briefs: Saudi Arabia*, Nov. 2009.

21. *New York Times*, May 16, 2004; *Oil and Gas Journal*, Mar. 21, 2005, 5. See also *Oil and Gas Journal*, July 10, 2000, regarding an earlier such move by Saudi Arabia.

22. *Media Line*, Feb. 10, 2010.

23. *Media Line*, Mar 14, 2010.

24. For further information, see www.kaust.edu.sa/.

25. See Pampanini 1997.

26. *ArabianBusiness.com* (UAE), Mar. 1, 2008.

27. For further information on the new routes, see www.saudirailexpansion.com/saudirailexpansion/ default.aspx and www.saudirailways.org/portal/page/ portal/PRTS/root/Home/04_Expansion_Specification/ 02Expansion.

28. *Arab News* (Riyadh), Dec. 6, 2006. The considerable nonpetroleum resources in the kingdom clearly have been a prime motivation in the surge of interest in railway construction.

29. *Economist*, Apr. 23, 2009.

30. *BBC News*, Feb. 11, 2009.

31. *Arab News*, Nov. 10, 2009.

32. *Arab News*, Feb. 5, 2009

33. There is a third museum in Damascus, housed in the former northern terminus of the Hejaz railway.

34. Turkey is also a member of the G-20.

35. *New York Times*, July 26, 1998.

36. In 2007, the two countries agreed to demarcate their maritime border (*Arab News*, Dec. 17, 2007).

37. For further details, see the SFD Web site, www .sfd.gov.sa/english/.

38. Through the end of 2006, Saudi Arabia had provided $26.9 billion to multilateral agencies. See www .sfd.gov.sa/english/appen1.htm.

39. Harbison 1990.

40. Abdullah had met with Pope John Paul II in 1999 before he was king.

41. Remarks of King Abdullah at the Culture of Peace Conference at the United Nations, Nov. 12, 2008. For the full speech, see www.saudi-us-relations .org/articles/2008/ioi/081113p-un-speech.html.

15

The Gulf and Its Oil States

AN OVERVIEW

The body of water almost enclosed by the Arabian Peninsula and the Iranian coast is variously designated as the Persian Gulf, Arabian Gulf, Persian/Arabian Gulf, or, increasingly, simply the Gulf. By whatever name, it is now well known because of its oil resources and its place in news headlines during the wars of 1980–1988, 1990–1991, and 2003 onward. Whatever else may be said of them, Desert Shield, Desert Storm, and Operation Iraqi Freedom left no doubt about the explosive significance of Gulf geopolitics. But before the 1930s, the region was little known in the West other than by a few British officials and adventurers. Remote, isolated, and poverty ridden, the area was characterized by one British official in 1928 this way: "The amenities of life are few and far between. Nature is in her fiercest humour and man has done little to improve upon her handiwork."[1]

Then between 1960 and 1985, the span of one generation, the coast of the Arabian Peninsula from Kuwait to Muscat underwent a dramatic transformation. Fishing villages mushroomed into cities with populations 50, 100, and 150 times those of 1928, including Kuwait, Dammam/al-Khobar, Doha, Abu Dhabi, Dubai, Sharjah, and Muscat-Matrah. Once impoverished indigenous peoples along that coast now have some of the highest per capita incomes in the world.

Although "nature is in her fiercest humour" even yet, "man" has done much recently to improve upon nature's handiwork. Billions of petrodollars built new cities and ports and, even more amazing, found (or "manufactured") water for urban domestic supplies and for irrigating parks and gardens. With enormous amounts of energy available, air-conditioning tames the temperature. Although most commodities and much of the labor are imported, few of the conveniences and comforts of modern living are lacking along the Gulf.[2] Oil has given these states a much improved standard of living, as can be seen from the gains in the Human Development Index, computed by the UNDP and embodying measures of health, education, and income. In 2007, the global rankings were 31st, 33rd, 35th, and 39th out of 182 countries (and 2nd, 4th, 5th, and 6th regionally) for Kuwait, Qatar, the United Arab Emirates (UAE), and Bahrain, respectively.[3] All have enjoyed the benefits of oil for more than a generation, but their HDI scores have continued to rise—by an average of about 15 percent since 1990, largely on gains in life expectancy and school enrollment.

Earlier chapters covered several functional aspects of the Gulf: its physical characteristics, influence on climate, role in the petroleum industry, strategic aspects, organization in the Gulf Cooperation Council (GCC), and maritime function. Now it is time to examine the regional characteristics of the individual smaller states along the western coast of the Gulf: Kuwait, Bahrain, Qatar, and the UAE.[4]

A Glance at History

In addition to several Paleolithic (Old Stone Age) sites, a number of Neolithic sites have been found in several locations, and artifacts from rather intensive explorations can be seen in handsome museums in all the littoral states. The artifacts and other evidence testify to the vigor of the sea traffic through the Gulf and eastward to the Indus Valley from about 2300 BCE, with another peak during Babylonian times. With its gushing artesian springs, Bahrain was an important way station for ancient mariners sailing between the Indus Valley and Mesopotamia. Nearchus, Alexander the Great's military commander, transited this sea-lane while returning from Alexander's expedition to the Indus Valley in 325 BCE. Romans mastered the art of sailing with the monsoons to and from India, via the Red Sea rather than the Gulf.

Islamic civilization and its maritime trade reinvigorated the Gulf's economic role after the eighth century, as we can see from the tales of Sinbad the Sailor, woven around voyages that originated in the Gulf. The basin's importance revived when the Portuguese arrived in 1514 after opening the route around Africa. Drawn by the wealth of Persia under Abbas the Great, the Dutch and British supplanted the Portuguese. Expanding Ottoman power coalesced with European bridgeheads in the Gulf, and Basrah, Bushehr (Bushire), Bahrain, Bandar-e Abbas, Hormuz, and other ports were thriving trade centers and entrepôts after the early 1600s. Two centuries later, Britain's economic, military, and political dominance extended along almost the entire littoral in connection with its Indian interests.

By the end of the 1920s, southwestern Iran was a British "sphere of influence," Iraq was a British mandate, and Kuwait, Bahrain, Qatar, the Trucial States, and Muscat and Oman were all under some form of British control or influence. The British installed navigational aids (Persian Gulf Lighting Service) and undertook surveying, charting, and mapping of both the Gulf and its coasts and of the Tigris and Karun rivers. The evolving British role, as well as the emergence of independent Gulf states, is discussed in Chapter 8 and below.

A Note on Gulf Oil

In 2010, the eight petroleum producers facing the Gulf had reserves of 747.8 bn bbl, 55 percent of the world total, and their average daily output during 2009 was 14.1 mn bbl, 20 percent of world output. The four states discussed in this chapter had reserves of 227.3 bn bbl (17 percent of world reserves) and an average production of 5.35 mn bpd (7.6 percent of world output). Natural gas reserves of the eight states totaled 74.5 bn m³ and of the four totaled 33.41 bn m³, about 40 percent and 18 percent of global reserves, respectively.[5] The oil and gas fields in and around the Gulf are seen in Map 6.2; those that are completely or partially offshore are identified. Also shown are the many oil terminals, several ranking among the world's largest: Ras Tanura, Juaymah, Mina al-Ahmadi, and Kharg Island. A general discussion of the petroleum industry is in Chapter 6; additional details are found in Chapter 14 and below.[6]

A Geopolitical Perspective

Intra-Gulf Relations. The Gulf has long been both an arena of contention and conflict and a theater of peaceful trade and regional intercourse. For most of the past 150 years, partly under the Pax Britannica, the littoral states have usually sought nonmilitary solutions. Most clashes that have taken place have occurred in the hinterland—over water sources, grazing rights, dynastic disputes, or territorial consolidation—rather than over the Gulf as such. Wells and springs in the desert have occasionally been contested, and Bahrain and Qatar contended for two centuries over dynastic and territorial questions. The Buraymi Oasis dispute is a classic modern example of mediated conflict.

Gulf states have periodically disputed control over offshore islands and pearl beds as well as freedom of navigation. Some oil fields straddle political boundaries, onshore and offshore, but differing claims over these boundaries have been settled surprisingly amicably. Britain sometimes served as arbiter, and the United States conducted a cross-Gulf survey in the mid-1960s, delineating a median line in the central Gulf. Bahrain and Qatar agreed in 2001 to a mediated split of islands and waters separating them. One unsettled offshore boundary is that of Kuwait, Iraq, and Iran at the head of the Gulf.

By far, three modern clashes have been the most serious: the protracted Iran-Iraq War in the 1980s, the Gulf crisis of 1990–1991 (both sparked by Iraqi aggression), and the controversial Iraq War beginning in March 2003. The first continued the historic conflict along the line of disjunction between the Zagros Mountain belt and the Mesopotamian Basin, two major regional power foci. The second was more complicated, but, inter alia, it manifested the resurgence of the Mesopotamian focus. The third has been the most bitterly debated conflict since Vietnam.

Global Perspective. However, because the Gulf Basin countries possess 55 percent of the world's petroleum resources and produce nearly one-third of the world's daily oil output, its geopolitical interactions extend to virtually every part of the world. This was clearly demonstrated when nearly forty countries contributed in some way to Kuwait's liberation in 1990–1991. The trou-

bled waters of the Gulf are an unstable chessboard on which every energy-dependent country must try for checkmate—hence the intensity of the polemics over the U.S.-led invasion and subsequent occupation of Iraq. This subject has been examined in Chapters 6 and 8 and will be touched on again in this chapter.[7]

KUWAIT

Kuwait Fort and Port

Originally a small port and trade center, Kuwait ("little fort" from Arabic *kut*, "fort") historically used its location on a small bay at the head of the Gulf for maritime activities and modest overland trade (Map 15.1). Landward, trade and pastoralism supported 10,000–15,000 townspeople and several thousand Bedouin.[8] More important economically were pearling, fishing, boat building, and trade with India and Gulf coastal towns. Kuwait's greatest asset was its excellent harbor, its greatest drawback a lack of fresh water. Considering this, its population of 50,000 after World War I was surprisingly large.

The world depression of the 1930s and competition from Japanese cultured pearls undermined Kuwait's traditional livelihood. By 1937, its economic future looked bleak. The 700 pearling dhows of 1921 decreased to 125 in 1939, and 40 in the 1940s.[9] Many of them joined the fleet of "booms" bringing fresh water from the Shatt al-Arab, supplying up to 100,000 gal/378,500 l each day. But the economy recovered and expanded dramatically when the discovery of large petroleum resources in 1938 led to steadily increasing exports after World War II and immense wealth and rapid development in little more than a decade.[10]

With economic and political viability, Kuwait gained independence in 1961 from Britain, its protector since 1899. However, sovereignty for the amirate, including withdrawal

KUWAIT

Long-form official name, anglicized: State of Kuwait

Official name, transliterated: Dawlat al-Kuwayt

Form of government: constitutional monarchy with one legislative body (National Assembly)

Area: 6,880 mi²/17,818 km²

Population, 2008: 3,530,000; Literacy (Latest): 84.4%

Ethnic composition (%): Arab 80, of which Kuwaiti 40, Bedouin 4, other Arab 36; South Asian 10; Iranian 4; other 6

Religions (%): Muslim 80, of which Sunni 60, Shii 20; Christian 10; others 10

Demography: Life expectancy—75.9 yr (M), 77.9 yr (F); Birthrate (per 1,000)—17.1; Fertility rate—3.00

GDP, 2009: $114.9 billion; purchasing power parity: $148.7 billion; per capita: $55,800

Currency: Kuwaiti dinar, US$1 = 0.288 dinars, 1 dinar = $3.446 (March 2010)

Energy reserves: oil—101.5 bn bbl; natural gas—63 tn ft³; coal—nil

Main exports (% of total value, 2006): crude petroleum 67.3; refined petroleum 23.2; liquefied petroleum gas 4.5; ethylene product 2.0

Main imports (% of total value, 2006): industrial requirements 31.0; capital goods 24.2; consumer durables 11.1; food 10.0

Capital city: Kuwait City (agglomeration) 1,810,000; other cities: Qalib ash-Shuyukh 179,264; Salimiyah 145,328; Hawali 106,992

---

of British protection, brought problems; because independent Kuwait was extremely wealthy but small and weak, its long-covetous neighbor, Iraq, immediately renewed its often-stated claim to its territory. Britain responded promptly, and its protection was then taken over by Arab League forces—and Iraq withdrew both threat and troops. But the claim was periodically renewed, provoking several border incidents—the most serious in 1973.

For three decades, independent Kuwait saw almost unparalleled development. Billions of dollars allowed it to hire outside expertise and labor and to import goods and equipment. The Iran-Iraq War had brought eight years of problems and fears to Kuwait,

which negotiated for and bought what it needed, including security. Then, on August 2, 1990, Kuwait's complacency was shattered when Iraq invaded. The formerly obscure amirate suddenly dominated world television screens, radio, and headlines.

Although the 1990–1991 crisis is discussed in Chapter 8, the impact on Kuwait will be examined briefly here. Significantly, at the time of the invasion (early August), as is true every year, thousands of Kuwaiti residents were on vacation in cooler lands and many expatriates were in their homelands, making invasion easier for Iraq but complicating the situation for Kuwaitis unable to return home.

Destruction was extensive and often savagely senseless. Iraqis looted transportable

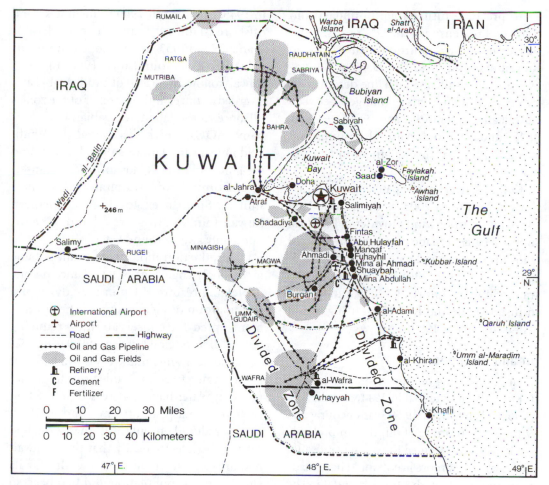

MAP 15.1 General and economic map of Kuwait. The Divided Zone is the former Saudi Arabia–Kuwait Neutral Zone, delineated with dashed-line boundaries.

items and sabotaged fixed facilities—an estimated $70–$100 billion loss.[11] Some valuable items were later returned under UN cease-fire resolutions,[12] but the sabotage of oil facilities was not so easily overcome. This caused not only direct financial and infrastructural losses but also environmental havoc. In an act variously called "environmental terrorism," "ecoterrorism," or "ecocide," Iraq blew up 749 of 935 wellheads, leaving more than 690 wells afire or blowing wild; millions of barrels flowed into the desert, while millions more burned.[13] In late January 1991, Iraq dumped 150,000 bpd from storage tanks into the Gulf, a spill that eventually exceeded 4 mn bbl.

Stopping the destruction was the most prolonged firefighting exercise in history; the last fire was extinguished November 6, 1991.[14] Meanwhile, in response to pressures that built from the early days of the occupation, government and public attention was devoted to social and political reforms. Various levels of Kuwaiti reaction to the invasion and to the brutality of the occupation had revealed serious weaknesses and deficiencies in the body politic; the imperative for reform was patent, and pressures were exerted from within and without. Change was slow in coming, but Kuwait had achieved progress by the late 2000s.

To preclude future Iraqi boundary and territorial pretensions, the UN precisely demarcated the long-controversial line between Kuwait and Iraq in 1992–1993. The boundary generally confirmed the line described in two earlier documents exchanged between Kuwait and Iraq, in 1932 and 1963 (see Chap. 8, "Boundary and Territorial Disputes"),[15] and Iraq accepted this judgment in November 1994.

Kuwait actively participated in the U.S. actions in Iraq from 2003, as the ground base for coalition troops and provider of logistical support. Later, it made peace with the elected Iraqi government and renewed formal diplomatic relations in 2008, having supported Iraqi rebuilding efforts. In 2009, the foreign minister made the first Kuwait high-level visit to Iraq since 1990.

Oil and Oil Industry

A surface showing of asphalt spurred interest in Kuwait's oil potential in 1911, and the first geological survey, in 1914, was encouraging. Without the promise of oil, Britain probably would not have retained Kuwait separate after World War I but more likely would have made it become part of the Iraqi mandate. The Anglo-Persian Oil Company and the Gulf Oil Corporation of the United States, in a jointly owned local subsidiary, Kuwait Oil Company (KOC), obtained a concession in 1934.[16] KOC struck a gusher in the Burgan Dome in 1938; with oil in several relatively shallow horizons, it was the world's biggest field up to that time. It is still the second-largest (after Saudi Arabia's Ghawar) and the world's richest field for its areal extent, with 70 bn bbl. Delayed by World War II, exports were first lifted in 1946. Exploration in the 1950s opened more fields—Ahmadi, Magwa (both in the Greater Burgan field), Raudhatain, Bahra, Sabriya, and Minagish. Into the 2000s, new discoveries continued, like Kara al-Marou in the west.

Concessions went to Aminoil (United States) for Kuwait's share in the Neutral Zone in 1945, extended in 1949 to include several offshore islands. It found the considerable Wafra field in 1953 and developed Umm Gudair after KOC found it in 1966. In 1958, Kuwait followed the lead of Saudi Arabia and awarded a concession for its half of the zone's offshore to the Japanese Arabian Oil Company (AOC), which discovered the Khafji field in 1960 and Hout in 1963. It also found the Lulu and Dorra fields in 1967; the unsettled maritime border with Iran has kept these shut in. Spanish exploration in northern Kuwait found both more oil and the amirate's only sweet groundwater in 1955.

As production mounted, Kuwait became increasingly cognizant of its reliance on one depletable resource. Upon the advice of a young group of "technocrats," the government opted for conservation by reducing output. It also reined in wasteful flaring (because no economic market was available) of gas separated from the crude prior to further handling. After having increased production each year to a peak of 3 mn bpd in 1972, Kuwait reduced output to less than 2 mn bpd during the late 1970s. By that time, Kuwait had amassed such enormous wealth for its small size and population and had been so intensively developed that conserving its oil was more logical than accumulating additional billions of dollars.

Like other OPEC countries, Kuwait sought participation in its concessionary companies and by 1975 controlled KOC. It nationalized Aminoil and its operations in the Neutral Zone (by that time termed the Divided Zone) in 1977. In 1980, Kuwait Petroleum Corporation (KPC) was created to serve as the umbrella for upstream and downstream operations as well as tanker transportation. Now a completely vertically integrated corporation, it competes with the multinationals, owning refineries in western Europe and North America and downstream operations in South Asia and the Pacific Rim. In Kuwait, three main refineries at Mina al-Ahmadi (the largest, with a capacity of 466,000 bpd), Mina Abdullah, and Shuaybah have a combined capacity of about 936,000 bpd throughput (see Table 6.2).

By the late 2000s, Kuwait's 103 bn bbl of reserves (including half of Divided Zone reserves of 5 bn bbl) were the fourth largest in the world—7.7 percent of the world total, and an average of 2.3 mn bpd was produced from 790 wells. Project Kuwait is drilling a modest number of new wells in some fields, constructing new gathering centers to handle more output, increasing production capacity from 2.4 mn bpd to 4.0 mn bpd by 2020,[17] relaxing policies on foreign company activities to gain outside expertise, and expanding the petrochemical industry. (Nationalists and Islamists oppose allowing foreign companies into the sector.) Overall, the sector accounts for half of GDP, 95 percent of export revenues, and 80 percent of government income. Record high oil prices in 2008 meant record export earnings—$80.2 billion. The amirate's rapid recovery after the 1991 Gulf War was based on its huge resources, the intelligent use of outside expertise, and a resilient indigenous population.

Other Industry and Trade

Development goals focus on capital- and energy-intensive industries (rather than labor-intensive manufacturing) like petroleum and by-products, construction materials, consumer goods, and electronics. Diversification and domestic production of traditionally imported basic commodities are deterred by the small size of the consuming population,[18] despite high per capita GDP—$57,500 in 2008. The relatively few nonpetroleum industries include cement, pharmaceuticals, nonalcoholic beverages, processed foods, milled flour, plastics, paper products, and furniture.

With less than 4.5 in/114 mm of annual rainfall, no surface streams, and only small amounts of underground water, Kuwait once imported its water and "manufactures" it

now. Plentiful energy desalinates water[19] and simultaneously generates electric power; it produces close to 50 gigawatt hours (GWh) annually, while supplying more than 330 mn gals/1.25 mn m^3 of sweet water per day. Per capita electricity consumption is among the highest in the world (and second only to Qatar in the region) at heavily subsidized prices. A 50 percent expansion in generating capacity is planned, along with a shift to using mostly natural gas as the fuel for the plants; in the late 2000s, oil was still being used for about 70 percent of its generating needs.[20] It will probably have to both import liquefied natural gas (LNG) and further develop its own deposits of nonassociated gas.[21]

Kuwait has a consumer economy matching the oil sector. With a tradition of trading and shipping, prescient merchants moved rapidly into importing, retailing, appliance service, electronic products, household furnishings, and automobiles. The old *suqs* have long since been replaced by modern shopping centers and individual outlets. Some of the country's banks ranked among the world's leading independent financial houses by the 1970s, when investors wealthy from the booming economy sought to place surplus funds. However, four events during the 1980s seriously impacted Kuwait economically and politically: (1) the scandalous collapse in 1982 of the extraofficial *Suq al-Manakh* "stock market," resulting in more than 500 bankruptcies; (2) the 50 percent drop in oil prices during the early 1980s; (3) the Iran-Iraq War, which depressed economic activity in the region; and (4) most traumatic of all, the devastating Iraqi occupation.[22]

Having largely recovered from the occupation in the ensuing decade, Kuwait profited substantially from the oil price rises in 2004–2005 and 2008. The amirate served as a staging area, coalition partner, contractor, and supplier in the buildup to and execution of Operation Iraqi Freedom in 2003. After the invasion, many companies working in Iraq established offices in the amirate and contracted with local agencies for goods and services—so it both benefited from and contributed to the operation.

In 1976, when Kuwait decided to reduce oil production to extend the life of its main resource, it set up the Reserve Fund for Future Generations, to which 10 percent of ordinary revenues is allocated each year. This fund is complemented by a portfolio of normal investments, the General Reserve Fund. Of the $100 billion of the two funds invested abroad by 1990, the government drew on about half during and right after the Iraqi occupation for operational and reconstruction expenses.

The Kuwait Fund for Arab Economic Development, created in 1961, was the first Arab bilateral aid agency. Through 2008 it had financed some 760 projects in 103 countries ranging from Belize to the Solomon Islands and from Kazakhstan to Swaziland.[23] The government also has made huge grants to the "frontline states" of Egypt, Syria, and Jordan, as well as—ironically—loans of $4 to 5 billion (never repaid) to Iraq during its war with Iran. Kuwait has also contributed to the resources of several multilateral agencies, such as the World Bank, the Islamic Development Bank, the African Development Bank, and the International Fund for Agricultural Development.

Indicating how globalized Middle Eastern economies have become, the Kuwaiti economy felt the impact of the world economic crisis of 2008 both quickly and emphatically. Over the course of the year, the Kuwait Stock Exchange—second largest regionally—saw a loss of close to 40 percent of market capitalization. Further, the government was one of the first to invest surplus oil revenues internationally, and those very sizable investments were adversely affected, at least in the short term, by the downturn in global financial and real estate markets. In 2007, Kuwait ended its long-established practice of linking the dinar

only to the dollar, switching to a basket of the currencies of its major trading partners—thus somewhat shielding its domestic economy from vagaries in the dollar's exchange rate. Record oil prices in 2008 gave it its tenth straight budget surplus; unfortunately, this lessened pressure on the government to take some needed economic and fiscal reforms. Revenues in 2009 fell by more than 40 percent to $46 billion from the previous year's high of $79 billion.

From the beginnings of settlement in the Kuwait area, there has never been much agricultural activity; today, the amirate imports 95 percent of its food. The 12,000–15,000 Bedouin of a century ago supplied meat, but the few remaining ones contribute little to current food supply. Small date groves persist around brackish wells, and new dairy and chicken farms, along with limited hydroponic vegetable production, add to the fresh food supply. A negligible number of workers are in agriculture, while 50 percent are in public administration, 40 in services, and 9 in industry; 80 percent of the workforce is non-Kuwaiti.

In an effort to further diversify the economy, the government announced a $77 billion plan in 2008 to build the "City of Silk," a 77-mi^2/200-km^2 planned community at Subbiya near the Iraqi border across Kuwait Bay from the capital and to be linked to it by a 16-mi/26-km causeway. The new city would have quarters for embassies and international institutions, university and research facilities, leisure and recreational attractions, and, most important, commercial and financial services;[24] the aim is to secure for Kuwait some of the business activities in these two sectors that have grown so rapidly in Dubai, Abu Dhabi, and Bahrain. The parliament approved a $107 billion economic diversification program in 2010, about half of which will be spent in the expanding hydrocarbon production and downstream activities. Raising oil production by 10 percent by 2015 is intended to provide the additional funding for this program.[25]

The conservative Fraser Institute rates Kuwait highest in the region as far as economic freedom is concerned and 19th of 141 countries globally in 2008,[26] but it lags its small Gulf neighbors (and Saudi Arabia) in economic competitiveness, 39th of 133 globally.[27] A World Bank report on the ease of doing business in 178 countries ranked Kuwait 40th globally and 3rd in the region.[28]

Society and Settlements

The town of Kuwait was settled in the early eighteenth century by Arabs from Najd, in central Arabia. Although the environment was niggardly, with its shortage of water, the benefits of the excellent harbor sustained a tenacious seafaring population. Gradually, other Arabs from Mesopotamia and the peninsula, as well as Iranians, joined the small settlement, ruled by Al Sabah shaykhs. In the early 1900s, the population was perhaps 35,000, doubling by 1946 when oil exports began. Increasing production and development attracted immigrants by the thousands, until the population reached 206,473 in the first census in 1957, and an estimated 3.5 million—some seventeen times that of the first census—in the late 2000s.

By 1965, non-Kuwaitis, including both immigrants and expatriates, outnumbered native Kuwaitis, and an alarmed state imposed criteria that restricted citizenship to residents prior to 1920 and their offspring. Conditions for naturalization effectively precluded it for immigrants, except for about 50 per year.[29] In the late 2000s, only the citizen third of the population was entitled to the full range of social benefits. Suffrage was even more restrictive. Only adult male citizens, about 113,000, were enfranchised until 1996. Since then, male citizens naturalized for thirty years or more also could vote. In 1999, the ruler gave the vote to women in the same categories for the 2003 legislative elections.

Exercising its constitutional right, the National Assembly refused to recognize this and other decrees; it eventually enfranchised women in 2005. Shortly thereafter, the first woman was appointed to the cabinet as planning and development minister; by the end of the 2000s, a second ministry went to a woman. Kuwaiti women voted for the first time in the 2006 elections, then again in 2008 and 2009, when three women won seats.

After liberation in late February 1991, scores of thousands of citizens and expatriates sought reentry, but many lifelong resident expatriates were turned away. Further, many who had remained during the occupation were expelled. Seizing the opportunity for sociopolitical restructuring, the government embraced "Kuwait for the Kuwaitis," announcing a population goal of about 1.2 million. This was unrealistic, however, severely hindering a return to national viability and prosperity, and the government later admitted or readmitted workers from countries that had supported Iraq. As a result, by 2008, there were an estimated 2.3 million expatriates, some 68 percent of the population.

Especially numerous among expatriates before 1991 were Palestinians, who came by the thousands in search of livelihoods and homes following their loss of both to Israel. As Arabs, mostly Muslims, educated, and motivated, they became available just as Kuwait had a critical need for their skills, and by the late 1980s they and their descendants in the state numbered nearly 400,000. They were civil servants, engineers, technicians, middle managers, and teachers. Some Palestinians became politically active, however, making the entire group suspect. During the Iraqi occupation, the perceived support for Saddam Husayn—or at least for his expressed ideals—among many Palestinians in Jordan and some in Kuwait created bitter resentment among Kuwaitis (and other peninsula and Gulf Arabs); this led to the expulsion of hundreds of thousands until fewer than

40,000 remained.[30] In 2001, the government announced there were no longer any special restrictions on Palestinians; in 2009, there were perhaps 80,000, counting those with Jordanian citizenship.

The Al Sabah have furnished the ruling shaykhs since the 1750s. The latest, Sabah al-Ahmad al-Jabir Al Sabah, became amir in 2006. Under the 1962 constitution, the ruler enjoys broad powers, including the final word on most policies. However, the National Assembly—the first elected parliament in the Arab Gulf states—exercises real power. Although the amir suspended parliament in 1976–1981 and again in 1986–1992, parliaments elected after the national trauma of 1990–1991—in 1992, 1996, 1999, 2003, 2006, 2008, and 2009—have grown stronger. This was dramatically shown when the amir, Shaykh Jabir, died in 2006; the assembly refused to acquiesce in the elevation of the then crown prince, who was in poor health, resulting in the accession of Shaykh Sabah.

Ideological representation in the assembly is broad; a large percentage has an "opposition" orientation, and candid criticism of the government and proposals of different policies in its meetings are common. Of the Shii 35–40 percent of the population, many of Iranian descent were attracted to Islamic revolutionary ideology before 1990. Some were deported, but in the reformist atmosphere after 1991 Shii were given a greater role in government, and they now enjoy increasing equality. In recent elections both Sunni and Shii Islamists polled strongly for the assembly.

Citizens have profited especially from the rapidly expanding political and economic systems of the state; however, expatriates have also enjoyed great benefits, though they are not entitled to certain privileges. Full benefits include virtually guaranteed employment, free medical service, housing subsidies, marriage bonuses, free education at all levels, and sizable pensions. Thousands of Kuwaitis, mostly men, have gone abroad for free university education, although most students now attend the impressive University of Kuwait, opened in 1967. In a sharp break with tradition, increasing numbers of Kuwaiti women both serve on the staff of and also attend the university, outnumbering men there since the early 1980s.

Once a small port, Kuwait City is now an elaborately planned metropolis with many ultramodern buildings echoing traditional Islamic architecture (Fig. 15.1). Each of its sectors suggests traditional urban quarters, with a mosque and shopping area reminiscent of the traditional *suq*. The city's symbol, the three Kuwait Towers on the tip of Ras Ajuzah, is a dominant feature of the urban landscape (Fig. 15.2). The southwest-northeast axis of the built-up area follows the coastline forming the city's northwestern boundary. Although the historic mud wall was dismantled with expansion of Kuwait City in the late 1950s, two old gates have been preserved. The Central Business District covers most of the old *madinah* (see Fig. 4.13). Three harbors retain features of the old Kuwait along the bay, and traditional dhows anchor inside the breakwaters. Concentric ring roads centered on the old town carry residential sectors southeastward and industrial sectors southwestward. Kuwait's main general cargo port is an extensive state-of-the-art facility at Shuwaykh on the western side of the city.

At the end of the 2000s, Kuwait was reportedly close to beginning construction of a new 322-mi/518-km rail network that would tie in with that of Iraq and extend south to the Saudi Arabian border, linking to that country's national network now being expanded; eventually, the lower Gulf states are to be tied into this system. A 106-mi/171-km urban rapid-transit system for Kuwait City and its suburbs is part of the overall plan.

Relations

Like the shaking of a kaleidoscope, the disarray of the 1990–1991 crisis forced Kuwait

FIGURE 15.1 Sawabar Residential Complex, Kuwait City, a modernistic adaptation of Islamic architectural themes.

FIGURE 15.2
Water towers, Kuwait. The capital's hallmark, the colorful towers serve an identifying function similar to that of the Eiffel Tower in Paris. The decorated spheres store municipal water, and the tower on the right includes a luxury rotating restaurant. Trees indicate scale.

into new patterns of regional and world relations. Bonds with such traditional friends as Saudi Arabia and other GCC neighbors, Britain, the United States, and Japan were greatly strengthened. Links to Iraq fell to a nadir after the invasion, improved little during the following decade, then fell further with Operation Iraqi Freedom in 2003. Relations with Jordan and Yemen were strained after their ambivalent reactions to Iraq's assault. Diplomatic relations with Jordan were restored in 1999, and those with Iran have improved from the low level of the 1980s. Ties to the United States have become extraordinarily close, building on the U.S. Navy's convoying of Kuwaiti tankers in 1987–1988. After the coalition rescued it in 1991, Kuwait recognized that its security ultimately depended on Western military power. It pragmatically acquiesced to cooperative security measures and was a major base for and supporter of U.S. and British air operations against Iraq in the 1990s, hosting as well thousands of U.S. ground troops. As noted earlier, it played a key role both before the invasion of Iraq in 2003 and during the ensuing occupation;[31] as a result, relations with the United States became even closer during the 2000s. It joined the World Trade Organization in 1995 and, as member of the Gulf Cooperation Council, is a participant in the GCC Customs Union that was to become fully operational in 2009.

BAHRAIN

An Overview

Bahrain (Arabic for "two seas") is the largest of a group of thirty-three low-lying islands that constitute the kingdom. Smallest of the sixteen Middle East states,[32] it is located 15 mi/24 km off the east coast of Saudi Arabia, to which it is connected by a causeway, and 18 mi/29 km from the Qatar Peninsula (Map 15.2). Only six islands are inhabited; the four main ones are linked by causeways. Of the

archipelago's total area, Bahrain Island is 80 percent. Second most important is Muharraq, with the state's second-largest city (also called Muharraq), an international airport, and a dry dock, connected to Bahrain with an expanded causeway. Other islands include Sitra, locus of the state's large refining and oil-export terminal, linked to Bahrain by a causeway; Nabih Salih, well watered by artesian springs; Umm Nasan, the ruler's private property; and Jiddah, with the state prison. Awarded to Bahrain in 2001, the Hawar Islands off the western coast of Qatar had long been disputed between the two states, poisoning relations for decades until Qatar took its claim to the World Court, which divided the contested territory. Most urban development is on the *sabkhahs* of northern Bahrain and southern Muharraq; these areas are surrounded by oases, which give way southward to rocky and gravelly barren desert.[33]

Bahrain is very hot in the summer, with regular afternoon temperatures exceeding 106°F/41°C, with the heat made especially uncomfortable by consistently high humidity. November to March marks a milder season, when there is an average annual 3 in/76 mm of rainfall.

The main island is fringed by a shallow rock platform and by extensive coral reefs. It is a surface expression of a breached asymmetrical anticline with a north-south axis in which oil and gas are trapped at several depths. Erosional breaching of the anticline has produced a shallow basin in the center of the island surrounded by a low, oval-shaped inward-facing escarpment of resistant limestone. Several remnant hills that mark the former crest of the arch rise 100–200 ft/30–60 m above the inner basin. Most prominent is Jabal Dukhan, near the center of Bahrain's oil field, the highest elevation at 440 ft/134 m. Oil company headquarters are at Awali in the northern part of the basin.

Important as oil became after 1932, it was another liquid resource that attracted visitors

BAHRAIN

Long-form official name, anglicized: Kingdom of Bahrain

Official name, transliterated: Mamlakat al-Bahrayn

Form of government: constitutional monarchy with a parliament comprising two bodies (Council of Representatives, Shura Council)

Area: 276.4 mi^2/715.8 km^2

Population, 2008: 1,084,000; Literacy (Latest): 90.0%

Ethnic composition (%): Bahraini Arab 63.9; Indo-Pakistani 14.8; Persian 13.0; Filipino 4.5; British 2.1; other 1.7

Religions (%): Muslim 82.4, of which Shii 58.0, Sunni 24.0; Christian 10.5; Hindu 6.3; other 0.8

Demography: Life expectancy—71.7 yr (M), 76.8 yr (F); Birthrate (per 1,000)—21.0; Fertility rate—2.63

GDP, 2009: $19.36 billion; purchasing power parity: $28.0 billion; per capita: $38,400

Currency: Bahraini dinar, US$1 = 0.376 dinars, 1 dinar = $2.644 (March 2010)

Energy reserves: oil—125.0 mn bbl; natural gas—3.25 tn ft^3; coal—nil

Main exports (% of total value, 2006): petroleum products 79.1; aluminum 12.1; iron ore agglomerates 1.2; urea 1.1

Main imports (% of total value, 2006): crude petroleum products 54.7; machinery and apparatus 9.3; vehicles 7.0; metals and scrap 4.6; food and live animals 4.5

Capital city: Manama 143,035; other major cities: Muharraq 91,307; Rifa 79,550; Madinat Hammad 52,718; Ali 47,259; Madinat Isa 36,833

---

and settlers as early as the Neolithic period and especially during the Bronze Age: the plentiful supply of sweet artesian water from numerous *ayns* in northern Bahrain Island and on adjacent islands. Other freshwater springs erupt from the floor of the Gulf between Bahrain and Saudi Arabia and have supplied mariners with drinking water for centuries. Its central location on the Gulf's long axis, and being the largest and best-watered of the islands south of Kuwait, made it a transit point for Sumerians sailing between Mesopotamia and the Indus Valley. The same basic advantages pertain today.

Excavations near the ruins of Bahrain Fort uncovered an ancient temple complex with artifacts linking it with Sumer and the Indus Val-ley. Archaeologists conclude that it is the Dilmun mentioned in Sumerian inscriptions[34] and that it also had ancient cultural links with Faylakah Island in Kuwait Bay and with settlements in Abu Dhabi. Grave mounds, numbering more than 100,000 in a huge necropolis in the northwest, date from as early as 2400 BCE and from every period after that through the Sassanian. Such prominent landscape features have caught the attention of visitors for 2,300 years. Unfortunately, thousands of the tumuli have been bulldozed for highways and new and expanding settlements.

Transit trade, dhow building, fishing, and pearling underpinned the island's economy for centuries as Bahrain was occupied or controlled by Sassanians, Umayyads, Abbasids,

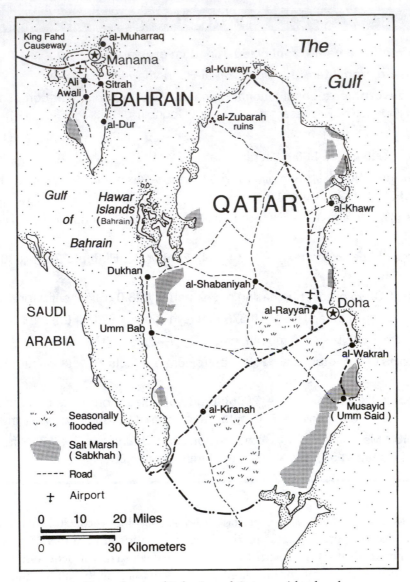

MAP 15.2 General map of Bahrain and Qatar, an island and a
peninsula in the middle Gulf.

Hormuzis, Portuguese, Persians, mainland
Najdis, and Ottomans. The leading shaykhs,
Al Khalifah—with tribal affiliations to the Al
Sabah in Kuwait—were accepted as rulers in
the eighteenth century, throwing off Iranian
control in 1783. Soon after, they came under
the British protective umbrella, which continued for 150 years. The decline of pearling
during the 1930s coincided, fortuitously, with
the discovery of oil. In 1971 Bahrain gained

independence, 40 years after it became the
first oil producer on the west side of the Gulf,
just in time to enjoy an economic boom as a
sovereign state.

With escalating oil prices and explosive
development in the Gulf during the first
decade of independence, Bahrain profited in
many ways from its geographical location,
relative stability, diplomatic finesse, and able
workforce. As its economy expanded, its tra-

ditional strategic importance also increased. A balancing act during the Iran-Iraq War of the 1980s preserved its links with all sides, and during the Gulf War in 1990–1991 it was headquarters for the U.S. Fifth Fleet and a British-U.S. air base. Bahraini pilots also flew strike missions in Iraq. Like Kuwait and Qatar, Bahrain also supported surveillance of Iraq during the 1990s, and it provided a base for U.S. aircraft in 2003.

Descendants of the Khalifah family continue to rule the state. Shaykh Isa bin Sulman Al Khalifah led impressive economic development during the two Gulf crises in 1980–1988 and 1990–1991. A new constitution in 1973 allowed more political participation in an experimental National Assembly, but it was disbanded by the ruler in 1975, and afterward he gave no date for reintroduction of representative institutions. He did appoint a thirty-member Consultative Council in 1993 and made other overtures, but opposition Shii and liberal demands continued, and occasional violence indicated sustained defiance. In 1999, he died and was succeeded by his son, Hamad bin Isa Al Khalifah.

Soon afterward, the new ruler offered relatively democratic reforms and conciliation to the Shii majority. By a 2001 referendum, Bahrain changed from a hereditary amirate to a constitutional kingdom, and Hamad became king. He then set municipal and legislative elections for 2002, in which women cast more than half the votes. In 2006, another round of elections saw Shii parties emerge as the largest bloc, a woman elected for the first time, and a Shii named a deputy prime minister. Shii unrest remained a problem through the decade, partly because the powers of the elected Chamber of Deputies are balanced by the equal status of the still royally appointed upper house.

People and Population

In Bahrain's long history as a center for traders and seafarers, many ethnic groups settled there, producing a unique indigenous mixture. Iranian influence is seen in the 70 percent adherence of Bahrainis to Shii Islam, although the ruling family and most members of the power structure are Sunni, and governing dominance by a minority religious group has long caused tensions. The three main Shii groups are the Baharna, descended from the island's original inhabitants; the Hassawi, originally from oases in eastern Saudi Arabia; and the Ajami, who came from Iran more recently. The Hawala are Sunnis from Arabia who migrated to Iran and then to Bahrain. The ethnically complex population includes large numbers of Indians, Pakistanis, other Gulf Arabs, some Europeans and Americans, and a few Jews and Africans; about one-third of the population is non-Bahraini. Although not socioeconomically stratified, the groups tend to concentrate in certain areas of the island or city quarters.

Bahrain's population has increased steadily since World War II. Rising from 90,000 in 1941 to more than 1 million by the end of the 2000s, it is even so probably the smallest in the region, since Qatar's population has grown even more rapidly. The main concentration is around the capital Manama and its suburbs, with a secondary node on the island of Muharraq (see Fig. 4.12). Manama displays an interesting mixture of old and new, as its Indian-style bazaars are surrounded by new high-rise office buildings and luxury hotels (Fig. 15.3). A few miles southwest of Manama is Isa Town, begun in 1968 as a model town. Hamad Town, in western Bahrain, was added in 1982 and has expanded rapidly. In eastern Muharraq Island, the Shii city of al-Hidd is now developing as an industrial area. In central Bahrain, the amir's palace and its appurtenances have evolved into the desert town of al-Riffa. The oil company center Awali in the central basin has developed much like a small American suburban town.

FIGURE 15.3 Newer buildings in Manama, capital of the island kingdom of Bahrain. Compare with earlier view in Fig. 4.12. (Photograph courtesy of the Bahraini Ministry of Information)

Like other parts of the Gulf region, Bahrain in the 2000s began to seriously consider rail-based transportation as a way to relieve growing urban traffic. In 2009, plans for a light-rail metro system were announced, with the first two lines to be completed by 2013. There are also plans for a high-speed railway using the causeway that will link the kingdom to Qatar as part of the GCC-wide rail project.

Economic Patterns

The petroleum industry and related activities have dominated the economy since the 1930s, but such traditional activities as trade, shipping and servicing Gulf shipping (including entrepôt services), dhow building, fishing, and agriculture are still important. Only pearling—Bahrain led the world in the early 1900s—has virtually disappeared, although the pearl trade is still important in the Manama *suq*. In the 1950s, the government saw how limited oil reserves were, prompting diversification, especially by attracting activities not based on natural resources or a large labor supply. Planning was well conceived and by the 1980s was paying high dividends. Even so, oil and gas are still dominant, providing about 60 percent of government revenue, with surging prices in the 2000s a windfall. The sector is responsible for 10 percent of GDP and 60 percent of export earnings.

Oil. The first oil well in Bahrain, and the first in the Gulf area outside Iran, was drilled by Bahrain Petroleum Company (Bapco) in 1931–1932 at Jabal Dukhan and produced 9,600 bpd from 2,008 ft/612 m. It is still producing. The refinery opened in 1936 and has grown to handle a throughput of 262,000 bpd, mostly Saudi crude received through undersea pipelines as feedstock to produce more than eighty products, most of them exported. Saudi oil constitutes 36 percent of Bahraini imports.

Holding at 30,000 bpd for many years, production rose steadily to a peak of 76,600 bpd in 1970 before declining to 40,000 bpd in the 1980s. Output statistically tripled in the 1990s, when Saudi Arabia assigned Bahrain all of the 140,000 bpd output from their joint offshore field of Abu Safah. Output there is being doubled, although it is likely that Bahrain's share will not be increased. Its onshore oil reserves are expected to be exhausted in ten to fifteen years; however, depending on production, nonassociated gas reserves in the deep (about 10,000 ft/3,048 m) Khuff formation should last for several decades, supplying new industries. With its Hawar Islands claim confirmed, offshore exploration may expand production, and two companies received licenses to drill there in 2008.

Bapco, which held the Bahrain concession for more than four decades, was incorporated in Canada but was originally a wholly owned subsidiary of Standard Oil of California (Socal), now Chevron. In 1936, Texaco bought 50 percent of Bapco and joined Socal in the California-Texas Oil Corporation, which became Caltex Petroleum Corporation in 1968 and owned Bapco as a subsidiary. The company was for many years the main employer in the islands. It enjoyed an amicable partnership with the government and played a vital role in the country's development. In 1975, Bahrain assumed 60 percent participation in Bapco, and it took over the other 40 percent in 1980, administering control through Banoco (Bahrain National Oil Company), founded in 1976.[35] After some shuffling during the 1980s, the government bought out Caltex in 1997; in 1998, it merged all oil operations into a single company, renamed the Bahrain Petroleum Company BSC in 2002. In addition to the Sitra refinery, which has been extensively modernized and expanded, it operates a liquefaction plant and a sizable petrochemical plant; plans for a larger plant were reportedly under consideration in the late 2000s.

Other Industry. ALBA, a large aluminum complex 77 percent government owned, opened in 1971. It utilizes Bahraini gas and Australian alumina for a smelting operation with annual output that has steadily increased to more than 850,000 mt in the late 2000s. The complex includes several downstream facilities, including a rolling mill, an extrusion plant, a cable plant, and factories producing aluminum powder, wire-mesh screening, and automobile wheels. Plans to add up to 350,000 additional mt in production capacity require locating a dedicated source of gas beyond the country's current output.[36] Another large installation is the Arab Ship Repair Yard (ASRY), completed in 1977 on an artificial island linked to Muharraq. Owned jointly by Bahrain and six OAPEC states,[37] ASRY's huge facility services supertankers up to 500,000 deadweight tons. It was of great value during the tanker war of the 1980s, the 1990–1991 crisis, and Operation Iraqi Freedom. The large industrial area near Mina Salman has a score of smaller plants. The formal opening of Salman Industrial City saw the commitment of investments of $3.5 billion in plants and facilities. Electric power and desalination capacity is increasing, with a large installation in al-Hidd; about 95 percent of the electricity is generated using gas.[38] Power and water production are the focus of privatization efforts: The Al-Hidd plant was sold to an international consortium in 2006, and a second private power plant began operations the same year. Elsewhere are food-processing plants, clothing factories, potteries, and similar light industries. Dhows are still constructed for both commercial and recreational use.

Other Economic Sectors. By the 1960s, Bahrain sought to supplement its modest petroleum industry with service-centered economic sectors, particularly entrepôt facilities, trade of various categories, financial services, education and training, and tourism. Coincidentally, regional dynamics directed billions of petrodollars toward Bahrain when Beirut was hit by domestic turmoil. The government and private capital built infrastructure for the expected commercial boom: state-of-the-art communications and information technology, a modern and efficient international airport, spacious modern office quarters, luxury hotels and upscale residential areas, a broad choice of restaurants, good roads and automotive maintenance facilities, and a hospitable administrative climate. Reasonable regulation is complemented by a stable currency, no personal or corporate taxation, unrestricted capital flows, and a capable labor force. The atmosphere is cosmopolitan yet informal in Manama's business district.

Bahrain is now a major regional financial center, with more than 350 offshore banking units and representative offices in the late 2000s. Its financial sector is the largest contributor to GDP (30 percent); especially prominent is the presence of Islamic banking and insurance institutions. Three of the Arab world's 20 largest banks are Bahraini, and some 65 U.S. companies have regional headquarters here. By the end of the 2000s, the economy had seen the benefit of several years of generally high oil prices, but as in other regional states the global economic crisis of 2008–2009 was sharply felt.

Tourism has grown along with commercial development; most of Bahrain's millions of annual visitors arrive by the 15.5-mi/25-km causeway from Saudi Arabia. The more relaxed atmosphere and availability of alcohol and female companionship are attractive to mainlanders. Since Saudis are such a large share of visitors, the island was more insulated than, for example, Dubai, when the 2008 economic crisis impacted world tourism, and about 4.9 million visitor arrivals were recorded in 2008. The government sees the provision of educational services to GCC members as a growth area of significant promise, and it is actively pursuing policies to this end.

Relations

Despite its small size and population, Bahrain has complex foreign relations. Its most intimate connections are with its neighbors through the GCC, complemented by its close relations with Britain and the United States. Most obviously, it has good rapport with Saudi Arabia. For many years, 75 percent of the feedstock for the Bapco refinery has come from the mainland. Saudi Arabian money paid for the causeway connecting the two kingdoms and fuels much of Bahrain's industrial development, banking operations, retail trade and entrepôt operations, tourism, and even its basic budget, since much of the revenue derives from Saudi-produced oil from the offshore Abu Safah field. With many Persian families among its Shii population having ties to Iran, Bahrain has maintained correct relations with revolutionary Iran, hoping that it will continue to honor the late shah's repudiation of Iran's long-standing claim to the archipelago. The kingdom is cautious about involvement with Arab and Islamic issues and maintains strict control over militant groups on the islands, whether pro-Palestinian, pro-Arab nationalist, or pro-Iranian. After the World Court settled the Bahrain-Qatar territorial dispute in 2001, relations between the two neighbors became quite amicable; in 2009, the contract was signed to build a $3 billion 24.9-mi/40-km causeway connecting them; it will carry both rail and road traffic.[39]

Links with Britain dating to when Bahrain was a British-protected state have continued in political, commercial, and cultural relations. Ties with the United States have been extensive, beginning with the American Mission Hospital, established more than a century ago. In 2008, Houa Nanoo, a Bahraini Jewish woman, became the kingdom's ambassador to the United States. Economic links date to the 1930s with Bapco, U.S. owned though operating under British (Canadian) charter. Bahrain has been a base for U.S. Navy activity in the Gulf since 1947; it still hosts the U.S. Fifth Fleet and receives modest military aid. It assisted U.S. and European convoys during the 1987–1988 tanker war, actively participated in the coalition against Iraq in 1990–1991, and supported the 2003 invasion. Afterward, it offered humanitarian assistance and provided technical training for reforming Iraq's banking sector.

In 2004, Bahrain raised some ripples with its neighbors, especially Saudi Arabia, when it signed a Free Trade Agreement with the United States, part of the U.S. initiative to create a Middle East Free Trade Area.[40] It went into effect in August 2006, resulting in greater U.S. commercial interest in the kingdom and a one-year increase of 60 percent in bilateral trade. The kingdom has major sources of imports in the EU, Australia, and Japan, and it joined the World Trade Organization in 1995.

QATAR

Peninsula State

The State of Qatar lies on a mitten-shaped peninsula midway on the eastern Gulf coast (see Map 15.2). Formed by a broad, gentle anticlinal upfold, it is a generally flat, low-lying area of mostly barren Tertiary carbonate rocks (primarily Middle Eocene limestones, dolomites, and marls), with much of the surface overlain by aeolian sheet and dune sands and *hamadah* (gravel-like desert pavement). Elevations for the most part are less than 130 ft/40 m, with limestone ridges in the west and Miocene-Pliocene mesas in the south. The main western ridge is Jabal Dukhan, the surface expression of a tight north-south anticlinal fold that lies parallel to the main upwarp

and to the similar Bahrain and Dammam folds to the northwest. The ridge also reflects the subsurface structure that contains Qatar's major Dukhan oil and gas field, the amirate's only onshore producer. Sterile sand dunes and *sabkhahs* characterize the base of the peninsula. The remarkable northwest-southeast lineation of aeolian sand ridges in all parts of the peninsula connotes the prevailing northwest wind, the *shamal*.[41]

Of the several islands included in the state, Halul, east of the peninsula, is of particular importance in oil operations. As mentioned above, the Hawar Islands off the west coast were awarded to Bahrain in 2001. The long-running dispute between Qatar and Saudi Arabia over their boundary at the base of the peninsula was finally resolved in 2008, and the border is finally de jure (see Chap. 8).

The desert climate is reflected in the widely spaced and stunted flora, and temperature and precipitation are similar to Bahrain's. Qatar has no surface streams or springs, although in recent years modestly productive underground aquifers have been found. Groundwater is pumped to scattered small agricultural plots that utilize generally circular surface depressions (*rawdahs*; often *rodas*) that are surface expressions of underground collapse of solution structures in limestone and evaporites. Irrigation of the *rawdahs* has led to dangerous overpumping, diminishing the capital's water supply and necessitating desalination of seawater.[42]

Gulf waters in the bay to the west are quite shallow; thus, maritime activities, including modern port and urban development, have always been on the east coast, despite the location of the Dukhan field just inland from the west coast. Land has also been reclaimed north and south of the capital city, Doha (Dawhah), which takes its name from the Arabic word for a small crescent bay.

Several Neolithic sites have been found in northern Qatar, but later occupation appears to have been limited, presumably because of

QATAR

Long-form official name, anglicized: State of Qatar

Official name, transliterated: Dawlat Qatar

Form of government: constitutional amirate with one advisory body (Advisory Council)

Area: 4,412 mi^2/11,427 km^2

Population, 2008: 1,448,000; Literacy (Latest): 89.0%

Ethnic composition (%): Arab 40, of which Qatari 12, Palestinian 11, Lebanese 9, Syrian 8; Indo-Pakistani 36; Persian 10; other 14

Religions (%): Muslim 78, of which Sunni 69, Shii 9; Christian 8; other 14

Demography: Life expectancy—74.4 yr (M), 75.8 yr (F); Birthrate (per 1,000)—12.8; Fertility rate—2.8

GDP, 2009: $92.51 billion; purchasing power parity: $101.7 billion; per capita: $121,400

Currency: Qatari rial, US$1 = 3.638 rials, 1 rial = $0.275 (March 2010)

Energy reserves: oil—25.4 bn bbl; gas—899 tn ft^3; coal—nil

Main exports (% of total value, 2006): crude petroleum 46.9; liquefied natural gas 34.8; refined petroleum 4.6; liquefied propane 3.4; polyethylene 3.3; urea 2.0

Main imports (% of total value, 2006): nonelectrical machinery and equipment 23.5; iron and steel 13.7; electrical machinery 8.6; road vehicles 6.8; chemicals and chemical products 5.1; fabricated metals 4.9

Capital city: Doha (Ad-Dawhah) 339,847; other major cities: Rayyan 258,193; Wakrah 26,993; Umm Salal Muhammad 25,413; al-Khawr 18,036

---

increasing desiccation of the climate. By the eighteenth century, Qatar was controlled by the family of Al Khalifah in the west and the Al Thani clan, originally Bedouin from Najd, in the east. When the Al Khalifah moved to Bahrain, the Al Thani assumed control in Qatar, and it is still the ruling family there today. Qatar became a British protectorate in 1916 and regained sovereignty in 1971, when the British withdrew from the Gulf.[43]

From Poverty to Prosperity

Qatar was isolated, sparsely populated, and poor before the 1930s. Limited fishing and pearling with some irrigation agriculture supported fewer than 20,000 people on the entire peninsula. Petroleum Development

(Qatar), renamed the Qatar Petroleum Company (QPC) in 1963, an Iraq Petroleum Company subsidiary, received a concession in 1935, found oil in the Dukhan fold in 1940, and began exporting in 1949. Shell received the concession for the offshore areas in 1952 and discovered the Idd al-Shargi field in 1960. Deep drilling, especially in Dukhan, increased reserves from 3.7 bn bbl in 2000 to 25.4 bn bbl in the late 2000s in Dukhan and six offshore fields. In 1971, Shell exploring offshore 44 mi/70 km north of the peninsula drilled into the Khuff zone in water 165 ft/50 m deep and discovered the fabulous North Field gas reservoir. Its proven reserves have rapidly mounted to between 600 and 750 tn ft^3/17 and 21.2 tn m^3, making it the largest-known single nonassociated gas reservoir in the world. Including all known reserves of gas, Qatar has 899.3 tn ft³/25.5 tn m³, third largest in the world after Russia and Iran.[44]

Qatar assumed ownership of QPC in stages through 1976, added 100 percent of Shell operations in 1977, and consolidated both in the Qatar General Petroleum Company. It shares with Abu Dhabi production from the offshore Bunduq field, located astride the median line between the two amirates. Its oil output rose to 765,000 mn bpd by 2009 in response to unprecedented world demand (and prices); thus, by the late 2000s, Qatar's small population enjoyed the world's highest per capita income.

In modernizing and industrializing, Qatar faced shortages of almost everything except energy. To gain access to technical and managerial skills for industrial diversification, it arranged joint ventures with the Norwegians, Japanese, French, and others for a fertilizer plant, a direct-reduction iron and steel plant, and a petrochemical complex that is one of the largest in the Middle East. All were constructed in a heavy-industry park at Umm Said (Musayid), 25 mi/40 km south of Doha. This ever-expanding concentration has a sizable refinery, upgraded from 57,500 bpd throughput in the late 1990s to 200,000 bpd by 2008; two joint-venture natural gas liquids plants utilizing North Field gas that are among the world's largest; an extensive bulk-handling port; and several support activities.

After expanding processing capacity, Qatar will account for one-third of the world's liquefied natural gas by 2010; it was the world's leading exporter by 2007, supplying customers from Britain to South Korea. It has invested heavily in delivery systems—a large fleet of state-of-the-art LNG ships—and in Europe's largest and most advanced LNG import terminal, opened in Wales in May 2009. Aberrations in gas deliveries to Europe from Russia, at least partly politically motivated, have made Qatar a more reliable potential future source for many countries. Further output growth has been put on hold through 2010 while the world market's future for its LNG is reassessed. A major question at the beginning of the new decade is whether technical, economic, and environmental obstacles to the development of major deposits of natural gas held in shale beds in the United States and Europe can be overcome in the medium-term future, and, thus, possibly radically reshape the global gas market. Oil and gas account for more than 60 percent of GDP, 85 percent of export earnings, and 70 percent of government revenues. Gas-fired plants now generate all of the country's electricity,[45] and Qataris lead the region in annual per capita use of electric power, topping Americans by nearly 30 percent.

Financing its share of the North Field gas infrastructure in the 1980s made heavy demands on Qatar's capital resources just as oil prices dropped sharply and the Asian economic crisis occurred, but subsequent higher oil prices and production and the rapid growth of the natural gas sector have brought the amirate great wealth. Because of the supergiant scale of the North Field, numerous large-scale projects to exploit its resource have been undertaken. A mammoth venture ultimately to cost $10 billion—the Dolphin Project—was partly complete at the end of the 2000s. In Phase 1, gas is being piped under the Gulf to Abu Dhabi and Dubai for use in gas-supply projects and large gas-based industries there and then to Suhar, Oman. Plans envision the Dolphin net's reaching Pakistan by pipeline under the Gulf of Oman, but this high-risk phase remains on hold, since Pakistan may buy gas from Iran.[46] In a related procedure, gas-to-liquids (GTL)—producing liquid fuels like low-sulfur diesel and naphtha from gas—progress has been slower; a GTL complex jointly owned with Shell is due to begin production in 2010. In 2007, construction of a 585,000 mt/yr aluminum smelter began; full operation of the

FIGURE 15.4 Royal Palace, Doha, Qatar, one of several structures in the capital with striking architecture.

plant is scheduled for 2010;[47] Qatalum is the largest aluminum plant ever launched.[48] The late 2000s saw concrete steps toward private-sector participation in the gas-powered electricity and desalination sectors. Despite its massive gas reserves, in 2010 Qatar initiated plans for building a $1 billion solar-power plant to cope with rapidly growing domestic energy demand and to preserve gas for export and other uses.[49] A light-industrial zone near Doha supplies processed foods and small manufactured items for the limited consumer market.

Qatar's small population has increased more than fiftyfold since the 1930s, rising to almost 1.5 million by the late 2000s as it attracted thousands of Pakistanis, Indians, Iranians, and Baluch, as well as Arabs from Egypt, Jordan, Lebanon, and Yemen to swell its labor force.[50] In consequence, citizens may now constitute only one-tenth of the population. The vast majority of the population live in and around Doha, which was little more than a fishing village before World War II but which, like Kuwait City, has become a modern capital with high-rise buildings of original design. The new palace of the ruler sits amid scores of handsome structures on

the shore of Doha Bay (Fig. 15.4). An older traditional palace now houses the national museum. In November 2009, Qatar signed a $25 billion contract with Deutsche Bahn to build a rail system that will include a metro system for Doha and international links to Bahrain and Saudi Arabia.[51]

Remote in location, Qatar had no air connections until the early 1950s, when it first joined its neighbors in the Gulf Aviation (later Gulf Air) operation. It inaugurated its own Qatar Airways in 1994 and has financed its rapid expansion to a seventy-plane fleet and plans to more than double aircraft in operation. Because petrorevenues have long exceeded its current budgetary needs, it has invested heavily in international markets, and thus it was adversely affected, at least in the short run, by the global economic crisis of 2008–2009. Foreigners doing business in Qatar generally find a hospitable atmosphere; in 2009, the international ratings group Transparency International judged Qatar to be the least-corrupt country in the Middle East, ranking it 22nd out of 180 countries rated and above such developed economies as France and Spain. Also, the World Economic Forum rates it as the most competitive economy in the region; in 2009, its Global Competitiveness Index value ranked it 22nd of 133 countries considered.[52]

The current amir, Amir Hamad bin Khalifa, deposed his father, Shaykh Khalifa bin Hamad, in 1995 in a bloodless coup amid accusations of diversion of too much national revenue to the latter's personal accounts. The more progressive new amir has encouraged democratic institutions, with a new constitution approved in a 2004 referendum. Municipal elections were held in 2003 in which women voted and one was elected to office; a third round of municipal elections took place in 2007, and these are supposed to be precursors of elections to the now wholly appointed Advisory Council.[53] There are growing numbers of Christians among the expatriate labor force, and the amir has encouraged construction of several churches. More dramatic is Aljazeera (formally al-Jazirah), the Qatar-based television network, which galvanized regional and world attention when it opened in 1996 under the amir's sponsorship. It introduced a unique medium without censorship and with liberal programming for Arab audiences;[54] the network has often run afoul of regional governments with its generally frank reporting, but it treads notably more carefully in reporting on Qatari events.

Qatar sees a first-class educational system as critical if it is to continue its economic progress, and as part of its efforts in this regard it has built the Education City complex in the Doha area. The facility has attracted several major U.S. universities that now conduct graduate and undergraduate programs, including Cornell University's local degree-granting medical school. Qatar conducts a lively foreign trade, with Japan its biggest customer, and the chief sources of its imports are the EU, the United States, and Japan; it has been a member of the World Trade Organization since 1996. It hosted forty-five nations for the Asian Games in 2006 and is bidding to be the site for international football's World Cup in 2018 or 2022.[55]

Relations

Having emerged from isolation with its oil resources, Qatar has recently found itself on the world stage economically with its gas reserves, politically with its role in the GCC, and socially with Aljazeera. Long-standing boundary disputes with Bahrain and Saudi Arabia were settled amicably and have resulted in greatly improved relations with these neighbors. As mentioned above, a causeway linking Qatar to Bahrain is being built. Economic cooperation in the Dolphin Project with Oman and the UAE has strengthened its links with both states. Relations with Britain, the former protecting power, have remained cordial since independence. In the late 2000s, Qatari diplomats were quite active as mediators: in Lebanon between the government and Hizballah (and by breaking a deadlock in 2008, allowing the election of a new president [see Chap. 10]), in Sudan regarding Darfur, and in nearby trouble spots like Yemen, Eritrea, and Ethiopia.

Amir Hamad has joined his GCC neighbors in relying on U.S. military protection and in supporting U.S. military operations in the region. He has also cooperated with U.S. efforts to smooth incorporation of Israel into the region's economic and political structure, allowing the Jewish state to open a trade office in Doha in 1994. Qatar hosted the Middle East/North Africa Summit—including Israel—in November 1997; however, this virtually collapsed before it opened owing to Arab anger over Israeli intransigence in the peace process at the time. The onset of the second intifadah and, subsequently, Israeli actions in Lebanon and Gaza rather halted Qatari efforts, and ties with Israel were severed in 2009 with the closing of the trade office.[56] The amirate has hosted a "United States–Islamic World Forum" annually since 2004, sponsored by the U.S. Saban Center; at

UNITED ARAB EMIRATES

Long-form official name, anglicized: United Arab Emirates (UAE)

Official name, transliterated: Al-Imarat al-Arabiyah al-Muttahidah

Form of government: federation of seven hereditary amirates with one advisory body (Federal National Council)

Area: 32,280 mi²/83,600 km²

Population, 2008: 4,660,000; Literacy (Latest): 90.4%

Ethnic composition (%): Arab 43, of which UAE 19, Bedouin 10, Egyptian 6, Omani 4, Saudi 4; South Asian 40; Persian 5; Filipino 3; European 2; other 7

Religions (%): Muslim 62 (mostly Sunni, perhaps Shii 10); Hindu 22; Christian 10; other 8

Demography: Life expectancy—73.2 yr (M), 78.3 yr (F); Birthrate (per 1,000)—16.1; Fertility rate—2.43

GDP, 2009: $228.6 billion; purchasing power parity: $200.4 billion; per capita: $41,800

Currency: UAE dirham, US$1 = 3.672 dirhams, 1 dirham = $0.272 (March 2010)

Energy reserves: oil—97.8 bn bbl; natural gas—214.4 tn ft³; coal—nil

Main exports (% of total value, 2006): crude petroleum 40.8; re-exports 32.3; free-zone exports 14.4; natural gas 5.0; domestic nonpetroleum exports 4.1; refined petroleum products 3.4

Main imports (% of total value, 2006): emirate imports 78.7, free-zone imports 21.3

Capital city: Abu Dhabi 633,136; other major cities: Dubai 1,225,137; Sharjah 584,286; al-Ayn 444,331; Ajman 250,808

---

the seventh forum in 2010, U.S. secretary of state Hillary Clinton delivered a major policy speech building on the points made by President Obama in his Cairo University speech in April 2009.[57] More significantly, it permits the United States to operate a large air force base at al-Udayd and hosts the U.S. Central Command Forward Headquarters, which coordinated Operation Iraqi Freedom. In a gesture of solidarity, Qatar established the Qatar Katrina Fund in 2005 to disburse $100 million to assist the victims of the disastrous storm that hit the U.S. Gulf coast that year.[58] Thus it is that the remote, sparsely populated, and poverty-stricken desert peninsula has found itself intimately connected with modernity

and supporting a vigorous population with wealth beyond exceptional dreams.

UNITED ARAB EMIRATES

A Survey

Most recent of the Middle East states to achieve independence, the United Arab Emirates[59] comprises seven component polities, including, on the Gulf, Abu Dhabi, Dubai, Sharjah, Ajman, Umm al-Qaywayn, and Ras al-Khaymah, and, on the Indian Ocean, Fujayrah (see Map 15.3). Thus, the UAE occupies coasts on both sides of the Musandam Peninsula (the "Horn of Arabia"). Formerly an aggregation of British-protected tribal

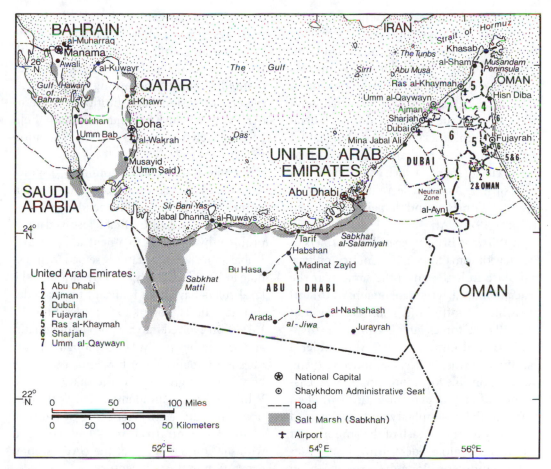

MAP 15.3 General map of the seven United Arab Emirates, with neighboring Bahrain and Qatar. Numbers in the UAE refer to exclaves belonging to the respective amirates. See maps in Chapter 6 for petroleum and gas fields. UAE boundaries are now de jure.

shaykhdoms known as the Trucial States, the amirates moved abruptly from isolation and poverty in the 1950s to oil wealth and dramatic development in the 1970s and 1980s and to world-famous spectacular development in the 1990s and 2000s.[60]

Several Neolithic sites have been found in the area, but recent excavations have also uncovered a Paleolithic presence in Sharjah many thousands of years older. The findings will influence the "out of Africa" hypothesis that traces hominoid migrations out of Africa and across Arabia. Neolithic and Bronze Age settlements and tombs, found especially in Abu Dhabi, Dubai, and Ras al-

Khaymah, reveal ties with the Dilmun, Harrapan, early Persian, and Sumerian cultures in Mesopotamia, the northern Gulf, and neighboring areas. The coastal area became familiar to Europeans—the Portuguese in the early 1500s and then the British in the 1700s—after the route around the Cape of Good Hope opened. A series of coastal islands and indentations, dotted with villages, offered shelter at that time to fishing and pearling dhows. Following several naval operations in the southern Gulf, the British imposed the first coastwide maritime truce in 1820 and followed it with other treaties and imposed agreements in 1835, 1839, and 1847.[61] The

Treaty of Maritime Peace in Perpetuity (1853) gave the British navy supervision over maritime relations in the lower Gulf, leaving land relations to the shaykhdoms.[62] From this 1853 truce evolved the official designation of the coastal settlements as the Trucial States (sometimes Trucial Shaykhdoms, Trucial Coast, or even Trucial Oman), a designation that lasted for more than a century. Out of these "village states," which had shifting patterns of independence as ruling families altered relationships and domains, developed the post-1971 UAE.

In 1951, the British persuaded the rulers of the shaykhdoms to create a Council of Trucial State Rulers, and in the same year the Trucial Oman Levies were organized to suppress slave traffic and maintain law and order. These forces later became the storybook Trucial Oman Scouts, who, under a handful of British officers seconded to them, were responsible for security in the area. Disbanded after independence, they supplied cadres to the new military units maintained separately at first in each of the amirates but later merged into a federal army.

The landscape along the coast has been dramatically transformed in one generation. Cross-country tracks and wadi bottoms served as roads until the mid-1960s (see Fig. 7.4A); a few small generators supplied electricity part-time in the towns. When pearling declined, the hardy inhabitants relied on a subsistence economy of fishing, herding, date culture, and a growing dhow trade. In the early 1960s, the oil boom began in Abu Dhabi, later in Dubai, and then in the other amirates. Within a few years of independence, the UAE achieved a level of economic development that could be described only as spectacular, its people enjoying one of the world's highest per capita incomes.[63]

Before withdrawing from the Gulf, the British delineated shaykhdom boundaries for the first time, partly to inhibit later boundary conflicts and partly to prevent dissension over oil and gas exploration. With British warnings against political fragmentation, the Trucial States explored confederation with Bahrain and Qatar (which in the end remained separate), becoming independent under a provisional constitution in December 1971. Ras al-Khaymah originally held back but relented and joined the federation in February 1972.

Despite British efforts, boundary disputes jeopardized the success of federal integration in the early months of independence. However, Dubai and Abu Dhabi resolved their problem by agreeing to a neutral zone, and Dubai and Sharjah tentatively settled their dispute in 1976 and finally in 1997. Although the local rulers have been reluctant to surrender their traditional powers to the federation, the UAE soon evolved into a vigorous, pragmatic, and prosperous polity. For the long term, the question remains about how much they will be willing to give up for the sake of unity. While Emiratis still identify first with their home amirate, a stronger sense of national identity—"Emiratization"—has emerged with the coming of age of the UAE's second generation in the new century.

To the relief of both neighbors and the British, centripetal forces have proved stronger than centrifugal ones. The UAE emerged as a political-geographical oddity, a republic in which the federal units are monarchies.[64] With its seven constituents, it is the region's most complex polity. Yet, remarkably, over nearly forty years a balance has been reached in the allocation of powers (and funds) between the principalities and federal institutions. Criteria for distributing offices proved acceptable, and in June 1996, the Federal National Council (FNC) approved a permanent constitution and designated Abu Dhabi the permanent capital. In 2006, elections were held for half the 40 members of the FNC; the electoral college (nominated by the rulers) consisted of 6,689 Emiratis (about 18 percent women, one of whom was elected to the council, joining 7 women appointed members). The other 20 FNC members are still directly appointed by the rulers.[65]

Population

Development led population to grow from about 75,000 in 1950 to about 223,000 in 1970; then there was an explosive twentyfold increase—to more than 4.6 million by 2008. Main concentrations are in the capital city of Abu Dhabi and in the coalescing cities of Dubai and Sharjah. Additional nodes of population mark the other amirate capitals and several oasis towns—especially the merging villages and towns in al-Ayn, the UAE part of the Buraymi Oasis. The ethnic composition of the population is noteworthy, not only because it is the most complex of the varied population mixtures of the Gulf states but also because no more than 20 percent of the population is indigenous Emirati.

The sparse population of the early 1960s, although intelligent and energetic, could not possibly meet the demand for labor, either in numbers or in technical skills, of the early boom years; not only expertise and materials had to be imported, but also scores of thousands of workers. This created housing shortages, forcing many workers, some with families, into *barasti* (palm frond) huts, tents, and other makeshift housing until the wealthier amirates erected extensive housing blocks. Like all the major Arab petroleum producers, the UAE is trying to reduce its need for outside personnel—still more than 90 percent of the workforce. Various regulations call for more "Emiratization" at managerial levels, but despite restrictions on further immigration, the pressing need for expatriates continues.

Economic Development

Petro-industries dominate the economy of the UAE but not to the extent that they do in Qatar and Kuwait. Exports of crude and processed oil and gas supply 50 to 60 percent of export earnings, and 90 percent of government revenues are from oil. However, only 25 percent of GDP is from oil revenues, and economic diversification is being pursued aggressively.[66] It is noteworthy that Abu Dhabi produces 82 percent of the UAE's oil and contributes three-fourths of the federal government's income. As in the other Gulf oil producers, especially Bahrain, the UAE has followed a vigorous program of industrialization along both energy-related and other lines. Although most of the plants are export oriented, some of them cater to the affluent population of the union and neighboring countries.

However, as important as the oil industry is, most related facilities are in remote areas. Thus, the emphasis several amirates put on traditional economic activities—trade and transit trade, shipping, and modest but increasingly important agriculture (including dairy and poultry production), horticulture, animal herding, and fishing—is significant. Successful diversification has helped cushion low-oil-price recessions and has burgeoned dramatically during booms. Even more important is the role of administrative, financial, commercial, and personal services—government, banking, insurance, export-import, retailing, hotel and restaurant operation, and, since the 1980s, tourism.

Thus, a diversified and vigorous economy across a larger territory gives the UAE an outward and genuine air of energy and bustle. Different centers have developed specializations and characteristics: Abu Dhabi is an oil, financial, industrial, and administrative center (Fig. 15.5); Dubai is a lively recreational, trade, industrial, financial, and shipping center, perhaps profligate in self-promotion; Sharjah focuses on cultural amenities with two universities and natural gas exports, complementing Dubai with commercial, transportation, and manufacturing activities; Fujayrah is a beach resort and small port; and

FIGURE 15.5 Typical street in downtown Abu Dhabi, capital of the United Arab Emirates. In 1964, the city had fewer than a dozen permanent structures, none more than two stories high.

al-Ayn is a productive agricultural oasis, as are Sharjah's Dhayd and Ras al-Khaymah's Diqdaqah (Digdagga) oases.

Oil, Gas, and Related Industries. Ranking fifth in both the Middle East and the world in proven petroleum reserves, the UAE has a known 97.8 bn bbl, about 7.2 percent of the world's resources. It is close behind Kuwait (see Table 6.1), with far more reserves than any of the next three oil giants—Venezuela, the Former Soviet Union, and Mexico. It has about five times the oil of the United States and could produce 2 mn bpd for 135 years, although it is expanding its average daily output to 3 mn bpd. In addition, as a result of the new discoveries in the 1980s, it has the seventh-largest gas reserves in the world.[67] Abu Dhabi alone has 94 percent of the federation's oil reserves and 92 percent of the gas. Each member of the federation retains full rights to its own oil and gas resources, sharing with other states only that income unanimously agreed upon. In practice, Abu Dhabi and Dubai help support the less wealthy amirates through the federal budget; Abu Dhabi came to Dubai's aid in the credit crunch of 2009.

Petroleum Development (Trucial States), an Iraq Petroleum Company subsidiary (Abu Dhabi Petroleum Company from 1962), conducted initial explorations in southwestern Abu Dhabi in 1939, found oil in 1958, but exported only in 1963. Produced in the great Bab field (originally Murban), the oil was lifted from a new terminal at Jabal Dhanna in extreme western Abu Dhabi. Meanwhile, oil had been found by Abu Dhabi Marine Areas (ADMA) in the offshore Umm Shaif field; production began in 1962. A second offshore field, Zakum, went on stream in 1967, pumping to the Das Island terminal, along with output from Umm Shaif and from Bunduq, jointly owned with Qatar.

By the late 2000s, more than a score of fields had been found in Abu Dhabi waters (all are not yet on stream), along with ten major onshore fields. One crosses the Saudi border, an extension of the large Shaybah light-oil reservoir. Deep drilling for nonassociated gas in the Khuff zone below already producing oil horizons discovered immense reservoirs beneath Umm Shaif and Abu al-Dukhush offshore and Bab onshore. Khuff gas gave Abu Dhabi the huge reserves mentioned earlier, sufficient for 160 years at the present rate of production. Even so, Abu Dhabi and Dubai are pursuing the Dolphin Project to bring Qatari gas to the UAE and Oman (discussed under Qatar, above). Using Dolphin gas to generate power for several huge desalination plants and industries will permit the UAE to devote its own gas to the extraction of natural gas liquids and gas reinjection to maintain reservoir pressure. In the late 2000s, nearly all of the federation's electricity was being generated using gas,[68] but nuclear energy is in the offing.[69] The Abu Dhabi National Oil Company, operating mainly onshore, and ADMA, mainly offshore, are the principal operating and service companies.

In Dubai, Petroleum Development (Trucial Coast) began exploration in 1937 without success. Not until 1966 did Dubai Marine Areas (a consortium of U.S. and European companies) find the moderately large field of Fateh, 56 mi/90 km offshore (see Fig. 6.2). Other fields were found a few years later, and total production rose to 469,000 bpd in 1990 before declining to 100,000 bpd in the late 2000s. A new offshore field was confirmed in 2010.[70] Dubai imports gas from both Sharjah and Abu Dhabi to feed its industries.

Sharjah and Ras al-Khaymah found oil still later. After onshore wells in Sharjah proved dry, a new concessionaire (Crescent Petroleum Company, with Buttes Gas and Oil of the United States as operator) found the small Mubarak field near Abu Musa Island, 45 mi/72 km offshore, in 1972. Oil from there was first exported in 1974; revenues were shared with Iran (which asserts claim to the island and its territorial waters). Production rapidly declined from 38,300 bpd to less than 2,000 bpd by the early 2000s. However, onshore, a deep gas condensate field found (by Amoco and Sharjah Petroleum Department) in 1980 at Saja, along with later condensate and dry gas discoveries, are bringing Sharjah significant revenues, and it is now supplying gas to several of its neighbors. Ras al-Khaymah also produces small amounts of gas condensate from its offshore Saleh field, opened in 1983–1984 26 mi/42 km into the Gulf. Exploration in Ajman, Umm al-Qaywayn, and Fujayrah has been commercially unsuccessful, but some gas has been found in Umm al-Qaywayn.

The UAE operates five refineries and is steadily expanding other energy-related industries. The largest refinery, with a capacity of 350,000 bpd, operates in the western Abu Dhabi industrial zone of al-Ruways, near Jabal Dhanna, which also includes expanding petroleum-based plants for petrochemicals, fertilizers, and, increasingly, natural gas liquids. As the UAE steadily exploits its enormous gas reserves, gas-processing plants using 3 bn ft³/85 mn m³ per day are being developed offshore and onshore. The increasing condensate exports are not subject to OPEC quotas. Record prices in 2008 took oil export earnings to an all-time high of $90.9 billion, but with the drop in demand in 2009 revenues declined by more than 42 percent to about $52 billion. In its pursuit of alternate energy sources, the UAE is building the first carbon-free city, Masdar City, in Abu Dhabi.

Other Industries.   In addition to the petroleum-processing plants, the al-Ruways industrial zone includes a steel mill producing iron bars for construction. In the mid-1970s, Dubai developed a man-made port, industrial area, and free-trade zone at Jabal Ali in an isolated desert area southwest of Dubai City that eclipses al-Ruways. Despite skepticism, an imaginative and enterprising ruler of Dubai, the late Shaykh Rashid bin Said Al Maktum, deep-dredged a channel and constructed a major port, put in a large power plant and desalination facility, invited dozens of industrial companies, and opened a free port area. As the ingenious Rashid predicted, thirty-five years later, Jabal Ali is a multibillion-dollar regional economic node.

Like Bahrain and Qatar, the UAE has turned to aluminum smelting using the region's plentiful gas reserves as fuel. Current and future facilities in Dubai (in Jabal Ali) and Abu Dhabi will put total output at 2.3 mn mt/yr, close to half the total production of the GCC countries.[71] The main power plant, regularly expanded, not only feeds the smelter but also desalinates tens of millions of gallons of water daily. The booming zone includes other power and water plants; hundreds of factories, including refineries and gas-processing facilities, petrochemical plants, cement plants, steel fabrication plants, fertilizer and paint factories, food-processing establishments, grain silos, tank farms, and metal fabricators; an ever-expanding free zone with comprehensive private rights of operation for 2,400 companies from seventy-five countries; and the world's largest man-made port, a state-of-the-art facility that is the third busiest in the world in volume handled—after Singapore and Hong Kong. Modest industrial parks have also been developed in Sharjah and tiny Ajman.

As in other energy-rich Gulf states, desalination is a major and expanding industry. More than forty-five plants generate large amounts of electricity plus 550 mn gal/2.08 mn m³ per day of desalted water. Desalination plants provide more than three-fourths of nonagricultural water in the UAE. Nearly all of the amirates have made impressive plantings of flowering shrubs along boulevard medians and highways. However, overuse of groundwater has caused aquifers to drop significantly, and many wells have run dry; encroaching seawater has caused other groundwater to become saline.

Trade and Transportation.   Crude petroleum and refined products are the bulk of exports, and the biggest customers are Japan and Taiwan. However, re-exports and UAE-fabricated products like aluminum are becoming increasingly important and constitute more than one-fourth of exports. Each amirate operates at least one free-trade zone; there are twelve all together. Dubai has a highly developed re-export system in free zones at both main seaports and the airport. Shipments between Europe and the Far East are sent to Dubai, where they are offloaded, broken down, and reloaded as re-exports for specific destinations. Machinery, much of it for oil operations, and consumer goods constitute more than half of imports. Centuries-long traditions continue regional maritime trade and extensive commerce with India, Iran, and East Africa. The picturesque dhows operating from Dubai Creek (Khawr Dubai) smuggle gold and consumer goods to Iran and the subcontinent.

Vigorous local retail trade satisfies lively demand for consumer goods by a wealthy upper class and an affluent middle class; most imported goods are customs free or are taxed at a flat 5 percent in accordance with GCC practice, and there is no tax on retail sales. Sharjah and Dubai are crowded with vacation shoppers who come on charter flights from areas with shortages of consumer products (especially parts of the Former Soviet Union). They come specifically to buy large quantities of electronic items, watches, jewelry, photographic equipment, and other low-bulk, high-value goods for resale back home at handsome profits. The trade is highly organized—special flights, discount hotel rates, and shopping buses to the huge new *suqs* of Sharjah, Dubai, and Ajman. These extraordinary malls feature world-class architecture (Fig. 15.6) and are brimming with broad selections of consumer goods. Large profits also accrue from trade in contraband, including weapons, which arrive on nighttime flights for repackaging and re-export.

Each amirate has its own seaport. Large planned ports in Dubai, Abu Dhabi, and Sharjah contrast with their tiny predecessors, used only by dhows for Gulf and Indian trade, fishing, and pearling. Port Rashid in Dubai is one of the largest ports in the Middle East—more than 500 ac/200 ha within its breakwater. East of Port Rashid, a large container port with efficient roll-on/roll-off facilities that have attracted additional cargo traffic has been built. Jabal Ali port in southern Dubai has steadily increased its cargo handling until it now has world rank. Even

so, the small-scale facilities in Dubai Creek (Khawr Dubai) still attract scores of dhows each day. The number of vessels calling at the amirate's ports has increased exponentially, as has the amount of cargo handled.

In a manner typical of the competitiveness among member amirates, Abu Dhabi has expanded its Port Zayid, especially the container facilities. It is also installing a large free-zone facility on Saadiyat Island, adjacent to Abu Dhabi Island, to compete with Jabal Ali. Sharjah has vigorously pushed its smaller Port Khalid in Sharjah town, its east coast container port of Khor Fakkan on the Indian Ocean, and a port at Hamriyah with a free trade zone. Khor Fakkan—as well as the small port of Fujayrah—has grown steadily in response to its major locational asset: its situation on the Gulf of Oman, outside the Straits of Hormuz. An international cargo ship can save up to twenty-four hours, and high insurance costs, by avoiding the trip through the straits. Ajman and Ras al-Khaymah also promote their small ports on the Gulf.

Like the other GCC countries, in the late 2000s the UAE embarked on railway development projects tying all the peninsular nations and the seven amirates together. The Union Railways Company was established in 2009 to oversee the planned system,[72] and tenders for construction were due in 2010. The initial 357-mi/574-km phase will run from the Saudi Arabian border to Jabal Ali port near Dubai. Altogether, the network is envisioned to stretch 684 mi/1100 km, terminating at Khor Fakkan on the Gulf of Oman, with a link between Abu Dhabi and al-Ayn and on into Oman.

Of the federation's four larger airports (Abu Dhabi, Dubai, Sharjah, and Ras al-Khaymah), the first three vie for handling the most aircraft and passengers. They have spacious and impressive terminals with large duty-free shopping areas. Dubai has gained first rank with its extravagant terminal facilities and service, which received top approval

FIGURE 15.6 Sharjah City's old *suq* (*top*, 1964) with palm-frond (*barasti*) roof for shade, and one of the city's newer *suqs* (*bottom*, 1979). In the background in the bottom photo, the high-rise buildings of the city's Central Business District can be seen. In the past decade several "new new" suqs have opened in Sharjah and adjacent Dubai, some of them of world-class opulence.

by the more than 4 million passengers visiting Dubai in 2003. Large numbers arrive in Sharjah at its aesthetically attractive terminal on shopping vacations, and Abu Dhabi receives governmental and business travelers. Again, competitiveness led Ras al-Khaymah and Fujayrah each to open its own airport. The UAE is oversupplied with both seaports and airports, yet all of them are either crowded or reasonably utilized. Although the UAE was formerly a constituent owner of Gulf Air, three of its amirates have opened their own airlines: Dubai inaugurated Emirates Airline in 1985, and in a little more than twenty years it boasted the largest fleet in the region (see Chap. 7); Abu Dhabi is rapidly expanding its competing carrier, Etihad, started in 2003; and also in 2003, Sharjah began the budget airline Air Arabia, which in 2009 was named "Low-Cost Carrier of the Year."[73] All towns and villages of the UAE are integrated into an excellent national highway network (see Fig. 7.4B).

Finance and Tourism. As global financial markets moved to twenty-four-hour operations in the 1970s, the Gulf was uniquely positioned geographically between established centers in the Far East like Tokyo and Hong Kong and in Europe like London and Frankfurt. This largely explains the growing presence of international banks and financial institutions in the region—in Dubai particularly and Abu Dhabi to a lesser extent. Loose regulation at first led to problems bordering on (or worse) the fraudulent—like the infamous Bank of Credit and Commerce International (BCCI) based in Abu Dhabi, once the world's seventh-largest bank. BCCI was created in 1972 with capital from the then Abu Dhabi ruler Shaykh Zayid and the Bank of America; its management specifically located it to avoid regulatory oversight. Predictably, the result was financial fraud—on a scale never seen until then; it was finally forced into liquidation in 1991. The bright

side for the UAE was considerable tightening of oversight mechanisms and a healthier environment in which the sector continued to flourish. Electronic money transfers, believed by the United States in the aftermath of 9/11 to be used by international terrorist groups and by Iraqi and Afghan insurgents, came under heavy regulation from 2005. By the late 2000s, the country had almost fifty banks, both foreign and domestic in ownership. Seven of the Arab world's thirty largest banks are headquartered in Abu Dhabi and Dubai. Many other firms in this sector—brokerages, investment houses, insurance companies— are also represented.

Of course, the global economic crisis of the late 2000s first appeared in this sector, and the effects were evident in the UAE. To avoid panic, the government injected $6.8 billion into local banks in 2008.[74] By late 2009, Dubai's sovereign investment fund, Istithmar, had suffered a steep decline in asset values; it froze investment activities while it tried to refinance short-term debt of perhaps as much as $6 billion, more than its portfolio was worth.[75] Then Dubai World, also government related, had to ask creditors for an extension on its repayments.[76] Without actually classifying the debt as a government obligation, the amirate did eventually announce it would provide $9.5 billion to help Dubai World with its efforts to restructure what it owes to creditors.[77]

As the crisis snowballed, the possible bankruptcy of not just these companies but Dubai itself and even the UAE loomed large, and something resembling panic was evident, at least briefly, on local and world markets.[78] With the nation as a whole threatened, Abu Dhabi stepped in with funding to give Dubai some breathing space.[79] There was speculation that the senior amirate might place conditions on Dubai that would permanently dampen the frenzied pace of the latter's development in the previous decade.[80] Whether Abu Dhabi's assistance will carry the day, whether Dubai will recover, and whether it will be a more staid place if it does are all questions unanswered at the onset of the new decade.[81] At the very least, the symmetry in the power relations between the two amirates has changed.

Generally, the UAE has a strong business environment with a good reputation relative to corruption: In 2009, Transparency International ranked it 30th out of 180 countries worldwide and 3rd regionally, behind Qatar and Cyprus and ahead of Israel. The World Economic Forum rates the UAE as the 2nd most competitive regional economy and 23rd out of 133 countries globally. Regarding economic freedom, the Fraser Institute ranks the UAE 2nd in the region, behind only Kuwait, and 26th of 141 countries globally in 2008.[82] However, a World Bank report on the relative ease of doing business in 178 countries, ranked the UAE only 68th, well behind neighboring Saudi Arabia, Kuwait, and Oman.[83]

As recently as twenty years ago, a Gulf state, with its notoriously hot, humid climate, aspiring to be a major year-round tourist destination would have seemed quite ridiculous. In the previous section, shopping tourism was mentioned, and this is where it all began. For many years, duty-free shops at Gulf airports (beginning with Bahrain) flourished as long-haul flights between Europe and the Far East discharged their passengers while they refueled. Airport installations led to new malls with more shops and hotels for the shoppers. With luxury resorts (including the world's only seven-star hotel, the Burj al-Arab), Dubai added attractions like world-class sporting events (golf, tennis, cricket, auto racing), top-name entertainers, amusement parks, and even an indoor ski slope. Again, as with the financial sector, global tourism was hit hard by the 2008 economic turndown, and as the decade ended there were serious concerns that Dubai had also overextended its investments in tourism.

Agriculture and Fishing.   Although their relative contribution is now minor, fishing (including pearling) and agriculture (including nomadic herding) were, along with trade, the main bases of the economy prior to World War II. Agriculture in this desert environment was then confined to small oases and date-palm groves around the coastal villages, and the limited water resources were minimally developed. After the mid-1960s, the greatly increased availability of capital and the greater demand for fresh foods stimulated development of the few potentially productive agricultural areas.

Increased production has come from the three extensive oases of al-Ayn in eastern Abu Dhabi (see Map 15.3); Dhayd, east of Sharjah City; and Diqdaqah in Ras al-Khaymah. All three lie at the foot of the Oman Mountains and tap aquifers fed by runoff from the slopes. In use for at least four millennia, al-Ayn is exceptionally extensive and, as the original bailiwick of the first UAE president, the late Shaykh Zayid, has been intensively developed to produce a variety of dates, fruits, and vegetables.[84] Dhayd, somewhat farther away from the mountains, uses groundwater irrigation; it produces crops from strawberries to lemons. Diqdaqah, south of Ras al-Khaymah, has an agricultural experiment station established in 1956. Fruits and vegetables from the oases supply many of the needs of UAE cities. All three exemplify the marvels that can be wrought with huge inputs of capital and technology. Large dairy farms also operate in all the large oases, as do air-conditioned chicken farms marketing several million chickens each year. More than fifty date-palm groves extend along an arc of tiny oases in the isolated al-Jiwa (or al-Liwa) in southwestern Abu Dhabi.

Relations

With some of the world's largest petroleum and gas reserves in a crucial location, yet with a small population and negligible military strength, the vulnerable UAE must walk a strategic tightrope. Locally, it places much of its diplomatic emphasis on the GCC (though in 2009 it opted out of the GCC common currency) and regionally and cautiously on the Arab League. It follows a pragmatic balancing act by maintaining, for example, mutually beneficial "correct" relations with Iran on one side and Saudi Arabia on the other. Since its inception, the federation has disputed with Iran over ownership of three small Gulf islands (Abu Musa and the Greater Tunb and Lesser Tunb) just inside the Strait of Hormuz. The boundary with Saudi Arabia has been declared de jure, that with Oman was agreed to in 2004 and is now de jure, and there are no serious disputes on any land borders (see Chap. 8). Abu Dhabi, the richest of the amirates, has built strong links for the UAE with developing countries through the activities of the Abu Dhabi Fund for Development which from its founding in 1971 up to 2008 extended $3.4 billion in assistance to forty-nine countries for 188 projects.[85]

Unlike Qatar and Oman, the UAE never initiated overt quasi-diplomatic links with Israel; however, with the onset of the Oslo peace process, ties on the commercial,[86] touristic, and athletic levels grew quietly and steadily, especially with Abu Dhabi and Dubai. But in 2009, an incident involving the assassination of a Hamas official in a Dubai hotel, allegedly by the Israeli intelligence agency Mossad, brought these to a crashing halt. The clumsy actions of more than twenty-five agents using the pilfered identities and passports of dual nationals resident in Israel were repeatedly caught on surveillance cameras at various Dubai locales. Local authorities claimed that Israel had violated the amirate's reputation as a neutral place to do business and had acted with arrogance and disdain, as though the amirate was an unsophisticated backwater.[87]

Once a British protectorate, the UAE maintains numerous links with Britain. Since independence, it has built good relations with the United States—close private commercial ties and friendly government-to-government relations, including security assistance. Ties became much closer after the Iraqi invasion of Kuwait, and the UAE contributed more than $4 billion, as well as a contingent of troops, to the 1990–1991 coalition. It opposed the U.S.-led invasion of Iraq, but was discreetly supportive of Iraqi recovery, and large communities of Iraqi refugees sought safe haven in Dubai and Sharjah. In 2008, it returned its ambassador to Baghdad and canceled all of Iraq's debt due from the Iran-Iraq War. Its military has also participated in peacekeeping missions, such as those in Somalia, Kosovo, and Lebanon. Like other members of the GCC with high oil income but incapable of mounting their own military defense, it has opted to place defense of its territory and resources with the United States. In 2004, the UAE signed a Trade and Investment Framework Agreement with the United States, and the two countries agreed to undertake negotiations aimed at concluding a Free Trade Agreement. The UAE joined the World Trade Organization in 1996.

In May 2009, France opened its first military facilities outside its own territories in fifty years in Abu Dhabi; three locations have been made available for army, navy, and air force use. The newest major intergovernmental entity—the International Renewable Energy Agency (IRENA)—designated Abu Dhabi as its interim headquarters in June 2009; by March 2010, IRENA had 142 signatory members, including 14 of the 16 countries in this study.[88]

Sketches of Individual Amirates

Abu Dhabi. The largest (86 percent of the total area) and by far the wealthiest of the seven amirates, with a third of total population, Abu Dhabi (or Abu Zaby) is the dominant member of the UAE. It is the southernmost and possesses the longest coastline.

Located on a low near-shore island of *sabkhah* and sand, Abu Dhabi City, the population core, grew from a small village of *barasti* huts and a fort in the 1950s to a wealthy, bustling, planned city. With high-rise office buildings, luxury hotels and palaces, divided boulevards, mosques and schools, housing estates, and irrigated plantings ornamenting the boulevards and traffic circles (see Fig. 15.5), it serves as the UAE capital. Enhancing its international stature has been the construction of branches of the Louvre and Guggenheim museums. A secondary core is the oasis of al-Ayn, seat of the UAE's first university, and other clusters are in the al-Ruways–Jabal Dhanna oil and industrial area and in the arc of the al-Jiwa oases (see Map 15.3). As part of the UAE's railway plans, the Abu Dhabi Metro Project envisions an 81-mi/131-km light-rail system to serve the capital city by 2016; bids for the endeavor were invited in 2009.[89] By 2010, the amirate had made several major investments that made clear its commitment to rival Dubai in attracting the regional headquarters of media and entertainment companies.[90]

Dubai.   The next-largest polity, also with a third of the UAE's population, and the next to the north of Abu Dhabi, is Dubai (sometimes Dubay or Dubayy), with about 45 mi/72 km of sand and *sabkhah* coastline. Even before independence, its rulers were the most imaginative and aggressive of the ruling shaykhs, skillfully balancing the various cultural and economic factors affecting the development of the amirate and the area. The commercial and shipping center of the city developed on both sides of Dubai Creek, which affords an ideal harbor for dhows engaged in fishing, pearling, smuggling, and other maritime trade.

Dubai proper lies south of the Creek and near the shore in the Batakia sector has a carefully preserved group of older structures topped by *badgirs*, Persian wind towers (see Fig. 2.10); Dayrah, with more of the original commercial and tourism functions, developed north of the inlet. The two are connected not only by four bridges and a tunnel but also by *abras*, picturesque small passenger ferries. With a laissez-faire commercial philosophy, Dubai is the commercial center of the UAE, and with "hustle, imagination, and a willingness to indulge a degree of hedonism," it has opened superluxury theme malls, nightclubs, golf courses, racetracks, world-class hotels, an information-technology center, a diamond exchange, theme parks, a Media City (which includes the main studios of Al-Arabiya, a television network competing with Aljazeera), and other facilities utilizing the latest technology.[91] The 2000s saw Dubai becoming renowned for innovative architecture and extravagant facilities, some of which were considered overly flamboyant. The extensive use of colored lighting illuminating the city's skyline has evoked comparisons (not always favorable) with Las Vegas. Nevertheless, it has added to the city's touristic drawing power.

With the charming but cramped Dubai Creek business center constricting commercial and tourist facility growth, the audacious ruler founded a completely new Central Business District well to the south of the Creek along Shaykh Zayed Road. Development exploded. In January 2010, Dubai opened the world's tallest building so far at about 2,717 ft/828 m,[92] with a surprise renaming of the tower to Burj Khalifa, in honor of the Abu Dhabi ruler and UAE president who had recently come to Dubai's aid financially (Fig. 15.7). An eighty-story apartment building, every floor of which can pivot separately around a central core so that it is constantly changing its appearance, was in the planning stages, but with the onset of Dubai's financial crisis its future was uncertain. September 2009 saw the inauguration of the Gulf's first metro system (Fig. 15.8); innovative as the world's longest driverless system, it will cover 45 mi/73 km when complete.

FIGURE 15.7 Dwarfing the normal high-rise buildings surrounding it in Dubai, Burj Khalifa (Khalifa Tower) opened in early 2010 as the world's tallest structure. Its opening came at the height of the economic downturn, raising questions about the tower's viability. (Dr. John Fox, American University of Sharjah)

Beginning in 2002, Dubai relaxed its rules on foreign property ownership and thus attracted many buyers for luxury villas and apartments, including those built on imaginative man-made islands that are in the pattern of palm trees, the first of which opened for occupancy in 2006. Another off-shore residential project was designed to resemble a giant world map. The mid-2000s saw a housing boom take off in Dubai despite warnings that speculation was driving prices too high; the boom went bust in 2008, and within a year a well-known index of housing prices was down almost 50 percent over the previous year.[93] The collapse of the real estate market preceded the crescendo of problems that built up in Dubai in 2009, and at the end of the decade it seemed that, at best, the market's recovery would be slow.

Sharjah. The third-largest amirate, Sharjah (al-Shariqah), with a fifth of the UAE's people, is adjacent to and north of Dubai; the two are coalescing into one urban area following agreement on the sandy no-man's-land between them. Despite this proximity, Sharjah is distinctly more conservative than its neighbor.[94] Its 10-mi/16-km coastline included a small dhow harbor that developed into a modest modern port after 1970. Its territory is the most fragmented of the amirates (see Map 15.3). With three exclaves on the Batinah coast of the Gulf of Oman (Diba, Khor Fakkan, and Kalba), it thus has common borders with all

FIGURE 15.8 Dubai's incredible southern Central Business District sprang from the almost empty desert in an explosive development along Shaykh Zayed Road, seen here in a view looking north. Note elevated metro system to lower right, as well as the variety of architecture in the high-rise buildings. (Dr. John Fox, American University of Sharjah)

six of the federation's polities. Dhayd Oasis and irrigation along the Batinah give it a plentiful supply of fruits and vegetables.

Sharjah has become the industrial heartland of the UAE, with more than 1,600 enterprises employing more then 75,000 workers; the amirate accounts for about half of the industrial portion of the country's GDP. The Industrial City Development had already attracted more than $1.3 billion in infrastructural investment by early 2010 and offers some 2.7 mi^2/7 km^2 for plant and facility expansion.[95]

With only limited hydrocarbon resources, Sharjah pursued a vigorous program of tourism tied to shopping. As the fever of shopping by East European traders subsided, the present ruler, Shaykh Sultan bin Muhammad Al-Qasimi, has encouraged cultural facilities, including two universities that opened in 1997. The impressive American University of Sharjah (AUS) is U.S. accredited and has 5,000 students; the University of Sharjah caters to evening and part-time students. Farther into the desert beyond AUS is the Desert Park and Natural History Museum, with world-class exhibits. He has also been restoring the *suqs*, houses with *badgirs*, and a mosque in the old city center, along with the encircling wall. The historic area is mostly used for cultural events. Nearby are the Sharjah Art Museum with a collection of Orientalist and contemporary Arab art and the Islamic Arts Museum.

Two Gulf islands, Abu Musa and Sir Abu Nuayr, are claimed by Sharjah and Iran (which occupies them). They share revenues from the offshore Mubarak oil field in Abu Musa's territorial waters. Sharjah City was the site of the coast's first airfield; it also hosted a Royal Air Force unit and the headquarters of the Trucial Oman Scouts. Sharjah International Airport is heavily utilized for cargo transport and intraregional traffic, especially the flights of Sharjah-based budget airline Air Arabia.

Ajman. Next up the coast is the amirate of Ajman, the smallest unit in the UAE: While it has only 5 percent of the UAE's population, it was growing rapidly in the late 2000s. It includes Ajman town, a strip of desert behind it, and two tiny interior exclaves; it has a small but lively industrial park in its port area. A new interconnecting highway system has facilitated the merging of Ajman, Sharjah, and Dubai into a single metropolitan area.[96] It retains seafaring traditions with a large dhow-building yard and a fish-trap fabricating facility. In 2006, it followed Dubai in relaxing its rules on foreign property ownership.

Umm al-Qaywayn. North of Ajman is the second-smallest and the least populated (about 1.1 percent of the total) of the amirates, Umm al-Qaywayn. The town occupies the tip of a narrow peninsula, reached by a spur from the coastal highway. With negligible energy resources, Umm al-Qaywayn has lagged behind the other members of the federation in industrial growth. Adding to its traditional fishing, it has attracted clothing-manufacturing and printing establishments. As with Ajman, the expanding UAE highway network has promoted rapid population growth in the late 2000s.

Ras al-Khaymah. Northernmost of the polities and occupying a triangular area west of a mountain spur that reaches the sea, Ras al-Khaymah (with about 5 percent of the UAE's people) is quite diverse. The capital itself lies on a peninsula and has a long seafaring tradition. It has the Diqdaqah agricultural station and half a dozen other towns and villages. In the mountains at the northern tip lives a small but interesting non-Arab ethnic group, the Shihuh (or Shikuh). Two offshore islands—Greater Tunb and Lesser Tunb—are claimed by Ras al-Khaymah but were seized by Iran in 1971. Its only known oil comes from its offshore field of Saleh, but it also has some modest gas reserves. Requisite raw materials for cement are near at hand, and three large plants operate between the mountains and the north-south highway. Like Dubai and Ajman, it now allows some foreign property ownership.

Fujayrah. The only UAE member located on the eastern, or Gulf of Oman, side of the peninsula, Fujayrah, with about 3 percent of the population, was isolated until federal highways made it easily accessible and encouraged beach-resort development. It had only a limited fishing economy and a few date palms until the 1960s; now, its successful resort facilities include stretches of clean, sandy, and still-uncrowded beaches, making it unrecognizable compared to that period. The amirate is also developing its port to compete with Sharjah's exclave, Khor Fakkan. Huge chicken farms with air-conditioned hen houses and a major dairy have also been developed inland from the coast.

It is truly difficult to comprehend the explosive development of primitive fishing villages along desert coasts into a succession of spectacular, diversified cities in one lifetime, but such is now the story of the amirates of the Gulf.

NOTES

1. L. S. Amery, in his foreword to S. Wilson 1928, ix.
2. After development in the Gulf boomed, many studies on the subject appeared. For development and general coverage, see Cottrell 1980; Niblock 1980; Netton 1986; Crystal 1990; Zahlan 1998; *Persian Gulf*

States Country Studies 1993; Balfour-Paul 1994; D. Long 2002; and Potter and Sick 2002. Netton also contains an excellent essay on source materials. The Gulf Cooperation Council is analyzed in Twinam 1992.

3. United Nations Development Programme 2009.

4. See Scoville 1979 and Lorimer 1915.

5. Statistics are from *Oil and Gas Journal*, Dec. 22, 2009.

6. Gulf petroleum is discussed in the studies already cited and also PennWell's annual *International Petroleum Encyclopedia*; Yergin 1991; and U.S. Department of Energy, Energy Information Administration, *Country Analysis Briefs: Persian Gulf Oil and Gas Exports Fact Sheet*, Sept. 2004.

7. Many studies understandably link oil and Gulf security. In addition to the works cited in notes 2 and 4, see Peterson 1983; Cordesman 1997; Ramazani 1979; Doran and Buck 1991; Sindelar and Peterson 1989; and Fox, Mourtada-Sabbah, and al-Mutawa 2006.

8. The classic work on the old Kuwait is the massive compendium Dickson 1949, followed by his *Kuwait and Her Neighbors* (1956).

9. Crystal 1990, 39.

10. See Middle East Research Institute report on Kuwait (1985); Al-Sabah 1980; *Persian Gulf States* Country Studies 1993; Crystal 1990; and U.S. Department of State, *Background Note: Kuwait*, Feb. 2009, and *Country Commercial Guide: Kuwait*, 2007.

11. *Christian Science Monitor*, Mar. 19, 1991. An "inside story" of the invasion and occupation is Levins 1997.

12. Return of the stolen items is discussed in the *Washington Post Weekly*, Mar. 1, 1992; and *Christian Science Monitor*, June 17, 1991.

13. One of the authors, in Riyadh (500 km away) at the time, remembers smoke-darkened skies for weeks.

14. Among the many articles on the environmental catastrophe engendered by the oil spills and well fires in Kuwait, useful and easily available coverage, including ground photographs and space imagery, is given in R. Williams et al. 1991 and Earle 1992. An authoritative assessment with more perspective is given in *International Petroleum Encyclopedia* 1992, 222–229.

15. See note 21, Chap. 8, especially Schofield 1993 and H. Rahman 1997.

16. Much of the following account is based on Crystal 1992 and EIA, *Country Analysis Briefs: Kuwait*, Apr. 2009.

17. For 2010, the government announced spending plans of $3 to $4 billion in pursuit of this goal (*Maktoob Business*, Feb. 2, 2010).

18. This situation could change if Kuwait becomes part of a larger free-trade bloc like GAFTA (see Chap. 8).

19. Reliance on desalination plants does bring vulnerability, as happened when Iraq emptied crude oil into the waters surrounding Kuwait in 1991 and when a malfunctioning sewage plant leaked pollution, as reported in *Kuwait Times*, Aug. 25, 2009.

20. IEA, "2006 Energy Balance for Kuwait."

21. USGS, "The Mineral Industry of Kuwait," in *Minerals Yearbook* 2008.

22. The costs have been estimated at nearly $200 billion. Iraq was required by the UN to pay reparations (see Chap. 13).

23. Kuwait Fund for Arab Economic Development, *Annual Report, 2007–2008*.

24. Agence France Presse, Feb. 6, 2008.

25. *Oil and Gas Journal*, Feb. 8, 2010.

26. Fraser Institute 2008.

27. World Economic Forum 2009a.

28. World Bank and the International Finance Corporation, "Doing Business, 2008," www.doingbusiness.org/features/DB2008Report.aspx.

29. A group called the *Bidoon jinsaya* (Arabic for "without nationality") or just *Bidoon* are longtime residents of Kuwait who for various reasons have been unable to claim citizenship; they are estimated by the government to number more than 100,000. The antecedents of many but not all of them were nomadic tribesmen who roamed the Arabian desert before modern political boundaries existed. They are subject to a fair amount of discrimination because of their indeterminate legal status.

30. The problem is examined in detail in A. Lesch 1991 and in articles in *Christian Science Monitor*, Mar. 26, Apr. 17, June 26, Aug. 2, 1991, and Feb. 27, 1992. See also Le Troquer and al-Oudat 1999.

31. See *New York Times*, Nov. 20, 2002, and Feb. 11 and Mar. 17, 2003.

32. The main island was called al-Awal in the past, hence the name Awali for the oil field and town. Believed to have been the ancient Dilmun, Bahrain was the classical Tylos, and, to add to the confusion, the name Bahrain was long applied to eastern Arabia as well as to the islands.

33. See Brunsden et al. 1979. For more detailed examinations, see *Persian Gulf States* Country Studies 1993; Lawson 1989; Nugent and Thomas 1985; and U.S. Department of State, *Background Note: Bahrain*, Jan. 2010. Current information is also drawn on the *Country Commercial Guide: Bahrain*, Aug. 2004.

34. Bibby 1969. The finds are on display in the small but interesting Bahrain museum.

35. A. Clarke 1990 covers the history and status of Bahrain oil in minute detail and includes very useful appendixes and a bibliography.

36. USGS, "The Mineral Industry of Bahrain," in *Minerals Yearbook* 2008.

37. Iraq, Kuwait, Libya, Qatar, Saudi Arabia, and the UAE.

38. IEA, "2006 Energy Balance for Bahrain."

39. *The National* (Abu Dhabi), Nov. 22, 2009.

40. *New York Times*, Dec. 24, 2004.

41. See the detailed Landsat images in Yehia 1983, which also includes sectional topographic and geologic maps of Qatar.

42. Batanouny 1981 gives good, concise coverage of the Qatar environment, as well as detailed scientific coverage of the flora. Yehia 1983 discusses and illustrates the *rawdahs* and coastal features.

43. Among the studies on Qatar, see Zahlan 1998; Crystal 1990; *Persian Gulf States* Country Studies 1993; and Cottrell 1980. For Qatar's development efforts, see *New York Times*, Dec. 2, 2004. Some of this section has also been drawn from U.S. Department of State, *Background Note: Qatar*, Jan. 2010.

44. In 2008, the three held initial talks aimed at forming a cartel for natural gas. See *The Guardian*, Oct. 22, 2008. Exact total reserves vary slightly by source and date.

45. IEA, "2006 Energy Balance for Qatar."

46. See *Oil and Gas Journal*, July 19, 1999, 28, and Oct. 27, 2003, 8. For information on Qatar's oil and gas industry and other economic developments, see *Country Commercial Guide: Qatar*, 2009; EIA, *Country Analysis Briefs: Qatar*, Dec. 2009; and *International Petroleum Encyclopedia* 2003, 104.

47. USGS, "The Mineral Industry of Qatar," in *Minerals Yearbook* 2008.

48. For further information, see www.qatalum .com/en/.

49. *Media Line*, Jan. 8, 2010, www.themedialine .org/news/news_detail.asp?NewsID=27646.

50. See Berrebi, Martorell, and Tanner 2009.

51. *BBC News*, Nov. 22, 2009.

52. Transparency International 2009; World Economic Forum 2009a.

53. A less optimistic view of the evolution of Qatari political institutions is found in Kamrava 2009.

54. See *New York Times*, July 4, 1999; *Christian Science Monitor*, Dec. 25, 2002; and *New York Times*, Aug. 16, 2004. An interesting and thorough treatment of the network is found in El-Nawawy and Iskandar 2002.

55. *The Observer* (UK), June 8, 2008; *Arabian Business*, Mar. 17, 2009, www.arabianbusiness.com.

56. A comprehensive view of Qatar's relations with Israel is found in Rabi 2009; see *Ha'aretz*, Jan. 16, 2009, for details on the breaking of relations.

57. The complete text is available from the Council on Foreign Relations, www.cfr.org/publications/21438/html.

58. Within fifteen months of its establishment, all of the funds had been committed to some eighteen projects in education, health care, and housing. See http://qatarkatrinafund.org/ for details.

59. Although "amir" and "amirate" are the preferred transliterations and are generally used in this book, "Emirates" is the official English name for the UAE, and so it is, at the risk of some confusion, used in this specific application. As for the "most recent" Middle East state, unified Yemen might claim that distinction, since its two components combined in 1990, whereas the UAE became independent in 1971. However, each of the constituents of the new Yemen had previously been independent.

60. See Middle East Research Institute report on the UAE (1985); Peck 1986; Taryam 1987; Vine 1996; Zahlan 1998; Heard-Bey 1999; Al Sayegh 2004; Fox, Mourtada-Sabbah, and al-Mutawa 2006; and U.S. Department of State, *Background Note: United Arab Emirates*, June 2007. Our thanks go to Dr. John W. Fox for his suggestions about this section on the UAE and for his photographs.

61. The traditional claim that the British assumed control of the Gulf to suppress Arab piracy is disputed in al-Qasimi 1988.

62. Britain's relations with the shaykhdoms, like those with Kuwait, Bahrain, Qatar, Oman, and Aden, were conducted from India, not London.

63. See Al-Fahim 1997 for an excellent account of the transition.

64. Malaysia has a similar political structure—nine of its thirteen states are hereditary monarchies, and the country's head of state is elected from among these rulers for a five-year term. It is also a parliamentary democracy.

65. U.S. Department of State, *Background Note: United Arab Emirates*, June 2007.

66. For further details, see EIA, *Country Analysis Briefs: United Arab Emirates*, Nov. 2009, and *Country Commercial Guide: United Arab Emirates*, 2007; and Gabriel 1988.

67. After Russia, Iran, Qatar, Turkmenistan, Saudi Arabia, and the United States.

68. IEA, "2006 Energy Balance for United Arab Emirates."

69. *The Daily Star* (Beirut), Dec. 28, 2009. A $20 billion contract went to a Korean combine to build and operate four reactors.

70. *Gulf News* (Dubai), Feb. 5, 2010.

71. USGS, "The Mineral Industry of the United Arab Emirates," in *Minerals Yearbook* 2008.

72. *The National*, July 8, 2009.

73. *Khaleej Times* (Dubai), Dec. 8, 2009.

74. *New York Times*, Nov. 24, 2008.

75. *New York Times*, Sept. 15, 2009.

76. *BBC News*, Nov. 25, 2009.

77. *BBC News*, Mar. 25, 2010.

78. *BBC News*, Nov. 27, 2009; *New York Times*, Nov. 28, Nov. 30, and Dec. 3, 2009. Some British banks were thought to have particularly large exposures to Dubai.

79. Associated Press, Dec. 14, 2009.

80. *New York Times*, Dec. 1, 2009.

81. *New York Times*, Nov. 30, Dec. 14, and Dec. 15, 2005; National Public Radio, Dec. 4 and Dec. 7, 2009.

82. Transparency International 2009; World Economic Forum 2009a; Fraser Institute 2008.

83. World Bank and the International Finance Corporation, "Doing Business, 2008," www.doingbusiness.org/features/DB2008Report.aspx.

84. See Shahir and Nasr 1999.

85. ADFD, *Annual Report, 2007/2008*, www.adfd.ae/.

86. For example, Abu Dhabi has contracted with an Israeli-owned satellite communications company for photographic imagery since 2006 (*DefenseNews*, Feb. 23, 2009, www.defensenews.com/story.php?i=3958937).

There had been a small office in Abu Dhabi representing Israeli commercial interests until it was closed in early 2009 in the aftermath of Israel's Operation Cast Lead against Gaza.

87. For an outline of the events as they unfolded, see *BBC News*, Mar. 29, 2010.

88. The Federal Government [of Germany], "Founding an International Renewable Energy Agency (IRENA)"; IRENA, "Report of the Conference on the Establishment of the International Renewable Energy Agency," Jan. 2009, www.irena.org/.

89. *Arabian Business*, Feb. 18, 2009, www.arabianbusiness.com.

90. *The Daily Star*, Mar. 9, 2010.

91. *New York Times*, Feb. 12, 2004.

92. Even at its opening, the building's owners were secretive about its exact height (Associated Press, Jan. 3, 2010).

93. *New York Times*, Aug. 3, 2009.

94. For example, it has and enforces a law against men wearing conspicuous jewelry. See *Gulf News*, July 21, 2009, http://gulfnews.com/news/gulf/crime/.

95. Oxford Business Group, Mar. 30, 2010.

96. It is worth noting that up until 1971, a passport was needed for going from one amirate to another.

16

Oman and Yemen
The Southern Fringe

Extending from the Strait of Hormuz to the Bab el-Mandeb along the southern fringe of the Arabian Peninsula are Oman and Yemen, the two largest of the six peripheral states of the peninsula. Since 1971, Oman has developed increasingly close relations with the Gulf states (with which it is often grouped because of its exclave on the Strait of Hormuz) and with neighboring Saudi Arabia. In 1990, North Yemen and South Yemen merged into the Republic of Yemen.

Oman and the two formerly separate parts of Yemen maintain individually distinct characters physically, culturally, economically, and politically. Oman is a sultanate, with the once almost absolute monarch now advised by two councils. Conservative and stable, it maintains cautious links with the West and has had forty years of well-planned development financed by moderately large oil income. The Republic of Yemen, in contrast, unified the Marxist former People's Democratic Republic of Yemen (South Yemen) and the more traditional Yemen Arab Republic (North Yemen). The new state reaffirmed its raison d'être following a 1994 civil war and haltingly tries to evolve the necessary institutions of a politically viable entity and to develop economically from a low baseline while faced with insurrection, secessionist elements, and the increasing presence of terrorist cadres.

OMAN

Termed "Muscat and Oman" prior to 1970, the Sultanate of Oman was sometimes confused with Trucial Oman, an alternate name for the Trucial States, now the UAE. Among other things, the several names reflect the regionalization of Oman into two basic parts: Inner Oman, west of the mountains, and the Batinah coast along the Gulf of Oman (Map 16.1).

The only sultanate in the Middle East, Oman has modernized in ways similar to those of the oil states of the Gulf, but with some unique characteristics and while keeping much of its traditional culture. Caution and moderate conservatism characterize its approach to development, and it deliberately pursues modest growth rather than allowing the explosive expansion that has occurred in Kuwait, Qatar, Abu Dhabi, and Dubai.[1] For example, the population is estimated to have grown by about fivefold between 1950 and 2000, compared with more than twentyfold in the UAE during the same period.

Oman, on the Tropic of Cancer, is notably hot in summer and warm even in winter. It is a desert land except in a few higher elevations and in the uplands of southern Dhufar. Muscat, the capital, has an average annual temperature of 84°F/29°C, with less than 4 in/100 mm of rain. Like Yemen's mountains,

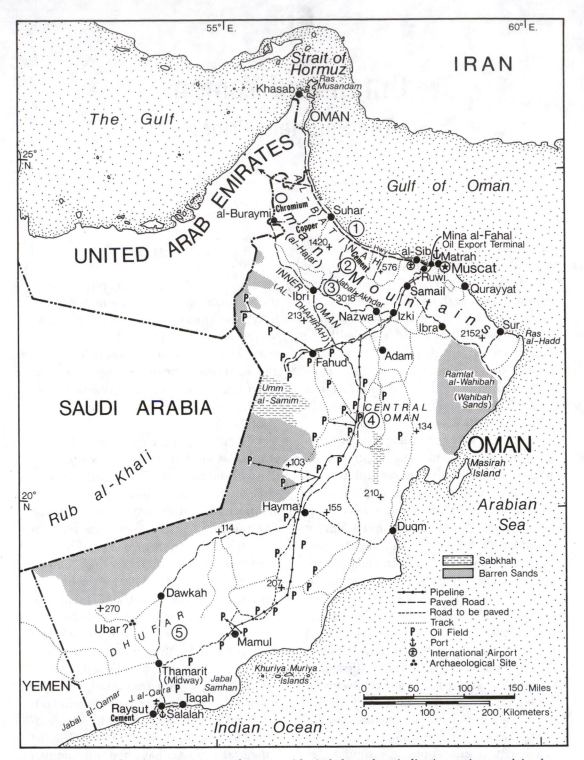

MAP 16.1 General and economic map of Oman, with circled numbers indicating regions explained in text. Note the widespread distribution of petroleum fields, most of them small. Oman's boundaries with all three neighbors are now de jure, a historic achievement.

OMAN

Long-form official name, anglicized: Sultanate of Oman

Official name, transliterated: Saltanat Uman

Form of government: monarchy with two advisory bodies (State Council, Consultative Council)

Area: 119,500 mi²/309,500 km²

Population, 2008: 2,651,000; Literacy (Latest): 75.8%

Ethnic composition (%): Omani 48.1; Indo-Pakistani 31.7; other Arab 7.2; Persian 2.8; Zanzibari 2.5; other 7.7

Religions (%): Muslim 89, of which Ibadiyah 75, Sunni 8, Shii 6; Christian 5; Hindu 5; other 1

Demography: Life expectancy—70.4 yr (M), 73.6 yr (F); Birthrate (per 1,000)—25.0; Fertility rate—5.84

GDP, 2009: $52.34 billion; purchasing power parity: $69.43 billion; per capita: $20,300

Currency: Omani rial, US$1 = 0.3835 rials, 1 rial = $2.588 (March 2010)

Energy reserves: oil—5.5 bn bbl; natural gas—30 tn ft³; coal—122 mnt

Main exports (% of total value, 2007): crude petroleum 58.5; liquefied natural gas 12.4; refined petroleum 4.9; re-exports 10.6, of which vehicles and parts 8.3

Main imports (% of total value, 2007): vehicles and parts 24.1; nonelectrical machinery and equipment 17.8; food and live animals 8.3; iron and steel 8.2; chemicals and chemical products 6.4

Capital city: Muscat (agglomeration) 785,515; other major cities: Sib 268,259; Bawshar 193,778; Salalah 185,780; Suhar 119,983

---

highland Oman receives summer monsoon rain, particularly in the mountains around Salalah in the south, as well as orographically enhanced winter cyclonic storm rain, exceeding 18 in/457 mm in its northern ranges. Runoff from such rains there supplies the irrigation water for crops along the Batinah coast and in interior oases.

Physical Regions

Oman comprises five distinct physical regions, each of which has its individual cultural character: [1] the Batinah coast; [2] al-Hajar (or Oman Mountains); [3] Inner Oman; [4] Central Oman; and [5] Dhufar. (See circled numbers on Map 16.1.)

[1] Batinah Coast. The Batinah is a coastal plain 6–18 mi/10–30 km wide extending 168 mi/270 km along the Gulf of Oman. The name implies "front" or "belly," as opposed to "al-Dhahirah" (Inner Oman), which suggests "back." Composed primarily of coalesced alluvial fan deltas of gravel, sand, and silt, the plain is squeezed between mountain chain and seashore and is Oman's primary agricultural area, cultivated for millennia. Crops are irrigated in a strip about 1.8 mi/3 km wide, using groundwater stored in the sandy gravels of the fans at the stream mouths. Date, citrus, and banana groves line the road, alternating with "strip settlements" one house deep on each side of the road—the

FIGURE 16.1 High-speed boats in Khasab harbor, Oman, at northern tip of the Musandam Peninsula ("Horn of Arabia"). Most of the boats engage in smuggling and take on loads of cigarettes, electronic goods, and other small high-demand items in Oman, then make a dash at night across the Strait of Hormuz to avoid Iranian customs. Note the steep sides to these inlets, often described as "fjords," although their origin is quite different.

Omani version of the classic *strassendorf*. At the debouchment of the larger wadis, major fans support extensive agriculture and, usually, more populous settlements. Some towns are of considerable antiquity; Suhar, the largest, and many coastal settlements still engage in fishing. After the Capital Area, the Batinah is the sultanate's most densely populated region, with steadily developing commerce and industry. Sib International Airport is at the southern end of the plain; major industrial estates lie at each end, one at Rusayl, near Sib, the other a new one near Suhar in the north.

[2] Al-Hajar. Often called the Oman Mountains, al-Hajar (literally, "the Rock") is a high rugged chain of mountains paralleling the Batinah in a 435-mi/700-km arc from the northern tip of the Musandam Peninsula (Horn of Arabia) to Ras al-Hadd. The mountains form the "backbone" between the Batinah "belly" and the "back" of Inner Oman.

Their northern end overlooks the Strait of Hormuz; this is Ras Musandam, a striking desert fjord-type land that forms a maze of isthmuses and islands with coastal cliffs dropping sharply to sea-filled valleys (Fig. 16.1). Politically, it is an Omani exclave, separated from the rest of the sultanate's territory by UAE territory and recently connected to Muscat by high-speed ferry. As such, it may be considered a subregion of al-Hajar. Much of the mountain chain exceeds 4,800 ft/1,463 m, with elevations of nearly 10,000 ft/3,048 m in the central block, the very rugged Jabal al-Akhdar (Green Mountain), a name sometimes mistakenly applied to the entire Hajar range.

The Oman Mountains are a virtually unique geomorphic feature, both scientifically and scenically. Two nappe complexes, one of ophiolite oceanic crust, have been thrust from former ocean deeps into stacked thrust sheets thousands of feet thick. Gigantic "windows" (*fenêtres*) carved into the nappes

FIGURE 16.2 Air view of Muscat, showing the capital crowded into the small pocket between rugged lava mountains and the sea, so that primarily only the older quaint houses remain. Growth has been in Matrah, Ruwi, and other developments beyond the mountains. The center building along the coast is the sultan's palace. (Tor Eigeland, *Saudi Aramco World*, SAWDIA)

through erosion have exposed multiple over-folded strata of different ages, origins, and colors. Some almost vertical window walls are more than 6,500 ft/2,000 m high.[2] The one major pass through the chain is the Samail Gap, just east of Jabal al-Akhdar, traversed by the main route connecting Muscat with Inner Oman. Large oil and gas pipelines parallel the road, carrying the sultanate's entire production to the export terminal west of Matrah. Created by erosion along a major tectonic fault, the trough divides the Hajar range into the larger scenically rugged Western Hajar (Hajar al-Gharbi) and the smaller Eastern Hajar (Hajar al-Sharqi).

The northern end of the Samail Gap intersects the southern end of the Batinah coastal plain, where al-Hajar pushes to the coast, embracing two harbors. Muscat, on the eastern bay, evolved as the main port and capital, but its small basin in the rugged ophiolites and

pillow lavas curtailed development (Fig. 16.2). Matrah, in the next depression westward, has a larger basin and is now the main port. Urban development has leapfrogged over the lava ridges and has spread up the southern Batinah to Sib airport and beyond. Thus, the Greater Capital Area is a second subregion of al-Hajar.

[3] Inner Oman. Inner Oman (al-Dhahirah—"the back") is an amorphous foreland area extending southwestward from al-Hajar to the sands of the Rub al-Khali. The pattern of picturesque, long-settled villages—Izki, Nazwa, Bahlah, Ibri, Dank, and the oasis town of Buraymi—along the internal piedmont and belt of alluvial fans resembles the string of settlements on the eastern side of al-Hajar. Watered by hundreds of small canals and *aflaj* (singular: *falaj*), extensive date-palm groves, deep green against the barren

mountains, mark the several oasis towns and dozens of villages on the alluvial fans along the al-Hajar piedmont. However, the interior is less endowed with water and has traditionally been isolated, wedged between rugged mountains to the east and barren sands to the west. It has had ties with the Gulf shaykhdoms through the Buraymi Oasis and with the Batinah via the Samail Gap.

Subregional designations reflect variety in this seemingly uniform area. The northern extension of Inner Oman toward Buraymi is al-Jaw, with Ibri—the largest town in al-Dhahirah—as the center. The subregion of the Jabal Akhdar piedmont is the traditional heart of Inner Oman, al-Dakhiliyah, with the major oases of al-Hamra, Bahlah, Nazwa, and Izki. All have extensive date groves and are diversifying into fruits and cotton. Nazwa, with its well-preserved fort, is the major town, the political and cultural capital for centuries. East of the Samail Gap, the piedmont of the Eastern Hajar is usually referred to as al-Sharqiya (the East) with a string of oasis towns in Ibra, al-Mudayrib, al-Mintirib, and al-Kamil, as well as the ancient port of Sur and the eastern tip of Oman at Ras al-Hadd. Modern roads and excellent telecommunications now facilitate closer relations in both directions, integrate the interior economically, and strengthen political ties with the sultanate core around Muscat. Inner Oman is associated with a distinct Islamic sect, the Ibadhis, who enjoyed a militant autonomy under their own imam for several decades prior to 1959. It is also the location of Oman's main producing oil fields.

[4] *Central Oman.*   Central Oman, locally called al-Wusta (literally, "the middle"), extends from Inner Oman southward. A large barren area, it has for centuries been the realm of fewer than a dozen small Bedouin tribes. In the east, wedged between the Arabian Sea and the eastern Oman Mountains, is an unusual dune field, the Wahibah Sands. It

contains a range of dune formations, including fossil sand seas, of such interest that it was the object of an intensive multidisciplinary investigation by the Royal Geographical Society (London) and Omani counterparts in 1985–1987. Otherwise, Central Oman is a monotonous land of sand and gravel, much of it dissected by wadis in former pluvial periods, with little to offer until more than a score of oil fields were discovered beneath its surface (see Map 16.1). Continued exploration found another sixty small pocket fields, some of which are actually in Dhufar. A high-speed highway completed in 1986 traverses the region, connecting Muscat and Salalah. This formerly remote and isolated area has also been carefully mapped and is intensively crisscrossed by the tracks of oil-exploration and well-maintenance vehicles, although it is still devoid of significant settlements.

[5] *Dhufar.*   Dhufar (sometimes Dhofar) is an ill-defined area that merges with Central Oman to the northeast and Yemen to the west. A rough, barren, sparsely inhabited desert area inland, it has mountains just back of the coast with green slopes and monsoon woodlands, some producing frankincense, contrasting spectacularly with the inland desert. It was poorly known until exploration opened more than a dozen oil fields centered 100 mi/160 km northeast of Salalah, the provincial capital. It appeared in world headlines when it was contested between Dhufari rebels and Oman in the late 1960s and early 1970s (see next section). Mountain areas and some coastal villages are inhabited by a complex of ethnolinguistic groups, some believed to predate Arab presence in the area. In 1991, amateur archaeologists, guided by satellite imagery, discovered the ruins of an ancient city 93 mi/150 km north-northeast of Salalah that is believed to be Ubar, famed center of frankincense trade from 2000 BCE to late Roman times.[3] Salalah is the southern anchor of administration, commerce, transporta-

tion, and, recently, tourism. Its unusual summer weather, unique in the sultanate, attracts thousands of Omanis to enjoy the cool, misty midsummer monsoons on the mountain slopes. The recently developed Port Salalah is one of the few ports between Europe and Singapore able to handle the largest container vessels. Lying offshore are the Khuriya Muriya Islands, officially named al-Hallaniyat.

A Historical Sketch

Although incompletely studied, the antiquity of human occupation has long been recognized in sites along the coast, in Inner Oman, and in Dhufar. Tombs in the village of Bat, near Ibri, contain artifacts similar to those found in Abu Dhabi, suggesting a relationship with Sumer from about 3000 BCE. In the extreme east, in the Ras al-Hadd area, Phoenician artifacts found in the port of Sur link it with the ancient Phoenician port of Sur (Tyre). Dhufar was a major source of frankincense, with significant trade for millennia.

Like the rest of the peninsula, Oman adopted Islam in the seventh century, but the theologically distinct Ibadhi sect, neither Sunni nor Shii, evolved here from the eighth century and remains dominant. Ibadhis are spiritual descendants of the Khariji (seceders), a group that first supported Ali in his claim to be caliph but then separated from him during his conflict with the Umayyads. Oman has the only concentration of Ibadhis in the region, although there are small communities in Zanzibar and North Africa.

Even more than in the Gulf amirates, Portuguese control for 142 years left its mark after 1508 in forts and towers still seen especially around Matrah and Muscat. Britain supplanted Portugal and Holland in regional control, and its influence remained strong for 300 years. The sultanate was technically independent after 1650, and Britain formally recognized its sovereignty in 1951. Isolated from fellow Arabs by mountains and formidable deserts, Omanis ventured into the Indian

Ocean as able seafarers and colonists. They established political control over Zanzibar and the neighboring African coast as well as over the exclave of Gwadar on the Baluchi coast, near the present Iran-Pakistan border. Oman held Gwadar until 1958 and, indirectly, Zanzibar until 1964.

The Al Bu Saids, an Ibadhi dynasty, have held the sultanate since 1744. Inner Oman and the coast have periodically been disunited, suffering a particularly sharp division in the nineteenth and early twentieth centuries, when the interior Ibadhis chose a theocracy ruled by the Ibadhi imam. The dispute subsided in 1920 when the Treaty of Sib granted the imam autonomy but recognized the sultan's nominal sovereignty. However, when Ghalib ibn Ali became imam in 1954, he rebelled against the sultan and was defeated and exiled, with British help, in 1959. The then sultan, Said bin Taimur Al Bu Said, was rather eccentric—prohibiting private vehicles, bicycles, and sunglasses; refusing to expand the small electricity and telephone net in the capital area; and maintaining a nighttime curfew in Muscat, with the city gates locked soon after dark. He isolated himself in Salalah, never returning to the capital after 1958. Oman at that time was the region's most backward and isolated area.

Four developments have dominated Oman's history since 1960. First, petroleum was discovered (1964), eventually bringing annual income of billions of dollars. Second, Marxist rebels—the Dhufar Liberation Front (DLF)—revolted in 1965. Third, the old sultan was forced to abdicate in favor of his son, the present ruler, Qabus (or Qaboos) ibn Said, in 1970. Fourth, the new sultan soon abolished many of his father's antiquated restrictions, urged educated Omanis to return home, oversaw the defeat of the Dhufar rebellion, united the country, and launched a major development program.

The Dhufar rebellion aimed at overthrowing not only the sultan but all conservative

Gulf regimes. The original DLF later merged with the Marxist-dominated Popular Front for the Liberation of Oman and the Arab Gulf (PFLOAG), which proclaimed revolution against all traditional regimes in the Gulf region. In mid-1974, PFLOAG, renamed the Popular Front for the Liberation of Oman, was defeated and finally driven out of Dhufar by the combined efforts of Omanis, British officers, an Iranian task force, Jordanian military forces, and others, with logistical help from Abu Dhabi.

Replacing his father's medieval practices, Qabus faced not only the Dhufar insurgency but also long-endemic diseases, illiteracy, and poverty. As the new sultan, he led Oman in an entirely new direction, both economically and politically: While retaining ultimate secular authority, he brought leaders of various segments of the complex society into the political process to balance tribal, regional, ethnic, and economic interests. In 1996, he approved Oman's first written constitution. In 1997, a limited electorate chose eighty-two members of the Majlis al-Shura; it has some powers to propose legislation. Then he appointed forty members, including four women, to the new Majlis al-Dawlah (with advisory powers only); in the mid-2000s, this body was expanded to fifty-nine members, nine of whom were women. He declared universal suffrage for the 2003 elections, and two women were elected to serve with eighty men. In 2007, no women candidates were successful, but fewer than half the incumbents were reelected.

In general, Oman, with its stable, moderately conservative institutions, has had the region's lowest level of politico-economic tensions,[4] but in the late 2000s some problems emerged. Inroads by Saudi ultraconservative Wahhabi Islam brought a strong reaction from the heterodox Ibadhi Omani regime. As many as 40,000 Pakistani workers were deported in the mid-2000s, allegedly for illegal entry, but suspicions of religious extremism may have also played a part. Last, Oman has a very young population, and with its having benefited from education and electronic links to the outside world, there are signs that the younger generation feels constrained by the sultan's paternalistic authoritarianism.

The Omanis

The 2003 census found nearly one-fourth of the population concentrated in the Muscat-Matrah-Ruwi core, the rest scattered mostly throughout a belt of Batinah towns and in the string of inner villages paralleling the southwestern piedmont of al-Hajar. Major population outliers include the area of Salalah-Raysut and surrounding villages on the southern Dhufar coast and Sur at the eastern corner of the country. The sultanate's first census, in 1993, and its successor a decade later statistically confirmed population distribution patterns that had been previously suspected. By the late 2000s, probably more than 55 percent of the population lived in the Capital Area and along the Batinah.

Ethnic boundaries are generally defined by language or sect (or both) rather than by territory, occupation, or even class.[5] Because of the links with peoples on nearby coasts, ethnic groups are numerous, with at least a dozen languages spoken as mother tongues. Ethnic and especially tribal affiliation plays a role in employment and other social interactions. However, long accustomed to a complex society, Omanis have few intergroup tensions.

Oman's basic Arab population differs perceptibly from that of neighboring Saudi Arabia and the UAE. The distinction arises partly because southern Asian and East African influences entered along the coast and partly because Arab influences from the interior diminished as they diffused into this easterly projection of the peninsula. Furthermore, fragmented by mountain ranges, highland masses, and desert belts, Oman has many different remnant ethnolinguistic and religious minorities, some still surviving from pre-Islamic centuries in isolated mountain refuges. Strong tribal affiliations further diversify the people.

Oman's maritime connections with southern Asia and East Africa and its control of Gwadar and Zanzibar attracted immigrants from those areas. Indians, Baluch, Iranians, Somalis, and other East Africans settled in Oman, with many of the Africans being brought as slaves. Baluch are especially numerous and are the largest non-Arab community. Omanis with an East African connection are called Zanzibari as returnees from Zanzibar and the adjoining mainland after the 1964 independence of those areas. Swahili-speaking East Africans, originally slaves, were freed by Sultan Qabus.

The Shii Khojas (Liwatiyya), a prominent minority, are a close-knit community of Hindu converts to Islam originally from India but resident in Oman as merchants for more than two centuries. They occupy a separate walled quarter in Matrah but also live in other Batinah towns. Other Shii include the Baharinah and the Ajam, of Persian background. Several minor groups, including some unassimilated pre-Arab peoples, occupy mountain areas in Dhufar. To the above must be added the nearly 600,000 expatriates—close to a fifth of the population. As other Gulf states are doing, it is reducing the expatriate presence with a program of "Omanization."

Although Islam is the predominant religion, the sultanate's major sect, the Ibadhi, is distinct from other branches of Islam. Oman was established as an Ibadhi state and has evolved an Ibadhi particularity. Although Inner Oman has long been the main concentration and theological stronghold of the sect, the ruling dynasty is also Ibadhi. Conservative, fundamentalist, and simple in their principles without being extremist, Ibadhi norms have strongly shaped Omani culture. Sunnis are the largest non-Ibadhi sect—the 250,000 Baluch are Sunni—and dominate in Salalah. Shii form the third-largest group and are concentrated in the Batinah, especially in Muscat-Matrah, with the Khojas.

Most Omanis of both sexes can be easily differentiated from their neighbors by their national dress. The standard male attire is the white, calf-long *dishdashah*, comparable to the *thawb* in Saudi Arabia. Headgear is of two types: Dominant is the *kumma*, a fitted, brimmed cap often colorfully and expensively embroidered and unique to Oman. More formal is the elaborate turban, the *amamma*, a square of light Kashmir wool artfully wound around the head. The well-dressed male traditionally wore a *khanjar*, a curved dagger with a highly decorated scabbard. Women also dress distinctively, echoing both Arabia and India. Under a colorful *dishdashah* they wear ankle-length trousers, the *surawal*, and usually add one or more filmy decorated scarves or shawls.

Economy

Oman's preindustrial economy of seafaring, fishing, and irrigation agriculture rested on a broader base and supported a larger population than did the economies of the four Gulf shaykhdoms. For example, it has nearly twice the cropland of the four combined, with most of its agricultural area divided between the Batinah coast and the inner piedmont of the Hajar. Two-thirds of that area is in permanent crops, primarily dates, bananas, mangoes, and limes. Fishing remains significant, much of it still traditional, although increasingly it is being modernized to take advantage of the rich fisheries along the coast.

Petroleum. Though last in the region to discover oil,[6] Oman's economy has been revolutionized by its oil industry. The original concession holder, the Iraq Petroleum Company had no success in the 1950s and abandoned its concession, later taken up by Petroleum Development (Oman) (PDO) with Shell as its major partner. The associates made initial strikes at Natih, Fahud, and Yibal, 140–185 mi/225–300 km southwest of Muscat in 1962–1964. A pipeline from the discovery area was laid through the Samail Gap to an export terminal at Mina al-Fahal, west of Matrah; and all subsequent production has been linked to this same terminal, where Oman's single refinery is as well (see Table 6.2). Intensive exploration by PDO and a score of other companies has found more than 110 fields, but many are too small to tie into the system. Output is still mainly from the original area—Yibal, al-Khuwayr (Lekhwait), and Fahud fields—but it also comes from fields in Central Oman and Dhufar (see Maps 6.1 and 16.1).

The sultanate's very complex geology makes exploration, drilling, and production difficult and expensive. Reservoirs are scattered, small, less productive, and quickly exhausted, so production per well is much less than in the UAE and Saudi Arabia. As Table 6.1 shows, 50 percent more wells than in Saudi Arabia yield only 8 percent as much oil. Enhanced oil recovery (EOR) techniques— for example, horizontal and multiple drilling and water and gas injection—are increasingly used; some 2,000 new wells are being drilled in the EOR program. By the end of the decade, successful results were apparent; output rose in both 2008 and 2009.[7] Petroleum provides 70 percent of government revenue, 75 percent of exports, and about 48 percent of GDP. In the late 2000s, reserves were a moderate 5.5 bn bbl, sixth largest in the region and comparable to those of the Divided Zone; production was about 715,000 bpd, peaking at 964,000 bpd in 2001. Since Oman is not an OPEC (or OAPEC) member, it is not subject to quotas, but it coordinates closely with the group.

Oman emphasizes the production, use, and export of the growing finds of natural gas. The Dolphin Project (see Chap. 15) links Oman with Qatar and the UAE with a natural gas pipeline. Qatar has very large gas deposits, and although both its partners have gas in more modest amounts, the project aims to distribute gas around the region to broadly diversify its uses; in Oman, imports began in October 2008 and initially are to be added feedstock in the EOR program. The sultanate tripled its production of natural gas over the decade since 1999, but new discoveries from stepped-up exploration slowed in the late 2000s. It is used domestically as petrochemical feedstock, in the EOR program, and for generating electricity. Liquefied natural gas (LNG) is produced at three joint venture facilities. Most LNG exports in the 2000s went to the Far East, but the reduced pace of new discoveries has led observers to question whether Oman is overcommitting itself with long-term export obligations.

Few of the many minerals found in the complex rocks of al-Hajar have historically been of much worth commercially; however, ancient copper workings near Suhar, in the northern Batinah, have been reopened and mined for several years, and new deposits found in 2001 should maintain copper output for several years. Also recently exploited are some small coal seams and deposits of chromite, manganese, asbestos, and marble. In the late 2000s, output of ores of chromium, copper, gold, and sulfur increased markedly, and in 2010 Oman opened its first chromite concentration plant close to a mine in Wadi Mahram.[8]

An intriguing future mineral possibility for Oman arises from geoengineering research related to global warming and aimed at literally scrubbing carbon dioxide from the atmosphere and selling it commercially. A study project under way proposes to build "artificial trees"—towers covered with filters containing ultramafic rock, which captures the CO_2 from moving air, then holds it until it is processed and stored.[9] It seems that Oman has the world's largest deposit of this type of rock.

Other Economic Aspects

After the 1970 coup, Sultan Qabus moved deliberately, with guidance from experienced consultants, toward systematic development of Oman. Following a series of five-year plans that began in 1976, he made basic infrastructure the first priority. Then came improved agriculture and fishing, educational and social programs, modern communications, and finally a modest import-substitution industrial program. By the mid-2000s, some 400,000 vehicles of all types traveled on about 10,000 mi/16,000 km of well-surfaced roads. Installed generating capacity was nearly 3.0 gigawatts electric, and gas supplied the plants with more than 80 percent of their fuel needs.[10]

As one major step in industrialization, an industrial estate was established in 1983 in Rusayl, near the airport at Sib (see Fig. 7.3). More than 100 privately owned factories now produce a wide range of basic products for the local market, from car batteries to air-conditioning units. Industrial estates have opened at opposite ends of Oman: one in Suhar, in the northern Batinah, and one in Raysut, west of Salalah. Plans include others at Nazwa, Buraymi, Khasab, and Sur.

Because of the small size of Muscat's picturesque harbor, a modern and more spacious port—Mina Qabus—was constructed in Matrah, a few miles west, in the early 1970s. Development of the south included a new port at Raysut, near Salalah. Now called Port Salalah, it has been expanded to dominate container transit traffic on the Indian Ocean coast, competing with Khor Fakkan and Aden. In 1974, the Sib airport was opened west of Matrah; the only other airport with scheduled service had been Salalah's, but new ones to service tourism have opened recently. The sultanate participates in the regional Gulf Air but in 1993 inaugurated its own airline, Oman Air. At the end of 2009, it was announced that bids for carrying out the preliminary studies for a rail network would soon be sought. Initially, a 122-mi/200-km line connecting Sohar and Muscat is envisioned, but this would be only part of a $60 billion GCC network that could also be extended southwestward through Oman to Yemen.[11]

While pushing modernization aggressively, Oman has taken remarkable care to preserve important archaeological and cultural monuments. Notable are the striking sixteenth-century Portuguese forts overlooking Muscat and Matrah, Muscat's fine old mansions, and the splendid forts of Rustaq (the old capital), Nazwa, and Bahlah (Fig. 16.3). Worthy in themselves, these conservation measures also serve expanding tourism. Excellent hotels cater to tourists, and al-Bustan Palace Hotel, in a spacious setting east of Muscat, is one of the most sumptuous hostelries in the region. The Capital Area has greatly expanded westward toward the airport, with a commercial and banking center in Greater Matrah-Ruwi, residences in Qurum and Madinat Qabus, and ministries and embassies in al-Khuwair. Many of the more affluent residents of the traditional houses in the old "inner cities" of Muscat and Matrah have moved to new upscale suburbs, leaving older sections to poorer families.

The seventh five-year economic plan (2006–2010) illustrates the determination to lessen dependence on petroleum. The goal is for petroleum to be no more than 20 percent of GDP in 2020. It stressed more investment in natural gas–related activities, as mentioned above, as well as industrial and geographic diversification, job creation for Omanis, and growth in the private sector. Of particular importance has been the tourism sector—particularly significant when it is recalled that through the late 1980s, Oman did not even issue tourist visas. By 2009, citizens of some sixty countries could obtain visas upon arrival, and the Tourism Ministry had set an ambitious goal of 12 million visitors by

FIGURE 16.3 Ruins of the splendid old mud fort in Bahlah, in Inner Oman. The structure has been restored since this 1997 photo.

2020.[12] The improvements brought to Omanis by oil revenues can be seen in the sultanate's Human Development Index as computed by the UNDP: In 2007, it ranked 56th among 182 countries and 7th regionally, and since 1990 its HDI had risen by 41 percent on the strength of gains in all three of the index's components—health, education, and per capita income.[13]

Relations

While the sultanate was a British protectorate, most of its relations were handled by Britain. With British withdrawal from the Gulf in 1971, Qabus expanded Oman's international presence. In the West, it retained its friendship with Britain but turned also to the United States, with which it has maintained fairly close ties. Relations with the United States actually date to a treaty of friendship and navigation signed in 1833;

they culminated in a Free Trade Agreement (FTA) negotiated and ratified by each in 2006. Oman joined the World Trade Organization in 2000. It has long supported efforts toward Israeli-Arab peace, and was the only Arab country to support the Camp David accords in 1978 and to maintain diplomatic relations with Egypt afterward. Like Qatar, it allowed Israel to open a trade office in the sultanate, but this was closed in 2000 after the outbreak of the second intifadah.

Facing Iran across the Strait of Hormuz, Oman pursues balance in the uneasy Gulf. It maintains a correct posture with Iran and in the late 2000s was particularly concerned by the growing confrontation between Iran, on the one hand, and the United States and Europe, on the other. It cooperated with the Gulf states, Britain, and the United States during the Iran-Iraq War and quietly but firmly supported the coalition against Iraq in

YEMEN

Long-form official name, anglicized: Republic of Yemen

Official name, transliterated: Al-Jumhuriyah al-Yamaniyah

Form of government: multiparty republic with two legislative houses (Consultative Council and House of Representatives

Area: 214,300 mi²/555,000 km²

Population, 2008: 23,013,000; Literacy (Latest): 53.0%

Ethnic composition (%): Arab 92.8; Somali 3.7; Black African 1.1; Indo-Pakistani 1.0; other 1.4

Religions (%): Muslim 99, of which Sunni 57, Shii 42; others 1

Demography: Life expectancy—60.6 yr (M), 64.5 yr (F); Birthrate (per 1,000)—42.7; Fertility rate—6.49

GDP, 2009: $26.24 billion; purchasing power parity: $58.2 billion; per capita: $2,500

Currency: Yemeni rial, US$1 = 203.3 rials, 1 rial = $0.0048 (March 2010)

Energy reserves: oil— 3.0 bn bbl; natural gas—16.9 tn ft³; coal—nil

Main exports (% of total value, 2006): crude and refined petroleum 91.7; food and live animals 3.9; machinery and apparatus 1.3; transport equipment 1.0

Main imports (% of total value, 2006): crude and refined petroleum 24.8; food and live animals 19.2; machinery and apparatus 13.7; base and fabricated metals 10.2; transport equipment 9.3

Capital city: Sana 2,006,619; other major cities: Aden 588,938; Taizz 466,968; Hudaydah 409,994; Ibb 212,992; Mukalla 182,478

1990–1991, allowing Britain and the United States use of Masirah Island. It grounds much of its moderate foreign policy on its membership in the GCC; it belongs to the Arab League, the Organization of the Islamic Conference, and the Nonaligned Movement, and continues a centuries-long friendship with India. Long cordial relations with the UAE have become more so with the delineation of their mutual border in 2003. It has drawn increasingly close to Saudi Arabia and has negotiated de jure status of its long-uncertain boundaries with its larger neighbor and with Yemen as well.[14] At the end of the decade, a growing concern was the increase in piracy in the Indian Ocean south of Oman and Yemen and east of Somalia. This has already increased insurance costs for shipping to and from ports near this area (see Chap. 8).

YEMEN

The Republic of Yemen (ROY) is the most recent state to appear in the Middle East, with the contemporary state emerging in 1990 with the fusion of the Yemen Arab Republic (YAR—North Yemen) and the People's Democratic Republic of Yemen (PDRY—South Yemen).[15] The ROY is second largest in area and population on the Arabian Peninsula. Indeed, its population exceeds the number of indigenous Saudi Arabs.

Yemen occupies the general area of classical Arabia Felix (Fortunate Arabia), the southwest corner of the Arabian Peninsula. Like Oman, it has been semi-isolated, with a tenuous, millennia-old link between the northwest of the country and both the coastal plain and the upper plateau. With connections to Africa across the Red Sea and to Indian Ocean rimlands from its south coast, it has evolved a distinctive and interesting culture, including remarkable architecture.

The PDRY was the poorest Middle East country and, as a radical client of the former Soviet Union, was virtually a pariah state in the region; the YAR was the second-poorest country and was ambivalent in its East-West relations. United Yemen remains poorest in the region. Indeed, unification left many problems unsolved and created new ones. However, it had many benefits: It reduced many redundant expenses, numerous inter-Yemeni conflicts (such as control over Karaman Island and Perim Island), and other obstacles to economic and social development.

Republican Yemen started at a low level and still has a long way to go—with limited capital—to emerge from grinding poverty. Petroleum discoveries raised cautious optimism, but actual development has been moderate. The challenges are obvious: extraordinarily rugged topography, limiting communications; weak government control and insecurity in many areas, even growth of terrorist activity and training; poor integration among half a dozen geopolitical cores; endemic tribal rivalry; alarmingly high population growth rate; and increasingly serious water shortages. But Yemeni living standards have improved in the past two decades, as can be seen from the UNDP's Human Development Index. Yemen's HDI has risen steadily by more than 150 percent from the first time it was computed for the united republic; the HDI's components representing both health and education registered notable gains. Still, in the 2009 report, it ranks last in the region and 140th among the 182 coun-

tries studied (lack of reliable data precluded including Iraq).[16]

Another measure, the Global Hunger Index (GHI, published annually by the International Food Policy Research Institute) illustrates Yemen's problems; it is a simple average of three key indicators: the percentage of the undernourished in the population, the percentage of underweight children under age five, and the mortality rate of under-five children. Any GHI above 10.0 indicates a serious problem; alone in the region above this level, Yemen's GHI in 2009 was 27.0, down only slightly from 30.7 in 1990, and ranking 11th worst of 121 lower-income countries considered.[17] The FAO estimates that from the early 1990s to the mid-2000s, the percentage of undernourished Yemenis in the population rose from 30 to 32 percent—to a total of 6.7 million people—and that average caloric intake per capita is only about 65 percent of what it is in the neighboring states.[18]

Five Regions

Yemen extends from the Omani border on the east along the southern peninsula coast, around the corner at the strategic Bab el-Mandeb, and northward along the Red Sea to Saudi Arabia. With greatly contrasting rocks and rock structures, as well as sharp variations in relief, its dramatically rugged volcanic landscapes (including craters of extinct volcanoes as in Aden) vary greatly from the flat-lying limestones of the Hadramawt Plateau. Most spectacular is the steep but highly dissected escarpment towering over the Tihamah. Circled numbers on Map 16.2 show the five geographic regions.

[1] *Tihamah.* The Red Sea coastal plain, al-Tihamah, is part of the coastal fringe along the western edge of the peninsula. Averaging some 40 mi/65 km wide and sandy-gravelly for most of its length, it extends 325 mi/523 km from the Saudi border to the Bab el-Mandeb. Climatically a desert, the extremely

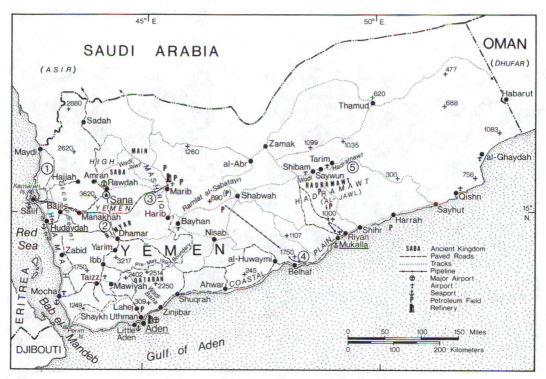

MAP 16.2 General and economic map of the Republic of Yemen. Note former boundary between North Yemen and South Yemen. Circled numbers indicate regions discussed in the text.

hot and humid Tihamah is traversed by large wadis with heavy runoff after spring and fall monsoon rains on the high escarpment. The broad wadi bottoms and alluvial fans are cultivated for cotton, melons, bananas, papayas, and similar crops; underground water in the wadi gravels is tapped for domestic use and irrigation. Smaller settlements are distinctly African in appearance, with round dwellings built of thatch and populations of Ethiopians and Sudanese from across the Red Sea. Formerly isolated from the rest of Yemen, Tihama now connects two highways with the Highlands. The centuries-old port of Mocha and the growing modern port and airport of Hudaydah have given the coastal plain new vitality, as has the oil-export facility at Salif.

[2] Central Highlands. From the Tihamah, a spectacular escarpment rises abruptly and steeply through block-faulted and ruggedly eroded topography to plateaus and shallow, flat-floored basins in the Central Highlands. Elevations commonly exceed 7,000 ft/2,135 m; southwest of Sana, a summit only 80 mi/130 km from the coast reaches 11,877 ft/3,620 m. The west-southwest-facing slopes intercept monsoon winds in April–May and August for 20–35 in/500–900 mm of orographically enhanced rainfall; more than 40 in/1,000 mm falls on the southern highlands around Ibb. The escarpment is almost vertical in places, but elsewhere slopes permit terraced agriculture (see Fig. 16.4), making this scenic subregion Yemen's most productive, with surprisingly high population.

The High Yemen varies in width from 40 to 75 mi/65 to 120 km. It is an extended plateau from the northern border to the former boundary of the two Yemens. Broken toward both ends, irregular mountain masses rise above it near Sana and in the south. The

FIGURE 16.4 Typical village and terraced agriculture in the ruggedly dissected escarpment of western Yemen. Terracing is one effort to utilize steep slopes where rainfall is adequate for crops.

relatively dense population concentrates in and around Sana, capital and largest city of united Yemen. With the highest elevation of any Middle East capital—7,250 ft/2,210 m—it has moderate temperatures with a large diurnal range and cool nights year-round. More accessible and better known than the distinctive architecture of the Wadi Hadramawt (see [5] below) is the building and ornamental style well preserved in Sana's walled core, a World Heritage site (Fig. 16.5). Whitewashed surrounds of windows and doors give a unique character to multistory houses of basalt dimension stone or mud.

Noteworthy towns are population nodes along the backbone, all of them with the distinctive architectural styles and most with picturesque old walls, towers, forts, and mosques. From north to south, they include Sadah (center of rebel activity in 2009–2010), with heavy road traffic to Saudi Arabia in normal times; Amran, with picturesque walls; Sana, anchoring the center; Dhamar, an old Himyaric city and agricultural center; Yarim near a breathtaking pass; Ibb, an especially scenic old city, now a major development center; and Taizz, the former capital, clinging to a rugged volcanic slope. Indeed, evidence of volcanism is rarely out of sight anywhere on the plateau. Much of the highland itself is built up of successive lava flows, and northward from Sana extends a striking series of cinder cones. This is the southern end, in Arabia, of vulcanism related to the tectonic rifting that extends from East Africa up the Red Sea trough and Jordan Valley well into northwestern Syria (see Chap. 2).

From the plateau summit, the eastern escarpment descends to the interior less steeply and with much less relief than on the western escarpment. It steps down from more than 7,000 ft/2,135 m to the eastern desert at a

FIGURE 16.5 View of traditional central Yemen buildings just inside the Bab al-Yemen of the Old City of Sana with their unique architectural styles. Note the painted (whitewashed) surrounds of the windows. The Old City of the capital has been declared a World Heritage Site by UNESCO.

general level of 3,300 ft/1,000 m. Lying in the rain shadow of the Central Highlands, it contrasts with the west and is dry and sunny. It also contrasts lithologically and primarily displays dissected Jurassic and Cretaceous sedimentary strata—mostly limestones—as opposed to the lava flows that predominate on the west. Like the vegetation, population is sparse.

[3] Mashriq. Toward the bottom of the escarpment, volcanic forms reappear, and then both the sedimentary layers and the lavas lose themselves under the sands of the Rub al-Khali; locally, the dune fields are known as the Ramlat al-Sabatayn. This region, the Mashriq ("the east"—not to be confused with the same term used for the entire eastern Arab world), was well developed 3,000–1,500 years ago, when Marib was on the Incense Trail during a more pluvial period and the Sabaeans maintained the famed Marib Dam system. It retained floodwaters in a large wadi, permitting intensive irrigation. Shifts in trade patterns, collapse of the main dam, and declining Sabaean vigor ended this civilization in the sixth century; the area was isolated and little known during the following millennium. Excavations in the 1950s revealed temples from Marib's heyday, but it was the discovery of substantial oil fields in the early 1980s that opened the Mashriq once again. A new Marib Dam now impounds floodwaters; extensive irrigation has created a green oasis in the otherwise barren landscape.

[4] Indian Ocean Coastal Plain. The coastal plain along the Indian Ocean is separated from Tihamah by volcanic masses at Aden and the right-angle intersection of two sets of ocean-spreading rifts (see Chap. 2, especially Map 2.2). It is a generally flat, sandy coastal strip varying from 5 to 10 mi/8 to 16 km in

width. Reddish black volcanic hills—some actual craters—and ragged, barren masses of lava frequently rise above and interrupt the plain, overlooking fishing villages that fringe the shore. Occasional wadis cross the plain, bringing runoff from the inland hills; along them are irrigated, cultivated plots. The entire coast formerly supported only occasional villages and a small port at Mukalla. Development since 1985 has stimulated growth along the coast, especially in Bir Ali, west of Mukalla and terminus of the pipeline from the Shabwah fields; Balhaf, west of Bir Ali, with a multibillion-dollar LNG plant; Riyan, east of Mukalla, the regional airport; Shihr, east of Riyan and terminus of the pipeline from the Masila fields; and in Mukalla itself.

With its complex of harbors created by its location on one side of an old volcanic crater, Aden has been a port and an entrepôt for centuries. The modern city's sections—Crater, Maala, Khormaksar, Steamer Point, Tawahi, and Little Aden with its refinery—play hide-and-seek with one another behind dark, barren, pockmarked volcanic masses. Nearly 300 mi/480 km to the east, Mukalla has been an important port, serving the Wadi Hadramawt, with which it is connected by a well-surfaced road up and over the intervening plateau. Facilities have been expanded and upgraded since the 1990s. The large island of Socotra, 215 mi/346 km off the coast (not included on Map 16.2, but see Map 2.1), is of particular interest: A separate fragment formed during the tectonic separation of Arabia from Africa, it displays a biological complex differentiated from the mainland since Tertiary times.[19]

[5] *Hadramawt.* Stretching over most of eastern Yemen inland from the coastal plain is the extensive Hadramawt, including several plateaus and the great flat-floored valley famed as the Wadi Hadramawt. Lying between the wadi and the coastal plain is the Jawl plateau, a broad tableland of flat-lying,

reddish brown limestones, dissected by wadis from a few feet to 200–500 ft/60–150 m deep. They were eroded mostly during earlier pluvial periods, seeming oversized for the water now being drained. The Jawl flats lie at 3,300 ft/1,000 m; on the south, they fall abruptly to the coastal plain 10–12 mi/16–20 km back from the shore, and on the north they drop vertically to the Wadi Hadramawt.

After the valley was initially eroded, silt, sand, and gravel partially filled the wadi bottom, giving it a flat floor that has been irrigated and cultivated along its course for thousands of years. Irrigation supports scores of small villages and several towns. Neighboring Shibam, Saywun (locally Sayoun), and Tarim are remarkable settlements with mud-brick architectural treasures constructed by local builders (see Saywun palace, Fig. 16.6, *top*). Centuries-old "skyscraper" mud-brick houses in Shibam were added to the UNESCO World Heritage list in 1982 (Fig. 16.6, *bottom*). Although rare, devastating floods can play havoc with the mud structures, as happened in 1989.

Wadi Hadramawt was little known even when it was theoretically accessible under the British; it was virtually a closed area under the PDRY. As a result, it retained its special character, unique architecture, distinctive ethnic mix, and social and religious conservatism. Now opened to tourism, modernization seems inevitable. It customarily sent young men to Malaysia, Indonesia, and East Africa to work for and with fellow Hadramis established there. Most retired to the wadi, many of them wealthy, building mansions in a mixed Hadrami-Malay-Javanese style. Many such handsome homes contribute to the special character of the town of Tarim.

Historical Sketch

During the first millennium BCE up until the sixth century CE, southwestern Arabia saw many kingdoms: Saba (Sheba), with the famous dam at its capital of Marib; Main

FIGURE 16.6 Remarkable mud architecture in the Wadi Hadramawt, eastern Yemen: palace of the former sultan of Kathiri (*top*), in Saywun (Sayoun), built entirely of mud that has been painted white, and western facade of the all-mud city of Shibam (*bottom*). These unique mud "skyscrapers" earned Shibam inclusion on the UNESCO World Heritage list in 1982.

(Minaea), farther north; Himyar, still flourishing into the sixth century, south of Saba; Qataban, southeast of Himyar; and Hadramawt, to the east. All (see Map 16.2) thrived on the flourishing and long-lived transit trade. Islam swept the region during the time of Muhammad and remains virtually the only religion. Local rulers, Ethiopians, Persians, Muslim empires, Egyptians, Portuguese, and Ottoman Turks controlled part or all of the area before the British took Aden in 1839[20] and gradually extended control up the wadis and across the plateaus. Through 1990, the south and the High Yemen then developed separately.

The South.   As with its Gulf interests, Britain's relations with local rulers north of Aden and in the Hadramawt were overseen from India, not directly from London. In the southern hinterland, a patchwork of as many as twenty-one shaykhdoms and sultanates composed the Western Aden Protectorate, with another six or so in the Eastern Aden Protectorate of Hadramawt. Aden and its environs became a crown colony in 1937. This three-way pattern continued until the late 1950s, as Britain prepared to withdraw from the area.

The PDRY evolved through a complicated series of political and name changes. Preparatory to its leaving the region, Britain cajoled the traditional leaders into merging in a loose—and weak—Federation of Arab Amirates of the South in 1959, but radical nationalist groups caused the federation to collapse. After independence in 1967, rival groups contended for domination in South Yemen in a costly civil war. Renamed the People's Republic of South Yemen, the new state became more radical and reemerged as the PDRY, heavily influenced by the Soviet Union and China. Internally, it adopted regionally incongruous, radically centralized control over political and social structures. Partly reflecting the centuries-old mosaic of tribal loyalties tied to tiny quasi-independent polities, bitter

enmities fueled a series of attempted coups. Although it pursued some progressive paths unique within the region (particularly with regard to women's rights), development was constrained by poverty and the gradual shrinkage of external assistance, and it increasingly became isolated from its neighbors.

The North.   The historical evolution of the north followed a quite different course over the past two millennia. Although both north and south grew wealthy from early trade between Aden and the Levant, particularly in frankincense and myrrh, the north had better climate and soil, and hence it had a more developed agriculture and a larger population.

Highland Yemenis embraced Islam in the mid-seventh century, serving in Muslim armies from North Africa to Central Asia. In 897, having been under control of the Hijaz, Damascus, and Baghdad, the High Yemen came under the rule of a descendant of Zayd, great-grandson of Ali. For most of the next 1,100 years, until 1962, a Shii Zaydi[21] dynasty ruled all or part of the area as imams. At times in the Middle Ages, the region was fragmented into scores of petty shaykhdoms, sultanates, and kingdoms perched on mountainsides or peaks. Ottoman Turks exercised varying degrees of suzerainty with full Turkish occupation from 1872 to 1918. Elevated and protected contemporary villages, though picturesque and even spectacular in today's landscape, reflect long periods of disorder and insecurity (see Figs. 4.11, 5.5, and 16.4). Tribal feuds and disputes over lands, water, and political influence have persisted into the new century.

Two very conservative Zaydi imams, Yahya (1904–1948) and Ahmad (1948–1962), resisted outside influence, but Arab nationalism, especially of the Nasserist variety, increasingly appealed to many Yemenis. Trying to forestall this, Ahmad led the country into a loose and basically meaningless link to Egypt and Syria[22] in 1958. But when Ahmad died in 1962,

Nasserist army officers opposed the succession of his son Badr and, with Egyptian support, declared the Yemen Arab Republic (YAR).

Revolutionary republican forces, mainly from the Sunni Shafei population south of Sana, were joined by thousands of Egyptian troops in a civil war against Badr's forces. Royalists, primarily tribesmen and other Zaydi groups, were in turn aided by Saudi Arabia[23] and Jordan. More than 200,000 were killed as war dragged on until 1969, although Nasser withdrew his forces in 1967. Significantly, in the mid-1960s the political capital was shifted back from Taizz, in the southern plateau, to Sana, in the more neutral center, where the capital had been before 1948.

In 1971, the YAR's first nationwide elections marked reconciliation between republicans and royalists. During the twenty following years, it walked tightropes internally, externally, and with the "other Yemen." With moderately large capital transfers and technical assistance from many countries—including Saudi Arabia, the United States, China, Britain, the Soviet Union, and Kuwait—it built basic infrastructure, especially a highway net, that moved it beyond the level of the PDRY and stood it in good stead when development accelerated in the 1980s.

Republic of Yemen

Yemen to the north and Aden and the Hadramawt to the south and east have opposed and resisted control by the other for centuries. After the north declared itself a republic in 1962 and the British left an independent south in 1967, the two states outwardly declared for unity but in reality sparred for dominance, with the north much more populous[24] and the south much more radical politically. They engaged in brief but savage bilateral warfare in 1972 and 1976, further wasting both human and financial resources already depleted by a decade of fighting in both states.

The PDRY's Marxist ideology promoted secularization, and "progressivism"—espe-

cially in Greater Aden—altered the traditional status of religion, social classes, women (less so in the Hadramawt), education, and, of course, government. The influence of the Soviet Union, China, and North Korea increased as that of the West plummeted. Revolution brought sharp departures to the YAR from imamate days, but many conservative customs remained. It sought political nonalignment and took aid from all quarters. A higher percentage of women remained veiled there than in the PDRY.

Despite the obvious advantages of unity, practical obstacles remained, especially merging scores of disparate elements with their respective ambitions, ideologies, and traditions. After long discussions, preparation of a draft constitution, and votes in each parliament, the two united in May 1990, creating the Republic of Yemen.[25] Inevitably, compromises and adjustments were necessary. Some obstacles were external: Shortly after unification, the ROY made the costly decision not to condemn Iraq's invasion of Kuwait. Many donors withdrew support, and Saudi Arabia and other Gulf states expelled more than 800,000 Yemeni guest workers; the expellees returned home to 40 percent unemployment. Sizable numbers still work abroad, many illegally in Saudi Arabia; in the late 2000s, annual remittances were estimated to be about $1.3 billion or about 7 percent of GDP; this figure is likely understated.

With heightened friction, the south tried to withdraw from the union, and civil war raged from May to July 1994. The secessionists were defeated, the unified republic was restored—temporarily stronger than before—and it gradually emerged from its near-pariah status. A series of generally free and fair elections with universal adult suffrage began with multiparty parliamentary polling in 1997 and the first direct presidential election in 1999. These were followed by further elections in 2003 (parliamentary, returning two women to the lower house) and 2006 (presidential).

With internal strife mounting in the late 2000s, the parliamentary election scheduled for April 2009 was postponed until 2011 at almost the last minute. The announced reason was the need for a thorough review of election procedures, but regret at the delay was quickly expressed by the U.S. State Department.

Yemen's situation at the end of the 2000s was rather precarious.[26] Weak central government control means that large parts of the countryside offer dissident and even terrorist groups the opportunity to thrive. Its long and mostly unpatrolled land border and coastline make penetration by outside forces fairly easy. Secessionist sentiment has grown considerably in the former PDRY as southerners have increasingly complained of discrimination against them by the more numerous and conservative northerners. Across the narrow Bab el-Mandeb is Somalia, essentially without a government since 1991; Yemen continues its open-door policy for Somali refugees. Offshore is the notorious hunting ground of Somali pirates and smugglers, continuing to defy the stepped-up policing efforts of naval forces from the United States, Europe, and the Far East. In September 2008, a car-bomb attack on the American Embassy compound in Sana killed nineteen people; at the close of the decade, the United States was increasing support for the ROY's domestic antiterrorist efforts.[27]

There is a long history of friction between tribal/local elements and the government, but a dispute that began in 2004 in Sadah province in the northernmost part of Yemen had taken on international dimensions by the end of the decade. A Shii group, Shabab al-Mumineen (Believing Youth), led by Hussein al-Houthi, rebelled against perceived pro-Sunni and secularist tendencies of the ROY regime. Al-Houthi was killed by government forces in 2005, but the group continued its struggles. The ROY (supported by Saudi Arabia) accused Iran of supporting the rebels and in October 2009 claimed

to have intercepted a ship carrying Iranian weapons bound for the al-Houthis.[28] By the end of that year, it was estimated that as many as 175,000 civilians had fled the area of the fighting. A fragile truce was declared in early 2010.

The annual survey conducted by *Foreign Policy* and the Fund for Peace in 2009 placed Yemen high on its list of "failed states"—eighteenth, just ahead of North Korea.[29] In the region, only war-ravaged Iraq was rated in worse condition. Particularly troubling was the potential for the chaos in nearby Somalia—with two decades as a failed state—to boil over into Yemen, where more than 150,000 Somalis are registered with UNHCR as refugees and even more are in the country illegally.

The Yemenis

The population is estimated to be more than 23 million, with 83 percent in the north and a high growth rate everywhere. With the region's highest total fertility rate—an estimated 5.94, the number of children an average women will have—the population is on track to double in fewer than twenty years. The Sana area has the greatest concentration of inhabitants, the Aden area the second largest, and Taizz and Hudaydah the third and fourth largest. Ethnic uniformity is high: Yemeni Arabs are the overwhelming majority, but biological differences and descent characteristics differ appreciably across regions. For example, an upper-class inhabitant of Sana is shorter with lighter skin than an upper-class Hadrami. Many Hadramis are descended from dark-skinned migrants from the subcontinent; others have Arab blood mixed with Malay-Indonesian and East African strains. Many villagers in Tihamah are of black African descent. Accents and dialects may vary, but the mother tongue of nearly all Yemenis is Arabic. Tribal affiliations are paramount in the north and east. The remaining Bedouin are found primarily in the

Mashriq and the Jawl, and Bedouin tradition has even less influence than in the past.

A sizable minority of Jews once lived in the cities—especially Sana, Sadah, and Aden—some groups for more than 2,500 years. According to tradition, they came in several waves and were an integral part of Yemeni life. In 1949–1950, about 50,000 were airlifted to Israel on special flights, and only a few hundred remained in the country. In the late 2000s, regional events made this remnant's situation precarious; an effort to bring them to the United States by American Jewish groups was denounced by an official of the Jewish Agency in Israel who claimed that if they left Yemen, they should only go to Israel.[30]

Relative ethnic uniformity is partly offset by persistent tribal distinctions and conflicts (which, however, are slowly diminishing); by sectarian division of the north into two main areas—dominated by Zaydi Shii in the northern two-thirds and Shafei[31] Sunni south of Dhamar; and among political groupings in the south. The greater power in the highlands has traditionally been wielded by the tribally conscious Zaydi, from whom came the ruling imams; but the Sunni, with some ties to the south, have gained strength under the republican regimes. Always powerful, tribal leaders in the north periodically reassert their prowess, sometimes in outright rebellion, to remind the government of their needs and aspirations. Tribes have often kidnapped tourists or oil-company representatives to reinforce demands for government funds and projects—roads, housing, irrigation, vehicles, and similar items. Victims have rarely been harmed, although botched rescue attempts in 1998 and 2000 resulted in five deaths.[32]

The western escarpment and the Central Highlands exhibit a surprisingly dense pattern of villages distributed over landscapes that would appear to limit settlement. Although only a small percentage of the Yemenis continue to be nomadic, less than one-quarter of the population is urban. The half-dozen cities are growing rapidly, as urban pull attracts job seekers from the more impoverished rural areas. Another seventy towns have more than 2,000 inhabitants each. Yemen as a country of villagers is seen in the detailed data for the former YAR, which are also generally applicable to the south and are still broadly relevant: 11,000 villages had 100 to 500 inhabitants, and an astonishing 41,000 hamlets had fewer than 100 residents. This pattern of settlement is consistent with the topographic and climatic environments, which offer few sites for extensive settlement with adjacent cultivable area supporting agriculture. Further limiting settlement size was the traditional siting in medieval times of fortress-type villages on peaks and ridges for protection during the frequent local wars (see Fig. 16.4).

Like the landforms, historical evolution, and traditional architecture, Yemeni dress is distinctive. Unlike virtually all other Arabs, males wear a calf-length, patterned wraparound skirt (*lungi* or *futah*, or, in the Wadi Hadramawt, where Malay-Indonesian influence is considerable, *sarong*); a colorful turban headdress similar to the Omanis' but wrapped differently; and, often, a folded shoulder shawl, especially in the higher elevations where temperatures can suddenly drop below comfort levels. More than anywhere else in Arabia, men also traditionally wear a *janbiyah*, a curved dagger in a decorated scabbard, like the Omani *khanjar*. Western wear is gradually becoming more common, as it is in most of the Middle East. Female attire is similar to that in southwestern Saudi Arabia.

A particularly detrimental social problem, especially among Highland Yemenis, is the daily pastime of chewing qat (*Catha edulis*), a leafy shrub containing cathinone, a natural chemical similar to amphetamine. About 60 percent of men—and 20 percent of women—of all social classes participate in this deeply rooted ritual that is a socially accepted and prevalent custom. The consumer packs several leaves inside one cheek in early afternoon, sucking on the wad for two or three hours; lethargy generally ensues. Long-term effects are not clearly understood, but the reduced productivity during the *qat*-chewing period slows economic progress. The leaves must be picked fresh daily and rushed to the nearest *suq*, where they are quite expensive, especially those of premium quality. A daily supply can absorb one-third of a worker's earnings. The *qat*-chewing routine is receiving mounting criticism from national leaders who denounce it as destructive of both soil and society.

Emerging Economy

The more populous north has historically possessed the greater agricultural potential—recent findings indicate that irrigated farming in the Dhamar area dates from before 2500 BCE. In the south, Aden and its environs have been the overwhelming focus of economic activity for centuries. Its primary asset has been Aden's excellent harbor and its location at the junction of land and sea routes to and from several directions. The port gained particular primacy after Britain took control in 1839 and made it the regional coaling station for the increasing number of steamships plying the Indian Ocean.

Aden's importance was greatly enhanced when the Suez Canal opened in 1869, when it became the midway port of call for ships sailing between the Mediterranean and India and points east. When oil replaced coal to fuel steamships, Aden served as a key oil-bunkering port. Increasing regional production of petroleum added to the importance of routes passing Aden; Britain constructed a major refinery in 1954 on the western arm of the harbor. By the late 1950s, it was one of the world's busiest ports, with as many as 250,000 transit passengers annually generating a booming trade in the duty-free shops.

Ten years later, it was languishing; the Suez Canal was closed and civil conflict besieged the city. The port served only local interests during the PDRY years; it did not revive until unified Yemen designated Aden the "economic capital" of the ROY (Fig. 16.7).

More rural, and with less European influence before 1970, northern Yemen desperately needed, and sought, large-scale aid abroad; as a result, it received substantial help from its neighbors and from both the West and the Communist world. The Central Planning Organization coordinated foreign aid, focusing first on infrastructure, then on social services, public administration, and agriculture. With relations between Yemen and Saudi Arabia variable, aid from the Saudis was sometimes uncertain but in some years exceeded $100 million. U.S. assistance was modest, but it built Yemen's first modern highway up the escarpment. Chinese, British, Dutch, German, Swiss, Soviet, and especially UN technical assistance combined to endow northern Yemen with a badly needed basic network of paved highways, planned urban expansion, a number of small industries, and fair educational and health systems. China built a large cotton textile mill near Sana and, with Chinese labor, constructed the vital and scenic surfaced highway from Hudaydah up the escarpment to Sana, as well as roads in the south.

Much of the economic growth after 1975, especially in the north, was fueled by remittances from more than a million Yemenis working abroad, mainly in Saudi Arabia. Employment, salaries, and remittances rise and fall with oil prices. With union of the north and south approaching, several donors increased their assistance to encourage this beneficial step, but the newly unified republic's reaction to the 1990–1991 Gulf crisis prompted the economic penalties mentioned earlier.

Two sectors deserve special attention: agriculture, the traditional mainstay now chal-

FIGURE 16.7 Port of Aden, "economic capital" of Yemen. The Aden harbor is nestled in a breached volcanic crater.

lenged by water shortages, and oil, lately the driving force but a limited resource.

Agriculture. Highland Yemen and Tihamah have been overwhelmingly agricultural. Well into the 1950s, agriculture engaged 90 percent of the economically active population; it still engages some two-thirds in the 2000s, by far the region's highest level (see Table 7.1). Once self-sufficient in food, Yemen now imports large amounts of wheat, rice, and animal feed. Extensive rainfed agriculture is based on the centuries-long practice of terracing the slopes—thus conserving soil (virtually creating it in some ways) and maximizing use of seasonal rains (see Fig. 16.4). The degree of slope that has been terraced and the extent of the terraces are astonishing in parts of the escarpment. The terraces must be carefully maintained, especially after heavy rains, and the exodus of so many young men from the terraced farms is cause for concern.

More active irrigation is necessary in Tihamah, the south, and the extraordinary Wadi Hadramawt.

In addition to the expected crops of wheat, barley, maize, grapes, several fruits, and various vegetables, Yemen produces cotton and dates on the coastal plains and in the Wadi Hadramawt. It also produces three crops that are unusual among Middle East countries: sorghum (*durrah*), coffee, and *qat*. *Durrah* is especially well adapted to the double monsoon and formerly occupied up to three-fourths of the cropland. Yemen held a virtual world monopoly on coffee during the period 1500–1775, giving it appreciable local wealth. For many decades, most coffee was exported from the Red Sea port of Mocha—hence the popular name for coffee. Although coffee remains a premium product, output of less than 3,000 mt is negligible on the world market, and production continues to decline.

FIGURE 16.8 Young Yemeni roadside salesmen north of Aden offering fruits, vegetables, and *qat* to passersby. Note mixture of traditional and western clothing.

Unfortunately, coffee and *qat* have the same ecological demands; coffee trees have been uprooted on the high terraces of the western escarpment, replaced by *qat* bushes. Coffee requires several years to reach optimum yield, and there is only one crop a year. *Qat* leaves are produced in marketable amounts in a few months, and there is a high-value crop every day (Fig. 16.8), averaging twenty times the annual income of coffee.[33] Thus, Yemen loses the value of an export while bearing the social and economic costs linked to *qat*. Food crops are also being replaced by *qat*, so Yemen is becoming less and less able to feed itself. The country's water problems are exacerbated by the *qat* cultivators—it has been estimated that their illegal wells use 40 percent of the available water in Sana's water basin.[34] Agriculture in the 2000s has been responsible for an estimated 10 percent of GDP, although its share may actually be higher—good statistics about *qat* production and value are lacking. The loss

of land to *qat* also helps to explain why Yemen alone among the countries in the region showed a decline (about 12.5 percent) in food production per capita from the early 1960s to the mid-2000s.[35]

Water Resources. Yemen's renewable water resources of 1 mi³/4.1 km³ per year are inadequate for the needs of its population, and, unlike the even more water-deficit Gulf states, it does not have the financial capacity to supplement supply with large-scale desalination. Per capita freshwater availability—4,767.5 ft³/135 m³ per year—is only one-tenth the average across this region characterized by aridity.[36] The portion of this amount that is renewable (i.e., not mined or fossil water) is even more dire—3,235 ft³/91.6 m³ in 2008.[37] No perennial streams enter or rise in Yemen, so the unsustainable rates of groundwater withdrawal—more than 150 percent of replacement—are depleting the country's endowment.

Spate irrigation—the capture of flash floods resulting from unpredictable precipitation—has traditionally supported complex systems of terracing and runoff management. Given the scarcity of the resource, social organization supported a communal framework of rules governing access and control of water. Changes in technology, such as deep wells, not only have led to greater privatization of water resources but also mean that fewer landholders, with less social accountability, have access rights. With increased demand for water by *qat* cultivators, as mentioned earlier, and rapid population growth, Yemen is seeing both growing shortages and more conflict over access.

Agriculture accounts for about 90 percent of freshwater withdrawals; its contribution to GDP may be as high as 15 percent if the high cash value (but not the probably higher social costs) of *qat* is taken into consideration. The market distortion introduced by *qat* cultivation is accompanied by high demand for water for the crop. What is used from the spate by upstream growers obviously does not reach downstream farmers; what it takes from aquifers is not available for other crops or urban consumers. The result has been increasing local and interregional disputes over available supplies.

Water-distribution networks reach only 56 percent of city dwellers and 45 percent of rural residents, and sanitation provision is even lower—31 percent in urban areas, 21 percent in the countryside. Drinking-water provision is low, and attempts to improve the situation have led to problems. For example, in the 1990s, the government tried to increase Sana's supply by transferring water from al-Haima wadi, an agricultural area—wells there dried up, and crops failed. A similar attempt to provide Taizz with water diverted from Habir sparked armed conflict in the latter area. Plans to enhance storage with dams in al-Mahweet and Khawlan al-Tiyal intensified competition between potential benefici-

aries. In some tribal areas—like the Saada region, the Houthi stronghold—traditional leaders lost support when they were seen to have garnered the largest shares of water and the revenues thus generated.

Oil. With Yemen's GDP under pressure with reduced remittances and foreign aid, oil finds in the Mashriq and the adjacent Shabwah area of the south came at a particularly auspicious period. In the former YAR, the first strike came on July 4, 1984, in the Alif field in the Marib–al-Jawf Basin 37 mi/60 km east-northeast of the town of Marib in the Mashriq. The discovery was made by the Hunt Oil Company, a U.S. firm, which later, as Yemen Hunt Oil Company, became the operator of a production-sharing agreement with participation by Exxon and a Korean consortium. During the same period, exploration near Shabwah on the PDRY side of the border was under way by Soviet technicians, who were later joined by other companies and then replaced by an Arab group.

Marib production quickly reached 175,000 bpd, by which time a small 10,000 bpd refinery was in operation near the Alif field; meanwhile, a 24–26-in/61–64-cm pipeline with a capacity of 225,000 bpd was completed to Salif on the Red Sea, a total of 263 mi/423 km (see Map 16.2). Further exploration in the Mashriq led to the discovery of several new fields, some yielding significant amounts of nonassociated gas. Farther southeast, in the Ayad and Amal fields near Shabwah, early limited production increased after the completion in 1991 of a 20-in/51-cm pipeline to the small port of Bir Ali on the Gulf of Aden, 130 mi/210 km distant.

In the early 1990s, Canadian Occidental (Canoxy) discovered new fields in the Masila area. With completion of a 93-mi/150-km pipeline to Shihr in 1993, with a capacity of 300,000 bpd, the Masila fields became Yemen's most productive. A score of oil companies were exploring in the late 1990s under production-sharing agreements (PSAs). Production curves suggest that Marib output peaked in 1995 and that overall production may well have peaked (at 420,000 bpd) in 2003 unless there are significant new finds. Output dropped below 300,000 bpd by 2009.[38] Yemen's two refineries, already mentioned, have capacities of 120,000 bpd (Aden) and 10,000 bpd (Marib). Damaged during the 1994 civil war, the aging Aden plant has been upgraded to restore its design capacity of 170,000 bpd throughput. A third refinery is tentatively planned for Ras Isa (Salif), north of Hudaydah, the terminus of the Marib-Salif pipeline.[39]

Like its neighbors, Yemen is focusing its hydrocarbon hopes on nonassociated gas, which totals 16.9 trillion ft³/0.5 trillion m³ in the Marib Basin. A gas pipeline has been laid to a large joint-venture liquefied natural gas plant on the Gulf of Aden coast at Balhaf, and production was to begin in 2009. Competing with plants in neighboring countries, the multibillion-dollar venture, exporting to the United States and Asia, is the largest single industrial project. Natural gas is also critical in plans to increase generation of electricity, available in the mid-2000s to only about 40 percent of the population and at that time entirely fueled by oil.[40] The government has recently admitted failure to keep up with increasing demand and announced a $2.9 billion system expansion plan for 2009–2012 with incentives to attract private investment.[41] On a per capita basis, Yemenis use far less electricity annually than the citizens of any other regional country, and only about 1.5 percent of what Americans use.

Other Sectors. Finally, fishing is important for food and income along both seacoasts; Hudaydah has good processing facilities. Air transportation has opened Yemen's links with the world more than anything else. International airports operate in Sana, Taizz, Hudaydah, and Aden; they urgently need up-

grading with adequate navigational aids. Much of the infrastructure also needs improvement to sustain development. Increased tourism, for example, would boost the economy considerably. After its neighbors began to implement plans in the late 2000s to build or expand railway networks, the ROY announced it would undertake a feasibility study for a 1,560-mi/2,000-km coastal line running from the Omani to the Saudi border, connecting with rail systems in those countries and passing through Aden.[42] Foreign investment in nonhydrocarbon sectors is not helped by excessive government red tape or by the reputation for corruption: In 2009, the ratings group Transparency International placed Yemen far down on its list—154th out of 180 countries—ahead of only Iran and Iraq in the region.[43]

Relations

Unification eliminated the most persistent problems in foreign relations for both Yemens—those with each other—and the collapse of communism provided a more salutary climate for the merger. The unfortunate retribution that some of its financial supporters exacted from the state after 1990 gradually subsided, but now the republic critically needs external capital transfers. When oil prices are high as in 2003–2004 and especially 2008, Yemen's income rises without obviating its reliance on generous aid. The government's adoption in 2006 of a reform program designed to bolster the economy's non-oil sectors brought donor pledges of $5 billion in assistance. Since the ROY is much less integrated into the global economy than its Arab neighbors, its major concern regarding the economic downturn at the end of the 2000s is the prospect of less assistance from donor states in recession just as oil revenues fell sharply.[44]

Three territorial questions that plagued the country in the past have been resolved. First, Oman and Yemen definitively settled their boundary. Second, Eritrea and Yemen reconciled over the Hanish Islands after arbitration in 1998 divided the islands between them. Finally, and of signal importance, the long dispute over the border with Saudi Arabia east of the Asir, the last remaining seriously disputed border on the peninsula, was settled in 2000. Uncontested delineation of this border will permit secure exploration for and production of oil and gas in this promising area.[45]

U.S. relations with the former PDRY were uniformly bad; with the YAR, they were ambiguous and broken in 1967. Restored in 1972, relations segued with the unified ROY, were near the breaking point after the invasion of Kuwait, but warmed following U.S. support for unity during the 1994 civil war. The two governments coordinated on the search for those who attacked the U.S. Navy destroyer USS *Cole* in 2000, killing seventeen sailors, and worked even more closely in joint investigations after 9/11 and the attack on the American Embassy in Sana in 2008. At the end of the decade, the previously mentioned rebel activity in the northern reaches of the country was increasingly worrisome to the United States, as was the likelihood that al-Qaida affiliates were elsewhere at work.[46]

The U.S. Agency for International Development reestablished a modest presence in Yemen in 2003 in response to the ROY's cooperation in antiterrorism activities; in 2009, its program amounted to $24 million and was concentrated on projects in health, education, democracy and governance, and economic growth.[47] Yemen's strategic location and its growing internal problems could lead to greater U.S. assistance in the future.[48] In early 2010, more than twenty donors began to coordinate a major aid effort while pressing the government for major political and economic reforms.[49] Ignoring the triple political threat facing the country—the Houthi rebellion, southern secessionism, and the al-Qaida presence—along with the economic realities of declining oil revenues and increasing water shortages would be disastrous.[50]

NOTES

1. Sources for developing Oman include Townsend 1977; Allen 1987 (with good references for further reading); Anthony 1976; Zahlan 1998; Mandaville n.d.; O'Reilly 1998; Riphenburg 1998; *Persian Gulf States* Country Studies 1993; and U.S. Department of State, *Country Commercial Guide: Oman,* 2005, and *Background Note: Oman,* March 2010.

2. See details in Hanna 1995.

3. *New York Times,* Feb. 5, 1992; *Christian Science Monitor,* Feb. 19, 1992; Clapp 1998.

4. Al-Haj 1996; *Middle East Policy* 1995; Kechichian 1995; U.S. Department of State, *Background Note: Oman,* March 2010.

5. See the two excellent articles on "Oman's Diverse Society" by J. E. Peterson, both in 2004. Some of the following discussion is based on Peterson's detailed research.

6. For an authoritative study, see Al-Yousef 1995. See also the U.S. Department of Energy, Energy Information Administration, *Country Analysis Briefs: Oman,* Aug. 2008. Latest details are on www.pdo.co.om/PDO/, the official Web site of Oman's main oil company.

7. Oxford Business Group, "Oman: Boost Continues," Feb. 22, 2010. Earlier data in Table 6.1 understated Oman's 2008 daily average.

8. USGS, "The Mineral Industry of Oman," in *Minerals Yearbook* 2007; *Global Arab Network,* Feb. 24, 2010.

9. See *BBC News,* Aug. 27, 2009, for how this would work.

10. IEA, "2006 Energy Balance for Oman."

11. *The National* (Abu Dhabi), Oct. 14, 2009; *Arab News* (Riyadh), Dec. 9, 2009.

12. *Media Line,* Apr. 9, 2009, www.themedialine.org.

13. United Nations Development Programme 2009.

14. See Al Sayegh 2004, which is an intimate survey of UAE-Oman relations by a professor at the University of the UAE, al-Ayn.

15. The former North Yemen is covered in Steffen et al. 1978, which is highly geographical as well as demographic, and Daum 1987. *Yemen* Country Studies 1985 covers both former Yemens authoritatively; Dunbar 1992 examines the unification of the two Yemens. (Dunbar was U.S. ambassador to Sana at the time of the merger.) See also Dresch 1989. The former PDRY (South Yemen) is discussed in Stookey 1982.

For more current coverage of unified Yemen, see U.S. Department of State, *Background Note: Yemen*, Jan. 2010, and *Country Commercial Guide: Yemen* 2004. A good history is Dresch 2000.

16. United Nations Development Programme 2009.

17. International Food Policy Research Institute 2009.

18. United Nations Food and Agriculture Organization 2009.

19. See Mackintosh-Smith 1999.

20. Until 1937, Aden was ruled by the British from India, not London. Like Malta, Cyprus, the Suez Canal Zone, and the Gulf amirates, it was part of Britain's defense of the route to India. See Busch 1971.

21. The Zaydis (or Fivers) are one of the three main Shii sects (see Chap. 4).

22. The two then temporarily united as the United Arab Republic (see Chap. 8).

23. The very conservative Wahabbi Saudis disliked the secular and socialist Nasserists more than the Zaydi Shii.

24. At the time of unification the north had about five times the population of the south; this disproportion remains much the same.

25. See Dunbar 1992 and Dresch 2000.

26. *BBC News*, Dec. 15, 2009.

27. After the attempted Christmas 2009 bombing of a U.S.-bound airliner failed and the would-be bomber was linked to Yemen, the government arrested twenty-nine suspected al-Qaida members, and the U.S. presence in the antiterrorist campaign seemed to be quietly increasing (*The Daily Star* [Beirut], Dec. 28, 2009; *Wall Street Journal*, Dec. 30, 2009). Britain was similarly involved (*BBC News*, Jan. 3, 2010).

28. Former U.S. ambassador to Yemen Edmund J. Hull warned against portraying Yemen's internal problems in Shii-versus-Sunni terms, as in Iraq. See *New York Times*, Jan. 12, 2010.

29. *Foreign Policy*, www.foreignpolicy/articles/2009/06/22the_2009_failed_states-index.

30. *Jerusalem Post*, Mar. 18, 2009.

31. The Shafei school is one of four equally regarded Sunni schools of Islamic law (see Chap. 4, note 31).

32. U.S. Department of State, *Country Commercial Guide: Yemen* 2004; *The Daily Star*, Apr. 9, 2005.

33. An interesting exploration of the economics of *qat* cultivation is found in Leonard Milich and Mohammed Al-Sabbry, "The 'Rational Peasant' vs. 'Sustainable Development': The Case of *Qat* in Yemen," available at http://ag.arizona.edu/~lmilich/yemen.html.

34. *Christian Science Monitor*, Nov. 5, 2009.

35. FAO, various issues. Iraq could not be included in this regard because of a lack of recent data.

36. World Bank 2009.

37. FAO Aquastat 2009.

38. *Yemen Post*, Dec. 25, 2009.

39. See EIA, *Country Analysis Briefs: Yemen*, July 1999, July 2004, and Jan. 2010. Author Held is grateful to Yemen Hunt Oil Company for a briefing and for his visit to the offshore tanker at Salif in 1997.

40. IEA, "2006 Energy Balance for Yemen."

41. Global Arab Network, Jan. 3, 2010, www.english.globalarabnetwork.com.

42. *The Daily Star*, Jan. 17, 2010.

43. Transparency International 2009.

44. Oil revenues in 2009 were off almost 65 percent from the record level of 2008, as both prices and exports fell, according to the Central Bank of Yemen (*Global Arab Network*, Dec. 22, 2009).

45. *New York Times*, Oct. 14, 1998; Lefebvre 1998; and EIA, *Country Analysis Briefs: Yemen*, July 2004 and Oct. 2007.

46. *Boston Globe*, Dec. 13, 2009; *Washington Post*, Dec. 28, 2009; *Yemen Post*, Dec. 30, 2009; *The Independent*, Jan. 12, 2010.

47. See www.usaid.gov/locations/middle_east/countries/yemen/.

48. Gregory Johnsen in www.salon.com/opinion/greenwald/radio/2009/12/24/gjohnsen_transcript/ discusses the necessary delicacy of the U.S. involvement with the ROY in targeting al-Qaida elements in Yemen.

49. *Wall Street Journal*, Jan. 27, 2010.

50. For a recent comprehensive treatment of the Yemeni dilemma, see Boucek 2009. See also Dorsey 2010.

17

Egypt
A River and a People

A VIEW OF EGYPT

"Egypt is the gift of the Nile," wrote Herodotus 2,500 years ago. Kipling, in turn, described the Nile as "that little damp trickle of life." Both comments emphasize the role of a single river as the fundamental element in the existence of this ancient land.

In few countries are the basic geographical factors and their direct influences so plainly imprinted as in Egypt. The Nile Valley is unique in its singular symbiosis of people and environment and in its remarkable history and contemporary development. Flanked by desert ramparts, kingdoms have flourished in the valley for millennia, with only occasional major disruptions. Egypt's location on the nexus between Africa and Eurasia has long given it a pivotal position in the World-Island, whether in ancient, medieval, or modern times, right into the twenty-first century.

Inscriptions, carvings, bas-reliefs, statues, and monuments—all well preserved in the dry climate but now under serious stress from contemporary pollution—provide detailed documentation of everyday life and beliefs in Pharaonic and Ptolemaic Egypt. Both tourism and archaeological scholarship focus on such ancient works as well as on the numerous pyramids, temples, tombs, and colossi, with their hieroglyphics and distinctive arts. History is an essential ingredient of everyday life in the country (see Figs. 3.2 and 17.1).

Although the imperial domains of ancient Egypt were less extensive than those of Persia or Assyria, they often extended well into the Levant, and the Nile Valley persisted as one of the four power cores of the region (see Chaps. 3 and 8). Ensconced behind its desert glacis (buffer zone) and well supplied with military resources, it saw fewer conquerors than Fertile Crescent states. Domestic stability and protected location contributed to a historical continuum that, although several times disturbed, was never devastated in the same way that the civilizations of the Hittites, Assyrians, and Israelites were. Similarly, growing along a riverine ribbon made it a linear geographical unity that, once integrated in about 3000 BCE, has rarely been seriously ruptured. The city-states that were so adapted to the environments of mainland Greece, western Asia Minor, and Phoenicia contrast with the integrated polities of the Nile Valley and Delta. The productive agricultural economy along the river has always supported a relatively large population (see Table 4.1 and Graph 4.1).

Located near the center of the Islamic and Arab worlds, Egypt has long played an influential role in both realms, partly because of the influence of Cairo's al-Azhar University on religious affairs and partly because of the

EGYPT

Long-form official name, anglicized: Arab Republic of Egypt

Official name, transliterated: Jumhuriah Misr al-Arabiyah

Form of government: republic with two legislative houses (Shura Assembly and People's Assembly)

Area: 385,210 mi^2/997,690 km^2

Population, 2008: 74,085,000; Literacy (Latest): 56.1%

Ethnic composition (%): Arab 99.6; other 0.4

Religions (%): Sunni Muslim 89.5; Christian 10.0; other 0.5

Demography: Life expectancy—69.2 yr (M), 73.6 yr (F); Birthrate (per 1,000)—25.5; Fertility rate—2.83

GDP, 2009: $188.0 billion; purchasing power parity: $470.4 billion; per capita: $6,000

Currency: Egyptian pound, US$1 = 5.39 pounds, 1 pound = $0.180 (March 2010)

Energy reserves: oil—3.7 bn bbl; gas—58.5 tn ft^3; coal—23.1 mn t

Main exports (% of total value, 2006): petroleum 55.4, of which crude petroleum 17.4; finished goods 28.0; semimanufactures 6.4; raw cotton 0.8

Main imports (% of total value, 2006): petroleum 17.6; machinery and apparatus 10.9; food 9.7; metal products 7.3; chemicals and chemical products 6.0

Capital city: Cairo (agglomeration) 11,128,000; other major cities: Alexandria 4,085,000; al-Jizah (Giza) 2,891,000; Shubra al-Khaymah 1,026,000; Port Said 571,000; Suez 418,000

---

country's long intellectual tradition. Similarly, it has exercised a dominant influence in the Arab world, particularly since World War II, sometimes contending with Syria and Iraq (and occasionally with Saudi Arabia) for leadership. Its cultural output—films, radio, television, publications—has long exceeded that of all other Arab countries combined. In 1988, an Egyptian novelist, Naguib Mahfouz, received the first Nobel Prize for Literature awarded to an Arab writer.

Egypt moved from power core to colonial possession to political leader of the Arab world, became a regional pariah for several years after 1979, and, finally, regained a qualified political eminence in the 1990s. These changing roles have accompanied variations in Egypt's own stability and in the regional environment. In adapting to its changing roles, it has sought security and economic viability within new relationships and new internal and external patterns.[1]

A RICH HISTORY

Historic Continuity

Over the centuries, Egyptian civilization developed a stability that enabled it to survive, if not always to repel, foreign incursions. Although defeated occasionally, resilient Egypt not only preserved its population and sustained its culture but also absorbed newcomers, sometimes adapting their religious or political concepts, sometimes passing on Egyptian concepts to them—for example, to the Hebrews.

FIGURE 17.1 Abu Simbel monument in its repositioned setting. The monument was cut into segments and moved from its original cliffside location, which is now under the water of Lake Nasser. The mound behind the monument is an empty shell of disguised concrete. Note cruise ship in lower right and tourist facilities in right distance.

Once Lower Egypt (the Nile delta) merged with Upper Egypt (the valley south of the delta) around 3000 BCE, the two physically different but interdependent parts remained integrated through five millennia. Reunification of the two after a 200-year cleavage preceding and during the Hyksos invasions in 1720–1580 BCE was celebrated by many new symbols, including the form of the royal crown, and in thousands of hieroglyphic inscriptions. Unity prevailed even when incompatibilities between valley and delta with their cultural and environmental differences could not be entirely overcome. The centripetal-centrifugal relationships between Upper and Lower Egypt remain meaningful, although modern communications and increased interregional dependence have reinforced the sense of unity.

The movement of royal capitals and religious centers between north and south in ancient times reflected shifts in the political center of gravity. Memphis, the first capital of the united kingdom, was founded at an intermediate location near the apex of the delta, to which the capital returned periodically after shifts to Thebes (modern Luxor area) and other valley and delta cities (see Map 3.3). It is significant that Cairo, the political center for the past 1,300 years, is located—as was Memphis—at the junction of delta (Lower Egypt) and valley (Upper Egypt).

Despite periodic incursions over many centuries—Hyksos, Libyans, Nubians, Ethiopians, Assyrians, Persians—Egypt maintained a national character. The Persian conquest in 525 BCE was the first by more distant powers: Greeks under Alexander the Great, 332–323 BCE; Greek Ptolemies, 304–30 BCE; Romans, 30 BCE–476 CE; and their Byzantine successors, 476–640 CE (see Chap. 3). A major modification of the ancient culture came during the Roman-Byzantine hegemony: Christianity became the dominant religion (see Chap. 4). It persists today among the minority Copts.

Arab-Islamic Transformation

In 642 CE, the Muslim Arab conquest brought a momentous and permanent transformation of Egypt. The Arabs not only overwhelmed Egypt militarily but also immigrated into Egypt by the thousands, intermarrying with the indigenous population. Their intangible contributions included a proselytizing religion (Islam), a new language (Arabic), and a concept of strong ties between religion and government. Islam gradually supplanted Christianity—not for several centuries in the south—but by 706 Arabic had become the language of official transactions.

Once ingrained, Islam has never been challenged. Sunnism, however, gave way for two centuries to the Shii Fatimid state, 909–1171, which supplanted Abbasid control across North Africa. The Sunni Ayyubids reigned from 1171 to 1250; their dynasty included Salah al-Din (Saladin), a Kurd whose exploits against the Crusaders made him one of Arabdom's most honored heroes. The succeeding Mamluk (literally, "slave") sultans then ruled for more than 250 years, while Cairo gained architectural treasures, underwritten by the rich Red Sea–Mediterranean trade. Mamluk buildings, especially mosques with characteristic minarets and fluted domes, are some of the city's most distinctive monuments.[2] Portuguese merchantmen sailing around the Cape of Good Hope after 1497 deprived the Mamluks of their main revenues, and Egypt fell to the Ottoman Turks in 1517. Ottoman control was tenuous after the late 1700s, but technically it continued until 1914. From 1805, Egypt was locally ruled by the Muhammad Ali dynasty under Ottoman suzerainty; in fact, British control prevailed after 1882.

Contemporary Republic

Contemporary Egypt was born in a bloodless military coup on July 23, 1952, sending Faruq (Farouk), last of the Alid line, into exile. A republic emerged, led by a revolutionary junta, and the following two decades saw a sequence of events in Egypt that shook the Middle East and sometimes the world. Many were orchestrated by Gamal Abd al-Nasser (al-Nasir), the charismatic coup leader who became president in 1954. Not for centuries had any other leader fired the imagination of his fellow Arabs as much as did this extraordinary Air Force colonel, in word, image, or action.

Among his more memorable actions, he forced the withdrawal of Britain in 1954–1956, negotiated a Czech-Soviet arms deal in 1955, nationalized the Suez Canal in 1956, preached and promoted aggressive Arab nationalism, accepted controlled Soviet aid—including for the Aswan High Dam, merged with Syria in the United Arab Republic (UAR, from 1958 to 1961), and escalated tensions leading to Israel's invasion of Egypt in June 1967. Trying to reconcile the Palestine Liberation Organization and the Jordanian government in September 1970 ("Black September"), he suffered a fatal heart attack.

Nasser's successor, the more pragmatic Anwar al-Sadat, changed national policy directions. After downgrading Soviet relations, he led a joint Egyptian-Syrian surprise attack on Israeli lines at the Suez Canal and in the Golan Heights in 1973; afterward, he developed close ties with the United States. To counteract economic stagnation, he cut Nasserist socialism back with an economic "open-door" policy (*infitah*). To escape continued military entanglement and exploit promised U.S. support, he made a dramatic visit to Jerusalem in November 1977 to address the Israeli Knesset. Then, with help from President Carter, he signed the Camp David accords in September 1978 and the Egyptian-Israeli peace treaty in March 1979. Having championed resistance to Israel for thirty-five years, Egypt embittered its former allies by making peace with the Jewish state, and they expelled it from the Arab League (see Chap. 8). Domestically, the treaty was received with ambivalence, with some extremist opponents especially vocal. Although Sadat was praised in the West as a man of peace, receiving the Nobel Peace Prize (along with Israeli prime minister Begin) in 1978, he was assassinated by disaffected Egyptian extremists in October 1981.

Sadat's successor, President Husni Mubarak, has taken a low-key approach and, with his five six-year terms in office, has had the longest tenure among leaders of Egypt since Muhammad Ali. Pragmatic and politically shrewd, he skillfully maintained his power and the country's interests and security, engaging in a delicate balancing act. Acting under constitutional provisions for a strong executive, he maintained strict control of government policies, domestic and diplomatic. Egyptian politics have always included vigorous opposition elements, some of which periodically engage in militant practices; and increasing antigovernment militancy, seen in Sadat's assassination, continued under Mubarak. It became sustained terrorism during the 1990s until local terrorists in a climactic attack killed 62 tourists and Egyptians in Luxor in 1997. This was the last serious terrorist attack in Egypt until 2004, when a car bomb exploded at an Israeli-owned hotel in Taba, in Sinai, causing 34 deaths, including Egyptians, Israelis, and other foreigners. Attacks on other tourist sites in Sinai were carried out in 2005–2006 and killed 121, mostly Egyptians and Europeans. In 2009, Cairo's famed Khan al-Khalili *suq*, visited by thousands of tourists daily, was targeted, with 1 fatality.

For his part, Mubarak firmly asserted control, sometimes forcefully subduing normal protest along with antigovernment activity. Although domestic and international human rights agencies have objected to his suppression of freedom of expression[3] and have reproved him for political repression, Mubarak was commended for Egypt's relative economic openness and development. He has conducted foreign relations with considerable skill, balancing his role in the Arab and Muslim worlds with close ties with the West, especially the United States, and with his treaty relationship with Israel. At the end of the 2000s, the issue of succession to the octogenarian president came to the fore, especially with regard to the increased prominence in the ruling party of his son Gamal, a banker by background and an advocate of economic reform; opposition to a Syria-like scenario with the al-Asads has been quite vocal.

RIVER, DELTA, AND DESERTS

Egypt comprises five regions: [1] Nile River Valley; [2] Nile Delta; [3] Western Desert; [4] Eastern Desert; and [5] Sinai Peninsula (see circled numbers, Map 17.1). It is worth noting that while Egypt has generally been considered a seismically stable region, a 5.9 earthquake centered 20 mi/12 km southwest of Cairo occurred in 1992, causing more than 400 deaths and 3,000 injuries. Not built according to earthquake-resistant codes, many buildings collapsed; post-1950s structures especially showed damage and were condemned and sometimes razed. However, major ancient monuments seem to have escaped serious problems.[4]

[1] Nile River and the Aswan Project

Egypt is the Nile, and the Nile is Egypt. The Nile–Lake Nasser system provides Egypt with its only significant renewable surface water. The river's headwaters are far to the south, fed by runoff from heavy summer rains in the East African lake district and Ethiopia's highlands. These form the White Nile and Blue Nile, which join at Khartoum in the Sudan, whence the single Nile enters Egypt through Lake Nubia/Lake Nasser. It then flows 938 mi/1,510 km up the entire length of the country, including Lake Nasser, before debouching into the Mediterranean.[5]

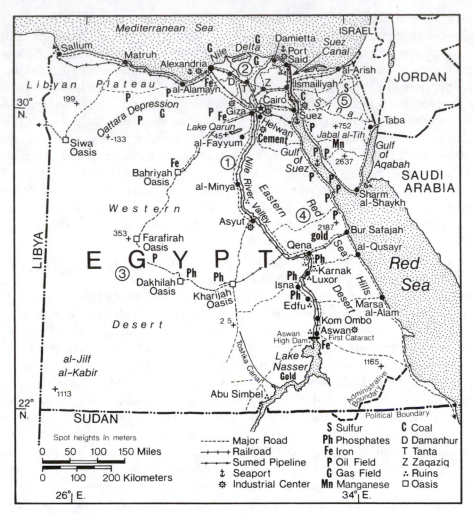

MAP 17.1 General and economic map of Egypt. The five major geographical regions are identified by circled numbers. Note concentration of cities and main transportation lines along the Nile and in the Delta.

Altogether, the complex of barrages, dams, canals, and water supply and wastewater treatment facilities is among the most extensive in the world. Because Egypt relies almost completely on water that passes through other countries—each of which has need for, and influence on, the waters of the two Niles—any change in the hydraulic infrastructure in upstream riparians affects water availability in Egypt and other downstream users. It has long held that its historic use of Nile waters, which dwarfs upstream withdrawals, have priority. As a downstream hegemon, it has

claimed that negative changes in the quantities reaching it as a result of agricultural or other hydraulic development in upstream countries would be a casus belli.

Water ministers of the ten countries in the river's basin and watershed formed the Nile Basin Initiative (NBI) in 1999,[6] creating a partnership among the riparians that has tried for the past decade to reach agreement through dialogue on an equitable utilization of the Nile's water resources. Although $1 billion in grants and loans has been committed to projects dealing with watershed management, flood control, and other issues of mutual interest and benefit, the Cooperative Framework Agreement establishing a permanent NBI commission had still not been signed in early 2010.

As the imperial power from the Mediterranean south through East Africa at the time, Britain secured Egypt's dominant position in the 1929 Nile Water Agreement with the then Anglo-Egyptian Sudan and in the 1959 Agreement for the Full Utilization of the Nile with the East African territories that were still British colonies. Essentially, these pacts gave Egypt the right to veto any upstream work affecting the river and about two-thirds of the river's annual flow (at least 55.5 bn m³), with the rest going to the Sudan. The East African states argue that, as colonies in 1959, they had no say in the agreement and therefore do not recognize its continued validity. Even more so, Ethiopia, the source of most of the river's water, was never involved in any discussions conducted by Britain and therefore does not acknowledge the current arrangement. For Egypt, maintaining the existing situation is a matter of national security—indeed, national survival—and any interference with the flow that it has not agreed to would be, as mentioned, a casus belli.

Nile Valley: Upper Egypt. North of the first cataract at Aswan, the Nile enters a narrow, flat-floored valley, eroded as much as 1,000 ft/300 m below the flanking plateau near Qena (Qina). The valley continues flat, broadening downstream below the Qena bend, until it is 6–11 mi/10–18 km wide approaching Cairo. The valley walls drop to less than 165 ft/50 m high at Giza, then disappear entirely as the river moves out onto its delta. It is the lush ribbon of irrigated, cultivated fields on the flat floodplain along the valley that is the quintessence of traditional Egypt (see Fig. 5.7).

Just upstream of the delta, a prominent feature west of the valley is the Fayyum (Fay-

oum), a circular depression in the limestone plateau of the Western Desert. Nile waters formerly poured into it, at least during flood, through the Hawara channel, feeding the large Lake Moeris. However, later diversion of the river from the basin reduced it to a remnant (now called Lake Qarun), with a surface 147 ft/45 m below sea level. Most of the old lake bed is now intensively cultivated and supports a dense population in this significant subregion.[7]

The evolution of the valley is extremely complex. Stream flow, valley erosion, and deposition of sediment both within the valley and in the delta have varied greatly with alternating periods of pluvial and arid conditions in the watershed. On top of thousands of feet of earlier valley fill, an average of 30 ft/9 m of silt has been deposited since beneficial deposition began approximately 10,000 years ago.[8]

Although some major archaeological sites are found in the delta and in the desert, the vast majority are located along the valley (see Map 17.1). Few stretches of the river between Aswan and Cairo lack ruins of some period or other, and remarkable new finds have recently emerged in Luxor and on the Giza Plateau. Modern cities, some with large populations, have developed around some of the monuments, including Aswan, Luxor, Qena, Asyut, al-Mina, Helwan, and Giza. Tourist records were set in the late 2000s (12.3 million in 2008); while this is good for the economy, it does cause problems for the sites themselves. The tombs can be damaged by overvisiting, which raises the humidity within, leading to fungal growth that destroys wall paintings. The Supreme Council on Antiquities has made major improvements in ventilating the most popular sites, but it is necessary to limit the number of visitors to some of these and to periodically close others. There are plans to build exact replicas of such attractions as the tombs of Tutankhamun, Nefertiti, and Seti I.

FIGURE 17.2 The Aswan High Dam, with large hydroelectric power station.

Aswan High Dam. Inaugurated in 1971 after more than a decade of construction, the Aswan High Dam (Sadd al-Aali) has had the most momentous physical and symbolic impact of any modern project in Egypt. Transforming the country's vital resource—water—the dam impounded the world's largest reservoir, altered the river's equilibrium below Aswan, changed the rhythm of valley life, and had significant impact on crucial aspects of valley ecology. One example is the effect of the dam and lake on the Nile's silt load: Now that the river empties into Lake Nubia (the Sudanese segment of Lake Nasser), the 50 million mt of silt once spread annually along the valley and into the Mediterranean is forming a new delta spreading northward in the lake.

The constricted valley of the Nile at Aswan, where it crosses resistant granites and other basement rocks, had long been considered as an ideal site for a high dam. The original low Aswan Dam, constructed in 1902 and raised in 1912 and 1934, showed the benefits of river control and promoted plans for a higher

structure. Work began on the multipurpose high dam in 1960, and specialists studied the potential environmental, historical, archaeological, and social effects of the project while it was under construction.[9]

The completed dam, power station, and reservoir are among the world's largest. A few statistics indicate the High Dam's impressive scale: It is 365 ft/111 m high, 2.36 mi/3.8 km long at the top, and 0.62 mi/1 km thick at the base; it contains seventeen times the volume of the Great Pyramid of Giza. The reservoir is 297 mi/478 km long, averaging 6 mi/10 km wide. The power station doubled Egypt's generating capacity in 1970; by the late 2000s with numerous new thermal plants, mostly natural gas powered, the dam's 2.1 gigawatt capacity was about 14 percent of the national total (see Fig. 17.2).[10] With plans to expand nationwide electrical output to 32 gigawatts by 2013, its contribution will fall to 6.5 percent.

On the positive side, the dam permits flood control and, by regulating river flow for optimum benefit to downstream agriculture, allows perennial irrigation, multiple cropping, and greatly increased crop output. Water storage mitigates the effect of poor rainfall years in the areas where the Nile rises. As mentioned, it generates considerable amounts of electricity. The lake supports both commercial and sport fishing, and the lake and the dam are major tourist attractions.

Negative impacts, many of which were known from feasibility studies, are of serious concern. The water table under cultivated fields in the floodplain has risen, and poor drainage threatens salination of productive valley and delta soils; although underground drains can minimize these risks, they require major projects. Fields once naturally fertilized by the annual flood now need artificial supplements, changing the valley's chemical balance. The extent of reclamation from the project has, disappointingly, been a third less than was projected.

The now-clear river no longer feeds the delta with silt, and the Mediterranean coast has eroded as much as a mile. The loss of nutrient-rich materials to the sea has reduced fish life, especially sardines, up to 90 percent. In the exceptionally dry climate of southern Egypt, evaporation from the extensive lake surface is enormous—several hundred bn m^3 each year. More manifest is the impact of periodically severe drought in the Nile's upper catchment basin, reducing river flow. In 1988, the lake level dropped as much as 75 ft/23 m following the drought that caused widespread starvation in Ethiopia. By contrast, good rains in the late 1990s overfilled the lake. Such variations have, of course, beset the watershed throughout history. The dam mitigates but does not eliminate cyclical rainfall effects, but the balance is now so delicate that the potential scale of catastrophe is much greater.[11]

[2] Nile Delta: Lower Egypt

The Nile Delta encompasses about 8,495 mi^2/22,000 km^2, more than half of Egypt's cultivated area (Fig. 17.3). A classic delta deposit, it was built up by continued sedimen-

tation of silt in a former embayment on the African coast (the earlier coastline reached to present-day Cairo). Although distributaries of the river have varied in number and course over thousands of years, there are two main branches at present: the Rosetta on the west and the Damietta on the east.

Typical of deltas, the alluvial area is very flat, with a low gradient to the distributaries crossing the plain. The low mounds scattered over the surface are tells marking the sites of ancient settlements. The delta is one of the world's most intensively cultivated areas, with thousands of villages and several of Egypt's larger cities: Alexandria, an ancient city at the delta's northwest corner, Egypt's second-largest city and most important port; the large central-delta textile cities of Mahalla and Tanta; and other such as Zagazig, Rashid (Rosetta), and Damietta. Rural densities are 3,500–4,000 people per mi^2/1,350–1,545 per km^2, among the highest in the world. Thousands of small settlements show as gray dots in the space photograph in Figure 17.3. Egypt made a major change in its own geographic environment with the completion of the High Dam—as mentioned above, the river no longer adds sediment to the delta with the annual flood, and the sea has already made extensive inroads along the coast. If climate change leads to higher sea levels, this low-lying area stands to be affected perhaps more than any other part of the Middle East: In the late 2000s, about a third of the country's people lived in the governorates along the delta coast from Alexandria to Port Said.

[3] Western Desert

The huge Western Desert covers 263,000 mi^2/681,000 km^2, slightly less than Texas and more than two-thirds Egypt's total area. Stretching west from the delta and valley, it is an extension of the Libyan Desert, itself part of the Sahara. Although the Western Desert is basically a low plateau with a cover of generally horizontal sedimentary rocks,

FIGURE 17.3 Image from space of the Nile Delta and the Sinai. The Suez Canal crosses the center of the photograph; sand-choked wadis crisscross the central Sinai. View looking southeast. Compare Fig. 2.2. (Photograph courtesy of National Aeronautics and Space Administration)

landforms vary moderately from section to section in response to changes in rock types, wind erosion, and occasional faulting. Nubian sandstones prevail in the south but are overlain by Tertiary limestones to the north, with the extensive Great Sand Sea in the west blanketing nearly half of the region. Several strata of the Nubian Formation under much of the northern Sahara serve as aquifers with large amounts of fossil water. Egypt plans to exploit these resources, as Libya does in its Kufrah Oasis, but budgetary constraints have limited progress.

Overlying the Nubian sandstone, the limestones form a barren plateau tableland extending eastward to the valley and sloping gently northward to the Mediterranean. Along their southern edges, they form prominent ragged escarpments 985–1,640 ft/300–500 m high. Embayments along the escarpments embrace several large semienclosed depressions watered by contact springs. Here lie five major oases: Siwa, al-Bahriyah, al-Farafirah, al-Dakhilah, and Kharijah (see Map 17.1). The last four inner oases lie along what is believed to be an ancient channel of the Nile and are currently being revitalized (see "Agriculture and Water" section below). Geomorphically, the Fayyum Depression mentioned above may be included in the same category as these oases.[12]

In the northwest is the largest of the depressions, the forbidding and uninhabited Qattara Depression, about the size of Delaware. With an irregular floor 436 ft/133 m below sea level in its lowest part, it has been considered for an ambitious but risky project to generate electricity. The plan, now in abeyance, proposes to pipe Mediterranean water to the depression's edge and then down through penstocks to drive turbines located halfway down the basin wall.

In addition to the Qattara Depression itself, towns along the northern coast became internationally known during World War II because of their roles in North African campaigns—Sallum, Sidi Barrani, Matruh, and al-Alamayn (el-Alamein). The stretch of shore west of Alexandria, toward al-Alamayn and beyond, developed in the 1990s as a mixed resort area with luxury summer villas. Such mansions were traditional in Alexandria in past decades, but these coastal estates permit extensive gardens and secluded swimming pools as well as inhibit the spread of planned resorts that might generate tourist revenues. Farther south, ongoing oil and gas exploration has opened several productive fields. In the far west and southwest is the vast emptiness of the Great Sand Sea, the Gilf Kabir, and the Uwaynat region, where cave petroglyphs testify to the one-time rainier and peopled history of the Sahara.

[4] Eastern Desert

The two deserts divided by the Nile are markedly different in character. In contrast to the Western Desert just described, the Eastern Desert consists essentially of a backbone of elevated and mostly rugged mountains running parallel to and just inland from the Red Sea coast. These Red Sea Hills are an elevated and faulted edge of the Nubian Shield composed of igneous and metamorphic rocks of the basement complex (see Chap. 2). Overlapping the western and northern portions of the hills is a relatively low, maturely dissected, extensive Eocene limestone plateau. Farther to the south, the resistant crystalline hills reach 7,175 ft/2,187 m.[13]

More elevated and slightly better watered than the Western Desert, the Eastern Desert is less inhospitable and is traversed by several routes between the valley and the Red Sea. The crystalline rocks of the Red Sea Hills contain numerous mineral occurrences; gold mining is discussed below. The coast—fringed by long stretches of pristine white-sand beaches—has a number of small ports, some dating from ancient times. To promote tourism, Egypt has developed several lively resorts with such activities as swimming, diving, fishing, and seashell collecting. Farther north, the Gulf of Suez coast also has diving attractions, its surrealistic offshore oil-production platforms and flares visible from shore.

[5] Sinai

The large triangular Sinai Peninsula, 23,590 mi^2/61,100 km^2 in area, belongs geomorphically to the Red Sea Hills but has been separated by sharp faulting along both sides of and beneath the Gulf of Suez (see Fig. 2.2). Such tectonics have in some stretches created structural conditions for petroleum. The southern extent of Sinai is composed of uptilted igneous and crystalline rocks that reach 8,650 ft/2,637 m in Jabal Katherina, the highest elevation in Egypt, and 7,495 ft/2,285 m in nearby Jabal Musa (Mount Sinai). Nestled in a dramatic site lies the famous Greek Orthodox Monastery of St. Katherine (Fig. 4.7), with its unique collection of ancient manuscripts.

FIGURE 17.4 Suez Canal, with freighter in transit.

Some dating from the fifth and sixth centuries, they are now being painstakingly digitally reproduced. The monastery is an important tourist destination and in 2002 was added to the UNESCO list of World Heritage Sites.[14]

Formerly remote and isolated, Sinai has increasingly been opened since 1980. It has undergone rapid development by oil companies in the west of the peninsula, and now has highly successful resort operations—complete with airfields—on both coasts. Solid mineral mining operations are under way, and new roads have been constructed. New national parks and natural protectorates encourage international tourism, protect the unique environment, and help raise the Bedouin standard of living. Though the efforts have achieved some success, there have been problems of inadequate financing.[15]

Sinai's landforms are seen in Figure 2.2: In the northern two-thirds of the peninsula, a great northward-draining limestone plateau rises from the Mediterranean coast and terminates southward in a high escarpment, Jabal al-Tih, on the northern flanks of the igneous core of Sinai. The backslope of the limestone is relatively open country that drains to the sea through numerous sand-choked tributaries, which merge into the Wadi al-Arish, the River of Egypt in the Old Testament. The northern reaches of the plateau have been crossed through the centuries by armies and migrating peoples, including Egyptian and Israeli armies in 1948–1949, 1956, 1967, and 1973. The peninsula is connected with Africa by the sandy Isthmus of Suez, through which the Suez Canal was cut by 1869 (see Fig. 17.4 and discussion under "Waterways" below). Anchoring the northern end of the canal is Port Said on the Mediterranean, at the southern end is Suez, and midway is Ismailiyah.

THE EGYPTIANS AND THEIR SOCIETY

Population

With an estimated 2008 population of 74.1 million, Egypt adds 1 million people every ten months. The population and rate of increase involve several significant geographical relationships. That so many people could mostly be supported (until recently) on such a limited amount of cultivable land is a tribute to the productivity of this great river and its people. However, increasing population is shrinking the amount of farmland per capita and, under foreseeable financial conditions, threatens to overwhelm the national capacity to supply basic services—even food and water. An increasing percentage of the food consumed is imported each year. A broad spectrum of projects to meet these daunting challenges, under way since the mid-1980s, is discussed below.

Peoples

The dominant group in the population, Egyptian Arabs, represents a mixture of the already mixed indigenous Egyptians and immigrant Arabs who entered the area during the seventh to ninth centuries. Egyptians long called the Bedouin "Arabs" and viewed the vast majority of the population as "real Egyptians." *Fellahin* (literally, "tillers of the soil") in many isolated valley villages have the features and many customs of ancient Egyptians, as seen in tomb paintings. By the late 1800s, Egypt increasingly identified with the Arab world, inspiring some of the main currents of Arab nationalism; after the mid-1950s, Arabism's impact in turn defined Nasserist Egypt and its regional relationships.

Egypt does not show the complexity of the distinct ethnolinguistic groupings of Iraq or Iran. Most of the ethnic groups that entered Egypt in the past have long been absorbed into the population, although some small groups have emigrated en masse. Significant minorities, including Greeks and Jews going back millennia and Europeans more recently, were at home in Egypt for centuries, but many left during the Nasser period. Prominent among Egypt's growing social and economic elite are descendants of the former Turkish ruling class.

Copts, by far the largest minority, genetically preserve an ancient Egyptian lineage, more so than any other group. Although many Copts display physical differentiations, their major distinction is religious as a remnant of a community that included most Egyptians prior to the Muslim conquest (see Chap. 4). The Coptic language, directly descended from Pharaonic Egyptian, is still used by the church. Estimates of their number vary, but Copts probably make up about 10 percent of the population; they are concentrated in Luxor and the Asyut and Minya provinces of Upper Egypt and in Cairo and Alexandria. They once held many influential positions in the government and in business, but they have been discriminated against since Nasserist days. Thousands have left to escape discrimination and even periodic violence against them,[16] and many who remain in Egypt have turned inward, cutting the close day-to-day personal ties that have bound Muslims and Christians for centuries.[17] After a Christmas service in January 2010, worshipers in Nag Hammadi were subjected outside their church to a drive-by shooting that left seven dead; local Copts believed that their bishop was the intended target.[18]

The Nubians are the second-largest minority: They number possibly 200,000, now concentrated around Kom Ombo, north of Aswan. Formerly, they lived in villages stretching south from Aswan into the Sudan and were resettled in the early 1960s as their homes were submerged in Lake Nasser after completion of the High Dam. Although compensated for their lost property and given new lands and new homes, they have found the dislocation and loss of their homeland culturally disruptive.

Egyptian Bedouin have been moving toward sedentarization for more than a century. Several thousand nomadic Beja people (non-Arabs) migrate into and out of southeastern Egypt from and into northeastern Sudan. A small Bedouin tribe, the Maaza, with probably 1,000 members, wanders the hills and wadis of the Eastern Desert.[19] The Jabaliyya and associated tribes in the southern Sinai are closely involved in tourism and other forms of economic development in the St. Katherine area. A few other small groups are also elements in the mixture of peoples. Berbers are found in the Western Desert, especially in Siwa Oasis in the northwest of the country, an area they have inhabited for many centuries. Several thousand Armenians and a small number of Greeks live mostly in Cairo and Alexandria.

Although the Bible recounts that Hebrews lived in Egypt in serfdom as *Bnai Yisrael* (Children of Israel) in about the thirteenth century BCE, they are also portrayed as having left in the emigration described in the book of Exodus. A thousand years later, in Ptolemaic times, Jews settled in Alexandria, founding a community that expanded with the arrival of Spanish and central European Jews. Zionism, the later emergence of the state of Israel, and periodic wars between Israel and Egypt created a backlash against Egyptian Jews, most of whom gradually emigrated to Israel and elsewhere. Of about 80,000 Jews in 1947, only about 1,000 remain in Egypt. The pluralistic coexistence in Egyptian society fractured during the revolutionary Nasser period, and the number of Westerners decreased at that time. However, the expatriate community was again expanding by the 1980s and by the end of the 2000s included thousands of oil and gas technicians, general contractors, aid personnel, diplomats, and consultants.

Egypt was further fragmented by increased Islamic fundamentalism beginning in the late 1960s. Sociopolitical readjust-ments under Sadat contributed to the growth of a number of militant opposition groups. The older Muslim Brotherhood (Ikhwan al-Muslimun), founded in 1928, agitated for an ultraorthodox society and government. The Brotherhood moderated its methods, but more extreme and clandestine associations emerged, an estimated fifty of them in the Islamic Fraternity (Jamaat al-Islamiyya). The most violent and secretive of the groups styled itself al-Jihad (literally, Arabic "struggle," often translated as "holy war"); it was this group that assassinated Sadat.

During the 1970s, Christian Copts were attacked by militants, evoking retaliation by Coptic students. The Mubarak administration generally rectified this problem, but terrorism by the *jamaa* against governmental authorities, and often against Western tourist groups—to weaken the economy and therefore the government—became critical between 1992 and 1998. During scores of terrorist attacks, more than 1,000 persons were killed, including security personnel, terrorists, and foreigners; 20,000 accused were imprisoned and dozens executed. The violence ceased when the country, the civilized world, and even many militants recoiled over a Jamaat al-Islamiyya atrocity in November 1997. In a surprise attack in the Temple of Hatshepsut in Luxor (see Fig. 3.2), fanatics massacred 58 European and Japanese tourists and 4 Egyptians before 6 perpetrators were shot.[20] The attack devastated the vital tourist industry for several months, but greatly increased government security gradually restored confidence, and by early 1999 tourism was virtually normal.

Egypt is also the temporary home of a considerable number of refugees; the exact number is hard to pin down, but estimates range as high as 3 million in the late 2000s. By far the largest contingent are Sudanese, many fleeing from long years of conflict in that country's southern and Darfur regions, but others are economically motivated migrants. There are also notable numbers of Palestinians, Ethiopians, Eritreans, and West Africans. More recently, Iraqis fleeing the chaos of their postinvasion homeland may number as many as 100,000.[21]

Settlements

In its population distribution, Egypt has historically and traditionally been predominantly a land of small villages. Despite steadily increasing urbanization, thousands of these are still scattered the length of the valley and in the delta. Valley villages are often just beyond the edge of irrigation, in order to conserve irrigable land. Most of these villages are linear in morphology. Until recently, houses were constructed of mud from the clay-silt once in plentiful supply along the Nile or from nearby canals. Two or three villages can be seen from any given point, and there is a regular pattern of market towns that are service centers for surrounding villages. In turn, cities of 150,000–200,000 population have evolved every 40–50 mi/65–80 km as hierarchical central places.

Villages in the delta, in contrast, display a nucleated morphology and, in the absence of the stone available on the valley fringes, were even more likely to be constructed of mud brick. Obviously, as rapidly increasing population meant greater demand for housing, the use of mud from nearby fields turned once productive plots into barren pits. A farmer could earn more from the sale of the top 3.3 ft/1 m of his land for making mud bricks than he could earn from the sale of the land. So much arable land was being lost that in 1982, a law was passed prohibiting mud construction.

The dominance of the village has been diminishing since the early 1950s, and the urban percentage has increased from less than one-third in 1950 to 45 percent in the early 2000s. But despite the marked growth of several cities, especially Cairo, social structure retains village roots more than urban migration

would indicate. Increasing hundreds of thousands of landless and displaced *fellahin* have flooded into the cities since the 1950s, often grouping themselves by place of origin, thus preserving village identity. Indeed, this kind of urbanization, the virtual displacement of village to city, has been referred to as the "ruralization" of Cairo. Incoming migrants typically have little education, almost no money, and few relevant skills.[22]

Cairo has for many years been the largest city in the Middle East and, indeed, in all of Africa. During some recent years, it has added a million people annually; by the late 2000s, the population of the Greater Cairo Region (GCR) plus fringe suburbs, was probably close to 19 million, about a quarter of Egypt's total. In contrast to the city's impressively modern front yard along the Nile in Garden City, Zamalak, and Qasr al-Nil (Fig. 17.5), seething squatter slums lie to the east and west. Hundreds of thousands of the poor have taken refuge in the tombs and monuments in the City of the Dead, the extensive cemeteries east of the capital.

Although unable to supply adequate municipal services, the government is making major efforts to clean up the slums and to reduce the serious pollution from automobiles, potteries, cement factories, and lead smelters. An especially notable transformation of the inner city opened 74 ac/30 ha of the diversified and attractive al-Azhar Park for public enjoyment in 2004. The $30 million project removed 80,000 truckloads of debris from a centuries-old rubbish heap, uncovering in the process a section of the medieval wall.[23] Traffic in the central business district was becoming virtually immobile until a new subway system, opened in 1987 and considerably expanded during the following years, appreciably relieved surface circulation. Engineered and partly financed by France, the Cairo Metro has been such a success that Alexandria was planning its own system in the late 2000s.

FIGURE 17.5 View down the Nile River at Cairo, with major bridges in foreground and buildings of Zamalak in center distance.

With nearly half of its population urbanized, Egypt has four cities with populations larger than 1 million, more than thirty-five exceeding 100,000, and more than twice as many with 50,000 to 100,000 inhabitants. Growth far outruns the census taker. With Cairo at the junction of valley and delta, relentless urban sprawl by it and other large cities mostly located in the delta consumes agricultural land at an alarming rate. As Cairo has grown historically, new urban quarters have expropriated more and more agricultural land to the south in the valley and to the north in the delta. As early as the 1960s, the government has had some success in steering urbanization along an east-west axis—that is, out into the deserts well away from Cairo and from farmland. At first people were reluctant to relocate to these satellite cities, but as amenities, transport links to Cairo, and, more importantly perhaps, jobs became available in new localities like Tenth of Ramadan City, Sixth of October City and Sadat City, they became much more attrac-

tive alternatives to the crowded and more expensive established parts of Cairo.[24] Conversely, in areas where progress on developing infrastructure and services has been uneven, many migrants prefer living in a Cairo slum with old village friends and relatives to adopting an unfamiliar lifestyle in a strange environment.[25]

CHANGING ECONOMIC PATTERNS

An Economic Perspective

The historical riches of Egypt are proverbial—the productivity of the soil, the creativity of its artisans, the gold from Pharaonic and Ptolemaic tombs, and the transit trade between Red Sea entrepôts and Mediterranean coastal states. However, now an ever-increasing population presses on the maximum limits of even these fabled resources. Agricultural productivity is many times greater today than even a few generations ago, but demography demands even more. Once a net food exporter, then at least self-sufficient, Egypt now imports much of what it needs—well over half by the late 2000s. The UNDP's Human Development Index (HDI), used to compare living standards globally, in 2007 ranked Egypt 123rd out of 182 countries and 15th of the 16 countries included in this book, with the HDI increasing by some 42 percent since 1980 on the strength of gains in the health and education components of the index. When the same calculations were done recently on a national basis, the urban governorates (Port Said, Suez, Alexandria, and Cairo) topped the list, while those in rural lower Egypt were at the bottom; the difference between the highest HDI (Port Said) and the lowest (Fayoum) was 12.6 percent.

The political revolution of 1952 brought a correlative economic revolution. Junta efforts included land reform, controls over agriculture, nationalization of industries and institutions (notably of the Suez Canal in 1956), sequestration of foreign businesses and agencies, an inflow of bilateral and multilateral loans and grants, and construction of the Aswan High Dam. Progress toward these well-intentioned goals was impeded by administrative problems, bureaucratic inefficiency, and Egypt's military buildup and three wars with Israel. Nasser's insistence on state management repelled both foreign and domestic investment. Originally, the statist approach had popular appeal, since land reform, widespread nationalization, and tight control over the economy broke the power of large landowners, foreign capitalists, and wealthy Egyptians.

Nasser's revolution was, indeed, a watershed event in modern Egyptian history. Some reforms brought long-term benefits, but many apparent gains soon revealed serious flaws. For example, his "social contract" improved the lot of the average Egyptian, but only through price controls, heavy subsidies, and unselective guaranteed employment. Such broad paternalism and free university education, along with ensuring jobs to all

graduates, seemed progressive. However, the bureaucracy and large public-sector enterprises were soon loaded with redundant employees, depressing the wage scale; the quality of education was degraded, and a downward economic spiral ensued.

President Sadat reversed the trend, opening the economy's doors with his moderate *infitah* policy of 1974, which reduced many restrictions. However, conditions in Egypt and in the Middle East as a whole countered many of his goals,[26] resulting in deindustrialization and increased indebtedness. Falling incomes and government austerity measures led to riots in Aswan and Alexandria, intensifying the immediacy of his initiative to settle with Israel and request the contingent greater aid from the United States in order to realize a "peace dividend." After Sadat's assassination, Mubarak cautiously opened the economy further. During the 1990s, the macroeconomy enjoyed a significant turnaround and became increasingly globalized. Some state-owned enterprises were privatized, government spending was reined in, and the financial sector was slowly rationalized. Generally, the environment facing the private sector improved noticeably.

In the new century, some of these reforms—floating the pound, simplifying import-export procedures, reducing personal and corporate tax rates, privatizing state-owned enterprises, cutting subsidies, and making it easier and more attractive for foreign investment—started to pay off, at least on the level of national statistics. Annual growth surged to 7 percent or better on average through 2008, before falling back to 4.7 percent in 2009 with the global recession as tourism and Suez Canal receipts slumped. Both these sectors began to rebound in the second half of 2009, and growth in 2010 was projected at 5.5 percent.

In a World Bank Group report, Egypt was cited as topping the worldwide list for making it easier to do business. Reforms prompted improvements in five areas—starting a business, dealing with licenses, registering property, getting credit, and trading across borders. There was, however, room for considerably more effort in this regard: The country still ranked only 106th globally and 11th in the region.[27]

But the benefits to average Egyptian are less clear, and serious problems remain. Despite considerable development, much of the infrastructure is obsolete, and improvements have not kept pace with population. Although adding to the budget deficit, many necessities of life are still subsidized because the burden of further cuts would fall on the poorest Egyptians and might unleash unacceptable instability, especially when, as in 2008, world grain prices doubled. Some Nasserist negatives act as constraints—a bloated bureaucracy and an overstaffed public sector—and corruption is significant at all levels. According to Transparency International, Egypt was seeing increasing corruption in the 2000s and in 2009 ranked 111th out of 180 countries worldwide and 11th of the 16 considered in this book.[28]

By the late 1990s, tourism was the leading foreign-exchange earner, and although it plummeted after the Hatshepsut's Temple massacre, following 9/11, and again with the invasion of Iraq, it has recovered as a major component of GDP. In 2008, there were 12.3 million visitor arrivals—second in the region after Turkey—but totals were off slightly in the face of global recession in 2009. Remittances from the 2 million or more Egyptians working abroad, mostly in the Arabian Peninsula, were estimated to be about $7.7 billion in 2007, or about 5.5 percent of GDP; the amount is subject to the effects of regional disturbances.[29] Suez Canal revenues surged to an all-time high of $5.1 billion in 2007 but fell back as the global economic crisis deepened at the end of the decade.[30]

Agriculture and Water

The Nile Valley has supported a flourishing agriculture for more than 8,500 years, and much of the valley and delta was under culti-

vation soon after the union of Upper and Lower Egypt in about 3000 BCE. When cultivable area had been cleared of forest and brush, increasing portions of what is now cropland were farmed using the natural flood-irrigation system that was dominant until after 1800 CE.

The irrigation system so long practiced was basically simple. It utilized the runoff from the heavy summer rains in East African highlands, which poured down the Nile and raised the water level 20–25 ft/6–8 m, covering the entire floodplain with several feet of silt-laden floodwaters. When these receded after several weeks, the silt loam soils, built up by past floods, were water soaked and were also covered with fresh millimeters of nutrient-rich silt. Thus, valley soils naturally were watered, fertilized, and renewed annually without human intervention. Crops were planted to mature before the soil dried out months later. Carefully sited perennial tree and vine crops—somewhat lower than village locations—were also cultivated; only one crop per flood season could be harvested. In later centuries, water was retained in basins to prolong irrigation; still later, canals were installed by Pharaonic engineers. As experience passed down generations, the *fellahin* of the valley became expert hydraulic farmers, and their traditional culture was as immutable as the annual flood.

For centuries, virtually all production was restricted to the annual flood area. Not until application of modern technology in the mid-1800s was the irrigable area significantly increased—through construction of barrages at the head of the delta in 1860 and later at Asyut. Completion of the first Aswan Dam in 1902, and later additions to its height, extended perennial irrigation. The High Dam was the single most momentous element furthering irrigation and attendant year-round cropping virtually everywhere in the "old" settled area; despite bringing several major problems, the dam set the stage for the potential engineering of major "new" settlement areas.

The Tahrir (Liberation) Project west of the delta in the 1950s failed to meet expectations, but lessons learned offered hope for other schemes. Most ambitious is the New Valley Project (al-Wadi al-Jadid) for revitalizing the once productive and even wealthy oases of the Western Desert described earlier. Discovery of a Roman-era necropolis in Bahriyah revealed evidence of a thriving community 2,000 years ago that prospered by making wine from dates and grapes.[31] After twenty years of planning and delay, agriculture has been vigorously expanded by using deep Nubian Formation groundwater; production focuses on high-value crops like dates, olives, fruits, and vegetables for Cairo and other urban markets. Complementary infrastructure has accompanied crop expansion, with roads, electricity, schools, and housing for new settlers, plus hotels for the growing number of tourists.

The New Valley Project is expected to receive enormous impetus during the new century as the program merges with the grandiose Toshka (or Tushka) Canal Project. After several years of study and planning, the Toshka Canal venture began construction in 1997. Unrelated to the Toshka Spillway (opened in 1980, to drain excess floodwaters from Lake Nasser into a desert depression southwest of Aswan), the canal venture began construction in 1997—amid considerable skepticism from outside observers, including the U.S. Agency for International Development (USAID), the leading donor to Egypt.[32] It includes one of the world's largest pumping stations to lift lake water 175 ft/53 m to the canal. The concrete-lined channel will extend 150 mi/240 km northwest across empty desert. It will be extended to Kharijah Oasis and possibly on up the arc of depressions sheltering the other Western Desert oases (see Map 17.1). Thus, the New Valley and Toshka Canal project will merge, eventually to open about 3.5 mn ac/

1.4 mn ha for irrigated cultivation. Completion will take twenty years and more than $80 billion in investment.

However, many outside experts consider government expectations highly optimistic[33]— for one thing, Egypt is already pretty close to using all its available water, and agriculture claims 88 percent of this while contributing only 25 percent to GDP. Siphoning water directly from Lake Nasser and pumping it into the Western Desert means less water for all users downstream. Complementing these projects is another major (and probably more realistic) reclamation scheme in the northeast, the North Sinai Agricultural Development Project. This will use Nile water delivered through the Peace (al-Salam) Canal, which in turn will be fed with water siphoned under the Suez Canal through four tunnels. Plans call for cultivated area of 170,000 ac/69,000 ha.[34]

Cropping patterns are complicated by two factors: cultivation of two or three crops a year on many plots and yield differences between "new lands" and "old lands." However, overall, the main crop in both area and tonnage is clover (*berseem*), although cereals continue to occupy 40–50 percent of cropped area. Wheat and maize lead in extent and weight, with new high-yield wheats increasing output per acre nearly 50 percent since 1985. Rice ranks third among cereals; the famous Egyptian cotton is the leading nonfood crop. Fruits such as citrus, dates, and grapes and a wide variety of winter and summer vegetables vie with rice in area, and all these crops are important exports. Sugarcane maintains its place as a major crop. Figure 17.6 shows a typical mix of crops in the valley. From the early 1960s to the mid-2000s, Egypt saw an increase of nearly 90 percent in food production per capita despite already realizing fairly high crop yields during the base period.[35]

Egyptian long-staple cotton has long been preferred on world markets since its

FIGURE 17.6 Typical scene in the timeless Nile Valley in Upper Egypt: intensive cultivation in the fertile alluvial soils, date-palm grove and fruit trees, sugarcane, village under the shade of trees, and *fellahin* still hand-laboring as they have for centuries.

development by a French agronomist in the 1820s. Although it is increasingly grown elsewhere, Egypt still produces more than one-third of the world crop. The main cotton area is in the central delta, where expertise and government extension work and controls ensure quality. With the more realistic pricing policies that have recently aided farmers, production and marketing changes have followed. Output is increasingly used downstream in the domestic textile industry, and cotton textiles and yarns are now the second-leading export by value, with raw cotton dropping in export importance. However, it was reported in 2009 that the year's long-staple output would be the lowest in a century—partly because of the difficulty in competing in the world market with the United States' subsidizing the export price of its Pima grade, long staple's most important competitor. From economic and commercial viewpoints, increased long-staple output supplied directly into the production in Egypt of high-quality cotton textiles and garments for export promises considerable benefit for both domestic employment and international trade.

Livestock have been an integral element on virtually every Egyptian farm since ancient times. Tomb paintings depict the role of cattle and other animals in early agriculture, and the cow and the bull were venerated in the ancient pantheon. Sheep, goats, and ducks have also been of prime importance for more than 4,500 years, as has the donkey. Cattle, buffalo, and donkeys are still multipurpose farm animals, pulling plows and carts, carrying loads (the donkey serving also for individual transportation), supplying manure for fields and fuel, and furnishing milk. Camels came later and are still common. The Indian buffalo (*gamus* or *gamush*) was imported in the Middle Ages and is now the most numerous farm animal. It has adapted well along the river and canals, yielding milk, meat, manure, and hides and serving as a plow animal.

Fishery production in Egypt was 982,000 mt in 2007, well surpassing that of Turkey, formerly the regional leader. The fish catch had doubled over the previous decade, with Lake Nasser replacing the Mediterranean as the main source, and it contributed about 20 percent of the country's consumption of animal protein. By 2009, Nile fishermen were reporting that toxicity in the river was not only killing off the fish population but in places was bad enough to damage their nets.[36]

Industry

Oil and Oil Processing. The first oil well in Egypt was drilled in 1886, although commercial production came only in 1913. After World War II, several companies, most of them American, conducted explorations, primarily under concession agreements. Operations in Egypt—which is not an OPEC member—expanded in the 1960s, and production averaged 795,000 bpd in 1999–2001, after an all-time high of 992,000 bpd in 1995. Output has steadily dropped each year for the past decade. Sorely in need of economic stimulus and export products, the country benefited from increasing petroleum production during the 1980s, and the growing industry has had a major impact on the export sector. By 1981–1982, with the price between twenty-nine and thirty-four dollars per barrel, oil was the leading export, and, with some variations, petroleum and petroleum products have constituted more than half of exports during the price spikes of the mid- and late 2000s.

The most important oil-field developments have been in and along the Gulf of Suez (see Map 17.1), which still supplies half of the country's production. Intensive exploration in the Western Desert has made new discoveries, especially of gas and condensates, some of world class.[37] But in the late 2000s, rising domestic consumption caught up with production, and Egypt's days as a net oil exporter were clearly drawing to a close, bar-

ring major new discoveries or a reversal of consumption trends.

Whatever may result from continued intense exploration for oil, discoveries and output of nonassociated natural gas have increased dramatically—offering not only enhanced export earnings but also some reversal of oil consumption patterns with gas substituting for oil in some domestic sectors. Gas reserves in 1991 were 12.4 tn ft^3, up by 2008 to 58.5 tn ft^3, the total still given for 2010. These are the largest reserves in the eastern Mediterranean, the third largest in Africa, and equivalent to one-fourth those of the well-endowed United States. When major gas fields were found in three different Tertiary zones in the northern delta, offshore exploration opened several more major fields. Thus, the northern delta and adjacent offshore area, now a world-class gas province (indicating still greater reserves), possess more than two-thirds of Egypt's reserves.

By using gas for power plants, industry, and even for vehicles, the country can export more of its crude oil and product. With resources so plentiful, it also looked for markets for gas and LNG both among its neighbors and farther afield. An underwater pipeline to Aqabah, Jordan, began operation in 2003. The line now extends northward to Amman and Syria where deliveries began in 2008 and to Lebanon in 2009. Turkey and Syria agreed in 2008 to tie the pipeline by 2011 into the existing Turkish network that is linked to European markets. Another underwater line connects al-Arish to Ashkelon in Israel, with exports to the Jewish state a politically sensitive subject. Despite increased opposition to the exports after Israel's campaign in Gaza in early 2009, by midyear the two parties announced agreement on a revised pricing schedule, and pumping at the rate of 60 bcf annually commenced. Two LNG export facilities on the Mediterranean coast were operative in the late 2000s, and exports, to Spain, began in 2004. A third installation is scheduled to come on line in 2011. In order to utilize the country's natural gas in additional ways, Shell has proposed building a gas-to-liquids processing plant, to be colocated with an LNG facility.

Egypt was credited in the late 2000s with having oil reserves of 3.7 bn bbl. About half of the oil production is from the Gulf of Suez, the oldest fields, and most of the remainder from the Western Desert. Exploration and production are carried out by more than thirty European and North American companies, particularly BP, British Gas, Agip (Italy), and Shell, under contract with the government, usually with the Egyptian General Petroleum Company.

Two Egyptian pipelines are noteworthy. The 200-mi/320-km Sumed (Suez-Mediterranean) line, from Ayn Sukhnah on the Gulf of Suez to Sidi Krir west of Alexandria, is a dual 42-in/107-cm line with an original capacity of 1.6 mn bpd, increased to 2.4 mn bpd in 1995 and 3.1 mn bpd by 2007s. Egypt owns it jointly with Saudi Arabia, Kuwait, the UAE, and Qatar. It was opened in 1977 to bypass the Suez Canal, both because the largest tankers exceeded the capacity of the canal and also because the canal had been shut down between 1967 and 1975 after the June War with Israel. As a competitor to the canal, the pipeline offers discounts to the largest class of tankers offloading and reloading at its terminals. The second line, opened in 1981, extends from Ras Shuqayr on the Gulf of Suez to refineries at Suez and Cairo. Ras Shuqayr is the export terminal for the adjacent offshore fields.

Of nine refineries processing a total of 726,250 bpd in 2009, the largest are at Mostorod near Cairo and at Suez, each with a throughput of more than 145,000 bpd. Noteworthy among refineries newly constructed is the MIDOR refinery in Alexandria, opened in 2001, with a throughput of 100,000 bpd. Originally an Egyptian-Israeli joint venture, it is now an all-Egyptian oper-

ation. Principal petrochemical plants are near Alexandria and Suez, and as gas production increases more such plants, as well as LNG trains, can be expected. Two large joint-venture LNG plants came on line in the early 2000s to produce export gas for the European market, one at Damietta on the eastern side of the delta in 2004 and a second at Idku on the western side in 2005. In 2008, Egypt exported almost 30 percent of its gas output by pipeline or as LNG.[38]

Other Mineral Industries. Contemporary commercial solid-mineral mining is extensive and involves a considerable range of minerals, but it is only a modest contributor to the national economy. Iron ore, manganese ore, and phosphate rock are the most important nonfuel minerals produced in Egypt. Iron ore from Aswan was used in the Helwan mill, south of Cairo, from 1958 until the mid-1970s; however, somewhat better and more plentiful sedimentary ore from al-Bahriyah Oasis now feeds the mill via a specially constructed railway. A recently discovered high-grade iron ore deposit 50 mi/80 km southeast of Aswan supplies a new Aswan Iron and Steel Company complex. Its products will include seamless tubing for export to the regional oil industry. In the late 2000s, a mini gold rush was in progress in the Eastern Desert inland from Marsa Alam. An Australian-Egyptian company, Centamin Egypt, after reopening Pharaonic workings, claimed that these had barely scratched the surface in antiquity and, in 2007, that it had discovered reserves estimated at more than 10 million ounces. An underground mining contract was awarded in early 2009.

Phosphate rock is mined near Isna (south of Luxor), near Bur Safajah on the Red Sea, and near al-Kharijah Oasis. Production averaged 2.2 mn mt in the late 2000s, about 40 percent that of Jordan, the region's largest producer. Other nonmetallic minerals produced were of relatively low value and included large tonnages of gypsum, fire clay, kaolin, and salt, as well as many types of dimension stone, including Aswan granite. As is true elsewhere in the region, cement production is a major industry. Egypt's first coal mine opened in 1995 at al-Maghara in the northern Sinai and despite early prospects, it and the national total production in the late 2000s was only 75,000 mt year.[39] The coal has been used to fire thermal power plants, but with the growing use of natural gas for this purpose in the 2000s, coal production decreased.

Other Manufacturing. Egypt experienced modest early industrialization under Muhammad Ali in the nineteenth century but then stagnated for decades. Development was uneven after the 1952 revolution. Unskilled labor supply was adequate, and skilled labor was moderately available; however, capital was limited, as were planning and management skills. Petroleum development, the benefits of the High Dam, *infitah* policies, strong donor support, and realistic economic and political policies after 1991 finally stimulated significant and consistent growth of the sector.

However, the policies of industrial development under state socialism meant that virtually all large and medium-size establishments were in the public sector. The most important establishments were saddled with bloated employee rolls, bureaucratic mismanagement, and inefficient administration. Economic reform in the 1990s had as one major aim their privatization, and 193 out of 314 had been shifted into the private sector by the early 2000s. Another goal is geographical diversification. At present, nearly half of Egypt's manufacturing is centered in the Shubra al-Khaymah industrial area north of Cairo and in Helwan south of the capital (Fig. 17.7), leading to serious air and water pollution in the Greater Cairo Region. Major industrial areas outside the GCR are Nag Hammadi (west of Qena, processing imported bauxite to produce aluminum), Tanta

and Muhallah al-Kubra (textiles) in the delta, Alexandria (refineries, petrochemicals, iron and steel, shipyards), Suez (fertilizers), and several mid-Nile cities. Medium-size armament industries, including the assembly of jeeps, tanks, helicopters, and other weaponry, are located in Lower Egypt. By 2007, industry supplied more than 38 percent of GDP and employed 17 percent of the workforce.

Traditional private-sector establishments are small and often artisan in character. They are located primarily in and around Cairo, especially in the old *suqs* of the Muski and Khan al-Khalili, but also in other main cities and towns. They produce food products, specialty textiles, leather goods, jewelry, artistic glass objects, copper and brass ornamental and utilitarian items, and furniture and other wood products, including intricately inlaid boxes and other household items. Under a 2004 agreement with the United States, Egypt can designate within its territory "Qualifying Industrial Zones" (QIZs) that then enjoy duty-free status in exporting zone production to the United States. By 2009, more than 750 companies were operating in numerous places in the Cairo, Alexandria, Delta, and Suez Canal regions.[40]

Transportation and Trade

Roads. With settlement being intense in the Nile Valley and Delta, transportation by river, road, and railroad is equally concentrated (see Map 17.1). On paved highways extending the full length of the Nile Valley between Cairo and Aswan, donkey carts share space with buses and trucks, but there are only limited numbers of long-distance travelers in private automobiles. Major highways also extend from Cairo to Alexandria, other points in the northern delta, and now along the valley's desert fringe. At right angles to the valley-delta routes is the Mediterranean coastal highway between the Libyan border on the west and the Israeli border on the east. Successive military operations in Sinai, and

FIGURE 17.7 Interior view of steel mill in Helwan, south of Cairo, one of Egypt's many varied industrial facilities. (John Riddle, *Saudi Aramco World*, SAWDIA)

increasing development of the area, have prompted the construction of transpeninsular and circumpeninsular roads there, opening an area isolated as late as the 1950s.

A north-south Red Sea coastal highway connects Suez and the Sudan border, accessing burgeoning beach resorts and secondary ports and relieving traffic on valley routes. The Suez Canal is paralleled on both sides by roads linked by the Ahmad Hamdi Tunnel under and a high bridge over the canal.[41] The main north-south routes, in the valley and along the mainland and Sinai coasts, are connected by several east-west roads. In the late 2000s, work on a $3 billion 31.1-mi/50-km causeway tying Egypt and Saudi Arabia across the Strait of Tiran was in its early stages.

Railroads. Railways are heavily used by passengers, giving Egypt half the total passenger kilometers in the Middle East. Indicative of

the pressure of the large, highly concentrated population on facilities, trains into and out of Cairo are often so overloaded that hundreds of passengers must either stand inside or cling precariously to the outside of trains. This hazard has been partially relieved by the new mass transit system between al-Marg, a northern suburb of Cairo, and Helwan to the south. A second metro line now connects Giza and downtown Cairo; a third line extending to the airport is in the planning stage, and a new system for Alexandria is being discussed.

Some tourists travel between Cairo and Aswan one way by air, the other by rail in order to enjoy at close hand scenes of everyday village and city life along the length of the valley. Railways share transport of low-priority heavy freight with large cargo *faluqas* (feluccas) on the Nile. A major construction project opened a 620-mi/1,000-km rail line in 1996 between Safajah on the Red Sea and al-Kharijah Oasis; it carries phosphate rock from Abu Tartu, just west of al-Kharijah, and bauxite for processing at Nag Hammadi. Double-tracking from Asyut to Aswan was completed in 2004. By 2010, a previously announced link to Libya had not progressed, but an $860 million upgrade of existing facilities was outlined that year.

Waterways.   In addition to the Suez Canal, Egypt has 2,175 mi/3,500 km of inland waterways, half along the river itself and half along several major canals, especially in the delta. Sailing the Nile was the only north-south method of travel until completion of the railway to Aswan and later construction of a drivable road. The river below Aswan to the Mediterranean is still used by hundreds of the typical Nile sailing boats, *faluqas*, which are a practical and inexpensive means of north-south shipment of heavy and nonperishable goods. On the picturesque stretch between Aswan and Luxor, rich in ancient monuments, more than 325 sizable cruise boats carry tourists on pleasant multiday trips.

Since its opening in 1869, the Suez Canal has been both a significant symbol and an integral economic element for Egypt (see Fig. 17.4). Operated by an Anglo-French company until dramatically nationalized by Nasser in 1956, the canal quickly became Egypt's leading foreign-exchange earner. When tanker traffic and revenues steadily declined for various reasons, the canal's earnings also declined, but they then rose to an all-time high of $5.1 billion in 2007–2008, when an average of 58 vessels transited it each day; with the onset of global recession and the threat from Somali pirates, revenues fell in 2008–2009 by 7.2 percent, and the decline continued through the end of 2009, when the average daily number of transits dropped to 47.[42] It was closed by the 1967 Arab-Israeli war but was reopened in 1975, then dredged in 1980 to a draft of 52 ft/16 m

to permit transit of larger tankers. By the end of 2009, dredging to a depth of 66 ft/20.1 m was completed, and to increase the pass-through rate, further widening is under consideration. (See additional details under "Suez Canal," Chap. 8.)

Ports.   Alexandria, Egypt's most important port, was founded by Alexander the Great, and for much of twenty-three centuries it has functioned as one of the largest and busiest general-cargo ports in the eastern Mediterranean. It fills so many functions—port, resort, industrial center, commercial center—that traffic is increasingly being spun off to satellite facilities in Dikhaylah and Marsa Matruh to the west and in Damietta to the east. Port Said and Suez, at opposite ends of the Suez Canal, are thriving industrial centers as well as major ports; they enjoy free zones, as do Alexandria and Damietta. A new state-of-the-art port under private management opened at Ayn Sukhnah in 2003–2004 to handle much of the maritime trade with South and East Asia. Located 25 mi/40 km south of Port Suez on the mainland coast of the Gulf of Suez, it is also the head of the Sumed crude oil pipeline. As mentioned above, Safajah on the Red Sea has export facilities for phosphates.

Air Transportation.   The state-owned airline, Egypt Air, was founded in 1932 and operated for many years as Misr Air (Arabic *Misr* = Egypt). It flies an extensive network from the United States and western Europe to the Far East and Africa, operating more than fifty jet aircraft; by several criteria it ranks in the top six lines in the region. Along with its civil fleet, Egypt has a large air force and maintains a large number of medium-size combined civil and military airports. Cairo's airport is one of the four busiest in the Middle East, with many international connections as well as frequent flights to the main tourist centers in Upper Egypt and Sinai—Luxor, Aswan, and Sharm al-Shaikh.

Trade. Almost entirely in the private sector, most retail trade follows Arab commercial traditions, in which outlets tend to be small, often operated only by the owner and perhaps one or two family members. Cairo and Alexandria do have several large Western-style shopping malls. Countrywide, food shops predominate, but other retail stores offer clothing, textiles, small household items, and jewelry and other items handcrafted in Egypt for the tourist trade. Such items include a wide range of inlaid wood pieces, hand-engraved brass and copper, turned and carved alabaster, jewelry, tooled leather, traditional screens of turned wood (*mashrabiyah*), and paintings on handmade papyrus.

Cairo preserves the traditional *suq* in addition to its modern Western-style central business district. The Khan al-Khalili, located in a fourteenth-century Mamluk caravansary, or *khan*, has been famous for centuries throughout the Middle East. Traditional Egyptian goods and certain types of specialty goods from around the world are on sale in the primarily small stalls. The adjacent Muski sells similar items but also has sections for utilitarian and lower-value items. Both bazaars are a paradise for leisurely shopping for the curious and the unusual, especially if the shopper is a skilled bargainer.

Foreign trade has been a major factor in the economy for thousands of years. Exchange between Lebanon and Egypt, for example, flourished before 2400 BCE, and medieval Cairo was probably the world's greatest trade center, relaying shipborne products from the Indian Ocean to the Mediterranean. Shifts in traded commodities and in trade direction, both historically and recently, reflect changes within Egypt as well as in its foreign relations. For example, long-staple cotton exports during the U.S. Civil War brought instant but short-lived prosperity, petroleum during the early 1980s offset increasing trade deficits until the world price collapsed, and its main trading partners shifted with its political orientation

between 1970 and 1980 and changed again in 1995 when Egypt joined the World Trade Organization. Its leading trade partner now is the EU, followed by the United States. In the year ending with March 2009, exports to the United States from Qualifying Industrial Zones amounted to $843 million, all entering the United States duty and quota free. Unlike other countries in the region—Israel, Jordan, Bahrain, and Oman—Egypt does not have a Free Trade Agreement with the United States.

For many years, Egyptian exports were overwhelmingly agricultural raw materials, chiefly food products and cotton. The share of agricultural products is now down to 10 percent of the value of exports but is up to about 20 percent of the value of imports. Agricultural exports to European markets, based on favorable seasonal availability of specialty crops and vegetables, could become more important, but many high-value products face difficulties in meeting the EU's strict phytosanitary standards for food products. Especially in the delta, irrigation water in 2010 is highly polluted with chemicals from upstream fertilizer use, thus contaminating output.[43] Prime Minister Ahmad Nazif has set an ambitious goal of increasing exports by more than 150 percent by 2015.[44]

RELATIONS

Egypt's relations, both with its neighbors and with the major powers, have been of crucial importance since 1947.[45] Under Nasser, relations were confrontational and erratic. Under Sadat, they involved complete reversals in policies with Israel, the USSR, and the United States. They then stabilized and have followed a fairly consistent policy under Mubarak from the 1980s.

When President Sadat turned away from the USSR in the early 1970s, established close ties with the United States, and signed a peace treaty with Israel in 1979, these were watershed events in Egyptian relations. His

Israeli policy prompted most Arab countries to break diplomatic relations and precipitated Egypt's expulsion from the Arab League (Chap. 8). Its regional role, however, was and is too vital to be denied: The Organization of the Islamic Conference reinstated it in 1984, most Arab states reestablished relations after the 1987 Arab Summit in Amman, and the Arab League accepted Egypt back in 1989, returning to its Cairo headquarters in 1990. Thus, outwardly, Egypt was welcomed back into the Arab fold, but its sustained diplomatic ties with Israel continued—and still continue—to inhibit restoration to its pre-1977 pinnacle among fellow Arabs. On the one hand, these links with Israel, established and maintained under U.S. auspices, earned Egypt massive financial support and indirect benefits in many ways. On the other hand, Sadat's policies left lingering suspicions among Egypt's Arab neighbors and sharply engendered domestic tensions.

Tensions have eased under President Mubarak. In 1989, he took the chair of the Organization of African Unity. Thus, Egypt received at least qualified restoration to both Arabism and Pan-Africanism and regained a position within Islamic world affairs. In the regional reaction to Iraq's invasion of Kuwait in 1990, Egypt led the opposition to the incursion and vigorously supported the international coalition to liberate Kuwait. In addition to its critical political efforts, Egypt contributed 35,000 men and a significant amount of equipment—making it the third-largest contributor after the United States and Saudi Arabia—to coalition forces. But, even with the regional tensions, Egypt's overall internal situation markedly improved with the financial support of the United States.

Egypt's relations with its upstream neighbor, the Sudan, have been important since the dawn of history. These long relations found expression in a friendly 1982 agreement, a ten-year Charter of Integration between the two, calling for close cooperation in foreign policy, security, and development. But relations deteriorated in the late 1980s under Sudanese threats to dam the Nile, with the ascendancy in 1989 of a confrontation-prone government in Khartoum, and because Sudan sided with Iraq after Saddam Husayn invaded Kuwait. In 1995, Egypt accused the Sudanese government of involvement in a failed assassination attempt on President Mubarak while he was visiting Ethiopia. Relations with Libya, its other Arab neighbor, under the quixotic President Qadhdhafi (Qaddafi), have been spasmodic. Plans for political unity in 1971 were abrogated in 1984, giving way to conflict and brief border warfare. After years of tension, the countries reconciled in 1989, although proof of détente—resumption of full diplomatic links—was slow in coming until Qadhdhafi dramatically returned Libya to normal global relations in 2004. With Iraq, Egypt's relations have been generally stormy since the 1960s when pro-Nasser elements were often involved in Iraqi coup attempts. Unlike Syria, though, Egypt supported Iraq in its war with Iran; however, it became an active member of the coalition to dislodge Iraq from Kuwait. Egypt was quietly critical of the U.S.-led invasion in 2003 and afterward renewed diplomatic relations with the post-Saddam government. Its envoy in Baghdad was kidnapped and presumed killed in 2005, and not until 2009 did it appoint a new ambassador. Like other predominantly Sunni Arab states, it has been uneasy about the possibility of the emergence of a "Shii Crescent" stretching from Iran through Iraq to Lebanon.

Egyptian-Israeli relations have been the mainspring of the post–World War II geopolitical evolution of the Levant and northeastern Africa (see Chap. 8). Despite having been Israel's main foe in four wars, Egypt was the first Arab country to sign a peace treaty. Although it suffered ostracism by most of its neighbors after 1979, it increasingly profited from the peace dividend. A disputed claim over the Taba enclave in Sinai was settled in Egypt's favor in 1988, increasing reciprocal confidence. As the Egyptian-Israeli relationship and Mubarak's role matured, Egypt has often mediated among diverse players in regional disputes. Not only did it strongly support the successive stages of the Palestinian/Arab-Israeli peace process, it found mutual benefits in its various dealings with Israel and the United States. During the first term of the highly controversial Israeli prime minister Binyamin Netanyahu, the relationship moved into a "cold peace," and just as relations were improving, Israeli actions during the second intifadah, under Prime Minister Ariel Sharon, introduced constraints. In the late 2000s, Egypt served as the mediator between Israel and Palestinian factions, particularly in Gaza. When Netanyahu returned as Israeli prime minister in 2009, official relations seemed likely to turn cool again, but Egypt continued mediating between Israel and the Hamas regime in control of Gaza, as well as between Hamas and the Palestinian Authority in pursuit of renewed peace negotiations between Israel and a united Palestinian representation. However, on a business level, relations are more "normal" (see above regarding QIZs[46] and exports to Israel of natural gas). Israeli tourists continue to visit Egypt annually, especially to resorts in the Sinai; terrorist attacks at Taba, Sharm al-Shaykh, and Dahab in 2004 caused temporary downturns, but the cheaper holiday prices in Egypt continue to attract visitors. The reverse flow of tourists is minimal, as few Egyptians enter Israel.

Relations with the United States after 1974 have been central to Egypt's political-economic position. Cut off by Nasser after the Israeli attack in 1967, they resumed in 1974 after Nasser's death and after the United States brokered the Sinai disengagement agreements. In other efforts to foster détente between Egypt and Israel, the United States established the Sinai Support and Field Missions after 1976 and sponsored the Camp David accords and the Egyptian-Israeli peace treaty. From 1974, the United States first supplanted, then supplemented, Arab financial support, with military grants, credits, and training and economic and food aid. Egypt continues to be the second-largest recipient (after Israel) of U.S. aid, receiving more than $2 billion in military and economic assistance annually through the 2000s.[47] The USAID mission in Cairo (at one point the largest in the world) has assisted Egypt to encourage economic reform and support development projects, especially in agriculture, education, and health; by the end of the 2000s, development aid totaled $30 billion. Egypt, in turn, maintains peace with Israel and has provided facilities for use by U.S. forces in the region and for joint military exercises. U.S.-Egyptian relations became particularly close during 1991–1992, when the United States forgave $7 billion in debt. It was not coincidence that led President Barack Obama to deliver a major reconciliatory speech to the Islamic world at Cairo University in June 2009.[48]

Relations between the former Soviet Union and Egypt are primarily of historical interest, although the Aswan High Dam remains a long-term testament to what Egypt gained. Seventeen years of close relations based on mutual advantage deteriorated when Sadat replaced Nasser. In July 1972, he expelled 15,000–20,000 Soviet advisers and repudiated the 1971 friendship treaty. Soviet-Egyptian relations had remained correct after the reestablishment of ties with the United States, but in September 1981 the Soviet ambassador and several aides were expelled on charges of espionage. Relations were restored in July 1984. After the breakup of the USSR, Egypt pursued good relations not only with Russia but also with the new Muslim republics—Azerbaijan and the five Central Asian "stans."

Despite having exercised imperialist control over Egypt after 1882 and having participated in the 1956 tripartite invasion of the

Suez, Britain now has good relations with Egypt. France also had imperialist interests in the area and assumed an especially important role in the construction and operation of the Suez Canal. Both Britain and France were involved in the 1956 Suez affair, leading to Nasser's sequestration of British and French properties. European cultural influence carries over, however, and both English and French are second languages for many educated Egyptians. In addition, the EU is Egypt's leading trading partner. Egypt and the EU signed an Association Agreement in 2004 according free-trade status to much of the two-way movement of goods between them.

Thus restored to a pivotal role in Arab and Islamic world affairs, and once again demonstrating the continuing advantages of its major power core location, Egypt strives to pursue a moderate course among its trilateral ties with the Arab world, the West, and Israel. President Mubarak also restored relations with Iran in 1991 after four years of mutual distrust, though at the end of the 2000s Egypt has made no secret of its concern over Iran's nuclear policies. With Naguib Mahfouz winning the Nobel Prize for Literature in 1988, and former Egyptian foreign minister Boutros Boutros-Ghali, a Coptic Christian, having served as secretary-general of the United Nations from 1992 to 1996, Egypt has achieved positive recognition on the world stage.

NOTES

1. Egypt is one of the best-analyzed countries in the Middle East. Recommended studies of post-1952 Egypt include Waterbury 1983; Hopwood 1982; Makram-Ebeid 1989; Lorenz 1990; Goldschmidt 2004; *Egypt* Country Study 1991; and U.S. Department of State, *Background Note: Egypt*, Mar. 2010, and *Country Commercial Guide: Egypt*, 2009.

2. See C. Williams 2002.

3. See *New York Times*, Dec. 4, 2002, and Dec. 26, 2003; *Christian Science Monitor*, June 20, 2003.

4. Although technical in many aspects, R. Said 1962 is useful for the landforms of Egypt. Dr. Said was formerly director of the Geological Survey of Egypt. For the 1992 Cairo earthquake, see *New York Times*, Oct. 13, 1992.

5. Details are given in Elhance 1999 and Rogers and Lydon 1994.

6. For further information, see www.nilebasin.org/.

7. Several studies of the Fayyum are outdated or difficult to find, but see Hewison 2001.

8. The evolution of the Nile is well covered in R. Said 1981, which is less technical than R. Said 1962. Even more readable is Collins 2002.

9. A good account of all these efforts is in Keating 1975. Keating was with UNESCO and was deeply involved with that organization's Nubian Campaign.

10. IEA, "2006 Energy Balance for Egypt."

11. See Benedick 1979; Waterbury 1979; and the current and excellent Collins 2002. Nile water problems and some details of the Aswan High Dam are discussed in Elhance 1999 and Collins 2002. See also Haynes and Whittington 1981.

12. An excellent account of the Western Desert, its oases, landmarks, and people, is found in Vivian 2000.

13. The excellent Hobbs 1989 discusses the physical environment of the Eastern Desert and focuses on the Bedouin of the area.

14. *New York Times*, Sept. 8 and Mar. 4, 2002.

15. Scholarly but readable accounts of these developments are in Hobbs 1996, 1999. An update is in *Christian Science Monitor*, Mar. 10, 2004.

16. See Nisan 2002, Chap. 7.

17. *Washington Post*, July 7, 2008.

18. *BBC News*, Jan. 7, 2010; *Asia News*, Jan. 8, 2010 at www.sprcroforum.com.

19. Hobbs 1989 is an in-depth study of the Maaza.

20. For a retrospect, see *Economist*, May 1, 1999.

21. U.S. Department of Defense, "Report to Congress: Measuring Stability and Security in Iraq," Nov. 2006.

22. Saqqaf 1987, 227, 234. Part 5 of Saqqaf analyzes urbanization in Egypt, especially Cairo. The readable Rodenbeck 1998 gives an intimate view of Cairo. See also Abu-Lughod 1971. Ghannam 2002 is a more recent examination of this unusual metropolis.

23. *Christian Science Monitor*, May 27, 2004; *New York Times*, Oct. 19, 2004.

24. See Goell et al. 2009 for a discussion of Egypt's experiences with desert urbanization, at www.idec .eg/Upload/Documents/175/EN/Sustainable%20Cities %20in%20Egypt.pdf.

25. Stewart 1996.

26. See C. Moore 1986 and Goldschmidt 2004.

27. World Bank and the International Finance Corporation, "Doing Business, 2008," www.doingbusiness .org/features/DB2008Report.aspx. See also *Global Arab Network*, Mar. 24, 2010.

28. Transparency International 2009.

29. Brain-drain concerns are discussed in *Al-Ahram Weekly On-line* (Cairo) 2004, 2005; and *Egypt Today* (Cairo) 2004.

30. This section draws partly from three U.S. Department of State publications: *Country Commercial Guide: Egypt*, 2003 and 2009; *Economic Policy and Trade Practices: Egypt*, 1998; and *Background Note: Egypt*, Aug. 2004 and Mar. 2010; and one from the U.S. Department of Agriculture: *Agricultural Situation Report: Egypt*, 1997.

31. Hawass 1999. The find is also reported in *New York Times*, Aug. 24, 1999.

32. USAID emphasized its skepticism by indicating its unwillingness to finance any aspect of the project. Despite the unfortunate fact that this seemed to echo the U.S. refusal to be involved in the High Dam in the 1950s, the Toshka abstention was grounded in technical, not political, concerns.

33. See additional details in *New York Times*, Jan. 10, 1997; U.S. Department of State, *Country Commercial Guide: Egypt*, 2003; article by David Hirst in *Washington Times*, Aug. 4, 1999; and Foreign Agriculture Service (FAS) report for Egypt for 1997, available at www.fas.usda.gov.

34. See FAS report for Egypt 1997, as well as *Christian Science Monitor*, Oct. 22, 1997.

35. FAO, various issues.

36. IRIN, "Egypt: River Pollution Hits Nile Fishermen," Dec. 13, 2009, www.irinnews.org/.

37. *Oil and Gas Journal*, July 12, 2004. See also *International Petroleum Encyclopedia* 2003, 1999, and earlier years. This section also draws on U.S. Department of State, *Country Commercial Guide: Egypt*, 2003 and 2009, and U.S. Department of Energy, Energy Information Administration, *Country Analysis Briefs: Egypt*, Feb. 2004 and Aug. 2008.

38. *International Petroleum Encyclopedia* 2009.

39. USGS, "The Mineral Industry of Egypt," in *Minerals Yearbook* 2008.

40. To gain duty-free status, these products must include a specified degree of Israeli inputs.

41. There is also a swing bridge for railway traffic crossing the Canal near Ismailiya.

42. Alibaba.com, Dec. 8, 2009. See www.suezcanal.gov.eg/ for further information on expansion plans.

43. IRIN, Dec. 13, 2009, at www.spiroforum.com/.

44. *Media Line*, Feb. 17, 2010.

45. Lorenz 1990 gives an excellent discussion of the subject, including an introductory chapter titled "The Geographic and Historical Setting." See also U.S. Department of State, *Background Note: Egypt*, Aug. 2004 and Mar. 2010.

46. Goods produced in QIZs must contain a certain percentage of Israeli content to qualify for duty-free treatment.

47. U.S. aid to Egypt increased dramatically after Camp David and is analyzed in D. Clarke 1997 and updated in *Christian Science Monitor*, Apr. 12, 2004.

48. See www.whitehouse.gov/the_press_office/Remarks-by-the-President-at-Cairo-University-6-04-09/ for the full text.

18

Turkey
Bridgeland in Anatolia

The preceding country surveys reveal the pronounced variety of physical and cultural elements among those fourteen states. The analyses showed notable contrasts between Jordan and the UAE, Yemen and Egypt, Israel and Iraq. Yet, twelve of the fourteen—Israel and Cyprus are the exceptions—have been Arab states, members of the Arab League, their peoples mainly speaking Arabic. Except for Cyprus and Lebanon, the landscapes have included or even been dominated by deserts, with all that implies. We now turn to two quite different countries, first Turkey and then Iran. Neither is Arab, and each differs from the other as greatly as it does from the other fourteen. And although both are Muslim, each practices Islam differently from the other and in many respects differently from the Arab countries. Certainly, Turkey makes a startling contrast with the state just considered, Egypt.

BETWEEN EUROPE AND THE MIDDLE EAST

With its geopolitically strategic bridgeland location, Asia Minor has long been a transit land. Traversing that bridgeland millennia ago, Europeans moved down the valleys and over the passes of the Balkans into the Anatolian basins and beyond. Others from the Caucasus and the Iranian Plateau crossed the rugged mountains of eastern Anatolia, mingling with Europeans in the central basins. Later empires were centered in Constantinople and ruled lands from the Atlantic to the Arabian Peninsula coasts. Post–World War I republican Turkey retained its tenacious foothold in Europe and, now with bridges over the Bosporus, links Europe with Asia. Contemporary Turkey is also a Middle East Muslim state that openly pursues Europeanization, uses a European (Roman) alphabet, and belongs to the North Atlantic Treaty Organization (NATO). Moreover, the European Union finally invited Turkey to accession talks in October 2005 on eventual EU membership.

Turkey's geographical assets include not only its location in the geopolitically Anatolian power center but also its control of the strategic Bosporus and Dardanelles straits. Facing imperial Russia, later the Soviet Union, and now the successor republics across the Black Sea and in the Caucasus, it has been in more wars with Russia over the past 500 years than any other nation. Its strategic position is evinced in its being the anchor on NATO's southeastern flank and simultaneously a key member of the Central Treaty Organization (CENTO) before the collapse of CENTO with the Iranian revolution. Soviet disintegration somewhat diminished the importance of its NATO role, but

TURKEY

Long-form official name, anglicized: Republic of Turkey

Official name, transliterated: Türkiye Cumhuriyeti

Form of government: multiparty republic with one legislative house (Turkish Grand National Assembly)

Area: 299,158 mi^2/774,815 km^2

Population, 2008: 71,002,000; Literacy (Latest): 88.1%

Ethnic composition (%): Turk 70; Kurd 18; Crimean Tatar 7; Arab 2; Azerbaijani 1; Yoruk 1; other 1 (Ethnic Turks sometimes said to be nearly 80%)

Religions (%): Muslim 97.5, of which Sunni 82.5, Shii 15.0 (most classified as Shii are likely to be Alevi); nonreligious 2.0; other 0.5

Demography: Life expectancy—69.3 yr (M), 74.2 yr (F); Birthrate (per 1,000)—19.4; Fertility rate—2.17

GDP, 2009: $608 billion; purchasing power parity: $859.8 billion; per capita: $11,200

Currency: Turkish new lira, US$1 = 1.543 new liras, 1 new lira = $0.647 (March 2010)

Energy reserves: oil—262.2 mn bbl; natural gas—215 mn ft^3; coal—2 bn t

Main exports (% of total value, 2007): textiles and clothing 21.4; transport equipment 17.0; machinery and apparatus 15.1; base and fabricated metals 14.6; vegetables and fruits 4.1

Main imports (% of total value, 2007): machinery and apparatus 21.1; mineral fuels 20.6; base and fabricated metals 15.2; transport equipment 8.5

Capital city: Ankara 3,763,591; other major cities: Istanbul 10,757,327; Izmir 2,606,294; Bursa 1,431,172; Adana 1,366,027; Gaziantep 1,175,042

---

its setting thrust it once again into a geopolitical vortex vis-à-vis the former Soviet satellites and successor republics in the Balkans, the Trans-Caucasus, and Central Asia. Moreover, Turkey is the only country that bordered both contestants in the 1980–1988 Iran-Iraq War. As one of Iraq's six immediate neighbors, it played an important part in the 1990–1991 Gulf crisis but, asserting its independence, limited its role in 2003. However, it has been active in postinvasion Iraq on several fronts.

Fourth in size among Middle East states, Turkey has a much greater proportion of habitable productive environments than has the larger Saudi Arabia, Iran, and Egypt. It has by far the longest coastlines among all regional states. It leads the area in a wide range of agricultural products and, with the notable exception of petroleum, of both mineral resources and production. It ranks first in extent of roads and railroads, in vehicle numbers, in GDP, in total value added by manufacturing, and in many military categories. Development efforts have focused on human, agricultural, mineral, and industrial resources; after progressing slowly for decades, Turkey began realizing its national potential more rapidly in the mid-1980s. Serious problems remain, but it has made considerable advances toward modernization, democratization, and Westernization.[1]

Physical reminders of Asia Minor's rich history are found not only in Istanbul and other cities but also along the coastlands and in the remote valleys. Sites of the numerous successive civilizations in the richly diverse environments of the peninsula are becoming increasingly accessible and well known.

For clarity in nomenclature, "Turkey" refers to the Republic of Turkey, including the 3 percent of its territory in Europe (eastern Thrace). "Asia Minor" refers to the peninsula that lies between the Black Sea and the northeastern Mediterranean east of the Aegean. "Anatolia" (Turkish: Anadolu), frequently considered synonymous with Asia Minor, technically refers to the interior plateau excluding the three coastlands of Asia Minor. Both Asia Minor and Anatolia exclude Turkey-in-Europe—Anatolia implies Europe's antithesis. "Ottoman," of course, refers to the multinationality empire or aspects of that empire (dynasty, culture, territory) that centered in Constantinople before 1918.

COMPLEX REGIONAL PATTERNS

A Physical Interlocation

The rugged and often picturesque landscapes of Turkey are the product of particularly complex and powerful earth forces that have shaped Anatolia for millions of years and still manifest themselves in frequent earthquakes and related seismic events (see Map 2.3). Like Iran, Asia Minor lay in the former Tethyan geosyncline, literally squeezed between the African and Eurasian tectonic plates (see Chap. 2). It is part of the huge belt of Alpine folding during the Tertiary period extending from the Atlantic to the eastern Himalayas. Anatolia and Iran are the two halves of the Mobile Belt Province (see Map 2.2); both exhibit exceedingly complex geomorphology that has a strong impact on other patterns.[2]

The massive tectonism that shaped Asia Minor created a virtually continuous belt of folded mountains across northern Anatolia

and a similar one across the south. This pattern is replicated in Iran. In both countries, the diastrophism and volcanism accompanying plate convergence induced widespread mineralization (see Map 6.5). Compression enclosed resistant blocks in between, and accompanying forces raised and depressed masses in the east and west. In the west, the alternating raised blocks (horsts) and depressed basins (grabens) create the irregular coastline along the Aegean. In the east, the confused mountain mass comprises some of the most rugged topography in the region (see Fig. 2.6), including lofty volcanoes, such as the well-known Mount Ararat. Other volcanic cones rise high above the central Anatolian Plateau in symmetrical grandeur.

At least three geomorphic blocks in southern Turkey are allochthonous terrains—segments of the earth's crust rafted in from some considerable distance over millions of years and literally rammed into place as the African and Eurasian plates compressed.[3] Thus, relatively recent folding, faulting, and volcanism combined with interrelated soils, vegetation, and climates to endow Turkey with a wide variety of environments. These, in turn, have been utilized and shaped by successive civilizations to produce the modern state.

A Mosaic of Regions

[1] Pontus and Black Sea Coast. The northern fold belt comprises principally the Pontic (or North Anatolian) Mountains, which include a variety of sedimentary rocks, some igneous intrusions, and large areas of lava flows (see Map 18.1; circled numbers indicate regions). Topographically, the mountains comprise long, narrow chains and lengthy troughlike valleys and basins; rivers follow the structures for part of their courses toward the Black Sea. Some of the trenches mark the strike of the North Anatolian Transform Fault. Slippage along this very active fault zone caused several devastating earthquakes in the twentieth century between Erzincan in

the east and the Marmara in the west. In addition to those mentioned below, the 7.4 magnitude quake in August 1999 on the Gulf of Izmit and its aftershocks, followed by another 7.2 quake at Düzce in November, were among Turkey's greatest natural disasters. More than 17,000 died, 50,000 were injured, and 500,000 were made homeless in this densely populated area. As much as 16 ft/5 m of right-lateral strike-slip displacement occurred along a 75-mi/120-km zone of the North Anatolian Fault between Karamürsel and Golyaka.

Several ridges in the west and one toward the east form an almost unbroken wall between the Black Sea and the interior, with elevations of 5,000–6,000 ft/1,525–1,830 m in the west and higher ones in the east, 10,000–13,000 ft/3,050–3,960 m (see Fig. 1.2). The upper and steeper slopes, especially those facing northwest, support Turkey's densest forests, primarily hardwoods in the west and evergreen softwoods in the east.

Features with major historical, economic, strategic, and seismic significance include the down-faulted basins now flooded by the Sea of Marmara and its eastern extensions into the gulfs of Izmit and Gemlik. Qualifying as a separate geographic region by some authorities, the eastern Marmara area has the greatest concentration of population in the country, including the historic city of Istanbul (formerly Constantinople) and its suburbs. Especially in Thrace, the countryside has orchards and market gardens near the cities, with fields of sunflowers beyond. This foothold in Europe holds an especially important symbolic significance for Turks.

North of the Pontic Mountains, a narrow coastal plain extends the length of the Black Sea shore, with the Kızıl and Yeşil rivers forming prominent deltas west and east of Samsun. Except where mountain shoulders push against the shore, the plain is densely populated, with the major coal-mining and industrial town of Zonguldak to the west and

one of Turkey's two tobacco areas to the east, around Samsun, which is the southern terminus of the underwater "Blue Stream" natural gas pipeline from Russia (see "Hydrocarbons," below). East of the tobacco belt lie citrus groves and, around the ancient city and port of Trabzon, the world's leading hazelnut area. Farthest east, beyond Rize, are extensive tea plantations; the southeastern Black Sea is Turkey's best fishery.

[2] Taurus, Anti-Taurus, and Mediterranean Coast.   Covering the southern third of Asia Minor, the Taurus Mountains (Toros Dağları) stretch from the southwestern corner of the peninsula east to the upper Seyhan River Basin north of Adana. From there, the Anti-Taurus extends to Lake Van. The complex Anti-Taurus also embraces extensive nappe structures, but it differs from the Taurus in having deep ocean crust masses (ophiolites, as in Oman), South Anatolian Suture structures, faulting along the South Anatolian Transform Fault, and thrust-faulted masses east of the transform fault. Mineralization in these complex structures enriches the area; around Ergani lies one of Turkey's most important mining and metallurgical areas. Around Elazığ and Malatya, the rugged topography, drained by the Euphrates and Tigris, is the focus of its most ambitious development scheme, the Southeast Anatolia Project (Turkish: Güneydoğu Anadolu Projesi—GAP) (see "*Étatisme* and After" later in this chapter). High atop the isolated peak of Nemrud Dağ stands the remarkable burial complex of a Commagene king from the middle of the first century BCE (Fig. 18.1). The eastern Anti-Taurus merges with the East Anatolian Accretionary Complex (see [5] below).

The upper elevations of the broad mountain belt of the Taurus vary from 7,000 to 9,000 ft/2,135 to 2,745 m. Primarily limestone, and including several nappes and fenêtres (see Glossary) like those in the Swiss

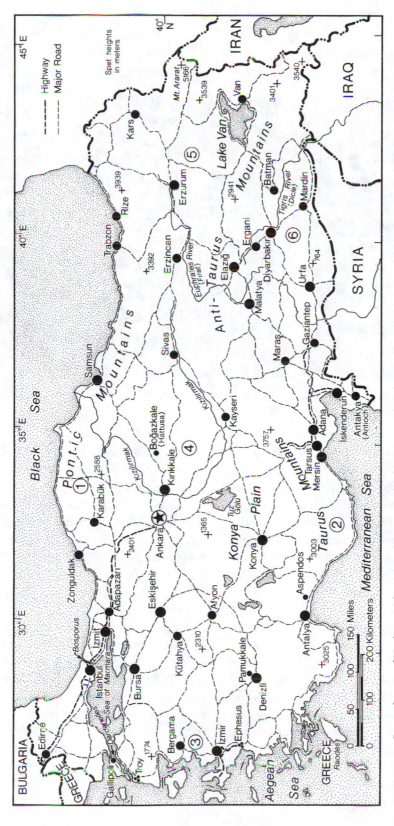

MAP 18.1 General map of Turkey, with major cities, main highways, spot heights, main mountain ranges, and geographic regions (identified by circled numbers).

FIGURE 18.1 Huge stone heads from a Commagene monument on remote Nemrud Dağ date from the second century BCE.

Alps, the maquis-clad highland separates the Mediterranean coast and the Anatolian interior. The few rivers that cut through the limestone mass follow almost vertically walled canyons, and only three or four major routes connect coast and interior. The most famous of them passes northwestward from Adana through the dramatic Cilician Gates (Gülek Boğazı), at 3,444 ft/1,050 m.

Along the southern coastal bulge from Alanya to Mersin, mountain shoulders drop steeply into the sea, separating eastern settlements from those to the west around Antalya. Impressive karst features are common—collapsed caverns, sinkholes, and dolines and poljes (larger solution basins). Several are spectacular tourist attractions. Many of the dolines and poljes are floored with alluvial soils; wheat, barley, grapes, and figs are grown. Where coastal plains exist, or on small deltas formed by rivers slicing through the

Taurus, citrus, bananas, early vegetables, and other tender plants are cultivated.

At the eastern end of the coast is the flat Çukurova (Çukur Plain) on the extensive coalesced deltas of the Seyhan and Ceyhan rivers. Sometimes called "smooth Cilicia," it is the best-developed agricultural area in Turkey, with large irrigated cotton fields. Cotton, cottonseed, textile mills, and clothing factories employ much of the plain's dense population. Adana is the fifth-largest city, and near it is the huge NATO air base of Incirlik (discussed in "Relations" below). The Gulf of Iskenderun, with a complex of ports for petroleum coming from three directions and agricultural products from the southeast, lies to the east of the Çukurova. Yumurtalık is the terminus for dual pipelines from Iraq and, perhaps more important, for the strategic Baku-Tbilisi-Ceyhan (BTC) pipeline from the Caspian, operational in 2005.

Dörtyol is the export terminus for Turkey's Batman oil fields. Iskenderun (formerly Alexandretta) is the main import-export facility for the southeast, including the GAP, and has a major iron and steel mill.

West of the Çukurova lies Turkey's largest port—Mersin. Still farther west as far as Manavgat is the "rough Cilicia" coast, and farther, to Antalya, is the Pamphylian coastal plain. Between Mersin and Antalya, along this Turkish Riviera, the ruins of ancient settlements, most from Hellenistic and Roman times, attest to a dense, rich, and thriving seaward-facing population in classical times. Castles, theaters, and other vestiges attract archaeologists and tourists to Anamur, Alanya, Side, Aspendos, Perge, Termessos, and, especially, to Antalya,[4] the western core of the coast and developed as a bustling tourist destination since the 1970s.

[3] Aegean Area. Turkey's Aegean area resembles much of Greece in topography, climate, soils, and even the ruins of numerous classical cities along the coast. Until the early 1920s, much of its population was Greek. The up-thrust horsts and down-dropped grabens follow the predominant east-west structure of Asia Minor, offering easy access to climatic and cultural influences. Grabens afford deep eastward penetration of valleys, some drowned by the sea, and horsts form extensions of the land westward as mountainous peninsulas. Rivers such as the Büyük Menderes drain the alluvium-filled grabens and have built deltas into the narrow bays. Some deltas advance several meters per year, and in doing so have silted up ancient harbors, leaving classical ports like Ephesus and Miletus several miles inland.

These and other Greco-Roman cities combine with modern resorts and scenery to give Turkey some of its most outstanding tourist attractions.[5] Major classical sites include Pergamum (modern Bergama, Fig. 3.4), Izmir (formerly Smyrna), Sardis, Colophon, Ephesus, Priene, Miletus, Didyma, and Halicarnassus (modern Bodrum). The focal point of the region is Izmir, Turkey's third-largest city, with NATO's largest naval base in the eastern Mediterranean and the annual International Trade Fair. Among the coastal resorts, Kuşadası is one of the best developed. The alluvial-filled grabens are prime agricultural areas, planted in olive groves next to the coast, then fruit and nut trees (citrus toward the south and almonds toward the north), tobacco, and cotton. Aegean tobacco complements Black Sea tobacco, supplying one of Turkey's traditional exports. The broad grabens have long provided access between the Aegean and the productive interior.

[4] Interior Anatolia. Immured between the Pontic wall on the north and the Taurus barrier on the south is the inner Anatolian Plateau, technically the true Anatolia. Its surface, except in the heart of the region around Tuz Gölü, displays greater variety of relief than the term "plateau" might suggest.

Western Anatolia, which is hilly to mountainous, exhibits evidence of continuing tectonism, with numerous earthquakes, lava flows, and hot springs. Thermal springs indicate molten rock intrusions close to the surface. Hot springs near Denizli were a spa for classical Hieropolis, and dramatic calcium-carbonate travertine terraces at Pamukkale attract scientists and tourists. Still more volcanism is seen in the city of Afyon, which developed around a prominent mountain that peaks in a volcanic plug. Wheat and corn are widely grown, and uncommon specialty crops are produced in selected localities—for example, opium poppies around Afyon (Turkish *afyon* = opium), tobacco in several areas, and roses near Isparta, north of Antalya. An essential oil for rose water, used both in desserts and for fragrant hand washing on special occasions throughout the Middle East, is derived from roses.

The transitional area between the Aegean and central Anatolia was the major battleground for the Greek-Turkish war in the early 1920s. The same area received many of the Turkish immigrants from the Balkans in the population exchange with Greece and Bulgaria in the 1920s. Industry developed steadily in the area, bringing factories to Isparta, Kütahya, Eskişehir, and Afyon. A scenic lake district between Isparta and Konya includes twelve sizable lakes in grabens and solution basins, serving as local sumps. Most are saline without outlets.

Farther east, in the central and eastern parts of the interior, lies quintessential Anatolia with its vast flat-to-rolling treeless steppes and characteristic grain fields. Climatic stress typical of steppes brings poor rain years and sharp yield reductions, as in 1928 with harvests less than one-tenth the average. This semiarid core, with less than 12 in/300 mm of rainfall, grows wheat and barley; the more humid periphery has fruits, cotton, sugar beets, grapes, and tobacco.[6]

Formerly poorly developed, central Anatolia was the focus of national attention when the Ottoman Empire broke up after World War I and the capital was shifted from Istanbul to Ankara. Then little more than an unprepossessing village in a hilly volcanic area, Ankara had a central, interior, protected location at a major route junction. Now the second-largest city, it is the central place for the Anatolian Plateau; it spread up the slopes of the original basin onto the surrounding plateau (Fig. 18.2). Economic growth brought infrastructure development like dams and highways. Hirfanlı Dam was built on the Kızılırmak northeast of the Tuz Gölü in the 1950s. Of special scholarly and touristic interest are Hattusa, the ancient Hittite capital east of Ankara; Göreme, with unique early Christian churches and homes hollowed out of volcanic ash pinnacles west of Kayseri (Fig. 18.3); remarkable underground cities, excavated in the soft volcanic tuff and used by

early Christians for refuge, at Derinkuyu and Kaymaklı; and Konya, the Seljuk capital. Tuz Gölü is a shallow salt lake at the bottom of the enclosed central Anatolian sump. With its surface near 3,000 ft/900 m, the lake's size varies greatly, depending on precipitation and runoff.

[5] Eastern Anatolia. The rugged eastern Anatolian Mountains at the eastern end of the Anti-Taurus show the complex folding and volcanism resulting from the junction of three tectonic units (see Map 2.2 and Fig. 2.6). Several extensive Tertiary lava flows and volcanic cones testify to vigorous volcanicity attending interplate compression, with Mount Ararat (Ağrı Dağı) towering to 16,948 ft/5,166 m. Several peaks reach 8,000–10,000 ft/2,440–3,050 m. Lake Van, largest of Turkey's lakes, has a surface elevation of 5,400 ft/1,646 m; it so completely blocks transit routes that the railway to Iran crosses it by ferry. Massive and frequent earthquakes here result from slippage along two fault systems (North and East Anatolian) intersecting west of the lake. Erzincan, near where they meet, has seen three disasters in the past seventy years—45,000 died in the 1939 quake, 1,330 in 1983, and 1,000 in 1992.

These rugged highlands have given refuge to several peoples, especially the Armenians (for whom the mountainous area of Armenia was named) and, to the south, the Kurds. Covered with heavy snow in the long winters, the mountains serve as a major hydrographic center, from which snowmelt and spring rains supply the headwaters of several rivers—the Tigris and Euphrates, flowing south to the Gulf; the Aras, flowing east to the Caspian; and several small streams emptying into the Black Sea or Lake Van.

Numerous villages lie in the valleys and on the steep slopes, but towns are widely separated. Erzurum has a large university and serves as a main station on the new BTC pipeline. To the northeast, Kars and Ardahan

FIGURE 18.2 View of Ankara, capital of Turkey, from the Hisar (ancient citadel), on a volcanic remnant in the center of the city. The view looks northeast along Etlik Caddesi to the northeastern suburbs of Ankara.

FIGURE 18.3 Hollowed-out volcanic-ash stacks in the Göreme Valley in Cappadochia were used as dwellings and churches by early Christians.

anchor territory often contested by Turks and Russians.

[6] The Southeast: The Arabian Platform. South of the Anti-Taurus and the Arabian Fold Belt is the Arabian Foreland, extending into Syria. The broad plateau surface exhibits gentle relief and elevations between 1,640 ft/500 m and 2,625 ft/800 m. The main center is Urfa (officially Şanlıurfa)—once the capital of the Crusader kingdom of Edessa. Gaziantep, one of Turkey's ten largest cities, serves as a center west of the Euphrates, as does Mardin to the east. Toward the northern edge of the platform, on the upper Tigris, is the ancient basalt-walled Kurdish city of Diyarbakır. Traditionally growing wheat and barley, the region saw only limited development until major new irrigation projects brought Euphrates water to the western section. The area is experiencing a boom in the transformation of the landscape through GAP, the Southeast Anatolia Project. About 600,000 Arabs inhabit the area, along with Kurds who have moved from mountain villages in the north to the southeastern cities. The insurrection led by the Kurdish Workers Party (PKK) destabilized the region for fifteen years after 1984, but development accelerated after a qualified resolution of the conflict (discussed under "Relations" and in Chap. 8).

A HISTORICAL TAPESTRY

Like Egypt and Iran, Asia Minor reflects a long history of cultures and empires (see Chap. 3), and recent intensified field research has pushed back both the beginning dates and the scope of early Anatolian cultures. The increasingly rich physical evidence of this may be seen in the thousands of tells (*hüyüks* or *tepes*), tumuli, towers, tombs, and ruins. World-class museums in Istanbul and Ankara contain superb collections of prehistoric implements and later pottery, statuary, cuneiform tablets, and other artifacts.

Caves near Antalya show evidence of Upper Paleolithic occupation. Hacılar, the earliest agricultural settlement in Asia Minor, dates to about 7040 BCE, and Çatal Hüyük, with its remarkable artworks, flourished in 6500–5650 BCE (see Map 3.1). The oldest man-made place of worship yet discovered is at Göberkli Tepe, where the earliest structures date as far back as 10,000 BCE.[7] Fabled Troy, guarding the entrance to the Dardanelles, has early layers predating 2500 BCE, although the legendary Trojan War was about 1200 BCE. The Hittites arose in central Anatolia and maintained a great capital at Hattusa, whose remarkable ruins are near Ankara. A score of other peoples waxed and waned in Anatolian fastnesses and along the rugged coastlines. Lydians in the west had Sardis as their capital and Croesus (fl. 550 BCE) their most famous king. Aeolian, Ionian, and Dorian Greeks ensconced themselves along the Aegean coast during classical times. Among the many peoples in the interior were the Galatians (Gauls), of European descent, to whom the apostle Paul wrote New Testament epistles. Indeed, Asia Minor nurtured first-century Christianity, harboring the "Seven Churches of Asia" addressed in the Book of Revelation—Pergamum, Smyrna, Ephesus, Sardis, Laodicea, Philadelphia, and Thyatira—and emerging as the area in which early Christianity then had its strongest foothold.

A watershed geopolitical event occurred in 330 CE, when Emperor Constantine transferred his capital from Rome to Byzantium, renaming it Constantinople. It was the capital of empires—Eastern Roman, Byzantine, and Ottoman—for nearly 1,600 years, putting its distinctive stamp on most of Asia Minor as well as on the Balkans and the Levant (see Chap. 3). With its steady decline, Arab Muslims from one direction and Seljuk Turkish Muslims from another carved away at its territories. Crusader efforts to protect the Christian Byzantines delayed, but hardly prevented, Turkish inroads. In central Anatolia, Seljuks established the Sultanate of Rum (Rum = Rome, that is, Europe), with other Turkish and Turkman principalities that rose and fell for two centuries. Finally, the Ottomans dominated and eventually gained control of Asia Minor and extensive areas beyond (see Chap. 3).[8] They seized Constantinople in 1453 and maintained it as their capital until their empire ended with World War I.

Contemporary republican Turkey arose on the ruins of the decayed Ottoman Empire, the "sick man of Europe," defeated in war against the Allies.[9] Led by the charismatic Mustafa Kemal, later surnamed Atatürk (Father of the Turks), the young republic asserted itself in the early 1920s.[10] It resisted partition of the Anatolian heartland, expelling British, French, and Greek forces, substituting the Treaty of Lausanne in 1923 for the onerous Treaty of Sèvres (1920). The aggressive Kemalist program called for republicanism, nationalism, populism, reformism, secularism, *étatisme* (state capitalism), and economic development.

This warrior-statesman insisted on Turkishness, the modernization of Turkey, and economic and cultural Europeanization. One fundamental and symbolic change, for example, was the abandonment of the Arabic alphabet and adoption of a modified Roman alphabet (1928). Also replaced were several items of traditional Turkish clothing, notably the fez (or tarbush) worn by men. Most adopted the visored cap, then common in America and Europe, headgear that still gives Turkish workingmen a characteristic appearance. The veil formerly worn by women was forbidden, angering conservative families, especially in inner Anatolia—an issue that was rekindled in the 1990s. The magnetic Atatürk served successive terms as president until his death in 1938. By then, Kemalism had been institutionalized into a quasi religion, countering some of Islam's conservativism. It continues to provide the state with an ideological base and is still the rationale for liberal policies.

Turkey was neutral until the final days of World War II, when, by declaring war on Germany, it became a charter member of the United Nations. Soviet assertiveness immediately after the war prompted a mutuality of interests between Turkey and the United States. Under the Truman Doctrine (1947), military and economic aid was extended to Greece and Turkey, and Turkey joined NATO in 1952. Most Turkish concerns for the next forty years focused chiefly on Soviet intentions. Lacking Atatürk-like authority, governments repeatedly failed in economic matters, and domestic conflict—often violent—flared between Left and Right. The Kemalist-minded military staged coups in 1960, "by memorandum" in 1971, and in 1980; each temporarily stabilized a disintegrating situation. Thus, for decades Turkish democracy was regularly marred by episodes of instability and authoritarian rule.

For fifteen years after 1984, the PKK insurrection in the southeast, the poorest and most neglected part of the country, became a quagmire for every administration.[11] Capture of PKK leader Abdullah Öcalan in February 1999 and his later death sentence provoked violent demonstrations. His request to his followers to cooperate with the state suppressed the level of domestic rebellion; pressure from the EU and other sources gained the commutation of his sentence to life in prison. With the conflict subdued, the state of siege in the southeast was lifted in November 2002. Political and juridical reforms begun in preparation for EU acceptance have smoothed Turkish-Kurdish tensions, although in the aftermath of the invasion of Iraq new problems have arisen regarding Kurdish aspirations there (see Chap. 13). In a similar sense, Turks are concerned with the situation of their ethnic kin, the Turkmans, in Iraqi Kurdistan.[12]

Meanwhile, beginning in the 1990s, basic shifts rapidly succeeded one another in Turkey's political orientation, structure, and electorate. Resurgent political Islamism dates to the 1960s and led to conflict with secularist elements, especially the ever-vigilant military. By fits and starts, a compromise was reached: Islamist politicians gained power by becoming increasingly moderate; from the mid-1980s, the military maintained watchfulness but mostly eschewed direct political involvement. Since 2002, the government has been in the hands of a temperate party, Justice and Development (AKP), with religious roots, headed by Prime Minister Recep Tayyip Erdoğan, a former reformist mayor of Istanbul. Making the qualifying for acceptance into the EU his top priority, he melded secularism and conservative Islam, coordinating an impressive overhaul of laws, policies, and procedures, even the constitution—modifying one-third of its provisions.[13] When the parliament refused a U.S. offer of billions of dollars for the use of Turkish bases to invade Iraq in 2003, he placated the United States by allowing use of Incirlik air base for troop rotations. Many Turkish observers saw this show of independence as strengthening the country's democracy.

Toward the end of the decade, partly as a result of the hostility of some European countries (France and Germany in particular) to Turkish EU membership, partly because of increased hostility toward Israel after the "Summer War" of 2006 and the Gaza campaign of 2009, partly because of Turkey's increased involvement with the petro-states to the east and south relative to transmission facilities, the government seemed to be reemphasizing its connections with its Muslim neighbors. Whether this would be at the expense of past links with Europe, the United States, and Israel was a subject receiving considerable attention at home and abroad.[14] Domestically, between the devout and the secular major issues remain, but through most of the decade, these were generally settled through compromise after periodic confrontation. In 2010, a sizable number of active and retired military officers were under arrest in connection with the alleged Ergenekon plot of ultranationalists against the AKP. Some secularists feared the government was using the investigation to consolidate one-party Islamist rule,[15] and many observers argued that the influence of the military—the historic guardian of the Kemalist secular state—was waning.[16]

THE TURKISH POPULATION

Turkey is second in population in the Middle East, and Turks are, after Arabs, the second-largest ethnolinguistic group in the region. Its population doubled from 1950 to 1975, exceeding growth in employment; thousands of jobless workers headed for labor-short Western Europe during the 1960s. Although migration later ceased, as many as 4 million Turkish citizens and their descendants, about one-quarter of them Kurds, remained there in the late 2000s.

Among the larger states of the region, Turkey has the most evenly distributed population geographically. Lacking deserts, it has low population densities only in the more rugged mountains and on the central steppe. Map 4.2 shows the highest densities are around Istanbul, along the Black Sea coast, along and inland from the Aegean coast, near Ankara, and on the highly developed Çukurova around Adana.

As a multiethnic empire, the Ottoman state followed a *millet* system that permitted ethnic groups autonomy. Inevitably, in more enlightened modern times, separatist sentiments evolved into anti-Turkish nationalism among some groups; and supported by European powers, many groups did gain independence. After the war, the republic sought greater homogeneity and renounced the multinational state; downplaying ethnic differences, it proclaimed "Turkey for the Turks and the Turks for Turkey." Having experienced centrifugal forces of separatism and foreign exploitation of minorities after World

War I, the government has adamantly enforced "Turkishness," and recognition of minorities and of special minority rights contradicts the policy's most basic tenets. Kurds and Armenians are seen as specific examples of minorities fragmenting the republic, and changing this core belief is an alteration that Turkey will find difficult in preparing for EU membership.

Ethnic Turks are descendants of Central Asiatic nomadic tribes who intermarried with more than a score of identifiable groups over many centuries. In the Ottoman golden age, "Turk" was a term of disdain for Anatolian peasants as opposed to the cosmopolitan "Ottomans" of Constantinople. But republican leaders proclaim Turkishness with national pride and have systematically "purified" the language of many Arabic and Persian loanwords.

Census reports minimize ethnolinguistic differences, grouping most citizens as Turks. As a result, the size of known minority groups can be only estimated. The obviously large Kurdish population is believed to be as much as 18 percent, and Arabs perhaps 2 percent. Smaller minorities include Circassians, Abkhaz (related to Circassians), Georgians, Laze, Armenians, Greeks, and Jews. Tatars, Turkmans, and Yörük are grouped with Turks.

An estimated 12-13 million Kurds, sometimes referred to as "mountain Turks," are firmly entrenched in the extension of their mountain homeland into southeastern Turkey. Kurds, Armenians, Turks, and Russians battled in eastern Anatolia in 1915, when Kurds and Armenians each sought independence from Turkey and Russia, sometimes fighting each other. Once Turkey had achieved stability in the mid-1920s, it specifically rejected Kurdish identity and checked any movement toward separatism, as it had earlier with Armenians. As Kurds in Iraq battled suppression under Saddam Husayn, the Marxist PKK initiated open rebellion in southeastern Anatolia in 1984. By the time of

the trial of its leader Öcalan, nearly 30,000 rebels, military, police, and civilians had died during fifteen years of insurgency. The southeast was under martial law, and use of the Kurdish language in schools, courts, publications, and broadcasting was illegal. In the early 2000s, restrictions were slightly eased, and in 2008 a twenty-four-hour state-owned television channel even started broadcasting in Kurdish, Farsi, and Arabic.

The war against Kurdish separatism has been one of Turkey's two costliest ventures, with GAP, also in the southeast, being the other. Turkey's human rights record, especially regarding the Kurds, evoked international censure and is a major issue in its preparation for EU membership. In late 2009, the government put forward a multifaceted peace initiative as the basis of negotiations with the Kurdish minority, including establishment of an independent human rights oversight commission, ratification of the UN Convention Against Torture, legalization of the use of the Kurdish language in political campaigning,[17] and restoring Kurdish names to places where Kurds are the majority. This bold move was soon complicated by a Constitutional Court ruling that outlawed the main Kurdish political party (with twenty-one parliamentary seats), a move then strongly criticized by Prime Minister Erdoğan;[18] within days, however, the government arrested eight mayors of Kurdish towns.[19] Turkey's Kurdish problem is unrelenting.

Also noteworthy in the southeast are the Alevi, a heterodox offshoot from Shiism and close kin to the Syrian Alawi sect (see Chap. 9). Because adherents to the sect often disguise their affiliation, the Alevi are sometimes mistakenly equated with all Shii, although in actuality the Alevi are only one—though the largest—of four Shii-related sects in Turkey. Alevi constitute a sizable percentage of the population and include Turks, Arabs, and Kurds. Although they were originally mostly in the southeast, many have migrated to urban areas in western Turkey and other parts of Anatolia. Yezidis, who may or may not be Kurds but definitely practice their own distinctive religion, were reported in the late 2000s to have mostly emigrated to Germany.[20]

Relatively small minorities from the Caucasus include Circassians and the related Abkhaz, with many Circassians living in the Adana area; Georgians, a group that actually comprises several different minorities; and the Laze, a small group in the southeastern Black Sea area, primarily fishermen.

Greeks and Armenians are the major Christian groups in Turkey. Both are heavily concentrated in Istanbul; they are tiny remnants of much larger pre–World War I groups (see Chap. 4). Armenians were formerly dominant in eastern Anatolia, generally referred to as "Armenia" but are now a small minority numbering about 40,000. Details of the tragic deaths of perhaps as many as 1.5 million are given in Chapter 4. Armenian militants attacked Turkish diplomats in Europe during the 1970s and early 1980s, but with their own neighboring independent state since the collapse of the USSR, Armenians now present their case nonviolently in world media.[21] Fewer than 5,000 Greeks remain, clustered in Istanbul around the Phanar, the seat of the ecumenical patriarch, Bartholomew, the first among equals of the heads of the Eastern Orthodox communities and their 300 million believers. The historic Patriarchate, dating to the fourth century, exists under a great deal of unofficial constraint, and some fear that it is in danger of either dying out or of having to leave its traditional seat for exile.[22] After decades of harassment, tiny remnants of Syrian Orthodox and Assyrian/Chaldean Christians that perhaps once numbered 200,000 remain in scattered locations in the southeast.

Of an estimated 90,000 Jews in Turkey after World War II, fewer than 25,000 remain. About 30,000 went to Israel in the late 1940s, and more have left since then—not all to Is-rael. Most remaining are in business or the professions in Istanbul or Izmir. Nonhomogeneous, they include Sephardim, speaking Ladino; Ashkenazim, speaking Yiddish; and Karaites, speaking Greek and often viewed by other Jews as heretics. All speak Turkish as a second or equal language. Dönme (a somewhat opprobrious term like "turncoat") are Jews who converted to Islam and now merged with the general population; they are considered neither Jews nor Muslims by most of their compatriots.

VILLAGE AND CITY

Although Turkey is becoming more urbanized, it is still very much village oriented, with more than 40,000 villages well distributed over the country. The widespread pattern of humid climates and rainfed agriculture situates villages on upper slopes and hilltops, thus presenting landscapes more typical of the humid Levant or Europe. Widely differing house materials appear in different environments: wooden in forested areas, masonry on barren limestone slopes, and mud brick or with mud walls in river bottoms.

Mosque, public bathhouse, small fruit and vegetable market, and the teahouse (*halkevi*—literally, "people's house") form the village center. The *halkevi* is ubiquitous in both city and village, where the clientele is virtually all male. Increasing numbers of them offer Internet links. Village attitudes remain conservative regarding women. Except where they have become enclaves of expanding cities, villages are politically conservative, religious, and stable. Important in rural life is the weekly market, conducted in larger centrally located villages.

Rapid rural population growth in the 1950s and 1960s sent millions of the landless to larger cities. Whereas rural population was nearly 80 percent in the early 1950s, it was only 32 percent by 2006. Migrants to Istanbul, Ankara, Izmir, and other cities found shelter in rapidly spreading *gecekondus* (literally, "built overnight"), squatter settlements enabled by a law prohibiting forced removal of habitations having completed roofs (see Chap. 4). The Muslim tradition of urban "quarters" for different groups carries over to the *gecekondus*, which cluster by ethnic and sectarian affiliation.[23]

The cities exhibit great variety, especially those that were once capitals of kingdoms or principalities. Istanbul, the imperial capital on a peninsula above Bosporus, Marmara, and Golden Horn waters, has a unique skyline of magnificent domes and minarets. Bursa, the Ottoman capital before Istanbul, preserves medieval monuments and is a major silk-producing center. The Seljuk capital of Konya, its ruins mixed with modern buildings rising from the Anatolian plain, preserves structures in the old Seljuk style. Turkey's modern capital Ankara has a core of contemporary government buildings and a picturesque old center clustered around the ancient *hisar* (fortress).[24]

ECONOMIC DEVELOPMENT

Étatisme and After

Having lagged economically in the declining Ottoman years, Turkey made slow progress after World War I. To counter private capital shortages and forestall dominance by foreign capital, Atatürk adopted *étatisme* (state capitalism) as his basic economic philosophy. Government participation in industry had advantages for planning purposes at the price of bureaucratic constraints. Though domestic capital was usually in short supply, persistence brought the country to an appreciable level of development with a series of five-year plans under the State Planning Organization, created in 1961.

Reforms during the 1980s under Prime Minister and (later) President Turgut Özal, an economist, led to a development-oriented investment climate.[25] The government grad-

ually abandoned Atatürk's policies and steadily reformed and privatized state economic enterprises (SEEs). Turkey achieved an enviable level of prosperity: It averaged an annual 5 percent GDP growth for fifteen years, became the world's eighteenth-largest economy, was the fastest-growing member of the Organization for Economic Cooperation and Development, was the largest Middle East economy, was rated as one of the world's top tourist destinations, was designated by the United States as a "big emerging market," became—as an original signatory to the General Agreement on Tariffs and Trade—a founding member of the World Trade Organization in 1995, and entered a customs union with the EU in 1996. The energy, telecommunications, transportation, and textile sectors of its economy were especially vigorous, and the labor-force share of manufacturing and services rose steadily.

On the economic downside in the 1990s, runaway inflation—averaging about 70 percent annually, peaking at more than 125 percent in 1995—resulted mostly from public-sector deficits. To illustrate the problem: The Turkish lira dropped from 9 to the dollar in 1957 to 2,618 in mid-1990, 624,000 in mid-2000, and a staggering 1,351,351 by the end of 2004. The situation demanded radical action, and a new lira dropping six zeros appeared on January 1, 2005 and remained reasonably stable through the rest of the decade. These problems manifested the urgency for accelerating privatization, especially since it was obvious that the dynamic private sector was driving overall development. A 1998 accord with the International Monetary Fund obligated Turkey to speed up sale of SEEs, reduce subsidies and price supports, raise the retirement age (which, under three separate systems, averaged forty-three), and cut the budget deficit. Despite general infrastructural adequacy, Turkey needed to upgrade its ports, some airports, and railways.[26] Its achievements were statistically impressive, as was noted earlier, and with the exception of its lack of petroleum, it was and is the most nearly balanced economy in the region.

That the new policies bore fruit can be seen in the rise in foreign direct investment from $982 million in 2000 to $22.2 billion in 2007. There has also been some improvement in investor perceptions of corruption in Turkey: By Transparency International's index, there has been slow, steady improvement over the past decade. In 2008, Turkey ranked 61st of 180 countries, 8th among the countries studied in this book—still low by European standards—but one place ahead of EU member Italy and eleven ahead of Greece.[27] By the European criteria Turkey aims to fulfill, living standards for its citizens still lag. Regarding other business-oriented measures, Turkey's standings need improvement if more and diversified foreign investment is to be increased significantly. By the World Economic Forum, Turkey was ranked 61st of 133 countries internationally (10th regionally, ahead of only Egypt and Syria) in global competitiveness in 2009.[28] The Fraser Institute in 2008 put Turkey in 90th place of 141 countries (and 11th regionally, ahead only of Syria) in economic freedom.[29] In a World Bank Group report on the ease of doing business, Turkey ranked 57th of 178 countries globally and 5th regionally, falling between Oman and the UAE.[30]

Using the Human Development Index (HDI) developed by the UNDP, Turkey's global rank was 79th of the 182 countries rated in 2007, 9th of the 16 Middle East countries, and below all the current and aspiring members of the European Union, even Albania. Still, its most recent HDI did show a gain of more than 28 percent over 1980, largely on the basis of rising per capita income.[31]

Turkey has the highest potential for hydroelectric power among all European countries except Norway and Sweden. Lacking petroleum resources, it turned to hydropower for energy.[32] Dams were constructed before 1970 in widely separated river basins—the Kızılırmak, Yeşil, upper Gediz, Sakarya, Seyhan—and smaller dams elsewhere. However, it was the ambitious program of constructing the giant Euphrates dams after 1965 that strongly established Turkey's impressive achievements in hydropower and large-scale irrigation. The keystone is the Southeast Anatolia Project.

Embracing thirteen interrelated subprojects distributed over 28,185 mi^2/73,000 km^2, GAP is one of the largest projects of its kind ever attempted. Included are twenty-two dams and nineteen hydroelectric installations—seven on the Euphrates and six on the Tigris. One goal is irrigating 4.2 mn ac/1.7 mn ha—equivalent to about half of Egypt's irrigated land. The Euphrates is dammed by three giant barrages, Keban (technically not part of GAP), Karakaya, and Atatürk (shown on Map 18.2). It exploits the steep gradients of the rivers descending from the well-watered east Anatolian Mountains through deep canyons. The Euphrates profile permits high dams forming successive reservoirs in stair-step configuration, with a difference in elevation of 495 ft/151 m from one reservoir to the next.

The first dam upstream is the Keban, completed before GAP in 1974 for power purposes only, 670 ft/204 m high. Located 103 mi/166 km farther on is the Karakaya, completed in 1987—also for power generation only. Downstream 112 mi/180 km is the showpiece of GAP, the Atatürk and its 2,400-MW power station (Fig. 18.4). This dam, near the southern margin of the Anti-Taurus, is to irrigate about 1.8 mn ac/730,000 ha of high-quality land in the Arabian Foreland north of Syria. Turkey's blocking the Euphrates flow and its increased consumption of water have greatly concerned the downstream riparian states, Syria and Iraq (see Chap. 8). Six subprojects are on the Tigris between Diyarbakır and the border; although

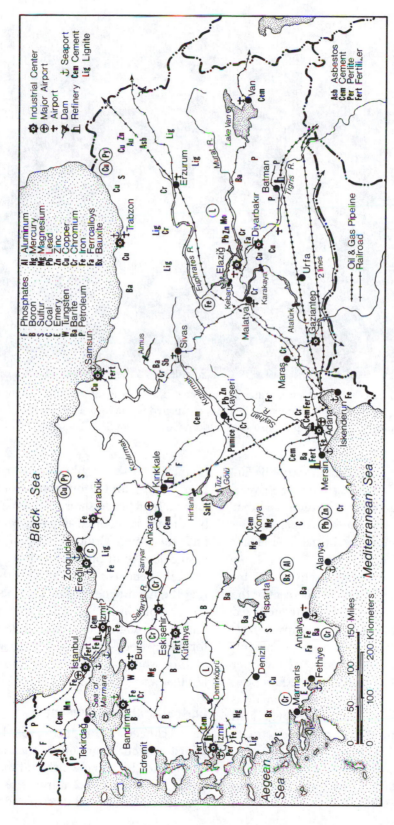

MAP 18.2 Economic map of Turkey, showing railways, ports, airports, numerous solid-mineral mining areas, pipelines, and other economic features. Note Atatürk Dam on the Euphrates River west of Urfa (see also Fig. 18.4).

FIGURE 18.4 Atatürk Dam on the Euphrates River. Each of the eight giant penstocks of the power station (center) is 24 ft/7.25 m in diameter. The dam, completed in the early 1990s, is the centerpiece of Turkey's GAP project. (Photograph courtesy of Turkish Government State Hydraulic Works [DSI])

all are on smaller scales than those on the Euphrates, they nevertheless affect the river's flow. Both Syria and Iraq have argued that Turkey is violating international law by claiming its absolute territorial sovereignty with regard to water.

If completed, GAP will generate 27 bn KW hours annually, about 25 percent of the national total. Turkey has greatly increased its gas-fired thermal power capacity in an effort to maintain its pace of development; still, Turks consumed electricity on a per capita basis in 2006 far below the European average—only in Moldova and Albania was the rate lower. Gas-fired plants generated about 45 percent of the nation's electricity and coal about 25 percent.

GAP ran into delays in the late 2000s because of budgetary, environmental, and lingering regional ethnic problems. European financing for the highly controversial Ilisu Dam planned for the Euphrates near the Syrian and Iraqi borders was canceled in 2009,[33] but China was reported as having some interest in the project. Critics have claimed that so far the poor southeastern provinces have yet to see the benefits claimed for the project and that the main beneficiaries have been electricity consumers in urbanized western Turkey; through 2008, the completion rate for the hydroelectric projects was about 85 percent, while that for irrigation projects was less than 25 percent.[34]

Agricultural Development

Varied climate and productive soils have sustained Anatolian agriculture for more than 3,000 years. Farming, which had made little technical progress in centuries, was encouraged to modernize and diversify after World

War II; Turkish agriculture is now a more productive sector. The most fruitful lands historically have been the Aegean and Marmara areas, but the irrigated Çukurova now vies with them. As more and more of the Arabian Foreland plains are irrigated in the GAP, they too will become prime areas. In the late 1990s, 123,550 ac/50,000 ha were devoted to irrigated crops, mostly cotton, in the Harran Plain (south of Urfa) alone. Overall, irrigated area has increased from 2.7 mn ac/1.1 mn ha in 1962 to 12.9 mn ac/5.2 mn ha by 2007.

Agricultural landholdings in the 4.5 million farms are generally small and fragmented, although wheat farms are medium size. Maintaining inherited land is traditional, and only Yemen in the region has a higher proportion of the workforce in agriculture. Mechanization, still-high rural birthrates, and urban attractions induce rural-to-urban and east-to-west migration.

Animal husbandry has long been essential in Anatolia, both on farms and with nomadic pastoralists and their sheep, goats, and camels (see Fig. 5.8). As with crops, animal breeds, breeding practices, feeds, processing, and marketing are all being improved. Cattle receive particular attention, and dairying is important in the high pastures of the northern mountains. Grazing dominates the mountainous eastern fourth of the country. As elsewhere in the Middle East, poultry raising has expanded markedly; Turkey is second, after the United States, in mohair production, from the famous Angora goat.

With its great environmental variety, Turkey produces a great range of crops: bananas, dates, grapes, citrus, and cotton along the southern coast; olives, cotton, tobacco, citrus, grapes, soft fruits, and figs in the west; tobacco, tea, rice, and hazelnuts along the Black Sea; and wheat and barley in central Anatolia. Potatoes, sugar beets, pulses, melons, onions, and other crops are widely distributed. Sunflowers flourish in the open landscapes of Thrace. An unusual aspect of Turkish agriculture is the regulated cultivation of opium poppies in the west-central basins. Maize is well adapted to the more humid areas of Anatolia (see Fig. 1.2) and is increasingly produced for both food and feed. Turkey leads the Middle East in the production of a score of crops, producing from 40 to 70 percent of the regional total in many cases (see Tables 5.2, 5.3, and 5.4). In 2007, agriculture's contribution to GDP was 8.9 percent, while it continued to provide a livelihood to 36 percent of the labor force. From the early 1960s through the mid-2000s, food production per capita grew by a modest 6 percent, notably less than most of the other countries in the region.[35]

Forestry and Fishing

Turkey and Iran are the only two countries in the Middle East with well-developed forest industries., and Turkey has the more extensive forests (45 million ac/18 million ha). Its production equals the roundwood output of the rest of the entire region. Forests cover the steeper slopes rimming the central Anatolian Plateau and basins, with particularly dense forests in the Pontic Mountains in the north.

Formerly the leading fishing country in the Middle East, Turkey is now second to Egypt. It increased its annual catch twelvefold from 1975 to 2006, to 662,000 mt. Fish exports, mostly to western Europe, include such specialty items as shrimp, lobsters, snails, eels, sponges, tortoises, and frog legs. Half of the catch is taken in eastern Black Sea waters, but virtually every town and village along all three coasts engage in fishing.

Industrial Development

An Overview.   As we have seen, Turkey leads the region with its range of industrial establishments and their total non-oil output. The variety and quantity of agricultural products support food processing and agribusiness, and the minerals industry—the most varied and highly developed in the region—further adds to manufacturing diversification. As they have from the early years of expansion, energy deficiencies (particularly petroleum and natural gas) challenge manufacturers to seek alternatives. Imported natural gas now supplies that energy at the cost of limited foreign exchange. However, Turkey's manufacturing sector has steadily increased its GDP share, reaching 22 percent by 2006.

As with agricultural production, mining operations, and population—all unusually uniformly spread over the country—industrial concentrations are likewise well distributed (see Map 18.2). The largest complexes, especially those producing consumer goods, are in the main population centers. As a consequence, the half-dozen largest cities are also the leading industrial centers: Istanbul (with more than half of all enterprises), Ankara, Izmir, Adana, Bursa, and Gaziantep. However, towns in specialty crop areas usually process foods, beverages, and industrial crops. Examples include Rize, tea packing; Trabzon, hazelnut shelling and packing; Tekirdağ, wine making; Afyon, opium processing; Bursa, silks; Isparta, rugs, using local wool; and Adana, cotton milling and textiles.

Mineral Industries.   The tectonic and structural conditions in the Mobile Belt, extending west-east across the Anatolian and Iranian plateaus, give rise to several zones of extensive mineralization. Unfortunately, Turkey possesses a sizable number of small deposits but few large ones. Reserves of most metals are not large by world standards, although those for bauxite (aluminum ore), chromite, copper, lead, iron ore, gold, and silver are appreciable.[36] Most significant in reserves and production are such industrial minerals as barite, boron, emery, feldspar, magnesite, perlite, pumice, and dimension stone. Sharing the Mobile Belt mineralization, Turkey and Iran rank first or second in the region in output of a dozen minerals, including bauxite, copper, iron ore, and silver. They also rank second and third after Saudi Arabia in gold and lead ore.

The public-sector Etibank had long controlled minerals and mining, but during the 1990s it steadily sold off its holdings under the privatization program. Sectoral profitability has now notably increased, and solid minerals production contributes appreciably to GDP. Mineral utilization has a long tradition in Anatolia: Ironworking—believed to have originated among the Hittites—was a profitable activity in their empire 3,700 years ago, the wealth of Croesus came from gold taken from the rivers of the Aegean region, and obsidian (volcanic glass) from the volcanic area of central Anatolia was traded in the Fertile Crescent during the Neolithic period.

Hydrocarbons.   Turkey's mineral fuels include coal, lignite, and small amounts of petroleum and natural gas. Although its coal and lignite production is more than 96 percent of the region's total, its oil output is by far the least of all Middle East producers and is less than one-fourth that of tiny Bahrain (see Table 6.1). Bituminous coal reserves, 1 bn mt, and lignite reserves, 8 bn mt, are sufficient for more than 200 years at the present rate of production. By contrast, petroleum reserves of 300 mn bbl indicate less than a twelve-year supply, even at the low rate of production. Recent natural gas discoveries, primarily in Thrace, improve the energy outlook modestly, but Turkey must import more than 90 percent of its petroleum needs and 50 percent of its total energy requirements. One of the benefits of allotting right-of-way for Iraqi pipelines to Yumurtalık is a share of the oil they carry (see Chaps. 6 and 13). The lines had to shut down in August 1990 for several years, but deliveries resumed in 1997–2003 under the UN Oil for Food program. A reported 50,000 bpd was also smuggled in from Iraq by tanker truck during this period.

In the aftermath of the 2003 invasion, Iraqi throughput was often interrupted by pipeline sabotage but was quite steady in early 2010.

As mentioned in Chapter 6 under "Pipelines," Turkey was deeply involved in the discussions over the controversial routing and financing of the Baku-Tbilisi-Ceyhan pipeline bringing Caspian oil to an export terminal. Agreements signed in Istanbul in 1999 selected the route through Turkey, strongly supported by the United States and Israel, over Russian and Iranian alternatives; after thirty-three months of construction, deliveries began in 2005. An engineering triumph, at 1,038 mi/1,670 km in length through Azerbaijan, Georgia, and Turkey, it is about as long as Tapline with a larger diameter (42 in/107 cm) and twice the capacity (1 mn bpd). After entering northeastern Turkey, it passes near Erzurum and reaches the terminal near Ceyhan, close to the Yumurtalık outlet of the Iraqi pipelines. Inter alia, Turkey opposed an eastern Black Sea terminus for the pipeline because tankers from there would pose a major environmental hazard transiting the narrow Bosporus to reach western markets.[37] Additionally, in the late 2000s, that passage is near its capacity and cannot safely accommodate many more ships than now.

Like other countries in the region and elsewhere, Turkey is vigorously ensuring sources of natural gas for power operation and domestic heating. Smog and other pollutants from widespread use of low-grade coal convinced it to use hydropower and imported gas to generate environmentally clean energy. Although it has imported Russian gas by pipeline through Bulgaria since 1986, it diversified its suppliers with two additional ones: In 2002, a long-delayed line from Tabriz, Iran, began deliveries, and later that year the twin Blue Stream 866-mi/1,394-km line was operational from Russia under the Black Sea. The line reaches Samsun and extends to the Ankara area, and it can deliver

565 bcf a year. Additional options for Turkey are a Caspian gas line and imports of Algerian LNG.

The country is increasingly crisscrossed by pipelines taking oil and gas to distant markets. In 2009, Turkey and the EU signed an $11 billion deal to build the 2,000-mi/3,220-km Nabucco gas pipeline to cross Anatolia, stretching from the Caspian to Austria and bypassing current supply lines through Russia.[38] But Azerbaijan reportedly was dissatisfied with the progress of negotiations on transit terms with Turkey and as a result was exploring other options for selling to Europe, including sending LNG to Bulgaria by ship, exporting via Russian pipelines, or even building a trans–Black Sea marine pipeline from Georgia to Romania; called White Stream,[39] this expensive option would certainly require its use by Central Asian producers as well to be economically feasible. Turkey, Italy, and Russia agreed in 2009 to construct a pipeline from Samsun to Ceyhan, allowing Russian exports (eventually 1.5 bb/day) to flow directly to tankers on the Mediterranean.[40] Thus, once again, Turkey's "bridgeland" function plays its role.

Although 45–60 million mt of lignite is mined in most years in several areas, especially in east-central Anatolia, hard coal comes almost entirely from the Zonguldak area on the western Black Sea coast (3 mn mt of anthracite in an average year). Although Turkey has 4.6 bn mt of coal resources, only 7 percent of which is anthracite, but because the veins are thin and contorted, extraction is increasingly costly, and coal is now imported for industrial use in the western and southern parts of the country.

Petroleum. The first encouraging oil strikes, in the Batman area between Diyarbakır and Siirt in southeastern Anatolia, were not made until 1940. Royal Dutch Shell and ExxonMobil have been the most successful of several operating companies, but the public-sector petroleum company, TPAO, produces about 80 percent of the output. Despite widespread exploration, discoveries have been virtually limited to the Fold Belt; fields are small, scattered, often deep, and found in complex geological structures. Production during the late 2000s averaged 41,000–45,000 bpd, having jumped to 90,000 bpd in 1991 after the Iraq pipeline was shut in. Output from the Batman fields moves by pipeline to Dörtyol on the Gulf of Iskenderun, but it satisfies less than 10 percent of Turkey's needs.

Oil Processing.   Of Turkey's seven refineries (see Map 18.2 and Table 6.2), with a total capacity of 714,000 bpd, the two largest are located at Izmit and Izmir and are supplied by imports by sea. The Kırıkkale refinery, opened in 1986, is fed by Iraqi crude brought by a dedicated pipeline from Yumurtalık; it has seen interrupted deliveries since 2003. Petrochemical production is limited, since feedstock has to be imported.

Metallurgy.   Many processing plants and manufacturing establishments that use mineral raw materials are mine oriented; mining areas and mineral industry concentrations are locationally related (see Map 18.2). Steel mills are located in three widely separated areas: around Zonguldak, with large plants at Karabük and Ereğli; Iskenderun; and around the eastern part of the Sea of Marmara, where three small plants mostly use scrap metal. A small plant in Izmir also uses scrap. Aluminum ore is mined and processed in a large new complex at Seydişehir, southwest of Konya.

More important on the world scale is Turkish production of several ferroalloys, none of which is plentiful on the world market. These include chromite (from Kütahya, Ergani, and Muğla), antimony (northwest of Sivas), manganese (Thrace, Eskişehir, Ereğli, and Denizli), and tungsten (near Bursa). Also significant are such nonferrous metals as copper (from several sources but especially from Ergani and Murgul), lead, and zinc (around Kayseri and Elazığ). Turkey produces significant amounts of the world's emery, boron, magnesite, perlite, and barite.[41] Near Eskişehir is the world's only commercial deposit of meerschaum, which is machined and carved in a cottage industry in and around the city for distinctive tobacco-pipe bowls.

Other Industries.   In addition to the crop-related and mineral industries, Turkey has developed perhaps the widest range of manufactures in the region, although Iran may be comparable. With a large domestic market, it produces consumer goods from automobiles through household appliances and electronic items. For its farms, it makes tractors (it has more tractors than all other Middle East countries combined), combines, milking machines, and fertilizers. For its large military forces, it manufactures weapons and ammunition, tanks, military vehicles, aircraft, and naval vessels. It also manufactures a wide variety of electrical equipment, railway rolling stock and other equipment, cement, and automotive parts. It makes steel from its own pig iron, coming from its own iron ore, and exports a growing amount of its manufactures. Tourism is not surprisingly a major sector in a country that boasts historic and religious sites spanning millennia, spectacular scenery, Mediterranean beaches, and major shopping opportunities. In 2008, there were 25 million tourist arrivals, leading all the sixteen countries detailed in this book, and placing fifth in Europe after France, Spain, Italy, and Britain; sectoral earnings were estimated at $20 billion. Not to be overlooked are its well-regarded traditional crafts—ceramic tiles from Iznik and pottery from Kütahya, brass and copper items, leather products and traditional hand-knotted rugs, as well as machine-made carpets.

Transportation

Turkey's large size plus its well-distributed development and detailed planning have resulted in an impressive transportation network. Although several links require improvement, the basic nets are the largest and best balanced in the region. By rail and road, it is well connected with five of its land neighbors. With the former Soviet republics, there was some traffic even before 1990, and since then there have been many improvements. Shipping and airlines link it with its neighbors and more distant states.

Railways. A trans-Anatolian rail line served Turkey as early as 1918, and an additional 2,052 mi/3,302 km of railway was completed by the end of World War II. Since then major additions have been made in the southeast and east, along the steadily developing Malatya-Elazığ-Diyarbakır-Siirt axis and on the line to Iran crossing Lake Van by ferry. All trackage is standard gauge (4.7 ft/1.435 m). Operated by Turkish State Railways (TCDD), the network has fallen far behind schedule for completing a badly needed overhaul of much of the system. Turkey's rail lines are especially adapted for shipping coal, other bulky minerals, and grain hundreds of miles to ports or internal markets. By the late 2000s, they made up one-third of the rail lines in the region. In 2009, Turkey and Saudi Arabia expressed the intention to rebuild the old Hijaz railroad as a standard-gauge line to connect at Madinah with a Saudi line now under construction.[42] Urban metro construction began in the 1990s, and by the end of the 2000s, Istanbul, Ankara, Bursa, and Izmir all had operating systems.[43]

Roads. After World War II, Turkey had a very limited road network, mostly poorly surfaced. Some of the Truman Doctrine financial aid to Turkey was devoted to road building for economic and political purposes as well as for security reasons. By 2008, it had 41 percent of the total length of all roads in the Middle East (see Table 7.2); every town had been integrated into a well-designed,

well-constructed, and serviceable network. Accelerated economic growth after 1985 overtaxed major routes, requiring construction of four-lane divided motorways. About 2,175 mi/3,500 km of motorways have been completed, approximately one-third of those planned. The Europe–Middle East route was first to be constructed: Edirne to Istanbul, across the second Bosporus bridge to Ankara, then to Adana and Gaziantep; sections around Izmir, Konya, and Ankara have also been completed. Turkey's goal is to build a net comparable to the German autobahns or the U.S. Interstate Highway system.

Despite an efficient and colorful ferry service across the Bosporus, heavy and rapidly increasing vehicular traffic by the late 1960s necessitated construction of a bridge across the strait. Spanning the narrowest part (about 0.6 mi/1 km) a few miles up the waterway from the old city and high above the water level, the suspension bridge linked Europe and Asia, enabling drivers to avoid long delays at ferry crossings. It was so successful at alleviating congestion that a wider second span opened in 1988 to carry long-distance routes, leaving the first bridge for local traffic. Despite early fears, the structures detract little from the beauty of the Bosporus (Fig. 18.5). As intercontinental traffic over the bridges (and on the ferries) continued to mount, the Marmaray project—a rail tunnel under the Bosporus—was undertaken. Completed in 2008, it links the commuter systems on the European and Asian sides of the metropolis, and it will carry a high-speed link to Ankara and beyond as well. A third bridge is planned at the Bosporus's northern end.

The Trans-European Motorway (TEM) enters Turkey at Edirne, crosses the Bosporus by bridge, and extends eastward through Ankara to the Iranian border opposite Maku, a stretch of 1,120 mi/1,800 km. Branches reach south to Adana (and beyond to Syria, Iraq, and the peninsula countries) and north to the Black Sea at Trabzon—a total of 2,235

FIGURE 18.5 Bosporus Strait, looking north toward the Black Sea. Rumeli Hisar, built in 1453 by Ottoman sultan Mehmet the Conqueror to facilitate his seizure of Constantinople, is to the left. The second Bosporus Bridge, opened in 1988 and named after Sultan Mehmet, spans the strait in the distance.

mi/3,600 km. Important for transiting traffic, especially tandem trailer trucks, between Europe and the Middle East, Turkey benefits appreciably from inclusion in the TEM network. Tourist facilities expect to attract larger numbers of Europeans from the northwest and Arabs from the southeast.

Ports and Shipping.   With 4,474 mi/7,200 km of coastline—longest in the Middle East— and intimate interrelations between land and sea in the west and northwest, Turkey has a long maritime history. It has numerous ports, some active since ancient times, and has a vigorous maritime trade. In addition to numerous small ports for coastal shipping, it has a half-dozen major and a score of secondary and minor ports for international trade. Although tonnage varies from year to year, leaders include Mersin and Iskenderun

on the Mediterranean, Izmir on the Aegean, Samsun on the Black Sea, and Bandırma, Derince, and Hydarpaşa (opposite Istanbul) on the Sea of Marmara. All are served by railway. Secondary ports from Alanya around to Trabzon are indicated on Map 18.2.

The total tonnage of general international cargo, excluding petroleum, through all ports exceeds that of any other Middle East country. Free zones were established at the Mediterranean ports of Mersin and Antalya in the mid-1980s. Turkey operates the third-largest merchant marine fleet in the region, about 890 ships, but deadweight tonnage is less than that of Iran and only a fifth that of the fleet registered in Cyprus under that country's flag of convenience.

Airways.   Turkish Airways (Türk Hava Yolları—THY), with more than 120 jet aircraft, ranks third in the Middle East after Emirates and Saudia. Turkey has more than forty airports with scheduled flights, and there are also several major military/NATO airfields, notably Incirlik (near Adana), Izmir, and Karamürsel (near Izmit). Istanbul's Atatürk International Airport opened a new international terminal in 2000; in 2008, it and Antalya's airport were the second and third busiest in the region. Turkey also has a number of private airlines (scheduled, charter, and cargo) operating internationally.

Trade

With its central location, lengthy coastline with numerous harbors, and range of resources, Asia Minor has historically engaged in extensive commerce and transit trade. Although some medieval trade routes from India, China, and East Africa ended at the Levant coast, others continued northward across Asia Minor to Trabzon or westward to the entrepôt of Constantinople or to lesser termini on the Aegean coast. European countries traded actively with the Ottoman Empire even as it declined.

During its early years, republican Turkey had little to export but agricultural products and specialty raw materials. By the late 1980s, manufactured products were more than two-thirds of exports. Exploiting the Arab League boycott of Egypt after 1979, Turkey increased its exports to Egypt and other Middle East countries as part of expanding economic and political ties with its neighbors to the south and southeast, most of whom were once Ottoman imperial possessions. However, its persistent vigorous efforts to strengthen relations with the EU have likewise targeted most foreign trade in that direction. All aspects of trade were sharply improved after economic liberalization beginning in the early 1980s and the lira was made fully convertible in early 1990. One evidence is the escalation in Turkey's exports from $2.28 billion in 1978 to $31 billion in 1998 and $107 billion in 2007. Textiles, apparel, machinery, and foodstuffs are the main exports.

RELATIONS

Turkey's location on the strategic bridgeland of Asia Minor with its geopolitical assets inevitably creates multidirectional reciprocal relationships; these exist not only between the republic and its neighbors but also with more distant powers concerned about this critical area. Interactions with imperial Russia were a mainspring of Ottoman foreign policy for centuries; periodically, they turned to Britain or France—and, later, Germany—to counterbalance Russia. After Atatürk's revival of his defeated country and his preservation of its Anatolian territory, Turkey and Western European states reached an uneasy détente. Though neutral for most of World War II, it eventually declared war on the Axis and became a charter UN member. As Soviet assertions after 1945 replaced historic Russian imperialism, it allied with the West, especially with the United States starting with the Truman Doctrine, against Soviet hegemonism.

With the Turkish Straits a critical focus (see Map 8.9), Turkey as a significant segment of the Northern Tier and the Eurasian Rimland, played a major geopolitical role during the Cold War. It participated in NATO after 1952, the Baghdad Pact, and then CENTO (headquartered in Ankara from 1958 to 1979) as a regional military anchor. It joined the Council of Europe in 1949, was a founding member of the Organization for Economic Cooperation and Development in 1961, linked with the European Free Trade Association in 1991, and entered into a customs union in 1996 with the EU. After years of ambivalence, the EU agreed to consider Turkey for membership in 2005—the only Muslim state so far accepted for consideration. Along with Saudi Arabia, Turkey is a member of the so-called G-20, increasingly the principal economic and financial forum of the world's wealthiest economies; a nonregional contributing member of the Asian Development Bank; and a borrowing member of the European Bank for Reconstruction and Development.

Turkey has made qualifying for the EU a priority, especially since that would, inter alia, finally bestow on it the cachet of a genuine European entity—one of Atatürk's main goals. In early discussions, the EU identified problem areas that Turkey must correct or greatly improve: human rights policies, military power in politics, treatment of minority ethnic and religious groups, and more open negotiation with Greece and Greek Cyprus. It has made strides toward some of these aims but, as mentioned above, has had difficulty with others, and there is open hostility in some EU countries to its admission to full membership. In recent years, it has shown some ambivalence about joining and has turned toward its Arab neighbors, Iran, and the newly independent states in the Caucasus and Central Asia.

Along with its important relations with Europe, Turkey's links with the United States remain close, although they have occasionally cooled. One time of stress was between 1975 and 1978, when the United States embargoed arms supplies consequent to Turkey's invasion of Cyprus in 1974; another, in early 2003, occurred when the parliament rebuffed U.S. efforts to employ Turkish bases for launching forces into Iraq. On the other hand, the United States has been a strong and consistent supporter of Turkey's quest for EU membership. Since 1947, U.S. military aid has totaled more than $14.5 billion. A large USAID mission coordinated more than $4 billion in an economic assistance program phased out in the mid-2000s,[44] a Joint Economic Commission guided economic development after 1993, and the Joint U.S. Military Mission for Aid to Turkey and the Turkish-U.S. Logistics Group coordinated military aid of equipment transfers. In return, Turkey gave the United States access to more than a dozen major facilities, including airfields, naval and communications bases and intelligence-gathering installations, and, until 1963, nuclear storage locales. The United States conducted major operations against the northern no-fly zone in Iraq from the Incirlik air base near Adana until 2003. At the end of the decade, a complicating factor in U.S.-Turkish relations was growing sympathy in Congress for declaring the tragic events affecting Armenians in Ottoman Turkey during World War I to be genocide;[45] in the late 2000s, the United States had been actively promoting reconciliation between Armenia and Turkey (see below), and the White House viewed congressional action on this matter as damaging to its efforts.

Turkey's focus on the Soviet threat during the Cold War contrasted with the Arab focus on the threat posed by Israel. Its alliances with Western powers put it further at odds with its neighbors. During this time, it discreetly disengaged from its Middle East environment and avoided involvement in inter-Arab disputes and in the Arab-Israeli and other regional conflicts. Yet it attempted to maintain cordial, if not close, political and diplomatic ties with all Arab regimes and Iran—usually with the exception of Syria.[46] The Cold War's end profoundly affected Turkey because its role in the Western alliance was suddenly ambivalent; it then sought a more participatory role in its own neighborhood—the Balkans, the Caucasus, Central Asia, and the Middle East.[47] At that same time, the Iraqi invasion of Kuwait forced it to adopt a proactive policy in regional affairs, while seeking links with the newly independent ex-Soviet republics, especially the five with which it had ethnolinguistic links.

Relations with its three Muslim neighbors—Syria, Iraq, and Iran—have varied markedly. With Syria they never have been warm, primarily because republican Turkey incorporated the Arabian Foreland plains inhabited by Arabs and because France unilaterally ceded it the disputed Hatay/Alexandretta area in 1938 (see Chap. 8). Two situations in the 1980s and 1990s heightened tensions dangerously: Syria's umbrage over Turkey's alleged overutilization of Euphrates water in the GAP and Turkish anger over Syrian support of Kurdish rebels, including harboring the PKK leader Abdullah Öcalan during 1984–1999. Details of both disputes are given in other chapters. Turkish-Syrian relations improved markedly in 2009.

Relations between Turkey and Iraq are of signal importance to both parties on several matters: their Kurdish minorities, the Kirkuk-Yumurtalık pipeline, the shared Euphrates and Tigris basins, and communications and commercial relations. Cooperation between them during the Iran-Iraq War was of great mutual benefit, but after Iraq invaded Kuwait, Turkey closed the pipeline from Kirkuk and joined the UN coalition. Both Iraq and Turkey benefited from the line's conditional reopening in 1997. They made tentative overtures for closer relations, but Turkey continued allowing U.S. aircraft to operate from Incirlik. Turkey's stance before and during the U.S.-led invasion attracted modest Arab approval. Since 2003, its interactions with and in Iraq have been complicated: On the one hand, it has been wary of the autonomy enjoyed by the Kurdish provinces in northern Iraq and on several occasions has skirmished with Kurds based there and engaging in hostile activities within Turkey; on the other hand, Turkish entrepreneurs have been very active—and very profitably so—in supplying a wide range of goods to Iraq, especially to the Kurdish north. Turkey has been actively supportive of Iraqi unity and of the government in Baghdad, which Prime Minister Erdoğan visited in 2008. It has also been increasingly vocal in backing the Turkman minority's rights in Kirkuk against Kurdish claims for the city.

Turkish-Iranian links were very close for twenty-five years under the Baghdad Pact/CENTO, and even more so under the Regional Cooperation for Development (RCD), but ties loosened somewhat with Iran's Islamic Revolution. Still, both are members of the RCD's successor, the Economic Cooperation Organization (ECO) founded in 1985 and expanded in 1992 to include Afghanistan and six former Soviet republics. ECO has a common market as its long-term goal. During the Iran-Iraq War, Turkey maintained links with both combatants; it still enjoys good, if not close, relations with the Islamic republic and has tried to mediate between Iran and the West regarding Iran's nuclear program.

Along with the more crisis-driven developments in Turkey's redirected foreign relations during the 1990s, links with Israel quietly evolved until they became a major regional concern. Turkey as a Muslim state—albeit secular—had been cautious in its attitude toward the Arab-Israeli conflict, but it recognized Israel in 1949 and maintained low-key diplomatic and economic relations over the next forty years. But with the sea change in regional dynamics after 1990, it de-emphasized links with Arab states and, strongly encouraged by the United States, pursued closer ties with Israel. After exchanging ambassadors in 1991, Turkey and Israel reached a series of agreements, including one in 1996 permitting Israel to use Turkish airspace for training flights. Turkey also contracted with Israel for missiles and F-4 fighter jet upgrades. U.S., Turkish, and Israeli naval units conducted joint maneuvers in 1998 off the Israeli coast. The two countries entered into a Free Trade Agreement in 2000. These moves, however, were not universally popular, and since the 2002 election installed a government with Islamic roots, there has been some pullback. Turkey was positioned to mediate in the late 2000s, promoting Israeli-Syrian rapprochement, although it reacted very negatively to Israel's 2008–2009 "Cast Lead" campaign in Gaza and later that year refused Israeli participation in a joint air force exercise in Turkish air space. By 2010, relations had frayed considerably, but both sides continued to show interest in Turkey's acting as mediator between Israel and Syria.

Across the Black Sea, in the Caucasus, and in Central Asia, the independent ex-Soviet republics immediately attracted attention, and Turkey quickly reached out to them—especially to the five that are both Muslim and Turkic: Azerbaijan, Kazakhstan, Kyrgyzstan, Turkmenistan, and Uzbekistan.[48] In 1992, Turkey hosted eleven nations, including six former Soviet republics, to create the Black Sea Economic Cooperation project; in 1999, Turkey, Azerbaijan, and Georgia pledged to cooperate on Caspian pipelines. Interestingly, in 2009 Turkey and Armenia announced that they would normalize relations after Turkish president Gul visited Yerevan after the brief war between Russia and Georgia; speculation was that Turkey wants to optimize its links with all the Caucasus states. Armenia reportedly was willing to postpone any discussion of the controversial events during World War I until diplomatic and trade relations were established. Rapprochement with Armenia, however, complicates links with Azerbaijan since part of its territory—Nagorno-Karabakh—is occupied by Armenia; Turkey has said full normalization will require settlement of this issue. The difficulty in attaining true rapprochement between the two neighbors was apparent by early 2010.

As important as the above relations may be, none are more critical than those with Greece and Cyprus. Dating from ancient times, antagonisms between Greece and Asia Minor revived more recently: the Greek war of independence from the Ottomans in the early 1800s, the Greek-Turkish war in the 1920s, conflict over Cyprus, and the dispute over the Aegean seabed (see Chap. 8). Among all the foreign relations problems, Cyprus has been the most acute and the most difficult to resolve. Turkey (along with the United States and the EU) supported the plan of Secretary-General Annan of the United Nations—a united republic of two states in confederation—and pressured Turkish Cypriots to vote in favor of it, which they did in 2004 by a 65 percent ma-

jority. Unfortunately, Greek Cypriots with a hard-line president rejected it by 75 percent. The year 2008 saw the hard-liner's defeat by a new president who pledged to restart negotiations. When the new Greek prime minister visited Turkey as his first overseas destination in 2009, the move was widely hailed in Greece. Perhaps a half century of conflict can move toward resolution in the coming years.

Enjoying similarities and differences vis-à-vis Turkey and sharing the Mobile Belt with that bridgeland, Iran remains as the last—but far from least—of the sixteen countries of the Middle East to be considered and now becomes the focus of our attention.

NOTES

1. Several good general studies of Turkey include *Turkey* Country Study 1995; B. Lewis 1968; Schick and Tonak 1987; Ahmad 1993; Mastney and Nation 1997; and Howe 2004.

2. A good, readable discussion is in Dewdney 1971, which also covers the general geography of Turkey. For technical geology, see Brinkmann 1976. For technical tectonics, see Dixon and Robertson 1984, which reveals the enormous complexity of Asia Minor's structure.

3. See Dixon and Robertson 1984, Sec. 3.

4. These and other sites are covered in Bean 1968 and Akurgal 1970.

5. For a detailed, scholarly, yet practical study of the many archaeological sites in Turkey, see Akurgal 1970.

6. Erinç and Tunçdilek 1952, which is still applicable.

7. *Archaeology* (Nov.–Dec. 2008).

8. See Pitcher 1972, a superb historical geography of the Ottoman Empire with excellent maps.

9. B. Lewis 1968 is a standard work on the evolution of modern Turkey. See also Ahmad 1993 and D. Howard 2001.

10. Numerous extensive biographies exist—for example, Mango 1999.

11. See *Turkey* Country Study 1995; U.S. Department of State, *Background Note: Turkey*, Mar. 2010; Kramer 2000; and D. Howard 2001.

12. See *New York Times*, Dec. 1, 2002, Feb. 21, 2003 (with chronology on the Kurdish problem), and Oct. 1, 2004. Istanbul hotel bombings are covered in *New York Times*, Aug. 11, 2004. For a complete study of Turkey's Kurdish problem, see Barkey and Fuller 1998.

13. *New York Times*, Oct. 24, 2004.

14. For example, Bacik 2009 and Meir 2009.

15. For a comprehensive treatment of the affair and of interactions among secularists, nationalists, and Islamists, see Jenkins 2009.

16. *New York Times*, Mar. 1, 2010.

17. *Today's Zaman*, Mar. 27, 2010. The new law still requires that Turkish be used in televised campaigning, but Kurdish and other minority languages can be used in rallies and written materials. It also bans the political use of the Turkish flag and of religious symbols.

18. *BBC News*, Dec. 11, 2009; Reuters, Dec. 14, 2009, www.reuters.com/article/idUSTRE5BD21V20091214.

19. *Today's Zaman*, Dec. 25, 2009, www.todayszaman.org/tz-web/.

20. Maisel 2008.

21. For opposing viewpoints on Turkish treatment of the Armenians, see Jernazian 1990 and Gürün 1985. See also *New York Times*, Mar. 6, 2004, regarding Turkish historians who advocate some Armenian claims. The budding rapprochement between Turkey and Armenia involves an understanding to put aside this dispute temporarily.

22. Following an interview aired on the U.S. television program *60 Minutes* on Dec. 17, 2009, in which he expressed his fear that "the Patriarchate is dying," he was interviewed by the Turkish press (see *Hurriyet: Daily News and Economic Review*, Dec. 24, 2009, www.hurriyetdailynews.com/; and *Today's Zaman*, Dec. 25, 2009, www.todayszaman/tz-web/). Political tensions between Greece and Turkey no doubt are at the root of the Patriarchate's problems—in the mid-1980s, the Greek government rescinded the provision of the Treaty of Lausanne that allowed its Muslim minority to elect its own religious leadership and began appointing it instead. The continued Cyprus dispute is also a factor.

23. For a detailed study of the Anatolian village, see Kolars 1968; for a study of the *gecekondu*, see Karpat 1976.

24. An excellent guidebook on Turkey, intelligently written and superbly illustrated, is *Turkey* 1989.

25. Development is concisely covered in G. Harris 1985. For more details and later coverage, see Schick and Tonak 1987 (Pt. 3); *Turkey* Country Study 1995; U.S. Department of State, *Background Note: Turkey*, Mar. 2010; and U.S. Department of Energy, *Energy Information Administration, Country Analysis Briefs*, May 2004.

26. See the U.S. Department of State's *Country Commercial Guide: Turkey*, 2008, and *Background Note: Turkey*, Oct. 2004 and May 2009.

27. Transparency International 2009.

28. World Economic Forum 2009a.

29. Fraser Institute 2008.

30. World Bank and the International Finance Corporation, "Doing Business, 2008," www.doingbusiness.org/features/DB2008Report.aspx. Compared to the members of the EU to which Turkey aspires, only Poland and Greece ranked lower.

31. United Nations Development Programme 2009.

32. This section is based on briefings by officials of the Turkish State Hydraulic Works (DSI) at Atatürk Dam in 1990 and in DSI headquarters in Ankara in 1997, as well as on Kolars and Mitchell 1991.

33. Spiegel OnLine International, July 8, 2009, www.spiegel.de/international/world/0,1518635054,00.html.

34. *Christian Science Monitor*, May 27, 2008.

35. FAO, various issues.

36. USGS, "The Mineral Industry of Turkey," in *Minerals Yearbook* 2008.

37. Aspects of the BTC are discussed in the *Oil and Gas Journal*, Nov. 15, 1999, 23–28, and Apr. 4, 2005, 10; *International Petroleum Encyclopedia* 2003; and EIA *Country Analysis Briefs: Turkey*, May 2004.

38. Reuters, July 13, 2009. The United States indicated its opposition to the proposed pipeline carrying Iranian gas (which it probably needs for the project to be financially viable) in the absence of U.S.-Iran rapprochement.

39. Socor 2009.

40. *Oil and Gas Journal*, Oct. 22 2009. Crude from Kazakhstan would also be involved.

41. USGS 2008.

42. *Arab News* (Riyadh), Feb. 5, 2009.

43. For further information, see www.urbanrail.net/.

44. Total U.S. economic assistance from 1947 on amounted to more than $12.5 billion (U.S. Department of State, *Background Note: Turkey*, Mar. 2010).

45. On March 4, 2010, the Foreign Affairs Committee of the House of Representatives approved sending the Armenian Genocide resolution to the House floor for a vote despite pleas from the White House and the U.S. State Department to defer action. In the past, the Israeli lobby had strongly opposed similar resolutions, but with the deterioration in Turkish-Israeli relation since 2008, the lobby withdrew its objections. See *BBC News* and *Huffington Post*, Mar. 5, 2010, and *Forward*, Mar. 10, 2010.

46. See a good study in Sayari 1997.

47. Abramowitz and Barkey 2009 question whether Turkey is really the regional power its government claims it to be.

48. Tajikstan's people are linguistically related to Iranians.

19

Iran
Complex Republic on the Plateau

YOUNG STATE, ANCIENT LAND

Iran's rankings serve as reminders of its importance: In the region, it is second in size, second in population, second in petroleum reserves, first in natural gas reserves, second in total area under cultivation, first in irrigated area, second in wheat production, first in copper output, and a major producer of other crops and minerals (see tables in Chaps. 4, 5, and 6). Gas reserves are second only to those of Russia, and those of petroleum second to Saudi Arabia, although it was one of the earliest producers with cumulative output of billions of barrels. Iran has been the core of Shii Islam for centuries and the leader of militant Shiism and even of militant Islam since 1979. Ensconced in one of the region's strongest power foci (see Map 3.6), it has often shown resiliency, as in the Iran-Iraq War of the 1980s. Of special historical-geopolitical significance is its persistent concept of *Iran-zamin*, "the land of Iran." Somewhat comparable to the idea of Greater Syria, this broadly comprises the former Iranian imperial domain, implanted Iranian culture, and its historical influence through millennia—an ancient relationship between a people and their cultural homeland.[1] Although contemporary sentiment regarding *Iran-zamin* may not lead to emotional irredentism, its efforts to extend the Islamic revolution to neighboring lands suggest that the idea is near the surface of its revolutionary consciousness.

Certain aspects of ethnicity and terminology also suggest Iran's individuality. One of the four states in the Middle East that is not Arab, it is the only major one in the region where the national language is neither Semitic nor Turkic. Migrating Aryans brought their Indo-European language to the plateau in the second millennium BCE, becoming ancestors of the Persians. The term "Iran" derives from "Aryan" and has always been preferred by the descendants of the Aryans as the name for the general area. Another toponym arose in the south-central part of the plateau—"Fars" became the root for both "Farsi," the designation for the main language, and "Persia," by way of Greek through a consonant shift. The area was best known in the West as Persia until Reza Shah in 1935 demanded that "Iran" be applied to the state and the oil company operating there. Thus, this official name is a reminder of the Aryans (literally, "nobles") who laid the foundations for the future state.

Entrenched on its high plateau, Iran has been a significant power for more than 2,500 years. Since Cyrus the Great built his empire, it has kept a vigorous national base century after century, even when temporarily succumbing militarily and politically to Greeks,

IRAN

Long-form official name, anglicized: Islamic Republic of Iran

Official name, transliterated: Jomhuri-ye Eslami-ye Iran

Form of government: unitary Islamic republic with one legislative house (Islamic Consultative Assembly)

Area: 629,315 mi^2/1,629,918 km^2

Population, 2008: 72,269,000; Literacy (Latest): 84.6%

Ethnic composition (%): Persian 50; Azerbaijani 20; Kurd 10; Gilaki and Mazanidarani 8; Afghani 3; Arab 2; Lur 2; Baluch 2, Turkman 2; other 1

Religions (%): Muslim 98.2, of which Shii 88.1, Sunni 10.1; Bahai 0.5; Christian 0.4; Zoroastrian 0.1; other 0.8

Demography: Life expectancy—68.6 yr (M),71.4 yr (F); Birthrate (per 1,000)—17.8; Fertility rate—1.82

GDP, 2009: $331.8 billion; purchasing power parity: $876.0 billion; per capita: $12,900

Currency: Iranian rial, US$1 = 9,715 rials, 1 rial = $0.0001 (March 2010)

Energy reserves: oil—137.6 bn bbl; natural gas—1.05 tn ft^3; coal—1.5 bn t

Main exports (% of total value, 2006): crude petroleum 73.1; chemical products 5.2; fruits and nuts 2.2; wool carpets 0.8

Main imports (% of total value, 2006): nonelectrical machinery 23.5; base metals 13.8; vehicles 13.0; chemical products 10.7

Capital city: Tehran 7,873,000; other major cities: Mashhad 2,469,000; Esfahan 1,628,000; Karaj 1,423,000; Tabriz 1,240,000

Arabs, or Mongols. Migrating peoples settled in less populated mountain basins and valleys, but, like the Chinese, it assimilated many of them; other groups were tolerated in isolated areas. Periodically absorbing powerful new influences that refreshed and reinvigorated it, the vibrant culture persevered and preserved its essence.

The Islamic revolution brought radical social change, none more radical than a shift in the ruling elite. Competing social groups have dynamized the body politic for decades: aristocracy, *bazaari* (merchants), clergy, tribal leaders, and army. Thought to be well under control, a highly politicized clergy asserted itself in the late 1970s, and the Iran of the

1980s reversed the sociopolitical trends of previous decades. People and environments once again interacted to search for identity and control.

Iran enjoyed many years of generally good relations with the rest of the world before 1979. Its status as a pariah afterward sometimes obscures its long cultural traditions, enduring geopolitical significance, petroleum wealth, economic potential, and human resources. As is true in any political-geographical evaluation of a state, the short-term conditions must be balanced with the enduring factors. This is difficult in Western estimates of Iran because of its direct and indirect involvement in hostage taking, terrorism, nuclear threat, and other abnormal behavior after the 1979. Nevertheless, Iran's abiding factors must be kept in focus, and those factors are emphasized in this chapter.

PLATEAU PALIMPSEST

The sequence of human occupancy over thousands of years is well preserved in the Iranian Plateau, and its antiquity is neither inconsequential nor academic. Evidence of ancient habitation is rarely out of sight in the more humid areas. More than 250,000 archaeological sites include some from the Middle Paleolithic (Mousterian) period about 40,000 years ago, during the last glacial period. Thousands of tells covering successive Neolithic villages dot the valleys, piedmonts, and plains. Also called *tepes* or *chegas*, mound sites of later villages are equally numerous,[2] and excavations have yielded elaborate pottery and ornaments of bronze, silver, and gold. On the Marv Plain (Marvdasht) before Persepolis, more than 1,000 tells have been identified, most from 6000–5500 BCE.

After a succession of powerful empires, the Arab Muslim invasion in the 630s led to momentous changes. The Sassanian collapse was at first staggering, but a national revival demonstrated vitality once again. Borrowed and exploited by the Arabs, Persian expertise, vigor, experience, and cultural vibrancy strengthened the Umayyad Empire and then were major factors in the Abbasid ascendancy in Mesopotamia. The Persian language diffused throughout the region, exchanging hundreds of loanwords with Arabic and, later on, Turkish. Although Islam was cradled in Arabia and brought by Arabs to Iran, the Islamic civilization that evolved over the centuries was highly Persianized.

Iran suffered political fragmentation, cultural disruption, and physical destruction after the Abbasid collapse in 1258; Mongols and Tatars threatened its identity for 300 years. But, as in the seventh century, it absorbed and integrated disparate ethnic and cultural influences, preserving "Persianality." Shii Islam became the state religion in the sixteenth century under the Safavids, one of whom gave Iran a golden age—Abbas the Great (1587–1629), whose lasting contributions to Persian culture are preserved in the splendid monuments of Esfahan. Safavid rule ended in 1736; the Zands followed until 1794, and then the Qajar mediocrities, with losses of both national vigor and territory. Reza Khan seized the throne in 1925, founding the Pahlavi dynasty and embarking on modernization. Emulating Atatürk's authoritarianism in Turkey, his policies were less successful. Considered pro-German, he was forced by Britain and the USSR to abdicate in 1941. The reign of his son, Mohammad Reza, was threatened by nationalist prime minister Mohammad Mossadegh, who embroiled Iran in a prolonged dispute with Britain over the oil concession. With controversial U.S. assistance, the shah regained power in 1953, ruling increasingly autocratically until forced into exile in January 1979.[3]

A THEOCRATIC REPUBLIC

Having sought political control in times past, Shii clerics joined laymen in the 1970s to fight foreign influence and widespread domestic corruption and repression. After the shah was ousted by Ayatollah Ruhollah Khomeini, however, many of his methods were no less harsh than those of the monarchy. Revolutionary courts condemned opponents on such a scale as to raise internal and external censure. As one Iranian scholar put it: "Iran's Islamic Republic is a religious oligarchy of intricately overlapping relationships among the leading clerics. . . . At the apex of the political pyramid is the Supreme Leader (*rahbar*) . . . the spiritual guide of the nation, the official head of state, the commander-in-chief of the armed forces and, as vali-e-faqih [Islamic jurist], the protector of the faith. . . . Since Islam is a polity ruled by God, disobedience toward God's surrogate rulers is seen as not only a sin against the Almighty but a crime against the state, leaving no room for criticism, disagreement or dissent."[4] Designating opponents as enemies of God[5] is only too common in the contemporary Middle East, from the Hizballah in Lebanon to Jewish extremists in Israel.[6]

Under Iran's complicated mixture of the clerical and the laical in its constitution, the supreme leader (Ayatollah Ali Khamenei since Khomeini's death in 1988) holds power for life, has the final say on all domestic and foreign policies, is the final arbiter of disputes between the various branches of government, and appoints key government officials, including the head of the judiciary. He has the power to remove the elected president (who has day-to-day executive responsibilities) and has ultimate command of the military. He is chosen by a popularly elected body of clerics, the Assembly of Experts, which is charged with reviewing his performance; theoretically, it can depose and replace him.

The revolutionaries thus replaced a secular monarchy with a complex theocracy, and the new politics required extensive domestic and international adjustments. National cohesion became a priority; when some ethnic groups reasserted separatist tendencies, suppression was ruthless. The regime reoriented its foreign relations, repudiating Western (especially U.S.) influences. The seizure of fifty-three American diplomats in November 1979 was an unprecedented violation of protocol and international norms and isolated Iran globally. The eventual release of the hostages did little to improve perceptions since hard-liners continued to flaunt world opinion.

The outbreak of the Iran-Iraq War in September 1980 (see Chaps. 8 and 13) led to as many as 1 million Iranian casualties and to tremendous destruction that required years of recovery. Although Iraq received greater outside aid, the Iranians received assistance at critical times, especially from Syria, Libya, Taiwan, and China, as well as, paradoxically, from and through Israel and the United States,[7] as was disclosed in the Iran-Contra ("Irangate") congressional hearings in Washington in 1986–1987.[8]

During the two years between the Iran-Iraq cease-fire and Iraq's invasion of Kuwait, the Islamic Republic reestablished stability despite eight years of bitter warfare—and, indeed, partly by using the war as a unifying factor. During that time, an unexpectedly smooth transition followed Khomeini's death. The new leaders, Ayatollah Khameni and President Ali Akhbar Hashemi-Rafsanjani, were more moderate and pragmatic than the zealous and charismatic Khomeini. The invasion of Kuwait created a dilemma for Iran—it condemned Iraq but detested the U.S.-led coalition. The situation did force Iraq to end their mutual hostilities on Iran's terms. During the 1990s, its internal and external dynamics often bewildered the rest of the world, with the "Janus face of the Islamic Republic" showing "unprecedented progress juxtaposed against regressive changes."[9]

Hashemi-Rafsanjani was succeeded in 1997 by another moderate, Muhammad Khatami, in a landslide ("the second revolution"), showing public aspiration for a more open society and economic reform. Riots in Tehran in 1992 and 1995 occasioned by the stagnant economy and the more significant university student riots in 1999 made the mood for change patently clear. Conservative elements suppressed the outbreaks, dampening Khatami's liberalization efforts.[10] In 2005, Hashemi-Rafsanjani was defeated by a relative unknown, Mahmud Ahmadinejad, supported by the most conservative elements among the clergy. A disputatious and rather demagogic former Teheran mayor, Ahmadinejad revealed more by rhetoric than policy discussion during his first term.

Dissatisfaction with his administration was expressed both in the Majlis and in frequent urban strikes and demonstrations, but he gained highly disputed reelection in 2009. Following this, Tehran's streets were several times filled by as many as hundreds of thousands, at first protesting irregularities in the polling and later in the year, after the death of dissident cleric Hoseyn Montezeri, the legitimacy of the Islamic Republic itself. The regime responded with increasing force, protesters and bystanders were killed and injured, and numerous opposition leaders (and their family members) were jailed and accused of operating with unspecified "foreign powers" to overthrow the republic. Over the rest of 2009, the regime seemed to be using Iran's nuclear dispute with the international community as further evidence of foreign conspiracies against the Islamic Republic. All this was happening as the national economy was at a crisis stage, not so much because of the global recession or the effects of UN sanctions, but because state subsidies on a wide range of goods—estimated to cost at least $90 billion annually and equal to the equivalent of 30 percent of GDP—were impeding growth, encouraging overconsumption, and hindering domestic production.[11]

Parliamentary elections during the decade also highlighted the paradoxes of contemporary Iran. Although the "mullahocracy" had evolved a genuine if quirky system of democratic elections, it contravened the arrangement in 2004 by bluntly ruling out the candidacies of hundreds of announced moderates; then hundreds of approved candidates resigned in protest. The result was that the hard-line winners gained a large majority. In the 2008 election, again with moderate participation kept to a minimum, the conservative majority increased, but many among this group were for various reasons opponents of Ahmadinejad, and conflict between the legislative and executive branches increased.

Iran faced numerous major domestic and international problems in the 2000s. Although regularly accused by the United States of sponsoring terrorism and included in President George W. Bush's "Axis of Evil," it condemned the 9/11 terrorist attacks and expressly rejected the extremism of Osama bin Laden's (Sunni) version of Islam. A month after 9/11, Iran signed a deal with Russia—six years after Russia, under U.S. pressure, had stopped supplying arms—for planes, missiles, and, significantly, nuclear reactors for the long-delayed Bushehr facility (the nuclear part of the deal led to a prolonged international crisis; see below under "Relations").

In 2003, the regime was embarrassed when an Iranian woman lawyer, Shirin Ebadi, was awarded the Nobel Peace Prize for her human rights work, carried out under very difficult circumstances; predictably, she became the target of much clerical opprobrium, but her international prominence as a Nobel laureate seemed to protect her from official retaliation despite her continued outspokenness. However, in December 2008, the offices of her organization were raided and closed by authorities, claiming it was the center of an illegal political organization. Later, regime-sponsored demonstrators accused her of being insufficiently critical of Israeli actions against Gaza; this prompted international concern (including a protest from the UN secretary-general[12] to the government) for her safety.

Inexplicable as the Islamic Republic often is, it has engendered political and social self-examination in all segments of society, which has engaged in tremendous intellectual ferment and dynamic debate over the Islamicization of politics, the role and status of women, pluralism, foreign relations, and the very essence and direction of the republic. The process has been very Iranian—sometimes painfully pronounced, sometimes subtly nuanced, always contradictory, oscillating between modernity and retrogression. With all its contradictions, Iran has seen some progress, often shrouded by abuses of human rights, rampant corruption, demagogic rhetoric, religious obscurantism, and challenges to norms of international behavior, especially regarding its nuclear program. There have been advances in rural development (electrification, water supply, road access, postal services), an almost doubled literacy rate, an increase in women's higher education and governmental employment (while paradoxically suppressing their role in society and enforcing a strict female dress code), and the reconstruction of cities damaged in the Iran-Iraq War. Living standards for the average Iranian, using the UNDP's Human Development Index as a guide, have improved, but remain relatively low—in 2007, Iran ranked 88th among 182 countries globally and 11th regionally. But compared to 1980, its index had registered a gain of nearly 40 percent, largely on the basis of improvements in the education component.[13]

A MOUNTAIN-RIMMED PLATEAU

Iranian Landscapes

Variety and Contrasts. Even in a region of contrasts, the diversity among landscapes is greater than those in any other Middle East country. Turkey and Israel display great variety, but only Iran ranges from lush subtropical environments, like the mountain-backed Caspian coast, to totally barren, salt-encrusted deserts, like the huge *kavirs* of the interior basins. Its landforms, climates, vegetation, and people all spread across a wide spectrum.[14]

Landforms. The Iranian Plateau is a region of intermontane plateaus and mountains, with high, rugged mountains providing walls on three sides (Map 19.1). It is shaped like a triangular bowl—the base runs from northwest to southeast, and the apex lies in the northeast near Mashhad. Coastlands and mountains framing the borders have historically served as ramparts.

Iran is the central segment of the Tethyan geosynclinal belt extending from Morocco to Indonesia. It is the eastern half of the Middle East's Mobile Belt, or Fold Belt (see Map 2.2), and was compressed between the Arabian Shield and the Russian Platform in the long period of intense folding from Triassic to Pliocene and Pleistocene times. The Zagros and Elburz-Kopet mountains buckled upward with tectonic compression, embracing between them a relatively inflexible block, a denuded shield forming vast interior *kavirs*. Eastern Iran has one of the most remarkable geomorphic features in the region, a huge rafted tongue of exotic terrain clearly visible from space. Compression and thrust faulting continue, with numerous seismic events on all sides; 100,000 people died in eleven major quakes during the past sixty years. The most disastrous hit Bam in December 2003, when 43,000 died.[15] Iran has so many mountains and high plateaus that its average elevation is an unusual 4,920 ft/1,500 m.

Drainage. Reflecting Mediterranean-type precipitation, runoff peaks in late winter and early spring with seasonal rains and melting snow. In April, the Karun River, Iran's largest river, has ten times its October flow. Farther east, the Zayandeh Rud, the largest river in the Esfahan watershed, has a spring maximum discharge of 1,680 m³/sec, loaded with meltwater and fifty times more than in late fall—it actually dried up during the severe drought of 2000–2001. Salty Lake Urmia, in a closed northwestern basin, covers one-third more area in May with snowmelt than in early October.

Several large dams impound seasonal runoff for use through the year, but many more are needed to increase irrigation and environmentally clean electricity. Scores of smaller streams carry runoff from upper slopes to piedmonts and alluvial fans on the inner sides of the many mountain chains and then dissipate in the sands, gravels, and saline

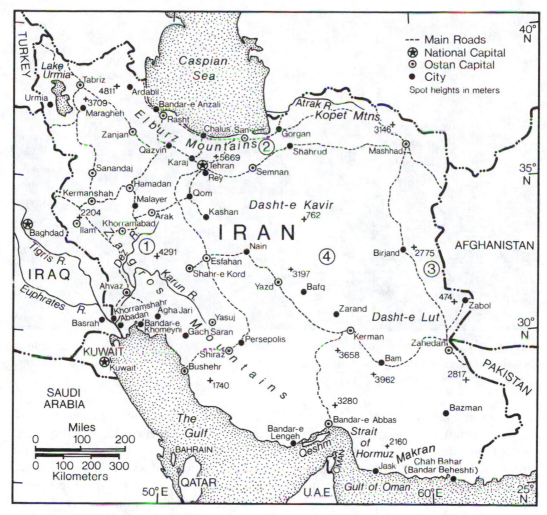

MAP 19.1 General map of Iran, with *ostan* (provincial) centers and other cities, highways, spot heights, and main mountain ranges. Regions are indicated by circled numbers.

crusts of interior basins. More than half of Iran's drainage area lies in these basins, from the vast *kavirs* to pocket-size valleys in the Zagros. It is, nevertheless, these interior streams that are exploited by thousands of subterranean *qanat* systems for irrigation. Table 2.1 shows the seasonality and yearly average of precipitation in Iran's four main climate areas.

Pattern of Regions

The pattern of regional physical and cultural features reveals especially significant contrasts, and some understanding of the regional design aids in appreciating Iran's general character and problems. For this reason, several representative central places that are notably differentiated both historically and regionally are included in the surveys below.[16]

[1] Zagros Mountains and Gulf Coast. Part of the southern arc of the great Alpine folding system, the Zagros Mountains extend northwest-southeast for 1,000 mi/1,600 km from Turkey to the Strait of Hormuz. Four parallel belts exhibit different lithology,

FIGURE 19.1 Masjid-e Shah (Royal Mosque), Esfahan, from the reign of Shah Abbas the Great in the early 1600s, now officially called Masjid-e Imam. With its beautiful blue tiles, it is considered one of the world's most splendid mosques.

structures, and landforms from west to east, and in the southeastern Zagros scores of salt domes pierce the folded sequence, forming prominent features in the desert climate (see Fig. 8.6). Many are domed-structure oil and gas reservoirs.

It is in the belts of the Zagros region that much of the population lives and most development has historically taken place. Winter precipitation intercepted by the considerable elevations irrigates in the succeeding season. Most oil fields are in the central-western folds (see Maps 6.1 and 6.2); many metallic minerals are found in the volcanic belt and thrust faulting of the eastern Zagros, along the interplate zone of contact. Most of Iran's major and more famous cities are nestled in the valleys or along the piedmonts of the folds and along the Gulf coastal plain to the west (see Map 19.1).

In the northwest is Tabriz, the fifth-largest city, a former imperial capital and now capital of Azerbaijan Ostan (Farsi *ostan* = province).

Its bustling old bazaar has the distinct atmosphere of a Turkic metropolis, but many ethnic groups jostle on its crowded streets. In the central Zagros valleys, basins, and eastern piedmont are several major centers, from Sanandaj and Qom in the north to Esfahan in the south. They include former capitals (Hamadan and Esfahan), noted carpet centers (Hamadan, Kermanshah, Qom, Kashan, Esfahan), and modern industrial concentrations. The important religious center of Qom was enhanced after the clergy gained power; Ayatollah Khomeini ruled like a sovereign from his home there. Esfahan preserves its former imperial status in its Safavid pavilions, picturesque main square or *maydan*, and blue-tiled royal mosque, Masjid-e Shah (now Masjid-e Imam; Fig. 19.1). The third-largest city, it is credited with half the globe's beautiful sites in the proverb "Esfahan nesf-e Jahan" (literally, "Esfahan is half the world"). In the south, Shiraz is the main center—yet another city with the special aura of a former imperial capital.

Climatic and soil conditions give it a particularly good ecology for growing roses, which crowd the hundreds of gardens adorning the city. Two of Iran's most famous poets, Hafez and Saadi, are memorialized in impressive tombs.

The Gulf coast of more than 800 mi/500 km once repelled human habitation and development, both by its topography and by its climate. Along most of the shore, Zagros ridges rise precipitously from the Gulf, leaving no room for settlement. Elsewhere, marshy flats dominate, and nowhere is fresh water plentiful. Nevertheless, Iran's extensive oil operations in the southwest require nearby export facilities, and imports need large-scale general-cargo ports. The main oil terminal is on Kharg (Khark) Island, 25 mi/40 km offshore, opposite Kuwait. Gulf cargo ports are Bandar-e Khomeini (originally Bandar-e Shahpur) in the north, Bandar-e Bushehr south of Kharg, and Bandar-e Abbas on the Strait of Hormuz (Farsi *bandar* = port). The coast is now more closely integrated with the rest of the country, especially as offshore oil and gas fields are developed (see "Ports" below). The small island of Kish has been transformed into a free port with a relatively liberal social atmosphere.

[2] Elburz Mountains and Northeast Chains. This region comprises not only the Elburz chain itself but also the eastern extension of the same compressional structures, plus the piedmonts or forelands that lie to the north and south. From the southwestern corner of the Caspian Sea to the far northeast beyond Mashhad, the range is part of the northern belt of Alpine folding, splaying from the Zagros structures west of Tehran. The eastern extension comprises several parallel ridges, usually called the Kopet Mountains (*Kopet Dagh*—the name of the northernmost ridge along the Turkmenistan frontier).

Averaging about 60 mi/97 km in width, the range has many summits above 12,000 ft/3,658 m. It culminates in the symmetrical volcanic cone of Mount Damavand, 18,600 ft/5,671 m, highest in the Middle East. The steep northern slopes descend to the Caspian plain and shore, which lies 92 ft/28 m below sea level. On the opposite side, the southern slopes terminate at plateau level, 5,000 ft/1,525 m at Tehran, so that the total relief is much less than on the northern side. Several small glaciers emphasize the elevation of the peaks. Except for a few high passes, traversed by three spectacular highways, the chain is a major impediment to transportation and to the flow of moisture-laden winds from the northwest. The range is tectonically active, as indicated by frequent sharp earthquakes.

In the northeast, the folded Kopet ridges of northern Khorasan are appreciably lower than the Elburz proper and more comparable to the folded Zagros. Open valleys are devoted to cereal cultivation and support a moderately dense population. Mashhad is not only Iran's second city but, like Tabriz, also a center of ethnic complexity, with Persians, Turkmans, Baluch, Kurds, Hazaras, and others mingling in the bazaars and mosques. Like Qom, Mashhad has one of the holiest Shii shrines—the tomb of the eighth imam, Ali Reza. The opening of the border between Iran and Turkmenistan and the other new republics of ex-Soviet Central Asia (historically, a region long influenced by Persian culture) in 1991 has produced an appreciable influx of visitors from these long-isolated lands.

The large population of the Caspian coast is distributed in many small towns and villages rather than in a few metropolitan areas. Rasht, in the west, is noteworthy, along with the port of Bandar-e Anzali (once Bandar-e Pahlevi). In the east are Gorgan and Bandar-e Torkeman (formerly Bandar-e Shah). Several coastal towns are much frequented resort centers, including Ramsar and Chalus.

The piedmont and foredeep south of the Elburz-Kopet belt support not only metropolitan Tehran but also Qazvin to the west,

FIGURE 19.2 Northern Tehran (Shemiran and Tajrish residential suburbs) nestled at the foot of the towering snow-covered Elburz Mountains.

the ancient city of Rey south of Tehran, and a series of towns along the Tehran-Mashhad railway, following the old Silk Road. Suburbs and peripheral villages have coalesced to form Greater Tehran, sprawling along the alluvial fans south of the Elburz. About 20 percent of the population resides around the metropolis. Upper-class residences (now often those of favored officials and clergy) are concentrated in northern Tehran's higher slopes, especially in the suburb of Shemiran (Fig. 19.2). These neighborhoods had first use of the water from the *qanats* that formerly supplied the city; they both avoided lower Tehran's smog and were cooler because of their elevation.[17] The city has an impressive concentration of government buildings, embassies, banks, schools, and office buildings. The streets of the central business district have some of the most congested traffic in all the Middle East, and the bazaar, in the crowded southern sector, is one of the region's major shopping centers, especially noted for gold jewelry, carpets, and decorative brass- and copperwares.

[3] Eastern Highlands. Several separate complex ridges form the eastern rim of the Iranian "bowl." Runoff supports scattered villages, some of which include ruins of ancient settlements. South of Zahedan, at the southern end of the highlands, is the only recently active volcano, Kuh-e Taftan. The eastern reaches of Khorasan, the largest province, share a long porous border with Afghanistan, most of which was part of *Iran-zamin* for centuries. During the Soviet occupation in the 1980s and later fighting, about 2 million Afghans sought refuge here, and many still remained in the late 2000s. After Pakistan, Iran has more refugees than any other country. The government gained control of the

frontier zone only in the 1960s; now it is a battleground between drug smugglers and the army.

[4] *Interior Basins.* This east central region is contained within the larger Iranian triangle. It includes several smaller basins, but its two major ones are Dasht-e Kavir in the north center and Dasht-e Lut in the southeast (Farsi *dasht* = desert or plain).[18] The lowest part of its watershed is the Great Kavir (*kavir* = playa or salt flat), an immense erosional surface with salt- and mud-filled depressions and extensive dune fields covering more than 20,000 mi²/51,800 km². Dasht-e Lut (*lut* = desert basin), the lowest sump in interior Iran at 672 ft/205 m above sea level, is somewhat smaller than the Great Kavir, separated from it by a low divide and quite different from it. The weird surface is etched by wind into *yardangs*, alternating ridges and grooves, some as high as 195 ft/60 m, and wind-eroded material is piled into dunes to the south and east.

Neither the great salt expanse of the Dasht-e Kavir nor the rough Dasht-e Lut is inhabited, even by nomads. Neither soil nor meager precipitation permits perceptible vegetation, although desert bush survives on the higher parts of the basins and in the courses of seasonal streams. These barren interior basins are the least-useful parts of Iran.

PEOPLE: DEMOGRAPHY AND ETHNOGRAPHY

Population

With one of the three largest populations in the Middle East,[19] Iran has more people than all the Gulf states combined, including Iraq and Saudi Arabia. Moreover, it has the region's most complex ethnic structure, both in the number of major groups and in concentrations of those groups. It has at least eight peoples numbering more than 1 million each and another half-dozen in the range of 100,000 to 1 million each (see Table 4.3 and Map 19.2).

The areas most favorable to habitation have long been densely populated: the Zagros valleys, Caspian coastlands, and inner piedmonts of the mountain frame. With socioeconomic change and a rising standard of living from the 1950s, faltering only in the late 1970s, Iran saw its net population increase to 4.6 percent annually, the highest in the region. Efforts initiated by the shah in the 1960s to slow the rate were showing modest success—2.9 percent by the mid-1970s—when the fundamentalists reversed course. It jumped to 3.9 percent before the regime reacted and again encouraged birth control; the rate was down to about 1.0 percent by the late 2000s.

As in other Middle East states and in most developing countries, the shift from rural to urban areas in Iran has been pronounced. Urban population, only 30 percent in the mid-1950s, reached 69 percent by the late 2000s. This increase notwithstanding, millions of Iranians continue to reside in more than 55,000 villages along the piedmonts and valleys of the countryside (see Fig. 4.8). Since they are concentrations of population, the pattern of village areal distribution correlates with patterns of available runoff and of higher rainfall. The Islamic city, as examined in Chapter 4, is clearly identifiable in Iran, where it also possesses its own "Persianality."[20]

Peoples of the Plateau

Ethnic Complexity. Iran exhibits the most complex ethnic mosaic in the region. Indeed, its pattern of peoples is so motley that the central government has done well to maintain the state's national unity through the centuries; this section emphasizes this complexity. Although ethnic Persians (as distinct from Iranians) have played the most prominent role in Iran's development, events have also often been influenced by minority peoples. Both its location and its complex

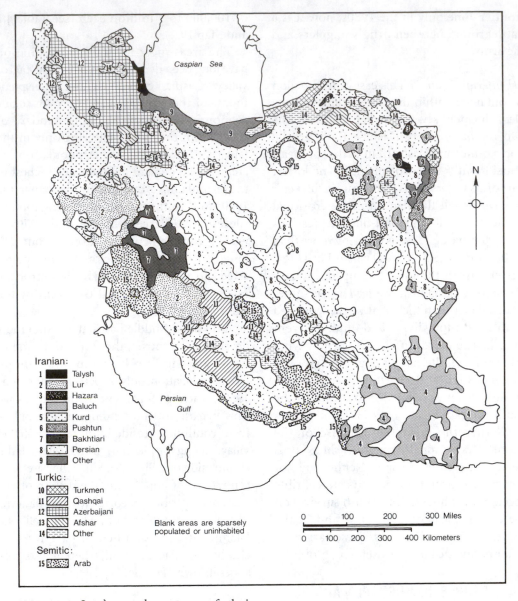

Caspian Sea

Lake Urmia

Persian
Gulf

Iranian:
1 ██ Talysh
2 ░░ Lur
3 ▓▓ Hazara
4 ▒▒ Baluch
5 ∴∴ Kurd
6 ▤▤ Pushtun
7 ██ Bakhtiari
8 ·.· Persian
9 ▦▦ Other

Turkic:
10 ⊠⊠ Turkmen
11 ╱╱ Qashqai
12 ▦▦ Azerbaijani
13 ╲╲ Afshar
14 ▤▤ Other

Semitic:
15 ▨▨ Arab

Blank areas are sparsely
populated or uninhabited

N

0   100   200   300 Miles

0   100 200 300 400 Kilometers

MAP 19.2 Iran's complex patterns of ethnic groups.

pattern of landforms have influenced the historical influx of various groups and the resultant ethnic pattern.[21]

Over the millennia, groups have invaded or migrated into the plateau from Asia Minor, the Caucasus, Central Asia, and the Indian subcontinent. Once they found themselves south of the barriers of the Black Sea, Caucasus Mountains, and Caspian Sea, migrants were forced through the mountain-

ribbed Iranian "throat" between the Caspian and the Gulf. Some westward-moving peoples pushed into and across Mesopotamia; others elected to settle in the basins of the rugged Zagros Mountains.

Landform complexity—elaborate patterns of parallel and sometimes interconnected linear valleys and irregular basins—imposed difficulties but also offered opportunities: for settlement, for survival where there was water, and for protection from neighbors as well as from central authority. Some migrants were partly or completely assimilated, but more than a score retain their identities in their own territories, like the Qashqai, Bakhtiari, and Lur. Several minorities have kept tribal organization, thus preserving their cultures. The preservation of minority languages provides a functional linguistic criterion to aid in distinguishing groups. In a few cases, religion becomes the main particularity.

Most of the peoples of Iran are discussed in Chapter 4 and are included in Table 4.3, hence only a few details need be added here to place them in more specific context. A few smaller groups are also mentioned. Map 19.2 shows the group patterns, and the identification numbers discussed below are keyed to that map.

Persians and Related Peoples. Persian/Farsi is the principal language in a subfamily of languages that includes Kurdish, Luri, Baluchi, Gilaki, Mazandarani, and the tongues of several smaller groups. Although ethnic Persians (8) are the third-largest people in the Middle East and the largest single group in Iran, they are less than half the population. The most widely distributed of Iran's peoples, they are found especially in an almost unbroken, broad ring around the interior basins. They comprise the great majority of ruling clerics, managerial and government workers, and the economic elite.

Kurds (5) concentrate in the Iranian segment of Kurdistan, in the western Zagros along the Turkish and Iraqi borders. Like their kin in those countries, Iranian Kurds have opted for separatism, rebelling unsuccessfully in 1919, during World War II (the short-lived Mahabad Republic suppressed in 1947), and again in 1979. They are mostly Sunnis—the largest group of Sunnis in the republic.

The Baluch (4), also mostly Sunni, dwell in the southeastern corner of Iran; still no-

madic, they are the least-economically and -socially integrated of the major minorities. Separatism has been a major issue in the 2000s; the government argues this is spearheaded by the Jundullah, which it terms a foreign-supported terrorist group (see Chap. 8, "Terrorism and Piracy"). After the capture of the group's leader, Abdolmalek Rigi, in February 2010, Tehran claimed that he was about to travel to a U.S. base in Central Asia.[22]

Divided by the main concentration of the Bakhtiari (7), the Lur (2) have two clusters in the central Zagros. Khorramabad is the center of the northern area, Lorestan; the oil center of Gach Saran lies on the southern edge of the southern concentration. The Bakhtiari, mostly between the oil center of Masjid-e Soleyman and Shahr-e Kord, are perhaps the most powerful southern tribe. Both groups are mostly Shii.

Secluded in high mountain valleys and basins in Khorasan, a few tens of thousands speaking several Indo-European languages spill over from neighboring Afghanistan and Central Asia. Other groups live in scattered locations southwest and south of the Caspian. The numerous Shii Hazara, or "Berberi" (3), around Mashhad, have many kin in central Afghanistan. The Aimaq, in the "Other" category on the map (9), include a score of groups, exemplifying the multiplicity in this rugged area of crisscrossing migrations.

Astride the northern part of the Iranian-Afghan border are many Pushtun (6), who have millions of kin farther east. West of the Caspian, on either side of the border, are several thousand Talysh (1). Groups subsumed in the "Other" category (9) include a few tens of thousands of Tajik in the northern part of the Zabol salient. Along the Caspian coast are the Gilani (sometimes Gilaki) in the west, around Rasht, and the Mazandarani farther east; both peoples are predominantly Shii. The Gilani have shown separatism several times, most notably in a short-lived socialist republic after World War II.

Turkic Peoples.   The Azeri, or Azerbaijani (12), Iran's largest ethnolinguistic minority, speak a Turkic language but are Shii and adhere to other Persian cultural traditions. Their center is Tabriz. While maintaining their identity and language, they join in Iranian nationalism, provided the government accepts their informal autonomy. Separatism emerged after World War II in a brief USSR-inspired republic. Thwarting this effort was one of the first effective acts of the UN. After the ex-Soviet republic of Azerbaijan became independent in 1991, Iranian Azeris—to the discomfit of the government—made tentative declarations of hope for union in an enlarged Azeri state.

The Qashqai (11) have perhaps the strongest nomadic tradition among the larger groups. In two large areas in Fars Province, to the north and south of Shiraz, and well organized in confederations, they have traditionally resisted government control. Like most Iranians, they are Shii.

Turkmans (10), mostly Sunni and tribally organized, are widely scattered in the northeast next to Turkmenistan. At one time a strong military cavalry cadre, but now they are nomadic pastoralists and settled farmers, known for hand-knotted carpets named after various subgroups—Tekke, Yomut, Salor, and Saryk. Separatism, strong until the 1920s, reasserted itself after the 1979 revolution but was suppressed by the government. Afshars (13) inhabit several areas in the northwest. In the "Other" category (14) for Turkic groups, there are fifty or more Ilsavan (formerly Shahsavan) nomadic groups occupying a dozen scattered areas from the Aras River southeastward to the steppes south of Tehran. Qajars have an enclave among the Mazandarani on the southeastern corner of the Caspian. Other small tribal Turkic groups are scattered in the mountains of Khorasan

and in the more rugged areas east of Shiraz, especially the Teymurtash and Qaragozlu.

Arabs.   More than a million Arabs (15) live primarily in Khuzistan, a plain at the head of the Gulf, which they refer to as Arabistan (land of the Arabs). They also live in the southern Zagros interior and in widely scattered areas northeast and east of the Dasht-e Kavir. Descendants of Arabs who invaded in the seventh century and of later settlers, they maintain their separateness and have not assimilated, although they are predominantly Shii.

Armenians and Assyrians.   Two quite different peoples constitute the largest Christian groups. The primarily Orthodox Armenians, whose sizable presence dates to the time of Shah Abbas, live in Tehran, Tabriz, and Esfahan. As in Lebanon and Syria, they maintain their separate language and schools and have achieved marked success in Tehran and in the Khuzistan oil fields. Some 300,000 at the revolution's onset in 1979, the community has seen considerable emigration since then. Only a tenth as many as Armenians, Assyrians concentrate west of Lake Urmia, maintain their cohesion, preserve their Syriac vernacular, and are divided into Nestorian and Catholic Chaldean branches. They are the remnant of an ancient branch of Christianity that dominated the region (and much of Central Asia) in pre-Islamic times. Iran's legal system based on Sharia discriminates in some ways against non-Muslims, but overt persecution has been directed mostly against converts from Islam to proselytizing evangelical sects. (The Bahai have been severely persecuted under the republic because they are treated as apostates from Islam; they are not a separate ethnic group. See Chap. 4.)

Jews.   Resident in Iran at least as early as the Babylonian Captivity, Jews numbered about 100,000 in the 1970s, when they prospered and were influential under the shah; along with Christians, they were respected as "people of the book." Much less favored after 1979, they maintain their identity in schools, synagogues, social institutions, and businesses. The government emphasizes that it draws a distinction between the Jewish state, Israel—which it reviles—and the Jewish faith. Even so, more than two-thirds have chosen gradually to emigrate, many to the United States, some to Israel.[23] The present community, about 25,000 and slightly larger than Turkey's, is still the largest in the Muslim world.

IRANIAN ECONOMIC PATTERNS

Perspective

As in neighboring Gulf countries, development and modernization have escalated in oil-wealthy Iran since 1950. However, economic patterns exhibit comparatively greater complexity and subtlety of structure because of its long economic history, its early start in petroleum production, and its combination—unique in the Middle East—of having a large population, a large area, arable land, and huge petroleum resources.[24] Patterns are further complicated by revolutionary ramifications.

Before petroleum, the economy was based on a varied agriculture, trade, and widespread and artistic craftsmanship. Agriculture continues to be a major sector; in many regions it is the only activity of significance. In the late 2000s, it contributed 11 percent to GDP; for the labor force, it provided livelihoods to 25 percent; of exports, its products were about 4 percent. Fabled hand-knotted carpets, ordinary and specialized hand-printed textiles called *qalamkar*, copper and brass artifacts, decorated gold and silver items, enamel and inlaid work, and hand-painted miniatures attracted buyers worldwide. Although these traditional items now form only a modest percentage of exports, demand remains high—carpets lead non-oil

exports—and for some tribal groups, they provide much of their cash income. These products, rather than petroleum, symbolize the country's traditions and creativity.

Assured in the 1950s of a major place in the oil market, the shah pursued economic development almost frenetically. From 1960 to 1977, real annual growth averaged 9.6 percent—about double the average of developing countries. The stable currency was virtually convertible. Every sector received attention, especially physical infrastructure—roads, railroads, ports, airports, communications, industry, urban development. However, his quests for military superiority, becoming an industrial power, a modern welfare state, and a secular Westernized society overloaded the base. Pervasive authoritarianism and denial of basic freedoms set the stage for 1978–1979. By coincidence and design, the republic reversed much of his program, especially Westernization. Nevertheless, the new regime coasted on his accomplishments for several years, especially in the military sphere when Iraq invaded.

The government's initial efforts are hard to evaluate because of the almost immediate impact of the Iran-Iraq War,[25] but it is clear that it had little comprehension of economic complexities. Major industries were taken from private owner-managers and placed in state hands. Thousands of firms were taken from alleged supporters of the monarchy; banking was rendered "Islamicized" (and unprofitable). Hindering growth were the war, the sharp decline of oil prices, the freeze on Iranian assets abroad, and economic sanctions. By the late 1980s GDP had fallen to pre-1973 levels. The revolution led to the exodus of many entrepreneurs, managers, and skilled professionals and provoked considerable capital flight. The former privileged class was largely broken, and a new elite arose—the clergy and their allies. The lot of the poor, for whom the revolution was theoretically launched, was little improved in urban areas, but rural development did enhance the quality of life in thousands of villages.

In its first five-year plan (1989–1994), the more moderate regime that succeeded Khomeini attempted to address economic reality. It reprivatized some establishments, attempted to restore confidence in government policies, invited selected foreign firms to enter the oil and manufacturing sectors, and sought foreign financing for industrial production. However, liberalization efforts were consistently derailed by conservative elements, so that, with mismanagement, corruption, inflation, and population growth, the economy stagnated. Indeed, per capita income decreased 57 percent between 1976 and 1994, and the gap between new rich and old poor widened alarmingly.

The second five-year plan (1995–2000) focused on the financial and fiscal sectors. However, there were inherent systemic problems. Unemployment was chronic, partly because many workers held two jobs as wages failed to keep pace with the cost of living. A major obstruction were the *bonyad*, independent monopolistic religious conglomerates that control enterprises with few constraints, little financial accountability, and less management expertise. Generous subsidies on basic items palliated the poor but magnified the budget deficit. Lack of meaningful reform and progress dampened enthusiasm for the otherwise popular President Khatami, who was nevertheless reelected in 2001.

The third five-year plan (2000–2005) focused on administrative reform, privatization, research and development, investment, human resources, and foreign policy—all of which badly needed rational attention. The need for capital and technical assistance in the petrosector was critical.

The fourth plan (2005–2010) emphasized increasing non-oil exports; establishing free-trade zones like those in the UAE, were seen as one way to do this. Domestically, the plan indicated the need for regulating markets, maintaining supplies of basic commodities, and reforming the subsidy system to relieve the government budget—aims that appeared to observers as contradictory. It was carried out under Ahmadinejad; as it neared its conclusion, progress toward fulfilling many of its goals was not apparent. Through the 2000s, efforts at reform had foundered in the face of the state's heavy hand and bloated bureaucracy—price controls, subsidies, and corruption led to shortages, inflation, and rationing—often provoking violent protests. Even if sanctions were not a problem, the strong perceptions of corruption would deter investors in any nonpetro sector of the economy: Transparency International ranked Iran 165th out of 180 countries, and 15th among the countries herein, ahead of only war-torn Iraq.[26] High oil prices in 2008 bolstered government revenues (to a record $82.5 billion) but also led to increased spending on temporary panaceas in advance of the 2009 presidential elections and to the postponement or halfhearted implementation of needed reforms. When demand dropped in 2009 with the global recession, Iran's oil revenues declined by more than 33 percent—to $54.6 billion, slightly below the earnings realized in 2006 and 2007.

If Iran has been, as is generally believed internationally, pursuing a nuclear weapons program, it would appear to be defeating its own developmental goals. If, however, it has actually been seeking peaceful nuclear power capability, as it has claimed, then greater transparency would certainly have resolved many of the tensions aroused by the program (discussed below in "Relations").

Agriculture and Water Control. Although only a limited proportion of Iran is suitable for rainfed agriculture, human ingenuity exploiting the environment over thousands of years has created a broad agricultural base. Finding, conserving, and channeling water to cultivable areas in linear valleys and piedmonts were the essential challenge and the main accom-

FIGURE 19.3 *Qanats* on Iran's northwestern plateau. These underground tunnels with their surface chain of wells have been the standard Iranian irrigation method for millennia.

plishment. Agricultural productivity, supplemented by imports, remained sufficient in the 1980s so that even under wartime conditions there was no widespread hunger. Despite oil's dominance, 25 percent of the economically active population still depends on agriculture, which contributes 11 percent to GDP.

As in Syria and Iraq, large landowners and tribal leaders held huge areas before 1960; peasants worked the land as sharecroppers. Indeed, landowners controlled entire groups of villages along with the land and the inhabitants. Two major land-reform programs transformed the system. One was the shah's highly publicized "White Revolution" in 1963; the other was the revolutionary government's land reform in 1982. These curbed landowner power and reduced the size of their landholdings.

Extensive areas in the northwest and northeast support rainfed cultivation and arboriculture, as well as specialty horticulture in the distinctive ecology of the Caspian coast. However, typically agriculture relies on water management. Several techniques are employed, but the ancient system of distributing water through the *qanat* network remains the most important (see Chap. 5). Ideally, these underground galleries, showing on the surface as a chain of wells, are constructed in alluvial fans that absorb runoff from adjacent watersheds on higher slopes receiving rain and snow. Scores of thousands of *qanats*, many constructed centuries ago and carefully maintained on northern and southwestern slopes, look like strings of beads on the long slopes of the fans from the air (Fig. 19.3). Although all irrigation requires local cooperation, *qanat*-watered basins demand an exceptionally high level of coordination and engender a complex and uniquely socioeconomic structure.

Crops. The four tables in Chapter 5 clearly show Iran's high rank in crop and livestock production. As noted earlier, in the region, it leads in irrigated area and in the production of oranges, combined fruits, dates, sheep, chickens, and goats, and ranks second or third for many other crops. Nearly everywhere, except in the barren interior and southeast, the dominant crops are wheat and barley, grown in both rainfed and irrigated areas. Much wheat is rough milled to make the unusual Iranian bread: large, flat, and dimpled from being baked on hot pebbles in a large oven. Rice, the third major cereal, is grown in paddies on the alluvial plains along the Caspian coast. Much of the excellent rice is consumed in the favorite national dish, *chelo kebab*—grilled lamb kebabs on a bed of rice. Wheat and rice production fail to meet demand, necessitating substantial imports. Potatoes are grown in large quantities. Melons are grown everywhere, along with a wide range of vegetables. Also widely distributed are grapes, consumed as raisins, table grapes, and, in the past, wine. From the early 1960s through the mid-2000s, Iran saw a spectacular increase in per capita food production—more than 120 percent—well beyond the achievement of any other country in this study.[27]

Tree crops, common on the lower Zagros slopes, yield a wide range of fruits and nuts, with pistachios a particular specialty. It ranks first globally for pistachios (the United States is second but with less than half Iran's output), and nuts rank third in exports. Almonds and walnuts grow well in subhumid areas. Fruits, from citrus on the Gulf to apples in higher elevations, include all but humid tropical varieties. Tea grows along the Caspian in the same conditions that produce rice and other subtropical crops. It is the popular social beverage, far surpassing coffee, and imports are needed to meet demand.

On the Caspian coast and in favored locations in the southern Zagros, cotton and tobacco are major industrial crops. Both sugarcane and sugar beets have been expanded in acreage, and mills process these crops at refineries in the center and northeast. Opium poppies, once prohibited, are grown under government supervision, as in Turkey.

Livestock, Fishing, and Forestry.   Vast areas are well suited for grazing sheep and goats, and cattle are of increasing importance. Besides dairy products, cattle supply manure for fertilizer and domestic fuel (see Fig. 4.8). Fishing is important both off the southern coast and on the Caspian, where fisheries are especially famous for their superior caviar, the roe of large sturgeon. Already very limited and therefore expensive, caviar supplies are threatened by chemical pollution, the fluctuating water level of the Caspian, and overexploitation. Ranking third in amount of fish caught (see Table 5.3), Iran ranks second in the export value because of caviar. Forests in the Elburz are the only commercially productive ones in the region other than in Turkey.

Hydrocarbons: A Major Producer

Iran became the first major petroleum country in the Middle East in 1908 with the discovery of the great Masjid-e Soleyman field in the folds of the middle Zagros, southeast of Dezful (see Chap. 6). Oil has long played a dominant role in the economy and has undergirded the country's economic development for decades.

Iran's reserves rose to 137.6 bn bbl with new finds in Khuzistan,[28] to place it second in the Middle East and in the world, ahead of Iraq. Even more impressive are its natural gas reserves of 1,045.7 tn ft^3/29.6 tn m^3, second globally after Russia. Like Egypt and neighboring countries, Iran is stressing gas, although it has vacillated about the details of allowing foreign investment. Oil output peaked in 1974 at more than 6 mn bpd before falling to a minimum of 1.37 mn bpd in 1981, early in the Iran-Iraq War. It returned to 3.6 mn bpd in the mid-1990s and then to about 3.7 mn bpd in 2009.

Historical Note. Early oil operations by Anglo-Persian (later Anglo-Iranian) Oil Company are traced in Chapter 6. After four decades of AIOC control, one of the first major crises in international oil history arose during the 1951–1953 dispute between the government, under Prime Minister Mohammad Mossadegh, and the company. It arose when he rejected a draft agreement between the AIOC and Iran and then nationalized the industry under the new National Iranian Oil Company (NIOC). During the ensuing dispute, oil sales fell to zero. In 1953, Mossadegh was ousted and the shah was restored, with covert U.S. help, and under a completely new accord the former concession passed to a new consortium of British, Dutch, French, and, just coincidentally, U.S. companies.

Under NIOC supervision, the consortium produced and refined most Iranian output for the next twenty-five years. However, NIOC partnered with several other U.S., Italian, and Canadian companies from the late 1950s for exploration and production outside the original concession area, including offshore. In the 1980s, it operated on its own in some areas and succeeded reasonably well under difficult wartime circumstances, finding giant nonassociated gas fields, especially offshore, the largest being South Pars, an extension of the supergiant North Field off Qatar (see Chaps. 6 and 15).

In the early 1990s, Iran acted to reinvigorate its hydrocarbon industry but faced two major obstacles: the deterioration of aging fields and facilities during the long spell of isolation and dramatic reductions in the availability of funding needed for implementation. Sanctions imposed by the United States exacerbated these obstacles, so the government actively sought foreign-company participation. Major projects included opening offshore gas fields (especially South Pars) and rejuvenating overexploited onshore oil fields using gas-injection techniques. Having neglected enhanced oil recovery (EOR) methods for two decades, NIOC initiated a vigorous program in several onshore fields. More than a dozen European companies have been interested in working in Iran, despite the U.S. government's extraterritorial attempt to preclude foreign companies from operating there. For a different reason—Iran's nuclear program—sanctions were a factor again later in the decade.

Fields and Facilities. Most oil fields are located in linear northwest-southeast reservoirs paralleling the Zagrosian fold structures in the original discovery belt (Map 19.3; see also Map 6.2). After a century of exploration, there are twenty-five onshore fields extending from west of Khorramabad to Bandar-e Abbas, a distance of 600 mi/966 km, and seven offshore fields widely scattered the full length of the Gulf on Iran's side of the median line. Onshore gas fields are concentrated at the northwestern and southeastern ends of the oil belt (Map 6.2). Virtually no onshore reservoirs have been found outside the Zagros folds. As in Saudi Arabia, overall central control of operations permits drilling only the optimum number of wells, so that in 2009 Iran produced from just 1,128 wells, some of which still yielded thousands of barrels a day after ninety years.

Oil and gas pipelines form a dense network in the closely packed fields of Khuzistan and adjacent areas. Most lines feed the Kharg Island export terminal northwest of Bushehr, which is, with Ras Tanura and Juaymah in Saudi Arabia, one of the world's three largest terminals. Other lines carry feedstock to the refinery on Abadan Island on the east bank of the Shatt al-Arab, one of the largest in the Gulf, processing 400,000 bpd. Among the country's nine refineries, with a total capacity of 1.5 mn bpd, the three next largest after Abadan are in Esfahan, Bandar-e Abbas, and Tehran. This is not enough to satisfy domestic demand for partly subsidized petroproducts; considerable gasoline, for example,

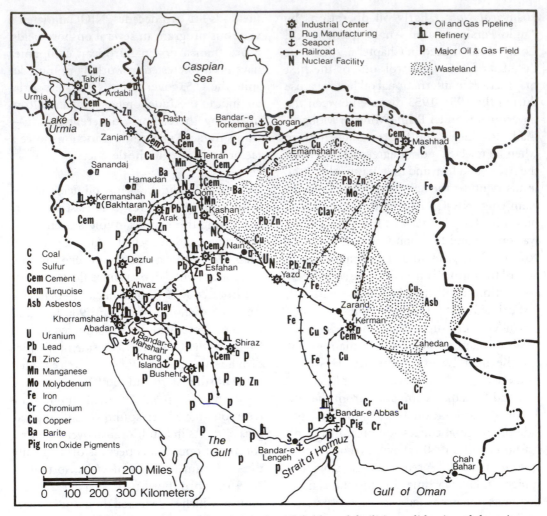

MAP 19.3 Economic map of Iran, showing major oil fields and facilities, solid-mineral deposits, industrial centers, ports, and railways.

must be imported (at market prices), and in late 2009 the government reported that its budget for the last quarter of the year for these imports was short by $3 billion.[29]

With almost unlimited natural gas production potential, Iran is seeking export customers and widespread domestic use for its gas. Following installation of only a skeletal pipeline net, gas could completely replace oil in electricity generation (in the late 2000s, gas-fired plants produced about 75 percent of the national supply), supply a major new export, and permit widespread distribution of bottled liquefied petroleum gas (LPG) for

domestic home and vehicle use; with more pipelines, gas could gradually be supplied to much of the country. Some of this potential has been realized: Most power plants now use gas. By the late 1990s, more than 300 cities were receiving piped gas, up from 6 before 1978. As one phase of the program to reduce serious pollution in the capital, many taxis run on LPG. Additionally, huge quantities of gas are reinjected into oil fields in EOR efforts. In 2010, a gas pipeline linking Iran and Turkmenistan was inaugurated.

As early as 1970, Iran opened a 40–42-in/ 102–107-cm pipeline, IGAT-1, from its southwestern fields into the Soviet Union. IGAT-2, from the Kangan gas field on the Gulf south of Shiraz to Astara, where the Azerbaijan border meets the Caspian Sea coast, opened in 1992. Its diameter is a huge 56 in/142 cm to Qazvin, northwest of Tehran, and 48 in/122 cm from Qazvin to Astara. IGAT-3, with the same diameter as IGAT-2, is under construction, and two more Iranian Gas Transport lines are in planning. An export line to Turkey opened in 2002—the precursor of many others in various states of planning to supply Iranian gas across Turkey to Europe. In 2008, Iran and Pakistan agreed to proceed with a pipeline that could be extended to India if the latter is satisfied with gas-price negotiations.[30] Further to utilize its plentiful hydrocarbon wealth, Iran has an extensive program to construct ten new petrochemical plants, with Bandar-e Khomeini (sometimes Bandar-e Imam) as a special petrochemical economic zone. The National Petrochemical Company is offering inducements to foreign companies to join the program over the next several years. Utilizing petroleum and natural gas to produce petrochemicals has many advantages, including adding considerable value to raw materials and avoiding restrictions imposed by OPEC production quotas.[31]

Non-Oil Resources

Scattered mineral deposits, especially copper, were mined in ancient times on the Iranian Plateau. However, few commercially significant deposits were identified until modern technology, including space imagery, was applied to the exploration of the highly mineralized volcanic belt in Iran near the tectonic plate boundary along the inner Zagros. Geologists discovered one deposit after another—copper, iron, chrome, lead, zinc, bauxite, manganese, coal, barite—approximately along the axis of the railway from Qom to Kerman. Numerous finds are now being exploited, some on a large scale. Thus, Iran possesses an array of mineral raw materials for domestic use and export (see Map 19.3).[32]

The most important discoveries were of copper along the entire length of the inner Zagros volcanic belt from the northwestern border to south of Bam in the southeast. Total reserves are more than 2.6 billion tons, with the largest deposits at Sar Cheshmeh, southwest of Kerman; some Western engineers claim these are the richest in the world. An integrated mining, smelting, and refining operation is based on the deposit; a new smelter has opened at Khatounabad, near Sar Cheshmeh. Mining at Ahar, north of Tabriz, has been expanded. Iran is aiming for an annual output of 250,000 mt of copper content a year but it is having difficulty reaching this goal.

Iran is first or second regionally in production of several other ores, including iron, chrome, zinc, lead, manganese, and aluminum. A remarkable concentration exists near Bafq, southeast of Yazd, with major deposits of iron and lead-zinc ores not far from large coal resources. Iron is transported to the Esfahan steel works by rail from Bafq; still richer ore resources of 1.13 bn mt at Gol-e Gohar, south of Sirjan, feed both Esfahan and Ahvaz plants. By 2012, Iran hopes to have total steel capacity of some 40 mn mt/yr.[33] Several major chrome deposits south and southeast of Kerman yield ores for export and for smelting near Bandar-e Abbas. The aluminum industry has burgeoned as bauxite production has increased, and in the late 2000s additional smelter capacity came on line at Arak, southwest of Hamadan, and at Bandar-e Abbas, bringing the total to more than 450,000 mt annually. Another 200,000 mt facility was being built by a Chinese company at Sarab.[34]

Important nonmetallic minerals include coal; the largest deposits are northwest of Kerman, but more than a score of collieries extend across northern Iran from Lake Urmia to Mashhad. Fine turquoise from Neyshabur,

FIGURE 19.4 Hand-knotting an especially large and fine rug in an Esfahan workshop (1964). Three young girls are guided by two adult women. Handmade carpets are the second-ranking export of Iran.

west of Mashhad, is used in locally crafted jewelry, and some turquoise is exported. Inexhaustible supplies of salt occur in numerous plugs near Bandar-e Abbas; native sulfur from many of the same structures supply an important export item. Near Qom, local kaolin is used in the large ceramics industry for the decorative tiles used in walls, floors, and even house facades.

Industries

Industrialization during the 1960s proceeded on a scale that observers considered unrealistic, demanding too much too fast—large-scale projects with inadequate infrastructure, provoking fundamentalist charges of "Westoxication" and anti-Islamic policies. Nevertheless, many different major industries were successfully established, from food processing to iron and steel production and automobile assembly. Joint ventures with foreign corpo-

rations brought technology transfers and training programs, even though few ventures achieved planned production levels. After the revolution, an unreliable labor supply and shortages of raw materials, spare parts, and other inputs meant few of these new enterprises could sustain production. The Iraq war turned the emphasis to military needs.

Industry is widely distributed in the western third of the country. Many plants are concentrated around Tehran; light industries and craft shops are found in dozens of towns and even villages. Major products include processed foods and beverages, cigarettes, home appliances, assembled automobiles, textiles, and machine tools. Iran is especially known for its excellent artisan work: handknotted rugs, jewelry, metalwares, inlay work, and decorated ceramic tiles (Fig. 19.4).

Greater Tehran dominates the manufacturing sector, with auto assembly, household

FIGURE 19.5 A one-man shop in the copper and brass bazaar of Esfahan. Traditional products such as these hand-hammered and hand-engraved trays are still major items of manufacture in several Iranian cities.

appliance, and clothing plants. Esfahan, the second-largest industrial center, has the major iron and steel plant, cotton mills, and numerous small shops producing metal household items, including brass and copper trays (Fig. 19.5). Tabriz, with a major machine tool plant, is the northwest's industrial focus. Arak, southwest of Qom, has one of Iran's aluminum smelters; about 60 percent of its output is exported. Still other cities with appreciable manufacturing are shown in Map 19.3, which illustrates the concentration in the western third, with Mashhad an outlier in the far northeast. Rug-making centers—Tabriz, Ardabil, Hamadan, Qom, Kashan, Esfahan, Nain, Shiraz, Kerman, and Mashhad—are world renowned. Some sophisticated plants, especially nuclear processing facilities, are off-limits, but foreigners have visited those in Natanz, Arak, and Bushehr, and in January 2005 the government let UN nuclear inspectors examine the facility at Parchin, southeast of Tehran, and a previously unknown enrichment plant near Qom in October 2009. Weapons plants are dispersed and are similarly classified.

Transportation and Trade

Land Routes. Development after World War II was constrained by infrastructural limitations, and construction of a transportation net was both difficult and expensive. Terrain, climate, and distance combine to inhibit construction, even when financing and engineering skills are available. By the 1980s, however, all cities had been integrated into a well-engineered highway network constructed by foreign companies under contract. The net covers all parts of the country except the virtually uninhabited interior basins (see Map 19.1).

The railway through the Zagros between Dezful and Qom was extended during World War II to Tabriz and the Soviet border to carry war matériel. As part of the CENTO- and RCD-sponsored railway from Istanbul to Karachi, a line was constructed to the Turkish border and from Qom through Kashan and Yazd to Kerman. An extension to Bam and on to Zahedan to finish the connection to Pakistan was at last inaugurated in July 2009. A major line ties Bafq (between Yazd and Kerman) through the mountains to the port of Bandar-e Abbas. An extension from Bafq to Mashhad was under way in the late 2000s, as were links to Basrah and Baghdad in Iraq (and thence to Syria) and to Herat in Afghanistan. In the far northeast, a short but strategic link in the late 1990s extended the Tehran/Mashhad line on to Sarakhs on the Turkmenistan border. From there, the Trans-Asian railway follows along the old Silk Road to Mary, Bukhara, Samarkand, and Tashkent; in 2010, Iran and Turkmenistan signed an agreement to link Iran with Kazakhstan to the north by rail. Iran has thus positioned itself to link Central Asia to the Gulf, the subcontinent, and the Levant. The 2000s saw the opening of parts of a three-line metro system in Tehran. Light-rail systems were under construction or in the planning stage in Ahvaz, Esfahan, Karadj, Mashhad, Shiraz, and Tabriz.[35]

Ports. Despite a coastline of 1,555 mi/2,500 km from the Shatt al-Arab to the Pakistan border, Iran has few good natural harbors. Since population and development centered near the head of the Gulf even in antiquity, most major ports lie in the arc from Khorramshahr to Bushehr, including the main oil-export terminal of Kharg Island. Bandar-e Khomeini (once Bandar-e Shahpur) was ex-

panded during the 1990s to serve the burgeoning petrochemical center. Farther south, Bandar-e Bushehr is the site of Iran's nuclear reactor, mentioned earlier. Bandar-e Abbas was expanded during the war with Iraq and is now connected by rail to the main line through the country's center. It is a major general-cargo port, a passenger port for cross-Gulf traffic, and the main naval base, guarding the Strait of Hormuz. Chah Bahar (sometimes Bandar Beheshti) on the Indian Ocean was also developed during the Iraq war (see Map 19.3). On the Caspian coast, Bandar-e Anzali is the leading port for fishing and trade with the littoral states.

Trade. In normal times Iran imports a range of modern industrial and consumer goods. Its exports are mostly petroleum, petroleum products, and related items, by both volume and value. Petroleum customers vary from year to year but regularly include Japan, Britain, South Korea, Germany, and Turkey. Imported products—machinery, iron and steel products, transport equipment, grains, textiles, and chemicals—come primarily from Germany, Japan, Italy, and the UAE. Weapons and ammunition have loomed large among imports during the past four decades, and armaments imports in the 1990s equaled the level reached under the shah in the 1970s. Despite its condemnation of the monarchy for squandering Iranian wealth on weapons, the republic has imported a wide range of armaments, as well as machine tools for producing armaments, from Russia, China, and North Korea. Russia and China also supplied nuclear technology, creating the international tensions noted earlier.

RELATIONS

Long before petroleum was found, the Iranian Plateau played an important geopolitical role both locally and internationally. On the contemporary scene, its geopolitical position, place in world oil and global finances, human resources, and aggressively idiosyncratic approach to internal and external relations converge to make Iran a vital partner or opponent in many global relationships. One scholar commented, "Iran is fortunate in its strategic situation. It has no historical enemies, no irredenta, no source of permanent tensions on its frontiers. It is well endowed with resources, material and human and well situated. . . . It has failed to capitalize on these assets due to an excessive cultivation of past grievances and . . . has thus squandered the country's potential."[36]

Regional

CENTO/ECO. Although revolutionary Iran withdrew from the Central Treaty Organization in 1979 and thereby precipitated the bloc's collapse, it maintained its ties with Turkey and Pakistan and continued some participation in the Regional Cooperation for Development, later the Economic Cooperation Organization (ECO; see Chap. 8). ECO was expanded in 1992 to include Afghanistan and six former Soviet republics; membership potentially provides these states with more direct access to the sea than they had as members of the USSR. Most members signed the agreement on the Trans-Asian railway mentioned above, and Iran is strongly attracted by the Silk Road concept.[37] The Caspian Basin states, resources, and problems are matters of priority in its grand strategy. Sunni and secular, Turkey contrasts with contemporary Iran, but Iran has been pleased by recent Turkish moves toward Islamism, even if these have been limited. They share the Kurdish problem but compete in independent Azerbaijan. Already well linked by rail and road, they have the gas pipeline mentioned earlier, although Iran objects to Turkish-Israeli military cooperation. In 2009, after meeting with President Obama, Turkish prime minister Erdoğan indicated opposition to fresh sanctions being imposed on Iran.

Similarly, Iran maintains good relations with the Islamic Republic of Pakistan, with which it has in common a domestic tug-of-war between conservatism and moderation. They also have a common minority problem on their border—the Baluch.

Iraq. It is with its western neighbor, Iraq, that Iran has long had the most persistent conflict, a prolongation of the millennia-old cleavage between the Iranian Plateau and the Mesopotamian Basin; the bloody eight-year war of the 1980s was a return to earlier battles. Relations eased after Saddam's overthrow; however, Iran condemned the U.S.-led invasion and occupation. It had been pleased when Iraq allowed pilgrims to visit Shii holy shrines in 1997 (for the first time since 1980), and Iranian Shii flooded into Najaf and Karbala after April 2003. While Iran has been playing a significant role in Iraqi reconstruction, its ties to certain Shii political parties and militias have been a cause for concern for many Iraqis. Since 2006, the Iraqi president and prime minister have made numerous visits to Tehran, and in 2008 Ahmadinejad was the first president of the Islamic Republic to travel to Baghdad. One boon to Iran of its improved relations with its neighbor: Iraq has become a major customer for its non-oil exports, buying at least $2.3 billion in 2008.

Gulf Cooperation Council. The GCC members are states with whom Iran should logically maintain close relations; these, however, have been strained from the foundation of the GCC. It was no secret that perceived Iranian threats were (and continue to be) in large part the group's raison d'être. Incidents involving Iranian pilgrims in Mecca have periodically marred relations with Saudi Arabia. The UAE and Iran have close trade ties but have contended over Abu Musa and the Tunb islands, discussed earlier. In the 2000s, all GCC members, to some degree, have been alarmed at the prospect of a nuclear-armed

Iran and the perceived "Shii Crescent" stretching across to Lebanon.

Syria, Egypt. Iran's curious ties with Syria have been cordial, and relations with arch enemy Egypt even warmed under the deft handling of President Khatami. Both the United States and Saudi Arabia have been actively wooing Syria away from Iran, and in the 2000s Egypt has become more concerned with Iran's influence with the Shii of other countries and with its nuclear program.

Israel. Israel, in contrast, is acrimoniously reviled in Iran, at least in public. This reverses the cordial relations that existed before 1979, when Israel sent technicians to Iran and Iran shipped petroleum to Elat, and their two intelligence services, Mossad and SAVAK, collaborated closely. During the 1990s, Israel battled Iranian-supported Hizballah guerrillas in its strip of occupation in south Lebanon. The "Summer War" of 2006, in which Israeli cities were attacked as they had not been since the 1940s, showed that Iran was still supplying Hizballah with sophisticated weaponry. As the crisis over Iran's nuclear program heightened, Israel increasingly pushed for military action.

Afghanistan. With close historic, cultural, and linguistic ties to Afghanistan, Iran has moved to bolster relations with the post-Taliban regime (it played a supportive role in overthrowing the Taliban),[38] despite the U.S. military presence. It is the largest regional donor to Afghanistan's recovery efforts, and the Kabul government has denied U.S. claims that Iran has been backing insurgent elements. However, Iran's links with Afghanistan are still tenuous and are likely to remain uncertain while that country remains fragmented. Iran has no affinity with the Sunni extremist Taliban and has a special interest in the welfare of Afghanistan's Shii Hazara, a long-mistreated minority.

Former Soviet Union. When the Soviet Union collapsed, Iran quickly found itself with a group of newly independent neighbors—from Armenia in the northwest on into Central Asia. In the Caucasus, two very different situations arose: First, Muslim Azerbaijan's leaders soon betrayed their irredentist ambition to attract Iran's Azerbaijan Ostan into a reunited republic; second, Christian Armenia, before independence came, was at war with Azerbaijan over the Armenian exclave of Nagorno-Karabakh. Despite religious differences, Iran essentially sided with Armenia, and although in the 2000s a semblance of cordiality was restored to Iran's relations with Azerbaijan, the early semialliance has remained in place. A bargaining chip for Iran is the Azerbaijani exclave of Nakhchivan—it has borders only with Iran and Armenia, and Iran often seems to treat it as an independent entity.

Farther east, two new Central Asian states—Turkmenistan and Kazakhstan—share the Caspian littoral with Iran (and Russia and Azerbaijan). Given the Caspian Basin's emerging importance both for its petroresources and as a key locus for the transmission of those resources to world markets, it is vital to Iran to maintain good relations with these two states east of the Caspian. Its rival for their goodwill is independent Russia. There is a long history of Iranian ethnic, cultural, and linguistic influence throughout Central Asia, and Tajikistan's people speak a closely related tongue (as mentioned in Chap. 18, the other republics have languages related to Turkish). Iran's quest for full membership in the Shanghai Cooperation Organization (Russia, China, and four of the "stans") has so far proved unsuccessful—largely because of the notoriety of the nuclear controversy.

Global

United States. Crucial as Iran's relations with Iraq and the GCC may be, those with the United States have been the most important for more than half a century.[39] The mutually hostile current attitudes stand in marked contrast to those of the twenty-five years following 1953, when the Central Intelligence Agency helped restore the shah to power. By the 1960s, Iran—an "island of stability" in the Middle East—became the United States' "chosen instrument," the eastern anchor of the U.S. geopolitical position in the region. Huge quantities of sophisticated military equipment poured into the country so it could play a leading role in the Gulf (and to earn billions of dollars for U.S. arms exporters). Some critics accused the United States not only of winking at widespread abuses of human rights but actually of contributing to them.

As the shah's main supporter, the United States became the main target of the Islamic revolution. In this backlash, the United States became the "Great Satan." The seizure of the American Embassy, the U.S. tilt toward Iraq during the Iran-Iraq War, and the downing of an Iranian civil aircraft in a case of mistaken identity by the U.S. Navy all deepened the rift even further. In the 1990s, the United States coupled Iran with Iraq in the "dual containment" policy, treating both as rogue supporters of terrorism and states seeking to develop weapons of mass destruction. There were attempts when Khatami and Clinton presided over their countries to broach détente, but one or another issue always revived mutual recriminations. With the onset of the Bush administration, an adversarial stance returned to the fore, with Iran declared part of the "Axis of Evil" with Iraq and North Korea; sanctions and embargoes (most trade with Iran is prohibited under various provisions of U.S. law) were regularly renewed. After the U.S. invasions of Afghanistan and Iraq, Iran felt surrounded. Since long-term instability in either of its neighbors is not in its best interests, it actually assisted in many aspects of postinvasion reconstruction, but underlying hostility on both sides made overt cooperation between them difficult. In 2009, the first approaches of the new U.S. administration to Iran did somewhat mute the stridency that had characterized most public statements of the previous decade (the nuclear dispute is discussed below).

Other States. Links with Russia are generally cordial, although remnants of historic suspicion no doubt remain. Both czarist and Soviet Russia eyed Iranian territories covetously, and Iran was a key element in efforts to contain Soviet expansionism. To offset its enmity with the United States, revolutionary Iran cautiously established a military-economic link with Russia, which supplies large amounts of heavy armaments and is engaged in (slowly) completing the Bushehr nuclear reactor. Iran maintains similar ties with China, which supplies arms and also constructs major industrial plants. Iran's long-standing, mutually beneficial relations with the EU as an entity seesawed during the 1990s but were strained by the mid-2000s with the cat-and-mouse game that Iran seemed to be playing regarding its nuclear program. Russia, China, and the EU all are involved in this controversy.

Nuclear Issue. In 2003, the International Atomic Energy Agency (IAEA) reported that Iran, a signatory of the Nuclear Non-Proliferation Treaty and a member of the IAEA, had contravened its obligations by concealing some of its nuclear activities since the 1980s. Responding to the agency's demand that it prove it was not pursuing a weapons program, Iran agreed to cooperate more fully and to suspend uranium enrichment. The IAEA concluded there was no evidence of nonpeaceful activity, but within months it complained Iran was not keeping its promises. These were the opening salvos in a diplomatic cat-and-mouse game that continued for the rest of the decade without resolution.

Essentially, over the following years, various combinations of international players—

the EU, Britain, France, Germany, the United States, Russia, China, the UN, and the IAEA—have alternatively cajoled and threatened Iran, seeking cessation of the enrichment efforts (but not of the parts of the nuclear program with nonmilitary ends) and full and transparent cooperation with IAEA inspectors. In return, various economic rewards (including nuclear assistance) and integration of Iran into global decision-making processes have been on offer, while tighter sanctions—like those imposed by the UN Security Council in 2006 and unilaterally by the United States in 2007—have been cited as the alternative. Meanwhile, Iran sometimes pursued further enrichment, sometimes suspended it; in 2008, it demonstrated its progress in weapons delivery systems with successful medium-range missile tests. Toward the end of the decade, military preemption has been publicly mentioned as a possibility. Israel, resolved to keep its regional monopoly of a nuclear weapons stockpile, has been particularly vocal in this regard, openly discussing various plans for air strikes on key Iranian targets.

The United States, even under the Bush administration, was aware that Iran would retaliate against any precipitous attack on its facilities by moving in various ways against the United States in Iraq and Afghanistan—and possibly undertake to hinder oil-tanker traffic in the Straits of Hormuz. Thus, the diplomatic approach prevailed through the end of the decade. Various solutions were offered for Iran's need of enriched uranium for scientific purposes; Iran at first seemed willing, then hedged. Observers concluded that within the government, there was conflict between hard-liners bent on a weapons program and others (possibly including the president and the supreme leader) looking for a resolution bringing practical economic gains. Russia indicated that, for "technical reasons," it would be unable to complete the Bushehr reactor[40] on schedule or supply Iran with the air-defense system that was on order.

Iran revealed it was building a second enrichment plant near Qom in September 2009, and while IAEA inspectors visited the site a month later, the agency rebuked Iran in November 2009 for not revealing its existence sooner. Then, seemingly in retaliation, Iran announced its intention to build up to ten new enrichment plants—necessary, claimed President Ahmadinejad, so that the country could produce 20 gigawatts of nuclear energy by 2020.[41]

As 2009 wore on, the nuclear issue became entangled domestically with the growing post-election opposition to the regime and the government's attempts to blame all its political and economic problems on external forces. International diplomacy had little success; Iran would sometimes show interest in negotiating and then retract its apparent agreements. While many, especially among U.S. and European conservatives and in Israel, have called for overwhelming military strikes against nuclear facilities, others argued such strikes would only delay the weapons program and, whether they were successful or not, would probably strengthen the regime against its nascent domestic opposition. It would allow a corrupt and weakening regime to appeal to its citizens' patriotism and sense of Persian identity. As mentioned before, the United States also has concerns about possible backlash against its forces in Iraq and Afghanistan, and it, the Europeans, and even China are aware what an Iranian blockade of the Strait of Hormuz could do to the world economy.

While diplomacy remained the preferred path in 2010 for the major international and regional powers, as well as of the UN and the IAEA, clearly their collective patience was wearing thin. Critical to forward movement was the need for agreement within the UN Security Council on the format and strength of additional sanctions, but the actions and reactions of the two unpredictable antagonists—

Iran and Israel—can easily trump any plans of the other parties. However this crisis plays out, it is obvious that the confrontation so far has interfered with Iran's developmental progress by diverting resources toward a military objective of doubtful strategic value and by subjecting the country to a rigid system of economic sanctions.[42]

NOTES

1. See Limbert 1987, Chaps. 1 and 2.

2. For a focus on Fars, see Summers 1986. For general coverage of archaeological sites, see Matheson 1976.

3. Limbert 1987 covers these developments as well as Iran in general, including *Iran-zamin*. The well-documented role of the CIA in the shah's restoration became and is still an issue of bitterness among Iranians, especially Khomeini revolutionaries.

4. Amuzegar 1995, 26, 22–23.

5. As a senior cleric did during the late 2009 riots when he called on the leaders of the opposition to repent or be declared enemies of God and face death (*The Daily Star* [Beirut], Dec. 31, 2009).

6. Like Israeli rabbi Yitzhak Shapiro, whose recent book states that God allows killing Gentile children who might grow up to be enemies of the Jews (*Jerusalem Post*, Nov. 11, 2009).

7. See Parsi 2007.

8. Summaries of the investigative reports from the Tower Commission and the U.S. Congress are available at www.presidency.ucsb.edu/PS157/assignment%20files%20public/TOWER%20EXCERPTS.htm and www.presidency.ucsb.edu/PS157/assignment%20files%20public/congressional%20report%20key%20sections.htm, respectively.

9. Boroujerdi 2001. See also Fairbanks 1997 and Amuzegar 1995. For later specific developments, see *Economist*, Aug. 21, 1999.

10. *New York Times*, July 15, 1999, covers the crisis in detail. See also *Economist*, May 15 and July 17, 1999. A serious retrospective study is Milani 2001.

11. Reuters, Nov. 9, 2009.

12. See www.un.org/apps/news/story.asp?NewsID=29459&Cr=human+rights&Cr1=iran#.

13. United Nations Development Programme 2009.

14. An excellent, comprehensive coverage of Iran's geography is in W. Fisher 1968. A concise treatment is given in Limbert 1987, Chap. 1.

15. See the National Geographic Society map, *Middle East*, Oct. 2002. It was movement along the western edge of the rafted terrain that produced the Bam earthquake. The disaster is reported in *New York Times*, Dec. 28, 2003, and is reviewed in *Christian Science Monitor*, Feb. 17, 2004.

16. In addition to the standard U.S. Department of Defense, Defense Mapping Agency 1985, see Adamec 1976–1988. Numerous place-names were changed by the revolutionary Iranian authorities (see "A Note on Transliteration" at the beginning of this book). Some names seem to have been changed back to the originals. Kermanshah (city) was renamed Bakhtaran, then re-renamed Kermanshah. Chah Bahar was renamed Bandar Beheshti but is now shown as Chabahar.

17. Montaigne 1999 discusses this topic and pictures northern Tehran.

18. Detailed technical studies are in Krinsley 1970.

19. The populations given for Egypt, Iran, and Turkey are all estimates, and actual totals almost certainly shift periodically among the three in rankings. The Table 4.1 population of 72 million is less than three later U.S. government figures. It might be said that Turkey, Iran, and Egypt all have populations of about 71–75 million.

20. Useful studies regarding Iranian settlements are Bonine 1979; English 1966; and Kheirabadi 1991.

21. Concise discussion of peoples and their distribution is given in Limbert 1987 and *Iran* Country Study 1989.

22. *New York Times*, Feb. 24, 2010; *BBC News*, Feb. 25, 2010.

23. *Economist*, Feb. 13, 1987; *Christian Science Monitor*, Feb. 3, 1998.

24. See Limbert 1987, Chaps. 1, 5, and 6; *Iran* Country Study 1989, esp. Chap. 3; and Hoogland 2002.

25. The intricacies of the Iranian economy in this period are followed in *Iran* Country Study 1989; Amirahmadi 1990; and Amuzegar 1992, a concise comparison of pre- and postrevolutionary conditions, updated in Amuzegar 1995 and 1999; and Khajehpour 2001. We have drawn from these works and U.S. Department of State, *Background Note; Iran*, various issues.

26. Transparency International 2009. Adding to Iran's unattractiveness for foreign investment (except for the oil sector) is the perceived low level of economic freedom. An alternative to the Fraser Institute's measure cited in earlier chapters (Iran was not included in that study) is the more subjectively based offering in Heritage Foundation, *2009 Index of Economic Freedom* (Washington, DC). In the most recent rankings from this source, Iran placed 168th of 179 countries globally and last of the 15 regional countries in the study (Iraq was excluded for lack of data).

27. FAO, various issues.

28. U.S. Department of Energy, Energy Information Administration, *Country Analysis Briefs: Iran*, Aug. 2004 and Jan. 2010; *International Petroleum Encyclopedia*. Much of the following section is based on these sources, plus *Oil and Gas Journal* articles.

29. *The Daily Star*, Dec. 8, 2009.

30. A route through Baluchistan was chosen for the line (*Oil and Gas Journal*, Aug. 25, 2009).

31. A detailed study is *Oil and Gas Journal*, Aug. 16 and Aug. 23, 1999.

32. USGS, "The Mineral Industry of Iran," in *Minerals Yearbook* 2008.

33. Steel production rose by 11 percent in 2009 to an annual rate of about 11 mn mt, and at least 6.4 mn mt capacity more is expected in 2010, but it would appear this goal is unlikely to be reached (*The Daily Star*, Dec. 28, 2009).

34. USGS 2008.

35. For further details, see www.tehranmetro.com/index.asp, www.subways.net/iran/, and www.shiraz metro.ir/english.html.

36. Chubin 2000, 10. The statement perhaps overlooks the long-running enmity between Mesopotamia and the Iranian Plateau.

37. For further information, see www.ecosecretariat .org/.

38. *USA Today*, June 9, 2009. Iran was close to open war with the Taliban after the murder of nine Iranian diplomats in Mazar-al-Sharif and a massacre of Afghan Shii in 1998.

39. For a penetrating study of these relations by a leading scholar, see Bill 1988 and Bill and Chavez 2002. *Middle East Policy* 1994 has a debate on "dual containment" among four experts. For later developments, see Amuzegar 1998; Monshipouri 1998; Ramazani 1998, 2001; Sick 2001; Murden 2002, Chap. 3; and Pollack 2004. Relations with Israel are discussed in Sobhani 1999.

40. *Christian Science Monitor*, Nov. 18, 2009.

41. *BBC News*, Nov. 29, 2009.

42. A thoughtful discussion of what the region's future with a nuclear-armed Iran might be like is found in Lindsay and Takeyh 2010.

Glossary

See Index for page number of main discussion of most terms. For names of geological time periods (Pleistocene, Cretaceous, etc.), see the Geological Time Chart after this glossary.

Abbasid: pertaining to the Muslim empire ruled by the Abbasid dynasty from Baghdad, 750–1258 CE.

Age-gender cohort: in demography, a group between two specified ages.

Ahl al-kitab: "people of the book," i.e., Jews, Christians, and others who have their own respective scriptures.

Al, al-(-el): uppercased and not hyphenated, connotes "family of, belonging to," as in Al Saud, Al Jabbar. Lowercased, represents definite article "the," as in al-Khalij, "the Gulf" (usually connected to the noun by a hyphen).

Aliyah: literally, "ascent, going up," the immigration of Jews to Eretz Yisrael, the Land of Israel (*see also olim*).

Allah: God.

Alluvial: pertaining to river-deposited materials, especially fine silt and silt-clay laid down on floodplains and deltas such as those of the Nile.

Amir (emir): commander, prince, ruler. May have, but need not have, territorial jurisdiction.

Amirate (emirate): realm of an amir. In lower Gulf, also called shaykhdom.

Ashkenazim: Jews from central or eastern Europe, directly or by descent.

Axis of Evil: designation used first in 2002 by President George W. Bush in his State of the Union address to designate Iraq, Iran, and North Korea. Later, Syria seemed to be added as a junior member.

Ayatollah: "the sign of God." Title of respect for upper-ranking Shii clergyman. One title for the late Ruhollah Khomeini, former Iranian revolutionary leader.

Ayn: flowing spring, open sinkhole water supply, or flowing artesian spring.

Baath: Arab Renaissance (Revival) Party, separate branches of which controlled the governments of Iraq and Syria until April 2003, when Baath in Iraq was ousted.

Basalt: a common type of lava—dark, fine-grained, extrusive volcanic rock. In original molten state, flows readily from fissures; covers large areas of the Levant and western Arabia.

Basement (or basement complex): massive, very ancient igneous and metamorphic rocks, usually Precambrian, very complex and underlying sedimentary strata.

Bbl: barrel, barrels. Standard barrel of oil contains 42 U.S. gallons (34.97 UK or imperial gallons).

Bedouin: pastoral Arab nomad of the desert; corruption of Arabic for "desert dweller."

Bpd: barrels per day (usually oil production).

C°: temperature in degrees Celsius or centigrade. Temperature in C° = Fahrenheit° minus 32 times 5/9. Temperature in F° = C° times 9/5 plus 32. Thus, 100°C = 212°F; 0°C = 32°F.

Caliph: from Arabic *khalifah*, "successor"—i.e., successor to Muhammad as head of the community of Islam, the *ummah* (q.v.).

Common Market: a group of countries with a common external tariff and no barriers to trade or the movement of inputs to production—labor, capital, and resources—among them; for example: the European Union.

Cuesta: linear ridge with steep escarpment on foreslope and with gentle backslope. Asymmetry results from erosion of outcrop of gently dipping resistant stratum. Successive cuestas are prominent features of central Arabia.

Customs Union: two or more countries with a common external tariff and no tariff barriers to their own trade; for example: Turkey and the EU.

Dağ (dagh): Turkish for "mountain."

Desert: any area with scanty rainfall, little vegetation, and therefore limited agricultural use. May be plain, plateau, or mountains at any latitude. Area in Koeppen's BWh group (see Map 2.6).

DFLP: Democratic Front for the Liberation of Palestine, one of the earlier more aggressive Palestinian guerrilla groups.

Dhow: general term for several types of traditional coastal sailing ships plying the waters around the Arabian Peninsula and parts of the Indian Ocean. The term is not used by Arabs, who employ specific names for different types: *boom, sambook,* and others.

Diaspora: dispersion. Usually refers to the dispersion of Jews from Palestine after 70 CE. Also, Jews now outside Palestine constitute the diaspora. Palestinian refugees sometimes apply the term to their dispersion and community outside Palestine. Used here for Lebanese and Cypriots as well.

Diastrophism: from Greek for "distortion, dislocation." Processes that have deformed the earth's crust, producing continents, ocean basins, mountains, folded strata, and other major features. Orogeny (q.v.) is one type of diastrophism.

Dirah: traditionally accepted tribal range of the Bedouin tribe.

Diurnal: daily, occurring daily, or having a daily cycle; e.g., the range of high and low temperatures during a twenty-four-hour period.

Dolomite: light-colored stratified sedimentary rock similar to limestone but high in calcium magnesium carbonate rather than the calcium carbonate of limestone.

Dunum: a unit of land area measurement common in Palestine and Jordan. Equivalency varies between 900 m^2 and 1,000 m^2 but is most commonly 919 m^2 (0.23 acre, 0.0919 ha).

Economic Union: a common market that also has a common currency, central bank, and monetary policy: for example, the Euro-zone within the EU (q.v.)—in 2010, sixteen members, including Cyprus.

EFTA: European Free Trade Area; in 2010—four members.

Emir/Emirate: *see* amir/amirate.

Enosis: union of Cyprus with Greece.

Entrepôt: center—usually a city and often a port city—that receives goods in transit, warehouses them, and reships them.

Ethnolinguistic: pertaining to a distinct people (ethnic group) whose distinguishing characteristic is especially language, although other criteria may also make them distinctive (e.g., Armenians).

EU: European Union, successor to European Community; in 2010—twenty-seven members, including Cyprus.

Expatriate: one who lives in a foreign country. Many Europeans, Americans, and South Asians work and live in several Middle East countries as expatriates (informally called "expats").

Extrusive: pertaining to pouring out of molten rock (lava) onto the earth's surface, where it solidifies; opposite is intrusive (e.g., granite). *See* basalt.

Falaj (**pl.** *aflaj*): *see* qanat.

Faluqa (**felucca**): traditional sailboat on the Nile and seas adjacent to Egypt, carries lateen sail.

Farsi: Persian, i.e., the language spoken by Persians; the official language of Iran.

al-Fatah (Fateh): palindromic acronym for Harakat al-Tahrir al-Filastiniya (Palestinian Liberation Movement), a guerrilla group formed several years before the PLO. Power base for the late Yasser Arafat, one of Fatah's founders.

Fault: surface of fracture in rock involving vertical or horizontal (or both) displacement of rock on either side of the fault plane; result of tectonic strain in earth's crust. Faulting is a major cause of earthquakes (seismic crustal tremors). With horizontal shearing, a fault is left-lateral if displacement is to the left of an observer looking across the fault line. *See also* transform fault.

Fedayeen (*fidayyin*): from Arabic for "sacrificers," usually applied to Palestinian guerrillas or to Shii fundamentalist fighters.

Feddan: a unit of land-area measurement used in Egypt, equal to 1.038 ac or 4,201 m^2.

Feedstock: raw material for a processing plant, often applied to crude oil or natural gas for a refinery or petrochemical plant.

Fellah (**pl.** *fellahin*): roughly equivalent to peasant, from Arabic for "tiller of the soil."

Fenêtre: French for "window." In geomorphology (q.v.), an opening or window caused by erosion in the upper limb of a nappe (q.v.) or overfolded strata. Comparable to a breach in an anticline (see Fig. 2.7), but a fenêtre floor has younger rocks than does the rim.

Fertile Crescent: modern term for arcuate area extending from Gaza northward and northeastward across northern Syria and southeastward along Zagros piedmont (see Map 3.1), believed to be where Neolithic farming evolved.

FTA: Free Trade Area (or Agreement); two or more countries retaining their own external tariffs but having no tariff barriers to their trade with each other; for example, Canada, the United States, and Mexico—NAFTA, and U.S. separate FTAs with Bahrain, Israel, Jordan, and Oman.

GAFTA: Greater Arab Free Trade Area; open to all the members of the Arab League; in 2009—eighteen members.

Garigue: stunted evergreen dry scrub vegetation on limestone in drier areas of Mediterranean climate in Asia Minor and the Levant (cf. maquis).

Gawr (gor, khawr, khor): river floodplain, narrow coastal indentation, or flat-bottomed valley.

GCC: Gulf Cooperation Council, short form of Cooperation Council for the Arab States of the Gulf, formed in 1981 and including Saudi Arabia, Kuwait, Bahrain, Qatar, the UAE, and Oman.

GDP: gross domestic product, total value of goods and services produced by residents and nonresidents within a given country in a given year.

Gecekondu: Turkish for "built overnight," applied to spontaneous settlements built illegally on the peripheries of Turkish cities.

Geomorphology: "earth form," the earth science dealing with the origin and development of earth landforms; somewhat related to the older term "physiography."

Gneiss: coarse-grained crystalline rock usually with streaked or banded black-white-gray appearance. The product of dynamic metamorphism of granites and other igneous rocks. *See also* schist.

GNP: gross national product, total value of goods and services produced both from within a given country and from external (foreign) transactions in a given year.

Gondwana: a conjectured single landmass in Paleozoic times from which the southern continents are theorized to have been formed. *See* plate tectonics.

GOSP: gas-oil separator plant, an oil-field facility serving several producing wells to separate dissolved natural gas from the crude petroleum.

Graben: narrow, down-dropped block of the earth's surface bounded by parallel faults; related to rift valley. *See* rift.

Granite: intrusive igneous rock of various colors and grain size.

Hajj: the Muslim pilgrimage to Mecca, an obligation required in the Quran and one of the pillars of Islam.

Halakha: Jewish religious law.

Hamadah: a rock desert with barren, wind-scoured bedrock surface and little sand. There is an extensive *hamadah* where Arabia, Jordan, and Iraq meet.

Hamas: acronym for Harakat al-Muqawama al-Islamiyya (Islamic Resistance Movement), extremist group, one of several Palestinian resistance groups in West Bank and Gaza Strip. Active in both intifadahs.

Hammam: bath, bathing facilities, and/or toilet facilities.

Harem: quarters in a Muslim household set aside for women and children.

Hashimite (Hashemite): pertaining to descent from Hashim or the Hashimite clan, which included Muhammad's family and was part of the Quraysh tribe; commonly pertaining to dynasty in Jordan and, before 1958, in Iraq.

HDI: Human Development Index; measure of the quality of life allowing comparisons among countries, devised and calculated by the United Nations Development Programme.

Hectare: international unit of land area measurement, 10,000 m^2 or 2.47 ac; abbr.= ha

Hegira (hejira): from Arabic *hijrah*, "flight"; the flight of Muhammad and his followers from Mecca to Yathrib (renamed Medina) in 622 CE, which marked the beginning of the Islamic calendar.

Hizb Allah **(Hizballah, from Arabic; Hezbollah, from Farsi):** Party of God, a group in Lebanon comprising Shii extremists who were involved in seizing hostages in the late 1980s and then conducted guerrilla warfare against Israelis and their proxy South Lebanon Army in the self-declared Israeli security zone, from which Israel withdrew in May 2000. Now an influential political party in Lebanon; listed as a terrorist organization by the U.S. Department of State.

Horst: opposite of graben (q.v.); an uplifted block roughly paralleled by faults.

Ibadhi: an Islamic sect distinct from both Sunni and Shii sects, dominant in Oman; descended from the Karijites (q.v.).

Igneous: pertaining to molten or formerly molten rock material, either extrusive (on the earth's surface) or intrusive (underground rock masses). Types include lava (extrusive) and granite (intrusive).

Imam: Shii religious or, sometimes, political leader; commonly, the leader of Muslim worship services; technically, one of the succession of Shii leaders who, beginning with Ali, are accepted by Shii as the legitimate successors of Muhammad.

Infitah: Arabic for "opening," i.e., economic opening in post-Nasserist Egypt.

Interfluve: linear area lying between roughly parallel rivers, e.g., the location of Baghdad between the Tigris and Euphrates rivers.

Intermontane: between mountains, usually a plateau between mountain ranges, e.g., the Anatolian and Iranian plateaus.

Intifadah: Arabic for "uprising," the rebellion of young rock-throwing Palestinians in the Gaza Strip (especially) and West Bank during the period late 1987 to late 1992. A "second intifadah," or "al-Aqsa Intifadah," erupted in September 2000 but died down in late 2004.

Iranian: pertaining to the country of Iran or to its citizens of whatever ethnic group (not equivalent to Persian).

Islam: "submission," the submission of the followers of Islam to the will of God (Allah).

Islamism: a complex ensemble of ideological extensions of Islam into political action, return to fundamentals ("Islamic fundamentalism"), resurgence or renaissance of Islamic ideals, revolutionary Islam, and others, sometimes through extremist and violent methods. A devotee is an Islamist.

Ismailis: the second-largest Shii sect, sometimes called the "Seveners"; ruled Fatimid Empire, tenth to twelfth centuries.

Isobar: line on a map connecting points of equal barometric pressure.

Isohyet: line on a map connecting points of equal precipitation (see Map 2.5).

Isotherm: line on a map connecting points of equal temperature (see Map 2.4).

ITCZ: Intertropical Convergence Zone, the "monsoon trough."

Jabal (*jebel*): Arabic for "hill," "mountain."

Jamii (*camii*): Arabic for "mosque," often for the main or Friday mosque in a city. *See masjid.*

Jihad: Arabic for struggle on behalf of righteousness, especially within Islam; translation as "holy war" is rather ambiguous and focuses on only one aspect.

Jundullah: "Soldiers of God"; Baluch separatist/terrorist group operating in Iran and Pakistan.

Karaites: an Islamic group that originally supported Ali as caliph, like the Shii, but turned against him.

Karajites: a Jewish sect that rejects the Orthodox position that Moses received oral law, as codified in the Talmud.

Karst: limestone or dolomite landscape subjected to carbonation-solution and having underground drainage, caverns, sinkholes, and other typical surface features.

Kavir: Persian for "salt flat," "salt waste," "playa." *Kavirs* are numerous and extensive in eastern, interior Iran.

Khalifah: *see* caliph.

Khawr (*khor*): *see gawr.*

Kilometer: international unit of distance measurement equaling 1,000 m, 0.6214 m, 0.5399 nautical m; abbr. = km

Knesset: Israeli parliament.

Kufiyah: common traditional male Arab headdress, a large square of cloth folded diagonally and worn with straight edge over the forehead. Usually white in Gulf area, red checkered or black and white in the Levant, but colors and patterns vary among localities. Called *ghutrah* in Saudi Arabia.

Lava: extrusive igneous rock that flows onto earth's surface while molten. *See* basalt.

Levant: eastern Mediterranean coastal region, roughly the maximum area held by the Crusader states; comprises western Syria, Lebanon, Palestine, and western Jordan.

Lingua franca: a language or composite language spoken as a common tongue among several language groups in a given region.

Lithosphere: outermost shell of the earth's layers, 10–30 mi/16–48 km thick, comprising several rigid "plates" floating on the partly molten asthenosphere. *See* plate tectonics.

Littoral: of or pertaining to the shore (of seas or lakes), sometimes to banks of rivers.

LNG: liquefied natural gas—that is, natural gas cooled to approximately—260°F/162°C and stored and shipped in special insulated containers. It is increasingly used in commercial transport. *See also* NGL.

Loess: fine, coherent, porous yellowish dust believed to have been picked up from barren areas by the wind and redeposited in amorphous layers nearby. Serves as parent material for fine-textured, deep, well-drained soils.

LPG: liquefied petroleum gas, primarily propane and butane, derived from NGL (q.v.).

Madrasa (*medrese*): Muslim school, originally one attached to a mosque for religious training. Now used more generally.

Maghrib (Maghreb): Arabic for "west" and applied to the western Arab states in northwestern Africa: Morocco, Algeria, Tunisia, and sometimes Libya.

Majlis (*mejlis*): from general Arabic-Persian term for gathering, gathering place, reception; hence, an official reception room or audience of a ruler or tribal shaykh. In some countries, the consultative or legislative assembly, e.g., Iran, Kuwait.

Mamluk: literally "slave," but applied to Turkish and Circassian slave military oligarchy that ruled Egypt 1250–1517; also architecture and other aspects of the period.

Mandate: in the Middle East, a commission awarded by the League of Nations to Britain or France to administer an assigned territory toward timely independence; also the polity so administered under this commission (Palestine, Transjordan, and Iraq by Britain; Syria and Lebanon by France).

Maquis: a low evergreen scrub vegetation typical of better Mediterranean climate areas of western and southern Asia Minor and the Levant; includes oleander, rosemary, myrtle, and similar plants and is a higher-order plant association than garigue (q.v.).

Mashriq: Arabic for "east" and sometimes applied to the eastern Arab states in the Middle East as defined in this book. Less common term than Maghrib (q.v.).

Masjid: Arabic-Persian for "mosque." *See jamii.*

Massif: general term applied to a compact upland mass.

Mawali: "clients"; non-Arab converts to Islam during early period of the Muslim conquests; soon outnumbered Arab Muslims (*ummah,* q.v.).

Maydan: Arabic-Persian for an urban open area or city square, typical of the traditional Islamic city.

Mesolithic: Middle Stone Age, sometimes called Epipaleolithic; transitional between Paleolithic and Neolithic periods and dated roughly 12,000–8,000 BCE.

Metamorphic: pertaining to rocks whose original structure has been altered by great earth pressures (dynamic metamorphism), heat (thermal metamorphism), or both, producing compact and resistant rock types (e.g., gneiss, schist, quartzite, marble).

Meter (metre): the basic international unit of measurement equaling 1,000 mm, 100 cm, or 3.28 ft.; abbr. = m

Metric Ton: 1,000 kg, or 2,204.6 lbs.

Millet: under the Ottomans, self-administered non-Muslim religious community (e.g., Armenians, Jews, Greek Orthodox), a logical extension of the early Muslim concept of "people of the book."

Mina: coastal inlet and, by derivation, port.

Minaret: tower associated with a mosque from which the call to prayer for the Muslim faithful is intoned at least five times daily by a muazzin (q.v.).

Mizrahim: Eastern or Oriental Jew, recently adopted term to distinguish Middle East and North African Jews in Israel from Ashkenazim (q.v.) and Sephardim (q.v.). Formerly grouped with Sephardim.

Monsoon: from Arabic word for "season"; the seasonal reversal of pressure and winds, especially across southern and eastern Asia; generally applied to rains typical of summer season in Asia and to winds in both summer and winter.

Muazzin (*muadhdhin, muezzin*): specially trained man who intones calls to prayer for the Muslim faithful from a minaret five times daily.

Muhammadan: loosely applied to follower of Muhammad, but correct term is Muslim (q.v.).

Muslim: an adherent of Islam (q.v.), "one who submits"—to the will of God.

Nakbah: Arabic for "catastrophe," the establishment of the state of Israel in Palestinian areas and the displacement of Palestinian Arabs from their lands and homes.

Nappe: in geomorphology (q.v.), a tightly folded recumbent anticline thrust over other rock strata. Sometimes nappe over nappe (fold upon fold) structures occur. Nappes usually extend over many square miles.

Neolithic: New Stone Age, beginning roughly 8,000 BCE and ending 4,000–5,000 years later as copper and bronze came into use for implements.

NGL: natural gas liquids, derived from natural gas and yielding ethane, propane, butane, natural gasoline, and related substances. *See also* LNG.

Nomad: member of a social group that regularly migrates over a traditional realm in search of pasture for their flocks. Bedouin (q.v.) are the best-known true nomads of the Middle East.

OAPEC: Organization of Arab Petroleum Exporting Countries (see Chap. 6).

Olim (sing. olah): "ascenders," Jewish immigrants to the Land of Israel (*see* aliyah).

OPEC: Organization of Petroleum Exporting Countries (see Chap. 6).

Orogeny: a major tectonic process of fold-mountain building.

Orographic: pertaining to mountains; e.g., orographic rainfall is caused by the uplift, hence cooling, of humid wind blowing up a mountain slope—the process producing virtually all heavier rains in the Middle East.

PA: Palestinian Authority.

PFLP: Popular Front for the Liberation of Palestine, extremist Marxist Palestinian group known for earlier aircraft hijackings.

Plate tectonics: theory that the earth's crust (lithosphere) comprises about six main and several other minor rigid "plates" that broke away from one main mass and are now "drifting" slowly in respective directions (see Chap. 2).

PLO: Palestine Liberation Organization, formed in 1964, which became the umbrella organization for Palestinian aspirations; the late Yasser Arafat was replaced as chairman by Mahmoud Abbas upon Arafat's death in November 2004. Finally accepted by Israel as legitimate representatives of Palestinians for negotiations over future of remaining Palestinian lands, first in Oslo then for continuing peace process and for administration of Palestinian Authority.

Pluvial: rainy—pertaining to moister periods during the recent geological past, with such periods in the Middle East usually correlating with glacial advances and related climatic changes; opposed to alternating dry periods.

PNC: Palestine National Council, the Palestinian parliament.

Preferential Trade Agreement (PTA): agreement under which two or more countries abolish tariff barriers to mutual trade on a specified group of commodities; for example, separate PTAs between the EU and Egypt, Israel, Jordan, Lebanon, and the Palestinian Authority.

Primate city: a city much larger—even many times larger—than any other city in the country and with a much greater range of economic and social activities. Term suggested by Mark Jefferson, 1939. Cairo, Baghdad, and Tehran are examples.

Ptolemaic: the Egyptian kingdom under the Hellenized dynasty of the Ptolemies, 323–30 BCE.

Purchasing Power Parity (PPP): a method used by international institutions like the World Bank to allow more realistic comparisons of the cost of living in countries with different currencies. It equalizes the purchasing power of these currencies in their home countries for a given basket of goods and services; cross-national comparisons are then made using the United States and the dollar as the base.

Qanat: an underground gallery water channel marked by a surface chain of wells; thousands of *qanats* are found on alluvial fans in Iran (see Fig. 19.3).

Qat: *Catha edulis,* a leafy shrub grown on terraced hillsides in northern Yemen. *Qat* leaves contain cathinone, an amphetamine-related chemical, and are chewed by Highland Yemeni men during afternoon hours for mild narcotic effect.

QIZ: Qualifying Industrial Zone; industrial area from which goods made there can enter the United States duty-free, if they have a certain percentage of Israeli inputs; these exist in Egypt and Jordan.

al-Quran (Koran): Arabic for "recitation"; Muslim holy scriptures, believed by Muslims to be the exact words of God revealed (or "recited") to the Prophet Muhammad through the angel Gabriel.

Ramadan: ninth month of the Islamic calendar, considered a holy month because Muhammad received the first revelations from Gabriel in Ramadan. During the entire month, Muslims are obligated to observe absolute fasting between dawn and dusk. Such fasting is one of the pillars of Islam.

Rift: a narrow linear trough between parallel faults or along linear fissuring, e.g., the Levant Rift, a segment of the great rift from northern Syria to southern Africa.

Riparian: pertaining to riverbanks, especially rights of access to the river ("riparian rights") or occurring along rivers ("riparian powers"). As noun, persons or polity along a river.

Sabkhah (*subkha*)**:** a flat area of salty silt, whether a tidal flat, salt flat between dunes, or former tidal flat now cut off from the sea (see Fig. 2.12).

Sabra: from Hebrew for "prickly pear," term for a native-born Israeli Jew.

Sanjak: provincial administrative district of the Ottoman Empire, administered by a sanjak bey, later by a mutassarif (e.g., Sanjak of Alexandretta).

Sassanian (Sassanid): pertaining to the Persian Empire or its ruling dynasty named after its founder, Sassan; 227–651 CE (see Map 3.4).

Saudi: concerning the central Arabian Peninsula dynastic family of Al Saud; the policies of that dynasty or the country it rules—Saudi Arabia; Arabia of the Sauds—the kingdom founded and ruled by the Al Saud.

Schist: fine-grained, foliated crystalline metamorphic rock of varying color. *See also* gneiss.

Sedimentary: formed of sediments—materials laid down usually in seawater but also in lakes and rivers or by wind—and usually stratified (e.g., limestone, shale, sandstone).

Seismic: pertaining to earth tremors or earthquakes.

Semitic: of or pertaining to the subfamily of the Afro-Asiatic language family that includes Arabic, Hebrew, and Aramaic languages; also pertaining to certain aspects of speakers of these languages, excluding racial characteristics.

Sephardim: technically, Jews from Spain or descended from Spanish Jews; by extension, "Oriental" Jews (from North Africa, Middle East, and southern and central Asia). However, *see* Mizrahim.

Shah: Persian for "king"; title of royal rulers of Iran until 1979.

Sharia: the right path; complex Muslim religious law and code of sociopolitical conduct and relations, derived primarily from the Quran and Sunna and secondarily from other traditions and opinions.

Shaykh (sheikh): literally "elder," but specifically a term of respect and rank given to an Arab tribal leader; extended to the ruler of smaller states, which are then referred to as shaykhdoms (e.g., Qatar, also sometimes called amirates [q.v.]); further, by extension, a learned Muslim.

Shield: rigid mass of stable, ancient (Precambrian) rocks, usually greatly metamorphosed, forming the nucleus of a continent or subcontinent—e.g., the Nubian-Arabian Shield of the southwestern Middle East (see Chap. 2).

Shii (Shiite): from Arabic for "partisan," i.e., partisan of Ali, Muhammad's kinsman and son-in-law. The Shii believe Ali should have succeeded to leadership of the *ummah* (q.v.) upon Muhammad's death and that Ali and his several successors (Shii imams) are the only true heads of the *ummah*. *See also* Sunni.

Steppe: grassland, especially land of short grasses, thus indicating subhumid or semiarid climate (Koeppen BS); in the Middle East, transitional between desert and Mediterranean climate areas or other more humid areas.

Sultanate: realm of a sultan (e.g., Oman), a secular ruler equivalent to a king or other dynastic ruler.

Sunna: Arabic for "habitual practice"; sometimes used in place of Sunni (q.v.).

Sunni (Sunnite): Muslim who accepts the legitimacy of Muhammad's successors. So-called after *Sunna,* the admonitions and examples of Muhammad regarding proper Muslim belief and conduct. *See also* Shii.

Suq: Ar. for "marketplace," comparable to Persian *bazaar.*

Tectonism (tectonic, tectonics): internal earth forces that build up, form, or deform the earth's surface or subsurface. *See* plate tectonics.

Tell: Arabic for "hill" or "mound" (Turkish: *hüyük*; Persian: *tepe*), specifically a characteristic surface mound made up of accumulated layers of debris from successive human occupations of a settlement site over many centuries (see Chap. 3).

Transform fault: a fault zone involving mostly horizontal displacement along an edge of a tectonic plate, e.g., the San Andreas fault in California and the North Anatolian and East Anatolian transform faults; displacement along such faults periodically involves disastrous earthquakes.

Ulama (*ulema*)**:** Arabic collective term for learned Muslim legal and religious leaders; theoretically, the ultimate repository of power in Saudi Arabia.

Umayyad (Omayyed): Arab Muslim dynasty of the Quraysh tribe and the empire it ruled from Damascus 661–750 CE; also the dynasty's continued rule in Spain until 1030.

Ummah: Arabic for the community of Muslims, an especially important concept pertaining to Arab Muslims in the early decades of the Muslim conquests.

UNDP: United Nations Development Programme, compiler of the annual Human Development Index (HDI—q.v.).

UNRWA: United Nations Relief and Works Agency, which since 1949 has operated emergency housing and food distribution for hundreds of thousands of registered Palestinian Arab refugees, usually in UNRWA-operated camps (see Map 8.6).

Vilayet: a province under the administrative pattern of the Ottoman Empire; term became crucial in post–World War I territorial settlements in the Levant.

Viticulture: cultivation of grapevines, almost a way of life in some specialized agricultural areas.

Volcanism (vulcanism): igneous activity processes in general, not just those associated with volcanoes; especially the processes by which molten materials and associated solids and gases are forced into the lithosphere or onto the earth's surface through craters or fissures. *See* basalt.

Wadi: widely used Arabic term for arid area stream basin (and, by extension, the stream), including major valleys and broad, hardly perceptible linear depressions, whether stream flow is perennial or periodic. Arabic for a major river (Nile, Tigris) is *nahr.*

Wahhabi: often misused term pertaining to reform puritan Muslim movement and group that evolved from the preachings of Muhammad ibn Abd al-Wahhab in the mid-1700s in central Arabia. Wahhabi puritanism is still strong in much of Arabia.

Waqf (wakf, vakf): Muslim religious endowment or trust involving land or other property; widespread in Islamic world but decreasing in more secular states such as Syria.

Xerophytic: pertaining to specialized vegetation of arid lands. Special adaptations include deep or long roots, waxy leaves, and tough bark (see Chap. 2).

Zaydis: Shii sect, sometimes called the "Fivers"; longtime rulers of Yemen.

Zionism: Jewish nationalism stressing unity of Jews and creation and maintenance of a Jewish state in Eretz Yisrael (Land of Israel) in greater Palestine as a territorial base for Jewry.

Geological Time Chart

EON	PERIOD		EPOCH	AGE	MILLIONS OF YRS AGO
CENOZOIC	QUATERNARY		Holocene (Recent)		0.01
			Pleistocene		1.6
	TERTIARY	Neogene	Pliocene		11.2
			Miocene		23.7
		Paleogene	Oligocene		36.6
			Eocene		57.8
			Paleocene		66.4
MESOZOIC	CRETACEOUS		Late	Maastrichtian	74.5
				Campanian	84.0
				Santonian	87.5
				Coniacian	88.5
				Turonian	91.0
				Cenomanian	97.5
			Early		144
	JURASSIC		Late		163
			Middle		187
			Early		208
	TRIASSIC		Late		230
			Middle		240
			Early		245
PALEOZOIC	PERMIAN				286
	CARBONIFEROUS				360
	DEVONIAN				408
	SILURIAN				438
	ORDOVICIAN				505
	CAMBRIAN				570

PRECAMBRIAN

	ERA				
PROTEROZOIC	Late				900
	Middle				1600
	Early				2500
ARCHEOZOIC	Late				3000
	Middle				3400
	Early				3800

In this simplified geological time chart, *Ages* are shown only for the late Cretaceous, although *Age* subdivisions exist for all *Epochs* after the Middle Cambrian. The Middle East surface geology is dominantly Mesozoic and Cenozoic, although the Nubian-Arabian Shield is Precambrian. Western Gulf oil fields are mainly Jurassic and Cretaceous, whereas Iranian and Kirkuk fields are Paleogene.

Bibliography

The following list of references includes virtually all the works cited in the Notes, a few other sources in English utilized in this book, and several additional works in English that are especially useful for a mid-level student or general reader. Most listings are reasonably available. More advanced sources and materials in languages other than English may be found in the bibliographies mentioned below. In response to the explosive use of the Internet, we have listed selected Web sites (URLs) that we have found useful and that readers will also find helpful. Most of them precede the main list of references below, some are supplied in the Notes, and a few appear in the main list itself.

The simplest way to stay abreast of the explosion of new literature on the Middle East is to refer to the listings in the quarterly *Middle East Journal*, which includes reviews, short notices, listings of literature received, and a bibliography of periodical materials. The autumn issue has an annual index and lists the periodicals regularly surveyed for the bibliography. Besides *Middle East Journal*, useful and commonly available periodicals include *Middle East Policy* (called *American-Arab Affairs* before March 1992) and *Journal of Palestine Studies*. These journal references may omit specialized geographical materials, most of which can be noted in one or another of the standard academic geographical journals (*Annals of the Association of American Geographers*, *Geographical Review*, *Professional Geographer*, *Geographical Journal*, *Arab World Geographer*, and others). References and articles in both the *International Journal of Middle East Studies* and the *Middle East Studies Association Bulletin* are useful. In the United States, the *New York Times* and the now weekly *Christian Science Monitor* report regularly on Middle East developments. Overseas, the Beirut *Daily Star* (URL below) is very useful, as are the Israeli *Ha'aretz* and *Jerusalem Post*. Every issue of *Saudi Aramco World* magazine covers some aspect of the Middle East. Several of the book references listed below have especially good bibliographies. Statistics may most easily be found in the Encyclopaedia Britannica yearbook's *Britannica World Data* and, more fully (and now on the Internet), in the standard United Nations yearbooks or other UN periodical statistical volumes. Their Web sites are given below.

For updated, authoritative information on countries, the following Internet sources are invaluable (and are given in other forms below under "United States Government"):

Central Intelligence Agency, *World Factbook:* www.cia.gov/library/publications/the-world-factbook/index.html

Department of Energy, Energy Information Agency (especially *Country Analysis Briefs*): www.eia.doe.gov/emeu/international/contents.html

Library of Congress, *Country Studies and Profiles*: http://lcweb2.loc.gov/frd/cs/profiles.html

U.S. Department of State, *Background Notes*: www.state.gov/r/pa/ei/bgn/

COUNTRY URLS

Bahrain: www.bahraingovernment.com/
Cyprus: www.cyprus.gov.cy
Egypt: www.sis.gov.eg/
Iran: www.mfa.gov.ir/
Iraq: www.iraqiembassy.us/
Israel: www.mfa.gov.il
Jordan: www.kinghussein.gov.jo/government.html

Kuwait: www.cbk.gov.kw
Lebanon: www.lebweb.com/dir/lebanese-government
Oman: www.omansultanate.com/
Palestine: www.minfo.ps/English
Qatar Central Bank: www.qcb.gov.qa/
Saudi Arabia: www.saudinf.com
Syria: www.moi-syria.com
Turkey: www.washington.emb.mfa.gov.tr/
UAE: www.government.ae/gov/en/index.jsp
Yemen Central Bank: www.centralbank.gov.ye/

DATA AND MAPS (SEE ALSO "UNITED STATES GOVERNMENT" BELOW)

British Petroleum: www.bp.com/home.do
Ethnologue, Languages of the World: www.ethnologue.com/
National Geographic: www.nationalgeographic.com/
Nation Stats: wwwNationMaster.com
Perry-Castaneda Library Map Collection (University of Texas, Austin): www.lib.utexas.edu/maps/
   index.html
World Climate: www.worldclimate.com/

JOURNALS AND OTHER PUBLICATIONS

Christian Science Monitor: www.csmonitor.com/
CIA World Factbook: www.odci.gov/cia/publications/factbook/index.html
Daily Star (Beirut): www.dailystar.com.lb/home.asp?edition_id=10
Economist: www.economist.com/
Foreign Affairs: www.foreignaffairs.org/
Foreign Policy: www.foreignpolicy.com/
Ha'aretz (Israel): www.haaretzdaily.com/
Jerusalem Post: www.jpost.com/
Jordan Times (Amman): www.jordantimes.com/mon/index.htm
Le Monde Diplomatique: http://mondediplo.com/
Media Line: www.themedialine.org/
National (Abu Dhabi): www.thenational.ae/
New York Review of Books: www.nybooks.com/
New York Times: www.nytimes.com/
Oil and Gas Journal: http://ogj.pennnet.com/home.cfm
Washington Post: www.washingtonpost.com/
Washington Report on Middle East Affairs: www.wrmea.com/

INSTITUTES, THINK TANKS, AND OTHER DATA SOURCES

American Israel Public Affairs Committee: www.aipac.org/
Americans for Middle East Understanding: www.ameu.org/
Arab.net: www.arab.net/
The Brookings Institution: www.brook.edu/
B'tsalem: www.btselem.org/English/index.asp
Council on Foreign Relations: www.cfr.org/
Encyclopedia of the Orient: http://i-cias.com/e.o/index.htm
Foundation for Middle East Peace: www.fmep.org/
Fraser Institute: www.fraserinstitute.org/
Institute for Research Middle Eastern Policy: www.irmep.org/
Israeli Democracy Institute: www.idi.org.il/sites/English/Pages/homepage.aspx

Jamestown Foundation: www.jamestown.org/
Jewish Virtual Library: www.jewishvirtuallibrary.org/index.html
Middle East Institute: www.mideasti.org/
Palestine Center: www.palestinecenter.org/
Palestine Facts: www.palestinefacts.org/
Pew Forum on Religion and Politics: http://pewforum.org/religion-politics/
Political Islam Online: www.politicalislam.org/
Saudi American Forum: www.saudi-american-forum.org/
Transparency International: www.transparency.org/
Washington Institute for Near East Policy: www.washingtoninstitute.org/
World Economic Forum: www.weforum.org/

SPACE PHOTOS

Digital Globe: www.digitalglobe.com/
Earth from Space: http://earth.jsc.nasa.gov/sseop/efs/
Earth Resources Observation System: http://edc.usgs.gov/
Gateway to Astronaut Photography of Earth: http://eol.jsc.nasa.gov/sseop/clickmap/

UNITED STATES GOVERNMENT

Central Intelligence Agency: www.cia.gov/
Department of Energy, Energy Information Administration (EIA), *Country Analysis Briefs*: www.eia.doe
    .gov/emeu/cabs/contents.html
Department of State: www.state.gov/
Federal Research Division, Country Studies: http://lcweb2.loc.gov/frd/cs/cshome.html
Geographic Names: http://geonames.nga.mil/ggmagaz/geonames4.asp
National Climatic Data Center Resources: www.ncdc.noaa.gov/oa/climate/ climateresourcesother.html
National Geospatial Intelligence Agency: www.nima.mil/portal/site/nga01/
NSGS Earthquakes: wwwneic.cr.usgs.gov/neis/bulletin/bulletin.html
Portals to the World from the Library of Congress: www.loc.gov/rr/international/portals.html
U.S. Agency for International Development: www.usaid.gov/
U.S. Energy Information: www.eia.doe.gov/emeu/international/contents.html
U.S. Geological Survey (USGS): www.usgs.gov/
USGS Middle East Mineral Information: http://minerals.usgs.gov/minerals/pubs/country/africa.html

UNITED NATIONS

International Fund for Agricultural Development: www.ifad.org/
International Monetary Fund: www.imf.org/external/index.htm
UN Economic And Social Commission For Western Asia: www.escwa.un.org/
UN Food and Agriculture Organization: www.fao.org/
United Nations Development Programme: www.undp.org/
United Nations Homepage: www.un.org/
World Bank Group: www.worldbank.org/
World Trade Organization: www.wto.org/

OTHER INTERNATIONAL ORGANIZATIONS

Abu Dhabi Fund for Development: www.adfd.ae/
Arab Fund for Economic and Social Development: www.arabfund.org/
Arab League: www.arableagueonline.org/
International Energy Agency: www.iea.org/

Islamic Development Bank: www.isdb.org/
Kuwait Fund for Arab Economic Development: www.kuwait-fund.org/
Nile Basin Initiative: www.nilebasin.org/
Organization of Petroleum Exporting Countries: www.opec.org/home/
Organization of the Islamic Conference: www.oic-oci.org/
Saudi Fund for Development: www.sfd.gov.sa/
U.K. Foreign and Commonwealth Office: www.fco.gov.uk/en/

USEFUL BIBLIOGRAPHICAL WORKS

ABC-Clio Information Services. 1985. *The Middle East in Conflict: A Historical Bibliography.* Clio Bibliography Series no. 19 [annotated]. Santa Barbara, CA: ABC-Clio Information Services. 302p.

Atiyeh, George N., comp. 1975. *The Contemporary Middle East, 1948–1973: A Selective and Annotated Bibliography.* Boston: G. K. Hall. 664p.

Collison, Robert L., editor in chief (individual compilers for each volume). 1979–1991. *World Bibliographical Series.* Includes no. 2, Lebanon; no. 5, Saudi Arabia; no. 27, Turkey; no. 28, Cyprus; no. 29, Oman; no. 36, Qatar; no. 42, Iraq; no. 43, UAE; no. 49, Bahrain; no. 50, The Yemens; no. 55, Jordan; no. 56, Kuwait; no. 58, Israel; no. 73, Syria; no. 81, Iran; and no. 86, Egypt. Santa Barbara, CA: ABC-Clio Press. Pages variable, from 162p. to 330p.

REFERENCES

Abbott, Kerry. 1994. "Lebanon: A Heritage to Restore." *Saudi Aramco World* (Mar.–Apr.).

Abdullah, Thabit A. J. 2006. *Dictatorship, Imperialism, and Chaos: Iraq Since 1989.* New York: Zed Books. 136p.

Abrahamian, Ervand. 2008. *A History of Modern Iran.* New York: Cambridge University Press. 228p.

Abramowitz, Morton, ed. 2000. *Turkey's Transformation and American Policy.* New York: Century Foundation Press. 298p.

Abramowitz, Morton, and Henric J. Barkey. 2009. "Turkey's Transformers." *Foreign Affairs* (Nov.–Dec.).

Abu-Lughod, Janet L. 1971. *Cairo: 1001 Years of the City Victorious.* Princeton: Princeton University Press. 284p.

Abu Odeh, Adnan. 1992. "Two Capitals in an Undivided Jerusalem." *Foreign Affairs* 71, no. 2 (Spring): 183–188.

Ackerman, Seth. 2001. "Al-Aqsa Intifada and the U.S. Media." *Journal of Palestine Studies* 30, no. 2 (Winter): 61–74.

Adamec, Ludwig W., ed. 1976–1988. *Historical Gazetteer of Iran.* Vol. 1, *Tehran and Northwestern Iran*; vol. 2, *Meshed and Northeastern Iran*; vol. 4, *Zahidan and Southeastern Iran.* Graz: Akademische Druck-u Verlagsanstalt. Vol. 1, 734p. + 62p. maps; vol. 2, 708p. + 150p. maps; vol. 4, 480p. + 48p. maps.

———. 2001. *Historical Dictionary of Islam.* Lanham, MD: Scarecrow. 417p.

Adams, Linda. 1996. "Political Liberalization in Jordan: An Analysis of the State's Relationship with the Muslim Brotherhood." *Journal of Church and State* (Summer).

Adams, Robert McC. 1981. *Heartland of Cities: Surveys of Ancient Settlement and Land Use on the Central Floodplain of the Euphrates.* Chicago: University of Chicago Press. 362p.

Agha, Hussein, and Robert Malley. 2001. "Camp David: The Tragedy of Errors." *New York Review of Books,* Aug. 9.

———. 2007. "The Road to Mecca." *New York Review of Books,* May 10.

———. 2009. "Israel & Palestine: Can They Start Over?" *New York Review of Books,* Dec. 3.

Aharoni, Yohanan. 1974. *The Land of the Bible: A Historical Geography.* Translated by A. F. Rainey. London: Burns and Oates. 409p.

Ahmad, Imad-ad-Dean. n.d. *Female Genital Mutilation: An Islamic Perspective.* www.minaret.org/fgm-pamphlet.htm.

Ahmad, Feroz. 1993. *The Making of Modern Turkey.* New York: Routledge. 252p.

Ajami, Fouad. 1993. *The Arab Predicament: Arab Political Thought and Practice Since 1967.* Updated ed. Cambridge: Cambridge University Press. 279p.

————. 2006. *The Foreigner's Gift*. New York: Free Press. 378p.

Akurgal, Ekrem. 1970. *Ancient Civilizations and Ruins of Turkey: From Pre-historic Turks Until the End of the Roman Empire*. Istanbul: Mobile Oil Turk. 375p.

Al Abed, Ibrahim, and Peter Hellyer, eds. 2001. *United Arab Emirates: A New Perspective*. London: Trident. 320p.

Al-Ahram Weekly On-line (Cairo). 2004. "Reversing the Brain Drain." No. 722. Dec. 23–29.

————. 2005. "The Brain Drain." No. 744. May 26–June 1.

al-Ansary, A. R. 1982. *Qaryat al-Fau: A Portrait of the Pre-Islamic Civilization in Saudi Arabia*. London: Croom Helm. 147p.

al-Fahim, Mohamed. 1995. *From Rags to Riches: A Story of Abu Dhabi*. London: Center of Arab Studies.

Alaolmolki, Nozar. 2001. *Life After the Soviet Union: The Newly Independent Republics of Transcaucasus and Central Asia*. Albany: State University of New York Press. 187p.

Allan, J. A. 2002. *The Middle East Water Question: Hydropolitics and the Global Economy*. London and New York: I. B. Tauris. 382p.

Allan, J. A., and P. D. Howell, eds. 1994. *The Nile, Sharing a Scarce Resource: A Historical and Technical Review of Water Management of Economic and Legal Issues*. Cambridge and New York: Cambridge University Press. 408p.

Allawi, Ali A. 2007. *The Occupation of Iraq: Winning the War, Losing the Peace*. New Haven: Yale University Press. 518p.

————. 2009. *The Crisis of Islamic Civilization*. New Haven: Yale University Press. 304p.

Allen, Calvin H., Jr. 1987. *Oman: The Modernization of the Sultanate: Profiler Nations of the Contemporary Middle East*. Boulder: Westview. 154p.

Alnajjar, Ghanim. 2000. "The Challenges Facing Kuwaiti Democracy." *Middle East Journal* 54, no. 2 (Winter): 242–258.

al-Qasimi, Sultan Muhammad. 1988. *The Myth of Arab Piracy in the Gulf*. 2d ed. New York: Routledge. 244p.

Al-Rasheed, Madawi. 2002. *A History of Saudi Arabia*. Cambridge, UK, and New York: Cambridge University Press. 255p.

Al Sayegh, Fatma. 2004. "Post-9/11 Changes in the Gulf: The Case of the UAE." *Middle East Policy* 11, no. 2 (Summer): 107–124.

Al Sayyad, Nezar. 1991. *Cities and Caliphs: On the Genesis of Arab Muslim Urbanism*. Westport, CT: Greenwood. 196p.

Altorki, Soraya, and Donald P. Cole. 1989. *Arabian Oasis City: The Transformation of Unayzah*. Austin: University of Texas Press. 266p.

Amery, Hussein A., and Aaron Wolf, eds. 2000. *Water in the Middle East: A Geography of Peace*. Austin: University of Texas Press. 293p.

Amirahmadi, Hooshang. 1990. *Revolution and Economic Transition: The Iranian Experience*. Albany: State University of New York Press. 420p.

————. 2000. *The Caspian Region at a Crossroad: Challenges of a New Frontier of Energy and Development*. New York: St. Martin's. 298p.

Amnesty International. 2009. *Troubled Waters: Palestinians Denied Fair Access to Water*. Oct.

Amuzegar, Jahanir. 1992. "The Iranian Economy Before and After the Revolution." *Middle East Journal* 46, no. 3 (Summer): 413–425.

————. 1995. "Islamic Fundamentalism in Action: The Case of Iran." *Middle East Policy* 4, no. 1–2 (Sept.): 22–33.

————. 1998. "Khatami's Iran, One Year Later." *Middle East Policy* 6, no. 2 (Oct. 1998): 76–94.

————. 1999. "Khatami and the Iranian Economy at Mid-Term." *Middle East Journal* (Autumn).

Andersen, Roy R., Robert P. Seibert, and Jon G. Wagner. 1990. *Politics and Change in the Middle East: Sources of Conflict and Accommodation*. 3d ed. Englewood Cliffs, NJ: Prentice-Hall. 331p.

Anderson, Ewan. 2000. *The Middle East: Geography and Geopolitics*. 8th ed. [Revision of older book by W. B. Fisher.] London and New York: Routledge. 342p.

————. 2003. *International Boundaries: A Geopolitical Atlas*. London and New York: Routledge. 941p.

Anthony, John Duke. 1976. *Historical and Cultural Dictionary of the Sultanate of Oman and the Emirates of Eastern Arabia*. Historical and Cultural Dictionaries of Asia no. 9. Metuchen, NJ: Scarecrow. 136p.

———. 2000. "Saudi-Arabian Gemeni Relations: Implications for U.S. Relations." *Middle East Policy* 7, no 3 (June): 78–96.

Antoniou, Jim. 1981. *Islamic Cities and Conservation.* Paris: UNESCO. 109p.

Antonius, George. 1938. *The Arab Awakening: The Story of the Arab National Movement.* New York: Hamilton. 471p.

Arabian American Oil Company (R. O. Williams, oceanographer). n.d. *Aramco Meteorologic and Oceanographic Data Book for the Eastern Province Region of Saudi Arabia.* Dhahran: Arabian American Oil Company, [ca. 1978].

Aras, Bülent, and Michael P. Croissant, eds. 1999. *Oil and Geopolitics in the Caspian Sea Region.* Westport, CT: Praeger. 305p.

Armour, Rollin S. 2002. *Islam, Christianity, and the West: A Troubled History.* Mary Knoll, NY: Orbis. 197p.

Armstrong, Karen. 1992. *Muhammad: A Biography of the Prophet.* New York: HarperCollins. 290p.

———. 1997. *Jerusalem: One City, Three Faiths.* Chicago: Ballantine Books. 512p.

———. 2000. *The Battle for God: Fundamentalism in Judaism, Christianity, and Islam.* New York: Alfred A. Knopf. 442p.

———. 2009. *The Case for God.* New York: Knopf. 406p.

Aruri, Naseer, ed. 2001. *Palestinian Refugees: The Right of Return.* London, UK, and Sterling, VA: Pluto. 294p.

Askari, Hossein, and John Thomas Cummings. 1976. *Middle East Economies in the 1970s: A Comparative Approach.* Praeger Special Studies in International Economics and Development. New York: Praeger. 581p.

Assiri, Abdul-Reda. 1996. *The Government and Politics of Kuwait: Principles and Practice.* Shaab, Kuwait: Al Watan. 235p.

Avishai, Bernard. 2002. *The Tragedy of Zionism: How Its Revolutionary Past Haunts Israeli Democracy.* New York: Helios. 384p.

Ayubi, Nazih N. 1995. *Over-Stating the Arab State: Politics and Society in the Middle East.* London: I. B. Tauris. 514p.

Bacevich, Andrew J. 2008. *The Limits of Power: The End of American Exceptionalism.* New York: Metropolitan Books. 206p.

Bacik, Gokhan. 2009. "Turkish-Israeli Relations After Davos: A View from Turkey." *Insight Turkey* 11, no. 2: 31–41.

Bahgat, Gawdat. 2003. *American Oil Diplomacy in the Persian Gulf and the Caspian Sea.* Gainesville: University Press of Florida. 213p.

Baker, William G. 2003. *The Cultural Heritage of Arabs, Islam, and the Middle East.* Dallas: Brown Books. 192p.

Balfour-Paul, Glen. 1994. *The End of Empire in the Middle East: Britain's Relinquishment of Power in Her Last Three Arab Dependencies.* Cambridge and New York: Cambridge University Press. 278p.

Ball, George W. 1992. *The Passionate Attachment: America's Involvement with Israel, 1947 to the Present.* New York: W. W. Norton. 382p.

Baly, Denis. 1957. *The Geography of the Bible: A Study in Historical Geography.* New York: Harper. 303p.

Bard, Mitchell Geoffrey. 1991. *The Water's Edge and Beyond: Defining the Limits to Domestic Influence on United States Middle East Policy.* New Brunswick, NJ: Transaction Publishers. 313p.

Barger, Thomas C. 2000. *Out in the Blue: Letters from Arabia—1937–1940: A Young American Geologist Explores the Deserts of Early Saudi Arabia.* Vista, CA: Selwa. 284p.

Barkey, Henri J., and Graham E. Fuller. 1998. *Turkey's Kurdish Question.* Lanham, MD: Rowman and Littlefield. 238p.

Barrett, David, et al. 2001. *World Christian Encyclopedia.* 2d ed. 2 vols. New York: Oxford University Press.

Barrett, Roby C. 2007. *The Greater Middle East and the Cold War: U.S. Foreign Policy Under Eisenhower and Kennedy.* New York: I. B. Tauris. 494p.

———. 2009. *The Arabian Gulf and Security Policy: The Past as Present, the Present as Future.* JSOU Report 09.04. Hurlbert Field, FL: Joint Special Operations University. 75p.

Basson, Philip, et al. 1979. *Biotopes of the Western Arabian Gulf: Marine Life and Environments of Saudi Arabia.* Dhahran: Aramco [Arabian American Oil Company]. 284p.

Batanouny, K. H. 1981. *Ecology and Flora of Qatar.* Doha: University of Qatar. 245p.

Bates, B. C., Z. W. Kundzewicz, S. Wu, and J. P. Palutikof, eds. 2008. "2008: Climate Change and Water." *Technical Paper of the Intergovernmental Panel on Climate Change.* IPCC Secretariat, Geneva. 210p.

Bates, Daniel, and Amal Rassam. 1983. *Peoples and Cultures of the Middle East.* Englewood Cliffs, NJ: Prentice-Hall. 288p.

Bean, George E. 1968. *Turkey's Southern Shore: An Archaeological Guide.* London: Ernest Benn. 188p.

Beattie, Kirk J. 2000. *Egypt During the Sadat Years.* New York and Basingstoke, UK: Palgrave. 340p.

Beaumont, Peter, Gerald H. Blake, and J. Malcolm Wagstaff. 1988. *The Middle East: A Geographical Study.* 2d ed. New York: Halsted. 623p.

Beaumont, Peter, and Keith McLachlan, eds. 1985. *Agricultural Development in the Middle East.* New York: John Wiley. 349p.

Beck, Lois. 1986. *The Qashqai of Iran.* New Haven, CT: Yale University Press. 384p.

Begin, Menachem. 1977. *The Revolt.* New York: Nash. 386p.

Beinin, Joel. 1998. *The Dispersion of Egyptian Jewry: Culture, Politics, and the Formation of a Modern Diaspora.* Berkeley and Los Angeles: University of California Press. 329p.

Belt, Don. 1998. "Petra: Ancient City of Stone." *National Geographic,* Dec., 117–133.

———. 1999. "Lawrence of Arabia: A Hero's Journey." *National Geographic,* Jan., 38–61.

———. 2009. "The Forgotten Faithful: Arab Christians." *National Geographic,* June, 78–97.

Benedick, Richard Elliot. 1979. "The High Dam and the Transformation of the Nile." *Middle East Journal* 33, no. 2 (Spring): 119–144.

Bengio, Ofra, and Gabriel Ben-Dor, eds. 1999. *Minorities and the State in the Arab World.* Boulder: Lynne Rienner. 223p.

Benjamin, Daniel, and Steven Simon. 2002. *The Age of Sacred Terror.* New York: Random House. 490p.

BenMeir, Alon. 1994. "The Israeli-Syrian Battle for Equitable Peace." *Middle East Policy* 3, no. 1: 70–83.

———. 1997. "Why Syria Must Regain the Golan to Make Peace." *Middle East Policy* 5, no. 3 (Sept.): 104–112.

Benvenisti, Meron. 1984. *The West Bank Data Projects: A Survey of Israel's Policies.* Washington, DC: American Enterprise Institute. 97p. Updated periodically.

———. 1996. *The Hidden History of Jerusalem.* Berkeley and Los Angeles: University of California Press. 274p.

———. 2000. *Sacred Landscape: The Buried History of the Holy Land Since 1948.* Berkeley and Los Angeles: University of California Press. 366p.

Bergen, Peter, and Alec Reynolds. 2005. "Blowback Revisited." *Foreign Affairs* (Nov.–Dec.).

Berkoff, Jeremy. 1994. *A Strategy for Managing Water in the Middle East.* Washington, DC: World Bank. 72p.

Berrebi, Claude, Francisco Martorell, and Jeffrey C. Tanner. 2009. "Qatar's Labor Markets at a Crucial Crossroad." *Middle East Journal* 63, no. 3: 421–442.

Betts, Robert Brenton. 1988. *The Druze.* New Haven, CT: Yale University Press. 161p.

Beyth, Michael. 2006. "Water Crisis in Israel." In *Water: Histories, Cultures, Ecologies,* edited by Marnie Leybourne and Andrea Gaynor. Perth: University of Western Australia Press. 254 pp.

Bibby, Geoffrey. 1969. *Looking for Dilmun.* New York: Knopf. 383p.

Bill, James A. 1988. *The Eagle and the Lion: The Tragedy of American-Iranian Relations.* New Haven, CT: Yale University Press. 520p.

Bill, James A., and Rebecca Bill Chavez. 2002. "The Politics of Incoherence: The United States and the Middle East." *Middle East Journal* 56, no. 4 (Autumn): 562–575.

Binder, Leonard, ed. 1999. *Ethnic Conflict and International Politics in the Middle East.* Gainesville: University Press of Florida. 396p.

Bisharah, Marwan. 2002. *Palestine/Israel: Peace or Apartheid: Occupation, Terrorism, and the Future.* 2d updated ed. London and New York: Zed. 173p.

Biswas, Asit K., et al. 1997. *Core and Periphery: A Comprehensive Approach to Middle Eastern Water.* New Delhi: Oxford University Press/Middle East Water Commission. 160p.

Black, Ian, and Benny Morris. 1991. *Israel's Secret Wars: A History of Israel's Intelligence Services.* New York: Grove Weidenfeld. 603p.

Blake, G. H., and Richard I. Lawless, eds. 1980. *The Changing Middle East City.* Croom Helm Series on the Arab World. London: Croom Helm. 273p.

Blake, G. H., and Richard N. Schofield, eds. 1987. *Boundaries and State Territory in the Middle East and North Africa.* Cambridgeshire, UK: Middle East and North African Studies Press. 167p.

Blake, G. H., et al. 1987. *The Cambridge Atlas of the Middle East and North Africa.* New York: Cambridge University Press. 132p.

Blau, Joseph L. 1966. *Modern Varieties of Journalism.* New York: Columbia University Press. 217p.

Bligh, Alexander, ed. 2003. *The Israeli Palestinians: An Arab Minority in the Jewish State.* London, UK, and Portland, OR: Frank Cass. 324p.

Blix, Hans. 2004. *Disarming Iraq.* New York: Pantheon. 285p.

Bobek, H. 1968. "Vegetation [of Iran]." Chap. 8 in *Cambridge History of Iran,* edited by William B. Fisher. Vol. 1, *The Land of Iran.* Cambridge: Cambridge University Press. 782p.

Bodanski, Yossef. 2002. *The High Cost of Peace: How Washington's Middle East Policy Left America Vulnerable to Terrorism.* Roseville, CA: Forum. 652p.

Bolukbasi, Suha. 1999. "Behind the Turkish-Israeli Alliance: A Turkish View." *Journal of Palestine Studies* 29, no. 1 (Autumn): 21–35.

Bonine, Michael E. 1977. "From Uruk to Casablanca: Perspectives on the Urban Experience in the Middle East." *Journal of Urban History* 3 (Feb.): 141–180.

———. 1979. "The Morphogenesis of Iranian Cities." *Annals* (Association of American Geographers) 69, no. 2 (June): 208–224.

Boroujerdi, Mehrzad. 2001. "The Paradoxes of Politics in Postrevolutionary Iran." Chap. 1 in *Iran at the Crossroads,* edited by John L. Esposito and Rouhollah K. Ramazani. New York: Palgrave. 248p.

Boucek, Christopher. 2009. *Yemen: Avoiding a Downward Spiral.* No. 102. Washington, DC: Carnegie Endowment for International Peace Middle East Program.

Bouillon, Markus. 2002. "Walking the Tightrope." Chap. 1 in *Jordan in Transition,* edited by George Joffé. New York: Palgrave. 378p.

Bournoutian, George. 2002. *A Concise History of the Armenian People (From Ancient Times to the Present).* Costa Mesa, CA: Mazda. 499p.

Brand, Laurie A. 1994. *Jordan's Inter-Arab Relations: The Political Economy of Alliance Making.* New York: Columbia University Press. 350p.

Breger, Marshall J., and Ora Ahimeir, eds. 2002. *Jerusalem: A City and Its Future.* Syracuse, NY: Syracuse University Press. 490p.

Bregman, Ahron. 2003. *A History of Israel.* New York: Palgrave Macmillan. 320p.

———. 2005. *Elusive Peace: How the Holy Land Defeated America.* New York: Penguin Books. 290p.

Bremer, L. Paul. 2006. *My Year in Iraq: The Struggle to Build a Future of Hope.* New York: Simon and Schuster. 417p.

Brinkmann, R. 1976. *Geology of Turkey.* New York: Elsevier Scientific. 158p.

Brockelmann, Carl. 1949. *History of the Islamic Peoples.* Translated by Joel Carmichael and Moshe Perlmann. New York: Putnam. 566p.

Bronson, Rachel. 2006. *Thicker Than Oil: America's Uneasy Partnership with Saudi Arabia.* Oxford: Oxford University Press. 262p.

Brown, Glenn F. 1972. "Tectonic Map of the Arabian Peninsula." Map AP-2. Jiddah: Kingdom of Saudi Arabia, Directorate General of Mineral Resources.

Brown, Glenn F., and R. G. Coleman. 1972. "The Tectonic Framework of the Arabian Peninsula." *Proceedings of the 24th International Geological Congress.* Section 3: 300–304.

Brown, L. Carl, ed. 1973. *From Medina to Metropolis: Heritage and Change in the Near Eastern City.* Princeton, NJ: Darwin. 343p.

———. 2000. *Religion and State: The Muslim Approach to Politics.* New York: Columbia University Press. 256p.

———, ed. 2004. *Diplomacy in the Middle East: The International Relations of Regional and Outside Powers.* London and New York: I. B. Tauris. 365p.

Browning, Iain. 1977. *Petra.* London: Chatto and Windus. 256p.

Brumley, Shawn, and Kart Campbell. 2007. "The FP Memo: The Endgame in Iraq." *Foreign Policy* (June 11).

Brunsden, Denys, et al. 1979. "The Bahrain Surface Materials Resource Survey and Its Applications to Regional Planning." *Geographical Journal* 145, no. 1 (Mar.): 1–35.

Bruton, Broncoyn E. 2009. "U.S. Policy Shift Needed in the Horn of Africa." New York: Council on Foreign Relations, Aug. 6.

———. 2010. "Disengaging from Somalia." New York: Council on Foreign Relations, Mar. 10.

Brzezinski, Zbigniew. 2004. *The Choice: Global Domination or Global Leadership.* New York: Basic. 242p.

Bulliet, Richard W. 1975. *The Camel and the Wheel.* Cambridge: Harvard University Press. 327p.

Bunzl, John., ed. 1993. *People of the Stone Age: Hunter-Gatherers and Early Farmers.* New York: Harper-Collins. 240p.

Burenhult, Goran, ed. 1994. *Old World Civilizations: The Rise of Cities and States.* New York: HarperCollins. 239p.

———. 2004. *Islam, Judaism, and the Political Role of Religions in the Middle East.* Gainesville: University Press of Florida. 202p.

Burke, Jason. 2003. *Al-Qaeda: Casting a Shadow of Terror.* London and New York: I. B. Tauris. 292p.

Busch, Briton C. 1971. *Britain, India, and the Arabs, 1914–1921.* Berkeley and Los Angeles: University of California Press. 522p.

Butler, Richard. 2000. *The Greatest Threat: Iraq, Weapons of Mass Destruction, and the Crisis of Global Security.* New York: Public Affairs. 262p.

Butzer, Karl W. 1976. *Early Hydraulic Civilization in Egypt: A Study in Cultural Ecology.* Chicago: University of Chicago Press. 134p.

Cairo Institute for Human Rights Studies. Annual. *Human Rights in the Arab Region.* Cairo: Cairo Institute for Human Rights Studies.

Caldwell, Dan. 1996. "Flashpoints in the Gulf: Abu Musa and the Tunb Islands." *Middle East Policy* 4, no. 3 (Mar.): 50–57.

Calotychos, Vangelis, ed. 1998. *Cyprus and Its People: Nation, Identity, and Experience in an Unimaginable Community, 1955–1997.* Boulder: Westview. 344p.

Carapico, Sheila. 2002. "Foreign Aid for Promoting Democracy in the Arab World." *Middle East Journal* 56, no. 3 (Summer): 379–395.

Carter, Jimmy. 2007. *Palestine Peace, Not Apartheid.* New York: Simon and Schuster. 264p.

Casey, Michael S. 2007. *The History of Kuwait.* Westport, CT: Greenwood. 141p.

Cassandra, Vivian. 2000. *The Western Desert of Egypt.* Cairo: The American University in Cairo. 423p.

Catherwood, Christopher. 2004. *Churchill's Folly: How Winston Churchill Created Modern Iraq.* New York: Carroll and Graf. 261p.

Central Intelligence Agency (CIA). 1973. *Issues in the Middle East: Atlas.* Washington, DC: U.S. Government Printing Office. 40p.

———. 1993. *Atlas of the Middle East.* Washington, DC: U.S. Government Printing Office. 76p.

———. Annual. *World Factbook.* www.odci.gov/cia/publications/factbook/index.html.

Champion, Daryl. 2003. *The Paradoxical Kingdom: Saudi Arabia and the Momentum of Reform.* New York: Columbia University Press. 392p.

Chandrasekaran, Rajiv. 2006. *Imperial Life in the Emerald City: Inside Iraq's Green Zone.* New York, New York: Vintage Books. 365p.

Chapman, Graham, and Kathleen M. Baker. 2003. *The Changing Geography of Africa and the Middle East.* London and New York: Routledge. 252p.

Chatty, Dawn. 2006. *Nomadic Societies in the Middle East And North Africa: Entering the 21st Century.* Boston: Brill. 1060p.

Chernichovsky, Dov. 2005. "The Jewish-Arab Divide in Life Expectancy in Israel." *Economics and Human Biology* 3, no. 1 (March): 123ff.

Chomsky, Noam. 2003. *Middle East Illusions: Including Peace in the Middle East? Reflections on Justice and Nationhood.* Lanham, MD: Rowman and Littlefield. 299p.

Christaller, Walter. 1966. *The Central Places of Southern Germany.* Translated by C. W. Baskin. Englewood Cliffs, NJ: Prentice-Hall. 230p.

Christison, Kathleen. 2001. *Perceptions of Palestine: Their Influence on U.S. Middle East Policy.* Updated ed. Berkeley and Los Angeles: University of California Press. 390p.

Chubin, Shahram. 2000. "Iran's Strategic Predicament." *Middle East Journal* 54, no. 1 (Winter): 10–24.

Chubin, Shahram, and Charles Tripp. 1988. *Iran and Iraq at War.* Boulder: Westview. 318p.

Clapp, Nicholas. 1998. *The Road to Ubar: Finding the Atlantis of the Sands.* New York: Houghton Mifflin. 342p.

Clarck, Arthur P., and Muhammad A. Tahlawi, eds. 2006. *A Land Transformed: The Arabian Peninsula, Saudi Arabia, and Saudi Aramco.* Dhahran, Saudi Arabia: Saudi Arabian Oil Company.

Clarke, Angela. 1990. *Bahrain Oil and Development, 1929–1989.* Boulder: International Research Center for Energy and Economic Development. 432p.

Clarke, Duncan L. 1997. "US Security Assistance to Egypt and Israel: Politically Untouchable?" *Middle East Journal* 51, no. 2 (Spring): 200–214.

Clarke, Richard A. 2004. *Against All Enemies: Inside America's War on Terror.* New York: Free Press. 304p.

Cleveland, William L. 2004. *A History of the Modern Middle East.* 3d ed. Boulder: Westview. 624p.

"Climate Change and Politics Threaten Water Wars in Bekaa." 2009. IRIN, Feb. 1. www.irinnews.org.

Cobban, Helena. 1984. *The Palestinian Liberation Organization: People, Power, and Politics.* Cambridge Middle East Library. Cambridge: Cambridge University Press. 305p.

———. 1985. "Thinking About Lebanon." *American-Arab Affairs,* no. 12 (Spring): 59–71.

Cockburn, Andrew, and Leslie Cockburn. 1991. *Dangerous Liaison: The Inside Story of the U.S.-Israeli Covert Relationship.* New York: HarperCollins. 416p.

Cohen, Avner. 1998. *Israel and the Bomb.* New York: Columbia University Press. 470p.

Cohen, Saul. 1988. *The Geopolitics of Israel's Border Question.* Jerusalem: *Jerusalem Post,* for the Jaffee Center for Strategic Studies, Tel Aviv University. Distributed by Westview Press, Boulder. 124p.

Cohen, Yoel. 2003. *The Whistleblower of Dimona: Israel, Vanunu, and the Bomb.* New York: Holmes & Meier. 381p.

Cole, Juan. 2003. "The United States and Shi'ite Religious Factions in Post-Ba'thist Iraq." *Middle East Journal* 57, no. 4 (Autumn): 543–566.

Collins, Robert O. 2002. *The Nile.* New Haven: Yale University Press. 260p.

Congressional Quarterly. 2007. *The Middle East.* 11th ed. Washington, DC: CQ Press. 663p.

"Contemporary Oman and U.S.-Oman Relations: A Symposium." 1996. *Middle East Policy* 4, no. 3 (Mar.): 1–29.

Cooley, John K. 2000. *Unholy Wars: Afghanistan, America, and International Terrorism.* London and Sterling, VA: Pluto. 299p.

Cordesman, Anthony H. 1997. *Bahrain, Oman, Qatar, and the UAE: Challenges of Security.* Boulder: Westview. 448p.

———. 2003. *Saudi Arabia Enters the Twenty-first Century: The Political, Foreign Policy, Economic, and Energy Dimensions.* Westport, CT, and London: Praeger. Published in cooperation with the Center for Strategic and International Studies, Washington, DC. 588p.

———. 2004. *Energy Developments in the Middle East.* Westport, CT: Praeger. 208p.

Cordesman, Anthony H., and Ahmed S. Hashim. 1997. *Iraq: Sanctions and Beyond.* Boulder: Westview. 394p.

Cottrell, Alvin, ed. 1980. *The Persian Gulf States: A General Survey.* Baltimore: Johns Hopkins University Press. 695p.

Cramer, Richard Ben. 2004. *How Israel Lost: The Four Questions.* New York: Simon and Schuster. 307p.

Cressey, George B. 1958. "Qanats, Karez, and Foggaras." *Geography Review* 48, no. 1 (Jan.): 27–44.

———. 1960. *Crossroads: Land and Life in Southwest Asia.* Chicago: Lippincott. 593p.

Crews, Robert C., and Amin Tarzi. 2008. *The Taliban and the Crisis of Afghanistan.* Cambridge: Harvard University Press. 430p.

Cristol, A. Jay. 2002. *The* Liberty *Incident: The 1967 Israeli Attack on the U.S. Navy Spy Ship.* Washington, DC: Brassey's. 295p.

Croissant, Michael P., and Bülent Aras, eds. 1999. *Oil and Geopolitics in the Caspian Sea Region.* Westport, CT: Praeger. 305p.

Crystal, Jill. 1990. *Oil and Politics in the Gulf: Rulers and Merchants in Kuwait and Qatar.* Cambridge Middle East Library, no. 24. Cambridge: Cambridge University Press. 210p.

———. 1992. *Kuwait: The Transformation of an Oil State.* Boulder: Westview. 194p.

Culbertson, Roberta, and W. Nathaniel Howell. 2001. *Siege: Crisis Leadership; The Survival of U.S. Embassy Kuwait.* Charlottesville, VA: VFH Press. 154p.

Cullen, Robert. 1999. "The Rise and Fall of the Caspian Sea." *National Geographic,* May, 2–35.

Curtis, Michael, ed. 1981. *Religion and Politics in the Middle East.* Westview Special Studies on the Middle East. Prepared under the auspices of the American Academic Association for Peace in the Middle East. Boulder: Westview. 406p.

Curtiss, Richard. 1996. *Stealth PACs: Lobbying Congress for Control of U.S. Middle East Policy.* 4th ed. Washington, DC: American Educational Trust. 278p.

Dargin, Justin. 2007. "Qatar's Natural Gas: The Foreign Policy Driver." *Middle East Policy* 14, no. 3 (Fall): 136–142.

Daum, Werner. 1987. *Yemen: 3000 Years of Art and Civilisation in Arabia.* Felix. Innsbruck, Austria, and Frankfurt/ Main, Germany: Pinguin-Verlag and Umschau-Verlag. 485p.

Davidson, Christopher M. 2008. *Dubai: The Vulnerability of Success.* New York: Columbia University Press. 376p.

————. 2009. *Abu Dhabi: Oil and Beyond.* New York: Columbia University Press. 244p.

Davison, R. H. 1960. "Where Is the Middle East?" *Foreign Affairs* 38: 665–675.

Dawisha, Adeed. 2003. *Arab Nationalism in the Twentieth Century: From Triumph to Despair.* Princeton: Princeton University Press. 340p.

————. 2008. "The Unraveling of Iraq: Ethnosectarian Preferences and State Performance in Historical Perspective." *Middle East Journal* 62, no. 2 (Spring): 219–230.

Day, Alan J., ed. 1982. *Border and Territorial Disputes.* Harlow, Essex, UK: Longman. 406p.

Day, Stephen. 2008. "Updating Yemeni National Unity: Could Lingering Regional Divisions Bring Down the Regime?" *Middle East Journal* 62, no. 3: 417–436.

de Bellaigue, Christopher. 2007. "The Uncontainable Kurds." *New York Review of Books,* Mar. 1, 34–36.

Dekmejian, R. Hrair. 1998. "Saudi Arabia's Consultative Council." *Middle East Journal* 52, no. 2 (Spring): 204–218.

Denktash, Rauf. 1982. *The Cyprus Triangle.* Boston: Allen and Unwin. 224p.

Detalle, Renaud, ed. 2000. *Tensions in Arabia: The Saudi-Yemeni Fault Line.* Baden-Baden: Nomas Verlagsgesellschaft. 181p.

Dewdney, John C. 1971. *Turkey: An Introductory Geography.* New York: Praeger. 214p.

Diamond, Larry. 2005. *Squandered Victory.* New York: Times Books. 369p.

Dickson, H. R. P. 1949. *The Arab of the Desert: A Glimpse into Badawin Life in Kuwait and Saudi Arabia.* London: George Allen and Unwin. 668p.

————. 1956. *Kuwait and Her Neighbors.* London: Allen and Unwin. 627p.

Dillman, Jeffrey D. 1989. "Water Rights in the Occupied Territories." *Journal of Palestine Studies* 19, no. 1 (Autumn): 46–71.

Dixon, J. E., and A. H. F. Robertson, eds. 1984. *The Geological Evolution of the Eastern Mediterranean.* Published for the Geological Society. Oxford: Blackwell Scientific Publications. 824p.

Dizard, John. 2004. "How Ahmed Chalabi Conned the Neocons." Salon, May 4. www.salon.com.

Dodd, Clement. 2002. *Storm Clouds over Cyprus: A Briefing.* 2d ed. Huntington, UK: Eothen. 121p.

Dolatyar, Mostafa, and Tim S. Gray. 2000. *Water Politics in the Middle East: Context for Conflict or Cooperation?* New York: St. Martin's. 255p.

Doran, Charles F., and Stephen W. Buck, eds. 1991. *The Gulf, Energy, and Global Security: Political and Economic Issues.* Boulder: Lynn Rienner. 275p.

Doran, Michael Scott. 2004. "The Saudi Paradox." *Foreign Affairs* 83, no. 1 (Jan.–Feb.): 35–51.

Dorsey, James M. 2010. "Letter from Sana'a." *Foreign Affairs,* Feb. 26. www.foreignaffairs.com/features/letters_from/letter_from_sanaa.

Dresch, Paul. 1989. *Tribes, Government, and History in Yemen.* Oxford: Clarendon. 440p.

————. 2000. *A History of Modern Yemen.* Cambridge: Cambridge University Press. 285p.

Dreyfuss, Robert. 2005. *Devil's Game: How the United States Helped Unleash Fundamentalist Islam.* New York: Metropolitan Books, Henry Holt. 388p.

Drysdale, Alasdair, and Gerald Blake. 1985. *The Middle East and North Africa: A Political Geography.* New York: Oxford University Press. 340p.

Dumper, Michael. 2002. *The Politics of Sacred Space: The Old City of Jerusalem in the Middle East Conflict.* Boulder: Lynne Rienner. 185p.

Dunbar, Charles. 1992. "The Unification of Yemen: Process, Politics, and Prospects." *Middle East Journal* 43, no. 6 (Summer): 456–476.

Dutton, R., and N. Winser. 1987. "The Oman Wahiba Sands Project." *Geographical Journal* 153, no. 1 (Mar.): 48–58.

Earle, Sylvia A. 1992. "Persian Gulf Pollution: Assessing the Damage One Year Later." *National Geographic,* Feb., 122–134.

Economist. 2009a. "A Mediterranean Maelstrom." Dec. 12, 56–58.

————. 2009b. "A Sticky Situation." Dec. 10.

Economist Intelligence Unit (EIU). 2008. *Democracy Index, 2008.* London: EIU.

Edwards, Mike, and Michael Yamashita. 1999. "Eyewitness Iraq." *National Geographic,* Nov., 2–27.

Efrat, Elisha. 1996. *Israel, a Contemporary Political Geography.* Bochum, Germany: Brockmeyer. 141p.

————. 2006. *The West Bank and Gaza Strip: A Geography of Occupation and Disengagement.* New York: Routledge. 206p.

Efron, Noah. 2003. *Real Jews: Secular Versus Ultra-Orthodox: The Struggle for Jewish Identity in Israel.* New York: Basic. 284p.

Egypt Today (Cairo). 2004. "Brain Drain." Aug.

Ehteshami, Anoushiravan. 2004. "Iran's International Posture After the Fall of Baghdad." *Middle East Journal* 58, no. 2 (Spring): 179–194.

Eickelman, Dale F. 1981. *The Middle East: An Anthropological Approach.* Englewood Cliffs, NJ: Prentice-Hall. 336p.

Elazar, Daniel J. 1989. *The Other Jews: The Sephardim Today.* New York: Basic. 236p.

Elhance, Arun. 1999. *Hydropolitics in the Third World: Conflict and Cooperation in International River Basins.* Washington, DC: U.S. Institute of Peace Press. 296p.

el Khazen, Farid. 2000. *The Breakdown of the State in Lebanon.* Cambridge: Harvard University Press. 432p.

———. 2003. "Political Parties in Postwar Lebanon: Parties in Search of Partisans." *Middle East Journal* 57, no. 4 (Autumn): 605–624.

Ellis, Kail C., ed. 2002. *Lebanon's Second Republic: Prospects for the Twenty-first Century.* Gainesville: University Press of Florida. 236p.

Ellis, Marc H. 2002. *Israel and Palestine: Out of the Ashes—The Search for Jewish Identity in the Twenty-first Century.* Sterling, VA: Pluto. 198p.

Elmusa, Sharif S. 1997. *Water Conflict: Economics, Politics, Law and the Palestinian-Israeli Water Resources.* Washington, DC: Institute for Palestine Studies. 408p.

El-Nawawy, Mohammed, and Adel Iskandar. 2002. *Al Jazeera: How the Free Arab News Network Scooped the World and Changed the Middle East.* Boulder: Westview. 228p.

Emmett, Chad F. 1996. "The Capital Cities of Jerusalem." *Geography Review* 86, no. 2 (Apr.): 233–258.

Encyclopaedia Britannica. Annual *Britannica World Data.* Part 2 of *Britannica Book of the Year.* Chicago: Encyclopaedia Britannica.

Enderlin, Charles. 2003. *Shattered Dreams: The Failure of the Peace Process in the Middle East, 1995–2002.* Albany: Other Press. 458p.

Engelmann, Kurt, and Vjeran Pavlakovi, eds. 2001. *Rural Development in Eurasia and the Middle East: Land Reform, Demographic Change, and Environmental Constraints.* Seattle: University of Washington Press. 284p.

Engineer, Asghar Ali. 1996. *The Rights of Women in Islam.* New York: St. Martin's. 188p.

English, Paul Ward. 1966. *City and Village in Iran: Settlement and Economy in the Kirman Basin.* Madison: University of Wisconsin Press. 204p.

Entessar, Nader. 1992. *Kurdish Ethnonationalism.* Boulder: Lynne Rienner. 207p.

Erinç, Sirri, and Necdet Tunçdilek. 1952. "The Agricultural Regions of Turkey." *Geography Review* 42, no. 2 (Apr.): 179–203.

Erlich, Haggai. 2002. *The Cross and the River: Ethiopia, Egypt, and the Nile.* Boulder: Lynne Rienner. 249p.

Esman, Milton J., and Itamar Rabinovich, eds. 1988. *Ethnicity, Pluralism, and the State in the Middle East.* Ithaca: Cornell University Press. Published in cooperation with the Dayan Center for Middle Eastern and African Studies, Tel Aviv University. 296p.

Esposito, John L., ed. 1990. *The Iranian Revolution: Its Global Impact.* Miami: Florida International University Press. 346p.

———, ed. 1995. *The Oxford Encyclopedia of the Modern Islamic World.* 4 vols. New York: Oxford University Press. 1,920p.

———, ed. 1999. *The Oxford History of Islam.* New York and Oxford: Oxford University Press. 749p.

———. 2002. *Unholy War: Terror in the Name of Islam.* New York: Oxford University Press. 196p.

Esposito, John L., and Rouhollah K. Ramazani, eds. 2001. *Iran at the Crossroads.* New York: Palgrave. 248p.

European Commission. 2007. "European Neighborhood Partnership Instrument, Syrian Arab Republic. Strategy Paper, 2007–2013." March. http://ec.europa.eu/world/enp/pdf/country/enpi_csp_nip _syria_en.pdf.

Facey, William. 1994. *The Story of the Eastern Province of Saudi Arabia.* London: Stacey International. 160p.

Fairbanks, Stephen C. 1997. "A New Era for Iran?" *Middle East Policy* 5, no. 3 (Sept.): 51–56.

Falah, Ghazi. 1996. "The 1948 Israeli-Palestinian War and Its Aftermath: The Transformation and De-Signification of Palestine's Cultural Landscape." *Annals* (Association of American Geographers) 86, no. 2 (June): 256–285.

———. 1992. "Land Fragmentation and Spatial Control in the Nazareth Metropolitan Area." *Professional Geographer* 44, no. 1 (Feb.): 30–44.

Fall, Patricia L., Lee Lines, and Steven E. Falconer. 1998. "Seeds of Civilization: Bronze Age Rural Economy and Ecology in the Southern Levant." *Annals* (Association of American Geographers) 88, no. 1 (Mar.): 107–125.

Farouk-Sluglett, Marion, and Peter Sluglett. 2001. *Iraq Since 1958: From Revolution to Dictatorship.* 3d ed. London: I. B. Tauris, 2001. 390p.

Farr, Warner. 1999. *The Third Temple's Holy of Holies: Israel's Nuclear Weapons.* The Counterproliferation Papers, Future War Series no. 2. Montgomery, AL: Air War College, Maxwell Air Force Base. Available at www.fas.org/nuke/guide/israel/nuke/farr.htm.

Farsi, Zaki M. A. 1989. *National Guide and Atlas of the Kingdom of Saudi Arabia.* Jiddah: n.p.

Farsoun, Samih K., and Christina E. Zacharia. 1998. *Palestine and the Palestinians.* Boulder: Westview. 400p.

Fathi, Schirin H. 1994. *Jordan: An Invented Nation? Tribe-State Dynamics and the Formation of National Identity.* Hamburg: Deutsches Orient-Institut. 296p.

Feitelson, Eran, and Marwan Haddad, eds. 2000. *Management of Shared Groundwater Resources: The Is-raeli-Palestinian Case with an International Perspective.* Boston: Kluwer Academic Publishers with International Development Research Center. 496p.

Feldman, Noah. 2008. *The Fall and Rise of the Islamic State.* Princeton: Princeton University Press. 189p.

Fernea, Elizabeth. 2000. "The Challenges for Middle Eastern Women in the 21st Century." *Middle East Journal* 54, no. 2 (Winter): 185–193.

Ferragina, Eugenia. 2002. "Social Adaptive Capacity to Water Crisis: The Case of Jordan." In *Jordan in Transition,* edited by George Joffé, 346–367. New York: Palgrave. 378p.

Fieldhouse, David. 2006. *Western Imperialism in the Middle East 1914–1958.* Oxford: Oxford University Press. 376p.

Findley, Paul. 1989. *They Dare to Speak Out: People and Institutions Confront Israel's Lobby.* 2d ed. Westport, CT: Lawrence Hill. 390p.

Finkelstein, Israel, and Neil Asher Silberman. 2001. *The Bible Unearthed: Archaeology's New Vision of Ancient Israel and the Origin of Its Sacred Texts.* New York: Free Press. 385p.

Finkelstein, Norman G. 2003. *Image and Reality of the Israel-Palestinian Conflict.* 2d ed. London: Verso. 287p.

Finnie, David H. 1992. *Shifting Lines in the Sand: Kuwait's Elusive Frontier with Iraq.* Cambridge: Harvard University Press. 221p.

Fischbach, Michael R. 2000. *State, Society, and Land in Jordan.* Leiden, Boston, and Kolu: Brill. 236p.

Fisher, Sydney Nettleton, and William Ochsenwald. 1997. *The Middle East: A History.* 6th ed. New York: McGraw-Hill. 780p.

Fisher, William B., ed. 1968. *Cambridge History of Iran.* Vol. 1, *The Land of Iran.* Cambridge: Cambridge University Press. 782p.

———. 1978. *The Middle East.* London: Methuen. 514p.

Fisk, Robert. 1990. *Pity the Nation: The Abduction of Lebanon.* New York: Atheneum. 678p.

Fleshler, Dan. 2009. *Transforming America's Israel Lobby: The Limits of Its Power and the Potential for Change.* Washington, DC: Potomac Books. 267p.

Fox, John W. 2003. "Solutions to Water Stress in the Middle East." *Journal of Social Affairs* 20, no. 77 (Spring): 83–99.

Fox, John W., Nada Mourtada-Sabbah, and Mohammed al Mutawa, eds. 2006. *Globalization and the Gulf.* London: Routledge. 298 p.

Fraser Institute. 2008. *Economic Freedom of the World: 2008 Annual Report.* Vancouver. www.fraserinstitute.org.

Frederiksen, Harald D. 2003. "Water: Israeli Strategy, Implications for Peace and the Viability of Palestine." *Middle East Policy* 10, no. 4 (Winter): 69–86.

Freedman, Lawrence. 2008. *A Choice of Enemies: America Confronts the Middle East.* New York: Public Affairs. 601p.

Freedman, Robert O., ed. 2000. *Israel's First Fifty Years.* Gainesville: University Press of Florida. 290p.

Freeman-Grenville, G. S. P., S. C. Munro-Hay, and Lorraine Kessel. 2002. *Historical Atlas of Islam.* Rev. ed. New York: Continuum International. 414p.

Freimuth, Ladeene, et al. 2007. *Climate Change: New Threat to Middle East Security.* Amman, Jordan: Friends of the Earth Middle East.

Friedman, Richard E. 1997. *Who Wrote the Bible?* San Francisco: Harper. 299p.

Friedman, Thomas L. 1989. *From Beirut to Jerusalem.* New York: Farrar, Straus, Giroux. 525p.

Frisch, Hillel. 1998. *Countdown to Statehood: Palestinian State Formation in the West Bank and Gaza.* Albany: State University of New York Press. 221p.

Fromkin, David. 2000. *Peace to End All Peace: The Fall of the Ottoman Empire & the Creation of the Modern Middle East.* London: Phoenix. 635p.

Frum, David, and Richard Norman Perle. 2003. *An End to Evil: How to Win the War on Terror.* New York: Random House. 284p.

Fuller, Graham E. 1991. *The Center of the Universe: The Geopolitics of Iran.* Boulder: Westview. 301p.

———. 2003. *The Future of Political Islam.* New York: Palgrave Macmillan. 227p.

Fuller, Graham E., and Ian O. Lesser. 1993. *Turkey's New Geopolitics.* Boulder: Westview. 197p.

Fuller, Graham E., and Rend Rahim Francke. 2001. *The Arab Shi'a: The Forgotten Muslims.* New York: Palgrave. 290p.

Fürtig, Henner. 2007. "Conflict and Cooperation in the Persian Gulf: The Interregional Order and US Policy." *Middle East Journal* 61, no 4 (Autumn): 627–640.

Gabriel, Erhard F. 1988. *The Dubai Handbook.* Ahrensburg, Germany: Institute for Applied Economic Geography. 243p.

Gaffney, Mark. 1989. *Dimona: The Third Temple? The Story Behind the Vanunu Revelation.* Brattleboro: Amana Publications. 236p.

Galbraith, Peter W. 2007. *The End of Iraq: How American Incompetence Created a War Without End.* New York: Simon and Schuster. 275p.

Galnoor, Itzak. 1995. *The Partition of Palestine.* Albany: State University of New York Press. 384p.

Gambill, Gary C. 2009. "The Pivotal Role of Lebanon's Armenian Christians." *Mideast Monitor,* July–Aug. www.mideastmonitor.org/issues/0907/0907_2.htm.

Gandolfo, K. Luisa. 2008. "The Political and Social Identities of the Palestinian Christian Community in Jordan." *Middle East Journal* 62, no. 3: 437–455.

Gause, F. Gregory, III. 1994. *Oil Monarchies: Domestic and Security Challenges in the Arab Gulf States.* New York: Council on Foreign Relations Press. 236p.

———. 2002. "Iraq's Decision to Go to War: 1980 and 1990." *Middle East Journal* 56, no. 1 (Winter): 47–70.

Gavin, Angus, and Ramez Maluf. 1996. *Beirut Reborn: The Restoration and Development of the Central District.* London: Academy Editions. 148p.

Gazit, Shlomo. 2003. *Trapped Fools: Thirty Years of Israeli Policy in the Territories.* London and Portland, OR: Frank Cass. 368p.

Gelber, Yoav. 2001. *Palestine, 1948: War, Escape, and the Emergence of the Palestinian Refugee Problem.* Brighton, UK, and Portland, OR: Sussex Academic Press. 399p.

Gelvin, James L. 2007. *The Israel-Palestine Conflict: One Hundred Years of War.* New York: Cambridge University Press. 296p.

Gerges, Fawaz A. 1999. *America and Political Islam: Clash of Cultures or Clash of Interests?* New York: Cambridge University Press. 282p.

Gerner, Deborah J. 1994. *One Land, Two Peoples: The Conflict over Palestine.* 2d ed. Boulder: Westview. 256p.

Gerner, Deborah J., and Jillian Schwedler, eds. 2004. *Understanding the Contemporary Middle East.* 2d ed. Boulder: Lynne Rienner. 477p.

Ghabra, Shafeeq. 1997. "Kuwait and the Dynamics of Socio-Economic Change." *Middle East Journal* 51, no. 3 (Summer): 358–372.

Ghadbian, Najib. 2001. "The New Asad: Dynamics of Continuity and Change in Syria." *Middle East Journal* 55, no. 4 (Autumn): 624–641.

Ghanem, As'ad. 2001. *The Palestinian-Arab Minority in Israel, 1948–2000: A Political Study.* Albany: State University of New York Press. 238p.

Ghannam, Farha. 2002. *Remaking the Modern: Space, Relocation, and the Politics of Identity in a Global Cairo.* Berkeley and Los Angeles: University of California Press. 214p.

Ghareeb, Edmund. 1981. *The Kurdish Question in Iraq. Contemporary Issues in the Middle East.* Syracuse: Syracuse University Press. 223p.

Gilbert, Martin. 2002. *The Routledge Atlas of the Arab-Israeli Conflict.* 7th ed. New York: Routledge. 156p.

Goell, Edgar, et al. 2009. *Sustainable Cities in Egypt Learning from Experience: Potentials and Preconditions for New Cities in Desert Areas.* Cairo: Center for Future Studies, the Egyptian Cabinet.

Goldberg, Jeffrey. 2008a. "After Iraq." *Atlantic,* Jan.–Feb., 68–79.

———. 2008b. "Unforgiven." *Atlantic,* May, 32–51.

Goldhill, Simon. 2009. *Jerusalem: City of Longing.* Cambridge: Harvard University Press, Belknap Press, 2009. 356p.

Goldscheider, Calvin. 2002. *Israel's Changing Society: Population, Ethnicity, and Development.* 2d ed. Boulder: Westview. 282p.

Goldschmidt, Arthur, Jr. and Lawrence Davidson 2004. *Modern Egypt: The Formation of a Nation-State.* 2d ed. Boulder: Westview. 242p.

———. 2010. *A Concise History of the Middle East.* 9th ed. Boulder: Westview. 555p.

Gonen, Amiram. 1993. *The Encyclopedia of the Peoples of the World.* New York: Henry Holt. 703p.

Goode's World Atlas. 2005. 21st ed. Chicago: McGraw-Hill. 371p.

Gordon, Aharon David. 1997. "Some Observations." In *The Zionist Idea: A Historical Analysis and Reader,* edited by Arthur Hertzberg. Rev. ed. Philadelphia: Jewish Publication Society. 648p.

Gordon, David C. 1983. *The Republic of Lebanon: Nation in Jeopardy.* Profiles: Nations of the Contemporary Middle East. Boulder: Westview. 171p.

Gore, Rick. 2004. "Who Were the Phoenicians?" *National Geographic,* Oct., 26–49.

Gorenberg, Gershom. 2003. "The One-Fence Solution." *New York Times Magazine,* Aug. 3, 34–37.

———. 2009. " The War to Begin All Wars." *New York Review of Books,* May 28.

———. 2009. "The Settlement Freeze That Isn't." *American Prospect,* Dec. 17. www.prospect.org/cs/articles?article=the_settlement_freeze_that_isnt.

Gradus, Yehuda, and Gabriel Lipshitz, eds. 1996. *The Mosaic of Israeli Geography.* Beer Sheva: Ben-Gurion University of the Negev Press. 516p.

Graicer, Iris. 1992. "Spatial Integration of Arab Migrants in a Jewish Town." *Professional Geographer* 44, no. 1 (Feb.): 45–56.

Grant, Michael. 1984. *The History of Ancient Israel.* New York: Scribner's. 317p.

Greenwood, Scott. 2003. "Jordan, the Al-Aqsa Intifada and America's 'War on Terror.'" *Middle East Policy* 10, no. 3 (Fall): 90–111.

Grill, N. C. 1984. *Urbanisation in the Arabian Peninsula.* Durham, UK: Centre for Middle Eastern and Islamic Studies, University of Durham. 113p.

Grimes, Barbara F., et al. 1996. *Ethnologue: Languages of the World.* 13th ed. Dallas: Summer Institute of Linguistics. 966p. www.sil.org/ethnologue.

Gubser, Peter. 1983. *Jordan: Crossroads of Middle Eastern Events.* Profiles: Nations of the Contemporary Middle East. Boulder: Westview. 139p.

Güçlü, Yücel. 2001. *The Question of the Sanjak of Alexandretta: A Study in Turkish-French-Syrian Relations.* Ankara: Turkish Historical Society Printing House. 368p.

Gulick, John. 1967. *Tripoli: A Modern Arab City.* Cambridge: Harvard University Press. 253p.

———. 1983. *The Middle East: An Anthropological Perspective.* Washington, DC: University Press of America, 1983. 244p.

———. 1997. *The Kurds and the Future of Turkey.* New York: St. Martin's. 184p.

Gunter, Michael M. 1999. *The Kurdish Predicament in Iraq: A Political Analysis.* New York: St. Martin's. 181p.

Gürün, Kamvran. 1985. *The Armenian File: The Myth of Innocence Exposed.* New York: St. Martin's. 323p.

Haas, Richard N. 2009. *War of Necessity, War of Choice: A Memoir of Two Iraq Wars.* New York: Simon and Schuster. 352p.

Haddad, Simon. 2003. *The Palestinian Impasse in Lebanon: The Politics of Refugee Integration.* Brighton, UK, and Portland, OR: Sussex Academic Press. 179p.

Haddad, Wadi D. 1985. *Lebanon: The Politics of Revolving Doors.* Washington Papers no. 114, published with the Center for Strategic and International Studies, Georgetown University New York: Praeger. 154p.

Al-Haj, Abdullah Juma. 1996. "The Politics of Cooperation in the Gulf Cooperation Council States: The Omani Consultative Council." *Middle East Journal* (Autumn).

Halliday, Fred. 2000. *Nation and Religion in the Middle East.* Boulder: Lynne Rienner. 251p.

Hammami, Rema, and Salim Tamari. 2001. "The Second Uprising: End or New Beginning?" *Journal of Palestine Studies* 30, no. 2 (Winter): 5–25.

Hanf, Theodor, and Nawwaf Salam. 2003. *Lebanon in Limbo: Postwar Society and State in an Uncertain Regional Environment.* Baden-Baden: Nomos Verglagsgesellschaft. 228p.

Hanieh, Akram. 2001. "The Camp David Papers." *Journal of Palestine Studies* 30, no. 2 (Winter): 75–97.

Hanna, Samir S. 1995. *Field Guide to the Geology of Oman.* Vol. 1, *Western Hajar Mountains and Musandam.* Ruwi, Oman: Historical Association of Oman. 178p.

Harbison, David K. 1990. "The U.S.-Saudi Arabian Joint Commission on Economic Cooperation: A Critical Appraisal." *Middle East Journal* 44, no. 2.

Harel, Amos, and Ari Issacharoff. 2009. *34 Days: Israel, Hezbollah, and the War in Lebanon.* New York: Macmillan. 304p.

Harris, George S. 1985. *Turkey: Coping with Crisis.* Profiles: Nations of the Contemporary Middle East. Boulder: Westview. 240p.

Harris, William. 2003. *The Levant: A Fractured Mosaic.* Princeton: Markus Wiener. 212p.

Hart, Parker T. 1998. *Saudi Arabia and the United States: Birth of a Security Partnership.* Bloomington: Indiana University Press. 383p.

Hartshorne, Richard. 1950. "The Functional Approach in Political Geography." *Annals* (Association of American Geographers) 40, no. 2 (June): 95–130.

Hawass, Zahi. 1999. "Oasis of the Dead." *Archaeology* 52, no. 5 (Sept.–Oct.): 38.

Haynes, Kingsley E., and Dale Whittington. 1981. "International Management of the Nile—Stage Three?" *Geographical Review* 71, no. 1 (Jan.): 17–32.

Hazleton, Lesley. 2009. *After the Prophet: The Epic Story of the Shia-Sunni Split in Islam.* New York: Doubleday. 239p.

Hazony, Yoram. 2000. *The Jewish State: The Struggle for Israel's Soul.* New York: Basic Books. 433p.

Heard-Bey, Frauke. 1999. "The United Arab Emirates." In *Middle East Dilemma: The Politics and Economics of Arab Integration,* edited by Michael C. Hudson. New York: Columbia University Press. 319p.

———. 2005a. *From Trucial States to United Arab Emirates: A Society in Transition.* London: Longman. 540p.

———. 2005b. "The United Arab Emirates: Statehood and Nation-Building in a Traditional Society." *Middle East Journal* 59, no. 3 (Summer): 357–375.

Held, Colbert. 2010. "Peoples and Cultures of the Middle East." In *The Contemporary Middle East,* edited by Karl Yambert. 2d ed. Boulder: Westview.

Held, Joanne D. [Cummings]. 1979. "The Effects of the Ottoman Land Laws on the Marginal Population and Musha Village of Palestine, 1858–1914." Master's thesis, University of Texas at Austin. 225p.

Helms, Christine Moss. 1984. *Iraq: Eastern Flank of the Arab World.* Washington, DC: Brookings Institution. 215p.

Hemmer, Christopher. 2003. "I Told You So: Syria, Oslo, and the Al-Aqsa Intifada." *Middle East Policy* 10, no. 3 (Fall): 121–135.

Herb, Michael. 2004. "Princes and Parliaments in the Arab World." *Middle East Journal* 58, no. 3 (Summer): 367–384.

Hersch, Seymour M. 1991. T*he Samson Option: Israel's Nuclear Arsenal and American Foreign Policy.* New York: Random House. 354p.

———. 2008. "A Strike in the Dark." *New Yorker,* Feb. 11 and 18.

Hertog, Steffen. 2007. "The GCC and Arab Economic Integration: A New Paradigm." *Middle East Policy* 14, no. 1 (Spring): 52–68.

Hertzberg, Arthur, ed. 1997. *The Zionist Idea: A Historical Analysis and Reader.* Rev. ed. Philadelphia: Jewish Publication Society. 648p.

———. 2003. *The Fate of Zionism: A Secular Future for Israel and Palestine.* San Francisco: Harper San Francisco. 194p.

Heun, Manfred, et al. 1997. "Site of Einkorn Wheat Domestication Identified by DNA Fingerprinting." *Science* 278, no. 5341: 1312–1314.

Hewison, R. Neil. 2001. *The Fayoum: A Practical Guide.* 3d ed. Cairo: American University of Cairo Press. 112p.

Hills, E. S., ed. 1966. *Arid Lands: A Geographical Appraisal.* London: Methuen; Paris: UNESCO. 461p.

Hilterman, Joost R. 2007. *A Poisonous Affair: America, Iraq, and the Gassing of Halabja.* New York: Cambridge University Press. 346p.

Hinnebusch, Raymond A. 2003. *The International Politics of the Middle East.* Manchester and New York: Manchester University Press and Palgrave, 2003. 262p.

Hinnels, John R. 2005. *The Zoroastrian Diaspora: Religion and Migration.* New York: Oxford University Press. 884p.

Hiro, Dilip. 2002a. *Iraq: A Report from the Inside.* London: Granta Books. 271p.

———. 2002b. *War Without End: The Rise of Islamist Terrorism and Global Response.* London and New York: Routledge. 513p.

———. 2004. *Secrets and Lies: Operations "Iraqi Freedom" and After.* New York: Nation Books. 467p.

Hirst, David. 2003. *The Gun and the Olive Branch: The Roots of Violence in the Middle East.* 3d ed. New York: Thunder's Mouth Press/Nation Books. 627p.

Hobbs, Joseph J. 1989. *Bedouin Life in the Egyptian Wilderness.* Austin: University of Texas Press. 165p.

———. 1996. "Speaking with People in Egypt's St. Katherine National Park." *Geography Review* 86, no. 1 (Jan.): 1–21.

———. 1999. "Sinai's Watchmen of the Wilderness." *Saudi Aramco World,* May–June, 12–21.

Hof, Frederic C. 1997. "The Water Dimensions of Golan Heights Negotiations." *Middle East Policy* 5, no. 2 (May): 129–141.

———. 1999. "The Line of June 4, 1967." *Middle East Insight,* Sept.–Oct., 17–23.

———. 2001. "A Practical Line: The Line of Withdrawal from Lebanon and its Potential Applicability to the Golan Heights." *Middle East Journal* 55, no. 1 (Winter): 25–42.

Holden, David, and Richard Johns. 1982. *The House of Saud: The Rise and Rule of the Most Powerful Dynasty in the Arab World.* New York: Holt, Rinehart, and Winston. 569p.

Holm, Donald August. 1960. "Desert Geomorphology in the Arabian Peninsula." *Science* 132, no. 3437: 1369–1379.

Hoogland, Eric. 2002. *Twenty Years of Islamic Revolution: Political and Social Transition in Iran since 1979.* Syracuse: Syracuse University Press. 193p.

Hopwood, Derek. 1982. *Egypt: Politics and Society, 1945–1981.* London: Allen and Unwin. 194p.

———. 1988. *Syria, 1945–1986: Politics and Society.* London: Unwin Hyman. 193p.

Hourani, Albert H. 1947. *Minorities in the Arab World.* London: Oxford University Press. 140p.

———. 1963. *Arab Seafaring in the Indian Ocean in Ancient and Early Medieval Times.* Beirut: Khayats. 131p.

———. 1991. *A History of the Arab Peoples.* Cambridge: Harvard University Press, Belknap Press. 551p.

Howard, Douglas A. 2001. *The History of Turkey.* Westport, CT: Greenwood. 241p.

Howard, Harry N. 1963. *The King-Crane Commission.* Beirut: Khayats. 369p.

———. 1974. *Turkey, the Straits, and U.S. Policy.* Baltimore: Johns Hopkins University Press, in cooperation with Middle East Institute. 337p.

Howe, Marvine. 2004. *Turkey: A Nation Divided over Islam's Revival.* New York: Basic Books. 310p.

Hoyland, Robert G. 2001. *Arabia and the Arabs: From the Bronze Age to the Coming of Islam.* London and New York: Routledge. 324p.

Hroub, Khaled. 2000. *Hamas: Political Thought and Practice.* Washington, DC: Institute for Palestine Studies. 329p.

Hudson, James. 1971. "The Litani River of Lebanon." *Middle East Journal* 25, no. 1 (Winter): 1–14.

Hudson, Michael C., ed. 1999. *Middle East Dilemma: The Politics and Economics of Arab Integration.* New York: Columbia University Press. 319p.

Hughes, Hugh. 1981. *Middle East Railways.* Harrow, UK: Continental Railway Circle. 128p.

Hunter, Shireen T. 1990. *Iran and the World: Continuity in a Revolutionary Decade.* Bloomington: Indiana University Press. 254p.

———. 1996. *Central Asia Since Independence.* Westport, CT: Praeger. 220p.

Hurriyet: Daily News and Economic Review. 2009a. "Crack in Northern Cyprus Gets Deeper as Turkish Side Fine Tunes Policy." Dec. 24. www.hurriyetdailynews.com/.

———. 2009b. "Cyprus Needs Turkey and Greece." Dec. 1. www.hurriyetdailynews.com/.

Index Islamicus, on CD-ROM. 1998. *A Bibliography of Publications on Islam and the Muslim World from 1906 to 1997.* Edited by G. J. Roper and C. H. Bleaney. Cambridge: Cambridge University Library, 1998.

Indyk, Martin. 2009. *Innocent Abroad: An Intimate Account of American Peace Diplomacy in the Middle East.* New York: Simon and Schuster. 494p.

International Energy Agency. Annual. "Energy Balances." www.iea.org/country/index.asp.

International Federation for Human Rights. 2003. "Migrant Workers in Israel." www.fidh.org.

International Food Policy Research Institute. 2009. *2009 Global Hunger Index: The Challenge of Hunger—Focus on Financial Crisis and Gender Inequality.* Washington, DC: International Food Policy Research Institute.

International Monetary Fund. 2009. "Macroeconomic and Fiscal Framework for the West Bank and Gaza: Fourth Review of Progress." Sept. 22.

International Petroleum Encyclopedia (IPE). Annual. Tulsa: PennWell.

International Rescue Committee. 2008. "Five Years Later, a Hidden Crisis: Report of the IRC Commission on Iraqi Refugees." Mar. www.ircuk.org/fileadmin/user_upload/Reports/iraq_report.pdf.

Ismael, Tareq Y., and Mustafa Aydin, eds. 2003. *Turkey's Foreign Policy in the 21st Century: A Changing Role in World Politics.* Aldershot, Hants, UK, and Burlington, VT: Ashgate. 224p.

Israel: The Historical Atlas. 1997. New York: Macmillan. 208p.

The Israeli Democracy Institute. "Israeli Democracy Index." Jerusalem. www.idi.org.il.

Israel Pocket Library. 1973. *Geography.* Compiled from material originally published in the *Encyclopaedia Judaica.* One of several volumes in this series (*Society; Religious Life and Communities; Immigration and Settlement; Economy;* and others). Jerusalem: Keter. 263p.

Issawi, Charles. 1982. *An Economic History of the Middle East and North Africa.* New York: Columbia University Press. 304p.

Ivereigh, Austen. 2008. "Bethlehem's Wall." *America* (Sept. 1): 15–17.

Jabbur, Jibrail S. 1995. *The Bedouins and the Desert: Aspects of Nomadic Life in the Arab East.* Translated by Lawrence I. Conrad. Edited by Suhay J. Jabbur and Lawrence I. Conrad. Albany: State University of New York Press. 670p.

Jaber, Hala. 1997. *Hezbollah: Born with a Vengeance.* New York: Columbia University Press. 240p.

Jaganathan, N. V., A. S. Mohammed, and A. Kremer. 2009. *Water in the Arab World: Management Perspectives and Innovations.* Washington, DC: World Bank.

Jenkins, Gareth H. 2009. *Between Fact and Fantasy: Turkey's Ergenekon Investigation.* Washington, DC: Silk Road Studies Program, John Hopkins University, Aug.

Jernazian, Ephraim K. 1990. *Judgment unto Truth: Witnessing the Armenian Genocide.* New Brunswick, NJ: Transaction. 163p.

Joffé, George. 2002. *Jordan in Transition.* New York: Palgrave. 378p.

Johanbakhsh, Forough. 2001. *Islam, Democracy, and Religious Modernism in Iran, 1953–2000: From Bazargun to Soroush.* Leiden and Boston: Brill. 201p.

Jones, Curtis F. 2006. *Divide and Perish: The Geopolitics of the Middle East.* Bloomington, IN: Authorhouse. 462p.

Jones, Stephen B. 1954. "A Unified Field Theory of Political Geography." *Annals* (Association of American Geographers) 44, no. 4 (Dec.): 111–123.

Joseph, John. 1983. *Muslim-Christian Relations and Inter-Christian Rivalries in the Middle East: The Case of the Jacobites in an Age of Transition.* Albany: State University of New York Press. 240p.

Joseph, Suad, and Susan Slyomovics, eds. 2001. *Women and Power in the Middle East.* Philadelphia: University of Pennsylvania Press. 203p.

Joyce, Miriam. 1998. *Kuwait, 1945–1996: An Anglo-American Perspective.* London and Portland, OR: Frank Cass. 182p.

Jungen, Christine. 2002. "Tribalism in Kerak: Past Memories, Present Realities." In *Jordan in Transition,* edited by George Joffé, 191–207. New York: Palgrave. 378p.

Kahan, David. 1987. *Agriculture and Water Resources in the West Bank and Gaza, 1967–1987.* Boulder: Westview Press. 181p.

Kahan Commission. 1983. *The Beirut Massacre: The Complete Kahan Commission Report.* With an introduction by Abba Eban. Princeton: Karz-Cohl. 107p.

Kahane, Meir. 1981. *They Must Go.* New York: Grosset and Dunlap. 282p.

Kahn, Muqtedar. 2003. "Prospects for Muslim Democracy: The Role of U.S. Policy." *Middle East Policy* 10, no. 3 (Fall): 79–89.

Kaikobad, Kaiyan Homi. 1988. *The Shatt al-Arab Boundary Question.* Oxford: Oxford University Press. 184p.

Kamrava, Mehran. 2009. "Royal Factionalism and Political Liberalization in Qatar." *Middle East Journal* 63, no. 3: 401–420.

Kaplan, Seth. 2008. "A New U.S. Policy for Syria: Fostering Political Change in a Divided State." *Middle East Policy* 15, no. 3 (Fall): 107–121.

Karasipahi, Sena. 2009. "Comparing Islamic Resurgence Movements in Turkey and Iran." *Middle East Journal* 63, no. 1: 87–107.

Kark, Ruth, ed. 1989. *The Land That Became Israel: Studies in Historical Geography.* New Haven: Yale University Press; Jerusalem: Magnes Press of Hebrew University. 332p. + plates.

Karouzis, George, and Christina G. Karouzis. 1997. *Touring Guide of Cyprus.* Rev. ed. Nicosia, Cyprus: Selas. 304p.

Karpat, Kemal H. 1976. *The Gecekondu: Rural Migration and Urbanization.* Cambridge: Cambridge University Press. 291p.

Karsh, Efraim. 1990. "Geopolitical Determinism: The Origins of the Iran-Iraq War." *Middle East Journal* 44, no. 2 (Spring): 256–268.

———. 1997. *Fabricating Israeli History: The "New Historians."* London: Frank Cass. 210p.

———. 1999. "Benny Morris and the Reign of Error." *Middle East Quarterly* 6, no. 1 (Mar.): 15–28.

Kastner, Ariel. 2008. "Israel-Syria Relations: Does America Have a Role in Ankara?" Brookings Institution, June 10. www.brookings.edu/opinions/2008/0610_peace_talks_kastner.aspx.

Kaufman, Asher. 2002. "Who Owns the Shebaa Farms? Chronicle of a Territorial Dispute." *Middle East Journal* 56, no. 4 (Autumn): 576–596

Kaufman, Burton I. 1996. *The Arab Middle East and the United States: Inter-Arab Rivalry and Superpower Diplomacy.* New York: Twayne. 291p.

Keating, Rex. 1975. *Nubian Rescue.* New York: Hawthorn. 269p.

Keay, John. 2003. *Sowing the Wind: The Seeds of Conflict in the Middle East.* New York: Norton. 506p.

Kechichian, Joseph A. 1995. *Oman and the World: The Emergence of an Independent Foreign Policy.* Santa Monica, CA: Rand. 409p.

———. 1999. "Trends in Saudi National Security." *Middle East Journal* 53, no. 2 (Spring): 232–253.

———. 2001. *Succession in Saudi Arabia.* New York: Palgrave. 287p.

———. 2002. *Iran, Iraq, and the Arab Gulf States.* New York and Basingstoke: Palgrave. 512p.

———. 2008. *Power and Succession in Arab Monarchies: A Reference Guide.* Boulder: Lynne Rienner. 555p.

Keddie, N. R. 1972. "Is There a Middle East?" *International Journal of Middle East Studies* 4: 255–271.

———. 2006. *Women in the Middle East: Past and Present.* Princeton: Princeton University Press. 193p.

Keddie, N. R., and Rudi Mathee, eds. 2002. *Iran and the Surrounding World: Interactions in Culture and Cultural Politics.* Seattle: University of Washington Press. 374p.

Keeley, Robert V. 2002. "Trying to Define Terrorism." *Middle East Policy* 9, no. 1 (Mar.): 33–39.

Kelly, J. B. 1980. *Arabia, the Gulf, and the West.* New York: Basic Books. 530p.

Kemp, Geoffrey, and Robert E. Harkavy. 1997. *Strategic Geography and the Changing Middle East.* Washington, DC: Carnegie Endowment for International Peace/Brookings Institution Press. 493p.

Kennan, George F. 1987. "The Sources of Soviet Conduct." *Foreign Affairs* 65, no. 4 (Spring): 852–868. Originally published in *Foreign Affairs* in July 1947 under the byline "X"; includes Kennan's updated comments.

Kennedy, David, and Derrick Riley. 1990. *Rome's Desert Frontier from the Air.* Austin: University of Texas Press. 256p.

Kepel, Gilles. 2002. *Jihad: The Trail of Political Islam.* Cambridge: Harvard University Press. 454p.

Kershner, Isabel. 1999. "Back to Haunt the Peacemakers." *Jerusalem Report,* Aug. 2, 20–26.

Keshavarzian, Arang. 2007. *Bazaar and State in Iran: The Politics of the Tehran Marketplace.* Cambridge Middle East Studies. New York: Cambridge University Press, 2007. 282p.

Kessler, Martha, Helena Cobban, and Hisham Melhem. 1999. "What About Syria?" *Middle East Policy* 7, no.1 (Oct.): 101–112.

Keyder, Caglar, ed. 1999. *Istanbul: Between the Global and the Local.* Lanham, MD: Roman and Littlefield. 201p.

Keyder, Caglar, and Frank Tabak, eds. 1991. *Landholding and Commercial Agriculture in the Middle East.* Albany: State University of New York Press. 260p.

Khadduri, Majid. 1988. *The Gulf War: The Origins and Implications of the Iraq-Iran Conflict.* New York: Oxford University Press. 236p.

Khadduri, Majid, and Edmund Ghareeb. 1997. *War in the Gulf, 1990–1991.* New York: Oxford University Press. 299p.

Khajehpour, Bijan. 2001. "Iran's Economy: Twenty Years After the Islamic Revolution." In *Iran at the Crossroads,* edited by John L. Esposito and Rouhollah K. Ramazani. New York: Palgrave. 248p.

Khalidi, Rashid. 2004. *Resurrecting Empire: Western Footprints and America's Perilous Path in the Middle East.* Boston: Beacon. 223p.

————. 2009. *Sowing Crisis: The Cold War and American Hegemony in the Middle East.* Boston: Beacon Press. 308p.

Khalidi, Walid, ed. 1971. *From Haven to Conquest: Readings in Zionism and the Palestine Problem Until 1948.* Beirut: Institute for Palestine Studies. 839p.

Khashan, Hilal. 2000. *Arabs at the Crossroads: Political Identity and Nationalism.* Gainesville: University Press of Florida. 187p.

Kheirabadi, Masoud. 1991. *Iranian Cities: Formation and Development.* An Iran-American Foundation Book. Austin: University of Texas Press. 160p.

Khoury, Phillip. 1987. *Syria and the French Mandate: The Politics of Arab Nationalism, 1920–1945.* Princeton: Princeton University Press. 698p.

Khoury, Rami G. 1988. *The Antiquities of the Jordan Rift Valley.* Amman: Al Kutba. 151p.

Kimball, Lorenzo Kent. 1972. *The Changing Pattern of Political Power in Iraq, 1958 to 1971.* New York: R. Speller. 246p.

Kimenyi, Mwangi S. 2010. "Fractionalized, Armed, and Lethal: Why Somalia Matters." Washington, DC: Brookings Institute. Feb 8.

Kimmerling, Baruch, and Joel S. Migdal. 2003. *The Palestinian People: A History.* Cambridge: Harvard University Press. 568p.

Kingdom of Saudi Arabia, Central Department of Statistics. Annual. *Statistical Year Book.* Riyadh.

Klare, Michael T. 2004. *Blood and Oil: The Dangers and Consequences of America's Growing Petroleum Dependency.* New York: Henry Holt. 265p.

Klieman, Aaron S. 1971. *Foundations of British Policy in the Arab World: The Cairo Conference of 1921.* Baltimore: Johns Hopkins University Press. 322p.

Kolars, John F. 1968. *Tradition, Season, and Change in a Turkish Village.* Research Paper no. 82, Department of Geography. Chicago: University of Chicago Press. 205p.

————. 1990. "The Course of Water in the Arab Middle East." *American-Arab Affairs* 33 (Summer): 57–68.

Kolars, John F., and William A. Mitchell. 1991. *The Euphrates River and the Southeast Anatolia Development Project.* Carbondale: Southern Illinois University Press. 325p.

Korn, David A. 1992. *Stalemate: The War of Attrition and Great Power Diplomacy in the Middle East, 1967–1970.* Boulder: Westview Press. 326p.

Kostiner, Joseph, ed. 2000. *Middle East Monarchies: The Challenge of Modernity.* Boulder: Lynne Rienner. 341p.

Kramer, Heinz. 2000. *A Changing Turkey: The Challenge to Europe and the United States.* Washington, DC: Brookings Institution Press. 304p.

Kreiger, Barbara. 1988. *Living Waters: Myth, History, and Politics of the Dead Sea.* New York: Continuum. 226p.

Krinsley, Daniel B. 1970. *A Geomorphological and Paleoclimatological Study of the Playas of Iran.* Pts. 1-2. Prepared for Air Force Cambridge Research Laboratories, U.S. Air Force, Bedford, MA. Washington, DC: U.S. Geological Survey, Department of the Interior, Aug. Pt. 1, 329p.; Pt. 2, 486p.

Kung, Hans. 2007. *Islam: Past, Present and Future.* Oxford: Oneworld Publications. 767p.

Lacroix, Stephane. 2004. "Between Islamists and Liberals: Saudi Arabia's New 'Islamo-Liberal' Reformists." *Middle East Journal* 58, no. 3 (Summer): 345–365.

Lagerquist, Peter. 2004. "Fencing the Last Sky: Excavating Palestine After Israel's 'Separation Wall.'" *Journal of Palestine Studies* 33, no. 2 (Winter): 5–35.

La Guardia, Anton. 2002. *War Without End: Israelis, Palestinians, and the Struggle for a Promised Land.* New York: Thomas Dunne. 408p.

Lapidus, Ira M. 1969. *Middle Eastern Cities: A Symposium on Ancient, Islamic, and Contemporary Middle East Urbanism.* Berkeley and Los Angeles: University of California Press. 206p.

————, ed. 2002. *A History of Islamic Societies.* 2d ed. Cambridge: Cambridge University Press. 970p.

Laqueur, Walter, and Barry Rubin, eds. 2001. *The Israel-Arab Reader: A Documentary History of the Middle East Conflict.* 6th ed. New York and London: Penguin. 580p.

Laron, Guy. 2009. "'Logic Dictates That They May Attack When They Feel They Can Win': The 1955 Czech-Egyptian Arms Deal, the Egyptian Army, and Israeli Intelligence." *Middle East Journal* 63, no. 1: 69–84.

Lawrence, T. E. 2004. *Seven Pillars of Wisdom: The Complete 1922 Text.* Edited by Jeremy and Nicole Wilson. New ed. Fordingbridge, UK: J. and N. Wilson. 870p.

Lawson, Fred H. 1989. *Bahrain: The Modernization of Autocracy.* Profiles: Nations of the Contemporary Middle East. Boulder: Westview Press. 150p.

———. 2007. "Syria's Relations with Iraq: Managing the Dilemmas of Alliance." *Middle East Journal* 61, no. 1 (Winter): 27–47.

Lees, G. M., and N. L. Falcon. 1952. "The Geographical History of the Mesopotamian Plains." *Geographical Journal* 118: 24–39.

Lefebvre, Jeffrey A. 1998. "Red Sea Security and the Geopolitical-Economy of the Hanish Islands Dispute." *Middle East Journal* 52, no. 3 (Summer): 367–385.

Lelyveld, Joseph. 2007. "Carter, Israel, and Apartheid." *New York Review of Books,* Mar. 29, 14–17.

Lenczowski, George. 1990. *American Presidents and the Middle East.* Durham: Duke University Press. 321p.

Le Renard, Amelie. 2008. "'Only for Women': Women, the State, and Reform in Saudi Arabia." *Middle East Journal* 62, no. 4: 610–629.

Lesch, Ann M. 1991. "Palestinians in Kuwait." *Journal of Palestine Studies* 20, no. 4 (Summer): 42–54.

Lesch, David W. 2003. *The Middle East and the United States: A Historical and Political Reassessment.* 3d ed. Boulder: Westview Press. 518p.

———. 2007. *The Arab-Israeli Conflict: A History.* New York: Oxford University Press. 460p.

Le Troquer, Yann, and Rozenn Hommery al-Oudat. 1999. "From Kuwait to Jordan: The Palestinians' Third Exodus." *Journal of Palestine Studies* 28, no. 3 (Spring): 37–51.

Levins, John. 1997. *Days of Fear: The Inside Story of the Iraqi Invasion and Occupation of Kuwait.* Dubai: Motivate Publishing. 672p.

Levitt, Matthew. 2002. *Targeting Terror: U.S. Policy Toward Middle Eastern State Sponsors and Terrorist Organizations, Post–September 11.* Washington, DC: Washington Institute for Near East Policy. 141p.

Lewis, Bernard. 1968. *The Emergence of Modern Turkey.* 2d ed. New York: Oxford University Press. 530p.

———. 1973. *Islam in History: Ideas, Men, and Events in the Middle East.* New York: Library Press. 349p.

———. 2002. *The Arabs in History.* 6th ed. Oxford and New York: Oxford University Press. 240p.

Lewis, Norman N. 1953. "Lebanon: The Mountain and Its Terraces." *Geography Review* 43, no. 1 (Jan.): 1–14.

———. 1987. *Nomads and Settlers in Syria and Jordan, 1800–1980.* Cambridge Middle East Library. Cambridge: Cambridge University Press. 249p.

Lewis, Peter G. 1982. "The Politics of Iranian Place-Names." *Geography Review* 72, no. 1 (Jan.): 99–102.

Lewis, Samuel W. 1999. "The United States and Israel: Evolution of an Unwritten Alliance." *Middle East Journal* 53, no. 3 (Summer): 364–378.

Liel, Alon. 2001. *Turkey in the Middle East: Oil, Islam, and Politics.* Boulder: Lynne Rienner. 253p.

Limbert, John W. 1987. *Iran: At War with History.* Profiles: Nations of the Contemporary Middle East. Boulder: Westview Press. 186p.

Lindsay, James M., and Ray Takeyh. 2010. "After Iran Gets the Bomb." *Foreign Affairs* (Mar.–Apr.).

Lippman, Thomas W. 2004. *Inside the Mirage: America's Fragile Partnership with Saudi Arabia.* Boulder: Westview Press. 390p.

Little, Douglas. 1990. "Cold War and Covert Action: The United States and Syria, 1945–1958." *Middle East Journal* 44, no. 1 (Winter): 51–75.

Long, David E. 1997. *The Kingdom of Saudi Arabia.* Gainesville: University Press of Florida. 154p.

———. 2005. *Culture and Customs of Saudi Arabia.* Westport, CT: Greenwood Press. 110p.

Long, David E., Bernard Reich, and Mark J. Gasiorowski 2007. *The Government and Politics of the Middle East and Northern Africa.* 5th ed. Boulder: Westview Press. 567p.

Long, Jerry M. 2001. "The Politics of Religion and the Persian Gulf War, 1990–1991." Ph.D. diss., Baylor University. 323p.

Long, Mark. 2009. "Ribat, al-Qa'ida, and the Challenge for Foreign Policy." *Middle East Journal* 63, no. 1: 31–47.

Lorentz, John H. 2006. *Historical Dictionary of Iran.* 2 ed. Lanham, MD: Scarecrow Press. 368p.

Lorenz, Joseph P. 1990. *Egypt and the Arabs: Foreign Policy and the Search for National Identity.* Boulder: Westview Press. 184p.

Lorimer, J. G. 1915. *Gazetteer of the Persian Gulf, Oman, and Central Arabia.* 4 vols. Calcutta: Superintendent of Government Printing.

Lucas, Russell E. 2004. "Jordan: The Death of Normalization with Israel." *Middle East Journal* 58, no. 1 (Winter): 93–111.

Lustick, Ian. 1980. *Arabs in the Jewish State: Israel's Control of a National Minority.* Modern Middle East Series no. 6. Austin: University of Texas Press. 385p.

———. 1988. *For the Land and the Lord: Jewish Fundamentalism in Israel.* New York: Council on Foreign Relations Press. 256p.

———. 1997. "Has Israel Annexed East Jerusalem?" *Middle East Policy* 5, no. 1 (Jan.): 34–45.

MacAdam, Henry Innes. 2002. *Geography, Urbanisation, and Settlement Patterns in the Roman Near East.* Aldershot, Hampshire, UK, and Burlington, VT: Ashgate and Variorum. 350p.

Mackinder, Sir Halford J. 1904. "The Geographical Pivot of History." *Geographical Journal* 23: 421–444.

———. 1919. *Democratic Ideals and Reality: A Study in the Politics of Reconstruction.* New York: Holt. 266p.

Mackintosh-Smith, Tim. 1999. "The Last Place in Yemen." *Saudi Aramco World,* Sept.–Oct., 8–21.

Mahoney, John, Jane Adas, and Robert Norberg. 2007. *Burning Issues: Understanding and Misunderstanding the Middle East—a 40-Year Chronicle.* New York: Americans for Middle East Understanding. 439p.

Maisel, Sebastian. 2008. "Social Change Amidst Terror and Discrimination of Yezidis in the New Iraq." *Middle East Institute Policy Brief no. 18,* Aug. www.mei.edu/Portals/0/Publications/Yezidis-in-the-New-Iraq.pdf.

Maisels, Charles Keith. 1993. *The Emergence of Civilization: From Hunting and Gathering to Agriculture, Cities, and the State in the Near East.* London: Routledge. 395p.

Makiya, Kanan. 1998. *Republic of Fear: The Politics of Modern Iraq.* 2d ed. Berkeley and Los Angeles: University of California Press. 323p.

Makram-Ebeid, Mona. 1989. "Political Opposition in Egypt: Democratic Myth or Reality?" *Middle East Journal* 43, no. 3 (Summer): 423–436.

Malinowski, Jon C., ed. 2004. *Geographic Perspectives: Iraq.* Guilford, CT: McGraw-Hill. 96p.

Malville, J. M., et al. 1998. "Megaliths and Neolithic Astronomy in Southern Egypt." *Nature* 392, no. 6675: 488–491.

Mandaville, James P., Jr. 1984. "Studies in the Flora of Arabia, XI: Some Historical and Geographical Aspects of a Principal Floristic Frontier." *Notes from the Royal Botanic Garden, Edinburgh* 42, no. 1: 1–15.

———. 1990. *Flora of Eastern Saudi Arabia.* London: Kegan Paul International. 482p.

———. n.d. "Plants [of the Oman Mountains]." In *The Scientific Results of the Oman Flora and Fauna Survey 1975.* A Journal of Oman Studies Special Report. Published by the Ministry of Information and Culture, Sultanate of Oman. 39p.

Mandelbaum, Judy. 2010. "Judy's World." *Open Salon,* Mar. 15, http://open.salon.com/blog/judy_mandelbaum.

Mango, Andrew. 1999. *Ataturk: The Biography of the Founder of Modern Turkey.* New York: Overlook Press. 666p.

Ma'oz, Moshe. 1999. *Middle East Minorities: Between Integration and Conflict.* Washington, DC: Washington Institute for Near East Policy. 111p.

Marlowe, John. 1962. *The Persian Gulf in the Twentieth Century.* London: Cresset. 278p.

Marr, Phebe. 2004. *The Modern History of Iraq.* 2d ed. Boulder: Westview Press. 392p.

Masalha, Nur. 2003. *The Politics of Denial: Israel and the Palestinian Refugee Problem.* Sterling, VA, and London: Pluto. 298p.

Mastney, Vojtech, and R. Craig Nation, eds. 1997. *Turkey Between East and West: New Challenges for a Rising Regional Power.* Boulder: Westview Press. 296p.

Matheson, Sylvia A. 1976. *Persia: An Archaeological Guide.* 2d rev. ed. London: Faber. 358p.

Mattar, Philip, ed. 2000. *Encyclopedia of the Palestinians.* New York: Facts on File. 514p.

Matthews, Weldon C. 2006. *Confronting an Empire, Constructing a Nation: Arab Nationalists and Popular Politics in Mandate Palestine.* New York: I. B. Tauris. 342p.

Mauger, Thierry. 1988a. *The Bedouins of Arabia.* Translated by Khia Mason and Igor Persan. Paris: Souffles. 139p.

———. 1988b. *Flowered Men and Green Slopes of Arabia.* Translated by Khia Mason. Paris: Souffles. 189p.

McCreal, Chris. 2006a. "Brothers in Arms: Israel's Secret Pact with Pretoria." *The Guardian,* Feb. 7.

———. 2006b. "Worlds Apart." *The Guardian,* Feb. 6.

McDowall, David. 2000. *A Modern History of the Kurds.* 2d rev. ed. London: I. B. Tauris. 515p.

McGowan, Daniel A., and Marc Ellis. 1998. *Remembering Deir Yassin: The Future of Israel and Palestine.* New York: Olive Branch Press. 150p.

McKee, Edwin D., ed. 1979. *A Study of Global Sand Seas.* U.S. Geological Survey Professional Paper 1052. Prepared in cooperation with the National Aeronautics and Space Administration. Washington, DC: U.S. Government Printing Office. 429p.

McManners, John, ed. 1990. *The Oxford Illustrated History of Christianity.* Oxford: Oxford University Press. 724p.

Meadows, Ian. 1994. "Lebanon: Up from the Ashes." *Saudi Aramco World,* Jan.–Feb.

Mearsheimer, Stephen M., and John J. Walt. 2008. *The Israel Lobby and U.S. Foreign Policy.* New York: Farrar Straus Giroux. 484p.

Mehr, Farhang. 1997. *A Colonial Legacy: The Dispute over the Islands of Abu Musa and the Greater and Lesser Tumbs.* Lanham, MD: University Press of America. 215p.

Meir, Alon ben. 2009. "Turkish-Israeli Relations: Mending a Strained Alliance," *Journal of Turkish Weekly,* Oct. 25. www.turkishweekly.net/.

Menashri, David, ed. 1998. *Central Asia Meets the Middle East.* London and Portland, OR: Frank Cass. 240p.

———. 2001. *Post-Revolutionary Politics in Iran: Religion, Society, and Power.* London and Portland, OR: Frank Cass. 356p.

Middle East and North Africa. 2003. 49th ed. London: Europa Publications. 1,353p.

Middle East Policy. 1994. "U.S. Policy Toward Iran and Iraq." Vol. 3, no. 1.

———. 1995. "Interview with Sultan Qaboos bin Said Al Said." Vol. 3, no. 4 (April): 1–6.

Middle East Policy Council. 2003. "Aftershocks of the Iraq War: What Purposes Have Been Fulfilled?" *Middle East Policy* 10, no. 3 (Fall): 1–21.

Middle East Quarterly. 1998. "Still Special? The U.S.-Israel Relationship." Vol. 5, no. 4 (Dec.): 53–65.

Middle East Research Institute (MERI), University of Pennsylvania. Mostly mid-1980s. Reports on most major Middle East states, titles with respective state names. London: Croom Helm.

Mideast Peace Pulse. 2009. "Syria Seeks U.S. Mediation in Peace Negotiations." *Israel Policy Forum,* Dec. 18.

Mikesell, Marvin W. 1969. "The Deforestation of Mount Lebanon." *Geography Review* 59, no. 1 (Jan.): 1–28.

Milani, Mohsen M. 2001. "Reform and Resistance in the Islamic Republic of Iran." In *Iran at the Crossroads,* edited by John L. Esposito and Rouhollah K. Ramazani. New York: Palgrave. 248p.

Miller, Aaron D. 2008. *The Much Too Promised Land: America's Elusive Search for Arab-Israeli Peace.* New York: Bantam. 407p.

Minerals Yearbook. Annual. U.S. Geological Survey, Bureau of Mines. http://minerals.er.usgs.gov/minerals/pubs/.

Ministry of Agriculture and Water [Saudi Arabia]. 1984. In cooperation with the Saudi Arabian–United States Joint Commission on Economic Cooperation. *Water Atlas of Saudi Arabia.* Riyadh: Saudi Arabian Printing. 112p.

Mitchell, William A. 1976. "Reconstruction After Disaster: The Gediz Earthquake of 1970." *Geography Review* 66, no. 3 (July): 296–313.

Mobley, Richard A. 2003. "The Tunbs and Abu Musa Islands: Britain's Perspective." *Middle East Journal* 57, no. 4 (Autumn): 627–645.

Monshipouri, Mahmood. 1998. "Iran's Search for the New Pragmatism." *Middle East Policy* 6, no. 2 (Oct.): 95–112.

Montaigne, Fen. 1999. "Iran: Testing the Waters of Reform." *National Geographic,* July, 2–33.

Moore, Clement Henry. 1986. "Money and Power: The Dilemma of the Egyptian Infitah." *Middle East Journal* 40, no. 4 (Autumn): 634–650.

Moore, John Norton, ed. 1974. *The Arab-Israeli Conflict.* 3 vols. Sponsored by the American Society of International Law. Princeton: Princeton University Press, 1974. Vol. 1, 1,067p.; vol. 2, 1,193p.; vol. 3, 1,248p.

Moore, Peter W., and Andrew Schrank. 2003. "Commerce and Conflict: U.S. Effort to Counter Terrorism with Trade May Backfire." *Middle East Policy* 10, no. 3 (Fall): 112–120.

Morgan, Adrian. 2007. "Women Under Islam: Female Genital Mutilation." *Spero,* July 9, www.speroforum.com/site/print.asp?idarticle=10250.

Morris, Benny. 1989. *The Birth of the Palestinian Refugee Problem, 1947–1949.* Cambridge: Cambridge University Press. 380p.

———. 1995. "Falsifying the Record." *Journal of Palestine Studies* 24, no. 3 (Spring): 44–62.

———. 1998. "Refabricating 1948." *Journal of Palestine Studies* 27, no. 2 (Winter): 81–95.

———. 2001. *Righteous Victims: A History of the Zionist-Arab Conflict, 1881–2001.* New York: Vintage. 784p.

———. 2004. *The Birth of the Palestinian Refugee Problem Revisited.* Cambridge: Cambridge University Press. 640p.

———. 2008. *1948: A History of the First Arab-Israeli War.* New Haven: Yale University Press. 420p.

———. 2009. *One State, Two States: Resolving the Israel/Palestine Conflict.* New Haven: Yale University Press. 256p.

Muasher, Marwan. 2008. *The Arab Center: The Promise of Moderation.* New Haven: Yale University Press. 312p.

Muhanna, Elias. 2009. "Deconstructing the Popular Vote in Lebanon's Election." *Mideast Monitor*, July–Aug. www.mideastmonitor.org/issues/0907/0907_3.htm.

Mundy, Martha, and Basim Musallam, eds. 2000. *The Transformation of Nomadic Society in the Arab East.* Cambridge: Cambridge University Press. 249p.

Murden, Simon W. 2002. *Islam, the Middle East, and the New Global Hegemony.* Boulder: Lynne Rienner. 235p.

Nabir, Mordechai. 1988. *Saudi Arabia in the Oil Era.* Boulder: Westview Press. 247p.

Nachmani, Amikam. 1998. "The Remarkable Turkish-Israeli Tie." *Middle East Quarterly* 5, no. 2 (June): 19–29.

Nakhleh, Emile A. 1988. "The West Bank and Gaza: Twenty Years Later." *Middle East Journal* 42, no. 2 (Spring): 209–226.

The National (Abu Dhabi, UAE). 2009. "Joint Statement of the Foreign Ministers of the UAE, Cape Verde, Costa Rica, Iceland, Singapore, and Slovenia." Dec. 9.

National Atlas of United Arab Emirates. 1993. Al-Ayn: UAE University.

National Geographic Society. 1983. *Exploring Our Living Planet.* Washington, DC: National Geographic Society. 366p.

———. 2001. *Peoples of the World.* Washington, DC: National Geographic Society. 304p.

———. 2003. *Atlas of the Middle East.* Washington, DC: National Geographic Society. 96p.

———. 2004. *National Geographic Atlas of the World.* 8th ed. Washington, DC: National Geographic Society. 137 double pages plus index.

Naval Intelligence Division [UK]. 1943. *Palestine and Trans-jordan.* Geographical Handbook Series BR 514. Oxford: Oxford University Press for H. M. Stationery Office. 621p.

Netton, Ian Richard, ed. 1986. *Arabia and the Gulf: From Traditional Society to Modern States.* Totowa, NJ: Barnes and Noble. 259p.

Newman, David. 1999. *The Dynamics of Territorial Change: A Political Geography of the Arab-Israeli Conflict.* Boulder: Westview Press. 256p.

Niblock, Tim. 1980. *Social and Economic Development in the Arab Gulf.* New York: St. Martin's. 242p.

———, ed. 2007. *The Political Economy of Saudi Arabia.* London: Routledge. 254p.

Nisan, Mordechai. 2002. *Minorities in the Middle East: A History of Struggle and Self-Expression.* 2d ed. Jefferson, NC: McFarland. 341p.

Norton, Augustus R. 1987. *Amal and the Shi'a: Struggle for the Soul of Lebanon.* Austin: University of Texas Press. 238p.

———. 2007. *Hezbollah: A Short History.* Princeton: Princeton University Press. 159p.

Norwich, John Julius. 1997. *A Short History of Byzantium.* New York: Knopf. 431p.

Nugent, Jeffrey B., and Theodore Thomas, eds. 1985. *Bahrain and the Gulf: Past Perspectives and Alternative Futures.* New York: St. Martin's. 221p.

O'Ballance, Edgar. 1999. *Civil War in Lebanon, 1975–92.* New York: St. Martin's. 240p.

Olsson, Tord, Elisabeth Ozdalga, and Catharina Raudvere, eds. 1998. *Alevi Identity.* Istanbul: Swedish Research Institute in Istanbul. 210p.

O'Reilly, Marc J. 1998. "Omanibalancing: Oman Confronts an Uncertain Future." *Middle East Journal* 52, no. 1 (Winter): 70–84.

———. 2008. *Unexceptional: America's Empire in the Persian Gulf, 1941–2007.* Lanham: Lexington Books. 300p.

Oren, Eliezer D., ed. 2000. *The Sea Peoples and Their World: A Reassessment.* Philadelphia: University Museum and University of Pennsylvania. 360p.

Oren, Michael B. 2002. *Six Days of War: June 1967 and the Making of the Modern Middle East*. Oxford: Oxford University Press. 446p.

———. 2007. *Power, Faith, and Fantasy: America in the Middle East: 1776 to the Present*. New York: Norton. 791p.

Orni, Efraim, and Elisha Efrat. 1980. *Geography of Israel*. 4th ed. Jerusalem: Israel Universities Press. 556p.

O'Shea, Maria T. 2003. *Trapped Between the Map and Reality: Geography and Perceptions of Kurdistan*. New York: Routledge. 258p.

Ottaway, David B. 2008. *The King's Messenger: Prince Bandar bin Sultan and America's Tangled Relationship with Saudi Arabia*. New York: Walker. 336p.

Owen, Roger. 1999. "Inter-Arab Economic Relations During the Twentieth Century." In *Middle East Dilemma: The Politics and Economics of Arab Integration*, edited by Michael C. Hudson. New York: Columbia University Press.

———, ed. 2000a. *New Perspectives on Property and Land in the Middle East*. Cambridge: Harvard University Press. 341p.

———. 2000b. *State, Power, and Politics in the Making of the Modern Middle East*. 2d ed. London and New York: Routledge. 259p.

Oz, Amos. 1993. *In the Land of Israel (Harvest in Translation)*. New York: Harcourt Brace. 275p.

Pacific Institute. n.d. "The World's Water: Water Conflict Chronology." www.worldwater.org/conflict.

Packer, George. 2005. *The Assassins' Gate: America in Iraq*. New York: Farrar, Straus, and Giroux. 467p.

———. 2007. "Betrayed." *New Yorker*, Mar. 26.

Palka, Eugene J., ed. 2004. *Geographic Perspectives: Afghanistan*. Guilford, CT: McGraw-Hill. 104p.

Palmer, Alan. 2009. *The Decline and Fall of the Ottoman Empire*. New York: Barnes and Noble. 354p.

Pampanini, Andrea. 1997. *Cities from the Arabian Desert: The Building of Jubail and Yanbu in Saudi Arabia*. Westport, CT: Praeger. 209p.

Pappé, Ilan. 1997. "Post-Zionist Critique on Israel and the Palestinians." *Journal of Palestine Studies* 26, no. 2 (Winter): 29–41.

———, ed. 1999. *The Israel/Palestine Question*. London: Routledge, 1999. 278p.

———. 2004. *A History of Modern Palestine: One Land, Two Peoples*. Cambridge: Cambridge University Press. 333p.

———. 2006. *The Ethnic Cleansing of Palestine*. Oxford: Oneworld Publications. 261p.

Parker, Richard B, ed. 1993. *The Politics of Miscalculation in the Middle East*. Indiana Series in Arab and Islamic Studies. Bloomington: Indiana University Press. 320p.

———, ed. 1996. *The Six-Day War: A Retrospective*. Gainesville: University Press of Florida. 345p.

———. 2001. *The October War: A Retrospective*. Gainesville: University Press of Florida. 396p.

Parsi, Trita. 2007. *Treacherous Alliance: The Secret Dealings of Israel, Iran, and the U.S.* New Haven: Yale University Press. 361p.

Pearcy, G. Etzel. 1964. *The Middle East: An Indefinable Region*. Department of State Publication 7684. Washington, DC: U.S. Government Printing Office. Updated from an article in the Department of State Bulletin, Mar. 23, 1959. 12p.

Peck, Malcolm C. 1986. *The United Arab Emirates: A Venture in Unity*. Profiles: Nations of the Contemporary Middle East. Boulder: Westview Press. 176p.

Pedahzur, Ami, and Arie Perliger. 2009. *Jewish Terrorism in Israel*. New York: Columbia University Press. 243p.

Peimani, Hooman. 2001. *The Caspian Pipeline Dilemma: Political Games and Economic Losses*. Westport, CT: Praeger. 134p.

Peretz, Don. 1994. *The Middle East Today*. 6th ed. Westport, CT: Praeger. 593p.

———. 1999. "The Significance of Israel." *Middle East Journal* 53, no. 3 (Summer): 357–363.

Peretz, Don, and Gideon Doron. 1997. *The Government and Politics of Israel*. 3d ed. Boulder: Westview Press. 308p.

Perthes, Volker. 1992. "The Syrian Economy in the 1980s." *Middle East Journal* 46, no. 1 (Winter): 37–58.

Peterson, J. E. 1983. *The Politics of Middle Eastern Oil*. Washington, DC: Middle East Institute. 529p.

———. 2001. "The Nature of Succession in the Gulf." *Middle East Journal* 55, no. 4 (Autumn): 580–601.

———. 2002. *Saudi Arabia and the Illusion of Security*. London: Oxford University Press. 104p.

———. 2004a. "Oman: Three and a Half Decades of Change and Development." *Middle East Policy* 11, no. 2 (Summer): 125–137.

———. 2004b. "Oman's Diverse Society: Northern Oman." *Middle East Journal* 58, no. 1 (Winter): 32–51.

———. 2004c. "Oman's Diverse Society: Southern Oman." *Middle East Journal* 58, no. 2 (Spring): 254–269.

Pew Forum on Religion and Public Life. 2009. *Mapping the Global Muslim Population*. Washington, DC: Pew Forum on Religion and Public Life.

Philby, H. St. John B. 1977. *Arabia of the Wahhabis*. New impression, with additions. 1928. Reprint, London: Cass, 1977. 422p.

Philippov, Michael. 2008. "Emigration from Israel: The Overlooked or Hidden Facts." Israel Democracy Institute, Nov. www.idi.org.il/sites/english/OpEds/Pages/EmigrationfromIsrael.aspx.

Phillips, David. 2005. *Losing Iraq*. Boulder: Westview Press. 292p.

Picard, Elizabeth. 1996. *Lebanon: A Sheltered Country*. New York: Holmes and Meier Publishers. 202p.

Pillar, Paul R. 2001. *Terrorism and U.S. Foreign Policy*. Washington, DC: Brookings Institution Press. 272p.

Pipes, Daniel. 1990. *Greater Syria: The History of an Ambition*. New York: Oxford University Press. 240p.

Pitcher, Donald Edgar. 1972. *A Historical Geography of the Ottoman Empire: From Earliest Times to the End of the Sixteenth Century*. Leiden: E. J. Brill. 171p. + 29 folded maps.

Plaut, Steven. 1999. "The Collapsing Syrian Economy." *Middle East Quarterly* 6, no. 3 (Sept.): 3–14.

Pollack, Kenneth M. 2002. *The Threatening Storm: The Case for Invading Iraq*. 1 ed. New York: Random House, 2002. 494p.

———. 2003. "Securing the Gulf." *Foreign Affairs* 82, no. 4 (July–Aug.): 2–16.

———. 2004. *The Persian Puzzle: The Conflict Between Iran and America*. New York: Random House. 539p.

Pope Benedict XVI. 2010. "If You Want to Cultivate Peace, Protect Creation." www.vatican.va/holy _father/benedict_xvi/messages/peace/documents/hf_ben-xvi_mes_20091208_xliii-world-day -peace_en.html.

Potter, Lawrence, and Gary G. Sick, eds. 2002. *Security in the Persian Gulf: Origins, Obstacles, and the Search for Consensus*. New York: Palgrave. 284p.

Potts, Daniel T. 1997. *Mesopotamian Civilization: The Material Foundations*. Ithaca: Cornell University Press. 366p.

———. 2000. *Ancient Magan: The Secrets of Tell Abraq*. London: Trident. 144p.

Preston, Zoe. 2003. *The Crystallization of the Iraqi State: Geopolitical Function and Form*. Oxford, UK: Peter Lang. 335p.

Pridham, B. R., ed. 1987. *Oman: Economic, Social, and Strategic Developments*. London: Croom Helm. 254p.

Quandt, William B. 2001. *Peace Process: American Diplomacy and the Arab-Israel Conflict Since 1967*. Rev ed. Washington, DC: Brookings Institution Press; Berkeley and Los Angeles: University of California Press. 488p.

Rabi, Uzi. 2009. "Qatar's Relations with Israel: Challenging Arab and Gulf Norms." *Middle East Journal* 63, no. 3: 443–459.

Rabil, Robert G. 2001. "The Ineffective Role of the U.S. in the U.S.-Israeli-Syrian Relationship." *Middle East Journal* 55, no. 3 (Summer): 415–438.

———. 2003. *Embattled Neighbors: Syria, Israel, and Lebanon*. Boulder: Lynne Rienner. 307p.

———. 2006. *Syria, the United States, and the War on Terror in the Middle East*. Westport, CT: Praeger Security International. 208p.

Rabinovich, Itamar. 1985. *The War for Lebanon, 1970–1985*. Ithaca: Cornell University Press. 262p.

———. 1998. *The Brink of Peace: The Israeli-Syrian Negotiation*. Princeton: Princeton University Press. 283p.

Radwan, L. 1998. "Water Management in the Egyptian Delta: Problems of Wastage and Inefficiency." *Geographical Journal* 164, no. 2: 129–138.

Ragette, Friedrich, ed. 1983. *The Beirut of Tomorrow: Planning for Reconstruction*. Beirut: American University of Beirut. 141p.

Rahman, H. 1997. *The Making of the Gulf War: Origins of Kuwait's Long-Standing Territorial Dispute with Iraq*. Berkshire, UK: Ithaca. 378p.

Rahman, Mushtaqur, ed. 1987. *Muslim World: Geography and Development*. Lanham, MD: University Press of America. 190p.

Ramazani, Rouhallah K. 1979. *International Straits of the World.* Vol. 3, *The Persian Gulf and the Strait of Hormuz.* Alphen aan den Rijn, Netherlands: Sijthoff and Noordhoff. 180p.

———. 1998. "The Shifting Premise of Iran's Foreign Policy: Towards a Democratic Peace." *Middle East Journal* 52, no. 2 (Spring): 177–187.

———. 2001. "Reflections on Iran's Foreign Policy: Defining the National Interest." In *Iran at the Crossroads,* edited by John L. Esposito and Rouhollah K. Ramazani. New York: Palgrave. 248p.

Randal, Jonathan C. 1998. *After Such Knowledge, What Forgiveness? My Encounters with Kurdistan.* Boulder: Westview Press. 368p.

Raschka, Marilyn. 1996. "Beirut Digs Out." *Archaeology* 49, no. 4 (July–Aug.): 44–50.

Raymond, Andre. 2000. *Cairo.* Translated by Willard Wood. Cambridge: Harvard University Press. 436p.

Reddaway, John. 1986. *Burdened with Cyprus: The British Connection.* London: Weidenfeld and Nicholson. 237p.

Redman, Charles L. 1978. *The Rise of Civilization: From Early Farmers to Urban Society in the Ancient Near East.* San Francisco: Freeman. 367p.

———. 1994. "Mesopotamia and the First Cities, 4000 BC–539 BC." In *Old World Civilizations: The Rise of Cities and States,* edited by Goran Burenholt. New York: HarperCollins.

Reich, Bernard, and Gershon R. Kieval. 1993. *Israel: Land of Tradition and Conflict.* 2d ed. Boulder: Westview Press. 236p.

Reiter, Yitzhak. 2004. "The Palestinian-Transjordanian Rift: Economic Might and Political Power in Jordan." *Middle East Journal* 58, no. 1 (Winter): 72–92.

Rempel, Terry. 1997. "The Significance of Israel's Partial Annexation of East Jerusalem." *Middle East Journal* 51, no. 4 (Autumn): 520–534.

Reston, James. 2007. *The Zionist Masquerade: The Birth of the Anglo-Zionist Alliance 1914–1918.* New York: Palgrave Macmillan. 155p.

Reuters. 2009. "Cyprus Peace Talks to Intensify in January: U.N." Dec. 21.

Richard, Suzanne, ed. 2003. *Near Eastern Archaeology: A Reader.* Winona Lake, IN: Eisenbrauns. 486p.

Richards, Alan. 2003. "'Modernity and Economic Development': The 'New' American Messianism." *Middle East Policy* 10, no. 3 (Fall): 56–78.

Richards, Alan, and John Waterbury. 1996. *A Political Economy of the Middle East.* 2d ed. Boulder: Westview Press. 464p.

Ricks, Thomas E. 2007. *Fiasco: The American Military Adventure in Iraq.* Boston: Penguin (Non-Classics). 492p.

———. 2009. *The Gamble: General David Petraeus and the American Military Adventure in Iraq, 2006–2008.* New York: Penguin. 394p.

Riphenburg, Carol J. 1998. *Oman: Political Development in a Changing World.* Westport, CT: Praeger. 248p.

Ritter, Scott. 1999. *Endgame: Solving the Iraq Problem—Once and for All.* New York: Simon and Schuster. 240p.

Rivlin, Paul. 2009. *Arab Economies in the Twenty-first Century.* New York: Cambridge University Press. 328p.

Roberts, Paul. 2004. *The End of Oil: On the Edge of a Perilous New World.* Boston: Houghton Mifflin. 389p.

Robins, Philip. 2004. *A History of Jordan.* Cambridge: Cambridge University Press. 243p.

Robinson, Andrew. 1995. *The Story of Writing.* London: Thames and Hudson. 224p.

Rodenbeck, Max. 1998. *Cairo: The City Victorious.* London: Macmillan. 395p.

Rogan, Eugene L. 2009. *The Arabs: A History.* New York: Basic Books. 532p.

Rogan, Eugene L., and Avi Shlaim, eds. 2001. *The War for Palestine: Rewriting the History of 1948.* Cambridge: Cambridge University Press. 234p.

Rogers, Peter, and Peter Lydon, eds. 1994. *Water in the Arab World: Perspectives and Prognoses.* Cambridge: Harvard University Press. 369p.

Rose, Euclid. 2004. "OPEC's Dominance of the Global Oil Market." *Middle East Journal* 58, no. 3 (Summer): 424–443.

Ross, Dennis. 2004. *The Missing Peace: The Inside Story of the Fight for the Middle East Peace.* New York: Farrar, Straus, and Giroux. 840p.

Rouyer, Alwyn. 2000. *Turning Water into Politics: The Water Issue in the Palestinian-Israeli Conflict.* New York: St. Martin's. 297p.

Rowley, Gwyn. 1992. "Human Space, Territoriality, Conflict: An Exploratory Study with References to Israel and the West Bank." *Canadian Geographer* 36, no. 3: 210–221.

———. 1999. "The Tragedy of the Common Waters: Towards the Deepening Crisis Within the Jordan Basin." *Arab World Geographer* 2, no. 1: 26–40.

———. 2008. "Continuing Conflict or Compromise? Water and Land in the Jordan Basin." *Arab World Geographer* 7, nos. 1–2: 70–95.

Roy, Olivier. 1999. "The Crisis of Religious Legitimacy in Iran." *Middle East Journal* 53, no. 2 (Spring): 201–216.

Roy, Sara. 1995. *The Gaza Strip: The Political Economy of De-development.* Washington, DC: Institute for Palestine Studies. 375p.

———. 2006. *Failing Peace: Gaza and the Palestinian-Israeli Conflict.* Ann Arbor: Pluto Press. 332p.

Rubenberg, Cheryl A. 2003. *The Palestinians: In Search of a Just Peace.* Boulder: Lynne Rienner. 485p.

Rubin, Barry, ed. 1999. *The Transformation of Palestinian Politics from Revolution to State-Building.* Cambridge: Harvard University Press. 277p.

———. 2003. *Revolutionaries and Reformers: Contemporary Islamist Movements in the Middle East.* Albany: State University of New York Press. 231p.

Rudloff, Willy. 1981. *World Climates.* Stuttgart: Wissenschaftliche Verlagsgesellschaft mbH. 632p.

Rugh, William A. 1996. "The Foreign Policy of the United Arab Emirates." *Middle East Journal* 50, no. 1 (Winter): 57–70.

———. 2004. *Arab Mass Media: Newspapers, Radio, and Television in Arab Politics.* Westport, CT: Praeger. 259p.

Runciman, Steven. 1954. *A History of the Crusades.* 3 vols. Cambridge: Cambridge University Press.

Ryan, Curtis R. 2002. *Jordan in Transition: From Hussein to Abdullah.* Boulder: Lynne Rienner. 159p.

———. 2006. "The Odd Couple: Ending the Jordanian-Syrian 'Cold War.'" *Middle East Journal* 60, no. 1 (Winter): 33–56.

Saad-Ghorayeb, Amal. 2002. *Hizb'ullah: Politics and Religion.* London: Pluto. 254p.

Al-Sabah. 1980. *The Oil Economy of Kuwait.* Boston: Kegan Paul. 166p.

Sachar, Howard M. 1976. *A History of Israel from the Rise of Zionism to Our Time.* New York: Knopf. 932p.

———. 1987. *A History of Israel from the Aftermath of the Yom Kippur War.* New York: Oxford University Press. 319p.

Safi, Omid. 2003. *Progressive Muslims: On Justice, Gender, and Pluralism.* Oxford: Oneworld Publications. 351p.

Saggs, H. W. F. 1989. *Civilization Before Greece and Rome.* New Haven: Yale University Press. 322p.

———. 1995. *Babylonians.* Vol. 1, *Peoples of the Past.* Norman: University of Oklahoma Press. 192p.

Said, Edward W. 1994. *The Politics of Dispossession: The Struggle for Palestinian Self-Determination, 1969–1994.* New York: Pantheon. 450p.

Said, Edward W., and Christopher Hitchens, eds. 1988. *Blaming the Victims: Spurious Scholarship and the Palestine Question.* London: Verso. 296p.

Said, Rushdi. 1962. *The Geology of Egypt.* Amsterdam: Elsevier. 377p.

———. 1981. *The Geological Evolution of the River Nile.* New York: Springer-Verlag. 151p.

Salamé, Ghassan, ed. 1987. *The Foundations of the Arab State.* London: Croom Helm. 260p.

Salameh, Elias. 1990. "Jordan's Water Resources: Development and Future Prospects." *American-Arab Affairs* 33 (Summer): 69–77.

Salhani, Claude. 2003. "Syria at the Crossroads." *Middle East Policy* 10, no. 3 (Fall): 136–143.

Salibi, Kamal. 1988. *A House of Many Mansions: The History of Lebanon Reconsidered.* Berkeley and Los Angeles: University of California Press. 247p.

———. 1998. *The Modern History of Jordan.* 2d ed. New York: I. B. Tauris. 298p.

Salt, Jeremy. 2008. *The Unmaking of the Middle East: A History of Western Disorder in Arab lands.* Berkeley and Los Angeles: University of California Press. 484p.

Samii, Abbas William. 2008. "A Stable Structure on Shifting Sands: Assessing the Hizbullah-Iran-Syria Relationship." *Middle East Journal* 62, no. 1 (Winter): 32–53.

Sand, Shlomo. 2009. *The Invention of the Jewish People.* New York: Verso. 332p.

Sandler, Shmuel, et al. 1999. "The Religious-Secular Divide in Israeli Politics." *Middle East Policy* 6, no. 4 (June): 137–145.

Sanjan, Ara. 2009. "Déjà Vu: Armenians and the 2009 Parliamentary Elections in Lebanon, 2009." June 29. arasan@ud.umich.edu.

Saqqaf, Abdulaziz Y., ed. 1987. *The Middle East City: Ancient Traditions Confront a Modern World*. New York: Paragon. 393p.

Sasser, Susan M. 2004. "Strangers in Our Midst." *Jewish Currents*, July. www.jewishcurrents.org.

Saudi Aramco and Its World: Arabia and the Middle East. 1995. Rev. ed. Dhahran: Saudi Arabian Oil Company. 291p.

Save the Children. Annual *State of the World's Mothers, 2009*. Westport, CT: Save the Children. wwwsavethechildren.org.

Sayari, Sabri. 1997. "Turkey and the Middle East in the 1990s." *Journal of Palestine Studies* 26, no. 3 (Spring): 44–55.

Sayigh, Rosemary. 1998. "Dis/Solving the 'Refugee Problem.'" *Middle East Report* 207 (Summer): 19–23.

Sayigh, Yezid. 1997. *Armed Struggle and the Search for State: The Palestinian National Movement, 1949–1993*. New York: Oxford University Press. 953p.

Schalt, Joel. 2009. *Israel vs. Utopia*. New York: Akashic Books. 253p.

Schick, Irvin C., and Ertugrul Ahmet Tonak, eds. 1987. *Turkey in Transition: New Perspectives*. New York: Oxford University Press. 405p.

Schiff, Zeev, and Ehud Yaari. 1989. *Intifada: The Palestinian Uprising—Israel's Third Front*. Edited and translated by Ina Friedman. New York: Simon and Schuster. 356p.

Schmandt-Bessarat, Denise. 1978. "The Earliest Precursor of Writing." *Scientific American* 238: 50–59.

Schnell, Izhak, Itzhak Benenson, and Michael Sofer. 1999. "The Spatial Pattern of Arab Industrial Markets in Israel." *Annals* (Association of American Geographers) 89, no. 2 (June): 312–337.

Schofield, Richard. 1993. *Kuwait and Iraq: Historical Claims and Territorial Disputes*. London: Royal Institute of International Affairs. 226p.

———. 1996. "Mending Gulf Fences." *Middle East Insight*, Mar.–Apr., 36–41.

Schulz, E., and J. W. Whitney. 1986. "Vegetation in North-Central Saudi Arabia." *Journal of Arid Environments* 10: 175–186.

Schwarzkopf, H. Norman, with Peter Petre. 1992. *It Doesn't Take a Hero*. New York: Bantam. 530p.

Scientific American. 1983. Special issue, "The Dynamic Earth." Vol. 249, no. 3 (Sept.).

Scott, Max. 2006. *The Kingdom of Saudi Arabia*. London: Stacey International. 247p.

Scoville, Sheila A., ed. 1979. *Gazetteer of Arabia: A Geographical and Tribal History of the Arabian Peninsula*. Vol. 1, *A.–E.* Graz, Austria: Akademische Druck-u. Verlagsanstalt. 742p.

Sela, Avraham, ed. 2002. *The Continuum Political Encyclopedia of the Middle East*. New York: Continuum. 944p.

Serjeant, R. B., ed. 1980. *The Islamic City*. Paris: UNESCO. 210p.

Shadid, Anthony. 2002. *Legacy of the Prophet: Despots, Democrats, and the New Politics of Islam*. Boulder: Westview Press. 340p.

———. 2005. *Night Draws Near Iraq's People in the Shadow of America's War*. New York: Henry Holt. 424p.

Shafik, Nemat. 1999. "Labor Migration and Economic Integration in the Middle East." In *Middle East Dilemma: The Politics and Economics of Arab Integration*, edited by Michael C. Hudson. New York: Columbia University Press.

Shahak, Israel, and Norton Mezvisky. 1994. *Jewish History, Jewish Religion: The Weight of Three Thousand Years*. London: Pluto. 127p.

———. 1999. *Jewish Fundamentalism in Israel*. London: Pluto. 176p.

Shaheen, Murad. 2000. "Questioning the Water-War Phenomenon in the Jordan Basin." *Middle East Policy* 7, no. 3 (June): 137–150.

Shahir, Issa M., and Ayman H. Nasr. 1999. "Using Satellite Images to Detect Land-Use Change in Al-Ain City, United Arab Emirates." *Arab World Geographer* 2, no. 2 (Summer): 139–148.

Shamekh, Ahmed A. 1975. *Spatial Patterns of Bedouin Settlement in al-Qasim Region, Saudi Arabia*. Lexington: University Press of Kentucky. 315p.

Sharan, Shlomo, ed. 2003. *Israel and the Post-Zionists: A Nation at Risk*. Brighton, UK, and Portland, OR: Sussex Academic Press. 261p.

Shaw, Stanford. 1976. *History of the Ottoman Empire and Modern Turkey*. Vol. 1. Cambridge: Cambridge University Press. 351p.

Shaw, Stanford, and Ezel Kural Shaw. 1977. *History of the Ottoman Empire and Modern Turkey*. Vol. 2. Cambridge: Cambridge University Press. 518p.

Shen, P., et al. 2004. "Reconstruction of Patrilineages and Matrilineages of Samaritans and Other Israeli Populations from Y-Chromosome and Mitochondrial DNA Sequence Variation." *Human Mutation* 24: 248–260.

Shindler, Colin. 2008. *A History of Modern Israel.* New York: Cambridge University Press. 350p.

Shipler, David K. 1986. *Arab and Jew: Wounded Spirits in a Promised Land.* New York: Times Books. 596p.

Shlaim, Avi. 1990. *The Politics of Partition: King Abdullah, the Zionists, and Palestine, 1921–1951.* New York: Columbia University Press. 465p.

———. 2000. *The Iron Wall: Israel and the Arab World.* New York: Norton. 670p.

Shohat, Ella. 1999. "The Invention of the Mizrahim." *Journal of Palestine Studies* 29, no. 1 (Autumn): 6–20.

Shoup, John A. 2008. *Culture and Customs of Syria.* Westport, CT: Greenwood. 165p.

Sick, Gary. 2001. "The Clouded Mirror: The United States and Iran, 1979–1999." In *Iran at the Crossroads,* edited by John L. Esposito and Rouhollah K. Ramazani. New York: Palgrave. 248p.

Sicker, Martin. 2001. *The Middle East in the Twentieth Century.* Westport, CT: Praeger. 293p.

Sifry, Micah, and Christopher Cerf, eds. 2003. *The Iraq War Reader: History, Documents, Opinions.* New York: Touchstone, published by Simon and Schuster. 715p.

Silverstein, Ken. 2007. "Six Questions for Joost Hillermann on Blowback from the Iraq-Iran War." *Harper's Magazine,* July 5.

Simon, Reeva S., Michael M. Laskier, and Sara Reguer, eds. 2003. *The Jews of the Middle East and North Africa in Modern Times.* New York: Columbia University Press. 549p.

Simon, Steven, and Jonathan Stevenson. 2004. "The Road to Damascus." *Foreign Affairs* (May–June).

Sindelar, H. Richard, III, and J. E. Peterson, eds. 1989. *Crosscurrents in the Gulf: Arab, Regional and Global Interests.* For the Middle East Institute. London: Routledge. 256p.

Slot, Ben J., ed. 2003. *Kuwait: The Growth of a Historic Identity.* London: Arabian Publishing. 129p.

Smith, Charles D. 2006. *Palestine and the Arab-Israeli Conflict.* 6th ed. Boston: Bedford/St. Martin's. 567p.

Smith, George Adam. 1935. *The Historical Geography of the Holy Land.* 25th ed. London: Hodder and Stoughton. 744p.

Smith, Huston. 1991. *The World's Religions: Our Great Wisdom Traditions.* San Francisco: HarperSanFrancisco. 399p.

Smith, Pamela Ann. 1986. "The Palestinian Diaspora, 1948–1985." *Journal of Palestine Studies* 15, no. 3 (Spring): 90–108.

Smith, William Cantwell. 1957. *Islam in Modern History.* Princeton: Princeton University Press. 317p.

Sobhani, Sohrab. 1999. "The Course of Iranian-Israeli Relations." *Middle East Insight* (Nov.–Dec.): 39–40.

Socor, Vladimar. 2009. "Southern Corridor, White Stream: The Strategic Rationale." *Eurasia Daily Monitor* 6, no. 200 (Oct. 30). www.jamestown.org/.

Soffer, Arnon. 1999. *Rivers of Fire: The Conflict over Water in the Middle East.* Translated by Murray Rosovsky and Nina Copaken. Lanham, MD: Rowman and Littlefield. 303p.

Soffer, Arnon, and Julian V. Minghi. 1986. "Israel's Security Landscapes: The Impact of Military Considerations on Land Uses." *Professional Geographer* 38 (Feb.): 28–41.

Solomon, Steven. 2010. *Water: The Epic Struggle for Wealth, Power, and Civilization.* New York: Harper. 608p.

Somer, Murat. 2004. "Turkey's Kurdish Conflict: Changing Context and Domestic and Regional Implications." *Middle East Journal* 58, no. 2 (Spring): 235–253.

Sosland, Jeffrey K. 2007. *Cooperating Rivals: The Riparian Politics of the Jordan River Basin.* Albany: State University of New York Press. 212p.

Spiegel, Steven L. 1985. *The Other Arab-Israeli Conflict: Making America's Middle East Policy, from Truman to Reagan.* Middle Eastern Studies, Monograph no. 1. Graduate School of International Studies, University of Miami. Chicago: University of Chicago Press. 522p.

Spykman, Nicholas John. 1944. *The Geography of the Peace.* New York: Harcourt, Brace. 66p.

Stager, Lawrence E., Joseph A. Greene, and Michael D. Coogan, eds. 2000. *The Archaeology of Jordan and Beyond: Essays in Honor of James A. Saver.* Winona Lake, IN: Eisenbrauns. 529p.

Stasis, Anastasios, and Michael Mavrocordatos. 1989. *Geography of Cyprus.* 3d ed. Larnaca, Cyprus: American Academy. 121p.

Stauffer, Thomas R. 2003. "The Cost of Middle East Conflict, 1956–2002: What the U.S. Has Spent." *Middle East Policy* 10, no. 1 (Spring): 45–102.

Steffen, Hans, et al. 1978. *Final Report on the Airphoto Interpretation Project of the Swiss Technical Cooperation Service, Berne.* Project carried out for the Central Planning Organisation, Sana. The major findings of the Population and Housing Census of February 1975. Zurich: Department of Geography, University of Zurich. Two parts in one volume: pt. 1, 164p; pt. 2, 231p. (Much of the same information appears in Hans Steffen, *Population Geography of the Yemen Arab Republic, Tubinger Atlas des Vorderen Orients,* suppl. ser. B. [Geisteswissenschaften], no. 39 [Wiesbaden: Ludwig Reichert, 1979], 132p.)

Stegner, Wallace. 2007. *Discovery! The Search for Arabian Oil.* Vista, CA: Selwa Press. 245p.

Stein, Leonard J. 1983. *The Balfour Declaration.* Jerusalem: Magnes Press of Hebrew University. 681p.

Sternhell, Zeev. 1998. *The Founding Myths of Israel: Nationalism, Socialism, and the Making of the Jewish State.* Princeton: Princeton University Press. 419p.

Stevens, Paul. 2000. "Pipelines or Pipe Dreams? Lessons from the History of Arab Transit Pipelines." *Middle East Journal* 54, no. 2 (Spring): 224–241.

Stewart, Dona J. 1996. "Cities in the Desert: The Egyptian New-Town Program." *Annals* (Association of American Geographers) 86, no. 3 (Sept.): 459–480.

———. 2009. *The Middle East Today: Political, Geographical, and Cultural Perspectives.* New York: Routledge. 213p.

Stiglitz, Joseph E., Amyarta Sen, and Jean-Paul Fitoussi. 2009. "Report by the Commission on the Measurement of Economic Performance and Social Progress." http://stiglitz-sen-fitouusi.fr/.

Stookey, Robert W. 1982. *South Yemen: A Marxist Republic in Arabia.* Profiles: Nations of the Contemporary Middle East. Boulder: Westview Press. 124p.

Stronach, David, and Stephen Lunsden. 1992. "The University of California Berkeley's Excavations at Nineveh." *Biblical Archaeologist* 55, no. 4 (Dec.): 227–233.

Summers, W. M. 1986. "Proto-Elamite Civilization in Fars." In *Gamdat Nasr: Period or Regional Style?* edited by Uwe Finkbeiner and Wolfgang Rollig, 199–211. Wiesbaden: Ludwig Reichert, 1986.

Survey of Israel. 1985. *Atlas of Israel.* 3d ed. Tel Aviv: Survey of Israel. Pages unnumbered.

Sussman, Gary. 2004. "The Challenge to the Two-State Solution." *Middle East Report* 34, no. 2 (Summer): 8–15.

Swagman, Charles F. 1988. *Development and Change in Highland Yemen.* Salt Lake City: University of Utah Press. 200p.

Swisher, Clayton E. 2004. *The Truth About Camp David.* New York: Nation Books. 455p.

Taha, M. F., et al. 1981. "The Climate of the Near East." In *World Survey of Climatology,* edited by K. Takahasha and H. Arakawa. Vol. 9, *Climates of Southern and Western Asia.* Amsterdam: Elsevier Scientific.

Takeyh, Ray. 2003. "Iran at a Crossroads." *Middle East Journal* 57, no. 1 (Winter): 42–56.

Talhami, Ghada Hashem. 2001. *Syria and the Palestinians: The Clash of Nationalisms.* Gainesville: University Press of Florida. 257p.

Tapper, Richard. 1997. *Frontier Nomads of Iran: A Political and Social History of the Shahsevan.* Cambridge: Cambridge University Press. 429p.

Tarnoff, Curt. 2009. *Iraq: Reconstruction Assistance.* Washington, DC: Congressional Research Service. 37p.

Taryam, Abdullah Omran. 1987. *The Establishment of the United Arab Emirates, 1950–85.* London: Croom Helm. 190p.

Tekin, Ali, and Iva Walterova. 2007. "Turkey's Geopolitical Role: The Energy Angle." *Middle East Policy* 14, no. 1 (Spring): 84–94.

Telhami, Shibley. 2002a. *The Stakes—America and the Middle East: The Consequences of Power and the Choice for Peace.* Boulder: Westview Press. 204p.

———. 2002b. "Understanding the Challenge." *Middle East Journal* 56, no. 1 (Winter): 9–18.

Tepe, Sultan. 2008. *Beyond Sacred and Secular: Politics of Religion in Israel and Turkey.* Stanford: Stanford University Press. 413p.

Terrill, W. Andrew. 2009. "The Continuing Problem of Iraq." *Middle East Journal* 63, no. 4: 661–667.

Tessler, Mark. 1994. *A History of the Israeli-Palestinian Conflict.* Bloomington: Indiana University Press. 906p.

Theroux, Peter. 1996. "Syria: Behind the Mask." *National Geographic,* July, 106–131.

———. 1997. "Beirut Rising." *National Geographic,* Sept., 100–123.

Thesiger, Wilfred. 1959. *Arabian Sands.* London: Longmans. 326p.

———. 1964. *The Marsh Arabs.* New York: Dutton. 242p.

Thomas, Michael. 2007. *American Policy Toward Israel: The Power and the Limits of Beliefs.* New York: Routledge. 192p.

Thompson, Eric V. 2002. "Will Syria Have to Withdraw from Lebanon?" *Middle East Journal* 56, no. 1 (Winter): 72–93.

Tower, John. 1987. *The Tower Commission Report.* New York: Bantam. 550p.

Townsend, John. 1977. *Oman: The Making of a Modern State.* New York: St. Martin's. 212p.

Transparency International. 2009. *Annual Report.* Berlin: Transparency International. www.transparency.org.

Tripp, Charles. 2002. *A History of Iraq.* 2d ed. Cambridge: Cambridge University Press. 346p.

Tubb, Jonathan N. 1998. *Canaanites, Peoples of the Past.* Norman: University of Oklahoma Press. 160p.

Turkey. 1989. 3d ed. Insight Guides. Hong Kong: Apa Publications. 404p.

Twinam, Joseph Wright. 1992. *The Gulf, Cooperation and the Council: An American Perspective.* Washington, DC: Middle East Policy Council, 1992. 294p.

United Nations Children's Fund. Annual. *The State of the World's Children, 2009.* www.unicef.org.

United Nations Development Programme. 2009. *Arab Human Development Report 2009.*

United Nations Educational, Scientific, and Cultural Organization. 1971–1981. "Soil Map of the World," 1:5,000,000. Rome: UN Food and Agriculture Organization (FAO).

United Nations Environment Program. 2003. *Desk Study on the Environment in Iraq.* 96p.

United Nations Food and Agriculture Organization. 2001. *The Mesopotamian Marshlands: Demise of an Ecosystem.* 46p. www.grid.unep.ch/activities/sustainable/tigris/report.php.

———. 2009. *The State of Food Insecurity in the World.* Rome: FAO.

———. Annual. *Production Yearbook.* Rome: FAO.

U.S. Department of Agriculture. Annual. *Agricultural Situation Report. Foreign Agricultural Service (FAS).* www.fas.usda.gov/.

U.S. Department of Defense, Defense Mapping Agency. 1985. *Gazetteer of Iran: Names Approved by the United States Board on Geographic Names.* 2 vols. 2d ed. Washington, DC: U.S. Government Printing Office. 1,827p.

U.S. Department of State. Periodic. *Background Notes.* www.state.gov/www/background_notes/.

———. Annual. *Country Commercial Guide.* http://lcweb2.loc._gov/x-ds-com.html.

———. Annual. *Economic Policy and Trade Practices: Country Reports.* Annual. Washington, DC: U.S. Department of State.

———. 2009. *2008 Report on International Religious Freedom (Israel and the Occupied Territories).* Washington, DC: U.S. Department of State.

U.S. Department of the Army. *Country Studies: Area Handbook Series.* Prepared by the Library of Congress, with various editors. A study is available on every Middle East country (combined volume on *Persian Gulf States*), with fourth and fifth editions of studies of major Middle East countries published 1988–1991. Washington, DC: U.S. Government Printing Office. www.lcweb2.loc.gov/frd/cs/.

U.S. Geological Survey. 1966–1967, 1975, and 1989. *Geology of the Arabian Peninsula.* Geological Survey Professional Papers, 560 series. Geology of the Arabian Peninsula: A, "Arabian Shield"; B, "Yemen"; C, "Aden Protectorate"; D, "Sedimentary Geology of Saudi Arabia"; E, "Bahrain"; F, "Kuwait"; G, "Southwestern Iraq"; H, "Eastern Aden Protectorate and Part of Dhufar"; and I, "Jordan." Washington, DC: U.S. Government Printing Office.

Vasiliev, A. M. 2000. *A History of Saudi Arabia.* New York: New York University Press. 576p.

Ventner, Al J. 1998. "The Oldest Threat: Water in the Middle East." *Middle East Policy* 6, no. 1 (June): 126–136.

Victor, Barbara. 1994. *Voice of Reason: Hanan Ashrawi and Peace in the Middle East.* New York: Harcourt. 310p.

Vidal, F. S. 1955. *The Oasis of al-Hasa.* Dhahran: Arabian American Oil Company. 216p.

Vine, Peter J., ed. 1996. *Natural Emirates: Wildlife and Environment of the United Arab Emirates.* London: Trident. 243p.

Vita-Finzi, C. 1986. *Recent Earth Movements: An Introduction to Neotectonics.* London: Academic Press. 226p.

Vivian, Cassandra. 2000. *The Western Desert of Egypt: An Explorer's Handbook.* Cairo: American University in Cairo Press. 423p.

Volcker, Paul, Richard Goldstone, and Mark Pieth. 2005. *Manipulation of the Oil-for-Food Programme by the Iraqi Regime.* New York: Independent Inquiry Committee into the United Nations Oil-for-Food Programme, Oct.

Wagstaff, J. M. 1985. *The Evolution of Middle Eastern Landscapes.* Totowa, NJ: Barnes and Noble. 304p.

Wall Street Journal. 2009. "U.S. Woos Damascus by Easing Export Ban." July 28.

Wasserstein, Bernard. 2008. *Divided Jerusalem: The Struggle for the Holy City.* 3 ed. New Haven: Yale University Press. 422p.

Waterbury, John. 1979. *Hydropolitics of the Nile Valley.* Syracuse: Syracuse University Press. 301p.

———. 1983. *The Egypt of Nasser and Sadat: The Political Economy of Two Regimes.* Princeton Studies on the Near East. Princeton: Princeton University Press. 475p.

Water for the Future. 1999. Washington, DC: National Academy Press. 226p.

Watkins, Eric, ed. 1995. *The Middle Eastern Environment: Selected Papers of the 1995 Conference of the British Society for Middle Eastern Studies.* Cambridge: St. Malo. 253p.

Waxman, Chaim. 2000. "Religio-Politics and Social Unity in Israel." In *Israel's First Fifty Years,* edited by Robert O. Freedman. Gainesville: University Press of Florida. 290p.

Weekes, Richard V., ed. 1984. *Muslim Peoples: A World Ethnographic Survey.* 2 vols. 2d ed. Westport, CT: Greenwood. 953p.

Wendorf, Fred, and Romuald Schild. 1980. *Prehistory of the Eastern Sahara.* New York: Academic Press. 414p.

Whalen, Norman M., and David W. Pease. 1992. "Early Mankind in Arabia." *Saudi Aramco World,* July–Aug., 16–23.

Whittlesey, Derwent. 1929. "Sequent Occupance." *Annals* (Association of American Geographers) 19: 162–165.

Wigoder, Geoffrey, et al., eds. 2002. *The New Encyclopedia of Judaism.* New York: New York University Press. 856p.

Wiktorowicz, Quintan, and John Kaltner. 2003. "Killing in the Name of Islam: Al-Qaeda's Justification for September 11." *Middle East Policy* 10, no. 2 (Summer): 76–92.

Wilkinson, John C. 1991. *Arabia's Frontiers: The Story of Britain's Boundary Drawing in the Desert.* London: I. B. Tauris. 422p.

Wilkinson, T. J. 2003. *Archaeological Landscapes of the Near East.* Tucson: University of Arizona Press. 260p.

Williams, Caroline. 2002a. *Islamic Monuments in Cairo.* Rev. ed. New York: American University in Cairo Press. 276p.

———. 2002b. "Transforming the Old: Cairo's New Medieval City." *Middle East Journal* 56, no. 3 (Summer): 457–475.

Williams, Richard S., et al. 1991. "Environmental Consequences of the Persian Gulf War, 1990–1991: Remote-Sensing Datasets of Kuwait and Environs." *Research and Exploration* (Special issue of National Geographic Society) 7: 1–48.

Wilson, Jeremy. 1990. *Lawrence of Arabia: The Authorized Biography of T. E. Lawrence.* New York: Atheneum. 1,188p.

Wilson, Mary C. 1987. *King Abdullah, Britain and the Making of Jordan.* Cambridge Middle East Library. Cambridge: Cambridge University Press. 289p.

Wilson, Sir Arnold T. 1928. *The Persian Gulf: An Historical Sketch from the Earliest Times to the Beginning of the Twentieth Century.* London: George Allen and Unwin. 327p.

Winrow, Gareth M. 2003. "Pivotal State or Energy Supplicant? Domestic Structure, External Actors, and Turkish Policy in the Caucasus." *Middle East Journal* 37, no. 1 (Winter): 76–92.

Wolf, Aaron T. 1995. *Hydropolitics Along the Jordan River: The Impact of Scarce Water Resources on the Arab-Israeli Conflict.* New York: United Nations University Press. 272p.

Woodward, Bob. 2004. *Plan of Attack.* New York: Simon and Schuster. 467p.

Woodward, Peter N. 1988. *Oil and Labor in the Middle East: Saudi Arabia and the Oil Boom.* New York: Praeger. 195p.

World Bank. 2009. *Assessment of Restrictions on Palestinian Water Sector Development.* Apr. Sector Note.

World Economic Forum. 2009a. *The Global Competitiveness Report, 2009–2010.* Geneva: World Economic Forum. www.weforum.org.

———. 2009b. *The Global Gender Gap Report, 2009.* Geneva: World Economic Forum. www.weforum.org.

Wright, Robin. 2000. "Iran's New Revolution." *Foreign Affairs* 79, no. 1 (Jan.–Feb.): 133–145.

———. 2001. *Sacred Rage: The Wrath of Militant Islam.* New York and London: Simon and Schuster. 330p.

———. 2008. *Dreams and Shadows: The Future of the Middle East.* New York: Penguin. 464p.

Wright, Steven. 2007. *The United States and Persian Gulf Security: The Foundations of the War on Terror.* Reading, UK: Ithaca Press. 208p.

Wurmser, Meyrav. 1999. "Can Israel Survive Post-Zionism?" *Middle East Quarterly* 6, no. 1 (Mar.).

Yamani, Mai. *Changed Identities: The Challenge of the New Generation in Saudi Arabia.* London: Royal Institute of International Affairs, 2000. 170p.

Yambert, Karl. 2010. *The Contemporary Middle East.* 2d ed. Boulder: Westview Press.

Yapp, Malcolm. 1987. *The Making of the Modern Near East, 1792–1923.* London: Longman. 404p.

———. 1996. *The Near East Since the First World War: A History to 1995.* 2d ed. London: Longman. 597p.

Yavuz, Hakan, and Michael Gunter, eds. 2004. "The Kurds in Iraq." Papers Presented at Middle East Studies Association, Nov. 8, 2003. *Middle East Policy* 11, no. 1 (Spring): 106–131.

Yazbeck, Haddad, and John L. Esposito, eds. 1998. *Islam, Gender, and Social Change.* Oxford: Oxford University Press. 259p.

Yehia, Mohamed Adel Ahmed. 1983. *Atlas of Qatar: From Landsat Images.* Doha: Centre of Scientific and Applied Research, Qatar University. 166p.

Yergin, Daniel. 1991. *The Prize: The Epic Quest for Oil, Money, and Power.* New York: Simon and Schuster. 917p.

Yesilada, Birol A. 2002. "Turkey's Candidacy for EU Membership." *Middle East Journal* 56, no. 1 (Winter): 94–111.

Yetiv, Steven A. 2008. *The Absence of Grand Strategy: The United States in the Persian Gulf, 1972–2005.* Baltimore: Johns Hopkins University Press. 250p.

Yiftachel, Oren, and Avinoam Meir, eds. 1998. *Ethnic Frontiers and Peripheries: Landscapes of Development and Inequality in Israel.* Boulder: Westview Press. 337p.

Al-Yousef, Mohammed bin Musa. 1995. *Oil and the Transformation of Oman, 1970–1995.* London: Stacey International. 144p.

Zahlan, Rosemarie Said. 1998. *The Making of the Modern Gulf States: Kuwait, Bahrain, Qatar, the United Arab Emirates, and Oman.* Rev. ed. Reading, UK: Ithaca. 200p.

Zamir, Meir. 1999. "From Hegemony to Marginalism: The Maronites of Lebanon." In *Minorities and the State in the Arab World,* edited by Ofra Bengio and Gabriel Ben-Dor. Boulder: Lynne Rienner. 223p.

Zangwill, Israel. 1901. "The Return to Palestine." *New Liberal Review* 2 (Dec.): 615–634.

Zinni, Tony. 2006. *Battle for Peace: A Frontline Vision of America's Power and Purpose.* New York: Palgrave Macmillan. 233p.

Ziser, Eyal. 2000. *Lebanon: The Challenge of Independence.* London and New York: I. B. Tauris. 297p.

Zohary, Michael. 1962. *Plant Life of Palestine: Israel and Jordan.* New York: Ronald. 262p.

Zunes, Stephen. 2002. *Tinderbox.* London: Zed Books. 278p.

———. 2004. "U.S. Policy Towards Syria and the Triumph of Neoconservatism." *Middle East Policy* 11, no. 1 (Spring): 52–69.

Index